Lecture Notes in Computer Science

Lecture Notes in Artificial Intelligence **16631**

Founding Editor

Jörg Siekmann

The series Lecture Notes in Artificial Intelligence (LNAI) was established in 1988 as a topical subseries of LNCS devoted to artificial intelligence.

The series publishes state-of-the-art research results at a high level. As with the LNCS mother series, the mission of the series is to serve the international R & D community by providing an invaluable service, mainly focused on the publication of conference and workshop proceedings and postproceedings.

Jianwei Niu · Meikang Qiu · Cungen Cao
Editors

Knowledge Science, Engineering and Management

19th International Conference, KSEM 2026 Beijing, China, July 17–19, 2026 Proceedings, Part I

Springer

Editors
Jianwei Niu
Beihang University
Beijing, China

Meikang Qiu
Augusta University
Augusta, GA, USA

Cungen Cao
Chinese Academy of Sciences
Beijing, China

ISSN 0302-9743 ISSN 1611-3349 (electronic)
Lecture Notes in Artificial Intelligence
ISBN 978-981-92-2758-7 ISBN 978-981-92-2759-4 (eBook)
https://doi.org/10.1007/978-981-92-2759-4

LNCS Sublibrary: SL7 – Artificial Intelligence

This Springer imprint is published by the registered company Springer Nature Singapore Pte Ltd.
The registered company address is: 152 Beach Road, #21-01/04 Gateway East, Singapore 189721, Singapore

Preface

This volume contains the papers presented at KSEM 2026: The 19th International Conference on Knowledge Science, Engineering, and Management, held on July 17–19, 2026, in Beijing.

There were 695 submissions. The review process was double blind, and each submission was reviewed by at least 3 reviewers, and on average 3.5 Program Committee members. The committee decided to accept 186 high-quality regular papers, with an acceptance rate of 26.8%. We also accepted 99 special track papers, with an acceptance rate of 14.2%. We separate the proceedings into seven volumes: LNAI 16631, 16632, 16633, 16634, 16635, 16636, and 16637.

KSEM 2026 was the 19th in this series of conferences started in 2006. The aim of this interdisciplinary conference is to provide a forum for researchers in the broad areas of knowledge science, knowledge engineering, and knowledge management to exchange ideas and to report state-of-the-art research results. KSEM is in the list of CCF (China Computer Federation) recommended Conferences (C series, Artificial Intelligence).

KSEM 2026 was held in Beijing, China, following the tradition of the 18 previous successful KSEM events in Guilin, China (KSEM 2006); Melbourne, Australia (KSEM 2007); Vienna, Austria (KSEM 2009); Belfast, UK (KSEM 2010); Irvine, USA (KSEM 2011); Dalian, China (KSEM 2013); Sibiu, Romania (KSEM 2014); Chongqing, China (KSEM 2015), Passau, Germany (KSEM 2016), Melbourne, Australia (KSEM 2017), Changchun, China (KSEM 2018); Athens, Greece (KSEM 2019), Hangzhou, China (KSEM 2020), Tokyo, Japan (KSEM 2021), Singapore (KSEM 2022), Guangzhou, China (KSEM 2023), Birmingham, UK (KSEM 2024), and Macau, China (KSEM 2025).

Moreover, we would like to express our gratitude to the honorary chairs and the KSEM Steering Committee chairs, Ruqian Lu (Chinese Academy of Sciences, China), Dimitris Karagiannis (University of Vienna, Austria), and the members of the Steering Committee, who provided insight and guidance during all the stages of this effort. We extend our heartfelt gratitude to the Program Committee members and external reviewers for generously volunteering their time to review and discuss the conference papers. Special thanks go to the General Chairs for their outstanding leadership, and to the Finance, Publication, Publicity, and Local Organization Chairs for their dedicated efforts in ensuring the success of KSEM 2026. Finally, we would like to express our appreciation to all the authors for presenting their invaluable work at KSEM 2026.

The objective of KSEM 2026 was to bring together researchers and practitioners from academia, industry, and government to advance the theories and technologies in Knowledge Science, Engineering, and Management. For regular papers of KSEM 2026, we focused on four broad areas, i.e., Knowledge Science with Learning and AI (Volume 1), Knowledge Engineering Research and Applications (Volume 2), Knowledge Management (Volume 3), and Optimization and Security for Big Knowledge (Volume 4). For special track papers, we divide them into Science (Volume 5), Engineering (Volume 6), and Management (Volume 7).

We would like to thank the conference sponsors: Springer LNAI and Beihang University, China.

We hope you enjoyed the conference in Beijing!

July 2026

Jianwei Niu
Meikang Qiu
Cungen Cao

Organization

Honorary General Chairs

Ruqian Lu	Chinese Academy of Sciences, China
Zhiming Zheng	Chinese Academy of Sciences, China
Dimitris Karagiannis	University of Vienna, Austria

General Chairs

Weifeng Lv	Beihang University, China
Jinhu Lv	Beihang University, China
Jianwei Niu	Beihang University, China
Meikang Qiu	Augusta University, USA

Program Committee Chairs

Mohsen Guizani	Mohamed Bin Zayed University of Artificial Intelligence (MBZUAI), UAE
Chunming Hu	Beihang University, China
Shui Yu	University of Technology Sydney, Australia
Cungen Cao	Chinese Academy of Sciences, China
Gerard Memmi	Télécom Paris, France
Yan Zhang	University of Oslo, Norway
Joel J. P. C. Rodrigues	Federal University of Rio Grande do Norte, Brazil

Steering Committee

Ruqian Lu (Honorary Chair)	Chinese Academy of Sciences, China
Dimitris Karagiannis (Chair)	University of Vienna, Austria
Bo Yang	Jilin University, China
Chengqi Zhang	University of Technology Sydney, Australia
Christos Douligeris	University of Piraeus, Greece
Claudiu Kifor	Lucian Blaga University of Sibiu, Romania
Gang Li	Deakin University, Australia
Hui Xiong	State University of New Jersey, USA

Jörg Siekmann	German Research Centre for Artificial Intelligence, Germany
Martin Wirsing	Ludwig-Maximilians-Universität München, Germany
Meikang Qiu	Augusta University, USA
Xiaoyang Wang	Zhejiang Gongshang University, China
Yaxin Bi	Ulster University, UK
Yoshiteru Nakamori	Japan Advanced Institute of Science and Technology, Japan
Yuncheng Jiang	South China Normal University, China
Zhi Jin	Peking University, China
Zili Zhang	Southwest University, China

Program Committee

Dimitris Apostolou	University of Piraeus, Greece
Rehan Bhana	Birmingham City University, UK
Yupeng Cao	Stevens Institute of Technology, USA
Yiming Chen	Beihang University, China
Wei Chen	Beihang University, China
Zhong Chen	Southern Illinois University, USA
Yifan Deng	University of Wisconsin-Madison, USA
Dalia El-Banna	Birmingham City University, UK
Ruibing Feng	Beihang University, China
Shaojing Fu	National University of Defense Technology, China
Keke Gai	Beijing Institute of Technology, China
Jiechao Gao	Stanford University, USA
Xiangyu Gao	Washington University, USA
Ningbo Gu	Hangzhou Innovation Institute, Beihang University, China
Jinguang Gu	Wuhan University of Science and Technology, China
Yixuan Guan	Beihang University, China
Zehua Guo	Beijing Institute of Technology, China
Qi He	Beihang University, China
Wei Hu	Wuhan University of Science and Technology, China
Zheyuan Hu	Beihang University, China
Miao Hu	Sun Yat-sen University, China
Cheng Huang	Sichuan University, China

Radu Tudor Ionescu	University of Bucharest, Romania
Linpeng Jia	Institute of Computing Technology, Chinese Academy of Sciences, China
Muhammad Mubashir Khan	NED University of Engineering and Technology, Pakistan
Olga Korableva	Saint Petersburg State University, Russia
Florin Leon	Gheorghe Asachi Technical University of Iasi, Romania
Qingfeng Li	Beihang University, China
Shunde Li	Beijing Union University, China
Mu Li	Beihang University, China
Chao Li	Beijing Jiaotong University, China
Yijing Lin	Beijing University of Posts and Telecommunications, China
Zhihui Lu	Fudan University, China
Jianming Lv	South China University of Technology, China
Andreas Martin	University of Applied Sciences Northwestern Switzerland, Switzerland
Fanan Meng	Shandong University, China
Takeshi Morita	Aoyama Gakuin University, Japan
Jianwei Niu	Beihang University, China
Weina Niu	University of Electronic Science and Technology of China, China
Ovidiu Noran	Griffith University, Australia
Norbert Pataki	Eötvös Loránd University, Hungary
Lian Peng	Augusta University, USA
Kemal Polat	Abant Izzet Baysal University, Turkey
Andrea Polini	University of Camerino, Italy
Meikang Qiu	Augusta University, USA
Qingsong Shi	Zhejiang University, China
Ruisheng Shi	Beijing University of Posts & Telecommunications, China
Xinming Song	Shandong University, China
Wentao Song	Beihang University, China
Qing Sun	Beihang University, China
Zhiyu Sun	Northwestern Polytechnical University, China
Heng Sun	Jinan University, China
Ruijie Tian	Liaoning Normal University, China
Daniel Volovici	University of Sibiu, Romania
Mingxi Wang	Beihang University
Danghui Wang	Northwestern Polytechnical University, China
Jihe Wang	Northwestern Polytechnical University, China
Jue Wang	Chinese Academy of Sciences, China

Yanxuan Wei	Shandong University, China
Yuan Wen	University of Aberdeen, UK
Hans Friedrich Witschel	University of Applied Sciences Northwestern Switzerland, Switzerland
Robert Woitsch	BOC Group, Austria
Linying Wu	Northwestern Polytechnical University, China
Di Wu	Sun Yat-sen University, China
Song Xia	Nanyang Technological University, Singapore
Yuanhua Xiao	Northwestern Polytechnical University, China
Shengmin Xu	Fujian Normal University, China
Tiechui Yao	China Electric Power Research Institute, China
Jianglin Yu	Beihang University, China
Hengshan Yue	Jilin University, China
Zhongliang Zhang	Shandong University, China
Chunxia Zhang	Beijing Institute of Technology, China
Zili Zhang	Deakin University, Australia
Litian Zhang	Beijing University of Posts and Telecommunications, China
Zexi Zhao	Beihang University, China
Bowen Zhao	Singapore Management University, Singapore
Jiaqi Zhu	Institute of Software, Chinese Academy of Sciences, China
Shaoying Zhu	York St John University, UK

Contents

Knowledge Representation, Reasoning, and Uncertainty

Knowledge Representation, Reasoning, and Uncertainty

Role-Uncertainty–Aware Structured Pruning for DETR: Task-Sharing Structural Priors and Deployable Inference Acceleration

Wei Jin[1,2], Ningyuan Yu[1,2], Qiming Zhao[3], and Jing Wu[1,2](✉)

[1] School of Computer Science and Technology, Wuhan University of Science and Technology, Wuhan 430065, Hubei, China
{wustjin,oldfish}@wust.edu.cn

[2] Hubei Province Key Laboratory of Intelligent Information Processing and Real-time Industrial System, Wuhan University of Science and Technology, Wuhan 430065, China
wujingecs@wust.edu.cn

[3] Central China Normal University, Wuhan, China

Abstract. *Detection Transformer* (DETR) provides an end-to-end set prediction paradigm for object detection. However, its backbone network and stacked Transformer layers introduce substantial computational overhead, making real-time deployment challenging. Existing structured pruning methods typically rely on weight magnitude or a single overall loss to induce sparsity and estimate importance, which may overlook gradient discrepancies between classification and localization objectives, thereby degrading localization metrics and undermining pruning stability. To address this issue, we propose a role-uncertainty-aware structured pruning framework for DETR. Specifically, we introduce role-uncertainty-weighted L1 sparsity regularization to encourage a prunable sparse distribution, and construct a structural importance ranking based on the respective contributions of classification and localization. Guided by this ranking, we prune modules including backbone bottleneck blocks, feed-forward networks (FFNs), and the regression head to obtain an accelerated model suitable for deployment. Experiments on VOC2007 show that our method reduces parameters by 29.70% and FLOPs by 34.85% while increasing inference FPS by 9.01%, with only a 3.78% relative decrease in AP. On the VOC2012 dataset, utilizing the same pruning ratio, the AP degradation is limited to just 4.30%. These results demonstrate a practical solution for deploying lightweight yet accuracy-stable DETR detectors in resource-constrained and latency-sensitive scenarios.

Keywords: DETR · structured pruning · role uncertainty · task decoupling · inference acceleration

J. Niu et al. (Eds.): KSEM 2026, LNAI 16631, pp. 3–14, 2027.
https://doi.org/10.1007/978-981-92-2759-4_1

1 Introduction

In recent years, with the rapid development of computing capability [3,12,18] and big data [4,5,17], object detection has evolved from two-stage region proposal–based frameworks and one-stage dense prediction frameworks centered around convolutional neural networks to Transformer-based end-to-end paradigms represented by DETR [19]. By introducing attention mechanisms and bipartite matching, DETR eliminates anchors and non-maximum suppression, simplifying the detection pipeline and enhancing global modeling capability. However, because DETR and its variants typically rely on ResNet as the backbone and stack multiple Transformer layers, they exhibit large computational complexity and parameter counts, making it difficult to meet the requirements of real-time applications [6,11,16]. Common deployment-oriented approaches include knowledge distillation, quantization, and model pruning; among them, structured pruning has attracted particular attention because it can directly translate into substantial hardware acceleration benefits.

Structured pruning removes redundant structures using channels or hidden dimensions as the pruning unit, based on importance estimation or sparsity induction, thereby reducing parameters and computation while keeping tensor shapes regular and amenable to inference backends [22]. Compared with unstructured sparsity, the compression results of structured pruning are more reliably converted into end-to-end latency reductions, and are therefore better suited to latency-sensitive deployment scenarios. Existing pruning strategies have been extensively validated on classification networks, but when directly applied to DETR they tend to deviate from the objectives of detection: the importance measures are insufficiently coupled with detection losses, and it is difficult to simultaneously satisfy both classification and localization requirements, leading to unstable pruning and increased fine-tuning costs [13].

This paper proposes a role-uncertainty–aware structured pruning method that models the discrepant driving forces of classification and localization on channels. The gradient contributions of classification and localization tasks are statistically analyzed across channel dimensions to calculate channel task sharing. This sharing information is then used as a sparsity constraint to adjust pruning priorities, thereby mitigating the instability caused by multi-task coupling. After the statistics stabilize, the gating mechanism is incorporated into the deployable parameters, followed by structured pruning and post-pruning fine-tuning to complete network compression. The proposed method achieves substantial computation reduction and structured acceleration on key DETR submodules, while yielding more controllable accuracy degradation and more stable pruning outcomes.

The overall organization of this paper is as follows. Section 1 serves as the introduction; Sect. 2 reviews related work and discusses the challenges of structured pruning for DETR; Sect. 3 introduces the proposed methodology and deployment strategies; Sect. 4 presents experimental results and ablation studies on the VOC2007 and VOC2012 datasets; and Sect. 5 concludes the paper and outlines future directions.

The main contributions of this paper are as follows:

- We propose a role-uncertainty–aware structured pruning approach. By statistically analyzing per-channel gradient contributions under classification and localization objectives, we construct a task-sharing degree metric and introduce a sharing-penalty form of sparsity regularization to guide channel-wise removal, improving stability and interpretability of pruning decisions in multi-task settings.
- We design an iterative structured pruning pipeline driven by task contribution statistics. Using multi-task gradient contribution statistics as the pruning signal, we achieve stable compression and practical inference acceleration for key DETR modules.
- On VOC2007 ($r = 0.4$) and VOC2012 ($r = 0.4$), we demonstrate that our method reduces AP by only 3.78% and 4.30%, respectively, while reducing parameters by 29.70%, FLOPs by 34.85%, and improving inference FPS by 9.01%, respectively-substantially lowering computation and improving deployment efficiency.

2 Related Work

2.1 Improvements to DETR

As the first framework to introduce Transformers into object detection [1], DETR formulates detection as a set prediction problem and performs end-to-end training via Hungarian matching, thereby reducing reliance on hand-crafted components such as proposal generation and non-maximum suppression. Nevertheless, DETR still suffers from limitations in training efficiency and detection performance, and its reliance on multi-scale representations makes it less sensitive to small objects. To address these issues, prior work improves DETR mainly along two directions: (i) faster convergence and higher accuracy, and (ii) architectural optimization for improved efficiency.

Zhu et al. proposed Deformable DETR, which introduces multi-scale deformable attention to improve the utilization efficiency of high-resolution features while preserving global modeling capability [21]. Li et al. proposed DN-DETR, which constructs denoising queries to stabilize the one-to-one matching process and alleviate sparse supervision, thus accelerating convergence and improving localization accuracy [8].

Beyond work that improves convergence and detection performance through architectural and training-strategy modifications, another line focuses on computational efficiency. Zhang et al. proposed Efficient-DETR, adopting a lightweight feature pyramid and a simplified decoder to reduce redundant computation and memory usage [14]. Li et al. proposed RT-DETR, combining backbones and decoder designs tailored for real-time scenarios [20], achieving low latency on common benchmarks.

2.2 Structured Pruning

Structured pruning is a model compression method operating at the network-structure level. Its core idea is to prune convolution kernels, channels, attention heads, or entire layers as basic units, thereby directly reducing parameter counts and FLOPs while maintaining dense tensor operators. Compared with unstructured sparsity, structured pruning is more likely to deliver actual acceleration on general hardware and deep learning frameworks.

For structured pruning in convolutional neural networks, Li et al. proposed an importance measure based on weight norms [2], performing filter-level pruning by removing convolution filters with small norms, and significantly reducing computation on ImageNet classification and detection tasks. He et al. designed a channel pruning strategy by minimizing feature reconstruction error [7], compressing deep convolutional networks while preserving representation quality. Liu et al. applied sparse regularization to BatchNorm scaling factors [9], adaptively learning channel importance and enabling automatic pruning, achieving near-lossless compression across various backbones.

For structured pruning in Transformer-based models, Michel et al. studied redundancy in multi-head self-attention and proposed attention-head pruning based on importance scores [10], showing that many attention heads can be removed with only minor performance drops in tasks such as machine translation. Fan et al. introduced learnable gating and sparse constraints for network depth and FFN width [15], enabling joint pruning of encoder-layer depth and FFN dimensions, significantly reducing inference latency and memory while maintaining sequence modeling capability. Overall, existing work mostly targets backbone networks or local Transformer modules; systematic collaborative pruning and evaluation of the encoder, decoder, and query mechanism under object detection constraints remain insufficient.

3 Method

We propose a role-uncertainty–based pruning framework. The framework introduces a unified differentiable gating mechanism to enable learnable sparsification over structural dimensions, explicitly decomposes detection learning signals into classification and localization components, and constructs a role-uncertainty–weighted regularization term to characterize and adjust how channels allocate contributions across multi-task objectives. Based on the sparse structure and accumulated statistics learned during training, the pruning stage performs structured removal to obtain a deployable compressed model with accelerated inference. The overall pruning pipeline is illustrated in Fig. 1.

3.1 Unified Differentiable Gating

Structured pruning typically uses channel counts or hidden dimensions as the minimum pruning granularity to ensure that the pruned network maintains

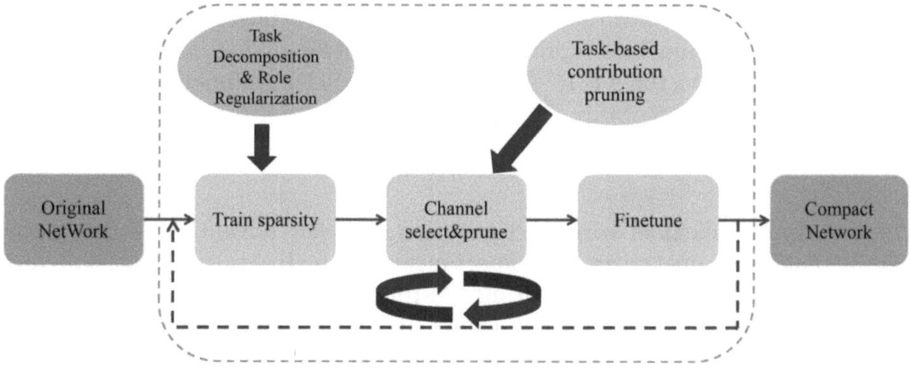

Fig. 1. Overall pruning pipeline.

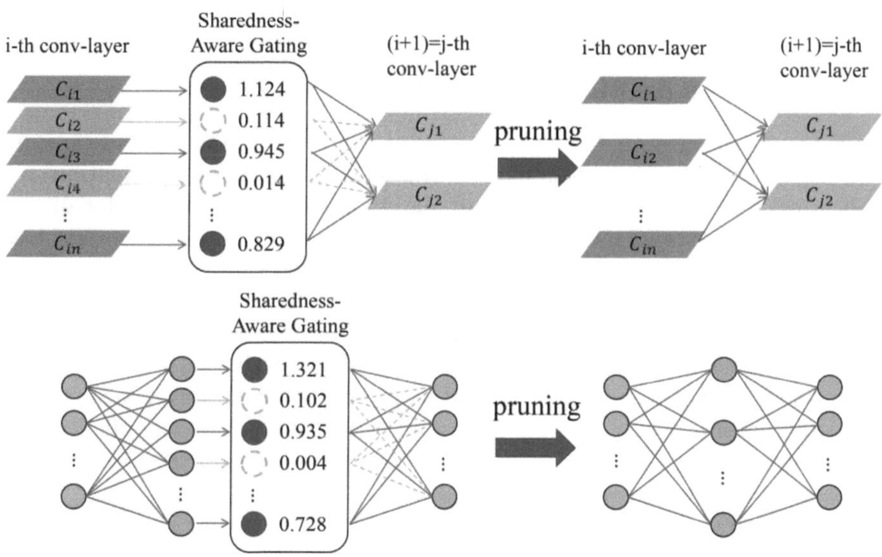

Fig. 2. Illustration of the structured pruning process for convolutional channels and hidden dimensions.

regular tensor shapes and achieves deployable operator-level acceleration. We adopt channel-wise structural units as the minimum pruning objects. Considering DETR's computation characteristics, we restrict pruning to key components that (i) occupy a large portion of computation and (ii) expose prunable structural dimensions. Specifically, we introduce a unified differentiable gating mechanism into the intermediate channels of bottlenecks in the backbone, the intermediate hidden dimension of FFNs in the Transformer, and the hidden-layer dimension of the bounding-box regression head. Each candidate structural dimension is associated with a learnable continuous gate parameter, enabling explicit modeling and differentiable optimization of its importance during training. Let the set of prunable structural dimensions in the network have size d, and let the corresponding intermediate representation be written as $h \in R^d$. We introduce a learnable gating vector $g \in R^d$ for this set of structural dimensions and apply element-wise scaling to obtain the pruned representation $\tilde{h}$ (Fig. 2):

$$\tilde{h} = g \odot h \tag{1}$$

where $\odot$ denotes element-wise multiplication. The key advantage of this gating form is that it parameterizes the importance of each structured dimension via a dedicated learnable coefficient. During end-to-end training, if the gate coefficient of a certain dimension continuously shrinks under the joint effects of optimization and sparsity constraints and approaches a small magnitude, the modulation effect of that dimension on the network output is systematically weakened. This indicates a small marginal contribution of the corresponding structural unit to the objective, providing a natural basis for subsequent structured pruning.

3.2 Task Decomposition and Role Regularization

DETR is optimized with multiple loss terms, and the corresponding optimization signals are often inconsistent in gradient space: the classification term emphasizes category discrimination and matching stability, while the localization term directly constrains geometric precision of bounding boxes. If one performs sparsification and importance estimation solely based on a "single total loss," the differential contributions of structural dimensions to different tasks can be obscured, causing pruning decisions to deviate from detection's multi-task objectives. To address this, we decompose the overall objective into a classification loss L_{cls} and a localization loss L_{loc}, and build gradient attribution statistics and role regularization over gate dimensions accordingly. Let the classification loss be L_{ce}, the bounding-box regression loss be L_{bbox}, and the geometric consistency loss be L_{giou}, with corresponding weights λ_{ce}, λ_{bbox}, and λ_{giou}. The two task losses are defined as:

$$L_{cls} = \lambda_{ce} L_{ce},\ L_{loc} = \lambda_{bbox}, L_{bbox} + \lambda_{giou} L_{giou} \tag{2}$$

We adopt a "parameter magnitude × gradient sensitivity" form to reflect each gate dimension's local first-order influence on the objective. For any gating vector $g \in R^d$, we compute its gradients under classification and localization. The contributions under classification and localization are:

$$S_{cls} = \left| g \odot \frac{\partial L_{cls}}{\partial g} \right|,\ S_{loc} = \left| g \odot \frac{\partial L_{loc}}{\partial g} \right| \tag{3}$$

Because single-step gradient attributions can be noisy and sensitive to samples and matching noise, we further maintain an exponential moving average for each gate to obtain a more stable long-term importance estimate:

$$\bar{S}_{cls} \leftarrow m\bar{S}_{cls} + (1-m)S_{cls}, \bar{S}_{loc} \leftarrow m\bar{S}_{loc} + (1-m)S_{loc} \tag{4}$$

where $m \in [0, 1)$ is the momentum coefficient and $\bar{S}$ denotes the accumulated contribution. Moreover, comparing contribution magnitudes alone is insufficient to characterize the "role type" of a structural unit in multi-task learning-i.e., whether it is more classification-oriented, localization-oriented, or shared by both. To capture this, we normalize the two contributions into task proportions and define a sharing degree. For any dimension $i, \varepsilon > 0$, let ε be a numerical stability constant; then:

$$p_{cls}^{(i)} = \frac{S_{cls}^{(i)}}{S_{cls}^{(i)} + S_{loc}^{(i)} + \varepsilon}, p_{loc}^{(i)} = \frac{S_{loc}^{(i)}}{S_{cls}^{(i)} + S_{loc}^{(i)} + \varepsilon} \tag{5}$$

Subsequently, role uncertainty is defined:

$$U^{(i)} = 4p_{cls}^{(i)} p_{loc}^{(i)} \tag{6}$$

When $U^{(i)}$ is close to 1, the dimension exhibits strong cross-task sharing; when $U^{(i)}$ is close to 0, the dimension is strongly task-specialized. From the resource allocation perspective of channel role uncertainty, we construct a channel task-decoupling mechanism based on role uncertainty to separate and route task-relevant information in mixed-role channels, thereby reducing task interference and erroneous removal during compression and improving multi-task optimization stability. Concretely, we use U as a weight to impose a weighted L_1 regularization on gate magnitudes:

$$R_{role} = \sum_{\alpha \in G} \frac{1}{|g|} U^{(i)} \cdot |g^{(i)}| \tag{7}$$

The final training objective is:

$$L = L_{base} + \lambda_{role} R_{role} \tag{8}$$

where L_{base} denotes the original multi-term weighted DETR loss, and λ_{role} is the strength of the role regularization.

3.3 Structured Pruning

After obtaining a stable channel sparsity distribution and accumulated statistics during training, we base structured pruning decisions on each dimension's overall importance. For the i-th dimension of any gating vector, we define the importance score as the sum of accumulated classification and localization contributions:

$$I = \bar{S}_{cls} + \bar{S}_{loc} \tag{9}$$

Because gradient scales can differ significantly across layers and modules, direct comparisons may introduce scale bias. We therefore normalize the scores to improve cross-layer comparability and stabilize ranking:

$$\hat{I} = \frac{I}{max(I) + \epsilon} \tag{10}$$

Given a pruning ratio $r \in [0, 1)$, we sort gate dimensions by importance scores and retain the top-k dimensions via a top-k strategy, performing structured pruning by removing the corresponding structural dimensions. Since pruning outcomes are directly reflected in the model's structural size, this method yields deployable reductions in computation and inference latency without relying on runtime sparse acceleration mechanisms.

4 Experimental Results

4.1 Datasets and Metrics

We conduct experiments on PASCAL VOC 2007 and PASCAL VOC 2012. The graphics card model used in the experiment was the RTX 4090. Dataset information is summarized in Table 1. To ensure reproducibility and fair comparison, all experiments follow the original splits provided by the datasets and evaluated using AP as the metric.

Table 1. Dataset statistics for PASCAL VOC 2007 and PASCAL VOC 2012.

Type	PASCAL VOC 2007	PASCAL VOC 2012
Train	2501	5717
Valid	2510	5823
Test	4952	–
Number of target categories	20	20

We evaluate both accuracy and efficiency under a unified experimental setup. For accuracy, we use average precision (AP) as the primary metric and additionally report multi-scale AP: AP_S, AP_M, and AP_L. AP is computed as follows. First, the intersection-over-union (IoU) between a predicted box B_p and a ground-truth box B_g is:

$$IoU(B_p, B_g) = \frac{|B_p \cap B_g|}{|B_p \cup B_g|} \tag{11}$$

Given an IoU threshold t, we obtain a precision–recall curve $P_t(R)$ by sorting predictions by confidence, and define the area under the curve as the average precision at threshold t:

$$AP_t = \int_0^1 P_t(R)\, dR. \tag{12}$$

To aggregate performance under different overlap criteria, the main AP is defined as the mean over a set of thresholds $T = 0.50, 0.55, ..., 0.95$:

$$AP = \frac{1}{|T|} \sum_{t \in T} AP_t \tag{13}$$

For efficiency, we measure both static complexity and runtime performance. Static complexity is evaluated by parameter count and FLOPs, reflecting storage cost and theoretical computation, respectively.

4.2 Results

Table 2 compares detection accuracy and efficiency on VOC2007. The original DETR baseline achieves AP = 45.0. Under the same pruning ratio $r = 0.4$, the L1-Norm structured pruning method reduces parameters and FLOPs by 29.70% and 34.85%, respectively, and improves FPS by 9.01%, but incurs a more notable accuracy drop: the relative AP decrease reaches 8.89%, and degradation is more severe on AP75, which emphasizes localization quality. This indicates that magnitude-based pruning can easily weaken key representations related to high-IoU matching and bounding-box regression, thus harming fine-grained localization.

Table 2. Comparison of detection performance and efficiency on VOC2007 test.

Method	AP	AP50	AP75	APS	APM	APL	Params	FLOPs	FPS
DETR	45.0	69.4	47.5	6.9	28.1	57.4	36.7M	57.1G	32.2
DETR-DC5	41.2	63.6	43.7	4.1	23.6	54.0	36.7M	57.1G	32.2
Deformable-DETR	46.9	70.6	52.6	10.4	35.3	57.0	32.3M	56.6G	13.2
Sparse-DETR	41.9	68.6	44.5	11.6	28.5	48.9	38.3M	56.6G	10.2
PnP-DETR	21.1	39.6	19.7	3.2	4.1	27.7	36.8M	54.6G	28.7
L1	41.0	61.7	42.5	6.2	22.0	46.4	25.8M	37.2G	35.1
Ours	43.3	65.5	45.3	9.2	26.6	53.5	25.8M	37.2G	35.1

In contrast, under the same model size and computation constraints as L1-Norm, our method limits the relative AP drop to 3.78%, outperforming L1-Norm across main metrics and being more favorable for small objects. This suggests that our method can more accurately distinguish "redundant" channels from "task-critical" channels during structural removal, better preserving feature branches sensitive to localization precision and small-object details, thereby achieving a superior accuracy–efficiency trade-off at the same compression level. The accuracy comparison between the two structured pruning methods at r = 0.4 is shown in Fig. 3.

In addition to structured pruning comparisons, Table 3 also includes representative DETR variants as references. These methods show different accuracy–efficiency trade-offs due to architectural or training-strategy changes. The results indicate that some variants achieve higher accuracy but significantly lower inference speed; for example, Sparse-DETR yields higher AP but much lower FPS, and Deformable-DETR attains higher AP than our pruned model while being

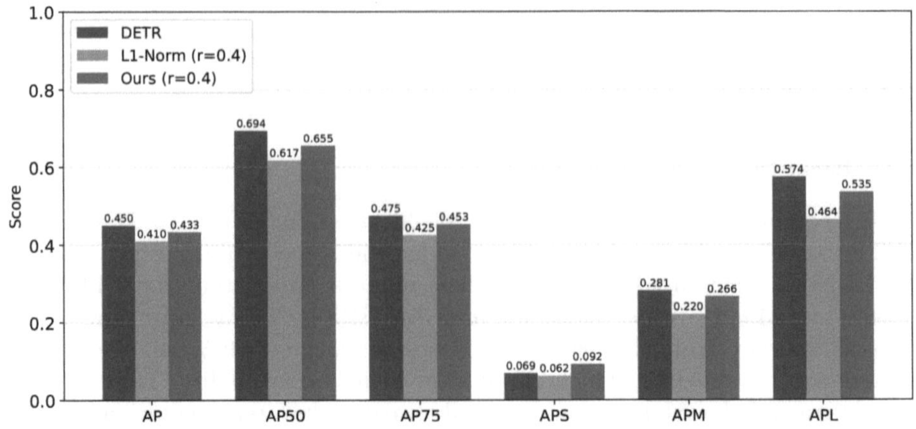

Fig. 3. A figure caption is always placed below the illustration. Please note that short captions are centered, while long ones are justified by the macro package automatically.

Table 3. Comparison of detection performance and efficiency on VOC2012 valid.

Method	AP	AP50	AP75	APS	APM	APL	Params	FLOPs	FPS
DETR	46.5	68.9	50.6	10.3	28.8	55.9	36.7M	57.1G	32.2
DETR-DC5	40.1	63.1	42.9	7.1	23.4	49.8	36.7M	57.1G	32.2
Deformable-DETR	49.1	72.8	56.5	17.8	37.5	55.5	32.3M	56.6G	13.2
Sparse-DETR	46.3	69.6	51.1	10.9	30.4	54.6	38.3M	56.6G	10.2
PnP-DETR	23.2	40.3	23.6	5.6	13.9	30.3	36.8M	54.6G	28.7
L1-Norm($r = 0.4$)	40.3	59.4	42.3	11.4	23.7	48.1	25.8M	37.2G	35.1
Ours($r = 0.4$)	44.5	66.7	48.2	11.6	26.6	54.5	25.8M	37.2G	35.1

slower. By contrast, our method delivers a deployment-friendlier balance between accuracy and efficiency without introducing additional structural complexity.

On VOC2012 valid, the results corroborate the same accuracy–efficiency trend observed on VOC2007. The original DETR achieves AP = 46.5. Under the same pruning ratio $r = 0.4$, L1-Norm causes a substantial accuracy degradation, resulting in a 13.33% relative AP drop to 40.3, along with evident declines in localization-oriented metrics, where AP50 decreases to 59.4 and AP75 decreases to 42.3. In contrast, under the same compression and inference-cost constraints, our method preserves detection performance more effectively, limiting the relative AP drop to 4.30% and achieving an AP of 44.5. Moreover, our method consistently outperforms L1-Norm on both AP50 and AP75, reaching 66.7 and 48.2, respectively, indicating stronger robustness under both coarse matching and high-IoU localization criteria.

4.3 Ablation Study

Table 4 shows the ablation results on the VOC2007 test dataset with a fixed pruning rate of $r = 0.4$. The experiments show that, under the same compression ratio, different pruning strategies can still lead to significant performance differences. Removing role regularization leads to the largest performance degradation, particularly harming small-object detection. Introducing the shared-channel mechanism mitigates the drop to some extent, but the overall improvement is limited. In contrast, our method achieves the best overall performance under the same pruning strength: overall AP is closer to the unpruned baseline; AP75 is nearly unchanged; and small-object performance is largely on par with the baseline. These results suggest that role-regularization–guided channel selection more effectively preserves key discriminative features, thereby improving post-pruning performance stability and scale robustness.

Table 4. Ablation study on different uncertainty-weighted sparsity designs.

Method	AP	AP50	AP75	APs	APM	APL
Unpruned baseline	45.0	69.4	47.5	6.9	28.1	57.4
Uniform L1 ($U = 1$)	41.0	61.7	42.5	6.2	22.0	46.4
Inverse-U ($1 - U$)	41.8	62.3	43.5	7.1	24.2	49.3
Ours (U-weighted)	43.3	65.5	45.3	9.2	26.6	53.5

5 Conclusion

To address the high computational overhead of DETR in deployment and the tendency of conventional magnitude-based pruning to mistakenly remove critical structures and degrade localization under the multi-task constraints of object detection, we propose a role-uncertainty-driven structured pruning method. Our approach introduced an L1 sparsity regularizer weighted by role uncertainty to recalibrate and sparsify prunable structural dimensions, thereby producing a more discriminative distribution of structural importance. Guided by training-time statistics that quantify the respective contributions of classification and localization objectives, we performed structured pruning to obtain a dense, compact model that can be deployed directly and achieves inference acceleration.

Acknowledgments. This work was supported by the Adult Continuing Education Scientific Research Planning Project of the China Adult Education Association (No. 2025-0121Y) and the 2025 Special Open Project for Applied Journals (No. CACJ202508ZZ).

References

1. Carion, N., Massa, F., Synnaeve, G., Usunier, N., Kirillov, A., Zagoruyko, S.: End-to-end object detection with transformers. In: Vedaldi, A., Bischof, H., Brox, T., Frahm, J.-M. (eds.) ECCV 2020. LNCS, vol. 12346, pp. 213–229. Springer, Cham (2020). https://doi.org/10.1007/978-3-030-58452-8_13
2. Filters'Importance, D.: Pruning filters for efficient convnets. arXiv preprint arXiv:1608.08710 (2016)
3. Gai, K., Du, Z.: Efficiency-aware workload optimizations of heterogeneous cloud computing for capacity planning in financial industry. In: IEEE CSCloud (2015)
4. Gai, K., Xu, K., et al.: Fusion of cognitive wireless networks and edge computing. IEEE Wireless Comm. **26**(3), 69–75 (2019)
5. Gai, K.: Proactive attribute-based secure data schema for mobile cloud in financial industry. In: IEEE 17th HPCC (2015)
6. He, K., Zhang, X., Ren, S., Sun, J.: Deep residual learning for image recognition. In: CVPR, pp. 770–778 (2016)
7. He, Y., Zhang, X., Sun, J.: Channel pruning for accelerating very deep neural networks. In: IEEE International Conference on Computer Vision, pp. 1389–1397 (2017)
8. Li, F., Zhang, H.: DN-DETR: accelerate DETR training by introducing query denoising. In: CVPR, pp. 13619–13627 (2022)
9. Liu, Z., Li, J.: Learning efficient convolutional networks through network slimming. In: IEEE International Conference on Computer Vision, pp. 2736–2744 (2017)
10. Michel, P., Levy, O., Neubig, G.: Are sixteen heads really better than one? Adv. Neural Inf. Process. Syst. **32** (2019)
11. Qiu, H., Dong, T., et al.: Adversarial attacks against network intrusion detection in IoT systems. IEEE Internet Things J. **8**(13), 10327–10335 (2020)
12. Qiu, M., Sha, E., et al.: Energy minimization with loop fusion and multi-functional-unit scheduling for multidimensional DSP. JPDC **68**(4), 443–455 (2008)
13. Sun, H., Zhang, S., Tian, X., Zou, Y.: Pruning DETR: efficient end-to-end object detection with sparse structured pruning. Signal Image Video Process. **18**(1), 129–135 (2024)
14. Yao, Z., Ai, J.: Efficient DETR: improving end-to-end object detector with dense prior. arXiv preprint arXiv:2104.01318 (2021)
15. Yu, F., Huang, K., Wang, M., Cheng, Y., Chu, W., Cui, L.: Width & depth pruning for vision transformers. In: AAAI, vol. 36, pp. 3143–3151 (2022)
16. Zeng, Y.: DeepVCM: a deep learning based intrusion detection method in VANET. In: IEEE BigDataSecurity (2019)
17. Zhang, K., et al.: Multimedia layout adaptation through grammatical specifications. Multimedia Syst. **10**(3), 245–260 (2005)
18. Zhao, H., Chen, M., et al.: A novel pre-cache schema for high performance android system. FGCS **56**, 766–772 (2016)
19. Zhao, J., Ding, Z., Zhou, Y., et al.: Orientedformer: an end-to-end transformer-based oriented object detector in remote sensing images. IEEE Trans. Geosci. Remote Sens. (2024)
20. Zhao, Y., Lv, W.: DETRs beat YOLOs on real-time object detection. In: CVPR, pp. 16965–16974 (2024)
21. Zhu, X., Su, W.: Deformable DETR: deformable transformers for end-to-end object detection. arXiv preprint arXiv:2010.04159 (2020)
22. Zhuang, Z., Tan, M.: Discrimination-aware channel pruning for deep neural networks. Adv. Neural Inf. Process. Syst. **31** (2018)

Adaptive Post-hoc Knowledge Consistency for Meteorological Prediction Under Extreme Uncertainty

Tang Huanrong, Li Jian, and Ouyang Jianquan(✉)

Xiangtan University, Xiangtan, Hunan, China
{throng,oyjq}@xtu.edu.cn

Abstract. Meteorological forecasting under extreme uncertainty remains challenging because purely data-driven models often produce unstable and physically implausible predictions in rare and severe weather events. Although physics-informed machine learning (PIML) has been introduced to alleviate this issue, most existing methods incorporate physical constraints directly into model architectures or training objectives, limiting flexibility across heterogeneous forecasting models. To address this problem, we propose the Adaptive Post-hoc Knowledge Consistency (APKC) framework, a lightweight and model-agnostic method that imposes temporal, spatial, and physical consistency directly on model outputs without modifying backbone structures. In addition, APKC employs an adaptive weighting mechanism to adjust constraint strength under different uncertainty levels. Experiments on the ERA5 reanalysis dataset, including extreme-event subsets, show that APKC consistently improves prediction stability, numerical accuracy, and physical plausibility across diverse time-series forecasting models, with negligible or even positive impact under normal conditions.

Keywords: Meteorological prediction · Extreme uncertainty · Knowledge consistency · Adaptive weighting · Physics-informed machine learning

1 Introduction

Accurate meteorological prediction under extreme uncertainty remains a fundamental challenge in atmospheric science and artificial intelligence. Recent advances in deep learning, fueled by large-scale reanalysis datasets such as ERA5, have enabled data-driven forecasting models to achieve remarkable improvements in spatiotemporal accuracy [9]. Large-scale neural weather models, including FourCastNet [13], Pangu-Weather [3], and FuXi-Weather [6], now demonstrate competitive or even superior performance compared to traditional numerical weather prediction (NWP) systems in global medium-range forecasting.

Despite these empirical successes, purely data-driven models often exhibit limited physical plausibility. Without explicit domain knowledge regulation, their

J. Niu et al. (Eds.): KSEM 2026, LNAI 16631, pp. 15–27, 2027.
https://doi.org/10.1007/978-981-92-2759-4_2

predictions can violate fundamental physical principles—such as energy conservation, temporal smoothness, and spatial continuity [17]—particularly in rare extreme events where data sparsity and inherent uncertainty are pronounced. This lack of physical generalization has emerged as a central bottleneck for deploying deep learning in safety-critical scientific applications [11,20].

To mitigate these issues, physics-informed machine learning (PIML) and physics-informed neural networks (PINNs) have gained increasing attention [16]. These approaches integrate physical priors to improve model stability and interpretability, with notable applications in precipitation modeling [19], long-term climate projections [2], and other geophysical domains. However, most existing methods embed physical constraints directly into model architectures or training objectives, limiting their flexibility and applicability across heterogeneous forecasting backbones.

To overcome these limitations, we reformulate meteorological prediction under extreme uncertainty as an adaptive post-hoc knowledge consistency regulation problem. We propose the Adaptive Post-hoc Knowledge Consistency (APKC) framework, which enforces temporal, spatial, and physical consistency directly on model outputs without modifying backbone structures. Through hierarchical coupling and an attention-guided adaptive weighting mechanism, APKC dynamically adjusts constraint strengths according to predictive uncertainty. Unlike existing physics-informed approaches that rely on static training-time constraints, APKC provides a lightweight, model-agnostic, and uncertainty-aware post-hoc solution for improving robustness and physical reliability in extreme weather forecasting.

2 Related Work

2.1 Deep Learning for Meteorological Prediction

Data-driven meteorological forecasting has advanced rapidly with large-scale neural models trained on reanalysis datasets. In addition to global medium-range forecasting, deep learning has been applied to task-specific problems such as visibility nowcasting, ocean surface wind estimation, and river temperature prediction [5,7,14]. These studies demonstrate the potential of deep learning for meteorological applications, but extreme events remain challenging because data sparsity and strong nonlinearity often lead to unstable and physically inconsistent predictions.

2.2 Physics-Informed and Knowledge-Guided Learning

Physics-informed machine learning (PIML) improves physical plausibility by incorporating domain knowledge into deep learning models. Recent studies have introduced constraint-aware forecasting, physics-informed graph neural networks, and physics-guided spatiotemporal modeling [1,10,18]. Although these methods improve interpretability and compliance with physical laws, most rely on static constraint embedding in architectures or training objectives, which limits adaptability under varying uncertainty and reduces compatibility across heterogeneous backbones [12].

2.3 Extreme Weather Prediction Under Uncertainty

Extreme weather prediction is particularly difficult because of long-tailed distributions, distribution shifts, and strong uncertainty. Existing efforts include uncertainty quantification for climate science [8], physics-aware generative modeling [4], and Newton's laws-integrated deep learning for compound flood modeling [15]. However, many existing methods still adopt fixed constraints or static weighting, which often become suboptimal in highly uncertain conditions. This motivates the need for an adaptive and model-agnostic consistency regulation framework.

3 Method

3.1 Problem Formulation and Unified Objective

Meteorological forecasting is formulated as a multivariate time-series prediction problem. Given a historical observation sequence

$$X = \{x_1, x_2, \ldots, x_T\}, \quad x_t \in \mathbb{R}^C, \tag{1}$$

the objective is to predict future meteorological states

$$Y = \{y_{T+1}, y_{T+2}, \ldots, y_{T+K}\}. \tag{2}$$

A forecasting model learns a mapping $f : X \mapsto \hat{Y}$. Conventional deep learning approaches optimize a purely data-driven objective

$$\mathcal{L}_{\text{pred}} = \frac{1}{K} \sum_{k=1}^{K} \|y_{T+k} - \hat{y}_{T+k}\|_2^2, \tag{3}$$

which prioritizes numerical accuracy but does not explicitly encode the spatiotemporal continuity and physical constraints inherent in atmospheric systems. As a result, predictions with low pointwise error may still exhibit non-physical behaviors, particularly under extreme and high-uncertainty conditions.

To address this limitation, we introduce a post-hoc consistency-regularized learning objective that enforces temporal, spatial, and physical coherence directly on model outputs. The overall optimization objective is defined as

$$\mathcal{L} = \mathcal{L}_{\text{pred}} + \lambda_{\text{time}}\mathcal{L}_{\text{time}} + \lambda_{\text{space}}\mathcal{L}_{\text{space}} + \lambda_{\text{phys}}\mathcal{L}_{\text{phys}}, \tag{4}$$

where $\mathcal{L}_{\text{time}}$, $\mathcal{L}_{\text{space}}$, and $\mathcal{L}_{\text{phys}}$ denote temporal, spatial, and physical consistency losses, respectively. The weighting coefficients $\lambda_{\cdot}$ are adaptively scheduled, and the consistency terms are hierarchically coupled to enable synergistic propagation across different constraint layers. The detailed formulations of each constraint and the coupling mechanism are introduced in the following subsections (Fig. 1).

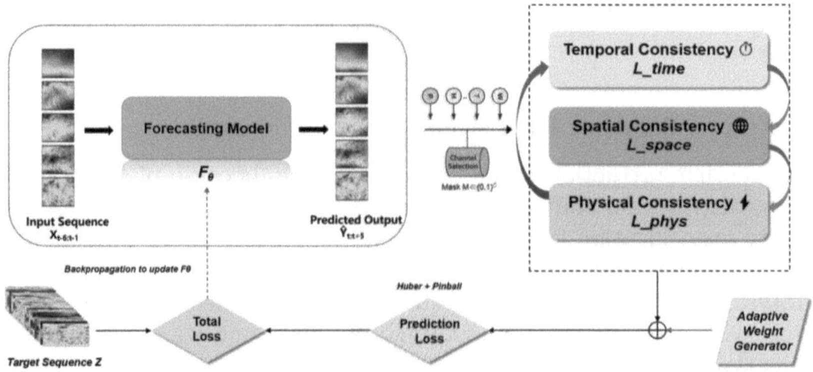

Fig. 1. Overall architecture of the Adaptive Post-hoc Knowledge Consistency (APKC) framework.

3.2 Adaptive Post-hoc Knowledge Consistency Framework Design

The Adaptive Post-hoc Knowledge Consistency (APKC) framework introduces a structured consistency regularization mechanism that jointly constrains temporal continuity, spatial coherence, and physical validity. Instead of treating these constraints as independent penalties, APKC enables adaptive interlayer interactions to guide stable and physically plausible prediction trajectories.

Temporal Consistency. Temporal consistency suppresses non-physical oscillations along the prediction horizon by penalizing abrupt temporal variations:

$$\mathcal{L}_{\text{time}} = \frac{1}{K-1} \sum_{k=1}^{K-1} \|\hat{y}_{T+k+1} - \hat{y}_{T+k}\|_2^2. \tag{5}$$

This constraint enforces temporal smoothness and provides stability cues for subsequent spatial and physical consistency propagation.

Spatial Consistency. Spatial consistency captures local coupling structures in meteorological fields through divergence–vorticity regularization:

$$\mathcal{L}_{\text{space}} = \gamma \|\nabla \cdot \mathbf{u}\|_F^2 + (1-\gamma) \|\nabla \times \mathbf{u}\|_F^2, \tag{6}$$

where $\mathbf{u}$ denotes the wind field, and γ balances mass conservation and rotational smoothness. This formulation suppresses spatial oscillations while remaining physically interpretable.

Physical Consistency. Physical consistency constrains model outputs to satisfy basic thermodynamic and dynamic principles. The overall physical loss is defined as

$$\mathcal{L}_{\text{phys}} = \mathcal{L}_{\text{energy}} + \mathcal{L}_{\text{humidity}} + \mathcal{L}_{\text{wind}} + \mathcal{L}_{\text{ideal}} + \mathcal{L}_{\text{range}}. \tag{7}$$

Specifically,

$$\mathcal{L}_{\text{energy}} = \left\| c_p \frac{\partial \hat{T}}{\partial t} - \hat{Q}_{\text{net}} \right\|_F^2, \tag{8}$$

$$\mathcal{L}_{\text{humidity}} = \left\| \frac{\partial \widehat{RH}}{\partial t} - k(\hat{P} - \hat{E}) \right\|_F^2, \tag{9}$$

$$\mathcal{L}_{\text{wind}} = 2 \left\| \nabla \cdot \mathbf{u} \right\|_F^2 + \left\| \nabla \times \mathbf{u} \right\|_F^2, \tag{10}$$

$$\mathcal{L}_{\text{ideal}} = \left\| \hat{p} - \hat{\rho} R_d \hat{T}(1 + 0.608\hat{q}) \right\|_F^2, \tag{11}$$

$$\mathcal{L}_{\text{range}} = \sum_v \left[\sigma(l_v - v) + \sigma(v - u_v) \right], \tag{12}$$

where $\sigma(z) = \frac{1}{\kappa}\log(1 + e^{\kappa z})$ is a smooth boundary penalty. These differentiable constraints jointly enforce approximate energy balance, moisture continuity, wind conservation, thermodynamic consistency, and physically valid variable ranges (Fig. 2).

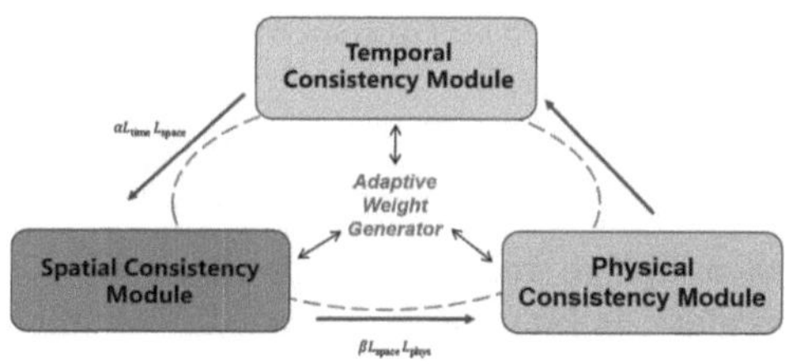

Fig. 2. Hierarchical coupling among temporal, spatial, and physical consistency constraints in APKC.

Interlayer Coupling and Unified Objective. To enable adaptive knowledge flow across consistency layers, APKC introduces interlayer coupling coefficients:

$$\alpha = \tanh\left(\eta \frac{\mathcal{L}_{\text{space}}}{\mathcal{L}_{\text{time}} + \epsilon} \right), \quad \beta = \tanh\left(\eta \frac{\mathcal{L}_{\text{phys}}}{\mathcal{L}_{\text{space}} + \epsilon} \right), \tag{13}$$

where η controls sensitivity and ϵ ensures numerical stability. Larger spatial inconsistencies activate stronger temporal guidance, while increased physical violations enhance spatial feedback.

The overall training objective is formulated as

$$\mathcal{L} = \mathcal{L}_{\text{pred}} + \lambda_{\text{time}}\mathcal{L}_{\text{time}} + \lambda_{\text{space}}(\mathcal{L}_{\text{space}} + \alpha\mathcal{L}_{\text{time}}\mathcal{L}_{\text{space}}) + \lambda_{\text{phys}}(\mathcal{L}_{\text{phys}} + \beta\mathcal{L}_{\text{space}}\mathcal{L}_{\text{phys}}). \tag{14}$$

Through this unified objective, temporal, spatial, and physical constraints form a dynamically coupled consistency flow, enabling adaptive co-evolution of prediction smoothness, structural coherence, and physical plausibility across training stages.

3.3 Attention-Guided Adaptive Weighting Mechanism (AG-APW)

The effectiveness of consistency constraints varies across samples and training stages, particularly under extreme and high-uncertainty conditions. To enable sample-wise adaptive regulation, we introduce an Attention-Guided Adaptive Weighting mechanism (AG-APW), which dynamically schedules consistency strengths based on model uncertainty and prediction difficulty.

Specifically, for each training sample, we construct a compact feature vector:

$$\mathbf{f} = [e, s_{\text{ext}}, g, H_{\text{att}}]^\top, \tag{15}$$

where e denotes prediction error intensity, s_{ext} represents an extremity score based on exceedance statistics, g measures gradient magnitude, and H_{att} is the entropy of the model attention distribution, serving as an uncertainty proxy.

After normalization, $\mathbf{f}$ is fed into a lightweight two-layer perceptron to generate adaptive consistency weights:

$$[\lambda_{\text{time}}, \lambda_{\text{space}}, \lambda_{\text{phys}}]^\top = \sigma\left(W_2 \tanh(W_1\mathbf{f} + b_1) + b_2\right), \tag{16}$$

where $\sigma(\cdot)$ is the sigmoid function. To preserve fundamental physical validity, a minimum lower bound is enforced on λ_{phys}.

The overall training objective is computed as a sample-wise weighted average:

$$\mathcal{L} = \frac{1}{N}\sum_{i=1}^{N}\left(\mathcal{L}_{\text{pred}}^{(i)} + \lambda_{\text{time}}^{(i)}\mathcal{L}_{\text{time}}^{(i)} + \lambda_{\text{space}}^{(i)}\mathcal{L}_{\text{space}}^{(i)} + \lambda_{\text{phys}}^{(i)}\mathcal{L}_{\text{phys}}^{(i)}\right). \tag{17}$$

AG-APW enables adaptive reinforcement of physical and structural constraints in high-uncertainty or extreme samples. Moreover, the generated weights implicitly modulate the interlayer coupling dynamics in APKC, forming a feedback loop between uncertainty perception and consistency regulation.

3.4 Stabilized Training with Soft Constraints

To jointly ensure predictive stability and tail sensitivity, we adopt a Huber–Pinball hybrid loss as the primary prediction objective:

$$\mathcal{L}_{\text{pred}}^{\text{hybrid}} = (1-\tau)\mathcal{L}_{\text{Huber}} + \tau\mathcal{L}_{\text{Pinball}}, \tag{18}$$

where the Huber term mitigates outlier-induced instability, while the Pinball term emphasizes extreme quantile learning.

All consistency constraints are implemented using soft penalty functions:

$$\mathcal{L}_{\text{soft}} = \frac{1}{\kappa}\log\left(1 + e^{\kappa(v-\text{bound})}\right), \tag{19}$$

ensuring smooth gradients near constraint boundaries.

During training, consistency weights are gradually increased from small initial values, allowing the model to first learn stable representations before progressively enforcing stronger physical and structural regularization. This strategy ensures that adaptive consistency regulation does not destabilize early-stage representation learning (Fig. 3).

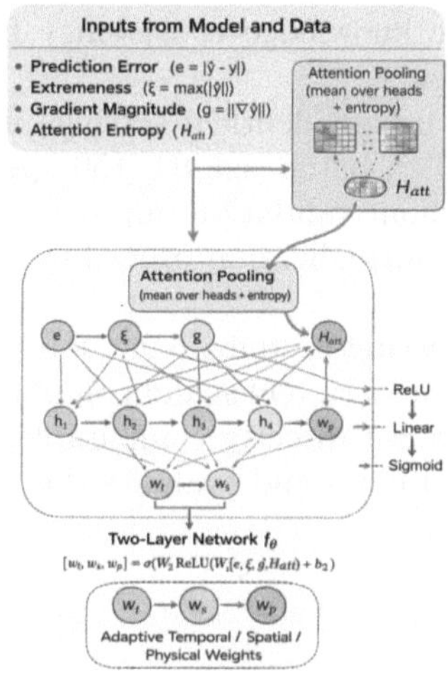

Fig. 3. Attention-guided adaptive weighting (AG-APW) for sample-wise consistency scheduling.

4 Experimental Setup

4.1 Datasets and Preprocessing

We evaluate the proposed APKC framework under three scenarios with increasing data scale and uncertainty: **WS-Beutenberg**, hourly in-situ observations from the Beutenberg station, Jena, Germany (2017–2022), including temperature, dew point, relative humidity, pressure, 10 m wind, precipitation, and radiation (20 variables), representing sparse and noisy real-world conditions; **ERA5-Std**, hourly ERA5 reanalysis data ($0.25° \times 0.25°$) over central Germany (48°–52°N, 8°–12°E), covering 2 m temperature, dew point, 10 m wind, surface pressure, total precipitation, and net radiation, with sliding windows of 96 h input and 24 h output; and **ERA5-Ext**, an extreme-event subset extracted from ERA5-Std (2018–2022), consisting of samples exceeding the 95th percentile of temperature anomalies or precipitation.

All datasets are unified to a 0.25° resolution using inverse distance weighting (IDW). ERA5-Ext is further categorized by event type (e.g., heavy precipitation and heat extremes) based on seasonal percentile thresholds. Identical input/output variables, temporal resolutions, and per-variable z-score normalization are applied across datasets to ensure fair comparison.

4.2 Models and Experimental Configuration

To assess cross-model generality, five representative time-series backbones are selected: Transformer, PatchTST, TimesNet, Autoformer, and LSTM.

We evaluate three variants for each backbone: **Baseline**, which minimizes prediction error without consistency constraints; **APKC-Fix**, which uses three-layer consistency constraints with fixed weights; and **APKC + AG-APW**, the proposed adaptive post-hoc knowledge consistency framework with attention-guided adaptive weighting.

All models are trained under identical settings using the Adam optimizer (initial learning rate 1×10^{-3}, batch size 64, 150 epochs). The learning rate is halved after five epochs without validation improvement. Input/output lengths, data slicing strategies, and normalization procedures are kept consistent across all experiments.

Large-scale global forecasting systems (e.g., Pangu-Weather or GraphCast) require substantially different data scales and computational resources. As their experimental conditions are not directly comparable, we focus on reproducible time-series architectures to isolate and evaluate the proposed consistency regulation mechanisms.

4.3 Evaluation Metrics

Performance is evaluated from two complementary perspectives: prediction accuracy and physical compliance.

Prediction Accuracy. We report root mean square error (RMSE) and mean absolute error (MAE).

Physical Compliance. We report physical violation rate (PVR), equivalent physical reliability (EPR), energy smoothness (ES), spatial divergence (SD), the dynamic responses of α and β, and attention entropy.

Statistical significance is assessed using paired t-tests ($\alpha = 0.05$). Improvements in PVR and EPR consistently achieve $p < 0.01$ with large effect sizes, indicating robust gains beyond random variation.

5 Results and Discussion

To provide an intuitive and comprehensive evaluation of the proposed Adaptive Post-hoc Knowledge Consistency (APKC) framework, we first visualize the distributional behavior of model predictions under extreme weather conditions. Figure 4 compares the normalized distributions of predicted variables against the ground truth on the ERA5-Ext subset.

Compared with the baseline models, APKC better captures the true heavy-tail distributions in high-impact regions, alleviating the underestimation and truncation effects commonly observed in extreme-event forecasting.

5.1 Overall Performance Comparison

Table 1 summarizes the overall performance of different backbone architectures under three configurations: Baseline, fixed-weight consistency (APKC-Fix), and the full APKC framework.

Across all backbones and datasets, APKC consistently reduces physical violation rate (PVR) while maintaining comparable or improved numerical accuracy.

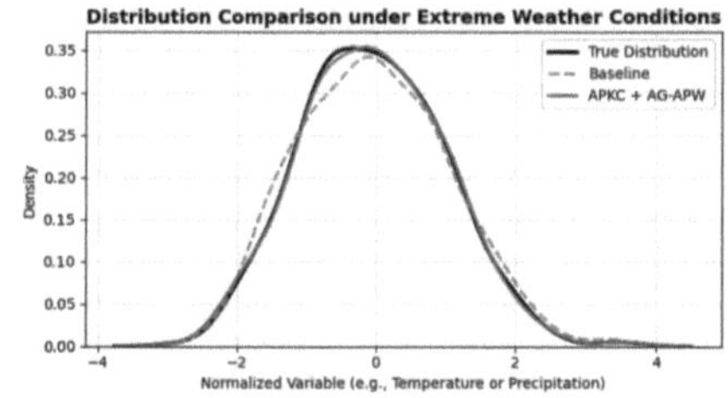

Fig. 4. Distribution comparison under extreme weather conditions.

The gains are especially evident for Transformer and LSTM, indicating that APKC effectively compensates for weaker intrinsic inductive biases. More structured models such as PatchTST and TimesNet also show consistent improvements, suggesting that APKC complements existing temporal modeling capabilities rather than overriding them (Table 2).

Table 1. Overall performance comparison of Baseline, APKC-Fix, and full APKC frameworks.

Backbone	Variant	WS MAE↓	Std MAE↓	Ext PVR↓ (%)	Avg EPR↑	Avg Impr (%)
PatchTST	Baseline	0.073	0.085	3.20	0.983	
PatchTST	APKC-Fix	0.077	0.077	2.10	1.000	+1.7
PatchTST	APKC+AG-APW	**0.073**	**0.076**	**0.50**	**1.005**	**+2.2**
Transformer	Baseline	0.127	0.100	18.70	0.513	
Transformer	APKC-Fix	0.136	0.138	12.30	0.642	+25.1
Transformer	APKC+AG-APW	**0.124**	**0.099**	**4.20**	**0.765**	**+49.1**
TimesNet	Baseline	0.047	0.048	4.20	0.922	
TimesNet	APKC-Fix	0.050	0.052	2.80	0.953	+3.4
TimesNet	APKC+AG-APW	**0.046**	**0.046**	**0.45**	**0.988**	**+7.2**
Autoformer	Baseline	0.367	0.303	15.30	0.787	
Autoformer	APKC-Fix	0.303	0.256	10.70	0.834	+6.0
Autoformer	APKC+AG-APW	**0.275**	**0.248**	**3.80**	**0.875**	**+11.2**
LSTM	Baseline	0.108	0.116	11.60	0.598	
LSTM	APKC-Fix	0.070	0.090	7.80	0.765	+27.9
LSTM	APKC+AG-APW	**0.069**	**0.085**	**1.80**	**0.825**	**+38.0**

Results on the ERA5-Ext subset further highlight the robustness of APKC under highly nonlinear and uncertainty-dominated regimes. Compared with both the baseline and fixed-weight variants, APKC achieves the lowest PVR and the highest EPR across all backbones. Relative improvements range from +7.2% to +49.1%, and PVR reductions exceed 75% in several cases, confirming the advantage of adaptive post-hoc consistency regulation under highly uncertain regimes.

5.2 Dynamic Evolution of Coupling Coefficients

Figure 5 shows the dynamic evolution of α and β. The coefficient α increases rapidly at early stages to stabilize spatiotemporal alignment, whereas β grows more gradually and dominates later, supporting the intended co-evolution mechanism of APKC.

Table 2. Performance of APKC and baselines under extreme weather conditions (ERA5-Ext).

Backbone Model	Model Variant	RMSE↓	PVR(%)↓	EPR↑	ES↓	SD↓	Rel. Impr. vs Baseline (%)
PatchTST	Baseline	0.1685	3.20	0.9125	0.1736	0.0412	
PatchTST	APKC-Fix	0.1562	2.10	0.9418	0.1628	0.0365	+3.1
PatchTST	APKC+AG-APW	**0.1480**	**0.50**	**0.9820**	**0.1450**	**0.0302**	**+7.6**
Transformer	Baseline	0.2156	18.70	0.5132	0.2085	0.0526	
Transformer	APKC-Fix	0.2483	12.30	0.6415	0.1967	0.0478	+25.1
Transformer	APKC+AG-APW	**0.2080**	**4.20**	**0.7650**	**0.1720**	**0.0385**	**+49.1**
TimesNet	Baseline	0.1083	4.20	0.9216	0.1765	0.0289	
TimesNet	APKC-Fix	0.1148	2.80	0.9532	0.1689	0.0257	+3.4
TimesNet	APKC+AG-APW	**0.1035**	**0.45**	**0.9880**	**0.1520**	**0.0210**	**+7.2**
Autoformer	Baseline	0.6847	15.30	0.7865	0.1124	0.0638	
Autoformer	APKC-Fix	0.6185	10.70	0.8342	0.0986	0.0574	+6.0
Autoformer	APKC+AG-APW	**0.5980**	**3.80**	**0.8750**	**0.0820**	**0.0485**	**+11.2**
LSTM	Baseline	0.2789	11.60	0.5983	0.1542	0.0463	
LSTM	APKC-Fix	0.2364	7.80	0.7645	0.1428	0.0417	+27.9
LSTM	APKC+AG-APW	**0.2200**	**1.80**	**0.8250**	**0.1280**	**0.0355**	**+38.0**

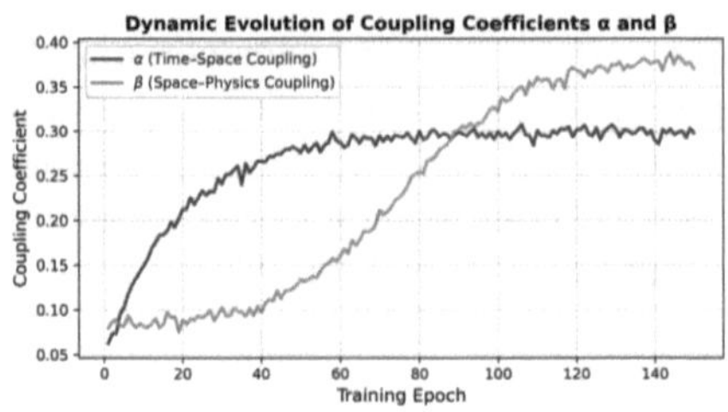

Fig. 5. Dynamic evolution of coupling coefficients α and β in APKC.

5.3 Attention Entropy and Adaptive Weighting Response

Figure 6 shows that regions with higher uncertainty receive stronger physical regulation, whereas low-uncertainty regions are only weakly constrained. This confirms that APKC enhances physical consistency in a targeted rather than uniformly aggressive manner.

5.4 Ablation Study

Table 3 evaluates the contribution of temporal (T), spatial (S), and physical (P) consistency components. Removing any single layer degrades performance, while the full APKC configuration consistently achieves optimal results across all backbones. This confirms that the three consistency layers are complementary and jointly necessary.

Overall, the results demonstrate that APKC significantly enhances physical plausibility while preserving numerical accuracy, with particularly strong advantages under extreme and uncertainty-dominated conditions.

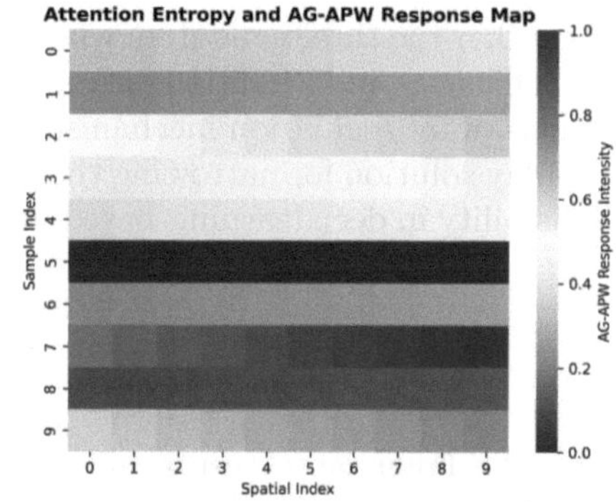

Fig. 6. Attention entropy and adaptive physical weighting response in APKC.

Table 3. Ablation results of temporal, spatial, and physical consistency components in APKC.

Model Family	Variant	Weight (T/S/P)	Pred. Acc.		Phys. Compl.			Effect.
			MAE↓	RMSE↓	EPR↑	Cons.Err↓	EPR_ext↑	
PatchTST	Baseline	0.0/0.0/0.0	0.1045	0.1864	0.9259	0.1881	0.7778	
	NoTime (No T)	0.0/1.0/1.0	0.0920	0.1480	0.9500	0.1720	0.8800	Eff.
	NoSpace (No S)	1.0/0.0/1.0	0.0950	0.1520	0.9300	0.1780	0.8200	Eff.
	NoPhys (No P)	1.0/1.0/0.0	0.0980	0.1580	0.8000	0.1900	0.7000	Part.
	Full (Ours)	1.0/1.0/1.0	**0.0850**	**0.1350**	**0.9800**	**0.1580**	**0.9500**	Opt.
Transformer	Baseline	0.0/0.0/0.0	0.1413	0.2149	0.6667	0.0939	0.0000	
	NoTime (No T)	0.0/1.0/1.0	0.1450	0.2200	0.6800	0.1300	0.0500	Ineff.
	NoSpace (No S)	1.0/0.0/1.0	0.1500	0.2300	0.6700	0.1500	0.0000	Ineff.
	NoPhys (No P)	1.0/1.0/0.0	0.1420	0.2150	0.6900	0.1400	0.0000	Ineff.
	Full (Ours)	1.0/1.0/1.0	**0.1300**	**0.2000**	**0.7200**	**0.1100**	**0.1500**	Opt.
TimesNet	Baseline	0.0/0.0/0.0	0.0415	0.0824	1.0000	0.1566	1.0000	
	NoTime (No T)	0.0/1.0/1.0	0.0420	0.0850	1.0000	0.1500	1.0000	Eff.
	NoSpace (No S)	1.0/0.0/1.0	0.0430	0.0870	1.0000	0.1520	1.0000	Eff.
	NoPhys (No P)	1.0/1.0/0.0	0.0500	0.0950	1.0000	0.1600	1.0000	Part.
	Full (Ours)	1.0/1.0/1.0	**0.0400**	**0.0780**	1.0000	**0.1450**	1.0000	Opt.
Autoformer	Baseline	0.0/0.0/0.0	0.3403	0.6530	0.6667	0.0709	0.0000	
	NoTime (No T)	0.0/1.0/1.0	0.3100	0.5900	0.7000	0.0900	0.1000	Part.
	NoSpace (No S)	1.0/0.0/1.0	0.3300	0.6300	0.6800	0.0800	0.0500	Ineff.
	NoPhys (No P)	1.0/1.0/0.0	0.3200	0.6100	0.6900	0.0950	0.0000	Ineff.
	Full (Ours)	1.0/1.0/1.0	**0.2900**	**0.5600**	**0.7800**	**0.1000**	**0.3000**	Opt.
LSTM	Baseline	0.0/0.0/0.0	0.0721	0.1280	0.7037	0.1455	0.1111	
	NoTime (No T)	0.0/1.0/1.0	0.0700	0.1200	0.7300	0.1400	0.1500	Eff.
	NoSpace (No S)	1.0/0.0/1.0	0.0710	0.1220	0.7200	0.1420	0.1300	Eff.
	NoPhys (No P)	1.0/1.0/0.0	0.0730	0.1250	0.7100	0.1480	0.1000	Part.
	Full (Ours)	1.0/1.0/1.0	**0.0680**	**0.1150**	**0.7500**	**0.1380**	**0.1800**	Opt.

6 Conclusion

We proposed the Adaptive Post-hoc Knowledge Consistency (APKC) framework, a lightweight and model-agnostic method for mitigating non-physical behaviors in deep meteorological forecasting models. APKC jointly enforces temporal, spatial, and physical consistency through a hierarchical coupled formulation and an attention-guided adaptive weighting mechanism.

Experiments across multiple time-series backbones and heterogeneous datasets show that APKC substantially reduces physical violation rates, especially under extreme regimes, while consistently improving equivalent physical reliability and maintaining comparable or improved numerical accuracy. The gains are particularly evident for architectures with weaker intrinsic inductive biases, such as Transformer and LSTM.

Ablation studies confirm that the three consistency layers are complementary, and analyses of coupling coefficients and attention entropy support the proposed co-evolution and uncertainty-aware regulation mechanisms. Overall, APKC provides a practical plug-and-play solution for narrowing the gap between predictive accuracy and physical plausibility in deep learning-based meteorological forecasting.

References

1. Ahmed, A., Mahboob, M.: Potential of using physics with artificial intelligence: physics-infused machine learning and neural networks for spatiotemporal analysis of hydro-climatic events. In: Rahman, M.R., Rahman, A., Saha, S.K. (eds.) Advanced GIScience in Hydro-Geological Hazards. GIScience and Geo-environmental Modelling, pp. 59–71. Springer, Cham (2025). https://doi.org/10.1007/978-3-031-76189-8_3
2. Beucler, T., Pritchard, M., Rasp, S., Ott, J., Baldi, P., Gentine, P.: Enforcing analytic constraints in neural networks emulating physical systems. Phys. Rev. Lett. **126**(9), 098302 (2021)
3. Bi, K., Xie, L., Zhang, H., Chen, X., Gu, X., Tian, Q.: Pangu-weather: a 3D high-resolution model for fast and accurate global weather forecast. arXiv preprint arXiv:2211.02556 (2022)
4. Bihlo, A.: A generative adversarial network approach to (ensemble) weather prediction. Neural Netw. **139**, 1–16 (2021)
5. Castillo, M.C.: Physics-informed lightweight machine learning for aviation visibility nowcasting across multiple climatic regimes. arXiv preprint arXiv:2512.16967 (2025)
6. Chen, L., et al.: Fuxi: a cascade machine learning forecasting system for 15-day global weather forecast. NPJ Clim. Atmos. Sci. **6**(1), 190 (2023)
7. Figueredo, M.B., de Jesus Ferreira, M., Monteiro, R.L.S., do Nascimento Silva, A., Murari, T.B., et al.: Hybrid PINN-LSTM model for river temperature prediction: a physics-informed deep learning approach. J. Comput. Commun. **13**(6), 115–134 (2025)
8. Gneiting, T., Katzfuss, M.: Probabilistic forecasting. Annu. Rev. Stat. Appl. **1**(1), 125–151 (2014)
9. Hersbach, H., et al.: The era5 global reanalysis. Q. J. R. Meteorol. Soc. **146**(730), 1999–2049 (2020)
10. Inam, S.A., Hashim, H., Ashraf, S.N., Naim, S.W., Rajput, H., Umer, S.: Ai-driven physics informed neural network for daily temperature forecasting with constraint aware learning and explainable feature attribution. VFAST Trans. Softw. Eng. **13**(4), 53–67 (2025)
11. Karniadakis, G., Kevrekidis, I., Lu, L., Perdikaris, P., Wang, S., Yang, L.: Physics-informed machine learning: nature reviews physics (2021)
12. Kashinath, K., et al.: Physics-informed machine learning: case studies for weather and climate modelling. Phil. Trans. R. Soc. A **379**(2194), 20200093 (2021)
13. Pathak, J., et al.: FourCastNet: a global data-driven high-resolution weather model using adaptive fourier neural operators. arXiv preprint arXiv:2202.11214 (2022)
14. Qiao, X., Yan, Q., Huang, W.: Hybrid CNN-transformer network with a weighted MSE loss for global sea surface wind speed retrieval from GNSS-R data. IEEE Trans. Geosci. Remote Sens. (2025)

15. Radfar, S.: Integrating newton's laws with deep learning for enhanced physics-informed compound flood modelling. arXiv:2507.15021 (2025)
16. Raissi, M., Perdikaris, P., Karniadakis, G.E.: Physics-informed neural networks: a deep learning framework for solving forward and inverse problems involving non-linear partial differential equations. J. Comput. Phys. **378**, 686–707 (2019)
17. Reichstein, M., et al.: Deep learning and process understanding for data-driven earth system science. Nature **566**(7743), 195–204 (2019)
18. Taghizadeh, M., Zandsalimi, Z., Nabian, M.A., Shafiee-Jood, M., Alemazkoor, N.: Interpretable physics-informed graph neural networks for flood forecasting. Comput.-Aided Civ. Infrastruct. Eng. (2025)
19. Teufel, B., et al.: Physics-informed deep learning framework to model intense precipitation events at super resolution. Geosci. Lett. **10**(1), 19 (2023)
20. Willard, J., Jia, X., Xu, S., Steinbach, M., Kumar, V.: Integrating physics-based modeling with machine learning: a survey. arXiv preprint arXiv:2003.04919, vol. 1, no. 1, pp. 1–34 (2020)

DynGS-Pro: Dynamic Scene Rendering Using Progressive Gaussian Splatting and Deformation Fields

Iqra Asghar[1], Sara Ali[2(✉)], Muhammad Sohaib Younis[1], Aqib Pervaiz[3], and Muhammad Baber Sial[4(✉)]

[1] National University of Sciences and Technology (NUST), Islamabad, Pakistan
muhammad.sohaib@smme.nust.edu.pk

[2] Suzhou Industrial Park Monash Research Institute of Science and Technology, Suzhou 215000, People's Republic of China
sara.sial@monash.edu

[3] College of Electrical and Mechanical Engineering (EME), National University of Sciences and Technology (NUST), Islamabad 44000, Pakistan

[4] School of Automation Science and Electrical Engineering, Beihang University, Beijing 100191, China
babersial@buaa.edu.cn

Abstract. Dynamic 3D scene reconstruction for real-time rendering is a challenging problem at the intersection of computer vision and graphics. Traditional neural radiance field approaches can model static scenes with high fidelity but struggle with dynamic content performance in real-time. Recent advances in 3D Gaussian splatting have enabled fast rendering of static scenes by employing probabilistic primitives to represent 3D point clouds, offering a balance between computational efficiency and visual quality. In this paper, we present DynGS-Pro, a novel framework that extends Gaussian splatting to dynamic scenes by integrating progressive Gaussian densification with learned deformation fields. Our approach maintains temporal coherence by smoothly propagating and updating Gaussian primitives over time, rather than re-estimating them independently per frame. A lightweight deformation field network drives non-rigid motions of the progressive-Gaussians, ensuring the model can capture complex motion while preserving scene structure. We demonstrate on both synthetic benchmarks and real-world multi-view datasets that DynGS-Pro achieves state-of-the-art reconstruction quality, improving PSNR by up to 12% and reducing loss compared to prior methods while rendering at real-time rates. The results confirm that bridging explicit progressive scene updates with deformation fields provides an effective solution for high-fidelity, real-time dynamic scene rendering.

Keywords: Dynamic Scenes · Neural Rendering · Gaussian Splatting · Temporal Coherence · Real-Time Rendering · Deformation Fields

J. Niu et al. (Eds.): KSEM 2026, LNAI 16631, pp. 28–39, 2027.
https://doi.org/10.1007/978-981-92-2759-4_3

1 Introduction

Real-time rendering of dynamic 3D scenes is crucial for interactive applications in augmented/virtual reality and robotics, yet remains challenging due to the need to capture both *geometric detail* and *temporal coherence* under motion. While Neural Radiance Fields (NeRF) [18] have revolutionized static scene capture, they typically require lengthy per-scene optimization and struggle with moving objects. Recent neural methods for dynamic scenes (e.g., D-NeRF [21], HyperNeRF [20]) handle moderate motions by learning deformation fields, but they incur hours of training and cannot render in real time due to their implicit volumetric representations. In contrast, explicit point-based representations have shown promise for speed: 3D Gaussian Splatting (3DGS) represents a scene as a set of elliptical Gaussians splatted onto the image plane, achieving real-time rendering (5090 FPS) for static scenes with competitive quality [15].

In this work, we propose Dynamic Gaussian Splatting with Progressive Refinement (DynGS-Pro), a method that bridges the gap between fast static renderers [15] and dynamic scene representations. Our key insight is to integrate a GaussianPro technique: Progressive Gaussian propagation, [9] a strategy for continually densifying and refining the set of Gaussians, as more of the scene becomes visible with Learned 4D deformation fields, a compact neural model that displaces each Gaussian in space-time to account for motion [10,26]. By *propagating existing Gaussians forward in time* (instead of re-initializing each frame) and applying smooth deformations, DynGS-Pro maintains a persistent scene model that updates gradually, thereby enforcing temporal coherence. Deformation fields alone fail at severe disocclusions because they cannot create geometry out of nowhere. Gaussian growth alone fails at continuous motion because spawning new points for every moving frame causes a memory explosion. Our method requires both: growth handles new geometry, and deformation handles continuous tracking.

A central challenge in dynamic view synthesis is the fundamental tension between topological evolution and temporal consistency. Previous approaches treat these as mutually exclusive: methods either optimize a fixed set of moving primitives (which fails at disocclusions) or independently optimize primitives per frame (which destroys temporal smoothness). A naive hybridization, simply adding new points into a continuous deformation field, disrupts temporal gradients and leads to severe ghosting. The core algorithmic insight of DynGS-Pro is a joint-optimization framework that allows a discrete point cloud to structurally evolve (via progressive densification) without breaking the continuous mathematical flow of the 4D deformation field. This enables the scene representation to dynamically 'grow' into newly revealed regions while perfectly maintaining smooth, jitter-free trajectories for existing geometry.

1.1 Contributions

Our main contributions are:

- **Dynamic Gaussian Splatting Framework:** We propose DynGS-Pro, a dynamic Gaussian splatting framework that combines explicit, densified Gaussians with a learned 4D deformation field, bridging the gap between fast static point-based renderers and slower dynamic radiance fields.
- **Progressive, Temporally Coherent Updates:** We introduce a progressive propagation scheme that carries Gaussians forward in time, adding or adjusting primitives only when new surfaces are revealed or move, which mitigates flicker and jitter common in per-frame or dynamic NeRF-style reconstructions.
- **Compact Deformation Representation:** We use a HexPlane-based voxel deformation field [4] to encode complex non-rigid motion efficiently, enabling accurate tracking of dynamic content without the cost of dense 4D grids or large networks.
- **State-of-the-Art Performance:** DynGS-Pro attains higher PSNR (by 1.5 dB) and better perceptual quality than recent dynamic methods such as 4DGS [26], HyperNeRF [20], and time-aware voxel grids [10], while maintaining interactive rendering speeds on commodity GPUs.

Novelty and Impact: DynGS-Pro shows that coupling *explicit* Gaussian primitives with *learned* deformations is a powerful recipe for dynamic scene reconstruction, extending static 3DGS-style representations to time-varying settings. A key novelty is our progressive, data-driven temporal update strategy: the Gaussian set grows and adapts over time rather than being fixed per frame, yielding strong temporal coherence and the ability to capture newly visible content. Because Gaussians persist and are smoothly deformed rather than reinitialized, DynGS-Pro naturally produces temporally stable renderings, suggesting a promising direction for future explicit dynamic models.

The remainder of this paper is structured as follows. Section 2 reviews prior work on dynamic scene rendering. Section 3 presents the DynGS-Pro pipeline, including progressive Gaussian propagation and the deformation field. Section 4 outlines our experimental setup, and Sect. 5 reports quantitative and qualitative results. Section 6 concludes with a summary and future directions.

2 Related Work

Neural Rendering of Dynamic Scenes: Dynamic NeRF variants extend radiance fields with time and deformation. D-NeRF [21] warps a canonical field with a learned deformation, and HyperNeRF [20] embeds time in a higher-dimensional space to handle topology changes. These implicit volumetric models capture non-rigid motion but are computationally heavy, with slow training and rendering, and their latent scene representation is difficult to edit [7]. Efficiency-focused methods such as NeRFPlayer [24] reduce runtime at some cost in quality, while NeRF-to-splat hybrids [14] explore bridges between implicit and explicit representations.

3D Gaussian Splatting (Static): Gaussian splatting replaces implicit fields with explicit 3D Gaussians parameterized by position, anisotropic covariance, color, and opacity. Kerbl *et al.* [15] showed that $\sim 10^5$ Gaussians can match NeRF quality for static scenes while rendering in milliseconds. Recent surveys summarize advances and open challenges in this line of work [3], but standard 3DGS is inherently static.

Progressive Refinement of Point-Based Representations: High-quality Gaussian sets often start from sparse SfM points. GaussianPro [9] progressively *propagates* Gaussians into under-reconstructed regions, turning a coarse model into a dense one. We adopt this idea of progressive densification but extend it to dynamic settings, updating the Gaussian set over time as new surfaces become visible.

Dynamic Gaussian Splatting and Fast Dynamic Representations: 4DGS uses a time-conditioned deformation network to move Gaussians per frame, achieving real-time rendering on dynamic scenes. SuperPoint Gaussian Splatting [25] clusters Gaussians into groups to support fast updates, and other works further explore dynamic Gaussian-based modeling [13,17,23]. Complementary explicit grid methods, such as TiNeuVox (time-aware neural voxels) [10], use 4D voxel features or latent codes to accelerate dynamic radiance fields. Recently, the decoupling of spatial and temporal patterns [16] has also been introduced to achieve better reconstruction and consistency.

3 Methodology

3.1 Pipeline Overview

DynGS-Pro represents a dynamic scene as a time-varying set of Gaussian primitives that are optimized to reproduce calibrated multi-view video frames over time. We first obtain a sparse 3D point cloud from SfM [22] and convert it into an initial Gaussian set S with parameters $(\mu_i, \Sigma_i, c_i, \alpha_i)$. These Gaussians are differentiably rasterized to depth and normal maps, and a patch-based propagation scheme identifies under-reconstructed regions. New Gaussians S_p are created by back-projecting unmatched patches, and the union $S \cup S_p$ is iteratively refined, following the progressive densification strategy of GaussianPro [9] as described in Fig. 1.

Motion is then modeled by a deformation field F_Θ defined in a canonical frame. For each Gaussian with canonical position $\mu_i^{(0)}$, the field predicts a time-dependent offset $\Delta\mu_i(t)$ so that $\mu_i(t) = \mu_i^{(0)} + \Delta\mu_i(t)$. F_Θ is implemented using a HexPlane-style 4D voxel grid [4,10,26]: an encoder H interpolates features at the Gaussian's spatial coordinates and time [5,6], and a lightweight MLP decoder maps these features to position (and optionally covariance) updates. At each time step, the deformed Gaussians are splatted to the image plane with standard 3D Gaussian accumulation, yielding a fully differentiable, GPU-friendly renderer.

3.2 Rendering and Optimization

DynGS-Pro is trained by minimizing a combination of reconstruction and regularization terms. For each frame t and camera view, we render the scene and

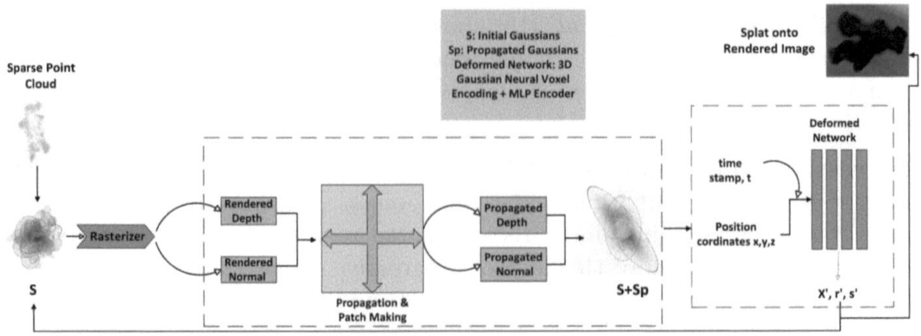

Fig. 1. Overview of the DynGS-Pro; The pipeline begins with the initial Gaussian scene, followed by a rasterization stage to render depth and normal maps. These are then processed through a propagation and patch-making module, producing propagated depth and normal outputs. A deformed Gaussian network (comprising 3D Gaussian neural voxel encoding and an MLP decoder) updates the Gaussian representation. Finally, the refined Gaussians are rendered to generate the final output image with enhanced geometric and texture fidelity.

optimize an L1 loss together with SSIM and LPIPS to encourage structural and perceptual fidelity. The full objective is

$$\mathcal{L} = \mathcal{L}_{\text{L1}} + \lambda_s \mathcal{L}_{(1-\text{SSIM})} + \lambda_p \mathcal{L}_{\text{LPIPS}} + \lambda_t \mathcal{L}_{\text{temp}}, \tag{1}$$

where λ_s=0.1, λ_p=0.01, and λ_t=0.1. Temporal smoothness is encouraged via

$$\mathcal{L}_{\text{temp}} = \sum_i \|\Delta\mu_i(t) - \Delta\mu_i(t-1)\|^2, \tag{2}$$

which discourages abrupt motion changes, and can additionally push static Gaussians toward $\Delta\mu_i(t) \approx 0$ [1].

Both Gaussian parameters and the deformation field are optimized jointly using gradient descent. The complete joint-optimization process is summarized in Algorithm 1 We employ a differentiable Gaussian splatting renderer that accumulates per-Gaussian contributions at each pixel to generate the final synthesized image [12]. Although the model is trained on discrete frames, the deformation field naturally supports continuous time: any intermediate t can be queried to obtain interpolated motion [4,8,20]. This enables flexible temporal sampling, such as slow-motion playback or frame interpolation.

3.3 Gaussian Initialization and Progressive Densification

We initialize Gaussians from an input point cloud or depth map of the first frame [2]. Each point yields a Gaussian centered at that location. The algorithm is: render the current Gaussian model to each training view to get depth and normal maps [9]. For each view, perform patch matching with neighboring views to find

Algorithm 1. DynGS-Pro Optimization Pipeline

Input: Multi-view video sequence, Sparse Point Cloud
Output: Optimized Gaussian set $\mathcal{S}$, Trained Deformed Network
Initialize Gaussian set S from Sparse Point Cloud
for *step* $= 1$ to N_{iters} **do**
    Sample frame at time stamp t and camera view v
    // **1. Rasterization and Propagation Phase**
    Pass S through Rasterizer to extract Rendered Depth and Rendered Normal
    if propagation condition met (e.g., *step* (mod 50) == 0) **then**
        Pass through Propagation & Patch Making module
        Generate Propagated Depth and Propagated Normal
        Create new Gaussians S_p and update set: $S \leftarrow S \cup S_p$
    end if
    // **2. Deformation Phase**
    for each Gaussian in S **do**
        Extract Position coordinates x, y, z and time stamp t
        Pass into Deformed Network (Neural Voxel Encoding + MLP)
        Predict updated parameters: X', r', s'
        Apply spatial and geometric updates to the Gaussian
    end for
    // **3. Rendering and Optimization Phase**
    Splat the deformed Gaussians onto the Rendered Image
    Compute unified loss (Eq. 1) combining L1, SSIM, LPIPS, and temporal warping
    Backpropagate and update Gaussian parameters and Deformed Network weights
end for

regions that lack consistent depth support. For each such region, back-project the patch's center to 3D using the depth from the other view or using multiple views triangulation, and create a new Gaussian at that location. We give new Gaussians a small initial size and infer their color from the images. After adding these Gaussians, we re-render and repeat if necessary. The result of this stage is a much denser Gaussian set that covers the scene surfaces thoroughly. This serves as a strong foundation for subsequent deformation learning.

3.4 Deformation Fields for Motion

To model motion over time, we use a deformation field $F_\Theta(\mathbf{x}, t)$ that maps a canonical 3D point $\mathbf{x}$ at time t to a displacement $\Delta\mathbf{x}$. In DynGS-Pro, F_Θ is implemented as a HexPlane-style latent grid with a small MLP decoder [4,10]. We maintain feature grids on dynamic planes XY–T, YZ–T, XZ–T and static planes XY, YZ, XZ. For a Gaussian at $\mu_i = (x, y, z)$ and time t, we sample features from these planes, concatenate them into $f_{i,t}$, and feed $f_{i,t}$ to the MLP to predict $\Delta\mu_i(t)$ (and optionally opacity changes $\Delta\alpha_i(t)$).

The canonical position of each Gaussian is then updated by the time-dependent offset:

$$\mu_i(t) = \mu_i + \Delta\mu_i(t) = \mu_i + F_\Theta(\mu_i, t), \tag{3}$$

and the MLP further outputs rotation and scale updates,

$$(\Delta\mu_i(t), \Delta r_i(t), \Delta s_i(t), \Delta\alpha_i(t)) = \text{MLP}(f_{i,t}), \tag{4}$$

where $\Delta r_i(t)$, $\Delta s_i(t)$, and $\Delta\alpha_i(t)$ control time-varying orientation, size, and opacity. This compact parameterization allows each Gaussian to follow complex, smooth trajectories in response to scene dynamics.

Table 1. Quantitative comparison of D-NeRF's [21] dynamic scene rendering methods. Arrows indicate the direction of better performance.

Method	SSIM ↑	PSNR ↑ (dB)	LPIPS ↓	Storage ↓ (MB)	Time ↓ (min)	FPS ↑
D-NeRF [21]	0.9761	31.14	0.0464	—	52	0.97
K-planes [11]	0.9699	31.41	0.0470	418	52	0.97
3DGS [15]	0.9293	23.39	0.0867	10	10	170
TiNeuVox-B [10]	0.9700	32.67	0.0400	48	28	1.5
4DGS [26]	0.9841	35.31	**0.0148**	18	20	82
SPGS [25]	0.9876	37.98	0.0185	—	—	227
DynGS-Pro (Ours)	**0.9908**	**39.67**	0.015	39	19.25	83.6

Table 2. Qualitative comparison on Mutant and Lego datasets. Each image shows a full view and zoom-in. Our method recovers more detail.

Dataset	Ground Truth	Ours	4DGS	K-Planes	3DGS
Mutant	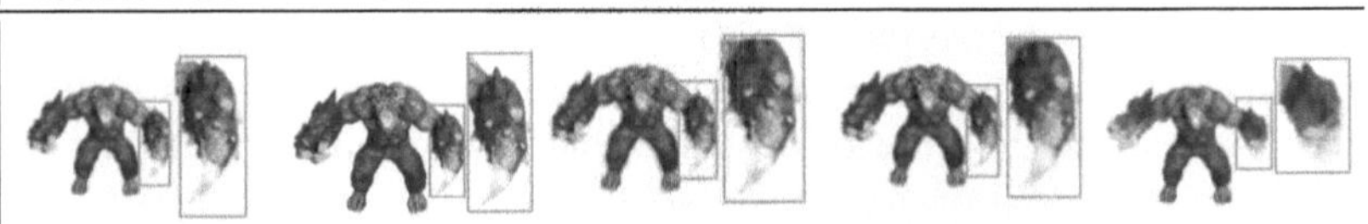				
Lego					

4 Experiments

4.1 Implementation Details

Our method is implemented in PyTorch on top of the 3D Gaussian Splatting (3DGS) codebase [15]. We train synthetic scenes for 20k iterations and real scenes for 14k iterations, following standard 3DGS settings with added progressive propagation every 50 iterations (three steps, $\sigma = 0.8$) and planar regularization ($\beta = 0.001$, $\gamma = 100$). We periodically prune points (threshold 8000), use voxel plane resolution [64, 64], set the Gaussian feature dimension to 32, and use an MLP hidden size of 64. All experiments run on a single NVIDIA RTX 4070 GPU. Real sequences are initialized from COLMAP sparse geometry for the first frame, while synthetic scenes use ground-truth depth. Baselines are taken from public code or reported numbers in [10,11,20,21,25,26].

Table 3. Quantitative results across different methods for real-time. Arrows indicate the desired direction for each metric.

Method	SSIM ↑	PSNR (dB) ↑	LPIPS ↓	Time ↓
HyperNeRF [20]	0.814	22.4	—	32h
Nerfies [19]	0.803	22.2	—	hours
3DGS [15]	0.680	19.7	—	**40 mins**
TiNeuVox [10]	0.836	24.3	—	48 mins
4DGS [26]	0.845	25.2	0.2915	54 mins
SPGS [25]	0.8404	25.61	0.2073	—
DynGS-Pro (Ours)	**0.862**	**26.65**	**0.197**	92 mins

4.2 Datasets

We evaluate DynGS-Pro on synthetic and real dynamic benchmarks. For controlled experiments with ground-truth geometry and appearance, we use the Synthetic-NeRF dataset [21], which provides multi-view sequences with known camera poses and predefined object motion. For real data, we use the HyperNeRF dataset [20], consisting of 58 synchronized cameras (30 FPS) capturing humans and objects under diverse motions. All available views are used for training; images are downsampled to around 800×800 pixels, and we rely on the provided calibrations.

5 Results

5.1 Synthetic Scene Results

Table 1 reports results on the D-NeRF synthetic benchmark. **DynGS-Pro attains the best scores across all metrics**, with SSIM = 0.9908 and

PSNR = 39.67 dB, clearly surpassing SPGS (37.98 dB, 0.9876 SSIM) and 4DGS. Our LPIPS (0.011) is also lowest (vs 0.0185 for SPGS and 0.0148 for 4DGS), indicating better perceptual fidelity. Qualitatively, DynGS-Pro's advantage is evident. In Table 2, we show a frame from the "Mutant" scene. Our method reproduces the sharp-edged arm shape and its specular highlight with high fidelity. 4DGS has slight fringing around the pointed corner (zoomed inset shows a faint edge), indicating minor temporal misalignment.

Table 4. Qualitative comparison on HyperNeRF's [20] **3D-Printrt**, **Banana**, and **Chicken** scenes using 3DGS, HyperNeRF, and our method.

Scene	Ground Truth	3DGS	HyperNeRF	4DGS	Ours
Banana					
Chicken					

5.2 Real-World Scene Results

Table 3 presents results on the HyperNeRF sequences. DynGS-Pro again ranks first, with SSIM = 0.862 and PSNR = 26.65 dB, compared to 4DGS (0.845 SSIM, 25.2 dB PSNR). The ~1 dB PSNR gain is notable given the difficulty of these real captures. HyperNeRF and Nerfies achieve SSIM around 0.81 and PSNR in the 2224 dB range, showing the limitations of implicit methods on noisy, fast-motion data. Our LPIPS (0.197) is also lower than SPGS (0.2073) and 4DGS (0.2915). While DynGS-Pro requires approximately 90 min of training per real scene, slightly slower than our 4DGS implementation (1 h), due to the progressively growing number of Gaussians, but still far below HyperNeRF's ~32 h and Nerfies' multi-hour training, making it practically usable.

We present visual examples in Table 4. One example is the "chicken" sequence, and other is a peeling-banana sequence. HyperNeRF, which aims to handle topology change, still blurs the boundary and has a floating artifact because it struggles with the quick appearance of new surfaces. 4DGS does better, showing two halves, but the cut region's texture is a bit smeared as it had limited Gaussians there from the start.

Table 5. Ablation study on DynGS-Pro (real-world). Arrows ↑/↓ indicate desired direction. Bold font marks the best score and underline marks the second-best.

Model Variant	SSIM ↑	PSNR (dB) ↑	LPIPS ↓	Time (min) ↓
w/o Densification	0.820	24.70	0.310	**35**
w/o Temporal Coherence	0.861	26.35	0.197	56
w/o Deformation Field	0.8	26.24	0.204	<u>40</u>
MLP-Depth-4 (2 layers)	0.851	26.02	0.199	95
MLP-Depth-3 (3 layers)	0.860	25.94	0.205	92
SiLU Activation	0.832	25.50	0.218	73
Leaky-ReLU Activation	0.847	26.63	<u>0.190</u>	81
GELU Activation	0.859	26.04	0.209	108
DynGS-Pro (Ours)	**0.862**	**26.65**	**0.197**	92

5.3 Discussion

Overall, the experiments confirm that DynGS-Pro delivers both high visual quality and real-time performance. The largest gains appear in scenarios with strong occlusions and disocclusions, where progressive propagation can introduce new Gaussians to capture previously unseen content. In more mildly dynamic scenes, 4DGS comes closer, yet DynGS-Pro still benefits from its more flexible per-Gaussian motion model. We performed ablations, described in Table 5, to justify our design choices and to evaluate the contribution of each component in our framework

A current limitation is the dependence on the initial geometry: if SfM fails to reconstruct an object (e.g., a textureless wall), we start without Gaussians there and must rely entirely on propagation, which can cause a brief lag in reconstruction quality. Integrating learned monocular depth priors (e.g., Depth Anything) or geometric priors is a primary direction for future work to bypass this initialization bottleneck. Additionally, DynGS-Pro inherits the well-documented limitations of 3DGS regarding highly specular surfaces. Because we rely on Spherical Harmonics to model view-dependent appearance, extreme lighting conditions or mirror-like reflections remain difficult to capture accurately using purely spatial deformations.

6 Conclusion and Future Work

In this paper, we presented DynGS-Pro, a dynamic scene reconstruction approach that achieves high-fidelity rendering of non-rigid scenes with unprecedented visual quality. By integrating the strengths of progressive, explicit scene representation with learned 4D deformation fields, our method addresses the twin challenges of geometric accuracy and temporal coherence in a unified framework. DynGS-Pro can reconstruct challenging dynamic scenes and consistently delivers superior visual fidelity across a range of evaluation metrics such as SSIM, PSNR, and LPIPS, outperforming prior state-of-the-art approaches.

Our findings demonstrate that high-quality, temporally coherent rendering of dynamic scenes is achievable through a hybrid representation that combines the explicit primitives with the flexibility of learned deformations. This work demonstrates a promising route to combining computer vision (multi-view geometry) and graphics (real-time rendering) techniques for dynamic scenes. In future work, we aim to make DynGS-Pro faster, more automated, and more robust by incorporating learned motion priors for quicker convergence and adapting continuously to streaming data. We also plan to extend the framework to additional modalities such as dynamic point clouds and event cameras.

Funding Statement. This work was supported by the Leadership Talent Program (Science and Education) of SIP under Project Code KJQ2025204. The funding body provided financial support for the research, authorship, and publication of this study.

References

1. Alfonso-Arsuaga, M., García-González, J., Castiella-Aguirrezabala, A., Alonso, M.A., Garcés, E.: Dynerfactor: temporally consistent intrinsic scene decomposition for dynamic nerfs. Comput. Graph. **122**, 103984 (8 2024). https://doi.org/10.1016/J.CAG.2024.103984
2. Bai, C., Fu, R., Gao, X.: Colmap-pcd: An open-source tool for fine image-to-point cloud registration. In: Proceedings - IEEE International Conference on Robotics and Automation, pp. 1723–1729 (2024). https://doi.org/10.1109/ICRA57147.2024.10611582
3. Bao, Y., et al.: 3D Gaussian splatting: survey, technologies, challenges, and opportunities. IEEE Trans. Circuits Syst. Video Technol. (2025). https://doi.org/10.1109/TCSVT.2025.3538684
4. Cao, A., Johnson, J.: Hexplane: A fast representation for dynamic scenes (2023). https://caoang327.github.io/HexPlane
5. Chan, E.R., et al.: Efficient geometry-aware 3D generative adversarial networks (2022). https://github.com/NVlabs/eg3d
6. Chen, A., Xu, Z., Geiger, A., Yu, J., Su, H.: TensoRF: Tensorial radiance fields. In: European Conference on Computer Vision, vol. 13692 LNCS, pp. 333–350 (2022). https://doi.org/10.1007/978-3-031-19824-3_20
7. Chen, G., Wang, W.: A survey on 3D Gaussian splatting. arXiv preprint arXiv:2401.03890 (1 2024). https://arxiv.org/abs/2401.03890v6

8. Chen, J., et al.: Animatable neural radiance fields from monocular RGB videos. arXiv preprint arXiv:2106.13629 (2021) (6 2021). https://arxiv.org/abs/2106.13629v2
9. Cheng, K., et al.: Gaussianpro: 3D gaussian splatting with progressive propagation (2024). https://github.com/kcheng1021/GaussianPro
10. Fang, J., et al.: Fast dynamic radiance fields with time-aware neural voxels. In: Proceedings - SIGGRAPH Asia 2022 Conference Papers (11 2022). https://doi.org/10.1145/3550469.3555383
11. Fridovich-Keil, S., Meanti, G., Warburg, F.R., Recht, B., Kanazawa, A.: K-planes: Explicit radiance fields in space, time, and appearance, (2023)
12. Fülöp-Balogh, B.E., Tursman, E., Tompkin, J., Digne, J., Bonneel, N.: Dynamic scene novel view synthesis via deferred spatio-temporal consistency. Comput. Graph. **107**, 220–230 (10 2022). https://doi.org/10.1016/J.CAG.2022.07.019
13. Guo, Z., Zhou, W., Li, L., Wang, M., Li, H.: Motion-aware 3D Gaussian splatting for efficient dynamic scene reconstruction. IEEE Trans. Circ. Syst. Video Technol. (3 2024). https://doi.org/10.1109/TCSVT.2024.3502257,
14. He, S., Osman, Z., Chaudhari, P.: From nerfs to gaussian splats, and back. arXiv preprint arXiv (5 2024). https://arxiv.org/abs/2405.09717v3
15. Kerbl, B., Kopanas, G., Leimkühler, T., Drettakis, G.: 3D Gaussian splatting for real-time radiance field rendering. ACM Trans. Graph. (2023). https://darkpgmr.tistory.com/77
16. Li, Z., et al: STDR: Spatio-temporal decoupling for real-time dynamic scene rendering (5 2025). https://arxiv.org/pdf/2505.22400
17. Luiten, J., Kopanas, G., Leibe, B., Ramanan, D.: Dynamic 3D gaussians: Tracking by persistent dynamic view synthesis. In: Proceedings - 2024 International Conference on 3D Vision, 3DV 2024, pp. 800–809 (2024). https://doi.org/10.1109/3DV62453.2024.00044
18. Mildenhall, B., Srinivasan, P.P., Tancik, M., Barron, J.T., Ramamoorthi, R., Ng, R.: Nerf. Commun. ACM **65**, 99–106 (12 2021). https://doi.org/10.1145/3503250
19. Park, K., et al.: Nerfies: Deformable neural radiance fields (2021)
20. Park, K., et al.: Hypernerf: A higher-dimensional representation for topologically varying neural radiance fields. ACM Trans. Graph. **40** (6 2021). https://doi.org/10.1145/3478513.3480487
21. Pumarola, A., Corona, E., Pons-Moll, G., Moreno-Noguer, F.: D-NeRF: Neural radiance fields for dynamic scenes (2021)
22. Schonberger, J.L., Frahm, J.M.: Structure-from-motion revisited (2016). https://github.com/colmap/colmap
23. Shi, C., et al.: Sparse4DGS: 4D gaussian splatting for sparse-frame dynamic scene reconstruction (11 2025). https://arxiv.org/pdf/2511.07122
24. Song, L., et al.: NeRFplayer: a streamable dynamic scene representation with decomposed neural radiance fields. IEEE Trans. Visual. Comput. Graph. **29**, 2732–2742 (5 2023). https://doi.org/10.1109/TVCG.2023.3247082
25. Wan, D., Lu, R., Zeng, G.: Superpoint Gaussian splatting for real-time high-fidelity dynamic scene reconstruction. Proc. Mach. Learn. Res. **235**, 49957–49972 (6 2024). https://arxiv.org/abs/2406.03697v1
26. Wu, G., et al.: 4D gaussian splatting for real-time dynamic scene rendering. In: Proceedings of the IEEE/CVF Conference on Computer Vision and Pattern Recognition (CVPR) (10 2023). https://doi.org/10.1109/CVPR52733.2024.01920,

RILEE: Reasoning-Intensive Legal Element Extraction via Hierarchical Re-answering

Lixuan Wang[1], Jikun Hu[1], Yali Ying[2], Zeyang Liu[1,3], Quan Zhou[1,2], Dongsheng Guo[1(✉)], and Cheng Luo[1,2]

[1] Quan Cheng Laboratory, Jinan, Shandong, China
sr-guodsh@qcl.edu.cn
[2] MegaTech.AI Inc., Beijing, China
[3] Shandong University, Jinan, Shandong, China

Abstract. Traditional Legal Element Extraction (LEE) tasks often treat legal elements as isolated labels, failing to capture the logical reasoning used in judicial decisions. In this paper, we propose a Reasoning-intensive Legal Element Extraction (RILEE) framework, which organizes legal elements into a hierarchical knowledge tree to model their logical dependencies. By using a specialized dataset of Chinese civil loan disputes with 89 expert-defined elements, we further introduce a hierarchical re-answering method. This approach allows Large Language Models (LLMs) to iteratively refine their judgments through legal rationales and structural context. Experimental results demonstrate that RILEE can significantly outperform general-purpose LLMs in both accuracy and logical consistency, offering a more interpretable and reliable solution for legal AI.

Keywords: Reasoning-intensive legal element extraction · Legal reasoning tree · Hierarchical re-answering · Structured legal knowledge · Large language models

1 Introduction

The core of legal adjudication lies in identifying and applying "legal elements", the essential conditions that bridge raw case facts with statutory norms. These elements are not just labels; they are the analytical foundation of judicial reasoning. When a case involves complex or ambiguous facts, resolving these elements requires a sophisticated synthesis of law and logic. However, current **Legal Element Extraction (LEE)** methods treat elements as isolated text spans or labels, ignoring the inferential steps behind judicial decisions.

Supplementary Information The online version contains supplementary material available at https://doi.org/10.1007/978-981-92-2759-4_4.

J. Niu et al. (Eds.): KSEM 2026, LNAI 16631, pp. 40–53, 2027.
https://doi.org/10.1007/978-981-92-2759-4_4

Existing LEE research generally follows two paradigms. The first treats the task as a standard information extraction problem [1]. These methods use expert-defined rules or schemas to identify specific text segments, such as dates in commercial contracts [2] or factual components in criminal cases [3]. They rely on textual patterns rather than legal logic. The second paradigm frames LEE as a classification task. Popular benchmarks like CAIL-2019 [4] and LEVEN [5] require models to map case descriptions to predefined categories across various legal domains, which reduce legal analysis to a simple matching problem. This approach identifies what is present in a case but fails to explain how those elements were derived from the facts or how they interact to reach a verdict.

Both paradigms treat legal elements as isolated entities, whereas in reality they are interdependent and emerge from coherent reasoning. Current methods thus offer limited support for high-stakes decisions or explainable legal AI. We propose **Reasoning-intensive Legal Element Extraction (RILEE)**, which shifts focus to adjudicative reasoning via three core principles. First, we adopt value-oriented selection, focusing on elements that are central to resolving difficult, real-world legal disputes. Second, we implement a structured knowledge representation by organizing elements into a hierarchical "knowledge tree" that encodes their logical dependencies. Finally, we introduce reasoning-aware inference, framing the extraction process as a hierarchical question-answering task. This mirrors the way legal experts deliberate, ensuring that the model's outputs are both logically sound and practically useful for the legal community.

We build a general framework modeling legal reasoning as a hierarchical knowledge tree, where parent-child nodes and dependencies reflect judicial deliberation. To test it, we construct the RILEE dataset of Chinese civil loan disputes (a common, complex type), defining 89 high-value elements with logical relationships in collaboration with legal experts. To help Large Language Models (LLMs) navigate this structure, we introduce a hierarchical re-answering method. Using depth-first traversal, the model generates initial answers and then refines them through a unified loop. This process integrates legal explanations and context from ancestor nodes, allowing the model to correct inconsistencies and produce results that are both accurate and legally sound.

In contrast to traditional LEE approaches, Our innovation lies in two key shifts. First, we replace flat labels with a structured, traversable reasoning tree that captures logical dependencies. Second, we transform the task from simple classification into a hierarchical question-answering process. This new formulation allows LLMs to simulate the stepwise verification used in real judicial practice. By connecting case facts with legal elements through structured reasoning, RILEE provides a more interpretable and reliable framework for computational judicial analysis. Figure 1 shows the difference between them.

Our main contributions are as follows:

- **A New Paradigm for Legal Element Extraction**: We introduce RILEE, redefining LEE from a shallow pattern-matching task into a structured, reasoning-intensive process. By integrating value-oriented selection, hierarchical knowledge representation, and reasoning-aware inference, RILEE captures the logical dependencies essential for professional judicial deliberation.

- **A High-Quality Expert-Annotated Benchmark**: We present a high-quality expert-annotated dataset of 89 fine-grained elements organized as a hierarchical knowledge tree on Chinese civil loan disputes. While focused on loan disputes, the framework is designed to be domain-agnostic and serves as a blueprint for scaling structured legal reasoning to other legal areas.
- **Hierarchical Re-answering Mechanism**: We propose an iterative hierarchical re-answering method that enables LLMs to navigate complex legal trees. By utilizing depth-first traversal and a self-refinement loop, the model incorporates legal rationales and structural context to ensure that its outputs are not only accurate but also logically consistent and legally auditable.

The remainder of this paper is organized as follows. Section 2 reviews related work. Section 3 defines the RILEE task and dataset. Section 4 presents our hierarchical re-answering framework. Section 5 reports experiments. Section 6 concludes the paper and discusses future directions.

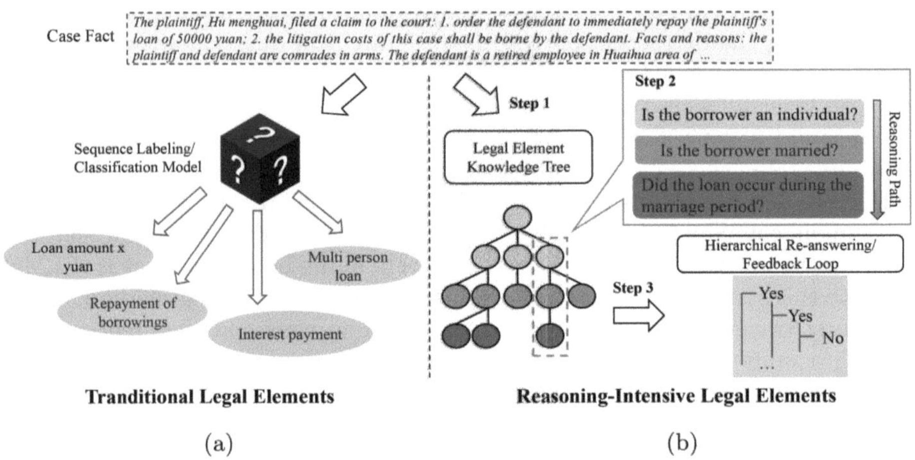

Fig. 1. Comparison between Traditional LEE and RILEE. (a) Traditional methods treat legal elements as isolated labels, failing to capture logical dependencies. (b) RILEE models the extraction as a hierarchical reasoning process over a knowledge tree, ensuring logical consistency and interpretability closer to judicial decision-making.

2 Related Work

2.1 Legal Element Extraction

LEE aims to identify the factual and normative conditions required for legal rules to apply. Existing approaches fall into two paradigms. The first treats LEE as information extraction, identifying surface spans or entities using expert-defined schemas. Chalkidis et al. [2] extract structural fields from contracts, and LEEC [3] is a criminal dataset with 159 annotated element labels. These methods are effective for factual grounding but produce outputs tied to lexical patterns and lack analytical depth. The second paradigm frames LEE as classification or event detection, assigning entire case texts to predefined legal categories, as in CAIL-2019 [4] and LEVEN [5], typically using BERT-based models [6]. While scalable, this approach reduces legal analysis to label matching and ignores logical dependencies among elements and their inferential links to legal norms. Related tasks such as legal summarization [7] and legal question answering [8] address broader comprehension but do not model the structured reasoning underlying element satisfaction. LEE is also commonly used as an intermediate step in judgment prediction [9–11] and case retrieval [12–15], yet without reasoning awareness, the resulting explanations remain shallow. In contrast, RILEE models elements as interdependent components of judicial reasoning, emphasizing logical structure, hierarchical dependencies, and law-grounded inference.

2.2 LLM Self-correction Mechanism

Self-correction methods refine LLM reasoning via response-feedback [16]. They are categorized by feedback timing: post-hoc correction revises completed responses [17,18], while generation-time correction guides intermediate steps [19]. Another line uses self-rewarding iterative refinement [20], often needing specialized training. Our approach uses lightweight post-hoc prompting without fine-tuning. Feedback quality is crucial; external/enriched information [21,22] outperforms internal signals alone [16], and smaller models struggle with feedback [17]. Our hierarchical re-answering adopts a streamlined post-hoc strategy combining feedback and refinement in one step, reducing instruction complexity while preserving efficiency. Inspired by chain-of-thought prompting [23,24], which decomposes complex tasks into sequential reasoning steps, our prompt design explicitly separates rationale generation from the final answer by first eliciting a law-grounded explanation and then the binary judgment to improve both consistency and explainability of model responses.

3 Reasoning-Intensive Legal Element Extraction

3.1 Task Definition

RILEE is a novel task that extracts high-value legally relevant elements from case texts to support judicial reasoning. Unlike general LEE, RILEE has two core characteristics. First, it focuses on elements central to adjudicative difficulty rather than surface frequency. Second, it models logical hierarchy and reasoning dependencies via a legal element knowledge tree. RILEE performs systematic hierarchical yes/no reasoning along this tree. For example, joint marital debt requires answering whether the borrower is an individual and married.

The output is structured QA pairs revealing element existence and its reasoning path.

Formally, let d denote the unstructured fact document of a legal case (e.g., the factual narrative from a judgment), and $\mathcal{T} = (Q, E)$ be a predefined legal element knowledge tree, where $Q = \{q_i\}_{i=1}^{N}$ is the set of nodes, each representing a yes/no legal question, and $E \subseteq Q \times Q$ defines parent-child dependencies: q_{child} is activated only if q_{parent} is `Yes`. The ground-truth annotation for d is a logically consistent, answer-labeled subtree $\mathcal{T}_d \subseteq \mathcal{T}$, where each node q_i is assigned a label from $\{\texttt{Yes}, \texttt{No}, \texttt{Not involved}\}$. Since `Not involved` and `No` are often indistinguishable in practice, we follow [3] and merge them into a single `No` label. The goal of RILEE is to learn a reasoning function $\mathcal{F}$ that, given d and $\mathcal{T}$, outputs a predicted subtree $\hat{\mathcal{T}}_d$ that best matches the ground-truth $\mathcal{T}_d$ while respecting the logical constraints of $\mathcal{T}$. Specifically, F assigns an answer $a_i \in \{\texttt{Yes}, \texttt{No}\}$ to each q_i in topological order, conditioned on d and the inferred answers of its ancestor nodes. The output is the maximal consistent subtree:

$$\hat{\mathcal{T}}_d = \mathcal{F}(d, \mathcal{T}) = \{(q_i, a_i) \in \mathcal{T} \mid a_i = \texttt{Yes}\}. \tag{1}$$

3.2 Dataset Construction

To support the RILEE task, we construct a high-quality dataset centered on Chinese civil loan cases.

Data Source. To ensure legal relevance and temporal validity, we collect 89 civil loan judgments published by the Supreme People's Court of China[1] from 2022 to 2023, covering diverse provinces. Additionally, we include 16 second-instance cases (2017–2023) that feature more complex factual scenarios. From each judgment, we extract only the factual narrative section, which serves as the input document d. The average length of d is 1,134 words.

Construction of the Legal Element Knowledge Tree. The legal element knowledge tree $\mathcal{T} = (Q, E)$ serves as the structural backbone of RILEE. We designed $\mathcal{T}$ in collaboration with four serving judges from intermediate and high courts in China, resulting in a hierarchy of 89 yes/no questions. Questions originate from legal norms, judicial practice, and empirical observation, and each follows four standards: judgment relevance, binary answerability, statutory grounding, and fact orientation.

$\mathcal{T}$ is built on a hierarchical reasoning principle: complex legal elements are decomposed into fine-grained binary questions organized under high-level categories. Level-0 contains 8 macro modules aligned with judicial frameworks. Levels 1–3 implement RILEE's core reasoning by breaking abstract concepts into fact-dependent verification steps. For example, determining joint marital debt follows the chain: "Is the borrower an individual?" → "Is the borrower married?" →

[1] https://wenshu.court.gov.cn/.

"Was the loan used for joint spousal life?", where each child question is activated only if its parent is answered `Yes`. This captures the conditional dependencies formalized in E. We employed an iterative, bidirectional methodology with legal experts. The top-down phase began with the 8 level-0 categories derived from civil law doctrines and trial procedures, followed by systematic logical decomposition to generate reasoning chains for well-defined legal issues (e.g., conjugal debt). Complementarily, the bottom-up phase emerged from pilot annotation of real cases: nuanced but recurring factual questions not initially covered were identified, clustered by shared adjudicative purpose, and integrated as new sub-branches under appropriate parent nodes. This dual approach ensured that $\mathcal{T}$ is both legally rigorous and empirically grounded, fully supporting the hierarchical, dependency-aware reasoning demanded by RILEE. The final tree has 3 levels: Level-1 comprises 30 questions, Level-2 contains 46, Level-3 includes 13.

Annotation. Manual annotation is done in two stages: (1) two law students independently annotated each case (2–3 h) with expert support; (2) joint review by annotators and a supervising judge resolved discrepancies. The final dataset contains 89 documents, one unified 89-node tree, 7,921 validated ⟨*Fact*, *Question*, *Answer*⟩ triplets, offering significantly finer granularity, hierarchical reasoning structure, and trial-oriented relevance than flat-label benchmarks. This systematic approach is reproducible and portable across legal domains.

4 Hierarchical LLM Re-answering for RILEE

Given a case fact document d and the legal element question set $Q = \{q_i\}_{i=1}^{89}$ defined by the knowledge tree $\mathcal{T} = (Q, E)$, our goal under the RILEE task is to generate a consistent answer sequence $A = \{a_i\}_{i=1}^{89}$, where each $a_i \in \{\texttt{yes}, \texttt{no}\}$. To respect the hierarchical judicial reasoning encoded in $\mathcal{T}$, we propose a *hierarchical re-answering* framework that integrates (1) structured traversal of $\mathcal{T}$, (2) context-aware multi-turn questioning with a LLM $\mathcal{F}(\cdot)$, and (3) an iterative re-answering to refine the output. Figure 2 illustrates the overall pipeline.

4.1 Dependency-Aware Hierarchical Questioning

We perform a depth-first traversal of $\mathcal{T}$, dynamically deciding which questions to pose based on prior answers. Specifically, for any node q_i, we only query the LLM $\mathcal{F}(\cdot)$ if its parent q_j has been answered as `yes`; otherwise, q_i and its entire subtree are automatically assigned `no`. This pruning strategy ensures computational efficiency and enforces logical soundness by construction.

For each active question q_i, we construct a contextualized prompt that incorporates: (1) the case fact d, the current question q_i, its category c_i, and the QA history $H_j = [(q_j, a_j)]$ from its ancestor nodes. Input to LLM is:

$$I_i = p \,\|\, d \oplus q_i \oplus c_i, \tag{2}$$

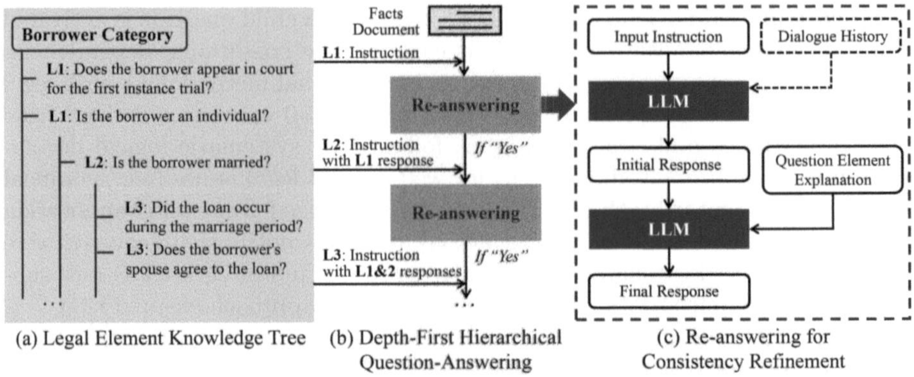

Fig. 2. Overview of the hierarchical re-answering framework, comprising three components: (a) the legal element knowledge tree $\mathcal{T}$, (b) depth-first hierarchical question-answering with conversation history, and (c) re-answering for consistency refinement.

and the answer is generated as:

$$a_i = \begin{cases} \mathcal{F}(I_i) & \text{if } q_i \text{ is a root node,} \\ \mathcal{F}(I_i, H_j) & \text{if } (q_i, q_j) \in E \text{ and } a_j = \texttt{yes}, \end{cases} \tag{3}$$

where p is a fixed instruction template, $\|$ separates system prompt from content, and $\oplus$ denotes textual concatenation. By feeding parent QA pairs as dialogue history, we enable the LLM to maintain reasoning continuity across levels of $\mathcal{T}$.

This dependency-aware questioning is operationalized via a recursive depth-first traversal of the three-level tree $\mathcal{T}$. Starting from Level-1 root nodes, we proceed to children only when parent is yes, else skip subtree. Current QA pair appended to history H for subsequent calls. Recursion ends on `no` or at depth 3. This procedure fully exploits the LLM's multi-turn dialogue capability to preserve logical continuity across hierarchical questions.

4.2 Re-answering for Consistency Refinement

To enhance the logical consistency and factual reliability of the LLM's judgments, we propose a fully automated re-answering mechanism that enables self-correction grounded in legal knowledge. Each element question q is paired with a machine-generated explanation e, which distills relevant statutory provisions and judicial criteria into plain language. These explanations are produced automatically by a strong LLM (Qwen3-Max [25]). During the initial reasoning stage, the model receives e together with the case facts d, the question q, and its category c, ensuring a fair comparison baseline as advocated by [16]. In the re-answering stage, the initial answer a^{init} is embedded as a prior dialogue turn (e.g., "User: q? Assistant: a^{init}"), and the model is prompted to reassess this response in light of d, c, and e, revising it if inconsistencies are detected.

This process is entirely end-to-end automatically. By presenting the initial answer as part of a simulated conversation rather than the model's current output, we reduce anchoring bias and encourage independent re-judgment. Both stages share the same objective: producing a legally valid binary answer, which minimizes instruction ambiguity during self-correction. The final re-answered result a^{re} is generated via $\mathcal{F}(I^{\text{re}})$, and this instruction Ire is constructed as

$$I^{\text{re}} = p^{\text{re}} \,\|\, d \oplus \texttt{[User: } q\texttt{? Assistant: } a^{\text{init}}\texttt{]} \oplus c \oplus e. \quad (4)$$

5 Experiments

5.1 Experiment Setting

Dataset. The dataset description is provided in Sect. 3.2. All data are used for validation, totaling 7921 question-answer pairs.

Metrics. Given that the final responses are binary (`yes` or `no`), we use following 4 metrics to evaluate the performance of models: precision (Prec.), recall (Rec.), F1 score (F1) and accuracy (Acc.). Among these, precision is a more important metric than recall, as it describes which legal elements are present in the cases.

Models. We choose different sizes of four widely used Chinese general LLMs (ChatGLM4 [26], Llama3 [27], Baichuan2 [28], and Qwen3 [25]), as well as two legal LLMs (LexiLaw [29] and Fuzi-Mingcha [30] which perform well on the LawBench [31]), on their performance in the RILEE task. All model weights are downloaded from their official websites or Hugging Face[2]. The experiments are conducted using the initial reasoning hyper-parameters of the models.

Reasoning Enhancement Methods. To evaluate the effectiveness of our re-answering method, we compare it with the following four methods, including Zero-shot Chain-of-Thought (CoT) [24], Self-consistency [32], Chain of Verification (CoVe) [18], Self-refine [17], Retrieval-Augmented Generation (RAG) [33]. All subsequent experiments are conducted using Qwen3-8B model.

5.2 Comparison of LLMs

This experiment regards RILEE as a document-based QA task, with all models using the same prompt. The experimental results are shown in Table 1. The results suggest that the legal LLMs performed inadequately in this task, potentially because these models were not exposed to similar tasks during their

[2] https://huggingface.co.

supervised fine-tuning phase, and their specialized tuning reduces instruction-following ability outside their training scope. Among the general-purpose models, Qwen3-8B model achieves a better balance between the size and performance metrics. To validate the effectiveness and generalizability of our proposed method, we applied the hierarchical re-answering framework on GLM4-9B-Chat and Qwen3-8B-Instruct. For Qwen3-8B-Instruct, the precision increase from 70.54% to 83.28%, and the F1 score improve from 73.91% to 80.51%. For GLM4-9B-Chat, we also observed notable gains, with precision increasing by 9.09 points and F1 by 11.43 points. These results demonstrate that our hierarchical re-answering method effectively enhances the legal reasoning capabilities of different LLMs.

Table 1. Performance (%) of LLMs on RILEE QA task. For rows with "w/ our method", values in parentheses denote performance improvement relative to baseline. The best performance is highlighted in **bold** and the second best is marked with underline.

Purpose	Model	Prec.	Rec.	F1	Acc.
General	GLM4-9B-Chat [26]	56.78	65.43	60.80	82.96
	Llama3-8B-Instruct [27]	45.79	54.21	49.65	71.33
	Baichuan2-7B-Chat [28]	47.42	56.80	51.69	72.14
	Baichuan2-13B-Chat [28]	59.21	64.15	61.58	80.31
	Qwen3-1.7B-Instruct [25]	60.04	77.30	67.59	74.60
	Qwen3-8B-Instruct [25]	70.54	77.62	73.91	89.12
	Qwen3-14B-Instruct [25]	71.12	86.59	78.10	90.35
	Qwen3-32B-Instruct [25]	73.07	81.45	77.03	90.33
	Qwen3-235B-Instruct [25]	70.67	**87.48**	78.18	90.30
Legal	LexiLaw [29]	25.36	30.01	27.49	49.95
	Fuzi-Mingcha [30]	24.88	32.61	28.23	58.26
w/ our method	GLM4-9B-Chat	65.87 (+9.09)	79.94 (+14.51)	72.23 (+11.43)	87.68 (+4.72)
	Qwen3-8B-Instruct	**83.28** (+12.74)	77.93 (+0.31)	**80.51** (+6.60)	**92.39** (+3.27)

5.3 Comparison of Reasoning Enhancement Methods

This experiment compares our re-answering method with five widely used reasoning enhancement methods. All methods are evaluated under the same hierarchical QA setup, using the un-enhanced hierarchical QA as the baseline. Table 2 shows the experimental results, which indicate that the self-correction methods CoVe [18] and Self-refine [17] not only fail to improve performance in this task but also show a decline compared to baseline, likely because their extra reasoning steps complicate instruction following. The zero-shot CoT [24] achieve the best result in recall, indicating that the prompt leads the model to answer `Yes` more often. The Self-consistency [32] method shows negligible improvement. RAG [33] offers only modest improvement, indicating that retrieval alone cannot meet the deep reasoning demands of RILEE. In contrast, our hierarchical re-answering method, which integrates explanation-guided reflection within the reasoning tree, proves to be the most effective approach for enhancing LLM-based legal reasoning. Given that precision is critical in LEE to avoid erroneous case analysis, our method's superior precision is particularly significant.

Table 2. Performance of reasoning methods on hierarchical QA reasoning tasks.

Method	Prec.	Rec.	F1	Acc.
Baseline	74.36	77.71	76.01	90.10
Zero-shot CoT [24]	<u>81.40</u>	**79.20**	<u>80.29</u>	<u>91.40</u>
Self-consistency [32]	73.09	77.68	75.32	89.77
CoVe [18]	68.20	74.60	71.25	87.60
Self-refine [17]	69.50	76.50	72.85	88.50
RAG [33]	75.63	77.74	76.66	90.69
Ours	**83.28**	<u>77.93</u>	**80.51**	**92.39**

5.4 Analysis of Hierarchical Re-answering

We conduct an ablation study to examine the contributions of our two core components: the hierarchical QA framework (including the knowledge tree $\mathcal{T}$, question categories C, and conversation history H) and the re-answering mechanism with explanation integration. Results are summarized in Table 3.

The hierarchical tree $\mathcal{T}$ enforces logical dependency: if a parent answer is `No`, all descendants are automatically assigned `No`, reducing query count by about one-third and speeding up inference. Removing $\mathcal{T}$ hurts performance significantly. Within the hierarchical framework, adding C and H further improves F1/accuracy, with H contributing more; using both gives the best scores. We next evaluate the impact of re-answering mechanism by incrementally applying it to different levels of the question tree (see the "Used Level" column in

Table 3). Applying re-answering only to level-1 questions (row 6) already yields improvements over the full hierarchical-QA baseline (row 5). While the combined accuracy for levels 2 and 3 (L2+3) rises from 90.23% to 93.47%. This distinction aligns with the nature of the questions: L1 questions are fact-based and can often be answered directly from the document, whereas L2 and L3 questions are inference-intensive and require deeper legal reasoning. The substantial boost in L2+3 accuracy demonstrates that our method, which integrates legal explanations and allows for reflective revision, is especially effective for the more complex, reasoning-intensive elements that are central to judicial decision-making.

Table 3. Ablation study of the hierarchical re-answering framework. ✓/× indicates whether the legal element knowledge tree ($\mathcal{T}$), question category ($\mathcal{C}$), or conversation history (H) is used. "Used Level" specifies which tree levels receive re-answering step.

$\mathcal{T}$	$\mathcal{C}$	H	Used Level	Prec.	Rec.	F1	Acc.	L1 Acc.	L2+3 Acc.
×	×	×	×	70.54	77.62	73.91	89.12	89.33	89.01
✓	×	×	×	71.83	77.90	74.73	89.41	89.45	89.32
✓	✓	×	×	72.62	78.10	75.25	89.65	89.32	89.82
✓	×	✓	×	73.51	<u>78.40</u>	75.87	89.92	90.14	89.81
✓	✓	✓	×	74.36	77.71	76.01	90.10	89.85	90.23
✓	✓	✓	$L1$	<u>76.20</u>	**78.80**	<u>77.48</u>	90.95	**90.33**	<u>91.26</u>
✓	✓	✓	$L1, L2, L3$	**83.28**	77.93	**80.51**	**92.39**	<u>90.27</u>	**93.47**

6 Conclusion and Future Work

In this study, we present RILEE, redefines legal element extraction by prioritizing structured reasoning over simple pattern matching. By organizing legal elements into a hierarchical knowledge tree, we move beyond flat classification to capture the logical dependencies used in actual judicial deliberation. Our hierarchical re-answering method further ensures that LLMs produce consistent and legally sound results through iterative self-refinement. Experimental results on Chinese civil loan disputes demonstrate that RILEE achieves a high accuracy of over 92% while providing clear, interpretable pathways for its decisions.

While our current evaluation focuses on loan disputes, the RILEE framework is flexible and can be adapted to various legal domains such as labor or family law. We acknowledge that the current dataset limits direct claims of generalizability and future work will validate on broader domains and languages. Looking ahead, we aim to explore the automated construction of reasoning trees to reduce the need for manual expert design. We also plan to integrate RILEE's structured outputs into downstream judicial tasks, such as automated judgment prediction and legal document generation, to better support legal practitioners. Furthermore, we believe this reasoning-intensive approach provides a more transparent and reliable foundation for the next generation of intelligent judicial systems.

Acknowledgments. This work was supported by the Key R&D Program of Shandong Province (SYS202201), the Research Project of Quan Cheng Laboratory (QCL20250105), and the Young Scientists Fund of the National Natural Science Foundation of China (62502282).

Disclosure of Interests. The authors have no competing interests to declare that are relevant to the content of this article.

References

1. Hogenboom, F., Frasincar, F., Kaymak, U.: An overview of event extraction from text. DeRiVE@ ISWC 48–57 (2011)
2. Chalkidis, I., Androutsopoulos, I., Michos, A.: Extracting contract elements. In: Proceedings of the 16th Edition of the International Conference on Articial Intelligence and Law, pp. 19–28 (2017)
3. Xue, Z., Liu, H., Hu, Y. et al.: LEEC for judicial fairness: a legal element extraction dataset with extensive extra-legal labels. In: Proceedings of the Thirty-Third International Joint Conference on Artificial Intelligence, IJCAI- 24, pp. 7527–7535 (2024)
4. Shu, Y., Zhao, Y., Zeng, X., et al.: CAIL2019-fe. Tech. Rep. (2019)
5. Yao, F., Xiao, C., Wang, X., et al.: LEVEN: a large-scale Chinese legal event detection dataset. In: Findings of the Association for Computational Linguistics: ACL 2022, pp. 183–201 (2022)
6. Devlin, J., Chang, M.-W., Lee, K., et al.: BERT: pre-training of deep bidirectional transformers for language understanding. In: Proceedings of the 2019 Conference of the North American Chapter of the Association for Computational Linguistics: Human Language Technologies, Volume 1 (Long and Short Papers), pp. 4171–4186 (2019)
7. Polsley, S., Jhunjhunwala, P., Huang, R.: Casesummarizer: a system for automated summarization of legal texts. In: Proceedings of COLING 2016, the 26th International Conference on Computational Linguistics: System Demonstrations, pp. 258–262 (2016)
8. Zhong, H., Xiao, C., Tu, C., et al.: JEC-QA: a legal-domain question answering dataset. In: Proceedings of the AAAI Conference on Artificial Intelligence, vol. 34, pp. 9701–9708 (2020)
9. Lyu, Y., Wang, Z., Ren, Z., et al.: Improving legal judgment prediction through reinforced criminal element extraction. Inf. Process. Manage. **59**(1), 102780 (2022)
10. Zhao, J., Guan, Z., Xu, C., et al.: Charge prediction by constitutive elements matching of crimes. In: Proceedings of the Thirty-First International Joint Conference on Artificial Intelligence, IJCAI-22, pp. 4517–4523 (2022)
11. Feng, Y., Li, C., Ng, V.: Legal judgment prediction via event extraction with constraints. In: Proceedings of the 60th Annual Meeting of the Association for Computational Linguistics (Volume 1: Long Papers), pp. 648–664 (2022)
12. Wang, Z.: Legal element-oriented modeling with multi-view contrastive learning for legal case retrieval. In: 2022 International Joint Conference on Neural Networks (IJCNN), pp. 01–10. IEEE (2022)
13. Tang, Y., Qiu, R., Li, X.: Prompt-based effective input reformulation for legal case retrieval. In: Bao, Z., Borovica-Gajic, R., Qiu, R., Choudhury, F., Yang, Z. (eds.) Databases Theory and Applications. ADC 2023. Lecture Notes in Computer

Science, vol. 14386, pp. 87–100. Springer, Cham (2023). https://doi.org/10.1007/978-3-031-47843-7_7
14. Deng, C., Dou, Z., Zhou, Y., et al.: An element is worth a thousand words: enhancing legal case retrieval by incorporating legal elements. In: Findings of the Association for Computational Linguistics ACL 2024, pp. 2354–2365 (2024)
15. Dan, J., Yang, D., Wang, Y.: Enhancing Chinese similar case retrieval based on key-fact and multi-legal-element joint augmentation. Artif. Intell. Law 1–31 (2026)
16. Kamoi, R., Zhang, Y., Zhang, N., et al.: When can LLMs actually correct their own mistakes? A critical survey of self-correction of LLMs. Trans. Assoc. Comput. Linguist. **12**, 1417–1440 (2024)
17. Madaan, A., Tandon, N., Gupta, P., et al.: Self-refine: iterative refinement with self-feedback. In: Advances in Neural Information Processing Systems, vol. 36 (2024)
18. Dhuliawala, S., Komeili, M., Xu, J., et al.: Chain-of-verification reduces hallucination in large language models. In: Findings of the Association for Computational Linguistics: ACL 2024, pp. 3563–3578 (2024)
19. Paul, D., Ismayilzada, M., Peyrard, M., et al.: Refiner: reasoning feedback on intermediate representations. In: Proceedings of the 18th Conference of the European Chapter of the Association for Computational Linguistics (Volume 1: Long Papers), pp. 1100–1126 (2024)
20. Xiong, W., Zhang, H., Ye, C., et al.: Self-rewarding correction for mathematical reasoning. CoRR (2025)
21. Shinn, N., Cassano, F., Gopinath, A., et al.: Reflexion: language agents with verbal reinforcement learning. In: Advances in Neural Information Processing Systems, vol. 36 (2024)
22. Gou, Z., Shao, Z., Gong, Y., et al.: CRITIC: large language models can self-correct with tool-interactive critiquing. In: International Conference on Representation Learning, vol. 2024, pp. 57734–57811 (2024)
23. Wei, J., Wang, X., Schuurmans, D., et al.: Chain-of-thought prompting elicits reasoning in large language models. In: Advances in Neural Information Processing Systems, vol. 35, pp. 24824–24837 (2022)
24. Kojima, T., Gu, S.S., Reid, M., et al.: Large language models are zero-shot reasoners. In: Advances in Neural Information Processing Systems, vol. 35, pp. 22199–22213 (2022)
25. Yang, A., Li, A., Yang, B., et al.: Qwen3 technical report. arXiv preprint arXiv:2505.09388 (2025)
26. Glm, T., Zeng, A., Xu, B., et al.: ChatGLM: a family of large language models from GLM-130B to GLM-4 all tools (2024). arXiv: 2406.12793
27. Grattafiori, A., Dubey, A., Jauhri, A., et al.: The Llama 3 herd of models. arXiv preprint arXiv:2407.21783 (2024)
28. Yang, A., et al.: Baichuan 2: Open large-scale language models. arXiv preprint arXiv:2309.10305 (2023)
29. Haitao, C.: LexiLaw: a legal text processing toolkit (2024)
30. Wu, S., Liu, Z., Zhang, Z., et al.: fuzi.mingcha. https://github.com/irlabsdu/fuzi.mingcha (2023)
31. Fei, Z., Shen, X., Zhu, D., et al.: Lawbench: benchmarking legal knowledge of large language models. In: Proceedings of the 2024 Conference on Empirical Methods in Natural Language Processing, pp. 7933–7962 (2024)
32. Wang, X., Wei, J., Schuurmans, D., et al.: Self-consistency improves chain of thought reasoning in language models. In: The Eleventh International Conference on Learning Representations (2023)

33. Shi, W., Min, S., Yasunaga, M., et al.: REPLUG: retrieval-augmented black- box language models. In: Proceedings of the 2024 Conference of the North American Chapter of the Association for Computational Linguistics: Human Language Technologies (Volume 1: Long Papers), Mexico City, Mexico, June 2024, pp. 8371–8384 (2024)

Complexity-Aware and Response Time Enhanced Knowledge Tracing

Wangqian Li, Weiqi Wu, Jingwei Sun, Guangzhong Sun, and Yu He(✉)

University of Science and Technology of China, Hefei, China
liwqian@mail.ustc.edu.cn, {weiqiwu,sunjw,gzsun,heyu3761}@ustc.edu.cn

Abstract. With the widespread deployment of intelligent tutoring systems, Knowledge Tracing (KT) has become essential for modeling students' latent knowledge states to enable personalized learning. However, existing models often fail to capture true student proficiency due to the interference of confounders-objective question-intrinsic attributes (e.g., inherent complexity and required time costs) that remain entangled with subjective learner characteristics (e.g., natural forgetting behaviors and individual response speeds). To separate these question-induced confounders, we propose **C**omplexity-**A**ware and **R**esponse **T**ime Enhanced KT (cartKT). First, to disentangle complexity from natural forgetting, cartKT incorporates a complexity-aware attention mechanism that dynamically adjusts forgetting rates based on question difficulty. Second, to deepen the modeling of the answering process, cartKT decouples overall response time into student-specific response speed (RS) and question-specific average response time (ART). By introducing RS and ART predictions as auxiliary tasks, the model successfully isolates the interference of question-intrinsic time costs. Experiments on real-world datasets demonstrate that cartKT effectively alleviates these limitations and outperforms state-of-the-art methods.

Keywords: Knowledge tracing · Multi-task learning · Forgetting behavior · Attention mechanism

1 Introduction

Intelligent tutoring systems (ITS) like Khan Academy rely heavily on assessing students' evolving knowledge states to enable personalized learning. Knowledge Tracing (KT) addresses this by utilizing historical interaction logs to predict future performance [3]. Accurate KT empowers systems to provide targeted feedback, helping students focus on unmastered knowledge concepts (KCs) while assisting teachers with data-driven instructional guidance.

KT models have evolved from traditional methods like BKT [3] to sophisticated deep learning-based (DLKT) architectures. These include autoregressive [14,16,18,24], memory-augmented [28], attention-based [1,4,8,25], and graph-based models [17,23]. Many DLKT frameworks further enhance performance by

J. Niu et al. (Eds.): KSEM 2026, LNAI 16631, pp. 54–66, 2027.
https://doi.org/10.1007/978-981-92-2759-4_5

incorporating side information such as question text [9], similarity [10], difficulty [4,10], and response time [19,20]. Despite these advances, a critical limitation remains: existing models often fail to isolate the student's true proficiency from question-intrinsic properties.

Specifically, current models largely ignore how question-specific factors act as *confounders* during the dynamic learning process. First, they oversimplify temporal decay by neglecting the impact of question complexity on forgetting rates. According to cognitive theories [2,21], information complexity directly influences memory retention; failing to decouple question complexity from natural forgetting skews knowledge state estimation. Second, existing models underutilize response time (RT). RT is typically treated merely as an enriched embedding or behavioral feature. However, it is jointly influenced by a student's latent proficiency and the intrinsic time cost of the question itself. Failing to properly handle this question-induced confounding limits the model's ability to extract pure representations of learner mastery.

To address these limitations, we propose **C**omplexity-**A**ware and **R**esponse **T**ime Enhanced KT (cartKT), a novel model designed to mitigate question-induced confounding in time-dependent signals. cartKT introduces a complexity-aware attention mechanism to dynamically adjust temporal decay, explicitly disentangling question complexity from the forgetting process. Furthermore, it employs a multi-task learning framework that decouples overall RT into two auxiliary prediction tasks: student response speed and question-level average response time.

The main contributions of this paper are summarized as follows:

- We propose cartKT, a novel framework that improves knowledge tracing by disentangling question-induced confounding effects from the modeling of students' true cognitive states.
- We design a complexity-aware attention mechanism that dynamically adjusts temporal decay, enabling precise modeling of forgetting behaviors under varying question complexities.
- We introduce a response time decoupling strategy via multi-task learning, explicitly separating individual student speed from question-intrinsic time costs to acquire purer proficiency representations.
- Extensive experiments on real-world datasets demonstrate that cartKT significantly outperforms state-of-the-art baselines, with ablation studies confirming the efficacy of its core components.

2 Related Work

2.1 Forgetting Modeling in Knowledge Tracing

Modeling student forgetting behavior is crucial for achieving accurate knowledge tracing, as it reflects the natural decay of knowledge over time. To capture student forgetting behavior in KT, researchers have developed multiple modeling strategies. Among these, utilizing time interval information is a common strategy. Representative works include DKT-Forget [16] and SAINT+ [20]. Another effective approach is to utilize recurrent mechanisms, relying on their internal forgetting gates to dynamically adjust knowledge states, such as LPKT [19] and LBKT [22]. Models like AKT [4], on the other hand, perform explicit modeling based on psychological theories. Inspired by the Ebbinghaus forgetting curve, researchers introduce exponential decay functions to simulate the natural decay of knowledge. Im et al. [6] introduced a "forgetting-aware linear bias" to model forgetting behavior as a linear penalty that increases with relative distance. Bai et al. [1] contributed a "Relative Forgetting Attention" framework to flexibly capture different forgetting decay patterns, including linear and exponential types, and addressed the issue of forgetting patterns being conflated with problem relevance.

2.2 Knowledge Tracing with Response Time

Response time is a natural indicator of cognitive processes. Luce [15] first used it to quantify mental processing. Zhan, Jiao et al. [26] modeled attributes and response speed jointly, and Zhan, Liao et al. [27] integrated response time and accuracy into testlet cognitive diagnosis. Krishnan et al. [7] suggested that shorter response time may reflect higher mastery, showing its close link with cognitive state. In KT, response time is used mainly as auxiliary information. Shin et al. [20] added it to the decoder sequence, Shen et al. [19] treated it as a basic element, and Liu et al. [10] used average response time as an exercise difficulty feature. Huang et al. [5] introduced a multi-task learning framework that integrates response speed prediction with answer prediction. Given its ubiquity in online learning, response time can supplement response results and describe response processes. Thus, exploring its relation to learners' knowledge states is necessary.

3 Problem Formulation

In an intelligent tutoring system, assume that there is a student set $S = \{s_1, s_2, \ldots, s_I\}$ containing I distinct students, a question set $Q = \{q_1, q_2, \ldots, q_J\}$ containing J distinct questions, and a knowledge concept set $KC = \{c_1, c_2, \ldots, c_M\}$ containing M distinct knowledge concepts. Given the historical sequence

$$X_t = \{(q_1, c_1, r_1), (q_2, c_2, r_2), \ldots, (q_{t-1}, c_{t-1}, r_{t-1})\}$$

of a particular student, where $r_{t-1} \in \{0, 1\}$ represents the student's answer (1 for correct, 0 for incorrect), KT aims to track the evolution of the student's knowledge state throughout the question-solving process. It predicts the probability $p(r_t \mid X_t, q_t, c_t)$ that the student will answer the question q_t correctly at time t, based on their current knowledge state at time $t-1$.

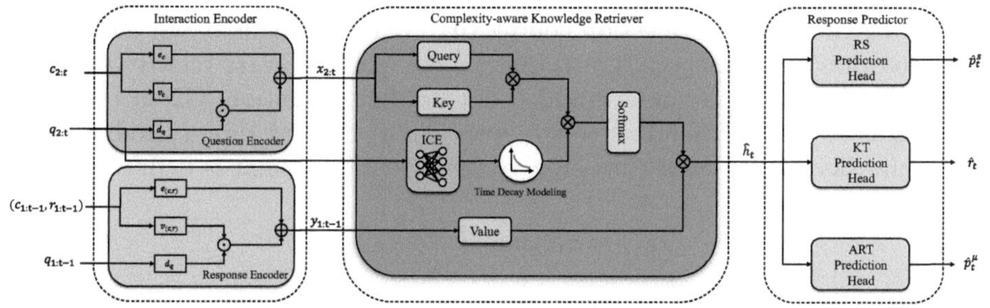

Fig. 1. The overview of the proposed cartKT framework.

4 The cartKT Method

In this section, we will provide a detailed introduction to the proposed cartKT model, with its overall architecture illustrated in Fig. 1. cartKT consists of three parts: an Interaction Encoder, a Complexity-Aware Knowledge Retriever, and a Response Predictor with auxiliary tasks. Specifically, when predicting a learner's future performance: (1) the Interaction Encoder first encodes the questions and interactions in the response sequence to obtain initial representations. (2) Next, the Complexity-Aware Knowledge Retriever, based on an attention mechanism, models the historical interaction sequence to extract latent representations of the knowledge state. (3) Finally, the Response Predictor guides the model's optimization direction through a multi-task objective function, thereby achieving fine-grained knowledge tracing.

4.1 Interaction Encoder

Questions mapped to the same KCs can vary in difficulty, so it is crucial to model studentquestion interactions effectively. Following AKT [4], simpleKT [12], and DTransformer [25], we encode the interaction sequence $\{(q_1, c_1, r_1), \ldots, (q_T, c_T, r_T)\}$ as:

$$\mathbf{x}_t = \mathbf{d}_{q_t} \odot \mathbf{v}_{c_t} \oplus \mathbf{e}_{c_t}, \qquad \mathbf{y}_t = \mathbf{d}_{q_t} \odot \mathbf{v}_{(c_t,r_t)} \oplus \mathbf{e}_{(c_t,r_t)}. \tag{1}$$

Here, $\mathbf{x}_t$ is the latent representation of question q_t and its associated KC c_t at time t. $\mathbf{d}_{q_t}$ denotes a learnable question-difficulty vector. $\mathbf{v}_{c_t}$ captures the KC variation, and $\mathbf{e}_{c_t}$ is the n-dimensional one-hot embedding of c_t. The operators $\odot$ and $\oplus$ indicate element-wise multiplication and addition, respectively.

$\mathbf{y}_t$ augments $\mathbf{x}_t$ by conditioning on the response r_t to q_t. $\mathbf{e}_{(c_t,r_t)}$ is the joint embedding of c_t and r_t, and $\mathbf{v}_{(c_t,r_t)}$ models the KCresponse variation of q_t for KC c_t with response r_t.

4.2 Complexity-Aware Knowledge Retriever

In this subsection, we introduce the Complexity-Aware Knowledge Retriever, which aims to model the evolution of students' knowledge states by additionally considering the factor of question complexity. This module is based on a multi-head attention mechanism and introduces a complexity-aware relative distance.

We first review the standard scaled dot-product attention. Given the query vector $\mathbf{q}_t \in \mathbb{R}^{D_k}$ corresponding to the question at current time t, and the key-value pairs $(\mathbf{k}_\tau, \mathbf{v}_\tau)$ at each time step τ, the attention weight is defined as:

$$\alpha_{t,\tau} = \text{Softmax}\left(\frac{\mathbf{q}_t^\top \mathbf{k}_\tau}{\sqrt{D_k}}\right), \tag{2}$$

where D_k is the dimension of the key vectors. In this model, both encoders utilize self-attention: the question encoder uses input sequence $\{\mathbf{x}_1, \ldots, \mathbf{x}_t\}$, and the response encoder uses $\{\mathbf{y}_1, \ldots, \mathbf{y}_{t-1}\}$.

However, directly applying standard attention is insufficient to capture the temporality in KT, as learning possesses sequential characteristics and memory naturally fades. Accordingly, following AKT [4], we introduce a learnable exponential time decay to the attention score:

$$\alpha_{t,\tau} = \text{Softmax}\left(\exp(-\theta \cdot d(t,\tau)) \cdot \frac{\mathbf{q}_t^\top \mathbf{k}_\tau}{\sqrt{D_k}}\right), \tag{3}$$

where θ is a learnable scalar parameter controlling the global decay rate, and $d(t,\tau)$ is the temporal distance measure between time steps t and τ.

Regarding the design of the distance metric function $d(t,\tau)$, this paper adopts a method distinct from previous studies. Considering that problems of varying complexity may lead to different forgetting rates, we incorporate a complexity factor into the design of $d(t,\tau)$. Specifically, instead of relying solely on the time interval, we integrate the question's intrinsic complexity information. This allows attention weights to decay at differentiated rates. The complexity-aware distance function is defined as:

$$d(t,\tau) = \beta_\tau \cdot |t-\tau|^\gamma, \tag{4}$$

where $|t-\tau|$ represents the relative time interval, and $\gamma \in [0,1]$ is a tunable hyperparameter that controls the smoothness of the time decay. The term β_τ serves as the *complexity amplification factor.* A larger β_τ accelerates the forgetting speed for complex questions, while a smaller β_τ for simple questions slows down the decay, aligning with the cognitive pattern that "simpler information is retained longer."

To obtain the scalar complexity factor β_τ for each question, we design a specialized module termed **Intrinsic Complexity Extractor (ICE)**, which is implemented via a lightweight feed-forward network (FFN). An exponential function (exp) is applied to the ICE module's output to ensure the factor is non-negative:

$$\beta_\tau = \exp\left(w_2^\top \text{ReLU}(W_1 \, \text{ReLU}(q_\tau) + \mathbf{b}_1) + b_2\right), \tag{5}$$

where $q_\tau \in \mathbb{R}^D$ is the question embedding, $\text{ReLU}(\cdot)$ is the Rectified Linear Unit activation, $W_1 \in \mathbb{R}^{H\times D}, \mathbf{b}_1 \in \mathbb{R}^H, w_2 \in \mathbb{R}^H$, and $b_2 \in \mathbb{R}$. This formulation keeps the network fully differentiable and allows the ICE module to be learned jointly with the main model.

4.3 Response Predictor

Response time carries information about both students and questions, but has rarely been fully exploited in previous studies. Inspired by FKT [5], we propose a response time enhanced Response Predictor based on multi-task learning. Besides predicting answer correctness, our model adds two auxiliary tasks on response time: response speed and average response time. Unlike FKT, which only models the learner's response speed, we decompose the observed response time into a learner-specific speed term and a question-specific average time and predict them separately.

Formally, let τ_t denote the learner's response time at step t on question q_t, and let $\bar{\tau}_{q_t}$ be the average response time of q_t estimated from historical data. We define the response speed as

$$s_t = \frac{\tau_t}{\mu_{q_t}}. \tag{6}$$

Both s_t and μ_{q_t} are continuous. In practice, we discretize s_t into C_s bins and μ_{q_t} into C_μ bins, and cast their prediction as multi-class classification instead of regression. Empirically, classification-based auxiliary heads yield better performance on the main KT task than their regression counterparts.

Let $\hat{h}_t \in \mathbb{R}^{d_h}$ be the comprehensive knowledge state from the complexity-aware knowledge retriever at step t. The predictor module feeds $\hat{h}_t$ into three parallel two-layer feed-forward networks (FFNs):

1. **Response Speed (RS) Prediction:** This head outputs the probability distribution over response speed bins:

$$\hat{p}_t^{\mathrm{s}} = \mathrm{Softmax}\Big(W_2^{\mathrm{s}}\mathrm{ReLU}\Big(W_1^{\mathrm{s}}\hat{h}_t + b_1^{\mathrm{s}}\Big) + b_2^{\mathrm{s}}\Big), \tag{7}$$

   where $W_1^{\mathrm{s}} \in \mathbb{R}^{d_{\mathrm{s}} \times d_h}$, $W_2^{\mathrm{s}} \in \mathbb{R}^{C_{\mathrm{s}} \times d_{\mathrm{s}}}$, $b_1^{\mathrm{s}} \in \mathbb{R}^{d_{\mathrm{s}}}$, and $b_2^{\mathrm{s}} \in \mathbb{R}^{C_{\mathrm{s}}}$. The vector $\hat{p}_t^{\mathrm{s}} \in \mathbb{R}^{C_{\mathrm{s}}}$ is the predicted distribution over speed bins.
2. **Average Response Time (ART) Prediction:** This head predicts the distribution over average response time bins:

$$\hat{p}_t^{\mu} = \mathrm{Softmax}\Big(W_2^{\mu}\mathrm{ReLU}\Big(W_1^{\mu}\hat{h}_t + b_1^{\mu}\Big) + b_2^{\mu}\Big), \tag{8}$$

   where $W_1^{\mu} \in \mathbb{R}^{d_\mu \times d_h}$, $W_2^{\mu} \in \mathbb{R}^{C_\mu \times d_\mu}$, $b_1^{\mu} \in \mathbb{R}^{d_\mu}$, and $b_2^{\mu} \in \mathbb{R}^{C_\mu}$. The vector $\hat{p}_t^{\mu} \in \mathbb{R}^{C_\mu}$ is the predicted distribution over average-time bins.
3. **Knowledge Tracing (KT) Prediction:** The main head outputs the probability of a correct response:

$$\hat{r}_t = \sigma\left(W_m^{(2)}\mathrm{ReLU}\left(W_m^{(1)}\hat{h}_t + b_m^{(1)}\right) + b_m^{(2)}\right) \in [0,1], \tag{9}$$

   where $W_m^{(1)} \in \mathbb{R}^{d_{\mathrm{main}} \times d_h}$, $W_m^{(2)} \in \mathbb{R}^{1 \times d_{\mathrm{main}}}$, $b_m^{(1)} \in \mathbb{R}^{d_{\mathrm{main}}}$, and $b_m^{(2)} \in \mathbb{R}^1$.

4.4 Objective Function

To train the model, we jointly optimize the main task of answer prediction and the two auxiliary tasks: RS prediction and average response time prediction. The overall objective is defined over a learning sequence of length T.

First, for the main task of predicting answer correctness, we utilize the binary cross-entropy loss between the true response r_t and the predicted probability $\hat{r}_t$ across all time steps:

$$\mathcal{L}_{main}(\Theta) = -\sum_{t=1}^{T} \left[r_t \log \hat{r}_t + (1 - r_t) \log(1 - \hat{r}_t) \right]. \tag{10}$$

For the auxiliary tasks, since the targets are discretized into categorical bins, we employ the multi-class cross-entropy loss. Let s_t and μ_{q_t} denote the ground-truth categorical labels for the student's response speed and the question's average response time, respectively. The model outputs the corresponding predicted probability distributions $\hat{p}_t^s \in \mathbb{R}^{C_s}$ and $\hat{p}_t^\mu \in \mathbb{R}^{C_\mu}$. The losses are calculated as:

$$\mathcal{L}_s(\Theta) = -\sum_{t=1}^{T} \sum_{k=1}^{C_s} \mathbb{I}(s_t = k) \log(\hat{p}_{t,k}^s), \tag{11}$$

$$\mathcal{L}_\mu(\Theta) = -\sum_{t=1}^{T} \sum_{k=1}^{C_\mu} \mathbb{I}(\mu_{q_t} = k) \log(\hat{p}_{t,k}^\mu), \tag{12}$$

where $\mathbb{I}(\cdot)$ is the indicator function, and $\hat{p}_{t,k}$ denotes the predicted probability for the k-th bin.

The final training objective $\mathcal{L}(\Theta)$ combines these three components, balanced by weighting coefficients λ_1 and λ_2:

$$\mathcal{L}(\Theta) = \mathcal{L}_{main}(\Theta) + \lambda_1 \mathcal{L}_s(\Theta) + \lambda_2 \mathcal{L}_\mu(\Theta). \tag{13}$$

We minimize $\mathcal{L}(\Theta)$ to learn the model parameters Θ.

5 Experiments

5.1 Datasets

To evaluate the effectiveness of our model, we employ three widely used public real-world educational datasets that include the response time feature: ASSIST2012[1], ASSISTChall[2] and Junyi[3]. The dataset statistics are summarized in Table 1. ASSIST2012 records logs from the ASSISTments online tutoring system's skill-builder problem sets in the 2012–2013 school year with affect

1 https://sites.google.com/site/assistmentsdata/2012-13-school-data-withaffect.
2 https://sites.google.com/view/assistmentsdatamining/.
3 https://pslcdatashop.web.cmu.edu/DatasetInfo?datasetId=1198/.

annotations. ASSISTChall provides a benchmark dataset for the 2017 ASSISTments data mining competition and tracks students who use the ASSISTments blended learning platform in middle school between 2004 and 2007. Junyi contains learner interaction data collected in 2015 on the Junyi Academy platform, an educational website that offers learning materials and exercises across various academic subjects.

Table 1. Details of the three datasets.

Dataset	Interactions	Students	Exercises	KCs
Junyi	13,101,058	191,766	715	39
ASSIST2012	2,711,813	29,018	53,091	265
ASSISTChall	942,816	1709	3,162	102

5.2 Baselines

We compare our model with the following 9 baselines: DKT [18], DKVMN [28], AKT [4], AT-DKT [11], simpleKT [12], DTransformer [25], extraKT [8], FKT [5], LefoKT [1].

5.3 Experimental Setup

Following standard practices in KT, the maximum learning sequence length was set to 200, with longer sequences split into subsequences. We adopted 5-fold cross-validation for all datasets, using an 8:2 split for training/validation (80%) and reserving 20% for testing. Model performance was evaluated using Area Under the Curve (AUC) and Accuracy (ACC). All models were implemented in PyTorch and trained on a Linux server with an NVIDIA GeForce RTX 3080Ti GPU. Training employed the Adam optimizer (learning rate = 0.001), a batch size of 128, a dropout rate of 0.2, and early stopping with a patience of 10. Baseline model parameters were taken from the pyKT library [13] or their original papers. For our proposed cartKT, hyperparameters were determined through sensitivity analysis and validation results. The complexity-aware time decay factor was set to $\gamma = 0.3$. The auxiliary task weights were $\lambda_1 = 0.7$ (student response speed) and $\lambda_2 = 0.1$ (average question response time). The numbers of discretization bins were $C_s = 10$ for student response speed and $C_\mu = 5$ for average question response time.

5.4 Overall Performance

The prediction performance of the models is shown in Table 2. Based on the results, we observe the following: (1) cartKT achieves the best results on three datasets. Specifically, compared with the state-of-the-art model on each dataset, the AUC of cartKT is 0.64% higher on Junyi, 0.38% higher on ASSIST2012, and 1.76% higher on ASSISTChall. The results show that cartKT can effectively improve the accuracy of response answer prediction with great advantages. (2) The superiority of cartKT on ASSISTChall is more evident compared to ASSIST2012 and Junyi, which may be due to our model's better generalization ability on small-scale datasets. (3) Transformer-based models such as AKT, extraKT, and LefoKT generally perform well, as they all adopt improved attention mechanisms tailored for KT rather than a plain vanilla attention, enabling them to better capture complex dependencies within learning sequences.

Table 2. Performance comparison of different methods on Junyi, ASSIST2012, and ASSISTChall datasets.

Method	Junyi		ASSIST2012		ASSISTChall	
	AUC	ACC	AUC	ACC	AUC	ACC
DKT	0.7334	0.8399	0.7335	0.7381	0.7194	0.6876
DKVN	0.7327	0.8401	0.7317	0.7376	0.7081	0.6817
AKT	<u>0.7959</u>	0.8490	0.7769	<u>0.7593</u>	0.7659	0.7132
ATDKT	0.7310	0.8395	0.7321	0.7370	0.7226	0.6870
simpleKT	0.7950	<u>0.8494</u>	0.7756	0.7531	0.7611	0.7119
DTransformer	0.7783	0.8455	0.7765	0.7569	0.7421	0.7022
extraKT	0.7253	0.8326	0.7753	0.7566	<u>0.7669</u>	<u>0.7148</u>
LefoKT	0.7779	0.8401	<u>0.7771</u>	0.7565	0.7445	0.7040
FKT	0.7921	0.8492	0.7703	0.7515	0.7651	0.7131
cartKT	**0.8010**	**0.8534**	**0.7801**	**0.7608**	**0.7804**	**0.7249**

5.5 Ablation Study

We analyzed the impact of three key components in cartKT: the Complexity-Aware Knowledge Retriever (C), RS Prediction (S), and ART Prediction (T). Table 3 presents the performance of variants with different component combinations, where ✓ indicates the inclusion of a component.

Based on the results, all three components contribute consistently to model improvements. The full model (final row) achieves the highest AUC and ACC across all datasets, indicating that complexity-aware forgetting modeling and the dual-time auxiliary tasks provide complementary benefits. Among individual components, the C module offers the most pronounced gain, demonstrating that incorporating question complexity into attention computation effectively captures differentiated forgetting rates. The S and T modules yield smaller but stable improvements, showing that decomposing response time allows the model to extract finer-grained cognitive signals.

Furthermore, removing any single module (rows 5–7) leads to performance drops. Notably, jointly using S and T consistently outperforms variants that include only one of them, highlighting the synergy between the two auxiliary timing tasks. Specifically, replacing the complexity-aware mechanism with a standard Transformer encoder (removing C) results in a noticeable degradation, underscoring its central role in modeling forgetting dynamics. In summary, the three components reinforce one another and collectively drive the superior performance of cartKT.

Table 3. Ablation experiments on key components (C: Complexity-Aware Knowledge Retriever, S: RS Prediction, T: ART Prediction).

C	S	T	Junyi		ASSIST2012		ASSISTChall	
			AUC	ACC	AUC	ACC	AUC	ACC
-	-	-	0.7955	0.8493	0.7748	0.7569	0.7610	0.7134
✓	-	-	0.7971	0.8502	0.7776	0.7564	0.7722	0.7195
-	✓	-	0.7965	0.8510	0.7757	0.7564	0.7626	0.7188
-	-	✓	0.7969	0.8506	0.7757	0.7561	0.7617	0.7165
-	✓	✓	0.7995	0.8521	0.7766	0.7571	0.7653	0.7201
✓	-	✓	0.7982	0.8516	0.7783	0.7580	0.7743	0.7206
✓	✓	-	0.7994	0.8524	0.7782	0.7584	0.7759	0.7212
✓	✓	✓	**0.8010**	**0.8534**	**0.7801**	**0.7608**	**0.7804**	**0.7249**

5.6 Parameter Sensitivity Analysis

To investigate the impact of critical hyperparameters on model performance, we conducted a sensitivity analysis on the ASSISTChall dataset for the loss function weights λ_1 and λ_2, the time decay smoothing factor γ, and the number of discretization bins for auxiliary tasks C_s and C_μ. As shown in Fig. 2, the weights of the two auxiliary tasks exhibit distinct trends: λ_1 (weight for student response speed) shows an upward trend in performance in the range of 0.01 to 0.7, indicating that appropriately increasing the focus on personalized response speed significantly assists the main task. In contrast, performance declines when λ_2 (weight for average question response time) exceeds 0.1, suggesting that this auxiliary task should not dominate the optimization process. Regarding the time decay factor γ in Fig. 2(b), the AUC metric rises sharply from 0 to 0.3 before reaching its peak, confirming the effectiveness of the proposed complexity-aware time decay mechanism. However, as γ continues to increase toward 1.0, performance gradually declines, suggesting that an overly fast decay rate leads to the loss of long-term dependency information. Therefore, $\gamma = 0.3$ represents the optimal balance between forgetting and memory. Finally, Fig. 2(c) demonstrates the model's robustness to the number of categories. Specifically, the student response speed (C_s) performs best when the number of categories reaches 9–10, implying that a finer-grained division of speed is more conducive to capturing the student's latent state, while the average question response time (C_μ) saturates around 5 categories, which validates the selection of $C_s = 10$ and $C_\mu = 5$ in our experimental setup.

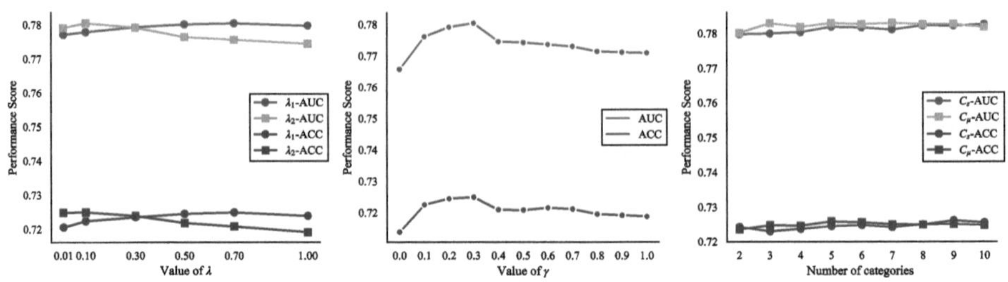

(a) Sensitivity of λ_1 and λ_2 (b) Sensitivity of γ (c) Sensitivity of C_s and C_μ

Fig. 2. Sub-figures (a)-(c) show the sensitivity of parameters λ_1, λ_2, γ, C_s and C_μ on dataset ASSISTChall.

6 Conclusion

In this paper, we propose to enhance the KT process with both a complexity-aware attention mechanism and a decoupled response time multi-task framework. With these designs, our cartKT approach is able to finely simulate the differentiated forgetting rates induced by question-specific complexity and effectively decouple response time to reduce question-induced confounding and obtain a more faithful mapping from latent knowledge states to observable performance. Experiment results on three real-world educational datasets demonstrate that cartKT outperforms the state-of-the-art approaches in terms of both AUC and ACC metrics. In the future, we plan to investigate the integration of our complexity-aware mechanism with other cognitive modalities to further improve model interpretability.

References

1. Bai, Y., Li, X., Liu, Z., Huang, Y., Tian, M., Luo, W.: Rethinking and improving student learning and forgetting processes for attention based knowledge tracing models. In: AAAI, vol. 39 (2025)
2. Chen, O., Paas, F., Sweller, J.: A cognitive load theory approach to defining and measuring task complexity through element interactivity. Educ. Psychol. Rev. **35**(2), 63 (2023)
3. Corbett, A.T., Anderson, J.R.: Knowledge tracing: modeling the acquisition of procedural knowledge. User Model. User-Adap. Inter. **4**, 253–278 (1994)

4. Ghosh, A., Heffernan, N., Lan, A.S.: Context-Aware Attentive Knowledge Tracing. In: SIGKDD (2020)
5. Huang, T., et al.: Response speed enhanced fine-grained knowledge tracing: a multi-task learning perspective. Expert Syst. Appl. **238**, 122107 (2024)
6. Im, Y., Choi, E., Kook, H., Lee, J.: Forgetting-aware linear bias for attentive knowledge tracing. In: CIKM (2023)
7. Krishnan, R., Singh, J., Sato, M., Zhang, Q., Ohkuma, T.: Incorporating wide context information for deep knowledge tracing using attentional bi-interaction. In: L2D@ WSDM (2021)
8. Li, X., et al.: Extending context window of attention based knowledge tracing models via length extrapolation. In: ECAI (2024)
9. Liu, Q., et al.: EKT: exercise-aware knowledge tracing for student performance prediction. IEEE Trans. Knowl. Data Eng. **33**(1), 100–115 (2019)
10. Liu, Y., Yang, Y., Chen, X., Shen, J., Zhang, H., Yu, Y.: Improving knowledge tracing via pre-training question embeddings (2020). arXiv:2012.05031 arXiv preprint
11. Liu, Z., et al.: Enhancing deep knowledge tracing with auxiliary tasks. In: www (2023)
12. Liu, Z., Liu, Q., Chen, J., Huang, S., Luo, W.: simplekt: A simple but tough-to-beat baseline for knowledge tracing. In: ICLR (2023)
13. Liu, Z., Liu, Q., Chen, J., Huang, S., Tang, J., Luo, W.: pyKT: a python library to benchmark deep learning based knowledge tracing models. Adv. Neural. Inf. Process. Syst. **35**, 18542–18555 (2022)
14. Long, T., Liu, Y., Shen, J., Zhang, W., Yu, Y.: Tracing knowledge state with individual cognition and acquisition estimation. In: SIGIR (2021)
15. Luce, R.D.: Response times: Their role in inferring elementary mental organization (1991)
16. Nagatani, K., Zhang, Q., Sato, M., Chen, Y.Y., Chen, F., Ohkuma, T.: Augmenting knowledge tracing by considering forgetting behavior. In: WWW (2019)
17. Nakagawa, H., Iwasawa, Y., Matsuo, Y.: Graph-based knowledge tracing: modeling student proficiency using graph neural network. In: IEEE/WIC/ACM International Conference on Web Intelligence, pp. 156–163. (2019)
18. Piech, C., et al.: Deep knowledge tracing. In: Advances in Neural Information Processing Systems, vol. 28 (2015)
19. Shen, S., et al.: Learning process-consistent knowledge tracing. In: SIGKDD (2021)
20. Shin, D., Shim, Y., Yu, H., Lee, S., Kim, B., Choi, Y.: Saint+: Integrating temporal features for ednet correctness prediction. In: LAK (2021)
21. Sweller, J.: Cognitive load during problem solving: effects on learning. Cogn. Sci. **12**(2), 257–285 (1988)
22. Xu, B., et al.: Learning Behavior-oriented Knowledge Tracing. In: SIGKDD (2023)
23. Yang, Y., et al.: GIKT: a graph-based interaction model for knowledge tracing. In: ECML PKDD (2021)
24. Yeung, C.K., Yeung, D.Y.: Addressing two problems in deep knowledge tracing via prediction-consistent regularization. In: Proceedings of the Fifth Annual ACM Conference on Learning at Scale, pp. 1–10 (2018)
25. Yin, Y., et al.: Tracing knowledge instead of patterns: stable knowledge tracing with diagnostic transformer. In: WWW (2023)
26. Zhan, P., Jiao, H., Liao, D.: Cognitive diagnosis modelling incorporating item response times. Br. J. Math. Stat. Psychol. **71**(2), 262–286 (2018)

27. Zhan, P., Liao, M., Bian, Y.: Joint testlet cognitive diagnosis modeling for paired local item dependence in response times and response accuracy. Front. Psychol. **9**, 607 (2018)
28. Zhang, J., Shi, X., King, I., Yeung, D.Y.: Dynamic key-value memory networks for knowledge tracing. In: WWW (2017)

Estimating Representation Drift for Prompt-Based Class-Incremental Learning

Yuting Hou, Rongyu Zhu, Junjie Liu, and Kedian Mu(✉)

School of Mathematical Science, Peking University, Beijing, China
{houyuting2000,zhurongyu}@pku.edu.cn, liujunjie@stu.pku.edu.cn, mukedian@math.pku.edu.com

Abstract. Exemplar-Free Class-Incremental Learning (EFCIL) aims to mitigate catastrophic forgetting while sequentially learning new tasks without access to previous data. Recently, prompt-based methods, which train only a small set of parameters known as prompts and use a query-key mechanism to retrieve corresponding prompts for each input, have received much attention. However, most of the prompt-based learners retrieve imprecise prompts during the testing phase due to the limitations in the representation capacity of the pre-trained model, which leads to a mismatch between classifiers and features. Secondly, without samples from past tasks, classifiers tend to classify the test data as the classes of the new task. To solve these two problems, we propose a novel prompt-based method called Adaptive Representation Drift Prompt (ARD-Prompt). We first utilize the samples from the current task to estimate a projection from the old to the new representation space, enabling the migration of the features of old classes into the new space. Then these migrated features are used to train a more effective classifier. Furthermore, we incorporate task-related information into the query-key mechanism to retrieve more appropriate prompts during testing. Experiments on Split CIFAR-100 and Split ImageNet-R show that our approach achieves state-of-the-art results.

Keywords: Incremental learning · Continual learning · Lifelong learning · Catastrophic forgetting · Prompt learning · Class-incremental learning

1 Introduction

Deep neural networks are known to suffer from catastrophic forgetting [4,15] when they learn tasks sequentially. Incremental Learning [1,25], which learns new tasks while preserving old knowledge, has received widespread attention. There are two main scenarios for incremental learning: Class-Incremental Learning

K. Mu—This work was partly supported by the National Natural Science Foundation of China under Grant No. 62576014.

J. Niu et al. (Eds.): KSEM 2026, LNAI 16631, pp. 67–83, 2027.
https://doi.org/10.1007/978-981-92-2759-4_6

(CIL) and Task-Incremental Learning (TIL) [26]. The main difference between them is that task identities of test samples are available during inference in TIL but not in CIL. Therefore, CIL is the more challenging of the two scenarios. Replay-based methods [16,17,21], one of the typical paradigms for CIL, aim to utilize an additional replay buffer to store a subset of past samples to mitigate forgetting. However, past data are usually unavailable due to memory limitations and data privacy in real-world scenarios. Thus, it is necessary to consider Exemplar-Free Class-Incremental Learning (EFCIL) [13,22].

Recently, with the widespread use of Large Language Models (LLMs) [10,34] and Vision Transformers (ViTs) [3], prompt-based methods [23,27,29–31] have shown attractive results in EFCIL. Differing from traditional deep learning methods that update network parameters directly, prompt-based methods freeze the backbone and focus on training a limited number of task-specific parameters for downstream tasks, known as prompts. Then they employ a query-key mechanism to retrieve appropriate prompts during testing. These approaches achieve state-of-the-art performance on several benchmark datasets and they exhibit reduced training time and computational resource requirements compared to traditional CIL methods.

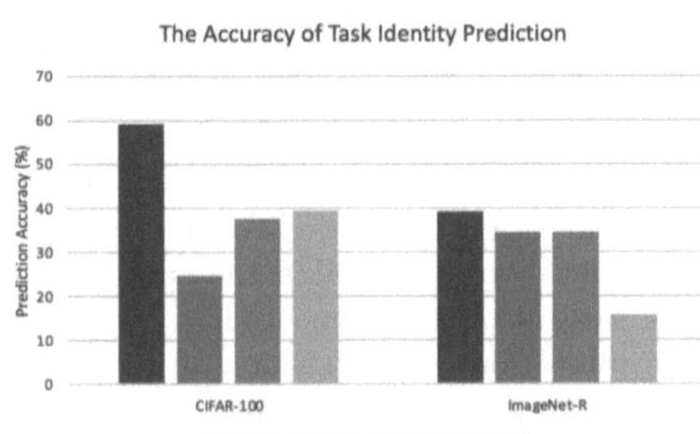

Fig. 1. S-Prompt's accuracy of task identity prediction using different pre-trained models on Split CIFAR-100 and Split ImageNet-R.

However, there are still two issues that limit the performance of these prompt-based models. Firstly, most of the methods do not consider the negative effect of the usual query-key mechanism. Note that the query is only gained by pre-trained models which are task-agnostic. If the domain of tasks differs from the pre-trained dataset, the prompts gained by query might be unsuitable. Inappropriate prompts further lead to degradation of the model's performance. To illustrate this, we consider the accuracy of task identity prediction of S-Prompt [29] using different pre-trained models on Split CIFAR-100 and 10-task Split ImageNet-R, which are shown in Fig. 1. Obviously, as the pre-trained dataset changes, the accuracy of task identity prediction varies widely. Secondly, due to the unavailability of past data in EFCIL scenarios, models are more likely to label incoming data as newly introduced classes. Consequently, this phenomenon leads to a notable decline in the accuracy of old tasks, thereby undermining the stability and performance of the models across different tasks.

In this paper, we propose a new prompt-based method, named Adaptive Representation Drift Prompt (ARD-Prompt). As mentioned above, most prompt-based methods cannot classify data from old tasks well. To alleviate this challenge, we estimate the representation of the old samples in the representation space with the new prompts embedded. Then we utilize the representation of old and new data to train a more adaptive classifier. In this way, we achieve better classification results even if the prompts are unsuitable. In addition, to improve the prompt retrieval process, we introduce an improved prompt retrieval mechanism without additional training. Specifically, we take advantage of the information associated with the prompt to retrieve the appropriate prompts. For each prompt, in addition to the cosine similarity between the query and the key, we also consider the maximum output associated with the corresponding task as an evaluation metric. This dual-criterion approach enables more accurate and contextually relevant prompt retrieval, thereby improving the overall performance of the model.

Our main contributions can be summarized as follows:

(1) The empirical experiments show that inappropriate prompts and incomplete classifiers of the existing prompt-based methods lead to the sub-optimality of the models.
(2) To tackle the problem of models favoring new classes, we propose Representation Drift Estimator (RDE) to estimate the representation of the old samples in the new representation space.
(3) To retrieve a more appropriate prompt, we propose a new self-calibration prompt retrieval mechanism called Prompt Retriever (PR). Compared to the traditional query-key mechanism, PR takes advantage of task-specific information associated with the prompt, which makes the prompt retrieval process more reliable.
(4) On Split CIFAR-100 and Split ImageNet-R, ARD-Prompt achieves state-of-the-art performance, as demonstrated by experimental results. Additionally, the ablation study confirms the effectiveness of RDE and PR.

The rest of this paper is organized as follows. We introduce related work in Sect. 2. Then we present problem formulation, empirical analysis and structure of ARD-Prompt in Sect. 3. Experiments and conclusions are shown in Sects. 4 and 5, respectively.

2 Related Work

2.1 Class-Incremental Learning

In general, the existing class-incremental learning methods can be divided into three categories: replay-based methods, regularization-based methods and parameter isolation methods.

Replay-based methods [16,17,21] use a replay buffer to store a small number of selective past samples and leverage them to prevent catastrophic forgetting. Although these approaches achieve impressive performances, they are limited by memory limitations and data privacy in real-world scenarios. Regularization-based methods [2,12] constrain changes in parameters which are important to past tasks by adding regularization terms to the loss function. These methods still have limitations due to the difficulty in assessing the significance of network parameters and widely known stability-plasticity dilemma. Parameter isolation methods [11,28] adapt to new learning tasks by dynamically modifying the model structure or incorporating new network parameters. These approaches can completely prevent catastrophic forgetting by fixing task-wise parameters, but they come with high training costs and increased memory as the number of tasks grows.

2.2 Prompt-Based Class-Incremental Learning

As large language models receive widespread attention, Visual Prompt Tuning (VPT) [8] is proposed and applied to various vision tasks. Prompt-based methods have achieved state-of-the-art results in EFCIL. Unlike the classical CIL methods, they freeze the parameters of pre-trained ViTs and train a few parameters called prompts inserted into the multi-head self-attention layers instead. Prompt-based methods can be further divided into two categories: prompt-pool methods and pool-free prompt methods.

Prompt-pool methods construct a learnable prompt pool and retrieve prompts through the query-key mechanism. L2P [31] was the first to apply prompts to incremental learning. It builds a pool of prompts and retrieves the appropriate prompt for each sample. Dual-Prompt [30] designs two types of prompts, general-prompt and expert-prompt, to capture both sharing and task-specific features simultaneously. CODA-Prompt [23] designs an end-to-end prompt, which is represented as a linear combination of task-related prompts. While the prompt-pool methods have achieved surprising results, they are severely limited by the relevance of the pre-trained dataset and downstream tasks.

Pool-free prompt methods train a prompt generator to generate instance-level prompts for each sample. DAP [9] optimizes an adaptive prompt generator that creates instance-specific prompts for each sample. GPLS [32] regards prompts as Gaussian distributions and generates prompts from these distributions. These methods train additional parameters to generate prompts and achieve significant performance improvements. The prompt generator also suffers from the catastrophic forgetting, which limits the performance of pool-free prompt methods.

2.3 Representation Drift in Class-Incremental Learning

In class-incremental learning, the representation space changes as network parameters are updated. Therefore, it is an important problem to estimate the old representation in the new representation space. PRL [20] constructs an auxiliary space that compresses old classes while guiding new features to embed into the reserved space. ADC [6] generates pseudo samples and estimates the migration of prototype using the average migration of these pseudo samples. Adaguess [19] estimates the distribution of old classes through adapting the covariance matrix.

3 Adaptive Representation Drift Prompt

In this section, we first introduce the problem formulation of prompt-based CIL. Then we analyse the current challenges of prompt-based methods through empirical experiments. Inspired by the analysis, we present our approach.

3.1 Problem Formulation

In CIL setting, the model is designed to learn knowledge from a sequence of tasks $T_1, T_2, \cdots, T_N$. The training dataset of T_t can be represented as $D_t = \{(x_n^t, y_n^t)\}_{n=1}^{N_t}$. Here, N_t is the number of samples in training set D_t and $x_n^t \in X_t$ belongs to the class $y_n^t \in Y_t$, where X_t and Y_t represent the input space and the label space of task t. We use c_t^k to denote the k-th class of task T_t. Y_i and Y_j are non-overlapping for $i \neq j$ and $|Y_t| = n_t$. The model aims to learn a projection $h_\phi(f_\theta(\cdot))$ from $X = \cup_{i=1}^N X_i$ to $Y = \cup_{i=1}^N Y_i$ and predict the label of testing data x. The feature extractor $f_\theta(\cdot)$ is a frozen pre-trained model and $h_\phi(\cdot)$ is a learnable classifier. Let $f_\theta(\cdot, p)$ represent the feature extractor with the prompt p embedded. Dataset D_t is only available in incremental session t and the task identity of data is unknown while testing. $\phi_i^{t,k}(i \leq t)$ is the prototype of the k-th class of task t in feature extractor with p_i embedded, i.e.,

$$\phi_i^{t,k} = \frac{1}{N_{t,k}} \sum_{j=1}^{N_t} f_\theta(x_j^t, p_i)\mathbf{I}(y_j^t = c_t^k), \tag{1}$$

where, $N_{t,k} = \sum_{j=1}^{N_t} \mathbf{I}(y_j^t = c_t^k)$ is the number of samples of the k-th class of task t. We use $|\Sigma_i^{t,k}|(i \leq t)$ to denote the determinant of the covariance matrix of the k-th class of task t in feature extractor with p_i embedded, which will be used to sample the old representation.

In this paper, we separately use new prompts and old prompts to express prompts related to new and old tasks. Similarly we denote new representation and old representation, new representation space and old representation space.

In our work, we use the technical foundations of prompting from DualPrompt [8]. In prompt-based CIL, frozen ViTs are usually regarded as the feature extractor. ViT includes an embedding layer f_e and multi-head self-attention (MSA) layers $f_1, f_2, \cdots, f_n$. We put prompts into part of these MSA layers and use prefix-tuning [8] to adapt the feature extractor.

Specifically, we define a prompt parameter $p \in \mathbb{R}^{L_p \times D}$, where L_p is the prompt length and D is embedding dimension. In ViTs, for an MSA layer with input $h \in \mathbb{R}^{L \times D}$, the output of this layer is represented as:

$$\mathrm{MSA}(h_Q, h_K, h_V) = \mathrm{Concat}(h_1, h_2, \cdots, h_m)W^O, \tag{2}$$

where, $h_Q = h_K = h_V = h$ and

$$h_i = \mathrm{Attention}\left(h_Q W_i^Q, h_K W_i^K, h_V W_i^V\right). \tag{3}$$

We split prompt p into $\{p_K, p_V\} \in \mathbb{R}^{L_p/2 \times D}$ and attach them to MSA layer separately, i.e., $\mathrm{MSA}(h_Q, [p_K, h_K], [p_V, h_V])$. We freeze the backbone and only update prompt parameters while training. Apart from prompt p, we train a group of parameters called key for each prompt. The keys are matched with query function to retrieve prompts during forward propagation.

In this paper, we consider prompts in each block and tasks to be highly relevant. In other words, if we identify that a sample belongs to task T_t, prompts related to task T_t will be embedded in each block. In addition, we consider that the query of input x is the feature $f_\theta(x)$ and we use it to identify the task identity. We denote the representation space of the feature extractor with the prompt p_i embedded by S_i.

3.2 Empirical Study of Prompt-Pool Methods

As mentioned in Sect. 1, we speculate that the sub-optimality of the prompt-pool methods can be attributed to the following two points: (1) Inappropriate prompts lead to the inappropriate presentation in unsuitable representation space; (2) The classifier cannot simultaneously adapt to old and new representation spaces. We validated these two points through empirical experiments.

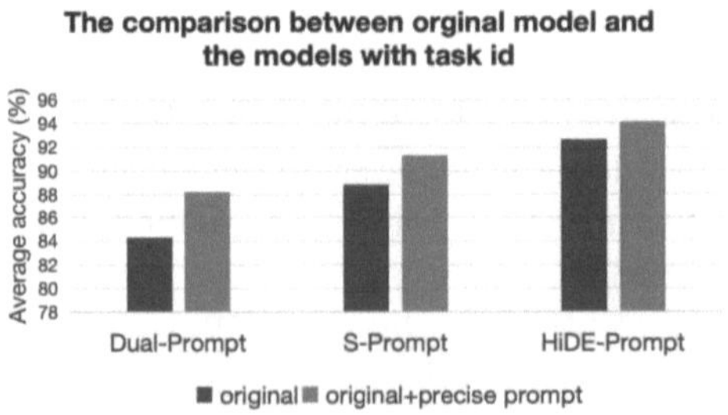

Fig. 2. The comparison between the original prompt-pool methods and the models with precise prompts.

First, we demonstrate that inappropriate prompts limit the performance of existing prompt-pool methods. On the one hand, we test the accuracy of task identity prediction. As shown in Fig. 1 in Sect. 1, the accuracy of task identity prediction of S-Prompt [29] on each pre-trained model is nearly all below 40 percent, which indicates that traditional query-key mechanism is difficult to retrieve precise prompts. On the other hand, we test the performance of the prompt-pool models with precise prompts. The comparison between original prompt-pool methods and these methods with precise prompts is shown in Fig. 2, which illustrates that with precise task-specific prompts, the models could perform better than original methods. Therefore, we conclude that the inaccurate prompt is an important cause of the sub-optimality of prompt-pool methods.

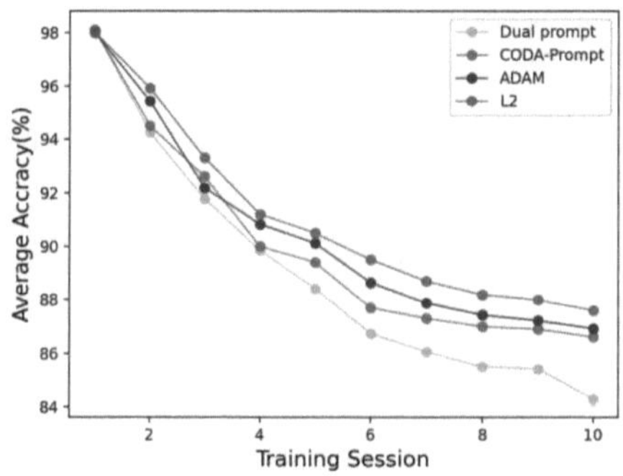

Fig. 3. The comparison of ADAM, L2, Dual-Prompt and CODA-Prompt.

Second, we compare prompt-pool methods with other approaches based on pre-trained models which mainly train classifiers [24,35]. The result is shown in Fig. 3, which validates that without any restriction on classifiers, the prompt-pool methods are inferior to other methods based on pre-trained models. We attribute this phenomenon to the fact that the classifiers are not adapted to all representation spaces. The classifiers are only trained on the new space and they may not work well on old spaces. Thus, no restriction on classifiers is another important reason for the sub-optimality of prompt-pool approaches.

In light of the empirical study presented above, it has been observed that there is a dual necessity: to enhance the accuracy of task identity prediction and to train a classifier that adapts to all representation spaces. Subsequently, we will introduce the Representation Drift Estimator (RDE) in Sect. 3.3 and the Prompt Retrieval (PR) in Sect. 3.4.

3.3 Representation Drift Estimator

Due to the unavailability of past data, we are unable to gain the distribution of past classes in the new space directly, which leads to a decrease in the accuracy of old tasks. Therefore estimating the distribution of the old class in the new representation space is an effective way to mitigate the decline in the performance of old tasks. While learning task T_t, we use one two-layer perception $g_{i\rightarrow t}(i =$

$1, 2, \cdots, t-1$), called Representation Drift Estimator (RDE), to estimate the drift from the old representation space S_i to the new representation space S_t. We use the following loss function as the optimization objective:

$$L_{i\to t} = \sum_{j=1}^{N_t} \|g_{i\to t}(f_\theta(x_j^t, p_i)) - f_\theta(x_j^t, p_t)\|_2^2, \tag{4}$$

where $x_j^t \in D_t$ is the sample in task T_t.

To avoid additional memory, we use one two-layer perception to estimate representation drift of all tasks sequentially.

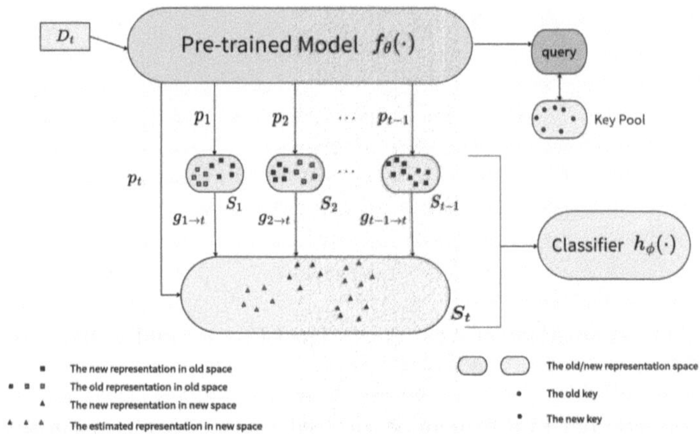

Fig. 4. Illustration of the training session of ARD-Prompt. During training session t, the model firstly trains the task-specific prompt p_t and its corresponding key k_t. For task $i(i < t)$, we utilize the representation of new samples in S_i and S_t to train the Representation Drift Estimator $g_{i\to t}$. Then we use $g_{i\to t}$ to generate the new representation of old classes in task i. With new representation of old classes, the model trains the classifier through minimize the cross entropy.

During incremental session t, after training prompts p_t and their corresponding keys k_t, we randomly initialize RDE and sequentially train $g_{i\to t}(i = 1, 2, \cdots, t-1)$ through minimizing the Eq. 4. After training $g_{i\to t}$, we generate the representation of the kth class in task i in new space S_t as follows:

$$D_t^{i,k} = \{r_m = g_{i\to t}(\pi(\phi_i^{i,k}, |\Sigma_i^{i,k}|))|m = 1, 2, \cdots, M\}, \tag{5}$$

where the definition of $\phi_i^{i,k}$ is shown in Eq. 1 and $\pi(\cdot,\cdot)$ denotes a prototype augmentation function, which is similar to PASS [36]. To be more specific, we consider the prototype ϕ as the center and the square root of the determinant of the covariance matrix $\sqrt{|\Sigma|}$ as the scale factor. We perturb the prototype by a scaled Gaussian noise $\hat{\phi} = \phi + \sqrt{|\Sigma|} * e$, where $e \sim \mathcal{N}(0, \mathcal{I})$ is a Gaussian distribution. We sample $M = 100$ samples and utilize these samples to estimate the prototypes of old classes in the new representation space.

In this process, we only store the determinant of the covariance matrix and use one two-layer perception as RDE, so there is almost no extra memory cost for this part.

RDE provides the representation of old data in the new representation space. Then we utilize the generated representation to train a better classifier and calculate the prototype of old classes in new space. We use $\phi_t^{i,k}$ and $|\Sigma_t^{i,k}|$ to represent the estimated prototype and the determinant of the covariance matrix of c_i^k in S_t.

3.4 Prompt Retriever

Limited by the representation capabilities of pre-trained models, the prompts selected by query-key mechanism are usually inappropriate. Apart from calculating the cosine similarity of query and key, we utilize the information contained in the prompts to assist in retrieving suitable prompts. Specifically, in ideal situation, if a sample belongs to task i, we tend to retrieve prompt p_i in the process of prompt retrieval. For prompt p_i, we regard the maximum output of the classes in task i as confidence level and combine it with cosine similarity between query and key as scoring function:

$$S(x, i) = \text{cosine}(q(x), k_i) + \beta \max_{y \in Y_i} h_\phi(f_\theta(x, p_i))[y], \tag{6}$$

where β is the balance hyper-parameter of cosine similarity and the confidence level of the classification results.

While testing, the model retrieves the index of the task with the maximum scoring function as the result of task identity prediction. Finally the model retrieves corresponding prompts as follows:

$$p = p_j, \ j = \arg\max_{1 \leq i \leq t} S(x, i). \tag{7}$$

After retrieving prompt p, we classify test data on all seen classes as follows:

$$y = \arg\max_{y \in \cup_{k=1}^{t} Y_k} \ h_\phi(f_\theta(x, p))[y]. \tag{8}$$

3.5 Overall Optimization Objective

In this section, we will introduce the main framework of our work.

As shown in Fig. 4, at the beginning of training session t, a classical cross entropy loss L_{CE}^t is first used to train the task-specific key k_t and prompt p_t. Then we train the Representation Drift Estimator and use it to generate representation sets $D_t^{i,k}$ $(i = 1, 2, \cdots, t-1; k = 1, 2, \cdots, n_i)$, which contain the representation of old data in new representation space as mentioned in Sect. 3.3. The cross entropy of past classes in new space is defined as follows:

$$L_{CE}^{past} = \sum_{i=1}^{t-1} \sum_{k=1}^{n_i} \sum_{r \in D_t^{i,k}} L_{CE}(h_\phi(r), c_i^k). \tag{9}$$

Next, to confirm the performance of the classifier in both old and new representation spaces, we propose the following loss function:

$$\begin{aligned} L_{CE}^{current} = \sum_{i=1}^{t-1} \sum_{n=1}^{N_t} L_{CE}(h_\phi(f_\theta(x_n^t, p_i)), y_n^t) + \\ \lambda \sum_{n=1}^{N_t} L_{CE}(h_\phi(f_\theta(x_n^t, p_t)), y_n^t), \end{aligned} \tag{10}$$

where λ is the hyper-parameter that balances old and new spaces.

Finally, to possibly ensure that old samples are not classified into new classes in old representation spaces, we consider the following loss function:

$$L_{CE}^{pf} = \sum_{m=1}^{t-1} \sum_{i=1}^{t-1} \sum_{k=1}^{n_i} L_{CE}(h_\phi(\pi(\phi_m^{i,k}, |\Sigma_m^{i,k}|)), c_i^k), \tag{11}$$

where the definition of $\pi(\cdot, \cdot)$ is the same prototype augmentation function as Eq. 5.

The overall optimization loss is represented as:

$$L = L_{CE}^{past} + \alpha_1 L_{CE}^{current} + \alpha_2 L_{CE}^{pf}, \tag{12}$$

where α_1 and α_2 are the hyper-parameters that balance different components.

During testing sessions, for each test point, the model calculates the score function for each prompt and selects the prompt with the maximum score as the corresponding prompt.

RDE provides pseudo samples of past classes for the model to train a better classifier, which helps PR determine the task identity for test points during the testing phase more accurately. Under the interaction of RDE and PR, ARD-Prompt alleviates the two problems raised in Sect. 3.2.

4 Experiments

4.1 Experimental Setup

We evaluate ARD-Prompt on two datasets: Split CIFAR-100 and Split ImageNet-R.

Split CIFAR-100 is a widely used incremental learning benchmark. It contains 100 classes which are randomly split into 10 incremental tasks of disjoint classes and each class has 500 training samples and 100 testing samples.

Split ImageNet-R [30] was first adapted for incremental learning by Dual-Prompt and is more relevant to real-life scenarios. Similarly, it contains 200 classes which are randomly split into 5, 10 or 20 incremental tasks of disjoint classes and each class has 120 training samples and 30 testing samples.

Evaluation Metrics: We repeat each method 3 times on two datasets and compare their average values with standard errors using two CIL metrics: **Average accuracy** and **Forgetting rate**.

The **Average accuracy** is the average prediction accuracy of T tasks after training process, i.e., $AA_T = \frac{1}{T}\sum_{i=1}^{T} A_{i,T}$, where $A_{i,T}$ is the average accuracy of all classes in task i after training task T.

The **Forgetting rate** of the model is the average forgetting rate of all tasks. The forgetting rate of task i is the gap between the best and the worst accuracy of task i, i.e.: $FR_T = \frac{1}{T-1}\sum_{i=1}^{T}(A_{i,i} - A_{i,T})$.

We compare our ARD-Prompt with five prompt-pool methods, L2P [31], Dual-Prompt [5], CODA-Prompt [23], S-Prompt [29], HiDe-Prompt [27], two methods based on pre-trained models, ADAM [35], SLCA [33] and two LoRA-based methods InfLoRA [14] and CL-LoRA [7] on above two benchmark datasets. **Upper Bound** is the average accuracy of joint training. All these baselines are class-incremental learning methods and based on ViTs.

In our experiment setup, we consider ViT-B/16 pre-trained on ImageNet-21K [18] as the backbone and Adam (β_1=0.9, $\beta_2 = 0.9$) with a learning rate of 0.001 as the optimizer. All the input images are resized to resolution of 224×224, normalized to $[0, 1]$ and with a batch size of 64. The length of the prompts in each layer is fixed at 10. The number of training epochs is 20 for Split CIFAR-100 and 30 for ImageNet-R. We set $\lambda = 1$ in Eq. 10. RDE is trained for 20 epochs in all experiments. We set $\alpha_1 = 1, \alpha_2 = 0.5$ for Split CIFAR-100; $\alpha_1 = 0.5, \alpha_2 = 0.2$ for 5-task ImageNet-R; $\alpha_1 = 1, \alpha_2 = 0.5$ for 10-task ImageNet-R; and $\alpha_1 = 2, \alpha_2 = 1$ for 20-task ImageNet-R. We run experiments on Split CIFAR-100 and Split ImageNet-R on 1×NVIDIA GeForce RTX 4090 GPU.

4.2 Main Results

The experimental results of ARD-Prompt and other class-incremental learning baselines on Split CIFAR-100 and Split ImageNet-R are shown in Table 1. The results show that the average accuracy of ARD-Prompt outperforms all existing prompt-based approaches by at least 1.38% and 1.23% on Split CIFAR-100 and Split ImageNet-R, and the forgetting rate of ARD-Prompt is lower than most of the baselines.

To be more specific, the improvement of ARD-Prompt on Split CIFAR-100 is not as significant as that on Split ImageNet-R. The reason for this phenomenon is that the pre-trained dataset we used is more similar to CIFAR-100 than ImageNet-R so that nearly all of the methods perform well enough on Split CIFAR-100. For Split ImageNet-R, Table 1 shows that as the number of tasks increases, the improvement of ARD-Prompt increases. We analyze that as the number of tasks grows, the more RDE need to be trained and representation of old classes will interfere with each other in the new representation space. Thus the gap between ARD-Prompt and the upper bound becomes larger when the number of tasks grows. In Table 1, we observe that the forgetting rate of ARD-Prompt is lower than other baselines, which indicates that the representation generated by RDE helps model to mitigate catastrophic forgetting effectively. In conclusion, ARD-Prompt performs better than existing CIL methods on Split CIFAR-100 and Split ImageNet-R.

Table 1. Experiment results (%) of class-incremental learning on Split CIFAR-100 and Split ImageNet-R. Here, L2P, Dual-Prompt, CODA-Prompt and HiDE-Promot are the state-of-the-art prompt-pool methods. ADAM and MOS are CIL methods based on pre-trained ViTs. InfLoRA and CL-LoRA are LoRA-based methods.

	Split CIFAR-100 (10-task)		Split ImageNet-R (5-task)		Split ImageNet-R (10-task)		Split ImageNet-R (20-task)	
Method	Avg.Acc.	Forgetting	Avg.Acc.	Forgetting	Avg.Acc.	Forgetting	Avg.Acc.	Forgetting
L2P	83.06 ± 0.17	6.58 ± 0.40	70.83 ± 0.58	3.36 ± 0.18	69.29 ± 0.73	2.03 ± 0.19	65.89 ± 1.30	1.24 ± 0.14
Dual-Prompt	84.29 ± 0.19	4.45 ± 0.16	73.05 ± 0.50	2.64 ± 0.17	71.32 ± 0.62	1.71 ± 0.24	67.87 ± 1.39	1.07 ± 0.14
CODA-Prompt	86.60 ± 0.63	4.04 ± 0.18	75.19 ± 0.47	3.65 ± 0.15	73.93 ± 0.49	1.64 ± 0.10	70.53 ± 1.24	1.00 ± 0.15
S-Prompt	88.81 ± 0.18	3.87 ± 0.05	74.85 ± 0.23	2.49 ± 0.12	73.98 ± 0.25	1.98 ± 0.13	70.65 ± 0.22	1.43 ± 0.19
Hide-Prompt	91.84 ± 0.28	3.16 ± 0.10	76.77 ± 0.14	2.37 ± 0.23	74.57 ± 0.12	2.17 ± 0.19	71.85 ± 0.23	2.62 ± 0.15
ADAM	87.26 ± 0.27	4.42 ± 0.41	75.45 ± 0.21	2.92 ± 0.31	74.34 ± 0.17	2.08 ± 0.20	71.35 ± 0.17	1.53 ± 0.27
SLCA	91.43 ± 0.16	3.69 ± 0.32	76.51 ± 0.29	2.73 ± 0.13	74.21 ± 0.42	1.76 ± 0.25	71.72 ± 0.20	1.12 ± 0.14
InfLoRA	87.31 ± 0.79	4.21 ± 0.41	75.35 ± 0.31	3.45 ± 0.27	74.01 ± 0.24	2.24 ± 0.28	70.00 ± 0.45	1.70 ± 0.24
CL-LoRA	87.65 ± 0.10	3.32 ± 0.22	75.68 ± 0.37	2.34 ± 0.20	74.55 ± 0.23	1.69 ± 0.33	72.61 ± 0.31	1.26 ± 0.19
Upper Bound	94.45	–	82.15	–	82.15	–	82.15	–
ours	**93.22 ± 0.43**	**2.38 ± 0.32**	**78.31 ± 0.42**	**1.83 ± 0.25**	**75.99 ± 0.16**	**1.58 ± 0.20**	**73.08 ± 0.17**	**0.85 ± 0.07**

4.3 Ablation Study

To verify the effectiveness of each component of the model, we perform an ablation experiment on different pre-trained models on Split CIFAR-100. We first consider a naive model which only has task-specific prompts and relies on query-key mechanism to retrieve prompts as baseline, i.e. "ours/PR+RDE" in Table 2. Then we express the naive model with RDE in terms of "ours/PR" and express the naive model with Prompt Retriever in terms of "ours/RDE". The results of ablation experiment are shown in Table 2.

The results show the effectiveness of Prompt Retriever and Representation Drift Estimator. Removing Prompt Retriever performs much better than removing Representation Drift Estimator, which indicates that Representation Drift Estimator plays a more important role in our model.

Table 2. The ablation experiment of ARD-Prompt on different pre-trained models on Split CIFAR-100.

	Sup-21k	iBOT-21k	Moco-1k
ours	93.22 ± 0.43	90.46 ± 0.36	91.08 ± 0.41
ours/PR	90.25 ± 0.65	87.22 ± 0.49	87.52 ± 0.53
ours/RDE	85.32 ± 0.74	81.41 ± 0.97	79.91 ± 0.76
ours/PR+RDE	81.34 ± 0.95	76.19 ± 0.84	74.14 ± 1.18

4.4 Further Experiments and Analysis

In addition to the above experiments, we first compare the accuracy of task identity prediction of S-Prompt, HiDE-Prompt, Dual-Prompt and ARD-Prompt on Split CIFAR-100 on pre-trained model Sup-21k, iBOT-21k and Moco-1k. The experiment result is shown in Fig. 5 and it shows that the accuracy of task identity prediction of ARD-Prompt is much higher than that of other prompt-pool methods, and without Prompt Retriever, the accuracy of task identity prediction of ARD-Prompt has no advantage over other methods. The result indicates that the Prompt Retriever indeed helps the model choose a more appropriate prompt.

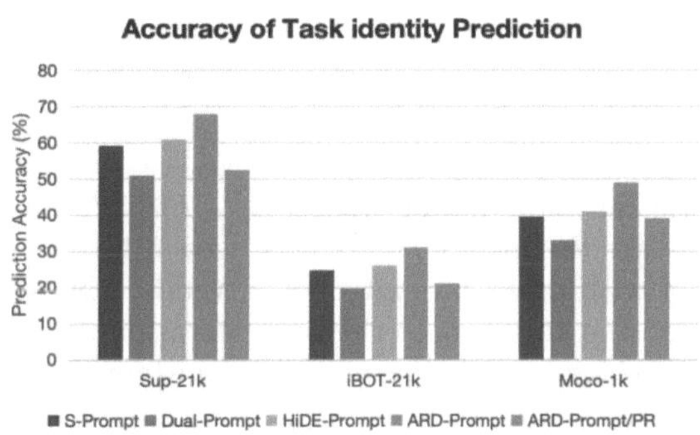

Fig. 5. Accuracy of task identity prediction on different pre-trained models on Split CIFAR-100.

Then we also provide an analysis of the impact of the hyper-parameters. We first adjust β in Prompt Retriever. The results of the experiment on the Split CIFAR-100 and 10-task Split ImageNet-R are shown in Table 3, which indicate that the value of β which is too high or too small can lead to degradation of the performance of the model and $\beta = 1$ is the most appropriate hyper-parameter.

Table 3. Impact of the hyper-parameter β in $L_{CE}^{current}$, which balances the cosine similarity and the confidence level of the classification results

	$\beta = 1$	$\beta = 3$	$\beta = 5$	$\beta = 0.5$	$\beta = 0.2$
Split CIFAR-100	93.22	92.7	92.27	92.34	91.89
Split ImageNet-R	75.69	74.82	74.26	74.23	73.65

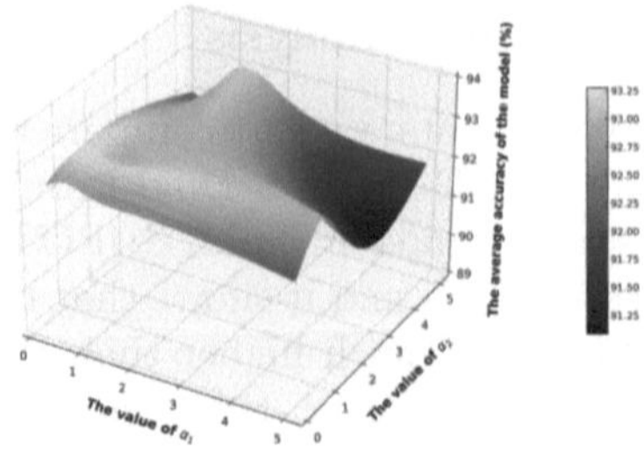

Fig. 6. Impact of the hyper-parameter α_1 and α_2. We test multiple sets of hyper-parameters and generated this fitted surface by interpolation.

Secondly, we analyze the impact of the hyper-parameters α_1, α_2. We assign five values to α_1, α_2 and compare the performance of models on Split CIFAR-100. The results are shown in Fig. 6, which indicate that the performance of models with different parameters does not differ much. The reason for this phenomenon is that there is little contradiction between L_{CE}^{past}, $L_{CE}^{current}$ and L_{CE}^{pf}.

Finally, we evaluate the memory resources needed for the training of ARD-Prompt. Compared with other prompt-pool methods, ARD-Prompt uses only one two-layer perceptron to estimate the representation drift and stores prototypes of old classes, which is negligible compared with other prompt-pool methods.

Table 4 shows the memory usage of different prompt-pool models on Split CIFAR-100. We observe that the GPU memory usage for ARD-Prompt and HiDE-Prompt is similar, whereas CODA-Prompt uses more GPU memory.

Table 4. The GPU memory of different prompt-based methods while training on Split CIFAR-100

	L2P	DualPrompt	CODA-Prompt	HiDE-Prompt	ARD-Prompt
GPU Memory	14.8 GB	15.2 GB	24.7 GB	15.8 GB	16.1 GB

5 Conclusion

In this work, we analyze the issues resulting in the sub-optimality of existing prompt-based EFCIL methods through empirical experiments. Then, to address these issues, we propose a novel prompt-pool method ARD-Prompt for EFCIL, which retrieves more accurate task-specific prompts and trains better classifiers through Prompt Retriever and Representation Drift Estimator. In evaluations, ARD-Prompt outperforms existing prompt-pool methods on CIFAR-100 and ImageNet-R. The ablation study verifies the effectiveness of RDE and PR. In future research, we aim to improve training efficiency of ARD-Prompt and explore theoretical foundations to support our work.

References

1. De Lange, M., et al.: A continual learning survey: defying forgetting in classification tasks. IEEE Trans. Pattern Anal. Mach. Intell. **44**(7), 3366–3385 (2021)
2. Dhar, P., Singh, R.V., Peng, K.C., Wu, Z., Chellappa, R.: Learning without memorizing. In: Proceedings of the IEEE/CVF Conference on Computer Vision and Pattern Recognition, pp. 5138–5146 (2019)
3. Dosovitskiy, A.: An image is worth 16 × 16 words: transformers for image recognition at scale. arXiv preprint arXiv:2010.11929 (2020)
4. French, R.M.: Catastrophic forgetting in connectionist networks. Trends Cogn. Sci. **3**(4), 128–135 (1999)
5. Goswami, D., Liu, Y., Twardowski, B., van de Weijer, J.: Fecam: exploiting the heterogeneity of class distributions in exemplar-free continual learning. In: Advances in Neural Information Processing Systems, vol. 36 (2024)
6. Goswami, D., Soutif-Cormerais, A., Liu, Y., Kamath, S., Twardowski, B., Van De Weijer, J.: Resurrecting old classes with new data for exemplar-free continual learning. In: Proceedings of the IEEE/CVF Conference on Computer Vision and Pattern Recognition, pp. 28525–28534 (2024)
7. He, J., Duan, Z., Zhu, F.: Cl-lora: continual low-rank adaptation for rehearsal-free class-incremental learning. In: Proceedings of the Computer Vision and Pattern Recognition Conference, pp. 30534–30544 (2025)
8. Jia, M., Tet al.: Visual prompt tuning. In: Avidan, S., Brostow, G., Cissé, M., Farinella, G.M., Hassner, T. (eds.) Computer Vision – ECCV 2022. ECCV 2022. Lecture Notes in Computer Science, vol. 13693, pp. 709–727. Springer, Cham (2022). https://doi.org/10.1007/978-3-031-19827-4_41
9. Jung, D., Han, D., Bang, J., Song, H.: Generating instance-level prompts for rehearsal-free continual learning. In: Proceedings of the IEEE/CVF International Conference on Computer Vision, pp. 11847–11857 (2023)
10. Kasneci, E., et al.: ChatGPT for good? On opportunities and challenges of large language models for education. Learn. Individ. Differ. **103**, 102274 (2023)
11. Ke, Z., Liu, B., Ma, N., Xu, H., Shu, L.: Achieving forgetting prevention and knowledge transfer in continual learning. In: Advances in Neural Information Processing Systems, vol. 34, pp. 22443–22456 (2021)
12. Kirkpatrick, J., et al.: Overcoming catastrophic forgetting in neural networks. Proc. Natl. Acad. Sci. **114**(13), 3521–3526 (2017)
13. Li, Z., Hoiem, D.: Learning without forgetting. IEEE Trans. Pattern Anal. Mach. Intell. **40**(12), 2935–2947 (2017)
14. Liang, Y.S., Li, W.J.: Inflora: interference-free low-rank adaptation for continual learning. In: Proceedings of the IEEE/CVF Conference on Computer Vision and Pattern Recognition, pp. 23638–23647 (2024)
15. McCloskey, M., Cohen, N.J.: Catastrophic interference in connectionist networks: the sequential learning problem. In: Psychology of Learning and Motivation, vol. 24, pp. 109–165. Elsevier (1989)
16. Rebuffi, S.A., Kolesnikov, A., Sperl, G., Lampert, C.H.: ICARL: incremental classifier and representation learning. In: Proceedings of the IEEE Conference on Computer Vision and Pattern Recognition, pp. 2001–2010 (2017)
17. Rolnick, D., Ahuja, A., Schwarz, J., Lillicrap, T., Wayne, G.: Experience replay for continual learning. In: Advances in Neural Information Processing Systems, vol. 32 (2019)

18. Russakovsky, O., et al.: ImageNet large scale visual recognition challenge. Int. J. Comput. Vision **115**, 211–252 (2015)
19. Rypeść, G., Cygert, S., Trzciński, T., Twardowski, B.: Task-recency bias strikes back: adapting covariances in exemplar-free class incremental learning. In: Advances in Neural Information Processing Systems, vol. 37, pp. 63268–63289 (2024)
20. Shi, W., Ye, M.: Prospective representation learning for non-exemplar class-incremental learning. In: Advances in Neural Information Processing Systems, vol. 37, pp. 995–1018 (2024)
21. Shin, H., Lee, J.K., Kim, J., Kim, J.: Continual learning with deep generative replay. In: Advances in Neural Information Processing Systems, vol. 30 (2017)
22. Smith, J., Hsu, Y.C., Balloch, J., Shen, Y., Jin, H., Kira, Z.: Always be dreaming: a new approach for data-free class-incremental learning. In: Proceedings of the IEEE/CVF International Conference on Computer Vision, pp. 9374–9384 (2021)
23. Smith, J.S., et al.: Coda-prompt: continual decomposed attention-based prompting for rehearsal-free continual learning. In: Proceedings of the IEEE/CVF Conference on Computer Vision and Pattern Recognition, pp. 11909–11919 (2023)
24. Smith, J.S., Tian, J., Halbe, S., Hsu, Y.C., Kira, Z.: A closer look at rehearsal-free continual learning. In: Proceedings of the IEEE/CVF Conference on Computer Vision and Pattern Recognition, pp. 2410–2420 (2023)
25. Thrun, S.: A lifelong learning perspective for mobile robot control. In: Intelligent Robots and Systems, pp. 201–214. Elsevier (1995)
26. Van de Ven, G.M., Tuytelaars, T., Tolias, A.S.: Three types of incremental learning. Nat. Mach. Intell. **4**(12), 1185–1197 (2022)
27. Wang, L., Xie, J., Zhang, X., Huang, M., Su, H., Zhu, J.: Hierarchical decomposition of prompt-based continual learning: rethinking obscured sub-optimality. In: Advances in Neural Information Processing Systems, vol. 36 (2024)
28. Wang, P., Bo, H., Hong, J., Liu, W., Mu, K.: AdaHAT: adaptive hard attention to the task in task-incremental learning. In: Bifet, A., Davis, J., Krilavičius, T., Kull, M., Ntoutsi, E., Žliobaitė, I. (eds.) Machine Learning and Knowledge Discovery in Databases. Research Track. ECML PKDD 2024. Lecture Notes in Computer Science(), vol. 14943, pp. 143–160. Springer, Cham (2024). https://doi.org/10.1007/978-3-031-70352-2_9
29. Wang, Y., Huang, Z., Hong, X.: S-prompts learning with pre-trained transformers: an Occam's razor for domain incremental learning. In: Advances in Neural Information Processing Systems, vol. 35, pp. 5682–5695 (2022)
30. Wang, Z., et al.: DualPrompt: complementary prompting for rehearsal-free continual learning. In: Avidan, S., Brostow, G., Cissé, M., Farinella, G.M., Hassner, T. (eds.) Computer Vision – ECCV 2022. ECCV 2022. Lecture Notes in Computer Science, vol. 13686, pp. 631–648. Springer, Cham (2022). https://doi.org/10.1007/978-3-031-19809-0_36
31. Wang, Z., et al.: Learning to prompt for continual learning. In: Proceedings of the IEEE/CVF Conference on Computer Vision and Pattern Recognition, pp. 139–149 (2022)
32. Yang, C., Liu, W., Chen, S., Qi, J., Zhou, A.: Generating prompts in latent space for rehearsal-free continual learning. In: Proceedings of the 32nd ACM International Conference on Multimedia, MM '24, pp. 8913–8922. Association for Computing Machinery, New York, NY, USA (2024). https://doi.org/10.1145/3664647.3681003
33. Zhang, G., Wang, L., Kang, G., Chen, L., Wei, Y.: SLCA: slow learner with classifier alignment for continual learning on a pre-trained model. In: Proceedings of

the IEEE/CVF International Conference on Computer Vision (ICCV), pp. 19148–19158 (2023)
34. Zhao, W.X., et al.: A survey of large language models. arXiv preprint arXiv:2303.18223 (2023)
35. Zhou, D.W., Cai, Z.W., Ye, H.J., Zhan, D.C., Liu, Z.: Revisiting class-incremental learning with pre-trained models: generalizability and adaptivity are all you need. Int. J. Comput. Vis. 1–21 (2024)
36. Zhu, F., Zhang, X.Y., Wang, C., Yin, F., Liu, C.L.: Prototype augmentation and self-supervision for incremental learning. In: Proceedings of the IEEE/CVF Conference on Computer Vision and Pattern Recognition, pp. 5871–5880 (2021)

Enhancing Document-Level Event Causality Identification via Event Semantic Consistency and Causal Hypergraph Modeling

Weiying Chen[1,2,3], Po Hu[1,2,3(✉)], and Guanyi Chen[1,2,3(✉)]

[1] Hubei Provincial Key Laboratory of Artificial Intelligence and Smart Learning, Central China Normal University, Wuhan, China
weiyingc@mails.ccnu.edu.cn
[2] School of Computer Science, Central China Normal University, Wuhan, China
[3] National Language Resources Monitoring and Research Center for Network Media, Central China Normal University, Wuhan, China
{phu,g.chen}@ccnu.edu.cn

Abstract. Document-level Event Causality Identification (DECI) aims to determine whether a causal relationship exists between two events within a document. Existing approaches typically construct document-level event graphs to facilitate cross-sentence reasoning over long contexts. However, these methods often struggle to effectively represent both events and their causal relationships. In particular, they fail to ensure consistent representations for different surface realizations of the same event and overlook the dependencies among causal relationships. To address these challenges, we propose a novel DECI framework, Event Semantic Consistency and Causal Hypergraph (ESCCH). For each event, ESCCH generates two complementary representations. The first representation is obtained using a language model enhanced with adaptive contrastive learning, which improves the semantic consistency of event representations while increasing their discriminability across different events. The second representation is derived from a causal hypergraph that explicitly models the interdependencies among causal relationships via causal hypergraph learning. Finally, experimental results show that ESCCH consistently achieves state-of-the-art performance on multiple benchmark datasets.

Keywords: Event Causality Identification · Event Representation · Contrastive Learning · Hypergraph Modeling

1 Introduction

Event Causality Identification (ECI) is a fundamental task in Natural Language Processing (NLP), aiming to identify whether a causal relationship exists between two events within texts. It can facilitate a wide range of applications,

J. Niu et al. (Eds.): KSEM 2026, LNAI 16631, pp. 84–100, 2027.
https://doi.org/10.1007/978-981-92-2759-4_7

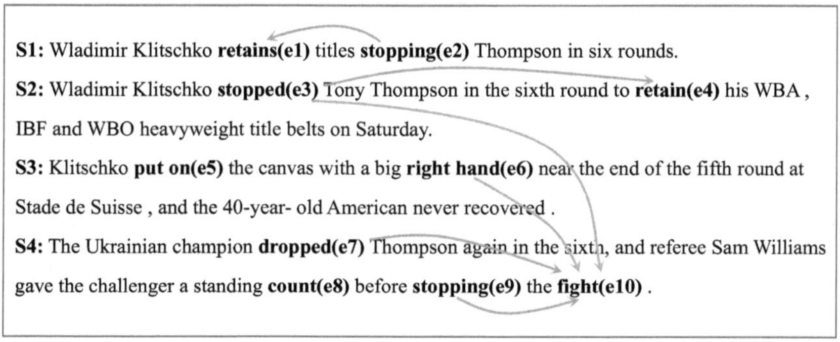

Fig. 1. An example document from the EventStoryLine dataset, where events highlighted in the same color represent similar events. Intra-sentence and inter-sentence causal relations are denoted by blue and green lines, respectively. (Color figure online)

including question answering and event prediction. According to whether two events appear in the same sentence, ECI can be classified into sentence-level ECI (SECI) and document-level ECI (DECI). As shown in Fig. 1, ⟨ *e3, cause, e10* ⟩ illustrates a pair of causal events between sentences, typically spanning greater textual distances and often lacking explicit causal indicators. Such causal pairs are more challenging to identify due to the absence of explicit indicators and the increased contextual distance between the events.

Recent studies [5,17,26] typically construct document-level event interaction graphs and formulate DECI as either a node classification or an edge prediction task. However, this approach to learning event representations has two major limitations.

First, existing methods often rely on local sentence-level context when learning event representations, neglecting the need for representational consistency across different surface realizations of the same event. As illustrated in Fig. 1, events highlighted in the same color correspond to the same underlying event but appear in different forms within the document. For example, *"stopping(e2)/stopped(e3)/stopping(e9)"* differ in surface realization but describe the same stop event. If the causal relationship between *stopping(e9)* and *fight(e10)* is identified, this causality should be transferred to the relationship between *stopped(e3)* and *fight(e10)*, as they represent the same event.

Second, existing graph-based DECI methods typically model only one-to-one binary causal relations, paying insufficient attention to the interdependencies among these relations. As a result, event representation learning (i.e., node representation learning[1]) benefits little from existing relations. In reality, causal relations within a document are often interdependent rather than isolated. A single causal event may lead to multiple effect events, and conversely, a single

[1] Events are represented as nodes in graphs, and learning event representations corresponds to learning node representations.

effect event may be caused by multiple causal events. Consequently, identifying one causal relationship can provide valuable structural cues for discovering other related causal pairs involving the same events. For example, as shown in Fig. 1, *fight(e10)* can be caused by four events: *stopped(e3)*, *dropped(e7)*, *stopping(e9)*, and *right hand(e6)*. Identifying the causal relationship between *fight(e10)* and *stopped(e3)* can help infer other causal relationships such as $\langle$ *e7*, *cause*, *e10* $\rangle$, $\langle$ *e9*, *cause*, *e10* $\rangle$, and $\langle$ *e6*, *cause*, *e10* $\rangle$, as they share the same effect event. A corpus analysis of the EventStoryLine and Causal-TimeBank datasets further shows that such complex causal relations account for 22% and 90% of instances, respectively, underscoring the necessity of explicitly modeling these interdependencies.

To address these limitations, we propose *Event Semantic Consistency and Causal Hypergraph* (ESCCH), an enhanced DECI framework that jointly models semantic consistency and the dependency structure among causal relations to learn more effective event representations. To improve semantic consistency, ESCCH employs adaptive contrastive learning. Specifically, it extracts negative examples from the dataset and leverages large language models (LLMs) to augment positive examples, thereby fine-tuning a RoBERTa model to produce consistent representations for different surface realizations of the same event. To capture interdependencies among causal relations, ESCCH constructs a causal hypergraph for each document, where hyperedges connect multiple causal relations associated with the same event. A hypergraph attention network is then applied to propagate structural information across these interdependent relations. Finally, ESCCH adopts a gating mechanism to dynamically fuse the event representations obtained from the fine-tuned RoBERTa model and the causal hypergraph. The fused representation is subsequently used for causal relation prediction.

2 Related Work

2.1 Event Causality Identification

Determining the causal relationship between events has gained considerable attention in recent years, demonstrating great potential for diverse applications. Early studies have evolved from rule-based methods [9], which relied on manual patterns for explicit causality, to feature-based methods [12] that integrated syntactic and semantic information.

Recently, Pre-trained Language Models (PLMs) have driven significant advancements. To capture implicit causality, recent studies incorporate external knowledge [18,29] or leverage prompt learning [19,23] with tailored templates. Additionally, graph-based methods [5,6,17] reformulate ECI as node or edge prediction, using relational graphs and iterative reasoning to model interactions. However, existing methods are typically limited to modeling one-to-one binary causality. In contrast, our work models the complex dependencies among causal relations by constructing a hypergraph.

2.2 Event Representation Learning

Effective event representation is fundamental for tasks like relation extraction and event prediction, grounded in the principle that similar events should share nearby positions in the embedding space. Early approaches [15, 24] utilized structural concatenation or bilinear tensor operations to model component interactions and surface variations. While recent semantic-enhanced methods [27] leverage event relationships, they often incur high costs due to their reliance on external expert knowledge. To address this, subsequent studies have incorporated sentiment information [28] or exploited document-level co-occurrence [11] to refine representations. Inspired by these works, our work improves event representation by exploiting consistency across different surface realizations of the same event to better support DECI.

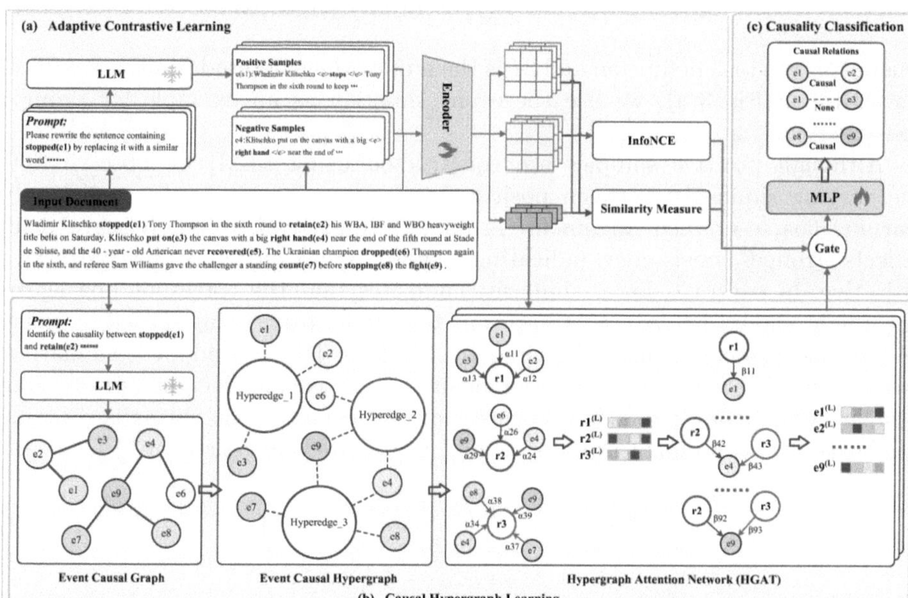

Fig. 2. The framework of our proposed ESCCH.

3 Method

The overall framework of our proposed method for DECI (i.e. ESCCH) is illustrated in Fig. 2, which has three components: (1) an adaptive contrastive learning module, which learns consistent event representations from different surface realizations of the same event; (2) a causal hypergraph learning module, which constructs a causal hypergraph to model the dependency structure between causal relations within the document; (3) a causal relation classification module that fuses the above event representations via a gating mechanism for final causal relation classification.

3.1 Adaptive Contrastive Learning

The same event is often referenced through multiple surface realizations, establishing coreference relationships among these different event mentions. Therefore, to improve model understanding of representational consistency across coreferential event mentions, we introduce adaptive contrastive learning to enhance event representation. Specifically, given the sparsity of coreferential mentions in single documents, we first leverage LLM to generate diverse positive samples. For an event e_i in sentence s_i, the generation process is formulated as:

$$\mathrm{P}(e_i) = \{e_1^s, \cdots, e_M^s\} = \mathrm{LLM}(\mathrm{I}_s, e_i, s_i, M) \tag{1}$$

where I_s is the task definition and M is the number of generated positive samples. As shown in Fig. 3(a), we use the event *stopping* as an example for prompt construction.

Although positive samples are constructed using LLM, we observe that the varying similarity between positive samples can result in the model only learning coarse-grained alignment. A higher similarity between positive pairs reflects stronger consistency, indicating a greater contribution to the contrastive objective. In contrast, lower similarity indicates that the corresponding learning weight should be reduced to prevent the model from being misled by noisy or less informative samples. Inspired by LLM-CL [10], we adopt a similarity-aware weighting mechanism to dynamically adjust learning weights, prioritizing samples with stronger semantic consistency. We compute the normalized cosine similarity between representations h_i and h_i^+ of an event pair (e_i, e_i^+):

$$\mathrm{SM}(h_i, h_i^+) = \frac{1}{2}\left(\frac{h_i \cdot h_i^+}{\|h_i\| \cdot \|h_i^+\|} + 1\right) \tag{2}$$

For each event $e_i = \{w_a, \ldots, w_b\}$ in sentence $s_j = \{w_1, w_2, \ldots, w_n\}$, we utilize RoBERTa [20] to encode s_j and obtain the contextualized representation for all words. The representation of e_i is the average of its trigger word representations, with the encoding process as follows:

$$\begin{aligned} \{h_{w_1}, \ldots, h_{w_n}\} &= \mathrm{RoBERTa}(\{w_1, \ldots, w_n\}) \\ h_i &= \frac{1}{b-a+1}\sum_{j=a}^{b} h_{w_j} \end{aligned} \tag{3}$$

Finally, we revise contrastive loss by incorporating similarity-aware weights for fine-grained alignment. For an event e_i with a set of positive samples $\mathrm{P}(e_i)$

and a set of negative samples $\mathrm{N}(e_i)$, the adaptive contrastive learning loss function can be formulated as follows:

$$\mathcal{L}_{\mathrm{ACL}} = \sum_{i=1}^{|S|} \sum_{j \in \mathrm{P}(e_i)} \mathrm{SM}(h_i, h_j) \cdot \mathrm{InfoNCE}(h_i, h_j)$$
$$\mathrm{InfoNCE}(h_i, h_j) = -\log \frac{\exp(\mathrm{sim}(h_i, h_j)/\tau)}{\sum_{k \in \mathrm{N}(e_i)} \exp(\mathrm{sim}(h_i, h_k)/\tau)} \tag{4}$$

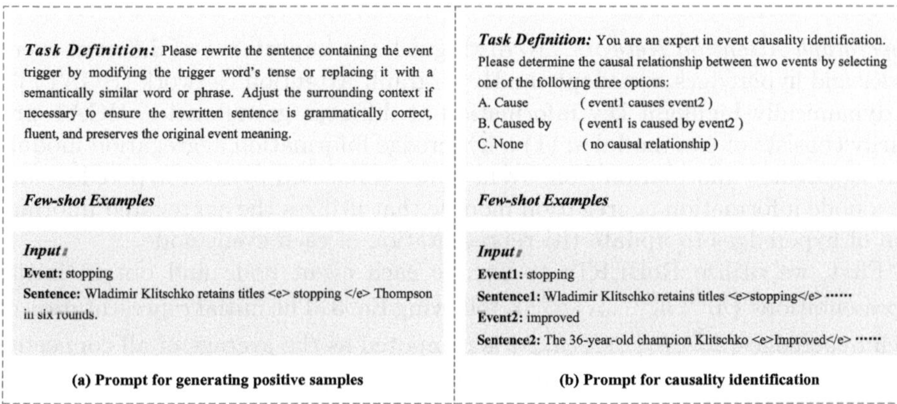

Fig. 3. An illustration of prompts for LLM. Each prompt consists of a task definition, few-shot examples and an input example.

where $\mathrm{sim}(\cdot, \cdot)$ is cosine similarity and τ is the temperature. The negative set $\mathrm{N}(e_i)$ consists of the three least similar events to e_i within the same document.

3.2 Causal Hypergraph Learning

Causal relations in a document are typically not isolated but demonstrate significant interdependencies. Therefore, to model the high-order dependency structure between causal relations, we construct a causal hypergraph for each document, where each node represents an event and the hyperedge connects all causal relations associated with the same event.

Causal Hypergraph Construction. For each event pair (e_i, e_j), we first design a single-choice template with three options (A: Cause, B: Caused by, C: None), prompting LLM to determine the initial causal relationship. Then we define a causal relation matrix $\boldsymbol{C} \in \mathbb{R}^{n \times n}$ to quantify the judgment of LLM, where n is the number of events in the document, specifically formulated as:

$$\mathbf{C}_{ij} = \begin{cases} 1, & \text{if } \mathrm{LLM}(\mathit{Prompt}) = A \text{ or } B \\ 0, & \text{if } \mathrm{LLM}(\mathit{Prompt}) = C \end{cases} \tag{5}$$

where *Prompt* includes task definition, e_i, e_j, s_i and s_j. A concrete example can be found in Fig. 3(b). If there exists causal relationship between e_i and e_j, then $\mathbf{C}_{ij} = 1$ and $\mathbf{C}_{ij} = 0$ otherwise.

Based on causal relation matrix $\boldsymbol{C}$, we construct the causal hypergraph $G = (\mathcal{V}, \mathcal{E})$, where $\mathcal{V} = \{e_1, \ldots, e_n\}$ is the set of event nodes and $\mathcal{E} = \{r_1, \ldots, r_m\}$ is the set of hyperedges. For each event node e_i, we connect it with all event nodes e_j that satisfy $\mathbf{C}_{ij} = 1$ through a hyperedge. Accordingly, we define an incidence matrix $H \in \mathbb{R}^{n \times m}$ to represent the constructed causal hypergraph, where $H_{ij} = 1$ if event node e_i is connected to hyperedge r_j, and $H_{ij} = 0$ otherwise.

Hypergraph Attention Network. To distinguish the importance of different event nodes and hyperedges, we adopt the Hypergraph Attention Network (HGAT) [3] to dynamically highlight key information at different granularities. HGAT primarily consists of two modules: (1) a hyperedge information aggregation module that aggregates information from event nodes connected by each hyperedge, and (2) a node information aggregation module that utilizes the aggregated information of hyperedges to update the representation of each event node.

First, we utilize RoBERTa to encode each event node and obtain initial representations $\{h_{e_1}^{(0)}, h_{e_2}^{(0)}, \ldots, h_{e_n}^{(0)}\}$, following Eq. 3. The initial representation of each hyperedge $\{h_{r_1}^{(0)}, h_{r_2}^{(0)}, \ldots, h_{r_m}^{(0)}\}$ is computed as the average of all connected event node representations. Let $\mathbf{m}_{i \to j}^{(1)}$ represent the information propagated from event node e_i to hyperedge r_j in the first HGAT layer. We adopt a multi-head attention mechanism to aggregate information from each event node connected to r_j, and derive its updated representation $h_{r_j}^{(1)}$ as follows:

$$
\begin{aligned}
h_{r_j}^{(1)} &= \Vert_{q=1}^{Q} \sum_{e_i \in \mathcal{N}_j} \mathbf{m}_{i \to j}^{(1)} \\
\mathbf{m}_{i \to j}^{(1)} &= \alpha_{ji}^{q} W_q^{(1)} h_{e_i}^{(0)} \\
\alpha_{ji}^{q} &= \frac{\exp\left(\sigma\left(a_q^T \cdot W_q^{(1)}\left(h_{e_i}^{(0)}, h_{r_j}^{(0)}\right)\right)\right)}{\sum_{e_u \in \mathcal{N}_j} \exp\left(\sigma\left(a_q^T \cdot W_q^{(1)}\left(h_{e_u}^{(0)}, h_{r_j}^{(0)}\right)\right)\right)}
\end{aligned}
\qquad (6)
$$

where Q is the number of attention heads, $\mathcal{N}_j$ denotes the set of all nodes connected to r_j, α_{ji}^{q} denotes the attention coefficient of node e_i in hyperedge r_j in the q-th attention head, σ is the non-linear activation function, a_q^T and $W_q^{(1)}$ are learnable parameters.

Second, we update the representation of each node by aggregating information from all hyperedges it connects to. Let $\mathbf{m}_{j \to i}^{(1)}$ represent the information propagated from hyperedge r_j to event node e_i in the first HGAT layer. The update of event node representation $h_{e_i}^{(1)}$ can be formulated as:

$$
\begin{aligned}
h_{e_i}^{(1)} &= \|_{q=1}^{Q} \sum_{r_j \in \mathcal{Q}_i} \mathbf{m}_{j \to i}^{(1)} \\
\mathbf{m}_{j \to i}^{(1)} &= \beta_{ij}^{q} W_q^{(1)} h_{r_j}^{(1)} \\
\beta_{ij}^{q} &= \frac{\exp\left(\sigma\left(a_q^T \cdot W_q^{(1)}\left(h_{e_i}^{(0)}, h_{r_j}^{(1)}\right)\right)\right)}{\sum_{r_f \in \mathcal{Q}_i} \exp\left(\sigma\left(a_q^T \cdot W_q^{(1)}\left(h_{e_i}^{(0)}, h_{r_f}^{(1)}\right)\right)\right)}
\end{aligned}
\tag{7}
$$

where $\mathcal{Q}_i$ represents the set of all hyperedges connected to e_i, and β_{ij}^{q} denotes the attention coefficient of hyperedge r_j on node e_i in the q-th attention head.

After l layers of HGAT, the final representation of each event node is obtained as $\{h_{e_1}^{(l)}, h_{e_2}^{(l)}, \ldots, h_{e_n}^{(l)}\}$, which is then used for subsequent causal relation classification.

Table 1. Details of EventStoryLine and Causal-TimeBank.

Dataset	Doc	Event	Causal Event Pair		
			Intra	Inter	Total
EventStoryLine	258	5,334	1,770	3,855	5,655
Causal-TimeBank	184	6,813	300	18	318

3.3 Representation Fusion and Causal Relation Classification

To better leverage the event representations derived from adaptive contrastive learning and causal hypergraph learning, we utilize a gating mechanism that dynamically fuses information from these two distinct aspects. The gating mechanism adaptively conducts optimal weighting between features from two different dimensions through training, and produces the final representation for each event, denoted as $h_{e_i}^{\text{final}}$.

$$
\begin{aligned}
\eta &= \text{sigmoid}(W_f h_{e_i}^{\text{ACL}} + U_f h_{e_i}^{\text{Hyper}} + b_f) \\
h_{e_i}^{\text{final}} &= \eta \odot h_{e_i}^{\text{ACL}} + (1 - \eta) \odot h_{e_i}^{\text{Hyper}}
\end{aligned}
\tag{8}
$$

where W_f and U_f are learnable parameters, b_f denotes the bias term.

We then feed the final representation of each event pair into a multi-layer perceptron to obtain the predicted probability of causal relation p_{ij}.

$$
p_{ij} = \text{softmax}(W_a(h_{e_i}^{\text{final}} \parallel h_{e_j}^{\text{final}}) + b_a) \tag{9}
$$

where W_a is the learnable parameter, b_a denotes the bias term, and $\parallel$ represents the concatenation operation.

For training, we employ focal loss to mitigate the class imbalance between positive and negative samples, where $\lambda \in [0, 1]$ represents a weight for the positive class, and $1 - \lambda$ for the negative class. The focal loss $\mathcal{L}_{\text{Focal}}$ is formulated as:

$$\mathcal{L}_{\text{Focal}} = - \sum_{e_i, e_j \in \mathcal{V}} \lambda_{ij} (1 - p_{ij})^{\tau} \log(p_{ij}) \tag{10}$$

where τ and λ are hyperparameters.

The final loss function combines adaptive contrastive learning loss and focal loss, where μ is a hyperparameter:

$$\mathcal{L} = \mu \mathcal{L}_{\text{ACL}} + \mathcal{L}_{\text{Focal}} \tag{11}$$

4 Experiments

4.1 Experimental Settings

Datasets and Evaluation Metrics. We evaluate the proposed method (i.e. ESCCH) on two benchmark datasets, with detailed statistics provided in Table 1. **EventStoryLine (ESL)** [2] is evaluated using 5-fold cross-validation on 20 topics, with the remaining two topics reserved as the development set following [1].

Table 2. Experimental results on the EventStoryLine (ESL) dataset. The best results are highlighted in **bold**, and the second-best results are underlined.

Model	Intra			Inter			Intra+Inter		
	P	R	F1	P	R	F1	P	R	F1
KnowDis(2020)	39.7	66.5	49.7	–	–	–	–	–	–
LearnDA(2021)	42.2	69.8	52.6	–	–	–	–	–	–
DPJL(2022)	65.3	70.8	**67.9**	–	–	–	–	–	–
GCKAN(2024)	50.9	60.6	55.3	–	–	–	–	–	–
DFP(2024)	55.9	69.8	62.1	–	–	–	–	–	–
BT-ESupCL(2025)	55.2	64.2	59.3	–	–	–	–	–	–
RichGCN(2021)	49.2	63.0	55.2	39.2	45.7	42.2	42.6	51.3	46.6
ERGO(2022)	57.5	**72.0**	63.9	51.6	43.3	47.1	48.6	53.4	50.9
CHEER(2023)	59.9	69.9	62.6	45.2	52.1	48.4	49.7	53.3	51.4
SENDIR(2023)	65.8	66.7	66.2	33.0	**90.0**	48.3	37.8	**82.8**	51.9
SIDL(2024)	63.7	70.3	66.8	50.6	53.2	51.9	55.2	59.2	52.5
GCI(2025)	51.3	65.6	57.6	57.3	47.9	52.2	56.1	53.7	54.7
MEA(2025)	60.1	71.7	65.4	50.4	63.7	56.3	51.2	69.6	59.0
ESCCH (Qwen-2.5-32B)	70.8	63.8	67.1	57.8	65.1	61.2	62.9	60.3	61.6
ESCCH (Llama-2-7B)	74.0	60.5	66.6	60.1	63.7	61.8	63.4	63.1	63.3
ESCCH (GPT-3.5-Turbo)	**74.2**	61.7	67.4	**61.6**	63.0	**62.3**	**64.7**	62.6	**63.6**

For **Causal-TimeBank (CTB)** [21], due to the extremely limited number of inter-sentence causal pairs, following previous work [19], we focus only on intra-sentence causality identification and employ 10-fold cross-validation.

Following previous studies [6], we use Precision (P), Recall (R), and F1-score (F1) as the evaluation metrics.

Parameter Settings. We use RoBERTa-base as the backbone, optimized via AdamW with learning rates of 1e-3 for HGAT and 1e-5 for other modules. The number of hypergraph layers l and attention heads Q are both set to 2. The number of positive samples (M) is set to 3. The hyperparameters λ and μ are set to 0.35 and 0.7, respectively. For positive sample generation, we employ GPT-3.5-Turbo-1106, Qwen-2.5-32B, and Llama-2-7B (temperature=0.8). Additionally, GPT-3.5-Turbo-1106 (temperature = 0.1) is used for initial causal relation prediction.

4.2 Baselines

We compare our ESCCH with the following baseline methods.

Table 3. Experimental results on the Causal-TimeBank (CTB) dataset. The best results are highlighted in **bold**, and the second-best results are underlined.

Model	P	R	F1
KnowDis(2020)	42.3	60.5	49.8
LearnDA(2021)	41.9	68.0	51.9
DPJL(2022)	63.6	66.7	64.6
GCKAN(2024)	52.2	60.7	56.1
DFP(2024)	53.7	64.2	58.5
BT-ESupCL(2025)	59.1	64.3	58.5
RichGCN(2021)	39.7	56.5	46.7
ERGO(2022)	62.1	61.3	61.7
CHEER(2023)	56.4	**69.5**	62.3
SENDIR(2023)	65.2	57.7	61.2
MEA(2025)	60.4	<u>68.5</u>	64.2
ESCCH (Qwen-2.5-32B)	66.7	64.8	<u>65.7</u>
ESCCH (Llama-2-7B)	<u>67.2</u>	63.6	65.4
ESCCH (GPT-3.5-Turbo)	**68.8**	65.3	**67.0**

SECI Baselines: (1) **KnowDis** [31] expands the training dataset for ECI via knowledge augmentation. (2) **LearnDA** [30] introduces a learnable knowledge-guided data augmentation framework. (3) **DPJL** [23] formulates two related tasks for ECI and designs prompt templates for joint learning. (4) **GCKAN** [8] integrates descriptive and relational knowledge via graph contrastive learning. (5) **DFP** [13] extracts reliable commonsense knowledge from ConceptNet and fuses it into PLMs for ECI. (6) **BT-ESupCL** [14] addresses data scarcity and class imbalance by combining back-translation with improved supervised contrastive learning.

DECI Baselines: (1) **RichGCN** [22] builds an event interaction graph to capture context-enhanced event representations. (2) **ERGO** [5] transforms ECI into an edge prediction problem by constructing an event-pair graph. (3) **CHEER** [6] incorporates central events into the event interaction graph for higher-order reasoning. (4) **SENDIR** [25] leverages distinct attention types to model events within or across sentences. (5) **SIDL** [7] separately models intra- and inter-sentence event pairs with hierarchical reasoning. (6) **GCI** [4] employs a dynamic grid tagging scheme to jointly extract mentions and relations. (7) **MEA** [16] enhances ECI by encoding context at four hierarchical levels to capture complex dependencies.

4.3 Results

Table 2 and Table 3 presents the experimental results on EventStoryLine and Causal-TimeBank.

Table 4. Ablation study on EventStoryLine.

Model	Intra	Inter	Intra+Inter
ESCCH	**67.4**	**62.3**	**63.6**
w/o ACL	66.1	60.3	61.8
w/o LLM-Aug	65.9	58.3	60.3
w/o SW	65.5	59.8	61.3
w/o CHL	65.8	56.0	58.5
w/o Gate	65.9	61.0	62.4

(1) Our ESCCH consistently outperforms all baselines on two datasets. Compared to state-of-the-art methods, it achieves improvements in F1 scores of 4.6% on EventStoryLine and 2.4% on Causal-TimeBank. These results demonstrate the effectiveness of our method for document-level event causality identification.
(2) It is obvious that all models perform better on intra-sentence compared to inter-sentence. This is because events within the same sentence often share the same semantic context. This also highlights the inherent difficulty of identifying inter-sentence causal relations, where events are more dispersed and lack explicit causal indicators. However, ESCCH achieves a

6.0% improvement over state-of-the-art methods on inter-sentence causality identification, while also demonstrating competitive performance on intra-sentence.

(3) Compared to the current state-of-the-art graph-based method (CHEER), our method achieves substantial performance improvements. Specifically, ESCCH improves overall F1 scores by 12.2% on EventStoryLine and 4.7% on Causal-TimeBank. On EventStoryLine, it further improves inter-sentence F1 scores by 13.9%. The reason may be that previous graph-based methods are limited to considering binary causal relations. This shows that our causal hypergraph can model high-order dependencies between multiple causal relations, enabling a more comprehensive understanding of document-level causal structures.

4.4 Ablation Study

Table 4 presents the ablation results for evaluating the individual contributions of each module.

(1) ESCCH w/o ACL, which removes the adaptive contrastive learning module. The removal of ACL results in a 1.3% decrease in overall F1 scores, highlighting the importance of fine-grained semantic alignment under different surface forms. Further breakdown shows that removing LLM-generated positive samples (w/o LLM-Aug) and similarity-aware weighting (w/o SW) also leads to a performance decrease. This indicates that diverse surface forms enrich event semantics, while adaptive weighting facilitates the model to focus on more informative positive pairs for fine-grained alignment.

(2) ESCCH w/o CHL, which removes the causal hypergraph learning module, results in the most notable decline in overall performance (5.1%). The 6.3% decrease in inter-sentence F1 scores further demonstrates the importance of using hypergraph to capture high-order dependencies between causal relations in the document. Furthermore, ESCCH w/o Gate, which removes the gating mechanism, shows a slight performance drop (1.2%). This indicates that the gating mechanism effectively balances semantic consistency and causal dependencies, thereby enhancing potential causality prediction.

4.5 Influence of Different Graph Neural Networks

To evaluate the impact of different graph neural networks on DECI performance, we select four types of graph neural networks for experiments. The experimental results are shown in Fig. 4. We can observe that hypergraph neural networks (HGAT and HGNN) significantly outperform conventional graph neural networks (GCN and GAT), particularly in the more challenging inter-sentence causal relations. This indicates that GCN and GAT operate on pairwise edges, which are inherently limited in modeling multi-event causal dependencies commonly found in document-level ECI. In contrast, hypergraph introduces hyperedges that can jointly connect multiple events, allowing the model to effectively

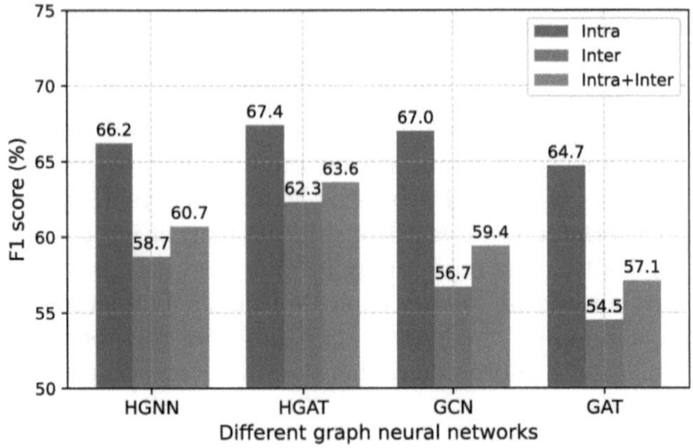

Fig. 4. The impact of different graph neural networks in EventStoryLine dataset on model performance.

learn one-to-many or many-to-one causal relations that are otherwise difficult to capture in conventional graphs. In addition, HGNN leads to a decrease in overall F1 scores compared to HGAT, indicating that although hypergraph is beneficial for DECI, attention-based aggregation in HGAT more effectively identifies and emphasizes informative event nodes during the message passing process.

4.6 Hyperparameter Analysis

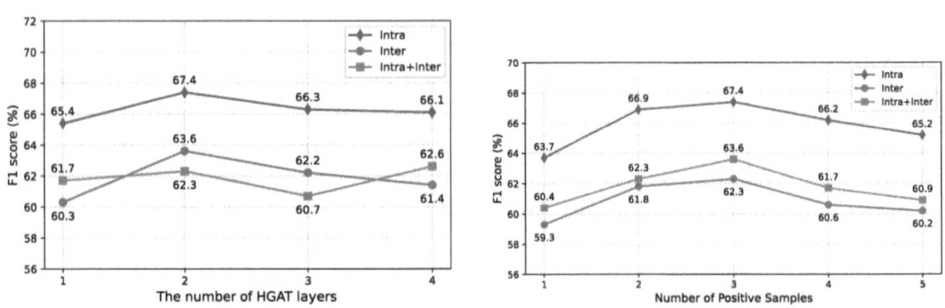

(a) Impact of HGAT layers **(b)** Impact of generated samples

Fig. 5. Hyperparameter sensitivity analysis on the EventStoryLine dataset. (a) illustrates the effect of HGAT depth, and (b) shows the impact of LLM-generated positive samples.

Influence of HGAT Layers. As shown in Fig. 5(a), using only one layer yields the worst performance, likely due to the limited depth of message passing and insufficient capacity to capture structural dependencies. Increasing the number of layers to two achieves the best performance. However, further increasing the depth to three or four leads to performance degradation. This decline can be attributed to the over-smoothing phenomenon inherent in hypergraph neural networks, where excessive aggregation from distant nodes obscures the discriminative features of individual events.

Influence of Generated Positive Samples. We investigate the impact of LLM-generated positive samples by varying the count from 1 to 5. Figure 5(b) shows that performance improves consistently as the sample count increases to 3. This suggests that as the number of positive samples increases, the model is able to capture more diverse event structures and contextual information, thereby enhancing its causal reasoning ability. Specifically, the model achieves the best performance with 3 positive samples, performing optimally across three tasks. However, as the number increases further, the performance begins to decline. This phenomenon may be attributed to the redundancy introduced by too many positive samples, leading to information conflicts and noise interference.

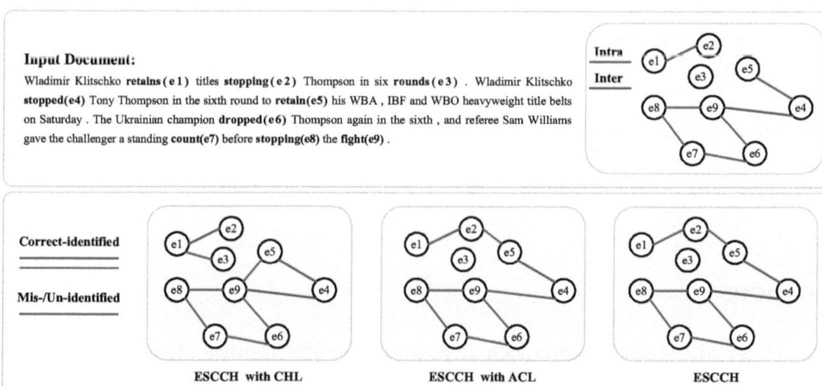

Fig. 6. A case to illustrate our proposed ESCCH on the EventStoryLine dataset. The top part shows the input document and the ground-truth event causal graph. The bottom part compares three model configurations: ESCCH with CHL, ESCCH with ACL, and the complete ESCCH.

4.7 Case Study

To further understand our proposed ESCCH, we present a case in Fig. 6. Overall, ESCCH with CHL (without adaptive contrastive learning) results in 2 mis-identified and 1 un-identified causal relations, while ESCCH with ACL (without causal hypergraph) leads to 1 mis-identified and 2 un-identified causal relations. In contrast, ESCCH accurately identifies nearly all causal relations, with only 1 causal relation mis-identified. Specifically, ESCCH correctly identifies the inter-sentence causal relation $\langle e_4$, *cause*, $e_9\rangle$, which can be attributed to the structural reinforcement from other correctly identified causal relations related to e_9, *such as* $\langle e_6$, *cause*, $e_9\rangle$ and $\langle e_8$, *cause*, $e_9\rangle$. Moreover, the high semantic similarity between e_4 and e_8 also contributes to identifying the shared causal relation with e_9. The mis-identified 1 causal relation $\langle e_2$, *cause*, $e_5\rangle$ can be attributed to the strong semantic similarity between e_5 and e_1, which caused an unintended transfer of the causal relation from $\langle e_2$, *cause*, $e_1\rangle$ to $\langle e_2$, *cause*, $e_5\rangle$.

5 Conclusion

In this paper, we proposed ESCCH, a novel method for document-level event causality identification. ESCCH captures event representation consistency and the complex dependencies in causal relations through adaptive contrastive learning and causal hypergraph learning. Extensive experiments on two datasets demonstrate that our model achieves significant improvements over current state-of-the-art baselines. Ablation studies further confirm the contribution of each component within the framework. In future work, we aim to incorporate richer external knowledge into hypergraph construction and extend our method to multilingual or low-resource scenarios.

Acknowledgement. This work was supported by the National Natural Science Foundation of China (No. 62476108) and the MOE (Ministry of Education in China) Project of Humanities and Social Sciences (Project No. 25YJC740005).

References

1. Cao, P., et al.: Knowledge-enriched event causality identification via latent structure induction networks. In: Proceedings of ACL-IJCNLP, pp. 4862–4872 (2021)
2. Caselli, T., Vossen, P.: The event storyline corpus: a new benchmark for causal and temporal relation extraction. In: Proceedings of the Events and Stories in the News Workshop, pp. 77–86 (2017)
3. Chen, C., Cheng, Z., Li, Z., Wang, M.: Hypergraph attention networks. In: Proceedings of TrustCom, pp. 1560–1565 (2020)
4. Chen, H.: Dynamic grid tagging scheme for event causality identification and classification. IEEE Trans. Audio Speech Lang. Process. (2025)
5. Chen, M., et al.: Ergo: event relational graph transformer for document-level event causality identification. In: Proceedings of COLING, pp. 2118–2128 (2022)
6. Chen, M., Cao, Y., Zhang, Y., Liu, Z.: Cheer: centrality-aware high-order event reasoning network for document-level event causality identification. In: Proceedings of ACL, pp. 10804–10816 (2023)
7. Deng, Y., Huang, W., Chen, T., Long, J.: Separate and integrate different level reasoning for event causality identification. In: Proceedings of IJCNN, pp. 1–8 (2024)
8. Ding, L., Chen, J., Du, P., Xiang, Y.: Event causality identification via graph contrast-based knowledge augmented networks. Inf. Sci. **656**, 119905 (2024)

9. Do, Q., Chan, Y.S., Roth, D.: Minimally supervised event causality identification. In: Proceedings of EMNLP, pp. 294–303 (2011)
10. Feng, Y., Li, L., Qin, X., Zhang, B.: Improving event representation learning via generating and utilizing synthetic data. Inf. Process. Manage. **62**(4), 104083 (2025)
11. Gao, J., Wang, W., Yu, C., Zhao, H., Ng, W., Xu, R.: Improving event representation via simultaneous weakly supervised contrastive learning and clustering. In: Proceedings of ACL, pp. 3036–3049 (2022)
12. Gao, L., Choubey, P.K., Huang, R.: Modeling document-level causal structures for event causal relation identification. In: Proceedings of NAACL, pp. 1808–1817 (2019)
13. Huang, P., Zhao, X., Hu, M., Tan, Z., Xiao, W.: Distill, fuse, pre-train: towards effective event causality identification with commonsense-aware pre-trained model. In: Proceedings of LREC-COLING, pp. 5029–5040 (2024)
14. Li, S., Zhou, G., Chen, J., Sun, Y., Huang, N., Peng, S.: Event-level supervised contrastive learning with back-translation augmentation for event causality identification. Neurocomputing **621**, 129232 (2025)
15. Li, Z., Ding, X., Liu, T.: Constructing narrative event evolutionary graph for script event prediction. In: Proceedings of IJCAI, pp. 4201–4207 (2018)
16. Liang, H., Zhou, Q., Gong, W., Li, X.: Multi-level encoder architectures for event causality identification. Neural Netw. 108356 (2025)
17. Liu, C., Xiang, W., Wang, B.: Identifying while learning for document event causality identification. In: Proceedings of ACL, pp. 3815–3827 (2024)
18. Liu, J., Chen, Y., Zhao, J.: Knowledge enhanced event causality identification with mention masking generalizations. In: Proceedings of IJCAI, pp. 3608–3614 (2021)
19. Liu, J., et al.: KEPT: knowledge enhanced prompt tuning for event causality identification. Knowl.-Based Syst. **259**, 110064 (2023)
20. Liu, Y., et al.: RoBERTa: a robustly optimized BERT pretraining approach. arXiv preprint arXiv:1907.11692 (2019)
21. Mirza, P., Tonelli, S.: An analysis of causality between events and its relation to temporal information. In: Proceedings of COLING, pp. 2097–2106 (2014)
22. Phu, M.T., Nguyen, T.H.: Graph convolutional networks for event causality identification with rich document-level structures. In: Proceedings of NAACL, pp. 3480–3490 (2021)
23. Shen, S., Zhou, H., Wu, T., Qi, G.: Event causality identification via derivative prompt joint learning. In: Proceedings of COLING, pp. 2288–2299 (2022)
24. Weber, N., Balasubramanian, N., Chambers, N.: Event representations with tensor-based compositions. In: Proceedings of AAAI, pp. 4946–4953 (2018)
25. Yuan, C., Huang, H.Y., Cao, Y., Wen, Y.: Discriminative reasoning with sparse event representation for document-level event-event relation extraction. In: Proceedings of ACL, pp. 16222–16234 (2023)
26. Zhang, J., Chen, T., Li, S., Zhang, M., Ren, Y., Wan, J.: A graph propagation model with rich event structures for joint event relation extraction. Inf. Process. Manage. **61**(5), 103811 (2024)
27. Zheng, J., Cai, F., Chen, H.: Incorporating scenario knowledge into a unified fine-tuning architecture for event representation. In: Proceedings of SIGIR, pp. 249–258 (2020)
28. Zhou, Y., Li, X.: Sentimental contrastive learning for event representation. Nat. Lang. Process. J. **4**, 100031 (2023)
29. Zuo, X., et al.: Improving event causality identification via self-supervised representation learning on external causal statement. In: Proceedings of ACL-IJCNLP, pp. 2162–2172 (2021)

30. Zuo, X., et al.: LearnDA: learnable knowledge-guided data augmentation for event causality identification. In: Proceedings of ACL-IJCNLP, pp. 3558–3571 (2021)
31. Zuo, X., Chen, Y., Liu, K., Zhao, J.: KnowDis: knowledge enhanced data augmentation for event causality detection via distant supervision. In: Proceedings of COLING, pp. 1544–1550 (2020)

Multimodal Named Entity Recognition via Semantic Reasoning and Knowledge Guidance

Xue Wang[1,2,3], Liping Zhang[1,2,3](✉), Sheng Yan[1,2,3], Min Hou[1,2,3], and Yu He[1,2,3]

[1] College of Computer Science and Technology, Inner Mongolia Normal University, Hohhot 010022, China
cieczlp@imnu.edu.cn

[2] Inner Mongolia Autonomous Region Key Laboratory for Ecological Environment Collaborative Intelligence, Hohhot 010020, China

[3] Inner Mongolia Autonomous Region Industrial Technology Engineering Center for Intelligent and Data in Ecological Environment, Hohhot 010020, China

Abstract. Primary school science educational resources present unique challenges for Multimodal Named Entity Recognition (MNER), including abstract visual information, logical isolation between entity tags, and severe class imbalance. To address these issues, we propose SRKG-MNER, a method based on semantic reasoning and knowledge guidance. First, we design a Deep Cross-Modal Semantic Reasoning Layer that employs a multi-layer iterative attention mechanism to align textual concepts with abstract visual symbols, enabling deep semantic reasoning. Second, we introduce a GCN Knowledge Injection Layer, which utilizes Graph Convolutional Networks to encode expert-constructed entity logic graphs, explicitly enforcing domain-specific logical constraints on predictions. Finally, an Inverse Frequency Weighted Loss Strategy is adopted to dynamically adjust class weights, effectively mitigating the long-tail effect. Additionally, we construct a manually annotated dataset, PSS-MNER, containing 2,778 image-text pairs. Experimental results show that SRKG-MNER achieves an F1-score of 89.57%, significantly outperforming state-of-the-art baselines.

Keywords: Multimodal named entity recognition · elementary school science education · semantic reasoning · knowledge-guided · class imbalance · graph convolutional neural network

1 Introduction

In the context of digital transformation in education, primary school science education in the intelligent era is endowed with the significant mission of cultivating students' scientific literacy and inquiry capabilities, making the intelligent processing of educational resources imperative [1]. With the rapid development of multimedia technologies, a vast amount of multimodal learning materials—ranging from experimental manuals to abstract schematic diagrams—has emerged in digital textbooks. However, these

J. Niu et al. (Eds.): KSEM 2026, LNAI 16631, pp. 101–113, 2027.
https://doi.org/10.1007/978-981-92-2759-4_8

resources contain a large number of unstructured text and images that vary greatly in abstraction and complexity, leading to difficulties in effective knowledge extraction and resulting in a "semantic gap" problem. Therefore, automatically identifying key scientific concepts to support the construction of educational knowledge graphs is an important trend for the future development of intelligent tutoring systems.

Multimodal Named Entity Recognition (MNER) is a key task for building such intelligent services and is one of the hot topics in the fields of Natural Language Processing (NLP) and educational data mining [2, 3]. It aims to identify entities with specific semantic categories by fusing visual and textual features, achieving the observation, representation, and understanding of multi-source information [4, 5]. However, the process of recognizing scientific entities not only requires the model to align visual objects with text superficially but also demands capabilities in deep semantic reasoning, understanding of abstract symbols, and organization of logical relationships between entities. This process involves multiple cognitive dimensions including observation, association, and logical verification. To enhance the accuracy and robustness of entity extraction in the education domain, it is necessary to consider factors influencing the recognition process from multiple perspectives by integrating domain knowledge.

Therefore, this paper, starting from the practical characteristics of primary school science education and integrating mechanisms of cognitive reasoning and domain logic, explores a deep multimodal named entity recognition method (SRKG-MNER) that comprehensively considers the abstract semantic gap, scientific logical constraints, and the long-tail distribution of data.

2 Related Work

Multimodal Named Entity Recognition (MNER) Early MNER research focused on feature fusion architectures to address the sparsity of social media text. Moon et al. [6] established the baseline using Bi-LSTM and CNNs, while subsequent works introduced visual attention mechanisms [7] and adversarial learning [8] to enhance cross-modal interaction. To mitigate visual noise, recent studies proposed uncertainty gating (e.g., UAMNer [9]) and explicit alignment strategies (e.g., MAF [10]). With the advent of Vision-Language Pre-training (VLP) [11], CLIP-based methods have shifted the research paradigm. Approaches like ITA [12] and PromptMNER [13] leverage image-text matching and prompt learning to unify semantic spaces, while AMLR [14] further optimizes multi-scale visual feature alignment.

Limitations in Scientific Education Domain Although effective in general domains, existing methods face significant challenges when transferred to primary school science education. First, most models rely on surface-level correlations in natural images, lacking the deep reasoning capability required to interpret highly abstract scientific diagrams (e.g., circuit schematics). Second, current approaches treat entity tags as isolated categories, ignoring the inherent logical constraints among scientific entities (e.g., the dependency between Instruments and Procedures). Finally, standard training objectives often fail to address the severe long-tail distribution of scientific entities. To address these gaps, this paper proposes the SRKG-MNER method. Unlike existing methods that rely on shallow fusion and isolated labels, our framework innovates by deeply coupling iterative visual reasoning for abstract gaps, explicit GCN-based logical constraints for domain rules, and dynamic inverse-frequency weighting for long-tail distributions.

3 Methods

Overall Architecture As illustrated in Fig. 1, the proposed SRKG-MNER framework consists of three core components: (1) a Dee Cross-Modal Semantic Reasoning Layer for aligning visual and textual semantics; (2) a GCN Knowledge Injection Layer for incorporating expert logic; and (3) an Inverse Frequency Weighted Loss Strategy to handle class imbalance. The details of each component are described below.

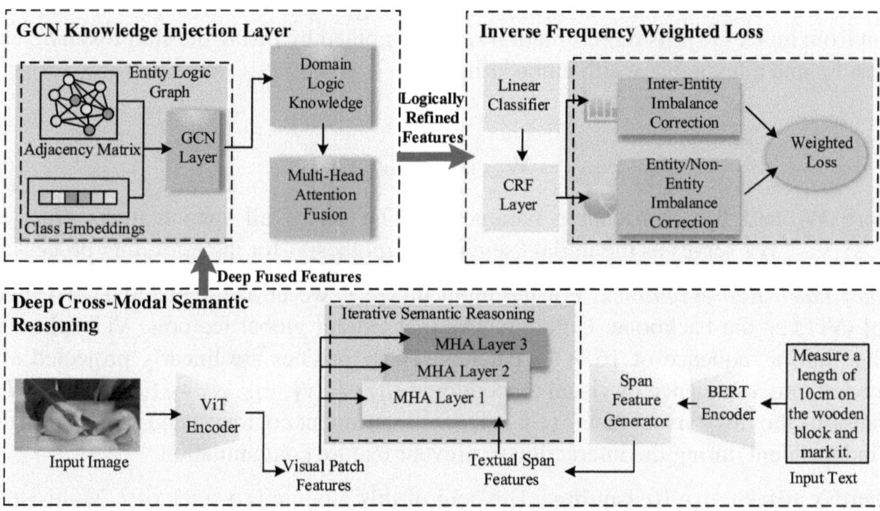

Fig. 1. The Architecture of SRKG-MNER

3.1 Problem Definition

Given a multimodal dataset $\mathcal{D} = \{(S, V, Y)\}$, where $S = \{w_1, w_2, \ldots, w_N\}$ represents the input text sequence of length N, and V represents the associated image. The goal of MNER is to predict a label sequence $Y = \{y_1, y_2, \ldots, y_N\}$, where each $y_i \in \mathcal{L}$ corresponds to a predefined category set (e.g., *B-BIO*, *I-SUB*, O) following the BIO tagging scheme.

3.2 Deep Cross-Modal Semantic Reasoning

In the context of primary school science, the association between textual entities and visual symbols is often abstract and non-intuitive. For instance, the word "circuit" corresponds to a topological structure of lines rather than a specific object shape. Standard single-layer attention mechanisms often fail to bridge this “abstract semantic gap.” To address this, we design the Deep Cross-Modal Semantic Reasoning Layer. Inspired by the “Hypothesis-Verification-Revision” cognitive chain in human learning, this module does not process visual information in a single pass. Instead, it employs an iterative interaction mechanism to allow textual concepts to repeatedly “consult” the visual evidence, progressively refining the semantic representation.

Multimodal Feature Extraction. Before reasoning, the model extracts structured feature representations from raw inputs.

Textual Span Representation. Given an input sentence $S = \{w_1, w_2, \ldots, w_N\}$, we first employ BERT [15] to generate contextualized token embeddings. Since scientific entities (e.g., “graduated cylinder”) often span multiple tokens, token-level features are insufficient. We introduce a Span Feature Generator to aggregate semantics. For a candidate span from index i to j, its representation $s_{i,j}$ is computed by fusing the start token h_i, end token h_j, and a learnable width embedding $w_{i,j}$:

$$s_{i,j} = \mathbf{W}_s \cdot [h_i; h_j; w_{i,j}] + \mathbf{b}_s \tag{1}$$

where $\mathbf{W}_s$ and $\mathbf{b}_s$ are trainable parameters. The set of all span features $H_{text} = \{s_1, s_2, \ldots, s_K\}$ serves as the initial “semantic hypothesis” for the reasoning process.

Visual Patch Representation. For the input image I, we utilize a Vision Transformer [16] (ViT) as the backbone. Unlike CNNs that extract global features, ViT splits the image into a sequence of 16×16 patches. These patches are linearly projected and encoded into a sequence of visual embeddings $H_{vis} = \{v_1, v_2, \ldots, v_M\}$. Crucially, H_{vis} represents the raw “visual facts” (e.g., arrows, instrument contours) and remains frozen or independent during the interaction to prevent feature contamination.

Iterative Interactive Reasoning. The core of this module is a stack of L Multi-Head Attention (MHA) [17] layers. Let $H^{(l)}$ denote the textual representation at the l-th layer, with $H^{(0)} = H_{text}$. In each iteration, the textual features act as Queries (Q) to search for supporting evidence from the visual features, which serve as Keys (K) and Values (V):

$$\mathbf{Q} = H^{(l)}\mathbf{W}_Q^{(l)}, \quad \mathbf{K} = H_{vis}\mathbf{W}_K^{(l)}, \quad \mathbf{V} = H_{vis}\mathbf{W}_V^{(l)} \tag{2}$$

$$A^{(l)} = \text{Softmax}\left(\frac{\mathbf{Q}\mathbf{K}^T}{\sqrt{d_k}}\right)\mathbf{V} \tag{3}$$

$$H^{(l+1)} = \text{LayerNorm}(H^{(l)} + \text{FFN}(A^{(l)})) \tag{4}$$

This iterative design implements a backtracking verification mechanism. In the first layer ($l = 1$), the model might only find superficial correspondences based on literal meanings. In subsequent layers ($l > 1$), the updated query $H^{(l)}$—which has absorbed initial visual cues—can perform more precise retrieval, focusing on fine-grained attributes or spatial relationships. After L rounds of reasoning, the final output $H_{reason} = H^{(L)}$ contains multimodal-grounded semantics that bridge the abstract gap.

3.3 GCN Knowledge Injection

Traditional NER models treat entity tags as isolated categories (e.g., SUB, TOO, STE), ignoring the rigorous logical system inherent in science. For example, a "Step" (e.g., heating) functionally requires a "Tool" (e.g., alcohol lamp). Predictions violating these constraints (e.g., labeling a tool as a Step) are scientifically invalid. To enforce these constraints, we introduce the GCN Knowledge Injection Layer, which transforms implicit expert knowledge into explicit logical priors.

Construction of Entity Logic Graph. We first construct a domain-specific Entity Logic Graph $\mathcal{G} = (\mathcal{V}, \mathcal{E})$. The node set $\mathcal{V}$ consists of the 9 entity categories defined in our dataset. The edge set $\mathcal{E}$ is defined by domain experts based on two criteria:

Co-occurrence Probability. An edge exists if two categories frequently appear in the same experimental context.

Functional Dependency. A directed edge exists if category A is a prerequisite for category B (e.g., Tool → Step).Based on $\mathcal{G}$, we generate a normalized adjacency matrix $\widetilde{\mathbf{A}} \in \mathbb{R}^{9\times 9}$, which hard-codes these logical relationships. Constructing this 9×9 macro-category matrix requires minimal expert annotation cost, ensuring high transferability across different science textbook editions.

Domain Knowledge Propagation. We initialize a learnable embedding matrix $\mathbf{E}^{(0)} \in \mathbb{R}^{9\times d}$ for the entity categories. A Graph Convolutional Network (GCN) is employed to propagate information across the graph, enabling each category to be aware of its logical neighbors. The update rule for the $(k+1)$-th GCN layer is:

$$\mathbf{E}^{(k+1)} = \sigma\left(\widetilde{\mathbf{D}}^{-\frac{1}{2}}\widetilde{\mathbf{A}}\widetilde{\mathbf{D}}^{-\frac{1}{2}}\mathbf{E}^{(k)}\mathbf{W}_g^{(k)}\right) \tag{5}$$

where $\widetilde{\mathbf{D}}$ is the degree matrix, $\mathbf{W}_g$ is the weight matrix, and σ is the ReLU activation function. The final output $\mathbf{E}_{logic}$ represents the logic-aware category prototypes, where each category embedding implicitly encodes the features of its compatible entities.

Knowledge-Guided Feature Refinement. Finally, we inject this domain logic into the instance-level features H_{reason} (from Sect. 3.2) using an attention-based fusion module. Here, the reasoned features serve as Queries, while the logic prototypes $\mathbf{E}_{logic}$ serve as Keys and Values:

$$H_{final} = \text{MultiHeadAttn}(Q = H_{reason}, K = \mathbf{E}_{logic}, V = \mathbf{E}_{logic}) + H_{reason} \tag{6}$$

This operation acts as a logical recalibration. If a span is visually ambiguous but semantically resembles a "Tool," the attention mechanism will pull its representation closer to the Tool prototype and its logically connected neighbors (e.g., Step), while distancing it from incompatible categories (e.g., Astronomy). The refined feature H_{final} is then passed to the decoding layer.

3.4 Inverse Frequency Weighted Optimization

In real-world educational scenarios, scientific entities exhibit a severe long-tail distribution. As shown in Table 1, common entities like Substance (301 samples) appear frequently, while rare but critical entities like Unit (21 samples) are scarce. Additionally, the number of non-entity tokens (Tag 'O') vastly outnumbers entity tokens. Standard Cross-Entropy (CE) loss treats all classes equally, causing the model to bias towards high-frequency classes and ignore the tail. To address this, we propose a dual-weighted loss strategy.

Inter-Entity Imbalance Correction. First, to mitigate the imbalance among the 9 entity categories, we assign a penalty weight to each class based on its inverse frequency. We define the weight α_c for category c as:

$$\alpha_c = \begin{cases} 1.0 & \text{if } c = \text{'O'} \\ \dfrac{\max_{j \in \mathcal{C}_{ent}}(N_j)}{N_c} & \text{if } c \in \mathcal{C}_{ent} \end{cases} \tag{7}$$

where $\mathcal{C}_{ent}$ denotes the set of entity classes (excluding 'O'), N_c is the number of samples for class c in the training set, and $\max(N_j)$ is the count of the most frequent entity class 2. This normalization ensures that the most frequent entity has a weight of 1.0, while rare classes (e.g., Unit) are assigned significantly higher weights ($\alpha_c > 1$). This forces the model to pay more attention to sparse samples during gradient updates, preventing them from being overwhelmed by dominant classes.

Entity-Non-entity Imbalance Correction. Second, to address the overwhelming dominance of the 'O' tag (background), we explicitly separate the loss contribution of positive entities from negative samples. Instead of down-sampling 'O' tags (which might lose context), we introduce a Positive Boosting Factor λ. The Weighted Cross-Entropy (WCE) loss for a single input sequence X of length L is formulated as:

$$\mathcal{L}_{WCE} = -\frac{1}{L}\sum_{i=1}^{L} w_i \log P(y_i|X) \tag{8}$$

where the final weight w_i for the i-th token with ground truth label y_i is defined as:

$$w_i = \begin{cases} \lambda \cdot \alpha_{y_i} & \text{if } y_i \neq \text{'O'} \\ 1 & \text{if } y_i = \text{'O'} \end{cases} \tag{9}$$

Here, λ is a hyperparameter (set to >1) that globally amplifies the gradients derived from entity spans. This "hard mining" strategy prevents the model from taking the shortcut of predicting 'O' for everything to minimize loss.

Joint Optimization Objective. The final training objective combines the token-level semantic discrimination capability of our WCE loss with the sequence-level structural constraints of the CRF layer.

As described in the CRF formulation, the CRF loss $\mathcal{L}_{CRF}$ maximizes the likelihood of the correct tag sequence. The total loss $\mathcal{L}_{total}$ is the weighted sum:

$$\mathcal{L}_{total} = \mathcal{L}_{WCE} + \mathcal{L}_{CRF} \tag{10}$$

By jointly optimizing these two objectives, SRKG-MNER not only learns to classify content accurately under imbalanced conditions but also ensures that the predicted label sequences are structurally valid.

4 Experiments

4.1 Dataset and Implementation

Dataset Construction and Annotation Since there is no publicly available dataset specifically for primary school science MNER, we constructed the PSS-MNER dataset. The raw data was collected from mainstream Chinese science textbooks (e.g., Su-Jiao version) and complementary digital resources. The construction process consists of three steps:

Data Cleaning. We filtered out images with low resolution and texts that were purely colloquial or irrelevant to scientific knowledge.

Semantic Alignment. We manually verified the correspondence between text sentences and illustrations to ensure that each pair contains complementary visual-textual information, rather than irrelevant decorations.

Annotation Scheme. Following strict cross-validation guidelines by two domain experts, we adopted the BIO tagging scheme (B-Begin, I-Inside, O-Outside). To ensure consistency, we first built a domain-specific entity dictionary containing 1,636 entries across 9 categories. For instance, entities like "microscope" were strictly labeled as Tool (TOO), while "heating" was labeled as Step (STE). The final dataset contains 2,778 high-quality image-text pairs with a diverse distribution of categories.

The 2,778 pairs are split into training (1,944), validation (556), and test (278) sets. Detailed sample distributions across the 9 entity categories are provided in Table 1.

Evaluation Metrics. Following standard practices in NER research, we use Precision (P), Recall (R), and F1-score (F1) as the primary evaluation metrics. We adopt the exact match criteria, where a predicted entity is considered correct only if both its boundary and semantic category match the ground truth exactly.

$$P = \frac{TP}{TP + FP} \times 100\% \tag{11}$$

$$R = \frac{TP}{TP + FN} \times 100\% \tag{12}$$

Table 1. Entity categories and descriptions in the PSS-MNER dataset.

Category	Count	Tag	Description
Substance	301	SUB	Refers to non-living matter used as "raw materials" or "objects" in nature or experiments (e.g., water, air, iron)
Tool	219	TOO	Refers to equipment, instruments, or tools used for experiments, measurements, or observation (e.g., magnifier, beaker)
Phenomenon	216	PHE	Refers to observable non-material events, states, or properties (e.g., rainbow, rusting, bubbling, shadow)
Organism	212	BIO	Refers to all living beings and their macroscopic components (e.g., animals, plants, seeds, leaves)
Step	188	STE	Refers to specific operations, actions, or methods in scientific inquiry activities (e.g., observing, heating, measuring)
Location	139	LOC	Refers to specific geographic locations or environments related to scientific phenomena (e.g., classroom, pond, water surface)
Sensory	75	SEN	Refers to body organs or parts used by humans (or animals) to perceive the world (e.g., eyes, nose, hands)
Astronomy	65	AST	Refers to astronomical objects (e.g., sun, moon)
Unit	21	UNI	Refers to standard units of measurement for quantifying physical properties (e.g., cm, gram, Celsius)

$$F1 = \frac{2 \times P \times R}{P + R} \times 100\% \tag{13}$$

The F1-score serves as the harmonic mean of Precision and Recall, providing a comprehensive assessment of the model's performance, especially under imbalanced class distributions.

Implementation Details. All experiments were conducted on an NVIDIA RTX 4090 (24G) GPU. We use BERT-base-chinese as the text backbone and ViT-B/16 as the visual backbone. The model is trained for 40 epochs with a batch size of 32 and a learning rate of 5e−5. The optimizer is AdamW.

4.2 Main Results

To comprehensively evaluate the performance of SRKG-MNER, we compare it with classic text-only baselines including BiLSTM-CRF [4] and BERT-BiLSTM-CRF [18]. We also compare with state-of-the-art multimodal methods: MAF [10] (explicit image-text alignment), VEC-MNER [19] (hybrid Transformer for filtering visual noise), and AMLR [14] (reinforcement learning for multi-scale visual alignment).

Analysis of Comparative Results. As presented in Table 2, SRKG-MNER achieves state-of-the-art performance. We analyze the results from three perspectives:

Table 2. Experimental results on the PSS-MNER dataset (%).

Modality	Model	Precision (P)	Recall (R)	F1-Score (F1)
Text-only	BiLSTM-CRF	80.86	80.31	80.61
	BERT-BiLSTM-CRF	81.95	80.98	81.46
Text + Image	MAF	83.67	86.70	84.73
	VEC-MNER	84.15	88.03	85.80
	AMLR	84.35	89.04	87.05
	SRKG-MNER (Ours)	**88.58**	**90.59**	**89.57**

1. Impact of Pre-trained Language Models: Comparing the text-only baselines, BERT-BiLSTM-CRF outperforms the traditional BiLSTM-CRF by 0.85% in F1-score. This improvement is attributed to the deep contextual representations learned by BERT from large-scale corpora. In the context of science education, where terms often have polysemous meanings (e.g., "cell" in biology vs. "cell" in a battery), BERT's dynamic embeddings provide better semantic disambiguation capabilities than static word vectors.
2. Impact of Visual Information: A crucial observation is that all multimodal models outperform text-only models. For instance, even the relatively simple MAF model surpasses BERT-BiLSTM-CRF by 3.27%. This empirical evidence strongly supports our hypothesis: primary school science resources are inherently multimodal. Textual descriptions like "The structure shown in the figure" are semantically incomplete without visual reference. Multimodal models successfully leverage visual cues (e.g., the shape of a beaker) to resolve textual ambiguities, thereby improving recall.
3. Superiority of SRKG-MNER: Our proposed method achieves the highest F1-score of 89.57%, significantly outperforming the latest SOTA methods. Specifically, SRKG-MNER surpasses VEC-MNER and AMLR by 3.77% and 2.52%, respectively. While existing methods focus on filtering visual noise or aligning features at a coarse level, they lack the capability for deep semantic reasoning. SRKG-MNER addresses this by: (1) iteratively refining features to bridge the abstract semantic gap; and (2) injecting explicit expert knowledge to eliminate logically invalid predictions. This confirms that for specialized domains like education, combining "reasoning" with "domain logic" is more effective than generic feature fusion.

4.3 Ablation Study

To verify the contribution of each component, we conduct ablation studies as shown in Table 3:

w/o SR (Removing Iterative Interaction): In this variant, the multi-layer iterative attention module was removed and replaced with a single-layer shallow feature concatenation. The F1 score dropped by 1.12%. This result strongly suggests that the single-layer shallow fusion used in baselines is insufficient to capture abstract image-text correspondences. The iterative reasoning design is crucial for enhancing the model's multimodal understanding at a deep semantic level.

Table 3. Ablation study results regarding different components (%).

Variant	Precision (P)	Recall (R)	F1-Score (F1)
w/o SR	86.82	90.15	88.45
w/o KG	87.78	89.78	88.77
w/o WL	85.74	89.45	87.56
SRKG-MNER (Full Model)	**88.58**	**90.59**	**89.57**

w/o KG (Removing Knowledge Injection): This variant removed the GCN module that encodes the expert-constructed Entity Logic Graph. The results show a 0.80% decrease in the F1 score. This indicates that a lack of domain logic constraints leads to predictions that violate scientific common sense. The GCN-based knowledge injection effectively achieves logical refinement of features, helping the model accurately define entity boundaries. Furthermore, replacing the expert graph with a data-driven co-occurrence graph drops the F1-score by 0.65%. Applying 15% random edge perturbations only causes a marginal 0.42% F1 drop, proving both the expert graph's superiority and our model's structural robustness.

w/o WL (Removing Weighted Loss): Removing the Inverse Frequency Weighted Loss strategy resulted in the most significant performance drop (2.01% in F1). This demonstrates the necessity of the strategy for addressing the severe class imbalance in scientific data. Without it, the model tends to favor high-frequency categories while ignoring rare but critical entities, leading to a substantial decline in overall robustness.

4.4 Qualitative Analysis and Case Studies

We visualize three representative cases in Fig. 2 to interpret how SRKG-MNER addresses specific challenges:

(a) Visual Complementarity in Short Texts: As shown in Case (a), the text description is extremely sparse: "Wildebeest fighting". Due to the lack of context, the pure text baseline (BERT-BiLSTM-CRF) struggles to determine whether "Wildebeest" refers to a biological entity or a mechanical device, incorrectly labeling it as a non-entity ('O'). However, SRKG-MNER utilizes the iterative reasoning mechanism to simulate the process of "repeatedly looking at the image." The model captures biological forms in the first round of interaction and focuses on the fighting action in subsequent layers. These progressive visual clues provide decisive logical support, successfully identifying "Wildebeest" as a BIO entity.

(b) Structured Logical Reasoning: In Case (b), the text describes the "Artificial Fog Experiment," involving a complex sequence of actions and objects: "Pour warm water into the cylinder...". Simple multimodal models like MAF often fail to distinguish the functional attributes of the "Cylinder" due to interference from rich visual objects, misclassifying it as a generic Substance. In contrast, thanks to the GCN Knowledge Injection layer, our model understands the logical association that the action "Pour (STE)" typically acts upon a "Container Tool (TOO)". Consequently,

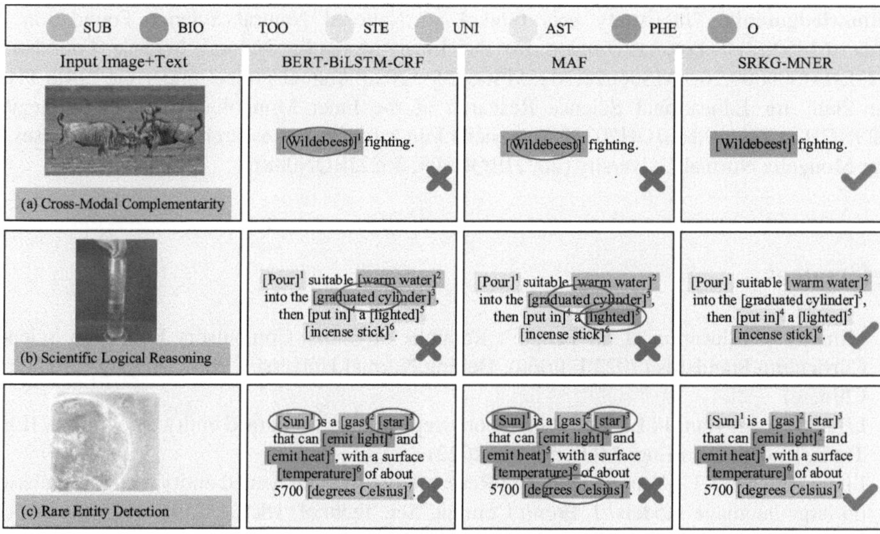

Fig. 2. Case Analysis

it accurately identifies the "Cylinder" as a TOO entity and correctly labels "Pour" and "Ignite" as Steps (STE).

(c) Robustness on Long-tail Entities: Case (c) describes the "Basic Properties of the Sun," containing extremely rare entities like "Celsius (UNI)" and "Sun (AST)". Conventional baselines, limited by sample imbalance, tend to predict high-frequency tags to reduce loss, leading to missed detections of rare entities. By introducing the Inverse Frequency Weighted Loss function, SRKG-MNER forces the model to pay attention to long-tail samples. Even under this extremely unbalanced distribution, it correctly identifies "Celsius" as a Unit (UNI) with 100% precision, verifying the effectiveness of our loss strategy.

5 Conclusion

In this paper, we address the unique challenges of Multimodal Named Entity Recognition (MNER) in primary school science education by proposing the SRKG-MNER framework. To bridge the abstract semantic gap, we design a Deep Cross-Modal Semantic Reasoning Layer that iteratively aligns visual and textual features. Furthermore, we introduce a GCN Knowledge Injection Layer to enforce explicit scientific logical constraints, ensuring predictions adhere to domain common sense. To tackle the severe long-tail data distribution, an Inverse Frequency Weighted Loss Strategy is applied. We also constructed a domain-specific dataset, PSS-MNER. Comprehensive experiments and case studies demonstrate that our method significantly outperforms existing state-of-the-art models. In the future, we plan to extend our framework to other educational subjects and explore the integration of Large Language Models (LLMs) to further enhance multimodal reasoning capabilities.

Acknowledgments. This study was funded by National Natural Science Foundation of China (61462071); Projects funded by the Inner Mongolia Natural Science Foundation (2023LHMS06009,2024MS06020,2025MS06055); 2023 Annual Project under the "14th Five-Year Plan" for Educational Science Research of the Inner Mongolia Autonomous Region (2023NGHZXZH119,NGJGH2023234);Special Funds for Basic Research Business Expenses of Inner Mongolia Normal University (2022JBQN108, 2022JBQN008).

References

1. Ministry of Education of the People's Republic of China: Compulsory Education Science Curriculum Standards (2022 Edition). Beijing Normal University Press, Beijing (2022). (In Chinese)
2. Li, J., Sun, A., Han, J., Li, C.: A survey on deep learning for named entity recognition. IEEE Trans. Knowl. Data Eng. **34**(1), 50–70 (2022)
3. Liang, J., Zhang, L., Yan, S., Hou, M.: Research progress on named entity recognition based on large language models. J. Front. Comput. Sci. Technol. **18**(10), 2594–2615 (2024). (In Chinese)
4. Lample, G., Ballesteros, M., Subramanian, S., Kawakami, K., Dyer, C.: Neural architectures for named entity recognition. In: Proceedings of NAACL-HLT, pp. 260–270 (2016)
5. Zhang, P., Chen, W.: Research progress of multimodal named entity recognition. Data Anal. Knowl. Discov. **8**(4), 50–63 (2024). (In Chinese)
6. Moon, S., Neves, L., Carvalho, V.: Multimodal named entity recognition for short social media posts. In: Proceedings of NAACL-HLT, pp. 852–860 (2018)
7. Lu, D., Neves, L., Carvalho, V., Zhang, N., Ji, H.: Visual attention model for name tagging in multimodal social media. In: Proceedings of the 56th Annual Meeting of the Association for Computational Linguistics, pp. 1990–1999 (2018)
8. Li, Q., Zheng, C., Wu, Z., Wang, T., Cai, Y.: Object-aware multimodal named entity recognition in social media posts with adversarial learning. IEEE Trans. Multimedia **23** (2021)
9. Liu, L., Wang, M., Zhang, M., Qing, L., He, X.: UAMNer: uncertainty-aware multimodal named entity recognition in social media posts. Appl. Intell. **52**(4) (2022)
10. Xu, B., Huang, S., Sha, C., Wang, H.: MAF: a general matching and alignment framework for multimodal named entity recognition. In: Proceedings of the 15th ACM International Conference on Web Search and Data Mining (WSDM), pp. 1215–1223 (2022)
11. Radford, A., et al.: Learning transferable visual models from natural language supervision. In: International Conference on Machine Learning (ICML), pp. 8748–8763 (2021)
12. Wang, X., Gui, M., Jiang, Y., et al.: ITA: Image-text alignments for multi-modal named entity recognition. In: Proceedings of the 2022 Conference of the North American Chapter of the Association for Computational Linguistics: Human Language Technologies, pp. 3176–3189 (2022)
13. Wang, X., Tian, J., Gui, M., et al.: PromptMNER: prompt-based entity-related visual clue extraction and integration for multimodal named entity recognition. In: International Conference on Database Systems for Advanced Applications, pp. 297–305 (2022)
14. Li, E., Li, T., Luo, H., et al.: Adaptive multi-scale language reinforcement for multimodal named entity recognition. IEEE Trans. Multimedia (2025)
15. Devlin, J., Chang, M.W., Lee, K., Toutanova, K.: BERT: pre-training of deep bidirectional transformers for language understanding. In: Proceedings of the 2019 Conference of the North American Chapter of the Association for Computational Linguistics: Human Language Technologies, pp. 4171–4186 (2019)

16. Dosovitskiy, A., Beyer, L., Kolesnikov, A., et al.: An image is worth 16x16 words: Transformers for image recognition at scale. In: International Conference on Learning Representations (2021)
17. Vaswani, A., et al.: Attention is all you need. In: Advances in Neural Information Processing Systems (NeurIPS), pp. 5998–6008 (2017)
18. Liu, S., Yang, H., Li, J.: Preliminary study on the knowledge graph construction of Chinese ancient history and culture. Information **11**(4), 186 (2020)
19. Wei, P., Ouyang, H., Hu, Q., et al.: VEC-MNER: hybrid transformer with visual-enhanced cross-modal multi-level interaction for multimodal NER. In: Proceedings of the 2024 International Conference on Multimedia Retrieval, pp. 469–477 (2024)

CatalogAgent: A Supervisor-Mediated Self-Learning System Enabling Context Engineering for GenAI Models

Zhu Cheng(✉), Zhenming Wang, Yu Tang, Dan Liu, Bryan Zhang, Athanasios N. Nikolakopoulos, Pranav Souri Itabada, Jing Zhang, Chih-Chi Chou, Peng Gao, Fatemeh Mansoori, Bharat Bojja, Sarath Chander, Sameer Thombare, Umit Batur, and Tarik Arici(✉)

Amazon, Seattle, USA
{zzcheng,aricit}@amazon.com

Abstract. Product catalogs are the backbone of e-commerce sites, yet a large number of structured attributes (SAs)—such as material, color, and shape often have missing values. Typically, SA values are extracted from product information, including titles and descriptions. While LLM-based generator-evaluator frameworks have demonstrated effectiveness for SA prediction—where an LLM generates SA values and another evaluates them—they face challenges when the Generator and Evaluator produce conflicting outputs, as either component can make mistakes. We introduce `CatalogAgent`, a novel agentic system that continuously improves Generator and Evaluator models for e-commerce catalog enrichment. When disagreements arise from (1) internal conflicts between the LLM-based Generator and Evaluator, or (2) external feedback from sellers on LLM outputs, a Supervisor Agent intervenes to mediate these conflicts and make final decisions. The system also incorporates a Memory Base and a Memory Summarizer that stores Supervisor Agent activities from individual cases and aggregates patterns into learnings. These learnings are fed back to the worker Generator and Evaluator LLMs, enabling self-improvement without human intervention. Through context engineering—injecting learnings and insights into worker LLMs' contexts—the system successfully transfers the Supervisor's capabilities to the Generator and Evaluator, improving their performance by 15.24% and 13.98%, respectively. Our experiments demonstrate a new paradigm of Supervisor Agent-mediated self-learning systems for improving generative AI model accuracy.

Keywords: Agent · Self-Learning · Context Engineering · GenAI · LLM

1 Introduction

Catalog enrichment plays a vital role in simplifying seller listing processes and enhancing customer shopping experiences in e-commerce. High-quality catalogs serve as crucial resources for customers and sellers.

J. Niu et al. (Eds.): KSEM 2026, LNAI 16631, pp. 114–130, 2027.
https://doi.org/10.1007/978-981-92-2759-4_9

A product consists of unstructured elements such as titles, descriptions, and images, and structured attributes (SAs) such as *material*, *color*, and *shape*. Each product belongs to a product type (PT), which defines the set of SAs applicable to that product. For example, the PT Shirt defines SAs such as *shirt form type*, *material*, *size*. We refer to a PT and one of its SAs as a PT-Structured Attribute pair (PT-A), and a specific product combined with one of its SAs as a Product-Attribute pair—the basic unit of a single enrichment task. Catalog enrichment is the process of filling in missing SA values in product catalogs. Major challenges include accurately predicting missing SA values from unstructured elements and verifying existing SA values against those elements to detect errors.

Large Language Models (LLMs) have gained significant traction for predicting or evaluating SA values [1–4]. However, several challenges remain: (1) It remains non-trivial to determine accurate SA values from unstructured elements, particularly given the diversity of SAs across different PTs. (2) With a vast set of SAs spanning a large volume of PTs in e-commerce catalogs, it is challenging to detect high-level error patterns or issue clusters (such as PT-level errors) that could simplify the enrichment problem and guide effective solutions. (3) Production-scale catalog enrichment requires lightweight, cost-effective LLMs that can process millions of products efficiently, making systematic context engineering essential for maximizing model performance without sacrificing scalability.

To address these challenges, we propose `CatalogAgent`, a novel Supervisor Agent-mediated self-learning system that performs **systematic context engineering** for worker Generator and Evaluator LLMs (Fig. 1). A **Generator** infers specific SA values from product title, descriptions, and structured data—for example, determining *battery type*, *material composition*, or *compatibility features*. An **Evaluator** verifies whether these values are accurate based on available evidence, creating an internal verification system. Both the Generator and Evaluator are designed as simple, efficient LLMs suitable for large-scale deployment: the Generator serves as the primary prediction model for attribute values, while the Evaluator acts as a quality control model to detect attribute value errors in catalog. This *LLM-as-a-judge* paradigm has gained traction as a practical and cost-effective alternative to human evaluation, enabling judgments that surpass traditional matching or embedding-based methods [5,6].

When both models agree on an attribute value, we have higher confidence in its accuracy. When they disagree, a **Supervisor** agent equipped with advanced reasoning capabilities and external tools arbitrates conflicts and determines the correct value. Such disagreements signal potential error patterns for specific structured attribute groups or product types, creating valuable learning opportunities for model improvement. A **Memory Base** stores these agent activities, and a **Memory Summarizer** extracts and aggregates learnings from this repository. These insights are validated through regression testing to ensure no degradation on existing performance, then fed back to the Generator and Evaluator models for targeted improvements through three types of context engineering: (1) prompt optimization to improve instruction clarity, (2) metadata refinement to identify incomplete value enumerations and propose additional valid values, and (3) image usefulness determination to identify which product images are most informative for specific PT-As.

This framework enables our system to autonomously monitor operations and enhance model quality through self-learning without human intervention. By engineering the right context—prompts, metadata, and input modalities—we can fully unleash the potential of lightweight worker LLMs. Moreover, the system is highly extensible and can incorporate additional signals from sellers or customers. For example, if sellers provide SA values that differ from the model-approved value, it may indicate a fundamental misunderstanding in a PT or its attribute definitions. Our system leverages such signals to autonomously self-improve.

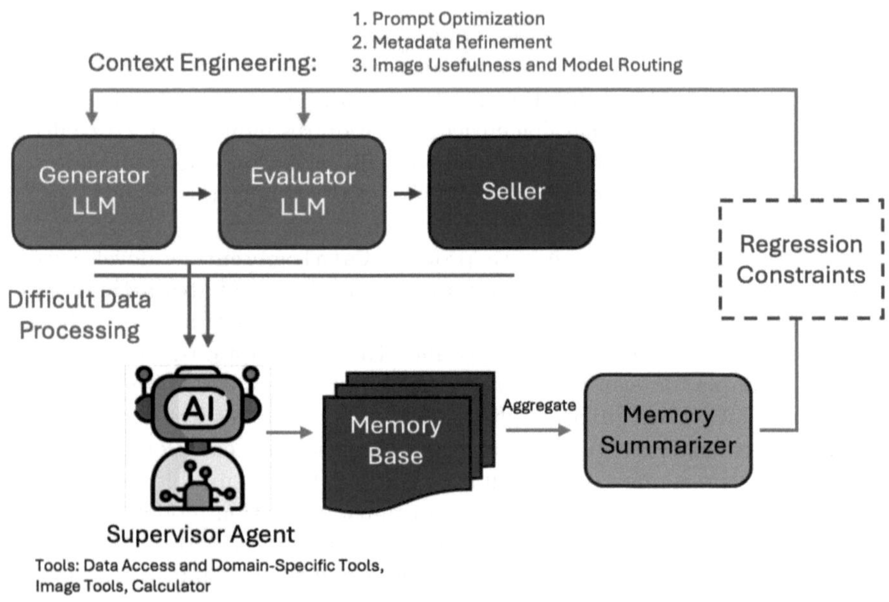

Fig. 1. Overview of CatalogAgent system. The Supervisor Agent intervenes when disagreements arise—either between the Generator and Evaluator, or between models and Sellers. Memory Base stores individual case learnings from Supervisor investigations, and the Memory Summarizer aggregates them into generalizable insights that are fed back to the Generator and Evaluator through context engineering, forming a closed-loop self-learning cycle. A Regression Constraints module validates that updates do not degrade performance before deployment.

Contributions: In this study, we introduce `CatalogAgent`—a novel supervisor agent-mediated self-learning system (Fig. 1). The system autonomously monitors individual model operations and enhances attribute value generation quality through systematic context engineering without human intervention. Our contributions are three-fold:

- We introduce a new paradigm—an agent-mediated self-learning system that achieves high accuracy on attribute prediction and evaluation tasks while providing context engineering feedback to Generator, Evaluator, and Seller in a self-learning manner.
- We present novel Memory Base and Memory Summarizer modules that create a self-improving feedback loop, capturing agent interactions and continuously feeding these learnings back to enhance the worker Generator and Evaluator models through context engineering.
- We propose a unique approach for model improvement by mining difficult cases in catalog data between Generator and Evaluator, Model and Seller. This approach efficiently identifies specific areas requiring context engineering, rather than applying broad untargeted optimizations.

2 CatalogAgent: A Supervisor-Mediated Self-Learning System

2.1 System Overview

Our system builds upon existing infrastructure where lightweight Generator and Evaluator LLMs process catalog enrichment at scale. These worker modules are standard LLMs optimized for high-volume batch processing.

We identify two critical signals that reveal model limitations: internal disagreements between Generator and Evaluator, and external conflicts where Sellers challenge the system-approved values. These challenging scenarios present opportunities for systematic improvement. To address these, we propose `CatalogAgent`, a novel Supervisor Agent-mediated self-learning system that performs systematic context engineering for Generator and Evaluator LLMs. `CatalogAgent` transforms difficult cases into continuous improvements by capturing failure signals, diagnosing root causes via the Supervisor's investigation, extracting generalizable patterns and insights, and injecting enhanced contexts back into worker models (Fig. 1). A theoretical analysis of the Supervisor's impact on catalog precision and accuracy is provided in Appendix A.

2.2 Supervisor Agent as Investigator and Arbitrator

The Supervisor Module operates as a high-reasoning agent that investigates difficult disagreement cases to generate granular, actionable insights. It arbitrates two types of conflicts: (1) *Generator-Evaluator disagreement*: When the Generator predicts an attribute value that the Evaluator rejects, the Supervisor analyzes both models' reasoning chains to determine the correct attribute value and diagnoses which model erred and why, producing individual case level learnings. (2) *Model-Seller disagreement*: When seller feedback conflicts with model-approved values, the Supervisor investigates the case to determine the accurate attribute value. In both scenarios, the Supervisor not only resolves the conflict but also generates insights that explain the root cause of errors and propose prompt refinements for Generator and Evaluator (Fig. 1).

The Supervisor Agent employs ReAct methodology [7] for iterative, tool-augmented reasoning, enabling multi-step investigations rather than one-shot predictions. The investigation process is supported by a comprehensive toolbox that provides multiple capabilities: Data Access Tools retrieve catalog metadata and attribute schemas; Domain-Specific Tools include category-specific validators (e.g., size charts for Apparel), image analysis that extracts and verifies visual attributes from product images. The modular design enables rapid integration of new feedback signals and tools, allowing the Supervisor to continuously expand its capabilities as new data sources and validation methods become available.

2.3 Memory Base: the Structured Foundation of Self-Learning

The system's self-learning capabilities are enabled by the Memory Base and Memory Summarizer modules. The Memory Base stores Supervisor Agent activities from processing individual cases using a carefully designed schema (Table 1).

Structured Schema for Context Engineering. The Supervisor Agent follows an output schema that captures three categories of insights for engineering better contexts for the worker Generator and Evaluator models.

(1) Prompt Improvements identify specific failure modes in the Generator and Evaluator. For instance, if the Evaluator consistently rejects accurate Generator predictions due to overly strict evidence requirements, the system updates the Evaluator's prompt to relax validation criteria for that PT-A.

(2) Metadata Refinement addresses gaps in attribute definitions that cause systematic errors. For example, if `button down shirt` is a valid *shirt form type* but absent from the predefined value set, neither the Generator nor the Evaluator can handle it correctly. Similarly, if an attribute definition is ambiguous—such as whether *fit type* describes a garment's relationship to the body or its length—models will produce inconsistent predictions. Metadata refinement addresses these issues by expanding value sets, clarifying definitions, or updating rules.

(3) Image Usefulness Analysis captures which images proved useful during the Supervisor's investigation for each product. For example, when investigating a handbag's inner capacity attribute, the schema records that secondary images showing the bag opened from above were necessary, whereas for a shirt's form type attribute, only the main image was needed. These individual case records accumulate in the Memory Base, providing the foundation for subsequent aggregation to identify systematic image usefulness patterns at the PT-A level.

2.4 Memory Summarizer: From Fine-Grained Insights to Generalizable Learnings

The Memory Summarizer processes records from the Memory Base to aggregate granular, case-specific insights into generalizable learnings at appropriate aggregation levels. For each PT-A pair, the Memory Summarizer retrieves all individual product-level suggestions from Supervisor investigations and identifies common patterns across failures at PT-A level. For example, for PT=Cellular Phone Case and Structured Attribute=*model name*, the Memory Summarizer fetches individual suggestions such as "be more cautious about assigning brand names as model names", "distinguish between pattern/design names and actual model names". By analyzing these recurring failure modes across multiple products, the Memory Summarizer synthesizes a consolidated prompt instruction: "When generating the model name attribute, focus on identifying a unique, specific identifier that distinguishes it within the manufacturer's lineup. Avoid using brand names, general product descriptions, color variants, pattern names, or compatibility information as model names. If no clear model name is provided, return Not Obtainable". For prompt improvements and metadata refinements,

Table 1. Supervisor Agent Output Schema for Context Engineering.

Field	Description
Case Identification	
`product_id`	Product identifier
`product_type`	Product Type
`attribute_name`	Attribute being analyzed
`current_value`	Existing attribute value
`disagreement_type`	Generator-Evaluator or Model-Seller
Arbitration Result	
`correct_value`	Supervisor-determined attribute value
`generator_correct`	Boolean: Whether Generator was correct
`evaluator_correct`	Boolean: Whether Evaluator was correct
Structured Schema for Context Engineering	
(1) Prompt Improvements	
`instructions_to_generator`	List of prompt refinements if G erred
`instructions_to_evaluator`	List of prompt refinements if E erred
(2) Metadata Refinement	
`metadata_clarification`	Clarifications to attribute definition
(3) Image Usefulness Analysis	
`image_analysis.useful`	Boolean: Whether images are predictive for this attribute List of image indices with predictive signal

the Memory Summarizer synthesizes common failure patterns into consolidated instructions and attribute definition updates.

The Memory Summarizer also aggregates individual image usefulness records to determine PT-A level patterns. When secondary images consistently proved necessary across cases—such as Handbag-*inner capacity*—the configuration includes secondary images in the model inputs. Conversely, when only the main image proved useful—such as Shirt-*form type*—the configuration optimizes to use only the main image, reducing input tokens and computational costs at scale.

2.5 Context Engineering Under Regression Constraints

While context engineering through prompt improvements and metadata refinements targets specific difficult failure cases, it is critical to ensure that these targeted new contexts do not degrade the Generator and Evaluator models' performance on the general population of well-understood cases. We express this dual objective—reducing difficult disagreement cases while preserving general performance—as a constrained optimization problem. Let θ denote the configuration (including prompt text, metadata), and let θ_0 represent the baseline configuration. We define:

- $\mathcal{D}(\theta)$: Disagreement rate under configuration θ, measured over Product-Attribute pairs where disagreements occur.
- $\mathcal{G}$: Golden dataset of Product-Attribute pairs with ground truth labels curated by human auditors, where $|\mathcal{G}| \ll |\mathcal{A}|$ and $\mathcal{A}$ represents all individual Product-Attribute prediction tasks in the catalog—each combination of a product and one of its PT-defined attributes constitutes a single task.
- $\mathcal{P}(\theta; \mathcal{G})$: Accuracy on the golden dataset $\mathcal{G}$ under configuration θ.

The optimization objective seeks to minimize disagreement rates while ensuring non-degradation on the general population as represented by $\mathcal{G}$:

$$\begin{aligned} \min_{\theta} \quad & \mathcal{D}(\theta) \\ \text{s.t.} \quad & \mathcal{P}(\theta; \mathcal{G}) \geq \mathcal{P}(\theta_0; \mathcal{G}) - \delta \quad \theta \in \Theta \end{aligned} \tag{1}$$

where $\delta \geq 0$ is a small tolerance threshold for acceptable performance degradation, and Θ represents the feasible space of configurations.

For completeness, we note that the Generator and Evaluator employ distinct configurations θ_G and θ_E respectively. The joint optimization becomes:

$$\begin{aligned} \min_{\theta_G, \theta_E} \quad & \mathcal{D}(\theta_G, \theta_E) \\ \text{s.t.} \quad & \mathcal{P}_G(\theta_G) \geq \mathcal{P}_G(\theta_G^0) - \delta_G \\ & \mathcal{P}_E(\theta_E) \geq \mathcal{P}_E(\theta_E^0) - \delta_E \\ & \theta_G \in \Theta_G, \ \theta_E \in \Theta_E \end{aligned} \tag{2}$$

where $\mathcal{D}(\theta_G, \theta_E)$ represents the disagreement rate under the joint configuration, $\mathcal{P}_G$ and $\mathcal{P}_E$ denote Generator and Evaluator accuracy on their respective golden datasets $\mathcal{G}_G$ and $\mathcal{G}_E$, with tolerance thresholds δ_G and δ_E.

The constraint ensures that any new configuration must maintain near-equivalent or better performance on the golden dataset, preventing regression on well-understood cases. The golden dataset $\mathcal{G}$, while necessarily limited due to human annotation costs ($|\mathcal{G}| \ll |\mathcal{A}|$), serves as a representative sample of the general catalog population and acts as a safeguard against overfitting to disagreement cases. This formulation captures the fundamental trade-off in production ML systems: aggressively optimizing for newly discovered failure modes while preserving gains on previously solved problems.

Regression Testing and Deployment. The Regression Test Module validates that aggregated learnings from the Memory Summarizer do not degrade performance on the golden dataset $\mathcal{G}$. We focus exclusively on regression testing because the disagreement cases triggering learnings are, by definition, edge cases not covered in $\mathcal{G}$—if they were present in $\mathcal{G}$, we would not observe these disagreements. Once validated, the improved prompt instructions and metadata refinements are integrated into the Generator and Evaluator configurations, completing the closed-loop learning cycle. The system then monitors online disagreement metrics $\mathcal{D}(\theta)$ in production as the primary indicator of improvement.

3 Experiments and Results

3.1 Dataset and Experimental Settings

We identified 4.89 million Product-Attribute pairs where the Evaluator rejected the Generator's predictions. We randomly sampled 50k Product-Attribute pairs for the Supervisor to investigate and generate learnings, and a separate 50k for testing whether the resulting context engineering enhanced the worker LLMs. The PT-A distribution is long-tailed, with the leading PT-As being Shirt-*shirt form type* and Cellular Phone Case-*subject character*. 23k Product-Attribute pairs from seller feedback were used—these represent cases where sellers provided different values from those generated and approved by Generator and Evaluator. The Supervisor Agent is equipped with tools including a metadata lookup function, image analysis, calculator function, with access to product data, and attribute definitions. The worker Generator and Evaluator use Mistral-NeMo, a lightweight LLM suitable for high-volume processing. Supervisor Agent is powered by Claude Sonnet, chosen for its reasoning and tool-use capabilities required for multi-step investigations.

3.2 Supervisor Agent as an Arbitrator

To resolve the conflict between Generator and Evaluator, Supervisor Agent monitors both models by analyzing their input and output. Acting as an arbitrator, the Supervisor Agent identifies true positives from each model and reveals domain-specific error patterns: Generator-dominant errors predominantly occur in the following PT-As: Shirt-*shirt form type*, Cellular Phone Case-*model name*. Evaluator-dominant errors are more common in *material*, *target gender* attributes (Table 2). This granular error attribution facilitates targeted improvements for Generator and Evaluator.

Table 2. Error attribution in Generator-Evaluator disagreements mediated by Supervisor Agent.

Product Type	Attribute	Generator error (%)	Evaluator error (%)
Shirt	shirt form type	97.78	2.22
Cellular Phone Case	model name	98.64	1.36
Shoe	model number	94.87	5.13
Boot	material	39.13	60.87
Shoe	material	30.23	69.77
Shirt	target gender	2.07	97.93
Shoe	shoe type	48.78	51.22
Boot	boot form type	62.22	37.78
Hat	fit type	23.81	76.19
Shirt	top style	56.25	43.75

Agreement between Generator and Evaluator does not guarantee accurate attribute prediction. We discovered this through seller feedback that challenge the potentially incorrect values produced by models. The Supervisor Agent serves as a judge, analyzing both model-generated and seller-proposed values to determine a correct value. Our analysis revealed that models were typically the source of errors (Table 3). For instance, in classifying *closure type* for leggings, the presence of a small zippered pocket misled the LLMs to incorrectly label the *closure type* as `zipper` instead of the correct value `pull-on`—an error that both Generator and Evaluator failed to catch. Interestingly, sellers were not always right either. Seller proposed values were incorrect in 76.60%, 42.86%, 48.98% of the feedback on *fit type*, *water resistance level*, *item form*, respectively (Table 3). Sellers were confused between certain attributes. They incorrectly submitted value `25" Inseam` as *fit type* of Pants, but rather attribute *inseam length* is an appropriate destination. These insights help target specific areas for model improvement while identifying opportunities for seller education. Supervisor Agent's output schema (Table 1) serves multiple purposes: it not only arbitrates errors (role-modeling for the Evaluator's assessment tasks), but also generates new attribute values after analyzing different conflicting view points, thereby acting as a role model for the Generator.

Table 3. Error attribution in Model-Seller disagreements mediated by Supervisor.

Attribute	Model error (%)	Seller error (%)
care instructions	81.08	16.22
fit type	14.89	76.60
closure type	91.67	4.17
material	85.71	4.08
water resistance level	53.06	42.86
directions	91.67	8.33
model number	87.76	10.20
recommended uses for product	89.80	8.16
compatible devices	71.43	20.41
number of items	73.91	23.91

3.3 Supervisor Agent Performance Benchmark

To validate the Supervisor Agent's effectiveness, we conducted human evaluations on both types of disagreement cases. For Generator-Evaluator disagreements, we randomly sampled 148 Product-Attribute pairs from cases where the Generator and Evaluator disagreed and compared the Supervisor's outputs against human assessment. The Supervisor achieved 97.26% accuracy when performing the Generator's role (SA value generation) and 94.56% accuracy when performing the Evaluator's role (SA value correctness assessment). For Model-Seller disagreements, human auditors evaluated 567 Product-Attribute pairs where sellers provided values differing from model-approved values. The Supervisor achieved 85.65% precision and 94.28% recall in arbitrating between model-approved and seller-proposed values (Table 4). The Supervisor Agent's performance can be attributed to its comprehensive approach: it considers both Generator and Evaluator perspectives, employs detailed multi-step reasoning via ReAct, and breaks down complex investigations into manageable sub-tasks.

Table 4. Supervisor Agent performance measured against human evaluation.

Generator-Evaluator disagreements ($n = 148$)	
Generation Accuracy	97.26%
Evaluation Accuracy	94.56%
Model-Seller disagreements ($n = 567$)	
Precision	85.65%
Recall	94.28%

3.4 Worker LLMs Self-Improve by Incorporating Aggregated Learnings from Supervisor

The Memory Summarizer and Regression Constraints modules are key to enabling self-improving capabilities of the system. It leverages stored agent activities from Memory Base to refine attribute metadata, improve Generator and Evaluator prompts, and determine LLM cascade configurations for various Product-Attribute tasks, routing each to the appropriate text-only or multi-modal model with the optimal image inputs. This creates a self-learning loop where the worker Generator and Evaluator LLMs constantly evolve and improve based on accumulated insights and learnings from Supervisor Agent (Fig. 1).

Learnings for Metadata Refinement. One of the key improvement opportunities identified by the Supervisor Agent is metadata enhancement. Analysis of Generator-Evaluator disagreements revealed that many classification errors occur when the Generator must select from a constrained set of predefined values that lack appropriate options. For example, the attribute *shirt form type* has predefined values such as `sport jersey`, `polo shirt`, and `t-shirt`, but lacks common styles like button down shirts, blouses, and henley shirts. When processing individual cases, the Supervisor Agent repeatedly observed that garments did not fit into any existing category, and systematically identified new values to add: `button down shirt`, `blouse`, `henley shirt`. These suggested additions undergo validation through a dedicated metadata agent before being integrated into the catalog schema.

As shown in Table 5, expanding the metadata values led to accuracy improvements of up to 5% for certain PT-As. These results demonstrate how systematic analysis can surface critical metadata gaps that, when addressed through coordinated efforts of Supervisor and metadata agents, significantly enhance classification accuracy across both Generator and Evaluator.

Table 5. Accuracy of generations from the worker LLM after metadata update.

Product Type	Attribute	Accuracy, Baseline (%)	Accuracy, with metadata update (%)
Shirt	shirt form type	87.95	92.54
Shoe	shoe type	92.75	95.09
Boot	boot form type	74.47	79.80
Pants	pants form type	87.69	90.35
Hat	hat form type	93.57	94.44

Learnings for Prompt Improvement. The schema of Supervisor Agent's output includes feedback messages from the Supervisor to Generator and Evaluator. Using Memory Summarizer, we compiled insights from individual cases handled by the supervisor. These consolidated learnings were then incorporated into the prompts for the Generator and Evaluator worker models. For example, in cases where a specific model name for a cellular phone case is not clearly identifiable, it should output Not Obtainable instead of attempting to create a model name from available information. Analyzing and aggregating from these agent activities led to a prompt update—"When generating the *model name* attribute, avoid using brand names, general product descriptions, color variants, pattern names, or compatibility information as model names, if no clear model name is provided, return Not Obtainable". Memory Summarizer identified that the problem lies in the hallucinated nature of worker Generator LLM—it tends to fabricate phone case model names rather than admitting when one is not available. After incorporating prompt updates from Memory Summarizer, the worker Generator achieved up to 15.01% improvement (Table 6).

Table 6. Worker LLM improved from prompt injection by Supervisor Agent.

Product Type	Attribute	Accuracy, Baseline (%)	Accuracy, with prompt update (%)
Cellular Phone Case	model name	69.20	84.21
Shoe	model number	65.39	78.80
Hat	material	70.47	83.68
Rug	care instructions	43.89	50.56
Cellular Phone Case	subject character	85.85	86.87

Prompt Improvement Under Regression Constraints. As formulated in Sect. 2.5, each new configuration θ must satisfy the constraint $\mathcal{P}(\theta; \mathcal{G}) \geq \mathcal{P}(\theta_0; \mathcal{G}) - \delta$, ensuring that targeted context engineering does not degrade performance on the general population represented by $\mathcal{G}$. For each PT-A where the Memory Summarizer produces updated prompts with injected learnings, we compare precision and recall against the baseline configuration θ_0 on the golden dataset. A prompt update is accepted if both metrics remain within the tolerance threshold δ. As shown in Table 7, most PT-As pass regression testing, with several showing notable improvements—for example, Nail Polish-*material type free* improved by +11.53% in precision and +17.50% in recall. A few PT-As exhibited degradation exceeding δ; their prompt updates are rejected, preserving hard-won gains on previously solved cases. This validates the constrained optimization formulation: the system aggressively optimizes for newly discovered failure modes while safeguarding performance on well-understood cases.

Learnings for Image Usefulness and LLM Model Selection. By studying the patterns stored in Memory Base from individual agent activities, we can further improve how we utilize images more effectively. For example, for a Wall Art product, the main image only displays the product details and features, making it unclear whether the product is intended for indoor or outdoor use, whereas the 2nd - 4th images show the Wall Art product displayed in dining and living rooms, which suggests the *indoor outdoor usage* to be indoor. Some PT-As are easily determined from the main image and text—like boot styles or

Table 7. Regression testing results on the golden dataset. New prompts with context engineering feedback are validated against golden dataset on both precision and recall.

Product Type	Attribute	Prec (θ_0)	Prec (θ)	Δ Prec	Rec (θ_0)	Rec (θ)	Δ Rec
Cellular Phone Case	compatible devices	78.57%	77.78%	-0.79%	96.25%	96.25%	0.00%
Shorts	fit type	28.07%	26.56%	-1.51%	20.00%	21.25%	+1.25%
Pants	care instructions	46.32%	45.00%	-1.32%	55.00%	56.25%	+1.25%
Pants	fit type	43.00%	44.00%	+1.00%	53.75%	55.00%	+1.25%
Essential Oil	product benefit	94.94%	97.47%	+2.53%	93.75%	96.25%	+2.50%
Electronic Cable	connector type	71.74%	71.28%	-0.46%	82.50%	83.75%	+1.25%
Nail Polish	material type free	48.89%	60.42%	+11.53%	55.00%	72.50%	+17.50%
Portable Electronic Device Cover	compatible devices	69.79%	71.13%	+1.34%	83.75%	86.25%	+2.50%
Pillow	fill material	83.54%	77.78%	-5.77%	83.54%	79.75%	-3.80%
Necklace	metal type	77.78%	83.78%	+6.01%	70.00%	77.50%	+7.50%
Headphones	noise control	72.22%	68.60%	-3.62%	81.25%	73.75%	-7.50%

shoe types. Specific details like a handbag interior material or its capacity to hold devices (attribute *maximum compatible device size*) often require secondary non-main images that show close-ups, inside views, or size comparisons. For example, a secondary image might show a top-down view of an open handbag revealing its fabric lining (attribute *inner material*). Certain PT-As benefit from the main image, whereas other PT-As benefit from non-main images (Table 8). We further used the insights and activities from Supervisor Agent and Memory Summarizer to route each PT-A to the appropriate text-only or multimodal model with the optimal image inputs.

Table 8. Top PT-As that benefit from predictive signals in main vs non-main image(s).

Predictive signals in **main** image		Predictive signals in **non-main** images	
Boot	boot form type	Clock	operation mode
Hat	hat form type	Handbag	inner material
Pants	pants form type	Rug	water resistance level
Sweatshirt	target gender	Handbag	compatible device size maximum
Pants	fit type	Wall Art	frame material
Shirt	shirt form type	Hat	fit type
Bracelet	bracelet form	Light Fixture	installation type
Coat	coat silhouette type	Wall Art	indoor outdoor usage

4 Related Work

Attribute prediction in e-commerce has evolved from rule-based [8] and NER-based extraction [9] to question-answering reformulations [10]. LLMs further expanded the scope by inferring values not explicitly stated in product text [1], and Zhang et al. [11–13] improve prediction by leveraging patterns from similar products as contextual guidance. More recently, LLM-based systems have been applied to broader e-commerce tasks: Huang et al. [2] orchestrate specialized LLM agents for automated product schema modeling, Cheng et al. [14] combine a fine-tuned domain expert with a general LLM for product categorization, Satyadharma et al. [3] develop a training-free LLM cascade for attribute value quality assessment, and Gao et al. [4] automate prompt specialization for thousands of attribute-specific prompts. Trabelsi et al. [15] investigate key design considerations for vision-language models applied to product image analysis. These works focus on individual tasks; our work addresses the complementary challenge of continuously monitoring and improving LLM-based attribute prediction through a self-learning manner mediated by Supervisor Agent.

Multi-agent architectures provide structured coordination for complex tasks. Supervisor-tool-calling [16,17] and hierarchical variants [18] enable agents to leverage external tools and decompose problems. Agent debate and critique have been applied in recommendation [19], legal [20], code generation [21], and general reasoning [22] domains. Multi-Expert Prompting [23] aggregates role-specific LLM responses to improve factuality. The *LLM-as-a-judge* paradigm [5,6] offers a cost-effective alternative to human evaluation; in our system, the Evaluator acts as a judge verifying Generator predictions, while the Supervisor serves as a higher-level judge with tool-augmented reasoning.

Recent work explores improving LLMs through feedback and context manipulation rather than weight updates. Self-Refine [24] uses iterative self-critique, Reflexion [25] maintains verbal reflections in episodic memory, and Malt [26] improves reasoning through multi-agent training. However, Huang et al. [27] show that self-correction without external feedback is unreliable—motivating our use of a tool-augmented Supervisor. In automatic prompt optimization, CriSPO [28] applies critique-suggestion modules, DSPy [29] compiles declarative modules into optimized pipelines, and ACE [30] evolves LLM contexts as self-improving playbooks. Our approach differs by mining *disagreement cases* between Generator, Evaluator, and Sellers as targeted improvement signals, aggregating case-level insights into generalizable learnings through the Memory Base and Memory Summarizer, and running the self-learning loop continuously with regression constraints to prevent quality degradation.

5 Conclusion and Discussion

We introduce a novel Supervisor Agent architecture within e-commerce catalog enrichment system that intervenes when two types of difficult disagreement cases occurred—Generator-Evaluator LLMs' conflicts, Seller corrections on LLM outputs. The system features a Memory Base and a Memory Summarizer that stores

Supervisor Agent activities from individual case processing, and aggregates patterns into learnings that are fed back into worker Generator and Evaluator LLMs to self-improve without human intervention. Future directions include using high quality labels generated from Supervisor Agent to finetune worker Generator and Evaluator LLMs.

A Appendix: Analysis of the Performance of Generator-Evaluator-Supervisor Framework

For a given *Product–Attribute* pair $(\mathtt{p}, \mathtt{a})$, let $\mathcal{X}_G := (T, I, M^G_{\mathtt{p,a}})$ and $\mathcal{X}_E := (T, I, M^E_{\mathtt{p,a}})$ denote the multimodal inputs to the Generator and Evaluator respectively, where T is textual information, I is image information, and $M^\bullet$ is the structured metadata visible to each role. The three pipeline components are:

$$G_\theta : \mathcal{X}_G \mapsto (V, R_G), \qquad E_\phi : \mathcal{X}_E \times V \mapsto (D, R_E), \qquad S_\psi : \mathcal{X}_G \times V \times R_G \times D \times R_E \mapsto (\widehat{V}, R_S),$$

with $D \in \{0, 1\}$ (Reject/Accept), free-text rationales R_G, R_E, R_S, and $V \subseteq S$ the attribute's value domain. The catalog publishes $\widehat{V}$ iff the last decision is Accept. The Supervisor is invoked on slices where the G–E pipeline identified an error. Since the Evaluator never sees R_G, we have $(D, R_E) \perp\!\!\!\perp R_G \mid (\mathcal{X}_E, V)$. This fact keeps the three roles statistically disjoint and will allow us to characterise the Evaluator with exactly two scalars, its true-positive and false-positive rates. Let Y be the (unknown) ground-truth value, we define $G_c := [V = Y]$, $p_g := \Pr(G_c = 1)$, $a := \Pr(D = 1 \mid G_c = 1)$ (Evaluator TPR), and $b := \Pr(D = 1 \mid G_c = 0)$ (Evaluator FPR). The Supervisor intervenes on three *residual slices*: $\mathcal{R}_1 : (G_c = 1, D = 0)$ **recovery**, with traffic mass $M_1 := p_g(1-a)$; $\mathcal{R}_2 : (G_c = 0, D = 1)$ **correction**, with traffic mass $M_2 := (1 - p_g)b$; $\mathcal{R}_3 : (G_c = 0, D = 0)$ **addition**, with traffic mass $M_3 := (1 - p_g)(1 - b)$.
For each slice, the Supervisor produces one of three outcomes: `ok` (correct value published), `bad` (incorrect value published), or `rej` (no value published), with slice-level rates $(p^{\mathtt{ok}}_{\mathrm{rec}}, p^{\mathtt{bad}}_{\mathrm{rec}}, p^{\mathtt{rej}}_{\mathrm{rec}})$, $(p^{\mathtt{ok}}_{\mathrm{cor}}, p^{\mathtt{bad}}_{\mathrm{cor}}, p^{\mathtt{rej}}_{\mathrm{cor}})$, $(p^{\mathtt{ok}}_{\mathrm{add}}, p^{\mathtt{bad}}_{\mathrm{add}}, p^{\mathtt{rej}}_{\mathrm{add}})$, with each triplet summing to 1. The baseline (time–t) precision is $\mathrm{Prec}_t = p_g a/(p_g a + M_2)$, and the post-Supervisor (time–$t{+}1$) precision is:

$$\mathrm{Prec}_{t+1} = \frac{p_g a + M_1 p^{\mathtt{ok}}_{\mathrm{rec}} + M_2 p^{\mathtt{ok}}_{\mathrm{cor}} + M_3 p^{\mathtt{ok}}_{\mathrm{add}}}{p_g a + M_1(p^{\mathtt{ok}}_{\mathrm{rec}} + p^{\mathtt{bad}}_{\mathrm{rec}}) + M_2(1 - p^{\mathtt{rej}}_{\mathrm{cor}}) + M_3(p^{\mathtt{ok}}_{\mathrm{add}} + p^{\mathtt{bad}}_{\mathrm{add}})}$$

We are now ready to state the following: inserting a Supervisor after the G–E pair can only improve catalog quality. Every residual slice lifts global precision in proportion to its traffic mass and the Supervisor's `ok` rate (Theorem 1), while each correct publication from any slice nudges overall accuracy upward and can never decrease it (Theorem 2).

Theorem 1 (Supervisor impact on Precision). *Define slice-specific precision advantages* $\ell_i := p^{\mathtt{ok}}_i - \mathrm{Prec}_t$ *for* $i \in \{\mathrm{rec}, \mathrm{cor}, \mathrm{add}\}$. *Then* $\Delta^{\mathrm{prec}} := \mathrm{Prec}_{t+1} - \mathrm{Prec}_t > 0 \iff M_1\ell_1 + M_2\ell_2 + M_3\ell_3 > 0.$

Corollary 1 (Sub–p_g Supervisor cannot lift precision). *If the Evaluator is non-trivial ($a \geq b$) and $p^{ok}_{\text{rec}}, p^{ok}_{\text{cor}}, p^{ok}_{\text{add}} \leq p_g$, then $\text{Prec}_{t+1} \leq \text{Prec}_t$, with strict inequality when any $M_i > 0$ and the corresponding slice precision is $< p_g$.*

Theorem 2 (Supervisor impact on accuracy). *Let $A_t := \Pr[\widehat{V} = Y]$ be catalog-wide accuracy and $\Delta_t := A_{t+1} - A_t = M_1 p^{ok}_{\text{rec}} + M_2 p^{ok}_{\text{cor}} + M_3 p^{ok}_{\text{add}}$.* ***(i) Non-regression:*** *$\Delta_t \geq 0$ for all admissible rate choices.* ***(ii) Strict improvement:*** *$\Delta_t > 0$ iff at least one slice has $M_i > 0 \wedge p^{ok}_i > 0$.*

References

1. Nikolakopoulos, A.N., Kaul, S., Gade, S.K., Dubrov, B., Batur, U., Khan, S.A.: Sage: structured attribute value generation for billion-scale product catalogs. arXiv preprint arXiv:2309.05920 (2023)
2. Huang, Y., et al.: AttributeForge: an agentic LLM framework for automated product schema modeling. In: Proceedings of EMNLP 2025, Industry Track, (2025)
3. Satyadharma, S., Sheikholeslami, F., Kaul, S., Batur, A.U., Khan, S.A.: Auto prompting without training labels: an LLM cascade for product quality assessment in e-commerce catalogs. In: Proceedings of EMNLP 2025, Industry Track (2025)
4. Gao, P., Nikolakopoulos, A., Cheng, Z., Scarinci, A., Batur, A.U., Khan, S.A.: Agentic prompt optimization for E-commerce catalog enrichment at scale. arXiv preprint (2026)
5. Li, D., et al.: From generation to judgment: opportunities and challenges of LLM-as-a-judge. arXiv preprint arXiv:2411.16594 (2025)
6. Gu, J., et al.: A survey on LLM-as-a-judge. arXiv preprint arXiv:2411.15594 (2024)
7. Yao, S., et al.: React: synergizing reasoning and acting in language models. In: The Eleventh International Conference on Learning Representations (2022)
8. Chiticariu, L., Krishnamurthy, R., Li, Y., Reiss, F., Vaithyanathan, S.: Domain adaptation of rule-based annotators for named-entity recognition tasks. In: Proceedings of EMNLP, pp. 1002–1012 (2010)
9. Yan, H., Gui, T., Dai, J., Guo, Q., Zhang, Z., Qiu, X.: A unified generative framework for various NER subtasks. arXiv preprint (2021)
10. Yang, L., et al.: Mave: a product dataset for multi-source attribute value extraction. In: Proceedings of WSDM '22, pp. 1256–1265 (2022)
11. Zhang, B., Khan, S.A., Walter, S.: Leveraging product catalog patterns for multilingual e-commerce product attribute prediction. In: Proceedings of EMNLP 2025, Industry Track (2025)
12. Zhang, B., Khan, S.A., Walter, S.: CatalogRAG: retrieval-guided LLM prediction for multilingual e-commerce product attributes. In: KDD 2025 Workshop on LLM4ECommerce (2025)
13. Zhang, B., Walter, S.: Don't just translate, summarize too: cross-lingual product title generation in e-commerce. In: LREC-COLING 2024 Workshop on e-Commerce and NLP (2024)
14. Cheng, Z., et al.: E-commerce product categorization with LLM-based dual-expert classification paradigm. In: Proceedings of the 1st Workshop on Customizable NLP (CustomNLP4U), pp. 294–304 (2024)

15. Trabelsi, A., Zontak, M., Qian, Y., Jackson, B., Khan, S., Batur, U.: What matters when building vision language models for product image analysis? In: IEEE Winter Conference on Applications of Computer Vision (WACV) Workshops (2025)
16. Schick, T., et al.: Toolformer: language models can teach themselves to use tools. Adv. Neural. Inf. Process. Syst. **36**, 68539–68551 (2023)
17. Parisi, A., Zhao, Y., Fiedel, N.: Talm: tool augmented language models. arXiv preprint arXiv:2205.12255 (2022)
18. Liu, P., Liu, X., Yao, R., Liu, J., Meng, S., Wang, D., Ma, J.: Hm-rag: hierarchical multi-agent multimodal retrieval augmented generation. arXiv preprint arXiv:2504.12330 (2025)
19. Cai, S., Zhang, J., Bao, K., Gao, C., Feng, F.: Flow: a feedback loop framework for simultaneously enhancing recommendation and user agents. arXiv preprint arXiv:2410 (2024)
20. ShengbinYue, S., et al.: Multi-agent simulator drives language models for legal intensive interaction. In: Findings of the Association for Computational Linguistics: NAACL 2025, pp. 6537–6570 (2025)
21. Hu, Y., et al.: Qualityflow: an agentic workflow for program synthesis controlled by llm quality checks. arXiv preprint arXiv:2501.17167 (2025)
22. Du, Y., Li, S., Torralba, A., Tenenbaum, J.B., Mordatch, I.: Improving factuality and reasoning in language models through multiagent debate. In: Forty-First International Conference on Machine Learning (2023)
23. Long, D.X., Yen, D.N., Luu, A.T., Kawaguchi, K., Kan, M.-Y., Chen, N.F.: Multi-expert prompting improves reliability, safety, and usefulness of large language models. arXiv preprint arXiv:2411.00492 (2024)
24. Madaan, A., et al.: Self-refine: iterative refinement with self-feedback. In: NeurIPS (2023)
25. Shinn, N., Cassano, F., Gopinath, A., Narasimhan, K., Yao, S.: Reflexion: language agents with verbal reinforcement learning. In: NeurIPS (2023)
26. Motwani, S.R., et al.: Malt: improving reasoning with multi-agent LLM training. arXiv preprint arXiv:2412.01928 (2024)
27. Huang, J., et al.: Large language models cannot self-correct reasoning yet. In: ICLR (2024)
28. He, H., et al.: CriSPO: multi-aspect critique-suggestion-guided automatic prompt optimization for text generation. In: Proceedings of the AAAI Conference on Artificial Intelligence, vol. 39, no. 22, pp. 24014–24022 (2025)
29. Khattab, O., Singhvi, A., Maheshwari, P., Zhang, Z., Santhanam, K.: DSPy: compiling declarative language model calls into self-improving pipelines. In: ICLR (2024)
30. Zhang, Q., et al.: Agentic context engineering: evolving contexts for self-improving language models. arXiv preprint arXiv:2510.04618 (2025)

Integration of Machine Learning and Knowledge Representation

Anisotropic Clustering via Adaptive Granulation

Duolin Xu[1], Zhijiang Chen[1], Yanmei Huang[1], Lijun Yang[1], Ke Gan[2], and Dongming Tang[1(✉)]

[1] College of Computer Science and Artificial Intelligence, Southwest Minzu University, Chengdu, China
tdm_2010@swun.edu.cn

[2] Sichuan Institute of Machinery Research & Design (Group) Co., Ltd., Chengdu, China

Abstract. While Granular Ball Clustering is efficient, it assumes isotropic distributions. Meanwhile, density-based methods suffer from parameter sensitivity on multi-density manifolds. To address this, we propose Anisotropic Granular Ball Clustering via Local Density-Adaptive Neighborhood and Variance-Driven Partitioning (GB-DSANN). First, a local density-adaptive mechanism constructs a mutual nearest neighbor graph. Second, dynamic secondary partitioning uses variance-based compactness. This generates anisotropic granules. Finally, Shared Nearest Neighbor spectral clustering merges these granules. This approach transforms non-convex clustering into efficient graph partitioning. Experiments on 28 datasets validate GB-DSANN. Outperforms state-of-the-art baselines in robustness and efficiency. Its complexity is $O(N \log N + m^3)$, where $m \ll N$. The source code is publicly available at https://github.com/xdlhhh/GB-DSANN.git.

Keywords: Clustering · Granular Computing · Anisotropic Granulation · Spectral Clustering · Local Density Adaptation

1 Introduction

Clustering analysis reveals latent structures in unlabeled data [9] by maximizing intra-cluster similarity and minimizing inter-cluster similarity. This method is widely applied in fields such as image segmentation, bioinformatics, and social network analysis [5].

Partitioning methods like K-means optimize intra-cluster squared errors [16] but assume spherical distributions, failing to capture complex manifold structures. To address this, Zhao et al. proposed AK-means [18], which adaptively selects centroids via density calculations yet still relies on convexity assumptions. Density-based methods like DBSCAN handle noise and arbitrary shapes [4] but struggle with heterogeneous data, where a single global parameter ϵ causes over-segmentation or incorrect merging. Although Shu et al.'s SDCHS-DDNDSA [10] replaces fixed ϵ distances with nearest neighbor k, it often fails in

J. Niu et al. (Eds.): KSEM 2026, LNAI 16631, pp. 133–143, 2027.
https://doi.org/10.1007/978-981-92-2759-4_10

high-dimensional sparse spaces. Additionally, hierarchical clustering faces cubic computational complexity [2].

Granulation and micro-cluster methods improve computational efficiency. For instance, Xu et al.'s MDMSC [14] builds micro-clusters using local density to accelerate spectral clustering but requires complex parameter tuning. Xia et al. proposed GBC [13] to reduce costs through hyperspherical granulation, yet it critically relies on an isotropic assumption. Since real data are locally anisotropic, spherical granulation mismatches the true topology, causing large clustering errors.

To address these drawbacks, we propose GB-DSANN to reduce computational overhead while preserving the intrinsic topological structure. The main contributions are:

- An adaptive local thresholding mechanism using k-NN statistics to handle multi-density parameter sensitivity.
- A variance-guided bisection strategy to form anisotropic granules aligned with local manifolds.
- A granule-based spectral clustering framework to efficiently capture non-convex structures.

2 Related Work

2.1 Local Density Estimation

Clustering based on density depends on the definition of local neighborhoods. A common metric for estimating local density uses the distance to the k-th nearest neighbor (k-NN), formulated as:

$$\rho_i = \left(\frac{1}{k} \sum_{j \in \mathcal{N}_k(i)} d(x_i, x_j) \right)^{-1} \tag{1}$$

where ρ_i represents the local density of the sample x_i.

Recent work refines Eq. (1) to vary the density of the clusters. Kernel estimators replace its linear sum with Gaussian weights, smoothing local noise [6]. Relative methods such as LOF further normalize ρ_i by neighbor densities in $\mathcal{N}_k(i)$ to separate boundary points from outliers [8].

2.2 Dynamic Segmentation Mechanisms

Segmentation algorithms decompose complex data into simpler substructures. Classical bisecting K-means recursively split clusters using Euclidean distance, assuming local isotropy, and chooses splits by minimizing the Sum of Squared Errors within a sub-cluster C.

$$J(C) = \sum_{x_i \in C} \|x_i - \mu_C\|^2 \tag{2}$$

where x_i represents a data point within the cluster C, and μ_C denotes the centroid of the cluster.

To overcome the spherical limitation of Eq. (2), the Mahalanobis distance uses covariance weights to capture elliptical shapes [3]. Infor-mation theoretic criteria add penalty terms to $J(C)$ to balance the complexity of the model [1].

2.3 Spectral Graph Partitioning

Spectral clustering resolves non-convex structures using graph eigenvalues [19].The core transformation utilizes the normalized Laplacian matrix L_{sym}:

$$L_{sym} = I - D^{-\frac{1}{2}} W D^{-\frac{1}{2}} \tag{3}$$

where L_{sym} is the normalized Laplacian matrix. I, D, and W represent the identity, degree, and adjacency matrices, respectively.

The high computational costs of building L_{sym} drive the approximation research. Nyström methods estimate eigenvectors without computing the full matrix W [17]. Landmark strategies use representative subsets to generate a sparse W. This significantly reduces the scale of eigen-decomposition [15].

3 Proposed Algorithm: GB-DSANN

The mathematical symbols and definitions utilized throughout the GB-DSANN framework are summarized in Table 1.

Table 1. Description of mathematical symbols

Symbol	Definition
ε_i	Adaptive local density threshold for sample x_i
$\mathcal{N}_k(x_i)$	Set of k-nearest neighbors for sample x_i
$\|x_i - x_j\|_2$	Euclidean distance between samples x_i and x_j
$\mathcal{N}_{\varepsilon_i}(x_i)$	Local neighborhood of x_i defined by the adaptive threshold
Comp(C)	Cluster compactness metric based on feature variance
d	Feature dimensionality of the dataset
$\|C\|$	Cardinality (total sample count) of cluster C
$x_{i,l}$	Value of the l-th feature for sample x_i
$\mu_{C,l}$	Mean value of the l-th feature within cluster C
S	Shared Nearest Neighbor (SNN) similarity matrix
D	Degree matrix associated with similarity matrix S
L	Normalized Laplacian matrix constructed for spectral clustering
δ	A small constant (e.g., 10^{-5}) to avoid division by zero

3.1 GB-DSANN Algorithm Framework

The GB-DSANN framework mitigates the sensitivity of global parameters while capturing manifold structures. The algorithm operates in three sequential stages: (1) construction of a local density-adaptive neighbor graph to capture density variations; (2) recursive dynamic segmentation to generate compact anisotropic granules; and (3) spectral merging of these granules to recover global topological structures. The overall workflow is illustrated in Fig. 1.

3.2 Local Density-Adaptive Neighborhood Construction

Density heterogeneity challenges fixed-radius methods. We derive a local density threshold ε_i for each sample x_i using BallTree queries to identify the nearest neighbors k (k-NN). Defined as the average distance to these neighbors:

$$\varepsilon_i = \frac{1}{k} \sum_{x_j \in \mathcal{N}_k(x_i)} \|x_i - x_j\|_2 \tag{4}$$

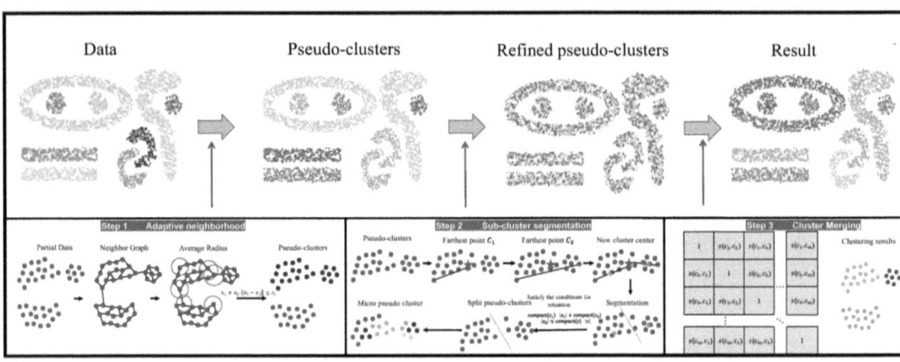

Fig. 1. The framework of the GB-DSANN algorithm

This local threshold ε_i reflects the sparsity of the region surrounding x_i. A robust mutual neighbor graph is constructed where there is an edge between x_i and x_j if and only if mutual neighborhood constraints are strictly met within $\min(\varepsilon_i, \varepsilon_j)$. This bidirectional verification filters accidental connections in sparse regions. UnionFind then extracts the initial connected components as raw clusters.

3.3 Dynamic Secondary Partitioning

Coarse-grained components require refinement via variance-driven dynamic segmentation. Unlike isotropic GBC or global error-minimizing Bisecting K-means, this strategy identifies principal local distributions to generate anisotropic granules. Cluster compactness is defined as the sum of variances across all feature dimensions:

$$\mathrm{Comp}(C) = \sum_{l=1}^{d} \frac{1}{|C|} \sum_{x_i \in C} (x_{i,l} - \mu_{C,l})^2 \tag{5}$$

Partitioning utilizes a farthest-point-driven bisection. Given centroid c, its farthest point p_1, and p_2 (farthest from p_1), the split centers are determined as:

$$c_1 = \frac{c + p_1}{2}, \quad c_2 = \frac{c + p_2}{2} \tag{6}$$

Samples are assigned to the nearest split center, and splits are accepted if the weighted sub-cluster compactness decreases. An atomic constraint ($|C| \geq 4$) ensures statistical stability for variance estimation in d-dimensional space, preventing trivial clusters.

3.4 Granule Merging and Noise Handling

The reconstruction of the connectivity of the multiplier is based on a similarity matrix of shared nearest neighbor (SNN) between the granules C_i and C_j:

$$s(C_i, C_j) = \frac{|\mathcal{N}(C_i) \cap \mathcal{N}(C_j)|}{1 + \mathrm{dist}(c_i, c_j)} \tag{7}$$

where $\mathcal{N}(C_i)$ is the aggregate neighbor set. The denominator acts as a regularization term, penalizing large centroid distances to prevent noise-induced "short-circuit" errors. Spectral clustering is performed on the resulting normalized Laplacian matrix $L = I - D^{-1/2}SD^{-1/2}$, reducing the problem to graph partitioning. Unassigned noise points are handled via distance-weighted voting:

$$\mathrm{label}(p) = \arg\max_{c} \sum_{q \in \mathcal{N}_k(p), \mathrm{label}(q)=c} \frac{1}{\|p - q\|_2 + \delta} \tag{8}$$

This ensures that the noise points are assigned to the most topologically relevant cluster, enhancing boundary integrity.

3.5 Time Complexity Analysis

The computational complexity of GB-DSANN involves three primary phases. First, constructing the BallTree index and querying k-nearest neighbors for N samples incurs $O(N \log N)$ time. Second, dynamic variance-driven partitioning under atomic constraints ensures a logarithmic-depth recursive segmentation, bounded by $O(N \log N)$. Third, spectral merging on m granules requires $O(m^3)$ operations to construct the similarity matrix and perform eigenvalue decomposition. Thus, the overall time complexity is:

$$T_{total} \approx O(N \log N + m^3) \tag{9}$$

Algorithm 1. GB-DSANN Complete Clustering Algorithm

Input: Dataset Data, Neighbor count k, Feature dimension d, Cluster number n_{clusters}
Output: Final clusters $\{K_1, \ldots, K_{n_{\text{clusters}}}\}$
Build BallTree index for Data to accelerate neighbor queries
Compute local ε_i and construct mutual neighbor graph
Extract initial components using UnionFind
for each component C **do**
    Recursively partition C based on variance reduction and atomic constraint $|C| \geq 4$
end for
Construct SNN similarity matrix S between anisotropic granules
Compute Normalized Laplacian L and perform spectral clustering
Assign noise points using inverse-distance weighted voting **return** Final cluster labels

Since granulation significantly compresses the data, the granule count m is typically much smaller than N ($m \ll N$). Consequently, for medium-scale datasets with complex structures, the $O(N \log N)$ term dominates the overall runtime, ensuring high computational efficiency.

4 Experiments and Analysis

The experiments were conducted on an Intel Core i5-14600KF using Python. Evaluation metrics include the adjusted Rand Index, Normalized Mutual Information, and Accuracy [12].

4.1 Experimental Parameter Configuration

Parameter tuning was standardized for fairness. K-means, AK-means, and Aggregation utilized the ground truth k. DBSCAN optimized ε and $MinPts \in \{3, 5, 10, 20\}$ via grid search to maximize ARI. MDMSC, SDCHSDDNDSA, and GB-DSANN tuned neighbors $k \in [5, 50]$ via grid search. Additionally, GB-DSANN set an atomic constraint $|C| \geq 4$, while GBC used its original defaults.

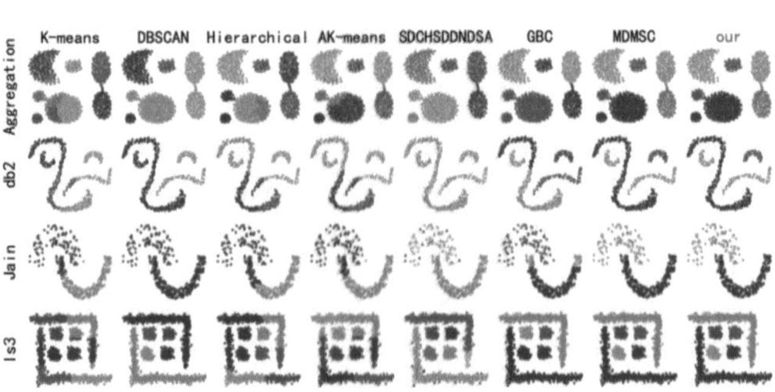

Fig. 2. Visualization of clustering results for shape datasets

Table 2. Details of Synthetic and Real-world Datasets

Dataset	N	D	K	Dataset	N	D	K	Dataset	N	D	K
Synthetic Datasets											
Aggregation	788	2	7	Gauss17-10	5100	2	17	Unbalance1	6500	2	8
db2	315	2	4	Gauss17-20	5100	2	17	Unbalance2	6500	2	8
Jain	373	2	2	Gauss17-30	5100	2	17	Unbalance3	1250	2	3
Ls3	1735	2	6	Gauss17-40	5100	2	17	Unbalance4	1710	2	15
Real-world Datasets											
biodeg	1055	41	2	crowdsourced	10545	28	6	glass	214	9	6
HAPT	2082	561	6	pengleukEW	72	7070	2	WDBC	569	30	2
balance	625	4	3	eeg	14980	14	2	GLI-85	84	22283	2
landsatEW	6435	36	6	raisin	900	7	2	Yale	164	1024	15
banknote	1372	4	2	energy-y2	768	8	3				
musk	6598	166	2	TOX-171	170	5748	4				

4.2 Performance Evaluation on Complex Manifolds

We evaluated 12 synthetic and 16 real-world datasets (Table 2) characterized by non-convex manifolds, varying densities, and high dimensionality.

Figure 2 illustrates that only GB-DSANN and MDMSC correctly identify clusters on complex manifolds. Other benchmarks frequently produce errors. Table 3 confirms that GB-DSANN consistently achieves optimal metrics. Unlike MDMSC, which neglects sparse connections, GB-DSANN handles density heterogeneity effectively. It attains near-perfect ARI (≈ 1.0) on these datasets. This validates that adaptive neighborhoods bridge sparse regions while anisotropic granules align with geometry. Real-world results further confirm the robustness of variance-driven partitioning in high-dimensional spaces.

4.3 Efficiency and Trade-Off Analysis

The scalability comparison in Fig. 3 reveals that GB-DSANN maintains high computational efficiency as dataset size increases, remaining significantly faster than Hierarchical clustering which approaches the timeout limit at $N \approx 12000$. Although MDMSC displays volatility and incurs higher runtime costs on medium-sized datasets ($N \approx 4000 - 8000$), GB-DSANN exhibits a stable, near-linear log-scale growth trend comparable to fast partitional methods, offering a superior balance between runtime feasibility and topological recovery accuracy.

Table 3. Performance comparison. Best results in red, second-best in **blue**.

Dataset	Metric	GB-DSANN	*K-means*	*DBSCAN*	*Hierarchical*	*AK-means*	*SDC...*	*GBC*	*MDMSC*
				Synthetic Datasets					
Gauss17-10	ARI	0.9790	0.9556	0.9306	0.9704	0.9486	0.8570	**0.9837**	0.9871
	NMI	0.9803	0.9648	0.9427	0.9777	0.9604	0.9151	**0.9819**	0.9872
	ACC	0.9900	0.9782	0.9522	0.9855	0.9747	0.8849	**0.9914**	0.9939
Gauss17-20	ARI	0.9555	0.9168	0.9019	**0.9554**	0.9078	0.7202	0.9333	0.9507
	NMI	**0.9613**	0.9363	0.9170	0.9638	0.9299	0.8418	0.8477	0.9599
	ACC	0.9786	0.9586	0.9267	0.9786	0.9539	0.7527	0.8606	**0.9763**
Gauss17-30	ARI	0.9249	0.8272	0.8065	0.8375	0.8476	0.3182	0.8041	**0.8934**
	NMI	0.9375	0.8820	0.8802	0.9044	0.8903	0.6664	0.4944	**0.9201**
	ACC	0.9635	0.9057	0.8925	0.8898	0.9208	0.3935	0.6214	**0.9469**
Gauss17-40	ARI	0.8680	0.8068	0.6756	0.8118	0.8141	0.2446	**0.8244**	0.8233
	NMI	0.9000	0.8687	0.7983	0.8804	0.8724	0.6593	0.6200	**0.8823**
	ACC	0.9341	0.8976	0.7561	0.9018	0.9020	0.2945	0.6629	**0.9098**
Unbalance1	ARI	0.9997	0.9982	**0.9995**	0.9997	0.8896	0.8971	0.8160	0.9913
	NMI	0.9980	0.9935	0.9926	**0.9975**	0.9083	0.8377	0.8422	0.9791
	ACC	0.9995	0.9986	0.9968	**0.9994**	0.8989	0.8909	0.8903	0.9837
Unbalance2	ARI	1.0000	0.9990	**0.9992**	1.0000	0.8578	0.8974	0.8179	0.9963
	NMI	1.0000	0.9971	0.9904	**0.9994**	0.9013	0.8379	0.8319	0.9869
	ACC	1.0000	0.9994	0.9954	**0.9998**	0.8328	0.8911	0.8826	0.9837
Unbalance3	ARI	**0.9360**	0.8401	0.8851	0.9354	0.8376	0.7823	0.6777	0.9433
	NMI	0.9015	0.8163	0.8408	**0.9032**	0.8141	0.7246	0.6115	0.9120
	ACC	**0.9784**	0.9416	0.9392	**0.9784**	0.9408	0.8704	0.7280	0.9808
Unbalance4	ARI	0.9994	0.8528	**0.9889**	0.9994	0.3857	0.8085	0.9239	0.8488
	NMI	**0.9964**	0.9433	0.9573	0.9969	0.7599	0.7871	0.9118	0.9453
	ACC	0.9982	0.8766	0.9573	0.9982	0.4702	0.7977	0.8673	0.8614
Average	ARI	0.9578	0.8996	0.8984	**0.9387**	0.8111	0.6906	0.8476	0.9293
	NMI	0.9594	0.9252	0.9149	**0.9530**	0.8795	0.7077	0.7677	0.9466
	ACC	0.9803	0.9445	0.9270	**0.9636**	0.8116	0.6807	0.8131	0.9546
				Real-world Datasets					
biodeg	ARI	**0.0822**	-0.0519	0.0939	-0.0522	-0.0009	-0.0028	0.0022	-0.0020
	NMI	0.0854	0.0782	0.1263	0.0749	0.0012	0.0036	0.0045	**0.0980**
	ACC	0.6967	0.5280	0.1194	0.5327	0.6616	0.6597	**0.6635**	0.6569
balance	ARI	0.2530	0.1605	0.0000	**0.1609**	0.1396	0.0858	0.0634	0.1224
	NMI	0.2165	0.1431	0.0000	0.1286	0.1240	**0.1725**	0.0032	0.0976
	ACC	0.5760	0.5376	0.4608	0.5392	0.5008	0.4608	0.4912	**0.5440**
banknote	ARI	0.8379	0.0223	**0.8263**	0.0978	0.0132	-0.0041	0.0068	0.4811
	NMI	0.7875	0.0174	**0.7375**	0.0990	0.0111	0.0184	0.0050	0.4190
	ACC	0.9577	0.5758	**0.9147**	0.6574	0.5590	0.5437	0.5015	0.8469
crowdsourced	ARI	0.2639	0.0769	-0.0248	0.1313	0.0769	0.0237	0.0713	**0.2633**
	NMI	**0.3051**	0.2600	0.0129	0.2961	0.2600	0.0308	-0.0318	0.3090
	ACC	0.7565	0.3779	0.6755	0.4514	0.3779	**0.7111**	0.3972	0.7006
eeg	ARI	0.0077	0.0000	-0.0004	0.0000	0.0000	0.0001	**0.0053**	0.0014
	NMI	0.0038	0.0002	**0.0104**	0.0002	0.0002	0.0266	0.0011	0.0005
	ACC	0.5596	0.5513	0.5310	0.5513	0.5513	0.5274	**0.5535**	0.5517
energy-y2	ARI	0.7111	0.6814	0.7058	0.4546	0.4263	0.4208	0.6625	**0.7065**
	NMI	0.6673	0.5814	0.6640	**0.6789**	0.5879	0.4647	0.7031	0.6644
	ACC	0.8164	0.7461	0.8073	0.5716	0.5065	0.5807	0.8021	**0.8099**
glass	ARI	0.2218	0.1688	0.2529	0.1589	0.2109	-0.0216	0.1608	**0.2024**
	NMI	0.3940	0.3266	**0.3925**	0.3169	0.3334	0.1596	0.0396	0.3302
	ACC	0.5000	0.4346	0.3505	0.4252	**0.5234**	0.3692	0.4065	0.5561
GLI-85	ARI	0.3857	0.1327	**0.2224**	0.0327	0.1327	0.0000	0.0061	0.1894
	NMI	0.2733	0.2338	**0.2611**	0.1732	0.2338	0.0000	0.0168	0.1317
	ACC	0.8214	0.6905	0.1071	0.6190	0.6905	0.7024	0.7024	**0.7262**
HAPT	ARI	**0.5885**	0.4574	0.3290	0.4558	0.4574	-0.0001	0.6538	0.5541
	NMI	0.6911	0.5824	0.4800	0.5941	0.5824	0.0050	0.4843	0.7151
	ACC	0.6902	0.5754	0.3353	0.5677	0.5754	0.1912	0.5524	**0.6076**
landsatEW	ARI	0.6174	0.5276	0.2788	0.5304	0.5276	0.0003	0.5663	**0.6172**
	NMI	0.6375	0.6020	0.4727	0.6015	0.6020	0.0127	0.5154	**0.6318**
	ACC	0.7829	0.6659	0.4917	0.6564	0.6659	0.2594	0.6824	**0.7731**
musk	ARI	**0.1051**	-0.0323	0.1314	-0.0334	0.0125	-0.0842	0.0027	0.0978
	NMI	0.0863	0.0285	**0.0788**	0.0274	0.0385	0.0417	0.0058	0.0513
	ACC	0.8577	0.5377	0.0252	0.5421	0.5489	0.7620	**0.8422**	0.8079
pengleukEW	ARI	0.5085	0.1621	0.0000	0.2112	0.1621	0.0000	0.1119	**0.3585**
	NMI	0.3887	0.1253	0.0000	0.1547	0.1253	0.0000	0.0769	**0.2509**
	ACC	0.8611	0.7083	0.0000	0.7361	0.7083	0.6528	0.6944	**0.8056**
raisin	ARI	0.4205	0.2767	0.1208	0.1274	0.2744	0.1048	0.0982	**0.3838**
	NMI	0.3933	0.3310	0.0915	0.2305	0.3293	0.1186	0.0219	**0.3780**
	ACC	0.8244	0.7633	0.3667	0.6789	0.7622	0.6556	0.5744	**0.8100**
TOX-171	ARI	0.2321	0.1254	0.0322	0.2548	0.1254	0.0000	0.0998	**0.2347**
	NMI	0.3712	0.2158	0.0834	**0.3704**	0.2158	0.0000	0.0038	0.3404
	ACC	0.5000	0.4412	0.2471	**0.4647**	0.4412	0.2647	0.3000	0.5059
WDBC	ARI	0.8112	0.7302	0.4562	0.5383	0.6536	-0.0386	0.0798	**0.7985**
	NMI	0.7266	0.6231	0.3576	0.4170	0.5324	0.0813	0.0383	**0.7087**
	ACC	0.9508	0.9279	0.5202	0.8682	0.9051	0.5395	0.5518	**0.9473**
Yale	ARI	0.3095	0.2707	0.0336	0.2584	0.2707	0.0000	0.4565	**0.2505**
	NMI	0.5649	0.5346	0.1202	**0.5423**	0.5346	0.0000	0.1805	0.5291
	ACC	0.5305	0.4756	0.0610	0.4512	0.4756	0.0671	0.3720	**0.4695**
Average	ARI	0.3972	0.2318	0.2161	0.2079	0.2177	0.0303	0.1905	**0.3287**
	NMI	0.4120	0.2927	0.2431	0.2888	0.2820	0.0710	0.1293	**0.3535**
	ACC	0.7301	0.5961	0.3758	0.5824	0.5909	0.4967	0.5680	**0.6950**

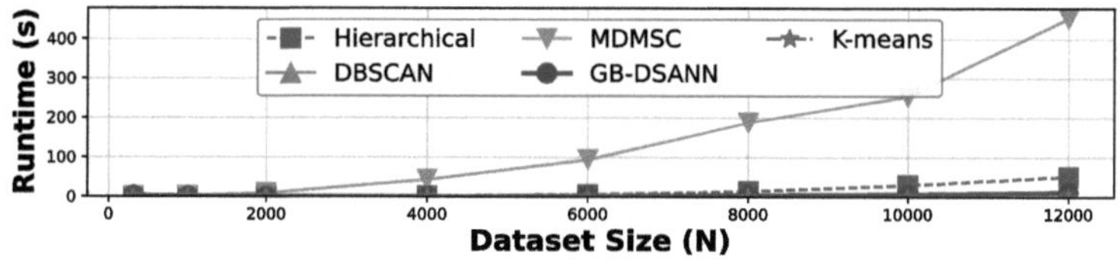

Fig. 3. Runtime comparison (log scale). GB-DSANN demonstrates scalability comparable to fast partitional methods.

4.4 Statistical Significance Analysis

Non-parametric tests on ARI results across 24 datasets confirm performance. The Friedman test ($p = 1.37 \times 10^{-14}$) rejects the null hypothesis. The Nemenyi test (Fig. 4) ranks GB-DSANN first (average rank 1.48), with a significant lead over MDMSC (rank 3.13), demonstrating consistent performance in diverse distributions.

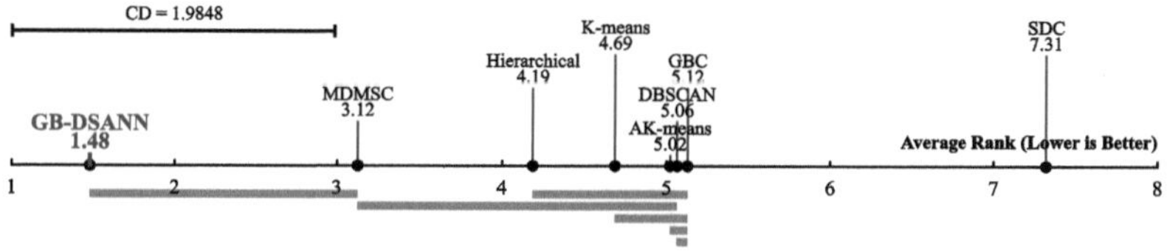

Fig. 4. Critical Difference (CD) diagram of the Nemenyi test ($\alpha = 0.05$)

4.5 Parameter Robustness and Sensitivity

Parameter stability experiments demonstrate consistent performance across key hyperparameters. As illustrated in Fig. 5, the algorithm maintains stability for neighbor count k provided $k > 10$. Regarding the atomic constraint, evaluations of $|C| \in \{2, 4, 8, 16\}$ indicate that $|C| = 4$ optimally balances statistical support with fine granularity; conversely, $|C| = 2$ induces expensive over-fragmentation, while $|C| > 10$ leads to coarse under-segmentation. Furthermore, the smoothing factor δ proves robust, yielding negligible ARI fluctuations ($< 0.1\%$) throughout the range 10^{-7} to 10^{-3}, validating its role as a numerical safeguard.

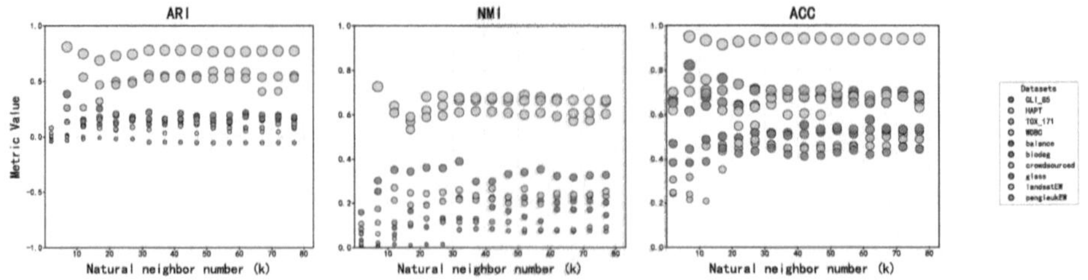

Fig. 5. Robustness experiment of natural neighbor number k

5 Conclusion

This paper proposed GB-DSANN to address structural complexity and parameter sensitivity in unsupervised learning. By synergizing local density-adaptive neighborhood estimation with variance-driven anisotropic granulation, we successfully overcome the isotropic limitations of traditional granular computing. Compared to leading micro-cluster methods such as MDMSC, GB-DSANN exhibits superior robustness on multi-density manifolds while maintaining a competitive computational complexity of $O(N \log N + m^3)$. Future work will focus on extending this approach to streaming data [7] and subspace learning [11] for high-dimensional spaces.

Acknowledgments. This work was supported by the Chengdu Science and Technology Project (Grant No. 2025-YF12-00017-RC).

References

1. Behrends, J., Béri, B.: The surface code beyond Pauli channels: logical noise coherence, information-theoretic measures, and errorfield-double phenomenology. PRX Quantum **6**(4), 040350 (2025)
2. Guan, W., Wang, P., Jiang, W., Zhang, Y.: HC3: a three-way clustering method based on hierarchical clustering. Cogn. Comput. **17**(1), 8 (2025)
3. Kadhim, M.N., Al-Shammary, D., Mahdi, A.M., Ibaida, A.: Feature selection based on mahalanobis distance for early Parkinson disease classification. Comput. Methods Programs Biomed. Update **7**, 100177 (2025)
4. Kazemi, U., Soleimani, S.: A new approach data processing: density-based spatial clustering of applications with noise (DBSCAN) clustering using game-theory. Soft. Comput. **29**(3), 1331–1346 (2025)
5. Miao, J., Zhang, X., Yang, T., Fan, C., Tian, Y., Shi, Y., Xu, M.: A comprehensive survey on subspace clustering: methods and applications. Artif. Intell. Rev. **58**(11), 346 (2025)
6. Mohammed, M.A.W., Jaber, A.G.: A new non-linear filter for image denoising. In: AIP Conference Proceedings, vol. 3264, p. 050061. AIP Publishing LLC (2025)
7. Punter, W.R., Papapetrou, O., Garofalakis, M.: OmniSketch: multi-dimensional update stream analytics with arbitrary predicates. VLDB J. **35**(1), 9 (2026)

8. Qin, Z., Li, L., Luo, Q., Yu, X., Zhang, Q.: Enhancing intrusion detection performance using GCN-LOF: a hybrid graph-based anomaly detection approach. Comput. Netw. 111606 (2025)
9. Raya-Tapia, A.Y., López-Flores, F.J., Ramírez-Márquez, C., Ponce-Ortega, J.M.: Machine learning and clustering for a sustainable future (2025)
10. Shu, H.: SDC-HSDD-NDSA: structure detecting cluster by hierarchical secdondary directed differential with normalized density and self-adaption. Inf. Sci. **702**, 121916 (2025)
11. Song, S., Li, R.: Manifold learning-based reconstruction and prediction of unsteady flow fields. Aerosp. Sci. Technol. 111631 (2026)
12. Warrens, M.J., Van Der Hoef, H.: Understanding the adjusted rand index and other partition comparison indices based on counting object pairs. J. Classif. **39**(3), 487–509 (2022)
13. Xia, S., Shi, B., Wang, Y., Xie, J., Wang, G., Gao, X.: GBCT: efficient and adaptive clustering via granular-ball computing for complex data. IEEE Trans. Neural Netw. Learn. Syst. **36**(7), 12159–12172 (2025). https://doi.org/10.1109/TNNLS.2024.3497174
14. Xu, Z., Long, Z., Meng, H.: Clustering by mining density distributions and splitting manifold structure. In: Proceedings of the AAAI Conference on Artificial Intelligence, vol. 39, no. 20, pp. 21842–21849 (2025). https://doi.org/10.1609/aaai.v39i20.35490
15. Yu, Y., Chen, X., Luo, J., Cheng, Y., Hao, Z.: Discriminative subspace clustering based on local hyperdisk for high-dimensional big data. Big Data Min. Anal. **9**(1), 57 (2026)
16. Zhang, Z., Chen, X., Wang, C., Wang, R., Song, W., Nie, F.: Structured multi-view k-means clustering. Pattern Recogn. **160**, 111113 (2025)
17. Zhao, Q., Thomas, A.H., Brin, A., Yu, X., Rosing, T.: Bridging the gap between hyperdimensional computing and kernel methods via the Nyström method. In: Proceedings of the AAAI Conference on Artificial Intelligence, vol. 39, pp. 22813–22821 (2025)
18. Zhao, S., Yang, R., Meng, F., Cai, L.: Optimizing cluster centroids with improved quadratic interpolation: an adaptive k-means algorithm. J. Comput. Appl. Math. **473**, 116921 (2026)
19. Zhao, Y., Bi, Z., Zhu, P., Yuan, A., Li, X.: Deep spectral clustering with projected adaptive feature selection. IEEE Trans. Geosci. Remote Sens. (2025)

Cross-View Interaction and Collaboration for Semi-supervised Time Series Classification

Maojing Shu, Xiaopeng Guo, and Jun Sun(✉)

Wangxuan Institute of Computer Technology, Peking University, Beijing, China
{shumaojing,jsun}@pku.edu.cn, xiaopeng.guo@stu.pku.edu.cn

Abstract. We study the problem of semi-supervised time series classification (SS-TSC), focusing on exploiting unlabeled time series data to enhance the performance of supervised learning with limited labeled time series examples. Recent studies demonstrate that leveraging spectral information alongside temporal features improves the generalization of SS-TSC models. Given temporal and spectral views, a common approach is to exchange confident pseudo-labels between classifiers. However, the performance gap across views may compromise the quality of pseudo labels, thus degrading SS-TSC performance. In this work, we devise a more effective cross-view pseudo labeling framework, implemented through **T**emporal-**S**pectral **IN**teraction and **C**ollaboration (**TSINC**). Specifically, we propose an efficient cross-view attention mechanism to integrate temporal and spectral representations into an auxiliary view for consensus pseudo-label prediction. Notably, the auxiliary view provides complementary predictions to the time-frequency ensemble under the tri-training strategy. To further mitigate the overfitting problem in SS-TSC, we introduce a diffusion-based augmentation scheme to balance the fidelity-diversity trade-off. Extensive experiments on 106 UCR datasets show that our framework consistently achieves state-of-the-art performance. Our code and appendix are available at https://github.com/MaojingShu/TSINC.

Keywords: Time Series · Semi-supervised Classification · Tri-training · Diffusion Augmentation

1 Introduction

Time series is a pervasive data format with widespread real-world applications across fields like financial risk control [18], traffic flow prediction [12], and medical sensor analysis [7], to name a few. This immense practical demand has driven increasing attention to time series analysis. A fundamental task within this domain is time series classification [8]. A natural way to establish an effective time series classification framework is to learn from a sufficient number of labeled time series examples. But in practice, the labeled examples may be

J. Niu et al. (Eds.): KSEM 2026, LNAI 16631, pp. 144–157, 2027.
https://doi.org/10.1007/978-981-92-2759-4_11

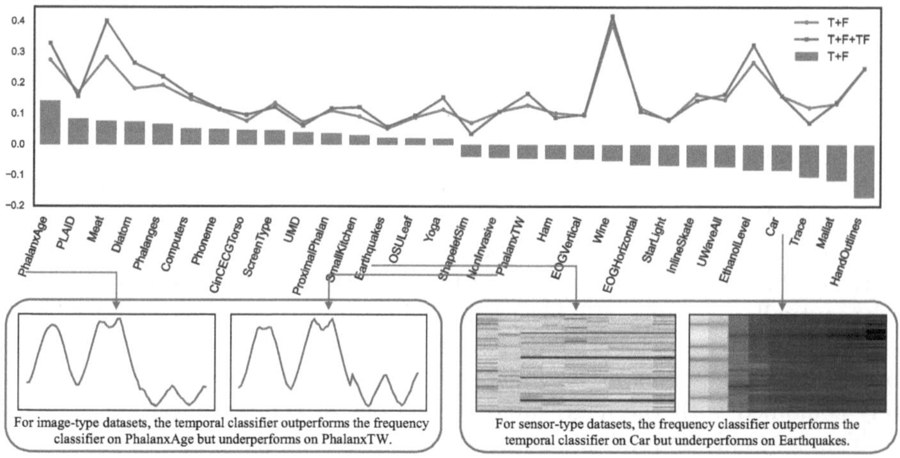

Fig. 1: Motivation of the proposed tri-training scheme. The bar chart illustrates the performance gap between individual temporal and frequency classifiers across 30 datasets under the co-training setting given 10% labeled samples. The line chart reveals that the proposed three-view collaboration achieves a higher error-correction proportion (i.e., the rate at which the ensemble rectifies single-view misclassifications), outperforming the two-view counterpart on 21 of 30 datasets.

scarce since labeling time series data usually requires domain-specific knowledge and is very time-consuming, especially in areas like biology and medicine [2]. By contrast, unlabeled time series data are far more abundant and easier to obtain. Semi-Supervised Learning (SSL) has therefore emerged as a key paradigm for leveraging unlabeled time series samples to achieve competitive performance with limited labeled data.

SSL is broadly categorized into consistency regularization and pseudo labeling. Specifically, for SS-TSC, MTL [9] and SemiTime [6] perform consistency regularization by treating different subsequences of the same time series as similar samples. TS-TFC [14] applies the co-training technique to transfer pseudo labels between temporal and frequency classifiers. Compared with vision and language data, time series data present unique temporal periodicity and spectral dependencies, motivating studies like MTFC [22] and TS-TFC [14] to jointly leverage temporal and frequency views for better performance.

Existing SS-TSC approaches leveraging temporal and spectral domains primarily exploit cross-view consistency [22] and complementarity [14]. However, inter-view performance discrepancies may yield biased pseudo-labels and hinder complementarity during co-training. The efficacy of co-training further hinges on the stringent assumption of sufficiently informative and redundant views [26]. As shown in Fig. 1, a pronounced time-frequency performance gap persists across 30 datasets under co-training, severely diminishing pseudo-label reliability. To address this limitation, inspired by tri-training paradigms [1,5], we propose a novel tri-training collaboration scheme. By integrating a hybrid view and employing three classifiers, our approach mitigates pseudo-label bias via majority consensus, achieving higher error-correction rates than two-view ensembles on 21 of 30 datasets in Fig. 1.

Based on these observations, our proposed framework, TSINC, aims to establish an efficient temporal-spectral interaction to derive the requisite auxiliary classifier for tri-training. Specifically, we develop a lightweight cross-view attention module based on efficient channel attention [20] to obtain the hybrid representation. Consequently, the temporal, spectral, and hybrid representations constitute three distinct views. During training, the temporal and spectral networks mutually exchange reliable pseudo-labels in a co-training manner, while their consensus pseudo-labels supervise the auxiliary network. At inference, the auxiliary network serves as an independent voter, whose output is collaboratively combined with the aggregated predictions of the temporal and spectral classifiers to yield the final decision.

Moreover, pseudo-label quality is inherently constrained by the scarcity of labeled data. Motivated by recent advances in generative augmentation [19,27], we incorporate a pretrained diffusion model to synthesize semantically consistent samples. By explicitly expanding the labeled dataset with high-fidelity variants, our approach facilitates the learning of smoother decision boundaries, thereby mitigating the risk of overfitting during the training process. Empirical results validate the effectiveness of diffusion-based augmentation, while sample visualizations illustrate the balance between fidelity and diversity.

Our contributions are as follows:

- We propose a novel cross-view pseudo labeling framework that treats temporal, spectral, and hybrid representations as three distinct views, leveraging a tri-training strategy to ensemble their predictions for robust SS-TSC.
- We introduce diffusion-based augmentation into SS-TSC to mitigate overfitting under limited labeled data. This versatile component empirically proves beneficial for both single-view and multi-view SS-TSC approaches.
- We conduct extensive experiments on 106 UCR datasets, demonstrating that TSINC consistently outperforms current state-of-the-art methods.

2 Related Work

Semi-supervised Time Series Classification. SS-TSC has attracted growing interest, spurring numerous label-efficient learning methods. These methods can be grouped into traditional methods and deep learning methods. Traditional methods typically include distance, graph, and shapelet-based techniques, while recent deep learning methods primarily capture temporal dynamics and spectral information. MTL [9] and SemiTime [6] devise diverse pretext tasks to capture temporal dependencies in unlabeled data, yielding effective representations for semi-supervised learning. Recently, several studies focus on incorporating multi-view information to enhance SS-TSC performance. MTFC [22] employs a multi-task learning framework to jointly learn temporal and frequency representations.

TS-TFC [14] presents temporal-frequency co-training, in which two classifiers learn from each other to alleviate single-view confirmation bias. In addition, DiffShape [15] utilizes shapelet matching and contrastive learning to improve the interpretability of SS-TSC models. While MTFC, TS-TFC, and our method share the spirit of multi-view learning, there are several distinct differences. In contrast to the shared-encoder design in MTFC, we assign a dedicated encoder to each view, which reduces the complexity of representation learning and leads to better performance. Different from TS-TFC, we further construct a hybrid auxiliary view and replace co-training with a tailored tri-training paradigm.

Data Augmentation for Time Series. Under label scarcity, effective data augmentation becomes critical for semi-supervised learning. Since the temporal semantics are prone to corruption, crafting label-preserving augmentations for time series is particularly challenging. Various works [13,25] tend to disturb the original sample directly, such as jitter and scaling. Several model-based methods, such as TimeVAE [4] and TimeGAN [23], employ generative models to synthesize more realistic samples. However, they may suffer from training instability or mode collapse. Furthermore, there exist some learning-based augmentation methods [16] for specific tasks. Inspired by advances in image augmentation, many label-efficient methods [19,27] leverage pretrained diffusion models to achieve superior performance. In this work, we apply diffusion-based augmentation to SS-TSC. The experimental results empirically validate its effectiveness in preserving temporal semantics while promoting augmentation diversity, which effectively mitigates the overfitting problem.

3 Methodology

In this section, we introduce our proposed method in detail. In what follows, we establish the problem formulation for SS-TSC. Then we explain the cross-view pseudo labeling framework. Subsequently, we present the cross-view collaboration mechanism applied during inference. Finally, we elaborate on the generative augmentation process utilizing pretrained diffusion models.

3.1 Problem Formulation

Let $\mathcal{D} = \mathcal{D}_l \cup \mathcal{D}_u$ denote a partially labeled time series dataset, where $\mathcal{D}_l = \{(X_i, y_i)\}_{i=1}^{M}$ is the labeled set and $\mathcal{D}_u = \{X_i\}_{i=1}^{N}$ refers to the unlabeled one. $X_i \in \mathbb{R}^{D \times L}$ represents a time series instance with dimension D and length L, and $y_i \in \{1, 2, 3, \dots, C\}$ is the corresponding label with C categories. M and N are the numbers of labeled and unlabeled time series, respectively, with $M \ll N$. Following these notations, the goal of SS-TSC could be formulated as learning a map Φ from time series instances to their corresponding categories, i.e., $\Phi : \mathbb{R}^{D \times L} \rightarrow \{1, 2, 3, \dots, C\}$ by using both the labeled set $\mathcal{D}_l$ and the unlabeled set $\mathcal{D}_u$.

3.2 Cross-View Pseudo Labeling

The key to tri-training lies in enabling three classifiers to guide each other with agreed-upon confident pseudo labels. We propose a novel cross-view pseudo labeling framework implemented through temporal-spectral interaction and collaboration. As shown in Fig. 2, our method, TSINC, consists of four components: **time-frequency encoding**, **temporal-spectral interaction**, **adaptive pseudo-label thresholding**, and **tri-view pseudo labeling**.

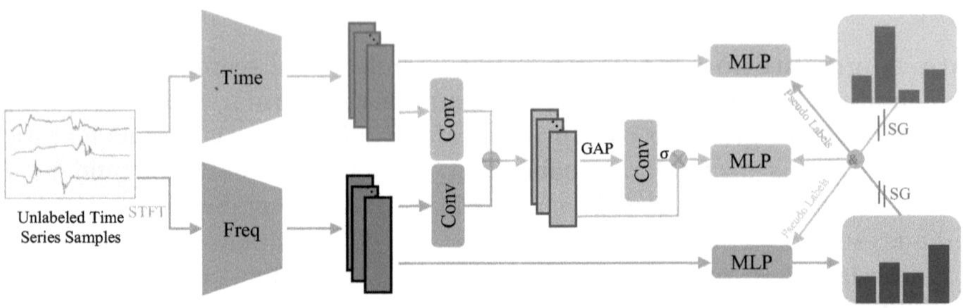

Fig. 2: Cross-view pseudo labeling framework across the time, frequency, and their hybrid representations.

Time-Frequency Encoding. Time series data inherently possess complementary temporal-domain and frequency-domain views. We employ the Short-Time Fourier Transform (STFT) to obtain the frequency-domain view of time series in this work. Formally, given a time-series sample $X = \{x_1, \ldots, x_n\}$, we obtain its spectrogram via $F = \mathrm{STFT}(X)$ by applying the Fourier transform over short overlapping windows. The STFT yields $F \in \mathbb{C}^{C_f \times L_t}$, where C_f and L_t denote the number of frequency channels and the temporal length, respectively. We then separate F into its real and imaginary components and concatenate them along the frequency dimension to form a real-valued input tensor of shape $(2C_f, L_t)$.

The time-frequency encoding component includes a temporal encoder $g(\cdot, \theta_t)$ and a spectral encoder $g(\cdot, \theta_f)$ with learnable parameters θ_t and θ_f. For an unlabeled mini-batch $\mathcal{X} = \{X_i\}_{i=1}^{B_u}$, we obtain the frequency view $F_i = \mathrm{STFT}(X_i)$ and $\mathcal{F} = \{F_i\}_{i=1}^{B_u}$. The two encoders then extract view-specific features:

$$Z_i^{time} = g(X_i, \theta_t), \quad Z_i^{freq} = g(F_i, \theta_f), \tag{1}$$

where Z_i^{time} and Z_i^{freq} denote time and frequency features, respectively.

Temporal-Spectral Interaction. While temporal and spectral features provide complementary perspectives on time series, effectively fusing these heterogeneous views to facilitate tri-training remains non-trivial. Standard fusion operations, such as concatenation or summation, often yield suboptimal results as they fail to capture cross-view interactions. To address this, we propose a lightweight cross-view attention mechanism based on Efficient Channel Attention (ECA) [20], which is a prominent lightweight module designed to enhance the representation of deep neural networks at a very low computational cost.

The primary challenge in adapting ECA for cross-view attention stems from the inherent heterogeneity across different domains. To overcome this, we first project the temporal Z_i^{time} and spectral Z_i^{freq} features into a shared representation space using convolutional kernels of size 1, as follows:

$$Z_i^{time'} = p(Z_i^{time}, \phi_t), \quad Z_i^{freq'} = p(Z_i^{freq}, \phi_f), \tag{2}$$

where $p(\cdot, \phi)$ denotes the projection function parameterized by learnable weights ϕ_t and ϕ_f. Because the projected feature maps may differ in dimension sizes, we align them via linear interpolation to ensure valid concatenation. Subsequently, we concatenate the aligned representations and perform channel mixing using another convolutional kernel $p(\cdot, \phi_m)$ of size 1, formulated as

$$\tilde{Z}_i^{fuse} = p(\text{Concat}(Z_i^{time'}, Z_i^{freq'}), \phi_m), \tag{3}$$

where $\tilde{Z}_i^{fuse}$ denotes a mixture of temporal and spectral views. Then we use global average pooling and score each channel with a convolutional kernel $p(\cdot, \phi_s)$ of size 3. The refined hybrid representation is then obtained via element-wise multiplication. Formally, the cross-view channel attention is formulated as

$$Z_i^{fuse} = p(\text{GAP}(\tilde{Z}_i^{fuse}), \phi_s) \cdot \tilde{Z}_i^{fuse}, \tag{4}$$

Finally, we obtain the integrated view Z_i^{fuse} derived from temporal and spectral views. Each view's feature vector is fed into a dedicated classification head h to produce the prediction probability $P_i = \text{softmax}(h(Z_i))$, where the view-specific notation is omitted for brevity.

Adaptive Pseudo-Label Thresholding. Recently, adaptive-threshold methods [21,24] have been proposed to replace fixed confidence cutoffs with dynamic thresholds that evolve continuously during training. To this end, we employ a view-specific adaptive threshold τ to filter out unconfident pseudo-labels. Following FreeMatch [21], the threshold for each view is updated at each training iteration using the Exponential Moving Average (EMA). The adaptively evolving threshold relies on the momentum hyperparameter λ_{ema}, which is consistently set to 0.99 across all datasets. Finally, for the time view, the pseudo-labeled set $\{\hat{X}^{time}, \hat{Y}^{time}\}$ for tri-training consists of unlabeled samples in $\mathcal{X} = \{X_i\}_{i=1}^{B_u}$ that satisfy $\max(P_i^{time}) > \tau^{time}$.

Tri-view Pseudo Labeling. After obtaining the pseudo-labels $\hat{Y}^{time}$ and $\hat{Y}^{freq}$ from the temporal and frequency classifiers, we perform tri-training on the temporal, frequency, and auxiliary classifiers to enhance the robustness of the unified model. To be specific, the auxiliary classifier retains pseudo-labels consistently predicted by both the time-domain and frequency-domain classifiers for pseudo-label supervision. The other two classifiers directly accept the pseudo labels provided by each other. Formally, the pseudo-label $\hat{y}_i^v$ assigned to supervise each view v is determined by:

$$\begin{cases} \hat{y}_i^{\text{time}} \leftarrow \arg\max(P_i^{\text{freq}}), & \text{if } \max(P_i^{\text{freq}}) > \tau^{\text{freq}} \\ \hat{y}_i^{\text{freq}} \leftarrow \arg\max(P_i^{\text{time}}), & \text{if } \max(P_i^{\text{time}}) > \tau^{\text{time}} \\ \hat{y}_i^{\text{fuse}} \leftarrow \arg\max(P_i^{\text{time}}), & \text{if } \arg\max(P_i^{\text{time}}) = \arg\max(P_i^{\text{freq}}) \end{cases}$$

With these assigned pseudo-labels acting as targets, the final training objective is optimized jointly across all views:

$$\mathcal{L}_{total} = \sum_{v \in \{\text{time,freq,fuse}\}} (\mathcal{L}_{sup}^v + \lambda_u \mathcal{L}_{unsup}^v), \tag{5}$$

where $\mathcal{L}_{sup}^v$ denotes the standard cross-entropy loss on the labeled data, $\mathcal{L}_{unsup}^v$ represents the cross-entropy loss computed against the filtered pseudo-labels on the unlabeled data, and λ_u is the unsupervised loss weight.

3.3 Cross-View Collaboration Mechanism

At inference, we devise a comprehensive collaboration mechanism that ensembles the predictions from all three classifiers to yield a more reliable final decision. Concretely, we first aggregate the outputs of the temporal and spectral encoders by averaging their prediction probabilities, generating an ensemble prediction $P_{agg} = \frac{1}{2}(P^{\text{time}} + P^{\text{freq}})$. We denote its corresponding categorical prediction as $y_{agg} = \arg\max(P_{agg})$ with confidence $c_{agg} = \max(P_{agg})$. Simultaneously, the hybrid auxiliary classifier produces its own prediction $y_{fuse} = \arg\max(P^{\text{fuse}})$ with confidence $c_{fuse} = \max(P^{\text{fuse}})$. To derive the final output category y_{final}, we compare the confidence scores of these two independent pathways and select the one with the higher certainty:

$$y_{final} = \begin{cases} y_{agg}, & \text{if } c_{agg} \geq c_{fuse} \\ y_{fuse}, & \text{otherwise.} \end{cases}$$

This confidence-based arbitration ensures that the model dynamically trusts the most definitive representation for each specific instance.

3.4 Diffusion Augmentation

As previously noted, the scarcity of labeled samples often leads to model overfitting. Compared to hand-crafted augmentation methods, generative data augmentation produces more realistic samples, effectively extending the size of the labeled dataset to mitigate the overfitting issue. Following Kollovieh et al. [10], we use the pretrained S4-based diffusion model to generate augmented samples.

As shown in Fig. 5, time series are prone to being corrupted by slight modifications that substantially alter the temporal semantics. Similar to DA-Fusion [19], the real time series x_0^{real} is corrupted with noise $\epsilon \sim \mathcal{N}(0, I)$ at time step sT, where T denotes the diffusion steps and the corruption strength s controls the noise injection level. With $\tilde{\alpha}_{sT}$ denoting the cumulative noise schedule, we have

$$x_{sT} = \sqrt{\tilde{\alpha}_{sT}}\, x_0^{\text{real}} + \sqrt{1 - \tilde{\alpha}_{sT}}\, \epsilon. \tag{6}$$

We then start the denoising process from x_{sT} and iterate the DDPM solver until the time step equals 0. The denoised samples are added to the training dataset. Following FreeMatch [21], we generate 10× instances for each original sample. The ratio of generated data in each mini-batch is 0.2 and the hyperparameter s is assigned values from $\{0.1, 0.2, 0.3\}$.

4 Experiments

4.1 Experimental Setup

Benchmark Datasets. UCR [3] is a commonly used archive for evaluating the performance of time series classification algorithms. There are 128 datasets in this archive, which vary drastically in terms of sample size, signal length, and class number. Similar to TS-TFC [14], we use 106 UCR datasets to comprehensively verify the effectiveness of our method.

Baseline Methods. We compare our proposed methods with six methods, including Pseudo-Labeling (PL) [11], MTL [9], SemiTime [6], MTFC [22], TS-TFC [14], and DiffShape [15]. Among them, PL is the general-purpose method, while MTL, SemiTime, MTFC, TS-TFC and DiffShape are currently state-of-the-art SS-TSC methods. These methods form a comprehensive benchmark for evaluating our approach.

Implementation Details. We perform 5-fold cross-validation on all datasets for each method. For each fold, the dataset is split into training, validation, and test sets at a ratio of 3:1:1. We report the averaged accuracy across 5 folds as the evaluation metric. A 4-layer 1D CNN is adopted as the time encoder, and the frequency encoder shares the same network architecture as the time encoder. For a fair comparison, we reproduce the experimental results of all baseline methods that adopt the same network architecture and training settings. Each method maintains the same set of hyperparameters across all datasets and labeled ratios. Following SemiTime [6], we use magnitude warping and time warping as data augmentations for all comparison methods except for the shapelet-based method, DiffShape. For our proposed method, we set the total number of epochs to 5000 and use the early stopping technique to monitor the classification accuracy on the validation set, stopping training when the accuracy no longer increases for 800 steps. We use SGD with an initial learning rate of 0.01 for optimization. B_l and B_u are set to 128 and 384, respectively. λ_u is set to 0.1.

4.2 Comparison with State-of-the-Art SS-TSC Methods

Table 1 presents the average quantitative results of various methods under the 10% and 20% labeled ratios.[1] Our method outperforms all baselines, achieving higher average accuracy and more wins under different labeled ratio settings. Both MTL and SemiTime perform well at the 10% labeled ratio but show a decline at the 20% labeled ratio, suggesting that jointly optimizing self-supervised and semi-supervised objectives is intrinsically challenging. Notably, MTFC exhibits suboptimal performance, even when compared to the vanilla supervised method. This outcome is likely due to the model's hyperparameter sensitivity, which is also reported in [14]. The results demonstrate the advantage of the tri-training strategy over the co-training approach leveraged in TS-TFC for pseudo labeling methods in SS-TSC. The notable performance achieved by DiffShape further confirms the benefit of diffusion models for SS-TSC. Furthermore, the Friedman and Nemenyi post hoc test [17] is used to analyze the significance of differences among various methods. As shown in Fig. 3, our method achieves statistically significant improvements under different label ratios. These quantitative results demonstrate that our method consistently outperforms current state-of-the-art approaches.

Table 1: The results compared with baselines across 106 UCR datasets in terms of accuracy, rank and win count. Averaged metrics across 5-fold cross-validation are reported. The best and second-best results are highlighted in **bold** and underline.

	10%				20%			
Method	Avg Acc	Avg Rank	Win	P-value	Avg Acc	Avg Rank	Win	P-value
Supervised	72.90	5.19	5	3.44E-11	77.95	4.97	6	1.28E-12
PL	72.45	4.80	8	3.93E-09	77.70	4.42	10	1.39E-09
MTL	73.47	4.32	10	2.31E-07	77.71	4.60	10	3.37E-09
SemiTime	73.26	4.55	5	8.78E-08	77.87	4.56	10	2.82E-09
MTFC	67.13	6.76	4	6.48E-16	70.87	6.97	4	1.35E-16
TS-TFC	73.79	3.49	30	7.52E-03	78.68	3.45	30	1.53E-03
DiffShape	73.55	4.08	23	8.81E-04	78.45	4.41	14	2.68E-05
TSINC(Ours)	**75.55**	**2.81**	**40**	N/A	**80.31**	**2.63**	**45**	N/A

[1] Detailed experimental results are provided in the appendix.

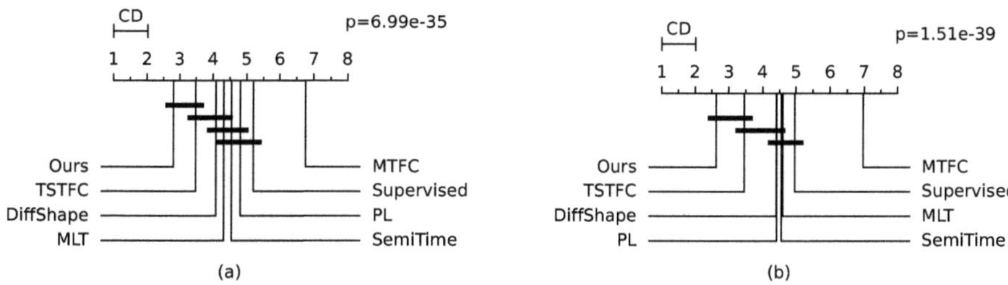

Fig. 3: Results of Friedman and Nemenyi post-hoc test in terms of label ratios. (a), (b) show the test results on accuracy under the label ratio of 10% and 20%.

4.3 Ablation Studies

In this section, we conduct thorough ablation studies to validate the effectiveness of the key components of our method, including the TSINC framework and the DiffAug strategy.

Effectiveness of TSINC. We conduct an ablation study on 106 datasets with a 10% labeled data ratio for our proposed framework. Table 2 quantifies the incremental gains brought by each module in our framework. Notably, vanilla co-training yields a substantial improvement over the single-view baseline, indicating the robustness of multi-view pseudo labeling in SS-TSC. Building on this, our proposed cross-view attention module, coupled with the tri-training strategy, delivers a marked performance increment, demonstrating the effectiveness of the introduced auxiliary view. By contrast, traditional augmentation contributes only modest gains, underscoring the limitations of hand-crafted time-series augmentation methods. However, replacing conventional augmentation with our diffusion-based augmentation produces a large improvement, indicating that generative augmentation is pivotal for achieving the strongest performance.

Table 2: Ablation on components in our proposed method. The notation TF refers to time-frequency hybrid view.

Components					Metrics		
Time	Freq	TF	WarpAug	DiffAug	Avg Acc ($\Delta \uparrow$)	Avg Rank ($\Delta \downarrow$)	Win ($\Delta \uparrow$)
✓					72.9 (N/A)	3.99 (N/A)	11 (N/A)
✓	✓				74.01 (+1.11)	3.43 (−0.56)	16 (+5)
✓	✓	✓			74.62 (+0.61)	2.69 (−0.74)	27 (+11)
✓	✓	✓	✓		74.85 (+0.23)	2.67 (−0.02)	36 (+9)
✓	✓	✓		✓	75.56 (+0.71)	2.23 (−0.44)	42 (+6)

Table 3: Results of time-series augmentation methods across 106 UCR datasets under the label ratio of 10%.

	MTL(single-view)				TSINC(multi-view)			
Method	Avg Acc	Avg Rank	Win	P-value	Avg Acc	Avg Rank	Win	P-value
none	71.52	3.11	13	4.35E-10	74.82	2.61	28	2.67E-03
Jitter+Scaling	73.21	2.58	27	5.65E-02	74.76	2.67	28	1.95E-03
WarpAug	73.47	2.19	41	8.64E-01	74.85	2.51	32	1.09E-02
DiffAug	73.80	2.12	41	N/A	75.56	2.20	41	N/A

Effectiveness of DiffAug. Table 3 presents an ablation comparing traditional augmentations, jitter+scaling, and warping with our approach. Our diffusion-based augmentation consistently improves both single-view and multi-view models, whereas jitter+scaling can even decrease performance in certain cases. These results highlight the robustness and potential applicability of diffusion-based augmentation for SS-TSC.

4.4 Resource Consumption

As shown in Fig. 4, we compare the resource consumption of our proposed methods in terms of runtime and GPU memory usage, with all experiments implemented in PyTorch and conducted on an RTX 3090 GPU. Larger datasets appear from left to right along the X-axis. The empirical analysis of computational complexity reveals that the extension from a two-view to our proposed three-view training paradigm incurs only a minor increase in resource consumption. These results demonstrate the efficiency of our cross-view attention module, as it provides a lightweight feature fusion mechanism between the temporal and frequency representations.

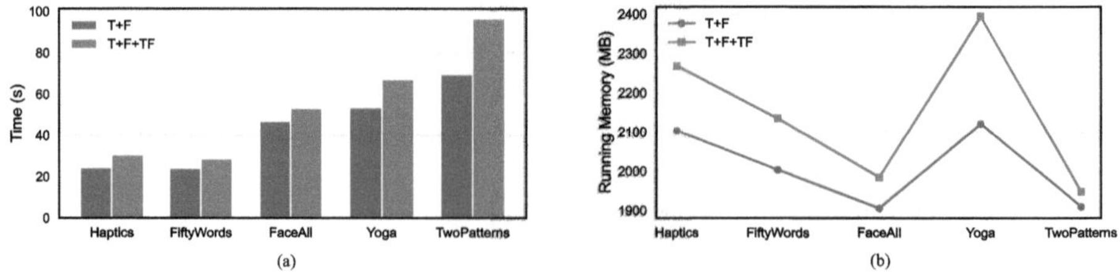

Fig. 4: Comparison of resource consumption between two-view and three-view.

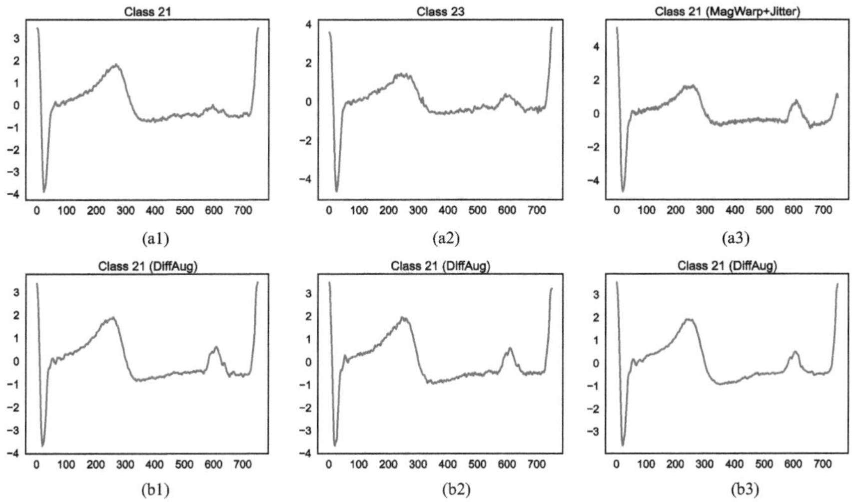

Fig. 5: Visualization for different augmentation methods on the dataset NonInvasiveFetalECGThorax1.

4.5 Visualization Analysis

The visualization of different augmentation methods is shown in Fig. 5. On the NonInvasiveFetalECGThorax1 dataset, the traditional augmentation techniques (Magnitude Warping + Jitter) exhibit a critical flaw: they can induce a severe temporal distribution shift. For instance, their augmented sample (a3) derived from an original Class 21 series (a1) risks being incorrectly warped into a series that resembles Class 23 (a2). In contrast, our proposed diffusion-based augmentation (b1–b3) preserves temporal dynamics while introducing controlled stochastic variation, thereby balancing fidelity and diversity. More t-SNE visualizations are provided in the appendix.

5 Conclusion

In this work, we propose TSINC, an efficient cross-view pseudo labeling framework for the SS-TSC task. We devise a lightweight cross-view attention mechanism to integrate temporal and spectral representations. The tri-training strategy, with temporal, frequency, and their integrated views, enhances model generalization in SS-TSC. We introduce diffusion-based augmentation to further alleviate the overfitting problem caused by scarce labeled data. Extensive experiments on 106 UCR datasets are conducted to evaluate our framework, and the results reveal that TSINC outperforms current state-of-the-art methods.

References

1. Chen, M., Wang, C.: Multi-head co-training: an uncertainty-aware and robust semi-supervised learning framework. Knowl.-Based Syst. **302**, 112325 (2024)
2. Ching, T., et al.: Opportunities and obstacles for deep learning in biology and medicine. J. R. Soc. Interface **15**(141), 20170387 (2018)
3. Dau, H.A., et al.: The UCR time series archive. IEEE/CAA J. Automatica Sinica **6**(6), 1293–1305 (2019)
4. Desai, A., Freeman, C., Wang, Z., Beaver, I.: TimeVAE: a variational auto-encoder for multivariate time series generation. arXiv preprint arXiv:2111.08095 (2021)
5. Dong-DongChen, W., WeiGao, Z.: Tri-net for semi-supervised deep learning. In: Proceedings of Twenty-Seventh International Joint Conference on Artificial Intelligence, pp. 2014–2020 (2018)
6. Fan, H., Zhang, F., Wang, R., Huang, X., Li, Z.: Semi-supervised time series classification by temporal relation prediction. In: ICASSP 2021-2021 IEEE International Conference on Acoustics, Speech and Signal Processing (ICASSP), pp. 3545–3549. IEEE (2021)
7. Huang, Y., Yen, G.G., Tseng, V.S.: Snippet policy network v2: knee-guided neuroevolution for multi-lead ECG early classification. IEEE Trans. Neural Networks Learn. Syst. (2022)
8. Ismail Fawaz, H., Forestier, G., Weber, J., Idoumghar, L., Muller, P.A.: Deep learning for time series classification: a review. Data Min. Knowl. Disc. **33**(4), 917–963 (2019)
9. Jawed, S., Grabocka, J., Schmidt-Thieme, L.: Self-supervised learning for semi-supervised time series classification. In: Lauw, H.W., Wong, R.C.-W., Ntoulas, A., Lim, E.-P., Ng, S.-K., Pan, S.J. (eds.) PAKDD 2020. LNCS (LNAI), vol. 12084, pp. 499–511. Springer, Cham (2020). https://doi.org/10.1007/978-3-030-47426-3_39
10. Kollovieh, M., Ansari, A.F., Bohlke-Schneider, M., Zschiegner, J., Wang, H., Wang, Y.B.: Predict, refine, synthesize: self-guiding diffusion models for probabilistic time series forecasting. In: Advances in Neural Information Processing Systems, vol. 36, pp. 28341–28364 (2023)
11. Lee, D.H., et al.: Pseudo-label: the simple and efficient semi-supervised learning method for deep neural networks. In: Workshop on Challenges in Representation Learning, ICML, vol. 3, p. 896 (2013)
12. Liao, B., et al.: Dest-ResNet: a deep spatiotemporal residual network for hotspot traffic speed prediction. In: Proceedings of the 26th ACM International Conference on Multimedia, pp. 1883–1891 (2018)
13. Liu, J., Chen, S.: TimesURL: self-supervised contrastive learning for universal time series representation learning. In: Proceedings of the AAAI Conference on Artificial Intelligence, vol. 38, pp. 13918–13926 (2024)
14. Liu, Z., Ma, Q., Ma, P., Wang, L.: Temporal-frequency co-training for time series semi-supervised learning. In: Proceedings of the AAAI Conference on Artificial Intelligence, vol. 37, pp. 8923–8931 (2023)
15. Liu, Z., Pei, W., Lan, D., Ma, Q.: Diffusion language-shapelets for semi-supervised time-series classification. In: Proceedings of the AAAI Conference on Artificial Intelligence, vol. 38, pp. 14079–14087 (2024)
16. Luo, D., et al.: Time series contrastive learning with information-aware augmentations. In: Proceedings of the AAAI Conference on Artificial Intelligence, vol. 37, pp. 4534–4542 (2023)

17. Pereira, D.G., Afonso, A., Medeiros, F.M.: Overview of Friedman's test and post-hoc analysis. Commun. Stat. Simul. Comput. **44**(10), 2636–2653 (2015)
18. Sawhney, R., Mathur, P., Mangal, A., Khanna, P., Shah, R.R., Zimmermann, R.: Multimodal multi-task financial risk forecasting. In: Proceedings of the 28th ACM International Conference on Multimedia, pp. 456–465 (2020)
19. Trabucco, B., Doherty, K., Gurinas, M., Salakhutdinov, R.: Effective data augmentation with diffusion models. arXiv preprint arXiv:2302.07944 (2023)
20. Wang, Q., Wu, B., Zhu, P., Li, P., Zuo, W., Hu, Q.: ECA-Net: efficient channel attention for deep convolutional neural networks. In: Proceedings of the IEEE/CVF Conference on Computer Vision and Pattern Recognition, pp. 11534–11542. (2020)
21. Wang, Y., et al.: Freematch: self-adaptive thresholding for semi-supervised learning. arXiv preprint arXiv:2205.07246 (2022)
22. Wei, C., Wang, Z., Yuan, J., Li, C., Chen, S.: Time-frequency based multi-task learning for semi-supervised time series classification. Inf. Sci. **619**, 762–780 (2023)
23. Yoon, J., Jarrett, D., Van der Schaar, M.: Time-series generative adversarial networks. In: Advances in Neural Information Processing Systems, vol. 32 (2019)
24. Zhang, B., et al.: Flexmatch: boosting semi-supervised learning with curriculum pseudo labeling. In: Advances in Neural Information Processing Systems, vol. 34, pp. 18408–18419 (2021)
25. Zhang, X., Zhao, Z., Tsiligkaridis, T., Zitnik, M.: Self-supervised contrastive pre-training for time series via time-frequency consistency. In: Advances in Neural Information Processing Systems, vol. 35, pp. 3988–4003 (2022)
26. Zhou, Z.H., Li, M.: Tri-training: exploiting unlabeled data using three classifiers. IEEE Trans. Knowl. Data Eng. **17**(11), 1529–1541 (2005)
27. Zhu, M., et al.: Unleashing the potential of the diffusion model in few-shot semantic segmentation. In: Advances in Neural Information Processing Systems, vol. 37, pp. 42672–42695 (2024)

Dynamic Curriculum Learning over Difficulty Heterogeneity for Text-to-SQL

Xiaoqi Zhang[1], Chongyang Tao[2(✉)], Shihao Xing[1], Zhengao Chen[1], and Shuai Ma[2(✉)]

[1] Henan University, Kaifeng, China
{zhangxq,shihaoxing,Chenza325}@henu.edu.cn
[2] Beihang University, Beijing, China
{chongyang,shuaima}@buaa.edu.cn

Abstract. Large language models (LLMs) have significantly advanced Text-to-SQL by enabling stronger semantic understanding and more accurate generation of executable queries. Recent progress has largely focused on synthesizing additional training data to further boost performance; however, the synthesis pipeline often incurs substantial computational and time costs, and can also suffer from distribution mismatch between synthetic and real-world queries. In this work, we explore a complementary direction: improving Text-to-SQL supervised fine-tuning under a fixed data and compute budget by better exploiting the inherent difficulty heterogeneity of existing data. We propose a Dynamic Curriculum Learning framework that constructs multiple difficulty-guided curriculum streams (data length, data loss, and SQL complexity) and dynamically selects training batches via a perplexity-based scheduler to maintain an adaptive easy-to-hard learning trajectory. To better align training stability with increasing difficulty, we further introduce a decreasing effective batch size schedule. Experiments on the BIRD benchmark show that our approach consistently improves execution accuracy over random shuffle tuning and representative static curriculum learning, achieving significant gains on more challenging queries.

Keywords: LLMs · Text-to-SQL · Curriculum Learning · SFT · Perplexity-Based Scheduler

1 Introduction

Text-to-SQL aims to translate natural language questions into executable SQL queries [3,5], enabling convenient data access. However, it remains challenging due to the need for fine-grained reasoning, precise schema alignment, and complex operations [15]. Recently, LLMs have propelled progress [8], primarily through prompting-based methods leveraging in-context learning [17,20,23,25] and supervised fine-tuning (SFT) [11,18,19]. Currently, SFT has become a

J. Niu et al. (Eds.): KSEM 2026, LNAI 16631, pp. 158–169, 2027.
https://doi.org/10.1007/978-981-92-2759-4_12

widely used mainstream method, which has motivated efforts to scale up data volume and improve data quality [9,10]. However, data synthesis often incurs substantial computational costs and distribution bias.

Instead of scaling data, our work investigates how to structure a fixed dataset to steer models along a rational trajectory—from simple to complex SQL. Text-to-SQL data exhibits significant difficulty heterogeneity, ranging from single-table queries to multi-table joins and nested subqueries. Traditional fine-tuning employs random shuffling [18,19], overlooking these differences. While Curriculum Learning (CL) organizes data easy-to-hard [1], heuristic curricula often cause catastrophic forgetting of foundational patterns [24]. To address this, inspired by CAMPUS [13], we propose a Dynamic Curriculum Learning (DCL) framework. DCL constructs a candidate curriculum pool via multi-perspective difficulty estimation and employs a perplexity-based dynamic scheduler for autonomous batch selection. Additionally, a Dynamic Effective Batchsize strategy gradually reduces batch size as difficulty increases, balancing stability and exploration. Experiments on BIRD [12] demonstrate that DCL significantly outperforms standard fine-tuning and static CL baselines.

The main contributions of this paper can be summarized as follows:

1. We propose a complexity-aware dynamic curriculum learning framework for Text-to-SQL to improve fine-tuned model performance on structured generation.
2. We design three complementary difficulty metrics for Text-to-SQL by combining database schema complexity, the model's comprehension level, and the intrinsic complexity of SQL queries.
3. Experiments on the BIRD dataset demonstrate that our method effectively exploits the utility of available data, significantly outperforming standard random baselines and static curriculum approaches.

2 Related Work

Recent advances in Large Language Models (LLMs) have significantly propelled this field forward, with mainstream approaches broadly categorized into prompting-based methods and supervised fine-tuning (SFT) based methods.

2.1 Prompting-Based Methods for Text-to-SQL

Prompting methods leverage carefully designed instructions and in-context examples to guide closed-source LLMs toward generating accurate SQL queries. DIN-SQL [17] decomposes complex questions through multi-stage prompting and self-correction, while DAIL-SQL [6] selects complexity-tailored few-shot examples. Recent works integrate specialized modules to enhance schema linking and reasoning: MAC-SQL [23] employs multi-agent collaboration; CHESS [22] utilizes agent-based schema pruning; E-SQL [2] enriches questions and predicates; RSL-SQL [4] introduces bidirectional pruning; and MCS-SQL [23] leverages multiple prompts to enhance robustness. Although achieving strong performance, these methods heavily depend on proprietary LLMs and incur significant inference costs, limiting their practicality in resource-constrained scenarios.

2.2 Supervised Fine-Tuning Based Methods for Text-to-SQL

To overcome prompting limitations, SFT-based methods distill task-specific knowledge into open-source LLMs, offering lower deployment costs and better data privacy. Beyond basic fine-tuning, advanced methods introduce specialized strategies: DTS-SQL [18] and DB-Explore [16] treat schema linking as a separate stage; ROUTE [19] unifies linking and generation within a multi-task framework; ExSL [7] proposes extractive schema linking; and JOLT-SQL [21] unifies linking and generation losses with noise-aware training. Other approaches incorporate advanced paradigms: CodeS [11] employs secondary pre-training on SQL corpora, and SENSE [26] applies reinforcement learning (DPO) to align model preferences. However, RL-based methods introduce training instability and overhead due to complex reward design. While effective, they represent a distinct paradigm separate from the data-centric curriculum improvements pursued in this work.

3 Method

3.1 Overall Framework

To enhance the performance of the model fine-tuning on Text-to-SQL tasks, we propose a curriculum learning–enhanced training framework specifically designed for Text-to-SQL tasks. The framework aims to guide the model to focus on samples with simpler structures and clearer semantics in the early training stages through an easy-to-hard data scheduling strategy, and then gradually transition to learning from more complex and longer-context queries. This progressive learning process improves the model's generalization capability and execution accuracy. The overall framework is illustrated in Fig. 1. Specifically, the instruction dataset is first sorted according to multiple difficulty metrics, and during training, a perplexity-based curriculum scheduler dynamically organizes the training data. The details of metrics and dynamic curriculum scheduler will be provided in Sects. 3.2 and 3.3.

3.2 Multi-perspective Difficulty Metric

To comprehensively assess the complexity of Text-to-SQL samples, we devise three complementary difficulty metrics.

Data Length d_1. Data length serves as an intuitive difficulty metric, reflecting both the amount of information contained in a sample and its processing complexity. Since the model input includes all table and column information from the database, data length also captures the difficulty of schema linking. Shorter

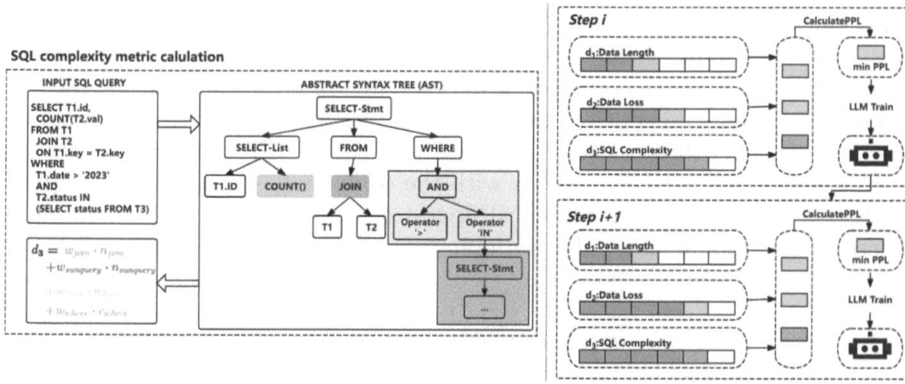

Fig. 1. Framework of our Dynamic Curriculum Learning for Text-to-SQL. The left panel summarizes the AST-based SQL complexity metric, while the right panel illustrates the training procedure.

samples typically correspond to simple query patterns and basic SQL structures, making them suitable for the early stages of training. In contrast, longer samples often involve complex multi-table joins and nested queries, which are more appropriate once the model has acquired fundamental reasoning capabilities. Therefore, we define the total token length of the instruction and output text as the data length metric d_1, which is defined as:

$$d_1 = \text{len}_{\text{token}}(\text{input}) + \text{len}_{\text{token}}(\text{output}) \tag{1}$$

Data Loss d_2. The perceived difficulty of data for a LLM is influenced by both the intrinsic complexity of the data and the model's own comprehension capacity. To this end, we introduce data loss, a simple yet effective metric for gauging model capability. For each data instance in the dataset, we compute the cross-entropy loss over the output segment using the base model (θ_{base}), formally defined as:

$$d_2 = -\sum_{t=1}^{N} \log p_{\theta_{\text{base}}}(y_t|x, y_{<t}) \tag{2}$$

where y is the output sequence corresponding to the input x, N denotes the length of y, and θ_{LLM} represents the parameters of the LLM. A high data loss value signifies greater model perplexity on a given sample, suggesting that its learning should be deferred in the

SQL Complexity d_3. To better capture the intrinsic structural difficulty of Text-to-SQL queries, we define a SQL complexity metric based on the abstract syntax tree (AST) of the target SQL. Given a SQL query, we first parse it into an AST where each node corresponds to a syntactic construct. Then, we calculate the complexity by aggregating interpretable statistical information on the AST.

Specifically, we consider: (i) the number of JOIN nodes in the FROM-subtree, which indicates multi-table composition; (ii) the maximum nesting depth of SELECT-subtrees, which corresponds to correlated or nested subqueries; (iii) the number of function-call nodes (e.g., COUNT, SUM, AVG), capturing aggregation reasoning; and (iv) the structural complexity of the WHERE-subtree, measured by the number of WHERE together with the complexity of the boolean expression tree (e.g., the number of logical operators and its nesting depth), which reflects compositional constraint reasoning. Formally, we score SQL complexity as:

$$d_3 = w_{\text{join}} \cdot n_{\text{join}} + w_{\text{subquery}} \cdot n_{\text{subquery}} + w_{\text{func}} \cdot n_{\text{func}} + w_{\text{where}} \cdot c_{\text{where}}, \tag{3}$$

where n_{join}, n_{subquery}, and n_{func} are counted from the AST, and c_{where} summarizes the complexity of the WHERE subtree. The coefficients w control the relative contribution of each structural factor. In our implementation, we set the feature weights to $w_{\text{join}} = 1.5$, $w_{\text{subquery}} = 2.0$, $w_{\text{func}} = 0.7$, and $w_{\text{where}} = 1.0$ (heuristically), reflecting the relatively higher difficulty introduced by subqueries and joins.

3.3 Dynamic Curriculum Scheduler

Based on the three difficulty metrics above, we formulate three distinct curricula, each providing a unique learning perspective and difficulty progression. During training, a dynamic scheduler leverages these curricula to determine the optimal data batch for each training step. Unlike traditional static curricula that follow a fixed, sequential order, our approach enables the model to autonomously pose the following question at each step: "Given my current knowledge, which upcoming batch from the data length, data loss, and SQL complexity curricula presents the least perplexing challenge?". The model answers this by evaluating the perplexity of the data, defined as:

$$\text{PPL}(B_i(t)) = \frac{1}{|B_i(t)|} \sum_{x \in B_i(t)} \exp\left(\frac{1}{N_x} \sum_{j=1}^{N_x} -\log p(w_j | w_{<j})\right) \tag{4}$$

where $\text{PPL}(B_i(t))$ calculates the perplexity of batch $B_i(t)$, which denotes the data samples selected from the i-th curriculum channel at training step t. $|B_i(t)|$ is the batch size. For each sample x, N_x is the number of tokens, w_j is the j-th token, $w_{<j}$ denotes the preceding context, and $p(w_j|w_{<j})$ is the model's predicted conditional probability of w_j given its history. The PPL measures the model's confusion with real data samples. A high PPL indicates that the LLM currently lacks the foundational ability to comprehend the sample, warranting its learning to be deferred. Consequently, the scheduler dynamically selects the training batch with the lowest PPL from the candidates, thereby maintaining a coherent and ascending difficulty progression throughout the training process.

At each scheduling step, we sample candidate chunks from the three curricula, compute their perplexities under the current model, and choose the chunk with the lowest PPL for the next update. The overall procedure is summarized in Algorithm 1. We additionally apply a three-stage effective batch-size schedule to match the easy-to-hard curriculum: a large batch stabilizes early learning on easy samples, while smaller batches later increase stochasticity and improve robustness on hard samples. Specifically, $B_{\text{eff}} \in \{128, 64, 32\}$ for the first, middle, and last third of training steps, and we set the evaluation chunk size to the current B_{eff}.

Algorithm 1. Dynamic Curriculum Learning Framework for Text-to-SQL

Require: Base model θ; Three sorted curriculum streams D_{len}, D_{loss}, D_{sql}; Effective batch size schedule Schedule(u); PPL evaluation batch size C.
Ensure: Fine-tuned model θ_T.

Initialize curriculum pointers: $p_{\text{len}} \leftarrow 0$, $p_{\text{loss}} \leftarrow 0$, $p_{\text{sql}} \leftarrow 0$.
for $u = 0$ to $T_{\max} - 1$ **do**
  // **Dynamic Scheduler Phase**
  if $p_k \geq |D_k|$ for all $k \in \{\text{len, loss, sql}\}$ **then**
  end if
  $B_{\text{eff}} \leftarrow \text{Schedule}(u)$
  Candidates $\leftarrow \{\}$
  for $k \in \{\text{len, loss, sql}\}$ **do**
    if $p_k < |D_k|$ **then**
      $C_k \leftarrow D_k[p_k : p_k + B_{\text{eff}}]$
      $\text{PPL}_k \leftarrow \text{CalculatePPL}(\theta, C_k)$
      $\text{Candidates}[k] \leftarrow \text{PPL}_k$
    end if
  end for
  $k^* \leftarrow \min(\text{Candidates}[k])$
  // **Training Phase**
  $D_t \leftarrow D_{k^*}[p_{k^*} : p_{k^*} + B_{\text{eff}}]$
  Train the LLM with the D_t
  $p_{k^*} \leftarrow p_{k^*} + B_{\text{eff}}$
end for

4 Experiments

4.1 Experiment Setting

Datasets. To evaluate the effectiveness of our proposed curriculum learning method, we conducted comprehensive experiments on the widely-used BIRD benchmark dataset. BIRD represents a pioneering, cross-domain dataset that examines the impact of extensive database contents on text-to-SQL parsing. BIRD contains over 12,751 unique question-SQL pairs [12], 95 big databases with a total size of 33.4 GB. Its Training/Dev/Test sets include 9,428/1,534/1,789 pairs, respectively. Given that BIRD's Test set is not public, we primarily report results on its Dev set. We employ the publicly released dataset from the Liu et al.

[14] study. This resource is built upon the BIRD training set, where each query is augmented with a reasoning trace generated by the GPT-4o-mini model. In our experiments, we directly utilize these augmented data samples.

Evaluation Metrics. We employ execution accuracy (EX) as our primary evaluation metric. EX measures whether the SQL query predicted by the model and the ground-truth query yield identical results when executed on the underlying database. This directly reflects the model's practical ability to generate correct SQL.

Baselines. We compare our method against three baseline approaches for comprehensive evaluation. The first is Supervised Fine-Tuning with Random Shuffling, which follows the standard practice of presenting training data in a completely random order. The second is Supervised Fine-Tuning with Fixed Ordering, where all training samples are pre-sorted by SQL complexity and then fed to the model in this static sequence throughout training. The third is Incremental Curriculum Learning, which implements a conventional four-stage training regimen: the dataset is first divided into Simple, Medium, and Difficult subsets based on SQL complexity, and the model is then trained sequentially on these subsets followed by a final fine-tuning stage using the entire dataset.

Implementation Details. We selected the widely-used open-source model, Qwen2.5-Coder-7B-Instruct, for our experiments. The model was fully fine-tuned on 4×A100 GPUs with a batch size of 32, a learning rate of 1e-5, and was trained for 3 epochs. During the inference stage, we employed a greedy decoding strategy by setting the temperature to 0.

Table 1. Results of the Model Performance on the BIRD Dev.

Model	Method	Dev EX(%)
Qwen2.5-Coder-7B-Instruct	–	53.00
	Random Shuffle Tuning	57.56
	Sequential Curriculum Learning	57.36
	Incremental Curriculum Learning	58.60
	Dynamic Curriculum Learning	**59.19**

4.2 Main Results

Table 1 presents the comparative experimental results based on the Qwen2.5-Coder-7B-Instruct model. We benchmark our proposed method against three baseline settings: standard Random Shuffle Tuning, Sequential Curriculum

Learning (based on static difficulty sorting), and phased Incremental Curriculum Learning.

Experimental results demonstrate that all fine-tuning strategies yield significant performance improvements over the original model. Specifically, the off-the-shelf Qwen2.5-Coder-7B-Instruct achieves an execution accuracy of 53.00% on this dataset, whereas standard Random Shuffle Tuning boosts performance to 57.56%. However, Sequential Curriculum Learning, which strictly follows an easy-to-hard training order, achieves an accuracy of only 57.36%, slightly underperforming the random baseline (−0.20%). This phenomenon suggests that a rigid curriculum strategy may induce catastrophic forgetting of early, simple patterns, thereby compromising overall generalization capabilities. In contrast, Incremental Curriculum Learning—which partitions the training process into four stages (Easy, Medium, Hard, and Mixed)—effectively mitigates this forgetting issue. By introducing a 'review' mechanism encompassing all data in the final stage, it outperforms the baselines with an accuracy of 58.60%.

Among all evaluated approaches, our proposed Dynamic Curriculum Learning achieves the highest performance, reaching an execution accuracy of 59.19%. This represents a substantial improvement of 1.63% over standard Random Shuffle Tuning and a further gain of 0.59% over the static phased Incremental Curriculum. These results strongly validate the superiority of our dynamic scheduling strategy.

4.3 Ablation Experiments

Ablation on Difficulty Metrics. Table 2 presents the results using individual difficulty metrics. To ensure a fair comparison and isolate the efficacy of each metric as a difficulty criterion, we uniformly employ the Incremental Curriculum Learning strategy across all single-metric experiments.

The results indicate that curriculum learning approaches based on any single difficulty metric consistently outperform the Random Shuffle Tuning baseline. Among the three individual metrics, SQL Complexity exhibits the most superior performance, achieving an execution accuracy of 58.60%. This result notably surpasses both Data Length (57.95%) and Data Loss (57.82%), thereby demonstrating the superiority of our proposed SQL Complexity metric.

Table 2. Ablation experiments on difficulty metrics.

Metrics	Dev EX(%)
Random Shuffle Tuning	57.56
Data Length	57.95
Data Loss	57.82
SQL Complexity	58.60
Dynamic Curriculum Learning	**59.19**

Ablation on Different Schedulers. In Table 3, we evaluate different dynamic curriculum scheduling strategies, including Random selection, Sequential (round-robin), Maximum Perplexity, and our proposed Minimum Perplexity. Specifically, the Random strategy uniformly samples from the three sub-curricula at each step, while the Sequential strategy cycles through them in a fixed order. Notably, the Sequential strategy performs poorly, achieving an execution accuracy of only 54.56%, which is even lower than the Random baseline (55.22%). We attribute this to the fact that strict sequential rotation disrupts the smooth, progressive nature of curriculum learning, causing drastic fluctuations in training difficulty. Interestingly, the PPL max strategy also achieves a relatively high score (58.90%). This is because its hard-to-easy training order makes the model particularly adept at simple instances; given that simpler samples dominate the test set, this proficiency yields higher test accuracy. Nevertheless, the results demonstrate that selecting the curriculum with the minimum perplexity constitutes the optimal strategy, aligning well with both core curriculum learning principles and human intuition.

Table 3. Comparison experiments on different curriculum scheduling strategies.

Scheduler	Dev EX(%)
Random	55.22
Sequential	54.56
PPL max	58.90
PPL min	**59.19**

Ablation on Removing Individual Difficulty Metrics. We further conduct an ablation study on removing individual curriculum streams under the dynamic curriculum framework. To ensure a fair comparison without changing the training budget or the number of candidate streams, we do not reduce the total number of curricula; instead, we replace the removed difficulty-ordered stream with a randomly shuffled stream while keeping the other two streams unchanged. As shown in Table 4, the full dynamic curriculum achieves the best Dev EX of 59.19%. Replacing the Data Length, Data Loss, and SQL Complexity streams with random ordering consistently degrades performance to 58.50, 58.41, and 58.89, respectively, indicating that the three difficulty signals are complementary. The smaller drop when replacing SQL Complexity (−0.30) suggests that the scheduler can partially compensate using the remaining ordered streams, but the best performance is still obtained when all three difficulty-guided curricula are jointly used.

Table 4. Ablation on removing individual difficulty metrics under the dynamic curriculum framework.

Setting	Dev EX(%)
Full Dynamic Curriculum	59.19
w/o Data Length curriculum	58.50
w/o Data Loss curriculum	58.41
w/o SQL Complexity curriculum	58.89

4.4 Performance Across Difficulty Levels

To examine how different training strategies behave under varying query difficulty, we report execution accuracy (EX) on the two difficulty levels (Simple and Moderate) provided by the benchmark. Following the benchmark setting, we merge the original Moderate and Challenging subsets due to the limited number of Challenging examples. We evaluate the original model, Random Shuffle Tuning, and our Dynamic Curriculum Learning under the same training budget.

Figure 2 shows a clear difficulty-dependent trend. On the Simple subset, the original model already achieves relatively strong performance (62.16%), leaving limited headroom for improvement. Random Shuffle Tuning and Dynamic Curriculum Learning yield modest gains to 64.32% and 65.08%, respectively (+2.16 and +2.92). In contrast, on the merged Moderate subset, the benefit of difficulty-aware training becomes much more pronounced: Dynamic Curriculum Learning reaches 50.08%, outperforming Random Shuffle Tuning (47.29%) by +2.79 and the original model (39.08%) by +11.00.

We attribute the larger gains on the harder subset to two components of our framework. First, our perplexity-based scheduler explicitly defers samples that the model currently finds confusing, selecting the candidate batch with the lowest PPL to maintain a coherent learning progression. Second, the decreasing effective

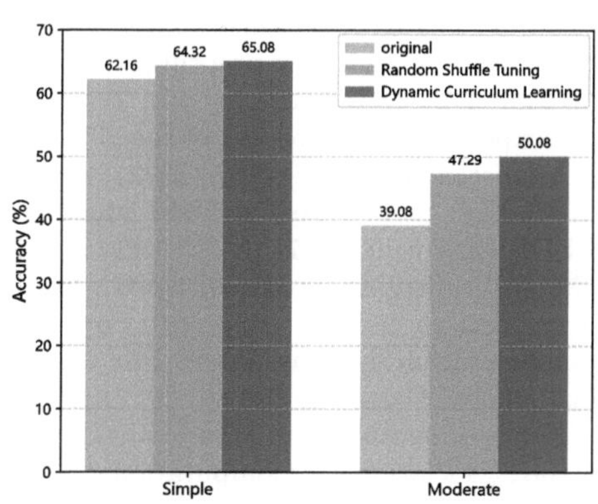

Fig. 2. Execution accuracy on different difficulty levels on BIRD dev set.

batch size schedule amplifies gradient stochasticity as training moves toward harder samples, which acts as an implicit regularizer and improves robustness on challenging distributions.

5 Conclusion

In this paper, we proposed a Dynamic Curriculum Learning framework for Text-to-SQL fine-tuning that combines multi-view difficulty signals (data length, data loss, and SQL complexity) with a perplexity-based scheduler and a decreasing effective batch size schedule. This design maintains an adaptive easy-to-hard training trajectory under a fixed training budget, improving learning efficiency beyond random shuffling and static curricula. Experiments on BIRD demonstrate consistent gains in execution accuracy, and achieving significant improvements on more challenging examples.

Acknowledgements. We thank the anonymous reviewers for their constructive comments and suggestions. This work was supported by the National Natural Science Foundation of China (Grant No. 62572034, U22B2021 and U24B20143), State Key Laboratory of Complex & Critical Software Environment (SKLCCSE), and CIE–Tianyi Cloud Research Program.

References

1. Bengio, Y., Louradour, J., Collobert, R., Weston, J.: Curriculum learning. In: Proceedings of the 26th Annual International Conference on Machine Learning, pp. 41–48 (2009)
2. Caferoğlu, H.A., Ulusoy, Ö.: E-SQL: direct schema linking via question enrichment in Text-to-SQL. arXiv preprint arXiv:2409.16751 (2024)
3. Cao, R., et al.: Spider2-V: how far are multimodal agents from automating data science and engineering workflows? In: Advances in Neural Information Processing Systems, vol. 37, pp. 107703–107744 (2024)
4. Cao, Z., Zheng, Y., Fan, Z., Zhang, X., Chen, W., Bai, X.: RSL-SQL: robust schema linking in Text-to-SQL generation. arXiv preprint arXiv:2411.00073 (2024)
5. Deng, N., Chen, Y., Zhang, Y.: Recent advances in Text-to-SQL: a survey of what we have and what we expect. In: Proceedings of the 29th International Conference on Computational Linguistics, pp. 2166–2187 (2022)
6. Gao, D., et al.: Text-to-SQL empowered by large language models: a benchmark evaluation. Proc. VLDB Endowment **17**(5), 1132–1145 (2024)
7. Glass, M., Eyceoz, M., Subramanian, D., Rossiello, G., Vu, L., Gliozzo, A.: Extractive schema linking for Text-to-SQL. arXiv preprint arXiv:2501.17174 (2025)
8. Hong, Z., et al.: Next-generation database interfaces: a survey of LLM-based Text-to-SQL. IEEE Trans. Knowl. Data Eng. (2025)
9. Hu, Y., et al.: Importance of synthesizing high-quality data for Text-to-SQL parsing. In: Findings of the Association for Computational Linguistics: ACL 2023, pp. 1327–1343 (2023)
10. Li, H., et al.: OmniSQL: synthesizing high-quality Text-to-SQL data at scale. arXiv preprint arXiv:2503.02240 (2025)

11. Li, H., et al.: Codes: towards building open-source language models for Text-to-SQL. Proc. ACM Manage. Data **2**(3), 1–28 (2024)
12. Li, J., et al.: Can LLM already serve as a database interface? A big bench for large-scale database grounded Text-to-SQLs. In: Advances in Neural Information Processing Systems, vol. 36, pp. 42330–42357 (2023)
13. Li, Y., et al.: Teaching according to talents! Instruction tuning LLMs with competence-aware curriculum learning. In: Findings of the Association for Computational Linguistics: EMNLP 2025, pp. 11724–11741 (2025)
14. Liu, H., et al.: Uncovering the impact of chain-of-thought reasoning for direct preference optimization: lessons from Text-to-SQL. arXiv preprint arXiv:2502.11656 (2025)
15. Liu, X., et al.: A survey of NL2SQL with large language models: where are we, and where are we going? arXiv preprint arXiv:2408.05109 (2024)
16. Ma, H., et al.: Db-explore: automated database exploration and instruction synthesis for Text-to-SQL. arXiv preprint arXiv:2503.04959 (2025)
17. Pourreza, M., Rafiei, D.: Din-SQL: decomposed in-context learning of Text-to-SQL with self-correction. In: Advances in Neural Information Processing Systems, vol. 36, pp. 36339–36348 (2023)
18. Pourreza, M., Rafiei, D.: DTS-SQL: decomposed text-to-SQL with small large language models. In: Findings of the Association for Computational Linguistics: EMNLP 2024, pp. 8212–8220 (2024)
19. Qin, Y., et al.: Route: robust multitask tuning and collaboration for Text-to-SQL. arXiv preprint arXiv:2412.10138 (2024)
20. Rajkumar, N., Li, R., Bahdanau, D.: Evaluating the Text-to-SQL capabilities of large language models. arXiv preprint arXiv:2204.00498 (2022)
21. Song, J., et al.: Jolt-SQL: joint loss tuning of Text-to-SQL with confusion-aware noisy schema sampling. arXiv preprint arXiv:2505.14305 (2025)
22. Talaei, S., Pourreza, M., Chang, Y.C., Mirhoseini, A., Saberi, A.: Chess: contextual harnessing for efficient SQL synthesis. arXiv preprint arXiv:2405.16755 (2024)
23. Wang, B., et al.: Mac-SQL: a multi-agent collaborative framework for Text-to-SQL. In: Proceedings of the 31st International Conference on Computational Linguistics, pp. 540–557 (2025)
24. Wang, X., Chen, Y., Zhu, W.: A survey on curriculum learning. IEEE Trans. Pattern Anal. Mach. Intell. **44**(9), 4555–4576 (2021)
25. Wei, J., et al.: Chain-of-thought prompting elicits reasoning in large language models. In: Advances in Neural Information Processing Systems, vol. 35, pp. 24824–24837 (2022)
26. Yang, J., Hui, B., Yang, M., Yang, J., Lin, J., Zhou, C.: Synthesizing Text-to-SQL data from weak and strong LLMs. In: Proceedings of the 62nd Annual Meeting of the Association for Computational Linguistics (Volume 1: Long Papers), pp. 7864–7875 (2024)

LogCraft: Pattern-Guided Iterative Clustering for Efficient Unsupervised LLM-Driven Log Parsing

Yantong Hao[1] and Yudan Tian[2](✉)

[1] Shanghai Key Laboratory of Trustworthy Computing, East China Normal University, Shanghai, China
[2] East China Normal University, Shanghai, China
ydtian@admin.ecnu.edu.cn

Abstract. Modern software systems generate vast amounts of logs, yet existing parsing methods struggle to balance accuracy and efficiency. Traditional approaches are efficient but inaccurate, while LLM-based methods suffer from high cost and low efficiency. To address this, we propose LogCraft, an unsupervised log parsing framework that integrates Pattern-Guided Iterative Clustering (PGIC) and Variable-Aware Sampling (VA) to construct consistent log clusters and guide template generation with minimal LLM usage. A multi-template generation and caching mechanism further reduces redundant calls. Experiments on 16 LogHub-2k datasets show that LogCraft achieves state-of-the-art performance (84.7% PA), outperforming existing methods. On LogHub-2.0, it reduces overhead by over 50% and token consumption by 13.7%. These results demonstrate that LogCraft effectively balances accuracy and efficiency for practical log parsing.

Keywords: Log Parsing · Large Language Models · Unsupervised Learning · Knowledge Extraction

1 Introduction

Modern software systems generate massive volumes of logs that serve as critical data sources for anomaly detection, fault diagnosis, and system reliability assurance [4]. As logs are typically semi-structured text, manual parsing is costly, making automated log parsing a fundamental step in log analysis [19]. Traditional log parsing methods mainly rely on heuristic rules, clustering techniques, or high-frequency pattern mining [5]. Although these approaches are computationally efficient, their dependence on manually designed heuristics and static assumptions limits robustness under evolving log formats and often results in insufficient parsing accuracy for complex systems. Common log parsing is shown in Fig. 1.

With the rapid advancement of large language models (LLMs), supervised log parsing methods based on LLMs-such as DivLog [16] and LILAC [7] have

J. Niu et al. (Eds.): KSEM 2026, LNAI 16631, pp. 170–183, 2027.
https://doi.org/10.1007/978-981-92-2759-4_13

significantly improved parsing accuracy by leveraging annotated examples or training data [10]. However, their reliance on human annotation limits scalability and practical applicability, resulting in suboptimal performance when handling diverse datasets. To reduce annotation costs and improve generalization, researchers have proposed a series of unsupervised LLM-based log parsing methods, such as SelfLog [13] and LogBatcher [15]. Although these methods formally eliminate annotation requirements [6], they still face challenges in practice: high invocation costs, inefficient processing, and excessive token consumption.

Overall, existing log parsing methods typically excel in either efficiency or accuracy, struggling to balance both under unsupervised and scalable conditions. This paper argues that, in addition to the slow inference speed of LLMs, the lack of a reasonable organization and sampling strategy for logs before inputting them into the model is also a key bottleneck in unsupervised LLM log parsing. Based on this insight, we propose LogCraft-a high-precision, high-efficiency unsupervised log parsing framework. The framework constructs structurally consistent log clusters through Pattern-Guided Iterative Clustering (PGIC) and employs Variable-Aware Sampling (VA) to cover key variables with minimal samples. By integrating multi-template generation and bucket caching strategies, it achieves high-accuracy parsing while significantly reducing redundant LLM invocations and token consumption, and substantially shortening grouping and sampling times.

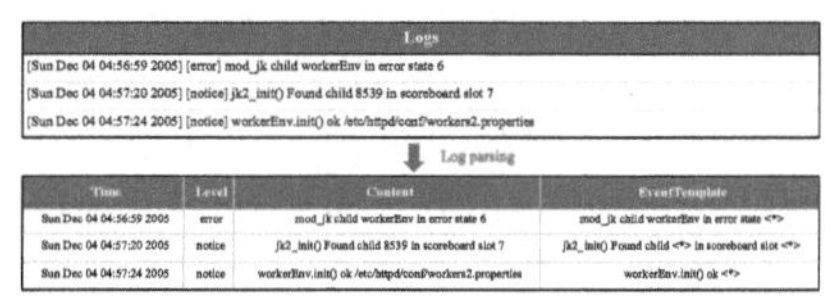

Fig. 1. Log Parsing Examples.

On 16 public datasets from LogHub-2k [18], LogCraft achieves 92.1% grouping accuracy and 84.7% parsing accuracy, substantially outperforming traditional methods and mainstream LLM baselines. On the LogHub-2.0 [8] dataset, LogCraft reduces grouping and sampling time overhead by over 50% and total token consumption by 13.7% compared to existing unsupervised parsers. Experimental results demonstrate that LogCraft achieves an effective balance of accuracy, efficiency, and cost in unsupervised log parsing tasks.

The main contributions of this paper are as follows:

- We propose Pattern-Guided Iterative Clustering (PGIC) to efficiently construct structurally coherent log clusters, providing high-quality contextual input for LLMs.
- We design Variant-Aware Sampling (VA) and a multi-template generation caching mechanism to significantly reduce token consumption while maintaining parsing accuracy.
- Extensive experiments on the LogHub-2k and LogHub-2.0 datasets demonstrate that LogCraft outperforms traditional methods and existing LLM parsers in both accuracy and efficiency.

The remainder of this paper is organized as follows. Section 2 reviews related work and background. Section 3 presents the proposed LogCraft framework, including the PGIC and VA modules. Section 4 describes the experimental setup, followed by results and analysis in Sect. 5. Finally, Sect. 6 concludes the paper and discusses future work.

2 Background and Related Work

Traditional log parsing methods rely on handcrafted rules or statistical features, mainly including three categories: rule-based methods (e.g., SPELL [3]) with high efficiency but poor adaptability to structural variations; clustering-based methods that group similar logs but tend to generate noisy clusters; and frequent pattern mining methods (e.g., SlCT [14]) that distinguish static/dynamic components via token frequency but suffer from data imbalance.

With the development of large language models (LLMs), LLM-based log parsing has emerged, divided into supervised and unsupervised approaches. Supervised methods (e.g., DivLog [16]) rely on labeled data for fine-tuning or in-context learning, achieving high accuracy but poor scalability. Unsupervised methods (e.g., LogBatcher [15]) reduce annotation costs via clustering and batch processing but face issues like unstable grouping, high preprocessing overhead, and inefficient LLM invocations due to lack of structural consistency modeling.

Current techniques face a trade-off between accuracy and efficiency: traditional methods are efficient but less capable; supervised LLM methods are accurate but data-dependent; unsupervised LLM methods are promising but immature in cost control. To address these, we propose LogCraft, which enhances grouping consistency via Pattern-Guided Iterative Clustering (PGIC) and improves sampling effectiveness via Variable-Aware Sampling (VA), enabling accurate and cost-efficient unsupervised log parsing.

3 LogCraft Framework

3.1 Framework Overview

In this section, we introduce the architecture of LogCraft and then elaborate on its key technical innovations. As shown in Fig. 2, LogCraft is an unsupervised intelligent log processing framework that automates the transformation from raw logs to structured templates through a multi-stage architecture. The specific modules and execution flow are as follows:

Cache Matching: Upon entering the system, logs first attempt to match against log templates in the cache. A successful match indicates successful parsing. Logs that do not match the cache are accumulated to a preset block size, triggering a batch processing workflow.

Preprocessing and Pattern-Guided Iterative Clustering (PGIC): Before entering PGIC, logs undergo preprocessing involving regular expression replacement and word segmentation. We use predefined common rules to uniformly replace variables like date and time with the placeholder "$< * >$". The log is

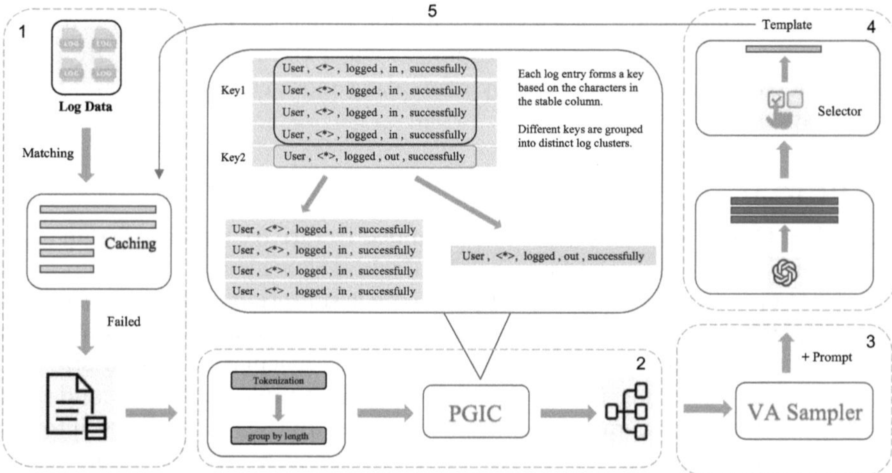

Fig. 2. LogCraft Framework. The sequence of numbers 1 to 5 in the diagram corresponds to the order of introduction.

then tokenized by spaces, converting the raw log into a structured sequence of tokens. Next, logs are preliminarily grouped based on their processed length. For each length-based group, PGIC is simultaneously applied for finer segmentation. The principles and implementation of PGIC will be detailed in the next subsection.

Variable-Aware Sampling (VA): After fine-grained grouping, each resulting cluster typically corresponds to a single template. Next, sampling is performed within each cluster to select representative samples for constructing prompts. The VA sampling algorithm first constructs the intra-cluster variable distribution, identifying the value ranges for each variable column. It then employs a greedy coverage strategy, prioritizing log samples that maximize variable gain until the specified number of samples is reached.

Multi-template Generation and Selection: The sampled representative logs are fed into an LLM for template generation. Experiments reveal that LLM responses may narrowly miss correct answers due to minor differences or uncertainties. Thus, the LogCraft framework employs an innovative multi-template generation strategy: during a single query, the LLM generates multiple candidate templates for each log cluster. All candidates undergo automated evaluation, with only the optimal template selected. Occasionally, the selected optimal template may not match all logs within a cluster. Unmatched logs from this cluster, along with cached logs that failed matching, accumulate to form new unmatched log blocks.

Dynamic Template Caching: Newly generated templates are added to the cache after validation. Templates in the cache pool are grouped by length rather than randomly arranged. During cache matching, logs are only matched against templates of similar length, enhancing matching efficiency. Caching also reduces uncertainty caused by inconsistent responses when the LLM repeatedly parses logs with identical templates, thereby generating more consistent templates for log generation.

3.2 PGIC-Based Grouping

Algorithm Overview. PGIC (Pattern-Guided Iterative Clustering) is an unsupervised pre-clustering method inspired by Brain [17], achieving precise grouping through column consistency (stability). Its core assumption is that logs from the same template should exhibit high token consistency at fixed positions, while variable columns show significant variation. PGIC calculates column stability, selects columns exceeding a stability threshold as "stable columns", and combines their values to generate grouping keys. Logs are then partitioned into distinct clusters based on these keys. Due to finite log lengths, stable-column-driven splitting iterations typically do not exceed five iterations.

Compared to traditional clustering methods (e.g., K-means, DBSCAN) requiring predefined cluster counts or complex density estimation, PGIC achieves near-linear time complexity without parameter tuning and scales effectively for large-scale log scenarios. Its pattern-guided grouping strategy produces highly consistent log clusters for subsequent LLM template generation, thereby balancing efficiency and accuracy in log parsing tasks.

Algorithm Formal Description and Workflow. Let the log cluster be defined as $G = \{L_1, L_2, ..., L_n\}$ where each log $L_i = \{t_{i,1}, t_{i,2}, ..., t_{i,m_i}\}$ represents a sequence of tokens after word segmentation. The stability coefficient for the j column is defined as:

$$S_j(G) = \frac{\max_{t \in T_j} count(t, T_j)}{|T_j|} \tag{1}$$

where $T_j = \{t_{i,j} \mid L_i \in G, j \leq m_i\}$ denotes the set of all valid tokens in column j, and $count(t, T_j)$ represents the occurrence count of token t within that column. Given a stability threshold $\theta_{\text{stability}}$, the set of stable columns is defined as:

$$SC(G) = \{j \mid S_j(G) \geq \theta_{\text{stability}}\} \tag{2}$$

For a log L_i and a set of stable columns SC, the grouping key is defined as $Key(L_i, SC) = (t_{i,j_1}, t_{i,j_2}, ..., t_{i,j_k})$, where $SC = \{j_1, j_2, ..., j_k\}$. The corresponding workflow is shown in Algorithm 1.

3.3 Variable-Aware Sampling

VA (Variable-Aware Sampling) is an intelligent sampling strategy specifically designed for structurally consistent clusters obtained after PGIC clustering. Its core principle is to prioritize samples that maximize coverage of variable value distributions while preserving log structural consistency, thereby providing the

Algorithm 1: PGIC

Input: logs $L = \{L_1, L_2, \ldots, L_n\}$, stability threshold $\theta_{\text{stability}}$
Output: clusters $C = \{C_1, C_2, \ldots, C_k\}$
// Preprocessing and initialization
$G \leftarrow$ TOKENIZE(L) ;
groups $\leftarrow$ GROUPBYLENGTH(G) ;
// Iterative splitting
repeat
  new_groups $\leftarrow \emptyset$;
  foreach *group* $G \in$ *groups* **do**
    // Calculate stability for each column
    $SC(G) \leftarrow \{j \mid S_j(G) \geq \theta_{\text{stability}}\}$;
    // Split by stable columns
    if $SC(G) \neq \emptyset$ **then**
      foreach $L_i \in G$ **do**
        $key \leftarrow Key(L_i, SC(G))$;
        subgroups[key] $\leftarrow$ subgroups[key] $\cup \{L_i\}$;
      new_groups $\leftarrow$ new_groups $\cup$ subgroups ;
    else
      new_groups $\leftarrow$ new_groups $\cup \{G\}$;
  groups $\leftarrow$ new_groups ;
until *no split occurred*;
return groups ;

most representative batches for the LLM template generation phase. VA work details are shown in Fig. 3.

Each cluster $G = \{L_1, L_2, ..., L_n\}$ obtained by the PGIC algorithm maintains consistent internal log structure, with differences between logs primarily manifesting in variable positions. VA first identifies variable columns within the cluster to be sampled. For each column, it performs token statistics to obtain the distinct values and occurrence frequencies of all variables in that column. This frequency distribution is stored as a dictionary for subsequent use. For each log to be sampled within the cluster, VA calculates whether its variables are present in their respective variable column sets. If absent, it increases the coverage gain score. Compared to methods like DPP that focus on increasing sample diversity, VA's variable-specific sampling approach ensures selected samples fully represent the original data's variable diversity. This helps LLMs observe sufficient patterns from limited log inputs to extract templates.

One point requires special clarification: the preprocessed results of logs with replaced content are used solely within the PGIC workflow. The corresponding original logs are still retained in their unmodified state. VA operates on the unprocessed original logs. The goal of VA is to select samples that cover variable diversity within structurally consistent clusters. PGIC provides these structurally consistent clusters, within which VA identifies variable diversity-explaining why the tokenization operation reappears in Fig. 3.

3.4 Multi-template Generation and Evaluation

LogCraft's multi-template generation mechanism is one of its core innovations. The multi-template evaluation system is based on two key dimensions: matching performance and template specificity. Matching performance measures how effectively a template successfully matches a given log collection. If a template correctly extracts variables from a log, that log is considered a successful match. This metric reflects the template's versatility and parsing capability; a higher matching rate indicates superior structural adaptability. Template specificity measures the ratio of fixed components to wildcard components within a template. Higher specificity indicates a more precise template structure, while excessively low specificity may lead to overgeneralization.

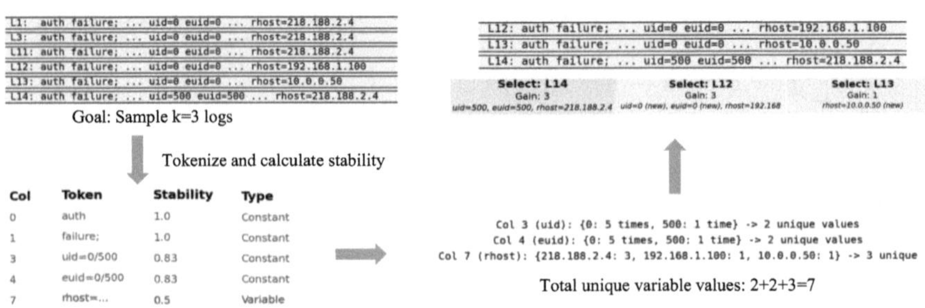

Fig. 3. VA Workflow.

$$Match\_Ratio = \frac{\text{Number of successfully matched logs}}{\text{Total number of logs}} \tag{3}$$

$$Specificity = \frac{L_{\text{fixed}}}{L_{\text{fixed}} + N_{\text{wild}}} \tag{4}$$

where L_{fixed} represents the fixed text length, i.e., the total number of characters in the template excluding the wildcard "$< * >$", and N_{wild} denotes the number of wildcards in the template. To balance match rate and specificity, the final result depends on the weighted sum of both factors.

$$Score = a \times Match\_Ratio + b \times Specificity \tag{5}$$

4 Experimental Setup

4.1 Datasets and Evaluation Metrics

We conducted experiments on 16 publicly available log datasets (**Loghub-2k** [18]) sourced from the LogPai project [19]. These datasets encompass logs from distributed systems, standalone software, supercomputers, personal computer operating systems, mobile systems, microservices, and more. However, it has been observed that the original labels contain some errors due to inconsistent annotation styles [8,9,18]. Therefore, drawing on prior research, we adopted the corrected version of LogHub provided by Khan et al. [9] as the default dataset for evaluation. Additionally, for subsequent processing time assessments, we utilized a subset of the large-scale dataset from **LogHub-2.0** [8].

Given the inherent difficulty in evaluating template correctness, various metrics exist. Commonly used metrics include Precision-Accuracy (PA) and Grouping Accuracy (GA). Following prior work, we primarily employ three standard accuracy metrics to evaluate LogCraft and baseline methods.

Group Accuracy (GA): Group Accuracy is a metric in log parsing that evaluates how well a parser correctly groups log messages belonging to the same template. GA is calculated as the number of correctly grouped logs divided by the total number of logs [19].

Parsing Accuracy (PA): A log message is considered correctly parsed if the template assigned to it perfectly matches the actual template after replacing variable placeholders. PA is calculated as the number of correctly parsed logs divided by the total number of logs [2].

Edit Distance (ED): The edit distance refers to the minimum number of operations-insertions, deletions, or substitutions-required to transform one string into another [12]. Here, it denotes the normalized edit distance [11], which calculates the average edit distance across all template pairs in the dataset.

4.2 Baseline Methods and Configuration

We compared LogCraft against three industry-leading approaches, including a traditional parser (Drain) and two LLM-based parsers (LILAC and Logbatcher).

Considering cost and model performance, we adopted GPT-4.1-mini as the underlying large language model, which has gained widespread favor among researchers as a recently released model. To ensure fairness and eliminate potential data discrepancies or fluctuations caused by model performance improvements, all LLM-based methods-including our LogCraft framework-were trained on the same LLM and run three times under identical conditions, with results averaged. For traditional non-LLM parsing method, we utilized empirically validated data from the SOK [1].

Experiments were conducted on a server running Python 3.9 and Ubuntu 24.04, equipped with a 32-core Xeon(R) Platinum 8352V CPU and 120 GB of memory. The large language model was invoked via Python libraries provided by OpenAI.

For LogCraft, the stability threshold was set to 0.8, with 5 logs input to the LLM. The multi-template selection parameters were configured as $a = 0.7$ and $b = 0.3$. All other baseline methods were implemented using the default configurations described in their respective original papers to ensure fair and accurate comparisons.

5 Results and Analysis

5.1 RQ1: How Does LogCraft Perform Compared to Baseline Methods in Terms of Parsing Accuracy?

Log parsing accuracy is a critical prerequisite for downstream log analysis tasks and is commonly evaluated using Group Accuracy (GA), Parsing Accuracy (PA), and Edit Distance (ED) [19]. To answer RQ1, we compare LogCraft with a representative traditional parser (Drain) and a state-of-the-art supervised LLM-based parser (LILAC) on 16 datasets from LogHub-2k [18]. The detailed results are reported in Table 1.

Overall, LogCraft demonstrates the strongest parsing performance across datasets, achieving an average PA of 84.7%, significantly outperforming Drain

Table 1. Performance on Loghub-2k Datasets (Drain/LILAC/LogCraft)

Dataset	Drain			LILAC			LogCraft		
	GA	PA	ED	GA	PA	ED	GA	PA	ED
Android	0.830	0.548	0.904	0.949	**0.705**	**0.914**	**0.956**	0.692	0.862
Apache	**1.000**	0.694	0.920	**1.000**	**1.000**	**1.000**	**1.000**	**1.000**	**1.000**
BGL	0.962	0.344	0.843	**0.979**	**0.966**	**0.993**	0.977	0.950	0.991
HDFS	0.998	0.626	0.933	**1.000**	0.583	0.989	**1.000**	**1.000**	**1.000**
HPC	**0.887**	0.654	0.957	0.875	**0.901**	**0.979**	0.869	0.858	0.974
Hadoop	0.948	0.514	0.786	**0.979**	0.951	**0.986**	0.974	**0.958**	0.983
HealthApp	0.780	0.230	0.607	**0.902**	**0.887**	0.959	0.897	**0.887**	**0.963**
Linux	0.422	0.182	0.776	0.300	0.342	0.861	**0.938**	**0.612**	**0.922**
Mac	0.786	0.218	0.757	0.803	**0.485**	**0.860**	**0.832**	0.436	0.829
OpenSSH	0.789	0.508	0.965	0.562	0.554	0.927	**0.996**	**0.997**	**0.999**
OpenStack	0.224	0.018	0.512	**0.492**	**0.445**	**0.819**	0.416	0.374	0.713
Proxifier	0.764	0.681	0.963	0.790	0.802	0.944	**1.000**	**1.000**	**1.000**
Spark	0.920	0.382	0.960	**0.925**	**0.885**	**0.980**	0.922	0.880	0.950
Thunderbird	0.955	0.046	0.812	0.964	0.922	0.980	**0.966**	**0.927**	**0.988**
Windows	**0.997**	0.462	0.864	0.688	0.521	0.767	0.996	**0.985**	**0.995**
Zookeeper	0.966	0.792	0.937	0.988	0.698	0.967	**0.994**	**0.988**	**0.999**
Average	0.827	0.431	0.844	0.825	0.728	0.933	**0.921**	**0.847**	**0.948**

(43.1%) and LILAC (72.8%). On structured datasets such as Apache, HDFS, and Proxifier, it achieves near-perfect PA, while on more complex datasets (e.g., Linux), it still shows substantial improvements over baselines. Although LILAC performs slightly better on a few datasets (e.g., HPC and OpenStack), LogCraft maintains competitive results and consistently achieves higher GA and ED scores, indicating more stable grouping. Overall, LogCraft attains the best PA on 14 out of 16 datasets, demonstrating strong robustness across diverse log characteristics.

These results confirm that LogCraft significantly improves parsing accuracy over traditional parsers and provides a strong, scalable alternative to supervised LLM-based approaches, especially in scenarios with complex log structures.

5.2 RQ2: How Does LogCraft Perform in Terms of Processing Efficiency?

The purpose of this section is to investigate the efficiency and cost of LLM log parsers while maintaining comparable parsing quality. Since LogCraft achieves higher accuracy than LILAC, we mainly compare with LogBatcher, which has similar performance (83.6% PA on Loghub-2k). Table 2 shows that LogCraft reduces total token consumption by 13.7% (from 13,683 to 11,804) and single-

Table 2. Token Consumption Comparison on Loghub-2k

System	$\mathbf{T}_{total}$		$\mathbf{T}_{invoc}$	
	LogBatcher	LogCraft	LogBatcher	LogCraft
Android	21429	**18672**	138	**124**
Apache	1049	**907**	175	**151**
BGL	19203	**16375**	163	**149**
Hadoop	18571	**16290**	164	**160**
HDFS	6515	**5715**	465	**408**
HealthApp	8278	**7153**	113	**99**
HPC	6129	**5334**	**130**	137
Linux	11359	**9277**	98	**81**
Mac	62809	**53725**	187	**173**
OpenSSH	4679	**3903**	187	**156**
OpenStack	14792	**11375**	361	**300**
Proxifier	3990	**3194**	362	**290**
Spark	5541	**5032**	179	**168**
Thunderbird	20425	**17932**	130	**121**
Windows	6765	**5937**	135	**129**
Zookeeper	**7393**	8049	**142**	178
Average	13683	**11804**	196	**177**

call tokens from 196 to 177 (9.7%), significantly lowering inference cost. For complex logs such as OpenStack, the reduction exceeds 20.

LogCraft also performs well on large-scale datasets (Loghub-2.0). Table 3 shows that on an 11.16 million-record HDFS dataset, $\mathbf{C}_{\text{time}}$(clustering time) decreases from 363.878 s to 119.275 s (67.2%), while $\mathbf{S}_{\text{time}}$(sampling time) drops by 79.4%. These gains are mainly due to the PGIC and VA strategies.

Despite reduced grouping and sampling time (excluding LLM calls), LogCraft maintains competitive accuracy (Table 4): it achieves 96.6% PA on HDFS and 92.0% on BGL, comparable to LogBatcher. This demonstrates a strong balance between efficiency and accuracy.

Table 3. Performance of LogBatcher and LogCraft on LogHub-2.0($C_{\text{time}}/S_{\text{time}}$)

Dataset	Log count	LogBatcher		LogCraft	
		$\mathbf{C}_{\text{time}}$	$\mathbf{S}_{\text{time}}$	$\mathbf{C}_{\text{time}}$	$\mathbf{S}_{\text{time}}$
HDFS	11167740	363.878	33.179	**110.275**	**6.833**
BGL	4631261	136.592	19.721	**57.328**	**2.126**
Apache	51977	3.779	0.230	**0.643**	**0.029**

Table 4. Performance of LogBatcher and LogCraft on LogHub-2.0(GA/PA/ED)

Dataset	Log count	LogBatcher			LogCraft		
		GA	PA	ED	GA	PA	ED
HDFS	11167740	**1.000**	**1.000**	**1.000**	**1.000**	0.966	0.999
BGL	4631261	0.966	**0.932**	**0.981**	**0.973**	0.920	0.975
Apache	51977	**1.000**	**0.989**	**0.991**	**1.000**	0.970	0.981

5.3 RQ3: How Do Different Modules Influence LogCraft?

We further evaluated the contributions of the three components-PGIC, VA, and multi-template generation-through ablation experiments (see Table 5).

Table 5. Performance Ablation of LogCraft

Configuration	GA		PA		ED	
	Score	Δ	Score	Δ	Score	Δ
Full LogCraft	0.921	–	0.847	–	0.948	–
w/o PGIC	0.792	↓14.0%	0.766	↓9.6%	0.862	↓9.1%
w/o VA	0.819	↓11.0%	0.733	↓13.5%	0.890	↓6.1%
w/o Multi-Template	0.902	↓2.1%	0.736	↓13.1%	0.913	↓3.7%

PGIC Grouping Module. As LogCraft's core innovation, PGIC plays a decisive role in parsing performance. When PGIC is removed and only length-based grouping is used, parsing performance significantly declines. GA shows the most pronounced drop, reaching up to 14%. This demonstrates that PGIC is crucial for precise log grouping and accurate parsing.

Variable-Aware Sampling (VA). The Variable-Aware Sampling mechanism critically impacts parsing performance. Replacing it with a random sampling strategy resulted in significant performance degradation: GA decreased by 11.0%, PA by 13.5%, and ED by 6.1%. This demonstrates that the VA module is a core component ensuring parsing accuracy. The key role of the VA mechanism lies in enhancing sample diversity compared to random sampling, enabling the LLM to observe different variables and thereby determine the log template format.

Multi-Template Generation. The multi-template generation mechanism plays a crucial role in ensuring parsing quality. Replacing it with single-template generation resulted in a 13.1% decrease in the PA metric, indicating this module's significant impact on parsing accuracy. Although GA only decreased by 2.1%, parsing accuracy (PA) is typically the core metric for evaluating log parsing tasks.

6 Conclusion

This paper presents LogCraft, an efficient unsupervised log parsing framework that balances parsing accuracy and processing efficiency without requiring labeled data or human demonstrations. By integrating Pattern-Guided Iterative Clustering (PGIC) with Variable-Aware Sampling (VA), LogCraft constructs structurally consistent and information-rich contexts for large language models, reducing redundant invocations and improving template generation stability. Experiments on the LogHub-2k and LogHub-2.0 datasets show that LogCraft achieves strong parsing performance while significantly reducing token consumption and computational overhead in the grouping and sampling stages, demonstrating its practical effectiveness for unsupervised LLM-based log parsing.

Future work may incorporate lightweight domain knowledge or adaptive strategies while preserving the unsupervised setting, to further enhance LogCraft's adaptability to diverse log patterns. Systematic evaluation of

LogCraft across different large language models, considering their varying reasoning capabilities and cost characteristics, also remains an important direction.

Acknowledgments. This research is supported by, National Science and Technology Major Project(No.2025ZD1606804), the Ministry of Industry and Information Technology of China, the Key Program of National Natural Science Foundation of China (No. 62432007) and Shanghai Trusted Industry Internet Software Collaborative Innovation Center.

References

1. Beck, V., Landauer, M., Wurzenberger, M., Skopik, F., Rauber, A.: System log parsing with large language models: a review. arXiv preprintarXiv:2504.04877 (2025)
2. Dai, H., Li, H., Chen, C.S., Shang, W., Chen, T.H.: Logram: efficient log parsing using n-gram dictionaries. IEEE Trans. Software Eng. **48**(3), 879–892 (2020)
3. Du, M., Li, F.: Spell: streaming parsing of system event logs. In: IEEE 16th International Conference on Data Mining (ICDM), pp. 859–864. IEEE (2016)
4. He, P., Zhu, J., He, S., Li, J., Lyu, M.R.: An evaluation study on log parsing and its use in log mining. In: 2016 46th Annual IEEE/IFIP International Conference on Dependable Systems and Networks (DSN), pp. 654–661 IEEE (2016)
5. He, P., Zhu, J., He, S., Li, J., Lyu, M.R.: Towards automated log parsing for large-scale log data analysis. IEEE Trans. Dependable Secure Comput. **15**(6), 931–944 (2017)
6. Huang, J., Jiang, Z., Chen, Z., Lyu, M.R.: Lunar: unsupervised LLM-based log parsing. arXiv preprint arXiv:2406.07174 (2024)
7. Jiang, Z., et al.: Lilac: log parsing using LLMs with adaptive parsing cache. Proc. ACM Software Eng. **1**(FSE), 137–160 (2024)
8. Jiang, Z., et al.: A large-scale evaluation for log parsing techniques: How far are we? In: Proceedings of the 33rd ACM SIGSOFT International Symposium on Software Testing and Analysis, pp. 223–234 (2024)
9. Khan, Z.A., Shin, D., Bianculli, D., Briand, L.: Guidelines for assessing the accuracy of log message template identification techniques. In: Proceedings of the 44th International Conference on Software Engineering, pp. 1095–1106 (2022)
10. Le, V.H., Zhang, H.: Log parsing: how far can ChatGPT go? In: 2023 38th IEEE/ACM International Conference on Automated Software Engineering (ASE), pp. 1699–1704. IEEE (2023)
11. Marzal, A., Vidal, E.: Computation of normalized edit distance and applications. IEEE Trans. Pattern Anal. Mach. Intell. **15**(9), 926–932 (2002)
12. Nedelkoski, S., Bogatinovski, J., Acker, A., Cardoso, J., Kao, O.: Self-supervised log parsing. In: Dong, Y., Mladenić, D., Saunders, C. (eds.) ECML PKDD 2020. LNCS (LNAI), vol. 12460, pp. 122–138. Springer, Cham (2021). https://doi.org/10.1007/978-3-030-67667-4_8
13. Pei, C., et al.: Self-evolutionary group-wise log parsing based on large language model. In: 2024 IEEE 35th International Symposium on Software Reliability Engineering (ISSRE), pp. 49–60. IEEE (2024)
14. Vaarandi, R.: Mining event logs with SLCT and LogHound. In: NOMS 2008-2008 IEEE Network Operations and Management Symposium, pp. 1071–1074. IEEE (2008)

15. Xiao, Y., Le, V.H., Zhang, H.: Free: towards more practical log parsing with large language models. In: Proceedings of the 39th IEEE/ACM International Conference on Automated Software Engineering, pp. 153–165 (2024)
16. Xu, J., Yang, R., Huo, Y., Zhang, C., He, P.: Divlog: log parsing with prompt enhanced in-context learning. In: Proceedings of the IEEE/ACM 46th International Conference on Software Engineering, pp. 1–12 (2024)
17. Yu, S., He, P., Chen, N., Wu, Y.: Brain: log parsing with bidirectional parallel tree. IEEE Trans. Serv. Comput. **16**(5), 3224–3237 (2023)
18. Zhu, J., He, S., He, P., Liu, J., Lyu, M.R.: LogHub: a large collection of system log datasets for AI-driven log analytics. In: 2023 IEEE 34th International Symposium on Software Reliability Engineering (ISSRE), pp. 355–366. IEEE (2023)
19. Zhu, J., et al.: Tools and benchmarks for automated log parsing. In: 2019 IEEE/ACM 41st International Conference on Software Engineering: Software Engineering in Practice (ICSE-SEIP), pp. 121–130. IEEE (2019)

A Dynamically Updatable Zero-Knowledge Proof Commitment Scheme for Cross-Shard Transactions

Xingguang Zhou[1,2](✉), Yizhong Liu[3](✉), and Boyu Zhao[3](✉)

[1] Civil Aviation Management Institute of China, Beijing 100102, China
zhouxingguang@camic.cn
[2] Key Laboratory of Civil Aviation Data Governance and Decision Optimization, Beijing 100102, China
[3] Beihang University, Beijing 100191, China
{liuyizhong,boyuzhao}@buaa.edu.cn

Abstract. While sharding technology enhances throughput by enabling parallel transaction processing, it introduces the critical challenge of efficiently and securely verifying state updates in cross-shard transactions. To address these issues, this paper proposes a lightweight and dynamically updatable zero-knowledge proof commitment scheme. The core innovation lies in a lightweight update protocol where the state change proof consists of only two group elements, and verification requires merely two bilinear pairing operations, reducing the verification complexity from *O(n)* to *O(1)*. Performance evaluations show that the proposed scheme obviously reduces the average computational overhead of the state change proof by over 70% and the maximum latency at peak throughput by 50% compared to existing schemes.

Keywords: Zero-Knowledge Proof · Blockchain · Updatable Commitment · Air Travel

1 Introduction

1.1 Background

Blockchain technology has revolutionized numerous industries, including supply chain, air travel, finance and digital identity, by leveraging its decentralization and immutable ledger properties [1–3]. As we enter the critical phase of transitioning from experimental architectures to large-scale infrastructure, the scalability limitation of traditional single-chain blockchain remains a core bottleneck, For instance, Ethereum [4] can only process 10–20 transactions per second (TPS). According to its official reports, Visa's peak processing capacity reaches 65,000 transactions TPS. To overcome this limitation, sharding technology has been proposed as a promising approach to improve blockchain scalability [5]. Its core idea is to partition the blockchain network into multiple shards, each capable of processing transactions and reaching consensus in parallel [6]. In the scenario

J. Niu et al. (Eds.): KSEM 2026, LNAI 16631, pp. 184–197, 2027.
https://doi.org/10.1007/978-981-92-2759-4_14

of aviation e-commerce, the customer (i.e. the airline's membership customer) payment contract and its balance state are deployed on one shard, while the airline's product management contract and its state reside on the other shard. To implement a complete order processing, two-way cross-shard contract shall be established. Then a dynamic state change mechanism is required to ensure credible verification of cross-shard transactions [7].

The adoption of the blockchain sharding architecture has enhanced the system's throughput and scalability [8]. However, it should be noted that while sharding technology disperses transaction data, it inevitably brings some challenges of cross-shard transactions. Firstly, credible verification of cross-shard transactions becomes a core issue. Due to the lack of a global unified state view among shards, efficient mechanisms are needed to ensure the legality and credibility of cross-shard state updates [9]. Secondly, existing state commitment schemes for sharding blockchains mostly adopt a static design paradigm, which is incompatible with the frequent state changes in practical applications [10]. These schemes may face the challenge of low verification efficiency and insufficient security during updates. The updatable encryption and commitment technologies provides new insights for addressing these issues [11]. For example, the work of updatable encryption could lay a foundation for dynamic commitment design [12]. Thus, designing an efficient, secure, and verifiable dynamic zero-knowledge proof commitment method for sharding blockchains is crucial to resolve the pain points and promote the large-scale application of blockchain technology [13].

1.2 Related Work

Early sharding schemes, such as Elastico, adopt the static sharding partitioning strategy, where nodes are fixedly assigned to each shard based on their hash values [5]. Each node would handle mutually disjoint transaction sets and does not support cross-shard transaction. OmniLedger utilizes the Atomix protocol to handle cross-shard transaction but relies on client-driven coordination [14]. When cross-shard transaction increases, the system's throughput significantly declines. RapidChain as a sharding blockchain protocol that allows up to 1/3 Byzantine nodes, improves efficiency by reducing data exchange for cross-shard transactions [15].

However, the intra-shard Byzantine Fault Tolerance (BFT) interaction cost surges with shard expansion, making it inefficient to support dynamic state iteration. Current research on blockchain sharding technology primarily revolves around the atomicity, processing efficiency, and fault tolerance of cross-shard transactions. In terms of cross-shard atomicity, schemes such as the buffer mechanism [16], two-phase commit protocol [17], and optimistic processing approach [18] contribute to achieving atomic cross-shard transaction processing. Regarding fault tolerance, an improved blockchain sharding scheme enhances fault tolerance by dynamically adjusting the number and size of shards [19]. In the aspect of processing efficiency, the CHERUBIM protocol significantly improves throughput and optimizes cross-shard consensus efficiency through a two-phase commit mechanism [20]. Additionally, hierarchical architectural designs, such as

PyloChain, boost local transaction throughput and reduce latency via a multi-level local chain and main chain structure [21]. Despite significant advancement in existing research aims at improving the performance of blockchain sharding, challenges such as the high overhead of cross-shard state verification and the low efficiency of data availability validation remain unresolved.

Therefore, the updatable zero-knowledge proof commitment mechanism emerges as a solution. It employs polynomial commitments to represent state updates as polynomials and verifies the correctness of state transitions by generating succinct proofs. Currently, general zero-knowledge proof (ZKP) schemes such as ZK-SNARK [22] and ZK-STARK [23] have been widely applied in state verification, transaction privacy protection, and other scenarios [24,25]. ZK-SNARKs require a trusted setup but have short proofs and fast verification, while ZK-STARKs do not require a trusted setup and are resistant to quantum computing but have larger proof sizes. Both approaches suffer from either complex preprocessing or high verification costs, making them difficult to adapt to the dynamic update requirements of sharding blockchains [26]. In terms of commitment schemes, existing research mainly focuses on the construction and optimization of static commitments, such as hash commitments and Pedersen commitments. They can bind and hide messages but do not support dynamic data updates. If the commitment content needs to be changed, a complete new commitment must be generated and synchronized across the network, resulting in excessive communication and storage overhead [27]. Schemes like static Pedersen commitments combine bilinear pairing technology to reduce computational overhead and enhance resistance to collusion attacks but still fail to address dynamic updates [28]. Some dynamic commitment schemes, such as updatable Pedersen commitments, support commitment updates by introducing additional key management mechanisms. However, they face challenges like potential privacy leaks and lack of consideration for cross-shard verification scenarios in a sharding architecture, making them difficult to apply directly to sharding blockchains. Since 2021, research on updatable encryption technology has made breakthroughs. Nishimaki proposes a directionless key update scheme based on updatable trapdoor smooth projective hash functions, enhancing the scheme's universality [29]. Boneh et al. design a post-quantum secure updatable encryption architecture based on RLWE, providing an important reference for the design of dynamic commitment schemes [12]. Song et al.propose a token-based open security model, further optimizing the privacy protection and access control capabilities of updatable encryption [30]. Gai and Qiu et al. [2] proposed differential privacy-based blockchain for industrial internet-of-things [31–33] and various computing systems [34–36].

In summary, when updatable zero-knowledge proof commitment mechanisms are adapted to cross-chain transaction scenarios, it is imperative that they not only provide verifiable proofs of state updates, but also balance the requirements for nodes lightweight design and privacy protection. This contradiction between privacy and verifiability is particularly prominent in transaction scenarios that require compliance with regulations and user privacy protection simultaneously.

Therefore, this study proposes the design of a lightweight, dynamically updatable zero-knowledge proof commitment scheme. Sharding nodes only need to generate concise proofs of state changes to complete update verification without revealing transaction details or storing the full state.

1.3 Contributions

(a) **A novel lightweight ZKP scheme for state updates.** We propose a ZKP commitment scheme specifically designed for dynamic state updates. The scheme achieves both privacy and verifiability by allowing sharding nodes to generate brief change proofs without revealing transaction details or maintaining the full state. This ensures that state updates are both efficient and confidential.

(b) **Lowering the communication and processing overhead in cross-shard transaction scenarios.** By leveraging bilinear mapping and polynomial commitment techniques, we transform the verification of the entire state into a constant-size change consistency proof, including only two group elements. This reduces the computational complexity of state change from *O(n)* to *O(1)* for both proof generation and validation.

(c) **Formal security analysis and extensive experimental validation.** Security analysis demonstrates that the proposed scheme satisfies semantic security and unforgeability, which is resilient to double-spending attacks. The experimental results demonstrate that our scheme reduces the average computational overhead of the state change proof by over 70% and the maximum latency by 50% at peak throughput.

2 Preliminaries

2.1 Bilinear Groups

Let G_1, G_2, G_T be three cyclic groups of prime order p. The generator of group G_1 is g_1, and the generator of group G_2 is g_2. A bilinear map e: $G_1 \times G_2 \rightarrow G_T$ satisfies the following properties:

- Bilinearity: For all $a, b \in Z_p^*$, $e(g_1^a, g_2^b) = e(g_1, g_2)^{ab}$.
- Non-degeneracy: $e(g_1, g_2) \neq 1$.
- Computability: There is a polynomial-time algorithm to compute $e(u, v)$ for any $u \in G_1$, $v \in G_2$.

2.2 Theoretical Assumptions

Decisional Bilinear Diffie-Hellman (DBDH) Assumption. Let G_1 and G_2 be two cyclic groups of prime order q, and let e: $G_1 \times G_1 \rightarrow G_2$ be a bilinear map. Given a tuple (g, g^a, g^b, g^c, T), where g is a generator of G_1, a, b, c are randomly chosen exponents, and T is an element in G_2. There is no polynomial-time algorithm that can distinguish between $e(g_1, g_2)^{abc}$ and T with non-negligible probability.

Computational Diffie-Hellman (CDH) Assumption. Given g^a,$g^b \in G$, there exists no probabilistic polynomial-time algorithm capable of computing g^{ab} with non-negligible probability.

3 System Model

3.1 System Architecture

The system usually includes five participating entities: the user, the initiating shard A, the relay, the receiving shard B, and the main chain. We assume them in an air travel scenario.

User: It is the initiator of a cross-shard transaction, submitting a transaction request to the associated shard. For example, the user could be a customer who belongs to an airline's membership company.

Initiating Shard (Shard A): It handles the initial validation of the transaction, locks the account state, executes the local state update, and generates a zero-knowledge proof for the state change. For example, Shard A could be the company which acts as the airline's membership customer.

Receiving Shard (Shard B): It is responsible for verifying the state update proof from the initiating shard and executing the corresponding state change. For example, Shard B could be the airline.

Relay: It is responsible for securely and reliably transmitting cross-shard messages between shards. It acts as the communication bridges.

Main Chain: It is responsible for providing the core infrastructure and rule framework for the cross-chain system, and maintaining a unified global state view. It ensures the final consistency of the entire system.

3.2 System Assumption

Basic Assumption. The threat model and the communication model used in our scheme are described as follows:

(a) Threat Model: We consider an adaptive adversary $\mathcal{A}$ who is restricted by the following limits:
   - $\mathcal{A}$ can dynamically adjust its attack strategy based on the information obtained during the protocol execution, such as public parameters, historical commitments, update proofs, etc.
   - $\mathcal{A}$ can corrupt nodes at any point during the protocol execution, causing them to behave in a Byzantine manner.
   - The proportion of malicious nodes controlled by the adversary within each shard does not exceed one-third, and the adversary cannot simultaneously control more than one-third of all shards.

– The honest node is considered as an challenger $\mathcal{C}$. It obeys rules of the whole system, but could do everything possible to spy on the transaction.

(b) Communication Model: A partially synchronous model is adopted, which allows for bounded message delays in the network, with a definite upper bound on latency.

Security Model. Our system is expected to meet the semantic security and unforgeability. The corresponding security models are described as follows:

(a) Semantic Security Model
Initialization: The challenger $\mathcal{C}$ runs $Setup\left(1^{\lambda}\right)$ to generate $pp = (G_1, G_2, G_T, e, p, g_1, g_2, pk, H)$ and sk, then sends pp and pk to the adversary $\mathcal{A}$.
Challenge: $\mathcal{A}$ submits two distinct messages $m_0, m_1 \in Z_p$. $\mathcal{C}$ randomly selects $b \in 0, 1$ and $r_0 \in Z_p^*$, computes $C_b = g_1^{m_b + \alpha r_0}$, then selects $m' \in Z_p$ and $r_1 \in Z_p^*$ to generate $\pi = (A, B)$ and C_b^*. Finally, $\mathcal{C}$ sends (C_b, π, C_b^*) to $\mathcal{A}$.
Guess: $\mathcal{A}$ outputs $b' \in 0, 1$. $\mathcal{A}$ wins if $b' = b$.

(b) Unforgeability Model
Initialization: The challenger $\mathcal{C}$ runs $Setup\left(1^{\lambda}\right)$ to generate pp, sk, and pk. It sends pp and pk to the adversary $\mathcal{A}$, and maintains a query list Q.
Query: $\mathcal{A}$ submits (m_i, m_i') pairs multiple times. $\mathcal{C}$ returns π_i and C_i^*, and records them in Q.
Forgery: $\mathcal{A}$ outputs (π', C_0', C_1'). $\mathcal{A}$ wins if $VerifyUpdate\ (pp, pk, C_0', C_1', \pi') = 1$ and $(\pi', C_0', C_1') \notin Q$.

Due to page limits, the detailed proof are included in the full version.

4 Proposed Approach

4.1 System Overview

Figure 1 takes the aviation e-commerce as an example. It shows the full process of protocol interaction among all participating entities during cross-shard transaction. In practical applications such as aviation e-commerce, a user's payment and balance state might be deployed in Shard A, while the recipient's payee state might be deployed in Shard B. Shard B and Shard A represent the airline company and the membership customer respectively. The account and transaction information of them are deployed in their own shards. To complete the aviation service, Shard A needs to initiate a cross-shard transaction call to Shard B. It consists of six phases.

Phase I: System Initializaton

(1) The user submits a cross-shard transaction (Tx) to Shard A. Shard A performs pre-checks, including balance verification and signature verification, and returns a processing voucher upon success.

Phase II: Initial Commitment Generation

(2) Shard A locks the outbound account status to prevent the account assets from being manipulated repeatedly during the transaction process.

(3) Shard A performs local deduction operations and updates the account status.

Phase III: Commitment Update Request

(4) Shard A generates a change certificate, proving that its deduction status has been legally updated.

(5) Shard A broadcasts cross-shard messages through the relay, including Tx details and existence proof.

Phase IV: Update Verification

(6) The relay forwards the message to Shard B.

(7) Shard B verifies the change proof, such as legality and validity of proof.

Phase V: Updated Commitment Confirmation

(8) Shard B verifies the changed state, such as the consistency with Shard A's latest commitment, and returns the verification result (success/failure).

(9) If the verification is successful, shard B performs the operation of adding balance to the payee. If the verification fails, the transaction is discarded.

(10) Shard B notifies Shard A of the verification result (success/ failure).

(11) If Shard A receives a successful notification, it permanently commits the status and releases the lock. If it receives a failed notification, it rolls back the status, releases the lock and processes the refund.

Phase VI: Commitment Opening (Optional)

(12) Shard A and B submit new blocks and state commitments to main chain.

(13) The main chain aggregates commitments from all shards to update the global state view, and completes the final synchronization.

4.2 The Construction of Our Scheme

In this section, we propose a dynamically updatable zero-knowledge proof commitment scheme for the cross-shard transaction. The construction steps matches the transaction processes which are described in Fig. 1.

System Initialization. It is executed by a trusted third party (TTP) or distributed nodes, outputting public parameters and a commitment key pair:

(a) The TTP selects a bilinear group system$(G_1, G_2, G_T, e, p, g_1, g_2)$.
(b) It randomly generates the committer's private key $sk \in Z_p^*$ and computes the public key $pk = g_2^{sk}$.
(c) It generates change constraint parameters. It selects $\alpha \in Z_p^*$ as the constraint coefficient and computes $H = g_1^{\alpha} \in G_1$ to bind the relationship between messages before and after changes.

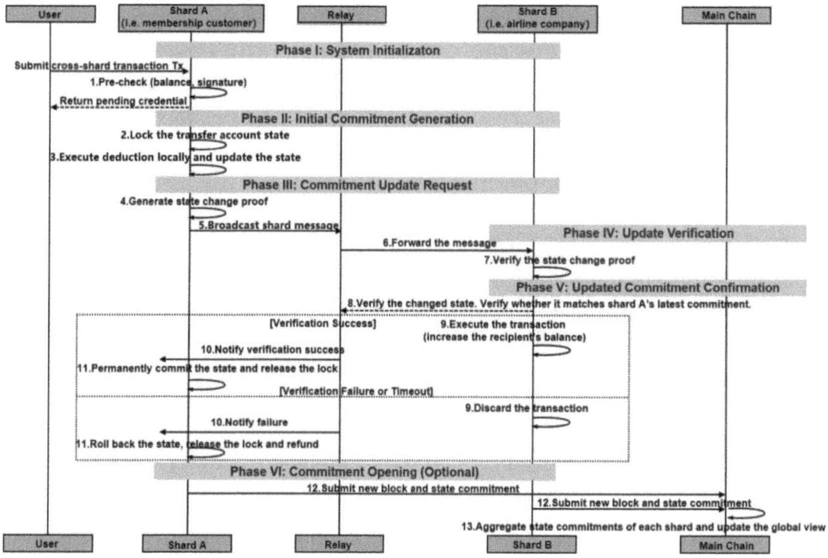

Fig. 1. Cross-Shard Transfer Transaction Process in aviation e-commerce scenario.

(d) It publishes public parameters $PP = (G_1, G_2, G_T, e, p, g_1, g_2, pk, H)$. The committer keeps *sk*, and the TTP can go offline after initialization (no participation in subsequent processes).

Initial Commitment Generation. The committer generates a commitment for the initial message $m_0 \in M$. The process is as follows.

(a) The committer randomly selects an initial random number $r_0 \in R$ to hide m_0 and enhance confidentiality.
(b) The committer computes the initial commitment $C_0 \in G_1$:

$$C_0 = g_1^{m_0} \cdot H^{r_0} = g_1^{m_0 + \alpha r_0}$$

where $H = g_1^{\alpha}$ is the constraint parameter generated in the initialization phase. This structure binds m_0 and r_0 to form an indistinguishable commitment.
(c) The committer publishes C_0 to the verifier and secretly stores (m_0, r_0) for subsequent updates or proofs.
(d) The verifier only receives C_0 without performing verification.

Commitment Update Request. When the committer needs to update the message from m_0 to $m_1 \in M$, a "change proof" is generated to prove the legality of the update. The process is as follows.

(a) Compute the variation.

Compute the message variation: The committer determines the new message m_1 and calculates the message variation $\Delta\mathrm{m} = m_1 - m_0 \in Z_p$.
Compute the random number variation: The committer randomly selects a new random number $r_1 \in R$ and computes $\Delta\mathrm{r} = r_1 - r_0 \in Z_p^*$.

(b) Generate the change proof $\pi = (A, B)$.
Compute the private key binding term $A : A = g_1^{sk\cdot(\Delta\mathrm{m}+\alpha\Delta r)} \in G_1$. It proves that the committer holds the legitimate private key sk and the committer is the initiator of the update.
Compute the change consistency term $B : B = g_1^{\Delta\mathrm{m}+\alpha\Delta r} \in G_1$. It proves that the update operation complies with the commitment structure.

(c) Compute the new candidate commitment C_1^*.

$$C_1^* = C_0 \cdot B = g_1^{m_0+\alpha r_0} \cdot g_1^{\Delta\mathrm{m}+\alpha\Delta r} = g_1^{m_1+\alpha r_1}$$

(d) The committer sends the update request package (C_0, C_1^*, π) to the verifier.

Update Verification. After receiving the update request, the verifier verifies the legality of π using public parameters. The process is as follows.

(a) Private key binding verification. Check if $e(A, g_2) = e(B, pk)$. The equation holds if the committer holds the legitimate private key and is the update initiator.

$$e(A, g_2) = e\left(g_1^{sk\cdot(\Delta\mathrm{m}+\alpha\Delta r)}, g_2\right) = e(g_1, g_2)^{sk\cdot(\Delta\mathrm{m}+\alpha\Delta r)}$$

$$e(B, pk) = e\left(g_1^{\Delta\mathrm{m}+\alpha\Delta r}, g_2^{sk}\right) = e(g_1, g_2)^{sk\cdot(\Delta\mathrm{m}+\alpha\Delta r)}$$

The validity of the equation indicates that the committer is indeed in possession of the legitimate private key sk.

(b) Change consistency verification: Check if $C_1^* = C_0 \cdot B$. The equation holds if the new candidate commitment is a legitimate update based on the old commitment, complying with the inherent consistency of the commitment structure $g_1^{m+\alpha r}$.

(c) Result determination: Accept C_1^* as the valid new commitment if both verifications pass. Otherwise, reject the update and keep C_0 valid.

Updated Commitment Confirmation. After successful verification, the verifier sends a "verification passed" feedback to the committer.

(a) The committer publicly confirms the new commitment $C_1 = C_1^*$ and secretly updates the stored private data from $(m_0, r_0)$to (m_1, r_1), securely discarding the old random number.

(b) The verifier records C_1 as the current valid commitment, and C_0 becomes invalid. It is usually marked as a "historical commitment" for auditing or traceability.

Commitment Opening (Optional). For the scenario such as auditing, the committer can open the commitment by publishing (m, r). The verifier verifies as follows:

$$e(C, g_2) = e(g_1^m \cdot H^r, g_2) = e(g_1, g_2)^m \cdot e(g_1^\alpha, g_2)^r = e(g_1, g_2)^{m+\alpha r}$$

The equation holds if C is legitimately generated by m and r according to the scheme's rules.

5 Performance Analysis

5.1 Theoretical Analysis

Table 1 shows the efficiency of our proposed scheme in detail. We denote t_e as one exponent operation time in G, t_m as one multiplication operation time in G and t_p as one pairing operation time. We ignore the addition operation time in G as they are relative fast. Table 2 shows the theoretical comparison results among different schemes. A comparative analysis reveals that our proposed scheme, which supports dynamic commitment updates, holds these advantages: it achieves the commitment generation and verification complexity of *O(1)*, and requires minimal storage overhead, which only needs to store the current commitment and keys, without the need for full historical commitments as other schemes. Furthermore, the scheme retains the privacy benefits of ZKPs while simultaneously avoiding the trusted setup requirement inherent in ZK-SNARKs and overcoming the static, non-updatable limitation of Pedersen commitments.

Table 1. The efficiency of the proposed scheme

Process	Computational Time	Computational Complexity
Setup	$2t_e$	*O(1)*
Initial Commit	$2t_e + t_m$	*O(1)*
Update Request	$2t_e + t_m$	*O(1)*
Update Verification	$2t_p + t_m$	*O(1)*
Confirmation	0	*O(1)*
Opening	t_p	*O(1)*

5.2 Experimental Performance

To verify the performance of the proposed dynamic updatable zero-knowledge proof commitment scheme for cross-shard transactions, we select general ZKP scheme (ZK-SNARK [22]), traditional static commitment scheme (Pedersen Commitment [28]), and typical sharding blockchain scheme (OmniLedger [14])

Table 2. The theoretical analysis of different schemes

Comparison Dimension	Proposed Scheme	ZK-SNARKs	Pedersen	OmniLedger
Commitment Generation Complexity	*O(1)*	*O(n)*	*O(1)*	*O(k)*
Verification Complexity	*O(1)*	*O(1)*	*O(n)*	*O(k)*
Storage Overhead	Low	Medium	Medium	High
Dynamic Update Support	Yes	No	No	Limited
Privacy Preservation Support	Yes	Yes	Limited	Limited

as comparison objects. The test environment is configured as follows: the host machine uses an Intel i9-12900KF processor, running an Ubuntu system in a virtual machine with 2 CPU cores and 4GB of RAM allocated. The test program is written in Golang and performs benchmarking tests on cryptographic schemes, evaluating two key metrics: commitment generation time and update verification time. Test results are shown in Table 3. The unit ms/op means milliseconds per operation. The commitment generation time of our proposal is only 5 ms/op. It is slightly slower than Pedersen, but far outperforming ZK-SNARK and OmniLedger. The proposed scheme obviously reduces the computational overhead of the state change proof by over 70% compared to existing schemes. Although the update verification time of 30 ms/op is higher than ZK-SNARK and Pedersen, its *O(1)* complexity ensures stable performance under high concurrency, vastly outperforming OmniLedger.

Table 3. The commitment generation and update verification time of different schemes

Scheme	Commitment Generation Time	Update Verification Time
Our proposal	5 ms/op	30 ms/op
ZK-SNARKs	750 ms/op	2.8 ms/op
Pedersen	12 ms/op	8 ms/op
OmniLedger	420 ms/op	185 ms/op

We also evaluate the performance through throughput and latency. The core parameters for the test are as follows: the test is set up with a transaction size of 128 bytes, a batch size ranging from 1k to 100k. It is conducted in a distributed network with 10 shards, each containing 32 nodes. Test results are shown in Fig. 2. Our proposed scheme achieves the highest throughput, with latency close to zero in the low-throughput range, showing only a slight increase to about 25 s at peak throughput. It demonstrates the high efficiency of our scheme in high-concurrency scenarios. The Omniledger has the lowest throughput, approximately 4 ktx/s, yet exhibits the highest latency due to its reliance on signature verification and 2PC, which causes communication and verification overheads increasing under high concurrency. ZK-SNARK still faces limited performance gains as its latency is significantly constrained by the high time cost of the zero-knowledge proof phase. The Pedersen offers balanced overall performance but lacks dynamic adaptability due to its static parameters, resulting in insufficient flexibility in complex scenarios.

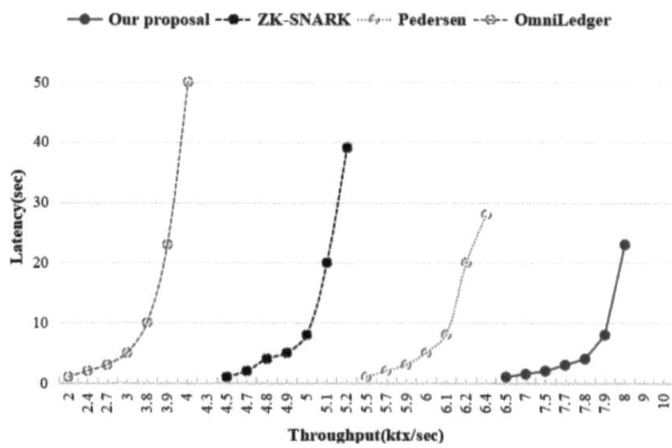

Fig. 2. The transaction throughput and latency of different schemes.

6 Conclusion

This paper proposed a dynamically updatable ZKP commitment scheme for cross-shard transactions in sharding blockchains. The scheme balances privacy protection and verifiability by converting full-state proofs into change consistency proofs. Security analysis confirms the scheme's security and unforgeability under standard cryptographic assumptions. Performance evaluations demonstrate its superiority over existing schemes in terms of computational overhead and transaction latency.

Acknowledgments. This paper is supported by Beijing Natural Science Foundation (L251003), and Research Foundation for Youth Scholars of Civil Aviation Management Institute of China (No. 23QN06).

References

1. Qiu, M., Qiu, H., et al.: Secure data sharing through Untrusted clouds with blockchain-enhanced key management. SmartBlock, 11–16 (2020)
2. Gai, K., Wu, Y., et al.: Differential privacy-based blockchain for industrial internet-of-things. IEEE TII **16**(6), 4156–4165 (2019)
3. Huang, J., Kong, L., et al.: BlockSense: towards trustworthy mobile crowdsensing via proof-of-data blockchain. IEEE T. Mob. Comput. **23**(2), 1016–1033

4. Buterin, V.: A next-generation smart contracts and decentralized application platform. In: Ethereum White Paper (2014)
5. Luu, L., Narayanan, V., Zheng, C.: A secure sharding protocol for open blockchains. In: ACM CCS, pp. 17–30 (2016)
6. Wang, S., Yuan, Y., Wang, X., et al.: An overview of smart contract: architecture, applications, and future trends. In: IEEE S & P, pp. 108–113 (2018)
7. Liu, A., Chen, J., He, K., et al.: DynaShard: secure and adaptive blockchain sharding protocol with hybrid consensus and dynamic shard management. IEEE Internet Things J. **12**(5), 5462–5475 (2025)
8. Li, M., Lin, Y., Wang, W., et al.: SP-chain: boosting intrashard and cross-shard security and performance in blockchain sharding. IEEE Internet Things J. **12**(5), 31737–31753 (2025)
9. Al-Bassam, M., Sonnino, A.: Chainspace: a sharding smart contracts platform. In: Proceedings ACM CCS, pp. 1202–1215 (2018)
10. Ben-Sasson, E., Chiesa, A., et al.: Zerocash: decentralized anonymous payments from bitcoin. In: IEEE S & P, pp. 459–474 (2014)
11. Boneh, D., Lewi, K.: Updatable encryption with keyword search. In: ACM CCS, pp. 1133–1144 (2013)
12. Boneh, D., Montgomery, H., Raghunathan, A.: Post-quantum updatable encryption. In: ACM CCS, pp. 2157–2171 (2022)
13. Gervais, A., Karame, G.O., et al.: On the security and performance of proof of work blockchains. IEEE TIFS **11**(9), 1914–1929 (2016)
14. Kokoris-Kogias, E., Jovanovic, P., et al.: OmniLedger: a secure, scale-out, decentralized ledger. In: 2018 IEEE S& P, pp. 583–598 (2018)
15. Zamani, M., Movahedi, M., Raykova, M.: Rapidchain: scaling blockchain via full sharding. In: ACM CCS, pp. 931–948 (2018)
16. Liu, Y., Zhao, Z., Zhao, B., et al.: Kronos: a secure and generic sharding blockchain consensus with optimized overhead. In: NDSS, pp. 1–15 (2025)
17. Zhiqiang, D., Zhang, W., et al.: Cross shard leader accountability protocol based on two phase atomic commit. Sci. Rep. **14**(1), 64945 (2024)
18. Lu, Y.: AdaptShard: an optimistic cross-shard transaction processing protocol for account-based blockchains. In: International Conference on Blockchain Technology and Applications, pp. 89–103 (2025)
19. Liu, Y., Liu, A., et al.: Realizing corrupted-shard tolerance: a sharding blockchain with preserving global resilience. In: ACM CCS, pp. 1–20 (2025)
20. Liu, A., Liu, Y., Wu, Q., et al.: CHERUBIM: a secure and highly parallel cross-shard consensus using quadruple pipelined two-phase commit for sharding blockchains. In: IEEE TIFS, pp. 3178–3193 (2024)
21. Jo, Y., Park, C.: A Hierarchical Sharded Blockchain Balancing Performance and Availability. arXiv preprint (2025)
22. Groth, J.: On the size of pairing-based non-interactive arguments. In: Fischlin, M., Coron, J.-S. (eds.) EUROCRYPT 2016. LNCS, vol. 9666, pp. 305–326. Springer, Heidelberg (2016). https://doi.org/10.1007/978-3-662-49896-5_11
23. Ben-Sasson, E., Chiesa, A., Trome, E., et al.: Scalable zero knowledge with no trusted setup. Commun. ACM **62**(11), 103–111 (2019)
24. Miers, I., Garman, C., Green, M., et al.: Zerocoin: anonymous distributed e-cash from bitcoin. In: IEEE S & P, pp. 397–411 (2013)
25. Zhou, X., Meng, Z., Liu, Y.: Fast settlement scheme of aviation business privacy preservation based on consortium blockchain. In: IEEE PDCA, pp. 1460–1468 (2021)

26. Kokoris-Kogias, E.: Enhancing bitcoin security and performance with strong consistency via collective signing. In: 25th SOSP, pp. 3–18 (2015)
27. Kate, A.: Constant-size commitments to polynomials and their applications. In: International Conference on TACIS, pp. 177–194 (2010)
28. Boneh, D., Naor, M.: Timed commitments. In: Bellare, M. (ed.) CRYPTO 2000. LNCS, vol. 1880, pp. 236–254. Springer, Heidelberg (2000). https://doi.org/10.1007/3-540-44598-6_15
29. Nishimaki, R.: Directionless updatable encryption. In: ACM CCS, pp. 1741–1758 (2020)
30. Song, D., Wagner, D., Perrig, A.: Practical techniques for searches on encrypted data. In: IEEE S & P, pp. 44–55. IEEE (2000)
31. Gao, Y., Iqbal, S., et al.: Performance and power analysis of high-density multi-GPGPU architectures: a preliminary case study. In: IEEE 17th HPCC (2015)
32. Zhao, H., Chen, M., et al.: A novel pre-cache schema for high performance Android system. Futur. Gener. Comput. Syst. **56**, 766–772 (2016)
33. Qiu, M., Sha, E., et al.: minimization with loop fusion and multi-functional-unit scheduling for multidimensional DSP. JPDC **68**(4), 443–455 (2008)
34. Qiu, H., Qiu, M., Lu, R.: Secure V2X communication network based on intelligent PKI and edge computing. IEEE Netw. **34**(2), 172–178 (2019)
35. Gai, K., Qiu, M., Elnagdy, S.: A novel secure big data cyber incident analytics framework for cloud-based cybersecurity insurance. IEEE BigDataSecurity (2016)
36. Zeng, Y., Pan, M., et al.: Narcissus: a practical clean-label backdoor attack with limited information. In: ACM CCS (2023)

Online Automatic Modulation Classification Based on Distributional Signal Representation

Xinpeng Li[1,2], Zile Jiang[1], Kai Ming Ting[1,2](✉), and Ye Zhu[3]

[1] State Key Laboratory for Novel Software Technology, Nanjing University, Nanjing 210023, China
lixp@lamda.nju.edu.cn, zilerion99@gmail.com

[2] School of Artificial Intelligence, Nanjing University, Nanjing 210023, China
tingkm@nju.edu.cn

[3] School of Information Technology, Deakin University, Geelong 3125, VIC, Australia
ye.zhu@ieee.org

Abstract. Automatic Modulation Classification (AMC), as a crucial technique in modern non-cooperative communication networks, plays a key role in various civil and military applications. However, existing AMC methods based on deep learning are often excessively complex and restricted to batch-mode processing due to their high computational overhead. Furthermore, they usually rely on indirect signal representations that can compromise performance. To address these issues, this paper introduces a new online AMC scheme based on a direct and lossless distributional representation of signals. It works well in online settings under realistic time-varying channel conditions. Through extensive experiments in online settings, we demonstrate the effectiveness of the proposed classifier. Our results indicate that the proposed approach outperforms existing baseline models, including two advanced deep learning classifiers. Moreover, it distinguishes itself as the first online classifier for AMC with linear time complexity, which marks a significant efficiency boost for real-time applications.

Keywords: Automatic modulation classification · Signal representation · Distributional kernel · Online learning · Time-varying channel conditions

1 Introduction

With the rapid development of next-generation communication technologies, automatic modulation classification (AMC) has come to play a significant role in modern communication networks. On the receiver side, AMC monitors and automatically recognizes the modulation format of incoming signals in real-time, ensuring correct demodulation and reliable data recovery [28].

X. Li and Z. Jiang—Equal contribution.

J. Niu et al. (Eds.): KSEM 2026, LNAI 16631, pp. 198–210, 2027.
https://doi.org/10.1007/978-981-92-2759-4_15

While deep learning (DL)-based classifiers have emerged as a popular paradigm for AMC, they are constrained by significant drawbacks that often compromise their effectiveness in practical applications. First, most DL-based models rely on indirect representations of signals, which require a separate data conversion step prior to classification that could potentially result in information loss. Second, their complex architectures make hyperparameter tuning and training a resource-intensive and time-consuming process [2]. Finally, their reliance on offline batch training makes them unable to adapt to realistic time-varying channel conditions, leading to significant performance degradation when a mismatch occurs between training and deployment environments. While integrating an online update mechanism could compensate for this, it introduces further complexity.

To overcome these issues, this paper introduces IDK-OGD, a novel online scheme for AMC. The main contributions are:

1. We introduce an insight that the constellation diagram of a baseband signal sequence can be losslessly represented as a distribution. This distributional representation of signals enables the use of a distributional kernel for both extracting knowledge from signals as high-dimensional embeddings and measuring similarity between signals. It offers a fundamentally new paradigm for understanding and extracting information from signals in AMC tasks.
2. We propose IDK-OGD, an online AMC scheme that integrates the Isolation Distributional Kernel (IDK) [19] to embed the distribution exhibited in a constellation diagram with the Online Gradient Descent (OGD) classifier [7,18]. IDK-OGD is the first kernel-based classifier with linear time complexity that works well in online AMC environments where there is a mismatch between the channel conditions of the training and testing data.
3. Through extensive experiments comparing IDK-OGD against advanced DL-based methods and other baselines, we demonstrate its effectiveness and practicality on both synthetic and real-world datasets, particularly under challenging mismatched and time-varying channel conditions.

2 Related Work

Over the past few years, with the remarkable advancement of DL, numerous DL-based AMC methods have been proposed [4,8,22]. These DL-based methods are generally categorized into four types based on their signal representation strategy, *i.e.*, engineered feature, image, sequence, and combined representations [14]. We analyze these representations below to examine how prior research has utilized different techniques to represent signals.

Engineered feature representations such as high-order cumulants can be calculated from the original baseband signals and are prevalent in DL-based AMC frameworks [6,21]. However, these features require manual extraction tailored to the candidate modulation formats and channel conditions, limiting their flexibility. *Image representation*: Inspired by the success of DL in processing images, some researchers have proposed converting signals into fixed-resolution images to facilitate the application of image-based DL methods in AMC [13,17]. While such methods benefit from the powerful capability of DL in extracting knowledge from images, the image conversion process inevitably introduces noise and causes information loss. *Sequence representation*: these methods operate on sequences: either the raw I/Q baseband signal sequences themselves [3,12], or some transformed versions of these signals [5,15]. The efficacy of these methods hinges on the model's ability to extract robust temporal features from the sequences. *Combined representations* try to exploit the advantages of multiple signal representations [23,27]. However, whether these combinations yield a synergistic effect, or simply increase computational overhead, remains poorly understood.

To summarize, most current DL-based methods rely on indirect representations that incur information loss during the data conversion. In contrast, we propose a direct, lossless distributional signal representation in the next section.

3 Distributional Signal Representation

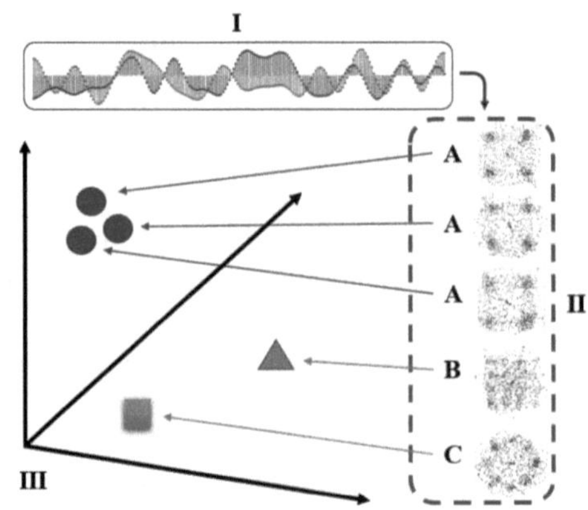

Fig. 1. Sketch of distributional signal representation for AMC (different letters, *i.e.*, A, B & C, stand for different modulation formats).

In this paper, we focus on digital amplitude-phase (A/P) modulated signals, *e.g.*, amplitude-shift keying (ASK), phase-shift keying (PSK), amplitude and phase-shift keying (APSK), and quadrature amplitude modulation (QAM). These modulation formats find widespread utilization in practical wireless communications and pose challenges for conventional AMC schemes.

In general, a baseband signal $r(t)$ received from a wireless channel can be expressed as:

$$r(t) = s(t) * c(t) + w(t) \tag{1}$$

where $s(t)$ denotes the transmitted baseband signal, $c(t)$ is the channel impulse response, $w(t)$ represents the additive noise, and $*$ is a convolution operator.

The transmitted A/P modulated baseband signal $s(t)$ with N symbols can be expressed as:

$$s(t) = \sum_{n=1}^{N} a_n \exp(j\varphi_n) g(t - nT_s) \tag{2}$$

and

$$a_n \exp(j\varphi_n) = a_n \cos\varphi_n + j \cdot a_n \sin\varphi_n = I_n + j \cdot Q_n \tag{3}$$

where a_n and φ_n are the amplitude and phase of the n-th symbol; $g(t)$ signifies the pulse shaping filter; T_s is the symbol duration; and I_n and Q_n denote the in-phase (I) and quadrature (Q) components of the n-th symbol, respectively.

In essence, the difference between two A/P modulation formats lies in the arrangements of A/P pairs (a_n, φ_n) of all N symbols [9].

As shown in Eq. 3, an A/P modulated signal consists of a sequence of complex data points, of which the real and imaginary components are the I and Q components of the signal, respectively. As shown in Fig. 1 from block I to II, this sequence can be seen as a scatter plot of a set of points in a two-dimensional complex space of I and Q axes, which is commonly referred to as a constellation diagram [1]. With Eq. 3, it is evident that the constellation diagram of an A/P modulated signal encompasses all the amplitude and phase information of the signal. Consequently, constellation diagrams are equivalent to the original signal sequences for AMC purposes, preserving all relevant information.

Our insight is that **a signal S in the I/Q space (or constellation diagram) can be treated as a set of independent and identically distributed (i.i.d.) points x drawn from an unknown probability distribution $\mathcal{P}_S$, *i.e.*, $x \sim \mathcal{P}_S$, without loss of information**.

With this insight, the task of AMC in identifying the unknown modulation format of a signal S can be achieved by maximizing the similarity between distribution $\mathcal{P}_S$ and the distribution $\mathcal{P}_{S_\alpha}$ of a modulation format α out of m candidate modulation formats $\{M_1, M_2, \cdots, M_m\}$. It is formally expressed as:

$$\mathrm{AMC}(S) = \underset{\alpha \in \{M_1, M_2, \cdots, M_m\}}{\arg\max} \mathcal{K}(\mathcal{P}_S, \mathcal{P}_{S_\alpha}) \tag{4}$$

where $\mathcal{K}$ is a distributional kernel which measures the similarity between two distributions; and S_α is the i.i.d. sample set of signals with modulation format α. Equation 4 returns the modulation format α of $\mathcal{P}_{S_\alpha}$ which is most similar to $\mathcal{P}_S$.

The task is made simple by using a feature mapping derived from $\mathcal{K}$ with an injective mapping guarantee [10,19] such that signals of the same modulation format are mapped into the same region in the high-dimensional feature space, while those of different modulation formats are mapped into different regions, as shown in Fig. 1 (from II to III). This ensures a higher similarity between signal distributions sharing the same modulation format.

Note that the choice of signal representation plays a pivotal role in determining the performance of an AMC classifier. The sequence and image representations commonly utilized in DL necessitate the transformation of the original signals into specific sequential or grid-based formats as input, which may result in unnecessary information loss and the introduction of noise. In contrast, our proposed distributional signal representation is a direct approach that preserves the original signals within their native I/Q domains in a two-dimensional I/Q signal space, eliminating the need for conversion, and thus the associated information loss and potential corruption.

4 Proposed Method

Kernel methods are widely employed in classification and pattern recognition tasks. With the above insight of distributional signal representation, we propose to use a recent Isolation Distributional Kernel (IDK) [19] to measure the similarity between two signals in their distributional representation. IDK is a well-established method that has already been applied in various applications, and detailed specifications can be found in [19]. The feature mapping of IDK, which maps a distribution $\mathcal{P}_S$ (from which the set of points $S \subset \mathbb{R}^d$ is drawn) to a single point in a high-dimensional feature space known as the Reproducing Kernel Hilbert Space (RKHS) $\mathcal{H}$ [16], is derived via kernel mean embedding [10] using the feature mapping $\Phi(x)$ of the point-wise Isolation Kernel (IK) [20,25]:

$$\widehat{\Phi}(\mathcal{P}_S) = \frac{1}{|S|} \sum_{x \in S} \Phi(x) \tag{5}$$

The similarity between two distributions $\mathcal{P}_S$, $\mathcal{P}_T$ measured by IDK is given as:

$$\mathcal{K}(\mathcal{P}_S, \mathcal{P}_T) = \left\langle \widehat{\Phi}(\mathcal{P}_S), \widehat{\Phi}(\mathcal{P}_T) \right\rangle \tag{6}$$

A key property of IDK is its finite-dimensional, data-dependent feature mapping derived directly from a given dataset to yield better task-specific performance [20]. The derivation is highly efficient as it bypasses an explicit learning process. Furthermore, IDK offers an injective mapping guarantee, ensuring that two distributions $\mathcal{P}_S$ and $\mathcal{P}_T$ are mapped to the same point in $\mathcal{H}$ only when they are exactly identical, *i.e.*, $\| \widehat{\Phi}(\mathcal{P}_S) - \widehat{\Phi}(\mathcal{P}_T) \|_{\mathcal{H}} = 0$ if and only if $\mathcal{P}_S = \mathcal{P}_T$ [24]. This is a significant theoretical advantage, as none of the existing representations used in DL-based methods can provide a similar guarantee.

Our proposed IDK-OGD classifier is designed for online AMC by integrating IDK for the embedding of signals with a large-scale online classifier Online Gradient Descent (OGD) [7]. It builds upon IK-OGD which has proven effective in conventional data stream contexts [18]. We adapt IK-OGD for the AMC task by substituting the point-wise IK with the distributional IDK to accommodate the distributional representation of I/Q baseband signals, and extending the binary classifier to a multi-class variant capable of discriminating between multiple modulation formats. This novel application is underpinned by the distributional signal representation we introduced, which makes these signals amenable to powerful distributional kernel-based online learning techniques.

Algorithm 1 IDK-OGD

Input:

m - The number of modulation formats
$\widehat{\Phi}_j$ - IDK feature mapping of modulation format j
η - Learning rate

Output:

Predicted modulation format $\widehat{c_i}$ for each signal S_i

1: Initialize weight vector $\mathbf{w}_j$ to $\mathbf{0}$ for $j = 1, \ldots, m$
2: **while** a new batch of signals $\mathcal{B}$ arrives **do**
3:     **for** $i = 1 : |\mathcal{B}|$ **do**
4:         **for** $j = 1 : m$ **do**
5:             $g_{i,j} = \left\langle \mathbf{w}_j, \widehat{\Phi}_j(\mathcal{P}_{S_i}) \right\rangle$
6:         **end for**
7:         $\widehat{c_i} = \arg\max_j \ g_{i,j}$
8:     **end for** ▷ Classification stage ends
9:     **if** ground-truth labels c_i for $S_i \in \mathcal{B}$ are available **then**
10:         **for** $i = 1 : |\mathcal{B}|$ **do**
11:             $k_i = \begin{cases} 1, & \text{if } c_i = \widehat{c_i} \\ -1, & \text{if } c_i \neq \widehat{c_i} \end{cases}$
12:             **for** $j = 1 : m$ **do**
13:                 $\mathbf{w}_j = \mathbf{w}_j - \eta \nabla L(g_{i,j}; k_i) k_i \widehat{\Phi}_j(\mathcal{P}_{S_i})$
▷ ∇L is the gradient of the hinge loss function L
14:             **end for**
15:         **end for**
16:     **end if** ▷ Online model update stage ends
17: **end while**

The operational workflow of the proposed IDK-OGD classifier is as follows. Suppose there are m candidate modulation formats denoted by $M_1, M_2, \cdots, M_m$. IDK-OGD is first initialized using a batch of training data to construct m distinct IDK feature mappings. Each feature mapping, $\widehat{\Phi}_j$, is derived exclusively from the training signals corresponding to a single modulation format M_j. During the classification stage, an incoming I/Q baseband signal is passed through all m feature mappings, and a corresponding set of m OGD classifiers generates a decision score for each class. The final prediction is determined by selecting the modulation format with the highest score. Subsequently, all OGD classifiers are updated simultaneously if the ground-truth labels for the signals are available. If labels are unavailable, the model suspends the update mechanism and functions as a robust static classifier.

Algorithm 1 provides the pseudo-code for the proposed IDK-OGD classifier, detailing the classification and online update stages. It is worth noting that the calculations for each modulation format (as shown in the for-loops at lines 4–6 and 12–14) are independent, allowing IDK-OGD to be implemented using a parallel architecture, which significantly improves its computational efficiency.

5 Experiments

5.1 Experimental Settings

Our experiments utilize the open-source RadioML2018.01A dataset [11] and synthetic datasets generated via MATLAB Communications Toolbox. The RadioML2018.01A dataset offers diverse 1024-point I/Q signals with various channel effects such as carrier frequency offset, multipath fading, sample rate offset, *etc.*, which make the task more challenging. However, it provides labels exclusively for signal-to-noise ratio (SNR), which quantifies additive white Gaussian noise (AWGN), lacking labels for other impairments such as phase noise or I/Q amplitude imbalance. Our synthetic data was generated to enable controlled studies under these effects. The evaluation focuses on ten modulation formats (4ASK, 8ASK, BPSK, QPSK, 8PSK, 16APSK, 32APSK, 16QAM, 32QAM, and 64QAM) for their widespread use and the challenges they pose to AMC.

Note that most existing AMC methods operate under the assumption that training and testing data share identical and fixed channel conditions. However, this assumption is often violated in real-world applications where channel conditions are time-varying and key parameters like SNR cannot be accurately estimated in real-time. Therefore, our experiments are designed to assess classifier performance under mismatched conditions, where the channel conditions of the testing data intentionally deviate from those of the training data. To simulate real-time data arrival, the testing set is organized into sequential batches of 100 signal samples, which are processed by the classifiers one by one; and to simulate time-varying channel conditions, every 10 batches are grouped together to share the identical channel conditions, while different groups of signal batches may exhibit different channel conditions.

We compare the proposed IDK-OGD classifier against various baselines for AMC, including fKNN [29], an online feature-based classifier using engineered high-order moments, and two advanced DL-based models: a Convolutional Neural Networks (CNN) using image for signal representation [17][1] and a Adaptive Wavelet Network (AWN) with sequence representations [26]. We also compare with IDK-SVM, a variant that pairs the IDK representation with a conventional, non-online Support Vector Machine (SVM) classifier, allowing for a direct evaluation of our method's effectiveness due to an online classifier. These methods illustrate three distinct adaptation strategies: incremental online update (IDK-OGD), retraining on cumulative data (fKNN), and static batch-learning (CNN, AWN, IDK-SVM)[2].

[1] While the CNN baseline [17] claims to have an online version involving a retraining process, only its no-retraining version is accessible. We therefore adopted the static version for comparison.

[2] For the IDK component, the hyperparameters are set to $\psi = 128$ and $t = 75$. Both OGD and SVM utilize a linear kernel, with the box constraint for SVM set to $C = 980$. For the fKNN baseline, the number of neighbors is set to $k = 15$. The hyperparameters for the CNN and AWN models are tuned according to the specifications provided in their respective original works [17,26].

The first two experiments are conducted on the RadioML2018.01A dataset. In both experiments, the testing sets are maintained at high SNR, while the training sets exhibit low SNR in the first case and medium SNR in the second. In the latter configuration, the training SNR range partially overlaps with that of the testing set. Furthermore, we design four additional experiments with mismatched training and testing channel conditions and different channel impairments, including AWGN, phase noise, I/Q amplitude imbalance, and a combination of all the three impairments. These experiments are conducted on synthetic datasets to facilitate controlled studies of the performance of the classifiers under different mismatched time-varying channel conditions. For initialization, all classifiers are trained on the identical dataset, of which the size matches the total testing set (110,000 samples in the first two experiments and 11,000 samples in the others).

5.2 Experimental Results

Table 1. Experimental results across six scenarios on the RadioML2018.01A and synthetic datasets, including: (a) mismatched and (b) overlapping SNR on RadioML2018.01A; and mismatched (c) SNR, (d) phase noise, (e) I/Q amplitude imbalance, and (f) all three impairments combined on synthetic datasets. In each plot, the parameters for the training and testing channel conditions are specified at the top.

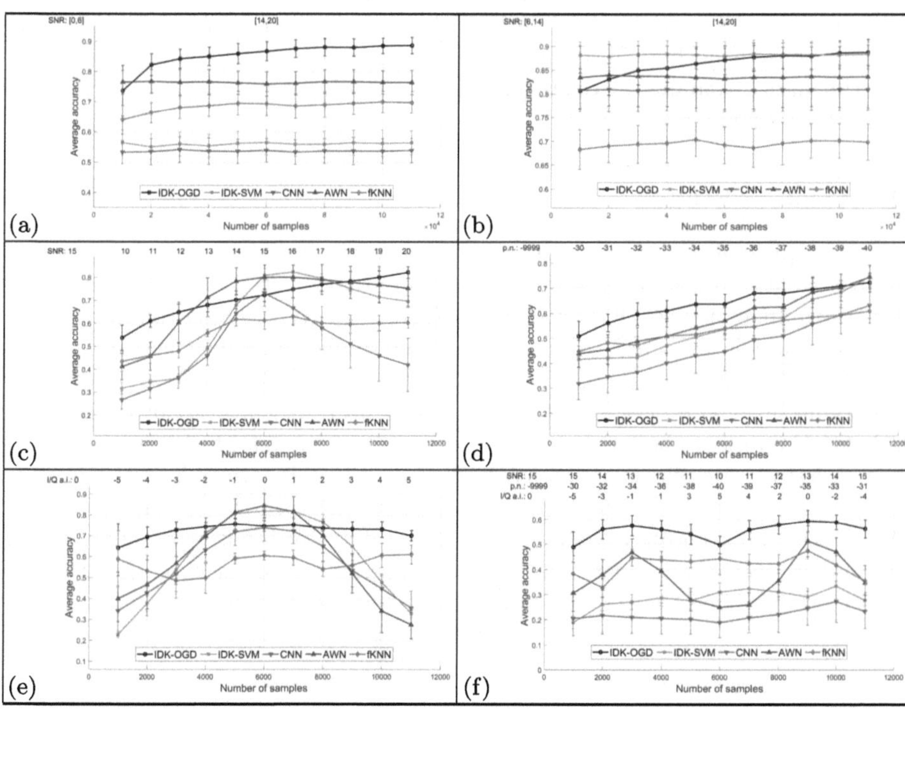

The experimental results are presented in Table 1, where classifier performance is evaluated based on the average prediction accuracy over 10 trials. Each subfigure illustrates a distinct experimental scenario, with the parameters listed at the top specifying the fixed training condition (leftmost) and the time-varying testing channel conditions. The curves below plot the corresponding accuracy of each method as the testing environment changes. Specifically, subfigures (a)–(b) show results on the RadioML2018.01A dataset for mismatched and overlapping SNR, while subfigures (c)–(f) use synthetic data to assess performance under mismatched SNR, phase noise, I/Q imbalance, and a combination of them all.

The primary finding from our experiments is the superior performance of the proposed IDK-OGD. As shown in Table 1 (a) and (b), IDK-OGD maintains high accuracy on the RadioML2018.01A dataset under both complete and partial SNR mismatch. While its initial accuracy is slightly below that of AWN in both cases, its online update mechanism enables rapid adaptation to new testing channel conditions. By learning from incoming signal batches, IDK-OGD quickly surpasses all other methods. This robustness is further validated on the synthetic datasets (subfigures (c)–(f)). In these scenarios, the performance of all baseline methods degrades significantly in the presence of mismatched impairments, whereas IDK-OGD consistently outperforms them by a large margin.

The batch-learning baselines (IDK-SVM, CNN, and AWN) exhibit similar performance trends. They achieve higher accuracy than IDK-OGD only when the testing channel conditions remain consistent with the initial training data. However, their performance degrades substantially as the mismatch between the environments increases, due to their lack of an adaptation mechanism. While the retraining-based method fKNN shows certain robustness to channel mismatch, its performance remains inconsistent and is significantly inferior to IDK-OGD across all experiments.

5.3 Ablation Study

Here we empirically demonstrate the superiority of our distributional representation over existing signal representations via an ablation study where we compare the performance of IDK-OGD with CNN-OGD and AWN-OGD (online-enabled DL-based models produced by combining the embeddings learned by the DL-based CNN/AWN with the OGD classifier). CNN-OGD utilizes the output of the pooling layer (*i.e.*, the result of the representation learning) in CNN, while AWN-OGD employs the latent embeddings prior to the final fully connected layers (*i.e.*, before classification) in AWN, for OGD classification. The result given in Fig. 2 shows that IDK-OGD almost always outperforms both CNN-OGD and AWN-OGD. This highlights the power of the distributional representation via IDK and its advantage over other signal representations used in the two DL-based methods (*i.e.*, the sequence and image representations).

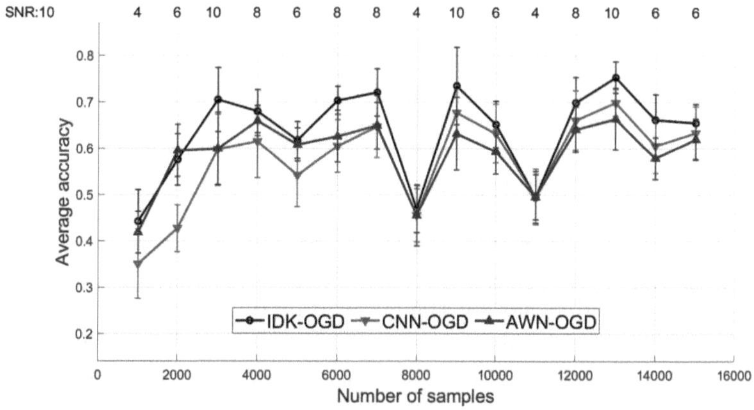

Fig. 2. The performance of IDK-OGD, CNN-OGD and AWN-OGD.

5.4 Runtime Comparison

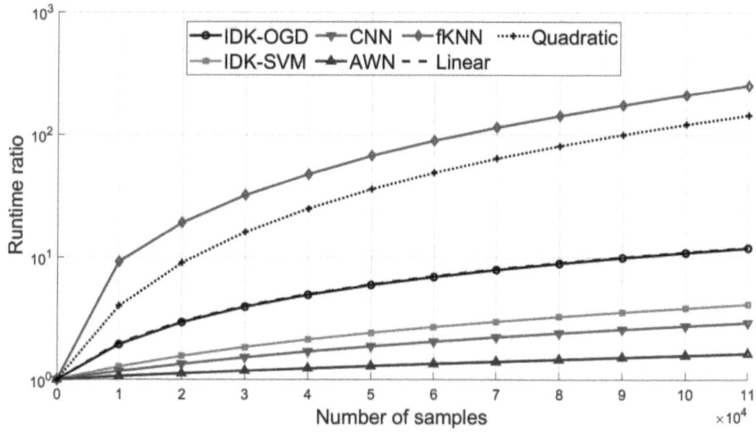

Fig. 3. Runtime ratio for the classifiers.

Figure 3 shows the ratio of the total runtime to the training time, where the IDK-OGD curve overlaps with the linear curve, demonstrating the superior scalability of IDK-OGD. Its runtime grows linearly with the input data size n, aligning with its complexity of $O(nmLt\psi)$. The other terms, *i.e.*, the number of modulation formats m, signal length L, and the IDK parameters t and ψ, are constants. In contrast, fKNN's retraining process results in quadratic complexity. While the batch-learning baselines (IDK-SVM, CNN, AWN) have rapid inference, they are non-adaptive, and retraining them would be computationally infeasible. The linear-time online update of IDK-OGD is, to our knowledge, unique among AMC methods, establishing its efficiency for real-time deployment.

6 Conclusions

In this paper, we introduce a novel distributional signal representation that bridges the conceptual gap between powerful distributional measures such as distributional kernels and AMC tasks.

Building on this, we propose the IDK-OGD classifier and conduct extensive evaluation to demonstrate that it is highly effective and robust as an online AMC method under realistic time-varying channel conditions, especially when a mismatch of environment occurs. Two key factors contribute to its success: a powerful distributional kernel for the embedding of signals, and a robust online learning algorithm that enables rapid adaptation. IDK-OGD is also the first online classifier with linear time complexity for AMC, as far as we know.

Looking forward, we believe the distributional signal representation presented in this work has far-reaching implications. It paves the way for a new class of solutions for AMC that has remained largely unexplored, encouraging the broader application of distributional measures, both existing and new, to this important domain.

Acknowledgments. This project is supported by the State Key Laboratory for Novel Software Technology at Nanjing University (Grant No. KFKT2024A01).

References

1. Carvalho, N.B., Schreurs, D.: Microwave and Wireless Measurement Techniques. The Cambridge RF and Microwave Engineering Series, Cambridge University Press, Cambridge, England (2013)
2. Dai, Y., Gao, X., Jing, K., Tian, B.: High-efficiency modulation classification with temporal-frequency analysis based on multi-channel filter bank. In: ICASSP 2025-2025 IEEE International Conference on Acoustics, Speech and Signal Processing (ICASSP), pp. 1–5. IEEE (2025)
3. Dong, B., et al.: A lightweight decentralized-learning-based automatic modulation classification method for resource-constrained edge devices. IEEE Internet Things J. **9**(24), 24708–24720 (2022)
4. Hu, X., Gao, G., Li, B., Wang, W., Ghannouchi, F.M.: A novel lightweight grouped gated recurrent unit for automatic modulation classification. IEEE Wirel. Commun. Lett. **13**(8), 2135–2139 (2024)
5. Khan, F.N., Zhong, K., Al-Arashi, W.H., Yu, C., Lu, C., Lau, A.P.T.: Modulation format identification in coherent receivers using deep machine learning. IEEE Photon. Technol. Lett. **28**(17), 1886–1889 (2016)
6. Lee, S.H., Kim, K.Y., Kim, J.H., Shin, Y.: Effective feature-based automatic modulation classification method using DNN algorithm. In: 2019 International Conference on Artificial Intelligence in Information and Communication (ICAIIC) (2019)
7. Lu, J., Hoi, S.C., Wang, J., Zhao, P., Liu, Z.Y.: Large scale online kernel learning. J. Mach. Learn. Res. **17**(47), 1–43 (2016)
8. Mao, Q., Hu, F., Hao, Q.: Deep learning for intelligent wireless networks: a comprehensive survey. IEEE Commun. Surv. Tutor. (2018)

9. Mao, Y., Dong, Y.Y., Sun, T., Rao, X., Dong, C.X.: Attentive Siamese networks for automatic modulation classification based on multitiming constellation diagrams. IEEE Trans. Neural Netw. Learn. Syst. (2021)
10. Muandet, K., Fukumizu, K., Sriperumbudur, B., Schölkopf, B.: Kernel mean embedding of distributions: a review and beyond. Found. Trends Mach. Learn. **10**(1–2), 1–141 (2017)
11. O'Shea, T., West, N.: Radio machine learning dataset generation with GNU radio. In: Proceedings of the GNU Radio Conference, vol. 1, no. 1 (2016)
12. O'Shea, T.J., Corgan, J., Clancy, T.C.: Convolutional radio modulation recognition networks. In: Jayne, C., Iliadis, L. (eds.) EANN 2016. CCIS, vol. 629, pp. 213–226. Springer, Cham (2016). https://doi.org/10.1007/978-3-319-44188-7_16
13. Peng, S., et al.: Modulation classification based on signal constellation diagrams and deep learning. IEEE Trans. Neural Netw. Learn. Syst. (2019)
14. Peng, S., Sun, S., Yao, Y.D.: A survey of modulation classification using deep learning: signal representation and data preprocessing. IEEE Trans. Neural Netw. Learn. Syst. **33**(12), 7020–7038 (2022)
15. Rajendran, S., Meert, W., Giustiniano, D., Lenders, V., Pollin, S.: Deep learning models for wireless signal classification with distributed low-cost spectrum sensors. IEEE Trans. Cogn. Commun. Network. (2018)
16. Schölkopf, B., Smola, A.J.: Learning with Kernels: Support Vector Machines, Regularization, Optimization, and Beyond. MIT Press, Cambridge (2001)
17. Teng, C.F., Chou, C.Y., Chen, C.H., Wu, A.Y.: Accumulated polar feature-based deep learning for efficient and lightweight automatic modulation classification with channel compensation mechanism. IEEE Trans. Veh. Technol. **69**(12), 15472–15485 (2020)
18. Ting, K.M., Wells, J.R., Washio, T.: Isolation kernel: the X factor in efficient and effective large scale online kernel learning. Data Min. Knowl. Disc. **35**, 2282–2312 (2021)
19. Ting, K.M., Xu, B.C., Washio, T., Zhou, Z.H.: Isolation distributional kernel: a new tool for point & group anomaly detections. IEEE Trans. Knowl. Data Eng. (2021)
20. Ting, K.M., Zhu, Y., Zhou, Z.H.: Isolation kernel and its effect on SVM. In: Proceedings of the 24th ACM SIGKDD International Conference on Knowledge Discovery and Data Mining, pp. 2329–2337 (2018)
21. Wang, H., Ding, W., Zhang, D., Zhang, B.: Deep convolutional neural network with wavelet decomposition for automatic modulation classification. In: 2020 15th IEEE Conference on Industrial Electronics and Applications (ICIEA) (2020)
22. Wang, Y., Gui, G., Ohtsuki, T., Adachi, F.: Multi-task learning for generalized automatic modulation classification under non-Gaussian noise with varying SNR conditions. IEEE Trans. Wirel. Commun. **20**(6), 3587–3596 (2021)
23. Wang, Y., Liu, M., Yang, J., Gui, G.: Data-driven deep learning for automatic modulation recognition in cognitive radios. IEEE Trans. Veh. Technol. **68**(4), 4074–4077 (2019)
24. Wang, Z.J., Zhu, Y., Ting, K.M.: Distribution-based trajectory clustering. In: 2023 IEEE International Conference on Data Mining (ICDM) (2023)
25. Xu, B.C., Ting, K.M., Zhou, Z.H.: Isolation set-kernel and its application to multi-instance learning. In: Proceedings of the 25th ACM SIGKDD International Conference on Knowledge Discovery and Data Mining, pp. 941–949 (2019)
26. Zhang, J., Wang, T., Feng, Z., Yang, S.: Toward the automatic modulation classification with adaptive wavelet network. IEEE Trans. Cogn. Commun. Network. **9**(3), 549–563 (2023)

27. Zhang, Z., Wang, C., Gan, C., Sun, S., Wang, M.: Automatic modulation classification using convolutional neural network with features fusion of SPWVD and BJD. IEEE Trans. Sig. Inf. Process. Netw. (2019)
28. Zheng, Q., Tian, X., Yu, L., Elhanashi, A., Saponara, S.: Recent advances in automatic modulation classification technology: methods, results, and prospects. Int. J. Intell. Syst. **2025**(1), 4067323 (2025)
29. Zhu, Z., Nandi, A.K.: Automatic Modulation Classification: Principles, Algorithms and Applications. Wiley, Hoboken (2015)

Hybrid Evolutionary-RL for Multi-objective Task Scheduling in Smart Grid Edge Computing

Runjing Zhang[1], Jinqian Chen[1], Qingfeng Li[2], Shaoyong Guo[1](✉), Zhengqiu Yang[1], and Chengkang Guan[1]

[1] Beijing University of Posts and Telecommunications (BUPT), Beijing, China
{rankingzhang,chen_jinqian,syguo,zqyang}@bupt.edu.cn, 2024010355@bupt.cn
[2] State Grid Information and Telecommunication Co., Ltd., Beijing, China

Abstract. In smart grid edge computing, the inherent conflict between global multi-objective optimization quality and real-time decision speed often leads to resource underutilization and task deadline violations, particularly under heterogeneous resource constraints. To bridge this gap, this paper proposes a hybrid Evolutionary-Reinforcement Learning framework based on an offline-to-online collaborative mechanism. Specifically, an improved NSGA-III is executed offline to construct a high-quality expert knowledge base comprising Pareto-optimal solutions. These expert demonstrations are then transferred to the online phase to initialize Multi-Agent Reinforcement Learning (MARL) policies, effectively solving the cold-start problem. In the offline phase, the optimizer incorporates a Global-Local-Random (GLR) initialization and a critical task block insertion strategy to enhance global search efficiency. On the online side, a Routing Agent (RA) and a Sequencing Agent (SA) are trained using Multi-objective Proximal Policy Optimization (MPPO), enabling rapid adaptation to task arrivals and node faults by imitating offline experts. Extensive simulations validate that the proposed method effectively mitigates the trade-off of single-paradigm approaches by maintaining over 98% SLA satisfaction with approximately 10ms decision inference latency, demonstrating superior comprehensive performance and robustness under dynamic disturbances compared to benchmark algorithms.

Keywords: Hybrid Evolutionary-RL · Power Grid Edge Computing · Multi-objective Optimization · Offline-to-Online Collaboration · Multi-Agent Reinforcement Learning

1 Introduction

With the continuous evolution of the smart grid, mission-critical power services such as distributed fault recovery and load control are increasingly manifested as computationally intensive tasks at the network edge, imposing strict requirements on real-time execution and reliability [13]. To support these sophisticated

J. Niu et al. (Eds.): KSEM 2026, LNAI 16631, pp. 211–225, 2027.
https://doi.org/10.1007/978-981-92-2759-4_16

services, Edge Intelligence, which integrates artificial intelligence with edge computing, has become a pivotal paradigm for the smart grid [6,24]. However, task scheduling in this environment faces significant challenges, including heterogeneous resource constraints (e.g., CPU, GPU, NPU), complex task dependencies, and dynamic disturbances such as node failures and load fluctuations. These characteristics align closely with the Dynamic Flexible Job-Shop Scheduling Problem (DFJSP) [10], necessitating the optimization of conflicting objectives-makespan, energy consumption, and load balance-under strict real-time decision constraints.

Existing research on heterogeneous resource scheduling primarily falls into two categories: evolutionary algorithms and learning-based methods. Evolutionary Algorithms, such as NSGA-II [4] and MOEA/D [22], are widely employed for their global search capabilities in multi-objective optimization. Recent studies have enhanced these algorithms by introducing hybrid initialization strategies [1,21] and specific neighborhood search structures [23] to improve solution quality. Despite their effectiveness in static scenarios, these iterative algorithms suffer from significant computational overhead, making them unsuitable for real-time response in dynamic grid environments where rapid decision-making is required.

Conversely, Deep Reinforcement Learning (DRL) methods, including Deep Q-Networks (DQN) and Multi-Agent RL (MARL), have gained attention for their ability to enable rapid, real-time inference [9,14,19]. Several studies have applied DRL to task offloading and resource allocation in edge computing, modeling the problem as a Markov Decision Process (MDP) [7,15,16]. However, pure DRL approaches often struggle with convergence instability and the "cold start" problem, tending to get trapped in local optima in high-dimensional multi-objective spaces without expert guidance [5,8]. While some hybrid approaches attempt to combine heuristics with RL [11,12], they often lack a unified closed-loop mechanism for continuous evolution and knowledge transfer tailored for grid edge scenarios.

To bridge the gap between the "global optimality" of evolutionary algorithms and the "real-time responsiveness" of reinforcement learning, this paper proposes a hybrid Evolutionary-RL framework based on an offline-to-online collaborative mechanism. Unlike previous works, we establish a closed-loop system where an improved NSGA-III [3,20] continuously generates expert knowledge to guide online MARL policies. The main contributions of this paper are summarized as follows:

- We propose a three-layer edge-end closed-loop scheduling framework that integrates offline global optimization with online event-driven decision-making, ensuring system robustness and real-time responsiveness.
- An improved NSGA-III algorithm is developed for the offline layer, incorporating a GLR hybrid initialization and a critical task block insertion strategy to generate high-quality expert demonstrations.
- A collaborative MARL algorithm (E-MPPO) is designed for the online layer. By utilizing behavior cloning and periodic knowledge distillation, the agents

can rapidly adapt to dynamic task arrivals and node faults while maintaining alignment with the global Pareto-optimal front.
- Extensive simulations, including convergence analysis and scalability tests, validate the superiority of the proposed method. E-MPPO achieves a $> 98\%$ SLA satisfaction rate with real-time decision-making capabilities, significantly outperforming baseline algorithms in makespan, energy consumption, and load balance under dynamic disturbances.

2 Problem Description and Model Establishment

2.1 Problem Description

The multi-objective optimization scheduling problem typically entails the simultaneous optimization of three or more conflicting objectives. Focusing on grid heterogeneous resource scheduling, we optimize the following key objectives:

- **Task Completion:** Total Makespan, Average Response Latency.
- **Resource Utilization:** Peak Resource Utilization, Load Balance.
- **Energy Consumption:** Peak Power, Total System Energy.
  QoS/Stability: Reliability, Task Deadline Satisfaction Rate.

Addressing the core challenges of edge computing while balancing model complexity, we select four objectives characterized by significant trade-offs: Makespan (C_{max}) representing efficiency, Total System Energy (E_{total}) representing cost, Load Balance Rate (L_b) representing stability, and SLA Satisfaction Rate (SLA) representing quality. The problem assumes that n tasks are processed on m heterogeneous nodes. Each task contains multiple operations with precedence constraints. The goal is to jointly optimize these four objectives by determining the optimal node assignment and processing sequence.

2.2 Model Establishment

Computing Power Quantification Model. We quantify the computing power of heterogeneous resources by considering computation, communication, and storage to map them to a unified dimension [7]. The processing capability F_j^{device} of a device is described by integer (c_i), floating-point (c_f), and hash (c_h) computing rates:

$$F_j^{device} = w_0 \cdot c_i + w_1 \cdot c_f + w_2 \cdot c_h \tag{1}$$

Similarly, communication capability B_j^{device} and storage capability S_j^{device} are modeled as weighted sums of their respective performance metrics (bandwidth, IOPS, etc.):

$$B_j^{device} = w_3 \cdot b_{net} + w_4 \cdot b_{cap} \tag{2}$$

$$S_j^{device} = w_5 \cdot s_{sto} + w_6 \cdot s_{iops} \tag{3}$$

where $\{w_i\}$ are training hyperparameters.

Objective Functions

a) Total Makespan (C_{max}): Defined as the maximum completion time among all tasks:

$$C_{max} = \max_{1 \leq i \leq n} (F_i) \tag{4}$$

where F_i is the actual completion time of task i.

b) Total System Energy (E_{total}): Considering the non-linear relationship between utilization and power [2], the total energy is calculated by integrating static and dynamic power over time:

$$E_{total} = \int \sum (P_{static} + P_{dynamic}(U_r))dt \tag{5}$$

where $P_{dynamic}$ typically follows a quadratic relationship with resource utilization U_r.

c) Load Balance (L_b): Measured by the utilization difference between the busiest and idlest nodes:

$$L_b = \frac{\max_i U_i - \min_i U_i}{\max_i U_i} \in [0, 1] \tag{6}$$

d) SLA Satisfaction Rate (SLA): The ratio of tasks completed within their deadlines D_t:

$$SLA = \frac{|\{t \in T \mid F_t \leq D_t\}|}{|T|} \in [0, 1] \tag{7}$$

Constraints. The scheduling is subject to:

- **Precedence constraints:** Sub-tasks must be processed in the strict topological order defined by the task graph.
- **Non-preemption:** Once a sub-task begins execution on a node, it occupies the resource continuously and cannot be interrupted until completion.
- **Single assignment:** Each sub-task must be assigned to exactly one eligible computing node.

3 Edge-End Three-Layer Closed-Loop Framework

3.1 Framework Overview

To solve the challenges of multi-objective conflicts and dynamic disturbances, we propose an edge-end autonomous three-layer closed-loop scheduling architecture, as shown in Fig. 1. The framework includes:

- **Offline Optimization Layer:** Periodically executes the improved NSGA-III [3, 20] on historical logs to generate Pareto-optimal solutions. These solutions constitute a set of expert demonstrations for guiding the online agents.

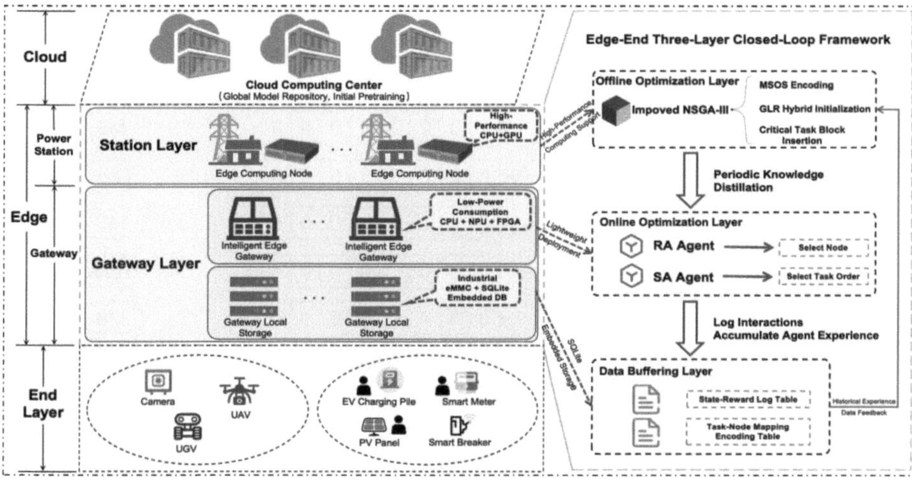

Fig. 1. Grid Edge Heterogeneous Computing Three-Layer Closed-Loop Scheduling Framework

- **Online Decision Layer:** Deployed on the intelligent edge gateway. It uses Routing Agent (RA) and Sequencing Agent (SA) for event-driven scheduling (handling new tasks, faults) and periodic rescheduling.
- **Data Cache Layer:** Stores state-reward logs and distributes policies, supporting data persistence.

This architecture achieves offline global optimization and online **rapid response**, with data staying locally to meet privacy requirements.

3.2 Improved NSGA-III

MSOS Encoding. We adopt MSOS encoding [20].

- **OS:** Length equals total sub-tasks. The gene value is the task ID. The k-th occurrence represents the k-th sub-task of that task.
- **MS:** Length equals OS. The gene value represents the assigned node ID.

GLR Hybrid Initialization Strategy To alleviate the initial load imbalance, the MS chromosome uses a hybrid strategy: 50% Global Selection (GS), 30% Local Selection (LS), and 20% Random Selection (RS). GS assigns tasks to the node with the minimum accumulated load. LS resets the load counter after each task is fully assigned [21].

Critical Task Block Insertion. For makespan compression, we introduce a local search mechanism based on Critical Task Block [10]. We move tasks within the block or to the front of the block to reduce the critical path length (Figs. 2 and 3).

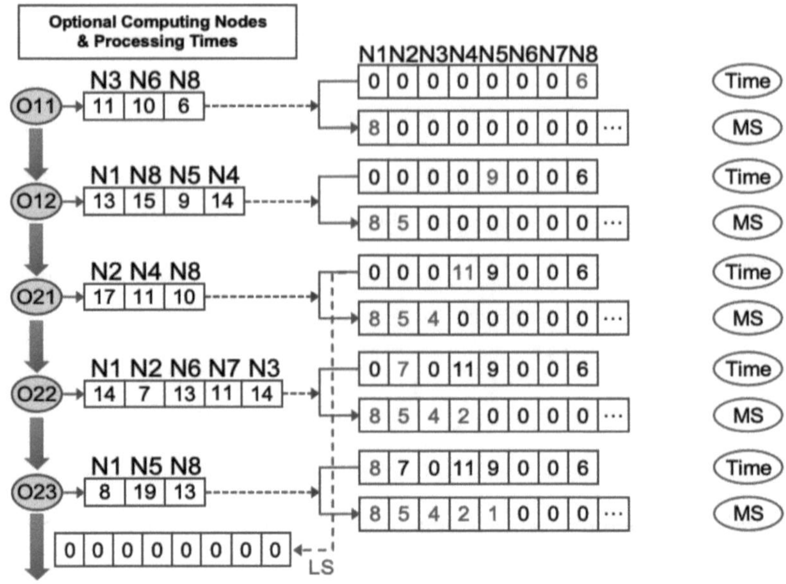

Fig. 2. Schematic Diagram of Global and Local Selection Initialization Strategies

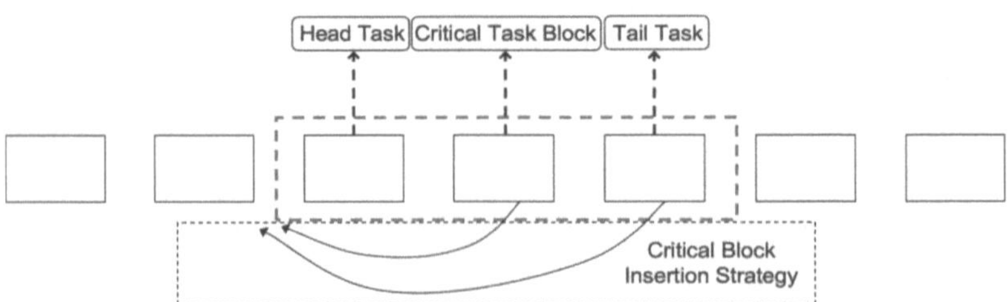

Fig. 3. Schematic of Critical Task Block Insertion Operation

3.3 MPPO-Based RA-SA Collaborative Scheduling

To address dynamic events with rapid responses, we deploy a lightweight MARL system driven by Multi-objective Proximal Policy Optimization (MPPO).

Problem Abstraction and State Space. The online scheduling timeline is discretized into decision steps t. The system state is modeled as a 5-tuple tensor $S_t = \{s_{sys}, s_{node}, s_{job}, \omega_i, e_t\}$, processed by a 1×1 convolution layer to extract features while maintaining low dimensionality:

- s_{sys}: System-level features (e.g., global makespan C_{max}, average latency).
- s_{node}: Node-level status matrix (utilization, queue length).
- s_{job}: New task attributes (FLOPs, deadline, data size).
- ω_i: Weight vectors for multi-objective decomposition.
- e_t: Event flags (0: Normal, 1: New Job, 2: Failure).

Agents and Network Architecture. We design two specialized agents that share a lightweight backbone to ensure deployment efficiency. To achieve decision decoupling, they operate under an event-driven mechanism:

- **Routing Agent (RA):** Activated upon task arrival, it performs task routing by selecting a computing node $a_{RA} \in M_{ij}$ for the current sub-task.
- **Sequencing Agent (SA):** Activated upon computing node availability, it performs task sequencing by prioritizing the next sub-task $a_{SA} \in Q_k$ from the waiting queue.

Lightweight Backbone: Both agents share a 3-layer MLP (32-64-32) encoder. Only the output heads are independent. This parameter sharing reduces the total model size to < 100k parameters, enabling < 2ms inference latency on embedded devices.

Reward Function Design. To guide the agents towards the Pareto front, we design decoupled reward functions:

RA Reward (r_{RA}). The RA targets node-level resource efficiency and responsiveness.

$$r_{RA} = \alpha \cdot \tanh\left(\frac{\overline{E} - E_{inc}}{\overline{E} + \epsilon}\right) + \beta \cdot \tanh\left(\frac{\overline{T}_{queue} - T_{est}}{\overline{T}_{queue} + \epsilon}\right) \tag{8}$$

where E_{inc} and T_{est} denote the estimated energy increment and latency, normalized by their respective historical moving averages $\overline{E}$ and $\overline{T}_{queue}$. ϵ is a smoothing factor, and α, β serve as weighting coefficients.

SA Reward (r_{SA}). The SA focuses on makespan and fairness. Its reward incentivizes critical path compression and prioritizes long-waiting tasks.

$$r_{SA} = \gamma \cdot \left(\frac{C_{max}^{prev} - C_{max}^{curr}}{C_{max}^{prev}}\right) + \delta \cdot \mathbb{I}(T_{wait} > \overline{T}_{wait}) \cdot \frac{T_{wait} - \overline{T}_{wait}}{\sigma_{wait} + \epsilon} \tag{9}$$

where C_{max} represents the global makespan, while T_{wait} and $\overline{T}_{wait}$ refer to the current and average task waiting times. σ_{wait} is the standard deviation used for normalization.

Offline-to-Online Knowledge Transfer. We introduce a hybrid training mechanism to mitigate the cold start problem and the inherent sample inefficiency of MARL.

Behavior Cloning Warm-up Before online interaction, the policy network π_θ is pre-trained using expert solutions generated by the offline NSGA-III. We minimize the cross-entropy loss L_{BC}:

$$L_{BC} = -\frac{1}{N}\sum_{i=1}^{N} \log \pi_\theta(a_{exp}^{(i)} | s^{(i)}) \tag{10}$$

Algorithm 1. Event-Driven E-MPPO for Grid Edge Scheduling

Input: Weight vector ω_i, Replay Buffer B, Batch size k, Clip ratio ϵ
Output: Updated policy $\pi_\theta = (\pi_\theta^{RA}, \pi_\theta^{SA})$

Initialize shared backbone θ, RA head θ_{RA}, SA head θ_{SA}
Warm-up: Pre-train θ using Behavior Cloning loss L_{BC} for N_{warm} epochs
for $t = 1$ to T **do**
    Observe system state s_t and **detect event type** e_t;
    if e_t is *Task Arrival* **then**
        Select RA: Sample action $a_t \sim \pi_\theta^{RA}(s_t)$
    else if e_t is *Node Availability* **then**
        Select SA: Sample action $a_t \sim \pi_\theta^{SA}(s_t)$
    end if
    Execute action a_t, observe reward r_t and next state s_{t+1}
    Store transition (s_t, e_t, a_t, r_t) into Buffer B
    if $|B| \geq k$ **then**
        Sample mini-batch of size k
        Compute GAE A_t and update θ via MPPO loss
    end if
    if $t \mod C = 0$ **then**
        Distillation: Inject offline expert samples into B (mix ratio 30%)
    end if
end for

where $(s^{(i)}, a_{exp}^{(i)})$ are expert state-action pairs derived from the offline Pareto set.

Online Policy Optimization. Following the warm-up phase, agents interact with the environment to continuously improve their policies. To balance the bias-variance trade-off in gradient estimation, we employ Generalized Advantage Estimation (GAE) [17]. The advantage function A_t is computed as:

$$A_t = \sum_{l=0}^{\infty} (\gamma\lambda)^l \delta_{t+l}, \quad \delta_t = r_t + \gamma V(s_{t+1}) - V(s_t) \tag{11}$$

where δ_t represents the TD-error, $V(s)$ is the value function estimated by the critic network, and $\lambda \in [0, 1]$ is the GAE smoothing parameter. The policy is then updated by minimizing the clipped PPO objective to ensure training stability [18].

Periodic Knowledge Distillation. During the online phase, updated expert samples are injected into the replay buffer periodically. The detailed online process is described in Algorithm 1.

4 Experiments and Analysis

4.1 Experimental Setup

The experimental evaluation is conducted on a hybrid benchmark dataset constructed from the widely used Google Cluster Trace (clusterdata-2011-2). To

Table 1. Experimental Settings and Hyperparameters

Parameter	Value
Environment Settings	
Standard Node Scale	30 (Heterogeneous Nodes)
Resource Types	Generic CPU, GPU, NPU
Scalability Test Range	10–120 Nodes
Task Operations	3 (Pre-process, Compute, Store)
Task Data Size	50 KB–500 MB
Initial Task Count (N_{init})	1,500–2,000
Dynamic Task Count (N_{dyn})	2,000–3,000
Breakdown Rate	30% Random Failure
Algorithm Hyperparameters	*(E-MPPO)*
Reference Points (H)	28 (Das and Dennis)
Training Episodes	2,000
Batch Size	128
Learning Rate (α)	3×10^{-4}
Discount Factor (γ)	0.99
Clip Range (ϵ)	0.2
Optimizer	Adam

simulate a realistic heterogeneous grid edge environment, we adopted a data augmentation strategy that bridges the gap between the trace's original data and modern hardware requirements. Specifically, while preserving the original task arrival timestamps and job duration distributions to capture authentic workload volatility, we extended the task attributes by synthetically generating resource demands for GPUs and DPUs following a Poisson distribution. We further map high-priority, latency-sensitive jobs to mission-critical grid services and long-duration batch jobs to data analysis tasks. This approach allows us to establish a comprehensive heterogeneous resource space comprising generic CPUs, GPUs, and DPUs, ensuring both the fidelity of workload dynamics and the applicability to heterogeneous accelerator scheduling. The hardware platform consists of a centralized server equipped with an NVIDIA RTX-4090 GPU for offline training, and multiple RK3568 edge gateways for online inference. The key parameters of the simulation environment and the hyperparameters of the proposed E-MPPO algorithm are detailed in Table 1. To systematically evaluate the performance of the proposed E-MPPO framework, we conducted a series of experiments focusing on convergence efficiency, multi-objective optimization quality, ablation studies, robustness under disturbances, and scalability.

4.2 Convergence Analysis

We first evaluate the training stability and learning efficiency of E-MPPO. Figure 4 illustrates the convergence curves of E-MPPO compared with baseline algorithms across four optimization objectives. As observed in Fig. 4, E-MPPO demonstrates significant advantages:

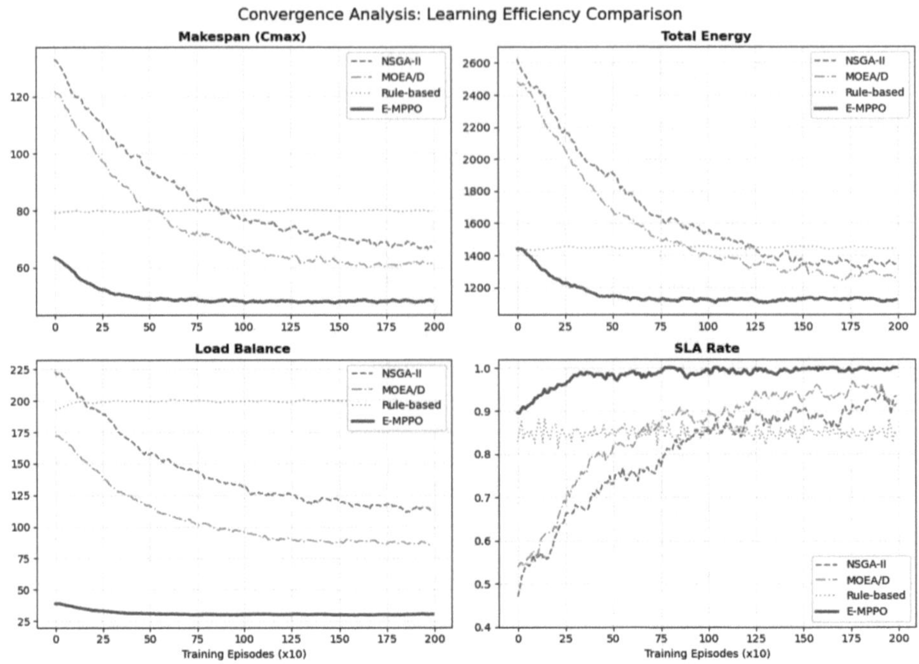

Fig. 4. Convergence Analysis of Multi-Dimensional Key Performance Indicators during Training.

- **Fast Start-up:** Benefiting from the expert demonstrations provided by the offline improved NSGA-III, E-MPPO exhibits a superior initial performance compared to the random initialization of NSGA-II and MOEA/D, achieving an effective warm start.
- **Efficiency and Stability:** Unlike the slow evolutionary search process, E-MPPO converges rapidly to a stable state within the first 20% of training episodes.
- **Final Performance:** E-MPPO converges to lower values in minimizing objectives (C_{max}, E_{total}, and Load Balance) and maintains a high SLA satisfaction rate (> 0.98), verifying the efficiency of multi-agent reinforcement learning in balancing complex objectives.

4.3 Multi-objective Performance Comparison

Figure 5 visualizes the Pareto front distribution obtained by E-MPPO and baselines under the standard scale of $30 \times 40 \times 60$. The visualization reveals a clear hierarchy in solution quality:

- **Pareto Dominance:** The solution set of E-MPPO (red circles) is densely concentrated in the lower-left region, strictly dominating NSGA-II, MOEA/D, and rule-based methods.
- **Continuous Trade-off in Extreme Regions:** The extreme solutions of E-MPPO exhibit a continuous concave morphology along the single-objective axes (C_{max}, E_{total}, and Load Balance), whereas baselines only form discrete scattered points. This indicates that the uniform λ vector effectively pushes the search towards extreme regions, forming a continuous trade-off band.
- **Seamless Offline-to-Online Transition:** E-MPPO samples better local solutions under single-objective weights than offline evolution, proving that online agents successfully inherit and surpass the offline global optimum. The concave profile implies that E-MPPO provides feasible solutions with lower extreme values.

4.4 Ablation Study on Collaborative Mechanism

To verify the necessity of the offline-guided online learning mechanism, we conducted an ablation study comparing the full E-MPPO with a Pure MPPO variant (trained from scratch without offline expert guidance). As shown in Fig. 6, the Pareto front of E-MPPO completely dominates that of Pure MPPO. This demonstrates that in the high-dimensional state space of heterogeneous scheduling, pure reinforcement learning without prior knowledge tends to get trapped in local optima. E-MPPO, leveraging knowledge distillation, successfully transfers the global search experience from the offline improved NSGA-III to online agents, effectively providing a global perspective that ensures correct search direction under complex constraints.

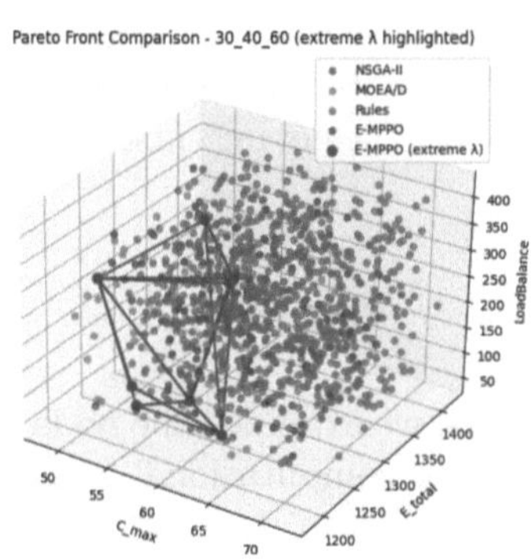

Fig. 5. Comparison of Pareto Optimization Performance and Front Distribution.

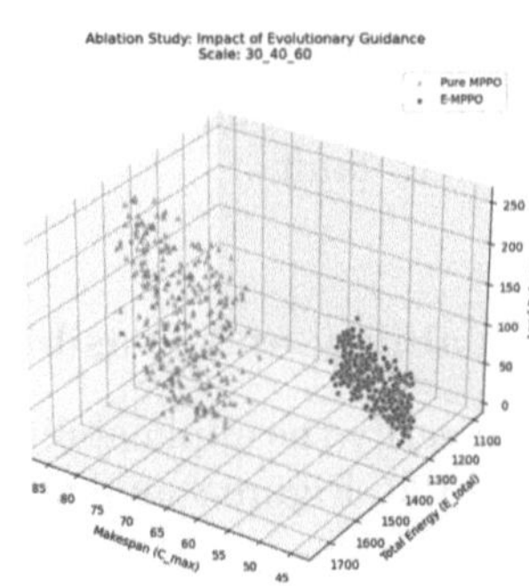

Fig. 6. Impact Analysis of Evolutionary Guidance on Pareto Optimization Quality.

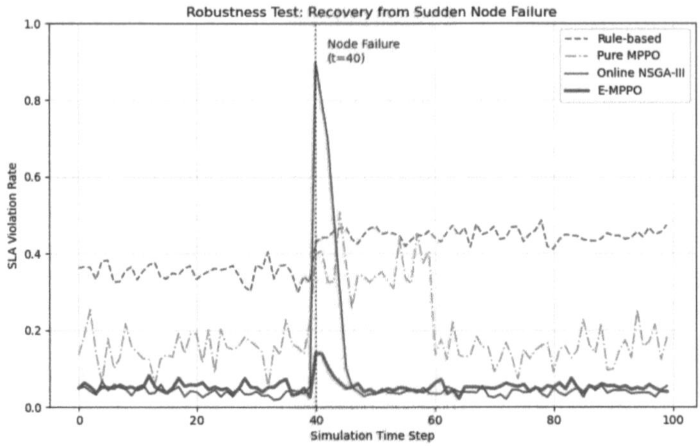

Fig. 7. Validation of Real-Time Response Capability Under Sudden Node Failure Scenarios.

4.5 Robustness Under Dynamic Disturbances

We simulated a sudden node failure scenario where 30% of computing nodes randomly go offline at time step $t = 40$. Figure 7 shows the real-time SLA violation rate response. The results highlight the difference in paradigm:

- **Comparison with Online Optimization:** Online NSGA-III suffers from a sharp spike in SLA violations immediately after the failure. This is attributed to the inherent computation latency of evolutionary algorithms during re-optimization (seconds level), causing task accumulation.
- **Comparison with Proposed Method:** E-MPPO demonstrates superior robustness, recovering rapidly with minimal fluctuation. Thanks to the millisecond-level inference of neural networks, agents can directly output adaptive scheduling actions without re-iteration, achieving instantaneous response to faults.

4.6 Scalability and Feasibility Analysis

Finally, to verify the applicability in large-scale grids, we extended the node scale from 10 to 120. Figure 8 analyzes the effectiveness and computational feasibility.

- **Effectiveness Stability:** As the scale increases, the search space expands exponentially. The SLA of traditional algorithms (NSGA-II/MOEA/D) drops significantly (below 0.85). In contrast, E-MPPO maintains a robust high SLA (> 0.98), proving the strong generalization ability of the learned policy.
- **Computational Feasibility:** While the computation time of evolutionary algorithms escalates significantly with scale, rendering them unsuitable for real-time dispatch, E-MPPO exhibits linear scalability. It maintains a stable

decision inference latency of approximately 10ms, verifying its feasibility for large-scale, real-time decision-making in heterogeneous clusters.

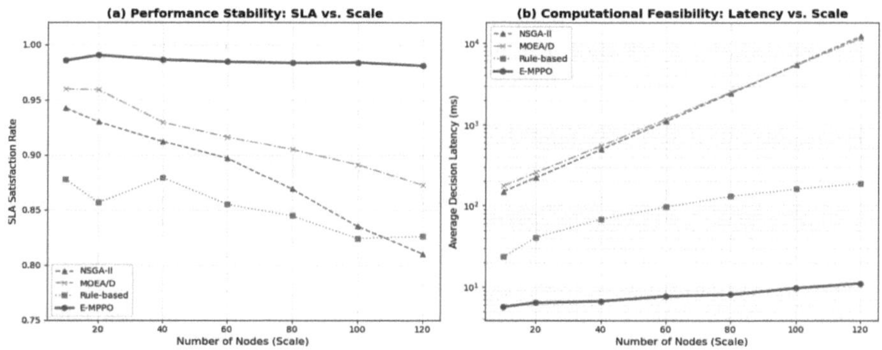

Fig. 8. Scalability and Computational Feasibility Analysis under Different Node Scales.

5 Conclusion

To address multi-objective conflicts in power grid edge computing, this paper proposes E-MPPO, a hybrid scheduling framework that synergizes the global search of Evolutionary Algorithms with the real-time responsiveness of MARL. We formulate the resource allocation problem as a multi-objective DFJSP and design a three-layer closed-loop mechanism to facilitate offline-to-online knowledge transfer. By utilizing improved NSGA-III to guide online agents, the proposed method achieves a balance between global optimality and inference speed. Simulation results validate that E-MPPO achieves superior Pareto trade-offs among makespan, energy, and load balance compared to state-of-the-art baselines, while maintaining high SLA satisfaction under dynamic disturbances. Future work will extend this framework to cross-domain federated evolution to enhance privacy, paving the way for autonomous edge intelligence in large-scale smart grids.

Acknowledgments. This work was supported by Key Technologies of Cloud-Edge-Terminal Collaborative Full-Stack Domesticated Power-Specific IoT Operating System (No. 2024ZD0803000).

References

1. Chen, G., Han, W.: Improved genetic algorithm based on minimum-load initialization to solve flexible job-shop scheduling problem. Inf. Control **50**(3), 374–384 (2021)
2. Cheng, M., Li, J., Bogdan, P., Nazarian, S.: H2O-cloud: a resource and quality of service-aware task scheduling framework for warehouse-scale data centers. IEEE Trans. Comput. Aided Des. Integr. Circuits Syst. **39**(10), 2925–2937 (2019)
3. Deb, K., Jain, H.: An evolutionary many-objective optimization algorithm using reference-point-based nondominated sorting approach, part I: solving problems with box constraints. IEEE Trans. Evol. Comput. **18**(4), 577–601 (2013)
4. Deb, K., Pratap, A., Agarwal, S., Meyarivan, T.: A fast and elitist multiobjective genetic algorithm: NSGA-II. IEEE Trans. Evol. Comput. **6**(2), 182–197 (2002)
5. Dulac-Arnold, G., et al.: Challenges of real-world reinforcement learning: definitions, benchmarks and analysis. Mach. Learn. **110**(9), 2419–2468 (2021)
6. Gai, K., Wu, Y., Zhu, L., Xu, L., Zhang, Y.: Permissioned blockchain and edge computing empowered privacy-preserving smart grid networks. IEEE Internet Things J. **6**(5), 7992–8004 (2019)
7. Hao, J., et al.: Heterogeneous resource scheduling in computing power networks: a method based on improved D3QN. In: 2024 IEEE 6th Advanced Information Management, Communicates, Electronic and Automation Control Conference (IMCEC), vol. 6, pp. 1561–1567. IEEE (2024)
8. Henderson, P., Islam, R., Bachman, P., Pineau, J., Precup, D., Meger, D.: Deep reinforcement learning that matters. In: Proceedings of the AAAI Conference on Artificial Intelligence, vol. 32 (2018)
9. Huang, L., Bi, S., Zhang, Y.J.A.: Deep reinforcement learning for online computation offloading in wireless powered mobile-edge computing networks. IEEE Trans. Mob. Comput. **19**(11), 2581–2593 (2019)
10. Jiang, Q., Wei, J.: Real-time scheduling method for dynamic flexible job shop scheduling. J. Syst. Simul. **36**(7), 1609–1620 (2024)
11. Khadka, S., Tumer, K.: Evolutionary reinforcement learning. In: Proceedings of the Genetic and Evolutionary Computation Conference, pp. 1388–1395 (2018)
12. Li, K., Zhang, T., Wang, R.: Deep reinforcement learning for multiobjective optimization. IEEE Trans. Cybern. **51**(6), 3103–3114 (2021)
13. Long, Y., Bao, Y., Zeng, L.: Research on edge-computing-based high concurrency and availability "cloud, edge, and end collaboration" substation operation support system and applications. Energies **17**(1), 194 (2023)
14. Lv, L., Zhang, C., Fan, J., Shen, W.: Deep reinforcement learning for job shop scheduling problems: a comprehensive literature review. Knowl.-Based Syst. 113633 (2025)
15. Mao, Y., You, C., Zhang, J., Huang, K., Letaief, K.B.: A survey on mobile edge computing: the communication perspective. IEEE Commun. Surv. Tutor. **19**(4), 2322–2358 (2017)
16. Min, M., Xiao, L., Chen, Y., Cheng, P., Wu, D., Zhuang, W.: Learning-based computation offloading for IoT devices with energy harvesting. IEEE Trans. Veh. Technol. **68**(2), 1930–1941 (2019)
17. Schulman, J., Moritz, P., Levine, S., Jordan, M., Abbeel, P.: High-dimensional continuous control using generalized advantage estimation. In: Proceedings of the International Conference on Learning Representations (ICLR) (2016)

18. Schulman, J., Wolski, F., Dhariwal, P., Radford, A., Klimov, O.: Proximal policy optimization algorithms. arXiv preprint arXiv:1707.06347 (2017)
19. Xiao, Y., Song, Y., Liu, J.: Collaborative multi-agent deep reinforcement learning for energy-efficient resource allocation in heterogeneous mobile edge computing networks. IEEE Trans. Wireless Commun. **23**(6), 6653–6668 (2023)
20. Xu, Y., Chen, Y., Wang, C.: Improving NSGA-III algorithm for solving high-dimensional many-objective green flexible job shop scheduling problem. J. Syst. Simul. **36**(10), 2314–2329 (2024)
21. Zhang, G., Gao, L., Li, P.: Improved genetic algorithm for the flexible job-shop scheduling problem. J. Mech. Eng. **45**(7), 145–151 (2009)
22. Zhang, Q., Li, H.: MOEA/D: a multiobjective evolutionary algorithm based on decomposition. IEEE Trans. Evol. Comput. **11**(6), 712–731 (2007)
23. Zhao, S.: Bilevel neighborhood search hybrid algorithm for the flexible job shop scheduling problem. J. Mech. Eng. **51**(14), 175–184 (2015)
24. Zhou, Z., Chen, X., Li, E., Zeng, L., Luo, K., Zhang, J.: Edge intelligence: paving the last mile of artificial intelligence with edge computing. Proc. IEEE **107**(8), 1738–1762 (2019)

An Unsupervised Contrastive Learning Approach for Cold-Start Question-Answering Systems

Wei Deng[1,2] and Zhe Cui[1,2](✉)

[1] Chengdu Institute of Computer Applications, Chinese Academy of Sciences, Chengdu 610041, China
dengwei211@mails.ucas.ac.cn, cuizhe@casit.com.cn
[2] University of Chinese Academy of Sciences, Beijing 101408, China

Abstract. In the current wave of digital transformation, Frequently Asked Questions (FAQ) answering systems have become a key technology for replacing traditional manual customer service and efficiently handling high-frequency user inquiries. This paper focuses on the cold-start phase of FAQ question-answering systems, aiming to ensure that such systems can be effectively initialized under no in-domain labeled data conditions. To this end, we investigate an FAQ question-answering system based on question semantic similarity, specifically designed for the cold-start scenario. To mitigate the anisotropy problem commonly observed in pre-trained language models, we propose an unsupervised text augmentation method to construct high-quality positive samples for contrastive learning. This approach enables the learning of a improved embedding geometry, which serves as a strong foundation for subsequent fine-tuning in low-resource downstream tasks. We refer to this method as LACSE (Large-model Augmented Contrastive Sentence Embeddings). Experimental results demonstrate that LACSE produces higher-quality sentence embeddings and effectively adapts to cold-start requirements across different business scenarios, providing a more robust semantic representation basis for subsequent supervised fine-tuning.

Keywords: Unsupervised Contrastive Learning · Sentence Embeddings · Semantic Similarity

1 Introduction

Frequently Asked Questions (FAQ) question-answering systems take users' natural-language inputs as the interaction interface and return standardized answers by rapidly locating, from a collection of question–answer pairs, the question that is most semantically similar to the user query, thereby helping users obtain relevant information efficiently. Such systems have been widely deployed in enterprise intelligent customer service platforms. The response accuracy of

J. Niu et al. (Eds.): KSEM 2026, LNAI 16631, pp. 226–237, 2027.
https://doi.org/10.1007/978-981-92-2759-4_17

FAQ question-answering systems largely depends on short-text semantic matching technologies [25–27].

With the emergence and success of pre-trained language models such as BERT [3] and the GPT series [4–6], the field of Natural Language Processing (NLP) has advanced rapidly. Pre-trained models are typically built upon the Transformer architecture [7] and exhibit strong transferability across a wide range of tasks. However, when applied to downstream tasks, existing pre-trained models usually require large amounts of labeled data for fine-tuning in order to obtain high-quality semantic representation models adapted to specific domains; moreover, without sufficient adaptation, the sentence embedding space may suffer from issues such as anisotropy and insufficient semantic isometry [13,14].

In practical business scenarios, labeled data are often scarce, while existing text augmentation methods remain limited in semantic fidelity and structural diversity, frequently leading to semantic drift or homogeneous generations [20, 21]. These limitations hinder the direct application of mainstream augmentation paradigms to the cold-start phase of question-answering systems.

To address this challenge, we propose an unsupervised contrastive learning approach based on open-source large-model text augmentation, aiming to learn a more uniformly distributed sentence embedding space. Our method targets scenarios with no in-domain labeled data and supports lightweight subsequent fine-tuning for downstream adaptation.

To simulate cold-start conditions, we randomly sample short sentences from Wiki1M [37] and construct positive pairs using meaning-preserving LLM rewrites under an unsupervised contrastive learning framework. This strategy improves embedding uniformity and yields high-quality universal sentence representations. Compared with conventional augmentation techniques, LLMBased augmentation offers stronger controllability and generation quality in few-shot settings [22–24].

The main contributions of this work are summarized as follows:

(1) In the cold-start phase, we propose an unsupervised contrastive learning method that effectively mitigates the anisotropy problem of pre-trained models using only a small amount of unlabeled data [9,13,19].
(2) Regarding text augmentation, we introduce an improved augmentation strategy based on open-source large models. Under the prerequisite of ensuring that data do not leak, our approach significantly improves the structural diversity of generated texts compared with traditional augmentation methods, and yields higher-quality sentence embeddings [20–23].
(3) We conduct experiments on multiple cross-domain semantic matching datasets, and the results indicate that the learned sentence representation space exhibits strong universality and transferability [9,15,16,18].

This method is intended to meet the cold-start requirements of question-answering systems across different business scenarios, and provides valuable practical experience and theoretical references for enterprises to build efficient and reliable intelligent question-answering platforms in the process of digital transformation [2,25].

2 Related Work

2.1 Text Augmentation

Text augmentation is often formalized as sampling meaning-preserving views $x^+ \sim q(\cdot \mid x)$ such that an encoder f_θ satisfies $f_\theta(x^+) \approx f_\theta(x)$ while reducing nuisance variations. Token-level edits are lightweight and effective in low-resource regimes [39]. Sentence-level transformations typically induce larger syntactic/length diversity with strong semantic fidelity [33,40]. For contrastive sentence representation learning, task-tailored augmentations often outperform dropout-only views on semantic similarity benchmarks [41]. More recently, LLM-Based paraphrasing expands the support of $q(\cdot \mid x)$ under label consistency and enables high-entropy, structure-diverse rewrites [22,42].

2.2 Contrastive Learning

Contrastive learning can be interpreted as jointly optimizing *alignment* (pulling positives together) and *uniformity* (spreading features on the hypersphere) [19]. In sentence embedding learning, SimCSE shows that simple stochastic views can already yield strong representations, while supervised variants further improve correlation and convergence [9]. Beyond two-view objectives, augmentation-enriched frameworks and supervised contrastive learning provide finer control of the alignment–uniformity trade-off and improve robustness under distribution shift [41,43].

3 Methodology

3.1 Overall View

Figure 1 illustrates the overall workflow of a typical question-answering system with continuous downstream fine-tuning.

In this system, frequently asked questions are first converted into vector representations, and an index is constructed in advance using SBERT. When a user submits a query, the system encodes the query into a sentence embedding and retrieves the most similar questions via semantic retrieval. If the retrieved question or any of the Top-k recommended questions matches the user query, the corresponding answer is returned; otherwise, the query is forwarded to human customer service.

During the initial system construction phase, to enable effective cold-start deployment, user queries are randomly sampled, augmented, and used for unsupervised contrastive learning to enhance the representation capability of the model. In subsequent system operation, user queries that are escalated to human agents can be manually aligned with corresponding frequently asked questions and treated as supervised training samples for continuous fine-tuning. This process enables sustained model updates, thereby progressively improving the system's adaptability and performance over time. The following sections provide a detailed description of the algorithms adopted in the cold-start phase of the FAQ system.

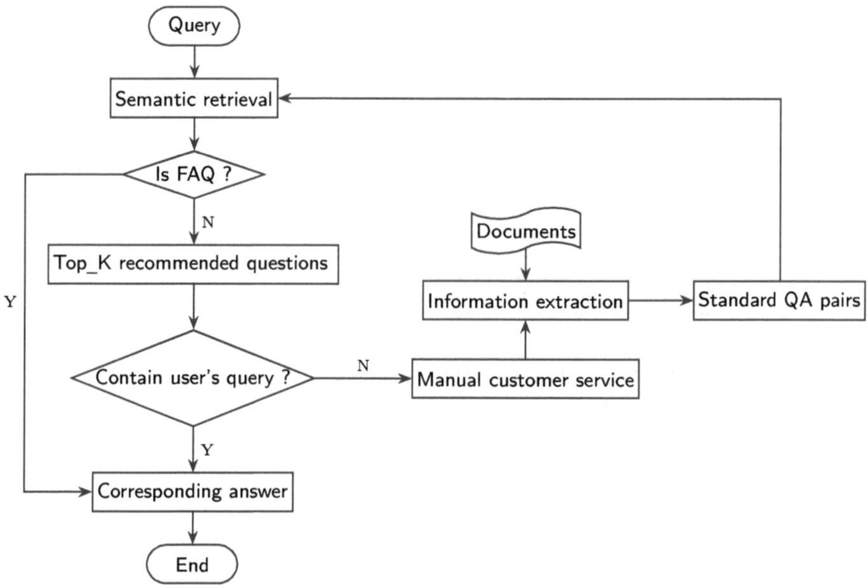

Fig. 1. A typical question-answering system with downstream fine tuning.

3.2 LLM–Based Text Augmentation

We observe that large language models (LLMs) exhibit strong generative capacity: under the guidance of few-shot prompting, they can produce outputs that are highly diverse in surface form while remaining semantically consistent, thereby substantially expanding the effective training set [6]. Motivated by this observation, we explore a few-shot, unsupervised text augmentation strategy to improve the geometry of sentence representations. Unlike conventional paraphrase-based augmentation, our approach explicitly encourages structural diversity while guarding against semantic drift, which is a known challenge in textual augmentation [20–22]. To balance effectiveness and cost, we adopt the open-source model **DeepSeek-V3** for augmentation [51]. We set the generation temperature to $T = 1$ and employ a carefully designed prompt template (Fig. 2) to maximize structural diversity under semantic fidelity constraints. A higher temperature encourages the model to explore alternative realizations, enriching the training distribution and reducing redundancy among augmented samples.

Compared with classical augmentation techniques, the proposed *controlled* LLMBased augmentation achieves a favorable trade-off: it preserves semantics while explicitly maximizing structural variation, yielding semantically stable and better-distributed positive pairs. These positives not only broaden coverage but also help stabilize the underlying representation space.

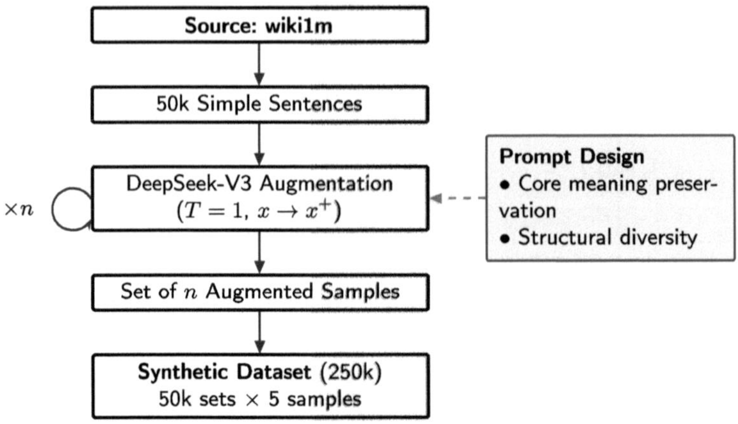

Fig. 2. The proposed data augmentation pipeline.

Rewriting Prompt

Rewrite the sentence with identical meaning.
Maximize structural variation (e.g., voice change, clause reordering), avoiding simple synonym substitution.
No long copied spans.
Output only the rewritten sentence.

From a geometric perspective, the augmentation encourages sentence embeddings to cluster more tightly around their semantic prototypes, improving the quality of the learned space in terms of compaction and separability. Such improvements are consistent with findings that contrastive learning benefits from better alignment and uniformity of representations [9,19]. As a result, this strategy can also provide secondary gains on related objectives, improving the overall quality of the resulting sentence representations.

In the cold-start stage, FAQ question-answering systems typically lack sufficient labeled data for effective fine-tuning of pre-trained encoders. If a pre-trained model is used without any task adaptation to generate sentence embeddings and cosine similarity is computed directly, semantic matching performance is often unsatisfactory due to the widely observed *anisotropy* of embedding spaces produced by pre-trained language models [13,14].

3.3 Unsupervised Contrastive Learning

As shown in the left panel of Fig. 3, for BERT-style encoders, embeddings tend to be concentrated in a narrow subspace: representations associated with frequent tokens are distributed densely near the origin, whereas those associated with rare tokens are distributed more sparsely and farther away. This imbalance induces a highly clustered geometry in which many sentence embeddings fall into

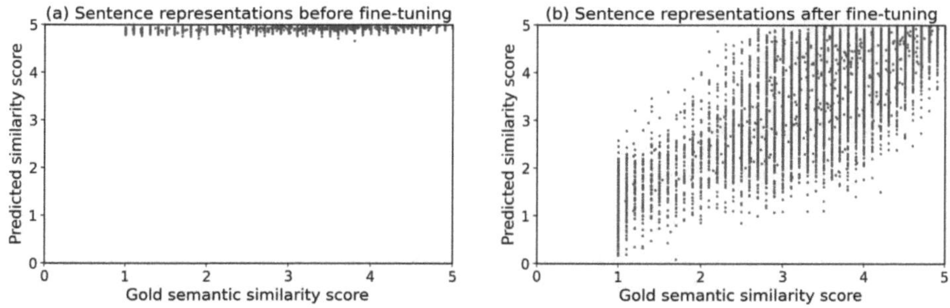

Fig. 3. Comparison between gold semantic similarity scores and predicted similarity scores before and after fine-tuning. Fine-tuning mitigates representation saturation and substantially improves alignment with human annotations.

a small number of dense regions, causing cosine similarities between arbitrary sentence pairs to be spuriously high and making it difficult to faithfully quantify true semantic relatedness [13,14]. To improve embedding geometry, prior work has proposed a variety of approaches, including flow-based transformation (BERT-flow) [13], whitening-based post-processing (BERT-Whitening) [24], and contrastive learning for sentence embeddings such as SimCSE and ConSERT [9,15]. These methods can improve the *uniformity* of representations; however, existing analyses also suggest that aggressively enforcing uniformity may come at the expense of *alignment* (i.e., bringing semantically equivalent pairs closer), potentially harming downstream performance [9,19].

To address semantic matching in the cold-start phase of FAQ systems, we adopt an *unsupervised contrastive learning* approach to directly reshape the representation space. Concretely, we construct contrastive signals from the training data itself: for each original text, we obtain a meaning-preserving rewrite via an LLMBased augmenter and encode the original and the rewrite into sentence embeddings v and v^+, respectively, treating them as a positive pair. Other samples in the same mini-batch serve as negative examples [9,22,23].

By optimizing the contrastive objective, the model is encouraged to minimize the distance between positive pairs, strengthening *alignment*, while simultaneously increasing the distance to negatives, improving *uniformity.* This training process can improve the geometry of the sentence embedding space under unlabeled data, thereby alleviating anisotropy and yielding more discriminative representations for semantic retrieval [9,19].

Specifically, for the i-th sample in a mini-batch, the loss is defined as:

$$\ell_i = -\log \frac{\exp\left(\cos\_sim\left(v_i, v_i^+\right)/\tau\right)}{\sum_{j=1}^{N} \exp\left(\cos\_sim\left(v_i, v_j^+\right)/\tau\right)}, \tag{1}$$

where $\cos\_sim(\cdot,\cdot)$ denotes cosine similarity, τ is a temperature hyperparameter controlling the sharpness of the similarity distribution, and N is the mini-batch size. Minimizing this loss promotes both alignment and uniformity, which helps reduce anisotropy in cold-start settings.

4 Experiments

4.1 Experiments Setup

Experiments are primarily conducted on a corpus of short sentences randomly sampled from a large-scale Wikipedia-derived dataset, where each sentence contains approximately 10 tokens. To evaluate the effectiveness of the proposed method, we conduct experiments on several standard semantic textual similarity benchmarks, including STS12–16, STS-B, and SICK-R.

All models are implemented using PyTorch and trained on four NVIDIA RTX 3090 GPUs with 24GB memory each. Model parameters are initialized from the RoBERTa_{base} checkpoint released by FAIR. We employ the AdamW optimizer to optimize the training objective. Following common practice in semantic textual similarity evaluation, Spearman's rank correlation coefficient is used as the primary evaluation metric (Table 1).

4.2 Semantic Matching Result

Table 1. Performance on STS tasks.

Method	STS12	STS13	STS14	STS15	STS16	STSb	SICKR	Avg.
NLI supervised baselines								
InferSent–GloVe†	52.60	66.52	61.90	72.58	66.70	67.85	65.50	64.81
Universal Sentence En†	64.20	67.65	64.50	76.70	73.00	74.70	76.50	71.10
$\text{SBERT}_{\text{base}}$-NLI (re-impl.)‡	69.70	75.65	72.20	78.40	73.55	76.60	72.60	74.10
$\text{SBERT}_{\text{large}}$-NLI (re-impl.)‡	72.55	78.60	75.00	80.85	76.70	79.40	73.10	76.60
$\text{BERT}_{\text{base}}$-CT†	68.65	74.45	**76.50**	79.60	77.00	–	–	–
$\text{BERT}_{\text{large}}$-CT†	69.70	75.35	76.35	81.20	78.00	–	–	–
ConSERT joint‡	70.40	79.85	74.75	81.35	76.60	78.70	**77.40**	77.10
Unsupervised baselines								
Avg. GloVe embeddings†	54.89	70.31	59.53	68.05	63.28	57.72	53.38	61.08
$\text{BERT}^{‡}_{\text{base}}$	34.86	59.15	49.05	63.06	62.40	47.90	58.37	53.64
$\text{BERT}^{‡}_{\text{large}}$	32.78	57.40	47.67	55.52	62.19	49.28	53.64	51.13
$\text{CLEAR}^{†}_{\text{base}}$	48.64	48.63	57.01	63.36	65.35	74.77	72.25	61.50
IS-$\text{BERT}_{\text{base}}$–NLI†	56.44	68.90	60.88	74.92	69.94	68.87	63.87	66.32
LACSE	**73.08**	**83.13**	75.62	**82.86**	**80.28**	**80.72**	75.46	**78.74**

We evaluate on STS12–STS16, STS-B, and SICK-R using Spearman's $\rho \times 100$. With `RoBERTa-base` (max sequence length 64), a batch size of 128, one LLM-enhanced sentence is used as the positive sample pair, a learning rate of 1×10^{-5}, temperature $\tau = 0.02$, and the AdamW optimizer, **LACSE** achieves an average score of **78.73**. Notably, LACSE even outperforms several commonly reported supervised baselines on STS benchmarks, demonstrating the effectiveness of the proposed approach for cold-start scenarios.

As shown in the right panel of Fig. 3, LACSE effectively mitigates the anisotropy of pre-trained models in cold-start scenarios, thereby significantly improving the accuracy of semantic matching.

4.3 Ablation Studies

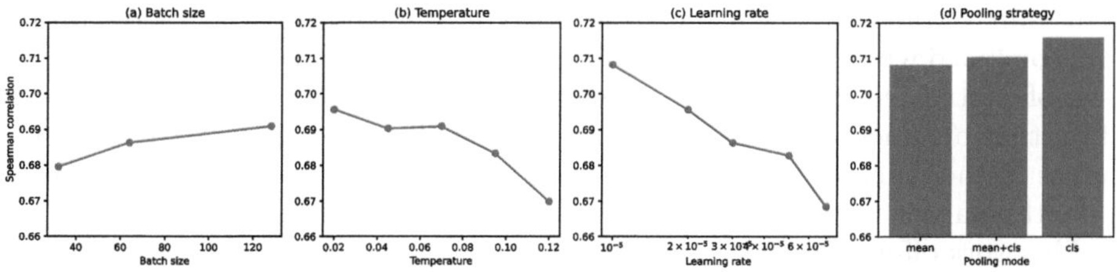

Fig. 4. Ablation study on key hyperparameters and architectural choices.

As shown in Fig. 4, we analyze the impact of key hyperparameters, including batch size, dropout rate, and pooling strategy, on unsupervised performance in order to select appropriate configurations.

First, batch size has a significant effect on model performance, with the best results achieved at a batch size of 128. This observation is consistent with the intuition that larger batches provide richer contrastive signals, leading to more informative representations. Second, the results indicate that a lower temperature amplifies subtle semantic distinctions; when combined with a small learning rate, it facilitates the formation of a more discriminative sentence embedding space. Based on this analysis, we set the temperature to 0.02. Finally, we compare different pooling strategies for sentence representations and adopt the [CLS] token as the final pooling method.

We further conduct ablation experiments to analyze how the proportion of original sentences and LLM-generated rewrites, as well as different positive-pair construction strategies, affect performance under identical hyperparameter settings. The best result is achieved when each training instance uses the original sentence as a stable semantic anchor and introduces only a single LLM-generated rewrite as a positive pair, yielding an average Spearman correlation of **0.7834**. Increasing the number of rewrites per instance leads to a slight performance drop (to 0.7794 and 0.7785), indicating that additional diversity also introduces semantic or stylistic noise. When training further enforces similarity among multiple LLM-generated sentences, performance degrades more noticeably (down to 0.7719), suggesting that excessive LLM–LLM constraints can harm semantic generalization. Finally, constructing positives solely from LLM-generated sentences performs worst (around 0.766), highlighting the importance of retaining original sentences as anchors. Overall, these results show that relying on original sentences with a small number of high-quality LLM rewrites provides the most effective and robust training signal.

5 Conclusion

This paper simulates real-world scenarios and proposes a cold-start method for FAQ question answering systems based on unsupervised contrastive learning. To address the cold-start challenge in FAQ systems, we employ a locally deployed open-source large language model to rewrite the original texts as data augmentation, combined with unsupervised contrastive learning to alleviate the anisotropy issue of pretrained models. Experimental results on multiple datasets demonstrate that our method consistently outperforms baseline approaches. Ablation studies further validate the effectiveness of the proposed method and provide an in-depth analysis of the impact of original texts on overall system performance.

This work offers valuable theoretical insights and practical guidance for enterprises deploying cold-start FAQ question answering systems during digital transformation.

References

1. LNCS Homepage. http://www.springer.com/lncs. Accessed 16 Jan 2026
2. Financial FAQ Question-Answering System Based on Question Semantic Similarity (SpringerLink). https://link.springer.com/chapter/10.1007/978-981-97-5498-4_12. Accessed 16 Jan 2026
3. Devlin, J., Chang, M.-W., Lee, K., Toutanova, K.: BERT: Pre-training of Deep Bidirectional Transformers for Language Understanding. https://arxiv.org/abs/1810.04805. Accessed 16 Jan 2026
4. Radford, A., et al.: Improving Language Understanding by Generative Pre-training (GPT-1). https://cdn.openai.com/research-covers/language-unsupervised/language_understanding_paper.pdf. Accessed 16 Jan 2026
5. Radford, A., et al.: Language Models are Unsupervised Multitask Learners (GPT-2). https://cdn.openai.com/better-language-models/language_models_are_unsupervised_multitask_learners.pdf. Accessed 16 Jan 2026
6. Brown, T., et al.: Language Models are Few-Shot Learners (GPT-3). https://arxiv.org/abs/2005.14165. Accessed 16 Jan 2026
7. Vaswani, A., et al.: Attention Is All You Need (Transformer). https://arxiv.org/abs/1706.03762. Accessed 16 Jan 2026
8. Reimers, N., Gurevych, I.: Sentence-BERT: Sentence Embeddings using Siamese BERT-Networks. https://aclanthology.org/D19-1410/. Accessed 16 Jan 2026
9. Gao, T., Yao, X., Chen, D.: SimCSE: Simple Contrastive Learning of Sentence Embeddings. https://aclanthology.org/2021.emnlp-main.552/. Accessed 16 Jan 2026
10. Gao, T., Yao, X., Chen, D.: SimCSE (arXiv version). https://arxiv.org/abs/2104.08821. Accessed 16 Jan 2026

11. Peng, H., et al.: CoSENT (TASLP 2024 PDF). https://penghao-bdsc.github.io/papers/CoSENT_TASLP2024.pdf. Accessed 16 Jan 2026
12. Sun, Y., et al.: Circle Loss: A Unified Perspective of Pair Similarity Optimization. https://arxiv.org/abs/2002.10857. Accessed 16 Jan 2026
13. Li, B., et al.: On the Sentence Embeddings from Pre-trained Language Models (BERT-flow). https://arxiv.org/abs/2011.05864. Accessed 16 Jan 2026
14. Is anisotropy really the cause of BERT embeddings not being semantic? (Findings of EMNLP 2022). https://aclanthology.org/2022.findings-emnlp.314/. Accessed 16 Jan 2026
15. Yan, Y., et al.: ConSERT: A Contrastive Framework for Self-Supervised Sentence Representation Transfer. https://aclanthology.org/2021.acl-long.393/. Accessed 16 Jan 2026
16. Giorgi, J., et al.: DeCLUTR: Deep Contrastive Learning for Unsupervised Textual Representations. https://aclanthology.org/2021.acl-long.72.pdf. Accessed 16 Jan 2026
17. Liu, F., Vulić, I., Korhonen, A., Collier, N.: Mirror-BERT (arXiv PDF). https://arxiv.org/pdf/2104.08027.pdf. Accessed 16 Jan 2026
18. Jiang, T., et al.: PromptBERT: Improving BERT Sentence Embeddings with Prompts. https://aclanthology.org/2022.emnlp-main.603/. Accessed 16 Jan 2026
19. Wang, T., Isola, P.: Understanding Contrastive Representation Learning through Alignment and Uniformity on the Hypersphere. https://arxiv.org/abs/2005.10242. Accessed 16 Jan 2026
20. Feng, S., et al.: A Survey of Data Augmentation Approaches for NLP. https://aclanthology.org/2021.findings-acl.84/. Accessed 16 Jan 2026
21. Shorten, C., et al.: A Survey on Data Augmentation for Text Classification. https://arxiv.org/abs/2107.03158. Accessed 16 Jan 2026
22. Data Augmentation using Large Language Models: Data Perspectives and Learning Paradigms (Survey). https://arxiv.org/abs/2403.02990. Accessed 16 Jan 2026
23. Empowering Large Language Models for Textual Data Augmentation (OpenReview PDF). https://openreview.net/pdf?id=JCuWXk9HGq. Accessed 16 Jan 2026
24. A unified framework of data augmentation using large language models (LLM-DA++) (Pattern Recognition 2025). https://www.sciencedirect.com/science/article/pii/S0031320325004157. Accessed 16 Jan 2026
25. Kang, D., et al.: Unsupervised FAQ Retrieval with Question Generation and BERT. https://aclanthology.org/2020.acl-main.74/. Accessed 16 Jan 2026
26. Sakai, T., et al.: FAQ Retrieval using Query-Question Similarity and BERT-Based Query-Answer Relevance. https://arxiv.org/abs/1905.02851. Accessed 16 Jan 2026
27. Feng, M., et al.: Question Similarity Calculation for FAQ Answering (PDF). https://www.researchgate.net/profile/Min-Feng-3/publication/4314910_Question_Similarity_Calculation_for_FAQ_Answering/links/54cff44a0cf29ca81100b7fd/Question-Similarity-Calculation-for-FAQ-Answering.pdf. Accessed 16 Jan 2026
28. Salton, G., Buckley, C.: Term-weighting approaches in automatic text retrieval (TF–IDF). https://www.cs.colostate.edu/~howe/cs640/papers/salton_termWeighting.pdf. Accessed 16 Jan 2026
29. Lin, C.-Y.: ROUGE: A Package for Automatic Evaluation of Summaries. https://aclanthology.org/W04-1013/. Accessed 16 Jan 2026
30. Papineni, K., Roukos, S., Ward, T., Zhu, W.-J.: BLEU: A Method for Automatic Evaluation of Machine Translation. https://aclanthology.org/P02-1040/. Accessed 16 Jan 2026

31. Miller, G. A.: WordNet: A Lexical Database for English. https://aclanthology.org/H94-1111/. Accessed 16 Jan 2026
32. Miller, G.A.: WordNet: A Lexical Database for English (1995 PDF). https://www.cis.upenn.edu/~danroth/Teaching/CS598-05/Papers/miller95.pdf. Accessed 16 Jan 2026
33. Sennrich, R., Haddow, B., Birch, A.: Improving Neural Machine Translation Models with Monolingual Data (Back-translation). https://arxiv.org/abs/1511.06709. Accessed 16 Jan 2026
34. Robertson, S., Zaragoza, H.: The Probabilistic Relevance Framework: BM25 and Beyond (PDF). https://www.staff.city.ac.uk/~sbrp622/papers/foundations_bm25_review.pdf. Accessed 16 Jan 2026
35. Chen, J., et al.: The BQ Corpus: A Large-scale Domain-specific Chinese Corpus For Sentence Semantic Equivalence Identification. https://aclanthology.org/D18-1536/. Accessed 16 Jan 2026
36. Google Research Datasets: WikiSplit (1M Wikipedia sentences for split-and-rephrase). https://github.com/google-research-datasets/wiki-split. Accessed 16 Jan 2026
37. Princeton-NLP (SimCSE datasets): `wiki1m_for_simcse.txt` (HuggingFace). https://huggingface.co/datasets/princeton-nlp/datasets-for-simcse/blob/main/wiki1m_for_simcse.txt. Accessed 16 Jan 2026
38. Loshchilov, I., Hutter, F.: Decoupled Weight Decay Regularization (AdamW). https://arxiv.org/abs/1711.05101. Accessed 16 Jan 2026
39. Wei, J., Zou, K.: EDA: Easy Data Augmentation Techniques for Boosting Performance on Text Classification Tasks. https://aclanthology.org/D19-1670/. Accessed 16 Jan 2026
40. Xie, Q., Dai, Z., Hovy, E., Luong, M.-T., Le, Q.V.: Unsupervised Data Augmentation for Consistency Training. https://arxiv.org/abs/1904.12848. Accessed 16 Jan 2026
41. Yan, Y., Zhang, R., Li, G., Zhang, Y., Chen, W., Peng, H.: ConSERT: A Contrastive Framework for Self-Supervised Sentence Representation Transfer. https://aclanthology.org/2021.acl-long.393/. Accessed 16 Jan 2026
42. Dai, Z., et al.: AugGPT: Leveraging ChatGPT for Text Data Augmentation. https://arxiv.org/abs/2302.13007. Accessed 16 Jan 2026
43. Gunel, B., Du, J., Conneau, A., Stoyanov, V.: Supervised Contrastive Learning for Pre-trained Language Model Fine-tuning. https://arxiv.org/abs/2011.01403. Accessed 16 Jan 2026
44. Agirre, E., Cer, D., Diab, M., Gonzalez-Agirre, A.: SemEval-2012 Task 6: A Pilot on Semantic Textual Similarity. https://aclanthology.org/S12-1051/. Accessed 16 Jan 2026
45. Gonzalez-Agirre, A., Agirre, E., Guo, W., Diab, M., Cer, D.: *SEM 2013 Shared Task: Semantic Textual Similarity. https://aclanthology.org/S13-1004/. Accessed 16 Jan 2026
46. Agirre, E., et al.: SemEval-2014 Task 10: Multilingual Semantic Textual Similarity. https://aclanthology.org/S14-2010/. Accessed 16 Jan 2026
47. Agirre, E., et al.: SemEval-2015 Task 2: Semantic Textual Similarity, English, Spanish and Pilot on Interpretability. https://aclanthology.org/S15-2045/. Accessed 16 Jan 2026
48. Agirre, E., et al.: SemEval-2016 Task 1: Semantic Textual Similarity, Monolingual and Cross-Lingual Evaluation. https://aclanthology.org/S16-1081/. Accessed 16 Jan 2026

49. Cer, D., Diab, M., Agirre, E., Lopez-Gazpio, I., Specia, L.: SemEval-2017 Task 1: Semantic Textual Similarity Multilingual and Crosslingual Focused Evaluation. https://aclanthology.org/S17-2001/. Accessed 16 Jan 2026
50. Marelli, M., Bentivogli, L., Baroni, M., Bernardi, R., Menini, S., Zamparelli, R.: SemEval-2014 Task 1: Evaluation of Compositional Distributional Semantic Models on Full Sentences through Semantic Relatedness and Textual Entailment. https://aclanthology.org/S14-2001/. Accessed 16 Jan 2026
51. DeepSeek-AI, et al.: DeepSeek-V3 Technical report. https://arxiv.org/abs/2412.19437. Accessed 16 Jan 2026

FedGAMA: Federated Learning on Heterogeneous and Long-Tailed Data via Group-Wise Asymmetric Masked Aggregation

Chenyue Xu[1,2], Zongwei Zhu[1,2](✉), Qianyue Cao[1,2], Rui Zhang[1,2], and Xuehai Zhou[1,2](✉)

[1] Suzhou Institute for Advanced Research, University of Science and Technology of China, Suzhou 215123, China
{xuchenyue,cqy_1999,ruizhang007}@mail.ustc.edu.cn, xhzhou@ustc.edu.cn
[2] University of Science and Technology of China, Hefei 230026, China
zzw1988@ustc.edu.cn

Abstract. Real-world Federated Learning (FL) deployments face the coupled challenges of data heterogeneity and long-tailed distributions. This creates a dilemma: prioritizing global long-tailed optimization yields a robust generic model but fails to adapt to client-specific heterogeneous distributions; conversely, relying solely on personalization is ineffective because the misalignment between global and local tail definitions prevents clients from learning critical shared representations. Existing approaches typically isolate these challenges, addressing either global imbalance or personalization on balanced data, thus failing to reconcile the conflict between generic robustness and local specificity. To address this, we propose **FedGAMA** (**Fed**erated **G**roup-wise **A**symmetric **M**asked **A**ggregation), a novel framework that decouples representation learning from classifier re-balancing to simultaneously enhance global and personalized performance. First, to resolve the misalignment of tail definitions, it employs a frozen Global Anchor Classifier (GAC) for robust feature extraction and a Global Probing Classifier (GPC) to estimate global distributions. Based on the GPC weight norms, it partitions head and tail classes to establish alignment of tail definitions for subsequent targeted optimization. Second, to reconcile the conflict between global and local optimization, it introduces Group-wise Asymmetric Masked Aggregation, which updates head classes universally while restricting tail updates to relevant clients, shielding tail knowledge from gradient noise. Extensive experiments demonstrate that FedGAMA outperforms state-of-the-art Federated Long-Tailed and Personalized FL methods.

Keywords: Federated Learning · Long-tailed Learning · Data Heterogeneity

J. Niu et al. (Eds.): KSEM 2026, LNAI 16631, pp. 238–251, 2027.
https://doi.org/10.1007/978-981-92-2759-4_18

1 Introduction

Federated Learning (FL) has emerged as a promising distributed computing paradigm to leverage distributed data for model training without compromising user privacy [6,16]. This paradigm has achieved remarkable success in various applications, ranging from natural language processing [5] to fraudulent credit card detection [33]. However, the practical deployment of FL is hindered by two coupled challenges: data heterogeneity [30] and long-tailed data distributions [32]. Specifically, real-world data across clients is not only non-independent and identically distributed (Non-IID) but also exhibits severe global class imbalance, where a few head classes dominate the sample space, while tail classes are extremely scarce. As shown in Fig. 1, local scarcity does not necessarily imply global scarcity. Given the data heterogeneity, a class residing in the local tail may actually be globally abundant due to the skewed label distributions across clients. For example, a specific disease might be globally rare (long-tailed) but locally abundant in a specialized medical center. Conversely, a regionally endemic disease might appear only in hospitals within a specific area, contributing to the global tail. Under such coupled challenges, a critical dilemma arises: prioritizing global generic optimization tends to produce a model that fails to adapt to client-specific heterogeneous distributions, whereas relying on pure personalization struggles to learn critical shared representations for globally rare classes due to the misalignment between global and local tail definitions.

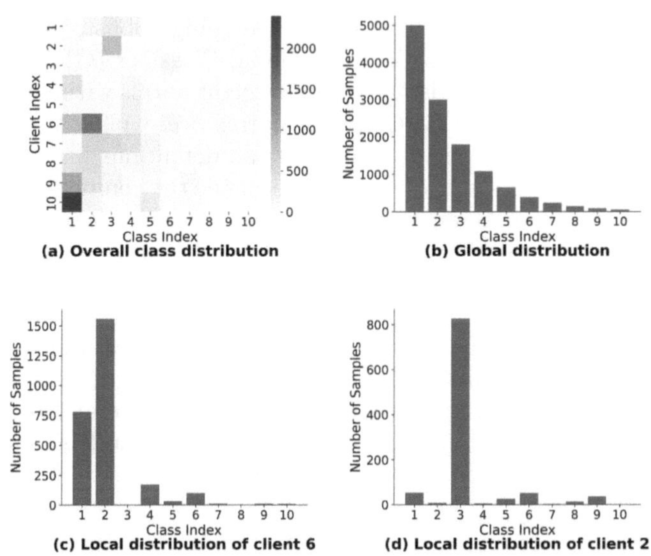

Fig. 1. An example of the joint problem of Non-iid data and long-tailed data, where the local distributions of each client and the global distribution exhibit inconsistent long-tailed class distributions. In subplot (a), darker colors in the heatmap represent a higher number of samples.

Recent works further investigate Personalized Federated Learning (pFL) [25] and Federated Long-Tailed Learning (Fed-LT) [22] to address this dilemma. pFL trains customized local models to prioritize the distinct data statistics of individual clients. However, traditional pFL methods [2,12] typically ignore global long-tailed distributions, failing to capture the critical shared representations required for globally rare classes. Conversely, existing Fed-LT works primarily prioritize global generic optimization to mitigate the bias caused by global class imbalance [29]. While effective in improving global performance, these generic models often fail to adapt to client-specific heterogeneous distributions. Although some attempts have been made to tackle both challenges [24,27], they cannot effectively decouple the optimization of head and tail classes. This often leads to a compromise where either the global model forgets tail knowledge due to gradient noise from head-dominated clients, or personalized models struggle to generalize due to the misalignment between global and local tail definitions. Therefore, how to construct a robust feature space and accurately perceive the global class distribution without transmitting private data, while effectively reconciling the conflict between generic robustness and local specificity, remains an open problem.

To address these challenges, we propose **FedGAMA**, a **Fed**erated **G**roup-wise **A**symmetric **M**asked **A**ggregation framework designed to decouple representation learning from classifier re-balancing. We introduce a two-phase training paradigm: the *Representation Learning and Distribution Calibration* phase and the *Group-wise Asymmetric Masked Aggregation* phase. In the first phase, to resolve the misalignment of tail definitions, we employ a frozen Global Anchor Classifier (GAC) to guide the backbone in learning robust, generic features, while simultaneously utilizing a Global Probing Classifier (GPC) to implicitly capture global distribution statistics through weight norms without transmitting private data. Based on these GPC weight norms, we explicitly partition head and tail classes to establish the alignment of tail definitions for subsequent targeted optimization. In the second phase, to reconcile the conflict between generic robustness and local specificity, we implement an asymmetric aggregation strategy that provides exclusive protection for global tail classes. By masking out updates from clients that do not possess tail samples, we ensure that the global tail performance is optimized solely by relevant clients, while head classes benefit from universal aggregation. Furthermore, during local training, our strategy enables clients to focus optimization exclusively on their local data distributions. By effectively shielding tail knowledge from gradient noise and negative transfer, this paradigm naturally yields superior personalized models tailored to local needs. Our main contributions are summarized as follows:

- We propose a decoupled training paradigm utilizing a frozen Global Anchor Classifier (GAC) to establish a robust representation space, alongside a Global Probing Classifier (GPC) to estimate global distributions via weight norms, effectively decoupling representation learning from classifier re-balancing.
- We introduce a consensus mechanism using the Elbow Method on GPC norms. This approach resolves the misalignment between global and local

tail definitions, enabling accurate identification of global tail classes without accessing private local data.
- We devise a Group-wise Asymmetric Masked Aggregation strategy to reconcile the conflict between generic robustness and local specificity. By shielding tail concepts from gradient noise via selective updates, this strategy simultaneously yields a superior generic global model and customized personalized models.
- We conduct extensive experiments on benchmark datasets with varying degrees of heterogeneity and imbalance. The results demonstrate that FedGAMA significantly outperforms state-of-the-art Fed-LT and pFL baselines in both global generic accuracy and local personalized performance.

2 Related Work

2.1 Federated Long-Tailed Learning

To tackle the Fed-LT problem, recent research has diverged into several strategic streams. Model decoupling approaches, such as classifier retraining [23] and prototype-based rebalancing [29], separate representation learning from classification. Complementary to these are methods focusing on calibration and distillation [22]. Furthermore, a wide array of optimization strategies has been proposed, ranging from meta-learning [19] and client selection [31] to re-weighting [27] and advanced aggregation [3]. Although these methods mitigate the global bias, they often focus solely on the generic model, neglecting the diverse local needs of individual clients.

2.2 Personalized Federated Learning (pFL)

pFL aims to resolve the tension between global consensus and local personalization. One established paradigm facilitates knowledge transfer from the global model to local learners [10]. Another major branch employs multi-task learning, implemented via client clustering [21] or model interpolation [11]. More recently, parameter decoupling has become a favored technique for neural networks. This can be achieved horizontally-by personalizing batch normalization layers [13], arbitrary components [18], or the last layer [4]. While effective in adapting to local distributions, existing pFL methods typically rely on a robust global prior and fail to support locally scarce tail classes that require shared global knowledge for effective learning.

3 Preliminaries

We consider an FL system with a server and K clients. The overall objective is to train one generic and K personalized models. Specifically, the generic model is parameterized by $w = \{\theta, \psi\}$, and the kth personalized model for each client $k \in [K]$ is denoted as w_k. We decoupled the neural network models into a feature extractor $f(x, \theta)$ and a set of classifiers. The feature extractor, parameterized by θ, transforms input x into features h. The generic classifier $g(h, \psi)$ and personalized classifiers $g(h, \phi_k)$ then map these features to the output labels. The global objective function can be expressed as:

$$\min_{w} \sum_{k=1}^{K} \frac{|\mathcal{D}_k|}{|\mathcal{D}|} \mathcal{L}_k \left(w_k, \mathcal{D}_k\right). \tag{1}$$

where $\mathcal{D} = \{\mathcal{D}_k\}_{k=1}^{K}$ is the global long-tailed dataset composed of K heterogeneous local datasets, each with size $|\mathcal{D}_k|$. The local objective function can be expressed as:

$$\min_{\{\theta, \phi_k\}} \mathcal{L}\left(\theta, \phi_k; \mathcal{D}_k\right). \tag{2}$$

The training is executed over T rounds. In each round t, the server distributes the current global model $w^{(t)}$ to all clients for local updates. Furthermore, given that c represents the class index, for $\forall c \in C$, the classifier vector is ψ_c, and the corresponding features are h_c.

4 Methodology

In this section, we introduce our proposed FedGAMA (see Algorithm 1), a simple yet effective framework for federated learning under data heterogeneity and long-tailed distributions. To construct a robust feature space and accurately perceive the global class distribution without privacy leakage, while effectively reconciling the conflict between generic robustness and local specificity, we introduce a two-phase training paradigm designed to decouple representation learning from classifier re-balancing: the Representation Learning and Distribution Calibration phase and the Group-wise Asymmetric Masked Aggregation phase.

4.1 System Overview

The overall framework of FedGAMA is illustrated in Fig. 2, which employs a decoupled two-phase training paradigm to simultaneously address feature collapse and gradient dilution. In the initial **Representation Learning and Distribution Calibration** phase, the system focuses on constructing a robust feature space and estimating global statistics without privacy leakage. To resolve the misalignment of tail definitions, the server initializes a dual-branch classifier structure: a frozen Global Anchor Classifier (GAC) and a trainable Global Probing Classifier (GPC). During local training, the backbone is optimized under the structural guidance of the fixed GAC to prevent overfitting to local head classes, while the GPC is updated in parallel to implicitly capture the global class distribution through its weight norms.

Upon completing the first phase, the server utilizes the geometric Elbow Method on the sorted GPC norms to objectively partition the label space into

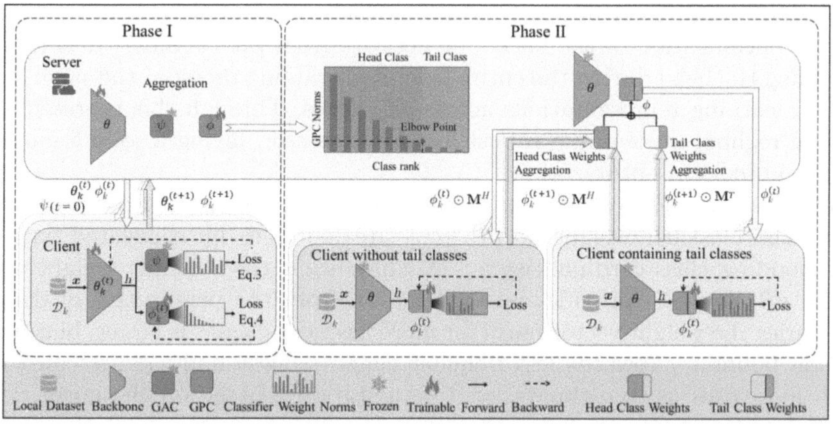

Fig. 2. The overall framework of FedGAMA. The training process is decoupled into two phases: (1) **Phase I:** Clients train the backbone guided by a frozen Global Anchor Classifier (GAC) while simultaneously estimating class statistics via a Global Probing Classifier (GPC). (2) **Phase II:** The server identifies the head-tail boundary using the Elbow Point of GPC norms. Clients are then grouped based on their local data composition to perform asymmetric updates, where tail-class weights are aggregated exclusively from relevant clients to prevent gradient dilution.

head and tail sets. The system then transitions to the **Group-wise Asymmetric Masked Aggregation** phase. In this stage, the backbone is frozen to preserve the learned generic representations, and the optimization focus shifts to classifier re-balancing. The server categorizes clients into two groups based on their local data composition and employs an asymmetric routing strategy: head class parameters are aggregated universally from all participating clients to ensure generalization, whereas tail class parameters are updated and aggregated exclusively from clients possessing tail samples. This selective mechanism effectively shields the vulnerable tail concepts from gradient noise and negative transfer caused by irrelevant clients.

4.2 Representation Learning and Distribution Calibration

Directly training a unified model on heterogeneous long-tailed data often leads to feature collapse, where the backbone overfits to local head classes and fails to generalize. To circumvent this, we conduct Representation Learning and Distribution Calibration Phase, decoupling the optimization of feature extraction from distribution estimation.

Initializing a classifier and subsequently freezing it during training has proven to be an effective strategy in federated learning [17]. Inspired by these findings, we introduce a Global Anchor Classifier (GAC) denoted by ψ to regularize the feature extraction process during the initial phase. Specifically, we initialize the classifier weights as a fixed matrix and freeze them throughout the Representation Learning and Distribution Calibration Phase. This design effectively decouples the optimization of the backbone network from the classifier. It is thought that fixing the head during the entire federated training provides the same guidelines on learning representations across all clients. Through this representation learning regime, we obtain a robust feature extractor, laying a solid foundation for the subsequent optimization.

To obtain a good estimation of class cardinality, in prior work such as [7, 14,26], the classifier weight norms $\|\psi_c\|$ are found to be correlated with the corresponding class cardinalities n_c, in which ψ_c is the classifier weight vector for the cth class. [8] provides an explanation from the perspective of decision boundaries the weight vector norm for more frequent classes is larger, biasing the decision boundary towards less frequent classes. These findings are consistent, which motivates us to estimate local data statistics based on the norm weight of the classifier.

Although the frozen GAC stabilizes representation learning, it is incapable of reflecting global class statistics, because its norm is randomly initialized and fixed. To address this, We design a new Global Probing Classifier(GPC) denoted by ϕ to obtain valid norms, which participate in gradient updates and weight aggregation alongside the backbone.

We have formally defined the three pivotal components of this phase: the feature extractor $f(x, \theta)$ parameterized by backbone θ, the Global Anchor Classifier (GAC), and the Global Probing Classifier (GPC).At the onset of training, the GAC is randomly initialized by the server and broadcast to all clients. In subsequent communication rounds, the server distributes the aggregated backbone and GPC parameters to the participating clients. During the local training, an input sample $\mathbf{x}_i$ is processed by the feature extractor to yield the representation $\mathbf{h}_i$. This feature $\mathbf{h}_i$ is then forwarded to both the GAC and GPC, computing two distinct losses. The loss function of backbone can be expressed as:

$$\mathcal{L}(\theta^t, \psi) = \ell_{CE}\left(\psi^\top \mathbf{h}_i, y\right). \tag{3}$$

where ℓ_{CE} denotes the cross-entropy loss function. The loss function of GPC can be expressed as:

$$\mathcal{L}(\theta^t, \phi_k^{(t)}) = \ell_{CE}\left(\phi_k^\top \mathbf{h}_i, y\right). \tag{4}$$

Crucially, we employ a decoupled optimization strategy via gradient manipulation: the gradient derived from $\mathcal{L}(\theta^t, \psi)$ back-propagates solely to update the backbone, keeping the GAC frozen; conversely, $\mathcal{L}(\theta^t, \phi^{(t)})$ updates exclusively the GPC parameters, with a stop-gradient operation applied to $\mathbf{h}$ to prevent it from affecting the backbone. After local updates, clients upload the backbone and GPC to the server for aggregation. After T rounds of such training, we obtain the converged global weights $\mathbf{w}^{(T_1)} = \{\theta^{(T_1)}, \phi^{(T_1)}\}$, where the backbone $\theta^{(T_1)}$ is robustly trained under the structural guidance of the GAC.

4.3 Group-Wise Asymmetric Masked Aggregation

Equipped with the robust feature extractor and the distribution prior encoded in the GPC norms from Phase I, we proceed to the Group-wise Asymmetric Masked

Algorithm 1. FedGAMA

Input: Clients $1 \dots K$ with datasets $\mathcal{D}_k$; Phase-I rounds T_1; Total rounds T; Learning rate η.

Output: Global model $\mathbf{w}^{(T)}$ and Personalized model $\mathbf{w_k}^{(T)} = \{\theta^{(T)}, \phi_k^{(T)}\}$.

Initialize: Backbone $\theta^{(0)}$, GPC $\phi^{(0)}$, and fixed GAC ψ.

// Phase I: Representation Learning and Distribution Calibration

for $t = 0, \dots, T_1 - 1$ **do**

  Server randomly select a set of active clients $\mathcal{S}_t$

  Clients $k \in \mathcal{S}_t$ receive $\theta^{(t)}, \phi^{(t)}$ and update in parallel:

   $\theta_k^{(t)} \leftarrow \theta_k^{(t)} - \eta \nabla_\theta \ell_{CE}(\psi^\top \mathbf{h}, y)$; $\phi_k^{(t)} \leftarrow \phi_k^{(t)} - \eta \nabla_\phi \ell_{CE}({\phi_k^{(t)}}^\top \mathrm{sg}(\mathbf{h}), y)$

  Server Aggregation: $\theta^{(t+1)}, \phi^{(t+1)} \leftarrow \sum_{k \in \mathcal{S}_t} \frac{|\mathcal{D}_k|}{|\mathcal{D}|}(\theta_k^{(t)}, \phi_k^{(t)})$

end for

// Phase II: Group-wise Asymmetric Masked Aggregation

Partitioning: Compute norms from $\phi^{(T_1)}$, find elbow c^* (Eq. 6-7), split $\mathcal{C}_H/\mathcal{C}_T$.

Grouping: Assign clients to $\mathcal{K}_H$ (head-only) or $\mathcal{K}_T$ (w/ tail); set masks $\mathbf{M}^H, \mathbf{M}^T$.

for $t = T_1, \dots, T - 1$ **do**

  Downlink: Send full $\phi^{(t)}$ if $k \in \mathcal{K}_T$, else send masked $\phi_H^{(t)}$ if $k \in \mathcal{K}_H$.

  Local Update: Clients fix θ, update $\phi_k^{(t)}$ on $\mathcal{D}_k$.

  Asymmetric Aggregation:

   $\phi_H^{(t+1)}$ via Eq. 9 (All clients); $\phi_T^{(t+1)}$ via Eq. 10 (Tail clients only).

   Global Update: $\phi^{(t+1)} \leftarrow \phi_H^{(t+1)} + \phi_T^{(t+1)}$.

end for

return $\mathbf{w}^{(T)} = \{\theta, \phi^{(T)}\}$ and $\mathbf{w_k}^{(T)} = \{\theta, \phi_k^{(T)}\}$.

Aggregation phase. In this stage, we leverage these insights to partition clients and enforce asymmetric gradient masking, thereby decoupling the optimization of head classes and tail classes.

To partition head and tail classes based on the positive correlation between the classifier weight norms and global class cardinality, relying on fixed thresholds is infeasible. This is because the precise mapping between norm magnitudes and cardinality is unknown in federated settings. Therefore, we treat the class partitioning as a signal detection problem on the classifier norm curve. Drawing upon the foundational Kneedle algorithm and the classical Elbow Method [20], this geometric approach provides a parameter-free and mathematically rigorous mechanism to detect the structural knee in discrete data, avoiding the bias introduced by manual heuristics. We utilize the Elbow Method to adaptively locate the inflection point where the marginal magnitude of weight norms diminishes significantly, serving as an objective divider between the well-represented head classes and the under-represented tail classes.

Specifically, we denote the weight matrix of GPC as $\phi = [\phi_{:,1}, \cdots, \phi_{:,C}] \in \mathbb{R}^{d \times C}$. We compute the L_2-norm for each class c and sort them in descending order to obtain a sequence of scalar values $\mathcal{V} = \{v_{(1)}, v_{(2)}, \dots, v_{(C)}\}$, where $v_{(c)} \geq v_{(c+1)}$. To geometrically identify the transition point (elbow), we map these sorted norms into a 2D coordinate system. Let P_i represent the coordinate of the c-th class rank:

$$P_c = (c, v_{(c)}), \quad \forall c \in \{1, \ldots, C\}. \tag{5}$$

We define a baseline segment connecting the head-most point $P_1 = (1, v_{(1)})$ and the tail-most point $P_C = (C, v_{(C)})$. This straight line represents the expected linear decay of norms. The vector representing this line segment is denoted as $\boldsymbol{V}_L = P_C - P_1$. To identify the elbow point, we calculate the perpendicular distance d_c from each point P_c to the baseline line. Using the point-to-line distance formula, d_c is given by:

$$d_c = \frac{|(v_{(C)} - v_{(1)}) \cdot c - (C-1) \cdot v_{(c)} + C \cdot v_{(1)} - v_{(C)}|}{\sqrt{(C-1)^2 + (v_{(C)} - v_{(1)})^2}}. \tag{6}$$

The optimal cut-off rank c^* is the index that maximizes this distance, corresponding to the point of maximum curvature:

$$c^* = \underset{c \in \{1, \ldots, C\}}{\arg\max}\ d_c. \tag{7}$$

Finally, the class space is partitioned based on this cut-off:

$$\mathcal{C}_H = \{\text{class } i \mid \text{rank}(i) \leq c^*\}, \quad \mathcal{C}_T = \{\text{class } i \mid \text{rank}(i) > c^*\}. \tag{8}$$

To facilitate focused optimization for tail classes, we categorize clients into two distinct groups based on their local data composition. Specifically, the server broadcasts the global head and tail class masks to all clients. Upon receiving these masks, each client inspects its local dataset labels to determine the presence of any global tail classes. Clients possessing tail samples are assigned to $\mathcal{K}_T$, while those containing exclusively head classes are assigned to $\mathcal{K}_H$.

We define two binary masks: the Head Mask $\mathbf{M}^H$ (where $\mathbf{M}_c^H = 1$ if $c \in \mathcal{C}_H$, else 0) and the Tail Mask $\mathbf{M}^T$ (where $\mathbf{M}_c^T = 1$ if $c \in \mathcal{C}_T$, else 0). The server aggregates the classifier weights ϕ separately for the head and tail components. We define N_H as the count of samples of clients in $\mathcal{K}_H$. N_H is denoted as $N_H = \sum_{k \in \mathcal{K}_H} |\mathcal{D}_k|$. We define N_T as the count of samples of clients in $\mathcal{K}_T$. N_H is denoted as $N_T = \sum_{k \in \mathcal{K}_T} |\mathcal{D}_k|$. For head classes $\mathcal{C}_H$, all participating clients contribute to ensure robustness:

$$\phi_H^{(t+1)} = \sum_{k \in \mathcal{K}_H \cup \mathcal{K}_T} \frac{|\mathcal{D}_k|}{N_H + N_T} \left(\phi_k^{(t)} \odot \mathbf{M}^H\right). \tag{9}$$

For tail classes $\mathcal{C}_T$, only clients in the tail group ($\mathcal{K}_T$) participate in aggregation:

$$\phi_T^{(t+1)} = \sum_{k \in \mathcal{K}_T} \frac{|\mathcal{D}_k|}{N_T} \left(\phi_k^{(t)} \odot \mathbf{M}^T\right). \tag{10}$$

The global backbone θ is frozen during this phase. The server splices the components to form the full global classifier $\phi^{(t+1)} = \phi_H^{(t+1)} + \phi_T^{(t+1)}$ and distributes it asymmetrically. The server sends the full global model $\{\theta^{(t+1)}, \phi^{(t+1)}\}$ to $\mathcal{K}_T$, and only sends the head-masked model $\{\theta^{(t+1)}, \phi_H^{(t+1)}\}$ to $\mathcal{K}_H$. Following this phase, local finetuning could be further conducted to boost the model performance. A summary of FedGAMA is given in Algorithm 1.

5 Experiments

5.1 Experimental Setup

Datasets and Metrics. We conduct experiments on three long-tailed datasets: CIFAR-10-LT, CIFAR-100-LT, and ImageNet-LT. CIFAR-10 [9] consists of 32 × 32 color images in 10 classes. CIFAR-100 [9] includes 100 classes images. They are sampled into a long-tailed distribution employing an exponential distribution governed by the Imbalance Factor (IF) [1]. We use IF = 50, 100 in CIFAR-10-LT and CIFAR-100-LT. ImageNet-LT contains 1000 classes, with the number of images per class ranging from 5 to 1,280. In order to induce a Non-IID in the training clients of each dataset, we partition the dataset using a Dirichlet distribution. The degree of Non-IID is controlled by the parameter α. We use $\alpha = 1, 0.5$ in CIFAR-10-LT and CIFAR-100-LT. We use $\alpha = 0.1$ in ImageNet-LT. A global balanced dataset is used for the calculation of test accuracy to evaluate global model (GM) performance. For personalized model (PM) evaluation, we use local test accuracy, and the local test set is sampled from the global test set. Each local test set has an identical distribution to the local training set. The accuracy of the PM is the arithmetic mean of local test accuracy across all clients.

Comparison Methods. In addition to FedAvg [16] and FedProx [12], we consider two types of state-of-the-art baselines: (1) pFL methods, including FedBN [13], FedRep [4], Ditto [11], and FedROD [2]. (2) Federated (Long-tailed) Representation learning, including FedBABU [17], FedETF [15], Ratio Loss [27] and FedLoGe [28].

Table 1. Test accuracies. CIFAR-10-LT,CIFAR-100-LT and ImageNet-LT with diverse imbalanced and heterogeneous data settings. GM/PM denotes Global/Personalized model.

Dataset	CIFAR-10-LT								CIFAR-100-LT								ImageNet-LT	
Non-IID	$\alpha = 0.5$				$\alpha = 1$				$\alpha = 0.5$				$\alpha = 1$				$\alpha = 0.1$	
Imbalance	IF = 50		IF = 100		IF = 50		IF = 100		IF = 50		IF = 100		IF = 50		IF = 100		-	
Model	GM	PM	GM	PM	GM	PM	GM	PM	GM	PM	GM	PM	GM	PM	GM	PM	GM	PM
FedAvg	79.54	87.35	71.89	86.41	79.12	89.31	72.58	89.21	42.93	60.42	38.39	62.29	42.01	61.12	37.75	62.88	32.89	53.68
FedProx	78.82	86.68	71.84	86.35	78.05	88.65	72.48	89.19	42.60	60.85	38.32	62.40	41.98	60.67	38.01	62.48	34.34	50.41
FedBN	76.21	88.52	69.65	88.69	76.18	89.02	70.51	89.43	43.15	66.72	39.08	67.24	42.45	63.89	38.29	65.81	32.05	50.18
FedRep	79.55	89.92	72.36	89.71	78.33	90.58	72.88	90.79	43.72	69.25	39.24	68.95	42.66	65.54	38.41	68.45	33.15	57.36
Ditto	78.29	89.05	71.95	88.92	78.25	89.45	71.98	89.86	43.28	64.57	38.61	65.71	41.71	62.05	38.38	63.34	34.22	67.14
FedROD	78.78	90.44	71.55	89.25	77.93	90.11	72.19	90.56	43.68	71.05	39.33	69.02	42.74	66.83	39.15	69.02	33.12	70.24
FedBABU	78.65	86.81	72.63	86.30	78.02	89.31	73.35	88.81	44.31	64.32	39.38	64.63	43.51	63.70	39.21	66.15	22.81	42.56
FedETF	80.72	74.65	67.25	73.08	74.71	81.25	65.98	79.35	42.38	60.39	38.08	64.38	42.61	63.18	42.94	64.91	21.95	41.69
Ratio Loss	80.12	87.75	72.74	87.41	78.75	89.54	73.28	89.19	43.41	61.68	39.27	63.31	42.67	62.29	38.52	63.29	35.15	52.08
FedLoGe	80.84	89.56	75.27	88.79	79.97	89.77	74.93	89.90	45.89	70.99	40.10	70.77	47.22	68.80	42.02	69.69	33.22	70.72
FedGAMA	**82.38**	**91.35**	**76.62**	**90.44**	**81.56**	**91.68**	**76.49**	**91.22**	**47.63**	**72.51**	**41.88**	**72.36**	**48.75**	**70.42**	**43.45**	**71.49**	**34.62**	**72.33**

Implementation Details. We implement the proposed method using PyTorch on NVIDIA Tesla V100 GPUs. We utilize ResNet-18, ResNet-34, and ResNet-50 as the backbone networks for CIFAR-10-LT, CIFAR-100-LT, and ImageNet-LT, respectively. For CIFAR-10-LT and CIFAR-100-LT, the system consists of $K = 40$ clients with a 100% participation rate in each round. For ImageNet-LT, we set $K = 20$ clients with a 40% participation rate. The global model is trained for $T = 500$ communication rounds. For local training, we employ the SGD optimizer with a learning rate of 0.03, a momentum of 0.5, and a batch size of 8. The number of local epochs is set to $E = 5$ for CIFAR datasets and $E = 3$ for ImageNet-LT.

5.2 Performance Comparison

As shown in Table 1, FedGAMA consistently outperforms all baselines across all settings, effectively breaking the inherent trade-off where existing pFL methods sacrifice global generalization and Fed-LT methods neglect local personalization. Attributable to FedGAMA's decoupled representation learning and group-wise asymmetric masked aggregation design, our framework yields superior performance for both generic and personalized tasks.

5.3 Ablation Study

To investigate the efficacy of each component, we conduct an ablation study on ImageNet-LT as shown in Table 2. Following standard protocols, we sort all classes based on the number of data samples in descending order and set two thresholds 75%, 95% to segregate the classes into head classes (Many), middle classes (Med), and tail classes (Few). We report Global Model (GM) accuracy on these class subsets. The removal of Asymmetric Masking results in a catastrophic drop in Few's accuracy and PM's accuracy, confirming that this strategy is crucial for shielding tail concepts from head-dominated gradients and preventing negative transfer to local models. Meanwhile, the 'w/o GAC' variant exhibits a skewed bias towards Many at the expense of tail categories, indicating that the frozen anchor effectively regularizes the backbone against overfitting. Ultimately, FedGAMA harmonizes these objectives, achieving the best trade-off between generic global performance and local personalization.

Table 2. Ablation study of different components in FedGAMA on ImageNet-LT. "w/o" denotes "without".

Method Variants	GM				PM
(Component Analysis)	Many	Med	Few	All	All
w/o GAC	**47.96**	30.28	16.03	32.97	52.30
w/o Asymmetric Masking	44.10	24.07	5.52	23.25	42.10
FedGAMA	42.85	**37.12**	**28.20**	**34.62**	**72.33**

5.4 Scalability Validation

To evaluate the scalability and robustness of FedGAMA under resource-constrained and large-scale settings, we conducted additional experiments on CIFAR-100-LT with a heterogeneity coefficient of $\alpha = 0.5$ and a reduced client participation rate of 30%. We varied the IF across 25, 50 and 100 and tested two scales of network size: a standard setup with $N = 40$ clients $N = 100$ clients.

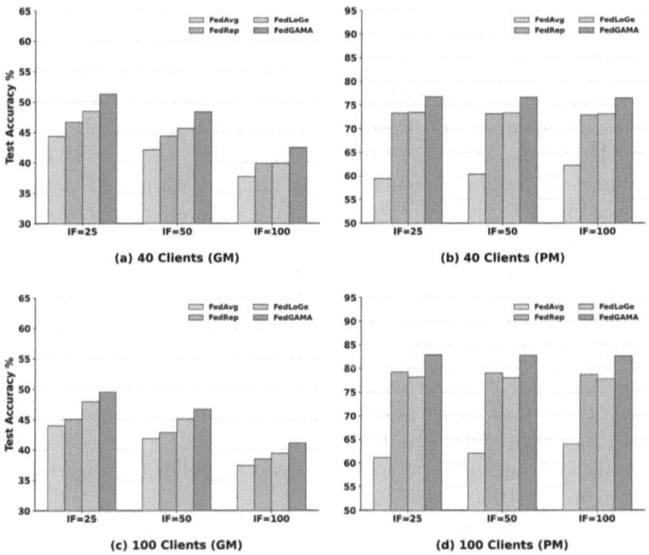

Fig. 3. Comparison of the performance of the methods under different number of client, client participation rate and imbalance factor.

Figure 3 demonstrates FedGAMA's superior resilience compared to strong baselines like FedRep and FedLoGe. Across both 40-client and 100-client settings, FedGAMA consistently achieves the highest global and personalized accuracy, maintaining significant margins even under severe imbalance (IF = 100). Notably, in the challenging 100-client scenario with partial participation, FedGAMA exhibits remarkable stability, contrasting sharply with the degradation observed in baselines. These results confirm FedGAMA's effective scalability and robustness against severe class imbalance and data heterogeneity.

6 Conclusion

In this paper, we proposed FedGAMA to address data heterogeneity and long-tailed distributions by decoupling representation learning from classifier rebalancing. Utilizing the Elbow Method to resolve the misalignment of tail definitions and group-wise asymmetric masked aggregation to reconcile the conflict between generic robustness and local specificity, our framework effectively shields tail optimization from gradient noise. Experiments demonstrate that FedGAMA outperforms state-of-the-art baselines in both global and personalized performance. Future work will extend the framework to diverse loss functions and tasks.

References

1. Cao, K., Wei, C., Gaidon, A., Arechiga, N., Ma, T.: Learning imbalanced datasets with label-distribution-aware margin loss. Adv. Neural. Inf. Process. Syst. **32** (2019)
2. Chen, H.Y., Chao, W.L.: On bridging generic and personalized federated learning for image classification. arXiv preprint arXiv:2107.00778 (2021)
3. Chou, Y.H., Hong, S., Sun, C., Cai, D., Song, M., Li, H.: GRP-fed: addressing client imbalance in federated learning via global-regularized personalization. In: Proceedings of the 2022 SIAM International Conference on Data Mining (SDM), pp. 451–458. SIAM (2022)
4. Collins, L., Hassani, H., Mokhtari, A., Shakkottai, S.: Exploiting shared representations for personalized federated learning. In: International Conference on Machine Learning, pp. 2089–2099. PMLR (2021)
5. Jiang, Z., Ren, Y., Lei, M., Zhao, Z.: Fedspeech: federated text-to-speech with continual learning. arXiv preprint arXiv:2110.07216 (2021)
6. Kairouz, P., et al.: Advances and open problems in federated learning. Found. Trends® Mach. Learn. **14**(1–2), 1–210 (2021)
7. Kang, B., et al.: Decoupling representation and classifier for long-tailed recognition. arXiv preprint arXiv:1910.09217 (2019)
8. Kim, B., Kim, J.: Adjusting decision boundary for class imbalanced learning. IEEE Access **8**, 81674–81685 (2020)
9. Krizhevsky, A., Hinton, G.: Learning multiple layers of features from tiny images (2009)
10. Li, D., Wang, J.: FedMD: heterogenous federated learning via model distillation. arXiv preprint arXiv:1910.03581 (2019)
11. Li, T., Hu, S., Beirami, A., Smith, V.: Ditto: fair and robust federated learning through personalization. In: International Conference on Machine Learning, pp. 6357–6368. PMLR (2021)
12. Li, T., Sahu, A.K., Zaheer, M., Sanjabi, M., Talwalkar, A., Smith, V.: Federated optimization in heterogeneous networks. Proc. Mach. Learn. Syst. **2**, 429–450 (2020)
13. Li, X., Jiang, M., Zhang, X., Kamp, M., Dou, Q.: FedBN: federated learning on non-IID features via local batch normalization. arXiv preprint arXiv:2102.07623 (2021)
14. Li, Y., et al.: Overcoming classifier imbalance for long-tail object detection with balanced group softmax. In: Proceedings of the IEEE/CVF Conference on Computer Vision and Pattern Recognition, pp. 10991–11000 (2020)
15. Li, Z., Shang, X., He, R., Lin, T., Wu, C.: No fear of classifier biases: neural collapse inspired federated learning with synthetic and fixed classifier. In: Proceedings of the IEEE/CVF International Conference on Computer Vision, pp. 5319–5329 (2023)
16. McMahan, B., Moore, E., Ramage, D., Hampson, S., Arcas, B.A.: Communication-efficient learning of deep networks from decentralized data. In: Artificial Intelligence and Statistics, pp. 1273–1282. PMLR (2017)

17. Oh, J., Kim, S., Yun, S.Y.: FedBABU: towards enhanced representation for federated image classification. arXiv preprint arXiv:2106.06042 (2021)
18. Pillutla, K., Malik, K., Mohamed, A.R., Rabbat, M., Sanjabi, M., Xiao, L.: Federated learning with partial model personalization. In: International Conference on Machine Learning, pp. 17716–17758. PMLR (2022)
19. Qian, P., Lu, Y., Wang, H.: Long-tailed federated learning via aggregated meta mapping. In: 2023 IEEE International Conference on Image Processing (ICIP), pp. 2010–2014. IEEE (2023)
20. Satopaa, V., Albrecht, J., Irwin, D., Raghavan, B.: Finding a "kneedle" in a haystack: detecting knee points in system behavior. In: 2011 31st International Conference on Distributed Computing Systems Workshops, pp. 166–171. IEEE (2011)
21. Sattler, F., Müller, K.R., Samek, W.: Clustered federated learning: model-agnostic distributed multitask optimization under privacy constraints. IEEE Trans. Neural Netw. Learn. Syst. **32**(8), 3710–3722 (2020)
22. Shang, X., Lu, Y., Cheung, Y.M., Wang, H.: FedIC: federated learning on non-IID and long-tailed data via calibrated distillation. In: 2022 IEEE International Conference on Multimedia and Expo (ICME), pp. 1–6. IEEE (2022)
23. Shang, X., Lu, Y., Huang, G., Wang, H.: Federated learning on heterogeneous and long-tailed data via classifier re-training with federated features. arXiv preprint arXiv:2204.13399 (2022)
24. Shuai, X., Shen, Y., Jiang, S., Zhao, Z., Yan, Z., Xing, G.: BalanceFL: addressing class imbalance in long-tail federated learning. In: 2022 21st ACM/IEEE International Conference on Information Processing in Sensor Networks (IPSN), pp. 271–284. IEEE (2022)
25. Tan, A.Z., Yu, H., Cui, L., Yang, Q.: Towards personalized federated learning. IEEE Trans. Neural Netw. Learn. Syst. **34**(12), 9587–9603 (2022)
26. Tan, J., Lu, X., Zhang, G., Yin, C., Li, Q.: Equalization loss v2: a new gradient balance approach for long-tailed object detection. In: Proceedings of the IEEE/CVF Conference on Computer Vision and Pattern Recognition, pp. 1685–1694 (2021)
27. Wang, L., Xu, S., Wang, X., Zhu, Q.: Addressing class imbalance in federated learning. In: Proceedings of the AAAI Conference on Artificial Intelligence, vol. 35, pp. 10165–10173 (2021)
28. Xiao, Z., et al.: FedLOGE: joint local and generic federated learning under long-tailed data. arXiv preprint arXiv:2401.08977 (2024)
29. Yang, W., Chen, D., Zhou, H., Meng, F., Zhou, J., Sun, X.: Integrating local real data with global gradient prototypes for classifier re-balancing in federated long-tailed learning. arXiv preprint arXiv:2301.10394 (2023)
30. Ye, M., Fang, X., Du, B., Yuen, P.C., Tao, D.: Heterogeneous federated learning: state-of-the-art and research challenges. ACM Comput. Surv. **56**(3), 1–44 (2023)
31. Zhang, J., et al.: Fed-CBS: a heterogeneity-aware client sampling mechanism for federated learning via class-imbalance reduction. In: International Conference on Machine Learning, pp. 41354–41381. PMLR (2023)
32. Zhang, J., Li, C., Qi, J., He, J.: A survey on class imbalance in federated learning. arXiv preprint arXiv:2303.11673 (2023)
33. Zheng, W., Yan, L., Gou, C., Wang, F.Y.: Federated meta-learning for fraudulent credit card detection. In: Proceedings of the Twenty-Ninth International Conference on International Joint Conferences on Artificial Intelligence, pp. 4654–4660 (2021)

Relation-Indicative Feature-Enhanced R-BERT for Entity Relation Classification

Shunran Duan, Meijuan Yin(✉), Xiangyang Luo, and Shengyuan Dai

Information Engineering University, Zhengzhou 450001, Henan, China
raindot_ymj@163.com

Abstract. Entity relation classification identifies the semantic relation between an entity pair mentioned in a sentence and is a cornerstone of information extraction. While BERT-based models perform well overall, they often underutilize relation-indicative signals such as entity-connecting word and entity type information, leading to misclassification or missed relations in complex contexts. We propose RIFER-ERC, a Relation-Indicative Feature-Enhanced R-BERT framework that strengthens both signals within a unified encoderclassifier architecture. First, dependency parsing is used to extract the connecting word that bridges the target entities; we explicitly mark their boundaries in the input so the encoder can model their full contextual semantics. Second, we insert entity type markers at entity boundaries to encode position and type priors, and further inject entity sememe information that captures deep type attributes via an attention-based enhancement of entity representations. To improve feature interaction, we design a residual classifier that fuses sentence-, entity-, and connecting-word representations for relation classification. Experiments on four public datasets (SanWen, DuIE, ACE 2005, and FinRE) show that RIFER-ERC consistently outperforms baselines in F1 and exhibits lower variance across runs, demonstrating both effectiveness and robustness.

Keywords: Entity relation classification · R-bert · Sememe enhancement · Attention mechanism · Feature fusion

1 Introduction

Relation Classification (RC) determines the semantic relation type of an entity pair based on its contextual information in a given text. As a core task in information extraction, RC plays a critical role in downstream applications such as knowledge graph construction, question answering, and text understanding. Early RC methods relied on hand-crafted features and statistical methods, but their performance was limited by feature engineering and poor domain transferability. With the rapid development of neural networks, deep networks such as CNNs [17,22] and RNNs [6,8] were introduced to model sequential texts for relation classification, substantially advancing the field.

J. Niu et al. (Eds.): KSEM 2026, LNAI 16631, pp. 252–267, 2027.
https://doi.org/10.1007/978-981-92-2759-4_19

Despite reducing reliance on manual feature design, CNN- and RNN-based approaches have intrinsic limitations. CNNs capture interactions via convolution kernels with a restricted receptive field, making it difficult to model long-range dependencies. RNNs process tokens sequentially and accumulate semantics step by step, which prevents them from explicitly modeling arbitrary token-to-token interactions. To further enhance semantic representations, researchers began adopting large-scale pre-trained language models as semantic encoders, gradually shifting RC from task-specific supervised learning to the pre-trainingfine-tuning paradigm.

Recent studies have shown that pre-trained language model based RC methods significantly outperform traditional neural approaches. The most commonly used pre-trained model is BERT [3], which learns general-purpose language representations from large unlabeled corpora. Compared with conventional neural networks, BERT better captures the semantics of entity pairs in context and has therefore been widely adopted for relation classification. Next, we briefly review BERT-based RC methods.

BERT-based relation classification methods can be roughly divided into two lines: (1) *in-text annotation enhancement*, which explicitly marks entity positions to strengthen BERT's entity awareness, e.g., R-BERT [21], BERT-MEI [9], and GSR-BERT [19]; and (2) *external knowledge injection*, which augments text representations with knowledge from knowledge graphs or label/entity semantics, such as KnowBERT [15] and KG-BERT [24].

While external knowledge can bring improvements, it may also introduce noise and error propagation (e.g., long-tail entities or cross-domain mismatch) and is less practical when reliable knowledge is unavailable. Therefore, annotation-based methods like R-BERT remain attractive due to their simplicity and effectiveness, and have been applied in finance [18], biomedicine [25], and ocean engineering [26].

However, R-BERT only marks entity positions and ignores other relation-indicative cues, notably entity types and entity-connecting word. Building on R-BERT, BERT-MEI [9] incorporates type identifiers and a connecting-word feature, but it extracts connecting-word from the shortest dependency path, which may disrupt alignment with the original sentence context and weaken contextual semantics. GSR-BERT [19] mitigates the limitation of mean pooling by learning type-related features for head and tail entities separately, yet it still falls short of capturing deep, attribute-level type semantics that are crucial for relation inference (e.g., "university" vs. "company" under the coarse type "organization"). In summary, R-BERT-style methods still face two key challenges: (i) context-preserving modeling of entity-connecting word and (ii) fully leveraging entities' deep attributes.

To address these limitations, we propose RIFER-ERC *(Relation-Indicative Feature-Enhanced R-BERT for Entity Relation Classification)*, which improves relation classification by strengthening two key relation-indicative signals: entity-connecting word and deep entity attribute information.

Our main contributions are summarized as follows:

(1) We extract the entity-connecting word that link the two target entities using dependency parsing and explicitly mark their boundaries in the original sentence, enabling the model to better capture the complete contextual semantics of the connecting word.

(2) We incorporate entity type tags to explicitly enhance type awareness, and further inject entity sememe information-reflecting deep entity attributes-into entity representations via an attention mechanism, strengthening deep entity feature modeling.

(3) Experiments on four public datasets demonstrate that our method achieves higher F1 scores than strong baselines and yields smaller performance variance, validating both the effectiveness and robustness of the proposed approach.

2 Preliminaries

This section reviews the R-BERT method and the sememe representation learning method used in this work.

2.1 R-BERT Overview

R-BERT marks the target entity pair by inserting two special boundary markers ($ and #) around two target entities and prefixes each sentence with `[CLS]`.

Suppose an input sequence for the model is $\boldsymbol{x} = \{x_0, x_1, x_2 \ldots, x_n\}$, which contains two entity spans $e_1 = \{x_i, \ldots, x_j\}$ and $e_2 = \{x_k, \ldots, x_m\}$. After BERT encoding, the corresponding contextual representations are $H = \{H_0, H_1, H_2, \ldots, H_n\}$. To obtain entity representations, R-BERT uses the average of token representations within each entity span as the initial entity representation. The two initial representations are then passed through a tanh activation and fed into the same affine layer to obtain the entity representations H_1' and H_2', as shown in Eq. 1:

$$
\begin{aligned}
H_1' &= W_1 \left[\tanh \left(\frac{1}{j-i+1} \sum_{t=i}^{j} H_t \right) \right] + b_1 \\
H_2' &= W_1 \left[\tanh \left(\frac{1}{m-k+1} \sum_{t=k}^{m} H_t \right) \right] + b_1
\end{aligned}
\tag{1}
$$

To obtain the sentence semantic representation, R-BERT applies a tanh activation to the first token `[CLS]` representation and feeds it into another affine layer, yielding the final sentence level representation H_0', as shown in Eq. 2:

$$
H_0' = W_0 \left(\tanh \left(H_0 \right) \right) + b_0 \tag{2}
$$

Finally, R-BERT concatenates H_0', H_1', and H_2' to perform relation classification using a affine layer followed by a softmax function, as shown in Eq. 3:

$$h'' = W_2\left[\text{concat}\left(H_0', H_1', H_2'\right)\right] + b_2$$
$$p = \text{softmax}\left(h''\right) \tag{3}$$

In Eqs. 1–3, W_0, W_1, and W_2 are the weight matrices of the affine layers, and b_0, b_1, and b_2 are the corresponding bias vectors. The output p denotes the predicted probability distribution over relation types. R-BERT is trained with cross-entropy loss, and dropout is applied before each affine layer to mitigate overfitting.

2.2 Sememe Representation Learning

In linguistics, a *sememe* is the smallest indivisible semantic unit [2]. The meaning of a word can be characterized as a composition of sememes from a finite, closed inventory. HowNet [5] is a widely used sememe knowledge base and has been applied to various NLP tasks such as sentiment analysis [20] and text representation learning [14]. Following prior work, we obtain sememe embeddings using the SE-WRL(SAT) approach [14].

SE-WRL(SAT) uses multiple context words around the target word as attention signals to dynamically select the most relevant sense(s) of the target word, thereby constructing a more accurate representation. Specifically, suppose a target word w has a set of context words $C(w)$. Each word corresponds to multiple senses, and each sense consists of a set of sememes. Each sememe, sense, and word is associated with an embedding vector. For each sense $s_j^{(w)}$ of the target word w, its embedding is computed as the average of the embeddings of the sememes it contains, as shown in Eq. 4:

$$\hat{\mathbf{s}}_j^{(w)} = \frac{1}{\left|X_j^{(w)}\right|} \sum_{k=1}^{\left|X_j^{(w)}\right|} \mathbf{x}_k^{(s_j)} \tag{4}$$

where $X_j^{(w)}$ denotes the set of sememes associated with sense $s_j^{(w)}$.

The "context representation" is computed as the average of word representations within a context window of size K' centered at the target word position i, as shown in Eq. 5:

$$\mathbf{w}_c' = \frac{1}{2K'} \sum_{k=i-K'}^{i+K'} \mathbf{w}_k, \quad k \neq i \tag{5}$$

The context representation is then used to compute an attention weight for each sense of the target word, as shown in Eq. 6:

$$\text{att}\left(s_j^{(w)}\right) = \frac{\exp\left(\mathbf{w}_c' \cdot \hat{\mathbf{s}}_j^{(w)}\right)}{\sum_{k=1}^{\left|S^{(w)}\right|} \exp\left(\mathbf{w}_c' \cdot \hat{\mathbf{s}}_k^{(w)}\right)} \tag{6}$$

This weight reflects the relevance of each sense under the current context. The final word representation is obtained as the weighted sum of sense representations, as shown in Eq. 7:

$$\mathbf{w} = \sum_{j=1}^{|S^{(w)}|} \text{att}\left(s_j^{(w)}\right) \cdot \mathbf{s}_j^{(w)} \tag{7}$$

With this mechanism, the representation of the target word is no longer a single vector; instead, it becomes a context-dependent mixture over multiple senses. The resulting representation is then used to predict context words and optimized via maximum likelihood. This training procedure yields representations for both words and sememes.

3 Method

3.1 Overview of RIFER-ERC

We present **RIFER-ERC**(*Relation-Indicative Feature-Enhanced R-BERT for Entity Relation Classification*), a concise R-BERT-based relation classification framework that strengthens modeling of *relation-indicative features* beyond entity position. As shown in Fig. 1, RIFER-ERC explicitly encodes three complementary signals: (i) sentence-level semantics from `[CLS]`, (ii) type-aware and sememe-enhanced representations for the target entity pair, and (iii) an entity-connecting word representation that highlights relation evidence. The overall architecture consists of three components: **input construction** that inserts type-aware entity boundary markers and entity-connecting word boundary markers; **feature extraction** that derives sentence level, sememe-enhanced entity level, and the connecting-word level features; and **entity relation classification** that fuses these features and predicts the relation type.

3.2 Input Sequence Construction

Entity types and entity-connecting word provide strong relation-indicative signals. To explicitly inject these priors into BERT, we insert type-aware boundary markers around the target entity mentions and mark the entity-connecting word span in the input sequence. Specifically, for a sentence $\boldsymbol{x} = \{x_0, x_1, x_2 \ldots, x_n\}$ containing an entity $e_1 = \{x_i, \cdots, x_j\}$ of type t_1, an entity $e_2 = \{x_k, \cdots, x_m\}$ of type t_2, and an entity-connecting word span $ecw = \{x_p, \cdots, x_q\}$, where $\{i, j, k, m, p, q\} \in [1, n]$ and $i \leqslant j, k \leqslant m, p \leqslant q$, we mark e_1 and e_2 with type-specific tags, i.e., "$< t_1 > e_1 < /t_1 >$" and "$< t_2 > e_2 < /t_2 >$". Meanwhile, we extract the connecting-word span by computing the shortest dependency path (SDP) between the two entities using a dependency parser, e.g. HanLP, and then explicitly mark the resulting span in the original sentence with "<e> *ecw* </e>" to expose relation evidence to the model.

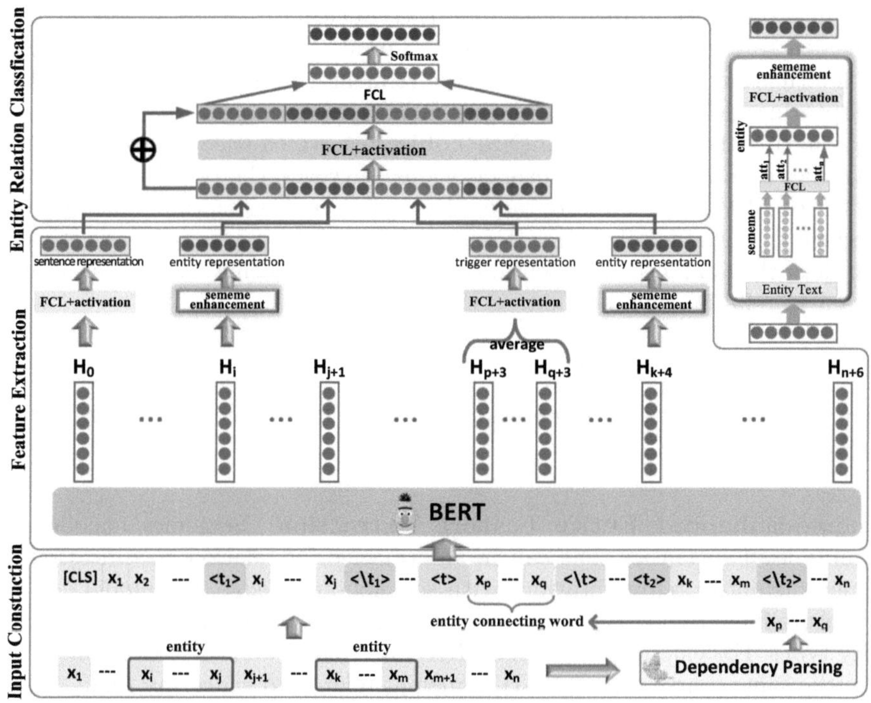

Fig. 1. Overall architecture of RIFER-ERC. The framework consists of three modules, and the inset in the upper-right corner depicts the sememe enhancement process. Compared with prior methods, RIFER-ERC differs in three key aspects: (1) explicitly marking the positions of entity-connecting word in the original sentence; (2) injecting entity sememe information into entity representations via an attention mechanism; and (3) introducing a residual structure in the classifier to yield more stable classification performance.

Marking entity-connecting word establishes a more direct dependency between two entities and encourages encoder to focus on relation-critical evidence. In long sentences or clause-heavy contexts, the explicit marking helps the model attend to the most direct semantic route between two entities, reducing interference from irrelevant semantics and thereby improving relation discrimination.

3.3 Feature Extraction for Entity Relation Classification

The feature for entity relation classification consists of three parts: (i) sentence-level semantic feature, (ii) sememe-enhanced entity feature, and (iii) entity-connecting word feature.

Sentence-Level Semantic Feature Extraction [CLS] is a special token prepended to the BERT input sequence. Through self-attention, it can aggregate information from all positions in the sequence, providing a structural basis for capturing global semantics. During BERT pre-training, [CLS] is optimized for the next sentence prediction (NSP) objective, which encourages it to encode global cues useful for sentence-level decisions. However, the [CLS] representation learned for NSP is not directly tailored to relation classification. Therefore, we introduce a learnable affine transformation followed by a non-linear activation to project the sentence representation into a task-specific space that is more relevant to relation classification, as shown in Eq. 8:

$$H_{sent} = \tanh\left(W_0 H_0 + b_0\right) \tag{8}$$

where H_0 denotes the representation of [CLS] from the last hidden layer of BERT.

Sememe-Enhanced Entity Feature Extraction. Sememes encode deep attribute-level semantics that can be informative for relation classification. By augmenting entity representations with sememe knowledge, the model can better capture fine-grained type attributes that are not distinguishable from coarse entity types. For example, although "XX University" and "XX Company" may share the same coarse type (ORG), sememes related to *education* (e.g., "education—", "study—", "teach—") are more indicative of relations such as *graduate-from* or *teach-at*, whereas sememes related to *commerce/economy* (e.g., "commerce—", "economy—") better support relations such as *investment* or *acquisition*. Based on this motivation, we enhance entity features via entity sememe information via sememe retrieval and attention-based fusion, as detailed next.

(1) Base Entity Feature Extraction

Our base entity representation differs from that of R-BERT. R-BERT averages the representations of all tokens inside an entity span and does not incorporate the representations of boundary marker tokens. This is because the boundary markers in R-BERT mainly serve as structural prompts: they provide entity position cues, occur frequently, and carry limited semantics. Averaging them with entity tokens may inject near-constant structural signals into semantic representations, introducing additional noise.

In contrast, we use type-aware boundary markers for different entity types, making boundary tokens more akin to learnable pointers. Following the practice of Soares et al. [1], we take the representation of the entity start marker (ENTITY-START) as the initial entity representation. These markers explicitly encode entity type and boundary information, and under BERT self-attention they can aggregate signals from entity-internal tokens and surrounding context, thereby capturing type-relevant and sentence-contextual semantics. Compared with mean pooling, using ENTITY-START as a stable "anchor" reduces the sensitivity of entity representations to entity length, alleviating representation bias caused by varying span sizes.

Assuming that the entity-connecting word appears between the two entities in the original sentence (as illustrated in Fig. 1), inserting boundary markers causes a position shift. In this case, the ENTITY-START of the first entity e_1 corresponds to the i-th contextual vector H_i, while the ENTITY-START of the second entity e_2 corresponds to the $(k+4)$-th contextual vector $H_{(k+4)}$. Therefore, we subsequently apply sememe enhancement to H_i and $H_{(k+4)}$ via an attention mechanism.

(2) Entity Sememe Retrieval

We retrieve the sememe set for each entity using OpenHowNet. OpenHowNet [16] is a sememe-based linguistic knowledge base developed by Tsinghua University based on HowNet, and it provides practical APIs for sememe access. We first attempt to segment the entity mention using a word segmentation tool. If the entity cannot be segmented, we query OpenHowNet using the whole entity as the keyword. If the entity can be further segmented, we use the last segment as the query keyword, because the core term that reflects the fine-grained domain of an entity phrase often appears at the end (e.g., "Apple · Company," "Tsinghua · University," "heart · disease"). For either case, if the queried keyword is not covered by OpenHowNet (e.g., person names, work titles, or other proper nouns), we fall back to using the entity type as the query keyword.

Although OpenHowNet organizes sememes in a hierarchical structure, the hierarchy mainly reflects conceptual abstraction relationships rather than context-specific relevance. Moreover, SE-WRL(SAT) [14] does not incorporate hierarchy when computing sememe embeddings. Accordingly, we also ignore the hierarchical structure in the subsequent fusion step: we treat the sememes of an entity as an unordered semantic set and integrate them into the entity representation via attention.

(3) Attention-Based Sememe Fusion

Let the sememe set of entity e_1 be $S_{e1} = \{s_1, \cdots, s_n\}$, and let the BERT representation of e_1's ENTITY-START be H_i. For each sememe $s_j \in S_{e1}$, we obtain a 768-dimensional sememe embedding following SE-WRL(SAT) [14] to match the dimensionality of BERT hidden states. Even with matched dimensionality, sememe embeddings and BERT representations may lie in different representation spaces: sememe embeddings capture context-independent static semantics, while H_i is a context-dependent dynamic representation; additionally, sememe embeddings are trained on corpora whose domain and distribution may differ from the relation classification datasets, potentially causing mismatched semantic emphasis. To mitigate both the "static–dynamic gap" and the "cross-domain distribution gap," we introduce a learnable affine transformation as a semantic adaptation layer to calibrate sememe representations toward the relation classification space.

After the affine transformation, each sememe embedding becomes $\tilde{h}_j^s$. We use the entity representation H_i as the query to compute attention weights $\mathrm{att}(\tilde{h}_j^s)$ over sememes, and then take the attention-weighted sum over S_{e1} to obtain the sememe-enhanced entity representation H_{e1}^s, as shown in Eq. 9:

$$\tilde{h}_j^s = W_s h_j^s + b_s$$
$$H_{e1}^s = \sum_{j=1}^{|S_{e1}|} \text{att}\left(\tilde{h}_j^s\right) \cdot \tilde{h}_j^s \tag{9}$$

where h_j^s denotes the embedding of the j-th sememe of entity e_1, and the attention weight $\text{att}(\tilde{h}_j^s)$ is computed as:

$$\text{att}\left(\tilde{h}_j^s\right) = \frac{\exp\left(H_i \cdot \tilde{h}_j^s\right)}{\sum_{k=1}^{|S_{e1}|} \exp\left(H_i \cdot \tilde{h}_k^s\right)} \tag{10}$$

The sememe-enhanced representation H_{e2}^s for entity e_2 is computed analogously. Finally, H_{e1}^s and H_{e2}^s are passed through an affine transformation and a non-linear activation (e.g., $\tanh(\cdot)$) to obtain the final entity representations H_{e1} and H_{e2}, as shown in Eq. 11:

$$H_{e1} = \tanh\left(W_1 H_{e1}^s + b_1\right)$$
$$H_{e2} = \tanh\left(W_2 H_{e2}^s + b_2\right) \tag{11}$$

Since H_{e1}^s and H_{e2}^s are designed to capture context-dependent semantic features rather than structural features (i.e., they are independent of relative entity positions), we share the same affine and activation layer for both entities by setting $W_1 = W_2$ and $b_1 = b_2$. This design (i) reduces the number of parameters and maps entity representations into a unified semantic subspace, and (ii) avoids hard-coding positional roles (e.g., head vs. tail) into entity representations, which could otherwise lead to shortcut learning (e.g., "W_1 implies subject and W_2 implies object"). As a result, the model becomes less sensitive to positional noise and more reliant on entity content and contextual evidence.

Entity-Connecting Word Feature Extraction. Unlike the entity boundary markers, which are designed to encode entity type information, the boundary markers for entity-connecting word serve only as *structural prompts* and do not carry semantic content. Therefore, we do not adopt the ENTITY-START representation strategy for the connecting-word span. Similar to the markers in R-BERT that purely function as structural hints, we construct the representation of entity-connecting word using mean pooling.

As shown in Fig. 1, let the start token of the entity-connecting word span correspond to index $(p+3)$ and the end token correspond to index $(q+3)$ after inserting the markers. We compute the initial connecting-word representation H'_{ecw} as the average of the contextual token representations within the span, as defined in Eq. 12:

$$H'_{ecw} = \frac{1}{q-p+1} \sum_{k=p+3}^{q+3} h_k, q \geqslant p \tag{12}$$

where h_k denotes the contextual representation of the k-th token from the last hidden layer of BERT.

We then pass H'_{ecw} through an affine transformation followed by a non-linear activation to obtain the final connecting-word representation H_{ecw}, as shown in Eq. 13:

$$H_{ecw} = \tanh\left(W_3 H'_{ecw} + b_3\right) \tag{13}$$

The affine-and-activation layer used here is *separate* from the one used for entity representations. This separation is motivated by two considerations: (1) the functional roles differ—entity representations emphasize semantic content, whereas connecting-word representation emphasizes *how* two entities are related; (2) their linguistic properties differ—entities are typically nouns, while connecting-word is more often a verb. Projecting connecting-word features with an independent layer allows the model to increase the separability between entity and connecting-word representations, and prevents relation evidence from being entangled with the entity semantic space.

3.4 Residual Entity Relation Classification Module

Many relation classifiers operate on a concatenation of different features followed by a linear Softmax layer, which provides limited capacity for non-linear reasoning and cross-feature interaction.

To address these limitations, we introduce an additional affine-and-activation layer before classification to model feature interactions. Since each feature has already been transformed by task-oriented affine-and-activation layers in previous steps, the concatenated feature vector only requires a *fine-grained correction.* To learn such corrections more efficiently and stably, we further adopt a residual structure with an "activate-then-add" design.

Specifically, let $H_{whole} = [H_{sent} : H_{e1} : H_{ecw} : H_{e2}]$, where [:] denotes vector concatenation. After an affine transformation and activation, we obtain H''_{cls}, and then apply a residual connection to produce H'_{cls}, as shown in Eq. 14:

$$\begin{aligned} H''_{cls} &= tanh\left(W_4 H_{whole} + b_4\right) \\ H'_{cls} &= H''_{cls} + H_{whole} \end{aligned} \tag{14}$$

We adopt an "activate-then-add" residual design to facilitate *fine-grained correction* on top of the already task-adapted features. Concretely, we initialize the transformation close to an identity mapping (e.g., $W_4 = 0$ and $b_4 = 0$), so the classifier starts from using the original concatenated representation and then learns small, incremental updates via backpropagation. This residual formulation reduces unnecessary feature re-construction, typically leading to faster convergence and more stable training.

We then map H'_{cls} to match the number of candidate relations and apply Softmax to obtain the final prediction, as shown in Eq. 15:

$$\begin{aligned} H_{cls} &= W_5 H'_{cls} + b_5 \\ p &= \text{softmax}\left(H_{cls}\right) \end{aligned} \tag{15}$$

In Eqs. 8,9,11, and 13, W_s, W_O, W_1, W_2, and W_3 share the same shape, i.e., $W_s, W_O, W_1, W_2, W_3 \in \mathbb{R}^{d\times d}$, where d is the hidden size of BERT. In Eq. 14, $W_4 \in \mathbb{R}^{4d\times 4d}$. In Eq. 15, $W_5 \in \mathbb{R}^{L\times 4d}$, where L denotes the number of relation types. b_s, b_O, b_1, b_2, b_3, b_4, and b_5 are the corresponding bias vectors.

During training, we optimize the model using the multiclass cross-entropy loss. Dropout is applied before each affine layer to randomly mask feature dimensions, mitigating overfitting and improving generalization.

4 Experiments

4.1 Datasets and Baseline Methods

We evaluate the proposed approach on four widely used public datasets: *SanWen* [23], a Chinese literary-domain dataset with 9 relation types; *DuIE* [11], a language understanding and reasoning dataset with 49 relation types; the Chinese portion of *ACE 2005 (LDC2006T06)*[1], which contains 18 relation types; and *FinRE* [13], a financial-domain relation extraction dataset with 44 relation types.

We compare our method with both classic relation classification approaches and recent representative methods, including BERT-CL-Biaffine [10], EINE [12], R-BERT [21], SEA-Attention [4], BERT-MEI [9], GSR-BERT [19], and TACNN [7].

4.2 Experimental Setup

All experiments are conducted on Ubuntu 22.04.4 LTS with two NVIDIA Quadro GV100 GPUs (32 GB memory each). Our method is implemented based on the PyTorch framework and the HuggingFace Transformers library. We set the batch size to 16 and use Adam with a learning rate of $5e-5$. The number of warmup steps is set to 10% of the total training steps, and the dropout rate is set to 0.1. We use `bert-base-chinese` as the underlying language model.

The sememe embeddings are trained following SE-WRL(SAT) [14]. The embedding dimension is set to 768 to match the hidden size of BERT. The training data of SE-WRL(SAT) include the 21 GB Sogou-T corpus as well as the training splits of the four experimental datasets (SanWen, DuIE, ACE 2005, and FinRE).

4.3 Comparative Experiments

To reduce the impact of randomness, we repeat each experiment 10 times and report the mean and variance of Precision (P), Recall (R), and F1. Notably, the reported mean F1 is computed as the average of F1 scores from 10 independent runs, rather than being derived from the mean P and mean R. The overall results are shown in Table 1. Figure 2 presents box plots of P/R/F1 (x-axis) across the

[1] https://catalog.ldc.upenn.edu/LDC2006T06.

Table 1. Comparative Experimental Results

Dataset	SanWen			DuIE			ACE 2005			FinRE		
	$\overline{P}$(%)	$\overline{R}$(%)	$\overline{F1}$(%)	$\overline{P}$(%)	$\overline{R}$(%)	$\overline{F1}$(%)	$\overline{P}$(%)	$\overline{R}$(%)	$\overline{F1}$(%)	$\overline{P}$(%)	$\overline{R}$(%)	$\overline{F1}$(%)
BERT-CL-Biaffine[10]	71.16 (±1.60)	72.35 (±1.52)	71.75 (±1.47)	76.09 (±2.90)	75.48 (±1.20)	75.78 (±1.79)	77.95 (±3.34)	79.51 (±1.55)	78.72 (±2.09)	63.89 (±3.41)	65.04 (±1.52)	64.45 (±1.94)
EINE[12]	70.28 (±2.34)	71.39 (±1.47)	70.83 (±1.74)	75.43 (±3.94)	76.87 (±0.92)	76.14 (±2.09)	78.65 (±4.94)	80.28 (±1.65)	79.45 (±2.81)	64.73 (±4.28)	66.83 (±1.91)	65.76 (±2.84)
R-BERT[21]	72.35 (±0.91)	73.64 (±1.50)	72.99 (±1.13)	75.84 (±1.17)	77.52 (±0.64)	76.67 (±0.69)	80.24 (±0.74)	81.23 (±1.27)	80.73 (±0.75)	65.21 (±2.46)	66.06 (±0.84)	65.63 (±1.50)
SEA-Attention[4]	74.62 (±2.92)	77.27 (±1.42)	75.92 (±2.00)	77.63 (±6.25)	79.84 (±2.12)	78.71 (±3.56)	79.64 (±4.33)	81.95 (±1.42)	80.77 (±2.27)	64.39 (±2.92)	66.57 (±1.50)	65.46 (±2.09)
BERT-MEI[9]	74.91 (±0.90)	77.68 (±0.51)	76.27 (±0.59)	78.21 (±0.41)	79.65 (±0.68)	78.92 (±0.44)	80.23 (±0.40)	82.07 (±0.61)	81.14 (±0.47)	65.42 (±0.98)	66.94 (±0.73)	66.17 (±0.63)
GSR-BERT[19]	75.17 (±1.19)	<u>78.34</u> (±0.29)	76.72 (±0.61)	78.16 (±1.13)	80.83 (±0.61)	79.47 (±0.82)	81.67 (±1.06)	<u>82.25</u> (±0.47)	<u>81.96</u> (±0.73)	67.17 (±1.19)	<u>68.26</u> (±1.05)	67.71 (±0.80)
TACNN[7]	**79.69** (±2.68)	78.15 (±0.98)	<u>78.91</u> (±1.57)	<u>82.32</u> (±1.91)	<u>81.27</u> (±0.56)	<u>81.79</u> (±1.05)	<u>82.41</u> (±1.57)	81.16 (±0.92)	81.78 (±1.18)	**68.83** (±0.65)	67.25 (±1.20)	<u>68.03</u> (±0.86)
RIFER-ERC	<u>79.21</u> (±0.87)	**81.14** (±0.53)	**80.16** (±0.63)	**83.68** (±1.10)	**85.36** (±0.50)	**84.51** (±0.75)	**83.22** (±1.51)	**84.37** (±0.47)	**83.79** (±0.77)	<u>68.73</u> (±1.11)	**70.81** (±0.53)	**69.75** (±0.69)

four datasets (y-axis), where circles denote mean values; the mean F1 values are connected by a magenta dashed line to illustrate the performance trend across methods.

The comparative experimental results demonstrate the following:

(1) **Overall effectiveness across datasets.** Our method achieves the best F1 on all four datasets. Compared with the baselines, it improves F1 by 1.25%–9.33% on SanWen, 2.72%–8.73% on DuIE, 1.83%–5.07% on ACE 2005, and 1.72%–5.30% on FinRE. The largest improvement over the second-best method is on DuIE, possibly because DuIE contains more relation categories (49 types), yielding a larger classification space. Explicitly introducing entity-connecting word as relation evidence can narrow the candidate relation space to some extent; meanwhile, sememe enhancement provides finer-grained semantics that helps reduce confusion among closely related relations.

(2) **Robustness and stability.** As reflected by the variances in Table 1 and the box-plot in Fig. 2, the proposed method exhibits smaller or comparable F1 fluctuations relative to baselines, suggesting robust performance across datasets. R-BERT and GSR-BERT also show relatively low variance, which may be attributed to explicit entity marking that provides stable and direct supervision signals, making fine-tuning less sensitive to random initialization and data perturbations.

(3) **Recall-oriented gains.** From Table 1, our method yields a modest gain in precision (+0.3975% on average) but a substantially larger gain in recall

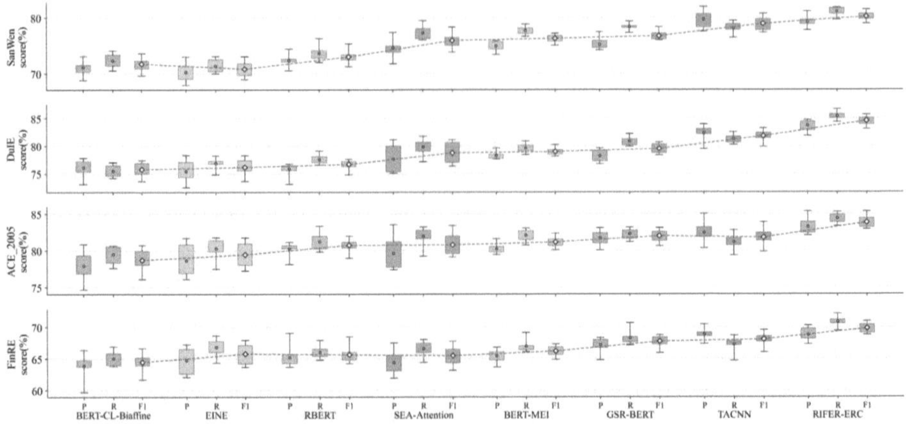

Fig. 2. The box plots of Precision (P), Recall (R), and F1, where the magenta dashed line connects the mean F1 scores of each method(x-axis) across the four datasets(y-axis).

(+2.89% on average) relative to the strongest baseline, indicating that the improvements are primarily recall-driven. This may be because explicitly marking entity-connecting words provides direct lexical evidence of relational events, which helps the model focus on relation-bearing regions and reduces false negatives. In addition, sememe enhancement decomposes entity semantics into finer-grained, compositional semantic units, which may further reduce missed detections.

4.4 Ablation Experiments

To assess the contributions of the sememe enhancement module and the entity-connecting word to the overall performance, we conduct an ablation study by removing key components from the full model one at a time. Specifically, we denote the variant without sememe enhancement as **-sememe**, the variant without entity-connecting word as **-ecw**, and the variant removing both components as **-s&e**. For each ablation setting, we repeat experiments 10 times. Table 2 reports the mean and variance of P/R/F1 on the four datasets.

From Table 2, we observe:

(1) **Both components consistently improve performance and stability.** Removing sememe information (**-sememe**) or removing entity-connecting word (**-ecw**) leads to a stable performance drop across all four datasets, demonstrating that both sememe information and connecting-word are effective for relation classification. Moreover, the variances of **-sememe** and **-ecw** generally increase, suggesting that these two components not only improve accuracy but also contribute to more stable training.

(2) **Sememes and entity-connecting word contribute differently to precision and recall.** After removing sememe information (**-sememe**), pre-

Table 2. Ablation Experiment Results

Method	SanWen			DuIE			ACE 2005			FinRE		
	$\overline{P}$(%)	$\overline{R}$(%)	$\overline{F1}$(%)	$\overline{P}$(%)	$\overline{R}$(%)	$\overline{F1}$(%)	$\overline{P}$(%)	$\overline{R}$(%)	$\overline{F1}$(%)	$\overline{P}$(%)	$\overline{R}$(%)	$\overline{F1}$(%)
RIFER-ERC	79.21 (±0.87)	81.14 (±0.53)	80.16 (±0.63)	83.67 (±1.10)	85.36 (±0.50)	84.51 (±0.75)	83.21 (±1.51)	84.37 (±0.47)	83.79 (±0.77)	68.73 (±1.11)	70.81 (±0.53)	69.75 (±0.69)
-sememe	75.14 (±1.37)	79.57 (±0.80)	77.29 (±1.00)	80.18 (±0.91)	83.84 (±0.92)	81.97 (±0.84)	80.85 (±1.38)	83.45 (±0.58)	82.13 (±0.88)	67.09 (±0.97)	69.35 (±0.92)	68.20 (±0.84)
-ecw	77.65 (±1.37)	76.44 (±0.64)	77.04 (±0.92)	82.16 (±1.17)	81.37 (±1.02)	81.76 (±0.88)	82.47 (±0.62)	82.19 (±0.84)	82.33 (±0.58)	68.35 (±1.54)	67.54 (±0.66)	67.94 (±1.00)
-s&e	73.17 (±2.04)	74.87 (±1.18)	74.01 (±1.44)	77.14 (±1.95)	78.56 (±1.55)	77.84 (±1.63)	80.54 (±2.21)	81.57 (±1.09)	81.05 (±1.42)	66.24 (±1.56)	67.17 (±1.07)	66.70 (±1.27)

cision and recall decrease by 2.89% and 1.37% on average, respectively. After removing entity-connecting word (**-ecw**), precision and recall decrease by 1.05% and 3.54% on average, respectively. This pattern is likely because sememe information models relations at a more abstract semantic level, enhancing discriminability among relations and thus improving precision, whereas entity-connecting word provide explicit evidence that a relation occurs, helping the model localize potential relation cues and reduce missed detections, thereby improving recall.

(3) **The two components are complementary.** When both sememe information and entity-connecting words are removed (**-s&e**), performance drops most substantially and the F1 scores reach the lowest on all four datasets. This indicates that the two components complement each other. Sememe information provides abstract and relatively stable semantic constraints on relations, while connecting-word offers concrete lexical evidence for relation judgment. Their combination yields synergistic gains across the semantic abstraction level and the surface textual expression level, improving overall relation classification performance.

5 Conclusion

We proposed a relation-indicative feature-enhanced R-BERT framework for entity relation classification. By explicitly marking entity types and entity-connecting word in the input and deeply integrating entity sememe information with contextualized entity representations, the proposed method improves relation discrimination. Experiments on four public datasets (SanWen, DuIE, ACE 2005, and FinRE) show that our approach consistently outperforms baselines in terms of F1 and achieves more stable performance. In future work, we plan to incorporate external domain-specific knowledge graphs to enhance performance in low-resource domains.

Acknowledgments. This study was funded by Key Program of the National Natural Science Foundation of China (No. U23A20305) and Zhongyuan Scholars Project(No. 254000510007).

References

1. Baldini Soares, L., FitzGerald, N., Ling, J., Kwiatkowski, T.: Matching the blanks: distributional similarity for relation learning. In: Korhonen, A., Traum, D., Màrquez, L. (eds.) Proceedings of the 57th Annual Meeting of the Association for Computational Linguistics, pp. 2895–2905. Association for Computational Linguistics, Florence, Italy (Jul 2019)
2. Bloomfield, L.: A set of postulates for the science of language. Int. J. Am. Linguist. **15**, 195–202 (1926)
3. Devlin, J., Chang, M.W., Lee, K., Toutanova, K.: BERT: Pre-training of deep bidirectional transformers for language understanding. In: Burstein, J., Doran, C., Solorio, T. (eds.) Proceedings of the 2019 Conference of the North American Chapter of the Association for Computational Linguistics: Human Language Technologies, Volume 1 (Long and Short Papers), pp. 4171–4186 Association for Computational Linguistics, Minneapolis, Minnesota (Jun 2019)
4. Ding, H., Xu, X.: Relation classification based on selective entity-aware attention. In: 2022 IEEE 25th International Conference on Computer Supported Cooperative Work in Design (CSCWD), pp. 177–182 (2022)
5. Dong, Z., Dong, Q.: Hownet - a hybrid language and knowledge resource. In: International Conference on Natural Language Processing and Knowledge Engineering, 2003. Proceedings, pp. 820–824 (2003)
6. Ebrahimi, J., Dou, D.: Chain based RNN for relation classification. In: Mihalcea, R., Chai, J., Sarkar, A. (eds.) Proceedings of the 2015 Conference of the North American Chapter of the Association for Computational Linguistics: Human Language Technologies, pp. 1244–1249 Association for Computational Linguistics, Denver, Colorado (2015)
7. Geng, Z., Li, J., Han, Y., Zhang, Y.: Novel target attention convolutional neural network for relation classification. Inf. Sci. **597**, 24–37 (2022)
8. Guo, X., Zhang, H., Liu, R., Ding, X., Tian, R., Wang, B.: Attention-based combination of CNN and RNN for relation classification. In: Cheng, L., Leung, A.C.S., Ozawa, S. (eds.) Neural Information Processing, pp. 244–255. Springer International Publishing, Cham (2018)
9. Hu, H., Liu, X., Yin, M., Li, L., Liu, F.: Improving relation classification with multi entity information. J. Inform. Eng. Univ. **23**(1) (2022)
10. Hu, S., Zhang, Z., Wang, H., Jiang, L.: Entity pair relation classification based on contrastive learning and biaffine model. IEEE Access **13**, 131289–131302 (2025)
11. Li, S., et al.: Duie: A large-scale Chinese dataset for information extraction. In: Tang, J., Kan, M., Zhao, D., Li, S., Zan, H. (eds.) Natural Language Processing and Chinese Computing - 8th CCF International Conference, NLPCC 2019, Dunhuang, China, October 9-14, 2019, Proceedings, Part II. Lecture Notes in Computer Science, vol. 11839, pp. 791–800. Springer (2019)
12. Li, X., Gao, R., Qin, H., Wen, B., Tian, Y., Ma, L.: EINE: relation classification by enhancing the impact of non-entity words. In: Proceedings of the 5th International Conference on Machine Learning and Natural Language Processing, MLNLP 2022, Sanya, China, December 23-25, 2022, pp. 68–73 ACM (2022)

13. Li, Z., Ding, N., Liu, Z., Zheng, H., Shen, Y.: Chinese relation extraction with multi-grained information and external linguistic knowledge. In: Korhonen, A., Traum, D., Màrquez, L. (eds.) Proceedings of the 57th Annual Meeting of the Association for Computational Linguistics, pp. 4377–4386 Association for Computational Linguistics, Florence, Italy (Jul 2019)
14. Niu, Y., Xie, R., Liu, Z., Sun, M.: Improved word representation learning with sememes. In: Barzilay, R., Kan, M. (eds.) Proceedings of the 55th Annual Meeting of the Association for Computational Linguistics, ACL 2017, Vancouver, Canada, July 30 - August 4, Volume 1: Long Papers, pp. 2049–2058 Association for Computational Linguistics (2017)
15. Peters, M.E., et al.: Knowledge enhanced contextual word representations. In: Wan, X. (ed.) Proceedings of the 2019 Conference on Empirical Methods in Natural Language Processing and the 9th International Joint Conference on Natural Language Processing (EMNLP-IJCNLP), pp. 43–54. Association for Computational Linguistics, Hong Kong, China (2019)
16. Qi, F., Yang, C., Liu, Z., Dong, Q., Sun, M., Dong, Z.: Openhownet: An open sememe-based lexical knowledge base. CoRR **abs/1901.09957** (2019)
17. Tran, V.H., Phi, V.T., Shindo, H., Matsumoto, Y.: Relation classification using segment-level attention-based CNN and dependency-based RNN. In: Burstein, J., Doran, C., Solorio, T. (eds.) Proceedings of the 2019 Conference of the North American Chapter of the Association for Computational Linguistics: Human Language Technologies, Volume 1 (Long and Short Papers), pp. 2793–2798 Association for Computational Linguistics, Minneapolis, Minnesota (Jun 2019)
18. Wang, X., Sun, Y., Chen, C., Cui, J.: A relation extraction model based on BERT model in the financial regulation field. In: 2022 2nd International Conference on Computer Science, Electronic Information Engineering and Intelligent Control Technology (CEI), pp. 496–501 (2022)
19. Wang, Y., Hu, J., Su, Y., Zhang, B., Sun, K., Zhang, H.: Modified R-BERT with global semantic information for relation classification task. Comput. Speech Lang. **89**, 101686 (2025)
20. Wen, Z., et al.: Sememe knowledge and auxiliary information enhanced approach for sarcasm detection. Inf. Process. Manag. **59**(3), 102883 (2022)
21. Wu, S., He, Y.: Enriching pre-trained language model with entity information for relation classification. In: Proceedings of the 28th ACM International Conference on Information and Knowledge Management, pp. 2361–2364. CIKM '19, Association for Computing Machinery, New York, NY, USA (2019)
22. Xiao, Q., Gao, M., Wu, S., Sun, X.: Attention-based improved BLSTM-CNN for relation classification. In: Tetko, I.V., Kůrková, V., Karpov, P., Theis, F. (eds.) Artificial Neural Networks and Machine Learning - ICANN 2019: Text and Time Series, pp. 34–43. Springer International Publishing, Cham (2019)
23. Xu, J., Wen, J., Sun, X., Su, Q.: A discourse-level named entity recognition and relation extraction dataset for chinese literature text. CoRR **abs/1711.07010** (2017)
24. Yao, L., Mao, C., Luo, Y.: KG-BERT: BERT for knowledge graph completion. CoRR **abs/1909.03193** (2019)
25. Zhao, Z., et al.: Tl-bert: A novel biomedical relation extraction approach. In: 2021 IEEE International Conference on Bioinformatics and Biomedicine (BIBM), pp. 797–800 (2021)
26. Zhu, R., Wu, X., Hu, Y., Chen, Y., Liu, B.: OEIS: Knowledge graph based intelligent search system in ocean engineering. In: 2022 Tenth International Conference on Advanced Cloud and Big Data (CBD), pp. 151–156 (2022)

Knowledge for Cognitive Analytics

RobotDiffuse: Diffusion-Based Motion Planning for Redundant Manipulators with the ROP Obstacle Avoidance Dataset

Xudong Mou[1], Xiaohan Zhang[1], Tiejun Wang[1], Tianyu Wo[2,3](✉), Cangbai Xu[1], Rui Wang[1], and Xudong Liu[1,3]

[1] School of Computer Science and Engineering, Beihang University, Beijing, China
[2] School of Software, Beihang University, Beijing, China
[3] Hangzhou Innovation Institute, Beihang University, Hangzhou, China
{mxd,zhangxh,wtj,woty,zy2306113,ruiking,liuxd}@buaa.edu.cn

Abstract. Redundant manipulators, with their higher Degrees of Freedom (DoFs), provide improved kinematic capability and versatility, making them well-suited to applications such as manufacturing, surgical robotics, and human-robot collaboration. However, motion planning for redundant manipulators remains challenging due to the increased dimensionality of the configuration space and the complexity of dynamic environments. Traditional motion planning algorithms often struggle to scale to such high-dimensional problems, while deep learning-based planners can be unstable or inefficient on complex tasks. This paper presents RobotDiffuse, a diffusion model-based motion planning framework for redundant manipulators. RobotDiffuse incorporates physical constraints through a point cloud encoder, and replaces the U-Net backbone with an encoder-only transformer to better capture temporal dependencies, producing smoother and more coherent motion plans. We evaluate the proposed method in a challenging simulator and release a new dataset, Robot-obstacles-panda (ROP), containing 35M robot poses and 0.14M obstacle-avoidance scenarios. RobotDiffuse achieves the highest overall score in our experiments, demonstrating both its effectiveness and the potential of diffusion models for motion planning. The dataset is available at https://github.com/ACRoboT-buaa/RobotDiffuse.

Keywords: Motion planning · redundant manipulators · diffusion model · obstacle avoidance dataset · higher degrees of freedom

1 Introduction

Redundant manipulators have garnered significant attention in academia and industry because of their ability to enhance kinematic performance, agility, and dynamic capabilities with higher Degrees of Freedom (DoFs). They can

J. Niu et al. (Eds.): KSEM 2026, LNAI 16631, pp. 271–282, 2027.
https://doi.org/10.1007/978-981-92-2759-4_20

be deployed in various applications [9], including advanced manufacturing, precision assembly, surgical robotics, autonomous material handling, and human-robot collaboration. Motion planning is crucial for optimizing the robot's tasks in real-world settings, ensuring stability and smooth operation while considering environmental constraints. Higher DoFs introduce challenges in inverse kinematics during motion planning. Additionally, the complexity and variability of obstacles and the diverse starting and ending points of tasks extend beyond a single, fixed environment.

Motion planning algorithms focus on building a path from the initial to the target position, avoiding environmental obstacles, and satisfying potential constraints while optimizing the path according to certain criteria [10]. Planning algorithms fall mainly into search-based, sampling-based, and intelligence-based. Search-based algorithms can find the theoretical optimal solution but suffer from node explosion in high-dimensional spaces. Sampling-based algorithms use probabilistic completeness to address high-dimensional spaces and have improved sampling strategies to reduce search space and enhance solution efficiency. However, they are still limited by high dimensionality and redundancy, requiring significant computation time for complex problems.

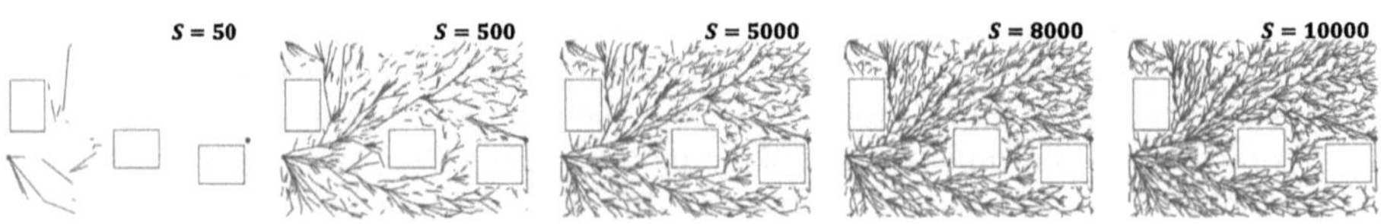

(a) Sample-based motion planning - RRT*

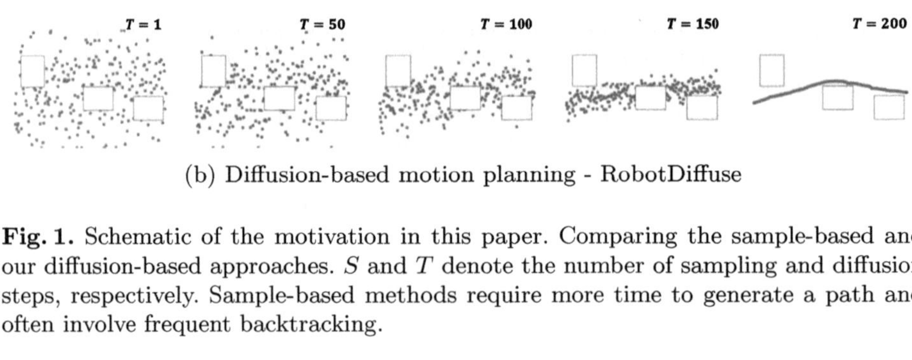

(b) Diffusion-based motion planning - RobotDiffuse

Fig. 1. Schematic of the motivation in this paper. Comparing the sample-based and our diffusion-based approaches. S and T denote the number of sampling and diffusion steps, respectively. Sample-based methods require more time to generate a path and often involve frequent backtracking.

Deep learning-based methods learn from experience and make quick decisions by leveraging problem similarities and prior knowledge. Mainstream deep learning motion planning approaches use neural networks to guide sampling directions, iteratively generating the next move until the robot reaches the target. While this simplifies motion planning, as movement is only determined by the target and environment, it has drawbacks: the solving time fluctuates with network modeling capacity and task complexity, and it overlooks previous directions while sampling points, leading to instability and unnecessary wear or inefficiency. Modeling motion planning as a motion generation task, where the neural network generates global movement in one step, offers an effective solution.

The Diffusion Model (DM) is a generative model derived from non-equilibrium thermodynamics [15]. In recent years, it has achieved excellent results in video, image, and speech generation, surpassing the Generative Adversarial Network (GAN). The core of the diffusion model is to simulate the evolution of data distribution. During training, it repeatedly adds noise and denoises to learn the transformation process from the Gaussian distribution to a complex distribution. As shown in Fig. 1, the sample-based methods require extensive exploration of the solution space and backtracking [7], whereas diffusion models proposed in this paper can quickly generate feasible solutions. The generated results have the advantages of strong generalization and high diversity. However, deploying DM on motion planning faces the following challenges: 1) The U-Net in DM excels at extracting local features but is weak in capturing temporal dependencies. 2) DM ignores physical world constraints and the unique motion characteristics of each robot. Recent attempts [1,14] employed physical guidance during DM sampling but have not directly addressed either of these challenges, which will be described in related work. This paper proposes a DM-based motion planning approach for redundant manipulators named RobotDiffuse. It describes the physical constraints during training with a well-trained point cloud encoder, accurately capturing obstacles regardless of rotations while filtering out redundant information. Then, it uses an encoder-only network to replace the U-Net structure in the DM to learn more temporal dependencies for longer motion planning. We deploy a PyBullet-based simulator [11] and generate a large and complex dataset, Robot-obstacles-panda (ROP), proposed in this paper. Experimental results demonstrate the effectiveness of our approach and the promise of diffusion models in motion planning tasks. The contributions are listed below.

- We propose a motion planning approach for redundant manipulators, RobotDiffuse, which generates more consistent moving directions than sample-based methods and, to the best of our knowledge, is the first DM-based method to introduce constraints during training.
- We leverage an encoder-only Transformer architecture to better capture temporal dependencies in movement sequences, enhancing trajectory coherence and improving the model's ability to navigate complex scenes.
- We release a challenging motion planning dataset, ROP, tailored for non-desktop scenarios, comprising 1.6 million frames of poses and 200 diverse obstacle-avoidance scenarios. Additionally, we provide the encoding methodology used for its generation.

2 Related Work

This section reviews robot motion planning research across search, sampling, and intelligence-based paradigms, with a focus on recent diffusion-based approaches. Classical Planning Paradigms Search-based algorithms, such as A^* [4] and

D^* [16], achieve global optimality by combining heuristic cost functions with actual distances. However, they suffer from the curse of dimensionality, where performance degrades sharply as search nodes increase in high-dimensional spaces. Sampling-based algorithms, including PRM and RRT, address high-dimensional challenges by connecting collision-free states in the configuration space. While RRT^* [7] and its variants (e.g., Informed RRT^*, RRT-Connect) introduce asymptotic optimality through path rewiring, they often struggle with narrow passages and the balance between path quality and computational efficiency in time-sensitive scenarios. Intelligence-based & Diffusion Models Learning-based methods like MPNet [12] utilize neural networks for multi-axis planning but frequently encounter cumulative prediction errors. Recently, diffusion models have emerged as a powerful alternative. While existing frameworks, such as MPD [1] and EDMP [14], incorporate task-specific priors or cost functions during inference, many still rely on traditional U-Net architectures and lack physical constraints during the training phase. This often leads to suboptimal performance in complex, physically-constrained 3D environments.

3 Preliminaries

3.1 Problem Definition

Notations. The posture state of the robotic arm is $x \in \mathbb{R}^D$, where D is determined by its DoF. A trajectory X is a sequence of joint states over N frames, i.e., $X \in \mathbb{R}^{D \times N}$. We use X_t to represent the trajectory at diffusion step t for $t \in \{1, \ldots, T\}$. The robot configuration space is defined as $CS \subset \mathbb{R}^D$, with obstacle space CS_{obs} and free space $CS_{free} = CS \backslash CS_{obs}$. The robot's workspace is denoted as $WS \subset \mathbb{R}^M$, where M is the workspace dimension. Similarly, the workspace can be divided into obstacle space WS_{obs} and free space $WS_{free} = WS \backslash WS_{obs}$. For a motion task, the robot moves in any state $x \in CS_{free}$. The obstacle point cloud is represented as $I \in \mathbb{R}^{K \times 3}$, where K is the number of points in the point cloud. We are interested in solving an optimization problem in the collision-free space $X \subset CS_{free}$ after a given task,

$$\min_{X} J(X; o, CS), \tag{1}$$

where the vector o represents the hyperparameter of the cost function J.

4 Method

The framework of our proposed RobotDiffuse is shown in Fig. 2. For robot motion generation, the dataset comprises pairs of (X, C), where C describes the motion sequence X, including the obstacle point cloud $I \in WS_{obs}$ and the robot's initial and final poses. The key idea is to generate high-quality and diverse robot motion sequences conditioned on C via three steps: embedding, training, and sampling. First, the task conditions are embedded in the latent space using

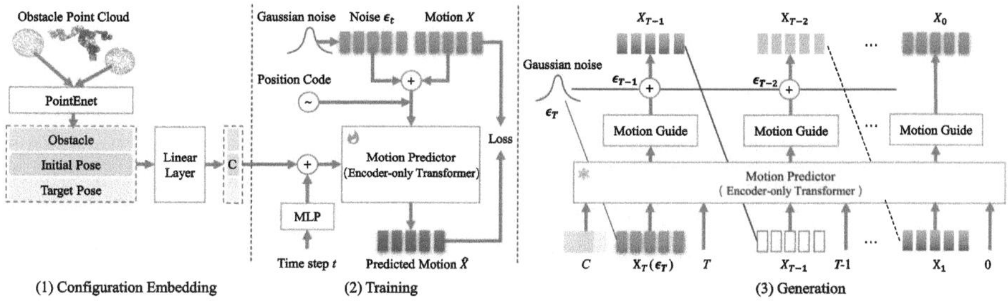

Fig. 2. RobotDiffuse overview. It contains three steps: embedding, training, and generation. (1) The obstacle point net is embedded into the latent space as z by the PointEnet component. Together with the initial pose CS_{init}, the target pose CS_{goal} comprises a condition code C. (2) C is randomly masked for classifier-free learning and then projected with t into the input token z_{tk}. Given a noise and motion X, the motion predictor based on an encoder-only transformer predicts the original clean motion $\hat{X}^{1:N}$. (3) Given a condition C, we sample random noise X_T at the dimensions of the desired motion, then iterate from T to 1. At each step t, the predictor predicts a clean sample $\hat{X}$ and then adds noise, bringing it back to X_{t-1}.

the pre-trained point-cloud encoder PointEnet, allowing the model to capture environmental and task characteristics. Then, Gaussian noise is added to the latent representation, and the denoising process is performed with a transformer network. The transformer encodes the environment embedding Z, initial pose CS_{init}, and target pose CS_{goal} with the parameter θ^p to generate a motion trajectory X. Finally, the reconstructed latent representations are restored to trajectories and are optimized with our guidance-based approach.

4.1 Condition Embedding

To eliminate the interference of irrelevant information (e.g., texture) during obstacle-avoidance motion planning and inspired by [8], we use a Compression AutoEncoder (CAE) as the point-cloud encoder for self-training. This architecture can learn a robust feature space for planning and control and performs better than other available coding techniques. CAE uses a reconstruction loss with regularization on the encoder parameters. To improve generalization, these parameters are frozen after pretraining and are not optimized in subsequent training.

$$l_{AE}(\theta^e, \theta^d) = \frac{1}{K} \sum_{i \in I} \|i - \hat{i}\|^2 + \lambda \sum_{ij} (\theta_{ij}^2)^2, \tag{2}$$

where θ^e and θ^d are the parameters of the encoder and decoder, λ is the regularization coefficient, and the output $\hat{x}$ represents the reconstructed point cloud. PointEnet, implemented with three-layer perceptrons, uses the parameter θ^e to compress the obstacle environment information $I \subset WS_{obs}$ into the latent space Z, i.e.,

$$Z \leftarrow PointEnet(I; \theta^e). \tag{3}$$

4.2 Diffusion Model for Motion Generation

Generative Adversarial Networks (GANs) are known for generating high-quality data through adversarial training, which can be effective when working with limited data. However, they often struggle to generalize under complex conditions. Moreover, predicting robot motion sequences based on tasks is not a simple one-to-one mapping, as multiple motion sequences can correspond to a given task. Inspired by the recent success of diffusion models in image generation, we apply a diffusion model to generate task-conditioned robot joint sequences. This probabilistic framework promotes diverse motion generation, and we leverage the denoising diffusion probabilistic model to facilitate this motion generation process.

RobotDiffuse uses an encoder-only Transformer instead of the common U-Net backbone in diffusion models [6,13], since it can better capture temporal dependencies in motion sequences of arbitrary length, as shown in prior work on human motion generation [17]. The Transformer takes two inputs: the time step t and the condition C. It predicts a denoised joint sequence from $X_1, \ldots, X_T$. We project the timestep t and condition C to the Transformer dimension via a feed-forward network and fuse them into a token z_{tk}. The noisy joint sequence X_t is also linearly projected to the Transformer dimension and added with standard positional encodings. The network output is then projected back to the original motion dimension to obtain the prediction $\hat{X}_0$. Given a task C, the pre-trained point cloud Enet encodes C as a potential space Z. Now, the forward diffusion process can be expressed as follows:

$$z_t = \sqrt{\overline{\alpha}_t} z_0 + \sqrt{1 - \overline{\alpha}_t} \epsilon_t, \epsilon_t \sim \mathcal{N}(0, \mathbf{I}). \tag{4}$$

z_T and the input X are fed into the diffusion model. After the reverse denoising process of step T, the final variable $\hat{z}$ is reconstructed into the robot motion path $\hat{X}$.

We optimize the diffusion model through a two-stage optimization process combined with motion feedback.

Optimize via Robot Feedback. Learning the mean can be reparameterized as learning to predict the original data x_0. Instead of predicting ϵ_t as formulated by [6], we follow [13] and predict the signal itself. The training loss is defined as a reconstruction loss of x_0:

$$\mathcal{L}_{simple} = \mathbb{E}_{x_0, n} \| \hat{x}_\theta(x_n, n, c) - x_0 \|_1. \tag{5}$$

As shown in Fig. 2, in the denoising step n, we concatenate joint pose condition c with the joint pose representation $X_1^n, ..., X_T^n$ at noise level n, combined with noise embedding as input to a diffusion model, and estimate x_0.

RobotDiffuse is trained using a composite loss function with 3 components: configuration space loss, geometric task space loss (to force accurate predictions), and collision loss (to prevent catastrophic behavior).

$$\mathcal{L} = \lambda_{joint} * \mathcal{L}_{simple} + \lambda_{point} * \mathcal{L}_{point} + \lambda_{collision} * \mathcal{L}_{collision}. \tag{6}$$

$\mathcal{L}_{simple}$ represents the L1 loss on joint angles, and $\mathcal{L}_{point}$ represents the L1 loss on the robot point cloud, where FK denotes forward kinematics, which computes the pose of each robot link given the joint angles.

$$\mathcal{L}_{joint} = \mathcal{L}_{simple} = \frac{1}{N}\sum_{i=1}^{N}\left\|\hat{x}_0^i - x_0^i\right\|^2, \tag{7}$$

$$\mathcal{L}_{point} = \frac{1}{N}\sum_{i=1}^{N}\left\|FK\left(\hat{x}_0^i\right) - FK\left(x_0^i\right)\right\|^2, \tag{8}$$

$\mathcal{L}_{collision}$ represents the collision loss of the point cloud,

$$\mathcal{L}_{collision} = \frac{1}{N}\sum_{i=1}^{N}\mathrm{h}\left(FK(\hat{x}_0^i), I\right). \tag{9}$$

The loss of configuration space has been extensively used in previous work [3]. Geometric task space loss can effectively capture the cumulative error of the motion chain. We construct a distance function D. During training, for a given closed surface, D computes the minimum distance between the robot's point cloud and the surface and returns a negative value if the point cloud is inside the closed surface

$$h(ws, I) = \begin{cases} S - D(ws, I) & if D(ws, I) \leq S \\ 0 & if D(ws, I) > S \end{cases}, \tag{10}$$

where S represents the safe distance, and $ws \in WS$ denotes a point corresponding to the robot link, including its position information in the 3-dimensional coordinates.

4.3 Motion Guided Generation

In addition, the motion sequence generated by DDPM is presented in its explicit form rather than being compressed into the latent space. Given a task, when sampling the model, the noise term $\epsilon_\theta(x_n, n, condition)$ determines the de-noising direction of the motion sequence in each iteration. Therefore, we apply physical constraints on the denoising process to guide the generation process and promote the trajectory to maintain kinematic validity. We combine several different cost functions to guide diffusion. Specifically, at each step of the denoising time, we modify the intermediate trajectory τ_t of the denoiser prediction under the first t diffusion time step. A "noise interpolation" method is proposed to control the initial and final attitude of the robot motion sequence; that is, the prefix frame and suffix frame of $\hat{x}_0$ are covered by the initial and final attitude of the task. This encourages motion generation to be consistent with the original input, solves the motion intermediate problem [5], and causes the network to produce a smooth trajectory in the start-goal pair.

5 Experiments

5.1 Datasets

To verify our approach in more complex obstacle-avoidance scenarios, we built a data generation pipeline and constructed the ROP dataset using PyBullet. ROP consists of more than 35 million frames of robot poses and more than 0.14 million obstacle-avoidance scenarios. Each scene contains challenging spherical and cubic obstacles placed at random positions. This setup is more challenging than the fixed obstacles used in most prior work.

We propose a Shared-Tree Informed RRT* algorithm to generate demonstration paths for the dataset, introducing a node security defense strategy and a shared spanning-tree strategy based on Informed RRT*. These innovations improve the performance and quality of traditional motion planning algorithms when applied to redundant manipulators. Each motion planning problem consists of three components: an obstacle scene, an initial pose CS_{init}, and a target end position WS_{goal}. Using inverse kinematics, a set of target poses CS_{goals} can be generated. A motion planning algorithm then computes a collision-free joint sequence from the initial pose to a target pose. The shared spanning-tree strategy enables a simultaneous search over CS_{goals}, allowing reuse of the generated tree and providing an efficient solution for multiple goals. The node security defense strategy addresses a limitation of traditional algorithms, which often generate paths too close to obstacles, by ensuring the robot maintains a safe distance from obstacles during motion. The dataset and visualizations are available at https://github.com/ACRoboT-buaa/RobotDiffuse.

5.2 Baselines

The proposed method is compared with several baselines, including the classical sampling-based RRT*, learning-based approaches, and diffusion-based methods. RRT* [7] is a sampling-based approach, widely recognized in path planning and known for its ability to provide asymptotically optimal paths in high-dimensional spaces. MPNet [12] uses autoencoders and multilayer perceptrons for learning-based sampling motion planning. MPINet [3] uses a PointNet++-based point-cloud network to model tasks with obstacle point clouds and robot end-effector point clouds, and uses a multilayer perceptron for motion planning. MPD [1] is diffusion-based: it pretrains an unconditional motion generator in a fixed multi-obstacle scenario and guides generation to meet task requirements via a cost function during sampling.

5.3 Evaluation Metrics

In addition to the commonly used success rate, we also consider collision rate and path length to evaluate the manipulator's trajectory more comprehensively.
Success Rate. A trajectory is considered successful if it avoids physical violations and exhibits stable motion, with the final task-space pose deviating by

no more than 1 cm and 15° from the target. Physical violations include collisions, exceeding joint limits, and erratic behavior (e.g., excessive twitching). **Collision Rate.** The rate of fatal collisions involving either the manipulator itself or surrounding obstacles. **Path length.** For redundant robots, the total path length is the sum of the link trajectories. **ComScore.** Considering that generation time should also be taken into account, we design a comprehensive metric that includes the three factors above and runtime. This metric normalizes each indicator and computes a weighted sum with equal weights. Specifically, for indicators like success rate, where higher values are better, we use

$$V_{norm} = \frac{V - V_{min}}{V_{Max} - V_{min}}, \tag{11}$$

and for indicators like collision rate, where lower values are better, we use

$$V_{norm} = \frac{V_{Max} - V}{V_{Max} - V_{min}}, \tag{12}$$

where V represents the value of each indicator, and V_{max} and V_{min} are the highest and lowest values across approaches. Finally,

$$ComScore = \sum_{i=1}^{n} w_i \cdot V_{norm,i}. \tag{13}$$

5.4 Results and Analysis

Table 1 and Fig. 3acompare performance on the ROP dataset. While RRT* and MPINet achieve high success rates at 10 min, their latency is impractical for real-time use. In contrast, the diffusion-based methods (MPD and RobotDiffuse) produce high-success trajectories in just 9–15 s. Specifically, RobotDiffuse reaches an 84.9% success rate in 15 s and outperforms all baselines within 5 min, showing an 11.6% improvement over traditional methods. Regarding path quality, RobotDiffuse produces trajectories that are 0.819 units shorter than the best sampling-based method, indicating better global optimization. Despite MPD's slight edge in smoothness, RobotDiffuse exhibits better scenario adaptability and achieves the highest overall ComScore, offering a reliable balance of efficiency and solution quality.

To provide an intuitive qualitative comparison, we visualize representative obstacle-avoidance trajectories in Fig. 3b

5.5 Ablation Studies

To systematically validate the effectiveness of our method across key components, including the point-cloud encoder, the diffusion backbone, and physics guidance, we conduct a series of ablation studies. All experiments are performed on the ROP dataset, and the results are summarized in Table 2.

Table 1. Main results on ROP dataset.

	Suc (%)↑[a]	Col (%)↓	Len↓	Time (s)↓	ComScore↑
RRT* [7]	73.3	**0**	15.037	600	0.4175
MPNet [12]	84.5	14.3	18.492	600	0.19
MPINet [3]	**87.4**	11.6	16.438	600	0.4175
MPD [1]	79.7	12.4	**14.142**	**9**	0.645
Ours	84.9	9.8	14.218	15	**0.765**

a) The arrows indicate that higher/lower values correspond to better performance.

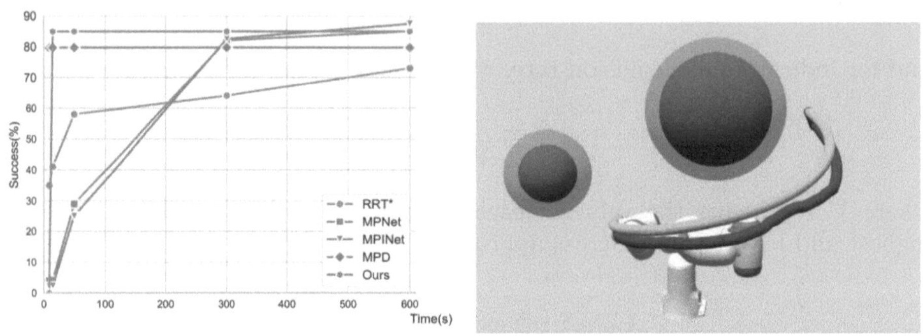

(a) Success rate (b) Visualization

Fig. 3. Comparison of success rates over time and visualization of robot obstacle avoidance trajectories.

The ablation results confirm that the CAE encoder extracts obstacle features more effectively than PointNet or DGCNN, which likely suffer from information loss when trained jointly with the planner. Regarding the diffusion backbone, the encoder-only Transformer performs best, leveraging bidirectional attention to capture long-range dependencies and global motion context while reducing computational overhead. Furthermore, adding the targeted loss components $\mathcal{L}_{\text{point}}$ and $\mathcal{L}_{\text{collision}}$ is crucial for reducing pose errors. The proposed diffusion guidance further improves the overall success rate by enforcing precise trajectory alignment in the middle stages of motion, achieving a favorable balance between collision rate and task completion.

Table 2. Ablation results.

	Suc (%)↑	Col (%)↓	Len↓	Time (s)↓
PointNet [2]	69.4	26.7	17.154	42
DGCNN [19]	73.4	22.5	16.864	64
U-Net [6]	59.3	29.7	17.358	27
Transformer [18]	69.0	16.5	17.137	32
Decoder-only	62.8	23.8	16.195	23
Noise	64.5	41.6	17.628	15
Joint-only	68.1	21.1	16.148	15
Joint&Point	74.0	19.5	14.762	15
JPC	79.1	9.2	14.571	15
Ours	**84.9**	**9.8**	**14.218**	15

6 Conclusion

In this work, we introduced RobotDiffuse, a diffusion-based motion planning approach for redundant manipulators that addresses the challenges of high-dimensional planning. By integrating physical constraints via a point-cloud encoder and using an encoder-only Transformer to capture temporal dependencies, RobotDiffuse improves both the efficiency and stability of motion generation. Our approach mitigates the computational inefficiency of traditional sampling-based methods while improving the coherence and quality of the generated trajectories. We validated the proposed method in a complex simulation environment on a large-scale dataset, and the results show promising feasibility and performance. These findings suggest that diffusion models have significant potential for motion planning, especially in dynamic and complex environments. In addition, we publicly release a trajectory-optimization dataset for non-desktop scenarios, which we hope will support and inspire further research.

In future work, we will explore fast diffusion methods to further improve planning efficiency. To better adapt RobotDiffuse to dynamic scenes (e.g., moving obstacles, changing goals, or partial observability), we will investigate online/receding-horizon replanning with streaming point-cloud observations, uncertainty-aware conditioning, and training strategies that incorporate temporal scene dynamics. We also plan to validate our approach on real manipulators with varying numbers of joints to further assess its practicality and robustness.

Acknowledgments. This work was supported by the National Key R&D Program of China (2024YFB4505604).

References

1. Carvalho, J., Le, A.T., Baierl, M., Koert, D., Peters, J.: Motion planning diffusion: Learning and planning of robot motions with diffusion models. In: IROS, pp. 1916–1923. IEEE (2023)
2. Charles, R.Q., Su, H., Kaichun, M., Guibas, L.J.: Pointnet: Deep learning on point sets for 3d classification and segmentation. In: CVPR, pp. 77–85. IEEE (2017)
3. Fishman, A., Murali, A., Eppner, C., Peele, B., Boots, B., Fox, D.: Motion policy networks. In: Conference on Robot Learning, pp. 967–977 (2023) PMLR
4. Hart, P.E., Nilsson, N.J., Raphael, B.: A formal basis for the heuristic determination of minimum cost paths. IEEE Trans. Syst. Sci. Cybern. **4**(2), 100–107 (1968)
5. Harvey, F.G., Yurick, M., Nowrouzezahrai, D., Pal, C.: Robust motion in-betweening. ACM Trans. Graph. (TOG) **39**(4), 60–1 (2020)
6. Ho, J., Jain, A., Abbeel, P.: Denoising diffusion probabilistic models. NeurIPS **33**, 6840–6851 (2020)
7. Karaman, S., Frazzoli, E.: Sampling-based algorithms for optimal motion planning. Int. J. Robot. Res. **30**(7), 846–894 (2011)
8. Liu, P., Zhong, L., Wang, R., Zhu, J., Zhai, X., Zhang, J.: Gram: geometric structure embedding into attention mechanisms for 3D point cloud registration. Electronics **13**(10), 1995 (2024)
9. Mu, Z., et al.: Hyper-redundant manipulators for operations in confined space: typical applications, key technologies, and grand challenges. TAES **58**(6), 4928–4937 (2022)
10. Mukadam, M., Dong, J., Yan, X., Dellaert, F., Boots, B.: Continuous-time gaussian process motion planning via probabilistic inference. Int. J. Robot. Res. **37**(11), 1319–1340 (2018)
11. Panerati, J., Zheng, H., Zhou, S., Xu, J., Prorok, A., Schoellig, A.P.: Learning to fly-a gym environment with pybullet physics for reinforcement learning of multi-agent quadcopter control. IROS, pp. 7512–7519 (2021) IEEE
12. Qureshi, A.H., Miao, Y., Simeonov, A., Yip, M.C.: Motion planning networks: Bridging the gap between learning-based and classical motion planners. IEEE Trans. Rob. **37**(1), 48–66 (2020)
13. Ramesh, A., Dhariwal, P., Nichol, A., Chu, C., Chen, M.: Hierarchical text-conditional image generation with clip latents **1**(2), 3 (2022). arXiv preprint arXiv:2204.06125
14. Saha, K., et al.: EDMP: Ensemble-of-costs-guided diffusion for motion planning. In: ICRA, pp. 10351–10358 IEEE (2024)
15. Sohl-Dickstein, J., Weiss, E., Maheswaranathan, N., Ganguli, S.: Deep unsupervised learning using nonequilibrium thermodynamics. In: ICML, pp. 2256–2265 PMLR (2015)
16. Stentz, A.: Optimal and efficient path planning for partially-known environments. In: ICRA, pp. 3310–3317 IEEE (1994)
17. Tevet, G., Raab, S., Gordon, B., Shafir, Y., Cohen-or, D., Bermano, A.H.: Human motion diffusion model. In: ICLR (2023)
18. Vaswani, A., et al.: Attention is all you need. NeurIPS **30** (2017)
19. Wang, Y., Sun, Y., Liu, Z., Sarma, S.E., Bronstein, M.M., Solomon, J.M.: Dynamic graph CNN for learning on point clouds. ACM Trans. Graph. (tog) **38**(5), 1–12 (2019)

MEMBERT: Inductive-Bias-Driven Modeling of Depression Emotions

Zibin Chen and Yu He(✉)

Zhuhai College of Science and Technology, Zhuhai, China
1033434803@qq.com

Abstract. Early detection of depression via social media texts is crucial for timely intervention. However, detecting such expressions is challenging due to their subtle, multi-granular, and unevenly distributed nature. While pre-trained models show promise, their high computational cost hinders deployment in resource-limited clinical settings. To address this, we propose MEMBERT, a lightweight inductive-bias-driven framework. It integrates MobileBERT with Mamba-2 modules for long-range emotional evolution modeling and an ECA-style gating mechanism for emotion-sensitive feature fusion, enhancing fine-grained modeling with minimal overhead. Experiments show MEMBERT achieves a Macro-F1 of 0.7666 and a False Negative Rate of 0.2068, outperforming its lightweight backbone and achieving competitive performance with BERT under efficiency constraints while increasing parameters by only 23.1%. This indicates a practical path for accurate, efficient, and risk-sensitive depression detection in low-resource environments.

Keywords: Depression Detection · Inductive Bias · MobileBERT · Sequence Modeling Enhancement · Emotion-Sensitive Modeling · Lightweight

1 Introduction

Detecting depression from social media texts is crucial for early intervention, as depressive expressions are often more subtle, multi-granular, and unevenly distributed than general sentiments [1]. These signals are embedded in scattered semantic cues and evolve over context, frequently appearing in short, informal texts [2]. From a knowledge-driven perspective, capturing these subtle and long-range emotional patterns is critical for early detection [3], imposing simultaneous demands on fine-grained sensitivity and long-range modeling, which are not jointly addressed by existing approaches.

To address this, we propose a lightweight architecture in which each component is designed to target a specific modeling requirement in depression emotion detection. Specifically, our contributions are:

1. We serially connect MobileBERT with three layers of Mamba-2 [4] to model long-range emotional evolution efficiently. The model captures the gradual

J. Niu et al. (Eds.): KSEM 2026, LNAI 16631, pp. 283–295, 2027.
https://doi.org/10.1007/978-981-92-2759-4_21

accumulation and transformation of depressive emotional signals across discourse spans, with a 23.1% increase in parameters.
2. We design an ECA-style gating mechanism for the Mamba-2 output, which integrates Efficient Channel Attention (ECA) [5] with a gating modulation operation [6]. This mechanism emphasizes emotion-sensitive channels while suppressing less relevant features at negligible computational cost.
3. Experiments on a multi-label depression emotion dataset confirm that the proposed framework achieves competitive performance with BERT-base on selected metrics while maintaining significantly higher efficiency and preserving efficiency close to MobileBERT, demonstrating improved task adaptability and potential clinical relevance.

2 Related Work

2.1 Traditional Feature-Based Methods

Early work on depression detection relied on hand-crafted lexical features (e.g., n-grams, TF-IDF) with classifiers like SVM [7–9]. While interpretable, these methods inherently assume emotional signals are explicit and uniformly distributed, thus failing to capture the implicit, context-dependent, and unevenly distributed cues that characterize depressive expressions.

2.2 Neural Sequence Models and Emotion-Aware Mechanisms

Neural sequence models, such as LSTMs [10] and their bidirectional variants [11], improved contextual representation learning. Hybrid architectures like C-LSTM [12] and attention mechanisms, including emotion-aware designs (e.g., EAN [13]), further enhanced sensitivity to salient cues. However, these models often struggle with two inherent challenges of depressive language: capturing extremely multi-granular emotional shades, and modeling long-range contextual dependencies efficiently, leaving room for more specialized architectures.

2.3 Pre-trained Language Models and the Efficiency-Performance Trade-Off

The advent of Transformer-based [14] pre-trained language models, particularly BERT [15], marked a significant leap in semantic understanding for depression detection. However, their substantial computational cost hinders practical use in resource-constrained scenarios. To address this issue, MobileBERT [16] adopts bottleneck and inverted bottleneck structures together with knowledge distillation from a BERT-base teacher model, reducing the model size from approximately 110M parameters in BERT-base to around 25M parameters, achieving a more favorable balance between efficiency and performance. Nevertheless, the compressed architecture of MobileBERT constrains its capacity to model complex emotional dynamics and long-range dependencies, motivating the need for lightweight enhancement mechanisms tailored to depression detection tasks.

3 Proposed Method

The proposed **MEMBERT** framework is shown in Fig. 1. This model integrates the global semantic representation of MobileBERT with the sequence modeling capability of Mamba-2 and introduces the efficient ECA-style gating mechanism, thereby achieving finer emotional feature capture in the multi-label depression emotion recognition task.

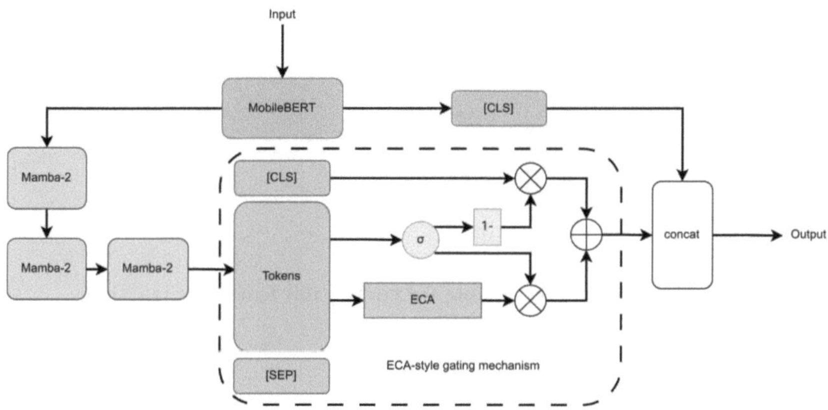

Fig. 1. Overview of the MEMBERT framework.

3.1 MobileBERT Feature Extractor

MobileBERT is adopted as the lightweight backbone for initial text representation, as illustrated in Fig. 2. Given an input sequence $X = x_1, x_2, \ldots, x_n$, MobileBERT encodes it into contextual token representations of dimension d, producing a sequence of hidden states for downstream processing:

$$H^{(\mathrm{MB})} = \mathrm{MobileBERT}(X) \in \mathbb{R}^{n \times d}, \tag{1}$$

where d denotes the hidden dimension. For downstream fusion, the global semantic representation is captured by the CLS token:

$$c_{\mathrm{MB}} = H_0^{(\mathrm{MB})} \in \mathbb{R}^d, \tag{2}$$

which serves as a compact summary of the input sequence for dual-branch integration.

Compared with BERT-base, MobileBERT introduces paired bottleneck and inverted bottleneck structures around both the self-attention and feed-forward sublayers. Specifically, hidden representations are first projected to a lower-dimensional bottleneck space ($d_b < d$) for computation, and then projected back to the original dimension. This design substantially reduces parameter count and computational cost while preserving stable cross-layer information flow.

In addition, MobileBERT reduces the number of attention heads (typically $h = 4$), allocating a larger subspace dimension to each head. While this configuration improves efficiency and maintains strong representation capacity, it also constrains the model's ability to capture complex semantic interactions and long-range emotional dependencies, which motivates the introduction of subsequent enhancement modules.

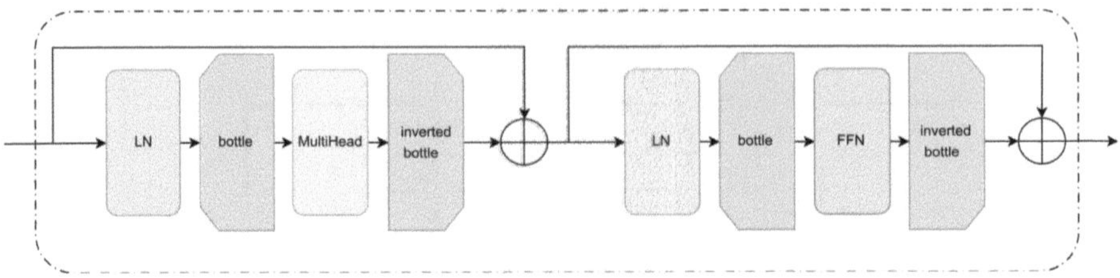

Fig. 2. MobileBERT backbone for contextual feature extraction.

3.2 Mamba-2 Sequence Modeling Enhancement

To compensate for MobileBERT's limited capacity in modeling long-range dependencies, we further enhance its representations using stacked Mamba-2 layers. Specifically, the final hidden states produced by MobileBERT, $H^{(\mathrm{MB})} \in \mathbb{R}^{n \times d}$, are fed into three sequential Mamba-2 blocks to model long-range emotional evolution.

Let the hidden state after the l-th Mamba-2 layer be:

$$H^{(\mathrm{M},l)} = \mathrm{Mamba} - 2_l(H^{(\mathrm{M},l-1)}), \quad H^{(\mathrm{M},0)} = H^{(\mathrm{MB})}, \tag{3}$$

and the final Mamba-2 output sequence is

$$H^{(\mathrm{M})} = H^{(\mathrm{M},3)} \in \mathbb{R}^{n \times d}. \tag{4}$$

where $H^{(\mathrm{M},l)}$ denotes the hidden state produced by the l-th Mamba-2 layer.

The sequence-level global semantic representation can be captured via the CLS token of Mamba-2:

$$c_{\mathrm{M}} = H_0^{(\mathrm{M})} \in \mathbb{R}^d, \tag{5}$$

which will later participate in the ECA-style gating mechanism.

Mamba-2 is built on a structured state space duality that enables linear-time complexity with respect to sequence length, while retaining powerful global context modeling. Its core innovation lies in an input-dependent selective state update mechanism. For clarity, we provide a conceptual simplified formulation to illustrate this selective behavior, rather than the full state-space parameterization of Mamba-2:

$$s_t = g_t \odot s_{t-1} + (1 - g_t) \odot \tilde{s}_t, \quad g_t = \sigma(W_g x_t + b_g), \tag{6}$$

where s_t denotes the hidden state at position t, $\tilde{s}_t$ is the candidate update derived from the current token embedding x_t, $g_t \in [0, 1]^d$ is an input-dependent gating vector, and σ is the sigmoid function. This formulation allows the model to selectively retain or update information across long sequences, which can effectively capture progressive emotional dynamics.

By stacking multiple Mamba-2 layers, the model incrementally refines sequence representations, allowing gradual accumulation and transformation of emotional signals across discourse spans. From a task perspective, this dynamic selectivity and sequence-level modeling behavior directly supports modeling the implicit, progressive, and context-dependent nature of emotional expression in depression-related texts.

3.3 ECA-Style Gating Mechanism

The sequence representations produced by Mamba-2 contain abundant fine-grained emotional cues at the token level. However, depression-related emotional cues are often sparse and unevenly distributed across feature channels, where only a subset of channels and semantic subspaces play a decisive role in emotion discrimination. To selectively emphasize emotion-sensitive features while suppressing redundant information, we introduce an ECA-style gating mechanism, as illustrated in Fig. 3.

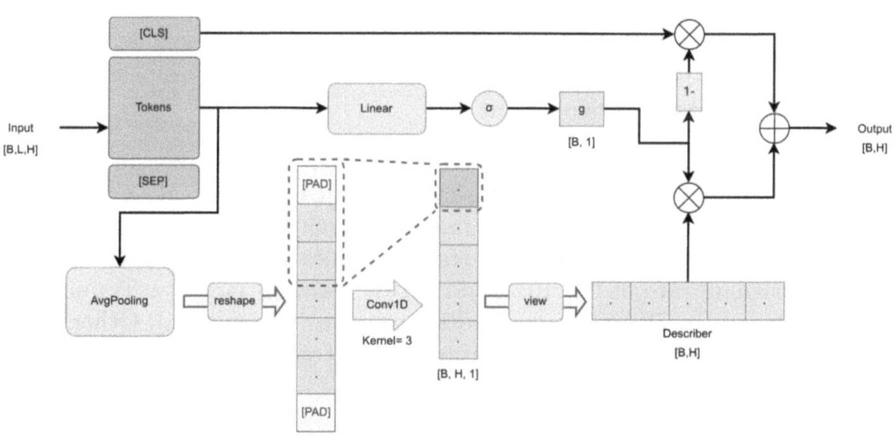

Fig. 3. ECA-style gating mechanism for integrating emotion enhancement.

Specifically, given the Mamba-2 output sequence $H^{(\mathrm{M})} \in \mathbb{R}^{n \times d}$, we first exclude the CLS and SEP tokens and feed the remaining sequence into the

ECA module to compute a channel-wise descriptor:

$$d_{\text{ECA}} = \text{ECA}(H_{1:n-1}^{(\text{M})}) \in \mathbb{R}^d, \tag{7}$$

where $H_{1:n-1}^{(\text{M})}$ denotes the token-level hidden states excluding special tokens, and d_{ECA} represents the channel-attention-enhanced descriptor.

Next, an adaptive scalar gating mechanism is applied to balance the contribution between the CLS token output by Mamba-2 $c_{\text{M}} = H_0^{(\text{M})}$ and the ECA descriptor d_{ECA}:

$$c_{\text{gated}} = g \odot d_{\text{ECA}} + (1 - g) \odot c_{\text{M}}, \quad g = \sigma(W_g \cdot \text{AvgPool}(H_{1:n-1}^{(\text{M})})), \tag{8}$$

where $g \in [0, 1]^d$ is the learnable gating vector computed from the average-pooled token representations, $\odot$ denotes element-wise multiplication, W_g is a learnable linear projection, and σ is the sigmoid function.

Finally, to preserve the global semantic information from the backbone, the gated Mamba-2 CLS token is concatenated with the MobileBERT CLS token c_{MB} to form the final feature representation for downstream classification:

$$h_{\text{final}} = [c_{\text{gated}}; c_{\text{MB}}] \in \mathbb{R}^{2d}. \tag{9}$$

This fusion allows MEMBERT to integrate fine-grained emotional cues from Mamba-2 with the global semantic representation from MobileBERT, enabling improved sensitivity to subtle depressive cues while preserving global contextual representations.

4 Experiment

4.1 Experimental Environment

All experiments were conducted in a Linux environment running under WSL2, using the PyTorch framework on a single NVIDIA GeForce RTX 4060 Laptop GPU (8GB). The batch size and maximum sequence length were set to 16 and 256, respectively. The model was trained using the AdamW optimizer with an initial learning rate of 2×10^{-5} and a 10% warmup strategy. Training was performed for up to 75 epochs with early stopping (patience=5). Other hyperparameters followed standard Transformer-based training settings.

4.2 Dataset

We evaluate our method on the DepressionEmo dataset [17], which is designed for multi-label depression emotion recognition based on social media texts. Each sample may express multiple emotions simultaneously, requiring the model to capture overlapping and fine-grained emotional patterns.

The dataset covers a wide range of text lengths, from very short posts to longer narratives, reflecting the high heterogeneity of depression-related expressions on social media. This variability poses challenges for both implicit emotion detection in short texts and long-range emotional evolution modeling in longer texts.

DepressionEmo includes eight emotion categories: anger, brain dysfunction (forget), emptiness, hopelessness, loneliness, sadness, suicide intent, and worthlessness. The distribution of each emotion across the training, validation, and test sets is reported in Table 1. As shown in the table, substantial label imbalance exists across emotion categories, and individual samples typically contain multiple emotion labels, highlighting the composite and overlapping nature of depressive emotional expression.

Table 1. Emotion category distribution in the DepressionEmo dataset

Emotion Type	Training Set		Validation Set		Test Set	
	Samples	Proportion	Samples	Proportion	Samples	Proportion
anger	1754	(41%)	346	(38%)	345	(38%)
brain dysfunction (forget)	813	(19%)	164	(18%)	171	(18%)
emptiness	1573	(37%)	358	(39%)	341	(37%)
hopelessness	2919	(69%)	640	(70%)	634	(70%)
loneliness	1929	(45%)	453	(50%)	420	(46%)
sadness	3260	(77%)	708	(78%)	697	(76%)
suicide intent	1035	(24%)	224	(24%)	232	(25%)
worthlessness	2095	(49%)	462	(51%)	434	(47%)

Following standard practice, we split the dataset into training, validation, and test sets with a ratio of 70%:15%:15%. The three subsets exhibit highly consistent statistics in terms of text length distribution and average number of emotion labels per sample, ensuring a stable data foundation for model training and evaluation. As a multi-label task, we adopt the binary cross-entropy loss with logits, treating each emotion as an independent label.

To further evaluate the generalizability of MEMBERT, we additionally conduct experiments on the Emotion Dataset [18], a widely used benchmark for single-label emotion classification containing approximately 417k samples. We adopt the standard six-class variant (joy, sadness, anger, fear, love, and surprise) from Hugging Face. For this single-label task, the standard softmax cross-entropy loss was used.

4.3 Evaluation Metrics

Due to the severe label imbalance, the multi-label nature of depression emotion recognition, and the high clinical cost of missed detections, a single metric is insufficient to comprehensively assess model performance. Therefore, we adopt a combination of standard multi-label classification metrics and clinically relevant indicators to evaluate both predictive effectiveness and safety-related behavior.

Specifically, we report Accuracy, Macro-F1 and Micro-F1 to measure overall prediction consistency and label-level performance. Accuracy is defined as subset accuracy, where a sample is considered correct only if all emotion labels are predicted correctly; as a result, its absolute value is typically low in this task and is used mainly to reflect global prediction consistency rather than as a primary optimization objective. Macro-F1 is emphasized to ensure balanced performance across all emotion categories, particularly for low-frequency but high-risk emotions. Micro-F1 complements this by reflecting the model's overall predictive capacity under label imbalance.

In addition, we introduce Recall, False Negative Rate (FNR), and Negative Predictive Value (NPV) as clinical risk indicators. Recall reflects the model's ability to capture positive emotional signals, while FNR directly measures the proportion of missed positive cases and is particularly critical in depression-related screening scenarios. NPV further evaluates the reliability of negative predictions, which is important for safe exclusion in clinical applications [19].

Macro-F1 and FNR are treated as the most important evaluation criteria in this study, as they jointly reflect the model's balanced emotion modeling capability and its sensitivity to clinically high-risk emotional states.

For the single-label Emotion Dataset, we employ the standard metrics, namely Accuracy and Macro-F1, to assess generalization performance.

5 Results and Analysis

5.1 Baseline Comparison and Ablation Analysis

To evaluate the overall effectiveness and clinical risk indicators of our framework, we compare it with representative baselines across traditional machine learning methods, neural sequence models, and pre-trained language models. Subsequently, we conduct systematic ablation studies to analyze the contribution of each architectural component and the associated efficiency-performance trade-offs. For efficiency evaluation, model parameters are counted as trainable weights, FLOPs are computed with batch size 1 and sequence length 256, and latency/FPS are measured on a single NVIDIA GPU and averaged over 100 warm-up runs. All reported results are averaged over five runs.

Based on the results reported in Table 2, MEMBERT consistently outperforms traditional machine learning approaches (SVM+TF-IDF) and neural sequence models (BiLSTM, C-LSTM, and EAN) across all major evaluation metrics. Compared with its lightweight backbone MobileBERT, MEMBERT achieves consistent improvements in both multi-label classification metrics and clinical risk-oriented indicators, indicating that the introduced Mamba-2-based sequence modeling and ECA-style gating mechanism effectively enhance the model's ability to capture complex emotional patterns.

From a macro-level perspective, MEMBERT approaches the performance of the larger BERT-base model on several metrics under strict efficiency constraints. Although BERT-base attains a slightly better performance on multi-label classification metrics, MEMBERT exhibits superior recall (0.7932 vs. 0.7874) and a lower false negative rate (0.2068 vs. 0.2126), while maintaining an equivalent negative predictive value (0.8319). Notably, these results are achieved with approximately 3.6× fewer parameters than BERT-base (30.3M vs. 109.8M), highlighting a substantially more favorable efficiency-performance trade-off. This indicates that MEMBERT is more sensitive to high-risk emotional signals, which is particularly desirable in depression emotion detection scenarios where missed positives are costly.

Table 2. Performance comparison with baseline models on the DepressionEmo dataset

Models	Params	Multi-label Classification Metrics			Clinical Risk Indicators		
		Acc.	Macro-F1	Micro-F1	Recall	FNR	NPV
SVM + TF-IDF	–	0.1104	0.6561	0.6970	0.6732	0.3268	0.7451
BiLSTM	6.4M	0.0784	0.5747	0.6080	0.5345	0.4655	0.6802
C-LSTM	6.3M	0.0762	0.5916	0.6575	0.6384	0.3616	0.7157
EAN	7.3M	0.1049	0.6129	0.6572	0.5984	0.4016	0.7116
MobileBERT	24.6M	0.2219	0.7530	0.7877	0.7608	0.2392	0.8134
BERT-base	109.8M	**0.2483**	**0.7713**	**0.8079**	0.7874	0.2126	**0.8319**
MEMBERT (ours)	30.3M	0.2263	0.7666	0.7998	**0.7932**	**0.2068**	**0.8319**

Overall, these results suggest that incorporating structured long-range sequence modeling and emotion-adaptive feature modulation under task-consistent priors enables MEMBERT to achieve a favorable balance between predictive effectiveness, risk sensitivity, and computational efficiency.

According to the ablation results in Table 3, the Mamba-2 module serves as the primary contributor to performance improvements by modeling long-range dependencies of MEMBERT. As the number of Mamba-2 layers increases from 0 to 2, both multi-label classification performance and clinical risk indicators improve steadily, with Macro-F1 increasing from 0.7530 to 0.7636 and the false negative rate (FNR) decreasing from 0.2419 to 0.2233. When three Mamba-2 layers are employed, the growth rate of the Macro-F1 score slows down, while the FNR further decreases to 0.2068, indicating that deeper sequence modeling primarily improves sensitivity to implicit and context-dependent depression-related cues rather than overall label discrimination.

From an efficiency perspective, increasing the Mamba-2 depth from 0 to 3 leads to moderate growth in model size and computational cost, whereas inference latency and throughput remain largely stable. In contrast, further increasing the depth to 4 layers results in marginal gains in Macro-F1 but a noticeable degradation in FNR and inference efficiency. This suggests that excessively deep

Table 3. Ablation study on architectural components and efficiency

Models	FNR	Macro-F1	Params	FLOPs	Latency (ms)	FPS
MobileBERT	0.2392	0.7530	24.6M	5.18G	42.42	**23.57**
MEMBERT (ours)	**0.2068**	0.7666	30.3M	6.10G	49.88	20.05
Mamba layers = 0	0.2419	0.7530	25.1M	5.18G	48.89	20.45
Mamba layers = 1	0.2315	0.7589	26.8M	5.49G	49.02	20.00
Mamba layers = 2	0.2233	0.7636	28.6M	5.79G	49.37	19.99
Mamba layers = 3	**0.2068**	0.7666	30.3M	6.10G	49.88	20.05
Mamba layers = 4	0.2187	**0.7710**	32.0M	6.40G	53.07	18.84
w/o ECA (Max pooling)	0.2502	0.7432	30.3M	6.10G	53.65	18.64
w/o ECA (Mean pooling)	0.2193	0.7576	30.3M	6.10G	52.53	19.04

sequence modeling may bias the model toward dominant or explicit emotional patterns while offering limited benefits for detecting weak or implicit depressive signals, which is inconsistent with the task's emphasis on minimizing false negatives. Therefore, three Mamba-2 layers represent a more appropriate trade-off between sensitivity and efficiency under task-specific priors.

The ablation results for the fusion strategy also highlight the importance of the ECA mechanism. Replacing ECA with max pooling leads to a substantial degradation in both Macro-F1 and FNR, indicating severe information loss caused by overly aggressive feature compression. Sequence-wise average pooling partially alleviates this issue but still underperforms the attention-based fusion. By modeling lightweight cross-channel interactions, ECA enables more effective selection of implicit and discriminative emotion-sensitive features, achieving superior Macro-F1 and lower FNR with only marginal additional computational overhead. These results confirm that ECA mechanism provides an efficient and effective mechanism for fine-grained emotional feature modulation in MEMBERT.

5.2 Cross-Dataset Generalization Analysis

The results on the Emotion dataset (Table 4) show that MEMBERT achieves an accuracy of 0.9009, outperforming its lightweight backbone MobileBERT (0.8891) and closing the gap with the much larger BERT-base model (0.9157), while maintaining a low parameter count of 30.3M.

This result indicates that the structured biases for capturing long-range dependencies and salient features are effective across different task formulations, confirming the robustness of our architecture.

5.3 Confusion Matrix and Label-Wise Performance of MEMBERT

Through the confusion matrix shown in Fig. 4, the overall discriminative behavior of MEMBERT in the multi-label depression emotion detection task can be

Table 4. Performance comparison on the Emotion dataset

Models	Params	Acc.	Macro-F1
MobileBERT	24.6M	0.8891	0.8548
BERT-base	109.5M	**0.9157**	**0.8724**
MEMBERT (ours)	**30.3M**	0.9009	0.8583

systematically analyzed. The matrix aggregates prediction outcomes over all sample-label pairs and reflects the model's global decision characteristics. The dominance of true positives (TP = 2,597) and true negatives (TN = 3,351) indicates that MEMBERT forms a relatively stable decision boundary for identifying depressive-related emotional cues, enabling effective detection of positive emotion samples while maintaining reliable exclusion of non-depressive texts.

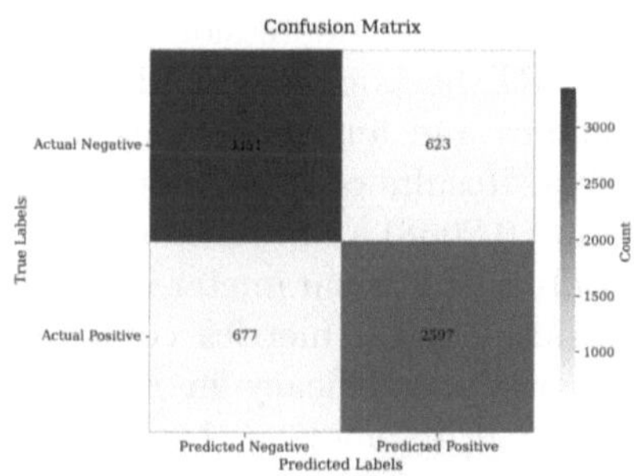

Fig. 4. Confusion matrix.

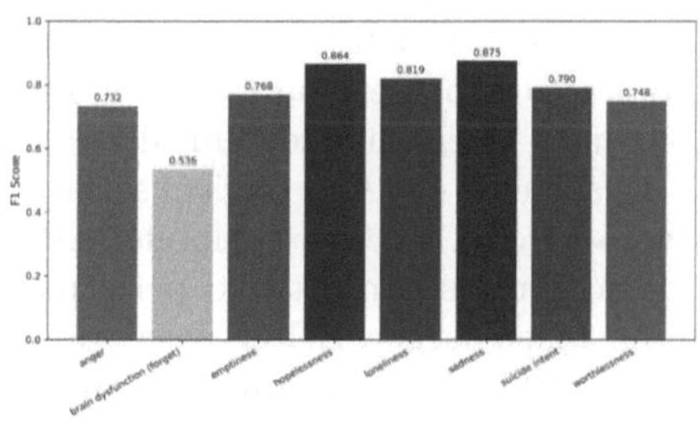

Fig. 5. Label-wise F1 scores.

From a clinical risk perspective, the number of false negatives (FN = 677, corresponding to an FNR of approximately 20.7%) remains within a controllable range. This suggests that the proposed architecture improves sensitivity to depression-related emotions and reduces the risk of missing potential high-risk samples. Nevertheless, the existence of false negatives also highlights the inherent difficulty of capturing extremely subtle, indirect, or semantically ambiguous emotional expressions, indicating that further reduction of FNR remains a meaningful direction for future improvement.

Figure 5 further illustrates the label-wise performance of MEMBERT across different emotion categories. The model achieves strong performance on core depressive emotions such as sadness (0.875) and hopelessness (0.864), demonstrating its effectiveness in modeling explicit and semantically salient emotional patterns. For high-risk emotions including loneliness (0.819) and suicide intent (0.790), MEMBERT also maintains competitive F1 scores, indicating robust sensitivity to clinically relevant emotional states.

In contrast, brain dysfunction (0.536) shows the lowest performance, likely due to the indirect, subtle, and weakly localized nature of its emotional expressions, which often lack explicit affective markers. Similarly, anger (0.732) and worthlessness (0.748), present higher semantic ambiguity, reflecting the complex and nuanced nature of these emotions. Their subtle emotional signals and varying expressions may require more intricate modeling to accurately distinguish them. Additionally, the emotion of emptiness (0.768) also shows relatively low F1 scores, as its linguistic markers are more abstract and harder for the model to interpret. These observations suggest that the perceptibility and expression explicitness of different depressive emotions have a substantial impact on recognition difficulty. Future improvements may focus on more fine-grained or knowledge-guided modeling strategies to better capture the subtle emotional categories that are harder to identify.

6 Conclusion

This paper presented MEMBERT, a lightweight framework for modeling depression emotions under efficiency constraints for multi-label depression emotion recognition. MEMBERT enhances the MobileBERT backbone with Mamba-2 modules to capture long-range emotional dynamics and an ECA-style gating mechanism to emphasize clinically-salient features. Results confirm that MEMBERT achieves superior clinical sensitivity (FNR of 0.2068) and robust accuracy (Macro-F1 of 0.7666) over MobileBERT. With only a 23.1% parameter increase, it demonstrates competitive performance on safety-critical metrics compared to the much larger BERT-base, validating its practical efficacy in resource-constrained settings. Additional validation on a separate emotion classification dataset confirms the generalizability across different task formulations, offering an effective approach for balancing performance and efficiency in depression detection tasks. Future work will explore the integration of emotional hierarchy priors and low-resource learning strategies to further enhance fine-grained depression emotion modeling.)

References

1. Choudhury, D., Gamon, M., Counts, M., Horvitz, S., E.: Predicting depression via social media. In: Proceedings of the 7th International AAAI Conference on Web and Social Media (ICWSM), pp. 128–137 (2013)
2. Yan, Z., Peng, F., Zhang, D.: DECEN: A deep learning model enhanced by depressive emotions for depression detection from social media content. Decis. Support Syst. **191**, 114421 (2025)
3. Chen, C., Li, F., Chen, H., Lin, Y.: Heterogeneous subgraph network with prompt learning for interpretable depression detection on social media. Knowl.-Based Syst. **315**, 113215 (2025)
4. Dao, T., Gu, A.: Transformers are SSMs: Generalized models and efficient algorithms through structured state space duality. In: Proceedings of the 41st International Conference on Machine Learning (ICML) (2024)

5. Wang, Q., Wu, B., Zhu, P., Li, P., Zuo, W., Hu, Q.: ECA-Net: Efficient channel attention for deep convolutional neural networks. In: Proceedings of the IEEE/CVF Conference on Computer Vision and Pattern Recognition (CVPR), pp. 11534–11542 (2020)
6. Cho, K., van Merriënboer, B., Gulcehre, C., Bahdanau, D., Bougares, F., Schwenk, H., Bengio, Y.: Learning phrase representations using RNN encoder-decoder for statistical machine translation. In: Proceedings of the 2014 Conference on Empirical Methods in Natural Language Processing (EMNLP), pp. 1724–1734 (2014)
7. Jurafsky, D., Martin, J.H.: Speech and Language Processing, Prentice Hall (2000)
8. Salton, G., Buckley, C.: Term-weighting approaches in automatic text retrieval. Inform. Process. Manage. **24**(5), 513–523 (1988)
9. Cortes, C., Vapnik, V.: Support-vector networks. Mach. Learn. **20**(3), 273–297 (1995)
10. Hochreiter, S., Schmidhuber, J.: Long short-term memory. Neural Comput. **9**(8), 1735–1780 (1997)
11. Graves, A., Schmidhuber, J.: Framewise phoneme classification with bidirectional LSTM and other neural network architectures. Neural Netw. **18**(5–6), 602–610 (2005)
12. Zhou, C., Sun, C., Liu, Z., Lau, F.: A C-LSTM neural network for text classification. In: Proceedings of the 2015 Conference on Empirical Methods in Natural Language Processing (EMNLP), pp. 2267–2276 (2015)
13. Ren, L., Lin, H., Xu, B., Zhang, S., Yang, L., Sun, S.: Depression detection on Reddit with an emotion-based attention network. JMIR Med. Inform. **9**(7), e28754 (2021)
14. Vaswani, A., et al.: Attention is all you need. In: Advances in Neural Information Processing Systems (NeurIPS) (2017)
15. Devlin, J., Chang, M.-W., Lee, K., Toutanova, K.: BERT: Pre-training of deep bidirectional transformers for language understanding. In: Proceedings of the 2019 Conference of the North American Chapter of the Association for Computational Linguistics: Human Language Technologies (NAACL-HLT), pp. 4171–4186 (2019)
16. Sun, Z., Yu, H., Song, X., Liu, R., Yang, Y., Zhou, D.: MobileBERT: A compact task-agnostic BERT for resource-limited devices. In: Findings of the Association for Computational Linguistics: ACL 2020, pp. 2158–2170 (2020)
17. Rahman, A.B.S., Ta, H.-T., Najjar, L., Azadmanesh, A., Gönül, A.S.: DepressionEmo: a novel dataset for multilabel classification of depression emotions. J. Affect. Disord. **366**, 445–458 (2024)
18. Saravia, E., Liu, H.-C.T., Huang, Y.-H., Wu, J., Chen, Y.-S.: CARER: Contextualized affect representations for emotion recognition. In: Proceedings of the 2018 Conference on Empirical Methods in Natural Language Processing (EMNLP), pp. 3687–3697 (2018)
19. U.S.: Preventive Services Task Force: Screening for depression and suicide risk in adults: U.S. Preventive Services Task Force recommendation statement. J. Am. Med. Assoc. **328**(20), 2050–2060 (2022) JAMA

AEFTS-Net: Period-Aware Spectral-Temporal Co-design for Efficient Multivariate Time Series Forecasting

Guang-fei Yang[1], Zhen-dong Liu[2(✉)], and Li-li Geng[3]

[1] School of Economics and Management, Dalian University of Technology, Dalian 116024, China

[2] School of Computer Science and Technology, Dalian University of Technology, Dalian 116024, China
lzd@mail.dlut.edu.cn

[3] Department of Infectious Diseases, Central Hospital of Dalian University of Technology, Dalian 116000, China

Abstract. Multivariate time series forecasting benefits from combining time-domain and frequency-domain approaches, as the former captures local irregularities while the latter reveals global periodicities. However, effectively integrating these two perspectives remains challenging, particularly in a lightweight and adaptive manner. To address this gap, we propose AEFTS-Net, a novel framework that unifies spectral analysis and temporal prediction through period-aware co-design. Our method first extracts denoised global features via a learnable frequency filter; it then introduces a trainable instantiation of the Wiener-Khinchin-based framework under Priestley's local stationarity assumption: by coupling learnable spectral filtering with autocorrelation peak projection, we enable reliable period discovery even under non-stationarity, transforming a classical spectral heuristic into a noise-robust, end-to-end architectural controller. Crucially, this period serves dual roles: (1) it guides adaptive fusion of global features into the time domain via a learnable scalar gate; (2) it directly structures the prediction layer via PGLF, a framework of two lightweight modules. Extensive experiments on seven benchmark datasets demonstrate that AEFTS-Net achieves state-of-the-art accuracy with computational efficiency comparable to linear baselines, offering an exceptional accuracy-efficiency trade-off for real-world deployment.

Keywords: Multivariate Time Series Forecasting · Spectral-temporal Fusion · Period-aware Modeling · Low-rank Forecasting · Frequency-domain Analysis

1 Introduction

Multivariate time series (MTS) forecasting supports decision-making in climate science [15], energy production [17], finance [1], and industrial systems [9]. Effective modeling requires balancing the capture of local irregularities with global

J. Niu et al. (Eds.): KSEM 2026, LNAI 16631, pp. 296–310, 2027.
https://doi.org/10.1007/978-981-92-2759-4_22

periodicities. Time-domain models, including RNNs and Transformers [8,10], capture temporal dynamics but often overlook spectral regularities. Frequency-domain approaches [13,20] capture periodic structures but typically treat frequency analysis as a static preprocessing step. This separation leads to suboptimal performance where local models overfit noise and spectral models oversmooth aperiodic shifts.

Linear models like DLinear [18] offer efficiency but lack mechanisms to exploit periodicity. Hybrid methods [16] introduce spectral filters but do not use the cleaned spectrum for structural guidance. We propose AEFTS-Net (Adaptive Efficient Frequency-Temporal Synergy Network) to address these limitations. Our framework uses an end-to-end spectral pipeline to produce denoised global features and a data-driven period token p^*. The global features enhance time domain representation via a learnable scalar gate. The period token p^* guides the Period-Guided Low-Rank Forecasting (PGLF) modules. Specifically, PGLF-LR conditions block segmentation on p^* rather than a fixed window [3]. PGLF-FFN adapts the Low-Rank Adaptation (LoRA) technique [2] by grounding the bottleneck dimension in p^* to impose domain-informed constraints.

Accurate periodicity detection is vital for robust forecasting. The Wiener-Khinchin theorem (WKT) links autocorrelation and spectrum but assumes wide-sense stationarity (WSS), which real-world signals often violate. We propose a learnable generalization inspired by Priestley's evolutionary spectral theory [11], which relaxes WSS to local stationarity. Our method treats periodicity estimation as a trainable spectral denoising problem. A learnable filter suppresses high-frequency noise, which is most vulnerable to non-stationary transients, while preserving low-frequency structure where dominant cycles reside. This yields robust differentiable period estimates even when the input violates strict WSS.

Experiments on seven benchmarks show that AEFTS-Net balances accuracy and efficiency. It matches frequency-aware SOTA models in accuracy while maintaining efficiency comparable to linear baselines. Our contributions are:

1. A frequency-first framework where spectral analysis provides both feature enhancement and structural control signals.
2. A differentiable period discovery module based on Wiener-Khinchin theory, made robust via learnable spectral filtering.
3. A period-guided low-rank predictor (PGLF) that achieves favorable accuracy-efficiency trade-offs through signal-informed architectural constraints.

2 Related Work

Our work intersects three active research strands: efficient linear modeling, frequency-aware forecasting, and parameter-efficient adaptation. We position the AEFTS-Net as the first period-guided spectral-temporal co-design framework that unifies these directions.

Efficient Linear and Decomposition-Based Models. The success of DLinear [18] demonstrates that linear projections with seasonal-trend decomposition can rival complex models, which highlights the power of inductive bias over architecture. Follow-ups like RLinear [7] reinforce this trend. While AEFTS-Net adopts linear mappings in embedding and PGLF layers, it fundamentally departs by explicitly modeling periodic structure. Our low-rank prediction is not generic but period-conditioned: PGLF-LR restructures sequences into p^*-length blocks; PGLF-FFN sets bottleneck dimension to p^*. This allows AEFTS-Net to retain high accuracy under limited lookback window length, where linear models struggle due to insufficient historical context.

Frequency-Aware and Hybrid Models. FEDformer [20] integrates Fourier bases for low-rank attention; TimesNet [13] reshapes 1D series into 2D via FFT-detected periods. FilterNet [16] introduces learnable frequency filters to suppress noise, which is a key inspiration for our denoising stage. However, existing works treat frequency analysis as a preprocessing or auxiliary step. FEDformer's spectral branch does not influence model structure; TimesNet adopts the frequency component with the largest FFT magnitude as the significant period, which is a strategy highly sensitive to noise; FilterNet focuses on feature denoising but does not exploit the cleaned spectrum for period-guided prediction. AEFTS-Net closes this loop. Our WKT-based estimator yields a differentiable period estimate that actively restructures prediction via PGLF. It also produces a denoised global representation that adaptively enriches temporal features via a learnable scalar gate. This enables true spectral and temporal co-design in a single pipeline. Unlike prior works applying FFT or ACF heuristically, our approach formalizes period discovery as a trainable approximation to the WKT-based estimator under non-stationarity. This connects spectral theory and architectural design.

Parameter-Efficient Adaptation. MTS-Mixers [6] exploits the intrinsic low-rankness of multivariate time series through factorized decomposition. TimeBase [3] applies low-rank decomposition to time series forecasting. PGLF-LR and PGLF-FFN extend these ideas by grounding rank or bottleneck selection in domain-specific period knowledge. PGLF-LR uses p^* to discover natural temporal atoms. PGLF-FFN sets latent dimension to p^*, making rank signal-informed. This principled alignment with temporal structure is absent in prior work, where ranks are hyperparameters chosen by validation performance.

In summary, while existing literature has advanced time-domain expressivity, frequency-domain insight, or model efficiency in isolation, AEFTS-Net is the first to unify them under a period-guided co-design, where the signal's intrinsic rhythm dictates both feature representation and model structure.

3 Methodology

3.1 Overview

Figure 1 illustrates the architecture of AEFTS-Net. The framework establishes a dynamic and end-to-end collaboration between time and frequency domains to capture local interactions and global periodic dependencies. The pipeline consists of three stages: Input Embedding, Frequency Domain Global Analysis, and Synergistic Fusion and Prediction.

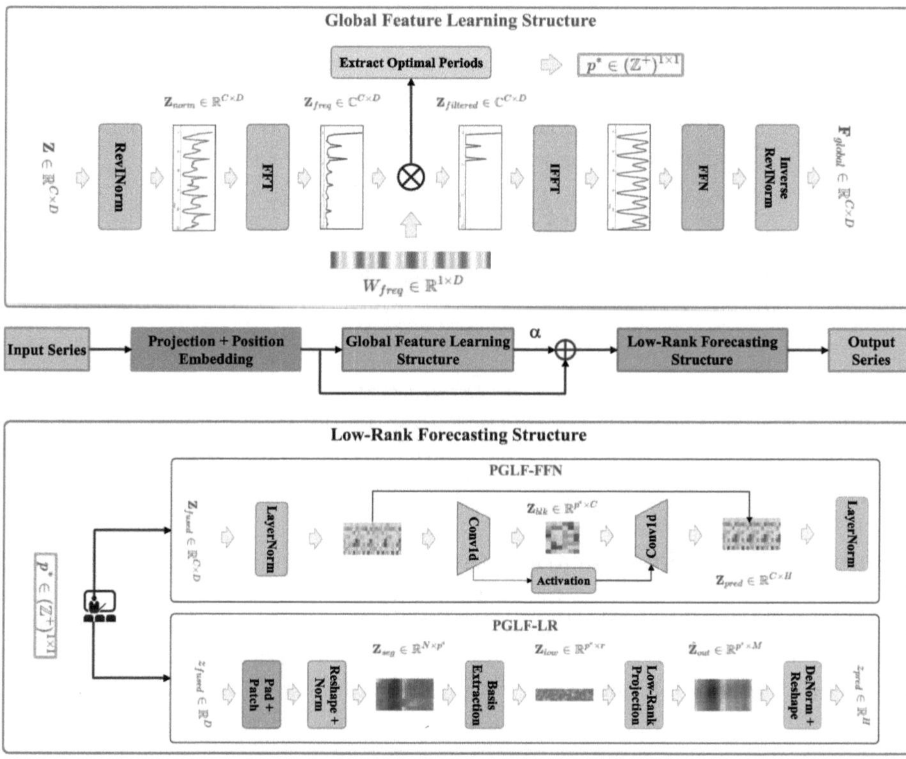

Fig. 1. Overall architecture of AEFTS-Net. (i) Projection+Position Embedding: An input projection and position embedding to map the input sequence into embeddings and incorporate temporal order. (ii) Global Feature Learning Structure: A frequency-domain global analysis module to extract dependencies and identify dominant periods via spectral operations. (iii) Low-Rank Forecasting Structure: A synergistic fusion and prediction module to integrate time and frequency features and generate forecasts using a period-guided low-rank mechanism.

3.2 Input Embedding

Let the input multivariate time series be $\mathbf{X} \in \mathbb{R}^{B \times C \times L}$, where B, C, and L denote batch size, number of variables, and sequence length. We first apply channel-wise standardization to remove scale bias while preserving statistical properties. The standardized input is projected into a D-dimensional embedding space via a learnable linear layer. We add sinusoidal positional encoding to incorporate temporal order [12]. The final embedded representation $\mathbf{Z} \in \mathbb{R}^{B \times C \times D}$ serves as the input for subsequent modules.

3.3 Frequency-Domain Global Analysis

Normalization and Spectral Filtering. To address distribution shifts, we apply Reversible Instance Normalization (RevIN) [4] to $\mathbf{Z}$, yielding $\mathbf{Z}_{norm}$. This removes trend and scale shifts that dominate the spectrum. We then perform real-valued FFT along the time axis:

$$\mathbf{Z}_{freq} = \text{FFT}(\mathbf{Z}_{norm}) \in \mathbb{C}^{B \times C \times D} \tag{1}$$

A learnable complex-valued filter $\mathbf{W}_{freq} \in \mathbb{C}^{D}$ is applied via element-wise multiplication:

$$\mathbf{Z}_{filtered} = \mathbf{Z}_{freq} \odot \mathbf{W}_{freq} \tag{2}$$

This acts as spectral attention, amplifying task-relevant frequencies while suppressing noise. The signal is transformed back to the time domain via IFFT to obtain global features $\mathbf{Z}_{global}$. An FFN projects these features to the original space, followed by inverse RevIN to obtain $\mathbf{F}_{global}$.

Dominant Period Identification. Accurate period identification is essential for effective temporal pattern modeling. We propose a hybrid algorithm combining spectral analysis with projection onto semantically meaningful candidate periods. Given $\mathbf{X} \in \mathbb{R}^{B \times C \times L}$, we first demean the series along the temporal dimension to remove DC bias:

$$\tilde{\mathbf{X}}_{b,c,t} = \mathbf{X}_{b,c,t} - \frac{1}{L}\sum_{t'=1}^{L} \mathbf{X}_{b,c,t'} \tag{3}$$

We then compute the autocorrelation function (ACF) efficiently in the frequency domain via the FFT, leveraging the WKT, which states that the autocorrelation of a WSS process is the inverse Fourier transform of its power spectral density. To eliminate circular convolution bias, we zero-pad the series to length $2L$. The autocorrelation is the inverse FFT of the power spectral density:

$$\mathbf{R} = \text{IFFT}\left(\left|\text{FFT}(\tilde{\mathbf{X}}_{pad})\right|^{2}\right) \tag{4}$$

We retain only the first N lags to form a causal ACF profile. We then average the ACF across batch and feature dimensions to stabilize period detection:

$$\mathrm{ACF}_{\mathrm{mean}}[k] = \frac{1}{BC}\sum_{b=1}^{B}\sum_{c=1}^{C}\mathbf{R}_{b,c}[k], \quad k = 0, 1, \ldots, N-1 \tag{5}$$

The search for the dominant period is constrained to a plausible lag interval to suppress spurious peaks. Let $P = \{p_1, p_2, \ldots, p_K\}$ be a predefined set of candidate periods. We define the search bounds as:

$$k_{\min} = \max(2, \lfloor \min(P)/2 \rfloor), \quad k_{\max} = \min(N-1, \lceil \max(P) \cdot 2 \rceil) \tag{6}$$

The raw estimate τ maximizes the averaged ACF within this interval:

$$\tau = \underset{k \in \{k_{\min}, \ldots, k_{\max}\}}{\operatorname{argmax}} \mathrm{ACF}_{\mathrm{mean}}[k] \tag{7}$$

To ensure interpretability, we project τ onto the nearest candidate period in P:

$$p^* = \underset{p \in P}{\operatorname{argmin}} |p - \tau| \tag{8}$$

This approach relaxes the wide-sense stationarity assumption via learnable spectral filtering, providing robust period estimates under non-stationarity.

3.4 Synergistic Fusion and Prediction

Feature Fusion. Time and frequency domain features are integrated via a learnable residual connection:

$$\mathbf{Z}_{fused} = \mathbf{Z}_{norm} + \alpha \cdot \mathbf{F}_{global} \tag{9}$$

where α is a learnable scaling parameter. This preserves local details while incorporating global dependencies.

Period-Guided Low-Rank Forecasting (PGLF). We propose PGLF to inject period knowledge into the forecasting backbone via structured low-rank inductive biases. Given p^*, PGLF restructures temporal modeling around period-aligned segments. We instantiate PGLF in two forms: PGLF-LR (explicit low-rank decomposition) and PGLF-FFN (implicit bottleneck projection).

PGLF-LR. This module explicitly factorizes temporal dynamics into period-aligned segments. First, the input is zero-padded to length L' divisible by p^* and segmented into $N = L'/p^*$ non-overlapping blocks:

$$\mathbf{X}_{seg} = \mathrm{Reshape}(\mathbf{Z}_{fused}, [B, C, N, p^*]) \tag{10}$$

For prediction, blocks are transposed and flattened to treat each as an independent sequence:

$$\mathbf{X}_{flat} = \mathrm{Flatten}\left(\mathrm{Transpose}(\mathbf{X}_{seg})\right) \in \mathbb{R}^{BC \times p^* \times N} \tag{11}$$

This is the period-aware insight: By aligning the model's internal computation with the discovered period p^*, we explicitly factor out periodicity, turning a complex long-horizon prediction into a simpler problem of predicting the next few period tokens, a strategy inspired by how humans reason about cyclical phenomena such as next Tuesday's traffic.

We project the flattened input to a low-rank basis space of dimension $r \ll N$:

$$\mathbf{Z}_{low} = \mathbf{X}_{flat}\mathbf{W}_{basis} \in \mathbb{R}^{BC\times p^*\times r}, \quad \mathbf{W}_{basis} \in \mathbb{R}^{N\times r} \tag{12}$$

$$\hat{\mathbf{Z}}_{out} = \mathbf{Z}_{low}\mathbf{W}_{map} \in \mathbb{R}^{BC\times p^*\times M}, \quad \mathbf{W}_{map} \in \mathbb{R}^{r\times M} \tag{13}$$

where r is the rank hyperparameter. Let H be the prediction horizon. $M = \lceil H/p^* \rceil$ is the number of output segments. This enforces $\text{rank}(\hat{\mathbf{Z}}_{out}) \leq r$, effectively modeling the future as a linear combination of learned periodic basis functions. Finally, the output is denormalized and reshaped back to $\mathbb{R}^{B\times C\times H}$.

Theoretical Justification for Padding. Zero-padding does not negatively affect forecasting. The low-rank projection operates on a global basis space, where padding tokens contribute minimally to the learned basis vectors $\mathbf{W}_{basis}$ since they carry much less energy than valid signal segments. Moreover, residual connections preserve original boundary information, ensuring structural benefits are maintained without compromising edge integrity.

PGLF-FFN. This module induces low-rank behavior implicitly through a period-aware bottleneck. Given $\mathbf{Z}_{fused}$, we apply LayerNorm and project the temporal dimension to a bottleneck of size $d_{ff} = p^*$ using a 1×1 convolution:

$$\mathbf{Z}_{blk} = \sigma\left(\text{Conv1d}_{D\to p^*}(\text{LayerNorm}(\mathbf{Z}_{fused})^\top)\right) \tag{14}$$

where σ is ReLU. Tying the representational capacity of the hidden layer to p^* limits the effective rank of the transformation based on intrinsic periodicity. The output is reconstructed via a second convolution and residual connection:

$$\mathbf{Z}_{pred} = \text{LayerNorm}(\mathbf{Z}_{fused} + \text{Conv1d}_{p^*\to H}(\mathbf{Z}_{blk})^\top) \tag{15}$$

This design crucially grounds the bottleneck dimension in domain-specific period knowledge rather than arbitrary rank selection. PGLF-FFN is a period-informed bottleneck module that bridges parameter-efficient adaptation with time series modeling. Its design enables plug-and-play deployment without requiring architectural modifications.

4 Experiments

4.1 Experimental Setup

Datasets. We evaluate AEFTS-Net on seven real-world datasets including ETT [19] (4 subsets), Traffic, Electricity (ECL), Weather, Solar-Energy (Solar) [5], PM2.5, and Temp [3]. All datasets are split into training, validation, and test sets with a 7:2:1 ratio.

Baselines and Implementation Details. We compare AEFTS-Net against representative SOTA models: FilterNet [16] (using PaiFilter which has better comprehensive performance for fairness), TimeBase [3], TimesNet [13], DLinear [18], Autoformer [14], FEDformer [20], and iTransformer [8]. Experiments are conducted in PyTorch 2.5 on a single NVIDIA RTX 4080. We use MSE as the loss function and report MAE and MSE as evaluation metrics.

4.2 Main Results

Tables 1 and 2 show that AEFTS-Net achieves state-of-the-art or comparable performance across all datasets. Compared to previous SOTA methods, AEFTS-Net demonstrates significant advancements. On the Solar dataset with a 96-step horizon, AEFTS-Net-FFN reduces MSE by 4.4% (from 0.203 to 0.194) compared to iTransformer. On the Temp dataset with a 720-step horizon, AEFTS-Net-LR achieves an 18.2% reduction in MSE (from 0.176 to 0.144) relative to TimeBase. These results confirm the effectiveness of AEFTS-Net in capturing complex dependencies in multivariate time series.

4.3 Model Analysis

Efficiency Analysis. We evaluate computational efficiency across four dimensions: parameter count, Multiply-Accumulate Operations (MACs), training time per epoch, and inference time per batch. Using the Electricity dataset (lookback window length 720, batch size 16), we compare AEFTS-Net-LR with iTransformer, Autoformer, and others, as shown in Fig. 2. AEFTS-Net substantially reduces parameters and computational complexity. Compared to DLinear and FilterNet, AEFTS-Net reduces parameters by up to 16% and MACs by over 17%. It also trains faster (28% reduction vs. DLinear, 59% vs. FilterNet) and infers faster (3% reduction vs. FilterNet, 17% vs. DLinear). These results demonstrate that AEFTS-Net maintains strong predictive performance while offering superior efficiency for resource-constrained environments.

Robust Period Detection Analysis. This experiment validates the learnable frequency-domain filter, which enhances the dominant mode in autocorrelation while suppressing noise. Figures 4aand 4bcontrast the raw input with the filtered reconstruction. In Fig. 4a, the raw autocorrelation is noisy. Noise at lag 6 creates a relative maximum mistaken for the period, leading to a selected candidate of 12 despite the true period being 24. In Fig. 4b, filtering sharply amplifies spectral power at the true period of 24 and attenuates noise at lag 6. The algorithm then unambiguously identifies lag 24. Figure 3 further shows that periods identified after adaptive filtering align with actual data periods across other datasets.

These results confirm two key innovations. First, the differentiable period-discovery module transforms periodicity analysis from a noise-corrupted process into a reliable procedure grounded in WKT. Second, a clean period signal p^* is necessary to guide PGLF modules. An erroneous period would misguide segment

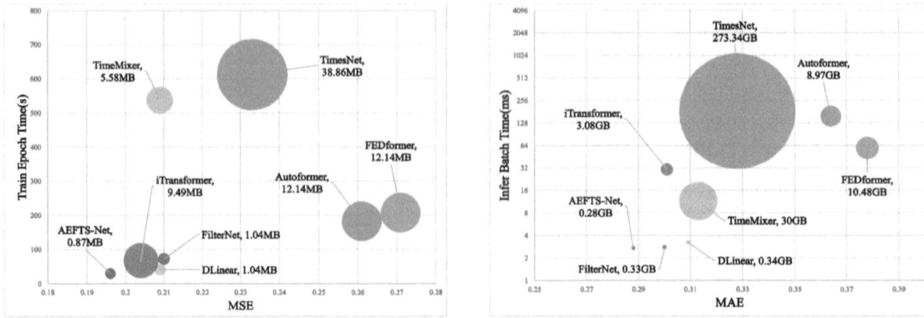

(a) (b)

Fig. 2. Efficiency comparison of AEFTS-Net-LR and other SOTA models on the Electricity dataset with a forecasting horizon of 720. MACs here indicate the computational cost for processing a single sample, and memory usage is measured with batch size of 16 for all models.

alignment in PGLF-LR and rank selection in PGLF-FFN. Our frequency-first paradigm delivers a denoised foundation, ensuring architectural decisions driven by p^* are semantically meaningful.

4.4 Ablation Study

Influence of Global Features. Fig. 5 illustrates MSE results with and without global feature fusion. Including the global features consistently improves performance across all datasets, with gains up to 0.054 in MSE. This indicates that global features help the model learn more representative basis components, enhancing both the model's representational capacity and predictive performance. The positive impact across multiple datasets and horizons demonstrates the value of incorporating global features.

Analysis of PGLF Strategies. We analyze PGLF strategies on Temp (lookback 720, prediction 720) and ETTm1 (lookback 96, prediction 96) datasets. Figure 6 shows that the optimal strategy depends on the inherent characteristics of the data, which confirms the value of our model's modular design. For Temp, which has more channels and longer context, PGLF-LR achieves better performance (Fig. 6a). Its low-rank structure extracts key periodic components from high-dimensional data, mitigating overfitting with fewer parameters. For ETTm1, which has fewer channels and shorter lookback, PGLF-FFN excels (Fig. 6b) by leveraging stronger nonlinear mapping to capture fine-grained dependencies. This validates our modular design: interchangeable period-guided modules allow the model to adapt to data properties. PGLF-LR captures dominant trends in high-dimensional series, while PGLF-FFN suits scenarios requiring expressive modeling of detailed patterns. Together, they enable robust and efficient forecasting across diverse applications.

Table 1. Forecasting results for prediction horizon $H \in \{96, 192, 336, 720\}$ with look-back window length $L = 96$. The best results are shown in **bold** and the second best are <u>underlined</u>.

Models		AEFTS-Net LR		AEFTS-Net FFN		FilterNet		TimeBase		iTransformer		DLinear		TimesNet	
Metrics		MSE	MAE	MSE	MAE	MSE	MAE	MSE	MAE	MSE	MAE	MSE	MAE	MSE	MAE
ETTh1	96	<u>0.374</u>	**0.392**	**0.371**	<u>0.394</u>	0.377	0.396	0.399	**0.392**	0.386	0.405	0.386	0.400	0.384	0.402
	192	<u>0.436</u>	<u>0.425</u>	**0.431**	<u>0.425</u>	0.442	0.429	0.455	**0.423**	0.441	<u>0.436</u>	0.437	0.432	0.436	0.429
	336	0.485	0.449	**0.474**	**0.440**	0.485	<u>0.448</u>	0.500	**0.440**	0.487	0.458	<u>0.481</u>	0.459	0.491	0.469
	720	<u>0.492</u>	0.476	**0.479**	<u>0.466</u>	0.498	0.476	0.501	**0.460**	0.503	0.491	0.519	0.516	0.521	0.500
ETTh2	96	0.294	**0.342**	**0.290**	**0.342**	<u>0.292</u>	<u>0.344</u>	0.325	0.370	0.297	0.349	0.333	0.387	0.340	0.374
	192	<u>0.378</u>	<u>0.396</u>	**0.370**	**0.395**	0.379	0.397	0.402	0.409	0.380	0.400	0.477	0.476	0.402	0.414
	336	0.426	0.434	**0.418**	**0.429**	<u>0.421</u>	0.435	0.436	0.445	0.428	<u>0.432</u>	0.594	0.541	0.452	0.452
	720	0.438	0.451	**0.427**	**0.445**	<u>0.430</u>	<u>0.446</u>	0.440	0.459	**0.427**	**0.445**	0.831	0.657	0.462	0.468
ETTm1	96	<u>0.318</u>	<u>0.354</u>	**0.314**	**0.352**	<u>0.318</u>	0.358	0.418	0.412	0.334	0.368	0.345	0.372	0.338	0.375
	192	<u>0.362</u>	<u>0.379</u>	**0.359**	**0.377**	0.364	0.383	0.434	0.416	0.377	0.391	0.380	0.389	0.374	0.387
	336	<u>0.395</u>	<u>0.403</u>	**0.392**	**0.402**	0.396	0.406	0.462	0.437	0.426	0.420	0.413	0.413	0.410	0.411
	720	0.464	<u>0.443</u>	**0.455**	**0.440**	<u>0.456</u>	0.444	0.525	0.469	0.491	0.459	0.474	0.453	0.478	0.450
ETTm2	96	**0.172**	**0.255**	<u>0.174</u>	**0.255**	0.176	<u>0.257</u>	0.213	0.291	0.180	0.264	0.193	0.292	0.187	0.267
	192	<u>0.239</u>	**0.298**	**0.237**	**0.298**	0.240	<u>0.300</u>	0.272	0.326	0.250	0.309	0.284	0.362	0.249	0.309
	336	<u>0.300</u>	<u>0.339</u>	**0.296**	**0.337**	0.302	0.341	0.335	0.368	0.311	0.348	0.369	0.427	0.321	0.351
	720	<u>0.397</u>	0.398	**0.392**	**0.394**	<u>0.397</u>	<u>0.395</u>	0.426	0.411	0.412	0.407	0.554	0.522	0.408	0.403
Weather	96	**0.163**	<u>0.209</u>	**0.163**	**0.208**	<u>0.164</u>	0.210	0.170	0.216	0.180	0.222	0.196	0.255	0.172	0.220
	192	**0.207**	<u>0.251</u>	<u>0.208</u>	**0.250**	0.214	0.252	0.216	0.258	0.221	0.254	0.237	0.296	0.219	0.261
	336	**0.263**	<u>0.291</u>	<u>0.264</u>	**0.290**	0.268	0.293	0.274	0.300	0.278	0.296	0.283	0.335	0.280	0.306
	720	**0.344**	**0.342**	**0.344**	**0.342**	**0.344**	**0.342**	0.352	0.348	0.358	<u>0.347</u>	<u>0.345</u>	0.381	0.365	0.359
Solar	96	0.214	0.262	**0.194**	<u>0.244</u>	0.234	0.268	0.616	0.496	<u>0.203</u>	**0.237**	0.290	0.378	0.250	0.292
	192	0.241	0.283	**0.225**	<u>0.267</u>	0.269	0.290	0.640	0.504	<u>0.233</u>	**0.261**	0.320	0.398	0.296	0.318
	336	0.273	0.302	**0.242**	<u>0.279</u>	0.298	0.305	0.636	0.495	<u>0.248</u>	**0.273**	0.353	0.415	0.319	0.330
	720	0.294	0.321	**0.246**	<u>0.281</u>	0.259	0.303	0.583	0.460	<u>0.249</u>	**0.275**	0.356	0.413	0.338	0.337

Analysis of Period-Adaptive Capability. We evaluate adaptive performance under different candidate periods on the ECL and ETTh1 datasets. Figure 7 shows that prediction error exhibits clear minima at specific periods rather than fluctuating randomly, and combining multiple periods consistently achieves higher accuracy than using a single period. This validates the period-identification module, which accurately captures intrinsic periodicities to guide model configuration. In terms of efficiency, training and inference times vary with the candidate period but remain relatively stable. Crucially, periods delivering the highest accuracy do not incur disproportionately high computational cost. This confirms that our period-adaptive framework balances high forecast-

Table 2. Forecasting results for prediction horizon $H \in \{96, 192, 336, 720\}$ with look-back window length $L = 720$. The best results are shown in **bold** and the second best are underlined.

Models		AEFTS-Net LR		AEFTS-Net FFN		FilterNet		TimeBase		iTransformer		DLinear		TimesNet	
Metrics		MSE	MAE	MSE	MAE	MSE	MAE	MSE	MAE	MSE	MAE	MSE	MAE	MSE	MAE
PM2.5	96	**0.423**	**0.427**	0.426	0.428	0.435	0.436	0.432	0.435	0.466	0.474	0.437	0.441	0.462	0.467
	192	**0.424**	**0.425**	0.429	0.428	0.433	0.435	0.429	0.432	0.505	0.511	0.454	0.458	0.452	0.456
	336	**0.413**	**0.421**	0.428	0.427	0.427	0.432	0.426	0.433	0.461	0.467	0.449	0.451	0.490	0.492
	720	**0.388**	**0.416**	0.402	0.422	0.409	0.433	0.425	0.448	0.489	0.514	0.457	0.479	0.461	0.484
Temp	96	**0.138**	**0.281**	0.141	0.286	0.143	0.289	0.142	0.286	0.155	0.310	0.165	0.329	0.155	0.309
	192	**0.146**	**0.296**	0.150	0.298	0.158	0.304	0.155	0.305	0.168	0.324	0.174	0.335	0.187	0.358
	336	**0.144**	**0.296**	0.187	0.329	0.190	0.334	0.176	0.323	0.232	0.395	0.246	0.417	0.236	0.400
	720	**0.264**	**0.393**	0.420	0.480	0.469	0.517	0.274	0.437	0.652	0.663	0.584	0.590	0.636	0.642
ECL	96	**0.130**	0.226	**0.130**	**0.225**	0.135	0.233	0.139	0.231	0.135	0.233	0.141	0.244	0.202	0.308
	192	0.152	0.242	**0.148**	**0.240**	0.153	0.249	0.153	0.245	0.155	0.253	0.155	0.258	0.218	0.322
	336	**0.164**	**0.259**	0.165	**0.259**	0.169	0.266	0.169	0.262	0.169	0.267	0.170	0.275	0.232	0.332
	720	**0.196**	**0.288**	0.202	0.293	0.207	0.300	0.207	0.294	0.204	0.301	0.209	0.309	0.299	0.375
Traffic	96	0.364	0.257	**0.363**	**0.255**	0.372	0.267	0.394	0.267	0.374	0.273	0.396	0.272	0.605	0.325
	192	0.378	0.263	**0.375**	**0.261**	0.389	0.276	0.403	0.271	0.393	0.283	0.404	0.275	0.627	0.340
	336	0.392	**0.270**	**0.390**	**0.270**	0.404	0.281	0.417	0.278	0.409	0.292	0.417	0.283	0.631	0.349
	720	0.432	0.291	**0.430**	**0.289**	0.441	0.302	0.456	0.298	0.450	0.314	0.457	0.310	0.700	0.371

ing accuracy with operational efficiency, providing a fundamental advantage for processing real-world non-stationary time series.

4.5 Discussion

On Candidate Period Set Flexibility. Our current implementation projects the estimated period onto a predefined candidate set P to ensure stability and semantic interpretability. While this design prevents overfitting to noise-induced spurious peaks, we acknowledge it may limit adaptability to non-standard or dynamically drifting periods. To address this in future work, the candidate set P could be generated dynamically via clustering the peaks in the autocorrelation function without predefined constraints. Despite the current fixed set, our experiments show that covering common periodicities suffices for most real-world benchmarks, providing a robust trade-off between flexibility and generalization.

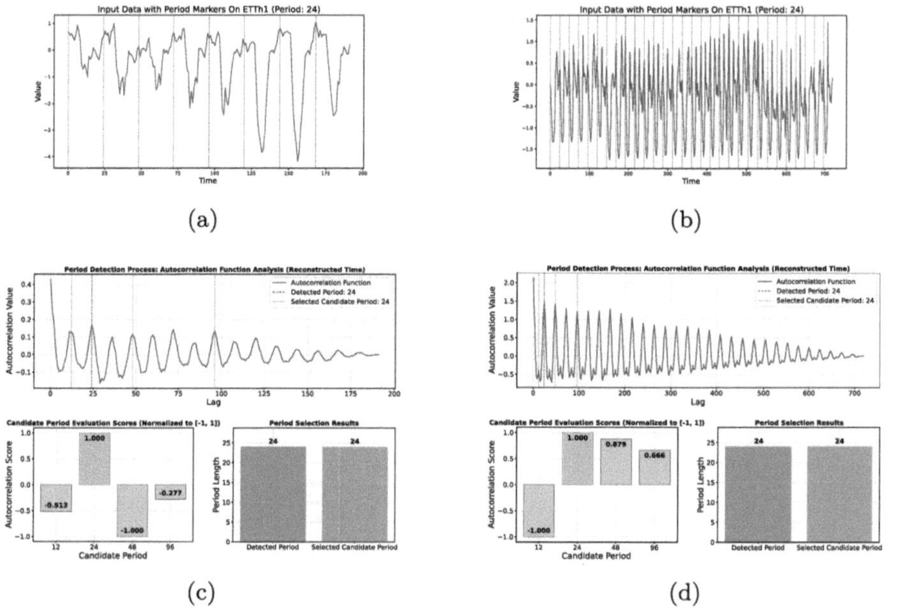

Fig. 3. Illustration of Period Identification on ETTh1 (left) and ECL (right) datasets with candidate period of $\{12, 24, 48, 96\}$. From top to bottom are the original input data, the ACF plot after our adaptive frequency-domain filtering and the period detection result. It demonstrates that the detected period aligns with the underlying periodicity of the data.

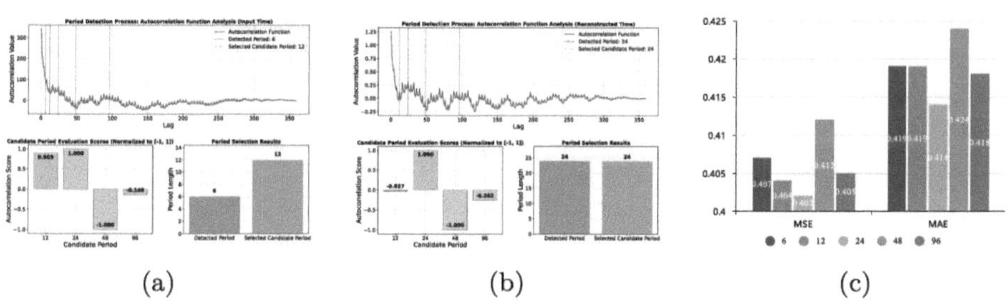

Fig. 4. Optimal period selection on the PM2.5 dataset with lookback length of 360, forecasting horizon of 360, candidate period of $\{12, 24, 48, 96\}$ and train epoch of 10. (a) and (b) show signals from Channel 1 before and after filtering. (c) shows prediction accuracy with fixed candidate period on PM2.5 dataset. Accuracy peaks at $p = 24$, exactly matching the period discovered in (b).

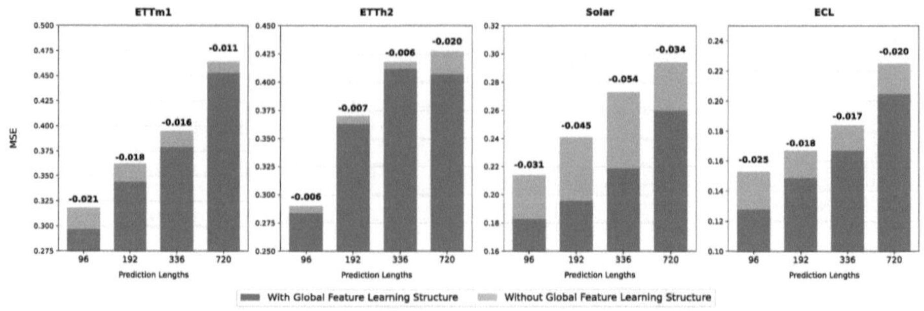

Fig. 5. MSE comparison with and without global features across different prediction horizons for ETTm1 and Solar datasets on AEFTS-Net-LR, ETTh2 and Electricity datasets on AEFTS-Net-FFN with lookback window length of 96.

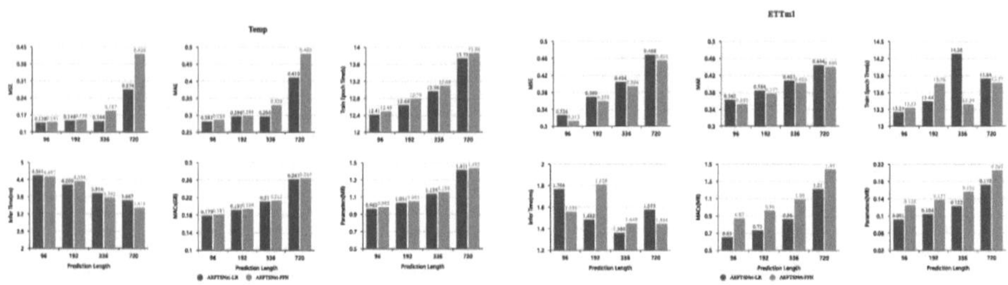

(a) (b)

Fig. 6. Comparison of forecasting performance under different prediction horizons between PGLF-LR and PGLF-FFN strategies.

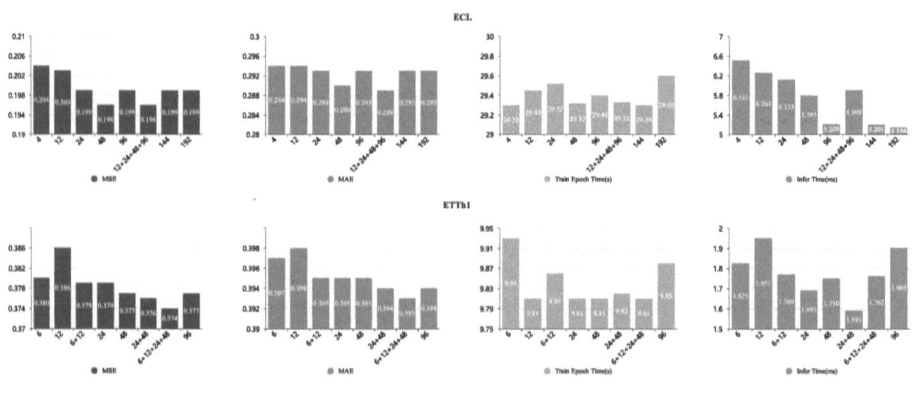

Fig. 7. Comparison of forecasting performance under different candidate periods.

5 Conclusion

In this work, we proposed AEFTS-Net, a frequency-first yet time-conscious framework for multivariate time series forecasting that bridges spectral insight and temporal prediction. The model grounds the pipeline in a learnable dominant period estimated via a noise-robust, differentiable generalization of Wiener-Khinchin theory. This design enables adaptive scalar-gated injection of global frequency features and period-structured low-rank prediction via PGLF. Experiments demonstrate AEFTS-Net establishes a new balance between accuracy and efficiency. It outperforms frequency-aware SOTA models while maintaining linear-method efficiency, particularly in data-scarce regimes and under distribution shifts. Beyond performance, AEFTS-Net offers a general principle where the signal's intrinsic rhythm dictates model structure. While the current framework utilizes a predefined candidate period set for stability, future work will explore adaptive period discovery to further enhance generalization on datasets with unknown distributions. This paradigm shift toward signal-informed architectural design facilitates efficient and adaptive time series modeling.

References

1. Ariyo, A.A., Adewumi, A.O., Ayo, C.K.: Stock price prediction using the Arima model. In: UKSim-AMSS 16th International Conference on Computer Modelling and Simulation, pp. 106–112. IEEE (2014)
2. Hu, E.J., et al.: Lora: low-rank adaptation of large language models. ICLR **1**(2), 3 (2022)
3. Huang, Q., Zhou, Z., Yang, K., Yi, Z., Wang, X., Wang, Y.: Timebase: The power of minimalism in efficient long-term time series forecasting. In: International Conference on Machine Learning, pp. 26227–26246. PMLR (2025)
4. Kim, T., Kim, J., Tae, Y., Park, C., Choi, J.H., Choo, J.: Reversible instance normalization for accurate time-series forecasting against distribution shift. In: International Conference on Learning Representations (ICLR) 2022, pp. 1–25 (2022)
5. Lai, G., Chang, W.C., Yang, Y., Liu, H.: Modeling long-and short-term temporal patterns with deep neural networks. In: The 41st International ACM SIGIR Conference on Research & Development in Information Retrieval, pp. 95–104 (2018)
6. Li, Z., Li, X., Rao, Z., Pan, L., Xu, Z.: Mts-mixers: Multivariate time series forecasting via factorized temporal and channel mixing. In: 2025 International Joint Conference on Neural Networks (IJCNN), pp. 1–8 IEEE (2025)
7. Li, Z., Qi, S., Li, Y., Xu, Z.: Revisiting long-term time series forecasting: An investigation on linear mapping. arXiv preprint arXiv:2305.10721 (2023)
8. Liu, Y., Hu, T., Zhang, H., Wu, H., Wang, S., Ma, L., Long, M.: itransformer: Inverted transformers are effective for time series forecasting (2023). arXiv:2310.06625 arXiv preprint
9. Mehdiyev, N., Lahann, J., Emrich, A., Enke, D., Fettke, P., Loos, P.: Time series classification using deep learning for process planning: a case from the process industry. Proc. Comput. Sci. **114**, 242–249 (2017)
10. Nie, Y., Nguyen, N.H., Sinthong, P., Kalagnanam, J.: A time series is worth 64 words: Long-term forecasting with transformers (2022). arXiv:2211.14730 arXiv preprint
11. Priestley, M.B.: Evolutionary spectra and non-stationary processes. J. Roy. Stat. Soc.: Ser. B (Methodol.) **27**(2), 204–229 (1965)
12. Vaswani, A., et al.: Attention is all you need. In: Advances in Neural Information Processing Systems, vol. 30 (2017)

13. Wu, H., Hu, T., Liu, Y., Zhou, H., Wang, J., Long, M.: Timesnet: Temporal 2d-variation modeling for general time series analysis (2022). arXiv:2210.02186 arXiv preprint
14. Wu, H., Xu, J., Wang, J., Long, M.: Autoformer: Decomposition transformers with auto-correlation for long-term series forecasting. Adv. Neural. Inf. Process. Syst. **34**, 22419–22430 (2021)
15. Wu, H., Zhou, H., Long, M., Wang, J.: Interpretable weather forecasting for worldwide stations with a unified deep model. Nature Mach. Intell. **5**(6), 602–611 (2023)
16. Yi, K., et al.: Filternet: harnessing frequency filters for time series forecasting. Adv. Neural. Inf. Process. Syst. **37**, 55115–55140 (2024)
17. Yi, K., et al.: Deep coupling network for multivariate time series forecasting. ACM Trans. Inform. Syst. **42**(5), 1–28 (2024)
18. Zeng, A., Chen, M., Zhang, L., Xu, Q.: Are transformers effective for time series forecasting? In: Proceedings of the AAAI Conference on Artificial Intelligence, vol. 37, pp. 11121–11128 (2023)
19. Zhou, H., Zhang, S., Peng, J., Zhang, S., Li, J., Xiong, H., Zhang, W.: Informer: Beyond efficient transformer for long sequence time-series forecasting. In: Proceedings of the AAAI Conference on Artificial Intelligence, vol. 35, pp. 11106–11115 (2021)
20. Zhou, T., Ma, Z., Wen, Q., Wang, X., Sun, L., Jin, R.: Fedformer: frequency enhanced decomposed transformer for long-term series forecasting. In: International Conference on Machine Learning, pp. 27268–27286 (2022) PMLR

Enhancing Multivariate Time-Series Class Incremental Learning with Informative Spatiotemporal Consolidation

Maojing Shu, Xiaopeng Guo, and Jun Sun(✉)

Wangxuan Institute of Computer Technology, Peking University, Beijing, China
{shumaojing,jsun}@pku.edu.cn, xiaopeng.guo@stu.pku.edu.cn

Abstract. We study the problem of Multivariate Time-Series Class Incremental Learning (MTSCIL), a critical sub-task within the domain of Class Incremental Learning (CIL). The primary objective of CIL is to adapt to unseen patterns of new classes while retaining old knowledge. Recent works have reported promising progress by effectively preserving learned temporal dynamics to avoid catastrophic forgetting. However, these methods lack the exploitation of inter-variable dependencies, hindering their capacity to track the evolution of spatial relationships. Moreover, coping with non-stationary spatiotemporal distributions remains a critical bottleneck. To overcome these limitations, we propose InfoTS, an InfoMax-guided Temporal-Spatial architecture for MTSCIL. Specifically, InfoTS employs a single graph convolutional layer to capture inter-series dependencies. Meanwhile, it enforces mutual information maximization between node embeddings and input variables to preserve holistic spatial information. Furthermore, we introduce a Confidence-aware Temporal feature Replay (CTR) strategy that effectively maintains feature-level stability. Extensive experiments demonstrate that our method consistently outperforms all baselines, while the proposed architecture delivers further improvements to numerous replay-based methods. Our code is available at https://github.com/MaojingShu/InfoTS-CTR.

Keywords: Multivariate Time Series Classification · Class Incremental Learning · Graph Neural Networks · Mutual Information Maximization

1 Introduction

Multivariate Time Series (MTS) are ubiquitous in real-world scenarios, such as activity recognition [10] and healthcare diagnosis [9]. In the open environment, MTS samples belonging to unseen classes appear continuously over time. When learning incremental tasks, deep neural networks are prone to catastrophic forgetting [24]. Distinct from vision and language tasks, MTS modeling relies on intra-series temporal periodicity and inter-series spatial dependencies, both of which may suffer from catastrophic forgetting in CIL, as shown in Fig. 1. Therefore, it is critical to develop tailored approaches for MTSCIL applications.

J. Niu et al. (Eds.): KSEM 2026, LNAI 16631, pp. 311–323, 2027.
https://doi.org/10.1007/978-981-92-2759-4_23

In recent years, numerous works [12,19,20] have aimed to address the dilemma between stability and plasticity in MTSCIL. However, existing methods often overlook the explicit modeling of inter-variable correlations, which may limit their capacity to preserve pivotal spatial structures across sequential tasks. In addition, most regularization methods utilizing feature distillation primarily maintain the stability of single-modality decision boundaries [24], which is inadequate for continual spatiotemporal representation learning. In this study, we aim to bridge the gap between MTS and CIL by jointly harnessing holistic temporal and spatial information while concurrently addressing the respective catastrophic forgetting of temporal dynamics and spatial dependencies.

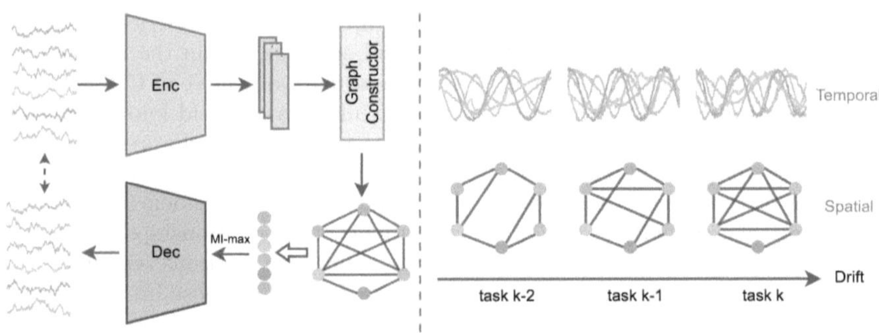

Fig. 1. Schematic of our proposed InfoTS framework and the dual distribution shifts in MTSCIL: Spatial Concept Drift arising from inter-variable variations and Temporal Concept Drift caused by evolving temporal patterns.

To address these problems, we propose an InfoMax-guided Temporal-Spatial architecture (InfoTS). Similar to [5], InfoTS transforms temporal embeddings into graph node vectors to learn spatial dependencies between pairwise variables. As the learnable graph evolves across incremental tasks, preserving task-biased graph topologies may hinder the acquisition of holistic spatial relationships. Inspired by Guo et al. [8], we propose to maximize the Mutual Information (MI) between graph node representations and corresponding input variables. To be specific, InfoTS aims to reconstruct the original variable features from their corresponding graph node vectors, as shown in Fig. 1, which effectively alleviates severe spatial concept drift. Compared with [5], the reconstruction mechanism establishes an explicit alignment between graph nodes and input variables, thereby significantly enhancing the interpretation of learned inter-variable relationships.

Moreover, to enforce the consolidation of essential temporal information, we introduce a Confidence-aware Temporal feature Replay strategy (CTR), as illustrated in Fig. 2. Specifically, CTR augments intermediate temporal prototypes from prior tasks and provides confident synthetic features to subsequent spatial layers. In contrast to conventional prototype-based approaches [27,28], CTR performs feature distillation at the intermediate temporal layers. This strategy not only preserves critical temporal dynamics but also promotes the stability of downstream spatial relationship acquisition. Empirical results show that CTR can effectively reduce catastrophic forgetting by recovering the statistics of confident temporal representations.

To sum up, the main contributions of this work are two-fold. First, we highlight the significance of integrating both temporal and spatial representations in MTSCIL. Second, we propose InfoTS-CTR, an effective graph-based temporal-spatial framework that mitigates catastrophic forgetting through informative spatiotemporal consolidation. Experimental results demonstrate that our method achieves superior performance.

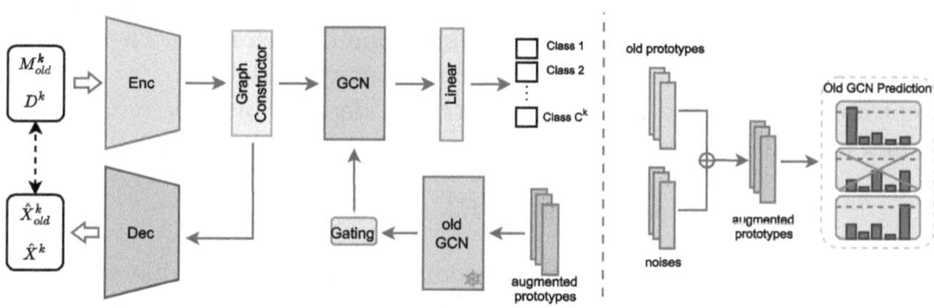

Fig. 2. Illustration of the overall pipeline (left). The Gating module performs confidence-aware feature selection for augmented temporal prototypes (right).

2 Methodology

In this section, we first introduce the problem formulation of MTSCIL. Then, we present the overall pipeline of our proposed temporal-spatial architecture, as depicted in Fig. 2. The framework is built upon two essential components: InfoMax-guided graph construction and confidence-aware temporal feature replay, both of which will be elaborated upon afterwards.

2.1 Problem Formulation

We focus on replay-based class incremental learning for multivariate time-series classification. The data stream arrives as a sequence of tasks $\{\mathcal{T}^1, ..., \mathcal{T}^K\}$. The task $\mathcal{T}^k$ involves training data $D^k_{\text{train}} = \{X^k_i, Y^k_i\}_{i=1}^{N_k}$, whose class set is disjoint from previous tasks. The input sample $x^k \in \mathbb{R}^{T \times N}$ is a multivariate time series with T timestamps and N variables. During task k, the model can only access the current data D^k and the replay buffer M^k that stores B exemplars of previous tasks. The learning objective is to achieve superior average accuracy on the cumulative test data $\bigcup_{i=1}^{K} \mathcal{D}^i_{\text{test}}$.

2.2 Graph-Based Temporal-Spatial Architecture

In the context of multivariate time series classification, jointly modeling temporal dynamics and cross-variable dependencies is crucial for learning comprehensive representations. Similar to [5,26], we introduce a learnable graph adjacency matrix to mine uni-directional inter-series correlations, while employing a MixHop [1] Graph Convolutional Network (GCN) g_ϕ to assimilate high-order dependencies propagated across multiple hops in the graph.

Given input data x, let $z_t \in \mathbb{R}^{d_f \times l_f}$ denote the feature map extracted by the temporal encoder f_θ. Following [5], the set of nodes $h^{(0)} \in \mathbb{R}^{N \times d_v \times l_f}$ is constructed from the feature map z_t through a linear transformation, defined as:

$$h^{(0)} = W z_t, \tag{1}$$

where $W \in \mathbb{R}^{N \times d_v \times d_f}$ is a trainable weight matrix. Note that the additional dimension d_v corresponds to the feature dimension of each node. The number of nodes N remains identical to the number of input variables.

According to [26], the adjacency matrix is derived by specifying the uni-directional associations between pairs of variables, formulated as:

$$A = \max\left(\tanh\left(\left(E_1 E_2^\top - E_2 E_1^\top\right)\right), 0\right), \tag{2}$$

where E_1 and $E_2 \in \mathbb{R}^{N \times e}$ are two randomly initialized learnable parameters. After obtaining the adjacency matrix, the MixHop layer aggregates cross-variable information to yield the spatial representation:

$$\begin{aligned} h^{(p)} &= \beta h^{(0)} + (1-\beta) h^{(p-1)} \tilde{A},\ p = 1, 2, ..., P \\ h_{\text{out}} &= \text{concat}(h^{(0)}, h^{(1)}, ..., h^{(P)}) W_{\text{out}}, \end{aligned} \tag{3}$$

Here, P is the depth of propagation, and β is a hyperparameter. $\tilde{A}$ represents the row-normalized matrix, calculated by $\tilde{A} = \tilde{D}^{-1}(A + I)$ and $\tilde{D}_{i,i} = 1 + \sum_j A_{i,j}$. Then, a fully connected layer projects h_{out} to z_s, conforming to the shape of z_t. Finally, average pooling is applied to the spatiotemporal feature $z = g_\phi(f_\theta(x)) = \text{ReLU}(z_t + z_s)$, which is then fed into the linear classifier m_ω for final prediction. We employ the standard cross-entropy loss as the training objective:

$$\mathcal{L}_{\text{ce}} = \sum_{(x,y) \in \mathcal{B}_X^k \cup \mathcal{B}_M^k} l(m_\omega(g_\phi(f_\theta(x))), y), \tag{4}$$

where $\mathcal{B}_X^k \cup \mathcal{B}_M^k$ is the mini-batch sampled from $D^k \cup M^k$. Next, we elaborate on the procedure of InfoMax-guided graph construction and confidence-aware temporal feature replay.

2.3 InfoMax-Guided Graph Construction

Based on the temporal-spatial architecture, we investigate the criteria of node construction under class incremental learning. Guo et al. [8] show that preserving sufficient mutual information is crucial to combating catastrophic forgetting in CIL. Therefore, we propose to enhance node embeddings through an information-theoretic lens to mitigate feature bias.

Let $X, H^{(0)}, Z_s, Y$ denote the random variables of input data, graph nodes, spatial representation, and labels, respectively. According to the data processing inequality [6], we have

$$I(X; H^{(0)}) \geq I(X; Z_s) \geq I(X; Y). \tag{5}$$

Training with the cross-entropy loss implicitly maximizes $I(X;Y)$, which serves as a loose lower bound on $I(X;H^{(0)})$; consequently, the set of nodes $H^{(0)}$ may fail to retain sufficient spatial information in X. As a result, we maximize MI $I(X;H^{(0)})$ between input data and node embeddings. According to [17], we seek to optimize the Barber and Agakov [3] lower bound on $I(X;H^{(0)})$:

$$I(X; H^{(0)}) \geq \mathbb{E}_{p(x,h^{(0)})}\big[\log q(x \mid h^{(0)})\big] + h(X). \tag{6}$$

Here, $h(X)$ is the differential entropy of X, which can be omitted from the training objective. As for the first term, we introduce an auxiliary decoder $q(x \mid h^{(0)})$ to maximize $I(X;H^{(0)})$ with the reconstruction loss. To be specific, we utilize an MLP decoder s_φ to reconstruct the corresponding input variable from individual node embeddings:

$$\hat{x}_i = s_\varphi(h_i^{(0)}),\ i = 1, 2, ..., N \tag{7}$$

Then, the MSE loss function is utilized as the reconstruction objective, thereby enforcing the InfoMax principle during graph construction.

$$\mathcal{L}_{\text{recon}} = \sum_{x \in \mathcal{B}_X^k \cup \mathcal{B}_M^k} \left\|x - \hat{x}\right\|_2^2. \tag{8}$$

2.4 Confidence-Aware Temporal Feature Replay

Inspired by Zhu et al. [28], we adopt a confidence-aware temporal feature replay mechanism that complements experience replay to maintain feature-level stability. First, knowledge distillation is applied to preserve the structure of the hidden space. According to [14], we minimize the feature discrepancy and constrain the prediction distribution as follows:

$$\mathcal{L}_{\text{kd}} = \sum_{x \in \mathcal{B}_M^k} \left\|z - z_{\text{old}}\right\| + \left\|m_\omega(z) - m_{\omega_{\text{old}}}(z_{\text{old}})\right\|, \tag{9}$$

where $z = g_\phi(f_\theta(x))$ denotes the feature from the current model and $z_{\text{old}} = g_{\phi_{\text{old}}}(f_{\theta_{\text{old}}}(x))$ denotes the corresponding feature from the previous model.

Subsequently, we aim to improve the stability of feature space, which is vulnerable to concept drift [11]. Similar to [28], we preserve class-wise temporal prototypes by averaging the feature maps $f_\theta(x)$ for each old class at task k.

When learning the new task $k+1$, the prototype p_j of each old class j is augmented with Gaussian noise e_j, which is derived from $\mathcal{N}(p_j, r_j^2)$. Given the set of temporal features $Z_t \in \mathbb{R}^{N_k \times d_f \times l_f}$, the Gaussian radius r_j is approximated by the average of channel-wise variance:

$$r_j = \lambda_{\text{scale}} \cdot \frac{1}{d_f} \sum_{c=1}^{d_f} (\text{Tr}(\text{cov}(Z_t(:, c, :)))/l_f)^{1/2}, \tag{10}$$

where Tr denotes the trace operation for the covariance matrix of Z_t^c, and λ_{scale} is a hyperparameter to control the sampling scale.

Considering the high-dimensionality of prototypes extracted from the intermediate layer, we selectively retain high-confidence augmented features and then regularize the subsequent graph layer via cross-entropy loss.

$$\mathcal{L}_{\text{proto}} = \sum_i \mathbb{1}(p_i > p_{\text{conf}})\ l(m_\omega(g_\phi(z_i)), y_i), \tag{11}$$

where $\mathbb{1}(\cdot)$ denotes the indicator function, p_i is the largest predicted probability output by $m_{\omega_{\text{old}}}(g_{\phi_{\text{old}}}(z_i))$, and p_{conf} is the confidence threshold.

2.5 Overall Objective

The overall objective function, which integrates InfoTS and CTR, consists of four terms:

$$\mathcal{L} = \mathcal{L}_{\text{ce}} + \lambda_{\text{recon}}\mathcal{L}_{\text{recon}} + \lambda_{\text{kd}}\mathcal{L}_{\text{kd}} + \lambda_{\text{proto}}\mathcal{L}_{\text{proto}}, \tag{12}$$

where λ_{recon}, λ_{kd} and λ_{proto} are hyperparameters weighting the loss terms.

Table 1. Summary statistics of the benchmark datasets.

Dataset	Tasks	Train Size	Test Size	Classes	Shape
HAR [10]	3	7352	2947	6	9 × 128
UWave [15]	4	896	3582	8	3 × 315
DSA [2]	6	6840	2280	18	45 × 125
GRABMyo [18]	5	36120	12040	16	28 × 128
WISDM [25]	6	18184	6062	18	3 × 200

3 Experiments

3.1 Experimental Setting

Benchmark Datasets. We conduct our experiments on five multivariate time-series datasets encompassing activity and gesture recognition. Table 1 summarizes the key characteristics of these datasets. For each dataset, every sample has a fixed sequence shape $C \times L$, where C is the number of variables and L is the sequence length. We split the whole dataset into a sequence of tasks. In line with [20], we shuffle the class order in advance of the task split and allocate 2 classes to each task. For DSA/GRABMyo/WISDM, the first three tasks are used for hyperparameter tuning, and the remaining tasks comprise the training stream; by contrast, all tasks are employed for evaluation and grid search on HAR and UWave.

Evaluation Metrics. For quantitative evaluation, we adopt two prevalent metrics: average accuracy and average forgetting [24]. Average accuracy is calculated by averaging the accuracy across all test sets of learned tasks. After learning task k, average accuracy $\mathcal{A}_k$ is defined as $\mathcal{A}_k = \frac{1}{k}\sum_{i=1}^{k} a_{k,i}$, where $a_{k,i}$ represents the accuracy evaluated on the learned task i after learning task k. Average forgetting evaluates the model's performance degradation on previously learned tasks. It is calculated as $\mathcal{F}_k = \frac{1}{k-1}\sum_{i=1}^{k-1} f_{k,i}$, where $f_{k,i}$ is $\max_{j\in\{1,\cdots,k-1\}}(a_{j,i} - a_{k,i})$. To assess overall performance, we report the final average accuracy $\mathcal{A}_K$ and forgetting $\mathcal{F}_K$, which are computed after the final task K.

Implementation Details. We employ a 4-layer 1D-CNN backbone for all baselines, following [20]. Similarly, our proposed model adopts this backbone as its temporal encoder. In all experiments, we utilize a single-head classifier for prediction and LayerNorm instead of BatchNorm for normalization [20]. We allocate the memory capacity equal to 5% of the training data across all tasks [20]. The input normalization layer is excluded in our proposed model, whereas we retain the configuration from [20] for the vanilla CNN backbone. Herding replay [21] is applied to our method. λ_{recon}, λ_{kd}, λ_{proto}, p_{conf} are set to 0.01, 0.1, 1, and 0.95, respectively. λ_{scale} is chosen from $\{0.5, 1, 2\}$, which is set to 1 for HAR, 2 for UWave, and 0.5 for the rest.

Table 2. Average accuracy of different methods on five datasets. The best and second-best results are highlighted in **bold** and underlined respectively.

Dataset	Herding	DER	ER	ASER	CLOPS	FastICARL	Ours
GRABMyo	60.26±4.93	<u>63.79</u>±4.30	60.28±4.49	58.32±2.88	51.55±5.20	52.91±4.83	**64.68**±5.23
WISDM	<u>68.79</u>±6.83	64.10±7.34	66.26±6.09	50.94±16.27	43.74±7.32	44.11±4.23	**71.41**±4.11
HAR	89.75±2.64	<u>90.02</u>±1.43	89.64±2.38	89.62±0.99	89.64±1.49	84.57±3.57	**91.75**±2.21
UWave	<u>86.75</u>±2.89	76.41±6.57	79.39±4.93	75.60±4.52	74.55±2.44	78.37±2.05	**89.84**±3.40
DSA	97.54±1.93	<u>98.17</u>±1.55	97.89±1.61	93.69±7.84	90.47±2.80	90.57±1.79	**98.83**±0.99

3.2 Quantitative Performance

We compare our method with the following popular exemplar-based baselines, consistent with the setup in [20] for a fair comparison: Herding [21], DER [4], ER [22], ASER [23], CLOPS [12] and FastICARL [13]. We report results averaged over five runs to mitigate random variation. As shown in Table 2, our

Table 3. Average forgetting of different methods on five datasets. The best and second-best results are highlighted in **bold** and underlined respectively.

Dataset	Herding	DER	ER	ASER	CLOPS	FastICARL	Ours
GRABMyo	42.33±5.68	**37.02**±4.42	41.89±5.13	44.38±3.29	52.61±4.89	52.04±5.41	38.55±5.48
WISDM	30.73±6.5	36.20±8.82	34.44±6.53	53.61±19.44	60.66±7.62	55.74±6.43	**27.58**±4.06
HAR	9.65±7.05	9.50±5.70	9.85±6.53	10.26±4.63	9.45±5.15	18.03±9.15	**7.28**±4.63
UWave	15.67±3.67	29.08±8.25	24.95±5.38	29.64±5.80	31.16±2.26	26.21±1.97	**11.74**±4.42
DSA	2.87±2.32	2.07±1.91	2.47±1.92	7.48±9.45	11.25±3.51	11.30±2.16	**1.35**±1.17

method consistently outperforms all baselines on five datasets, achieving superior average accuracy across all tasks. The impressive performance is largely attributed to its effective resistance to catastrophic forgetting. As demonstrated in Table 3, our framework adeptly retains previously acquired knowledge while continually adapting to new tasks. Furthermore, we investigate the impact of our proposed model on existing replay-based approaches. Figure 3 indicates that equipping these methods with our architecture yields consistent improvements on most datasets, even without any hyperparameter adjustment. These quantitative results provide compelling evidence of the efficacy of our method.

Table 4. The effectiveness of each separated component in our framework. InfoTS integrates an *InfoMax*-guided *Spatial* block, while CTR employs knowledge (*KD*) and prototype (*Proto*) distillation.

	GRABMyo		WISDM		HAR		UWave		DSA	
	$\mathcal{A}_K$	$\mathcal{F}_K$	$\mathcal{A}_K$	$\mathcal{F}_K$	$\mathcal{A}_K$	$\mathcal{F}_K$	$\mathcal{A}_K$	$\mathcal{F}_K$	$\mathcal{A}_K$	$\mathcal{F}_K$
Baseline	60.26	42.33	68.79	30.73	89.75	9.65	86.75	15.67	97.54	2.87
+Spatial	61.04	42.59	69.25	30.51	90.05	9.89	87.26	15.41	97.69	2.67
+InfoMax	62.39	41.44	70.85	28.39	90.05	10.04	87.91	14.29	98.08	2.28
+KD	63.23	40.19	70.88	28.12	91.24	8.22	87.95	14.34	98.61	1.35
+Proto	**64.68**	**38.55**	**71.41**	**27.58**	**91.75**	**7.28**	**89.84**	**11.74**	**98.83**	**1.35**

3.3 Model Analysis

Ablation Study. The proposed framework comprises two core components: InfoTS and CTR. Building upon the herding replay baseline, we incrementally incorporate each technique to assess its individual contribution. The ablation results in Table 4 demonstrate that the InfoMax mechanism is critical for improving the performance of the temporal-spatial architecture in the CIL setting. Additionally, it is worth noting that the temporal feature replay strategy provides further performance gains to our framework. As indicated by the forgetting

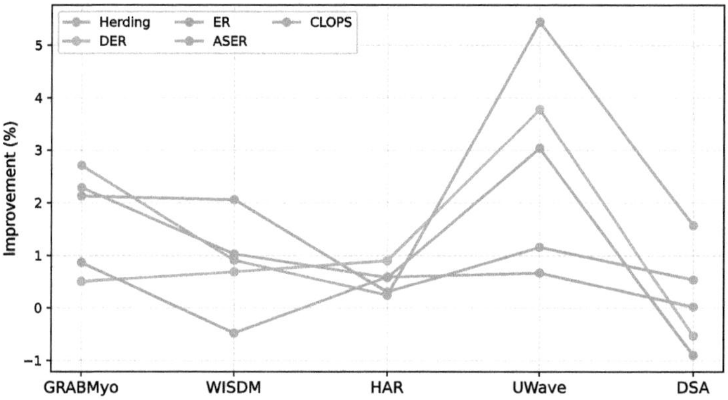

Fig. 3. Average accuracy improvements achieved by integrating the InfoMax-guided temporalspatial architecture into various methods.

metric $\mathcal{F}_K$, our proposed InfoTS and CTR significantly alleviate catastrophic forgetting from both spatial and temporal aspects.

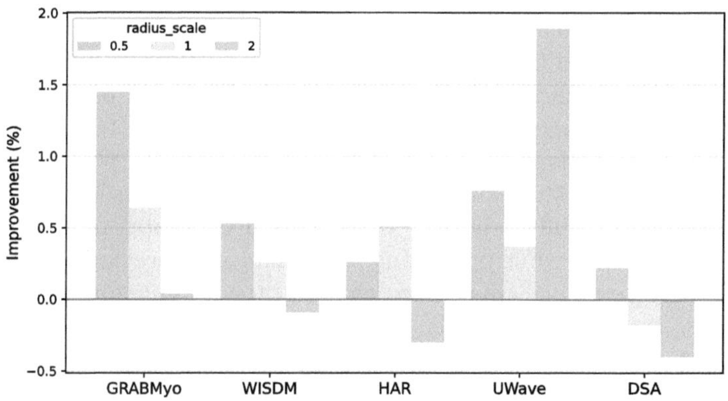

Fig. 4. Average accuracy gains brought by the CTR strategy under different hyperparameter settings.

Sensitivity Analysis. We investigate the impact of different hyperparameter settings on overall performance. λ_{scale} is a scaling factor for the Gaussian variance when augmenting memorized prototypes, and it is the only dataset-dependent hyperparameter. Figure 4 presents the results on five datasets by varying λ_{scale}. We observe that setting λ_{scale} to 0.5 consistently improves performance by 0.64% on average, suggesting that the proposed CTR strategy is not overly sensitive to the hyperparameter.

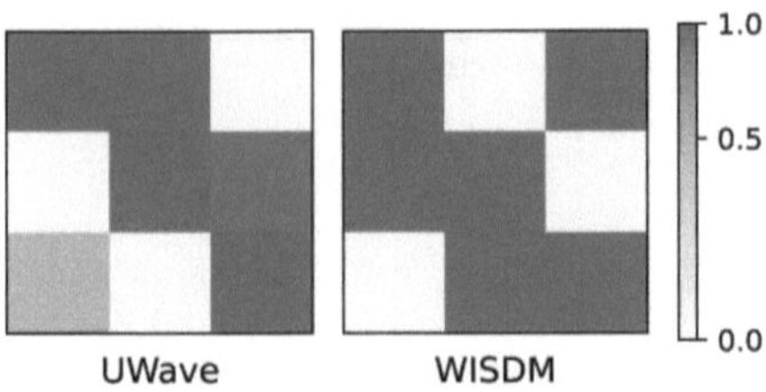

Fig. 5. Inter-variable dependencies learned by our model for UWave and WISDM.

Relationship Discovery. Figure 5 visualizes the inter-variable relationships captured by the learned adjacency matrices for UWave and WISDM. For WISDM, the model exhibits stronger inter-variable dependencies, consistent with the dataset's inherent complexity involving diverse activities and subjects. Conversely, UWave, characterized by simpler gestures, shows weaker correlations between the X and Z axes, as evidenced by the bottom-left entry of the adjacency matrix. This indicates that InfoTS is capable of learning adaptive spatial structures tailored to specific dataset properties.

4 Related Work

As a key problem in machine learning (ML), time series classification (TSC) has been extensively studied for decades. Recently, owing to the remarkable progress of deep learning (DL), the research paradigm in TSC has shifted from traditional ML-based methods to more effective DL-based approaches [16]. However, most DL-based TSC methods are developed for offline settings, where the training data are assumed to be static and i.i.d. In practice, time series samples and novel categories emerge continuously over time. This necessitates models capable of recognizing new classes while preserving performance on previously learned ones.

For MTSCIL, existing approaches can be broadly categorized into replay-free methods, represented by DT^{2}W [19] and ECG-CL [7], and replay-based methods, such as CLOPS [12] and FastICARL [13]. Replay-free approaches mitigate catastrophic forgetting without storing exemplars. For instance, DT^{2}W utilizes soft-DTW to align temporal feature maps, achieving shape-aware temporal distillation. ECG-CL employs a parameter-isolation strategy to retain previously learned knowledge while dynamically allocating available model capacity for subsequent tasks. In contrast, replay-based methods maintain an exemplar buffer containing representative samples from old tasks. CLOPS tailors memory mechanisms for streaming cardiac signals with importance-aware storage and uncertainty-based retrieval. FastICARL develops an efficient on-device CIL framework that incorporates quantization on exemplar sets in audio-based applications. While these methods effectively mitigate temporal forgetting, they tend to neglect intrinsic spatial dependencies. To address this problem, we explicitly model inter-variable relationships to retain relational knowledge, while employing an InfoMax-guided mechanism to capture holistic spatial dependencies.

In principle, replay-based methods generally achieve superior performance over replay-free approaches. Based on the preserved content, they are categorized into exemplar replay, generative replay, and feature replay [24]. Among them, feature replay excels in both memorycompute efficiency and privacy protection. Specifically, prototype-based replay [27,28] maintains compact class centroids to mitigate representation drift. However, conventional prototypes derived from the pre-classifier embedding are suboptimal for the entangled spatiotemporal representations of MTS. Therefore, we propose CTR, an adaptive temporal feature replay strategy that promotes temporal feature stability and facilitates subsequent spatial dependency modeling.

5 Conclusion

In this paper, we tackle MTSCIL by jointly alleviating spatial catastrophic forgetting and facilitating temporal retention. We propose to model inter-variable dependencies and maximize mutual information between node vectors and input variables to preserve holistic spatial information. Moreover, we introduce a confidence-aware prototype replay strategy, consolidating the latent temporal space. Extensive experiments show that the proposed architecture enhances the performance of numerous replay-based methods, demonstrating its versatility and broad applicability. The learned inter-variable relationships are also visualized to verify the effectiveness of our proposed approach in MTSCIL.

References

1. Abu-El-Haija, S., et al.: Mixhop: higher-order graph convolutional architectures via sparsified neighborhood mixing. In: International Conference on Machine Learning, pp. 21–29. PMLR (2019)
2. Altun, K., Barshan, B.: Human activity recognition using inertial/magnetic sensor units. In: Salah, A.A., Gevers, T., Sebe, N., Vinciarelli, A. (eds.) HBU 2010. LNCS, vol. 6219, pp. 38–51. Springer, Heidelberg (2010). https://doi.org/10.1007/978-3-642-14715-9_5
3. Barber, D., Agakov, F.: The IM algorithm: a variational approach to information maximization. Adv. Neural. Inf. Process. Syst. **16**(320), 201 (2004)
4. Buzzega, P., Boschini, M., Porrello, A., Abati, D., Calderara, S.: Dark experience for general continual learning: a strong, simple baseline. Adv. Neural. Inf. Process. Syst. **33**, 15920–15930 (2020)
5. Cai, W., Liang, Y., Liu, X., Feng, J., Wu, Y.: MSGNet: learning multi-scale inter-series correlations for multivariate time series forecasting. In: Proceedings of the AAAI conference on artificial intelligence, vol. 38, pp. 11141–11149 (2024)
6. Cover, T.M.: Elements of Information Theory. Wiley (1999)
7. Gao, H., Wang, X., Chen, Z., Wu, M., Li, J., Liu, C.: ECG-CL: a comprehensive electrocardiogram interpretation method based on continual learning. IEEE J. Biomed. Health Inform. **27**(11), 5225–5236 (2023)

8. Guo, Y., Liu, B., Zhao, D.: Online continual learning through mutual information maximization. In: Chaudhuri, K., Jegelka, S., Song, L., Szepesvari, C., Niu, G., Sabato, S. (eds.) Proceedings of the 39th International Conference on Machine Learning. Proceedings of Machine Learning Research, vol. 162, pp. 8109–8126. PMLR (2022). https://proceedings.mlr.press/v162/guo22g.html
9. Huang, Y., Yen, G.G., Tseng, V.S.: Snippet policy network v2: Knee-guided neuroevolution for multi-lead ECG early classification. IEEE Trans. Neural Networks Learn. Syst. **35**(2), 2167–2181 (2022)
10. Ismi, D.P., Panchoo, S., Murinto, M.: K-means clustering based filter feature selection on high dimensional data. Int. J. Adv. Intell. Inform. **2**(1), 38–45 (2016)
11. Jung, H., Ju, J., Jung, M., Kim, J.: Less-forgetful learning for domain expansion in deep neural networks. In: Proceedings of the AAAI Conference on Artificial intelligence, vol. 32 (2018)
12. Kiyasseh, D., Zhu, T., Clifton, D.: A clinical deep learning framework for continually learning from cardiac signals across diseases, time, modalities, and institutions. Nat. Commun. **12**(1), 4221 (2021)
13. Kwon, Y.D., Chauhan, J., Mascolo, C.: Fasticarl: fast incremental classifier and representation learning with efficient budget allocation in audio sensing applications. arXiv preprint arXiv:2106.07268 (2021)
14. Li, S., Su, T., Zhang, X., Wang, Z.: Continual learning with knowledge distillation: a survey. IEEE Trans. Neural Networks Learn. Syst. (2024)
15. Liu, J., Zhong, L., Wickramasuriya, J., Vasudevan, V.: UWave: accelerometer-based personalized gesture recognition and its applications. Pervasive Mob. Comput. **5**(6), 657–675 (2009)
16. Mohammadi Foumani, N., Miller, L., Tan, C.W., Webb, G.I., Forestier, G., Salehi, M.: Deep learning for time series classification and extrinsic regression: a current survey. ACM Comput. Surv. **56**(9), 1–45 (2024)
17. Poole, B., Ozair, S., Van Den Oord, A., Alemi, A., Tucker, G.: On variational bounds of mutual information. In: International Conference on Machine Learning, pp. 5171–5180. PMLR (2019)
18. Pradhan, A., He, J., Jiang, N.: Multi-day dataset of forearm and wrist electromyogram for hand gesture recognition and biometrics. Sci. Data **9**(1), 733 (2022)
19. Qiao, Z., Hu, M., Jiang, X., Suganthan, P.N., Savitha, R.: Class-incremental learning on multivariate time series via shape-aligned temporal distillation. In: ICASSP 2023-2023 IEEE International Conference on Acoustics, Speech and Signal Processing (ICASSP), pp. 1–5. IEEE (2023)
20. Qiao, Z., et al.: Class-incremental learning for time series: benchmark and evaluation. In: Proceedings of the 30th ACM SIGKDD Conference on Knowledge Discovery and Data Mining, pp. 5613–5624 (2024)
21. Rebuffi, S.A., Kolesnikov, A., Sperl, G., Lampert, C.H.: ICARL: incremental classifier and representation learning. In: Proceedings of the IEEE Conference on Computer Vision and Pattern Recognition, pp. 2001–2010 (2017)
22. Rolnick, D., Ahuja, A., Schwarz, J., Lillicrap, T., Wayne, G.: Experience replay for continual learning. Adv. Neural. Inf. Process. Syst. vol. 32 (2019)
23. Shim, D., Mai, Z., Jeong, J., Sanner, S., Kim, H., Jang, J.: Online class-incremental continual learning with adversarial shapley value. In: Proceedings of the AAAI Conference on Artificial Intelligence, vol. 35, pp. 9630–9638. (2021)
24. Wang, L., Zhang, X., Su, H., Zhu, J.: A comprehensive survey of continual learning: Theory, method and application. IEEE Trans. Pattern Anal. Mach. Intell. **46**(8), 5362–5383 (2024)

25. Weiss, G.M.: WISDM smartphone and smartwatch activity and biometrics dataset. UCI Machine Learning Repository: WISDM Smartphone and Smartwatch Activity and Biometrics Dataset Data Set **7**(133190–133202), 5 (2019)
26. Wu, Z., Pan, S., Long, G., Jiang, J., Chang, X., Zhang, C.: Connecting the dots: multivariate time series forecasting with graph neural networks. In: Proceedings of the 26th ACM SIGKDD International Conference on Knowledge Discovery & Data Mining, pp. 753–763 (2020)
27. Zhu, F., Cheng, Z., Zhang, X.Y., Liu, C.l.: Class-incremental learning via dual augmentation Adv. Neural. Inf. Process. Syst. **34**, 14306–14318 (2021)
28. Zhu, F., Zhang, X.Y., Wang, C., Yin, F., Liu, C.L.: Prototype augmentation and self-supervision for incremental learning. In: Proceedings of the IEEE/CVF Conference on Computer Vision and Pattern Recognition, pp. 5871–5880 (2021)

Knowledge in Complex Systems

IFHAGrec: Instruction-Finetuned Heterogeneous-Aware Graph Neural Network for Temporally Weighted Recommendation Model

Hongrui Wang[1], Shanchuan Yu[2(✉)], Xiaoyan Zhu[1], Guangtao Wang[1], Jiayin Wang[1], Jiaxuan Li[1], and Jindong Jiang[3]

[1] School of Computer Science and Technology, Xi'an Jiaotong University, Xi'an 710049, China
wanghongrui@stu.xjtu.edu.cn, {zhu.xy,wangguangtao, lijiaxuan}@xjtu.edu.cn, wangjiayin@mail.xjtu.edu.cn

[2] National Engineering and Research Center for Mountainous Highways, China Merchants Chongqing Communications Research and Design Institute Co., Ltd., Chongqing 400067, China
yushanchuan@cmhk.com

[3] China Research Institute of Radio-Wave Propagation, Qingdao 266107, China
jiangjd@crirp.ac.cn

Abstract. Nowadays, recommendation models based on their approaches to modeling user-item data, exhibit significant limitations in handling complex user behavior patterns and cannot be adaptively applied to multiple scenarios. To address the current algorithms' insufficient mining of auxiliary interaction information, this paper proposes **I**nstruction-**F**inetuned **H**eterogeneous-**A**ware **G**raph Neural Network for Temporally Weighted **Rec**ommendation Model (IFHAGrec). It models user semantic features through instruction fine-tuning, integrates the modeling of item features, and enhances recommendation performance via context learning, few-shot, and zero-shot learning. Then it constructs a **U**nified **S**entence **V**ector (USV) processed through a bidirectional GRU to identify item relationships within the heterogeneous graph. Subsequently, after encoding and decoding, it generates candidate sets for multiple item-related tasks under the instruction fine-tuned large model. This approach can capture users' dynamic interest changes during interactions, thereby more accurately modeling the representations of items within the heterogeneous graph. Extensive experiments on three real-world datasets demonstrate that the IFHAGrec model significantly outperforms state-of-the-art baseline recommendation methods.

Keywords: Recommendation Systems Heterogeneous-Aware Graph · Unified Sentence Vector · Large Language Model · User-Item

1 Introduction

With the rapid growth of "user-item" interaction data in the era of widespread internet adoption, personalized recommendation systems have become a core method for filtering and evaluating item information for users. Most recommendation systems are based on

J. Niu et al. (Eds.): KSEM 2026, LNAI 16631, pp. 327–340, 2027.
https://doi.org/10.1007/978-981-92-2759-4_24

user behavior data, item features, and social information. These systems analyze item attributes and user group behavior within social networks to capture users' interests. By leveraging historical user behavior, they predict future preferences, calculate the interaction probabilities between users and candidate items, and recommend the top-ranked items.

In previous recommendation systems, although they were able to make recommendations to some extent based on the association information between users and items, they suffered from a series of limitations due to their reliance on coarse-grained group recommendations and the lack of modeling for edge heterogeneity, illustrated in Fig. 1.

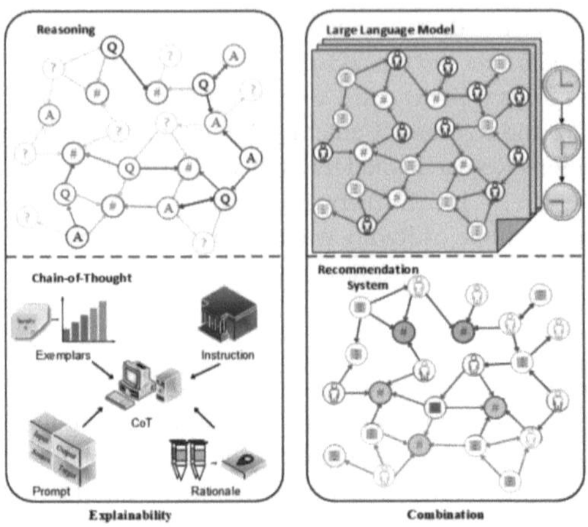

Fig. 1. Previous recommendation systems face the following challenges in terms of interpretability and integration with language models: limited reasoning capabilities (insufficient QA analysis for items), inadequate use and design of Chain-of-Thought (CoT) examples and instructions, and the lack of combined modeling for applying large language models to entire graph-based recommendation systems.

IFHAGrec model, through the integration of USV and T5-FLAN, establishes for the first time a unified modeling framework in recommendation systems that combines triadic vectorized information with natural language generation. This merges personalized recommendation information (graph relations, temporal dynamics, sentiment analysis) with language generation, advancing the task generalization capability of generative large-model recommendation systems: the prompt engineering and zero-shot capabilities of T5-FLAN empower the recommendation system with generalization abilities in new tasks and cold-start scenarios.

2 Related Work

Natural language is expressive but ambiguous, which can cause "hallucination" in recommendation systems (RS) [16]. For example, describing a vehicle as "black SUV" may confuse similar types, whereas unique identifiers like VIN avoid ambiguity [6]. Similarly, vague user inputs (e.g., "I like action movies") reduce accuracy; explicit descriptions ("action movies with intense fight scenes") improve understanding.

Text data (product descriptions, reviews) contains latent information. NLP techniques extract keywords, topics, or sentiment to enhance RS [1, 2]. User reviews help identify pros and cons. Transformer-based dialogue systems generate interactive responses and adjust recommendations based on user feedback [3]. BERT4Rec updates strategies when users dislike an item [13]. Multi-turn dialogues accumulate preferences for personalized suggestions. Contextual information (time, location, emotion) further improves precision [15].

New users lack historical data, making accurate recommendations difficult [18]. For item cold-start, CNNs analyze metadata (director, actors, genre) to infer similarity with existing items [20]. Large language models leverage social relationships, interest tags, or knowledge graphs to find relevant targets. Cross-domain knowledge transfer addresses cold-start, with emphasis on effective selection and adaptation of source-domain knowledge [10, 11].

Generative algorithms provide personalized recommendations using user behavior and preferences. GRUs model session-based sequences, with the last hidden state representing current interest [15]. Pre-trained models (BERT, GPT) enable zero-shot recommendation via powerful text understanding [16, 17]. Multimodal data (images, video descriptions) and data augmentation (expanding session sequences) improve training effectiveness [4, 16]. Prompt-based learning, popularized by GPT-3, solves NLP tasks using exemplar prompts [17].

3 Methodology

3.1 Heterogeneous Graph Structure: How Did Other Users Buy Items? (Space Weight)

In IFHAGrec, the heterogeneous graph consists of multiple types of nodes and edges. Nodes include Users, Items, and other entities (categories, tags). Edges represent different types of interactions (purchases between users and items, social connections between users).

The heterogeneous graph is represented as $G = (V, E)$ where V is the set of nodes, containing user nodes U and item nodes I, i.e., $V = U \cup I$. E is the set of edges, containing different types of edges representing user-item interactions, item similarities, and user social relationships. Heterogeneous Graph Edge Adjacency Matrices are used to represent edge relationships in the graph. With N_u user nodes and N_i item nodes, the following adjacency matrices are defined:

- Item-Item Adjacency Matrix $A_{ii} \in \mathbb{R}^{N_i \times N_i}$, ,, representing similarity between items (contentbased similarity).
- User-Item Adjacency Matrix $A_{ui} \in \mathbb{R}^{N_u \times N_i}$, where $a_{ui} = 1$ indicates an interaction (purchase, rating/review) between user u and item i.
- User-User Adjacency Matrix $A_{uu} \in \mathbb{R}^{N_i \times N_i}$, representing similarity and social relationships between users.

Building upon these heterogeneous relationships, Graph Convolutional Networks (GCNs) are used to aggregate neighbor information and update node representations. The node representation update is achieved through graph convolutional layers. The representation at layer l is denoted as $h(l)$. The update rule for node representation in IFHAGrec is given by Eq. (1):

$$h^{(l+1)} = \sigma\left(\sum_{v \in \mathcal{N}(u)} \frac{1}{\sqrt{|\mathcal{N}(u)|}} W_{uv} h^{(l)}\right) \tag{1}$$

where: $\mathcal{N}(u)$ is the set of neighbor nodes of node u. W_{uv} is the weight of the edge between node u and node v. σ is the activation function (ReLU).

Different types of edges have different weights, which can be learned through the graph. In IFHAGrec, the Space Weight corresponds to the weight of user-item interaction behaviors (ratings, clicks, purchases). Different behaviors have different levels of "importance," as in Eq. (2):

$$\hat{r}_{ui} = \boldsymbol{u}^T \boldsymbol{i} \tag{2}$$

Here, $\boldsymbol{u}$ and $\boldsymbol{i}$ are the vector representations of the user and item, respectively, and $\hat{r}_{ui}$ is the predicted rating.

3.2 Time Encoding: What Did the Users Previously Buy? (Time Weight)

Positional Encoding or Time Embedding is used to assign temporal information to each interaction. Specifically, for an interaction where user u interacts with item i at time t, the temporal information is represented as a vector $t_u \in \mathbb{R}^d$, where d is the dimensionality of the time embedding.

The temporal information is embedded into the feature vectors of users and items. Time Encoding is represented by Eq. (3):

$$\boldsymbol{t}_u = Time(t_u) \tag{3}$$

The temporal information is then combined with the representation of the useritem interaction, as in Eq. (4):

$$h^{(l+1)} = \sigma\left(\sum_{v \in \mathcal{N}(u)} \frac{1}{\sqrt{|\mathcal{N}(u)|}} W_{uv} (\boldsymbol{u} + \boldsymbol{t}_u)\right) \tag{4}$$

Behaviors from different time periods have varying impacts on recommendations. More recent behaviors are more representative of a user's current interests. This is achieved by weighting user behaviors with a time decay factor, as in Eq. (5):

$$\hat{r}_{ui} = \alpha(t) \cdot \boldsymbol{u}^T \boldsymbol{i} \tag{5}$$

Here, $\alpha(t)$ is the decay factor, representing the recency of the behavior relative to the current time.

3.3 Sentiment Analysis: Why Did the Users Recommend the Items? (Subjective Weight)

The goal of sentiment analysis is to analyze the sentiment tendency of users towards items. The IFHAGrec model employs the RoBERTa model for sentiment classification, modeling user reviews and extracting sentiment features. After classification, each review receives a sentiment score $s \in \{-1, 0, 1\}$, representing negative, neutral, and positive sentiment, respectively.

Based on the sentiment of user reviews, IFHAGrec adds weight to the user-item interaction. Positive reviews increase the user's interest in an item, while negative reviews decrease the likelihood of recommendation. IFHAGrec further adjusts the recommendation result as per Eq. (6):

$$\hat{r}_{ui}^{sentiment} = \boldsymbol{u}^T i + \omega_{sentiment} \cdot s \tag{6}$$

where $\omega_{sentiment}$ is the sentiment weighting coefficient, and s is the sentiment score of the review.

3.4 Unified Sentence Vector (USV)

Unified Sentence Vector (USV) is the framework used by IFHAGrec for recommendation text modeling. It passes through an adaptive preference gate bidirectional Bi-GRU (Bidirectional Gated Recurrent Unit) for reset and update operations, followed by Seq-to-Seq instruction finetuning, to generate sentence vectors rich in semantic information. USV is formed by concatenating the following three parts:

1. Spatial Vector (Graph-based Features): Edge weights calculated via graph attention on the user-item graph, denoted as $\boldsymbol{g_f}$.
2. Temporal Vector (Time Features): Temporal feature vector generated by the timeseries model RTE, denoted as $\boldsymbol{t_f}$.
3. Sentiment Vector (Sentiment Features): Sentiment feature vector generated based on sentiment analysis (Sentires) and quadruple extraction, denoted as $\boldsymbol{s_f}$.

The Unified Sentence Vector $\boldsymbol{u_f}$ is represented by Eq. (7):

$$\boldsymbol{u_f} = \left[\boldsymbol{g_f}; \boldsymbol{t_f}; \boldsymbol{s_f}\right] \tag{7}$$

where [; ;] denotes vector concatenation.

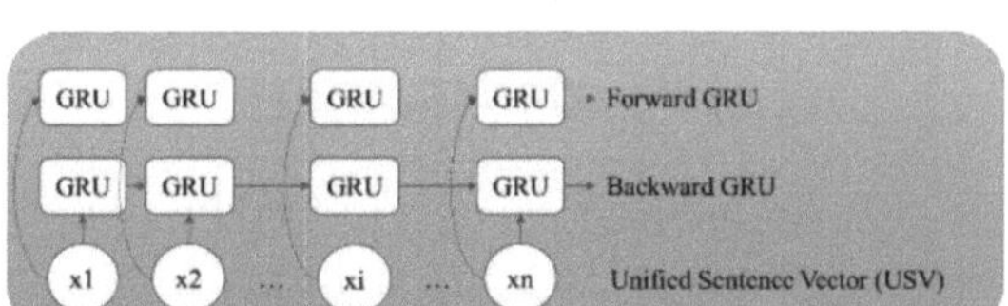

Fig. 2. Schematic of the Adaptive Preference Gate Principle.

As shown in Fig. 2, Bi-GRU is a commonly used Recurrent Neural Network (RNN) structure in natural language processing that can capture dependencies in both forward and backward directions of a sequence. Compared to the traditional GRU (Gated Recurrent Unit), the adaptive Bi-GRU in IFHAGrec enhances the model's memory capacity by running GRU units in both directions (forward and backward).

The adaptive preference gate consists of three gating mechanisms: reset gate, update gate, and candidate hidden state. The update formula for the hidden state h_t is given by Eq. (8):

$$\begin{cases} z_t = \sigma(W_z x_t + U_z h_{t-1}) \\ r_t = \sigma(W_r x_t + U_r h_{t-1}) \\ \tilde{h}_t = \tanh(W_h x_t + U_h(r_t \cdot h_{t-1})) \\ h_t = (1 - z_t) \cdot \tilde{h}_t + z_t \cdot h_{t-1} \end{cases} \tag{8}$$

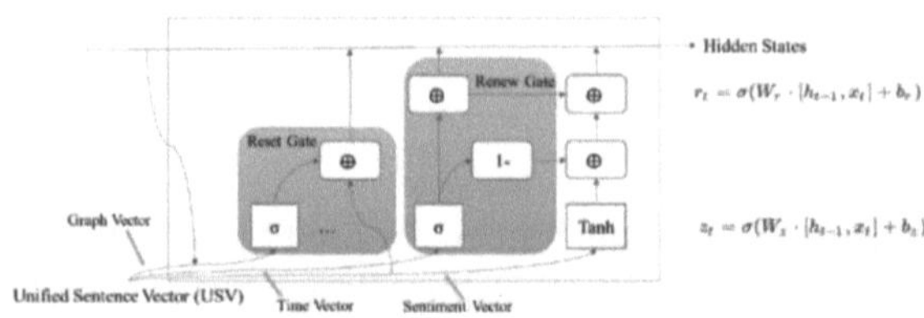

Fig. 3. Schematic of the Reset Gate, Update Gate, and Hidden State.

As shown in Fig. 3, z_t is the update gate, controlling the combination of the previous hidden state and the current candidate hidden state. r_t is the reset gate, controlling how the previous hidden state is reset. h_t is the candidate hidden state, computed via a nonlinear activation function (tanh). When the input USV sequence is $x_1, x_2, \ldots, x_T$, the adaptive preference gate Bi-GRU processes the input from front to back and back to front using two independent GRU networks, ultimately combining the hidden state information from both directions. From Eq. (8), for the outputs of the forward and reverse sequences, we have:

Forward sequence output as per Eq. (9):

$$h_t^{fwd} = GRU\left(x_t, h_{t-1}^{fwd}\right) \tag{9}$$

Reverse sequence output as per Eq. (10):

$$h_t^{bwd} = GRU\left(x_t, h_{t+1}^{bwd}\right) \tag{10}$$

From Eqs. (9) and (10), the hidden state h_t is formed by concatenating the forward and reverse hidden states, as in Eq. (11):

$$h_t^{bi} = \left[h_t^{fwd}, h_t^{bwd}\right] \tag{11}$$

This concatenated hidden state h_t^{bi} is the core representation used for further processing and generating the sentence vector. Subsequently, the model dynamically adjusts the focus on different features. An additional gating mechanism is introduced. At time step t, the update process of the preference gate is given by Eq. (12):

$$g_t = \sigma\left(W_g \cdot x_t + U_g \cdot h_{t-1}\right) \tag{12}$$

Here, g_t represents the output of the preference gate at the current time step, W_g and U_g are learnable weights, and x_t is the input at the current time step. Thus, the IFHAGrec model can selectively weight different features, enhancing focus on important features and suppressing the influence of irrelevant ones.

Instruction Fine-Tuning in IFHAGrec uses T5-FLAN to guide the model in performing specific recommendation tasks, enhancing the large model's generalization and task comprehension capabilities, and optimizing personalized recommendation effectiveness. In instruction finetuning, each recommendation task is described by an explicit natural language instruction P. Example instructions: "Recommend three sci-fi movies for the user," "Predict the next likely purchased item based on the user's purchase history." The input is divided into two parts:

Instruction Part: The task described in natural language $\boldsymbol{P}$.

Context Part: The user's historical behavior $\boldsymbol{H} = \{h_1, h_2, \ldots, h_T\}$ and the USV representation $\boldsymbol{u}$.

The final input sequence can be represented as per Eq. (13):

$$X = Concat(\boldsymbol{P}, \boldsymbol{H}) \tag{13}$$

where Concat(·) denotes sequence concatenation. T5FLAN employs an Encoder-Decoder architecture. The goal during instruction finetuning is to adjust model parameters to optimize its understanding of instructions and context. The encoder transforms the input sequence $\boldsymbol{X}$ into a contextual representation, as per Eq. (14):

$$\boldsymbol{H}_{enc} = Encoder(\boldsymbol{X}, \theta_{enc}) \tag{14}$$

where $\boldsymbol{H}_{enc}$ is the encoded contextual hidden representation, and θ_{enc} are the encoder parameters.

The decoder generates the recommendation result (recommendation list and predicted interaction) based on the encoder output, as per Eq. (15):

$$Y = Decoder(\boldsymbol{H}_{enc}, \boldsymbol{Y}_{<t}; \theta_{dec}) \tag{15}$$

where $\boldsymbol{Y}$ is the output sequence generated by the decoder (recommended item IDs), $\boldsymbol{Y}_{<t}$ is the decoder's output before time step t, and θ_{dec} are the decoder parameters. After incorporating the Unified Sentence Vector (USV), it is included as part of the context input to enhance the personalization of the task, as per Eq. (16):

$$X = Concat(\boldsymbol{P}, \boldsymbol{u}, \boldsymbol{H}) \tag{16}$$

3.5 Learning and Optimization Method

IFHAGrec uses a loss function $L = L_{soft}(Y, y) + \omega L_{sam}(\tilde{Y}, y)$. L_{soft} combines cross-entropy with L2 regularization to prevent overfitting, and applies Gaussian label smoothing to true labels Y. L_{sam} computes a cosine-similarity based loss on sampled user-item pairs where smoothed labels differ, encouraging separation of dissimilar embeddings. This dual loss enhances generalization and recommendation accuracy.

4 Experiments

4.1 Datasets and Parameter Settings

This study uses three public multitask datasets: MovieLens100K (100,000 ratings from 943 users on 1,682 movies), Retail Rocket (over 2 million user interaction logs including clicks, add-to-cart, and purchases), and Goodbooks10K (530,000 ratings from 53,414 users on 10,000 books). Table 1 summarizes the statistics of these datasets.

Table 1. Statistical Information of Datasets Selected for IFHAGrec

Dataset	#Train	#Validation	#Test	User	Item
MovieLens-100K	80000	10000	10000	943	1682
Retail Rocket	433648	59633	60858	15416	36968
Goodbooks-10K	975316	119867	121915	53414	10000

The sequence length for user-item interactions is set to 16, ensuring sufficient information capture without introducing excessive computational complexity. The model dropout rate is set to 0.3 to adapt to the loss function. To further optimize the training process, a dynamic learning rate adjustment strategy is adopted, where the learning rate is reduced to 20% of its previous value every three training epochs. The remaining hyperparameters are tuned using the last 10% of the training set split as a validation set, employing a grid search method to find the optimal parameter combination. Other parameters are set as shown in Table 2.

4.2 Experimental Environment

The reliability and reproducibility of the IFHAGrec experimental results depend on the model training conditions. The detailed hardware and software environment configurations are as follows.

Hardware Configuration: CPU: Intel® Core™ i9 Processors (14th gen) 14900K, 24 cores, with a processing speed of 6 GHz. Memory (RAM): 56 GB RAM. Graphics Processing Unit (GPU): NVIDIA RTX 4090 and NVIDIA RTX A100. Parallel computing using GPUs significantly accelerates the model training process.

Software Environment Configuration: Python Version: Python 3.12. Deep Learning Framework: PyTorch 2.5.1. Computing Platform: CUDA 12.6.

Table 2. IFHAGrec Dataset Parameter Settings

Hyperparameter	MovieLens-100K	Retail Rocket	GoodBooks-10K
optimizer	Adam	AdaMax	AdaDelta
learning rate	10^{-4}	10^{-4}	10^{-4}
dropout	0.3	0.3	0.3
weight decay	10^{-5}	10^{-5}	10^{-5}
hidden dim	512	512	512
L2 regularization	10^{-6}	10^{-6}	10^{-6}
batch size	128	128	128

4.3 Baseline Methods

This experiment employs various state-of-the-art baseline methods for comparison, categorized as follows.

S (Sequence): Represents sequential recommendation methods, such as BPR-MF, BPR-MLP, SASRec [16].

L (Language): Represents language model-based recommendation methods, such as Fair-Neg [7], Simple-X [8], NRT [9].

G (Graph): Represents graph model-based recommendation methods, such as TCSR [3], Attn2Seq [10], Caser [11].

LS: Represents methods utilizing both language models and sequential recommendation, such as S3-rec [12], BERT4Rec [13], U-BERT [14].

GL: Represents methods utilizing both graph models and language models, such as GCAN [2], M6-rec [15], PETER [16].

GS: Represents methods utilizing both graph models and sequential recommendation, such as FDSA , GC-SAN [19], CaSe4SR [18].

GLS: Represents methods utilizing all three: graph models, language models, and sequential modeling, such as Chat-rec [20], P5 [1], and the proposed IFHAGrec.

4.4 Main Results

We compare the performance of IFHAGrec with various existing recommendation methods on three public datasets. These experiments validate the effectiveness of IFHAGrec in different recommendation scenarios (movie, ecommerce, and book recommendation) and demonstrate its advantages over existing baseline methods. The experimental results are shown in Table 3. Each row in the table represents a recommendation model (the last row shows the results of the proposed IFHAGrec model), and each column represents the results on a specific evaluation metric for a given dataset.

For each dataset, the overall best result and the second-best result among the compared baseline methods are indicated in bold and underline, respectively. The significance of IFHAGrec's improvements over the baseline methods is verified using a paired t-test with $p < 0.01$.

Table 3. Performance Comparison of IFHAGrec and Other Recommendation Baseline Methods on MovieLens100K, Retail Rocket, and Goodbooks10K Datasets

Method		MovieLens-100K			Retail Rocket			Goodbooks-10K		
Model	Type	P@10	M@10	NDCG@10	P@10	M@10	NDCG@10	P@10	M@10	NDCG@10
BPR-MF	S	51.20	53.41	65.67	43.03	44.58	51.62	41.38	40.65	46.33
BPR-MLP	S	51.25	53.67	65.89	42.60	43.99	50.20	42.01	40.96	46.85
SASRec	S	51.87	55.64	68.92	44.40	44.95	53.68	43.90	41.78	47.63
Fair-Neg	L	73.40	67.56	61.23	69.54	67.13	68.58	69.14	68.24	69.43
Simple-X	L	65.79	62.41	60.98	70.18	72.32	70.99	68.98	68.20	68.78
NRT	L	75.12	77.06	77.31	66.04	60.44	63.43	47.32	48.99	48.60
TCSR	G	60.68	59.32	61.34	49.24	49.44	49.10	46.84	45.08	46.34
Attn2Seq	G	63.11	64.06	65.09	56.43	56.19	60.03	48.36	50.05	56.34
Caser	G	65.41	67.56	66.02	68.66	64.75	65.49	59.44	58.65	59.40
S3-rec	LS	81.44	80.86	83.68	71.31	70.42	70.18	51.23	53.24	52.50
BERT4Rec	LS	80.42	60.34	62.99	70.37	70.08	70.12	56.43	55.00	56.91
U-BERT	LS	65.41	67.56	66.30	58.98	51.21	53.88	49.04	48.95	49.51
FDSA	GS	61.04	60.47	60.94	68.96	69.09	67.92	48.03	48.22	48.90
GC-SAN	GS	75.58	76.81	80.95	69.04	69.43	70.98	49.97	50.14	52.36
CaSe4SR	GS	79.88	79.93	82.28	69.34	69.58	71.75	49.99	50.64	54.46
GCAN	GL	83.40	82.46	84.02	70.48	70.44	70.03	57.02	57.35	57.66
M6-rec	GL	70.23	75.34	66.60	71.40	71.66	70.60	68.40	68.13	68.64
PETER	GL	80.67	79.58	83.44	70.56	69.99	75.61	68.23	68.16	68.79
Chat-rec	GLS	53.55	62.81	60.11	65.92	66.45	67.18	69.21	**69.45**	69.08
P5-S	GLS	80.18	80.48	81.33	65.33	63.89	64.00	58.43	58.82	59.67
P5-B	GLS	82.36	84.01	83.46	70.00	69.94	72.01	69.14	68.43	**69.58**
IFHAGrec	GLS	**85.57**	**87.93**	**86.77**	**71.63**	**71.48**	**72.06**	**69.30**	68.54	68.06

IFHAGrec constructs a user-item heterogeneous graph using spatial vectors, employs GCN and GAT to compute edge weights, effectively characterizing the complex relationships between users and items, significantly outperforming G-type methods. Simultaneously, the temporal vector employs a relational time embedding method to reflect the dynamic evolution of user interests over time, significantly outperforming S-type methods. The sentiment vector analyzes users' emotional attitudes, thereby adding fine-grained expression to user interests, significantly outperforming L-type methods. These features are fused via USV, forming a high-quality user feature representation that enables the recommendation system to demonstrate powerful recommendation capabilities.

4.5 Recommendation Accuracy Experiment

The recommendation task is accomplished by the generative architecture of the T5FLAN framework. Its encoder-decoder structure efficiently handles diverse recommendation tasks. T5FLAN first utilizes a bidirectional encoder to encode the input user features (i.e., USV), mapping them into latent representations in a hidden space; then, it generates recommendation results through an autoregressive decoder. The comparison of recommendation accuracy between the IFHAGrec model and other methods is shown in Table 4.

Table 4. Comparison of Recommendation Accuracy between IFHAGrec and Other Baseline Methods on the MovieLens100K Dataset

Task	MovieLens 100K	RMSE	MAE
P5	P5-S	1.0198	0.6850
	P5-B	1.0043	0.7125
Prompt	Discrete Prompt	1.0383	0.8136
	Continuous Prompt	1.3621	0.7915
Baseline (Total: 10)	M6-rec	0.8653	0.6100
	U-Bert	0.6466	0.5972
	FairNeg	0.3130	0.2697
	Chat-Rec (3.5-turbo)	0.9688	0.7550
	BERT4Rec	0.8343	0.7985
	GPT-2	0.7129	0.5346
	SimpleX	0.7281	0.5403
	BPR-MLP	1.1134	0.9658
	BPR-MF	1.0436	0.7979
IFHAGrec	P5-S+FLAN-small	0.7035	0.5234
	P5-S+FLAN-base	0.6991	0.5108
	P5-B+FLAN-small	0.6604	0.5073
	P5-B+FLAN-base	0.6517	0.4991
	USV+P5-B+FLAN-base	0.5453	0.5016

IFHAGrec's performance on RMSE and MAE metrics is superior to models like FairNeg, BERT4Rec, and GPT2. On the RMSE metric, IFHAGrec's error is significantly lower than BERT4Rec and shows a 13.6% error reduction compared to FairNeg. On the MAE metric, IFHAGrec's error is 5.5% and 7.8% lower than BERT4Rec and GPT2, respectively. Significance analysis further indicates that IFHAGrec's performance advantages are statistically significant.

4.6 Ablation Study

To verify the effectiveness of each module in IFHAGrec, ablation experiments were designed by gradually removing key modules, including the user-item graph module (GCN/GAT generating spatial vectors), the temporal feature extraction module, and the sentiment vector module. The experiments were conducted on the MovieLens100K dataset, recording the changes in ACC and F1 scores, as shown in Table 5.

Table 5. Ablation Experiments on Module Effectiveness of IFHAGrec. (A preference gate for prioritizing spatial/temporal/sentiment vectors was set when passing through Bi-GRU)

Task	MovieLens 100K	ACC	F1
Space Weight	GCN	0.8413	0.6776
	GAT	0.7854	0.7296
	HGT	0.8676	0.8435

(*continued*)

Table 5. (*continued*)

Task	MovieLens 100K	ACC	F1
	R-GCN	0.9179	0.8938
Time Encoding	TGAT	0.7614	0.6965
Sentiments	TF-IDF	0.7718	0.7051
Bi-GRU	Prior Space	0.8967	0.8195
	Prior Time	0.8851	0.8203
	Prior Sentiments	0.8936	0.8014
IFHAGrec	Graph + P5-FLAN	0.8918	0.8137

From the ablation experiments, it can be observed that each module plays an important role in improving model performance. In particular, the introduction of the user-item heterogeneous graph (spatial vector) significantly enhances the modeling capability of complex associations between users and items, making the recommendation results more accurate.

Compared to other methods, the generative capability of T5-FLAN allows the optimization objectives of recommendation tasks to be unified as a sequence generation problem, eliminating the need to design separate optimization objectives for different tasks, thereby significantly improving the model's generalization ability and adaptability. Consequently, IFHAGrec completes effective parameter learning on largescale user behavior sequences, enabling it to maintain stable performance across various recommendation scenarios. The cross-validation sensitivity analysis for IFHAGrec is shown in Fig. 4.

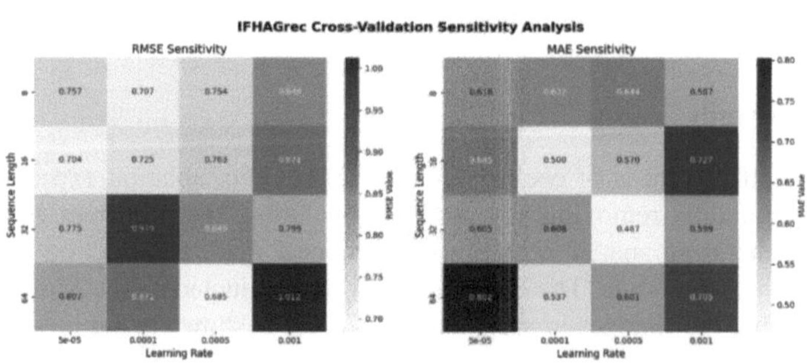

Fig. 4. Cross-Validation Sensitivity Analysis for IFHAGrec

5 Conclusions

This paper proposes the IFHAGrec model, a unified recommendation framework that deeply integrates heterogeneous graph structures, temporal dynamic encoding, and fine-grained sentiment analysis. By constructing a user-item heterogeneous graph and introducing spatial weights, it effectively models the complex interaction relationships among multiple types of nodes and edges, surpassing the limitations of traditional collaborative filtering and single graph models. Also, it innovatively incorporates temporal encoding and sentiment analysis as independent weighting dimensions into the model, capturing the temporal evolution patterns of user interests and subjective evaluation motivations, and it designs a Unified Sentence Vector (USV) generation mechanism and an adaptive preference gate Bi-GRU, which can adaptively fuse spatial, temporal, and sentiment features. However, this work still has certain limitations: the overall model architecture is relatively complex, potentially incurring high computational costs during training and inference. Additionally, the performance of the sentiment analysis module heavily relies on the quality and quantity of review texts.

Future research can regard model light-weighting, techniques such as knowledge distillation and model pruning can be explored to reduce the computational complexity of IFHAGrec, facilitating its deployment in resource-constrained environments or real-time recommendation systems. Also, the integration of multimodal information can be further expanded. By incorporating item image/audio features or users' cross-platform behavioral data to construct a more comprehensive user profile.

Disclosure of Interests. The authors have no competing interests to declare that are relevant to the content of this article.

References

1. Geng, S., Liu, S., Fu, Z., Ge, Y., Zhang, Y.: Recommendation as language processing (RLP): a unified pretrain, personalized prompt & predict paradigm (p5). In: Proceedings of the 16th ACM Conference on Recommender Systems, pp. 299–315 (2022)
2. Zhu, X., Zhang, Y., Wang, J., Wang, G.: Graph-enhanced and collaborative attention networks for session-based recommendation. Knowl. Based Syst. **289**, 111509 (2024)
3. Zhu, X., Zhang, Y., Li, J., Wang, J., Lai, X.: TCSR: self-attention with time and category for session-based recommendation. Comput. Intell. **40**(5), e12695 (2024)
4. Wang, Y., et al.: DPBPRMF: a rigorous differential privacy scheme with Bayesian personalized ranking for implicit recommendation. Neurocomputing, 131871 (2025)
5. Rendle, S., Freudenthaler, C., Gantner, Z., Schmidt-Thieme, L.: BPR: Bayesian personalized ranking from implicit feedback. In: Proceedings of the Twenty-Fifth Conference on Uncertainty in Artificial Intelligence, pp. 452–461 (2009)
6. Kang, W.C., McAuley, J.: Self-attentive sequential recommendation. In: 2018 IEEE International Conference on Data Mining (ICDM), pp. 197–206. IEEE (2018)
7. Chen, X., et al.: Fairly adaptive negative sampling for recommendations. In: Proceedings of the ACM Web Conference, pp. 3723–3733 (2023)
8. Mao, K., et al.: SimpleX: a simple and strong baseline for collaborative filtering. In: Proceedings of the 30th ACM International Conference on Information & Knowledge Management, pp. 1243–1252 (2021)
9. Rajput, S., et al.: Recommender systems with generative retrieval. Adv. Neural. Inf. Process. Syst. **36**, 10299–10315 (2023)
10. Dong, L., Huang, S., Wei, F., Lapata, M., Zhou, M., Xu, K.: Learning to generate product reviews from attributes. In: Proceedings of the 15th Conference of the European Chapter of the Association for Computational Linguistics: Volume 1, Long Papers, pp. 623–632 (2017)

11. Tang, J., Wang, K.: Personalized top-n sequential recommendation via convolutional sequence embedding. In Proceedings of the Eleventh ACM International Conference on Web Search and Data Mining, pp. 565–573 (2018)
12. Zhou, K., et al.: S3-REC: self-supervised learning for sequential recommendation with mutual information maximization. In: Proceedings of the 29th ACM International Conference on Information & Knowledge Management, pp. 1893–1902
13. Sun, F., et al.: BERT4Rec: sequential recommendation with bidirectional encoder representations from transformer. In: Proceedings of the 28th ACM International Conference on Information and Knowledge Management, pp. 1441–1450
14. Qiu, Z., Wu, X., Gao, J., Fan, W.: U-BERT: pre-training user representations for improved recommendation. In: Proceedings of the AAAI Conference on Artificial Intelligence, vol. 35, no. 5, pp. 4320–4327 (2021)
15. Cui, Z., Ma, J., Zhou, C., Zhou, J., Yang, H.: M6-REC: generative pretrained language models are open-ended recommender systems. arXiv preprint arXiv:2205.08084
16. Teo, T.W., Choy, B.H.: Personalized transformer for explainable recommendation. In: Tan, O.S., Low, E.L., Tay, E.G., Yan, Y.K. (eds.) Singapore Math and Science Education Innovation. ETLPPSIP, vol. 1, pp. 43–59. Springer, Singapore (2021). https://doi.org/10.1007/978-981-16-1357-9_3
17. Zhang, T., et al.: Feature-level deeper self-attention network for sequential recommendation. IJCAI, 4320–4326 (2019)
18. Liu, L., Wang, L., Lian, T.: CaSe4SR: using category sequence graph to augment session-based recommendation. Knowl. Based Syst. **212**, 106558 (2021)
19. Xu, C., et al.: Graph contextualized self-attention network for session-based recommendation. IJCAI **19**(2019), 3940–3946 (2019)
20. Gao, Y., Sheng, T., Xiang, Y., Xiong, Y., Wang, H., Zhang, J.: CHAT-REC: towards interactive and explainable LLMS-augmented recommender system. arXiv preprint arXiv:2303.14524

Ada-DVSA: Adaptive Dual-View Self-augmentation for Multi-behavior Recommendation

Yuxia Lei(✉), Yutao Gao(✉), Qing Zhang, Zhaoan Dong, and Jing Xiong

School of Computer Science, Qufu Normal University, Rizhao 276826, China
yx_lei@126.com, gaiyao81@163.com, {qingzhang,dzan,jingxiong}@qfnu.edu.cn

Abstract. Multi-behavior recommendation leverages auxiliary behaviors to mitigate the sparsity of target behaviors such as purchases. However, existing parallel modeling methods often overlook the quality of underlying representations, leading to unstable embeddings in sparse behavior graphs and ineffective knowledge transfer across behaviors. To address these challenges, we propose Ada-DVSA, an adaptive dual-view self-augmentation framework that enhances representation learning from both vertical and horizontal perspectives within a self-supervised paradigm. Specifically, a Vertical Structure Enhancement module stabilizes high-order node representations via cross-layer contrastive learning, while an Adaptive Relevance Gating mechanism dynamically weights auxiliary behaviors to filter noisy signals. Guided by this gate, Horizontal Semantic Alignment performs safe cross-behavior contrastive learning to facilitate robust knowledge transfer. Extensive experiments on real-world sparse datasets demonstrate that Ada-DVSA consistently outperforms state-of-the-art methods, highlighting the importance of robust representation learning and adaptive noise-aware alignment in multi-behavior recommendation.

Keywords: Multi-behavior Recommendation · Self-Supervised Learning · Graph Neural Network · Representation Drift · Adaptive Semantic Alignment

1 Introduction

With the rapid development of e-commerce platforms and online services, recommendation systems have become an indispensable component of modern information systems [10]. By modeling users' personalized preferences, recommendation systems can effectively alleviate information overload, improve user experience, and bring substantial economic benefits to online platforms. Early recommendation approaches mainly relied on collaborative filtering and matrix factorization

This article is partially supported by the Shandong Higher Education Undergraduate Teaching Reform Research Project (No. Z2024260).

J. Niu et al. (Eds.): KSEM 2026, LNAI 16631, pp. 341–352, 2027.
https://doi.org/10.1007/978-981-92-2759-4_25

techniques [11,13], while recent advances in deep learning and graph neural networks (GNNs) have enabled more expressive modeling of useritem interactions [2].

However, most traditional recommendation models focus on a single type of user behavior, which often suffers from severe data sparsity. To address this issue, multi-behavior recommendation (MBR) has been proposed, which leverages abundant auxiliary behaviors (e.g., clicks, carts) to enhance the modeling of sparse target behaviors. MBGCN combines graph convolutional networks for modeling [7], MBAGCN introduces an attention mechanism [12], KMCLR incorporates a knowledge graph, and MBCLRec uses contrastive learning [18,23]. By jointly exploiting multiple behavior signals, existing MBR methods have achieved notable performance improvements.

Despite these advances, multi-behavior recommendation still faces critical challenges. First, existing methods typically overlook the quality and stability of node representations learned from individual behavior graphs. In highly sparse settings, applying GCN-based propagation to single-behavior graphs may amplify noisy interactions, causing high-order node representations to drift away from their original semantic meanings. This representation drift limits the effectiveness of high-order structural information and degrades recommendation performance.

Second, multi-behavior recommendation models are prone to negative transfer caused by semantic fragmentation across behaviors. Different user behaviors often correspond to different stages and intensities of decision-making processes. Many existing approaches adopt parallel modeling or indiscriminate feature fusion strategies, which fail to explicitly align semantics across behaviors. As a result, auxiliary behaviors with weak or noisy correlations to the target behavior may be blindly transferred, introducing noise and harming model robustness. How to carry out effective knowledge transfer is an important issue.

To address the above challenges, we propose an Adaptive Dual-View Self-Augmentation framework (Ada-DVSA) for multi-behavior recommendation. Ada-DVSA enhances representation learning from two complementary perspectives: vertical (within-graph) and horizontal (across-graph). First, we introduce a Vertical Structure Enhancement (VSE) module that stabilizes high-order node representations by enforcing semantic consistency across GCN layers, thereby alleviating representation drift in sparse behavior graphs. Then, we design a Horizontal Semantic Alignment (HSA) module to reduce semantic discrepancies between auxiliary and target behaviors. To ensure safe and effective knowledge transfer, an Adaptive Relevance Gating (GATE) mechanism is further introduced to dynamically assess the semantic relevance between behaviors and regulate the alignment strength accordingly, effectively filtering noisy auxiliary signals.

Extensive experiments on real-world datasets, including Beibei, Tmall, and Taobao, demonstrate that Ada-DVSA consistently outperforms state-of-the-art multi-behavior recommendation methods, particularly in highly sparse scenarios.

Additional ablation studies further verify the effectiveness of each component in our framework. The main contributions of this work are summarized as follows:

- We propose Ada-DVSA, a dual-view self-augmentation framework that jointly enhances within-graph representation stability and cross-behavior semantic alignment, effectively mitigating representation drift and semantic fragmentation in multi-behavior recommendation.
- We design an adaptive relevance gating mechanism to regulate cross-behavior knowledge transfer based on semantic relevance, improving robustness and reducing negative transfer from noisy auxiliary behaviors.
- We conduct extensive experiments and ablation studies on multiple real-world datasets, demonstrating the superiority and robustness of the proposed method in sparse recommendation scenarios.

2 Related Work

2.1 Multi-behavior Recommendation

Multi-Behavior Recommendation (MBR) aims to alleviate the limitations of traditional recommendation methods that rely solely on target behaviors by jointly modeling multiple useritem interactions, such as clicking and collecting. By leveraging auxiliary behaviors, MBR methods can better capture users' latent preferences, thereby mitigating data sparsity and cold-start issues. Early MBR studies mainly adopt matrix factorization and multi-relational learning frameworks, such as MR-BPR, which show effectiveness in sparse settings but are limited in modeling high-order structures and inter-behavior relationships [8]. Recent methods shift toward graph-based representation learning. Models like MBGCN construct unified multi-behavior graphs to differentiate the influence of various behaviors [7], while LightGCN simplifies GCN architectures to improve efficiency and stability [6]. More recently, UIPL introduces invariant preference learning to disentangle behavior-specific and invariant user interests, effectively reducing noise from auxiliary behaviors [21]. Despite these advances, most existing methods primarily rely on supervised interaction signals and implicitly assume that the representations learned by underlying GNNs are stable and reliable, which may not hold in highly sparse and noisy scenarios.

2.2 Self-supervised Learning for Recommendation

However, the supervised learning methods is limited by data sparsity. Self-supervised learning uses the existing data itself to generate supervisory signal and has been introduced into recommendation [14]. Methods like SGL and SimGCL construct augmented views through random edge dropping or noise addition, then use self-supervised learning to model user interest [9,16]. S-MBRec uses a star-shaped contrastive learning model for target-auxiliary behavior similarity capture and self-supervised tasks for behavior importance differentiation

[5]. MBSSL is divided into two tasks: knowledge transfer between behaviors and denoising within behaviors, introducing adaptive learning to balance the two tasks [17]. NSED proposes a neighborhood enhancement module to alleviate data distribution imbalance issues [1]. However, most methods simply perform cross-behavior semantic alignment, lacking evaluation of auxiliary behaviors, which introduces noise into the target behavior.

3 Methodology

In this section, we will provide a detailed introduction to the Ada-DVSA framework. The overall architecture of the framework is shown in Fig. 1. We first introduce the basic concepts, and then elaborate on the three core components: (1) Vertical Structure Enhancement, (2) Adaptive Relevance Gating mechanism and (3) Horizontal Semantic Alignment. Finally, we describe multi-behavior preference learning and joint optimization objectives.

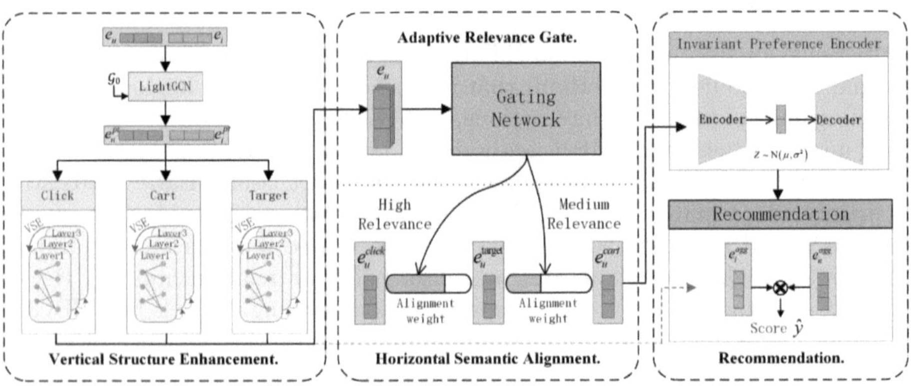

Fig. 1. Overall Architecture of the Ada-DVSA Framework.

3.1 Preliminaries

Multi-behavior Recommendation. In our framework, users and items are represented by u and i, respectively. The sets of users and items are defined as $U = \{u_1, u_2, \ldots, u_m\}$ and $I = \{i_1, i_2, \ldots, i_n\}$, where m and n represent the total number of users and items, respectively. We define the set of behavior types as $B = \{b_1, b_2, \ldots, b_K\}$, representing the set of all behaviors, where K is the number of behaviors. Each b_k represents a specific type of interaction (e.g., click, cart, purchase). Among these behaviors, a particular behavior (usually purchase) is designated as the target behavior b_{tar}, while the other behaviors are considered auxiliary behaviors $b_{\text{aux}} = B \setminus \{b_{\text{tar}}\}$.

We model multi-behavior data as a set of bipartite graphs representing specific behaviors, $G = \{G_1, G_2, \ldots, G_K\}$. For each behavior b_k, its graph is defined as $G_k = (U \cup I, E_k)$, where E_k represents the set of edges. An edge $(u, i) \in E_k$ exists if user u has interacted with item i under behavior b.

Backbone Encoder. We use LightGCN as the backbone to independently encode user and item representations in each behavior graph. For a specific behavior b_k, let $e^{(0)}$ be the initial embedding. The first layer of graph convolution aggregates neighbor information as follows:

$$e_u^{(l+1)} = \sum_{i \in N_u} \frac{1}{\sqrt{|N_u| \cdot |N_i|}} e_i^{(l)} \tag{1}$$

Unlike the standard LightGCN that uses only the final weighted sum, our framework retains embeddings from all intermediate layers $\{e^{(0)}, \ldots, e^{(l)}\}$ to facilitate vertical enhancement.

3.2 Adaptive Dual-View Self-augmentation

To address the issues of structural sparsity and semantic fragmentation in multi-behavior data, we designed the Ada-DVSA framework. This framework leverages self-supervised signals from both vertical and horizontal perspectives, and bridges them through a novel adaptive relevance gating mechanism to enhance representation learning.

Vertical Structure Enhancement. To address the representation drift problem in GCN-based multi-behavior recommendation methods, We introduce a hierarchical self-supervised learning objective to explicitly correct representation drift. Let $e_u^{(0)}$ represent the initial embedding of user u, which reflects the user's intrinsic identity. Let $e_u^{(l)}$ represent the embedding after l layers of graph convolution, which integrates contextual information.

We assume that a correct representation should include information from both neighbors and itself. Therefore, we maximize the mutual information between the initial and final layers to enhance semantic consistency. For a specific behavior graph G_k, we treat $e_u^{(0)}, e_u^{(l)}$ as positive examples, while embeddings of other users v in the same batch serve as negative samples. The vertical enhancement loss is formulated using InfoNCE as follows:

$$L_{\text{VSE}}^{(u,k)} = -\log \left(\frac{\exp\left(\frac{\text{sim}\left(e_u^{(0)}, e_u^{(l)}\right)}{\tau_1}\right)}{\sum_{v \in u_{\text{batch}}} \exp\left(\frac{\text{sim}\left(e_u^{(0)}, e_v^{(l)}\right)}{\tau_1}\right)} \right) \tag{2}$$

Here, u_{batch} represents the set of users in the current training batch, $sim(\cdot, \cdot)$ denotes cosine similarity, and τ_1 is a temperature parameter. By minimizing this loss, we impose a strong regularization constraint, forcing the GCN to filter out noisy neighborhood signals that would cause the high-level representation $e_u^{(l)}$ to deviate from its intrinsic feature $e_u^{(0)}$. This ensures that the learned embeddings remain robust and semantically consistent even in highly sparse graph environments.

Adaptive Relevance Gating Mechanism. Although cross-behavior semantic alignment can leverage auxiliary behaviors to enhance preference modeling, the relevance of different behaviors to the target behavior varies significantly across users. Applying uniform alignment constraints may result in negative transfer.

To address this, we introduce an adaptive relevance gating mechanism. This mechanism uses the target behavior representation as an anchor and adaptively learns the semantic relevance across behaviors, thereby dynamically adjusting the contribution intensity of auxiliary behaviors in the cross-behavior alignment process. In practice, for each user u, we denote the representations learned for the target behavior and a certain auxiliary behavior as e_u^{tar} and e_u^{aux}, respectively. To capture the semantic correlation between the two, we construct a gating function $g(\cdot)$ guided by the target behavior, whose input is the concatenated vector of the target behavior and auxiliary behavior representations:

$$z_u = \left[e_u^{\text{tar}} \parallel e_u^{\text{aux}}\right] \tag{3}$$

Here, $[\cdot \parallel \cdot]$ represents the vector concatenation operation. The gating function $g(\cdot)$ is implemented by a lightweight multi-layer perceptron and maps the output to the $(0, 1)$ interval through the sigmoid activation function, thereby obtaining the relevance gating coefficient corresponding to the auxiliary behavior:

$$\alpha_u = g(z_u), \alpha_u \in (0, 1) \tag{4}$$

This gating coefficient reflects the strength of the semantic correlation between auxiliary behaviors and target behaviors at the current user level. Subsequently, we use this coefficient to adaptively modulate the auxiliary behavior representation, obtaining a denoised auxiliary representation:

$$\tilde{e}_u^{\text{aux}} = \alpha_u \odot e_u^{\text{aux}} \tag{5}$$

Here, $\odot$ denotes element-wise multiplication.

Horizontal Semantic Alignment. Existing parallel modeling methods usually treat different behaviors as independent semantic spaces, overlooking the semantic correlations between auxiliary behaviors and target behaviors. To address this, we introduce an horizontal semantic alignment module. We use the target behavior as an anchor and achieve robust cross-behavior semantic alignment under the regulation of the gating mechanism.

Specifically, for each user u, we take the user representation under the target behavior e_u^{tar} as the anchor, and the auxiliary behavior representation $\tilde{e}_u^{\text{aux}}$ after adaptive relevance gating mechanism, as the positive sample. The auxiliary behavior representations of other users in the same batch are treated as negative samples. Based on this, we adopt a contrastive learning paradigm to align the representations of different users across behavior views, with the loss function defined as:

$$L_{\text{HSA}} = -\sum_{u \in \mathcal{U}_{\text{batch}}} \log \frac{\exp\left(\frac{\text{sim}\left(e_u^{\text{tar}}, \tilde{e}_u^{\text{aux}}\right)}{\tau_2}\right)}{\sum_{v \in \mathcal{U}_{\text{batch}}} \exp\left(\frac{\text{sim}\left(e_u^{\text{tar}}, \tilde{e}_v^{\text{aux}}\right)}{\tau_2}\right)} \tag{6}$$

Here, $sim(\cdot, \cdot)$ denotes dot-product similarity, and τ_2 is the temperature coefficient.

By combining an adaptive gating mechanism with cross-behavior contrastive learning, this module can adaptively adjust the influence intensity of auxiliary behaviors in the alignment process based on the semantic relevance between different behaviors.

3.3 Multi-behavior Preference Learning

Invariant Preference Disentanglement. To further capture users' inherently stable interests across behaviors, we follow the UIPL paradigm and input the fused user embeddings into a variational autoencoder (VAE). The VAE decouples user representations into invariant preferences e_{inv} and variant(behavior-specific) preferences e_{var}. This process is constrained by optimizing the KL divergence loss L_{KL}, an auxiliary orthogonal loss L_{Ort} and a contrastive loss $L_{(NCE\_VAE)}$, ensuring that the invariant preferences capture the users' interests.

Static Degree-Based Fusion. Since interaction frequency reflects behavioral importance, and to avoid overfitting from extra learnable parameters in sparse scenarios, we use a degree-based static fusion strategy. For item i, its final representation e_i is the weighted sum of embeddings from different behaviors.

$$e_i = \sum_{k=1}^{K} \alpha_k \, e_i^{(k)} \tag{7}$$

The weight α_k is determined by the number of interaction under this behavior.

3.4 Joint Optimization and Prediction

Prediction. The final predicted rating $\hat{y}_{ui}$ of the user for the item is calculated as follows:

$$\hat{y}_{ui} = \left(e_{u,\text{inv}} + e_{u,\text{var}}^{\text{tar}}\right)^{\top} e_i \tag{8}$$

where $e_{u,var}^{tar}$ is a variable preference for target behavior; e_u^{inv} is invariant preferences.

Joint Loss. The model is trained using a multi-task learning framework. The overall loss function as follow:

$$L_{\text{Total}} = L_{\text{Rec}} + \lambda_{\text{VSE}} L_{\text{VSE}} + \lambda_{\text{HSA}} L_{\text{HSA}} + L_{\text{VAE}} \tag{9}$$

where L_{Rec} is the recommendation loss, L_{VSE} and L_{HSA} are the proposed self-supervised enhancement losses, and L_{VAE} denotes the VAE regularization. The hyperparameters λ_{VSE} and λ_{HSA} balance different objectives.

4 Experiment

4.1 Datasets

We evaluate the proposed model on three publicly available real-world e-commerce datasets: Taobao, Tmall, and Beibei. In all datasets, purchase is treated as the target behavior, while other interactions are considered auxiliary behaviors. For detailed information about these three datasets, please refer to Table 1.

Table 1. Statistics of Evaluation Datasets

Dataset	User	Item	click	collect	cart	purchase
Taobao	48,749	39,493	1,548,162	–	183,747	211,022
Tmall	41,738	11,953	2,412,586	221,514	1,996	255,586
Beibei	21,716	7,997	1,681,430	–	642,622	304,576

4.2 Evaluation Metrics and Baseline

Following common practice, we adopt the leave-one-out evaluation protocol, where the most recent interaction of each user is held out for testing and the remaining interactions are used for training. We evaluate model performance using two widely adopted top-K ranking metrics: Hit Ratio ($HR@K$) and Normalized Discounted Cumulative Gain ($NDCG@K$). $HR@K$ measures whether the ground-truth item appears in the top-K recommendation list, while $NDCG@K$ reflects both ranking quality and user relevance.

To comprehensively evaluate the effectiveness of Ada-DVSA, we compare it with representative single-behavior and multi-behavior recommendation methods. For single-behavior baselines, we include MF-BPR [15] and LightGCN [6], which represent classical matrix factorization and GNN-based approaches. For multi-behavior recommendation, we select a diverse set of state-of-the-art models, including NMTR [4], MBGCN [7], CRGCN [19], MB-CGCN [3], BCIPM [22], UIPL [21], and MBLFE [20], covering multi-task learning, graph-based modeling, self-supervised learning, and invariant preference disentanglement.

Table 2. The overall performance comparison. Boldface notes the highest score and underline indicates the results of the best baselines.

Dataset	Tmall		Taobao		Beibei	
Metric	HR	NDCG	HR	NDCG	HR	NDCG
MF-BPR	0.0230	0.0230	0.0178	0.0101	0.0268	0.0139
LightGCN	0.0393	0.0393	0.0254	0.0138	0.0309	0.0161
NMTR	0.0517	0.0250	0.0409	0.0409	0.0315	0.0146
MBGCN	0.0549	0.0285	0.0434	0.0259	0.0470	0.0259
CRGCN	0.0840	0.0442	0.1152	0.0629	0.0459	0.0324
MB-CGCN	0.1073	0.0416	0.0989	0.0470	0.0579	0.0381
BCIPM	0.1414	0.0741	0.1292	0.0716	<u>0.0670</u>	<u>0.0331</u>
UIPL	0.1434	<u>0.0790</u>	0.1328	0.0782	0.0577	0.0301
MBLFE	<u>0.1452</u>	0.0787	<u>0.1343</u>	<u>0.0795</u>	0.0649	0.0345
Ours	**0.1880**	**0.1029**	**0.2057**	**0.1236**	**0.0987**	**0.0547**
Impr.	29.48%	30.25%	53.16%	55.47%	47.31%	65.26%

4.3 Overall Performance Comparison

Table 2 reports the overall performance of all methods on the Tmall, Taobao, and Beibei datasets in terms of HR@10 and NDCG@10. As shown, Ada-DVSA consistently outperforms all baseline methods across all datasets and evaluation metrics. Among single-behavior approaches, LightGCN achieves better performance than MF-BPR, while multi-behavior models generally yield substantial improvements over single-behavior baselines, highlighting the effectiveness of exploiting auxiliary behaviors. Compared with the strongest baseline methods, Ada-DVSA achieves notable gains on all three datasets, with particularly significant improvements observed in highly sparse settings. These results indicate that enhancing representation quality within individual behavior graphs and performing effective cross-behavior semantic alignment are both crucial for multi-behavior recommendation. By stabilizing high-order node representations and adaptively regulating cross-behavior knowledge transfer, Ada-DVSA is able to alleviate representation drift and semantic fragmentation, thereby reducing negative transfer from noisy auxiliary behaviors and improving recommendation accuracy under sparse interactions.

4.4 Ablation Experiment

To investigate the contribution of each component in Ada-DVSA, we conduct ablation experiments on three datasets using HR@10 and NDCG@10 as evaluation metrics. Several variants of Ada-DVSA are evaluated by selectively removing key modules. The ablation results are summarized in Table 3.

As shown in Table 3, both single-view variants, VSE-only (w/o HSA & GATE) and HSA-only (w/o VSE & GATE), consistently outperform the base-

Table 3. Ablation experiments for the individual components of the model.

method	VSE	HSA	GATE	tmall	taobao	beibei
Baseline	×	×	N/A	0.1434	0.1328	0.0577
w/o HSA&GA	✓	×	N/A	0.1787	0.2002	0.0773
w/o VSE&GA	×	✓	N/A	0.1742	0.1808	0.0594
w/o GA	✓	✓	×	0.1813	0.2046	0.0797
Full Model	✓	✓	✓	0.188	0.2057	0.0987

line across all datasets, confirming that the baseline performance is constrained by degraded representations in sparse interaction graphs. In particular, VSE effectively alleviates representation drift by enforcing cross-layer consistency, while HSA facilitates knowledge transfer by aligning semantic information across behaviors. When combining both enhancements, the w/o GATE variant consistently achieves better performance than either single-view setting, indicating that vertical structure enhancement and horizontal semantic alignment are complementary. Finally, the full Ada-DVSA model further improves performance over the w/o GATE variant, demonstrating the effectiveness of the adaptive gating mechanism. By dynamically modulating alignment strength based on the relevance between auxiliary and target behavior representations, GATE promotes reliable knowledge transfer.

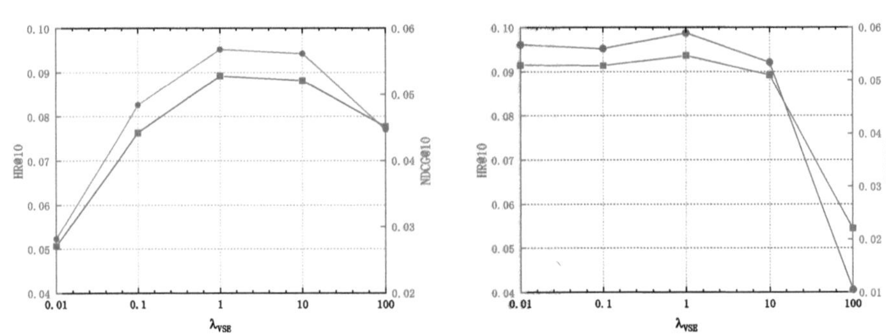

Fig. 2. Sensitivity Analysis of Hyperparameters λ_{VSE} and λ_{HSA} on Beibei.

4.5 Hyperparameter Analysis

Due to space limitations, we conduct hyperparameter sensitivity analysis on the Beibei dataset only, the results are shown in Fig. 2. We analyze the effect of the vertical structure enhancement weight λ_{VSE} and the horizontal semantic alignment weight λ_{HSA}. When fixing λ_{HSA} to 0.1, increasing λ_{VSE} from 0.01 to 0.1 leads to significant performance improvements, while further increasing it to 1 or 10 results in stable performance; however, an excessively large value, such as 100, causes performance degradation, indicating that overly strong structural constraints may hinder optimization. Similarly, when fixing λ_{VSE} to 1, model performance remains stable as λ_{HSA} varies from 0.01 to 1 and reaches its optimum at $\lambda_{\text{HSA}} = 1$, whereas larger values (e.g., 10 or 100) significantly degrade performance due to the introduction of noisy or weakly correlated auxiliary signals. Overall, Ada-DVSA exhibits robust performance within a reasonable range of both hyperparameters.

5 Conclusion

In this paper, we proposed Ada-DVSA, an adaptive dual-view self-augmentation framework for multi-behavior recommendation, aiming to address two fundamental challenges in sparse scenarios: representation drift within behavior graphs and negative transfer during cross-behavior knowledge fusion. Ada-DVSA enhances representation quality from both vertical and horizontal perspectives by jointly modeling intra-graph structural consistency and inter-behavior semantic alignment. In particular, the vertical structure enhancement module stabilizes high-order node representations under sparse conditions, while the adaptive relevance gating mechanism enables robust semantic alignment across behaviors. Extensive experiments on real-world datasets demonstrate that Ada-DVSA consistently outperforms state-of-the-art methods. These results highlight the importance of learning robust knowledge representations and transfer for effective multi-behavior recommendation.

References

1. Cai, W., et al.: Neighborhood structure enhancement and denoising method for multi-behavior recommendation. Neural Networks 107760 (2025)
2. Chen, L., Wu, L., Hong, R., Zhang, K., Wang, M.: Revisiting graph based collaborative filtering: A linear residual graph convolutional network approach. In: Proceedings of the AAAI Conference on Artificial Intelligence, vol. 34, pp. 27–34 (2020)
3. Cheng, Z., Han, S., Liu, F., Zhu, L., Gao, Z., Peng, Y.: Multi-behavior recommendation with cascading graph convolution networks. In: Proceedings of the ACM Web Conference 2023, pp. 1181–1189 (2023)
4. Gao, C., et al.: Learning to recommend with multiple cascading behaviors. IEEE Trans. Knowl. Data Eng. **33**(6), 2588–2601 (2019)
5. Gu, S., Wang, X., Shi, C., Xiao, D.: Self-supervised graph neural networks for multi-behavior recommendation. In: IJCAI, pp. 2052–2058 (2022)
6. He, X., Deng, K., Wang, X., Li, Y., Zhang, Y., Wang, M.: LightGCN: simplifying and powering graph convolution network for recommendation. In: Proceedings of the 43rd International ACM SIGIR Conference on Research and Development in Information Retrieval, pp. 639–648 (2020)
7. Jin, B., Gao, C., He, X., Jin, D., Li, Y.: Multi-behavior recommendation with graph convolutional networks. In: Proceedings of the 43rd International ACM SIGIR Conference on Research and Development in Information Retrieval, pp. 659–668 (2020)

8. Krohn-Grimberghe, A., Drumond, L., Freudenthaler, C., Schmidt-Thieme, L.: Multi-relational matrix factorization using bayesian personalized ranking for social network data. In: Proceedings of the Fifth ACM International Conference on Web Search and Data Mining, pp. 173–182 (2012)
9. Liu, C., Yu, C., Gui, N., Yu, Z., Deng, S.: SimGCL: graph contrastive learning by finding homophily in heterophily. Knowl. Inf. Syst. **66**(3), 2089–2114 (2024)
10. Liu, Q., Yu, M., Bai, M.: A study on a recommendation algorithm based on spectral clustering and GRU. Iscience **27**(2) (2024)
11. Patel, R., Thakkar, P.: IBCFAICDR: auxiliary data-driven item-based collaborative filtering in cross-domain RSS to address user cold start problem. Results in Engineering **24**, 103257 (2024)
12. Peng, X., Sun, J., Yan, M., Sun, F., Wang, F.: Attention-guided graph convolutional network for multi-behavior recommendation. Knowl.-Based Syst. **280**, 111040 (2023)
13. Qiu, H., Liu, Y., Guo, G., Sun, Z., Zhang, J., Nguyen, H.T.: BPRH: Bayesian personalized ranking for heterogeneous implicit feedback. Inf. Sci. **453**, 80–98 (2018)
14. Ren, X., Wei, W., Xia, L., Huang, C.: A comprehensive survey on self-supervised learning for recommendation. ACM Comput. Surv. **58**(1), 1–38 (2025)
15. Rendle, S., Freudenthaler, C., Gantner, Z., Schmidt-Thieme, L.: BPR: Bayesian personalized ranking from implicit feedback. arXiv preprint arXiv:1205.2618 (2012)
16. Wu, J., et al.: Self-supervised graph learning for recommendation. In: Proceedings of the 44th international ACM SIGIR Conference on Research and Development in Information Retrieval, pp. 726–735 (2021)
17. Xu, J., et al.: Multi-behavior self-supervised learning for recommendation. In: Proceedings of the 46th International ACM SIGIR Conference on Research and Development in Information Retrieval, pp. 496–505 (2023)
18. Xuan, H., Liu, Y., Li, B., Yin, H.: Knowledge enhancement for contrastive multi-behavior recommendation. In: Proceedings of the Sixteenth ACM International Conference on Web Search and Data Mining, pp. 195–203 (2023)
19. Yan, M., et al.: Cascading residual graph convolutional network for multi-behavior recommendation. ACM Trans. Inf. Syst. **42**(1), 1–26 (2023)
20. Yan, M., Cheng, Z., Han, Y., Wang, M.: Latent factor modeling with expert network for multi-behavior recommendation. IEEE Trans. Knowl. Data Eng. (2025)
21. Yan, M., Cheng, Z., Liu, F., Lyu, Y., Han, Y.: User invariant preference learning for multi-behavior recommendation. ACM Trans. Inf. Syst. (2025)
22. Yan, M., Liu, F., Sun, J., Sun, F., Cheng, Z., Han, Y.: Behavior-contextualized item preference modeling for multi-behavior recommendation. In: Proceedings of the 47th International ACM SIGIR Conference on Research and Development in Information Retrieval, pp. 946–955 (2024)
23. Zhao, Z., Tong, X., Wang, Y., Zhang, Q.: Multi-behavior contrastive learning with graph neural networks for recommendation. Knowl.-Based Syst. **300**, 112221 (2024)

LARK: Layer-Aware Routing with K-Ary Dynamic Pruning Tree for Self-speculative Decoding

Baizhou Xu, Zhaoning Zhang(✉), Zhen Huang, and Libo Zhang

National Key Laboratory of Parallel and Distributed Computing, College of Computer Science and Technology, National University of Defense Technology, Changsha, China
{xubaizhou23,zhangzhaoning,huangzhen}@nudt.edu.cn

Abstract. Accelerating large language model inference is critical due to the memory-bound nature of autoregressive decoding. Speculative decoding alleviates this bottleneck via a draft-then-verify approach, and self-speculative decoding (Self-SD) further eliminates the need for external draft models by reusing target model layers. However, existing Self-SD methods suffer from two primary limitations: feature misalignment induced by black-box layer selection and inefficient verification with local myopia. To address these challenges, we propose **LARK** featuring **L**ayer-**A**ware **R**outing with a **K**-ary dynamic pruning tree, a training-free method with no additional model weights. First, LARK introduces a layer-aware routing mechanism skipping less important layers to alleviate the feature misalignment. This mechanism relies on the offline computation of a *layer importance score* (LIS), which integrates perplexity impact and cosine similarity. Second, we design *K-ary dynamic pruning tree based on ancestor-aware path value* (PTPV), which adaptively adjusts the width and depth of the candidate tree based on global probability, achieving a balance between verification overhead and accept rate. Extensive experiments on LLaMA-2-13B and LLaMA-3-8B on three benchmarks demonstrate that LARK achieves the average speedup of 1.47× and accepted length of 8.2 without altering the original distribution of the generated text.

Keywords: LLM inference optimization · Self-speculative decoding · Layer importance · K-ary tree

1 Introduction

As the parameter scale of large language models (LLMs) [1,8] continues to expand, inference faces a severe memory-wall bottleneck [2]. The serial nature of auto-regressive decoding requires loading massive model parameters from memory for every single token generated. This results in low arithmetic intensity, causing GPU cores to idle while awaiting data transfer. Speculative decoding

J. Niu et al. (Eds.): KSEM 2026, LNAI 16631, pp. 353–366, 2027.
https://doi.org/10.1007/978-981-92-2759-4_26

[14,22] breaks the serial dependency of autoregressive decoding through a draft-then-verify paradigm, where multiple tokens are generated at low cost in a single forward pass and subsequently verified in parallel. This mechanism effectively amortizes the high memory access cost over a batch of tokens, shifting the workload from a memory-bound to a compute-bound regime, thereby accelerating inference while ensuring lossless generation.

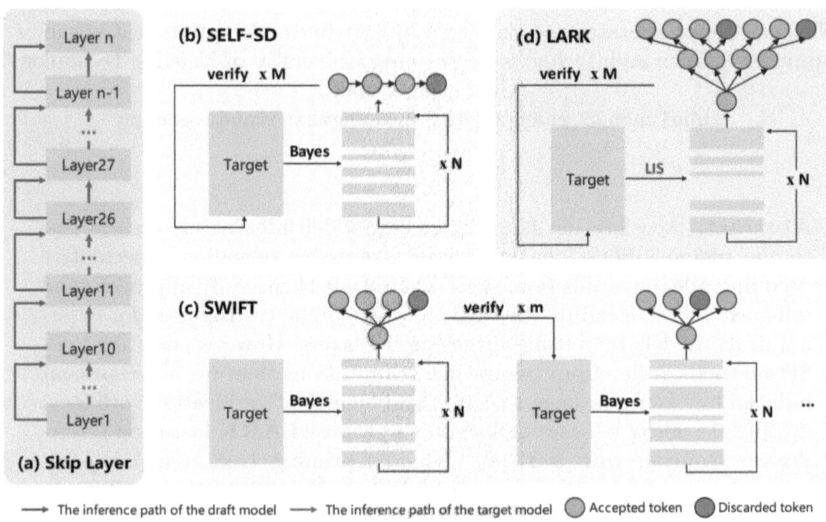

Fig. 1. Previous Self-SD methods vs. LARK. (a) Skip Layer depicts the foundational paradigm of Self-SD where drafting skips calculations (red path) while verification traverses all layers; (b) SELF-SD employs bayesian selection for fixed skip layers with chain verification; (c) SWIFT also adopts bayesian, but re-selects layers every m steps ($m \ll M$) using, and the candidate token sequence is constructed via a local probability tree; (d) LARK distinguishes itself by selecting fixed layers via LIS and employs global probability pruning and constructing a deeper dynamic tree.

Speculative decoding with independent draft models [17] has demonstrated potential, but introduces additional deployment complexity and training costs; moreover, training high-quality draft models poses nontrivial challenges, and such models exhibit poor generalization across different target models or datasets. To address these limitations, self-speculative decoding (Self-SD) skips certain layers of the target LLM and utilizes subset layers as the draft model, requiring no additional training or GPU memory overhead. Existing Self-SD approaches generally fall into two categories: online and offline layer selection. Online methods, such as SWIFT [23] and CLaSp [4], dynamically determine the skipping path during inference as shown in Fig. 1, introducing non-negligible computational costs and unstable acceleration during inference. In comparison, offline methods achieve both higher efficiency and stability. However, existing offline methods still suffer from the issue of feature misalignment, which denotes a distribution mismatch between the output of layer i and the expected input of layer j. This mismatch triggers abrupt fluctuations in the output of layer j and further disrupts the subsequent generation process (e.g., i=11, j=26 in Fig. 1(a)).

The main issues with current Self-SD are as follows:

1. **Feature Misalignment Induced by Skipping.** Existing methods formulate layer selection as a black-box problem via bayesian optimization and random search, which only prioritizes final inference speed metrics while ignoring the internal feature expression logic of neural networks. This results in heuristic attempts that disregard the importance of different network layers and feature distribution consistency.
2. **Inefficient Verification with Local Myopia.** Existing methods either use inefficient chain verification or construct candidate trees based solely on local node probability, disregarding the global probability of the entire generation path.

To address these issues, we propose **LARK**, a plug-and-play Self-SD framework featuring **L**ayer-**A**ware **R**outing with a **K**-ary dynamic pruning tree, which is shown in Fig. 2. We hypothesize that layer importance is proportional to the severity of feature misalignment caused by its removal. Consequently, we determine the layer importance score (**LIS**) quantified by Z-Score normalized sum of perplexity and similarity. Perplexity measures the model's predictive capability, and significant perplexity degradation upon skipping reveals important layers essential for preventing feature misalignment. High input-output cosine similarity means low importance due to negligible feature misalignment. Furthermore, to address inefficient verification with local myopia, we designed K-ary dynamic **P**runing **T**ree based on ancestor-aware **P**ath **V**alue (**PTPV**), that dynamically adjusts the tree width based on the probability of the input token and prunes the tree in depth based on the global path value, thereby achieving an optimal balance between acceptance length and verification overhead.

The main contributions of this paper are as follows:

1. **Layer-aware routing mechanism**. LARK selectively skips less important layers, thereby effectively mitigating the feature misalignment without any online search overhead.
2. **PTPV**. Overcoming the inefficient verification with local myopia, LARK dynamically constructs candidate trees based on global probability, significantly improving the accepted length of draft tokens.
3. **Efficient lossless acceleration**. Experiments on LLaMA-13B demonstrate that LARK, which is training-free and GPU Memory-efficient, achieves an average speedup of 1.47× and accepted length of 8.2.

2 Related Work

2.1 Speculative Decoding

SD is a decoding acceleration method that first generates multiple candidate tokens through draft model and then performs parallel verification via the target model. SD methods are primarily categorized into independent drafting and Self-SD. Independent drafting, such as EAGLE [15–17], generates candidate sequences by training a separate auxiliary draft model. Self-SD [9,24] reuses the parameters of the target model via layer skipping. Lookahead [11] utilizes the properties of Jacobi iteration to generate n-grams for verification, but it requires an additional memory retrieval pool that expands during decoding. Medusa [3] accelerates inference via multiple decoding heads or tree-based verification, though it relies on specific architectural modifications. SELF-SD [24] and SWIFT [23] use random search and interval bayesian optimization, while CLaSp [4] employs dynamic programming to determine optimal skipping strategies with minimal latency overhead. From the perspective of candidate sampling, SD can be divided into chain-based and tree-based strategies. Chain-based methods [24] typically employ probability-based early stopping mechanisms to terminate draft sequences. While simple to implement, they restrict candidate diversity. Tree-based methods like SpecInfer [20] pioneered token tree verification. EAGLE-2 [15] and ProPD [27] concentrate on tree pruning mechanisms, with ProPD additionally mitigating the computational overhead of sequence probability.

2.2 LLM Interpretability and Parameter Redundancy

LLM Interpretability refers to the research field dedicated to dissecting the internal operational mechanisms of LLMs. Chen et al. [5] systematically decomposed LLaMA layer functions, quantifying the perplexity (PPL) of each layer via probing tasks. Their results reveal that while removing middle layers causes PPL to rise in text coherence tasks, draft models have lower demands for such capabilities. Ju et al. [12] clarified the inter-layer distribution and dynamic characteristics of context knowledge in LLaMA through layer-wise probing. Liu et al. [18] found that lower layers in LLaMA-2 adapt to generation tasks while upper layers suit prediction tasks. Method [7] pointed out the low contribution of later layers, directly evidencing layer redundancy, while Shortened LLaMA [13] validated layer functional specialization through pruning. These layer-wise interpretability studies provide the core theoretical support for the redundancy of LLM layers.

In fact, layer redundancy in LLMs has been widely verified. Techniques such as quantization, pruning, knowledge distillation, and low-rank approximation have proven that massive redundancy exists in model parameters, allowing compressed models to maintain performance similar to the original. Specific research on decoder layer redundancy includes LayerDrop [10,26], LayerSkip [9], structured pruning [26], SkipDecode [6], and LayerSharing [25]. ShortGPT [19] and Shortened LLaMA [13] also analyzed LLaMA layer importance for pruning. These methods demonstrate that skipping or removing certain layers does not significantly affect model performance, serving as a theoretical foundation for Self-SD to accelerate inference by simply skipping parts of the target model without adding extra models.

3 Method

3.1 Overview

As illustrated in Fig. 2, the LARK framework comprises four core components: the target model, draft model, layer importance, and tree decoding. Although the draft model and target model share physical parameters, they are depicted separately to explicitly visualize the skip-layer data flow. The layer importance module evaluates layer importance by synthesizing the PIS indicated by the green flow and output distribution similarity (ODS) indicated by the orange flow. To address feature misalignment, the layer importance module implements a layer-aware routing mechanism that selectively skips less important layers as "Layer m" to "Layer M" in the draft model.

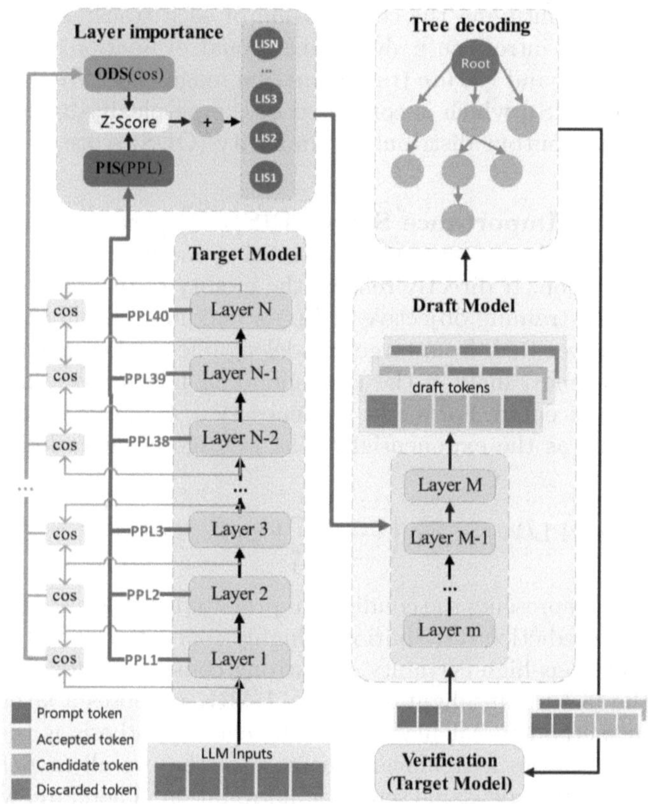

Fig. 2. Overview of LARK. The left panel illustrates draft model construction based on the layer importance module. The right panel depicts the tree-based inference loop.

During online inference, the draft model receives accepted tokens verified by the target model and performs multi-step auto-regressive generation, organizing high-probability candidate tokens (yellow nodes) into a tree structure while pruning low-probability ones (blue nodes). To overcome inefficient verification caused by local myopia, the tree decoding module utilizes PTPV to dynamically construct the candidate tree based on global probabilities rather than local probabilities, significantly improving the accepted length of draft tokens. Finally, the target model performs parallel verification on these candidate paths, closing the loop by feeding validated tokens back for the next iteration.

3.2 Layer-Aware Routing Mechanism

LARK proposes a layer importance evaluation framework as shown in Fig. 2 that fuses perplexity and cosine similarity to precisely select important layers for constructing a fixed Draft sub-network. To build an efficient Draft sub-network that maintains the generative capability of the original model, the core challenge lies in accurately quantifying the contribution of each transformer layer to the final prediction. We introduce a dual-dimensional evaluation system merging semantic uncertainty and feature transformation magnitude. We define the layer importance score (LIS), which is composed of the perplexity-based importance score (PIS) and the output distribution similarity (ODS) score.

Perplexity-Based Importance Score (PIS). Perplexity (PPL) is a classic metric for evaluating language models, measuring the uncertainty of the model in sequence prediction. It directly reflects the quality of the generated text and aligns with the pre-training objective of LLMs maximum likelihood estimation. Consequently, a lower PPL from target model signifies higher generation quality and better consistency, making the corresponding layers more important and more likely to be accepted. For a text sequence $\mathcal{W} = \{w_1, w_2, \ldots, w_N\}$ of length N, PPL is defined as the exponential of the average negative log-likelihood of the sequence:

$$\mathrm{PPL}(\mathcal{W}) = \exp\left(-\frac{1}{N}\sum_{i=1}^{N}\log p(w_i \mid w_{<i})\right),$$

where $p(w_i \mid w_{<i})$ represents the conditional probability. A low PPL value means that the model's prediction distribution is highly concentrated on the real token, that is, the model has high certainty and strong consistency for the sequence.

To solve the feature misalignment issue, LARK proposes a layer-wise sensitivity ablation method to calculate PIS. The core hypothesis is that if removing the l-th layer causes a significant increase in the overall model PPL, then that layer contains indispensable semantic information. Therefore, we define the importance of the l-th layer as the increment in PPL after its removal:

$$\mathrm{PIS}^{(l)} = \mathrm{PPL}(\mathcal{W})_{\mathrm{without\_l}} - \mathrm{PPL}(\mathcal{W})_{\mathrm{full}},$$

where $\mathrm{PPL}_{\mathrm{full}}$ denotes the PPL of the complete model, and $\mathrm{PPL}_{\mathrm{without\_l}}$ denotes the PPL after removing the l-th layer. A higher PIS value indicates that the layer is more important for maintaining semantic consistency.

Output Distribution Similarity (ODS) Based on Cosine Similarity. Cosine similarity measures the directional consistency between two vectors (such as hidden states or probability distributions). To evaluate whether feature mutation occurs in intermediate layers, we calculate the cosine similarity between the input and output vectors of the l-th layer. This quantifies the layer's regulation of the feature distribution. Lower similarity indicates greater feature transformation capability, implying greater importance. While PIS focuses on the prediction probability of the discrete sequence $\mathcal{W}$, ODS focuses on the geometric changes of the corresponding continuous feature vectors $\mathbf{w}$ in the feature space.

In the transformer architecture, if the input feature vector $\mathbf{w}_{in}$ and the output feature vector $\mathbf{w}_{out}$ of a layer are highly similar, it suggests that the layer performs only weak information transmission and can be considered redundant. Conversely, if a significant directional deviation occurs, it indicates that the layer performs important feature reconstruction. To intuitively quantify the magnitude of this feature transformation, we use the cosine distance metric. For the l-th layer, the ODS score is defined as:

$$\mathrm{ODS}^{(l)} = 1 - \mathrm{Cosine}(\mathbf{w}_{in}^{(l)}, \mathbf{w}_{out}^{(l)}),$$

where $\mathbf{w}_{in}^{(l)}$ and $\mathbf{w}_{out}^{(l)}$ represent the input and output vectors of the l-th layer, respectively, and $\mathrm{Cosine}(\mathbf{u}, \mathbf{v}) = \frac{\mathbf{u} \cdot \mathbf{v}}{\|\mathbf{u}\| \|\mathbf{v}\|}$ denotes the directional consistency between two vectors. The formula implies that when Cosine $\rightarrow 1$, input and output vectors almost overlap; when ODS $\rightarrow 0$, feature vectors are orthogonal, and the layer is judged as important. This definition $(1 - \mathrm{Cosine})$ ensures that ODS is positively correlated with layer importance, allowing for direct normalized fusion with the PIS metric (Fig. 3).

Layer Importance-Aware Skipping Mechanism. To comprehensively balance semantic integrity with the topological structure of the feature space, we perform a robust fusion of PIS and ODS to obtain LIS. Recognizing that PIS and ODS exhibit distinct physical scales and variance profiles, a simple linear combination would be dominated by the metric with a larger magnitude. Therefore, we employ Z-Score normalization to standardize both metrics into a common distribution space before aggregation:

$$\mathrm{LIS}^{(l)} = \frac{\mathrm{PIS}^{(l)} - \mu_{\mathrm{PIS}}}{\sigma_{\mathrm{PIS}}} + \frac{\mathrm{ODS}^{(l)} - \mu_{\mathrm{ODS}}}{\sigma_{\mathrm{ODS}}},$$

where μ and σ denote the mean and standard deviation of the respective metrics across all layers. Based on the standardized LIS, we adopt a Top-K routing strategy that selects the top-K layers with the highest scores to construct the draft model. This selection strategy ensures that we retain important layers while skipping redundant layers without causing feature misalignment.

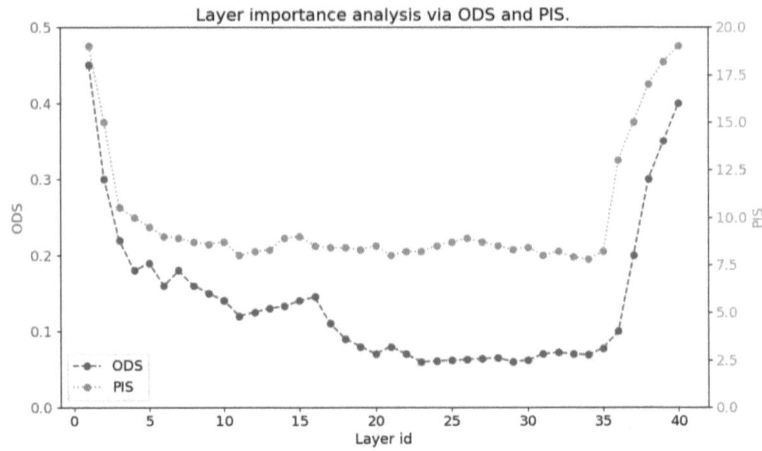

Fig. 3. Layer importance analysis of LLaMA-2-13B via ODS and PIS trends. Both curves exhibit a distinct U-shaped pattern, indicating that the initial and final layers encode important information while the intermediate layers are less important.

3.3 K-Ary Dynamic Pruning Tree Based on Ancestor-Aware Path Value

LARK proposes the K-ary dynamic pruning tree based on ancestor-aware path value (PTPV) as shown in Fig. 4, utilizing a tree structure that is adaptive in both width and depth. The width of the tree, which determines the degree of candidate diversity, is dynamically adjusted based on the probability of the input tokens provided to draft model. Redundant branches are effectively pruned through a global path value, which eliminates paths that exhibit high local probability but low overall global probability, thereby further enhancing inference efficiency. Furthermore, an attention masking mechanism is integrated to enable selective interaction among nodes within the tree, reducing unnecessary computations.

The width of the tree at any given node, denoted as K, is determined by the probability of the input token provided to the draft model. We define the probability distribution of the input token as $P = \text{Softmax}(z)$, where z represents the logits. And the local probability p constitutes the probability distribution. To balance generation diversity and computational overhead, the value of K is dynamically adjusted in segments based on the probability p: a preset threshold $\tau = 0.8$ is used, such that $K = 3$ when $p \leq \tau$, and $K = 6$ otherwise. These hyperparameters are determined based on empirical experience. This mechanism ensures that computational resources are concentrated on uncertain transitions while accelerating the generation of high-probability content.

The adaptive depth is achieved through ancestor-aware path value. For any node n located at depth l in the tree, let $P = [p_1, p_2, \ldots, p_l]$ denote the sequence of local probability along the path, where p_i is the local probability of the token

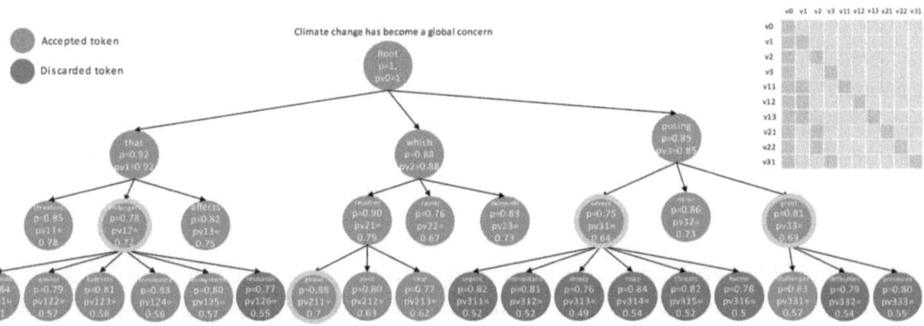

Fig. 4. Illustration of PTPV. The top-right corner displays the attention mask. **Nodes circled in yellow** with lower local probability are retained due to the high global probability of their ancestral paths (pv12 vs. pv33). For **nodes circled in red**, the deeper node (pv211) can exhibit a higher path value than the shallower node (pv31). Global path value allows pruning low-quality shallow branches early, thereby enabling efficient deep exploration.

at layer i. The path value (PV) is defined as the joint probability of the sequence as $PV(n) = \prod_{i=1}^{l} p_i$.

This global probability formulation aligns with the chain rule of autoregressive generation. In each generation step, the system retains only the top-D paths with the highest path values, while the remaining paths are pruned. The parameter D is determined by the maximum batch size capacity of the GPU memory limit. Specifically, the baseline value of D=30 is selected based on empirical practices in speculative decoding for LLMs.

4 Experiments

4.1 Experiments Setup

Implementation Details. To comprehensively evaluate model performance across diverse tasks, we selected three representative benchmarks: TinyStories, GSM8K, and CNN/DM, to assess logical reasoning capabilities, the coherence of long-text generation, and conditional generation quality, respectively. To calculate LIS which is the Z-Score normalized sum of PIS and ODS, we use the BookCorpus dataset (100 sampled entries, sequence length 128) that aligns with the distribution of target tasks and ensures reliable layer importance evaluation. Regarding the experimental setup, we employed the FP16 precision versions of LLaMA-2-13B [21] with 40 layers and LLaMA-3-8B [8] with 32 layers sourced from Hugging Face as target models. For the draft model, we constructed the sub-network by removing redundant layers based on the LIS analysis.

All experiments were implemented in pure PyTorch and conducted on a single NVIDIA H800 GPU. The batch size was set to 1, with a maximum generation length of 512 tokens. We employed a maximum tree depth of 25, incorporating a local confidence threshold of 0.8 and Top-D pruning (where $D = 30$). To mitigate the temporal overhead incurred by the SWIFT online search, the search process was configured to terminate after 300 steps. Consequently, performance was rigorously evaluated on 1,000 samples for the SWIFT method. In contrast, offline search baselines are unaffected by the accepted length fluctuations characteristic of early-stage searching and were therefore evaluated on a subset of 30 samples, which was sufficient to ensure assessment accuracy.

Evaluation Metrics. To simultaneously quantify generation quality and inference efficiency, we employ the following metrics: The **accepted length** is defined as the average number of tokens accepted by target model from the candidate sequences autoregressively generated by draft model. The **accept rate** is defined as the ratio of accepted tokens to the total number of draft steps. The **speedup ratio** is defined as the factor of improvement in end-to-end inference speed (tokens/s), calculated as $speedup = T_{target}/T_{ours}$, where T_{target} is the inference speed of the target model running independently without the assistance of a draft model, and T_{ours} is the inference speed with the assistance of a draft model.

4.2 Main Result

LARK achieves an average end-to-end speedup of 1.47 on LLaMA-2-13B as shown in Table 1, outperforming all baseline methods while maintaining lossless generation quality comparable to the original LLaMA. Notably, on the TinyStories dataset, the accepted length reaches 11.98, which is 47% higher than SWIFT and 73% higher than SELF-SD. This result demonstrates that the ancestor-aware path value pruning mechanism significantly improves candidate token utilization and breaks through the verification efficiency bottleneck of existing methods. On the CNN/DM dataset, the speedup reaches 1.57, which is 21% higher than SWIFT and 16% higher than SELF-SD. Compared with the other two tasks, the improvement in the speedup ratio of the GSM8K is not significant. When compared to SWIFT, LARK achieves a 12.2% higher average speedup, confirming the superior efficiency of layer skipping method.

For LLaMA-3-8B, LARK also shows prominent advantages: it achieves an average speedup of 1.24 and an average verification length of 5.08, which are 7.8% higher and 2.87× that of SELF-SD, and 19.2% higher and 1.98× that of SWIFT, respectively, further verifying the generalization of our proposed mechanisms.

4.3 Ablation

To validate the effectiveness of core components (LIS and PTPV) and the rationality of layer selection strategies, we conduct extensive ablation studies as shown in Table 2 on the CNN/DM dataset. To evaluate the contribution of the PTPV dynamic tree mechanism, we compare the full LARK model against a variant that removes the tree structure and reverts to chain-based verification (denoted as **LARK w/o tree**). And another that retains LARK's layer selection method while employing SWIFT's tree based solely on local probability (denoted as

Table 1. Main result. End-to-end performance comparison of LARK against state-of-the-art baselines across various LLaMA backbones and benchmarks.

Model	Method	CNN/DM		GSM8K		TinyStories		mean	
		length	speedup	length	speedup	length	speedup	speedup	length
LLaMA-2-13B	LOOKAHEAD	1.38	1.15	1.51	1.26	1.65	1.35	1.25	1.51
	SELF-SD	3.10	1.35	3.50	1.35	6.91	1.44	1.38	4.50
	SWIFT	4.47	1.30	3.60	1.27	8.13	1.36	1.31	5.40
	LARK	8.00	1.57	4.63	1.36	11.98	1.49	1.47	8.20
LLaMA-3-8B	SELF-SD	1.69	1.13	1.51	1.12	2.10	1.21	1.15	1.77
	SWIFT	2.30	1.05	2.71	1.04	2.67	1.02	1.04	2.56
	LARK	5.80	1.29	3.87	1.17	5.57	1.25	1.24	5.08

LARK w/ st). The experimental results indicate that removing the tree structure causes a significant drop in the average accepted length, from 8.00 to 4.31, while the speedup ratio decreases from 1.57× to 1.48×. This strongly validates the necessity of the PTPV mechanism: by maintaining diverse candidate paths and leveraging global value for pruning, the model effectively uncovers potential long sequences, thereby substantially enhancing token utilization efficiency.

Table 2. Ablation study quantifying the contribution of PTPV and LIS.

Method	length	speedup	accept rate
LARK	8	1.57	0.99
LARK w/ st	6.24	1.5	0.99
LARK w/o tree	4.31	1.48	0.98
SELF-SD	3.1	1.35	0.91
front w/ tree	4.54	1.37	0.97
last w/ tree	6.33	1.4	0.98
skip w/ tree	4.54	1.42	0.97

Furthermore, even without the tree structure, LARK w/o tree achieves a superior speedup compared to SELF-SD which also employs chain-based verification, demonstrating the superiority of our proposed layer skipping mechanism over the strategy used in SELF-SD. Finally, we design three fixed layer skipping strategies: **Front layer skipping**: Skips layers 6 to 23. This strategy exhibits poor performance because it excludes important layers—layers 6 to 15 were identified earlier as key for basic semantic encoding. **Last layer skipping**: Skips layers 20 to 37. **Inter-layer skipping**: Skips even-indexed layers (6, 8, 10, ..., 38). Comparing LARK against three fixed layer-skipping strategies (Front, Last, and Inter-layer skipping), the results demonstrate that LIS consistently outperforms these heuristic approaches across all metrics.

4.4 Hyperparameter Sensitivity Analysis

We analyze the sensitivity of the key hyperparameter k (number of top layers selected by LIS) on the CNN/DM dataset. k ranges from 19 to 24 (covering the optimal range of 22 layers), with results shown in Fig. 5.

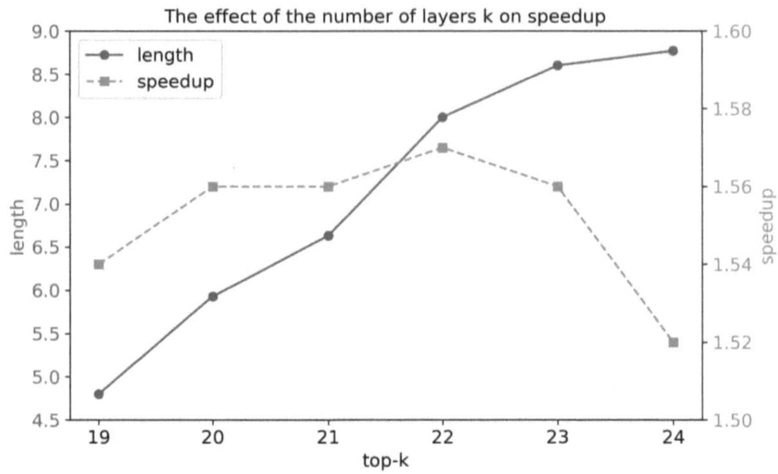

Fig. 5. The effect of the number of selected layers (hyperparameter k) on speedup and accepted length.

When $k = 22$, the method achieves the optimal balance of length and speedup. Fewer layers ($k < 22$) reduce computational overhead but sacrifice candidate quality, which is manifested as a shorter accepted length. More layers ($k > 22$) increase candidate quality slightly but introduce redundant computations with lower speedup. The performance remains stable within $k = 20 - -23$, demonstrating the robustness of the proposed method to small variations in k. This reduces the burden of hyperparameter tuning in practical applications.

5 Conclusion

We introduced **LARK**, an efficient Self-Speculative Decoding framework that overcomes the bottlenecks of feature misalignment and local myopia in LLM acceleration. By quantifying layer importance through our proposed layer importance score (LIS), which integrates perplexity and similarity metrics. To mitigate the feature misalignment, LARK implements a stable offline layer-aware routing mechanism skipping less important layers. Furthermore, to break the constraints of local greedy verification, we proposed the K-ary dynamic pruning tree based on ancestor-aware path value (PTPV). This strategy leverages global probabilities to dynamically adjust the draft tree structure, achieving an optimal trade-off between verification overhead. Extensive experiments on LLaMA series models demonstrate that LARK achieves an average speedup of 1.47× with a remarkable accepted length of 8.2. As a plug-and-play and GPU memory-efficient solution, LARK offers a robust paradigm for deploying large-scale generative models. Future work will explore extending this layer-aware philosophy to larger-scale models and multimodal architectures.

References

1. Achiam, J., Adler, S., A.: Gpt-4 technical report. arXiv preprint arXiv:2303.08774 (2023)
2. Agrawal, A., Panwar, A., Mohan, J., Kwatra, N., Gulavani, B.S., Ramjee, R.: Sarathi: Efficient LLM inference by piggybacking decodes with chunked prefills. arXiv preprint arXiv:2308.16369 (2023)
3. Cai, T., Li, Y., Geng, Z., et al.: Medusa: simple LLM inference acceleration framework with multiple decoding heads. In: ICML 2024 (2024)
4. Chen, L., Shan, R., Wang, H., et al.: Clasp: In-context layer skip for self-speculative decoding. In: ACL, vol. 2025, pp. 31608–31618 (2025)
5. Chen, N., Wu, N., S.L.: Is bigger and deeper always better? Probing llama across scales and layers, CoRR. abs/2312.04333 (2023)
6. Corro, L.D., Giorno, A.D., Agarwal, S., Yu, B., Awadallah, A., Mukherjee, S.: Skipdecode: autoregressive skip decoding with batching and caching for efficient LLM inference, (2023). arXiv:2307.02628 arXiv preprint
7. Csordás, R., Manning, C.D., Potts, C.: Do language models use their depth efficiently? CoRR: abs/2505.13898 (2025)
8. Dubey, A., et al.: The llama 3 herd of models. arXiv preprint arXiv:2407.21783 (2024)
9. Elhoushi, M., Shrivastava, A., L. et al.: LayerSkip: Enabling early exit Inference and Self-speculative Decoding, Bangkok, Thailand, pp. 12622–12642 (2024)
10. Fan, A., Grave, E., Joulin, A.: Reducing transformer depth on demand with structured dropout. In: 8th International Conference on Learning Representations, ICLR 2020, Addis Ababa, Ethiopia, April 26–30, 2020. OpenReview.net (2020)
11. Fu, Y., Bailis, P., Stoica, I., Zhang, H.: Break the sequential dependency of LLM inference using lookahead decoding. In: ICML (2024)
12. Ju, T., Sun, W., Du, W., et al.: How large language models encode context knowledge? A layer-wise probing study. In: COLING, pp. 8235–8246 (2024)
13. Kim, B., Kim, G., Kim, T., et al.: Shortened llama: a simple depth pruning for large language models. CoRR, abs/2402.02834 (2024)
14. Leviathan, Y., Kalman, M., Matias, Y.: Fast inference from transformers via speculative decoding. In: ICML, vol. 202, pp. 19274–19286 (2023)
15. Li, Y., Wei, F., Zhang, C., Zhang, H.: EAGLE-2: faster inference of language models with dynamic draft trees. arXiv preprint arXiv:2406.16858 (2024)
16. Li, Y., Wei, F., Zhang, C., Zhang, H.: EAGLE: speculative sampling requires rethinking feature uncertainty. In: Forty-first International Conference on Machine Learning, ICML 2024, Vienna, Austria, July 21-27, 2024. OpenReview.net (2024)
17. Li, Y., Wei, F., Zhang, C., Zhang, H.: EAGLE-3: scaling up inference acceleration of large language models via training-time test. CoRR, abs/2503.01840 (2025)
18. Liu, Z., Kong, C., Liu, Y., Sun, M.: Fantastic semantics and where to find them: investigating which layers of generative LLMs reflect lexical semantics. In: ACL, pp. 14551–14558 (2024)

19. Men, X., et al.: ShortGPT: layers in large language models are more redundant than you expect. In: ACL, pp. 20192–20204 (2025)
20. Miao, X., et al.: Specinfer: accelerating large language model serving with tree-based speculative inference and verification. In: ACM, vol. 3, pp. 932–949 (2024)
21. Touvron, H., et al.:: Llama 2: open foundation and fine-tuned chat models. arXiv preprint arXiv:2307.09288 (2023)
22. Xia, H., Ge, T., Wang, P., et al.: Speculative decoding: exploiting speculative execution for accelerating seq2seq generation. In: EMNLP, pp. 3909–3925 (2023)
23. Xia, H., Li, Y., Zhang, J., Du, C., Li, W.: Swift: on-the-fly self-speculative decoding for LLM inference acceleration. arXiv preprint arXiv:2410.06916 (2024)
24. Zhang, J., et al.: Draft& verify: lossless large language model acceleration via self-speculative decoding. In: Proceedings of the 62nd Annual Meeting of the Association for Computational Linguistics (Volume 1: Long Papers), pp. 11263–11282 (2024)
25. Zhang, K., Ding, N., Qi, B., et al.: CRaSh: clustering, removing, and sharing enhance fine-tuning without full large language model. In: EMNLP, pp. 9612–9637 (2023)
26. Zhang, M., He, Y.: Accelerating training of transformer-based language models with progressive layer dropping. In: Advances in Neural Information Processing Systems, vol. 33, pp. 14011–14023. Curran Associates, Inc. (2020)
27. Zhong, S., Yang, Z., Gong, R., Wang, R., Huang, R., Li, M.: ProPD: dynamic token tree pruning and generation for LLM parallel decoding, pp. 202:1–202:8. ACM (2024)

CasCM: Modeling Intra- and Inter-Community Evolution for Cascade Popularity Prediction

Yukun Zhou[1], Jiaxing Shang[1(✉)], Ruiyuan Li[1], and Fei Hao[2]

[1] College of Computer Science, Chongqing University, Chongqing, China
{shangjx,ruiyuan.li}@cqu.edu.cn
[2] School of Artificial Intelligence and Computer Science, Shaanxi Normal University, Xi'an, China

Abstract. Predicting the future popularity of information cascades is crucial for applications such as social recommendation and viral marketing. Existing methods mainly focus on individual users or cascade graphs, while largely ignoring community-level dynamics that play an essential role in information diffusion. To address this limitation, we propose **CasCM**, a hierarchical community-aware framework for cascade popularity prediction. CasCM first identifies community structures within each cascade graph and partitions the diffusion process into consecutive time segments. It then jointly models intra-community interactions and inter-community dependencies to capture both local structural patterns and global coordination signals. Community representations are aggregated into cascade embeddings via an attention mechanism, and their temporal evolution is further modeled through sequential learning. By integrating structural topology and temporal dynamics across node, community, and cascade levels, CasCM enables fine-grained and robust diffusion modeling. Experiments on three real-world datasets demonstrate that CasCM consistently outperforms state-of-the-art methods.

Keywords: Information diffusion · Cascade popularity prediction · Community structure · Graph neural network

1 Introduction

With the rapid growth of social media, users can easily create and share information, giving rise to information cascades. Understanding how information spreads in online networks has become a central topic in computational social science. Cascade popularity prediction seeks to forecast the future scale of diffusion based on early propagation patterns and is critical for applications such as social recommendation, fake news detection, and viral marketing [1]. To address this task, various approaches have been proposed to model propagation dynamics. Most existing studies treat a cascade as a temporal sequence and adopt models such

J. Niu et al. (Eds.): KSEM 2026, LNAI 16631, pp. 367–380, 2027.
https://doi.org/10.1007/978-981-92-2759-4_27

as Recurrent Neural Networks (RNNs) [2] or Neural Ordinary Differential Equations (Neural ODEs) [3] to capture dependencies among activated users.

Motivation. Although sequence-based models have shown strong performance in cascade popularity prediction, they mainly focus on individual users or cascade graphs, while overlooking community-level patterns. Grouping users with similar behavioral or structural characteristics into communities provides deeper insights into information diffusion within and across communities. As shown in Fig. 1, we perform community detection on a real cascade, where nodes of the same color indicate the same community. The early diffusion stage (left) shows information spreading primarily within the originating community, while the later stage (right) exhibits significant cross-community diffusion. This observation underscores the importance of modeling information cascades from a community-level perspective.

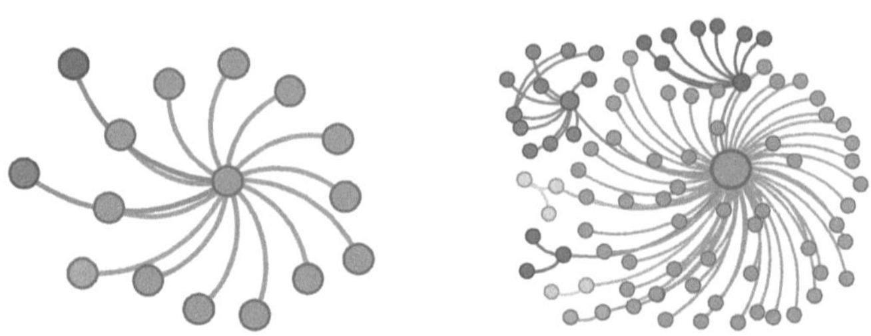

Fig. 1. The evolution of community structure for a real cascade.

Challenge. Incorporating community information into cascade popularity prediction introduces two major challenges. First, communities evolve continuously over time, requiring models to capture their temporal dynamics instead of assuming static structures. Second, cascade diffusion operates at multiple granularities, within communities and across them, making it essential, yet highly non-trivial, to jointly model intra- and inter-community interactions.

To address these challenges, we propose **CasCM**, a community-aware framework for cascade popularity prediction. The key idea of CasCM lies in the joint modeling of intra-community dynamics, inter-community interactions, and temporal evolution for more accurate cascade popularity prediction. Specifically, our main design and key contributions are summarized as follows:

- We model cascades from a community perspective, where a customized Graph Convolutional Network (GCN) [4] updates newly activated nodes to capture intra-community activation, while an edge-augmented Graph Attention Network (GAT) [5] assigns weights to inter-community edges to model cross-community influence.
- We design a hierarchical attention mechanism that first extracts community-level representations via multi-head attention pooling [6], and subsequently models cascade evolution with a bidirectional Gated Recurrent Unit (GRU) [7], jointly capturing local community signals and global diffusion patterns.

- We employ a joint optimization framework with the popularity growth labels at both community and cascade levels to enhance prediction performance. Extensive experiments on three real-world datasets demonstrate that CasCM significantly outperforms state-of-the-art baselines in prediction accuracy. The code is available at: https://github.com/CasModels/CasCM.

2 Related Work

Existing cascade popularity prediction approaches can be broadly classified into feature-driven methods, generative methods, and deep learning-based methods.

Feature-Driven Methods rely on manually designed features for popularity prediction. Tsur *et al.* [8] extracted textual features such as hashtags and emojis. Shulman *et al.* [9] utilized user-level features (e.g., the number of followers) to measure influence. Xu *et al.* [10] combined multimodal features (category, image, and text) for regression modeling. Although effective in various scenarios, feature-driven methods heavily depend on handcrafted features, limiting their generalization ability.

Generative Methods focus on modeling the intensity function of information diffusion. Most works are based on point process modeling. Zhao *et al.* [11] introduced a self-exciting point process to capture dynamic popularity evolution. Shen *et al.* [12] employed a reinforced Poisson process (RPP) for retweet behavior. Mishra *et al.* [13] utilized the Hawkes process to model self-excitation in diffusion. Rizoiu *et al.* [14] and the SIR-Hawkes model [15] integrated epidemic dynamics with Hawkes processes to explore correlations between endogenous and exogenous effects. While these methods provide good interpretability, they often rely on unrealistic assumptions, constraining their representational capacity.

Deep Learning-Based Methods automatically learn useful representations from data to model information cascades. DeepCas [16] was the first end-to-end deep model for popularity prediction, transforming cascade graphs into sampled diffusion paths. DeepHawkes [1] bridged the gap between interpretability and prediction accuracy by incorporating Hawkes process mechanisms. CasCN [2] jointly models cascade structure and temporal dynamics, whereas CasFlow [17] incorporates global network context into local cascade modeling. CTCP [18] introduced an evolutionary learning module to update user and cascade states, while CasDO [19] and ConCat [20] use ODEs to capture uncertainties associated with information cascades. Currently, community-level cascade popularity modeling remains largely unexplored.

3 Problem Formulation

To facilitate understanding, we first present several key definitions, followed by the formal formulation of the cascade popularity prediction task.

Definition 1 (Information Cascade Graph). *An information cascade graph is defined as* $G_c = (V_c, E_c)$*, where* $V_c = \{u_1, u_2, \ldots\}$ *represents the set of users who have participated in the diffusion process, and* $E_c = \{e_1, e_2, \ldots\}$ *denotes the propagation edges among these users. Each edge* $e_{i,j} = (u_i, u_j, t_n)$ *indicates that user* u_i *forwards or responds to the content of user* u_j *at timestamp* t_n.

Definition 2 (Global User Graph). *The global user graph* G_g *represents the overall network obtained by aggregating multiple cascade graphs. To prevent information leakage, we construct* G_g *using only the data within each cascade's own observation period.*

Definition 3 (Cascade Popularity Prediction). *For a cascade graph* $G_c(t_o)$ *observed over* $(0, t_o]$ *and a global user graph* G_g*, let* $|V_c(t)|$ *denote the number of users by time* t*. The goal is to learn a model that estimates the increase in participants from* t_o *to a future time* t_p*, defined as* $P(t_p) = |V_c(t_p)| - |V_c(t_o)|$.

4 The Proposed CasCM Model

The overall framework of CasCM is presented in Fig. 2, which consists of five logically connected modules. The following subsections provide detailed descriptions of each module.

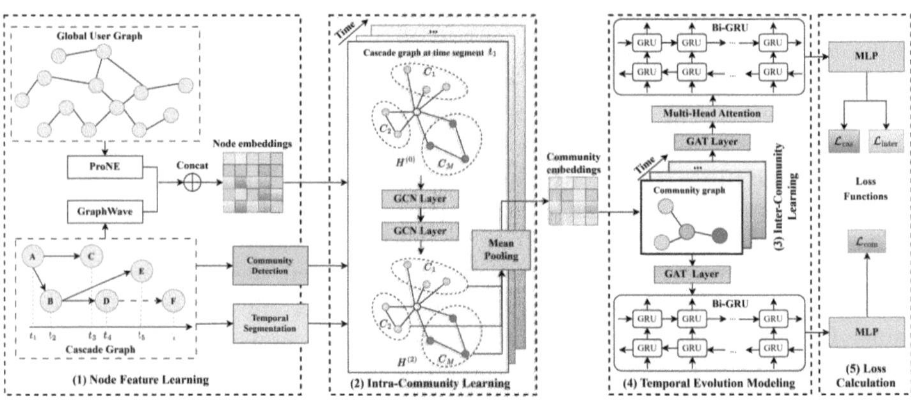

Fig. 2. The overall structure of the proposed CasCM model.

4.1 Node Feature Learning

To represent users participating in a cascade, we construct node features from two complementary views: (i) a *local* view that reflects a node's structural role within the observed cascade graph, and (ii) a *global* view that captures long-range connectivity patterns from the overall user interaction network. Given the observed cascade graph $G_c(t_o)$ and the global user graph G_g, we compute a cascade-local structural embedding using GraphWave [21] and a global embedding using ProNE [22]:

$$\mathbf{E}_c = \text{GraphWave}(G_c(t_o)), \quad \mathbf{E}_g = \text{ProNE}(G_g). \tag{1}$$

For each user node u_i, we concatenate the two embeddings as the initial node feature, i.e., $\mathbf{x}_{u_i} = [\mathbf{e}_c(u_i); \mathbf{e}_g(u_i)]$, where $\mathbf{e}_c(u_i)$ and $\mathbf{e}_g(u_i)$ denote the corresponding rows of $\mathbf{E}_c$ and $\mathbf{E}_g$. This initialization integrates cascade-specific structure with global user context, and serves as the input to subsequent community-aware structural encoding and temporal evolution modeling.

4.2 Intra-Community Representation Learning

After obtaining node features, we learn intra-community representations on the observed cascade graph. To avoid information leakage, we perform community detection *independently for each cascade* using only its observation window $[0, t_o]$. Given the observed cascade graph $G_c(t_o)$, we apply the Louvain algorithm [23] and obtain:

$$\mathcal{C} = \{C_1, C_2, \ldots, C_M\} = \text{Louvain}(G_c(t_o)), \tag{2}$$

where C_m denotes the node set of the m-th community and M is the number of detected communities.

Time-Segmented and Cumulative Subgraphs. We partition the observation window into K consecutive segments with endpoints $0 = t_0 < t_1 < \cdots < t_K = t_o$. For each community C_m, we construct a sequence of *cumulative* subgraphs: at segment k, the community subgraph $G_m^{(k)} = (V_m^{(k)}, E_m^{(k)})$ contains all nodes and edges within C_m that have appeared up to time t_k. We denote the corresponding node feature matrix and adjacency matrix as $\mathbf{X}_m^{(k)}$ and $\mathbf{A}_m^{(k)}$, respectively.

Masked GCN for Newly Added Nodes. Instead of updating all nodes at every segment, we emphasize incremental diffusion by updating representations mainly for newly appeared nodes, while earlier nodes provide structural context. Let $\mathbf{m}^{(k)} \in \{0,1\}^{|V_m^{(k)}|}$ be an indicator vector where $m_i^{(k)} = 1$ if node i first appears in segment $[t_{k-1}, t_k)$. We construct a mask matrix $\mathbf{M}_m^{(k)}$ as:

$$M_{ij}^{(k)} = \mathbb{I}\Big(m_i^{(k)} = 1 \vee m_j^{(k)} = 1\Big), \quad \mathbf{A}_m'^{(k)} = \mathbf{A}_m^{(k)} \odot \mathbf{M}_m^{(k)}, \tag{3}$$

so that message passing focuses on edges incident to new nodes. We then apply a GCN on the masked adjacency:

$$\mathbf{H}_m^{(k)} = \text{GCN}(\mathbf{A}_m'^{(k)}, \mathbf{X}_m^{(k)}). \tag{4}$$

Community Representation. After node updates, we obtain the segment-level representation of community C_m by mean pooling:

$$\mathbf{z}_m^{(k)} = \frac{1}{|V_m^{(k)}|} \sum_{u_i \in V_m^{(k)}} \mathbf{h}_{u_i}^{(k)}, \tag{5}$$

where $\mathbf{h}_{u_i}^{(k)}$ denotes the embedding of node u_i in $\mathbf{H}_m^{(k)}$. The community embeddings $\{\mathbf{z}_m^{(k)}\}_{m=1}^M$ are then fed into the inter-community relation modeling module.

4.3 Inter-Community Relation Modeling

Given the segment-level community embeddings $\{\mathbf{z}_m^{(k)}\}_{m=1}^M$, we model dependencies among communities to capture cross-community influence. At segment k, we construct a community graph $\mathcal{G}^{(k)} = (\mathcal{V}^{(k)}, \mathcal{E}^{(k)})$, where each node in $\mathcal{V}^{(k)}$ corresponds to community C_m, and $\mathcal{E}^{(k)}$ consists of inter-community edges determined by interactions or growth correlations.

Edge Feature Encoding. For an inter-community edge $(C_i, C_j) \in \mathcal{E}^{(k)}$, we define a raw edge feature vector:

$$\mathbf{e}_{ij}^{(k)} = [\text{count}_{ij}, \log_2(\text{count}_{ij} + 1), \text{decay}_{ij}, \text{out}_{ij}, \text{out}_{ji}, \text{common}_{ij}, \text{jac}_{ij}], \tag{6}$$

where count_{ij} denotes interaction frequency between communities, $\text{decay}_{ij} = \exp(-\Delta t_{ij}/\tau)$ is a temporal decay factor with time gap Δt_{ij} and decay scale τ, and common_{ij} and jac_{ij} denote the number of common neighbors and Jaccard similarity between communities, respectively. We project $\mathbf{e}_{ij}^{(k)}$ to a d_e-dimensional edge embedding through a learnable multi-layer perceptron, yielding $\mathbf{e}_{ij}^{\prime(k)} \in \mathbb{R}^{d_e}$.

Community Relation Modeling with GATv2. Let $\mathbf{H}_c^{(k)} = [\mathbf{z}_1^{(k)}; \ldots; \mathbf{z}_M^{(k)}] \in \mathbb{R}^{M \times d}$ denote the matrix of stacked intra-community embeddings at segment k, and let $\mathbf{E}_c^{\prime(k)} = \{\mathbf{e}_{ij}^{\prime(k)}\}$ denote the corresponding encoded edge features associated with $\mathcal{E}^{(k)}$. We model inter-community dependencies by applying two GATv2Conv layers over the community graph:

$$\begin{aligned} \mathbf{H}_c^{(k,1)} &= \text{ReLU}(\text{GATv2Conv}_1(\mathbf{H}_c^{(k)}, \mathcal{E}^{(k)}, \mathbf{E}_c^{\prime(k)})), \\ \mathbf{H}_c^{(k,2)} &= \text{GATv2Conv}_2(\mathbf{H}_c^{(k,1)}, \mathcal{E}^{(k)}, \mathbf{E}_c^{\prime(k)}). \end{aligned} \tag{7}$$

The resulting matrix $\mathbf{H}_c^{(k,2)} = [\mathbf{h}_1^{(k)}; \ldots; \mathbf{h}_M^{(k)}] \in \mathbb{R}^{M \times d}$ yields relation-aware embeddings, where each $\mathbf{h}_m^{(k)}$ captures intra- and inter-community information.

Cascade-Level Fusion. Based on $\mathbf{H}_c^{(k,2)}$, we obtain a cascade representation via multi-head attention pooling. Let $\mathbf{r}_h^{(k)}$ denote the pooled output of head h, and we concatenate all heads to form the pooled vector. The final cascade representation is computed with an MLP and a residual mean pooling:

$$\mathbf{z}_{\text{cas}}^{(k)} = \text{LayerNorm}(\text{MLP}_{\text{fusion}}([\mathbf{r}_1^{(k)}; \ldots; \mathbf{r}_H^{(k)}]) + \frac{1}{M}\sum_{m=1}^{M} \mathbf{h}_m^{(k)}). \tag{8}$$

This fusion adaptively emphasizes influential communities while preserving global statistics, producing a structure-aware cascade embedding for subsequent temporal modeling and growth prediction.

4.4 Temporal Evolution Modeling and Growth Prediction

Given the cascade representations $\mathbf{z}_{\text{cas}}^{(k)} \in \mathbb{R}^d$ at each segment k, we model temporal dependencies across segments to predict future popularity.

Growth-Aware Segment Representation. Structural snapshots alone may not fully reflect the instantaneous diffusion momentum. Therefore, for each segment k, we incorporate an observed growth statistic $g_{\text{cas}}^{(k)}$ within $[t_{k-1}, t_k)$ (e.g., the increment in adopters/retweets) as an additional signal. We map $g_{\text{cas}}^{(k)}$ to a learnable embedding $\mathbf{g}_{\text{cas}}^{(k)} \in \mathbb{R}^{d_g}$ via a lightweight non-linear projection, and concatenate it with the structural representation:

$$\mathbf{x}_{\text{cas}}^{(k)} = [\mathbf{z}_{\text{cas}}^{(k)}; \mathbf{g}_{\text{cas}}^{(k)}] \in \mathbb{R}^{d+d_g}. \tag{9}$$

The resulting sequence $\{\mathbf{x}_{\text{cas}}^{(k)}\}_{k=1}^{K}$ thus captures both the evolving cascade structure and the corresponding growth intensity.

Cascade-Level Temporal Modeling. To capture temporal dependencies and cumulative effects across segments, we employ a bidirectional GRU:

$$\overrightarrow{\mathbf{h}}_k = \overrightarrow{\text{GRU}}(\mathbf{x}_{\text{cas}}^{(k)}, \overrightarrow{\mathbf{h}}_{k-1}), \quad \overleftarrow{\mathbf{h}}_k = \overleftarrow{\text{GRU}}(\mathbf{x}_{\text{cas}}^{(k)}, \overleftarrow{\mathbf{h}}_{k+1}), \tag{10}$$

and define the segment representation as:

$$\mathbf{h}_k = [\overrightarrow{\mathbf{h}}_k; \overleftarrow{\mathbf{h}}_k] \in \mathbb{R}^{2d_h}. \tag{11}$$

This bidirectional encoding allows each segment representation to leverage contextual information from both earlier and later segments, which is beneficial for summarizing diffusion trajectories with irregular or bursty growth patterns.

Prediction and Auxiliary Supervision. We use the final hidden state $\mathbf{h}_K$ as a summary of the observed diffusion process up to t_o and feed it into a lightweight prediction head to estimate the future cascade popularity. To provide denser training signals over the observation window, we further introduce auxiliary supervision at intermediate steps, including segment-wise intermediate growth prediction and community-level growth prediction, as detailed below. All heads are implemented as lightweight MLPs and trained jointly with the objectives defined in the following section.

Intermediate Growth Supervision. We impose a segment-wise growth prediction objective on $\{\mathbf{h}_k\}_{k=1}^{K}$. Concretely, each $\mathbf{h}_k$ is mapped to a scalar growth estimate via a lightweight prediction head, and the corresponding supervision is incorporated into the training objective. This auxiliary signal regularizes temporal modeling by encouraging $\mathbf{h}_k$ to remain predictive of local diffusion progress, improving training stability and the quality of learned representations.

Community-Level Temporal Modeling. Beyond cascade-level temporal modeling, we introduce an auxiliary community-level temporal branch to capture fine-grained diffusion dynamics within individual communities. This mesoscopic supervision complements the cascade-level objective and helps learn more robust community representations.

Community Sequence Construction. For each community C_m in a cascade, we collect its segment-wise relation-aware representations produced by the inter-community module and form a temporal sequence:

$$\mathcal{S}_m = \{\mathbf{h}_m^{(1)}, \mathbf{h}_m^{(2)}, \ldots, \mathbf{h}_m^{(K)}\}, \tag{12}$$

where $\mathbf{h}_m^{(k)} \in \mathbb{R}^d$ denotes the relation-aware community embedding of C_m at segment k, obtained after inter-community modeling. For segments in which community C_m is not present or has no valid supervision signal, the corresponding loss terms are masked out in the community-level objective.

Community-Level BiGRU. We encode $\mathcal{S}m$ with a community-level bidirectional GRU to model temporal dependencies in community evolution:

$$\overrightarrow{\mathbf{s}}_{m,k} = \overrightarrow{\mathrm{GRU}}(\mathbf{h}_m^{(k)}, \overrightarrow{\mathbf{s}}_{m,k-1}), \quad \overleftarrow{\mathbf{s}}_{m,k} = \overleftarrow{\mathrm{GRU}}(\mathbf{h}_m^{(k)}, \overleftarrow{\mathbf{s}}_{m,k+1}), \tag{13}$$

$$\mathbf{s}_{m,k} = \left[\overrightarrow{\mathbf{s}}_{m,k}; \overleftarrow{\mathbf{s}}_{m,k}\right] \in \mathbb{R}^{2d_{\text{com}}}. \tag{14}$$

where d_{com} denotes the hidden dimension of the community-level BiGRU.

Community Growth Supervision. Let $g_m^{(k)}$ denote the observed growth of community C_m during segment k (e.g., newly activated nodes in $[t_{k-1}, t_k)$). A lightweight prediction head is applied to $\mathbf{s}_{m,k}$ to estimate community growth as an auxiliary supervision signal. This supervision encourages the model to capture community dynamics across diffusion stages, yielding more informative representations for cascade-level prediction.

4.5 Loss Function and Training Objective

CasCM is trained with a weighted multi-task objective aligned with its hierarchical modeling design. The primary objective predicts future cascade popularity, while two auxiliary objectives supervise segment-level and community-level growth dynamics. All losses are computed on $\log_2(\cdot + 1)$-transformed targets for consistency with evaluation.

Cascade-Level Loss. For each cascade n, let G_n and $\hat{G}_n$ denote the ground-truth and predicted future popularity, respectively. We minimize the mean squared error in the log space:

$$\mathcal{L}_{\text{cas}} = \frac{1}{N}\sum_{n=1}^{N}\Big(\log_2(\hat{G}_n + 1) - \log_2(G_n + 1)\Big)^2. \tag{15}$$

Intermediate Cascade Growth Loss. Let $g_{n,k}$ and $\hat{g}_{n,k}$ denote the ground-truth and predicted cascade growth at segment k of cascade n ($k = 1, \ldots, K$). Since supervision may be unavailable for some segments, we define $\Omega_{\text{cas}} = \{(n,k) \mid \text{valid supervision exists}\}$. The auxiliary loss is:

$$\mathcal{L}_{\text{inter}} = \frac{1}{|\Omega_{\text{cas}}|}\sum_{(n,k)\in\Omega_{\text{cas}}}\Big(\log_2(\hat{g}_{n,k} + 1) - \log_2(g_{n,k} + 1)\Big)^2. \tag{16}$$

Community-Level Growth Loss. Let $g_{n,m,k}$ and $\hat{g}_{n,m,k}$ denote the ground-truth and predicted growth of community m at segment k in cascade n. Since supervision is only available when a community is active, we define $\Omega_{\text{com}} = \{(n,m,k) \mid \text{valid supervision exists}\}$. The auxiliary loss is:

$$\mathcal{L}_{\text{com}} = \frac{1}{|\Omega_{\text{com}}|}\sum_{(n,m,k)\in\Omega_{\text{com}}}\Big(\log_2(\hat{g}_{n,m,k} + 1) - \log_2(g_{n,m,k} + 1)\Big)^2. \tag{17}$$

Total objective. The final objective is the weighted sum:

$$\mathcal{L}_{\text{total}} = \mathcal{L}_{\text{cas}} + \lambda_{\text{inter}}\mathcal{L}_{\text{inter}} + \lambda_{\text{com}}\mathcal{L}_{\text{com}}, \tag{18}$$

where λ_{inter} and λ_{com} are weighting hyperparameters.

5 Experimental Evaluation

5.1 Experimental Setup

Datasets. We employ three widely used real-world cascade popularity prediction datasets, including two social network datasets (Twitter[1] and Weibo[2]), and a citation dataset (APS[3]). Twitter and Weibo are obtained from public sources, while APS is released by the American Physical Society. Data processing and splits follow prior work [17], and dataset statistics are summarized in Table 1.

[1] https://carl.cs.indiana.edu/data/virality2013.
[2] https://bit.ly/weibodataset.
[3] https://journals.aps.org/datasets.

Table 1. Statistics of three datasets.

Dataset	Cascades	Nodes	Edges	Avg. popularity
Twitter	88,440	490,474	1,903,230	124
Weibo	119,313	6,738,040	15,249,636	240
APS	207,685	616,316	3,304,400	51

Baselines. We compare CasCM with state-of-the-art methods, including feature-based models and deep learning approaches. **Feature-based** methods extract handcrafted features (e.g., cascade size and temporal intervals) and employ an MLP for prediction. **Deep learning-based** methods include Hawkes-enhanced models (DeepHawkes [1]), graph neural network variants capturing structural-temporal dependencies (CasCN [2], CasSampling [24], CTCP [18]), diffusion-based frameworks leveraging local and global graphs (CasFlow [17]), sequential or hypergraph modeling approaches (MINDS [25]), and continuous-time models based on neural ODEs or probabilistic diffusion processes (CasDO [19], ConCat [20]). We also compare with DVCAE [26], which adopts dual variational autoencoders to jointly learn structural and temporal representations.

Implementation Details. All models are trained with Adam (learning rate = 0.001) for up to 100 epochs using early stopping (patience = 10). The weighting coefficients λ_{inter} and λ_{com} are selected from $\{0.1, 0.2, 0.5, 1\}$. We evaluate performance using two standard metrics: Mean Squared Logarithmic Error (MSLE) and Mean Absolute Percentage Error (MAPE), both computed on $\log_2$-transformed popularity values.

5.2 Overall Results

Table 2 reports the overall comparison (best in bold; second-best underlined). CasCM achieves the best performance in most settings across datasets and prediction horizons, and remains competitive otherwise, indicating consistent gains across heterogeneous diffusion scenarios. These improvements align with our community-aware modeling design. Unlike feature-based baselines and temporal-oriented approaches (e.g., DeepHawkes) that mainly rely on handcrafted statistics or temporal excitation patterns, CasCM integrates structural signals with temporal dynamics, yielding consistent improvements under both metrics. Compared with node- or cascade-level graph models (e.g., CasCN/CasFlow/MINDS), CasCM explicitly models mesoscopic community structure: the intra-community encoder captures fine-grained propagation patterns within communities, while the inter-community module captures cross-community influence that is hard to recover from a single cascade graph. Moreover, incorporating community-level evolution as auxiliary supervision complements cascade-level temporal modeling by refining intermediate representations and improving generalization across horizons. For example, on Twitter with a 2-day observation window, CasCM reduces MSLE from 4.4395 (CasDO) to 4.2521 (a 4.2% relative improvement) and improves MAPE from 0.3606 to 0.3573. Finally, against strong continuous-time and hybrid baselines (e.g., CasDO/ConCat/DVCAE), CasCM remains favorable overall, suggesting that explicitly modeling community-aware structural evolution and community growth patterns provides complementary predictive signals beyond purely node- or cascade-level formulations, leading to more accurate and stable cascade popularity prediction.

Table 2. Performance comparison between CasCM and the baseline methods.

Methods	Twitter				Weibo				APS			
	1 Day		2 Days		0.5 h		1 h		3 Years		5 Years	
	MSLE	MAPE	MSLE	MAPE	MSLE	MAPE	MSLE	MAPE	MSLE	MAPE	MSLE	MAPE
Feature-based	7.8392	0.5364	6.1542	0.4291	2.6183	0.2744	2.5918	0.2824	1.7242	0.2593	1.5862	0.2763
DeepHawkes	7.4192	0.5464	5.5164	0.5349	2.6284	0.2662	2.6351	0.2934	1.5396	0.2654	1.4157	0.2983
CasCN	7.1864	0.5864	5.5634	0.5296	2.8642	0.2567	2.7364	0.2618	1.6732	0.2519	1.3847	0.2637
CasFlow	7.0501	0.4440	5.1986	0.3782	2.4026	0.2250	2.2452	0.2449	1.3586	0.2547	1.3714	0.2591
CasSampling	6.7235	0.4619	4.6943	0.3964	2.6194	0.2362	2.5634	0.2673	1.5934	0.2634	1.4693	0.2764
CTCP	6.6256	0.4645	4.4698	0.3861	2.7232	0.2668	2.6252	0.2872	1.6959	0.2428	1.6212	0.2669
MINDS	6.4962	0.4384	4.6537	0.3752	2.5429	0.2376	2.4261	0.2457	1.3964	0.2453	1.3846	0.2673
CasDO	6.1033	0.4502	4.4395	0.3606	2.2154	0.2212	2.1306	0.2446	1.2658	0.2351	**1.1699**	0.2511
DVCAE	7.4246	0.4600	5.6090	0.4273	2.6705	0.2697	2.3822	0.2682	1.2685	0.2346	1.2913	0.2762
ConCat	6.2115	0.5064	4.5956	0.4044	2.3206	0.2598	2.1240	0.2744	1.2617	0.2294	1.2195	0.2648
CasCM	**5.9631**	**0.4361**	**4.2521**	**0.3573**	**2.2032**	**0.2168**	**2.1003**	**0.2438**	**1.2433**	**0.2255**	1.1770	**0.2463**

5.3 Ablation Studies

To assess the contribution of each component in CasCM, we conduct ablation studies by removing key modules. Specifically, **w/o Intra-Encoder** removes the intra-community encoder and directly averages node features within each community. **w/o Inter-Encoder** removes inter-community relation modeling and replaces it with mean aggregation across communities. **w/o Cas-Temporal** removes the cascade-level temporal module and performs prediction using only the structural representation. **w/o Com-Aux** removes the community-level branch and its auxiliary supervision. Results are reported in Table 3.

Removing the cascade-level temporal module yields the largest performance degradation, highlighting the importance of modeling temporal dependencies for cascade growth. Removing either intra-community encoding or inter-community relation modeling also degrades performance, indicating that both fine-grained intra-community structures and cross-community interactions contribute to effective cascade representations. Finally, removing the community-level auxiliary branch leads to a moderate drop, suggesting that the auxiliary supervision helps stabilize training and refine intermediate representations.

Table 3. Performance comparison between CasCM and its variants.

Methods	Twitter				Weibo				APS			
	1 Day		2 Days		0.5 h		1 h		3 Years		5 Years	
	MSLE	MAPE	MSLE	MAPE	MSLE	MAPE	MSLE	MAPE	MSLE	MAPE	MSLE	MAPE
w/o Intra-Encoder	6.5594	0.4710	4.6773	0.3859	2.4235	0.2341	2.3103	0.2647	1.3676	0.2435	1.2868	0.2773
w/o Inter-Encoder	6.4401	0.4623	4.5923	0.3787	2.3795	0.2298	2.2683	0.2638	1.3428	0.2390	1.2634	0.2722
w/o Cas-Temporal	6.6787	0.4797	4.7624	0.3930	2.4676	0.2385	2.3523	0.2696	1.3925	0.2481	1.3102	0.2825
w/o Com-Aux	6.2627	0.4502	4.3063	0.3791	2.3234	0.2299	2.1905	0.2539	1.3254	0.2317	1.2793	0.2815
CasCM	**5.9631**	**0.4361**	**4.2521**	**0.3573**	**2.2032**	**0.2168**	**2.1003**	**0.2438**	**1.2433**	**0.2255**	**1.1770**	**0.2568**

5.4 Parameter Sensitivity Analysis

We further analyze the sensitivity of CasCM to hidden dimensionality by varying the hidden size of three components: the intra-community encoder, the inter-community encoder, and the cascade-level temporal module. We report MSLE and MAPE on Twitter with a 1-day observation window. For each component, we vary the hidden size in $\{16, 32, 64, 128, 256\}$ while keeping the remaining hyperparameters fixed. As shown in Fig. 3, performance improves when increasing the dimension from small values (e.g., 16/32) and then slightly degrades at very large sizes (e.g., 128/256). Overall, CasCM shows stable performance within a moderate range, indicating limited sensitivity to the hidden size.

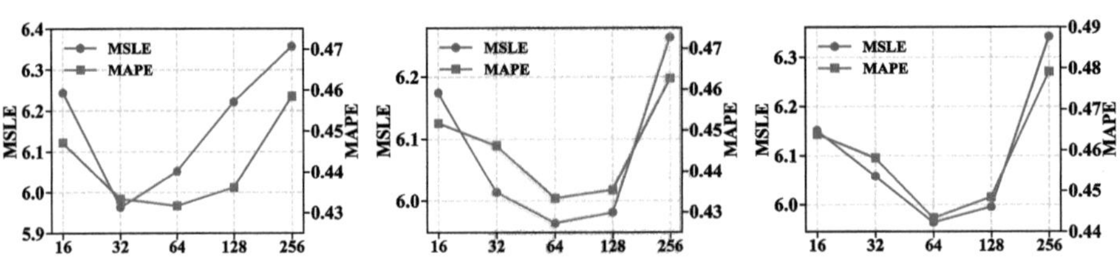

(a) d_{GCN} (b) d_{GATv2} (c) d_{BiGRU}

Fig. 3. Impact of three key hyper-parameters on the Twitter dataset.

6 Conclusion

In this paper, we proposed CasCM for cascade popularity prediction by jointly modeling intra-community dynamics, inter-community interactions, and temporal evolution. Extensive experiments showed that CasCM outperforms state-of-the-art baselines. Future work will investigate emerging communities beyond the observation window to improve adaptability to evolving diffusion patterns.

Acknowledgements. This work was supported in part by the National Natural Science Foundation of China (Nos. 62572086, 62477029) and the Sichuan Science and Technology Program (No. 2025YFHZ0025).

References

1. Cao, Q., Shen, H., Cen, K., Ouyang, W., Cheng, X.: DeepHawkes: bridging the gap between prediction and understanding of information cascades. In: Proceedings of the 2017 ACM on Conference on Information and Knowledge Management, pp. 1149–1158 (2017)
2. Chen, X., Zhou, F., Zhang, K., Trajcevski, G., Zhong, T., Zhang, F.: Information diffusion prediction via recurrent cascades convolution. In: 2019 IEEE 35th International Conference on Data Engineering (ICDE), pp. 770–781. IEEE (2019)
3. Jing, X., Jing, Y., Lu, Y., Deng, B., Chen, X., Yang, D.: CASFT: future trend modeling for information popularity prediction with dynamic cues-driven diffusion models. In: Proceedings of the AAAI Conference on Artificial Intelligence, vol. 39, pp. 11906–11914 (2025)
4. Kipf, T.: Semi-supervised classification with graph convolutional networks. arXiv preprint arXiv:1609.02907 (2016)
5. Brody, S., Alon, U., Yahav, E.: How attentive are graph attention networks? arXiv preprint arXiv:2105.14491 (2021)
6. Vaswani, A., et al.: Attention is all you need. Adv. Neural Inf. Process. Syst. **30** (2017)
7. Cho, K., et al.: Learning phrase representations using rnn encoder-decoder for statistical machine translation. arXiv preprint arXiv:1406.1078 (2014)
8. Tsur, O., Rappoport, A.: What's in a hashtag? content based prediction of the spread of ideas in microblogging communities. In: Proceedings of the fifth ACM International Conference on Web Search and Data Mining, pp. 643–652 (2012)
9. Shulman, B., Sharma, A., Cosley, D.: Predictability of popularity: gaps between prediction and understanding. In: Proceedings of the international AAAI Conference on Web and Social Media, vol. 10, pp. 348–357 (2016)
10. Xu, K., Lin, Z., Zhao, J., Shi, P., Deng, W., Wang, H.: Multimodal deep learning for social media popularity prediction with attention mechanism. In: Proceedings of the 28th ACM International Conference on Multimedia, pp. 4580–4584 (2020)
11. Zhao, Q., Erdogdu, M.A., He, H.Y., Rajaraman, A., Leskovec, J.: Seismic: a self-exciting point process model for predicting tweet popularity. In: Proceedings of the 21st ACM SIGKDD International Conference on Knowledge Discovery and Data Mining, pp. 1513–1522 (2015)
12. Shen, H., Wang, D., Song, C., Barabási, A.L.: Modeling and predicting popularity dynamics via reinforced Poisson processes. In: Proceedings of the AAAI Conference on Artificial Intelligence, vol. 28 (2014)
13. Mishra, S., Rizoiu, M.A., Xie, L.: Feature driven and point process approaches for popularity prediction. In: Proceedings of the 25th ACM International on Conference on Information and Knowledge Management, pp. 1069–1078 (2016)
14. Rizoiu, M.A., Xie, L., Sanner, S., Cebrian, M., Yu, H., Van Hentenryck, P.: Expecting to be hip: hawkes intensity processes for social media popularity. In: Proceedings of the 26th International Conference on World Wide Web, pp. 735–744 (2017)
15. Rizoiu, M.A., Mishra, S., Kong, Q., Carman, M., Xie, L.: SIR-Hawkes: linking epidemic models and Hawkes processes to model diffusions in finite populations. In: Proceedings of the 2018 World Wide Web Conference, pp. 419–428 (2018)
16. Li, C., Ma, J., Guo, X., Mei, Q.: DeepCas: an end-to-end predictor of information cascades. In: Proceedings of the 26th international conference on World Wide Web, pp. 577–586 (2017)

17. Xu, X., Zhou, F., Zhang, K., Liu, S., Trajcevski, G.: CasFlow: exploring hierarchical structures and propagation uncertainty for cascade prediction. IEEE Trans. Knowl. Data Eng. **35**(4), 3484–3499 (2021)
18. Lu, X., Ji, S., Yu, L., Sun, L., Du, B., Zhu, T.: Continuous-time graph learning for cascade popularity prediction. arXiv preprint arXiv:2306.03756 (2023)
19. Cheng, Z., et al.: Information cascade popularity prediction via probabilistic diffusion. IEEE Trans. Knowl. Data Eng. (2024)
20. Jing, X., Jing, Y., Lu, Y., Deng, B., Yang, S., Yang, D.: On your mark, get set, predict! modeling continuous-time dynamics of cascades for information popularity prediction. IEEE Trans. Knowl. Data Eng. (2025)
21. Donnat, C., Zitnik, M., Hallac, D., Leskovec, J.: Learning structural node embeddings via diffusion wavelets. In: Proceedings of the 24th ACM SIGKDD International Conference on Knowledge Discovery & Data Mining, pp. 1320–1329 (2018)
22. Zhang, J., Dong, Y., Wang, Y., Tang, J., Ding, M.: ProNE: fast and scalable network representation learning. In: IJCAI, vol. **19**, 4278–4284 (2019)
23. Blondel, V.D., Guillaume, J.L., Lambiotte, R., Lefebvre, E.: Fast unfolding of communities in large networks. J. Stat. Mech: Theory Exp. **2008**(10), P10008 (2008)
24. Cheng, G., Yan, X., Gao, S., Xu, G., Miao, X.: CasSampling: exploring efficient cascade graph learning for popularity prediction. In: Koutra, D., Plant, C., Gomez Rodriguez, M., Baralis, E., Bonchi, F. (eds.) ECML PKDD 2023. LNCS, vol. 14171, pp. 70–86. Springer, Cham (2023). https://doi.org/10.1007/978-3-031-43418-1_5
25. Jiao, P., Chen, H., Bao, Q., Zhang, W., Wu, H.: Enhancing multi-scale diffusion prediction via sequential hypergraphs and adversarial learning. In: Proceedings of the AAAI Conference on Artificial Intelligence, vol. 38, pp. 8571–8581 (2024)
26. Shang, J., Jia, X., Li, X., Hao, F., Li, R., Min, G.: DVCAE: semi-supervised dual variational cascade autoencoders for information popularity prediction. IEEE Trans. Knowl. Data Eng. (2025)

Kinematics-Inspired Behavioral Dynamics and Risk-Constrained Ensemble Learning for Student Performance Prediction in Blended Environments

Yinghe Li[1], Juan Chen[1,2,3], Zijun Yin[2], Haiyang Jia[1,2,3](✉), and Zhongbo Wu[1]

[1] College of Computer Science and Technology, Jilin University, Changchun 130012, China
{chenjuan,jiahy}@jlu.edu.cn

[2] College of Software, Jilin University, Changchun 130012, China

[3] Key Laboratory of Symbolic Computation and Knowledge Engineering of Ministry of Education, Jilin University, Changchun 130012, China

Abstract. With the proliferation of blended learning models, the accurate identification of academically at-risk students is pivotal for implementing personalized educational interventions and ensuring instructional quality. However, real-world educational data presents a dual challenge: extreme class imbalance (with failure rates below 10%) and distributional shifts (concept drift) across academic cohorts. Traditional approaches predominantly focus on static performance metrics, failing to capture the temporal evolution of learning behaviors. Furthermore, they often overlook the cost of false alarms (i.e., misclassifying low-risk students), leading to the misallocation of teaching resources.

To address these issues, this paper proposes a feature extraction and enhancement framework grounded in Temporal Motivation Theory (TMT) and psychological prior knowledge. Beyond extracting conventional Learning Engagement (LE) and Learning Stability (LS) features, we innovatively construct Learning Acceleration (LAcc) and Relative Procrastination Index (RPI) to deeply quantify the dynamics of learning pace and cohort-relative procrastination habits. Building upon these features, we construct a Recall-Constrained Heterogeneous Ensemble Learning model. This mechanism embeds a recall threshold into the Bayesian hyperparameter optimization process of base models. It enforces high sensitivity towards the minority class (failing students) while maximizing overall performance.

Validated on real-world cross-cohort data spanning six academic years (2020–2025), our proposed method effectively overcomes data distribution shifts and extreme imbalance. Supported by SHAP interpretability analysis, the model achieves a Recall of 82.35% for at-risk students and a Specificity of 71.82% for passing students, with a G-mean score of 0.7691.

This framework provides a highly reliable basis for precise pedagogical intervention.

Keywords: Student Performance Prediction · Ensemble Learning · Kinematics-Inspired Features · Class Imbalance · Concept Drift

J. Niu et al. (Eds.): KSEM 2026, LNAI 16631, pp. 381–391, 2027.
https://doi.org/10.1007/978-981-92-2759-4_28

1 Introduction

Academic Early Warning Systems (AEWS) constitute a pivotal branch of Educational Data Mining (EDM), aiming to timely identify academically at-risk students through data mining techniques to facilitate personalized intervention and enhance overall pedagogical quality. In recent years, with the rapid advancement of big data and machine learning, alongside the proliferation of blended learning in higher education, it has become increasingly critical to utilize multidimensional behavioral data to detect potential academic risks during the instructional process.

However, within real-world blended learning scenarios, we are confronted with Extreme Class Imbalance, where the proportion of failing students is typically less than 10%. Under conventional training paradigms, predictive models often fall into an "Accuracy Trap": they may achieve over 90% accuracy by trivially predicting all students as "passing," yet completely forfeit the essential function of identifying high-risk individuals. Furthermore, as academic cohorts evolve and pedagogical schemes are adjusted, student behavioral patterns exhibit Concept Drift, often rendering historical models obsolete in new semesters.

Existing solutions typically suffer from two primary deficiencies. First, in feature engineering, most studies focus solely on static statistical metrics (e.g., login frequency, assignment scores), failing to capture the Temporal Dynamics of learning behaviors, such as the acceleration in behavioral shifts from "regular study" to "abandonment." Second, regarding model optimization, standard oversampling techniques are susceptible to introducing severe noise into high- dimensional sparse data. Meanwhile, static cost-sensitive learning strategies often result in excessive False Alarms, thereby increasing the intervention burden on instructors.

To address these challenges, this paper proposes a Kinematics-Inspired and Risk-Constrained Ensemble framework rooted in psychological theory. First, we integrate physical kinematics and Temporal Motivation Theory (TMT) to construct Learning Acceleration (LAcc) and the Relative Procrastination Index (RPI), deeply quantifying the dynamic changes in student learning rhythms. Second, we design a Recall-Constrained mechanism embedded within Bayesian optimization, which compels the model to prioritize sensitivity towards minority class samples within the hyperparameter search space. Finally, through the Stacking fusion of heterogeneous models, we enhance the endogenous robustness of cross-cohort predictions.

The remainder of this paper is organized as follows: Section 2 reviews related work. Section 3 details the proposed framework and feature engineering methodology. Section 4 describes the experimental setup, datasets, and baselines. Section 5 presents our results, ablation studies, and SHAP-based interpretability analysis. Finally, Sect. 6 concludes this work and discusses its limitations.

2 Related Work

2.1 Prediction of Academic Performance Based on LMS Logs

With the proliferation of Learning Management Systems (LMS), early warning systems based on EDM have become a prominent research area. While early studies predominantly relied on static demographic characteristics or cumulative summary scores, recent advancements heavily emphasize the mining of fine- grained interaction logs. For instance, recent studies by Lagares Rodríguez et al. [1] and Khan et al. [2] demonstrated that utilizing deep learning ensembles on multi-dimensional LMS activity logs significantly enhances the predictive capacity for identifying at-risk students.

As the field progresses, researchers have shifted their focus to the temporal attributes of student behavior. Huang and Chen [3] proposed a temporal graph network to encode sequential interaction behaviors, while Shou et al. [4] introduced a multidimensional time-series approach using attention mechanisms. However, existing works remain largely limited in feature engineering: most studies focus on the "volume" or "frequency" of behaviors. Few studies integrate theories from physical kinematics to construct high-order dynamic features (such as acceleration) or employ Temporal Motivation Theory (TMT) [5] to reflect implicit psychological states.

2.2 Learning Strategies for Extremely Imbalanced Data

In real-world educational scenarios, failure rates are typically extremely low (<10%), constituting a classic class imbalance problem. Traditional strategies to address this issue fall into data-level resampling and algorithm-level cost- sensitive learning. Recent works have increasingly adopted hybrid methods, systematically evaluating the effects of imbalanced datasets on predictive algorithms [7, 8], and integrating SMOTE [12] with deep sequential models to improve recall [9, 10].

Despite these advancements, existing methods often fail in scenarios of extreme imbalance (<5% failure rate). Oversampling techniques easily introduce severe noise, leading to overfitting. Meanwhile, traditional cost-sensitive matrices often sacrifice excessive Specificity, resulting in numerous false alarms (known as the "Precision Paradox"). Currently, most optimization frameworks pursue global metrics like F1-score or AUC, lacking specific hard constraints to guarantee the identification of high-risk students.

2.3 Ensemble Learning and Concept Drift Adaptation

Educational data exhibits significant Concept Drift—student population distributions, pedagogical schemes, and course structures often vary across academic cohorts. Recent studies evaluated early student performance prediction under concept drift, proving that shifting learning behaviors across academic years severely biases predictive models [11].

To address this drift, existing studies often adopt adaptive sliding windows or online updating strategies. While Stacking strategies [13] based on heterogeneous models have proven effective, how to leverage the diversity between probabilistic models and boosting trees to construct an early warning system remains a key area of study [14]. Our framework addresses this gap by anchoring the decision boundary using kinematics-inspired dynamics.

3 Methodology

3.1 Overview of the Proposed Framework

The proposed early warning framework is designed to address extreme class imbalance and concept drift by integrating domain knowledge with robust ensemble learning. As illustrated in Fig. 1, the framework comprises three core modules: 1) **Data Governance and Augmentation**: Employs a penalty-based imputation strategy to encode "task abandonment" as a quantifiable behavior. 2) **Behavioral Dynamics Modeling**: Grounded in kinematics and TMT, this module extracts high-order dynamic features. 3) **Risk-Constrained Ensemble Prediction**: A heterogeneous ensemble model featuring a Bayesian optimization process with an asymmetric recall-penalty term for robust decision fusion across cohorts.

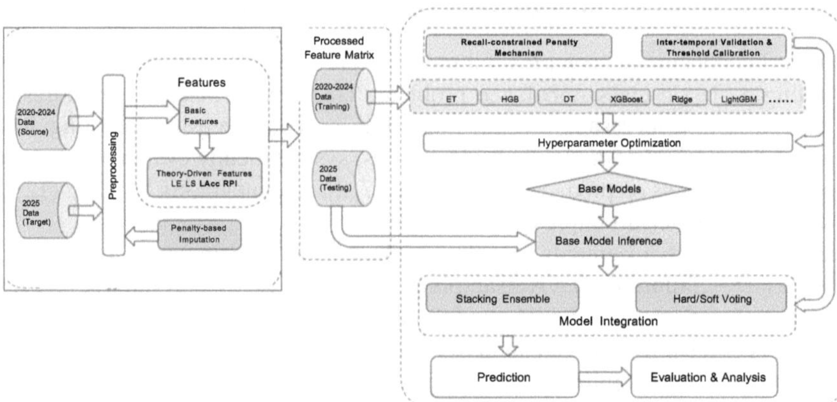

Fig. 1. Overview of the Proposed Framework.

3.2 Feature Engineering: Theoretical Basis and Preprocessing

In blended learning environments, student learning logs typically exhibit multi- dimensional, sparse, and unstructured characteristics. To address the challenges of quantifying raw behavioral data, we construct a feature extraction framework integrating Temporal Motivation Theory (TMT) and Self-Regulated Learning (SRL) theory.

Prior to feature construction, we implemented a **Penalty-based Imputation** strategy: timestamps for uncompleted tasks were set to 1.3 times the latest completion time in the cohort.

$$\text{Timputed} = 1.3 \times \text{Tmax} \tag{1}$$

The multiplier 1.3 is a heuristic value empirically derived from a pilot study on historical data distributions. It ensures that uncompleted tasks are mapped sufficiently beyond the maximum observed completion time to represent "abandonment," while remaining within a numerical range that does not induce extreme outlier distortion for tree-based splits.

3.3 Kinematics-Inspired Feature: Learning Acceleration (LAcc)

Traditional learning speed metrics rely on absolute timestamps, rendering them susceptible to fluctuations in task difficulty and release timing. Inspired by Kinematics, we propose **Relative Learning Acceleration (LAcc)** to deeply quantify the dynamic changes in student learning rhythms.

We define Relative Lag (Ls,i) as the time gap between student s and the cohort's fastest completer for task i. Let Tbest,i = minj∈Cohort(Tj,i) be the bench- mark time. The instantaneous acceleration as,i is derived from the second-order temporal difference:

$$\mathrm{Ls,\ i} = \mathrm{Ts,\ i} - \mathrm{Tbest,\ i} \tag{2}$$

$$\mathsf{a}_{\mathrm{s,i}} = \Delta^2 \mathsf{L}_{\mathrm{s,i}} = \left(\mathsf{L}_{\mathrm{s,i}} - \mathsf{L}_{\mathrm{s,i-1}}\right) - \left(\mathsf{L}_{\mathrm{s,i-1}} - \mathsf{L}_{\mathrm{s,i-2}}\right) \tag{3}$$

Unlike simple velocity, LAcc quantifies the "Rate of Detachment" between a student and the "leading group."

- **Positive LAcc:** Indicates that the lag relative to the benchmark is widening at an accelerating rate, signifying a collapse in learning discipline.
- **Negative LAcc:** Indicates that the student is accelerating to catch up, thereby narrowing the gap with the leaders.

For model training, calculated LAcc values are averaged within each phase and scaled to the [0, 1] range. By averaging LAcc, we transform the abstract trend of "falling behind" into a computable physical metric.

3.4 Psychology-Informed Features: RPI, LS, and LE

Drawing upon educational psychology theories, we extracted three dimensions to characterize learning habits:

Relative Procrastination Index (RPI): Drawing upon Temporal Motivation Theory (TMT) [5], which posits that procrastination is a direct manifestation of low utility, we construct RPI as a cohort-referenced metric to quantify this theoretical concept. Furthermore, guided by the focus theory of normative conduct [6], which emphasizes the influence of descriptive social norms on individual behavior, we establish the class median of completion time for each task as the "Social Norm." RPI is computed by calculating the cumulative sum of deviations between individual timestamps and this median.

$$RPI_s = \frac{1}{n}\sum_{i=1}^{n}(T_{s,i} - M_i)$$

An RPI > 0 indicates that the student is generally later than the cohort median, effectively isolating the impact of task release timing and focusing specifically on individual procrastination tendencies.

Learning Stability (LS): Grounded in SRL theory, we utilize Information Entropy to quantify the regularity of learning rhythms. We calculate the time intervals between adjacent tasks Ds,i = Ts,i - Ts,i-1 and convert them into a probability distribution Ps,i. The Learning Stability (LSs) is calculated using the normalized Shannon Entropy:

$$LS_s = -\sum_{i=2}^{n} P_{s,i} \frac{\log(P_{s,i})}{\log(n-1)}$$

A higher LS value implies a uniform distribution consistent with the "Distributed Learning" strategy; a lower LS value corresponds to an extremely uneven time distribution resulting from "Cramming" behaviors.

Learning Engagement (LE): To measure the relative active position of a student within the cohort, this indicator calculates the distance between the student's penalized timestamp and the latest completion time in the class, followed by reverse normalization.

3.5 Recall-Constrained Ensemble

Diversity of Base Learners: To construct a robust decision framework capable of navigating extreme class imbalance and concept drift across cohorts, we adopt a heterogeneous ensemble strategy. We categorize the selected base learners into three clusters: 1) **Gradient Boosting Frameworks** (e.g., XGBoost, LightGBM) to capture complex, non-linear interactions within behavioral dynamics. 2) **Parallel Randomized Trees** (e.g., ExtraTrees) to explicitly target variance reduction and provide resilience against the inherent noise in student logs. 3) **Probabilistic and Linear Models** (e.g., BNB, Ridge) to counterbalance the potential overfitting risk of tree-based models.

Recall-Constrained Ensemble Optimization: Real-world academic scenarios are characterized by high pass rates (>90%). To maximize Accuracy, algorithms tend to predict all students as "passing." To address this dilemma, we propose a Recall-Constrained Ensemble optimization strategy. We reformulate the objective function within the hyperparameter optimization process (Optuna- based Bayesian search) by embedding a hard constraint mechanism:

$$\text{J}(\theta) = \text{Metric} - \lambda \cdot \max(0, \text{Rmin} - \text{Rcurrent}) \tag{6}$$

where J(θ) is the objective score; Metric represents the base evaluation metric (G-Mean); Rmin is the preset safety threshold for Recall; Rcurrent is the Recall on the validation set; and λ is the penalty coefficient.

The hyperparameter Rmin is set to 0.8. This threshold is grounded in expert knowledge regarding educational interventions, which suggests that an early warning system must capture at least 80% of at-risk students to be considered pedagogically effective and reliable for classroom management. Furthermore, the asymmetric penalty coefficient (λ = 6.0) was empirically determined through a grid search on the validation set. Values below 5.0 failed to adequately penalize the objective to escape the "accuracy trap," while values above 8.0 caused extreme gradient distortion during the Bayesian search. If the Recall falls below 0.8, the final score incurs a severe penalty controlled by λ = 6.0. This asymmetric feedback creates a "strict penalty barrier," forcing the optimizer to abandon regions that yield high accuracy but high false-negative rates, redirecting the search towards subspaces that prioritize high Recall.

4 Experimental Setup

4.1 Datasets and Preprocessing

The datasets originate from the real-world blended learning logs of the "Fundamentals of Programming" course at a comprehensive university in China, spanning six consecutive cohorts from 2020 to 2025. As summarized in Table 1, the dataset presents extreme challenges:

- **Extreme Class Imbalance:** The overall failure rate is 4.81%, with the Imbalance Ratio (IR) peaking at 45.0:1 in the 2020 cohort.
- **Significant Concept Drift:** The failure rate increased significantly to nearly 10% in the 2024 and 2025 cohorts due to syllabus adjustments.

Data from the 2020–2024 cohorts served as the Source Domain for training, while the 2025 cohort was reserved as the unseen Target Domain.

4.2 Evaluation Metrics and Implementation Details

Traditional Accuracy fails to objectively reflect model performance under severe imbalance. Therefore, we adopted the following multi-dimensional framework:

1) **G-Mean**: $\sqrt{\text{Recall} \times \text{Specificity}}$. 2) **Recall**: Measures the model's ability to capture failing students (safety baseline). 3) **Specificity**: Measures the ability to exclude non-risk students. 4) **Balanced ACC** and **AUC** as comprehensive metrics.

Table 1. Statistics of the Dataset across Academic Cohorts (2020—2025).

Year	Role in Experiment	Total	Failed	Passed	Rate (%)	IR (Neg: Pos)
2020	Source Domain (Train)	919	20	899	2.18%	45.0:1
2021	Source Domain (Train)	882	26	856	2.95%	32.9:1
2022	Source Domain (Train)	913	23	890	2.52%	38.7:1
2023	Source Domain (Train)	859	24	835	2.79%	34.8:1
2024	Source Domain (Train)	871	78	793	8.96%	10.2:1
2025	Target Domain (Test)	880	85	795	9.66%	9.4:1

The experiments utilized an Inter-temporal Stratified 10-Fold Cross-Validation strategy. Threshold Moving within the $[0.01, 0.99]$ interval was utilized to identify the optimal boundary.

4.3 Baselines

To validate the effectiveness of our method, we compare it against three categories of baselines: 1. **Optimized Single Strong Classifiers**: State-of-the-art tabular classifiers (XGBoost, ExtraTrees) tuned via Optuna with standard mitigation strategies. 2. **Unconstrained Stacking Ensemble**: Utilizing the identical two-layer Stacking architecture, but optimized solely for standard global metrics (AUC or F1-score). 3. **Deep Sequential Baseline (Enhanced LSTM)**: A Long Short-Term Memory network optimized for imbalanced educational data, incorporating Weighted Cross-Entropy Loss to dynamically adjust loss weights, and Batch Normalization combined with L2 Regularization to suppress overfitting.

5 Results and Discussion

5.1 Main Results

As observed in Table 2, the proposed method achieves the best performance in G-Mean (0.7691) and Balanced-ACC (0.7709) on the unseen 2025 Target Domain.

Overcoming the Trade-off Dilemma: By embedding a hard constraint (Rmin = 0.8), our method finds an optimal equilibrium, locking the Recall at 0.8235 while maintaining a balanced Specificity (0.7182).

5.2 Ablation Study

To quantify the specific contributions of different theory-driven features, we systematically deconstructed the feature space (Fig. 2).

Table 2. Performance Comparison on the 2025 Test Set.

Metric	XGBoost	ET	LSTM	AUC-Stack	F1-Stack	Hard-Vote	**Ours**
G-mean	0.7384	0.6357	0.7029	0.5575	0.6983	0.7544	**0.7691**
Balanced-ACC	0.7417	0.6918	0.7030	0.6451	0.7174	0.7551	**0.7709**
Recall	0.8118	0.9647	0.6941	0.3205	0.5529	0.7882	**0.8235**
Specificity	0.6717	0.4189	0.7119	0.9697	0.8818	0.7220	0.7182
AUC	0.8269	0.8227	0.7321	0.9116	0.8323	0.8167	0.8283

Psychological Features as "Generalization Bridges": The Recall for removing LS and RPI dropped in the unseen test set. Without these, the model adopts a "conservative strategy," misclassifying at-risk students with subtle behavioral patterns as passing.

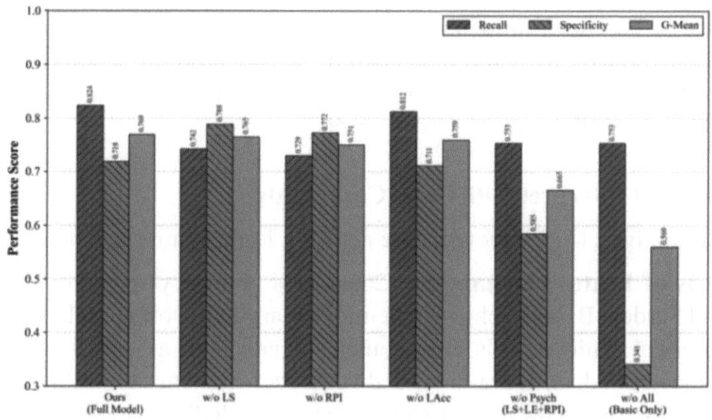

Fig. 2. Ablation Study results on the 2025 Target Domain.

Kinematics for Decision Equilibrium: The w/o LAcc results show that while Recall barely remains above the 0.8 constraint, both G-Mean and Specificity decline. This confirms that LAcc provides critical second-order dynamic information, helping the model distinguish between students "accelerating to catch up" and those "continuously detaching."

5.3 Longitudinal Robustness Analysis

To validate long-term stability and strictly prevent data leakage, we adopted a sequential rolling-window evaluation strategy for this specific analysis. When predicting the risk for a specific target cohort, the models were trained exclusively on the historical data strictly prior to that academic year (e.g., using 2020–2022 data to test the 2023 cohort). Under this rigorous setting, we evaluated the longitudinal performance on the 2023, 2024, and 2025 test cohorts (Fig. 3).

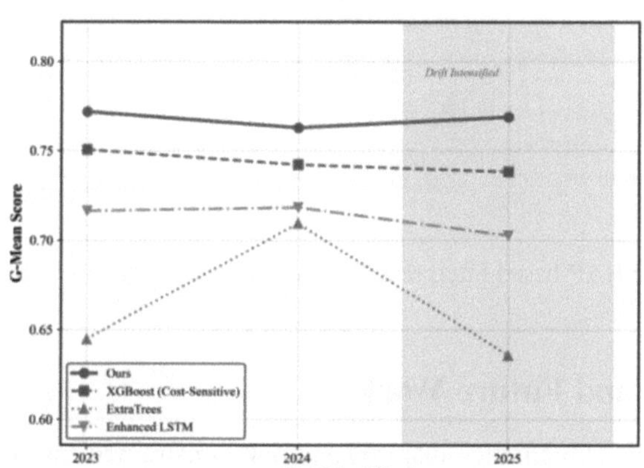

Fig. 3. Longitudinal Robustness Analysis across cohorts (2023—2025).

In contrast to baselines showing performance decay or high-variance fluctuations, Ours (Risk-Constrained) maintains high stability across the entire timeline. The "Recall-Constraint Mechanism" acts as an "anchor," compelling the model to learn essential academic risk patterns that persist across years.

5.4 SHAP-based Interpretability and Case Study

Global SHAP analysis (Fig. 4) reveals the decision logic behind risk prediction.

Case Analysis of Feature Dynamics: Consider a boundary scenario: Two students, Student A and Student B, both achieved identical, marginally low cumulative assignment scores. Traditional static models erroneously flagged both as equally high-risk. Our dynamic framework identified a critical divergence: Student A exhibited a Negative LAcc (accelerating to narrow the gap) and a decreasing RPI, indicating active recovery. Conversely, Student B exhibited a sharp Positive LAcc (continuously detaching) and an increasing RPI, signaling a collapse. Our model accurately calibrated Student A as "passing" and flagged Student B as "at-risk" weeks before failure, underscoring the early warning value of modeling the "rate of change." While Fig. 4 provides insights into individual feature contributions, we acknowledge that complex interdependencies between these dynamic features warrant further investigation. Therefore, future work will involve SHAP interaction plots to explicitly visualize the synergistic effects between dynamic features.

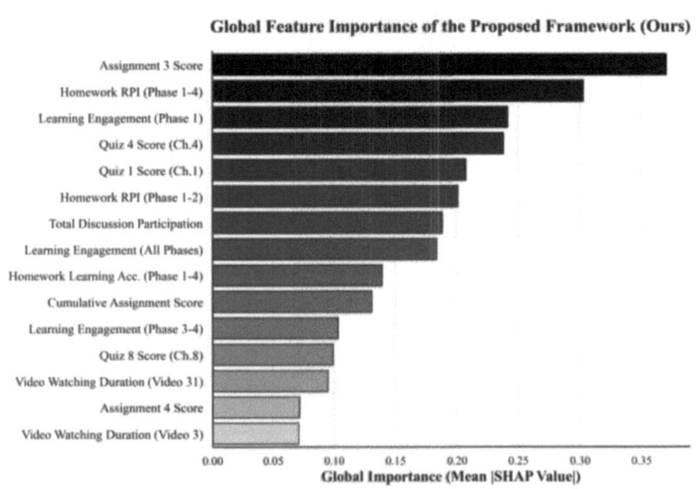

Fig. 4. SHAP-based Interpretability Analysis showing top 15 features.

6 Conclusion and Future Work

This paper proposed a kinematics-inspired and risk-constrained ensemble framework to address the dual challenges of extreme class imbalance and concept drift. Experiments spanning six academic cohorts demonstrated that our method significantly enhances the identification of high-risk students (Recall of 82.35%, G-Mean of 0.7691) while maintaining a low false alarm rate, exhibiting superior longitudinal robustness.

Limitations and Future Work: We acknowledge the following: First, the dataset is derived from a single course; cross-institutional validation is needed to ensure broader generalizability. Second, the selection of baseline models could be further expanded to incorporate more recent SOTA methods in EDM. Lastly, we aim to extend this analysis to uncover broader interaction patterns among behavioral indicators, providing deeper theoretical guidance for targeted pedagogical intervention.

Acknowledgement. This paper was supported by the Research Project on Higher Education Teaching Reform in Jilin Province (No. JLJY202262573244) and the Undergraduate "Digital-Intelligent Curriculum Program" Project of Jilin University (No. 24SZ089).

References

1. Lagares Rodríguez, J.A., et al.: A comparative analysis of student performance prediction: evaluating optimized deep learning ensembles against semi-supervised feature selection-based models. Appl. Sci. **15**(9), 4818 (2025)
2. Khan, M., et al.: Utilizing machine learning models to predict student performance from LMS activity logs. IEEE Access **11**, 86953–86962 (2023)
3. Huang, Q., Chen, J.: Enhancing academic performance prediction with temporal graph networks for massive open online courses. J. Big Data **11**, 52 (2024)
4. Shou, Z., et al.: Predicting student performance in online learning: a multidimensional time-series data analysis approach. Appl. Sci. **14**(6), 2522 (2024)
5. Steel, P.: The nature of procrastination: a meta-analytic and theoretical review of quintessential self-regulatory failure. Psychol. Bull. **133**(1), 65–94 (2007)
6. Cialdini, R.B.: The focus theory of normative conduct. In: Van Lange, P.A.M., Kruglanski, A.W., Higgins, E.T. (eds.) Handbook of Theories of Social Psychology, p. 295—312. Sage Publications Ltd. (2012)
7. Sujon, K.M., et al.: The effects of imbalanced datasets on machine learning algorithms in predicting student performance. JOIV: International Journal on Informatics Visualization **8**(3), 158—165 (2024)
8. Althaqafi, T., et al.: Enhancing student performance prediction: the role of class imbalance handling in machine learning models. Discover Comput. **28**, 79 (2025)
9. Nguyen Thi Cam, H., Sarlan, A., Arshad, N.I.: A hybrid model integrating recurrent neural networks and the semi-supervised support vector machine for identification of early student dropout risk. PeerJ Comput. Sci. **10**, e2572 (2024)
10. Jain, A., et al.: A PSO weighted ensemble framework with SMOTE balancing for student dropout prediction in smart education systems. Sci. Rep. **15**, 17463 (2025)
11. Sonnleitner, B., et al.: Evaluation of early student performance prediction given concept drift. Comput. Educ. Artif. Intell. **8**, 100369 (2025)
12. Chawla, N.V., et al.: SMOTE: synthetic minority over-sampling technique. J. Artif. Intell. Res. **16**, 321–357 (2002)
13. Wolpert, D.H.: Stacked generalization. Neural Netw. **5**(2), 241–259 (1992)
14. Chen, J., et al.: Student behavior analysis and performance prediction based on blended learning data. In: Memmi, G., Yang, B., Kong, L., Zhang, T., Qiu, M. (eds.) KSEM 2022. LNCS, vol. 13370, pp. 597–609. Springer, Cham (2022). https://doi.org/10.1007/978-3-031-10986-7_48

Physics-Informed Gaussian Process with Sequential Virtual Point Selection for Constrained Regression

Wang Yanlin[1], Cheng Zhijun[2(✉)], Wang Zichen[2], Pan Zhengqiang[2], and Liu Jiying[1]

[1] College of Science, National University of Defense Technology, Changsha 410073, Hunan, China
wangyanlin@nudt.edu.cn

[2] College of Systems Engineering, National University of Defense Technology, Changsha 410073, Hunan, China
chengzhijun@nudt.edu.cn

Abstract. To address the drawbacks of poor physical consistency and weak generalization in traditional purely data-driven modeling, physics-informed Gaussian process can incorporate constraints such as boundedness and monotonicity. By leveraging virtual points, global constraints are transformed into constraints imposed on a finite set of virtual points. In this paper, a novel sequential virtual point selection strategy is proposed. On the basis of the constraint violation probability criterion, a distance penalty term is introduced to enhance the diversity of virtual points, which not only avoids computational difficulties in matrix operations caused by point aggregation but also significantly reduces the computational burden arising from virtual point searching. The improved method is applied to predict robotic arm state functions, pipeline pressure-bearing capacity functions, and concrete strength using real-world datasets, verifying its effectiveness. Compared with unconstrained Gaussian processes and other existing methods, the proposed approach yields predictions with higher physical consistency and lower generalization errors. In terms of virtual point determination methods, it achieves higher accuracy than Latin hypercube sampling; compared with methods that only consider constraint violation probability, it cuts down computational time while maintaining model accuracy, thus demonstrating promising application prospects in other scenarios involving linear physical constraints.

Keywords: Gaussian process · Physics informed · Sequential sampling

1 Introduction

Surrogate models serve as effective tools for emulating expensive physical simulations or real-world experiments. They can replace original models to a certain

J. Niu et al. (Eds.): KSEM 2026, LNAI 16631, pp. 392–403, 2027.
https://doi.org/10.1007/978-981-92-2759-4_29

extent, providing support for further analysis and optimization. Gaussian process (GP) is a widely adopted surrogate modeling method, whose core advantage lies in the natural quantification of prediction uncertainty [12]. Gaussian process models have been applied to various high-cost fields where new data acquisition relies on experiments, such as materials science [2], aerospace engineering [13], marine engineering [14].

Machine learning methods represented by Gaussian processes hold considerable application prospects for problems where the physical processes are not yet fully understood and those where physical models incur excessive computational costs. However, as data-driven models are highly dependent on data, the generated results may violate physical laws and suffer from poor generalization capability [7,17]. Physics-informed knowledge reflects the characteristics of the real world and can be manifested in various forms, including monotonicity [11], boundedness [6], partial differential equations [5], and symmetry [4].

Cross [3] and Swiler [15] summarized how such physics-informed knowledge, namely constraints, can be incorporated into Gaussian processes. Recent studies have integrated monotonicity and boundedness constraints into a unified framework and embedded physics-informed knowledge into Gaussian processes. Among these efforts, a physics-informed Gaussian process based on splines was proposed in [10,11], which transforms constraints into coefficient constraints of basis functions. However, its validation was limited to problems with five or fewer dimensions [9].

Besides, the integration of constraints was achieved in [19] by truncating the conditional expectation of the multivariate normal distribution. A discrete location approximation strategy was adopted to convert global constraints into constraints on a finite set of virtual points, thus realizing a physics-informed Gaussian process. Building on this foundation, Agrell [1] established a unified linear representation for various types of constraints, further improving computational stability and efficiency. In such models, the selection of virtual points largely determines the model accuracy and computational cost. Both [1] and [16] adopted a sequential addition method that places points in regions with the lowest constraint satisfaction probability, which effectively enhances the efficiency of virtual point selection. Compared with virtual point selection methods such as Latin Hypercube Sampling (LHS), this sampling strategy allocates more constraint points in regions where constraints are violated, making it a non-blind approach.

However, this sampling process solely accounts for the constraint violation probability, which is prone to induce sample aggregation and subsequent information redundancy. As neighboring samples provide overlapping information, computational costs are inevitably escalated; furthermore, closely clustered samples can lead to the singularity of the covariance matrix, potentially resulting in the failure of Cholesky decomposition. In addition, this deficiency may also cause insufficient coverage of constraint-violating regions by virtual sample points, thereby overlooking constraint violations in other areas.

Accordingly, this paper proposes to integrate the constraint violation probability with a global exploration criterion, incorporating a distance penalty to enhance information diversity and reduce computational expenses. Following the validation of the proposed method on the robotic arm function and pipeline pressure-bearing capacity function, we further extend its application to real-world datasets. The experimental results confirm that the proposed method preserves the generalization capability of the model and physical consistency while simultaneously cutting down computational costs.

The remainder of this paper is organized as follows. Section 2 presents our proposed method; Sect. 3 describes the experimental setup and the results; Sect. 4 concludes the paper.

2 Physics-Informed Gaussian Process Modeling and Improvement

2.1 Original Gaussian Process

Gaussian Processes (GPs) are probability distributions defined over function spaces, characterized by a mean function and a covariance function. Their prior distribution is defined as:

$$f \sim \mathcal{GP}\big(\mu(x), K(x, x')\big) \tag{1}$$

where the mean function $\mu(x) = \boldsymbol{E}[f(x)]$ is typically set to a constant, and the covariance function $K(x, x') = \boldsymbol{E}\big[(f(x) - \mu(x))(f(x') - \mu(x'))\big]$. Given the observed dataset $D = (x_j, y_j)$, the predictive distribution of a new input X^* follows a Gaussian distribution:

$$f^* \mid X^*, X, Y \sim \mathcal{N}\big(\mu(x), \Sigma^2(x)\big) \tag{2}$$

$$\mu(X^*) = \mu(X^*) + K(X^*, X)\big[K(X, X) + \sigma^2 I\big]^{-1}\big(Y - \mu(X)\big) \tag{3}$$

$$\Sigma^2(X^*) = K(X^*, X^*) - K(X^*, X)\big[K(X, X) + \sigma^2 I\big]^{-1} K(X, X^*) \tag{4}$$

Here, $\mu(X^*)$ and $\Sigma^2(X^*)$ denote the predicted mean and variance, respectively. The variance directly quantifies the prediction uncertainty of the sample.

2.2 Physics-Informed Gaussian Process

Gaussian processes (GPs) possess a core property of closure under linear transformations. These linear transformations include boundedness ($\mathcal{L}f = f$), monotonicity ($\mathcal{L}f = \partial f / \partial x_i$), and convexity ($\mathcal{L}f = \partial^2 f / \partial x_j^2$). If $f \sim \mathcal{GP}\big(\mu(\boldsymbol{x}), K(\boldsymbol{x}, \boldsymbol{x}')\big)$, then the process $\mathcal{L}f$ (resulting from the linear operator $\mathcal{L}$ acting on f) remains a Gaussian process. Its mean can be expressed as $\mathbb{E}\big[\mathcal{L}f(\boldsymbol{x})\big] = \mathcal{L}\mu(\boldsymbol{x})$, and its covariance is given by $\mathrm{cov}\big(\mathcal{L}f(\boldsymbol{x}), \mathcal{L}f(\boldsymbol{x}')\big) = \mathcal{L}K(\boldsymbol{x}, \boldsymbol{x}')\mathcal{L}^T$. Common constraints can be transformed into the form $a(\boldsymbol{x}) \leq \mathcal{L}f(\boldsymbol{x}) \leq b(\boldsymbol{x})$.

The final prediction performance is illustrated in Fig. 1. The black sample points represent the training set, while the solid lines in different colors in each subplot denote the prediction results. Specifically, no constraints are imposed in Subplot 1, boundedness constraints are incorporated in Subplot 2, and monotonicity constraint is applied in Subplot 3.

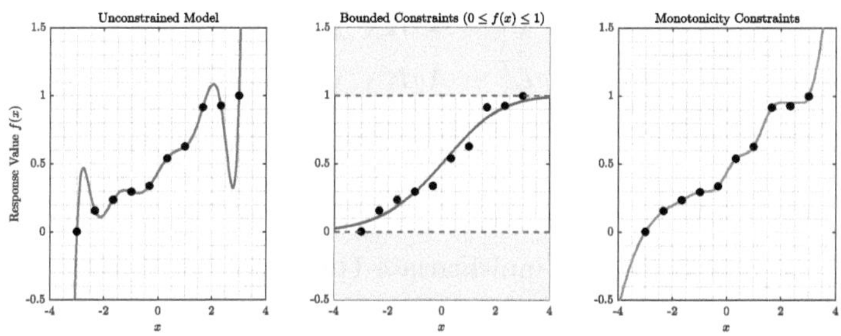

Fig. 1. Unconstrained modeling and modeling with physical information constraints

To avoid directly handling global constraints, a finite set of virtual observation points $\boldsymbol{X}^v = \boldsymbol{x}_1^v, \ldots, \boldsymbol{x}_S^v$ is introduced, and the constraints are required to hold at these points:

$$a(\boldsymbol{X}^v) \leq \mathcal{L}f(\boldsymbol{X}^v) + \varepsilon^v \leq b(\boldsymbol{X}^v) \tag{5}$$

where $\varepsilon^v \sim \mathcal{N}(0, \sigma_v^2 I)$ denotes virtual noise with variance σ_v^2 , and the constraints are expressed as $C(\boldsymbol{X}^v) = \bigcap_{i=1}^S \{a(\boldsymbol{x}_i^v) \leq \mathcal{L}f(\boldsymbol{x}_i^v) + \varepsilon^v \leq b(\boldsymbol{x}_i^v)\}$.

By jointly considering the real observations $\boldsymbol{Y}$ and the virtual observation constraints $C(\boldsymbol{X}^v)$, the target posterior distribution is $f \mid (\boldsymbol{X}, \boldsymbol{Y}, \boldsymbol{X}^v, C(\boldsymbol{X}^v))$. First, we derive the joint Gaussian distribution of $(f^*, \widetilde{\boldsymbol{C}}, \boldsymbol{Y})$, where $\widetilde{\boldsymbol{C}} = \mathcal{L}f(\boldsymbol{X}^v) + \varepsilon^v$ is the latent variable of virtual observations. $(f^*, \widetilde{\boldsymbol{C}}, \boldsymbol{Y})$ follows a joint multivariate Gaussian distribution. Its mean and covariance can be expressed as:

$$\boldsymbol{\mu}_{\text{joint}} = [\boldsymbol{\mu}^*, \mathcal{L}\boldsymbol{\mu}^v, \boldsymbol{\mu}]^T \tag{6}$$

$$\boldsymbol{\Sigma}_{\text{joint}} = \begin{bmatrix} K_{\boldsymbol{X}^*,\boldsymbol{X}^*} & K_{\boldsymbol{X}^*,\boldsymbol{X}^v}\mathcal{L}^T & K_{\boldsymbol{X}^*,\boldsymbol{X}} \\ \mathcal{L}K_{\boldsymbol{X}^v,\boldsymbol{X}^*} & \mathcal{L}K_{\boldsymbol{X}^v,\boldsymbol{X}^v}\mathcal{L}^T + \sigma_v^2 \boldsymbol{I}_{N_v} & \mathcal{L}K_{\boldsymbol{X}^v,\boldsymbol{X}} \\ K_{\boldsymbol{X},\boldsymbol{X}^*} & K_{\boldsymbol{X},\boldsymbol{X}^v}\mathcal{L}^T & K_{\boldsymbol{X},\boldsymbol{X}} + \sigma^2 \boldsymbol{I}_N \end{bmatrix} \tag{7}$$

where $\boldsymbol{\mu}^* = \mu(\boldsymbol{X}^*)$, $\mathcal{L}\boldsymbol{\mu}^v = \mathcal{L}\mu(\boldsymbol{X}^v)$, $\boldsymbol{\mu} = \mu(\boldsymbol{X})$ are prior means; N and N_v are numbers of training and virtual points; σ^2 is training noise variance.

Next, we obtain $\widetilde{\boldsymbol{C}} \mid \boldsymbol{Y} \sim \mathcal{N}(\boldsymbol{v}_c, \boldsymbol{\Sigma}_c)$, where the mean is $\boldsymbol{v}_c = \mathcal{L}\boldsymbol{\mu}^v + \boldsymbol{A}_1(\boldsymbol{Y} - \boldsymbol{\mu})$ and the covariance is $\boldsymbol{\Sigma}_c = \boldsymbol{B}_1 = \mathcal{L}K_{\boldsymbol{X}^v,\boldsymbol{X}^v}\mathcal{L}^T + \sigma_v^2 \boldsymbol{I} - \boldsymbol{A}_1 K_{\boldsymbol{X},\boldsymbol{X}^v}\mathcal{L}^T$. Conditioning on the real observations $\boldsymbol{Y}$, we derive the distribution of $(f^*, \widetilde{\boldsymbol{C}}) \mid \boldsymbol{Y}$:

$$(f^*, \widetilde{\boldsymbol{C}}) \mid \boldsymbol{Y} \sim \mathcal{N}\left(\begin{bmatrix} \boldsymbol{\mu}^* + \boldsymbol{A}_2(\boldsymbol{Y} - \boldsymbol{\mu}) \\ \mathcal{L}\boldsymbol{\mu}^v + \boldsymbol{A}_1(\boldsymbol{Y} - \boldsymbol{\mu}) \end{bmatrix}, \begin{bmatrix} \boldsymbol{B}_2 & \boldsymbol{B}_3 \\ \boldsymbol{B}_3^T & \boldsymbol{B}_1 \end{bmatrix}\right) \tag{8}$$

where $\boldsymbol{\mu}^v$ denotes the prior mean of virtual points. The matrices are defined as:

$$A_1 = \mathcal{L}K_{X^v,X}\left(K_{X,X} + \sigma^2 I_N\right)^{-1} \in \mathbb{R}^{N_v \times N}, \tag{9}$$

$$A_2 = K_{X^*,X}\left(K_{X,X} + \sigma^2 I_N\right)^{-1} \in \mathbb{R}^{M \times N}, \tag{10}$$

$$B_1 = \mathcal{L}K_{X^v,X^v}\mathcal{L}^T + \sigma_v^2 I_{N_v} - A_1 K_{X,X^v}\mathcal{L}^T, \tag{11}$$

$$B_2 = K_{X^*,X^*} - A_2 K_{X,X^*} \in \mathbb{R}^{M \times M}, \tag{12}$$

$$B_3 = K_{X^*,X^v}\mathcal{L}^T - A_2 K_{X,X^v}\mathcal{L}^T \in \mathbb{R}^{M \times N_v}. \tag{13}$$

After conditioning on $C(\boldsymbol{X}^v)$, it corresponds to interval truncation of $\widetilde{\boldsymbol{C}} \mid \boldsymbol{Y}$, so:

$$\widetilde{C} \mid (Y, C(X^v)) \sim \mathcal{TN}\left(\mathcal{L}\mu^v + A_1(Y - \mu), B_1; a(X^v), b(X^v)\right) \tag{14}$$

$\mathcal{TN}$ denotes the truncated multivariate Gaussian distribution, which filters valid samples via constraint events. After conditioning on the truncated $\widetilde{\boldsymbol{C}}$, we obtain the final predictive posterior $f^* \mid \boldsymbol{Y}, C(\boldsymbol{X}^v)$ by reusing the conditional Gaussian distribution formula to condition $(f^*, \widetilde{\boldsymbol{C}}) \mid \boldsymbol{Y}$ on the truncated $\widetilde{\boldsymbol{C}}$:

$$f^* \mid Y, C(X^v) \sim \mathcal{N}\left(\mu^* + A\left(\widetilde{C} - \mathcal{L}\mu^v\right) + B(Y - \mu), \Sigma\right) \tag{15}$$

The predictive distribution of the new input $\boldsymbol{X}^*$ is a compound Gaussian distribution :

$$f^* \mid Y, C \sim \mathcal{N}\left(\mu^* + A\left(C - \mathcal{L}\mu^v\right) + B(Y - \mu), \Sigma\right) \tag{16}$$

where $\boldsymbol{A} = \boldsymbol{B}_3\boldsymbol{B}_1^{-1}$, $\boldsymbol{B} = \boldsymbol{A}_2 - \boldsymbol{A}\boldsymbol{A}_1$, $\boldsymbol{\Sigma} = \boldsymbol{B}_2 - \boldsymbol{A}\boldsymbol{B}_3^T$.

2.3 Iterative Optimization of Virtual Points

In this process, the selection of virtual points directly determines the model quality. Works [20], [21] adopt the iterative confirmation method, whose core idea is analogous to that of active learning: in active learning, samples with large information content are selected iteratively while enhancing exploration of unknown regions, which can effectively improve sample selection efficiency and reduce the required sample size [22].

The selection of virtual points also relies on this adaptive iterative process: by sequentially selecting informative virtual sample points, rapid optimization is achieved. The core goal is to find the optimal $\boldsymbol{X}^v$ such that the probability of global constraint satisfaction is no less than p_{target}. To select effective virtual points, we introduce a distance penalty, balancing global exploration and local exploitation.

On one hand, the distance penalty prevents sample aggregation, which causes difficulties in covariance matrix computation. On the other hand, it ensures coverage of multiple constraints, enhancing the physical rationality of model predictions while improving model accuracy to some extent. Additionally, the distance penalty helps improve the efficiency of virtual point search. Thus, in the new virtual point determination workflow, the optimized objective is redefined.

- Calculate the constraint satisfaction probability $p_c(\boldsymbol{x}) = P(a(\boldsymbol{x}) \leq \mathcal{L}f(\boldsymbol{x}) \mid \boldsymbol{Y} \leq b(\boldsymbol{x}))$ for each point in the candidate set under the current $\boldsymbol{X}^v$. Further compute the global constraint satisfaction probability and new optimized objective:

$$\hat{p}_c(\boldsymbol{x}) = \frac{1}{m}\sum_{j=1}^{m} P\left(a(\boldsymbol{x}) - v < (\mathcal{L}f(\boldsymbol{x}) \mid \boldsymbol{Y}, C_j) < b(\boldsymbol{x}) + v\right) \tag{17}$$

$$\hat{p}_c'(\boldsymbol{x}) = \hat{p}_c(\boldsymbol{x}) - \frac{d_i^{min}}{d^{max}} \tag{18}$$

  where $v = \max\left(\sigma_v \Phi^{-1}(p_{target}), 0\right)$, $\Phi(x)$ is the normal cumulative distribution function. $d_i^{\min} = \min_{\boldsymbol{x}_v \in \mathcal{X}_v} \|\boldsymbol{x}_i - \boldsymbol{x}_v\|$ denotes the minimum distance between the i-th candidate virtual point and the existing virtual point set $\mathcal{X}_v$. $d^{\max}$ is the maximum of these minimum distances over all sample points.
- Identify the position $\boldsymbol{x}^*$ where $\hat{p}_c'(\boldsymbol{x})$ is minimized : $\boldsymbol{x}^* = \arg\min \hat{p}_c'(\boldsymbol{x})$.
- If $p^* < p_{target}$, add $\boldsymbol{x}^*$ to $\boldsymbol{X}^v$ and repeat until convergence.

The prediction performance is illustrated in Fig. 2. It can be observed that after introducing the distance constraint, sample aggregation in the original method is effectively alleviated, the diversity of virtual points is improved, computational costs are reduced, and matrix inversion difficulties are avoided. In the experiments of this paper, p_{target} is uniformly set to 0.8, and the maximum number of iterations is set to ten times the factor dimension. In CGP_LHS, sample points with a quantity of five times the factor dimension are generated for each constrained dimension.

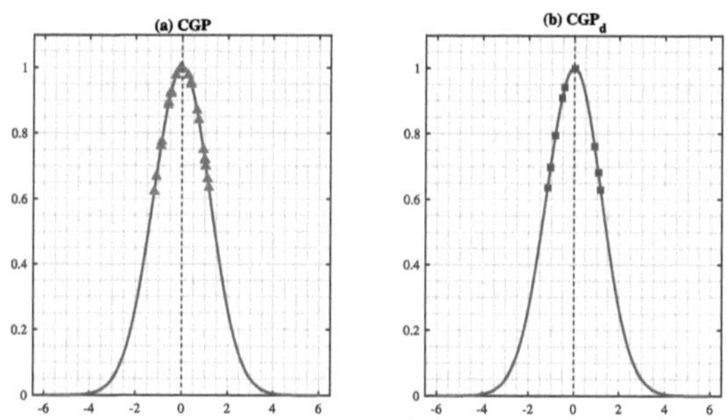

Fig. 2. Comparison of Virtual Point Determination Methods

For ease of reference, Table 1 summarizes the key symbols used throughout this paper.

3 Method Validation

3.1 Experimental Setup

We tested the proposed physics-informed modeling method on numerical examples from other papers and real-world regression datasets from the University of

Table 1. Summary of notation

Symbol	Description	Symbol	Description
f	Gaussian process	$\mathcal{L}$	Linear operator
$\mu(\boldsymbol{x})$	Mean function	$\mathcal{L}f$	Transformed GP
$K(\boldsymbol{x}, \boldsymbol{x}')$	Covariance function	$a(\boldsymbol{x}), b(\boldsymbol{x})$	Constraint bounds
$\boldsymbol{X}, \boldsymbol{Y}$	Training data (N samples)	$C(\boldsymbol{X}^v)$	Constraint event
σ^2	Observation noise	$\widetilde{\boldsymbol{C}}$	Latent virtual variable
$\boldsymbol{X}^v$	Virtual locations	p_{target}	Target probability
N_v	Number of virtual points	ν	Tolerance parameter
σ_v^2	Virtual noise	$p_c(\boldsymbol{x}), \hat{p}_c(\boldsymbol{x})$	Constraint probability
$\boldsymbol{X}^*, \boldsymbol{f}^*$	Test inputs & predictions	$\hat{p}_c'(\boldsymbol{x})$	Penalized acquisition

California, Irvine (UCI) Machine Learning Repository. The information is summarized in Table 2. Within the specific range of this dataset, it is known that concrete compressive strength increases with the cement content and decreases with the fly ash content.

The 4-dimensional function is derived from the robotic arm function [1], with the mathematical formulation expressed as:

$$f(\boldsymbol{x}) = \sum_{i=1}^{m} L_i \cos\left(\sum_{j=1}^{i} \tau_j\right) \tag{19}$$

The partial derivative constraints associated with L_1 and L_2 are introduced to quantify the movement trend of the robotic arm relative to the x-axis as the segment lengths vary.

The 5-dimensional function, adopted from [1], is formulated as:

$$P_{cap}(\sigma_u, D, t, d, l) = 1.05 \cdot \frac{2t\sigma_u}{D-t} \cdot \frac{1-d/t}{1-\frac{d/t}{Q}}, \quad Q = \sqrt{1 + 0.31 \cdot \frac{l^2}{Dt}} \tag{20}$$

The partial derivative constraints reflect the physical laws of the system: the pressure capacity increases with the increase of material strength and wall thickness, and decreases with the growth of pipe outer diameter, defect depth and defect length.

The methods compared with the proposed approach (CGP_d) include unconstrained Gaussian process(UGP), constraint Gaussian process using LHS (CGP_LHS), and the method considering only constraint violation probability from literature(CGP). CGP refers to the variant that maximizes only the constraint violation probability without the distance penalty term. The RBF kernel is adopted, as it satisfies the smoothness requirement needed for constraint implementation. To further verify the method's effectiveness, other machine learning methods including least squares support vector machine(LSSVR), linear regression(LR), Random Forest (RF), and XGBoost(XGB) are used.

For each dataset, to eliminate randomness caused by different data splits, we run 50 independent experiments under the condition of fixed training set size and test set size. The training set size is first set to 10 times the sample dimension [8]. The error metric is chosen as the normalized RMSE, with the specific expression:

$$\text{RMSE} = \frac{\sqrt{\frac{1}{n}\sum_{i=1}^{n}(y_i - \hat{y}_i)^2}}{y_{\max} - y_{\min}} \tag{21}$$

where n denotes the number of samples, y_i is the true value of the i-th test sample, $\hat{y}_i$ is the predicted value of the i-th test sample, and $y_{\max}$ and $y_{\min}$ are the maximum and minimum values of the true values in the test set, respectively.

Table 2. Configuration of test cases

Case	Test number	Dimension	Bound	Monotonicity
F4	2000	4	/	$\frac{\partial f}{\partial x_1} > 0$, $\frac{\partial f}{\partial x_2} > 0$
F5	2000	5	$[0, +\infty)$	$\frac{\partial f}{\partial x_1} > 0$, $\frac{\partial f}{\partial x_2} < 0$, $\frac{\partial f}{\partial x_3} > 0$, $\frac{\partial f}{\partial x_4} < 0$, $\frac{\partial f}{\partial x_5} < 0$
Concrete	900	8	$[0, 85]$	$\frac{\partial y}{\partial x_1} > 0$, $\frac{\partial y}{\partial x_3} < 0$

3.2 Experimental Results and Analysis

The prediction results of the 4-dimensional test case with 40 sample points are illustrated in Fig. 3. The statistical results of the data are presented using box plots. The bottom and top of each box plot represent the first quartile and the third quartile respectively. The black line in the center denotes the median of the indicator. The vertical lines at the ends of the box plot indicate the range of the remaining data relative to the first and third quartiles. The red dots represent outliers.

It can be observed from the box plot results that all four Gaussian process-based methods outperform the other comparative methods in F4. Among the four Gaussian process methods, the UGP ignoring physical constraints yields the worst performance, followed by the CGP_LHS. Compared with the aforementioned methods, both the median and mean values of the method proposed in this paper are significantly reduced.

It can be observed from the box plots of the 5d function in Fig. 4 that the method proposed in this paper maintains the same accuracy as the constrained Gaussian process. Compared with UGP and CGP_LHS, it has a slight advantage. Figure 4 presents the constraint satisfaction rate (CSR) of different methods, which is used to measure the proportion of predicted values of the final test set that satisfy the boundedness constraints. In engineering problems, predicted values exceeding the upper and lower bounds are not practically meaningful and thus should be avoided as much as possible. It can be seen that Random

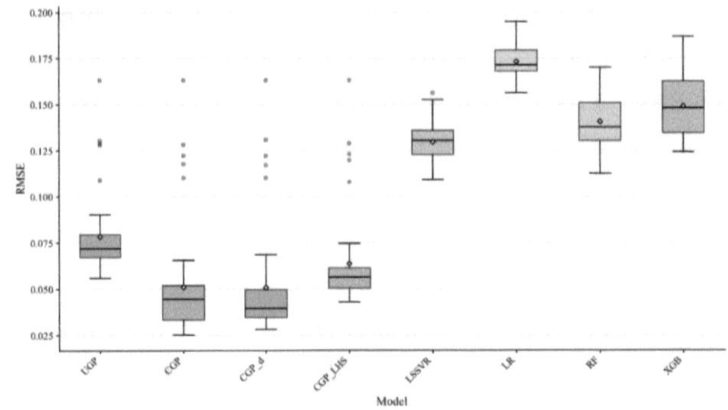

Fig. 3. RMSE results of f4

Forest and XGBoost achieve the best constraint satisfaction, but their accuracy is low and their generalization ability is insufficient. Among several constrained Gaussian process methods, the virtual point determination based on LHS fails to ensure a high constraint satisfaction rate, showing a similar performance to the unconstrained Gaussian process.

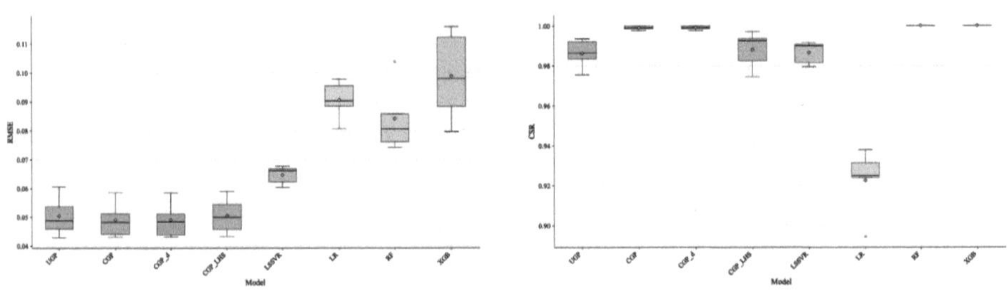

(a) RMSE results of f5 (b) CSR results of f5

Fig. 4. Performance comparison of f5

Figure 5 presents the computational time consumed by different virtual point selection methods. It can be observed that the method proposed in this paper achieves faster virtual point search. Combined with its accuracy performance, the improved method in this paper can save half of the model training time while ensuring prediction accuracy.

Next, the real-world dataset is analyzed. The modeling results of the Concrete dataset with 80 training samples are presented in Fig. 6. The improved method proposed in this paper also exhibits a slight overall advantage. In addition, the time statistics in Fig. 7 show that this method can save half of the computational time on average.

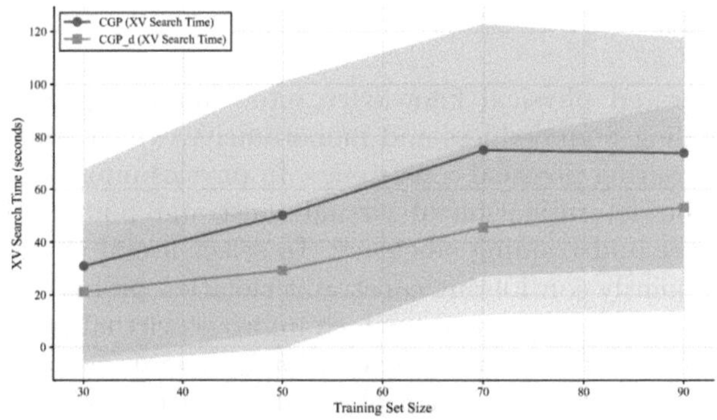

Fig. 5. Virtual points computational time of f5

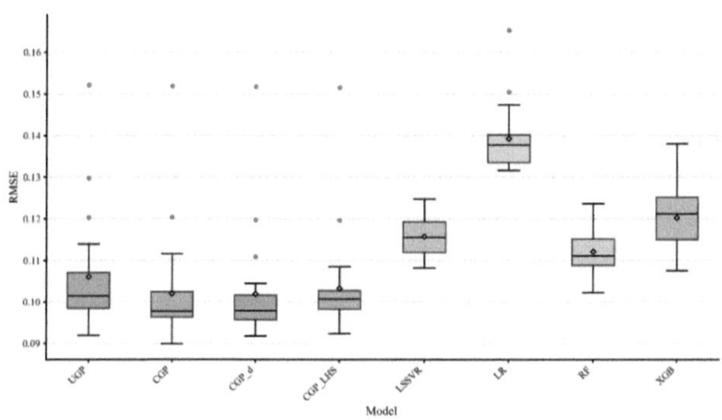

Fig. 6. RMSE results of Concrete dataset

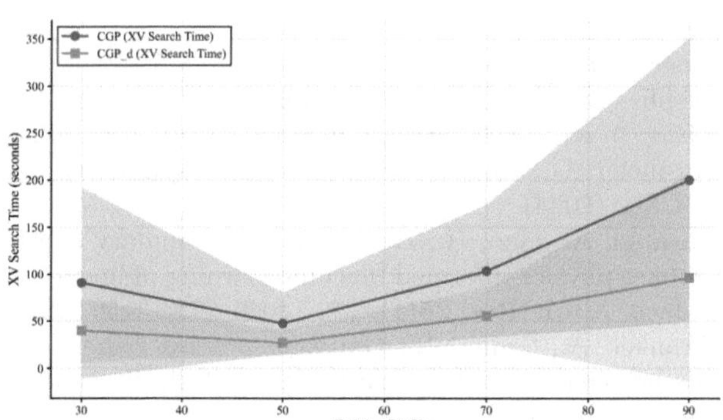

Fig. 7. Virtual points computational time of Concrete dataset

4 Conclusion

This paper integrated physical knowledge into Gaussian processes via linear constraints including boundedness and monotonicity, which enhances modeling accuracy while ensuring physical consistency. In physics-informed Gaussian process modeling, the determination of virtual constraint points critically affects model performance and training efficiency. To select useful virtual points effectively, a strategy jointly considering constraint violation probability and distance to existing virtual points is proposed, which improves virtual point optimization efficiency while preserving accuracy. Validation on two numerical examples and one real-world dataset confirms that physical knowledge integration enhances model accuracy and consistency.

Future work will focus on incorporating constraint information and virtual point position optimization into parameter estimation, investigating the effects of key parameters including maximum iterations and target constraint satisfaction on virtual point selection.

Acknowledgments. The authors acknowledge the support from Hunan Province Graduate Student Research Innovation Project under Grant No. CX20250012.

References

1. Agrell, C.: Gaussian processes with linear operator inequality constraints. J. Mach. Learn. Res. (2019)
2. Alvi, S.M.A.A., Janssen, J., Khatamsaz, D., Perez, D., Allaire, D., Arróyave, R.: Hierarchical gaussian process-based bayesian optimization for materials discovery in high entropy alloy spaces. Acta Materialia 120908 (2025). https://doi.org/10.1016/j.actamat.2025.120908
3. Cross, E.J., Rogers, T.J., Pitchforth, D.J., Gibson, S.J., Zhang, S., Jones, M.R.: A spectrum of physics-informed gaussian processes for regression in engineering. Data-Centric Eng. **5**, e8 (2024). https://doi.org/10.1017/dce.2024.2
4. Dalton, D., Husmeier, D., Gao, H.: Physics and lie symmetry informed gaussian processes. In: ICML (2024)
5. Dalton, D., Lazarus, A., Gao, H., Husmeier, D.: Boundary constrained gaussian processes for robust physics-informed machine learning of linear partial differential equations. J. Mach. Learn. Res. **25**(1), 272:13096–272:13156 (2025)
6. Gulian, M., Frankel, A., Swiler, L.: Gaussian process regression constrained by boundary value problems. Comput. Meth. Appl. Mech. Eng. **388**, 114117 (2022). https://doi.org/10.1016/j.cma.2021.114117
7. Karniadakis, G.E., Kevrekidis, I.G., Lu, L., Perdikaris, P., Wang, S., Yang, L.: Physics-informed machine learning. Nature Rev. Phys. **3**(6), 422–440 (2021). https://doi.org/10.1038/s42254-021-00314-5
8. Loeppky, J.L., Sacks, J., Welch, W.J.: Choosing the sample size of a computer experiment: a practical guide. Technometrics **51**(4), 366–376 (2009). https://doi.org/10.1198/TECH.2009.08040

9. López-Lopera, A.F., Bachoc, F., Durrande, N., Rohmer, J., Idier, D., Roustant, O.: Approximating gaussian process emulators with linear inequality constraints and noisy observations via MC and MCMC. In: Tuffin, B., L'Ecuyer, P. (eds.) MCQMC 2018. SPMS, vol. 324, pp. 363–381. Springer, Cham (2020). https://doi.org/10.1007/978-3-030-43465-6_18
10. López-Lopera, A.F., Bachoc, F., Durrande, N., Roustant, O.: Finite-dimensional gaussian approximation with linear inequality constraints. SIAM/ASA J. Uncertainty Quantif. **6**(3), 1224–1255 (2018). https://doi.org/10.1137/17M1153157
11. López-Lopera, A.F., Bachoc, F., Roustant, O.: High-dimensional additive gaussian processes under monotonicity constraints. In: NIPS (2022)
12. Marrel, A., Iooss, B.: Probabilistic surrogate modeling by gaussian process: a review on recent insights in estimation and validation. Reliab. Eng. Syst. Saf. **247**, 110094 (2024). https://doi.org/10.1016/j.ress.2024.110094
13. Menz, M., Dubreuil, S., Morio, J., Gogu, C., Bartoli, N., Chiron, M.: Variance based sensitivity analysis for monte Carlo and importance sampling reliability assessment with gaussian processes. Struct. Saf. **93**, 102116 (2021). https://doi.org/10.1016/j.strusafe.2021.102116
14. Pitchforth, D., Rogers, T., Tygesen, U., Cross, E.: Grey-box models for wave loading prediction. Mech. Syst. Signal Process. **159**, 107741 (2021). https://doi.org/10.1016/j.ymssp.2021.107741
15. Swiler, L., Gulian, M., Frankel, A., Safta, C., Jakeman, J.: A survey of constrained gaussian process regression: approaches and implementation challenges. J. Mach. Learn. Model. Comput. **1**(2), 119–156 (2020). https://doi.org/10.1615/JMachLearnModelComput.2020035155
16. Veiga, S.D., Marrel, A.: Gaussian process regression with linear inequality constraints. Reliab. Eng. Syst. Saf. **195**, 106732 (2020). https://doi.org/10.1016/j.ress.2019.106732
17. Willard, J., Jia, X., Xu, S., Steinbach, M., Kumar, V.: Integrating scientific knowledge with machine learning for engineering and environmental systems. ACM Comput. Surv. **55**(4), 66:1–66:37 (2022). https://doi.org/10.1145/3514228

A Surrogate Co-evolutionary Incremental Optimization Framework for Optical Cable Sheath Manufacturing

Yong Zhang, Senjie Xia, Jianzeng Song, and Jianfei Yin(✉)

Canghai Campus Nanshan District, Shenzhen University, Shenzhen, China
{zhangyong2023,xiasenjie2023,songjianzeng2023}@email.szu.edu.cn,
yjf@szu.edu.cn

Abstract. Process parameter optimization in optical cable sheath manufacturing is challenging due to highly nonlinear dynamics, strong parameter coupling, and expensive real-world evaluations. We propose a Surrogate Co-evolutionary Incremental Optimization (SCE-IO) framework that combines a task-specific multi-task surrogate model, namely the Optical Cable Sheath Objective Model (OCS-OM), with a Correlation-Guided NSGA-II (CG-NSGA-II) optimizer. To improve robustness under process drift, the framework further incorporates incremental updates using real production feedback. Experiments on real industrial datasets show that SCE-IO consistently outperforms representative baselines, achieving improvements of +38.61% in lean production and +43.63% in quality stability on the regular dataset. These results demonstrate the effectiveness of the proposed closed-loop optimization framework in dynamic manufacturing environments.

Keywords: Process parameter optimization · Multi-objective optimization · Surrogate-assisted evolutionary algorithm · Incremental learning · Optical cable sheath

1 Introduction

Process parameter optimization is a fundamental problem in manufacturing, as appropriate parameter configurations can significantly improve production efficiency, reduce material consumption, and enhance product quality stability [1,2]. In industrial scenarios such as optical cable sheath manufacturing, the relationship between process parameters and production quality is highly nonlinear and strongly coupled. Moreover, the true performance of a parameter configuration can only be verified through full production and inspection procedures, making real evaluations time-consuming and costly.

To alleviate the burden of expensive evaluations, surrogate-assisted optimization methods have been widely adopted. Black-box optimizers such as genetic algorithms (GA), differential evolution (DE), and Bayesian optimization (BO)

J. Niu et al. (Eds.): KSEM 2026, LNAI 16631, pp. 404–416, 2027.
https://doi.org/10.1007/978-981-92-2759-4_30

are commonly used to search for high-quality solutions under limited evaluation budgets [5,6]. However, these methods still face critical challenges in real industrial environments.

First, evolutionary algorithms are prone to premature convergence and local optima in strongly constrained and highly coupled parameter spaces. Second, most surrogate-assisted optimization frameworks rely on static surrogate models trained offline using historical data [3]. In practice, industrial processes often experience condition drift caused by equipment aging, material variability, and environmental fluctuations, which can significantly degrade surrogate reliability during optimization.

These issues are particularly severe in multi-objective process optimization, where conflicting objectives such as production efficiency and quality stability must be optimized simultaneously [4]. Static optimization strategies and fixed surrogate models often fail to maintain robust performance under such conditions.

To address these challenges, we propose a **Surrogate Co-evolutionary Incremental Optimization (SCE-IO)** framework for multi-objective process parameter optimization in optical cable sheath manufacturing. The proposed framework integrates surrogate-based objective evaluation, correlation-guided multi-objective evolutionary optimization, and real-feedback-driven incremental learning into a unified closed-loop process, enabling adaptive optimization under limited evaluation budgets and process condition drift.

Specifically, an **Optical Cable Sheath Objective Model (OCS-OM)** is constructed to approximate the multi-objective performance of candidate process parameter configurations. Based on OCS-OM, we develop a **Correlation-Guided NSGA-II (CG-NSGA-II)** algorithm that explicitly incorporates parameter correlation information into evolutionary operators, thereby reducing blind exploration and alleviating premature convergence. In addition, an incremental learning mechanism driven by real production feedback is employed to continuously refine OCS-OM during optimization.

The main contributions of this work are summarized as follows:

- We propose a Surrogate Co-evolutionary Incremental Optimization (SCE-IO) framework for multi-objective process parameter optimization in optical cable sheath manufacturing under limited evaluation budgets and process condition drift.
- We develop a Correlation-Guided NSGA-II (CG-NSGA-II) algorithm that integrates parameter correlation information into multi-objective evolutionary search, improving convergence behavior in strongly coupled parameter spaces.
- We design an Optical Cable Sheath Objective Model (OCS-OM), a task-specific surrogate evaluation model tailored for optical cable sheath manufacturing, to support reliable closed-loop multi-objective optimization.

2 Related Work

2.1 Traditional Black-Box Optimization Methods

Classical black-box optimization methods, including Bayesian Optimization (BO), Genetic Algorithms (GA), and Differential Evolution (DE), have been widely used for manufacturing parameter tuning. BO typically relies on surrogate models and acquisition functions to guide search, whereas GA and DE evolve candidate solutions through crossover, mutation, and selection [7,8]. However, these methods often struggle in highly nonlinear and strongly coupled industrial processes, especially under limited evaluation budgets. In contrast, our framework incorporates parameter correlation information from production data to guide search more effectively.

2.2 Regression and Machine-Learning-Based Frameworks

Regression- and learning-based frameworks aim to predict manufacturing outcomes or recommend process settings from historical data. Representative studies have been reported in extrusion, additive manufacturing, and process quality optimization [9–15]. Although these methods can capture parameter–quality relationships, their performance is often limited by small, imbalanced, or distribution-shifted industrial datasets. Our work instead builds a task-specific surrogate model for multi-objective optimization under such practical constraints.

2.3 Surrogate-Assisted Evolutionary Algorithms (SAEA)

Surrogate-assisted evolutionary algorithms (SAEA) reduce expensive evaluations by combining surrogate models with evolutionary search [3,16]. Existing studies have shown their effectiveness in industrial and multi-objective optimization scenarios [17–20]. However, most existing SAEA employ generic surrogate models and generic operators, which limits their ability to exploit process-specific parameter coupling. Our method integrates a task-oriented surrogate with correlation-guided evolutionary operators to improve robustness in complex industrial parameter spaces.

3 Problem Setting

3.1 Process Flow and Optimization Objectives

This study considers the extrusion-based production of optical cable sheaths in a batch manufacturing setting. Each batch is evaluated through quantitative inspections (e.g., sheath thickness and cable diameter) and qualitative pass/fail checks (e.g., fiber break and water penetration tests). The objective is to determine an optimal adjustable parameter vector $\mathbf{x} = [x_1, \ldots, x_5]$ under fixed production conditions so as to jointly optimize production efficiency and product quality. The task is therefore formulated as a multi-objective optimization problem.

3.2 Design of Evaluation Metrics

To quantitatively evaluate the performance of a given parameter configuration, two complementary and orthogonal evaluation metrics are designed: the *Lean Production Score* and the *Total Quality Score*. These metrics respectively capture the economic efficiency of the production process and the robustness of product quality, together forming the objective space of the multi-objective optimization problem.

Lean Production Score (S_{lean}). The Lean Production Score evaluates the cost-effectiveness of the manufacturing process by encouraging production outcomes that approach the lower bounds of allowable tolerance ranges while maintaining product qualification. This design reflects the industrial objective of minimizing material usage without violating quality constraints.

For quantitative inspection items with a bounded acceptance interval (e.g., $1.00 \le x \le 1.20$ mm for sheath thickness), the scoring function is based on a normal distribution model, where the score increases as the measured value approaches the lower tolerance limit:

$$s = 1 - \frac{\Phi(z) - \Phi(-3)}{\Phi(3) - \Phi(-3)}, \quad \text{where } z = \frac{x - \mu}{\sigma}, \tag{1}$$

where x denotes the measured value, μ and σ are the mean and standard deviation associated with the tolerance interval, z is the standardized score, and $\Phi(\cdot)$ represents the cumulative distribution function of the standard normal distribution.

For inspection items with a single-sided lower bound constraint (e.g., $x \ge L$), an exponential decay function is employed:

$$s = e^{-5d}, \quad \text{where } d = \frac{x - L}{L}. \tag{2}$$

The final Lean Production Score is computed as a weighted combination of the average inspection score $\bar{s}$ across all quantitative items and a base score:

$$S_{\text{lean}} = (1 - \omega_{\text{lean}}) + \omega_{\text{lean}} \cdot \bar{s}, \tag{3}$$

where ω_{lean} controls the relative contribution of inspection performance.

Total Quality Score (S_{qual}). The Total Quality Score provides a comprehensive assessment of product quality by jointly considering the stability of quantitative measurements and the reliability of pass/fail inspection outcomes. It consists of two components: a quantitative stability score (S_{quant}) and a robustness-aware pass-rate score based on the Wilson score interval (S_{wilson}).

Quantitative Stability Score (S_{quant}). For inspection items qualified by an acceptance interval, quality stability is evaluated by rewarding measurements closer to the center of the tolerance range, which indicates a well-controlled and stable process:

$$s = 1 - \frac{|\Phi(z) - \Phi(0)|}{\Phi(0) - \Phi(-3)}, \quad z = \frac{x - \mu}{\sigma}. \tag{4}$$

For single-sided or target-value inspection items, an exponential decay function is used to penalize deviations from the target value T:

$$s = e^{-5d}, \quad \text{where } d = \frac{|x - T|}{T}. \tag{5}$$

Wilson Score-Based Pass Rate (S_{wilson}). To robustly evaluate batch-level pass/fail inspections, the lower bound of the Wilson score confidence interval is employed. Compared with classical Wald intervals, the Wilson score provides more reliable estimates under small-sample and boundary conditions, which is critical in industrial quality assessment.

For k successful inspections out of n trials, the Wilson score lower bound is computed as:

$$W_{\text{lower}} = \max\left(0, \frac{\hat{p} + \frac{z^2}{2n}}{1 + \frac{z^2}{n}} - \frac{z}{1 + \frac{z^2}{n}} \sqrt{\frac{\hat{p}(1-\hat{p})}{n} + \frac{z^2}{4n^2}}\right), \tag{6}$$

where $\hat{p} = k/n$ and z denotes the standard normal quantile corresponding to the desired confidence level.

The final Total Quality Score is obtained by combining the two components:

$$S_{\text{qual}} = (1 - \omega_{\text{wilson}}) \cdot S_{\text{quant}} + \omega_{\text{wilson}} \cdot S_{\text{wilson}}, \tag{7}$$

where ω_{wilson} balances quantitative stability and pass-rate robustness.

3.3 Formal Multi-objective Problem Formulation

Given a set of fixed production conditions C, the process parameter optimization problem is formulated as a constrained multi-objective optimization task:

$$\max_{\mathbf{x}} \; \left(S_{\text{lean}}(\mathbf{x} \mid C), \; S_{\text{qual}}(\mathbf{x} \mid C)\right), \tag{8}$$

subject to

$$\mathbf{x}_{\text{min}} \leq \mathbf{x} \leq \mathbf{x}_{\text{max}}, \tag{9}$$

$$g_j(\mathbf{x}) \leq 0, \quad j = 1, \ldots, m, \tag{10}$$

where $\mathbf{x}_{\text{min}}$ and $\mathbf{x}_{\text{max}}$ denote parameter bounds, and $g_j(\cdot)$ represents process and safety constraints.

This formulation explicitly reflects the conflicting nature of economic efficiency and quality robustness, providing a principled foundation for the subsequent correlation-guided multi-objective optimization framework.

4 Methodology

4.1 Overall Framework of SCE-IO

The proposed Surrogate Co-evolutionary Incremental Optimization (SCE-IO) framework is established as a closed-loop system designed to achieve efficient multi-objective optimization under constrained evaluation budgets. As shown in Fig. 1, the architecture comprises two interconnected modules: the *surrogate search space* and the *offline verification space.*

In the surrogate search space, the OCS-OM provides rapid approximations of production objectives, while the CG-NSGA-II algorithm executes an efficient Pareto search to identify high-potential candidates. These solutions are subsequently processed in the offline verification space, where a subset is selected for real-world validation. The feedback from these inspections forms an incremental dataset used to update the OCS-OM online. This co-evolutionary mechanism ensures that the surrogate model adaptively aligns with actual production conditions, effectively mitigating performance degradation caused by process drift and ensuring long-term optimization reliability.

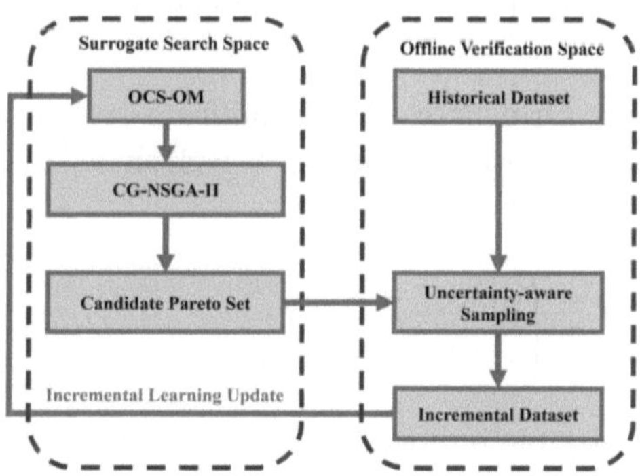

Fig. 1. Overall framework of the proposed SCE-IO.

4.2 Optical Cable Sheath Objective Model (OCS-OM)

To evaluate candidate configurations without the high cost of physical experiments, OCS-OM is developed as a high-fidelity surrogate model. It utilizes a Multi-Task Learning (MTL) architecture with a shared backbone for feature extraction and specialized output heads to capture the complex mappings between process parameters and heterogeneous production objectives.

The model takes process parameters $\mathbf{x} \in \mathbb{R}^d$ and production conditions $\mathbf{c}$ as inputs, outputting a multi-dimensional objective vector $\hat{\mathbf{y}} = [S_{lean}, S_{qual}]^T$. Here, S_{lean} represents the lean production score (characterizing economic efficiency) and S_{qual} represents the quality stability score (characterizing product robustness). By jointly modeling these conflicting objectives, OCS-OM captures the intrinsic physical coupling of the extrusion process, providing a continuous surrogate evaluation space for the subsequent evolutionary search.

4.3 Correlation-Guided Multi-objective Evolutionary Optimization

To solve the multi-objective optimization problem in strongly coupled parameter spaces, we adopt a correlation-guided extension of NSGA-II (CG-NSGA-II). CG-NSGA-II enhances standard evolutionary operators by incorporating process knowledge derived from historical data analysis.

1. Variable Importance Measure via GRA. To identify the critical variables dominating performance, we employ Grey Relational Analysis (GRA) to calculate a variable importance weight $w_i^{(k)}$ for the i-th variable at the k-th iteration:

$$w_i^{(k)} = \text{Normalize}\left(\frac{1}{m}\sum_{j=1}^{m}\xi_{i,j}^{(k)}\right) \tag{11}$$

where $\xi_{i,j}^{(k)}$ is the grey relational coefficient between the i-th variable and the j-th objective score.

2. Guided Crossover Operator. Unlike uniform crossover, our operator prioritizes the inheritance of critical features based on $w_i^{(k)}$. Given parents $\mathbf{x}^{(p_1)}$ and $\mathbf{x}^{(p_2)}$, the offspring's i-th variable $x_i^{(c)}$ is:

$$x_i^{(c)} = \begin{cases} x_i^{(p_1)}, & \text{if } r \leq w_i^{(k)}, \\ x_i^{(p_2)}, & \text{otherwise,} \end{cases} \qquad r \sim \mathcal{U}(0,1) \tag{12}$$

where r is a random variable uniformly sampled from $[0, 1]$.

3. Guided Mutation with Parameter Coupling. To maintain stability, we utilize Spearman correlation $\rho_{i,j}$ and historical standard deviation σ to perform coordinated mutations. When a primary parameter undergoes a perturbation Δx_i, its coupled parameter x_j is adjusted as:

$$\Delta x_j = \Delta x_i \cdot \rho_{i,j} \cdot \frac{\sigma_j}{\sigma_i} \tag{13}$$

Simultaneously, the mutation step size δ_i is constrained by the importance weight:

$$\delta_i \sim \mathcal{N}(0, (\alpha \cdot (u_i - l_i) \cdot w_i^{(k)})^2) \tag{14}$$

where $[l_i, u_i]$ denotes bounds and α is the mutation strength. This mechanism keeps the search focused on physically feasible and high-potential regions.

4.4 Incremental Learning and Co-evolution Mechanism

A key feature of the proposed SCE-IO framework is the co-evolution between the surrogate model and the optimization process. Instead of relying on a static surrogate trained offline, the framework incorporates an incremental learning mechanism driven by real production feedback.

At each optimization iteration, a subset of candidate solutions from the Pareto set is selected for offline verification based on model uncertainty and solution diversity. The corresponding true evaluation results are collected and appended to the incremental dataset. OCS-OM is then updated using both historical data and newly acquired samples, allowing the surrogate model to progressively refine its approximation accuracy in regions that are most relevant to the optimization task.

This closed-loop design effectively mitigates surrogate degradation caused by process condition drift and distribution mismatch. By continuously aligning the surrogate model with the evolving search trajectory, the proposed framework maintains reliable optimization guidance and supports long-term deployment in real industrial environments.

5 Experiments

5.1 Dataset Description

The dataset used in this study was obtained from an optical cable sheath manufacturing plant, containing real-world production data collected between June and December 2024. After rigorous data cleaning and aggregation, a total of 2,832 valid records were obtained, which we refer to as the **Regular Dataset**. To evaluate the performance of the proposed SCE-IO framework under limited evaluation budgets, the data is partitioned as follows: 1,556 records are used for the initial offline training of the surrogate model (OCS-OM), 389 records are allocated for testing, and an additional **500 records are reserved as a ground-truth pool for real production verification** during the co-evolutionary incremental learning process.

To investigate the optimization behavior under different manufacturing conditions, the Regular Dataset is divided into two subsets based on the median value of the quality stability score S_{qual}:

- **High-Quality dataset** (1,431 records): Represents stable operating conditions where the production process is already performing at a relatively high level.
- **Low-Quality dataset** (1,401 records): Represents operating conditions with significant room for optimization, where quality stability is currently below the median level.

The input vector for the optimization task is defined as $\mathbf{x}_{\text{in}} = [\text{MN, CD, SD, EN}]$, while the controllable process parameter vector is $\mathbf{x}_{\text{out}} = [\text{EIM, EOM, SS, SC, PS}]$.

5.2 Experimental Setup

To maintain consistency in industrial scenarios where evaluations are expensive, we set a unified **real evaluation budget** $B = 300$ for all iterative optimization methods. For population-based search, the configuration is standardized as **30/30/5**, representing a population size of 30, 30 evolutionary generations, and 5 co-evolutionary cycles. This setup ensures sufficient exploration of the parameter space while refining the surrogate model within the restricted budget.

5.3 Baseline Methods and Ablation Variants

To comprehensively evaluate the effectiveness of the proposed framework, we compare our method against representative baselines and its own ablation variants. For methods using static surrogate models without online updates, we use the prefix "SA-" (Surrogate-Assisted):

Regression and Static Optimization Baselines. We include process-specific models such as FDE for polymer flat-die extrusion [9], PEF for PLA extrusion parameter tuning [10], MAM for metal additive manufacturing surface roughness prediction [11], and CEF for cold extrusion optimization [12]. For advanced tabular learning, we compare with TabNet [21], SketchBoost [24], Condensed Gradient Boosting (CGB) [22], and JGPR for multi-target Gaussian process regression [23]. Furthermore, global search baselines using a static OCS-OM include SA-GA, SA-DE, SA-NSGA-II, and SA-MOEA/D.

The Proposed SCE-IO and Ablation Study. To analyze the contribution of each core component, we include the following three variants:

- **SCE-IO w/o Inc**: A variant that removes the incremental learning mechanism. It utilizes a static OCS-OM while retaining the correlation-guided search strategy.
- **SCE-IO w/o Cor**: A variant that retains incremental learning updates but removes the correlation-guided evolutionary operators (reverting to standard random mutation and crossover).
- **SCE-IO**: The full proposed framework, integrating both correlation-guided optimization and incremental learning to address process condition drifts.

5.4 Overall Performance Comparison

The experimental results on the three datasets are summarized in Table 1. Several key observations can be made from the comparison:

Superiority of SCE-IO. The proposed SCE-IO framework significantly outperforms all baseline methods across all datasets. On the Regular Dataset, SCE-IO achieves a **+38.61%** improvement in lean production (S_{lean}) and a **+43.63%** improvement in quality stability (S_{qual}), representing the best overall performance among all tested strategies. This confirms that the collaborative

Table 1. Performance improvement comparison on three datasets under a unified evaluation budget ($B = 300$).

Methods	Regular Dataset		HighQuality		LowQuality	
	S_{lean}	S_{qual}	S_{lean}	S_{qual}	S_{lean}	S_{qual}
FDE	+2.56%	+2.77%	+1.76%	-6.69%	+2.14%	+9.04%
PEF	+2.85%	+2.86%	+2.06%	-7.29%	+2.60%	+9.19%
MAM	+0.30%	+3.37%	+1.31%	-7.17%	+1.48%	+10.04%
CEF	+1.65%	+0.62%	+1.12%	-7.83%	+1.01%	+9.97%
CGB	+2.78%	+3.61%	+1.46%	-6.74%	+2.54%	+9.53%
TabNet	+2.53%	+2.47%	+1.88%	-7.90%	+1.97%	+9.35%
SketchBoost	+2.67%	+2.89%	+1.59%	-6.51%	+2.23%	+9.30%
JGPR	+2.06%	+3.29%	+1.53%	-6.99%	+2.25%	+9.75%
SA-GA	+18.56%	+4.29%	+20.16%	-9.97%	+18.27%	+15.48%
SA-DE	+18.56%	+4.57%	+20.19%	-9.67%	+18.42%	+15.89%
SA-NSGA-II	+19.32%	+9.42%	+20.78%	-5.61%	+19.23%	+21.04%
SA-MOEA/D	+19.23%	+8.34%	+20.52%	-6.15%	+19.22%	+19.64%
SCE-IO w/o Inc	+23.67%	+14.23%	+18.33%	-10.11%	+23.28%	+25.29%
SCE-IO w/o Cor	+27.04%	+32.12%	+19.56%	+8.49%	+22.34%	+34.75%
SCE-IO	**+38.61%**	**+43.63%**	**+34.70%**	**+15.03%**	**+29.84%**	**+49.36%**

mechanism between surrogate modeling and evolutionary search can effectively find superior process configurations within a limited evaluation budget.

Comparison with Static Baselines. Static optimization methods (SA-GA, SA-NSGA-II, etc.) show limited gains compared to SCE-IO. While they provide better results than simple regression-based recommendations, their performance is constrained by the initial offline surrogate. In contrast, SCE-IO leverages real production feedback to continuously refine its objective model, allowing it to navigate the search space more accurately.

5.5 Ablation Study and Mechanism Analysis

To investigate the contribution of the incremental learning and correlation-guided search, we analyze the performance of the ablation variants:

Impact of Incremental Learning (Inc). Comparing SCE-IO with *SCE-IO w/o Inc* reveals a substantial performance drop when the feedback loop is removed. On the Regular Dataset, the S_{qual} improvement decreases from 43.63% to 14.23%. This result demonstrates that incremental learning is crucial for correcting surrogate model bias and adapting to process condition drift, which is common in optical cable manufacturing.

Impact of Correlation Guidance (Cor). The variant *SCE-IO w/o Cor*, which uses standard mutation and crossover, achieves significantly lower improvements than the full SCE-IO. This confirms that explicitly incorporating parameter coupling (e.g., the physical link between screw speed and production velocity) helps the algorithm avoid blind exploration and focus on "physically feasible" high-potential regions, thereby accelerating convergence toward the true Pareto front.

5.6 Optimization Behavior Across Different Conditions

The optimization behavior varies notably between the **High-Quality** and **Low-Quality** datasets:

- **High-Quality Dataset:** In scenarios where the initial production state is already stable, most baseline methods struggle to improve S_{lean} without significantly sacrificing S_{qual} (showing negative gains as low as -10.11%). However, SCE-IO maintains a positive gain in both objectives (+34.70% and +15.03%), showing its robust trade-off capability.
- **Low-Quality Dataset:** For batches with poor initial quality, SCE-IO demonstrates a powerful "quality recovery" capability, boosting S_{qual} by **+49.36%**. This indicates that the knowledge-guided search is particularly effective at pulling the production state out of suboptimal zones and moving it toward the stable Pareto front.

6 Conclusion

This paper presented the SCE-IO framework for multi-objective process parameter optimization in optical cable sheath manufacturing. By coupling a task-specific surrogate model with correlation-guided search and incremental learning, the framework successfully addresses the limitations of expensive evaluations and process condition drift. Our experimental analysis across various production scenarios demonstrates that SCE-IO achieves a superior balance between material efficiency and quality robustness compared to static surrogate-assisted algorithms. Specifically, the correlation-guided operators effectively navigate the physically coupled parameter space, while incremental updates ensure the long-term reliability of the surrogate model. Future research will focus on improving the cross-equipment migration capabilities of the framework and incorporating additional safety constraints to further support industrial intelligent transformation.

References

1. Jones, J.: Big data analytics in industry 4.0: a systematic review of use cases, challenges, and future directions. Challenges Future Dir. (2024)
2. Tang, L., Meng, Y.: Data analytics and optimization for smart industry. Front. Eng. Manage. **8**(2), 157–171 (2021)

3. He, C., Zhang, Y., Gong, D., Ji, X.: A review of surrogate-assisted evolutionary algorithms for expensive optimization problems. Expert Syst. Appl. **217**, 119495 (2023)
4. Antony, J.: Design of Experiments for Engineers and Scientists. Elsevier (2023)
5. Storn, R., Price, K.: Differential evolution–a simple and efficient heuristic for global optimization over continuous spaces. J. Global Optim. **11**(4), 341–359 (1997)
6. Holland, J.H.: Adaptation in Natural and Artificial Systems: An Introductory Analysis with Applications to Biology, Control, and Artificial Intelligence. MIT Press (1992)
7. Snoek, J., Larochelle, H., Adams, R.P.: Practical bayesian optimization of machine learning algorithms. In: Advances in Neural Information Processing Systems, vol. 25 (2012)
8. Shahriari, B., Swersky, K., Wang, Z., Adams, R.P., de Freitas, N.: Taking the human out of the loop: a review of Bayesian optimization. Proc. IEEE **104**(1), 148–175 (2016)
9. Zhang, Y., Zhang, H., Long, T.: Implementation of machine learning in flat die extrusion of polymers. Molecules **30**(9), 1879 (2025)
10. Shah, M., Bianchi, A., Conti, L.: Machine learning-based time series analysis of polylactic acid bead foam extrusion. J. Appl. Polym. Sci. **141**(7), 1452 (2024)
11. So, M.S., Seo, G.J., Kim, D.B., Shin, J.-H.: Prediction of metal additively manufactured surface roughness using deep neural network. Sensors **22**(20), 7955 (2022)
12. Chen, L., Wang, J., Li, F.: A framework for prediction of extrusion responses using machine learning algorithms. Int. J. Adv. Manuf. Technol. **124**, 4159–4174 (2023)
13. Yin, X., Niu, Z., He, Z., Li, Z.S., Lee, D.: An integrated computational intelligence technique based operating parameters optimization scheme for quality improvement oriented process-manufacturing system. Comput. Ind. Eng. **140**, 106284 (2020)
14. Chia, H.Y., Wu, J., Wang, X., Yan, W.: Process parameter optimization of metal additive manufacturing: a review and outlook. J. Mater. Inf. **2**(4), (2022)
15. Panico, A., Corvi, A., Collini, L., et al.: Multi objective optimization of FDM 3D printing parameters set via design of experiments and machine learning algorithms. Sci. Rep. **15**(1), 16753 (2025)
16. Díaz-Manríquez, A., Nguyen, T.T., Sato, H., Ishibuchi, H.: A review of surrogate-assisted multi-objective evolutionary algorithms. Inf. Sci. **332**, 209–236 (2016)
17. Garate-Perez, E., de Calle-Etxabe, K.L., Ferreiro, S.: Data-driven differential evolution in tire industry extrusion: leveraging surrogate models. arXiv preprint arXiv:2507.11191 (2025)
18. Liang, J., Lou, Y., Yu, M., et al.: A survey of surrogate-assisted evolutionary algorithms for expensive optimization. J. Membrane Comput. 1–20 (2024)
19. Yu, M., Ye, S., Li, J.: A two-stage dominance-based surrogate-assisted evolution algorithm for high-dimensional expensive multi-objective optimization. Sci. Rep. **13**, 40019 (2023)
20. Aghaeipour, P., Hakanen, J., Hartikainen, M.: A surrogate-assisted a priori multi-objective evolutionary algorithm for constrained multiobjective optimization problems. J. Global Optim. **90**(2), 383–408 (2024)
21. Arik, S.Ö., Pfister, T.: Tabnet: attentive interpretable tabular learning. Proc. AAAI Conf. Artif. Intell. **35**(8), 6679–6687 (2021)
22. Emami, S., Martínez-Muñoz, G.: Condensed-gradient boosting. Int. J. Mach. Learn. Cybern. **16**(1), 687–701 (2025)

23. Nabati, M., Ghorashi, S.A., Shahbazian, R.: JGPR: a computationally efficient multi-target Gaussian process regression algorithm. Mach. Learn. **111**(6), 1987–2010 (2022)
24. Iosipoi, L., Vakhrushev, A.: Sketchboost: fast gradient boosted decision tree for multioutput problems. Adv. Neural. Inf. Process. Syst. **35**, 25422–25435 (2022)

SWDNet: Knowledge-Driven Cross-Modal Network with Sliding Window Difference Modeling

Junjie Huang and Renping Xie(✉)

School of Computer Science and Technology, Dongguan University of Technology, Dongguan 523808, China
{junjiehuang,xierenping}@dgut.edu.cn

Abstract. Effective representation and reasoning over cross-modal knowledge are essential for achieving reliable scene understanding in visually degraded environments. However, unimodal smoke segmentation models often fail to exploit the complementary characteristics of infrared and visible images, leading to suboptimal performance under smoke interference. To address this issue, we present SWDNet, a knowledge-driven cross-modal network equipped with sliding window difference modeling. Specifically, by leveraging the robustness of infrared images against smoke interference, we design a sliding window-based difference measurement module to capture semantic discrepancies between the infrared and visible modalities. Subsequently, we introduce a window attention mechanism to focus on and extract regions with significant inter-modal differences. Finally, we develop a ternary collaborative loss function to enhance cross-modal semantic consistency, thereby improving segmentation performance by fully utilizing complementary modality information. Experimental results show that the proposed method achieves superior performance over several compared methods on benchmark datasets, demonstrating its effectiveness and robustness in complex scenarios.

Keywords: Smoke segmentation · Infrared and visible images · Difference modeling · Sliding window

1 Introduction

Smoke segmentation is an important task in computer vision with applications in forest fire monitoring, industrial safety management, and urban emergency response. Since smoke typically emerges before open flames, accurately identifying smoke regions plays a critical role in early hazard awareness. Traditional visible-light–based approaches depend heavily on color or texture cues, but they often generalize poorly when smoke shares similar visual patterns with the background or exhibits low-contrast boundaries. Deep learning has improved adaptability and semantic understanding, yet remains limited by the inherent constraints of visible-light imaging alone. To obtain more reliable representations

J. Niu et al. (Eds.): KSEM 2026, LNAI 16631, pp. 417–429, 2027.
https://doi.org/10.1007/978-981-92-2759-4_31

of semi-transparent smoke, recent research has highlighted the importance of cross-modal knowledge integration, where different sensing modalities encode complementary aspects of scene information [1,2]. Infrared imagery preserves thermal radiation cues and is less susceptible to smoke-induced scattering, while visible images provide fine-grained textures and structural details that infrared lacks. However, most existing fusion methods rely primarily on shallow concatenation or decision-level integration, without explicitly modeling the cross-modal knowledge discrepancy or performing deep semantic reasoning about modality-specific information contributions.

To address these limitations, this paper proposes a knowledge-driven cross-modal smoke segmentation framework based on sliding-window difference modeling. The proposed SWDC module constructs a multi-dimensional difference metric function within local windows, effectively capturing the semantic difference features of smoke between infrared and visible images. Building upon this difference modeling, a window-based attention mechanism is employed to generate difference maps and attention weight maps, which guide the encoder and decoder to focus on regions with significant modality discrepancies. This guidance is further reinforced by a KL divergence-driven loss function that enforces consistency constraints on the differences, ultimately yielding accurate smoke segmentation with clear boundaries and detailed structural representations.

In this paper, our main contributions can be summarised in the following two aspects:

- This paper proposes the SWDC model, which constructs a multi-dimensional difference measurement function to capture the semantic difference features between infrared and visible modalities. This approach significantly enhances the segmentation accuracy of blurred areas at smoke boundaries.
- Based on cross-entropy loss, Dice loss, and semantic difference terms driven by KL divergence, a difference-aware ternary collaborative loss function is constructed. When combined with a dynamic optimization mechanism, this function enhances the capabilities of cross-modal semantic consistency representation.

The rest of the paper is structured as follows: Sect. 2 reviews related work. Section 3 presents the proposed method. The experimental analysis is given in Sect. 4, and Sect. 5 concludes the paper with future enhancement.

2 Related Works

2.1 Smoke Segmentation in Visible Images

Early smoke segmentation relied on handcrafted features and physical priors, but these methods lacked robustness in complex scenes. Deep learning-based approaches have addressed these limitations by automatically learning semantic representations. For instance, CCENet [3] introduces multidirectional convolutions and count-prior embedding to model global smoke distributions. Subsequent research has explored edge-aware optimization, multi-level feature fusion, and lightweight designs. EANet [4] enhances boundary precision through channel attention and boundary loss, while MsFireDNet [5] focuses on parameter efficiency for low-power platforms. Hybrid Transformer-CNN models [6] and multiscale frameworks such as MIFNet [7], further improve segmentation by integrating global context with fine-grained details. Nevertheless, key challenges remain in multimodal fusion, domain generalization, and adaptation to extreme conditions, necessitating continued innovation in this field.

2.2 Semantic Segmentation with Visible-Infrared Fusion

Visible-infrared image fusion has become essential for semantic segmentation, addressing the limitations of single-modality methods in complex environments characterized by lighting variations, occlusions, and blurred boundaries. Recent approaches leverage modality complementarity via structural modeling, generative strategies, and attention mechanisms. For instance, DSTCFuse [8] enhances fusion coherence through dual-cycle adversarial learning and structural tensor constraints, while SOSMaskFuse [9] introduces salient object masks and an IMV-F strategy to effectively mitigate infrared noise while preserving visible texture details. Beyond adversarial and attention-driven designs, architectural innovations such as dual-encoder frameworks and multiscale modeling have also shown promise. RTFNet [10] improves feature-level fusion, while physics-based and target-based methods, including TarDAL [11] and material-based CRF models [12] further enhance generalization in real-world scenarios. Nevertheless, many existing approaches still rely on shallow fusion and fail to effectively model deep semantic interactions between modalities [13].

2.3 Sliding Window-Based Approaches

The sliding window approach, a classical local modeling strategy, effectively captures localized spatial and temporal features, demonstrating broad applicability across image processing, computer vision, and sequential analysis. In image analysis, it has been utilized for multi-scale sub-sampling to enhance classification sensitivity in medical imaging [14], and integrated with frequency-domain modeling to improve image dehazing performance [15]. More recently, the sliding window paradigm has inspired architectural innovations such as the Swin Transformer [16], which employs hierarchical self-attention for dense prediction tasks. Beyond vision, sliding window strategies have improved sequential modeling and industrial monitoring, being combined with recurrent neural networks for energy disaggregation [17] or adaptive singular value decomposition for fault detection [18,19]. Despite these advances, sliding-window mechanisms remain unexplored in smoke segmentation.

3 The Proposed Method

To fully exploit the complementary advantages of infrared and visible modalities, we propose a sliding-window difference-driven cross-modal smoke segmentation network (SWDNet), whose overall framework is illustrated in Fig. 1. The network utilizes the classical U-Net [20] as its backbone and incorporates a difference measurement module (SWDC) to enhance the understanding of heterogeneous features between the infrared and visible modalities.

SWDNet adopts an encoder-decoder-based cross-modal smoke segmentation framework, in which a cross-modal difference modeling mechanism is incorporated as auxiliary guidance. The encoder takes the visible image as input and progressively extracts multi-scale semantic features via hierarchical downsampling to build robust structural and contextual representations. To leverage the structural robustness of the infrared modality, the proposed SWDC module jointly processes the visible image and the corresponding-scale infrared image. Within local sliding windows, the two modalities are spatially aligned, and their discrepancies are characterized in terms of magnitude difference, directional consistency, and structural sparsity, yielding a difference representation map.

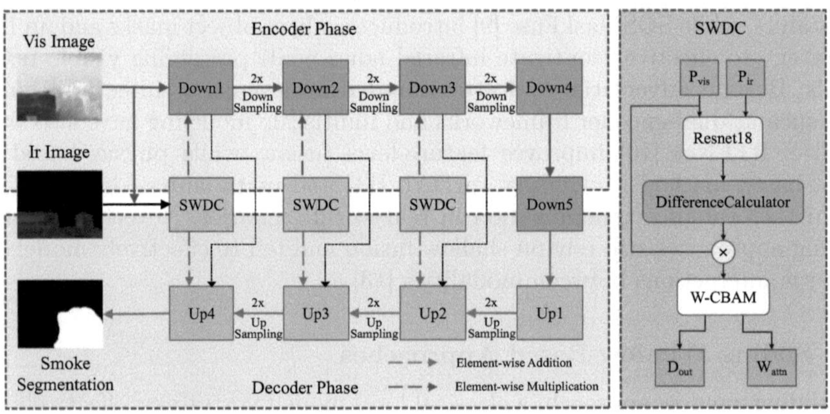

Fig. 1. The framework of the proposed smoke segmentation network.

On top of this difference modeling, a window-based cross-modal interaction enhancement module, W-CBAM [21], is embedded into the SWDC module. The difference map is used as guidance to perform localized attention modeling across channel and spatial dimensions. Through window partitioning and difference-guided interaction, it adaptively enhances the responses of regions with significant modality discrepancies and highlights structural details such as smoke boundaries and blurry textures. Finally, SWDNet feeds the enhanced difference representations and attention weights back into the encoder–decoder structure, where multi-scale semantic interaction and structural integration are achieved via skip connections, yielding more accurate smoke segmentation results.

3.1 SWDC Module

To capture the cross-modal semantic differences between visible and infrared modalities, this study proposes a difference measurement module based on a sliding window approach. The module adopts a sliding-window mechanism to model cross-modal semantic differences within local regions, enabling the network to identify modality inconsistencies related to smoke. The overall process is organized into two distinct stages.

Sliding Window Tri-Metric Difference Modeling. The SWDC module employs a sliding window strategy to characterize local modal differences across multiple semantic dimensions. Specifically, the module first receives visible and infrared feature maps F_{vis} and F_{ir} extracted by the ResNet18 backbone network. It simultaneously captures local regions P_{vis} and P_{ir} within a sliding window of size $S \times S$ and stride T. The values of the window size S and stride T are empirically determined through extensive experiments to achieve a balance between segmentation accuracy and computational efficiency. To characterize multi-dimensional semantic differences between different modalities, the module adopts a triadic metric formulation that jointly considers intensity variation, structural deviation, and directional inconsistency between modalities, allowing the difference representation to remain sensitive to both intensity degradation and spatial structural deformation commonly induced by smoke:

$$D_{i,j} = \alpha \cdot \|P_{\text{vis}}^{i,j} - P_{\text{ir}}^{i,j}\|_2 + \beta \cdot \|P_{\text{vis}}^{i,j} - P_{\text{ir}}^{i,j}\|_1 + \gamma \cdot \left(1 - \frac{P_{\text{vis}}^{i,j} \cdot P_{\text{ir}}^{i,j}}{\|P_{\text{vis}}^{i,j}\| \, \|P_{\text{ir}}^{i,j}\|}\right), \tag{1}$$

where α, β, γ are learnable weights that balance the contributions of the three difference metrics, optimized jointly with the network via backpropagation and constrained to be non-negative for stable modeling. $P_{vis}^{i,j}, P_{ir}^{i,j}$ denote the local feature patches of size $S \times S$ for visible and infrared modalities, respectively, extracted at sliding window position (i, j). The output $D_{i,j}$ represents the multi-dimensional semantic difference within the local window, providing the foundation for subsequent cross-modal interaction.

Sliding Window Cross-Modal Feature Fusion. To further emphasize cross-modal discrepancies in smoke regions, we extend the Convolutional Block Attention Module into a window-based cross-modal interaction enhancement module, denoted as W-CBAM. This module uses the difference map D as an interaction-guiding signal to implement local attention modeling in both channel and spatial branches. Specifically, in the difference injection pathway, the difference map is concatenated with the intermediate feature maps to provide explicit discrepancy cues, forming D_{out}. In parallel, the difference guidance pathway generates attention weights W_{attn} by modulating the feature responses based on difference-driven signals, enhancing the representation of regions with significant modal differences. By combining the element-wise product of W_{attn} and the original feature F with D_{out}, the network produces the updated feature representation F', expressed as:

$$F' = W_{attn} \odot F + D_{out}, \tag{2}$$

These enhanced features are then fed back to the encoder and decoder through skip connections, enabling multi-scale semantic interaction and structural integration, which allows the network to more accurately capture smoke boundaries and blurred textures for precise segmentation results.

3.2 Loss Function

For binary smoke segmentation, the entire optimization process is guided by a triadic collaborative loss that integrates cross-entropy, dice, and difference-aware constraints. The combined loss is defined as:

$$L_{Total} = \lambda_1 L_{CE} + \lambda_2 L_{Dice} + \lambda_3 L_{DAL}, \tag{3}$$

where the three components collectively enhance pixel-wise accuracy, structural fidelity, and cross-modal semantic consistency. The weighting factors λ_1, λ_2, and λ_3 modulate the relative importance of each loss term, enabling the overall objective to simultaneously maintain pixel-level accuracy, preserve structural completeness, and enhance modality-sensitive discrimination in regions influenced by smoke-induced degradation.

The cross-entropy loss L_{CE} provides a fundamental pixel-level supervision signal by penalizing deviations between the predicted probability and the binary ground truth label. It is formulated as:

$$L_{CE} = -\frac{1}{N} \sum_{i=1}^{N} \left[y_i \log(p_i) + (1 - y_i) \log(1 - p_i) \right], \tag{4}$$

where p_i denotes the predicted probability at pixel i, and $y_i \in \{0, 1\}$ represents the corresponding annotation.

The dice loss L_{Dice} complements the cross-entropy term by emphasizing global region-level coherence and mitigating the imbalance between smoke and non-smoke pixels. It is expressed as:

$$L_{Dice} = 1 - \frac{2 \sum_{i=1}^{N} p_i y_i + \epsilon}{\sum_{i=1}^{N} p_i + \sum_{i=1}^{N} y_i + \epsilon}. \tag{5}$$

To further incorporate cross-modal semantic cues derived from visible and infrared images, a difference-aware loss L_{DAL} is employed. This loss leverages the normalized modality-difference map as a spatial prior and enforces probabilistic alignment between this prior and the predicted confidence distribution. By adopting a KL-divergence–based formulation, the model adaptively focuses on ambiguity-prone regions exhibiting substantial modality discrepancies. The loss is defined as:

$$L_{DAL} = \sum_{i=1}^{N} D_i \log\left(\frac{D_i}{p_i + \varepsilon}\right), \tag{6}$$

where D_i denotes the normalized difference-map value at pixel i, and p_i is the predicted probability at that location.

4 Experimental Results and Analysis

4.1 Experiments Setup

Experiments were conducted on a server with an Intel® Xeon® Platinum 8352V CPU @2.10 GHz processor and two NVIDIA GeForce RTX 3090 GPUs. using the PyTorch 1.10.0 framework. We utilized the DSSR cross-modal dataset [22], which comprises 2000 aligned visible-infrared image pairs with pixel-level smoke segmentation annotations. The models were trained for 100 epochs using the SGD optimizer (momentum 0.9, weight decay 0.0001) with a batch size of 4 and an initial learning rate of 0.01. Segmentation performance and computational efficiency were evaluated using mIoU, mPA, Recall, F1-score, FPS, Params, and FLOPs.

4.2 Comprehensive Experiment

To validate the performance of SWDNet, we selected seven semantic segmentation models, including Semask-Maskformer [23], SmokeSeger [6], PIDNet [24], MDRNet [25], CAINet [26], SGFNet [27] and EAEFNet [28]. We conducted visual tests on the DSSR dataset [22] and a subset of M^3FD dataset. The M^3FD dataset contains 300 images, of which 26 include smoke. We selected 15 images with relatively clear smoke regions for evaluation to ensure reliable annotation.

Qualitative Comparison. In high-contrast scenarios (rows 1–2 of Fig. 2), most methods localize smoke regions, but SeMask and PIDNet show incomplete boundaries. Although MDRNet, CAINet, SGFNet, and EAEFNet show improved contour preservation, they still lack consistency in fine details. In comparison, our method demonstrate superior performance in edge retention and structural recovery, with predictions closely matching the ground truth.

In low-contrast or complex background scenarios (rows 3–5 of Figs. 2 and 3), SeMask, SmokeSeger, and PIDNet commonly suffer from misclassification or missed detection. While MDRNet, CAINet, SGFNet, and EAEFNet partially mitigate these issues by incorporating dual-modal features, their handling of transitional regions between smoke and background remains inadequate. By leveraging a cross-modal difference guidance mechanism, the proposed method effectively fuses visible and thermal infrared features, significantly improving

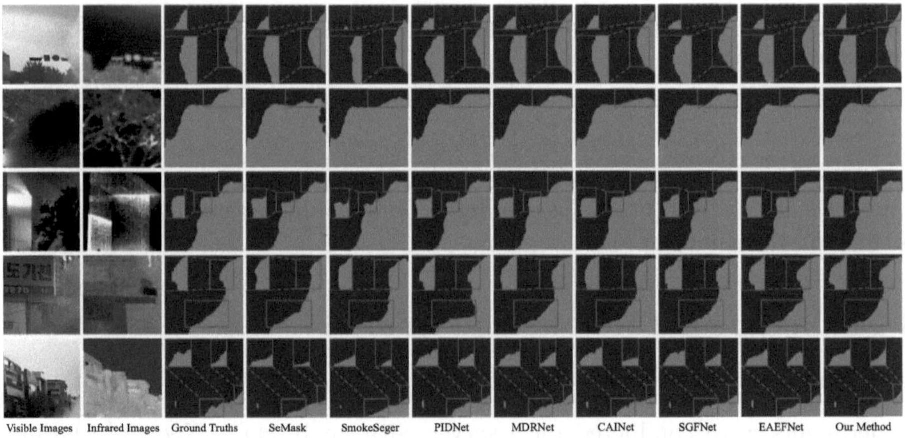

Fig. 2. Visual comparison of the proposed method with seven state-of-the-art methods on the DSSR dataset, and the purple mask indicates smoke pixels.

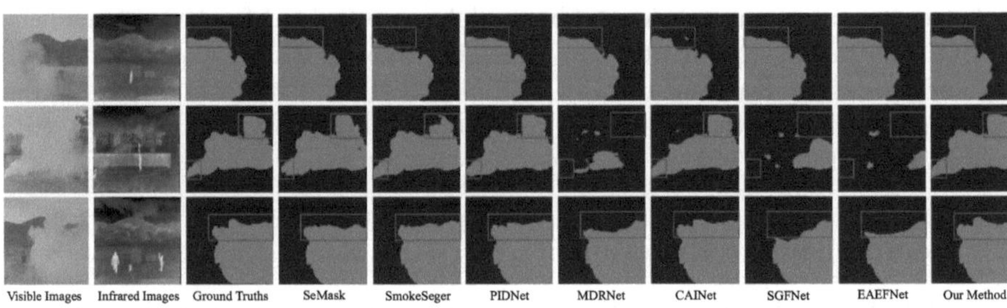

Fig. 3. Visual comparison of the proposed method with seven state-of-the-art methods on the M^3FD dataset.

boundary accuracy and regional integrity. In summary, the proposed method exhibits stronger robustness and segmentation accuracy across diverse scenarios, demonstrating notable advantages in addressing challenges such as blurred boundaries and semantic ambiguity.

Quantitative Comparison. Table 1 reports the results of the quantitative comparison on the DSSR dataset. In general, our proposed SWDNet performs the best in all four core metrics, reaching 84.5% in mIoU, 94.3% in F1-score, 97.9% in Recall and 87.6% in mPA, outperforming the other seven state-of-the-art methods. In terms of efficiency, SWDNet also demonstrates clear advantages: it achieves 121.6 FPS, only slightly lower than lightweight PIDNet, while significantly surpassing heavy models such as SeMask, MDRNet, and EAEFNet. Moreover, the model remains compact with only 15.6M parameters and 4.9G FLOPs, much smaller than SmokeSeger and CAINet.

Table 1. Performance comparison of metrics with state-of-the-art methods on the DSSR dataset.

Method	mIoU(%)	mPA(%)	F1(%)	FPS	Params(M)	FLOPs(G)
SeMask [23]	80.2	86.4	93.1	43.8	215.3	18.7
SmokeSeger [6]	81.0	85.1	92.4	93.2	31.6	50.9
PIDNet [24]	80.5	82.6	92.5	**137.8**	**7.7**	**0.4**
MDRNet [25]	81.2	86.5	93.6	27.4	210.8	30.0
CAINet [26]	80.2	86.6	93.1	87.8	23.8	61.8
SGFNet [27]	81.6	86.4	93.0	42.6	125.2	7.8
EAEFNet [28]	80.0	86.7	93.4	24.9	126.2	10.6
SWDNet	**84.5**	**87.6**	**94.3**	121.6	15.6	4.9

Table 2. Performance comparison of metrics with state-of-the-art methods on the M^3FD dataset.

Method	mIoU(%)	mPA(%)	F1(%)	FPS	Params(M)	FLOPs(G)
SeMask [23]	49.5	63.3	44.4	9.6	215.3	18.7
SmokeSeger [6]	47.6	58.1	42.6	7.3	31.6	50.9
PIDNet [24]	39.0	59.7	44.1	**88.5**	**7.7**	**0.4**
MDRNet [25]	36.9	50.0	35.6	5.2	210.8	30.0
CAINet [26]	**53.5**	**72.3**	**58.1**	37.0	23.8	61.8
SGFNet [27]	35.8	55.1	43.5	4.1	125.2	7.8
EAEFNet [28]	37.6	56.5	40.2	8.0	126.2	10.6
SWDNet	51.6	71.6	56.3	84.0	15.6	4.9

Similarly, Table 2 presents the quantitative comparison results on the M^3FD dataset. As shown, the proposed SWDNet achieves competitive performance across multiple evaluation metrics, demonstrating both high segmentation accuracy and strong computational efficiency. Specifically, SWDNet attains 51.6% mIoU and 71.6% mPA, surpassing several state-of-the-art models such as SGFNet and EAEFNet, and approaching the performance of the more complex CAINet. Meanwhile, the model maintains a balanced trade-off between accuracy and speed, achieving 56.3% F1-score with a real-time inference rate of 84.0 FPS. In terms of efficiency, SWDNet contains only 15.6 M parameters and requires 4.9 G FLOPs, which is significantly lower than most high-performing competitors including SeMask and CAINet, confirming its strong potential for deployment on edge and embedded devices.

4.3 Ablation Studies

To validate the contribution of the differential perception mechanism to cross-modal consistency, we designed ablation experiments from two perspectives: network structure and loss function.

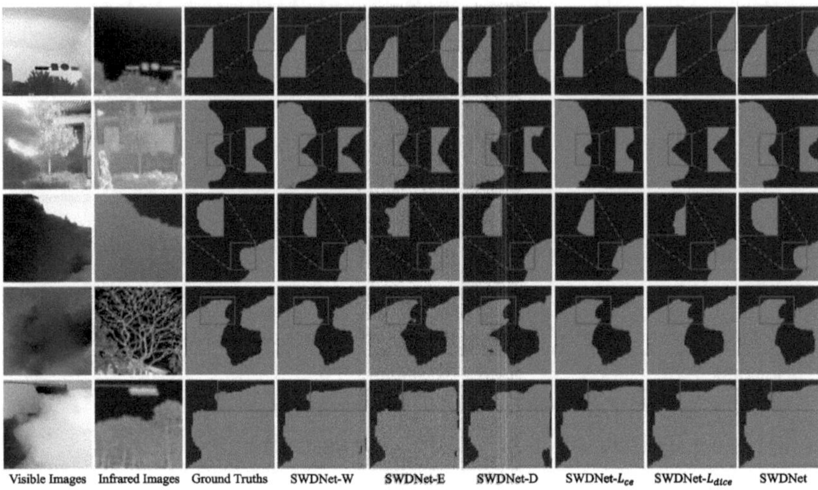

Fig. 4. Visual performance comparison for each ablation methods of the SWDNet framework on DSSR dataset.

Network Structure Analysis. At the architectural level, SWDNet-W denotes the variant without the W-CBAM module(W/o W), SWDNet-E removes the difference-map-guided component in the encoder(W/o E), and SWDNet-D excludes the attention-guided component in the decoder(W/o D). As illustrated by the qualitative results in Fig. 4, SWDNet demonstrates superior segmentation performance, especially in complex boundary regions. The red boxes highlight that SWDNet provides smoother and more accurate smoke boundaries compared to its variants. In contrast, SWDNet-W shows weaker response to detailed structures, while SWDNet-E and SWDNet-D yield less precise boundaries.

As shown in Table 3, the complete model SWDNet achieves the best performance in all accuracy-related metrics, with an mIoU of 84.5%, mPA of 87.6%, and F1-score of 94.3%, consistently outperforming all ablation variants. These results confirm that both the difference guidance and W-CBAM module significantly contribute to cross-modal consistency.

Table 3. Performance comparison for network structure and loss function ablation of the proposed SWDNet on the DSSR dataset.

Metric	Network Structure Ablation				Loss Function Ablation	
	W/o W	W/o E	W/o D	Ours	L_{CE}	$L_{CE} + L_{Dice}$
mIoU(%)	82.2	79.4	80.0	**84.5**	81.2	82.6
mPA(%)	84.2	85.6	85.7	**87.6**	–	–
F1(%)	92.7	93.2	93.3	**94.3**	91.6	92.6

Loss Function Analysis. At the loss-function level, three comparative experiments are designed to validate the effectiveness of the proposed triplet collaborative loss, including: using only the cross-entropy loss L_{CE}, jointly using L_{CE} and the dice loss L_{Dice}, and adopting the complete triplet loss. As shown in Table 3, when only using L_{CE}, the mIoU and F1-score are 81.2% and 91.6%, respectively. With the addition of the difference-aware loss L_{DAL}, the mIoU increases to 84.5% and the F1-score reaches 94.3%. From the qualitative results shown in Fig. 4, compared with SWDNet-L_{ce} (using only L_{CE}) and SWDNet-L_{dice} (using $L_{CE} + L_{Dice}$), the SWDNet achieves the best performance in terms of smoke boundary restoration and region integrity. The overall results indicate that the joint effect of difference map guidance and the KL divergence-based semantic discrepancy term reinforces cross-modal consistency modeling through both feature alignment and semantic constraint.

5 Conclusion

In this paper, we proposed SWDNet, a knowledge-driven sliding-window difference-modeling cross-modal smoke segmentation framework. The proposed model effectively leverages the complementary characteristics of both infrared and visible modalities. Specifically, it utilizes a sliding-window difference measurement module and a window attention mechanism to capture and emphasize cross-modal semantic discrepancies. To jointly promote cross-modal semantic consistency, we propose a difference-aware ternary loss function. Experimental results on the DSSR dataset and M^3FD dataset demonstrate that our method achieves superior performance over several compared methods, validating the effectiveness of the proposed difference measurement module in enhancing smoke segmentation accuracy. In future work, we will concentrate on model lightweighting and real-time optimization to enable efficient deployment in resource-constrained edge devices and large-scale intelligent perception systems.

References

1. Chen, Z., Tao, M., Xie, R., Nie, H., Chen, Q.: Mdp-eec: model distillation and partitioning enhanced end-edge collaboration computing for consumer electronics. IEEE Trans. Consum. Electron. (2025)
2. Tao, M., Su, L., Nie, H., Xie, R., Xu, X., Yu, J.: Collaborative neuro-fuzzy in edge-ai for industrial fault diagnosis with sensing data fusion. IEEE Trans. Comput. Soc. Syst. (2026)
3. Yuan, F., Dong, Z., Zhang, L., Xia, X., Shi, J.: Cubic-cross convolutional attention and count prior embedding for smoke segmentation. Pattern Recogn. **131**, 108902 (2022)
4. Zhang, L., Yuan, F., Xia, X.: Edge-reinforced attention network for smoke semantic segmentation. Multimedia Tools Appl. **82**(20), 31259–31284 (2023)
5. Hossain, F.A., Zhang, Y.: Msfired-net: a lightweight and efficient convolutional neural network for flame and smoke segmentation. J. Autom. Intell. **2**(3), 130–138 (2023)
6. Jing, T., Meng, Q.H., Hou, H.R.: Smokeseger: a transformer-cnn coupled model for urban scene smoke segmentation. IEEE Trans. Industr. Inf. **20**(2), 1385–1396 (2023)
7. Li, K., Yuan, F., Wang, C.: An effective multi-scale interactive fusion network with hybrid transformer and cnn for smoke image segmentation. Pattern Recogn. **159**, 111177 (2025)
8. Li, X., Chen, R., Wang, J., Ma, L., Cheng, L., Yuan, H.: Dstcfuse: a method based on dual-cycled cross-awareness of structure tensor for semantic segmentation via infrared and visible image fusion. In: Proceedings of the IEEE/CVF Conference on Computer Vision and Pattern Recognition, pp. 5558–5567 (2024)
9. Li, G., Qian, X., Qu, X.: Sosmaskfuse: an infrared and visible image fusion architecture based on salient object segmentation mask. IEEE Trans. Intell. Transp. Syst. **24**(9), 10118–10137 (2023)
10. Sun, Y., Zuo, W., Liu, M.: Rtfnet: Rgb-thermal fusion network for semantic segmentation of urban scenes. IEEE Robot. Autom. Lett. **4**(3), 2576–2583 (2019)
11. Liu, J., et al.: Target-aware dual adversarial learning and a multi-scenario multi-modality benchmark to fuse infrared and visible for object detection. In: Proceedings of the IEEE/CVF Conference on Computer Vision and Pattern Recognition, pp. 5802–5811 (2022)
12. Salamati, N., Larlus, D., Csurka, G., Süsstrunk, S.: Semantic image segmentation using visible and near-infrared channels. In: European Conference on Computer Vision, pp. 461–471. Springer (2012)
13. Tao, M.: Semantic ontology enabled modeling, retrieval and inference for incomplete mobile trajectory data. Futur. Gener. Comput. Syst. **145**, 1–11 (2023)
14. Haryanto, T., Suhartanto, H., Arymurthy, A.M., Kusmardi, K.: Conditional sliding windows: an approach for handling data limitation in colorectal histopathology image classification. Inf. Med. Unlocked **23**, 100565 (2021)
15. Feng, Y., Meng, X., Zhou, F., Lin, W., Su, Z.: Real-world non-homogeneous haze removal by sliding self-attention wavelet network. IEEE Trans. Circuits Syst. Video Technol. **33**(10), 5470–5485 (2023)
16. Liu, Z., et al.: Swin transformer: Hierarchical vision transformer using shifted windows. In: Proceedings of the IEEE/CVF International Conference on Computer Vision, pp. 10012–10022 (2021)

17. Krystalakos, O., Nalmpantis, C., Vrakas, D.: Sliding window approach for online energy disaggregation using artificial neural networks. In: Proceedings of the 10th Hellenic Conference on Artificial Intelligence, pp. 1–6. (2018)
18. Qin, Y., Yan, Y., Ji, H., Wang, Y.: Recursive correlative statistical analysis method with sliding windows for incipient fault detection. IEEE Trans. Industr. Electron. **69**(4), 4185–4194 (2021)
19. Taranco, R., Arnau, J.M., González, A.: Slidex: a novel architecture for sliding window processing. In: Proceedings of the 38th ACM International Conference on Supercomputing, pp. 312–323 (2024)
20. Ronneberger, O., Fischer, P., Brox, T.: U-net: convolutional networks for biomedical image segmentation. In: Medical image computing and Computer-Assisted Intervention–MICCAI 2015: 18th International Conference, Munich, Germany, 5–9 October 2015, proceedings, Part III 18. pp. 234–241. Springer (2015)
21. Woo, S., Park, J., Lee, J.Y., Kweon, I.S.: Cbam: convolutional block attention module. In: Proceedings of the European Conference on Computer Vision (ECCV), pp. 3–19 (2018)
22. Xie, R., Xu, H., Tao, M., He, C., Chen, M.: Data-driven smoke segmentation and removal for visible image. In: 2024 IEEE International Symposium on Parallel and Distributed Processing with Applications (ISPA), pp. 631–636. IEEE (2024)
23. Jain, J., et al.: Semask: semantically masked transformers for semantic segmentation. In: Proceedings of the IEEE/CVF International Conference on Computer Vision, pp. 752–761 (2023)
24. Xu, J., Xiong, Z., Bhattacharyya, S.P.: Pidnet: a real-time semantic segmentation network inspired by pid controllers. In: Proceedings of the IEEE/CVF Conference on Computer Vision and Pattern Recognition, pp. 19529–19539 (2023)
25. Zhao, S., Liu, Y., Jiao, Q., Zhang, Q., Han, J.: Mitigating modality discrepancies for rgb-t semantic segmentation. IEEE Trans. Neural Netw. Learn. Syst. **35**(7), 9380–9394 (2023)
26. Lv, Y., Liu, Z., Li, G.: Context-aware interaction network for rgb-t semantic segmentation. IEEE Trans. Multimedia **26**, 6348–6360 (2024)
27. Wang, Y., Li, G., Liu, Z.: Sgfnet: semantic-guided fusion network for rgb-thermal semantic segmentation. IEEE Trans. Circuits Syst. Video Technol. **33**(12), 7737–7748 (2023)
28. Liang, M., Hu, J., Bao, C., Feng, H., Deng, F., Lam, T.L.: Explicit attention-enhanced fusion for rgb-thermal perception tasks. IEEE Robot. Autom. Lett. **8**(7), 4060–4067 (2023)

EMS-GL: Adaptive Evict-then-Merge Strategy for KV Cache Compression Based on Global-Local Importance

Yingxin Li[1], Ye Li[1], Yuan Meng[2], Xinzhu Ma[3], Zihan Geng[1](✉), Shutao Xia[1], and Zhi Wang[1](✉)

[1] Shenzhen International Graduate School, Tsinghua University, Beijing, China
{liyx23,liye23}@mails.tsinghua.edu.cn,
{geng.zihan,xiast,wangzhi}@sz.tsinghua.edu.cn

[2] Department of Computer Science and Technology, Beijing, China
yuanmeng@tsinghua.edu.cn

[3] Chinese University of Hong Kong, Hong Kong, People's Republic of China

Abstract. KV Cache compression is critical for reducing memory overhead and accelerating inference in auto-regressive LLMs. Most existing methods compress the KV cache from two angles: identifying important tokens and developing compression strategies. However, these approaches often yield biased distributions of important tokens and fail to account for the sparsity and redundancy across different heads. To this end, we propose an adaptive Evict-then-Merge Strategy based on Global-Local score (EMS-GL) to overcome these limitations, while achieving superior KV cache compression under extreme compression ratios. Specifically, we introduce a hybrid Global-Local score that combines accumulated attention scores from both global and local KV tokens. For the compression strategy, we design an Evict-then-Merge Strategy that can account for both sparsity and redundancy across different heads. To achieve parallel compression, the merging and eviction are unified as the merging operation through a zero-class mechanism. Extensive experiments demonstrate our SOTA performance even under extreme compression ratios. EMS-GL improves the average score on LongBench by over 0.77 points across 4 representative LLMs under a cache budget of 256, preserves 96.8% retrieval accuracy with a cache budget less than 2% in the Needle-in-a-Haystack task, and achieves up to 10.75× throughput gains over the original FlashAttention2 implemented model.

Keywords: Large Language Models · KV Cache · Token Compression · Inference Optimization · Long Context

1 Introduction

Large Language Models (LLMs) [1–5] have demonstrated remarkable capabilities in handling complex tasks [6–8], driving an increasing demand for processing long

J. Niu et al. (Eds.): KSEM 2026, LNAI 16631, pp. 430–441, 2027.
https://doi.org/10.1007/978-981-92-2759-4_32

sequences efficiently [9–11]. To mitigate redundant computation, KV Cache is widely adopted in auto-regressive LLMs by storing previously generated key-value (KV) states, enabling faster inference. However, the size of the KV cache grows linearly with the length of the input sequence, which severely limits the applicability of LLMs [13]. Therefore, efficiently compressing the KV cache while preserving essential information has become a critical issue [14].

Existing work mainly approaches this issue from two perspectives: (*i*) identifying the importance of the generated KV tokens, and (*ii*) devising compression strategies to preserve more information. However, due to cumulative effects of attention weights and positional encoding, existing token importance exhibits former or recent bias. For compression strategies, existing approaches are generally categorized into evict-based and merge-based methods. However, a unified and effective approach that combines evict and merge for extreme KV cache compression is still largely unexplored. Based on the two limitations, we pose the following question:

Can we select important KV tokens in a more balanced manner while retaining information at a high compression ratio?

To answer this question, we decouple the compression of the KV cache into two stages: selecting important tokens and compressing the KV cache based on those selections. Under this workflow, we propose EMS–GL, a head-wise **E**vict-then-**M**erge **S**trategy based on **G**lobal-**L**ocal importance. We dynamically integrate the global- and local-aware importances and construct Global-Local score, which serves as the indicator for the subsequent compression. To bridge the scale gap, the score is calculated by aligning the accumulated attention scores of all KV tokens and local KV tokens. This approach not only ensures a more balanced selection of important KV tokens, but also mitigates biases caused by attention accumulation and positional encoding. In addition, to enhance the efficiency of getting the token importance indicator, we integrate the calculations of global and local scores into the FlashAttention2 [15] kernel. For the compression strategy, we propose a unified Evict-then-Merge strategy at the fine-grained head level to improve the storage density. In particular, the most irrelevant tokens will first be evicted, leaving only the tokens with higher importance scores for further compression. A subset of the remaining tokens is then selected as class centers based on their higher importance, with less important tokens being merged into these centers. However, as not all tokens are suitable for merging due to low redundancy, those with low similarity to important KV tokens are evicted to minimize output disturbance. To ensure parallel inference during head-wise merging and eviction, we introduce a zero-class center where evicted tokens are merged, treating the eviction process as a special case of merging. Additionally, this step allows for a dynamic merge ratio for each head, ensuring more adaptive and efficient compression. EMS–GL achieves extreme compression while preserving LLM capabilities, boosting the average score on LongBench by more than 1.28 points on 4 LLMs with a 256 cache budget, and retaining 95% retrieval accuracy using under 2% the context length in the Needle-in-a-Haystack task.

With 4096 prompt tokens and 8192 generated tokens, EMS–GL improves the throughput by 10.75× over the original FlashAttention2 implemented model. To summarize, our contribution can be generalized as:

(1) **We design a more balanced Global-Local score for important token selection.** The score automatically integrates global and local attention, reducing bias and ensuring more balanced token selection across tasks.
(2) **We propose a sparsity- and redundancy-driven Evict-then-Merge strategy.** Leveraging the characteristic of KV tokens, it significantly enhances the information retention even under low compression ratios.
(3) **We implement an efficient head-wise parallel compression for the KV cache.** We adapt the Global-Local score into the FlashAttention2 kernel and introduce a zero-class to unify the evicting and merging for efficiency.

2 Related Work

2.1 Important KV Selection

Recent work has focused on the selection of important KV tokens to preserve the performance of LLMs. StreamingLLM [16] discovers the sink mechanism and retains the first four tokens along with some local tokens, enabling streaming generation. Following it, ACT [17] further demonstrates that certain KV tokens in the middle also exhibit high attention weights. H2O [18] selects important KV pairs based on the accumulated attention score, leading to more concentration in the former context. SnapKV [19] chooses to calculate the accumulated attention score with a local window and retains more recent tokens. However, the valuable information is often spread across the contexts and the selection of important KV pairs should avoid former or recent preference caused by importance indicator.

2.2 KV Compression

KV cache compression can be categorized into evict and merge based strategies. Evict-based methods aim to retain only the important KV pairs under different token importance assumption [16–20]. DCP [23] introduces a lightweight attention block in each layer to dynamically decide which KV pairs to discard. FastGen [24] applies distinct compression strategies for each head through attention profilling in the prefilling stage. Compared to evict-only methods, merge-based approaches have the potential to retain more information. CAM [25] analyzes the attention output error caused by token eviction and only merges the evicted value tokens into the remaining ones to reduce performance loss. DMC [26] and LESS [27] merge tokens to the tail or the low-rank sidekick, but require additional training for performance gains. However, existing training-free methods overlook the head-wise characteristics of attention, leading to performance degradation, especially under low compression ratios.

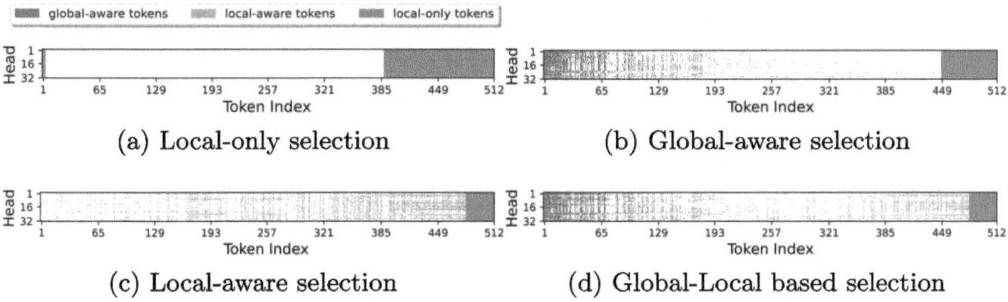

(a) Local-only selection

(b) Global-aware selection

(c) Local-aware selection

(d) Global-Local based selection

Fig. 1. Token selection patterns. The sample is taken from the *gov_report* [33] dataset, showing Top-128 selected tokens out of a total of 512 tokens.

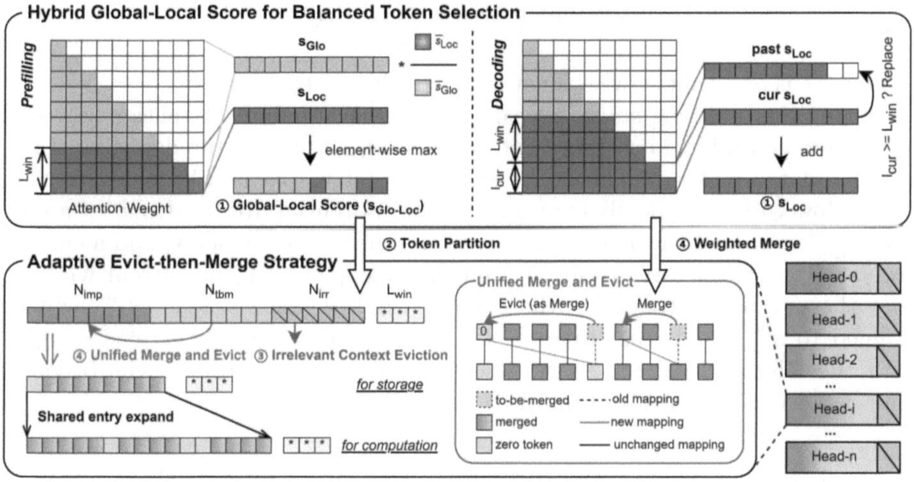

Fig. 2. The framework of EMS–GL.

3 Hybrid Token Selection Policy Based on Global-Local Score

3.1 Token Importance Bias

Existing methods for assessing the most essential KV tokens exhibit inherent biases, as illustrated in Fig. 1.

Local-only methods primarily focus on a few initial sink tokens and recent ones within a local window. Although they exhibit strong capabilities in local language modeling, their performance drops significantly in tasks requiring global semantic understanding. **Global-aware methods** [18,21] employ the global accumulated attention score to select important tokens. However, the cumulative effect of causal attention weight skews the importance distribution toward the earlier part. **Local-aware methods** [19,22] utilize local tokens as anchors to identify and retain tokens across the entire KV cache. However, the positional encoding causes nearby tokens to exhibit higher correlations, leading to a bias towards retaining more recent tokens.

3.2 Global-Local Score

To eliminate the influence of cumulative effects and positional encoding, we propose a Global-Local score to leverage both global and local information, which is shown in Fig. 2. Specifically, we convert $\mathbf{s}_{Glo}$ and $\mathbf{s}_{Loc}$ to similar magnitudes by mean-alignment, followed by the element-wise max to obtain the new score:

$$\boldsymbol{s}_{Glo-Loc} = \max\left(\boldsymbol{s}_{Glo} \times \frac{\sum \boldsymbol{s}_{Loc}/N}{\sum \boldsymbol{s}_{Glo}/N}, \boldsymbol{s}_{Loc}\right), \tag{1}$$

where max is an element-wise function, N is the context length.

During the prefilling stage, we calculate the accumulated attention scores of $\boldsymbol{A}$ from global and local scope to get $\boldsymbol{s}_{Glo}$ and $\boldsymbol{s}_{Loc}$. During the decoding stage, $\boldsymbol{s}_{Glo}$ is updated by accumulating the attention of new tokens. The local tokens in the window will dynamically change. To avoid potential overhead, we set a past score $\boldsymbol{s}_{Loc}^{past}$ to record the attention information in the last window, and a current score $\boldsymbol{s}_{Loc}^{cur}$ to accumulate attention from the new queries in the current window. Once the number of tokens in the current window reaches L_{win}, $\boldsymbol{s}_{Loc}^{cur}$ will be assigned to $\boldsymbol{s}_{Loc}^{past}$ and reset to zero. The final local score $\boldsymbol{s}_{Loc} = \boldsymbol{s}_{Loc}^{past} + \boldsymbol{s}_{Loc}^{cur}$. With the Global-Local score, the selection of important KV tokens becomes more balanced, as shown in Fig. 1d.

4 Head-wise Evict-then-Merge Strategy for KV Cache

4.1 Head-wise Sparsity and Redundancy

Sparsity. The sparsity rate of each attention head is determined by the minimum percentage of important tokens retained per head that can achieve over ζ of the total score:

$$\boldsymbol{p}_m = 1 - \frac{1}{N} \cdot_{N_k \in [1,N]} \left\{ N_k \mid \sum_{i=1}^{N_k} \boldsymbol{s}_i \geq \zeta \right\}, \tag{2}$$
$$\text{where } \boldsymbol{s} = \text{sort}(\boldsymbol{s}_{Glo-Loc}),$$

where $\boldsymbol{p}_m$ is the sparsity rate, m is the head index, sort($\cdot$) reorders the vector in descending way.

Redundancy. As shown in Fig. 3a, the similarity among key tokens is significantly higher, whereas the similarity among value tokens is relatively lower. We jointly consider the key similarity and the value similarity, and define the redundancy $R_{i,j}$ as the product of both. A token is considered redundant if it

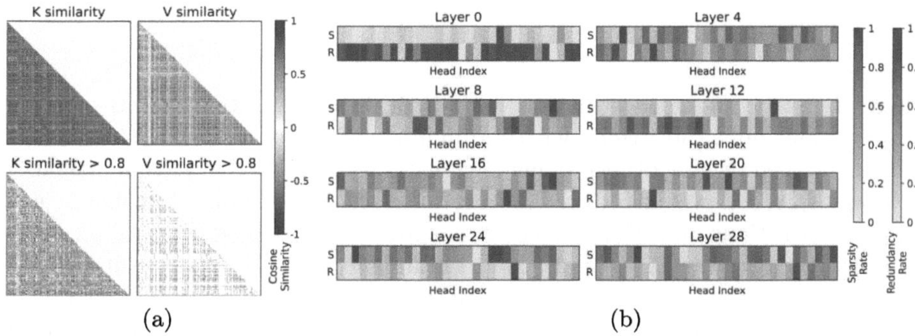

Fig. 3. Observations on sparsity and redundancy. (a) The distribution difference between key and value similarities. (b) The head-wise sparsity and redundancy. ζ and τ set to 0.95 and 0.6.

can find another token in the existing KV cache with redundancy exceeding the predefined threshold τ. The redundancy rate $\boldsymbol{r}_m$ of head m is given by:

$$\boldsymbol{r}_m = \frac{1}{N} \cdot \sum_{k=1}^{N} [\max(\boldsymbol{R}_{k,1:k}) \geq \tau] \, . \tag{3}$$

The head-level sparsity and redundancy rates for different heads are shown in Fig. 3b.

Head-wise Sparsity and Redundancy. From an overall perspective, different heads demonstrate varying degrees of sparsity and redundancy. Dynamically evicting and merging tokens based on the characteristic of each head can lead to a higher compression ratio. However, the challenge arises from the fact that all heads within a layer are stored and computed in parallel, making it difficult to manage fine-grained evict and merge decisions for each head.

4.2 Adaptive Evict-then-Merge Strategy

Token Partition. Based on the ranking of $\boldsymbol{s}_{Glo-Loc}$, KV tokens can be divided into three sets: N_{irr} irrelevant tokens, N_{tbm} to-be-merged (TBM) tokens, and N_{imp} most important tokens, except that L_{win} local tokens are always kept to preserve the local modeling capability. The most irrelevant tokens are first evicted to streamline the process and minimize the impact of irrelevant context [35]. Then, the most important tokens will serve as class centers based on the cache budget $N_{budget} = N_{imp} + L_{win}$, while N_{tbm} sub-important tokens will be merged into them to preserve as much valuable information as possible. The merge magnification factor $\gamma = (N_{budget} + N_{tbm})/N_{budget}$ indicates the extent to which tokens are merged relative to the cache budget.

Unified Evict-then-Merge Strategy. By calculating the redundancy between TBM tokens and class center tokens, the merge destinations for TBM tokens can be identified:

$$d_i = \arg\max_d (R_{i,d}), \quad (4)$$

where d_i is the merge destination for i-th TBM token. To minimize output perturbation, only the tokens with redundancy $R_{i,:d_i}$ exceeding a threshold τ will be merged, while others being evicted. Inspired by the virtual neighbor technique [28,29], we introduced a zero class center to unify the merge and eviction operations, and the evicted tokens are merged into it.

Moreover, the varying sparsity and redundancy of each head results in different eviction and merge ratios, as well as varying cache sizes. We choose to allocate an equal budget to each head, using a limited number of entries to store class centers. Based on this, the merged tokens share the same entry in the KV cache, reducing the overall size of the stored KV cache. A position look-up-table is carefully retained in the merging process. During the computation of each layer, a smaller cache is loaded and expanded with the help of this table, thus enlarging the context length. To ensure that more relevant tokens dominate the merged result, we apply a weighted merge based on their attention scores.

Table 1. Performance evaluation on LongBench.

	Method	Multi-Document QA			Single-Document QA			Summarization			Few-shot Learning			Synthetic		Code		Avg.
		HotpotQA	2WikiMQA	Musique	MF-en	NrtvQA	Qasper	GovReport	QMSum	MultiNews	TriviaQA	SAMSum	TREC	PRe	PCount	Lcc	RB-P	
	Full Cache	30.20	27.37	11.54	34.33	19.68	19.40	24.60	20.81	26.19	84.61	41.00	63.50	8.00	4.50	61.46	55.14	33.27
	StreamingLLM [16]	24.41	26.90	7.70	17.44	13.69	15.07	16.73	19.21	18.25	81.67	35.03	39.50	6.00	4.00	55.22	51.00	26.99
	H2O [18]	29.92	25.07	10.46	23.05	17.04	**18.45**	19.96	20.07	**24.12**	82.66	38.26	59.50	3.50	4.00	56.01	51.64	30.23
Llama-2-7B-Chat	CAM [25]	24.68	26.80	7.57	16.79	14.11	15.98	16.57	19.09	18.35	81.09	35.17	39.50	5.50	4.00	55.34	51.15	26.98
	SnapKV [19]	28.96	26.20	**11.14**	28.41	15.72	17.10	17.01	20.30	21.53	84.32	**38.62**	57.00	**8.50**	4.00	57.26	53.03	30.57
	EMS-GL (*w.o.* pos)	**31.12**	26.49	9.24	**30.45**	**18.07**	17.46	**21.91**	**20.55**	22.30	**84.86**	37.49	**60.50**	5.50	**4.50**	57.66	53.30	**31.34**
	EMS-GL (*w.* pos)	30.10	**26.45**	11.06	29.42	16.19	16.91	17.03	20.04	21.90	84.18	37.91	60.00	8.00	4.00	**58.33**	**53.33**	30.93
	Full Cache	44.93	37.92	24.10	41.89	22.84	39.26	28.69	23.57	26.58	90.31	42.67	74.50	67.00	6.48	57.13	51.34	42.45
	StreamingLLM [16]	37.64	25.25	16.94	22.61	16.58	18.73	18.42	20.15	19.25	78.43	39.29	53.00	65.08	7.25	56.83	53.72	34.32
	H2O [18]	43.74	34.06	20.65	27.71	20.34	26.67	21.27	20.58	**23.98**	88.52	38.50	58.50	66.50	**7.50**	57.14	52.11	37.99
Llama-3-8B-Instruct	CAM [25]	37.64	25.19	16.94	22.64	16.58	18.58	18.49	20.10	19.24	78.43	39.34	53.00	65.08	7.25	56.83	53.56	34.31
	SnapKV [19]	41.96	31.82	20.06	34.91	20.52	26.59	19.94	**21.72**	21.94	**90.47**	**39.55**	50.50	**67.00**	6.84	58.23	53.81	37.87
	EMS-GL (*w.o.* pos)	**44.52**	**36.54**	22.80	**36.43**	19.68	26.43	**22.05**	21.66	23.94	89.68	39.41	**61.50**	66.50	6.41	55.18	50.37	**38.94**
	EMS-GL (*w.* pos)	43.61	32.26	20.00	34.16	**20.38**	**26.73**	20.48	21.32	21.82	89.33	39.33	59.5	**67.00**	6.58	**59.52**	**55.94**	38.62
	Full Cache	31.26	22.52	12.16	43.92	18.33	28.81	31.29	22.57	26.32	82.41	40.06	66.00	31.50	0.00	53.02	55.28	35.34
	StreamingLLM [16]	13.06	9.62	1.97	4.48	4.02	8.64	1.00	3.18	0.92	4.72	6.96	20.50	2.96	0.50	2.16	5.93	5.66
	H2O [18]	11.33	10.37	1.20	7.13	4.04	8.59	2.42	9.52	2.92	23.26	7.11	27.50	2.45	0.15	9.30	8.24	8.47
LongChat-7B-v1.5-32k	CAM [25]	13.40	9.17	1.82	5.07	4.08	8.62	1.01	3.24	0.79	4.23	7.12	21.50	3.55	0.50	2.05	5.98	5.76
	SnapKV [19]	19.60	13.45	8.39	15.06	9.07	9.19	3.76	13.15	3.42	57.43	18.26	30.50	1.00	0.44	15.60	20.08	14.90
	EMS-GL (*w.o.* pos)	31.36	22.98	11.07	**39.44**	**15.25**	22.66	**23.53**	**20.79**	**23.49**	**79.48**	**36.76**	**61.00**	9.50	0.00	**54.96**	50.05	31.40
	EMS-GL (*w.* pos)	**31.51**	**23.60**	**11.27**	36.79	14.93	**22.80**	19.40	20.76	19.66	77.15	35.60	**61.00**	**27.50**	**0.60**	52.78	**51.48**	**31.68**
	Full Cache	36.42	21.77	19.13	47.12	21.02	29.62	32.57	24.02	27.09	86.23	42.99	71.00	89.33	3.07	54.00	51.87	41.08
	StreamingLLM [16]	21.60	13.24	10.25	26.35	13.72	11.58	17.98	19.73	18.92	80.67	40.26	50.50	24.80	**3.82**	50.57	44.04	28.00
	H2O [18]	23.31	14.07	10.32	33.42	14.29	16.75	**23.12**	21.09	23.73	83.22	38.74	63.00	31.50	3.44	49.17	44.66	30.86
Mistral-7B-Instruct-v0.2	CAM [25]	21.15	13.25	10.25	26.41	13.72	11.6	17.88	19.72	18.94	80.7	40.19	50.5	25.05	**3.82**	50.6	44.04	27.99
	SnapKV [19]	26.28	14.58	12.02	40.82	**16.88**	**18.87**	21.46	21.60	22.05	**84.82**	**40.79**	51.00	**70.08**	2.72	51.01	46.75	33.86
	EMS-GL (*w.o.* pos)	24.87	15.16	11.73	39.91	16.17	18.78	**22.80**	22.11	**23.59**	84.42	39.45	**63.00**	58.47	3.66	**51.48**	**47.28**	33.93
	EMS-GL (*w.* pos)	**26.29**	**15.47**	**12.12**	**41.13**	16.79	18.59	22.10	**22.34**	23.57	84.34	40.44	62.50	67.98	3.20	51.04	46.72	**34.66**

5 Experiment

5.1 Settings

In this paper, we use LLaMA-2-7B-Chat [31], LLaMA-3-8B-Instruct [4], LongChat-7B-v1.5-32k [30] and Mistral-7B-Instruct-v0.2 [5] models. All experiments can be conducted on a single NVIDIA A100 GPU with 40 GB of memory, except for the fully cached model. For common parameters, we set $L_{win} = 32$, kernel_size = 7 for perplexity and LongBench, and $L_{win} = 16$, kernel_size = 7 for Needle-in-a-Haystack task.

5.2 Performance Evaluation on LongBench

LongBench [32] is a comprehensive benchmark designed to assess long context modeling abilities across 6 categories of tasks. To demonstrate the effectiveness of EMS–GL under extreme compression ratios, we enforce a strict compression budget of 256, with τ and γ set to approximately 0.6 and 4. We present two versions of our method: one without position information to merge more aggressively and capture global information, and one with position information for tasks requiring precise token localization.

As shown in the Table 1, our method integrates the strengths of the baselines, achieving the state-of-the-art performance on nearly all tasks, with improvements of 1.28, 1.79, 17.64, and 1.28 across the four different LLMs. Notably, on LongChat-7B-v1.5-32k, while the performance of other compression methods breaks down, our method consistently maintains high performance, demonstrating its robustness under extreme compression ratios and long-context conditions. The results under more budgets can be found in Table 2. Across various budgets, EMS outperforms baselines on the four LLMs.

Table 2. Impact of varying cache budgets.

	Method	128	256	512	768	1024
Llama-2	StreamingLLM [16]	24.39	26.99	28.92	29.46	29.77
	H2O [18]	19.00	30.23	31.14	31.54	31.91
	SnapKV [19]	27.78	30.57	31.64	32.05	32.27
	EMS–GL (*w.o.* pos)	**29.41**	**31.34**	**32.26**	**32.71**	**33.00**
	EMS–GL (*w.* pos)	29.12	30.93	31.99	32.53	32.68
Llama-3	StreamingLLM [16]	32.42	34.32	36.18	37.27	38.80
	H2O [18]	36.02	37.99	39.55	40.20	40.62
	SnapKV [19]	35.54	37.87	39.78	40.57	40.95
	EMS–GL (*w.o.* pos)	**36.45**	**38.94**	**40.45**	**40.74**	**41.12**
	EMS–GL (*w.* pos)	36.14	38.62	40.12	40.73	41.10
LongChat	StreamingLLM [16]	5.77	5.66	5.45	8.51	13.98
	H2O [18]	5.71	8.47	17.71	26.25	31.19
	SnapKV [19]	6.04	14.90	32.08	33.27	33.63
	EMS–GL (*w.o.* pos)	**25.65**	**31.25**	33.00	33.05	33.36
	EMS–GL (*w.* pos)	18.85	31.10	**33.32**	**34.18**	**34.01**
Mistral	StreamingLLM [16]	26.97	28.00	29.90	30.74	31.37
	H2O [18]	29.89	30.86	32.02	33.38	34.24
	SnapKV [19]	31.15	33.86	36.16	37.24	37.91
	EMS–GL (*w.o.* pos)	31.16	33.93	35.37	36.30	37.14
	EMS–GL (*w.* pos)	**31.44**	**34.66**	**36.59**	**37.64**	**38.35**

5.3 Performance Evaluation on Needle-in-a-Haystack

Needle-in-a-Haystack [34] is a challenging task to assess the model's ability to retrieve specific information from a large volume of data. We test our method using Mistral-7B-Instruct-v0.2 with 10 depths, 40 lengths and maximum token limit 32k. The merge threshold τ and merge magnification factor γ are set to 0.55 and 4. As shown in Table 3, EMS–GL delivers the best retrieval performance across all three compression budgets. It retains 95.9% retrieval ability of the fully cached model, even surpassing SnapKV, which is specifically designed for retrieval tasks.

Table 3. The performance of Needle-in-a-Haystack across three budgets.

N_{budget}	128	256	512
H2O	0.312	0.335	0.384
SnapKV	0.802	0.893	0.956
EMS–GL	**0.818**	**0.896**	**0.959**

5.4 Efficiency Analysis

To assess the efficiency of EMS–GL, we measured the end-to-end latency on two RTX 4090 GPUs with the cache budget 256. As shown in Table 4, by compressing the KV cache, EMS–GL supports larger batch sizes, whereas the fully cached model encounters out-of-memory (OOM) errors with batch sizes of 2 or 4. Moreover, the efficiency gains of our method become more pronounced with

Table 4. Comparisons of the end-to-end latency (s) on long context settings.

$L_{prompt} + L_{gen}$	Method	Batch Size					Max Throughput
		1	2	4	8	16	(tokens/s)
128 + 4096	Full Cache	453.7	558.3	OOM	OOM	OOM	14.67
	EMS–GL	421.7	442.2	476.6	706.7	1299.2	50.44 (3.44×)
128 + 6144	Full Cache	657.7	1157.6	OOM	OOM	OOM	10.62
	EMS–GL	638.7	676.9	706.0	1080.2	2010.8	48.89 (4.61×)
4096 + 128	Full Cache	17.3	30.8	OOM	OOM	OOM	8.31
	EMS–GL	14.1	15.5	17.5	28.5	54.9	37.30 (4.48×)
4096 + 4096	Full Cache	751.5	1381.1	OOM	OOM	OOM	5.93
	EMS–GL	439.1	458.9	478.9	761.7	1432.8	45.74 (7.71×)
4096 + 8192	Full Cache	1918.6	OOM	OOM	OOM	OOM	4.27
	EMS–GL	980.0	910.7	959.8	1518.2	2855.7	45.90 (10.75×)

larger batch sizes and longer context length, leading to increased throughput. For example, with 4096 prompt tokens and 8192 generated tokens, our method achieves a 10.75× improvement in throughput compared to the fully cached model.

5.5 Ablation Study

We ablate the effectiveness of the Global-Local score and the Evict-then-Merge strategy using the LongBench average score on Llama-2-7B-Chat. Table 5 illustrates the effectiveness of our method. By incorporating the Evict-then-Merge strategy, the average score improves 0.61 points compared to the evict-only approach. Furthermore, integrating both global and local scores increases the average score by 0.37 and 2.62 points, respectively, compared to using either the global or local score alone. These results highlight the effectiveness of our method in token selection and compression strategy.

Table 5. KV cache compression using different token importance scores and compression strategies.

Score + Compression	Avg.
$\mathbf{s}_{Glo}$ + Evict-then-Merge	28.81
$\mathbf{s}_{Loc}$ + Evict-then-Merge	31.06
$\mathbf{s}_{Glo-Loc}$ + Evict-only	30.82
$\mathbf{s}_{Glo-Loc}$ + Evict-then-Merge	31.34

6 Conclusion

In this paper, we propose EMS–GL, a head-wise efficient KV cache management framework. By leveraging the proposed Global-Local attention score, EMS–GL addresses the biased distribution of important KV tokens caused by accumulated attention scores and positional encoding, leading to a more balanced selection of tokens. We further design a unified Evict-then-Merge strategy based on the redundancy and sparsity intrinsic of KV tokens across different heads. In particular, we implement a kernel and a zero-class mechanism to enable efficient compression. Extensive experiments on language modeling perplexity, LongBench, and Needle-in-a-Haystack tasks demonstrate the SOTA performance, validating the effectiveness of EMS–GL.

Acknowledgments. This study was funded by National Natural Science Foundation of China (Grant No. 92467204, 62472249 and 62402264), and Shenzhen Science and Technology Program (Grant No. KJZD20240903102300001).

References

1. Devlin, J.: Bert: pre-training of deep bidirectional transformers for language understanding. arXiv preprint arXiv:1810.04805 (2018)
2. Brown, T., Mann, B., Ryder, N., Subbiah, et al.: In: Larochelle, H., Ranzato, M., Hadsell, R., Balcan, M. F., Lin, H. (eds.) Advances in Neural Information Processing Systems, vol. 33, pp. 1877–1901. Curran Associates, Inc. (2020)
3. Anil, R., et al.: Palm 2 technical report. arXiv preprint arXiv:2305.10403 (2023)
4. Dubey, A., et al.: The llama 3 herd of models. arXiv preprint arXiv:2407.21783 (2024)
5. Jiang, A.Q., et al: Mistral 7B. arXiv preprint arXiv:2310.06825 (2023)
6. Ram, O., et al.: In-context retrieval-augmented language models. Trans. Assoc. Comput. Linguist. 1316–1331 (2023)
7. Wei, J., et al.: Chain-of-thought prompting elicits reasoning in large language models. In: Advances in Neural Information Processing Systems, pp. 24824–24837 (2022)
8. Roziere, B., et al.: Code llama: open foundation models for code. arXiv preprint arXiv:2308.12950 (2023)
9. Jin, H., et al.: Llm maybe longlm: self-extend llm context window without tuning. arXiv preprint arXiv:2401.01325 (2024)
10. Chen, Y., et al.: LongLoRA: efficient fine-tuning of long-context large language models. In: The Twelfth International Conference on Learning Representations (2024)
11. Chen, S., Wong, S., Chen, L., Tian, Y.: Extending context window of large language models via positional interpolation. arXiv preprint arXiv:2306.15595 (2023)
12. Lazaridou, A., Gribovskaya, E., Stokowiec, W., Grigorev, N.: Internet-augmented language models through few-shot prompting for open-domain question answering. arXiv preprint arXiv:2203.05115 (2022)
13. Yuan, Z., et al.: Llm inference unveiled: survey and roofline model insights. arXiv preprint arXiv:2402.16363 (2024)
14. Zhou, Z., et al.: A survey on efficient inference for large language models. arXiv preprint arXiv:2404.14294 (2024)
15. Dao, T.: FlashAttention-2: faster attention with better parallelism and work partitioning. In: International Conference on Learning Representations (ICLR) (2024)
16. Xiao, G., Tian, Y., Chen, B., Han, S., Lewis, M.: Efficient streaming language models with attention sinks. In: The Twelfth International Conference on Learning Representations (2024)
17. Yu, Z., Wang, Z., Fu, Y., Shi, H., Shaikh, K., Lin, Y.C.: Unveiling and harnessing hidden attention sinks: enhancing large language models without training through attention calibration. In: Forty-first International Conference on Machine Learning (2024)
18. Zhang, Z., et al.: H2O: heavy-hitter oracle for efficient generative inference of large language models. In: Thirty-Seventh Conference on Neural Information Processing Systems (2023)
19. Li, Y., et al.: Snapkv: Llm knows what you are looking for before generation. arXiv preprint arXiv:2404.14469 (2024)
20. Adnan, M., Arunkumar, A., Jain, G., Nair, P., Soloveychik, I., Kamath, P.: Keyformer: Kv cache reduction through key tokens selection for efficient generative inference. Proc. Mach. Learn. Syst. **6**, 114–127 (2024)

21. Wang, H., Zhang, Z.K., Han, S.: Spatten: efficient sparse attention architecture with cascade token and head pruning. In: 2021 IEEE International Symposium on High-Performance Computer Architecture (HPCA), pp. 97–110 (2021)
22. Liu, Z., et al.: Scissorhands: exploiting the persistence of importance hypothesis for LLM KV cache compression at test time. In: Thirty-seventh Conference on Neural Information Processing Systems (2023)
23. Anagnostidis, S., Pavllo, D., Biggio, L., Noci, L., Lucchi, A., Hofmann, T.: Dynamic context pruning for efficient and interpretable autoregressive transformers. In: Thirty-seventh Conference on Neural Information Processing Systems (2023)
24. Ge, S., Zhang, Y., Liu, L., Zhang, M., Han, J., Gao, J.: Model tells you what to discard: adaptive KV cache compression for LLMs. In: Workshop on Advancing Neural Network Training: Computational Efficiency, Scalability, and Resource Optimization (WANT@NeurIPS 2023) (2023)
25. Zhang, Y., et al.: CaM: cache merging for memory-efficient LLMs inference. In: International Conference on Machine Learning (2024)
26. Nawrot, P., Łańcucki, A., Chochowski, M., Tarjan, D., Ponti, E.: Dynamic memory compression: retrofitting LLMs for accelerated inference. In: Forty-first International Conference on Machine Learning (2024)
27. Dong, H., Yang, X., Zhang, Z., Wang, Z., Chi, Y., Chen, B.: Get More with LESS: synthesizing recurrence with KV cache compression for efficient LLM inference. In: Forty-first International Conference on Machine Learning (2024)
28. Li, Y., Liu, Z.X., Lan, G., Sader, M., Chen, Z.Q.: A DDPG-based solution for optimal consensus of continuous-time linear multi-agent systems. SCIENCE CHINA Technol. Sci. **66**(8), 2441–2453 (2023)
29. Liu, Z.X., Li, Y., Lan, G., Chen, Z.Q.: A novel data-driven model-free synchronization protocol for discrete-time multi-agent systems via TD3 based algorithm. Knowl.-Based Syst. **287**, 111430 (2024)
30. Li, D., et al.: How long can context length of open-source LLMs truly promise?. In: NeurIPS 2023 Workshop on Instruction Tuning and Instruction Following (2023)
31. Touvron, H., et al.: Llama 2: open foundation and fine-tuned chat models. arXiv preprint arXiv:2307.09288 (2023)
32. Bai, Y., et al.: Longbench: a bilingual, multitask benchmark for long context understanding. arXiv preprint arXiv:2308.14508 (2023)
33. Huang, L., Cao, S., Parulian, N., Ji, H., Wang, L.: Efficient attentions for long document summarization. In: Proceedings of the 2021 Conference of the North American Chapter of the Association for Computational Linguistics: Human Language Technologies, pp. 1419–1436. ACL (2021). https://doi.org/10.18653/v1/2021.naacl-main.112
34. Kamradt, G.: Needle in a Haystack-pressure testing LLMs (2023)
35. Shi, F., et al.: Large language models can be easily distracted by irrelevant context. In: International Conference on Machine Learning, pp. 31210–31227. PMLR (2023)
36. Yang, Z., et al.: HotpotQA: a dataset for diverse, explainable multi-hop question answering. arXiv preprint arXiv:1809.09600 (2018)

Knowledge Driven-Based Semantic Point Cloud Dataset for Multi-perception Tasks

Yuchen Zhang, Yiyin Yang, Yibo Zhou, Chang Zhang, Dongyu Li, and Zhenchao Ouyang(✉)

Hangzhou International Innovation Institute, Beihang University, Hangzhou, China
ouyangkid@buaa.edu.cn

Abstract. LiDAR point clouds, with their accurate ranging capability, serve as the core perception data source for carriers such as robots, autonomous vehicles and unmanned aerial vehicles, yet existing public point cloud semantic datasets are mostly collected and annotated by manually controlling carriers to randomly traverse target scenes, which suffer from drawbacks including low efficiency, poor pose generalization and time-consuming annotation, severely hindering the research on end-to-end models driven by semantic knowledge. To address this issue, this study proposes an efficient knowledge-driven workflow for constructing point cloud semantic datasets: it improves the efficiency of basic point cloud scanning in GPS-denied scenarios using rotating LiDAR, constructs fully scanned scene point cloud maps by combining M-detector and SLAM algorithms, optimizes point cloud registration results via interactive SLAM Human-in-the-loop and Graph-based optimization, and finally achieves per-point semantic annotation with relative pose by superimposing manual labels on whole scene maps. Based on this workflow, a dataset covering 5 huge real underground scenes is collected and annotated. Tests with multiple algorithms and deep learning models show that our dataset can not only support traditional tasks such as point cloud semantic segmentation, SLAM and autonomous exploration, but also enable knowledge-driven high-level fusion tasks including semantic SLAM and semantics-based autonomous exploration. Moreover, the annotated semantic data can extend the MARSim simulator to realize flexible point cloud data with semantic labels generation for multi-LiDAR models, providing support for in-depth research on relevant knowledge-driven algorithms.

Keywords: Semantic-driven Dataset · Panoramic LiDAR · 3D Point Cloud Perception · Semantic Segmentation · SLAM

1 Introduction

With the rapid development of robotics and autonomous driving, LiDAR has become a fundamental sensor for perception because of its robustness to illumination changes and active ranging capability. Among emerging LiDAR systems,

J. Niu et al. (Eds.): KSEM 2026, LNAI 16631, pp. 442–455, 2027.
https://doi.org/10.1007/978-981-92-2759-4_33

rotating panoramic LiDAR extends conventional designs with an additional rotational degree of freedom, offering a larger sensing field and stronger perception capability. Its effectiveness has been demonstrated in challenging applications such as the DARPA Subterranean Challenge [1,2]. However, despite the growing interest in this new sensing paradigm, the lack of dedicated datasets and simulation platforms has become a major bottleneck for advancing rotating panoramic LiDAR perception.

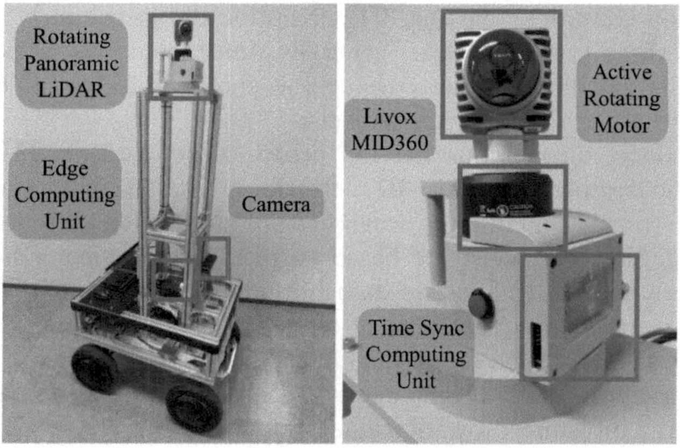

Fig. 1. Rotating Panoramic LiDAR Data Acquisition Platform.

This gap raises several important questions for data-driven perception: how to collect effective data for rotating panoramic LiDAR, what data distribution is required to improve model generalization, and how to evaluate its active perception capability without expensive hardware-dependent experiments. To this end, we build a rotating panoramic LiDAR data collection platform, analyze the impact of installation angle, sensor state, and carrier motion on data acquisition, and introduce the KRP-Perception Dataset, a knowledge-driven dataset collected in representative subterranean environments. The dataset contains 51,468 frames over 10.36 km, with accurate 6-DoF poses and comprehensive semantic annotations for semantic SLAM and point cloud segmentation. In addition, we develop a Marsim-based simulation environment for rotating panoramic LiDAR, providing compatible interfaces for downstream SLAM and navigation tasks. Together, these resources establish a foundation for future research on rotating panoramic LiDAR perception.

Our main contributions are summarized as follows: **a)** Analyzed the impact of LiDAR characteristics and carrier motion on dataset construction at both theoretical and experimental levels. **b)** Introduced a Knowledge driven-based semantic point cloud dataset for multi-perception tasks **c)** Constructed a semantic-driven data simulation and replay environment to support downstream task research.

2 Related Works

To support tasks such as semantic segmentation, 3D detection, and (semantic) SLAM, a large number of 3D perception datasets have been developed. However, most existing datasets are built around common configurations such as fixed-field-of-view vehicle-mounted LiDAR/cameras or indoor RGB-D sensors. For the novel sensing modality of rotating panoramic LiDAR investigated in this study, significant differences remain in terms of field-of-view coverage, observation geometry, and cross-scenario applicability. Based on data sources and application scenarios, existing 3D perception datasets can be broadly categorized into three types, yet they generally differ from this work in terms of sensor modality and field-of-view coverage, as shown in Table 1. These datasets exhibit limitations in the following aspects:

First, outdoor autonomous driving/urban scene datasets [3–6] primarily serve semantic segmentation or 3D detection tasks in road traffic environments. Their strengths lie in large scale, mature annotation systems, and ease of benchmarking. However, most are based on fixed-field-of-view vehicle-mounted LiDAR/camera setups, with scene distributions skewed toward outdoor roads and urban streets. Consequently, they often fall short in addressing occlusion resolution, loop closure, and cross-domain robustness analysis that require "full-coverage observation," and they struggle to directly reflect the changes in observation geometry introduced by rotational motion.

Second, simulation datasets [7] can generate controllable annotations at low cost and support synthetic-to-real transfer learning. Yet, their sensor noise, dynamic objects, and reflection characteristics often exhibit domain gaps compared to real hardware. Moreover, they typically rely on conventional perspective/field-of-view sensors, making it difficult to fully capture the sensing characteristics of rotating panoramic LiDAR.

Third, indoor datasets [8] are centered around RGB-D acquisitions or mesh shape libraries, respectively. While suitable for indoor semantic parsing and shape/part understanding, the former is limited by indoor scales and sensor range, while the latter lacks realistic noise and motion trajectories from actual data collection. As a result, they provide insufficient support for panoramic observation and localization and mapping of mobile robots in complex spaces.

To address these limitations, the KRP-Perception Dataset used in this work is designed for rotating panoramic LiDAR perception. By introducing an additional rotational degree of freedom to the LiDAR system, it achieves an REFOV(Expanded Rotational Field of View) The dataset provides per-point semantic annotations (13 categories) and high-precision poses optimized through backend processing. This enables more direct evaluation of the robustness and applicability of semantic segmentation and (semantic) SLAM under panoramic observation geometries and cross-domain conditions.

Table 1. Comparison of different datasets.

Dataset Type	Dataset	Sensor	Annotation Category	Classes	Frames	Mileage
Outdoor	SemanticKITTI [3]	LiDAR/Camera	Semantic	20	23,201	39.2 km
	Waymo Open [5]	LiDAR/Camera	Semantic/Bbox	30	230k	1750 km
	nuScenes [4]	LiDAR/Camera	Bbox	23	390k	242 km
	Semantic3D [9]	LiDAR/Camera	Semantic	8	–	–
	Paris-Lille-3D [6]	LiDAR (MLS)	Semantic	50	–	1.9 km
Simulation	Virtual KITTI [7]	RGB-D	Bbox	–	17,000	–
Indoor	ShapeNet [8]	CAD/mesh (no Sensor)	Object category/part	55	–	–
Underground	KRP-Perception	**Panoramic LiDAR**	Semantic	13	51,468	10.36 km

3 Data Acquisition and Analysis

While traditional LiDAR technology has advanced rapidly, with the number of laser beams continuously increasing and costs gradually decreasing, its mechanical structure suffers from inherent limitations, resulting in a fixed and restricted FOV (Field of View), which remains fixed and limited. Rotating panoramic LiDAR introduces an additional "head degree of freedom" to the LiDAR system. This "head degree of freedom" refers to the mechanism—illustrated in Fig. 2 (a)(b) where a LiDAR sensor with a fixed FOV is mounted at a tilted angle and actively rotated by a motor around its axis. This design enables the expansion of the sensor's intrinsic FOV, resulting in a larger REFOV.

3.1 Theory of Rotationally Expanded Field of View

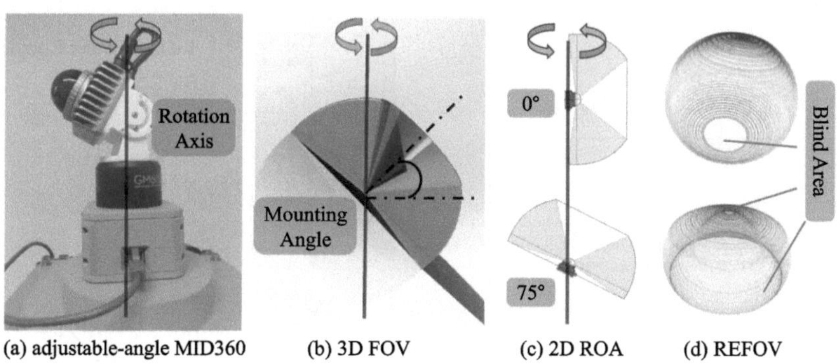

Fig. 2. Theoretical Schematic of Rotational Expanded Field of View.

Livox MID 360 LiDAR has a theoretical FOV that can be modeled as an elliptical cone with optical-intensity attenuation. After removing the region occluded by the LiDAR blind-zone cone, we introduce an azimuthal rotation-angle parameter $\alpha \in [-\alpha_{\max}, \alpha_{\max}]$, which represents a periodic rotation about a specific axis $\mathbf{n}$ (determined by the mounting direction).

This periodic rotation forms a ROA (Rotating Coverage Area). As shown in Fig. 2(c), it can be interpreted as the set of rotation surfaces generated by sweeping the boundary set V_b (the theoretical outer-boundary curve set of the fixed FOV on each cross-section through the rotation axis $\mathbf{n}$). The resulting set is

$$\mathcal{R}(\mathbf{v}_b) = \left\{ \bigcup_{\mathbf{v}_b \in \mathbf{V}_b} R_{\mathbf{n}}(\alpha) \cdot \mathbf{v}_b \mid \alpha \in [-\alpha_{\max}, \alpha_{\max}] \right\}$$

Here, $R_{\mathbf{n}}(\alpha) \in SO(3)$ is the rotation matrix for rotating about axis $\mathbf{n}$, V_b is the set of theoretical outer-boundary curves of the fixed FOV on each cross-section through $\mathbf{n}$, $v_b \in V_b$, and α is the rotation angle swept by the fixed FOV.

The final REFOV region is defined as the envelope of all ROA: $\mathcal{F}_{\text{REFOV}} = Envelop(\mathcal{R}(\mathbf{v}_b))$ where $\mathcal{F}_{\text{REFOV}}$ denotes the REFOV. For different mounting angles θ, the LiDAR rotation produces different REFOV areas. When the REFOV reaches its maximum, the corresponding mounting angle is the optimal mounting angle θ^*: $\theta^* = \arg\max_\theta \mathcal{F}_{REFOV}(\theta)$

From theoretical analysis, under ideal conditions, the relationship between the REFOV, the blind zone, and the ratio relative to the fixed-mount FOV is shown in Fig. 3. The results indicate that when the mounting angle is 0° (i.e., the LiDAR normal direction is parallel to the horizontal axis), the "head-free" rotation mode yields the maximum improvement in effective FOV, reaching 232% of the original FOV. When the LiDAR is mounted at nonzero angles, the REFOV range decreases; at 7° and 53°, laser-illumination blind zones appear in the lower and upper regions of the LiDAR, respectively, as illustrated in Fig. 2(d).

3.2 Real-World Experiment

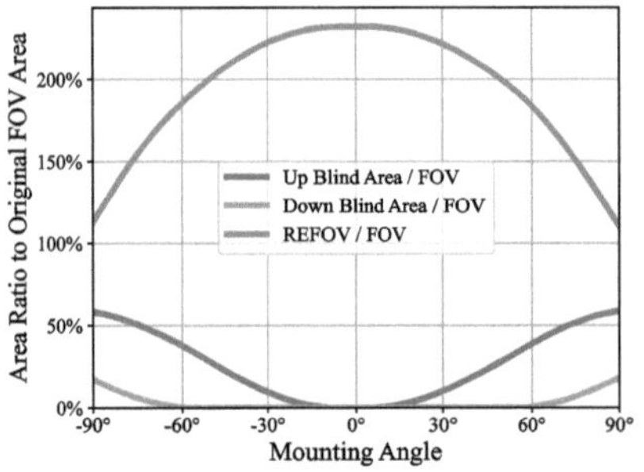

Fig. 3. The relationship between the REFOV and blind-zone area ratios to the FOV under different mounting angles.

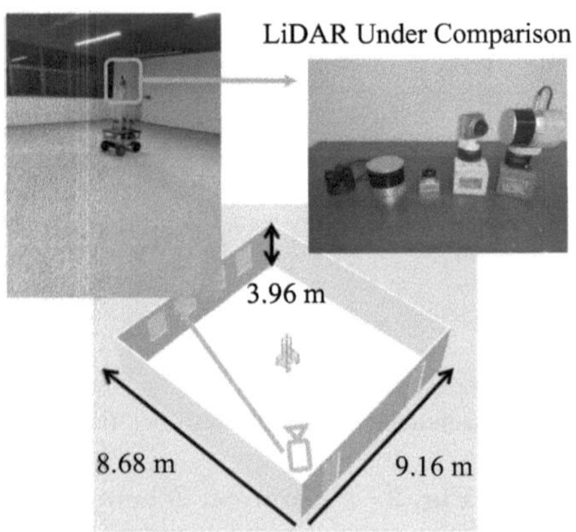

Fig. 4. Experimental Environment.

3.2.1 Experimental Conditions (a) Experimental setup: The experimental platform used in this study is the variable-angle LiDAR as shown in the Fig. 2(a). The variable-angle rotating panoramic LiDAR system consists of a Livox MID 360 LiDAR head, a DJI GM6020 active rotation motor, a time-synchronization and motor-control computing unit, and a LiDAR head connector equipped with precise angular markings.
(b) Ground-truth acquisition: To obtain a dense ground-truth point cloud, we employ the Hovermap ST MLS (mobile laser scanner) from Emesent, which can achieve millimeter-level accuracy [10]. Dense scans are collected by performing 6-minute stationary acquisitions at multiple locations within the environment. The captured data are then processed with the backend optimization software Aura to optimize the 3D map, register/merge the point clouds, and filter invalid noise points caused by glass penetration, ensuring a dense and complete ground-truth point cloud.
(c) Evaluation method: Following [11], we use *coverage* as the evaluation metric, defined as Coverage $= N_p/N_{gt}$, where N_p denotes the number of points in the ground-truth map that are covered, and N_{gt} is the total number of points in the ground-truth point cloud.

The evaluation pipeline is as follows. The evaluated and ground-truth point clouds are first aligned using ICP registration and then voxelized with the same grid. Given the centimeter-level accuracy of the Livox MID-360, the voxel size is set to 0.02 m. A KD-tree is built from the voxelized ground-truth point cloud, and nearest-neighbor search is performed for the evaluated points. If the nearest-neighbor distance is below a predefined threshold, the corresponding ground-truth voxel is considered covered. Then coverage is computed for each input frame, and both its temporal evolution and overall value are reported.

3.2.2 Mounting Angle Experiments To validate the real-world performance of different LiDAR head mounting angles, experiments were conducted in an unfurnished laboratory of size 9.16 m $\times$ 8.68 m $\times$ 3.96 m, as shown in Fig. 4. The LiDAR system with an adjustable mounting mechanism was fixed at one location in the enclosed space, while radar rotation and data acquisition were remotely controlled to avoid external interference. Data were collected for 5 min at each mounting angle. In total, 10 angles from $0°$ to $90°$ were tested at $10°$ intervals. Using the evaluation method in Sect. 3.2.1, the temporal evolution of spatial coverage under different mounting angles was obtained, as shown in Fig. 5, with the subplot reporting the final coverage at 270 s.

The experimental results generally agree with the theoretical analysis. Due to the symmetry of the mounting configuration, the $0°$ angle achieves the highest coverage, reaching 90.6%, or 177.9% of the original field of view. The remaining discrepancy between measured and predicted results mainly arises from the difference in observation conditions: the ground truth was generated by dense multi-view laser scanning, whereas the rotating panoramic LiDAR was fixed at a single viewpoint. In addition, the complex ceiling structure introduces occlusions, causing some points included in the ground truth to be unobservable from the LiDAR viewpoint and thus affecting the coverage estimation.

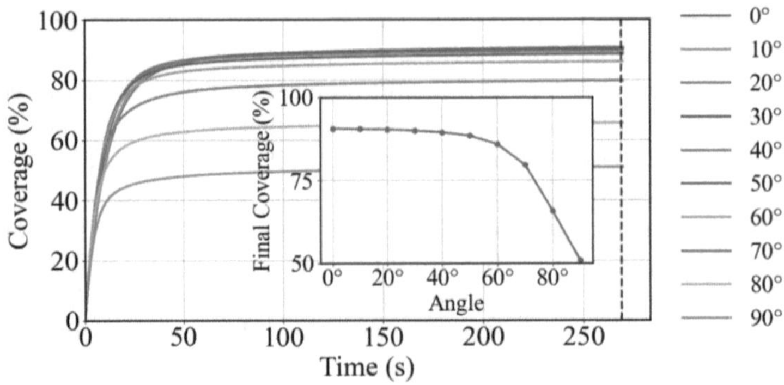

Fig. 5. Temporal Variation of Spatial Coverage Under Different Mounting Angles (LiDAR Rotation Speed: 30 rpm).

3.2.3 Comparative Study of Different LiDAR

This study, under the same experimental environment as in Sect. 3.2.2 and using the same data collection procedure, compared the coverage performance of different LiDAR sensors. The LiDARs involved in the comparison include the Hesai 16-beam, Hesai 32-beam, MID360, and Unitree L2. Figure 6 shows the coverage over time for different LiDARs. Figure 7 presents the final coverage achieved by different LiDAR types at 270 s.

The Hesai 16-beam and 32-beam LiDARs are repetitive-scanning sensors, and their spatial coverage in the test area is only 8.1% and 22.1%, respectively. The experimental results show that by equipping the Hesai LiDAR with a rotary mechanism, the LiDAR can rotate to expand its field of view, increasing the coverage to above 89.7%—an improvement of nearly tenfold. For the MID360, compared with the fixed installation, the coverage is also improved by 77.9%, which fully demonstrates the effectiveness of an active rotary mechanism. Figure 8 visualizes the coverage results of different LiDARs.

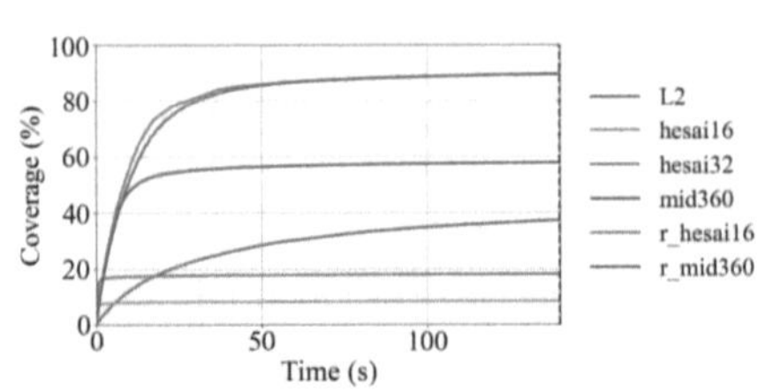

Fig. 6. Coverage over time for different LiDARs.

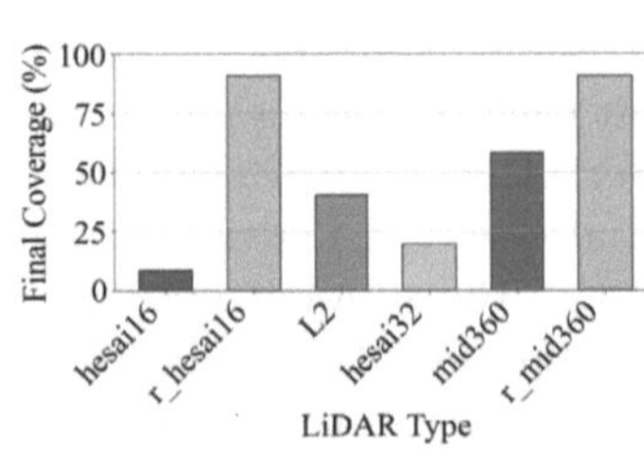

Fig. 7. Comparison of final coverage among different LiDARs.

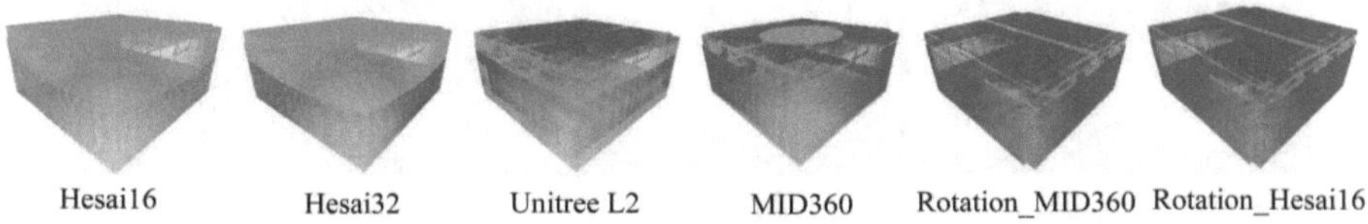

Fig. 8. Coverage performance of different LiDARs in the test area.

4 KRP-Perception Dataset

Based on the above analysis, we constructed the dataset with the LiDAR mounted at 0° and a rotational speed of 30 rpm. The platform speed was maintained at 2 m/s. Although higher platform speeds result in sparser point clouds, we still follow the platform's normal operating speed in real scenarios. Our data collection platform is shown in Fig. 1. The platform is equipped with an Orbbec camera to capture images for assisting semantic annotation, an Intel N100 computing unit for data acquisition, and the core sensing device—a rotating panoramic LiDAR with a Livox MID360 as the sensor head. The dataset includes five typical underground scenarios, as shown in Fig. 9. For each point-cloud frame, we apply HBA [12] for back-end optimization. We further introduce human-in-the-loop SLAM refinement to ensure map accuracy.

At the semantic perception level, we provide complete and fine-grained point-wise annotations for the dataset, covering 13 semantic classes such as walls, floors, and ceilings. Based on the high-precision map, we perform semantic annotation using PointLabeler [3]. The semantic categories are listed in Table 2.

Table 2. Comparison table of category examples in point clouds and images

Semantic	Color	Pointcloud	Image	Semantic	Color	Pointcloud	Image
wall				ceiling			
pillar				door			
floor				speed bump			
threshold ramp				car			
fire cabinet				wheel stopper			
person				charge pile			
other							

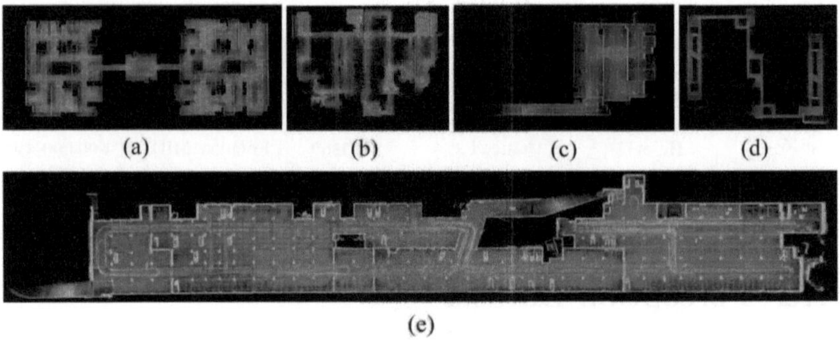

Fig. 9. Different underground environment scenes: (a)BHZF Garage (b) BFC Garage (c) BHZFL Garage (d) R1 Corridor (e) BHII Garage.

Benefiting from the REFOV provided by the rotating panoramic LiDAR, this dataset outperforms traditional fixed-FOV LiDAR datasets in both spatial coverage completeness and semantic consistency. It can effectively support perception and mapping research in complex environments. Meanwhile, the rotating sensing modality also introduces new challenges for map construction and semantic segmentation algorithms.

5 Dataset Perception Tasks

5.1 Point Cloud Semantic Segmentation

The core objective of point cloud semantic segmentation is to infer a semantic class label for every point in an environmental point cloud, thereby enabling human-like scene understanding. Semantic segmentation is an important upstream component in robotics and autonomous driving. Its outputs can serve as priors for multiple downstream tasks, providing semantic knowledge and accelerating other processes, including semantic-assisted real-time SLAM and semantic-guided autonomous exploration.

As a new sensor modality with high spatial coverage, panoramic LiDAR provides richer information for point cloud semantic segmentation, while also introducing substantially greater challenges. In this work, the semantic segmentation task is evaluated using the mean Intersection-over-Union (mIoU), defined as: $IoU_i = \frac{TP_i}{TP_i+FP_i+FN_i}$, where TP_i, FP_i, and FN_i denote the true positives, false positives, and false negatives of the i-th class, respectively. The mIoU is the average of IoU_i over all classes.

Using underground-environment data as an example, we benchmark several state-of-the-art point cloud semantic segmentation models. The results are reported in Table 3.

The best segmentation accuracy on the dataset is only 73.8%, indicating that this new LiDAR sensing modality poses significant challenges for point cloud semantic segmentation. For RangeMap-based methods, since a panoramic

Table 3. Performance Comparison of Different Models (%)

Category	Model	ALL	00	01	02	03	04	05	06	07	08	09	10	11	12
RangeMap	FIDNet [13]	54.2	72.6	99.2	80.7	88.0	78.2	32.3	72.2	37.4	87.9	0.0	0.0	55.9	0.0
	RangeNet++ [14]	44.0	71.4	97.1	35.4	59.0	90.0	4.9	15.7	46.4	53.1	77.4	13.1	6.0	2.7
Fusion	RPVNet [15]	73.8	89.3	98.5	81.4	84.0	98.3	27.5	79.8	62.8	88.5	97.1	60.1	43.7	48.1
	SPVCNN	73.8	89.3	98.5	81.4	84.0	98.3	27.5	79.8	62.8	88.5	97.1	60.1	43.7	48.1
Voxel	Cylinder3D [17]	71.7	89.3	99.0	80.1	81.2	98.2	30.8	82.7	45.6	88.7	96.8	58.1	43.1	38.2
	LPSF-LiDARNet [18]	67.0	87.9	96.8	78.3	77.4	96.6	24.9	68.7	48.2	86.8	93.5	44.3	44.4	22.9

*00: Wall, 01: Ceiling, 02: Pillar, 03: Door, 04: Floor, 05: Speed Bump, 06: Threshold Ramp, 07: Wheel Stopper, 08: Car, 09: Person, 10: Fire Cabinet, 11: Charging Pile, 12: Other.

rotating LiDAR differs from traditional fixed, repetitive-scanning LiDARs, converting the point cloud into a 2D range representation becomes more complex. Therefore, how to generate a panoramic RangeMap representation for such data is also a worthwhile problem to explore.

5.2 SLAM and Semantic SLAM

The core objective of SLAM is to enable a robot to estimate its own pose in real time while simultaneously perceiving the environment and constructing a map of the scene. After introducing a rotating mechanism, a panoramic LiDAR continuously rotates at high speed during mapping, while the platform itself is also moving. This coupled motion poses significant challenges to SLAM algorithms. In this study, we evaluate state-of-the-art SLAM methods on the KRP-Perception Dataset constructed in this paper. The evaluation metrics used are APE and RPE, whose formulations are as follows:

$$\mathrm{APE} = \sqrt{\frac{1}{N}\sum_{i=1}^{N}\left\|\left(\log\left(T_{\mathrm{gt},i}^{-1}T_{\mathrm{esti},i}\right)\right)^{\vee}\right\|_2^2},$$

$$\mathrm{RPE} = \sqrt{\frac{1}{N-\Delta t}\sum_{i=1}^{N-\Delta t}\left\|\left(\log\left(\left(T_{\mathrm{gt},i}^{-1}T_{\mathrm{gt},i+\Delta t}\right)^{-1}\left(T_{\mathrm{esti},i}^{-1}T_{\mathrm{esti},i+\Delta t}\right)\right)\right)^{\vee}\right\|_2^2}$$

In these formulas, N denotes the number of poses. T_{gt} is the ground-truth pose, and T_{esti} is the estimated pose to be evaluated. Each pose T is represented as a 4×4 homogeneous transformation matrix. Δt denotes the time interval.

We conducted experiments with SLAM algorithms on KRP-Perception Dataset, and the results are shown in Table 4.

Table 4. Comparison of Different LiDAR Odometry and SLAM Methods

Method	BHZF Garage		BHZFL Garage		R1		BHII Garage		BFC Garage		Average	
	APE	RPE	APE	RPE	APE	RPE	APE	RPE	APE	RPE	APE	RPE
FAST-LIO [19]	0.82	0.05	0.35	0.11	0.60	0.03	0.18	0.03	0.88	0.18	0.57	0.08
Point-LIO [20]	0.77	0.05	0.21	0.06	0.60	0.04	0.14	0.03	0.90	0.19	0.52	0.07
KISS-ICP [21]	73.34	0.17	27.08	2.01	70.90	7.44	37.24	4.75	1.57	0.18	42.03	2.91
LOAM [22]	–	–	–	–	–	–	–	–	–	–	–	–
LeGO-LOAM [23]	–	–	–	–	–	–	–	–	–	–	–	–

"–" indicates that the corresponding SLAM method failed (unable to construct a map), so no results are reported.

Traditional SLAM algorithms exhibit varying degrees of failure under the rotating LiDAR modality, indicating that the dataset poses significant challenges to existing methods.

With the rapid progress of point cloud semantic segmentation, a variety of semantics-driven downstream tasks have become feasible. Among them, the core objective of semantic SLAM is to leverage high-dimensional semantic information to enable efficient and fast SLAM-based map construction. Semantic SLAM requires complex training and deployment and is still under active development. Unfortunately, there is currently no effective semantic SLAM method available for panoramic rotating LiDAR.

We still take the 32-beam LiDAR underground parking garage data as an example and conduct training, deployment, and experimental evaluation of the SuMa++ algorithm. The results are reported in the Table 5.

The results indicate that incorporating semantics has a positive impact on map construction. However, semantic SLAM is still in its early stage, and SLAM on panoramic rotating LiDAR datasets also poses new challenges for semantic SLAM algorithms.

5.3 Semantics-Driven Panoramic LiDAR Simulation Environment

To address the hardware dependency issue in algorithm testing, we build upon [25] to implement panoramic LiDAR simulation and develop a semantics-driven data simulation pipeline. Specifically, annotated data can be imported into the simulator, and the system can output semantic point clouds under multiple LiDAR-head configurations (including fused multi-head setups). Moreover,

Table 5. Semantic SLAM.

Method	APE	RPE
LOAM [22]	4.43	0.04
LeGO-LOAM [23]	20.97	0.44
KISS-ICP [21]	4.64	0.03
SuMa++ [24]	2.45	0.36

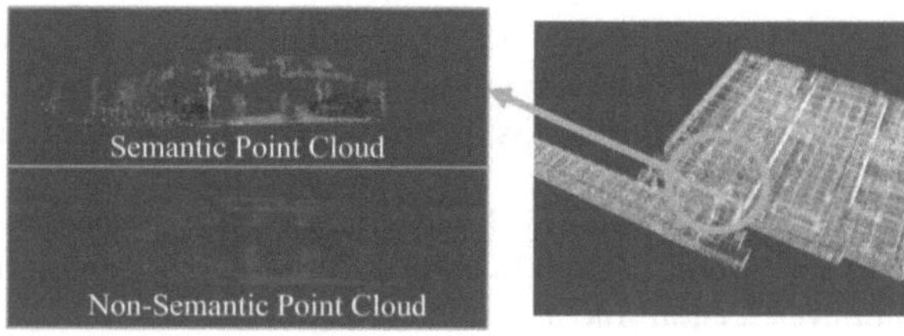

Fig. 10. Semantics-driven simulation environment.

we design an API framework in the ROS environment, enabling seamless integration with downstream mapping and navigation algorithms, and supporting semantics-driven SLAM as well as autonomous exploration tasks. As shown in Fig. 10, we compare the semantic point cloud and the non-semantic point cloud generated by the simulation environment.

6 Conclusion

In this study, we systematically investigate the coverage advantages of a panoramic rotating LiDAR and analyze how different factors influence its coverage performance. We further release a panoramic rotating LiDAR dataset, which is expected to benefit point-cloud semantic segmentation and a wide range of semantics-driven downstream tasks. In future work, we will continue to expand the dataset and progressively extend the downstream applications supported by the proposed semantics-driven simulation environment.

Acknowledgement. This research was fully supported by the National Natural Science Foundation of China (NSFC, Grant No. 62303036) and Zhejiang Provincial Natural Science Foundation of China under Grant No. LY23F020026.

References

1. Ramezani, M., Khosoussi, K., Catt, G., et al.: Wildcat: online continuous-time 3d lidar-inertial SLAM. CoRR **abs/2205.12595** (2022)
2. Cui, J., He, Y., Niu, J., et al.: α lidar: an adaptive high-resolution panoramic lidar system. In: Proceedings of the 30th Annual International Conference on Mobile Computing and Networking, MobiCom 2024, pp. 1515–1529. ACM, New York, NY, USA (2024)
3. Behley, J., Garbade, M., Milioto, A.: Semantickitti: a dataset for semantic scene understanding of lidar sequences. In: IEEE/CVF International Conference on Computer Vision (ICCV), pp. 9296–9306 (2019)
4. Caesar, H., Bankiti, V., Lang, A.H.: nuscenes: a multimodal dataset for autonomous driving. In: 2020 IEEE/CVF Conference on Computer Vision and Pattern Recognition (CVPR), pp. 11618–11628 (2020)

5. Sun, P., Kretzschmar, H., Dotiwalla, X., et al.: Scalability in perception for autonomous driving: waymo open dataset. In: Proceedings of the IEEE/CVF Conference on Computer Vision and Pattern Recognition (CVPR), pp. 2446–2454 (2020)
6. Roynard, X., Deschaud, J.E., Goulette, F.: Paris-lille-3d: a point cloud dataset for urban scene segmentation and classification. In: IEEE/CVF Conference on Computer Vision and Pattern Recognition Workshops (CVPRW), pp. 2027–2030 (2018)
7. Gaidon, A., Wang, Q., Cabon, Y., Vig, E.: Virtual worlds as proxy for multi-object tracking analysis. In: Proceedings of the IEEE Conference on Computer Vision and Pattern Recognition (CVPR), pp. 4340–4349 (2016)
8. Chang, A.X., Funkhouser, T., Guibas, L., et al.: Shapenet: an information-rich 3d model repository. Comput. Sci. (2015)
9. Hackel, T., Savinov, N., Ladicky, L.: Semantic3d.net: a new large-scale point cloud classification benchmark. ISPRS Annals of Photogrammetry, Remote Sensing and Spatial Information Sciences (2017)
10. Emesent: Hovermap accuracy report. Technical report Emesent (2024). Accessed 14 Jan 2026
11. Turkar, Y., Meshram, P., Aluckal, C.: Empir3D : A Framework for Multi-Dimensional Point Cloud Assessment. arXiv:2306.03660 (2024)
12. Liu, X., Liu, Z., Kong, F., et al.: Large-scale lidar consistent mapping using hierarchical lidar bundle adjustment. IEEE Robot. Autom. Lett. **8**, 1523–1530 (2022)
13. Zhao, Y., Bai, L., Huang, X.: Fidnet: lidar point cloud semantic segmentation with fully interpolation decoding. In: 2021 IEEE/RSJ International Conference on Intelligent Robots and Systems (IROS), pp. 4453–4458 (2021)
14. Milioto, A., Vizzo, I., Behley, J. et al.: Rangenet ++: fast and accurate lidar semantic segmentation. In: 2019 IEEE/RSJ International Conference on Intelligent Robots and Systems (IROS), pp. 4213–4220 (2019)
15. Xu, J., Zhang, R., Dou, J.: Rpvnet: a deep and efficient range-point-voxel fusion network for lidar point cloud segmentation. In: 2021 IEEE/CVF International Conference on Computer Vision (ICCV), pp. 16004–16013 (2021)
16. Fan, Y.C., Yan, W.Z., Liu, Y.S.: 3d large scene semantic segmentation system. In: 2023 International Conference on Consumer Electronics - Taiwan, pp. 85–86. ICCE-Taiwan (2023)
17. Zhou, H., Zhu, X., Song, X.: Cylinder3d: an effective 3d framework for driving-scene lidar semantic segmentation (2020)
18. Zhang, Y., Cui, J., Jia, H., et al.: Lpsf-lidarnet: log-polar spatiotemporal fusion-based lidar point cloud semantic segmentation for autonomous driving. In: Artificial Neural Networks and Machine Learning – ICANN 2025: 34th International Conference on Artificial Neural Networks. Kaunas, Lithuania, 9–12 September 2025, Proceedings, Part II, pp. 148–159. Springer, Heidelberg (2025)
19. Xu, W., Zhang, F.: Fast-lio: a fast, robust lidar-inertial odometry package by tightly-coupled iterated kalman filter. IEEE Robot. Autom. Lett. **6**(2), 3317–3324 (2021)
20. He, D., Xu, W., Chen, N. et al.: Point-lio: robust high-bandwidth light detection and ranging inertial odometry. In: Advanced Intelligent Systems, vol. 5 (2023)
21. Vizzo, I., Guadagnino, T., Mersch, B., et al.: Kiss-icp: In defense of point-to-point icp – simple, accurate, and robust registration if done the right way. IEEE Robotics and Automation Letters **8**(2), 1029–1036 (2023)
22. Zhang, J., Singh, S.: Loam: lidar odometry and mapping in real-time. In: Robotics: Science and Systems Conference (RSS), pp. 109–111 (2014)

23. Shan, T., Englot, B.: Lego-loam: lightweight and ground-optimized lidar odometry and mapping on variable terrain. In: IEEE/RSJ International Conference on Intelligent Robots and Systems (IROS), pp. 4758–4765 (2018)
24. Chen, X., Milioto, A., Palazzolo, E. et al.: Suma++: efficient lidar-based semantic slam. In: 2019 IEEE/RSJ International Conference on Intelligent Robots and Systems (IROS), pp. 4530–4537 (2019)
25. Kong, F., Liu, X., Tang, B., et al.: Marsim: a light-weight point-realistic simulator for lidar-based uavs. IEEE Robot. Autom. Lett. **8**(5), 2954–2961 (2023)

Agent and Embodied Intelligence

Structured Reinforcement Learning for Multi-agent Formation Target Tracking via Scalar Gain Scheduling

Shuangfei Ji, Yiquan Ren, Yingjie Guo, and Yazhou Hu(✉)

School of Computer and Artificial Intelligence, Zhengzhou University, Zhengzhou 450001, China
hooasia1990@outlook.com

Abstract. This work addresses the persistent challenge of post-capture drift in multi-agent formation tracking, where agents achieve positional consensus but suffer from residual velocity misalignment under acceleration limits. Traditional controllers struggle to balance aggressive long-range pursuit with precise near-field velocity coherence. We introduce a knowledge-guided, structured Reinforcement Learning (RL) framework that preserves interpretability while retaining a fixed-time consensus controller as the backbone. Instead of end-to-end policy learning, we restrict the RL agent to learning only a single bounded scalar gain that schedules a velocity-damping term. A novel distance–speed gating mechanism injects domain knowledge, dynamically activating this scheduler in the near-field regime to suppress drift while leaving far-field pursuit largely unaffected. This design preserves a clear fallback to the backbone when the learned term is suppressed. Extensive experiments show that our method substantially reduces post-capture drift (from 0.3427 ± 0.0106 m to 0.1937 ± 0.0413 m) and improves integrated absolute error in the primary benchmark (from 1.8198 ± 0.0290 to 1.0349 ± 0.1517 m·s), illustrating the value of embedding structural priors into multi-agent learning.

Keywords: formation control · target tracking · structured reinforcement learning · gain scheduling · fixed-time consensus · multi-agent systems

1 Introduction

Multi-agent formation tracking of a moving target is a core capability in robotics, supporting applications from environmental monitoring and search-and-rescue to automated warehousing and aerial swarms [1,2]. In formation target tracking, agents must pursue a dynamic reference while maintaining a prescribed geometry under strict physical limits, especially acceleration saturation.

In acceleration-limited second-order systems, position "capture" can occur before velocities synchronize with the reference motion. The resulting velocity mismatch causes persistent post-capture drift: residual motion and accumulated

J. Niu et al. (Eds.): KSEM 2026, LNAI 16631, pp. 459–471, 2027.
https://doi.org/10.1007/978-981-92-2759-4_34

displacement error after entering the capture region. This exposes a key trade-off: aggressive far-field pursuit and gentle near-field damping for velocity coherence are hard to achieve simultaneously with fixed gains.

Classical distributed controllers offer reliability and stability guarantees, but fixed gains can degrade under aggressive maneuvers, uncertainty, and tight saturation. CTDE-based RL enables adaptation, yet action-level or unconstrained residual policies often remain sample-inefficient, reward-sensitive, and harder to verify for deployment. We therefore restrict learning to a single bounded, non-negative scalar that schedules only a velocity-damping term inside a fixed-time consensus backbone; a distance–speed gate activates this scheduler mainly in the near field and otherwise recovers the backbone. The next section reviews related work and formalizes the problem.

2 Related Work and Problem Formulation

Our work lies at the intersection of distributed control theory and multi-agent reinforcement learning (MARL) for saturation-constrained formation tracking. We briefly review four related directions before formalizing the problem.

Distributed formation control and fixed-time consensus Distributed control provides a reliable basis for multi-agent coordination. Consensus and gradient-type controllers maintain formations using only local information, while fixed-time and prescribed-time protocols provide convergence bounds independent of initial conditions [3,4]. Extensions handle switching topologies, non-ideal dynamics, and robotic formation-tracking implementations [5–7], motivating our use of a fixed-time backbone that remains active when the learned component is gated off.

Multi-agent reinforcement learning and structured policies Multi-agent RL enables adaptive coordination in cooperative tasks. CTDE methods address non-stationarity and credit assignment [8–10], while graph-based representations and parameter sharing improve scalability. In target tracking, MARL has been used for dynamic formation reconfiguration, sometimes with demonstrations or prior knowledge [11,12]. However, many approaches still learn high-dimensional continuous actions directly, which increases sample complexity and weakens interpretability.

Residual-action reinforcement learning and structured parameter learning Residual-action RL improves a stable base controller by learning an additive correction [13]. More structured variants instead learn controller parameters, such as gains or scheduling variables, which improves interpretability and constrains the policy space [14]. This connects naturally to gain scheduling for regime-dependent dynamics [15,16]. Our method further simplifies this interface by learning a single bounded, non-negative scalar that schedules one damping-related gain.

Safety-/stability-aware learning control Safety in learning control is often addressed by embedding Lyapunov or barrier-function constraints into learning [17,18], or by safe model-based RL with stability-oriented guarantees [19]. Our approach follows this philosophy at the architecture level: we restrict learning to a bounded gain schedule that only adds dissipative velocity damping, acting as a tunable augment to a stable backbone and simplifying stability-oriented analysis.

2.1 Problem Formulation

This section defines the Multi-Agent Formation Target Tracking task, including agent dynamics, communication, target representation, and control objectives under strict saturation.

System Model and Notation. Consider a homogeneous team of N agents operating in $\mathbb{R}^3$. The state of agent i at discrete time step k is its position $p_{i,k} \in \mathbb{R}^3$ and velocity $v_{i,k} \in \mathbb{R}^3$. Each agent's motion is governed by a discrete-time, double-integrator model. The control input is a commanded acceleration $a_{i,k}^{\mathrm{cmd}} \in \mathbb{R}^3$, subject to actuator saturation.

Agents communicate locally over an undirected, connected graph $\mathcal{G} = (\mathcal{V}, \mathcal{E})$, where $\mathcal{V} = \{1, \ldots, N\}$ and $(i,j) \in \mathcal{E}$ if agents i and j can exchange state information. The neighbor set of agent i is $\mathcal{N}_i = \{j \mid (i,j) \in \mathcal{E}\}$. The target is represented by a rigid configuration of M reference points $\{q_{m,k}\}_{m=1}^{M}$ moving in $\mathbb{R}^3$. Its geometric center at time k is

$$c_k = \frac{1}{M} \sum_{m=1}^{M} \mathbf{q}_{m,k}. \tag{1}$$

Assume the target's translational velocity $v_{c,k}$ (e.g., its center velocity) is either known or can be estimated.

Target-Aligned Dynamic Coordinate Frame. To generate formation references that move with the target, we define a target-aligned orthonormal frame at each time step that follows the target's primary direction of motion.

Let $v_{c,k}$ be the estimated center velocity. We construct three orthonormal basis vectors $b_{1,k}$, $b_{2,k}$, $b_{3,k}$. (1) Primary axis $b_{1,k}$: aligned with the motion direction if $\|v_{c,k}\|_2$ exceeds a small threshold ε; otherwise, it defaults to a fixed axis (e.g., e_x).

$$b_{1,k} = \begin{cases} e_x, & \|v_{c,k}\|_2 < \varepsilon, \\ v_{c,k} / \|v_{c,k}\|_2, & \text{otherwise}. \end{cases} \tag{2}$$

(2) Secondary and tertiary axes $(b_{2,k}, b_{3,k})$: constructed via a Gram-Schmidt-like procedure to form a right-handed frame and improve numerical stability:

$$b_{2,k} = \frac{r_k - (r_k^\top b_{1,k}) b_{1,k}}{\left\| r_k - (r_k^\top b_{1,k}) b_{1,k} \right\|_2 + \varepsilon}, \tag{3}$$

$$b_{3,k} = \frac{b_{1,k} \times b_{2,k}}{\left\| b_{1,k} \times b_{2,k} \right\|_2 + \varepsilon}. \tag{4}$$

Here r_k is a deterministic reference vector for Gram–Schmidt: we set $r_k = e_z$ if $\left| e_z^\top b_{1,k} \right| \leq 0.9$, and otherwise $r_k = e_y$ to avoid near-collinearity.

The resulting rotation matrix $R_k = [b_{1,k}, b_{2,k}, b_{3,k}] \in \mathbb{R}^{3\times3}$ defines the transformation from the world frame to the target-aligned frame: for any world vector x, its coordinates in the target-aligned frame are $x^L = R_k^\top x$.

Formation Reference Generation. Given a predefined formation template defined by static offsets $\{p_i^{\mathcal{L}}\}_{i=1}^N$ in the target-aligned frame, the desired position for agent i in the world frame is:

$$p_{d,i,k} = c_k + R_k p_i^{\mathcal{L}} + p_{\text{off}}, \tag{5}$$

where p_{off} is an optional global offset. The corresponding desired velocity $v_{\text{ref},i,k}$ and acceleration $a_{\text{ref},i,k}$ are estimated via finite differences of the trajectory $\{p_{d,i,k}\}$:

$$v_{\text{ref},i,k} = \frac{p_{d,i,k} - p_{d,i,k-1}}{\Delta t}, \tag{6}$$

and

$$a_{\text{ref},i,k} = \frac{v_{\text{ref},i,k} - v_{\text{ref},i,k-1}}{\Delta t}, \tag{7}$$

respectively.

The core tracking error for agent i is then:

$$e_{i,k} = p_{i,k} - p_{d,i,k}. \tag{8}$$

Agent Dynamics and Actuator Saturation. We model agent dynamics with a discrete-time, acceleration-commanded point-mass model, incorporating norm-based saturation to reflect real-world actuator limits:

$$v_{i,k+1} = \text{clip}_{v_{\max}}\left(v_{i,k} + \text{clip}_{a_{\max}}\left(a_{i,k}^{\text{cmd}}\right) \Delta t \right), \tag{9}$$

$$p_{i,k+1} = p_{i,k} + v_{i,k+1} \Delta t. \tag{10}$$

where Δt is the control time step. The saturation function $\text{clip}_b(u)$ for a limit $b > 0$ is:

$$\text{clip}_b(u) = \begin{cases} u, & \|u\|_2 \leq b, \\ b\,u / \|u\|_2, & \text{otherwise.} \end{cases} \tag{11}$$

The saturation limits $a_{\max} > 0$ and $v_{\max} > 0$ are identical for all agents, representing a unified saturation constraint.

Control Objectives. Under the acceleration-limited dynamics, the primary objective is twofold: (1) drive all agents into a small-error capture region around their desired formation points $p_{d,i,k}$ as quickly as possible; (2) once captured, synchronize agent velocities $v_{i,k}$ with the reference motion $v_{\text{ref},i,k}$ to minimize post-capture drift, i.e., persistent displacement error caused by residual velocity mismatch.

3 Methodology

We consider acceleration-limited formation tracking, where agents must reach a moving formation reference under unified saturation. Performance is phase-dependent: far-field tracking favors aggressive pursuit to enter a capture region, while near-field tracking requires velocity coherence to suppress post-capture drift. Fixed-gain controllers are reliable but cannot adapt across phases; end-to-end RL adapts but is often sample-inefficient and difficult to validate for deployment.

We integrate learning through a constrained, interpretable interface (Fig. 1). A distributed fixed-time backbone outputs saturated acceleration commands. A TD3 policy does not output actions; it produces a single bounded nonnegative scalar $m_{i,k}^{\text{raw}}$ that schedules only the velocity-damping channel. A distance–speed gate restricts scheduling to the near-field, so far-field pursuit remains dominated by the backbone. When the gate suppresses scheduling, the learned term smoothly vanishes ($m_{i,k}^{\text{eff}} \to 0$), providing a transparent fallback.

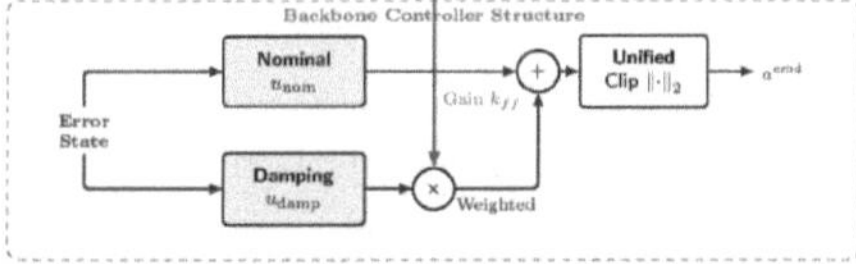

(a) Structured RL interface with gated scalar gain scheduling

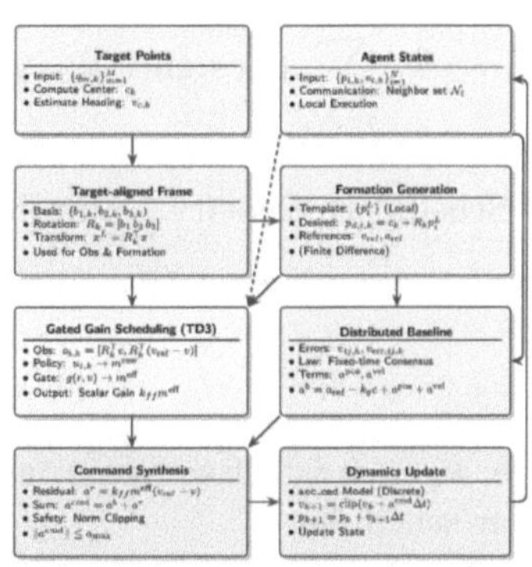

(b) End-to-end execution pipeline of the proposed framework

Fig. 1. Structured RL framework with gated scalar gain scheduling. (a) Constrained interface: a distance–speed gate activates a bounded scalar m_i^{eff} that schedules only the velocity-damping gain in a fixed-time backbone. (b) Execution pipeline.

The pipeline in Fig. 1(b) runs in discrete time with commanded acceleration $a_{i,k}^{\text{cmd}}$ under unified acceleration and velocity saturation. We describe the backbone controller, the phase-aware gate, the scalar scheduler, and the training objective.

3.1 Distributed Fixed-Time Backbone Controller

The foundation of our hybrid controller is a distributed, edge-based fixed-time consensus protocol adapted for acceleration-level control. Let $\mathcal{N}_i$ denote the neighbor set of agent i within an undirected, connected communication graph.

The edge position error and edge velocity error are defined as

$$e_{ij,k} = e_{i,k} - e_{j,k}, \quad j \in \mathcal{N}_i, \tag{12}$$

$$v_{\text{err},ij,k} = v_{\text{err},i,k} - v_{\text{err},j,k}, \tag{13}$$

where $v_{\text{err},i,k} = v_{i,k} - v_{\text{ref},i,k}$.

Using the element-wise signed power maps $\text{sign}(\mathbf{x}) \odot |\mathbf{x}|^{\alpha}$ and $\text{sign}(\mathbf{x}) \odot |\mathbf{x}|^{\beta}$ (where $\odot$ is the Hadamard product and $0 < \alpha < 1 < \beta$), the controller computes three acceleration components:

(1) Position Consensus Term (a_i^{pos}): Drives agents to the desired formation shape:

$$a_{i,k}^{\text{pos}} = -\sum_{j \in \mathcal{N}_i} \left(c_1 \, \text{sign}(e_{ij,k}) \odot (|e_{ij,k}|)^{\alpha} + c_2 \, \text{sign}(e_{ij,k}) \odot (|e_{ij,k}|)^{\beta} \right). \tag{14}$$

(2) Velocity Consensus Term (a_i^{vel}): Aligns agent velocities with each other:

$$a_{i,k}^{\text{vel}} = -k_v \sum_{j \in \mathcal{N}_i} \left(c_1 \, \text{sign}(v_{\text{err},ij,k}) \odot (|v_{\text{err},ij,k}|)^{\alpha} + c_2 \, \text{sign}(v_{\text{err},ij,k}) \odot (|v_{\text{err},ij,k}|)^{\beta} \right). \tag{15}$$

(3) Scheduled Velocity Damping Term (a_i^{ff}): The only term modified by RL. It provides damping relative to the reference velocity:

$$a_{i,k}^{\text{ff}} = -k_{ff} \, m_{i,k}^{\text{eff}} \, v_{\text{err},i,k}, \tag{16}$$

Here, $k_{\text{ff}} \geq 0$ is a fixed gain, and $m_{i,k}^{\text{eff}} \in [0, m_{\max}]$ is the learned, non-negative scalar scheduler.

The final commanded acceleration for agent i combines these terms with proportional feedback on the tracking error $e_{i,k}$ and the reference acceleration $a_{\text{ref},i,k}$:

$$a_{i,k}^{\text{cmd}} = a_{\text{ref},i,k} - k_g e_{i,k} + a_{i,k}^{\text{pos}} + a_{i,k}^{\text{vel}} + a_{i,k}^{\text{ff}}. \tag{17}$$

Here $k_g, k_v, c_1, c_2, k_{ff}$ are backbone gains, and only k_{ff} is scheduled by RL through the nonnegative scalar $m_{i,k}^{\text{eff}}$. The term a^{ff} acts as scheduled damping on the velocity error. The executed command is clipped by $\text{clip}_{a_{\max}}(\cdot)$ as defined in Eq. (11).

3.2 Phase-Aware Gating Mechanism

To activate scheduling primarily when it is beneficial (near-field tracking), we introduce a distance–speed gate that encodes the fact that strong velocity damping can hinder long-range pursuit. Let $r_{i,k} = \|e_{i,k}\|_2$ denote the distance to the desired formation point.

First, an effective look-ahead distance is computed by

$$r_{i,k}^{\text{eff}} = r_{i,k} + T_{\text{la}} \max\big(v_{i,k}^{\text{eff}},\, v_{\text{floor}}\big), \tag{18}$$

where $v_{i,k}^{\text{eff}} = \max\big(\|v_{i,k}\|_2,\, \|v_{\text{ref},i,k}\|_2\big)$. The term $T_{\text{la}} v_{i,k}^{\text{eff}}$ acts as a simple prediction horizon. We use a small speed floor $v_{\text{floor}} > 0$ to prevent vanishing look-ahead when $v_{i,k}^{\text{eff}} \approx 0$; in all experiments we set $v_{\text{floor}} = 0.2\,\text{m/s}$.

A piecewise-linear gate $g_{i,k} \in [0,1]$ is defined with thresholds $r_{\text{zero}} > r_{\text{full}}$:

$$g_{i,k} = \begin{cases} 0, & r_{i,k}^{\text{eff}} \geq r_{\text{zero}}, \\ 1, & r_{i,k}^{\text{eff}} \leq r_{\text{full}}, \\ \dfrac{r_{\text{zero}} - r_{i,k}^{\text{eff}}}{r_{\text{zero}} - r_{\text{full}}}, & \text{otherwise}. \end{cases} \tag{19}$$

An optional shaping exponent $p \geq 1$ can be applied for a nonlinear transition: $\tilde{g}_{i,k} = (g_{i,k})^p$.

3.3 Scalar Gain Scheduling via Reinforcement Learning

The learning agent's role is to produce the raw scheduling multiplier $m_{i,k}^{\text{raw}}$, which is then gated to yield the final effective scheduler:

$$m_{i,k}^{\text{eff}} = g_{i,k}^{p}\, m_{i,k}^{\text{raw}}. \tag{20}$$

Each agent's policy uses a compact, local observation in the target-aligned frame:

$$o_{i,k} = \left[\frac{(R_k^\top e_{i,k})^\top}{r_{\text{scale}}},\ \frac{\big(R_k^\top (v_{\text{ref},i,k} - v_{i,k})\big)^\top}{v_{\text{scale}}} \right]^\top \in \mathbb{R}^6. \tag{21}$$

The TD3 algorithm is employed to learn the policy. The actor network π_θ maps the observation $o_{i,k}$ to a scalar $u_{i,k} \in [-1, 1]$. During training, exploration noise ϵ_k is added. A dead-zone of width δ and linear scaling transform this output into the bounded, non-negative raw multiplier:

$$s_{i,k} = \text{clip}_{[0,1]}\left(\frac{\max(|u_{i,k}| - \delta, 0)}{1 - \delta} \right), \tag{22}$$

$$m_{i,k}^{\text{raw}} = m_{\min} + (m_{\max} - m_{\min})\, s_{i,k}. \tag{23}$$

This design ensures $m_{i,k}^{\text{raw}} \in [m_{\min}, m_{\max}]$, with $m_{\min} \geq 0$.

3.4 Training Objective and Implementation

A per-step reward function is utilized that explicitly targets the dual objectives of rapid capture and velocity coherence, while regularizing the scheduler for smoothness:

$$\mathcal{R}_{i,k} = -w_p \left\|e_{i,k}\right\|_2 - w_v \left\|v_{i,k} - v_{\text{ref},i,k}\right\|_2 - w_m \left(m_{i,k}^{\text{raw}} - 1\right)^2 - w_s \left(m_{i,k}^{\text{raw}} - m_{i,k-1}^{\text{raw}}\right)^2. \tag{24}$$

The first two terms penalize position error and velocity mismatch. The last two terms are optional regularizers for bounded and smooth scheduling. We use parameter sharing across homogeneous agents: a single actor and critic are trained on experiences pooled from all agents, while execution remains decentralized.

4 Experiments

4.1 Experimental Setup

We evaluate all methods in a custom multi-agent 3D simulator with unified saturation limits. Unless otherwise specified, the nominal setting uses $N = 5$ agents with a Ring topology, $\Delta t = 0.01$, and a 30 s horizon. Table 1 summarizes the simulator, controller, scheduler, and experiment matrix. Training uses 40k gradient steps with shared TD3 and standard MLPs: Actor [6 → 16 → 64 → 128 → 64 → 32 → 1], Critic [7 → 16 → 64 → 128 → 64 → 32 → 1], ReLU hidden layers, and Tanh actor output.

Table 1. Nominal evaluation setup and experimental matrix.

Category	Item	Value
Simulation	Horizon, Δt	30.0 s, 0.01 s
	World bounds (x, y, z)	$[-10, 10] \times [-10, 10] \times [-5, 5]$
Initialization	Mode, ranges	Random; $x, y \in [-3, 3]$, $z \in [-1, 1]$
Formation	Nominal template	Cube (scale 1.7, offset $(0, 0, 0)$)
Physics	Team and limits	$N = 5$, Ring; $v_{\max} = 5.0\,\text{m/s}$, $a_{\max} = 10.0\,\text{m/s}^2$
Observation	Scaling	Cartesian; $r_{\text{scale}} = 1.0\,\text{m}$, $v_{\text{scale}} = 5.0\,\text{m/s}$
Gating	Thresholds, look-ahead	$r_{\text{zero}} = 8.0\,\text{m}$, $r_{\text{full}} = 2.0\,\text{m}$; $T_{\text{la}} = 0.5\,\text{s}$; $v_{\text{floor}} = 0.2\,\text{m/s}$; $p = 2.0$
Scheduler	Range, dead-zone	$[m_{\min}, m_{\max}] = [0.0, 5.0]$, $\delta = 0.1$
Controller	Gains	$k_g = 4.0$, $k_v = 0.5$, $k_{ff} = 9.0$; $c_1 = c_2 = 0.8$
Experiments	Baseline comparison	$N = 5$, Ring, $v = 5, a = 10$; figure-eight, zigzag, spiral, circle; 5 seeds; 30 s
	Gate ablation	$N = 5$, Ring, $v = 5, a = 10$; figure-eight; 3 seeds; 30 s
	Generalization (topology)	$N = 8$, Chain/Star, $v = 5, a = 10$; figure-eight; 3 seeds; 30 s
	Robustness	$N = 5$, Ring, $v = 5, a = 10$; figure-eight; 3 seeds; 30 s

We report settling time T_{set} with $\varepsilon_{\text{set}} = 1.0\,\text{m}$ and a 1.0 s hold window, plus post-capture Drift_{5s}, IAE_{5s}, and Cos_v over the subsequent 5 s, together with full-horizon summaries (E_{avg}, $E_{\max}$). CVaR_{95} is used only in diagnostic tables. The learned scheduler is trained with TD3 using parameter sharing; Table 2 lists the hyperparameters.

Table 2. TD3 training hyperparameters used in our implementation.

Hyperparameter	Value	Hyperparameter	Value
Discount factor γ	0.99	Soft target update τ	0.005
Actor learning rate	1×10^{-3}	Critic learning rate	1×10^{-3}
Batch size	256	Replay buffer size	200,000
Warm-up steps	5,000	Target policy smoothing noise (std)	0.2
Noise clip	0.5	Policy delay	2
Action limit (scalar)	1.0	Training episodes	200
Updates per episode	200	Rollout exploration noise (std)	0.15

4.2 Baselines and Protocol

Primary baselines: We compare three methods that share the same backbone controller and unified saturation limits; they differ only in how the scalar scaling $m_{i,k}^{\text{eff}}$ is specified:

1. **Baseline (fixed-gain):** $m_{i,k}^{\text{eff}} \equiv 1$ (no scheduling).
2. **Handcrafted schedule:** $m_{i,k}^{\text{eff}}$ from a fixed heuristic mapping of tracking errors.
3. **Ours (learned schedule):** $m_{i,k}^{\text{eff}} = g\, m_{i,k}^{\text{raw}}$ with a learned scalar scheduler and distance–speed gate (Sect. 3).

Fair protocol: All methods share the same dynamics, saturation limits, formation templates, and target-trajectory generators; each table reports mean ± std over the seeds specified in its caption. We also tested action-level and residual-action TD3 baselines under the same saturation constraints; they were unstable or frequently timed out.

4.3 Experimental Results

Under unified saturation, Table 3 shows that the learned schedule achieves the lowest post-capture drift and also reduces IAE_{5s}. Relative to the fixed-gain baseline, Drift_{5s} drops from 0.3427 to 0.1937 m (about 43%), while saturation usage decreases from 57.8 to 52.2 and control energy from 3.32 to 3.23. The handcrafted schedule remains worse on post-capture metrics under the same constraints.

The gate keeps the learned scaling largely inactive in the far field and activates it near capture, so the main benefit appears in near-field drift suppression under clipping; IAE_{5s} may improve less when part of the drift reduction comes from short corrective transients around capture.

For long-horizon tracking, Table 4 reports lower tail-window error and drift than the handcrafted schedule ($\bar{e}_{\text{tail}}$: −20.7%, $\text{Drift}_{\text{tail}}$: −25.2%) together with reduced tail saturation ($\text{Sat}_{\text{tail}}\%$: 60.9 → 54.1), indicating that the short-horizon gains remain visible in several tail metrics, while some steady-state trade-offs relative to the fixed-gain baseline remain.

Table 3. Main quantitative results under unified saturation (N = 5, Ring; mean ± std over 5 seeds).

Method	T_{set} [s]	$Drift_{5s}$ [m]	IAE_{5s} [m·s]	Cos_v	J_u	Sat%
Baseline (Fixed Gain) [3]	7.05 ± 0.13	0.3427 ± 0.0106	1.8198 ± 0.0290	0.9900 ± 0.0000	3.3229 ± 0.0022	57.8360 ± 0.1304
Handcrafted Schedule [15]	9.97 ± 0.81	0.8600 ± 0.1600	4.5100 ± 0.8900	0.9700 ± 0.0300	3.3500 ± 0.0100	59.2000 ± 0.2000
Ours (Learned Schedule; TD3) [20]	7.69 ± 0.53	0.1937 ± 0.0413	1.0349 ± 0.1517	0.9800 ± 0.0100	3.2323 ± 0.0072	52.2240 ± 0.1186

Table 4. Long-horizon tracking (tail window $T_{\text{tail}} = 10\,\text{s}$, duration = 90 s). Δ: Ours vs Handcrafted.

Method	$\bar{e}_{\text{tail}}$ [m]	$\text{Drift}_{\text{tail}}$ [m]	$\text{Cos}_v^{\text{tail}}$	$\text{Sat}_{\text{tail}}\%$	J_u^{tail}	$\Delta\bar{e}_{\text{tail}}$	Δ $\text{Drift}_{\text{tail}}$
Baseline (Fixed Gain) [3]	1.74 ± 0.00	1.59 ± 0.00	0.77 ± 0.00	59.8 ± 0.0	3.39 ± 0.00	–	–
Handcrafted Schedule [15]	2.91 ± 0.00	2.82 ± 0.00	0.77 ± 0.00	60.9 ± 0.0	3.41 ± 0.00	–	–
Ours (Learned Schedule; TD3) [20]	2.31 ± 0.01	2.11 ± 0.01	0.58 ± 0.00	54.1 ± 0.2	3.37 ± 0.01	-20.7%	–25.2%

Figure 2 provides an illustrative additional-seed example in which the difference becomes more visible after capture, while far-field pursuit remains similar under the same saturation constraint.

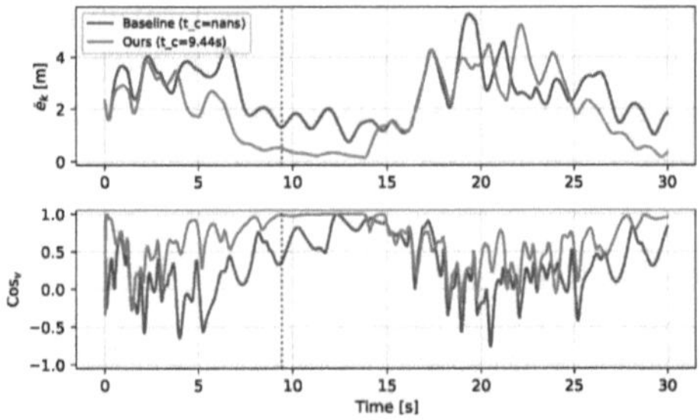

Fig. 2. Illustrative time-series example from an additional seed comparing Baseline vs. Ours. Top: mean tracking error $\bar{e}_k$. Bottom: velocity-direction coherence Cos_v (averaged). Vertical lines mark capture time t_c (undefined if not captured within the horizon).

4.4 Trajectory-Specific Qualitative Results

To complement the aggregate tables, we visualize representative rollouts under four maneuvers and formations. These showcased cases (Cases 1–4 in Fig. 3)

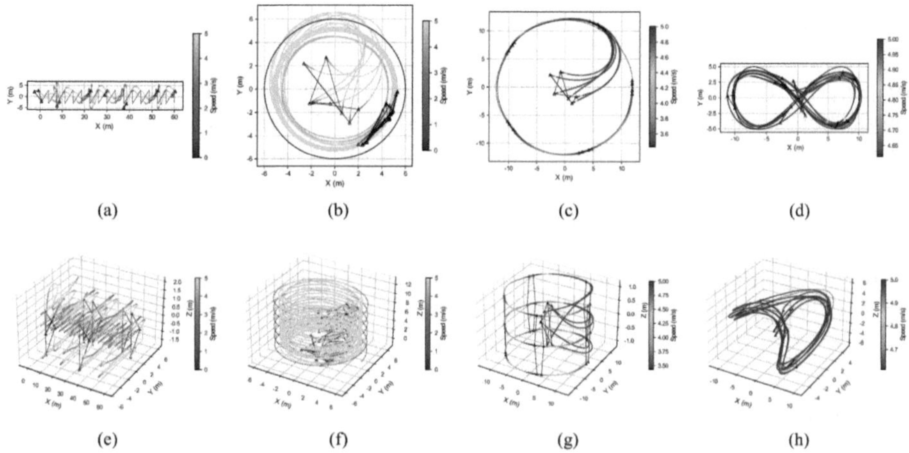

Fig. 3. Representative qualitative results for four trajectory cases. From left to right: Case 1, zigzag with variable speed and triangle formation; Case 2, expanding spiral with a small cube formation; Case 3, large-radius circle with a small hexagon formation; Case 4, large-scale figure-eight with a compact pyramid formation. Top: 2D views. Bottom: 3D trajectories.

Table 5. Per-trajectory metrics across showcased Cases 1–4 (3 seeds; mean ± std). Showcase runs are separate from Table 3.

Case	Method	Drift_{5s} [m]	IAE_{5s} [m·s]	Cos_v	Sat%
1	Baseline (Fixed Gain) [3]	3.0022 ± 0.0594	15.0993 ± 0.2381	0.5397 ± 0.0005	12.2 ± 0.0
1	Handcrafted Schedule [15]	2.4588 ± 0.0160	12.3143 ± 0.0802	0.6543 ± 0.0020	37.6 ± 0.6
1	Ours (Learned Schedule; TD3) [20]	2.2482 ± 0.2377	11.3647 ± 1.1585	0.6457 ± 0.0300	40.8 ± 0.8
2	Baseline (Fixed Gain) [3]	0.3717 ± 0.0016	1.8662 ± 0.0041	0.9982 ± 0.0001	1.2 ± 0.2
	Handcrafted Schedule [15]	0.6350 ± 0.0140	3.2271 ± 0.0148	0.9995 ± 0.0000	3.5 ± 0.0
2	Ours (Learned Schedule; TD3) [20]	0.3214 ± 0.0463	1.9147 ± 0.1726	0.9922 ± 0.0005	4.8 ± 0.2
3	Baseline (Fixed Gain) [3]	0.3933 ± 0.0008	1.9694 ± 0.0027	0.9995 ± 0.0000	2.3 ± 0.1
3	Handcrafted Schedule [15]	0.6488 ± 0.0019	3.2523 ± 0.0032	0.9998 ± 0.0000	3.3 ± 0.6
3	Ours (Learned Schedule; TD3) [20]	0.3215 ± 0.0842	1.7797 ± 0.3577	0.9974 ± 0.0006	3.6 ± 0.6
4	Baseline (Fixed Gain) [3]	1.8078 ± 0.0815	9.0831 ± 0.4110	0.9926 ± 0.0006	1.9 ± 0.1
4	Handcrafted Schedule [15]	1.8876 ± 0.0195	9.4877 ± 0.0913	0.9961 ± 0.0002	2.8 ± 0.4
4	Ours (Learned Schedule; TD3) [20]	1.7757 ± 0.0843	9.4105 ± 0.4678	0.9295 ± 0.0005	2.4 ± 0.2

are evaluated as separate 3-seed runs, so capture or timeout behavior can differ from Table 3; Table 5 therefore reports post-capture metrics only over captured rollouts.

Across showcased Cases 1–4, Ours yields the lowest Drift_{5s} and improves IAE_{5s} over the handcrafted schedule in all four cases; relative to the fixed-gain baseline, IAE_{5s} improves in 2/4 cases.

5 Conclusion

We propose a hybrid formation-tracking method for acceleration-constrained agents that retains a fixed-time backbone and uses RL only to schedule a damping gain, reducing post-capture drift under saturation through a constrained and interpretable interface. Further suppression of extreme error peaks and formal discrete-time guarantees remain future work.

Acknowledgements. This work was supported by the 2025 Undergraduate Innovation Training Program of Zhengzhou University (Grant No. S202510459233).

References

1. Oh, K.-K., Park, M.-C., Ahn, H.-S.: A survey of multi-agent formation control. Automatica **53**, 424–440 (2015)
2. Alexander Fax, J., Murray, R.M.: Information flow and cooperative control of vehicle formations. IEEE Trans. Autom. Control **49**(9), 1465–1476 (2004)
3. Polyakov, A.: Nonlinear feedback design for fixed-time stabilization of linear control systems. IEEE Trans. Autom. Control **57**(8), 2106–2110 (2012)
4. Ning, B., Jin, J., Zheng, J.: Fixed-time consensus for multi-agent systems with discontinuous inherent dynamics over switching topology. Int. J. Syst. Sci. **48**(10), 2023–2032 (2017)
5. Ma, L., Gao, Y., Li, B.: Distributed fixed-time formation tracking control for the multi-agent system and an application in wheeled mobile robots. Actuators **13**(2), 68 (2024)
6. Defoort, M., Polyakov, A., Demesure, G., Djemai, M., Veluvolu, K.: Leader-follower fixed-time consensus for multi-agent systems with unknown non-linear inherent dynamics. IET Control Theor. Appl. **9**(14), 2165–2170 (2015)
7. Parsegov, S.E., Polyakov, A.E., Shcherbakov, P.S.: Fixed-time consensus algorithm for multi-agent systems with integrator dynamics. In: 4th IFAC Workshop on Distributed Estimation and Control in Networked Systems (NecSys 2013), volume 46 of IFAC Proceedings Volumes, pp. 110–115, Koblenz, Germany, IFAC, Elsevier (2013)
8. Lowe, R., Yi, W., Tamar, A., Harb, J., Abbeel, P., Mordatch, I.: Multi-agent actor-critic for mixed cooperative-competitive environments. NeurIPS **30**, 6379–6390 (2017)
9. Rashid, T., Samvelyan, M., De Witt, C.S., Farquhar, G., Foerster, J., Whiteson, S.: QMIX: monotonic value function factorisation for deep multi-agent reinforcement learning. In: ICML, vol. 80. of PMLR, pp. 4295–4304 (2018)
10. Chao, Yu., Velu, A., Vinitsky, E., Jianfeng Gao, Yu., Wang, A.B., Yi, W.: The surprising effectiveness of PPO in cooperative multi-agent games. NeurIPS **35**, 24611–24624 (2022)
11. Wang, H., Li, J., Tao, H., Liu, J., Li, C., Wang, K., Xu, M.: Autonomous dynamic formation for maritime target tracking using multi-agent reinforcement learning. Eng. Appl. Artif. Intell. **154**, 110904 (2025)
12. Zhou, Y., Yue, Y., Yan, B., Li, L., Xiao, J., Yao, Y.: Collaborative target tracking algorithm for multi-agent based on MAPPO and BCTD. Drones **9**(8), 521 (2025)

13. Johannink, T., et al.: Residual reinforcement learning for robot control. In: 2019 International Conference on Robotics and Automation (ICRA), pp. 6023–6029, Montreal, QC, Canada, IEEE (2019)
14. Dogru, O., et al.: Reinforcement learning approach to autonomous PID tuning. In: 2022 American Control Conference (ACC), pp. 2691–2696, Atlanta, GA, USA, IEEE (2022)
15. Rugh, W.J., Shamma, J.S.: Research on gain scheduling. Automatica **36**(10), 1401–1425 (2000)
16. Timmerman, M., Patel, A., Reinhart, T.: Adaptive gain scheduling using reinforcement learning for quadcopter control. arXiv preprint (2024)
17. Chow, Y., Nachum, O., Duenez-Guzman, E., Ghavamzadeh, M.: A lyapunov-based approach to safe reinforcement learning. In: NeurIPS, vol. 31 (2018)
18. Cheng, R., Orosz, G., Murray, R.M., Burdick, J.W.: End-to-end safe reinforcement learning through barrier functions for safety-critical continuous control tasks. In: AAAI Conference on Artificial Intelligence, vol. 33, pp. 3387–3395 (2019)
19. Berkenkamp, F., Turchetta, M., Schoellig, A., Krause, A.: Safe model-based reinforcement learning with stability guarantees. In: NeurIPS, vol. 30 (2017)
20. Fujimoto, S., Hoof, H., Meger, D.: Addressing function approximation error in actor-critic methods. In: ICML, vol. 80 of PMLR, pp. 1587–1596 (2018)

M4EI: A Hierarchical Multimodal Memory Framework for Embodied Intelligence with Causal-Driven Retrieval

Zhaobo Zhang, Yunlong Hou, Donggang Cao(✉), and Hangqi Ren

Peking University, Beijing, China
{zhang_zb,caodg}@pku.edu.cn, {hyl18736691161,renhq}@stu.pku.edu.cn

Abstract. Embodied agents require memory to couple perception, reasoning, and action, yet many memory architectures remain flat, modality-specific, and reliant on shallow similarity search, hindering long-horizon, reasoning-intensive interaction. We introduce M4EI (Memory for Embodied Intelligence), a hierarchical, modular, and multimodal memory framework with short-term, long-term, and skill layers and perceptual, action, and cognitive indexing; modality-specific encoders project into a shared multimodal embedding space for unified retrieval. We build on a Causal Knowledge Graph (CKG) that stores embodied experiences as Episode nodes and extracts executable causal templates (GoalTemplate, CausalTemplate, Step/Condition nodes). Dual-key causal indexing performs two-stage retrieval—semantic matching, then executability filtering with causal gating and execution-aware ranking—to retrieve memories that are semantically aligned yet executable under current embodied states. Experiments in simulated embodied environments show that M4EI improves task success rates on long-horizon crafting tasks and reduces planning overhead in several settings, while causal indexing provides a structured basis for executable, context-aware retrieval.

Keywords: Embodied Intelligence · Embodied Memory · Knowledge Management

1 Introduction

Embodied intelligence—the ability of agents to perceive, reason, and act in the physical world—is a foundational capability for applications such as home service robots, autonomous vehicles, and assistive AI agents. These systems are expected to operate under real-world conditions, where tasks are long-horizon, contexts are uncertain, and inputs are inherently multimodal (e.g., visual, auditory, and proprioceptive signals). Under such settings, *memory* becomes essential: agents must remember past interactions, recognize situations, and adapt behaviors accordingly. As illustrated in Fig. 1, memory serves as a critical bridge connecting perception, reasoning, and action in embodied intelligence systems,

J. Niu et al. (Eds.): KSEM 2026, LNAI 16631, pp. 472–486, 2027.
https://doi.org/10.1007/978-981-92-2759-4_35

enabling agents to maintain context across time, integrate multimodal information, and make informed decisions based on past experiences.

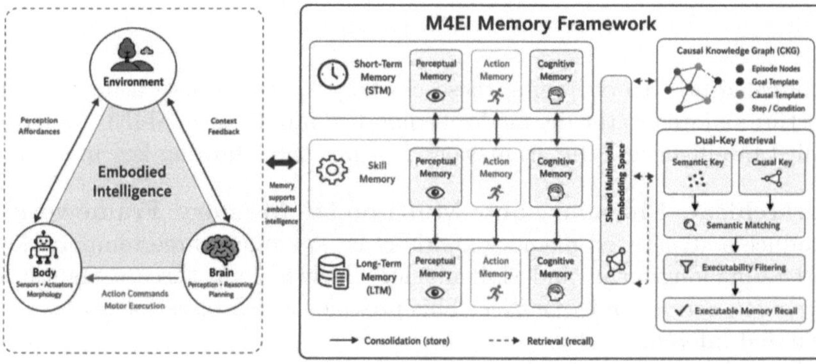

Fig. 1. The Role of Memory in Embodied Intelligence Systems. Memory acts as a central component that integrates perception, reasoning, and action, enabling agents to maintain context, learn from past experiences, and adapt to dynamic environments.

However, current memory mechanisms in embodied systems remain insufficient to meet these demands. Most existing designs exhibit several key limitations: they often utilize **flat or monolithic structures** that fail to distinguish between short-term and long-term memory, making it difficult to handle dynamic updates and durable knowledge simultaneously; adopt **modality-isolated storage**, where vision, language, and action data are stored and processed separately, resulting in fragmented semantic representations; and rely on **naive retrieval strategies** such as embedding-based similarity search [8] or static context windows [14], which lack the ability to reason over temporal and causal relations.

Progress in Memory-Centric Embodied Systems. Recent efforts have attempted to address these issues through more structured or centralized memory designs. For example, **MemoryEQA** [20] introduced a planner-free framework that organizes memory hierarchically into global and local modalities, enabling information to flow more freely across modules during embodied question answering (EQA) [3]. **FindingDory** [17] proposed a benchmark specifically targeting long-horizon memory tasks, exposing the limitations of large vision-language models (VLMs) [11] in retaining and utilizing long-term multimodal experience. **GraphPad** [1] took a step toward dynamic, updatable memory by introducing a mutable 3D scene graph that evolves through language-driven API calls at inference time.

While these works represent substantial progress, they still suffer from key limitations. First, most frameworks operate on coarse memory units (e.g., entire scenes or episodes) without explicit modeling of perceptual, action, and cognitive axes, resulting in limited structural granularity. Second, few systems leverage structured knowledge (e.g., causal/event graphs) to guide memory access or reasoning, indicating weak knowledge-driven retrieval capabilities. Third, memory usage remains sequential and often slow, making it hard to meet real-time constraints in interactive or robotic environments, highlighting the lack of retrieval efficiency.

Our Contribution. To overcome these challenges, we propose a novel memory architecture tailored to the demands of embodied intelligence, M4EI (Memory for Embodied Intelligence). Our framework features the following key innovations:

1. **Hierarchical, Modular, and Multimodal Memory Framework**: We introduce a structured memory architecture spanning three temporal layers: short-term, long-term, and skill memory layers along three semantic axes: *perceptual*, *action*, and *cognitive*. This provides a rich basis for context-aware recall and inference.
2. **CKG-Guided Executable Retrieval**: We store embodied experiences as Episode nodes in a Causal Knowledge Graph (CKG) [13] and extract executable causal templates (GoalTemplate, CausalTemplate, Step/Condition nodes). We propose a causal index with dual-key indexing (semantic and causal keys) that performs two-stage retrieval: semantic matching followed by executability filtering with causal gating and execution-aware ranking. This enables retrieval of memories that are not only goal-aligned in embedding space but also executable under current embodied states.

Together, these components enable embodied agents to form and use memory more effectively for long-horizon, multimodal, and context-sensitive tasks. Experimental results in simulated environments show that our method improves task success rates on long-horizon crafting tasks. We additionally report decomposition-induced changes in success rate, token usage, and average steps in our ablation study (Table 2). The results further indicate that causal indexing helps retrieve executable memories under current state constraints. Code is available[1].

The remainder of this paper is organized as follows. Section 2 reviews related work. Section 3 introduces the hierarchical multimodal memory framework. Section 4 presents CKG-based executable memory storage and causal indexing. Section 5 reports experimental results and ablation analysis. Section 6 concludes the paper.

2 Related Work

Memory mechanisms for embodied intelligence have received growing attention in recent years, especially as agents operate in dynamic environments that require long-term reasoning, cross-modal understanding, and context-aware behavior.

[1] https://github.com/syswonder/robonix.

We review related work in three key areas: (1) memory-centric designs for embodied tasks, (2) retrieval-augmented memory frameworks, and (3) structured and adaptive memory representations.

Memory-Centric Architectures for Embodied Tasks. A growing line of research repositions memory as a central control component in embodied agents. **MemoryEQA** [20] presents a hierarchical memory system with global and local modules so information flows to navigation, stopping, and answering without a central planner gate, improving embodied question answering that requires remembering and reasoning about multiple targets in large environments. **FindingDory** [17] proposes a long-horizon embodied memory benchmark; vision-language models succeed on short horizons yet struggle to use memory over extended interactions, and tasks require object permanence, cross-room navigation, and delayed goals.

Retrieval-Augmented Memory for Embodied Agents. Retrieval-augmented methods enhance embodied reasoning by recalling experience before acting. **Retrieval-Augmented Embodied Agents (RAEA)** [2] runs a two-stage pipeline that retrieves past trajectories and conditions generation on them, improving navigation and manipulation under sparse feedback. **Embodied-RAG** [15] introduces a multi-granularity forest memory with hierarchical querying so agents recall coarse context and refine it for instruction following and language-guided exploration.

Structured and Adaptive Memory Representations. Recent works seek structured memories that track environment and task state. **GraphPad** [1] pairs a 3D scene graph, navigation log, and task-specific scratchpad with online language-driven API calls at inference instead of static precomputation, improving alignment with evolving objectives without retraining. **KARMA** [12] combines long-term scene knowledge with short-term observations via memory-aware LLM prompting for household planning and low-level execution. **Episodic Memory Banks** [7] targets lifelong embodied learning by organizing visual, linguistic, and action sequences into episodic structures for retrieval and generalization across tasks and environments.

Limitations and Motivation. In summary, we address these challenges with a hierarchical memory over perceptual, action, and cognitive dimensions and a Causal Knowledge Graph (CKG) that stores experiences as Episode nodes and extracts executable causal templates, enabling two-stage retrieval (semantic matching + executability filtering) for reasoning-aware memory access.

3 Framework Overview

We propose a structured memory framework tailored for embodied agents operating in real-world, multimodal, and temporally extended environments, as shown in Fig. 2. The framework is composed of three key components: hierarchical memory layering, functional memory modules, and a modality fusion

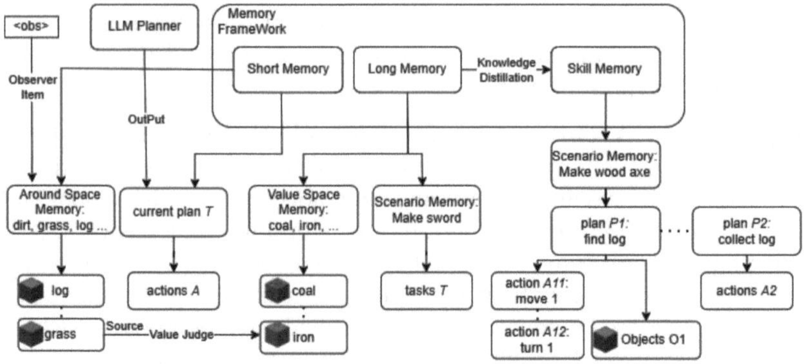

Fig. 2. Memory Architecture Overview

mechanism. Together, these components enable flexible memory storage, contextual alignment, and efficient memory recall.

3.1 Memory Layering

To manage memory across different time scales and task contexts, we organize memory into three layers:

Short-Term Memory (STM) captures the agent's most recent observations and internal states. It primarily consists of sensory buffers, temporary cognitive states, and immediate action feedback. This layer is volatile and frequently updated, playing a critical role in reflex-like behaviors and low-latency interactions.

Long-Term Memory (LTM) contains structured knowledge acquired over multiple tasks and environments, such as abstract task templates, semantic maps, and causal relations. It is designed for cross-task generalization and high-level planning and serves as a semantic backbone for reasoning and retrieval.

Skill Memory stores reusable action patterns, operation sequences, and skill templates. It allows the agent to quickly access and execute learned skills, supporting skill transfer and reuse across tasks. This layer bridges short-term perception and long-term knowledge, enabling the agent to match current observations with mastered skills.

Memory content flows dynamically between layers through consolidation and retrieval mechanisms. Short-term memory entries that demonstrate successful patterns or recurring structures are promoted to long-term memory through pattern extraction and abstraction processes. Specifically, frequently accessed short-term experiences with high success rates and consistent outcomes are consolidated into long-term memory as persistent knowledge structures. Conversely, well-established knowledge patterns in long-term memory that have been repeatedly validated and successfully applied across multiple tasks are further solidified into skill memory as executable skill templates. This hierarchical transformation ensures that recent successful experiences inform long-term knowledge acquisition, and validated long-term knowledge becomes automated skills that can be rapidly deployed in similar contexts. For example, when an agent searches for an apple and finds it in the kitchen (short-term memory), this experience is consolidated into long-term memory as knowledge that "apples are typically located in the kitchen" after multiple successful searches. When the agent repeatedly searches for various items across different contexts, this process forms a fixed cognitive workflow pattern that becomes a reusable skill template in skill memory, such as "retrieving a specific object", which can be rapidly applied to similar object retrieval tasks.

Each layer is temporally decoupled but remains semantically aligned through embedding synchronization and causal indexing mechanisms.

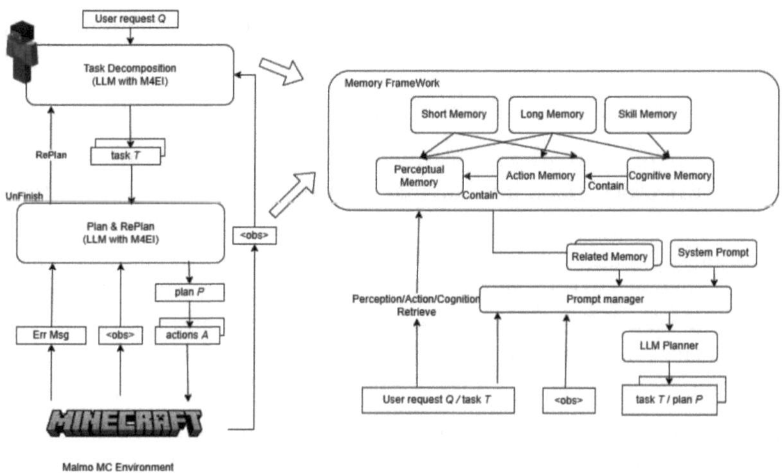

Fig. 3. WorkFlow Overview

3.2 Memory Modules

To support modular reasoning and interface with different subsystems of the embodied agent, memory content is organized into three modules:

Perceptual Memory stores multimodal sensory embeddings—vision, text, and proprioception. These representations are unified into a shared latent space, supporting fast querying by either modality or semantic condition (e.g., "where was the red mug last seen?"). We realize the shared space with modality-specific encoders followed by a common projection and similarity-based retrieval. Formally, a perceptual memory entry $m_p^{(t)}$ at time t is represented as:

$$m_p^{(t)} = \{e_v^{(t)}, e_t^{(t)}, e_{prop}^{(t)}\} \tag{1}$$

where $e_v^{(t)}$, $e_t^{(t)}$, and $e_{prop}^{(t)}$ denote visual, textual, and proprioceptive embeddings, respectively. For example, when the agent observes a red mug in the kitchen, the visual embedding $e_v^{(t)}$ encodes the object's appearance, while spatial coordinates are captured in $e_{prop}^{(t)}$. Cross-modal queries compare the query and memory entry after projection to the shared space:

$$\text{sim}(q, m_p^{(t)}) = \cos(z_q, z_p^{(t)}), \tag{2}$$

where z_q and $z_p^{(t)}$ are projected into the same shared multimodal embedding space.

Action Memory logs past actions, motion plans, and execution trajectories across various task domains. This enables the agent to review its interaction history, detect execution errors, or compare planned versus executed behaviors. An action memory entry $m_a^{(t)}$ captures both planned and executed actions:

$$m_a^{(t)} = \{a_{plan}^{(t)}, a_{exec}^{(t)}, \tau^{(t)}, \epsilon^{(t)}\} \tag{3}$$

where $a_{plan}^{(t)}$ and $a_{exec}^{(t)}$ represent planned and executed action sequences, $\tau^{(t)}$ denotes the trajectory (e.g., for navigation tasks: position coordinates, heading angles, waypoints; for manipulation tasks: joint angles, end-effector poses), and $\epsilon^{(t)} = \|a_{plan}^{(t)} - a_{exec}^{(t)}\|$ quantifies execution error. For instance, in navigation scenarios, when path planning fails or the agent gets stuck, the system can retrieve similar past failures by matching $\epsilon^{(t)}$ patterns and analyzing $\tau^{(t)}$ deviations to identify common failure modes such as obstacle collisions or incorrect route planning.

Cognitive Memory encodes internal beliefs, reasoning states, goal hypotheses, and agent intent. It is closely tied to planning and symbolic reasoning modules and acts as a high-level context anchor when performing long-horizon tasks or multi-step decision-making. A cognitive memory entry $m_c^{(t)}$ is structured as:

$$m_c^{(t)} = \{b^{(t)}, g^{(t)}, \mathcal{H}^{(t)}, \mathcal{I}^{(t)}\} \tag{4}$$

where $b^{(t)}$ represents belief states (e.g., probability distributions over world states), $g^{(t)}$ denotes current goal hypotheses, $\mathcal{H}^{(t)}$ captures reasoning history, and $\mathcal{I}^{(t)}$ encodes agent intentions. For example, during a multi-step task like "prepare breakfast", $g^{(t)}$ might contain sub-goals $\{g_1 : \text{find eggs}, g_2 : \text{heat pan}, g_3 : \text{cook eggs}\}$, while $b^{(t)}$ tracks the agent's confidence about object locations and task progress. The goal hypotheses $g^{(t)}$ and belief states $b^{(t)}$ serve as key inputs to the causal indexing mechanism (Sect. 4.2), enabling the system to retrieve executable memories that match stated goals and current state constraints.

Each module can be selectively queried and updated based on the demands of the retrieval or reasoning process, allowing flexible composition of memory content during downstream task execution.

3.3 Mission Decomposition Modules

The mission decomposition module (as shown in Fig. 3) decomposes user requests into sub-tasks that can be executed by combining successful action memory and cognitive memory. Both baselines use the same LLM-based decomposition interface. The difference is that the plain LLM decomposes tasks only from the current prompt, whereas M4EI retrieves successful historical cognitive and action patterns to guide decomposition.

4 Causal Knowledge Graph as Executable Memory: Storage and Indexing

This section introduces how we store embodied experiences in a **Causal Knowledge Graph (CKG)** [13] and propose a graph-enhanced indexing scheme that retrieves *executable* memories rather than semantically related but infeasible fragments.

4.1 CKG Storage: Episode-Centric Causal Consolidation

We store long-term memory as a typed directed graph $\mathcal{G} = (\mathcal{V}, \mathcal{E})$, where nodes represent reusable task structures and edges encode causal and control dependencies. To construct Episode nodes from the framework's memory modules (Sect. 3), we integrate information from perceptual memory $m_p^{(t)}$ (for context $\mathcal{C}$ and evidence $\mathcal{U}$), action memory $m_a^{(t)}$ (for procedure π and execution outcomes), and cognitive memory $m_c^{(t)}$ (for goal g and belief states). Each mission execution is summarized as an **Episode** node:

$$v_{\text{EPI}} = \{g, \pi, \mathcal{C}, y, f, \mathcal{U}\}, \tag{5}$$

where g is the sub-goal (extracted from $g^{(t)}$ in cognitive memory), π is the executed procedure instance (derived from $a_{exec}^{(t)}$ in action memory, e.g., a Behavior Tree (BT) subtree), $\mathcal{C}$ is a context signature (extracted from $e_{prop}^{(t)}$ in perceptual memory, encoding scene/region/sensor set) [10], y is the outcome (determined from execution error $\epsilon^{(t)}$ in action memory), f is a failure mode label (inferred when $\epsilon^{(t)} > \theta$), and $\mathcal{U}$ links to multimodal evidence (keyframes from $e_v^{(t)}$, trajectories from $\tau^{(t)}$, logs from $e_t^{(t)}$ in perceptual and action memory).

From each episode, we extract a **causal template** that compactly captures: (i) *control flow* (sequence/fallback/retry/timeout), (ii) *atomic skill steps*, and (iii) *verifiable predicates* as preconditions and effects. We then upsert into CKG:

- a **GoalTemplate** node (canonicalized goal form),
- a **CausalTemplate** node τ (executable procedure template),
- a set of **Step/Condition** nodes connected by control edges,

and connect templates to evidence via EVIDENCED_BY($\cdot \rightarrow v_{\text{EPI}}$) for context-aware reuse. Each CausalTemplate node τ maintains lightweight online statistics (success rate, per-episode execution duration, failure histogram) aggregated from its connected Episode nodes, which are used during retrieval for ranking and filtering.

4.2 Causal Indexing for Executable Recall

To enable efficient retrieval of the CausalTemplate nodes stored in CKG (Sect. 4.1), we build a **Causal Index** that indexes each template τ with dual keys for two-stage retrieval: semantic matching followed by executability filtering.

Indexing Structure. For each CausalTemplate node τ in CKG, we construct two indexing keys: (1) a semantic key z_τ obtained by encoding the associated GoalTemplate node and the template summary into a dense embedding, capturing the semantic meaning of the goal and procedure; (2) a causal key ϕ_τ extracted from the CausalTemplate's structure, encoding step types, required predicates (from Step/Condition nodes), constraints, and recovery branches. This dual-key structure enables both semantic search and executability checking during retrieval.

Specifically, we define the causal key of a template as

$$\phi_\tau = \langle T_\tau, P_\tau^{req}, C_\tau, E_\tau, R_\tau \rangle, \tag{6}$$

where T_τ denotes ordered step types, P_τ^{req} denotes required predicates, C_τ denotes resource, spatial, and temporal constraints, E_τ denotes expected effects, and R_τ denotes recovery branches. These fields are extracted from Step/Condition nodes in the CKG and represented as typed symbolic predicates for feasibility checking.

Two-Stage Retrieval Process. When retrieving memories, M4EI first extracts the current goal $g^{(t)}$ and belief state $b^{(t)}$ from cognitive memory. The retrieval proceeds in two stages:

Stage 1: Semantic Retrieval. The goal $g^{(t)}$ is encoded as a query embedding z_q, and we retrieve top-K candidate templates by semantic similarity [5]:

$$\mathcal{T}_K = \text{TopK}_{\tau \in \mathcal{T}} \cos(z_q, z_\tau). \tag{7}$$

Stage 2: Executability Filtering and Ranking. From the belief state $b^{(t)}$, we extract current state facts $\mathcal{S}_t$ (e.g., available objects, current location, task progress). We then filter candidates by checking if their required predicates are satisfied: $\text{Feasible}(\tau) = \mathbb{I}[\phi_\tau.\text{requires} \subseteq \mathcal{S}_t]$. Finally, we re-rank feasible templates by combining semantic similarity, success rate, risk, and execution time:

$$\text{Score}(\tau) = \alpha \cos(z_q, z_\tau) + \beta\, \text{SR}(\tau \mid \mathcal{C}_t) - \gamma\, \text{Risk}(\tau) - \delta\, \text{Time}(\tau), \tag{8}$$

where the scoring function combines four factors: (1) $\cos(z_q, z_\tau)$ is the semantic similarity between the query and template (ranging from -1 to 1), weighted by α; (2) $\mathrm{SR}(\tau \mid \mathcal{C}_t)$ is the context-conditioned success rate of template τ in similar contexts $\mathcal{C}_t$, maintained as online statistics in CKG and weighted by β; (3) $\mathrm{Risk}(\tau)$ quantifies the estimated failure probability based on constraint violations and historical failure patterns, subtracted with weight γ; (4) $\mathrm{Time}(\tau)$ is the estimated execution time derived from episode statistics and template complexity, subtracted with weight δ. The weights α, β, γ, and δ are hyperparameters that balance these factors, with $\alpha + \beta = 1$ and $\gamma, \delta > 0$ to penalize high risk and long execution time.

By integrating causal executability signals into indexing, the Causal Index prioritizes memories that score highly under semantic similarity while remaining *actionable* under the current embodied state, improving robustness for long-horizon tasks.

5 Experiments

To validate the effectiveness of our proposed hierarchical multimodal memory framework, we conducted experimental evaluations across multiple base models and Malmo-based task categories. The experimental design aims to test how different memory components enhance the capabilities of large language models (LLMs) in embodied intelligence tasks.

5.1 Experimental Setup

Base Models. We selected multiple mainstream large language models as base models for evaluation, including Qwen3 [18], and DeepSeek-V3.2 [4]. These models represent different architectural designs and capability levels, enabling us to comprehensively assess the generality and effectiveness of our memory framework.

Memory Component Configurations. To evaluate the overall effect of the memory framework, we compare the base LLM with its M4EI-augmented version.

- **Baseline. LLM:** Using only the base LLM without any memory mechanisms.
- **LLM with M4EI:** Enabling all memory components.

Evaluation Metrics. We adopt three metrics to evaluate system performance:

- **Success Rate:** $\frac{1}{N}\sum_{i=1}^{N} s_i \times 100\%$, where $s_i = 1$ if task t_i completes successfully, otherwise $s_i = 0$.
- **Average Steps:** $\frac{1}{N}\sum_{i=1}^{N} n_i$, where n_i is the step count for task t_i.
- **Token Length:** $\frac{1}{N}\sum_{i=1}^{N} l_i$, where l_i is the token count in context (retrieved memories and task descriptions).

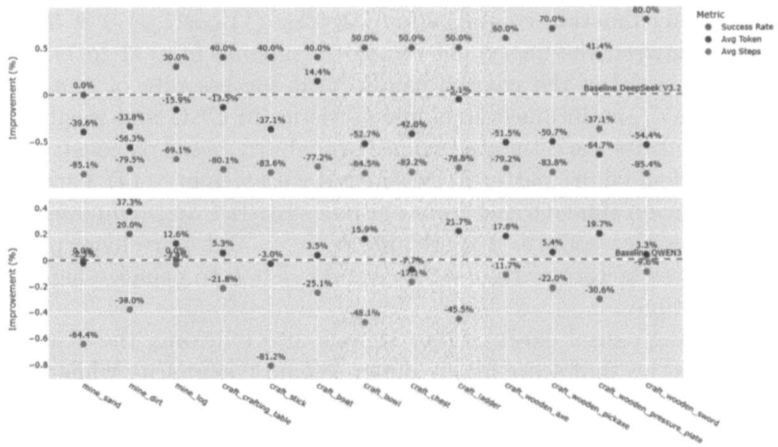

Fig. 4. Performance comparison of base LLMs with and without M4EI.

5.2 Evaluation on Malmo-Based Tasks

Malmo[2], originally released by Microsoft Research as a specialized evaluation platform for embodied intelligence, provides a simulated Minecraft (MC) world with rich multimodal interaction scenarios [6]. We designed the following tasks on the Malmo platform to evaluate our memory framework:

Task Design. Inspired by the evaluation setups of DEPS [16], Plan4MC [19], MP5 [9], and M2PA [21], we mirror their Malmo task coverage to stress long-horizon reasoning, recipe dependencies, and memory-guided recovery. We group tasks into three categories:

1. Resource collection scenarios that test perception-grounding, spatial recall, and short-horizon planning under varied terrain.
2. Dependency-aware crafting chains that probe multi-step sub-goal ordering and reuse of intermediate products.
3. Composite crafting goals that measure how quickly the agent composes skills, retrieves prior successes, and recovers from failed attempts when multiple items must be coordinated.

LLM with/without M4EI. Figure 4 reveals substantial improvements when augmenting the LLM baseline with our memory framework. On dependency-aware crafting tasks, M4EI achieves 100% success rate across 9 out of 10 tasks, compared to LLM's 20–70% range (e.g., `craft_wooden_sword`: 30.0% to 100%, `craft_crafting_table`: 60.0% to 100%). This demonstrates that hierarchical memory enables effective leverage of past successful patterns for task decomposition, particularly for complex multi-step tasks. On resource collection tasks,

[2] https://github.com/microsoft/malmo.

M4EI shows mixed results: 100% on `mine_log`, 70.0% on `mine_dirt` (up from 28.57%), but 60.0% on `mine_sand` (down from 93.75%). Overall, M4EI achieves 100% success on 10 out of 13 tasks, compared to LLM's 1 task, demonstrating the critical role of memory-guided task decomposition.

Table 1. Success Rate (SR%) Comparison Across Methods. Note that baseline methods (DEPS, Plan4MC, MP5, M2PA) only report success rate metrics.

Task Name	LLM(DS)	DEPS	Plan4MC	MP5	M2PA	M4EI
mine_dirt	28.57	96.67	80	96.67	**100**	70.0
mine_log	**100**	93.33	73.33	96.67	**100**	**100**
mine_sand	93.75	86.67	60	**100**	**100**	60.0
craft_crafting_table	60.0	86.67	53.33	**100**	**100**	**100**
craft_stick	20.0	86.67	56.67	**100**	**100**	**100**
craft_boat	60.0	86.67	43.33	86.67	**100**	**100**
craft_bowl	50.0	83.33	50	90	**100**	**100**
craft_chest	50.0	86.67	53.33	90	**100**	**100**
craft_ladder	70.0	80	33.33	86.67	**100**	**100**
craft_wooden_axe	40.0	76.67	43.33	80	96.67	**100**
craft_wooden_pickaxe	50.0	73.33	33.33	80	**96.67**	90.0
craft_wooden_plate	50.0	86.67	43.33	90	**100**	**100**
craft_wooden_sword	30.0	80	46.67	76.67	**100**	**100**

Experimental Results. Table 1 demonstrates that M4EI achieves 100% success rate on 10 out of 13 tasks, significantly outperforming baseline methods. The results validate two key aspects of our framework: the hierarchical memory structure's effectiveness and the superiority of knowledge-graph-guided retrieval over traditional approaches.

The hierarchical memory framework demonstrates its effectiveness in complex task execution, as evidenced by the substantial improvements shown in the LLM with/without M4EI comparison discussed above.

Beyond the framework structure, the CKG-guided retrieval mechanism with causal indexing demonstrates superior effectiveness compared to embedding-based approaches used in prior methods. M4EI compares favorably to DEPS, Plan4MC, and MP5 on most tasks, achieving 100% success on 10 tasks where these methods range from 33.33% to 96.67%. The key advantage lies in the two-stage retrieval process: first, semantic matching retrieves candidate CausalTemplate nodes by goal similarity; then, causal gating filters templates based on executability (checking if required predicates are satisfied by current state), and execution-aware ranking prioritizes templates with high success rates and low risk. This dual-key indexing approach enables retrieval of memories that are both goal-aligned under semantic similarity and executable under current embodied states, leading to more reliable task completion than methods that match tasks purely through embedding similarity.

The overall results demonstrate that the combination of hierarchical memory organization and CKG-guided retrieval with causal indexing provides a robust foundation for embodied intelligence tasks, particularly those requiring multi-step reasoning, dependency management, and adaptive skill composition.

5.3 Ablation Studies and Analysis

We investigate the role of successful memory-based decomposition by comparing LLM and M4EI baselines without mission decomposition modules (Table 2), reporting task-wise ΔSR, Δ token usage, and Δ average steps when decomposition is enabled. The ablation compares: (1) systems that retrieve past successful execution patterns from memory to decompose tasks; (2) systems without such memory-based decomposition.

Table 2. Performance changes introduced by memory-based decomposition for LLM and M4EI.

Task	LLM			M4EI		
	ΔSR(%)	ΔAvgTok	ΔAvgSteps	ΔSR(%)	ΔAvgTok	ΔAvgSteps
mine_dirt	28.57	28445.54	67.47	70	2491	34.2
mine_log	0	−1647.79	−15.66	0	−100	2
mine_sand	−6.25	−1505.28	70.66	−40	−49.5	12.4
craft_crafting_table	20	1049.8	−5.33	100	−4189.5	7.8
craft_stick	−60	3914.07	68.07	100	−4138.1	9.8
craft_boat	10	62.45	7.5	100	−5401	−86
craft_bowl	−50	−1502.4	37.5	100	−4215.73	9.33
craft_chest	−30	−26928	20.1	100	−10506.1	3.17
craft_ladder	−10	996.1	14.3	60	−7060.2	−9.2
craft_wooden_axe	20	−3719.3	−7.9	80	−1957.7	−68.3
craft_wooden_pickaxe	10	−24530.1	22.9	70	−3632.9	−28
craft_wooden_plate	−50	8857.1	61.6	0	1046.7	−5
craft_wooden_sword	5	−18438.4	69.8	66.67	−3379.57	−38.67

Results reveal significant performance gaps: LLM shows mixed gains (e.g., +28.57% SR on `mine_dirt`, −60% on `craft_stick`), indicating inconsistent benefit from decomposition without memory support, while M4EI demonstrates consistent improvements across most tasks (e.g., +70% SR on `mine_dirt`, +100% on `craft_crafting_table`), with corresponding changes in average token usage and step counts relative to the LLM-only baseline in our ablation. This indicates that memory-based decomposition is essential for M4EI to leverage hierarchical memory structures and CKG-guided retrieval with causal indexing. Without memory-based decomposition, M4EI cannot effectively utilize its memory components leading to reduced performance gains, while LLM relies on its inherent reasoning capabilities with inconsistent decomposition benefits across tasks.

A more fine-grained layer-wise ablation will be included in future work to further quantify the individual contribution of each memory layer.

6 Conclusion

In this work, we presented a hierarchical, modular, and multimodal memory framework for embodied intelligence. Our framework organizes memory across temporal layers (short-term, long-term, and skill) and indexes memory nodes along three semantic dimensions (perceptual, action, and cognitive). By incorporating a Causal Knowledge Graph (CKG) that stores experiences as Episode nodes and extracts executable causal templates, along with causal indexing mechanisms (dual-key indexing and two-stage retrieval), we enable retrieval of both goal-aligned and executable memories under current embodied states. Experimental results demonstrate substantial improvements in task success rate, token usage, and average steps compared to baselines, and our decomposition-focused ablation suggests that memory-guided task structuring contributes to M4EI's gains. Our evidence is Malmo-based, so broad embodied generalization is not claimed here; future work will stress-test the framework on real robotic platforms and richer environments, addressing robust memory retrieval under real-world variability, dynamic environment adaptation, and enhanced multimodal fusion in physical-world scenarios.

Acknowledgements. This work was supported in part by the National Key Research and Development Program of China under Grant No. 2024YFB3311904 and by the National Natural Science Foundation of China under Grant No. 6222780006.

References

1. Ali, M.: GraphPad: dynamic memory representation with mutable 3D scene graphs. In: Proceedings of the AAAI Conference on Artificial Intelligence (2025)
2. Chen, X.: Retrieval-augmented embodied agents: a two-stage memory pipeline for navigation and manipulation. In: Proceedings of the International Conference on Machine Learning (2024)
3. Das, A., Datta, S., Gkioxari, G., Lee, S., Parikh, D., Batra, D.: Embodied question answering. In: Proceedings of the IEEE Conference on Computer Vision and Pattern Recognition, pp. 1–10 (2018)
4. DeepSeek-AI: DeepSeek-v3.2: pushing the frontier of open large language models (2025)

5. Fan, Q., Wang, W., Wang, Y., Xie, H., Zhang, Y., Zhu, L.: DynaKiteQuery: top-k closest-vertex queries on dynamic attributed knowledge graphs for IIoT applications. In: Zhu, T., Zhou, W., Zhu, C. (eds.) KSEM 2025. LNCS, vol. 15921, pp. 294–306. Springer, Singapore (2025). https://doi.org/10.1007/978-981-95-3055-7_23
6. Johnson, M., Hofmann, K., Hutton, T., Bignell, D.: The Malmo platform for artificial intelligence experimentation. In: Ijcai, vol. 16, pp. 4246–4247 (2016)
7. Kumar, A.: Episodic memory banks: lifelong embodied learning through structured memory organization. In: Proceedings of the International Conference on Learning Representations (2024)
8. Mikolov, T., Chen, K., Corrado, G., Dean, J.: Efficient estimation of word representations in vector space. In: Proceedings of the 1st International Conference on Learning Representations (2013)
9. Qin, Y., et al.: MP5: a multi-modal open-ended embodied system in Minecraft via active perception. In: Proceedings of the IEEE/CVF Conference on Computer Vision and Pattern Recognition (CVPR), pp. 16307–16316 (2024)
10. Qiu, J., Song, A., Liu, T., Zhang, T., Wang, Y., Zhao, K.: Graph representation-aware online aggregations over knowledge graph. In: Zhu, T., Zhou, W., Zhu, C. (eds.) KSEM 2025. LNCS, vol. 15920, pp. 14–27. Springer, Singapore (2025). https://doi.org/10.1007/978-981-95-3052-6_2
11. Radford, A., et al.: Learning transferable visual models from natural language supervision. In: International Conference on Machine Learning (2021)
12. Shridhar, M.: KARMA: knowledge-aware reasoning for memory-augmented household task planning. In: Proceedings of the Conference on Robot Learning (2024)
13. Tan, F.A., Desai, J., Sengamedu, S.H.: Enhancing fact verification with causal knowledge graphs and transformer-based retrieval for deductive reasoning. In: Schlichtkrull, M., et al. (eds.) Proceedings of the Seventh Fact Extraction and VERification Workshop (FEVER), pp. 151–169. Association for Computational Linguistics, Miami (2024). https://doi.org/10.18653/v1/2024.fever-1.20, https://aclanthology.org/2024.fever-1.20/
14. Touvron, H., et al.: LLaMA: open and efficient foundation language models (2023)
15. Wang, L.: Embodied-RAG: retrieval-augmented generation for embodied agents with multi-granularity memory. In: Proceedings of the Conference on Neural Information Processing Systems (2024)
16. Wang, Z., Cai, S., Chen, G., Liu, A., Ma, X., Liang, Y.: Describe, explain, plan and select: interactive planning with large language models enables open-world multi-task agents. arXiv preprint arXiv:2302.01560 (2023)
17. Yadav, K.: FindingDory: a benchmark for long-horizon memory in embodied agents. In: Proceedings of the AAAI Conference on Artificial Intelligence (2025)
18. Yang, A., et al.: Qwen3 technical report (2025). https://arxiv.org/abs/2505.09388
19. Yuan, H., et al.: Plan4MC: skill reinforcement learning and planning for open-world minecraft tasks. arXiv preprint arXiv:2303.16563, vol. 2, no. 5 (2023)
20. Zhai, X.: Memory-centric embodied question answering: a planner-free framework with hierarchical memory. In: Proceedings of the AAAI Conference on Artificial Intelligence (2025)
21. Zhou, Y., et al.: M2PA: a multi-memory planning agent for open worlds inspired by cognitive theory. In: Findings of the Association for Computational Linguistics: ACL 2025, pp. 23204–23220. Association for Computational Linguistics, Vienna (2025). https://doi.org/10.18653/v1/2025.findings-acl.1191, https://aclanthology.org/2025.findings-acl.1191/

Textbook Content Moderation via Multi-agent Intergenerational Interaction

Yu Ji[1,2], Wen Wu[3(✉)], Xiang Liu[1], Qingchun Bai[4], Jiabao Zhao[5], Yunyu Shi[1], Zhe Huang[6], and Liang He[3]

[1] School of Electronic and Electrical Engineering, Shanghai University of Engineering Science, Shanghai 201600, China
{xliu,yunyushi}@sues.edu.cn
[2] NPPA Key Laboratory of Publishing Integration Development, ECNUP, Shanghai 200333, China
[3] School of Computer Science and Technology, East China Normal University, Shanghai 200333, China
wwu@cc.ecnu.edu.cn, lhe@cs.ecnu.edu.cn
[4] Shanghai Open Distance Education Engineering Technology Research Center, Shanghai Open University, Shanghai 200082, China
[5] School of Computer Science and Technology, Donghua University, Shanghai 201600, China
jbzhao@dhu.edu.cn
[6] School of Design and Arts, Shanghai Dianji University, Shanghai 201306, China

Abstract. Recently, agents powered by Large Language Models (LLMs) have proven effective in moderating online content by detecting harmful information such as abusive language and hate speech. However, when applied to textbook content that plays an important role in shaping students' values, these agents often show limitations in identifying problematic value orientations. This limitation stems from the inherent knowledge bases and value orientations embedded in LLMs. Inspired by the idea of intergenerational knowledge transfer in humans, we propose a Multi-Agent Intergenerational Interaction (MAII) method for textbook content moderation. Specifically, MAII method first constructs four generational agents with distinct value perspectives and assigns them to conduct independent moderation. MAII method then organizes these agents into intergenerational interaction, where they critique, reflect, and revise based on each other's opinions. After multiple rounds of interaction, MAII method produces a comprehensive moderation result by integrating the judgments of all generational agents. To support evaluation, we also construct and release a textbook illustration moderation dataset for Chinese primary and secondary schools, annotated by 40 professional editors. Experiments on our constructed textbook illustration moderation dataset demonstrate that MAII method significantly outperforms the baseline methods in moderation performance across various LLM configurations. Besides, both the incorporation of multi-generational perspectives and the intergenerational interaction mechanism have been proven

J. Niu et al. (Eds.): KSEM 2026, LNAI 16631, pp. 487–503, 2027.
https://doi.org/10.1007/978-981-92-2759-4_36

to enhance the accuracy and interpretability of textbook content moderation.

Keywords: Textbook content moderation · Multi-agents · Intergenerational interaction · Large language models · Intergenerational knowledge transfer

1 Introduction

Content moderation aims to identify potentially harmful information (e.g., illegal information) in given content [8]. It serves as an important approach for maintaining a healthy information environment. In recent years, Large Language Models (LLMs) have been widely applied in content moderation due to their strong general language understanding and reasoning capabilities [9,12,29]. By role-playing as professional editors, LLM-driven agents have improved both the accuracy and interpretability of content moderation [7].

Nevertheless, most existing methods have concentrated on moderating online content (e.g., Reddit posts) [11], while relatively little attention has been given to textbook content that plays a critical role in shaping students' values. In fact, there are substantial differences between the moderation of online content and that of textbook content. Concretely, online platforms are characterized by a high degree of expressive freedom and permit a certain level of diverse expression and value divergence [24]. However, as key educational resources for students, textbooks must convey positive and healthy values that are broadly acceptable across generations. For example, although some middle-aged and older groups may disapprove of the "Funeral Culture" (i.e., a cultural trend characterized by pessimism, passivity, and decadence) popular among younger groups [15], such content is still often tolerated and retained on online platforms. However, textbooks must strictly exclude similar content that reflects negative value orientations. This difference arises because people of different generations are shaped by diverse social environments and life experiences. As a result, they will emphasize different concerns and standards in value judgments [30]. Therefore, when current approaches employ LLM-driven agents to simulate the role of professional editors for content moderation, they often fail to incorporate generational factors into agent design and interactions. As a consequence, the agents tend to rely on the dominant values in the training corpora of LLMs, which results in a single and narrow perspective. This lack of multi-generational viewpoints makes them prone to blind spots in value judgment when moderating textbook content, ultimately reducing the accuracy of content moderation.

Inspired by the idea of intergenerational knowledge transfer in humans [3,25], we propose a Multi-Agent Intergenerational Interaction (MAII) method for textbook content moderation. Concretely, in organizational settings, intergenerational knowledge transfer refers to the process through which employees from different age groups share and assimilate knowledge and experience, thereby preserving organizational memory and supporting long-term success. As for our

MAII method, four generational agents with distinct generational value orientations are first created, and each generational agent performs independent moderation. These generational agents are then brought into an intergenerational interaction stage, where they critique the judgments of others, reflect on their own judgments in light of others' feedback, and revise their own judgments accordingly. After several rounds of intergenerational interaction, MAII method produces a final moderation result that integrates judgments from all generational agents. Experiments conducted on a real-world dataset show that our MAII method significantly outperforms the baseline methods in moderation performance across various LLM configurations. Besides, our MAII method provides stronger interpretability for the moderation process. We open the source code and dataset in GitHub[1].

The contributions of this study are threefold:

(1) We propose conducting textbook content moderation from a multi-generational perspective, effectively mitigating blind spots in value judgment caused by a single perspective and enhancing the moderation accuracy.
(2) We design an intergenerational interaction mechanism that simulates the process of intergenerational knowledge transfer in humans, enabling the integration of perspectives across generations and further improving both the accuracy and interpretability of textbook content moderation.
(3) We construct and release the first dataset for textbook illustration moderation in Chinese primary and secondary schools. Experiments conducted on the dataset demonstrate that our MAII method achieves higher accuracy than the baseline methods across various LLM configurations.

2 Related Work

In recent years, LLMs were applied to various fields (e.g., education [10] and healthcare [5]) and achieved remarkable performance. Hence, some researchers explored their potential in content moderation [17,21,22]. Compared with traditional methods that rely on keyword matching or fixed pattern recognition [6,23], LLMs demonstrated stronger contextual understanding and cross-modal reasoning capabilities [19], and can effectively identify complex harmful information with implicit expressions even under few-shot conditions [13]. In early explorations, researchers primarily sought to improve the moderation performance of LLMs through prompt optimization. For example, some studies guided LLMs to play the role of professional editors, combining predefined moderation rules with the target content as input to align outputs more closely with established standards [11]. In addition, researchers also explored retrieval-augmented generation with external knowledge bases [2], enabling LLMs to access domain-specific background knowledge and achieve stronger moderation performance [28]. More recently, some researchers began to explore multi-agent interaction

[1] https://github.com/jiyu0201/MAII.

methods based on LLMs [4,16,20]. These approaches normally assigned LLM-driven agents with different roles or perspectives to engage in interactive review around the target content. For example, Bao et al. constructed pro and con agents that debate the target content to reach a final conclusion, thereby improving both the accuracy and interpretability of moderation results [1].

Most existing studies concentrated on online content moderation, where the primary goal is to identify abusive language and hate speech. In contrast, relatively little attention was paid to textbook content, which plays a crucial role in shaping students' values. Unlike online spaces that allow for a certain degree of diverse viewpoints and value differences [24], textbooks must convey positive and healthy values that are broadly acceptable across generations. However, current approaches that employ LLMs for role-playing often failed to effectively incorporate generational factors into the design and interaction of LLM-driven agents. Due to differences in social environments and life experiences, people born in different eras prioritize different concerns and apply distinct standards in their value judgments [30]. Neglecting such generational differences may cause LLM-driven agents to rely on the dominant values in the training corpora of LLMs, leading to a single and narrow perspective. This can result in omissions where some value differences are overlooked and misjudgments where others are exaggerated. To address these issues, we attempt to introduce a multi-generational perspective into textbook content moderation to reduce blind spots caused by single-perspective value judgments. We are also interested in simulating the intergenerational knowledge transfer to design an intergenerational interaction mechanism that can more effectively integrate different generational viewpoints.

3 Method

For the textbook content moderation task, the objective is to determine whether a given textbook content C contains problematic value orientations. The moderation result is represented as a binary variable $y \in \{0, 1\}$, where $y = 1$ denotes the presence of problematic value orientations and $y = 0$ denotes their absence.

Figure 1 illustrates the overall framework of our proposed MAII method, which consists of three main stages. In the following, we will introduce the three main stages of our MAII method in detail.

3.1 Generational Agent Construction

In this stage, following the generational division method used in prior studies [14,27] (i.e., 18–25, 26–30, 31–40, and 41–50 years), our MAII method constructs four agents with specific generational perspectives. Formally, the set of generational agents is defined as $G = \{g_1, g_2, g_3, g_4\}$, where g_i $(1 \leq i \leq 4)$ denotes an agent with a specific generational perspective. This design ensures that multi-generational perspectives are incorporated into the subsequent moderation process. Concretely, each agent is powered by LLMs and initialized with

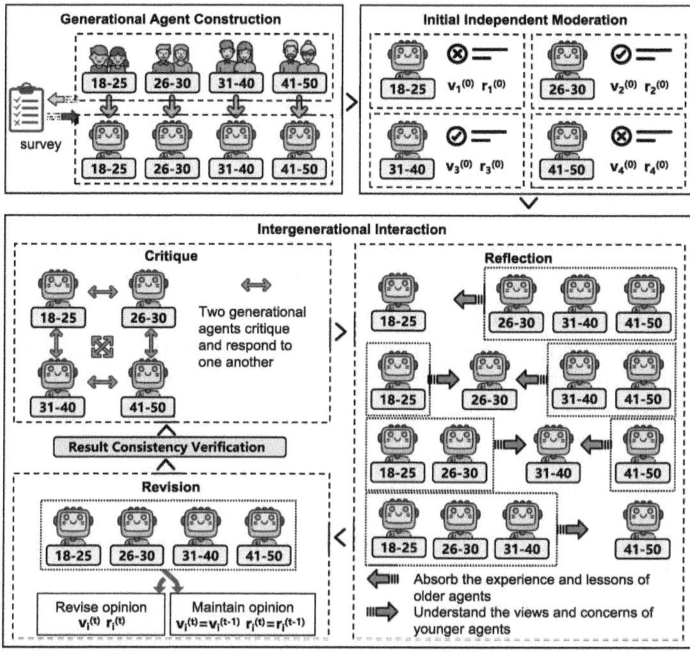

Fig. 1. The whole framework of our MAII method.

a prompt that encodes the value-oriented characteristics of its corresponding generational group. This prompt guides the agents to conduct textbook content moderation from the corresponding generational perspective. As for the value-oriented characteristics, they were obtained through a questionnaire survey conducted with 40 professional editors, who also contributed to the dataset construction. Specifically, we first collected the personal opinions of the 40 professional editors and summarized 10 categories of problematic value orientations in primary and secondary school textbooks: gender stereotypes, equating success with wealth, regional and cultural bias, single-family structure, neglect of disabled groups, weakened national identity, biased aesthetic values, glorification of violence, age-inappropriate sexual implications, and power worship. We then asked the editors to select from the 10 categories they focused on in textbook content moderation. Note that, multiple selections were allowed. Besides, an *Other* option was also provided, though none of the editors chose it. For each generational group, we further calculated the selection proportion of the 10 categories and identified the three with the highest proportions as the value-oriented characteristics of that generational group. For example, suppose the top three categories for the 18–25 group are category 1, category 2, and category 3. Accordingly, the prompt is formulated as follows:

"You are a professional textbook editor aged 18–25, and you are particularly concerned about whether textbook illustrations contain the following three problematic value orientations: category 1, category 2, and category 3."

3.2 Initial Independent Moderation

Before entering the intergenerational interaction stage, each generational agent g_i $(1 \leq i \leq 4)$ first conducts an initial independent moderation of the given textbook content C. Each generational agent generates an initial moderation result $v_i^{(0)} \in \{0, 1\}$ along with an explanation $r_i^{(0)}$. The purpose of this stage is to ensure that each generational agent forms its preliminary judgment without being influenced by other generational perspectives, thereby providing sufficient diversity of opinions for subsequent intergenerational interaction.

3.3 Intergenerational Interaction

During the intergenerational interaction stage, all generational agents engage in a three-step cycle of critique, reflection, and revision around each other's viewpoints. After at most T rounds, our MAII method produces the final moderation result by integrating the judgments of all generational agents. This stage helps avoid blind spots in value judgment caused by a single generational view. Specifically:

Critique: In the t-th round $(1 \leq t \leq T)$, each generational agent g_i reads the previous round $(t-1)$ moderation result $v_j^{(t-1)}$ and explanation $r_j^{(t-1)}$ produced by other agents g_j $(j \neq i)$, and provides critique $p_{i \to j}^{(t)}$ on their viewpoints, including both the supplementation and questioning of viewpoints. Meanwhile, generational agent g_i also receives responses from other generational agents g_j $(j \neq i)$ to its own critiques, denoted as $q_{j \to i}^{(t)}$. Hence, the intergenerational interaction record of generational agent g_i in the t-th round is represented as: $I_i^{(t)} = \{(p_{i \to j}^{(t)}, q_{j \to i}^{(t)}) \mid j \neq i\}$.

Reflection: After the critique step, each generational agent g_i reflects on the intergenerational interaction records and selectively absorbs reasonable information to update its judgment. We design intergenerational-dependent reflection prompts that guide agents to examine potential biases introduced by their generational standpoint and to incorporate complementary perspectives from other generational groups. Specifically, older agents are encouraged to attend to viewpoints emphasized by younger agents, younger agents are guided to integrate experiential knowledge from older agents, and middle-aged agents are instructed to balance both perspectives during reflection.

Revision: After the reflection step, each generational agent g_i either generates an updated moderation result $v_i^{(t)} \in \{0, 1\}$ together with an explanation $r_i^{(t)}$, or retains its previous output (e.g., $v_i^{(t)} = v_i^{(t-1)}$ and $r_i^{(t)} = r_i^{(t-1)}$).

If all generational agents agree in any round, the moderation process stops and outputs a consensus conclusion. If disagreements remain after T rounds of interaction, a one-vote veto rule applies: if any generational agent judges that the given textbook content C contains problematic value orientations, the final moderation result is set to 1 (i.e., problematic) to minimize the risk of missing potential issues. Conversely, the final moderation result is set to 0 (i.e., non-problematic) only if all generational agents judge that the given textbook content C does not contain problematic value orientations.

4 Experiments

In this section, we conduct experiments on a real-world dataset to validate the effectiveness of our MAII method. Specifically, we aim to answer the following research questions (RQs):

RQ1: Does our proposed MAII method outperform other baseline methods? (see Sect. 4.6)
RQ2: Does incorporating multi-generational perspectives help improve the moderation accuracy? (see Sect. 4.7)
RQ3: Does the intergenerational interaction mechanism contribute to enhancing both the accuracy and interpretability of textbook content moderation? (see Sect. 4.8)

4.1 Dataset

Given the absence of publicly available datasets for textbook content moderation, we constructed a dataset consisting of 20 positive samples and 20 negative samples, all of which were derived from illustrations in Chinese primary and secondary school textbooks. The positive samples are textbook illustrations without problematic value orientations, while the negative samples are those containing problematic value orientations. Concretely, we invited 40 professional editors with at least one year of editing experience to assist in obtaining the negative samples. Following the generational division method used in prior studies [14, 27], these editors were divided into four generational groups: 18–25 years (7 editors), 26–30 years (11 editors), 31–40 years (16 editors), and 41–50 years (6 editors). Specifically, we first systematically collected news reports and publicly available materials on problematic textbook incidents from the past five years and initially selected textbook illustrations that potentially contained harmful information. After that, the 40 editors independently judged whether each candidate textbook illustration contained problematic value orientations. We then obtained the final judgments by aggregating the independent judgments in two stages (i.e., intra-group stage and inter-group stage). To be specific, at the intra-group stage, we aggregated the independent judgments of all editors within each generational group to obtain the generational group's judgment on each textbook illustration. If more than half of the members judged a textbook illustration as problematic, the group's conclusion was recorded as problematic; otherwise, it was recorded as non-problematic. At the inter-group stage, these group-level results were further combined: a textbook illustration was included as a negative sample if any generational group judged it problematic, and only those judged non-problematic by all generational groups were excluded. Following this process, 20 high-quality negative samples were obtained. To ensure balance in the dataset, an additional 20 positive samples were randomly selected from Chinese primary and secondary school textbooks published by the People's Education Press, all of which were verified to comply with current publishing regulations.

4.2 Baselines

Based on our literature research, we compare our MAII method with several representative content moderation methods. These methods can be divided into two categories: methods with single-agent/multi-agents.

(1) Methods with single-agent

LLM-Mod [11]: inputs the target content along with the predefined moderation rules into LLMs, requiring LLMs to determine whether the content violates these rules and to produce explanatory outputs.

OPO [28]: retrieves the most relevant moderation rules from a pre-constructed external rule base for the target content, and then inputs both the retrieved rules and the content into LLMs, guiding LLMs to make judgments under the constraints of these retrieved rules.

(2) Methods with multi-agents

DMAC [1]: construct a pro-, a con-, and a judge-agent, where the pro- and con-agents debate the target content and the judge agent determines whether it is problematic.

MAII-I: is a variant of our MAII method that removes the intergenerational interaction stage from our MAII method. It relies solely on the initial moderation results independently generated by each generational agent and applies a one-vote veto rule to produce the final moderation result.

4.3 Implement Details

For LLM configurations, we select four representative domestic and international LLMs. The domestic LLMs include Doubao (version: doubao-1.5-vision-pro-250328) and Qwen (version: qwen-vl-max-2025-01-25), while the international LLMs include GPT-4o (version: gpt-4o-2024-11-20) and Gemini (version: gemini-2.0-flash). All four LLMs possess multimodal processing capabilities, enabling them to understand mixed text-image information and support multi-turn interactions. All LLMs are accessed via their official APIs, with the temperature parameter set to 0. In addition, prompt templates are kept consistent across LLMs to ensure the comparability of evaluation results.

For our MAII method, due to an initial independent moderation round, the maximum number of intergenerational interaction rounds is set to 2 (i.e., $T = 2$). For LLM-Mod method, Articles 25 and 26 of China's Regulations on the Administration of Publishing (2024 revision) are used as predefined moderation rules.

For OPO method, these same articles are used to construct an external rule base. Given that the content under review is in the form of images (i.e., textbook illustrations), we first guide LLMs to generate descriptive text of the textbook illustrations. OPO method then retrieves the most relevant rules from the rule base according to the generated descriptions. In addition, we adopt OpenAI's Text-Embedding-3-Large model [26] for text encoding. For DMAC method, considering that the original paper does not strictly require the judge-agent to make a definitive decision, we allow the judge-agent to refrain from declaring a winner before the preset maximum number of interaction rounds is reached, in order to improve experimental comparability. However, once the maximum number of interaction rounds is reached, the judge-agent must explicitly decide whether the pro-agent or the con-agent is the winner. Besides, the maximum number of interaction rounds is set to 3.

Table 1. Proportion of attention to problematic value orientations among different generational groups

Generational Group	Problematic Value Orientation	Proportion
18–25	equating success with wealth	85.7%
	biased aesthetic values	71.4%
	power worship	71.4%
26–30	equating success with wealth	63.6%
	gender stereotypes	45.5%
	biased aesthetic values	36.4%
31–40	biased aesthetic values	62.5%
	equating success with wealth	56.2%
	regional and cultural bias	43.8%
41–50	regional and cultural bias	50.0%
	biased aesthetic values	50.0%
	power worship	50.0%

4.4 Evaluation Metrics

Similar to the study [13], we adopt *Accuracy* (the higher the better) and *F1-Score* (the higher the better) [18] as the evaluation metrics.

4.5 Questionnaire Survey Results

The results of the questionnaire survey conducted with 40 professional editors are summarized in Table 1, which presents the top three categories of problematic value orientations that each generational group focuses on most in textbook content moderation. As shown in Table 1, editors from different generational groups indeed exhibit certain differences in their focus during textbook content moderation. For example, the 18–25 group shows high sensitivity to problematic value orientations such as "equating success with wealth" (selection proportion: 85.7%) and "power worship" (selection proportion: 71.4%), reflecting a concern for social fairness and anti-utilitarian values. Notably, "biased aesthetic values" is a frequent concern shared by all four generational groups, showing clear cross-generational consensus. This may be because aesthetic problems in textbook illustrations have recently attracted much public attention, making editors highly sensitive to such issues in textbook content moderation. The generational agents are initialized using prompts that incorporate these statistical findings.

4.6 Experimental Results and Analysis for RQ1

Table 2 presents the performance of different methods under four LLM configurations. As shown in Table 2, across all LLM settings, our MAII method achieves the best results in both accuracy and F1 score compared with both methods with single-agent and multi-agents. For example, under GPT-4o configuration, our MAII method achieves 77.5% accuracy, outperforming LLM-Mod (70.0%), OPO (72.5%), and DMAC (52.5%). Concretely, methods with single-agent (i.e., LLM-Mod and OPO) rely only on a single perspective for judgment, which can cause oversights in value judgment and reduce overall detection capability. In contrast, our MAII method incorporates multi-generational perspectives, enabling more comprehensive identification of potential problematic value orientations in textbook illustrations. As for DMAC (i.e., method with multi-agents), its performance is even lower than that of methods with single-agent. The possible reason is that DMAC adopts an overly rigid binary opposition, where the pro-agent must argue that problematic value orientations exist and the con-agent must argue that no problematic value orientations exist. This forced stance causes

Table 2. Overall experimental results. Bold indicates the best result among all methods, underline indicates the best result among the baseline methods, and * denotes statistical significance compared with the best baseline method ($p < 0.01$)

Method	Doubao		Qwen		Gemini		GPT-4o	
	Acc.	F1.	Acc.	F1.	Acc.	F1.	Acc.	F1.
Methods with single-agent								
Baseline: LLM-Mod	<u>55.0%</u>	<u>0.436</u>	<u>62.5%</u>	<u>0.564</u>	<u>57.5%</u>	<u>0.481</u>	70.0%	0.670
Baseline: OPO	<u>55.0%</u>	<u>0.436</u>	60.0%	0.524	55.0%	0.436	<u>72.5%</u>	<u>0.703</u>
Methods with multi-agents								
Baseline: DMAC	–	–	55.0%	0.487	50.0%	0.333	52.5%	0.486
Our Variant: MAII-I	57.5%	0.481	62.5%	0.564	70.0%	0.699	77.5%	0.763
Ours: MAII	**65.0%***	**0.601***	**65.0%**	**0.627***	**72.5%***	**0.725***	**77.5%***	**0.771***

both agents to stick to their own positions during the debate, limiting cross-side information use and weakening detection of problematic values. In contrast, our MAII method introduces an intergenerational interaction mechanism that enables each generational agent to selectively absorb and integrate reasonable information from other generational agents, yielding more accurate moderation results.

It is worth noting that when running DMAC under Doubao configuration, Doubao refused to perform the relevant task, and thus no corresponding results were obtained. A possible reason is that the forced requirement for the pro-agent to assert the presence of problematic value orientations may have triggered Doubao's response restrictions, leading it to refuse to make such a judgment without sufficient evidence (e.g., "I cannot provide you with a corresponding answer to this question"). In comparison, our MAII method imposes no predefined stances, allowing generational agents to explore issues across generational perspectives. If the given textbook content does not contain such issues, generational agents can naturally provide the judgment of "no problematic value orientations". Therefore, our MAII method better aligns with the response mechanisms of LLMs and exhibits greater generality and adaptability.

4.7 Experimental Results and Analysis for RQ2

Before addressing RQ2, we first examine the consistency of the moderation results produced by the four generational agents in the initial independent moderation stage under different LLM configurations. The results are shown in Fig. 2. It can be seen that under different LLM configurations, there is always a certain proportion of inconsistent results (refer to intergenerational divergence), with the proportion exceeding 35% under the GPT-4o configuration. This finding indicates that generational agents indeed differ in their value judgments. Furthermore, Table 2 shows that under three LLM configurations (i.e., Doubao, Gemini, and GPT-4o), MAII-I method achieves the best performance compared with the baseline methods (i.e., LLM-Mod, OPO, and DMAC). Under the Qwen configuration, the performance of MAII-I method is also on par with the best-performing baseline method (i.e., LLM-Mod). These results confirm that incorporating multi-generational perspectives can indeed improve the accuracy of

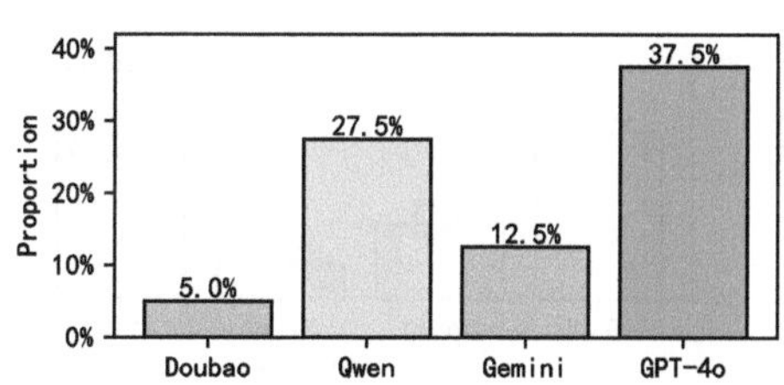

Fig. 2. Proportion of initial opinion disagreements among generational agents under different LLM configurations.

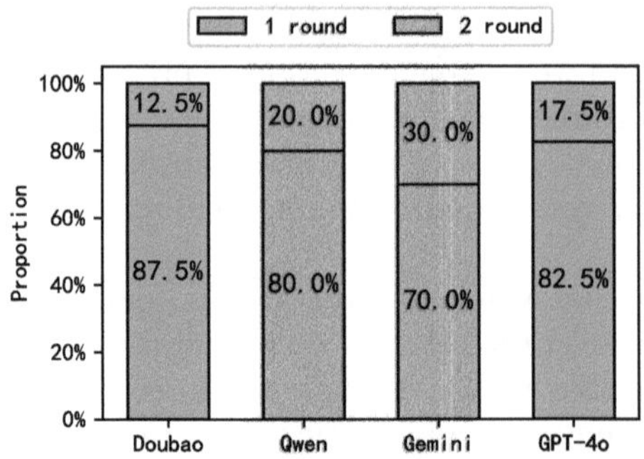

Fig. 3. Proportion of cases corresponding to different numbers of intergenerational interaction rounds under different LLM configurations.

textbook content moderation. As for the reason, relying solely on a single generational perspective for textbook content moderation may cause blind spots in value judgments, making it difficult to comprehensively identify potential problematic value orientations. In contrast, introducing multi-generational perspectives into the moderation process and integrating them can overcome the limitations of a single perspective.

However, MAII-I method only aggregates the independently generated moderation results of different generational agents through a one-vote veto rule. It does not promote further interaction among generational agents, which makes it prone to retaining initial biases in complex value judgments. In contrast, our MAII method introduces an intergenerational interaction mechanism that

Table 3. Opinion revisions after intergenerational interactions under different LLM configurations

	Doubao	Qwen	Gemini	GPT-4o
Opinion Revision (%)	5.0	17.5	5.8	5.6
Positive Revision (%)	100.0	57.1	57.1	55.6
Negative Revision (%)	0.0	42.9	42.9	44.4

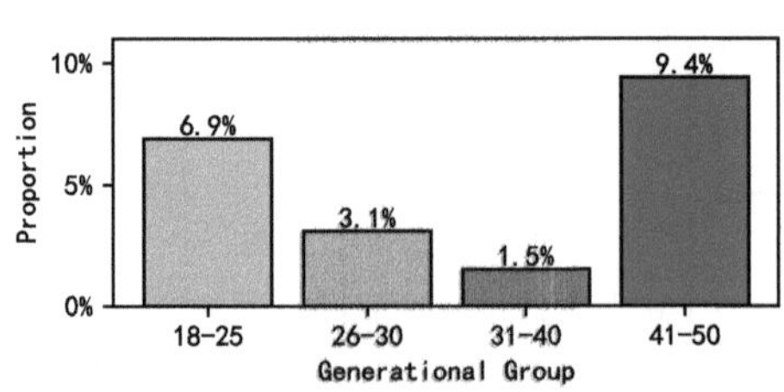

Fig. 4. Average opinion revision proportion of different generational agents under all LLM configurations.

encourages generational agents to exchange and complement one another's perspectives, thereby producing more robust moderation results. We will further discuss the intergenerational interaction mechanism in the next section.

4.8 Experimental Results and Analysis for RQ3

Before addressing RQ3, we first calculate the proportion of cases corresponding to different numbers of intergenerational interaction rounds under different LLM configurations (see Fig. 3). It can be seen that 70.0%–87.5% of moderation processes are completed in the first round. A possible reason is that incorporating multi-generational perspectives provides relatively sufficient coverage of viewpoints during the initial independent moderation. If the textbook illustrations do not contain significant controversies, the generational agents are more likely to reach a consensus in the first round, resulting in relatively robust moderation results. However, 12.5%-30.0% of the moderation processes enter the second round, indicating that in some contentious cases, there are relatively large differences and conflicts among generational agents, requiring further interactions to eliminate disagreements. Furthermore, Table 2 shows that under different LLM configurations, our MAII method consistently outperforms MAII-I method, indicating that the intergenerational interaction mechanism indeed plays a positive role in textbook content moderation. Compared with MAII-I method, our MAII method introduces this mechanism to guide generational agents in selectively absorbing and integrating reasonable information from other generations, thereby producing more comprehensive and robust moderation results.

In addition, we calculate the proportion of differences between the final moderation results of generational agents after intergenerational interaction and their initial independent moderation results under different LLM configurations. These differences are further classified into positive revisions (i.e., the revised final result is consistent with the ground-truth label) and negative revisions (i.e., the revised final result is inconsistent with the ground-truth label). The results are shown in Table 3. Taking Qwen as an example, after intergenerational interaction, 17.5% of the moderation results across all generational agents are revised compared with the initial independent moderation results, among which 57.1% are positive revisions. Overall, under different LLM configurations, the proportion of positive revisions is consistently higher than that of negative revisions, indicating that the intergenerational interaction mechanism generally guides viewpoints to converge toward the ground-truth label, thereby improving the accuracy and robustness of moderation results. It should be noted that a certain proportion of negative revisions also occur during intergenerational interactions. A possible reason is that the inherent safety sensitivity of LLMs makes them more inclined to focus on negative viewpoints in the interaction process. As a result, even if an agent initially judges that the target content contains no problematic value orientations, once other agents raise potential issues, it often pays extra attention out of caution, which increases the likelihood of miscorrecting an originally correct judgment. For this reason, in DMAC method, once the pro-agent raises a challenge or problem, the judge-agent tends to rule in favor of the pro-agent in most cases, which leads to overall poor performance. In contrast, our MAII method employs the intergenerational interaction mechanism, allowing agents to incorporate multi-generational viewpoints, thereby reducing single-view bias and improving robustness and performance.

Another interesting finding is that generational agents show certain differences in their tendency to revise viewpoints during the intergenerational interaction process. Figure 4 presents the average opinion revision proportions of different generational agents across all LLM configurations. The results show that the 41–50 generational agent has the highest average revision proportion. A possible reason is that when simulating the 41–50 group, the generational agent reflects their typically rich social and professional experience, which makes them more inclined to reflect on and reconcile diverse opinions, thereby showing a stronger willingness to revise. In contrast, the generational agents corresponding to the 26–30 and 31–40 groups exhibit relatively lower revision proportions. This may be because they occupy an intermediate stage in value development: they need to understand the ideas and demands of younger agents while also drawing on the experiences of older ones. Consequently, they tend to strike a balance across generational perspectives, which makes them more stable and less likely to change their original positions.

4.9 Case Study

To further show the intergenerational interaction mechanism in textbook content moderation, we select a positive sample (see Fig. 5) from the dataset.

Taking Gemini as an example, in the initial independent moderation stage, the four generational agents reached divergent conclusions. The 26–30 generational agent judged the illustration to be problematic, reasoning that the boy occupies the questioning and leading role while the girl merely smiles and watches from the side, which may imply a potentially problematic value orientation that boys are smarter and girls are more dependent. In contrast, during the intergenerational interaction stage of our MAII method, the three generational agents (i.e., 18–25, 31–40, and 41–50) questioned the viewpoint proposed by the 26âĂŞ30

Fig. 5. An illustration example without problematic value orientations.

generational agent. Specifically, the 18–25 generational agent pointed out that the girl's expression is more consistent with a thinking scenario. The 41–50 generational agent notes that the purpose of textbook illustrations is essentially to convey a learning atmosphere in mathematics, and a single image should not be over-interpreted as reflecting gender value differences. After one round of intergenerational interaction, the 26–30 generational agent revises its viewpoint. Finally, all generational agents agree that the textbook illustration does not contain problematic value orientations.

This case demonstrates that without intergenerational interaction, relying solely on the one-vote veto rule is prone to misjudgment due to the sensitive interpretations of one agent. By contrast, the intergenerational interaction mechanism enables generational agents to complement and reflect on one another's viewpoints, helping them avoid over-interpretation or narrow judgments. As a result, the process reaches a more reasonable conclusion and significantly enhances the robustness of the moderation results.

5 Conclusion

Existing methods that employ LLM-driven agents for textbook content moderation often fall into the blind spots of value moderation due to neglecting generational differences in value judgment. To address this issue, we proposed a textbook content moderation method based on Multi-Agent Intergenerational Interaction (MAII). This approach constructs agents representing different generational value orientations and introduces an intergenerational interaction mechanism to generate more comprehensive moderation results. Experimental results show that under various LLM configurations, our MAII method significantly outperforms baseline methods. Moreover, incorporating multiple generational perspectives improves the accuracy of moderation results, while the intergenerational interaction mechanism further enhances both accuracy and interpretability.

As for the future work, we plan to introduce viewpoint weighting in the intergenerational interactions stage to prevent individual sensitive opinions from being overly amplified and skewing overall judgments. In addition, we will consider integrating real feedback from frontline teachers and students to dynamically optimize the value configuration of generational agents.

Acknowledgments. This work was supported by New Generation Artificial Intelligence-National Science and Technology Major Project (2025ZD0124103) in collaboration with Shanghai Artificial Intelligence Laboratory. It is also supported by National Natural Science Foundation of China (under Project No. 62377013 and 62307028), the Fundamental Research Funds for the Central Universities, the Lab for Educational Big Data and Policymaking, and the Open Research Fund of NPPA Key Laboratory of Publishing Integration Development, ECNUP.

Conflict of Interest. The authors have no conflicts of interest to declare that are relevant to the content of this article.

References

1. Bao, Z., Ji, Y., Wu, W., Chen, X., He, L.: Supervisor alignment framework: enhancing LLM alignment with query-ignoring strategy and multi-agent interaction. In: ICASSP, pp. 1–5 (2025)
2. Fan, W., et al.: A survey on rag meeting LLMs: towards retrieval-augmented large language models. In: ACM SIGKDD, pp. 6491–6501 (2024)
3. Fasbender, U., Gerpott, F.H.: Knowledge transfer between younger and older employees: a temporal social comparison model. Work Aging Retirement **8**(2), 146–162 (2022)
4. Fillies, J., Mitsikas, T., Schäfermeier, R., Paschke, A.: Agent-based hate speech moderation approach. In: CALM, pp. 107–125 (2024)
5. Goyal, S., et al.: HealAI: a healthcare LLM for effective medical documentation. In: WSDM, pp. 1167–1168 (2024)
6. Hashmi, E., Yayilgan, S.Y., Yamin, M.M., Abomhara, M., Ullah, M.: Self-supervised hate speech detection in Norwegian texts with lexical and semantic augmentations. ESWA **264**, 125843 (2025)
7. Huang, T.: Content moderation by LLM: from accuracy to legitimacy. AIR **58**(10), 1–32 (2025)
8. Karabulut, D., Ozcinar, C., Anbarjafari, G.: Automatic content moderation on social media. MTA **82**(3), 4439–4463 (2023)
9. Karanikolas, N., Manga, E., Samaridi, N., Tousidou, E., Vassilakopoulos, M.: Large language models versus natural language understanding and generation. In: PCI, pp. 278–290 (2023)
10. Kohn, T.: From imitation games to robot-teachers: a review and discussion of the role of LLMs in computing education. JCAL **41**(3), e70043 (2025)
11. Kolla, M., Salunkhe, S., Chandrasekharan, E., Saha, K.: LLM-mod: can large language models assist content moderation? In: CHI EA, pp. 1–8 (2024)
12. Kuang, J., et al.: Natural language understanding and inference with MLLM in visual question answering: a survey. ACM Comput. Surv. **57**(8), 1–36 (2025)
13. Kumar, D., AbuHashem, Y.A., Durumeric, Z.: Watch your language: investigating content moderation with large language models. In: AAAI, vol. 18, pp. 865–878 (2024)
14. Liu, C., et al.: The combined impact of gender and age on post-traumatic stress symptoms, depression, and insomnia during covid-19 outbreak in China. Front. Public Health **8**, 620023 (2021)
15. Liu, Y.: "funeral culture" from the perspective of marxism. Adv. Soc. Sci. **12**, 3083 (2023)
16. Ma, J., Wang, C., Rong, L., Wang, B., Xu, Y.: Exploring multi-agent debate for zero-shot stance detection: a novel approach. Appl. Sci. **15**(9), 4612 (2025)
17. Masud, S., Singh, S., Hangya, V., Fraser, A., Chakraborty, T.: Hate personified: investigating the role of LLMs in content moderation. In: EMNLP, pp. 15847–15863 (2024)
18. Obi, J.C.: A comparative study of several classification metrics and their performances on data. WJAETS **8**(1), 308–314 (2023)
19. Pang, Y., Yang, B., Tu, H., Cao, Y., Zhang, Z.: Language models can see better: visual contrastive decoding for LLM multimodal reasoning. In: ICASSP, pp. 1–5 (2025)
20. Park, S., Kim, J., Jin, S., Park, S., Han, K.: Predict: multi-agent-based debate simulation for generalized hate speech detection. In: EMNLP, pp. 20963–20987 (2024)

21. Qiao, W., et al.: Scaling up LLM reviews for google ads content moderation. In: ACM International Conference, pp. 1174–1175 (2024)
22. Rajput, R.S., Shah, S., Neema, S.: Content moderation framework for the LLM-based recommendation systems. JCET **14**(3), 104–17 (2023)
23. Sun, H., Ni, W.: Design and application of an ai-based text content moderation system. Sci. Program. **2022**(1), 2576535 (2022)
24. Tang, Y., Tang, C.: Research on the allocation of platform liability for network information content governance. Res. Financ. Econ. Issues **6**, 59–72 (2023)
25. Wang, C., Dong, Y., Ye, Z., Feng, J.: Linking online and offline intergenerational knowledge transfer to younger employees' innovative work behaviors: evidence from Chinese hospitals. JKM **27**(3), 762–784 (2023)
26. Wang, L., Yang, N., Huang, X., Yang, L., Majumder, R., Wei, F.: Improving text embeddings with large language models. In: ACL, pp. 11897–11916 (2024)
27. WANG, L., SHI, K., LUO, D.Y.: Research on the influence mechanism of work-family conflict and ruminant thinking on subjective well-being. J. Northeastern Univ. (Soc. Sci.) **21**(5), 480 (2019)
28. Xu, C., et al.: Align on the fly: adapting chatbot behavior to established norms. arXiv preprint arXiv:2312.15907 (2023)
29. Yuan, L., et al.: Improving natural language understanding for LLMs via large-scale instruction synthesis. In: AAAI, pp. 25787–25795 (2025)
30. Zhou, Y.: New paths in the study of emerging generation values and behavior patterns. Acad. Monthly 130–141 (2022)

A Fairness-Aware Multi-agent Deep Deterministic Policy Gradient for Dynamic Scheduling

Xiaotong Chen[1,2], Linfu Sun[1,2(✉)], and Tong Gu[1,2]

[1] School of Computing and Artificial Intelligence, Southwest Jiaotong University, Chengdu, China
sunlf@163.vip.com

[2] Manufacturing Industry Chain Collaboration Industrial Software Key Laboratory of Sichuan Province, SWJTU, Chengdu, China
{c0672,gutong}@my.swjtu.edu.cn

Abstract. Dynamic scheduling is critical for enhancing performance, resource utilization, and adaptability in complex computational and industrial systems, especially within networked and cybersecurity environments where fairness and security are paramount. While the Multi-Agent Deep Deterministic Policy Gradient (MADDPG) algorithm demonstrates strong performance in decentralized scheduling, it often suffers from incentive conflicts among agents, leading to unfair resource allocation and instability during policy learning—issues that are particularly acute in networked systems prone to adversarial behaviors and security threats. To address these challenges, we propose Fair-MADDPG, a novel extension that seamlessly integrates fairness constraints into the policy gradient update. This approach ensures an equitable reward distribution among agents, thus promoting both robust system-level optimization and resilience against potential security vulnerabilities arising from unfair collaboration. Extensive experiments on eight diverse and challenging scheduling benchmarks, including scenarios inspired by network resource allocation and secure multi-agent coordination, demonstrate that Fair-MADDPG consistently achieves high task completion rates. Compared to state-of-the-art baselines, our method reduces decision latency by up to 67% and yields total rewards 3 to 36 times higher than MADPG, DQN, and Q-learning, all while maintaining inter-agent reward variance below 2%, thus ensuring fairness and stability.

Keywords: Dynamic scheduling · MADDPG · Fairness

1 Introduction

3 Dynamic scheduling has become a cornerstone technology in the field of knowledge science and engineering as applied to network systems and cybersecurity. In these environments, dynamic scheduling not only optimizes the allocation

J. Niu et al. (Eds.): KSEM 2026, LNAI 16631, pp. 504–518, 2027.
https://doi.org/10.1007/978-981-92-2759-4_37

of computational and communication resources, but also supports intelligent decision-making processes essential for knowledge-driven applications such as automated threat detection, adaptive security policy enforcement, and collaborative defense mechanisms. Using advanced methodologies, such as reinforcement learning [12] and twin-based digital simulation [2] enables the integration of domain-specific knowledge, real-time data and predictive analytics to continuously refine scheduling strategies under uncertain and dynamic conditions typical of complex networks.

A substantial body of literature explores the development of dynamic scheduling, particularly as it relates to knowledge science and engineering within network and cybersecurity contexts. The main approaches can be summarized as follows: (i) *Metaheuristic optimization algorithms.* For example, Fred Glover [3] introduced the tabu search algorithm, pioneering metaheuristic methods, while Kirkpatrick *et al.* [5] established simulated annealing, providing a foundation for optimizing large-scale and complex systems. (ii) *Reinforcement learning.* Chen *et al.* [1] developed an improved metaRL-based dynamic scheduling algorithm, and Yuan *et al.* [15] formulated a new Markov decision process model to enhance learning effectiveness. (iii) *Hybrid algorithms.* Liu *et al.* [7] proposed a knowledge- and data-driven dynamic job shop scheduling framework, while Guo *et al.* [4] presented a variable-fidelity surrogate-assisted hyper-heuristic algorithm. Despite these advances, existing methods still face challenges related to the integration and fair utilization of knowledge resources, often resulting in **unfairness** and **instability** during strategy learning, particularly in dynamic and uncertain network environments.

To address the aforementioned challenges, we propose Fair-MADDPG, a fairness-aware Multi-Agent Deep Deterministic Policy Gradient algorithm. Built upon a centralized training and decentralized execution framework, our approach incorporates an entropy regularization mechanism to enhance policy stability and prevent premature convergence. Also, we integrate fairness constraints directly into the objective function to ensure equitable resource allocation. Coupled with an online learning strategy, the proposed method enables real-time adaptation to load fluctuations through dynamic weight adjustment.

Contributions. In summary, our contributions are summarized as follows.

- We propose Fair-MADDPG, a fair multi-agent deep deterministic policy gradient algorithm that explicitly incorporates fairness as a first-class objective. By aligning individual agent incentives with global system goals through a novel fairness-aware credit assignment mechanism, Fair-MADDPG overcomes inequitable outcomes commonly observed in standard decentralized learning paradigms.
- To address the intrinsic instability of strategy training in dynamic multi-agent environments, we introduce a regularized entropy learning framework that integrates fairness-aware optimization and online adaptation mechanisms. This formulation not only stabilizes learning through entropy regularization, but also ensures robust real-time responsiveness to shifting workloads, effec-

tively resolving the volatility that plagues conventional decentralized training schemes.
– Extensive experiments across eight heterogeneous scheduling datasets demonstrate that our approach consistently achieves near-optimal task completion rates, reduces scheduling steps by up to 67% compared to baselines, and yields total rewards 3 to 36× higher than state-of-the-art multi-agent and single-agent methods, while maintaining strict reward fairness between agents.

2 Related Work

2.1 Dynamic Scheduling

Dynamic scheduling in complex, stochastic environments remains a fundamental challenge due to non-stationary task arrivals, partial observability, and competing objectives such as latency, energy efficiency, and load balance. Yuan et al. [15] propose an MDP framework that captures temporal learning dynamics to improve strategy convergence in real-time control. Sun et al. [11] introduce O3-DDQN, a dueling DQN variant using asynchronous state-action representations to handle non-stationary and partial observability. For multi-objective settings, Wang et al. [13] enhance NSGA-III with variable neighborhood search to better approximate Pareto fronts in hybrid static-dynamic scenarios. In railway operations, Yang et al. [14] unify nominal and disruption-aware railway scheduling via a shared DRL formulation. In heterogeneous computing, Cai et al. [6] propose Urgency-based List Scheduling (ULS), which prioritizes deadline-sensitive workflows using slack-aware urgency metrics. Liu et al. [8] present CrowdHMTware, a middleware that dynamically selects and deploys DNN models on edge devices by balancing latency, accuracy, and energy through online profiling.

2.2 Multi-agent Deep Deterministic Policy Gradient (MADDPG)

Multi-Agent Deep Deterministic Policy Gradient (MADDPG) has become a prominent approach for decentralized scheduling in dynamic, multi-agent environments. Recent works extend MADDPG to distributed task orchestration: Nimmala et al. [9] propose a multi-agent reinforcement learning framework for joint resource allocation and fault-tolerant job dispatching; Sun et al. [10] apply MADDPG to design incentive-compatible, distributed pricing mechanisms for mobile crowdsensing under strategic agent behavior; and Zhang et al. [16] introduce MATS, a scalable MADDPG-based scheduler for coordinating heterogeneous edge nodes. However, these methods share a critical limitation in that they fail to adequately address issues of learning stability and reward fairness.

3 System Model and Design Goals

3.1 System Model

Consider a typical single-processor real-time system composed of an occasional real-time task set $T = \tau_1, \tau_2, ..., \tau_n$. Each task τ_i is formally described using the classical triplet model (C_i, D_i, T_i), where C_i denotes the worst-case execution time, D_i represents the relative deadline satisfying $D_i \leq T_i$, and T_i indicates the minimum release interval. Each task τ_i periodically generates a sequence of job instances $J_{i,1}, J_{i,2}, \ldots$, where each job $J_{i,j}$ possesses three critical time attributes: The release time $r_{i,j}$ denotes when the job first becomes scheduled for execution. The absolute deadline $d_{i,j} = r_{i,j} + D_i$ defines the upper bound for the job's completion time, while the actual execution time $c_{i,j}$ is a dynamic variable satisfying $0 \leq c_{i,j} \leq C_i$. This model captures the fundamental temporal characteristics of real-time systems, providing a theoretical foundation for subsequent dynamic scheduling strategies.

At any given time t, each job in the system is in one of the following five mutually exclusive states:

1. **Ready.** $J_{i,j} \in R(t) \iff (r_{i,j} \leq t) \wedge (c_{i,j}^{\text{rem}} > 0) \wedge (J_{i,j}\text{unblocked})$
2. **Executing.** $J_{i,j} \in E(t) \iff J_{i,j}\text{running}$
3. **Blocked.** $J_{i,j} \in B(t) \iff (r_{i,j} \leq t) \wedge (c_{i,j}^{\text{rem}} > 0) \wedge (J_{i,j}\text{waiting})$
4. **Completed.** $J_{i,j} \in C(t) \iff c_{i,j}^{\text{rem}} = 0$
5. **Unreleased.** $J_{i,j} \in U(t) \iff r_{i,j} > t$

3.2 Problem Formulation

The dynamic scheduling problem is formalized as a constrained optimization problem. The decision variable is the scheduling function $S(t) \rightarrow J_{i,j}$, which determines which job should be executed at each time step. The objective function aims to minimize the weighted cost, comprising the degree of deadline violation for urgent tasks, the ultimate slack time loss for delayable tasks, and context switching overhead. The problem is subject to five classes of constraints: ① dispatchability constraints ensure that all urgent tasks meet their deadline requirements; ② resource constraints guarantee a single-processor platform executes at most one job at a time; ③ priority constraints ensure urgent tasks always precede non-urgent ones; ④ non-preemption constraints (optional) reduce context switching overhead; ⑤ causal constraints prevent jobs from executing before being released. This formal framework explicitly captures the multi-objective optimization nature of scheduling problems and the practical constraints of real-world systems.

$$\text{minimize} \quad \left\{ \omega_1 \cdot \sum_{J_{i,j} \in T_E} \max(0, F_{i,j} - d_{i,j}) + \omega_2 \cdot \sum_{J_{i,j} \in T_D} l_{i,j}(F_{i,j}) + \omega_3 \cdot N_{\text{switch}} \right\} \tag{1}$$

$$\begin{cases} \text{Schedulability constraint:} \quad \forall J_{i,j} \in T_E, \quad F_{i,j} \leq d_{i,j} \\ \text{Resource constraint:} \quad \forall t, \quad |\{J_{i,j} \mid J_{i,j} \in E(t)\}| \leq 1 \\ \text{Priority constraint:} \quad \forall J_{i,j} \in T_E, J_{k,l} \in T_D, \quad \text{Priority}(J_{i,j}) > \text{Priority}(J_{k,l}) \\ \text{Causality constraint:} \quad \forall J_{i,j}, \quad S_{i,j} \geq r_{i,j} \end{cases} \tag{2}$$

where $F_{i,j}$ is the job completion time, N_{switch} is the number of context switches, ω_1, ω_2, ω_3 are weight coefficients.

3.3 Design Goals

Dynamic scheduling in real-world cyber-physical production systems must reconcile three fundamental yet often conflicting requirements: responsiveness to stochastic disturbances, optimality with respect to multiple performance objectives, and scalable coordination under partial observability. Unlike static scheduling paradigms that assume deterministic workloads and fixed resource configurations, dynamic environments—such as flexible manufacturing workshops, edge computing infrastructures, or urban rail networks—are subject to unpredictable job arrivals, machine failures, deadline constraints, and heterogeneous agent capabilities. Consequently, an effective scheduling framework must be designed with the following objectives in mind:

- **Adaptivity.** The policy should continuously adjust decisions in response to real-time state changes without requiring offline retraining.
- **Multi-objective Pareto efficiency.** It must balance competing metrics.
- **Learning stability and convergence guarantees.** Especially in multi-agent settings, the learning dynamics must avoid policy oscillations and ensure convergence to robust equilibrial under non-stationary interactions.
- **Fairness-awareness.** Individual agents or tasks should receive equitable access to resources over time, preventing starvation or reward monopolization that could degrade system cohesion.

4 Methodology

4.1 Overview

The process of mapping dynamic scheduling problems to the MADDPG framework is best achieved by decomposing individual and global scheduling decisions into a system composed of multiple cooperative agents, as provided in Fig. 1. Specifically, each ready job instance $J_{i,j}$ is instantiated as an independent agent. The number of agents scales dynamically based on task arrival and completion, thereby naturally aligning with the time-varying characteristics of real production environments. To achieve efficient centralized training and distributed execution, all agents share the global system state s_t, which includes job attributes, real-time progress, and processor utilization information. Each agent i local observation s_t^i also enhances its perception of its own urgency. The agent's action space is designed as a continuous bid signal $a_t^i \in \mathbb{R}^+$, representing the virtual cost incurred to acquire processor resources. A central coordinator determines resource allocation via the $argmax_i(a_t^i)$ rule based on real-time bids from all active agents, ensuring strict adherence to the single-processor constraint. The reward function r_t^i employs a hierarchical design, agents receive instantaneous rewards that are positively correlated with their task value during execution. Successful completion before deadlines yields substantial completion rewards, while failures incur severe late penalties, driving strategy convergence towards minimizing overall weighted delay. To guarantee scheduling semantic correctness, critical constraints are enforced through hybrid mechanisms.

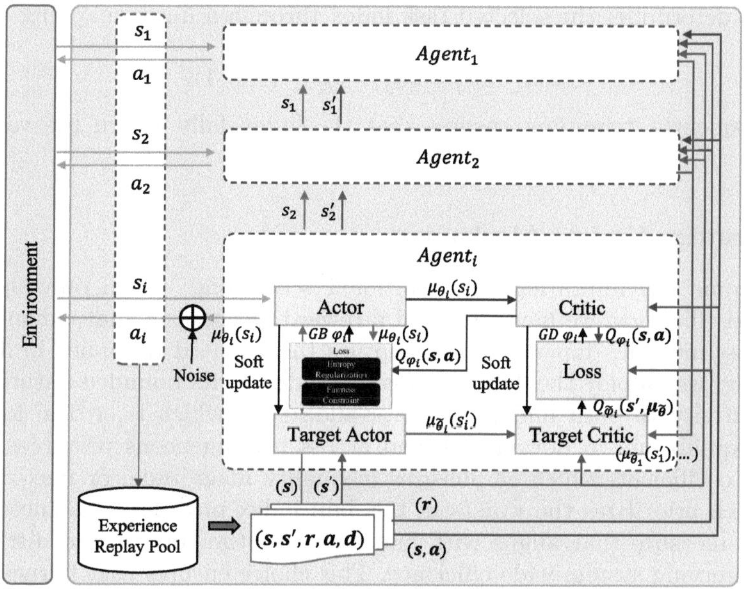

Fig. 1. Multi-agent deep reinforcement learning for dynamic scheduling framework.

4.2 State and Action Space Design

Consider a collaborative, dynamic scheduling environment consisting of N heterogeneous agents. At each time step t, the environment contains a set of uncompleted tasks, $\mathcal{T}_t$, where each task, $\tau_i \in \mathcal{T}_t$, has a processing time, $p_i \in \mathbb{R}^+$, and a priority weight, w_i, where $0.5 \leq w_i \leq 2.0$. Each agent a_j has a fixed efficiency factor of η_j belonging to the range $[0.8, 1.2]$, resulting in an actual processing time of p_i/η_j. The objective is to maximize the weighted task completion benefit while minimizing the total scheduling time, subject to load balancing and resource allocation fairness constraints.

The design of the state and action spaces takes into account the dynamic nature of the task, agent heterogeneity and the characteristics of temporal evolution. The global state vector $s_t \in \mathbb{R}^{d_s}$ is carefully constructed to encompass three types of information. For each task $i \in \{1, \ldots, T\}$, it incorporates normalized processing time $p_i/10$, priority $w_i/2$, and a binary indicator variable indicating whether it is assigned. For each agent $j \in \{1, \ldots, N\}$, it records the normalized current load $L_j/50$, efficiency factor $\eta_j/1.2$, and idle status $\mathbf{1}\{C_j \leq t\}$. Additionally, a normalized timestamp $t/200$ is introduced to enhance temporal modeling capabilities. Thus, the state dimension is

$$d_s = 3T + 3N + 1. \tag{3}$$

Regarding the action space, each agent outputs a continuous action a_j from $[1, 1]$ and determines the selected task index through a linear mapping

$$task\_idx_j = (a_j + 1)/2 \cdot (T - 1). \tag{4}$$

Subsequently, trimming ensures that the index falls within the valid task range.

4.3 Strategy Update Mechanism

To overcome the limitations of traditional scheduling, which only optimizes individual efficiency, we have designed a reward mechanism that enhances fairness across multiple dimensions. To capture the nuanced trade-offs in dynamic scheduling, we employ the Jain fairness index due to its bounded nature ($[0, 1]$) and sensitivity to both under- and over-allocation, which is critical for maintaining equilibrium in normalized load across heterogeneous resources. Unlike the Gini coefficient, which emphasizes inequality magnitude, or max-min fairness, which prioritizes the worst-off, the Jain index provides a balanced, scale-invariant measure that aligns with our goal of optimizing reward distribution while preserving system-wide efficiency. This choice ensures that fairness evaluations remain interpretable and responsive to real-time load fluctuations, a key requirement for adaptive scheduling frameworks.

$$J = \frac{\left(\sum_{j=1}^{N} \tilde{L}_j\right)^2}{N \sum_{j=1}^{N} \tilde{L}_j^2}, \quad \tilde{L}_j = \frac{L_j}{\eta_j}. \tag{5}$$

The range of values is $[1/N, 1]$, where higher values indicate a more fair distribution. Next, the Gini coefficient (G) is used to quantify load distribution inequality, with the aim of minimizing G. Furthermore, a load variance penalty term $(1/(1+Var(\widetilde{L})))$ is introduced to encourage load dispersion. Concurrently, we design an efficiency compensation mechanism to provide additional incentives for inefficient agents,

$$r_j^{\text{comp}} = \alpha \cdot \frac{\min_k \eta_k}{\eta_j}. \tag{6}$$

Ultimately, the reward function for agent j integrates the aforementioned elements and incorporates a time penalty to incentivize rapid completion

$$r_j = r_j^{\text{efficiency}} + \beta_1 J + \beta_2 (1 - G) + \beta_3 \frac{1}{1 + \text{Var}(\widetilde{L})} + r_j^{\text{comp}} - \gamma t, \tag{7}$$

where γ is the time penalty coefficient.

To enhance training stability, we introduce online reward normalization $\hat{r}_j = \frac{r_j - \mu_r}{\sigma_r + \epsilon}$, where the mean μ_r and standard deviation σ_r are dynamically updated via exponential moving averages

$$\mu_r \leftarrow (1-\alpha)\mu_r + \alpha \cdot \mathbb{E}[r_j], \quad \sigma_r \leftarrow (1-\alpha)\sigma_r + \alpha \cdot \mathrm{Std}(r_j). \tag{8}$$

During the strategy optimization phase, the actor's loss function incorporates two regularization terms beyond the standard MADDPG framework. First, an entropy regularization term $H(\pi_j) = -\mathbb{E}[\mathrm{Var}(a_j)]$ to enhance exploration. Second, a coordination constraint term $C_j = \sum_{k \neq j} \|\mu_j(s) - \mu_k(s)\|_2^2$ to encourage strategy convergence among agents and foster cooperation. The ultimate actor loss is defined as

$$\mathcal{L}_j^{\text{actor}} = -\mathbb{E}_{s \sim \mathcal{D}}[Q_j(s,a)] - \lambda_{\text{ent}} \cdot H(\pi_j) + \lambda_{\text{fair}} \cdot C_j, \tag{9}$$

where the fairness weight is set to a fixed value $\lambda_{fair} = 0.3$, while the exploration weight λ_{ent} decays exponentially with the training step count. The training process employs empirical replay and soft updates for the target network, sequentially updating the Critic and the improved Actor at each step.

5 Experiment and Evaluation

5.1 Datasets

Virtual. In this study, we employ a synthetically generated yet representative dynamic scheduling environment "DynamicSchedulingEnv" designed to emulate a multi-agent system where heterogeneous agents collaboratively allocate and execute stochastic tasks. Each episode features $N = 5$ tasks, each characterized by a discrete processing time $p_i \sim \mathcal{U}\{1, \ldots, 9\}$ and a continuous priority weight $w_i \sim \mathcal{U}(0.5, 2.0)$. The system comprises $M = 2$ agents with heterogeneous execution efficiencies $\eta \sim \mathcal{U}(0.8, 1.2)$, such that the actual processing duration of task i by agent j is p_i/η_j. The global state vector (dimensionality: $3N + 3M + 1 = 22$) encodes normalized task attributes (processing time, priority, assignment status), agent states (load, efficiency, availability), and elapsed time.

Public. The benchmark dataset[1] is specifically developed for evaluating robust optimization approaches in dynamic scheduling within stochastic remanufacture job shops. It consists of eight structured instances denoted as $Jn - Mm - Ss$, where $n \in \{10, 20, 30, 50, 60, 80, 100\}$ is the number of jobs, $m \in \{6, 10, 15, 20, 30\}$ the number of machines, and $s \in \{10, 20\}$ the number of discrete uncertainty scenarios used to model variability in processing times, release dates. Each instance is accompanied by two standardized files: (i) it contains scenario-wise operational data including stochastic processing times and temporal constraints across all s realizations; (ii) it defines the deterministic process plan for each job, specifying its machine routing and nominal operation sequence.

[1] https://doi.org/10.6084/m9.figshare.22774976.v1.

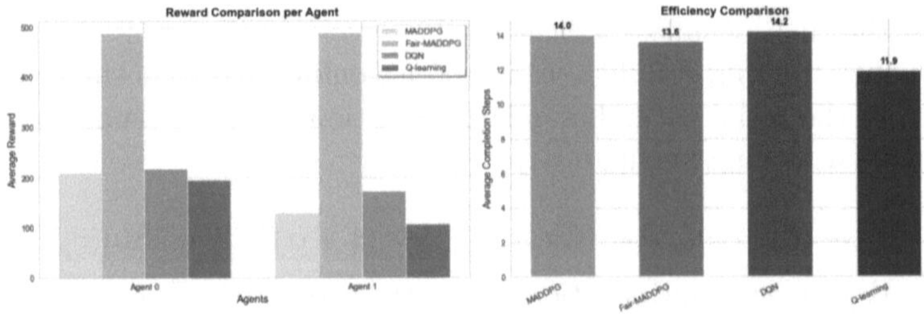

Fig. 2. Comparison of optimality gap with Fair-MADDPG baseline on virtual dataset.

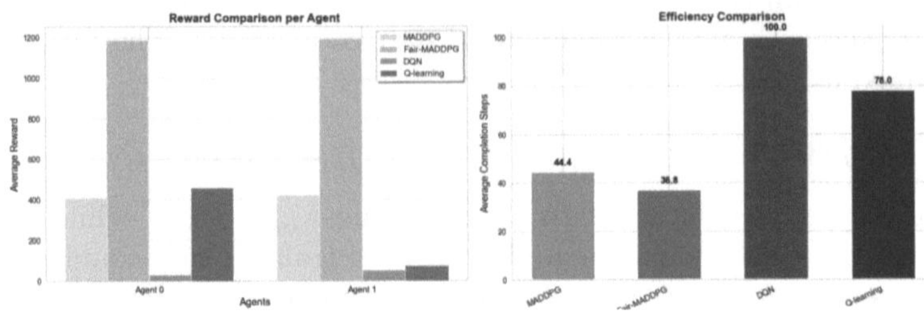

Fig. 3. Comparison of optimality gap with Fair-MADDPG baseline on public dataset.

5.2 Baselines

We evaluate Fair-MADDPG against three established baselines (MADDPG, DQN, and Q-learning) in a two-agent cooperative environment, assessing both reward performance and task efficiency (Fig. 2). As shown in the left panel, Fair-MADDPG yields substantially higher and more balanced cumulative rewards. Agent 0 achieves $\sim$ 490, and Agent 1 attains $\sim$ 485, outperforming all baselines. In contrast, MADDPG exhibits pronounced reward asymmetry, with a marked degradation for Agent 1, indicative of unbalanced strategy learning or reward allocation. The consistent performance of Fair-MADDPG among agents underscores its enhanced fairness and coordination capabilities. The right panel reports task completion efficiency ($lowersteps = higherefficiency$). DQN is most efficient (14.2 steps), followed closely by MADDPG (14.0) and Fair-MADDPG (13.6). Q-learning requires only 11.9 steps but achieves significantly lower rewards, suggesting premature convergence to suboptimal, poorly coordinated policies. Despite its fairness-aware objective, Fair-MADDPG maintains competitive efficiency while delivering superior and equitable rewards, demonstrating its effectiveness in complex multi-agent settings.

5.3 Result and Analysis

We evaluate Fair-MADDPG against three established multi-agent reinforcement learning baselines in a standard cooperative multi-agent environment. As shown in the left panel of Fig. 3, Fair-MADDPG achieves substantially higher and

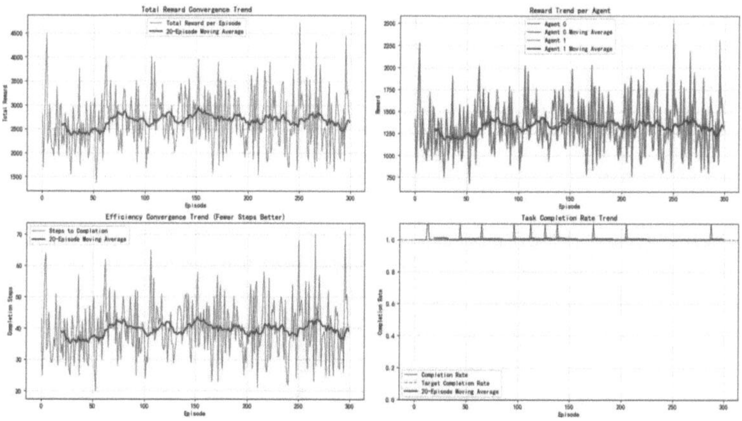

Fig. 4. Comprehensive convergence analysis.

more equitable per-agent rewards. Both agents attain an average return of 1190, markedly outperforming all baselines. In contrast, standard MADDPG exhibits significant reward disparity despite its cooperative design, while DQN and Q-learning yield substantially lower returns, reflecting their inability to cope with partial observability and environmental non-stationarity inherent in multi-agent settings. The right panel of Fig. 3 reports task completion efficiency (measured in steps). Although DQN and Q-learning complete tasks fastest, they do so at the cost of poor reward performance due to uncoordinated policies. Notably, Fair-MADDPG reduces the average completion steps from 44.4 (MADDPG) to 36.8, demonstrating enhanced coordination efficiency, while simultaneously ensuring good reward parity and superior long-term returns through joint strategy optimization under fairness constraints.

As shown in Fig. 4, experimental results demonstrate the effectiveness and convergence of the proposed multi-agent dynamic scheduling framework across multiple performance dimensions. While the total reward per round exhibits significant periodic fluctuations, the 20-round moving average stabilizes within the range of 2,700 to 2,800 after approximately 100 rounds, indicating that the strategy successfully converges despite environmental noise and random task dynamics. Individual agent rewards reveal balanced performance between Agent 0 and Agent 1, with both achieving long-term average earnings of approximately 1,400. This indicates fair task allocation and cooperative behavior that is free from free-riding tendencies. Notably, efficiency metrics show a marked decline in the number of steps required to complete tasks, ultimately converging to an average of about 40 steps. This reflects the algorithm's ability to learn more efficient execution strategies over time. Most critically, the task completion rate remained consistently close to 1.0 throughout training, with only negligible failures, highlighting the high reliability and robustness of the learned strategy. The introduction of fairness constraints does not compromise convergence stability, as evidenced by the steady-state behavior in the latter training stages,

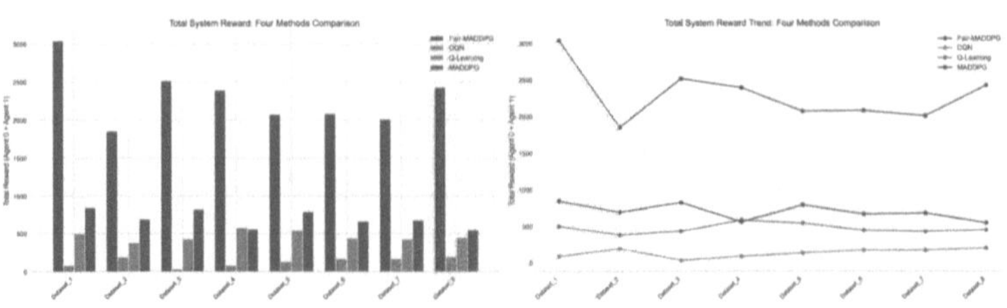

Fig. 5. Total reward comparison and trend.

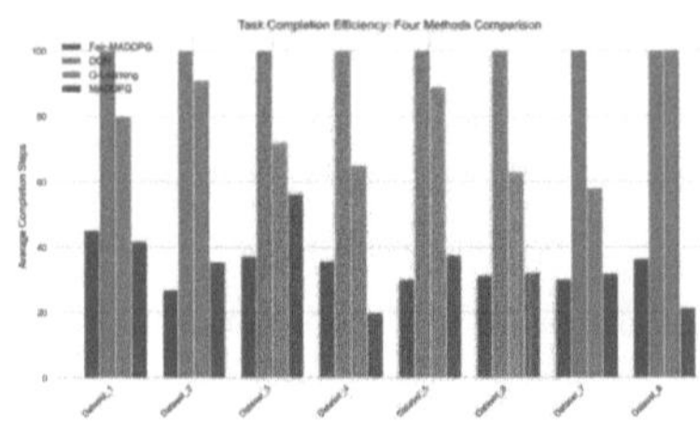

Fig. 6. Average completion steps.

where the smoothing effect of the moving average confirms the algorithm's ability to maintain performance equilibrium. Collectively, these results validate that the proposed method achieves an optimal balance between profit maximization, operational efficiency, and task reliability in multi-agent environments.

As shown in Fig. 5, Fair-MADDPG significantly outperforms the other three methods across all eight datasets, with its average total reward substantially higher than the remaining algorithms. On Dataset_1, Fair-MADDPG achieved a peak reward approaching 3000, approximately 3.5 times that of the second-place MADDPG. Meanwhile, on Dataset_8, the total reward remained around 2400, demonstrating the method's strong robustness and generalization capabilities. As shown in the line chart, although the reward curve of Fair-MADDPG exhibits fluctuations, it rapidly recovers and consistently remains above 2000 in subsequent datasets, demonstrating excellent long-term stability and adaptability. This is attributed to its introduced fairness mechanism, which prevents cooperative imbalances caused by excessive dominance of individual agents. In contrast, the MADDPG curve exhibits a "rise-then-fall" trend, gradually declining after Dataset_4. This may stem from the absence of explicit fairness constraints, potentially enabling free-rider behavior among agents and thereby reducing overall system gains. Q-learning and DQN exhibit smaller fluctuations but lower absolute values, indicating their difficulty in achieving efficient cooperation within multi-agent environments, particularly in the presence of competition or resource sharing.

Figure 6 illustrates the task completion efficiency of four multi-agent reinforcement learning methods across eight datasets, measured by the average number of steps required to complete tasks. Lower values indicate faster task

Table 1. Performance comparison across datasets and methods.

Dataset	Method	Ave. Reward		Dif. Reward	Steps	CompRate
		Agent 0	Agent 1	(%)		
Dataset_1	DQN	30.99	53.56	26.69	100.00	0.28
	Q-Learn	441.42	59.00	76.42	80.00	0.89
	MADDPG	448.56	397.67	6.01	41.80	**1.00**
	Fair-MADDPG	1521.88	1520.71	**0.04**	45.20	**1.02**
Dataset_2	DQN	80.37	110.68	15.86	100.00	0.62
	Q-Learn	366.77	11.80	93.77	91.00	0.77
	MADDPG	349.91	344.55	0.77	35.40	**1.04**
	Fair-MADDPG	924.36	928.27	**0.21**	26.80	**1.02**
Dataset_3	DQN	44.85	-14.54	195.97	100.00	0.16
	Q-Learn	369.01	60.60	71.79	72.00	0.87
	MADDPG	439.81	385.39	6.59	56.20	**1.00**
	Fair-MADDPG	1248.62	1267.36	**0.74**	37.20	**1.00**
Dataset_4	DQN	25.64	58.56	39.09	100.00	0.40
	Q-Learn	446.58	137.00	53.05	65.00	**1.00**
	MADDPG	282.38	277.42	0.89	19.80	**1.04**
	Fair-MADDPG	1190.66	1201.98	**0.47**	35.60	**1.02**
Dataset_5	DQN	-1.14	131.82	101.74	100.00	0.48
	Q-Learn	470.82	72.20	73.41	89.00	0.93
	MADDPG	391.83	400.89	1.14	37.60	**1.00**
	Fair-MADDPG	1045.35	1028.54	**0.81**	30.00	**1.00**
Dataset_6	DQN	139.34	28.17	66.37	100.00	0.44
	Q-Learn	380.80	62.40	71.84	63.00	0.88
	MADDPG	319.14	348.27	4.36	32.00	**1.00**
	Fair-MADDPG	1045.76	1037.30	**0.41**	31.20	**1.02**
Dataset_7	DQN	62.37	108.32	26.92	100.00	0.54
	Q-Learn	335.06	93.40	56.40	58.00	0.88
	MADDPG	341.87	340.48	**0.20**	31.80	**1.00**
	Fair-MADDPG	986.66	1024.99	1.91	30.00	**1.00**
Dataset_8	DQN	56.83	141.43	42.67	100.00	0.50
	Q-Learn	470.37	-20.00	108.88	100.00	0.69
	MADDPG	265.25	282.28	3.11	21.20	**1.00**
	Fair-MADDPG	1212.47	1215.00	**0.10**	36.40	**1.02**

completion and higher efficiency. Results show that Fair-MADDPG and MADDPG achieve the fewest completion steps (approximately 20 to 45 steps) across most datasets, demonstrating more efficient strategies. In contrast, DQN and

Q-Learning typically require nearly 100 steps, indicating that they often fail to complete tasks early and may even reach the maximum step limit without success.

We conducted a comprehensive comparative analysis of the proposed Fair-MADDPG algorithm against three representative baseline methods across eight heterogeneous scheduling datasets (Dataset_1 to Dataset_8). As shown in Table 1, the evaluation metrics included individual cumulative rewards per agent, total system reward, average scheduling steps and task completion rate. Experimental results demonstrate that Fair-MADDPG achieves optimal or near-optimal overall performance across all datasets. Specifically, its total system reward consistently exceeds 2000, significantly outperforming the second-best method, MADDPG, and single-agent approaches. Notably, Q-Learning exhibited Agent 1 rewards of -14.54 and -20.00 in Dataset_3 and Dataset_8, respectively, reflecting its strategy instability in non-stationary environments. In contrast, Fair-MADDPG consistently maintained positive and balanced individual reward distribution (difference between Agent 0 and Agent 1 $< 2\%$), validating its effectiveness in modeling fairness within multi-agent systems. Fair-MADDPG achieves high scheduling efficiency, completing tasks in just 30 to 45 steps on average demonstrating superior strategy convergence and action economy. Its task completion rate (CompRate) remains stable at 1.00 to 1.02; the slight excess over the theoretical optimum reflects occasional over-completion in dynamic settings, highlighting its ability to exploit latent scheduling capacity. In contrast, while MADDPG attains a comparable CompRate, it yields significantly lower total reward and exhibits high step-count variance, indicating poor alignment between individual policies and global scheduling objectives.

6 Conclusion and Future Work

In summary, we have demonstrated that strategy learning can significantly enhance both the efficiency and robustness of dynamic scheduling in symmetric cooperative environments. The proposed Fair-MADDPG achieves superior performance by aligning individual incentives with system-level objectives, thereby avoiding the coordination failures common in standard decentralized approaches. In the future, several areas warrant further investigation: (i) the extension of the fairness mechanism to heterogeneous agent settings through capability-aware or priority-weighted reward allocation, which would allow the framework to adapt to systems with varying computational capacities and task priorities; (ii) the integration of partial observability and communication constraints to better reflect real-world deployment conditions; (iii) the scaling of the framework beyond two agents via factorized or hierarchical architectures; and (iv) the validation of the approach in online, non-stationary environments with evolving task distributions. Taking these steps will be essential to bridge the gap between theoretical multi-agent coordination and practical, large-scale scheduling systems.

Acknowledgments. We thank the reviewers for their insightful comments. This work was supported in part by National Key R&D Project of China (No. 2023YFB3308501).

Disclosure of Interests. The authors have no competing interests to declare that are relevant to the content of this article.

References

1. Chen, Z., et al.: Multi-workflow dynamic scheduling in product design: a generalizable approach based on meta-reinforcement learning. J. Manuf. Syst. **79**, 334–346 (2025). https://doi.org/10.1016/j.jmsy.2025.01.010
2. Geng, S., et al.: Digital twin driven dynamic scheduling of discrete manufacturing workshop with transportation resource constraint using multi-agent deep reinforcement learning. Robot. Comput.-Integr. Manuf. **95**, 103042 (2025). https://doi.org/10.1016/j.rcim.2025.103042
3. Glover, F.: Tabu search–part I. ORSA J. Comput. **1**(3), 190–206 (1989)
4. Guo, H., Liu, J., Zhuang, C., Dong, H., Zhang, F.: A hyper-heuristic for dynamic integrated process planning and scheduling problem with reconfigurable manufacturing cells. IEEE Trans. Syst. Man Cybern. Syst. **55**(6), 3892–3905 (2025). https://doi.org/10.1109/TSMC.2025.3548120
5. Kirkpatrick, S., Gelatt, C.D., Vecchi, M.P.: Optimization by simulated annealing. Science **220**(4598), 671–680 (1983). https://doi.org/10.1126/science.220.4598.671
6. Kun, C., Wu, Q., Zhou, M., Chen, C., Wen, J., Wang, S.: Dynamically scheduling deadline-constrained interleaved workflows on heterogeneous computing systems. IEEE Trans. Serv. Comput. **18**(2), 758–769 (2025). https://doi.org/10.1109/TSC.2025.3536317
7. Liu, L., Thürer, M., He, S., Qu, T., Ma, L., Zhang, Z.: Scheduling features selection enhanced dispatching decision for dynamic job shop scheduling: a knowledge and data-based approach. Comput. Oper. Res. **186**, 107299 (2026). https://doi.org/10.1016/j.cor.2025.107299
8. Liu, S., et al.: Crowdhmtware: a cross-level co-adaptation middleware for context-aware mobile dl deployment. IEEE Trans. Mob. Comput. **24**(8), 7615–7631 (2025). https://doi.org/10.1109/TMC.2025.3549399
9. Nimmala, S., Sena, P.V., Inturi, S., Janbhasha, S., Narsimhulu, P., Manoranjini, J.: Multi-agent deep reinforcement learning for intelligent industrial iot networks. In: 2025 9th International Conference on Inventive Systems and Control (ICISC), pp. 455–459 (2025). https://doi.org/10.1109/ICISC65841.2025.11187915
10. Sun, J., Wu, D.: Maddpg based distributed multirequest pricing mechanisms for sensing tasks. IEEE Trans. Hum.-Mach. Syst. **55**(4), 569–578 (2025). https://doi.org/10.1109/THMS.2025.3580554
11. Sun, M., Ding, J., Zhao, Z., Chen, J., Q., H.G., Wang, L.: Out-of-order execution enabled deep reinforcement learning for dynamic additive manufacturing scheduling. Robot. Comput.-Integr. Manuf. **91**, 102841 (2025). https://doi.org/10.1016/j.rcim.2024.102841
12. Vitale, V.N., Tulino, A.M., Molisch, A.F., Llorca, J.: Delay-constrained dynamic network control with multi-agent deep reinforcement learning. In: 2025 IEEE International Conference on Communications Workshops (ICC Workshops), pp. 1942–1947 (2025). https://doi.org/10.1109/ICCWorkshops67674.2025.11162202
13. Wang, M., Zhang, P., Zhang, G., Sun, K., Zhang, J., Jin, M.: A resilient scheduling framework for multi-robot multi-station welding flow shop scheduling against robot failures. Robot. Comput.-Integr. Manuf. **91**, 102835 (2025). https://doi.org/10.1016/j.rcim.2024.102835

14. Yang, W., Liu, L., Yuan, H., Song, S.: Unified scheduling model for high-speed train timetable optimization and rescheduling based on deep reinforcement learning. IEEE Trans. Intell. Transp. Syst. **26**(6), 8178–8193 (2025). https://doi.org/10.1109/TITS.2025.3547473
15. Yuan, E., Wang, L., Song, S., Cheng, S., Fan, W.: Dynamic scheduling for multi-objective flexible job shop via deep reinforcement learning. Appl. Soft Comput. **171**, 112787 (2025)
16. Zhang, G., Song, J., Hu, Y., Fan, P., Li, C., Zhou, X.: Distributed task scheduling algorithm based on maddpg in mec emergency networks. IEEE Internet Things J. **12**(21), 44692–44704 (2025). https://doi.org/10.1109/JIOT.2025.3581514

DP-QMIX: Enhanced QMIX with Adaptive Death Prediction Model for Multi-agent Reinforcement Learning

Qi Zhang and Li Li(✉)

College of Computer and Information Science, School of Software, Southwest University, Chongqing, China
lily@swu.edu.cn

Abstract. Multi-agent reinforcement learning (MARL) faces significant challenges in unshaped scenarios where the state and action spaces dynamically change due to agent deaths or other environmental factors. Traditional methods either ignore these changes or employ hard masking techniques, leading to unstable learning and suboptimal policies. To address these limitations, we propose DP-QMIX, a novel approach that integrates a Death Prediction Model with the QMIX framework. Our method introduces three key innovations: (1) a multi-task DP-Model that jointly predicts agent survival probabilities and next states using LSTM networks, enabling progressive decay of dying agents' action-values; (2) a self-weighted mixing network architecture that dynamically adjusts agent contributions based on survival probabilities; and (3) a soft elimination mechanism that stabilizes the learning environment by smoothly transitioning state spaces. Extensive experiments on StarCraft II micromanagement scenarios demonstrate that DP-QMIX achieves faster convergence (approximately 28% improvement in complex scenarios) and higher win rates (up to 52% in challenging maps like 3s5z_vs_3s6z compared to 22% for QMIX+) while maintaining the Individual Global Maximization principle. Our approach effectively addresses the non-stationarity challenges in unshaped scenarios and provides a robust solution for dynamic multi-agent systems. The source code is available at https://github.com/Vergissmeinncht/DP-QMIX.

Keywords: Multi-Agent Reinforcement Learning · Centralized Training With Decentralized Execution · StarCraft II

1 Introduction

Multi-agent reinforcement learning (MARL) studies how multiple agents learn coordinated behaviors through trial-and-error interaction with a shared environment. It has been applied to diverse domains such as drone swarms [15,18,20], game micromanagement [4,8], traffic signal control [10], and autonomous driving [22]. However, MARL remains challenging due to non-stationarity from concurrently learning agents, poor scalability in team size and joint action spaces, and instability under partial observability and delayed credit assignment.

J. Niu et al. (Eds.): KSEM 2026, LNAI 16631, pp. 519–531, 2027.
https://doi.org/10.1007/978-981-92-2759-4_38

We focus on *unshaped* cooperative scenarios [2], where the effective set of active agents and feasible actions change over time (e.g., unit deaths in real-time strategy games). Such events abruptly alter the effective state–action space and the trajectory distribution in experience replay, violating stationarity assumptions commonly used by value-based and off-policy methods, and often leading to unstable optimization and low sample efficiency.

Existing MARL methods typically address agent deaths in two ways: (i) ignoring termination and continuing to evaluate inactive agents, which introduces invalid actions/targets; or (ii) hard elimination via masking/removal, which changes the effective agent set and can cause discontinuities and brittle training when replaying trajectories with varying survivability. These issues motivate a survivability-aware approach that stabilizes value estimation under dynamic agent availability.

To this end, we propose DP-QMIX, which replaces hard post-death masking with a soft attenuation mechanism guided by predicted death risk. DP-QMIX: **(1)** trains a multi-task Death Prediction Model (DP-Model) to estimate each agent's one-step-ahead death probability p_d^i (together with next observations), and uses the survival weight $(1 - p_d^i)$ to down-weight individual utilities; **(2)** introduces a self-weighted mixing network that incorporates p_d^i to adaptively modulate agent contributions while preserving the IGM property; and **(3)** achieves faster convergence and higher final win rates than strong baselines on SMACv2 [3] (Fig. 4). Our experiments on SMACv2 show that DP-QMIX improves the learning efficiency of QMIX [14] across multiple scenarios and outperforms several benchmark methods.

The remainder of this paper is organized as follows. Section 2 reviews related work. Section 3 introduces preliminaries on MARL and value decomposition. Section 4 presents the DP-Model, the self-weighted mixing network, and DP-QMIX. Section 5 reports experimental results. Section 6 concludes the paper.

2 Related Work

2.1 MARL Training Paradigms

MARL training is commonly categorized into three paradigms. Distributed training with decentralized execution (DTDE) [21] (e.g., IQL) learns each agent independently, which exacerbates non-stationarity and often yields weak cooperation. Centralized training with centralized execution (CTCE) [9] mitigates non-stationarity by sharing global information, but is frequently impractical due to partial observability and communication constraints. Centralized training with decentralized execution (CTDE) [9] balances both: agents can leverage global state or teammate information during training to stabilize learning, while executing independently from local observations to avoid centralized communication. CTDE has become a standard framework for complex tasks such as StarCraftII micromanagement (SMACv2), and supports both value-based methods [2,14,17,19] and policy-based methods [11]. Our method follows CTDE.

2.2 Value Decomposition Method

Value decomposition methods are widely used under CTDE. VDN [17] factorizes the joint action-value by summation, which is efficient but limited in capturing complex interactions. QMIX [14] uses a mixing network with a monotonicity constraint, enabling decentralized greedy action selection but potentially restricting expressiveness in challenging scenarios; QTRAN [16] relaxes this constraint. ASN [19] introduces attention to model state-dependent relationships, but can be computationally expensive at scale. These methods generally struggle when the effective state/action space changes over time, as in Unshaped scenarios. UNMAS [2] addresses agent deaths via binary action masking, whereas DP-QMIX performs survivability-aware pre-death probability weighting and maintains gradient flow for dying agents through $1 - p_d^i$ attenuation. To this end, DP-QMIX introduces a DP-Model for stabilizing learning under survivability dynamics and a self-weighted mixing network for improved value decomposition.

3 Background

3.1 Decentralized Partially Observable Markov Decision Process

We consider fully cooperative multi-agent tasks under partial observability, modeled as a Decentralized Partially Observable Markov Decision Process (Dec-POMDP) [1] defined by $G = \langle S, U, P, r, Z, O, n, \gamma \rangle$, which extends POMDPs [12] with joint actions and joint observations. Here $s \in S$ denotes the global state and $A = \{a_1, \ldots, a_n\}$ the set of n agents. At time t, agents select individual actions u_t^i to form the joint action u_t, inducing transitions according to $P(s_{t+1} \mid s_t, u_t)$ and a shared reward $r(s_t, u_t)$ with discount factor γ. Each agent observes only a local observation $z^i \in Z$ through $O(s, i)$, yielding an action–observation history $\tau^i \in T = (Z \times U)^*$. A decentralized policy is $\pi^i(u^i \mid \tau^i)$ and the joint policy π induces the joint action-value function $Q^\pi(s_t \mid u_t) = \mathbb{E}[R_t \mid s_t, u_t]$, where $R_t = \sum_{k=0}^{\infty} \gamma^k r_{t+k}$. Our goal is to optimize this joint action-value function.

3.2 QMIX

VDN [17] factorizes the joint action-value $Q_{tot}(\tau, u)$ as a sum of individual utilities:

$$Q_{tot}(\tau, u) = \sum_{i=1}^{n} Q_i(\tau^i, u^i; \theta^i) \tag{1}$$

with the standard TD target and loss:

$$y_i^{tot} = r + \gamma \max_{u'} Q(s', u'; \theta^-) \tag{2}$$

$$Loss(\theta) = \sum_{i=1}^{b} \left[\left(y_i^{tot} - Q(s, u; \theta) \right)^2 \right] \tag{3}$$

where b is the batch size and θ^- denotes target-network parameters periodically copied from θ. While efficient, VDN restricts the representable centralized value function and does not exploit additional training-time state information.

QMIX represents more expressive value functions than VDN while enabling decentralized execution. It combines agent networks with a mixing network parameterized by hypernetworks [5] to produce Q_{tot}, and enforces a monotonicity constraint via non-negative mixing weights:

$$\frac{\partial Q_{tot}}{\partial Q_a} \geq 0 \quad \forall a \tag{4}$$

which guarantees consistency between centralized and decentralized greedy action selection, i.e., the Individual Global Maximization (IGM) principle [16]:

$$\underset{u}{\text{argmax}} Q^*(\tau, u) = \begin{pmatrix} \underset{u^1}{\text{argmax}} Q_1(\tau^1, u^1) \\ \vdots \\ \underset{u^n}{\text{argmax}} Q_n(\tau^n, u^n) \end{pmatrix} \quad \forall \tau, u \tag{5}$$

However, QMIX typically assumes a fixed set of agents, which limits its robustness in unshaped scenarios with dynamic agent survivability.

4 Methodology

In this section, we present DP-QMIX, an enhanced QMIX framework for unshaped scenarios with dynamic agent deaths. DP-QMIX integrates a Death Prediction Model (DP-Model) that estimates each agent's death probability and uses it to softly attenuate individual Q-values. Meanwhile, a hypernetwork-based mixing network generates state-conditioned mixing weights to form the joint action-value Q_{tot} while preserving the monotonicity (IGM) property. Together, these designs stabilize learning under changing state/action spaces via a soft elimination mechanism.

4.1 DP-Model

In unshaped multi-agent scenarios, agent deaths change the effective state/action space over time and can destabilize value estimation. To address this, we propose a Death Prediction Model (DP-Model; Fig. 1) that predicts each agent's one-step-ahead death probability p_d from its observation–action history, and uses the survival probability $(1 - p_d)$ as a soft weight to attenuate high-risk agents, avoiding hard elimination.

The DP-Model takes the agent's local observation z_t and action u_t as inputs. For supervision, we construct a binary death mask m_t from environment-provided information in SMAC: each agent observation includes health points and shield points, and

$$m_t = \begin{cases} 0 & \text{if agent's health + shield } \leq 0 \text{ (agent is dead)} \\ 1 & \text{otherwise (agent is alive)} \end{cases} \tag{6}$$

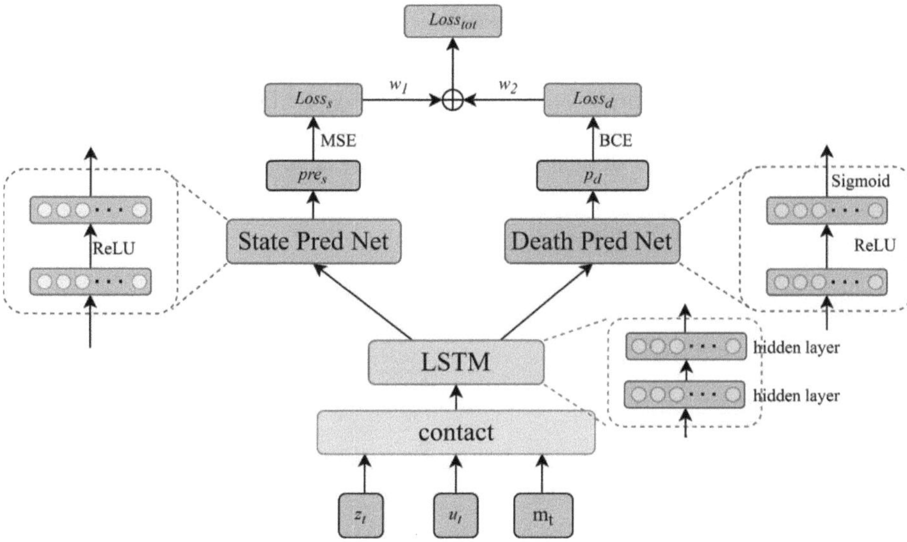

Fig. 1. Structural diagram of the DP-Model.

The mask m_t is used only as the training label for the death prediction loss $Loss_d$ (Eq. 8); during execution, the model outputs $p_d(t)$ from z_t and u_t.

At each timestep t, the DP-Model estimates $p_d^i(t)$, the probability that agent i will be dead at $t+1$. We adopt one-step prediction to match the Bellman update in Q-learning, keeping computation simple while allowing temporal context through an LSTM [6].

The LSTM features are fed into two branches. The State Prediction Network predicts the next-moment state s_t' and is trained with an MSE loss:

$$Loss_s = \frac{1}{T-1}\sum_{t=1}^{T-1}(s_t' - s_t)^2 \tag{7}$$

The Death Probability Prediction Network outputs $p_d(t) \in [0, 1]$ via a sigmoid layer and is trained with a BCE loss against m_t:

$$Loss_d = -\frac{1}{T-1}\sum_{t=1}^{T-1}\left[m_t \log(p_d(t)) + (1 - m_t)\log(1 - p_d(t))\right] \tag{8}$$

Finally, we combine the two objectives:

$$Loss_{tot} = w_1 Loss_s + w_2 Loss_d \tag{9}$$

where w_1 and w_2 balance the tasks (ablation in Sect. 5.3). The predicted p_d is then used as a survivability-aware weight in our self-weighted mixing network as shown in Fig. 2.

4.2 Self-Weighted Mixing Network

The self-weighted mixing network takes individual utilities Q_i, the global state s_t, and the per-agent death probability p_d^i predicted by the DP-Model as inputs. We adopt a two-layer hypernetwork to generate state-conditioned mixing weights, where the non-negativity of weights is enforced by a softplus activation:

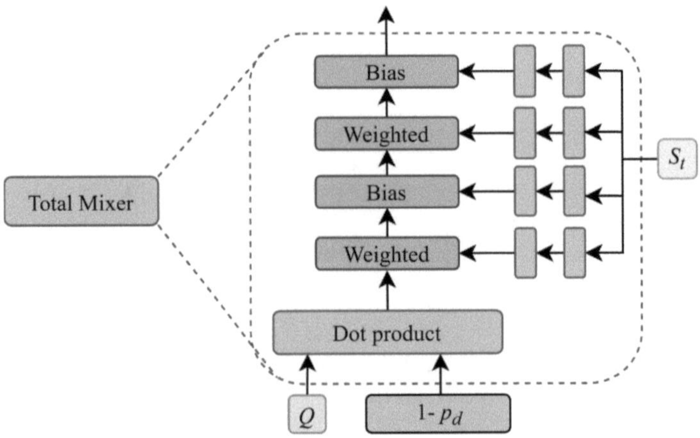

Fig. 2. Our self-weighted mixing network architecture diagram.

$$\begin{aligned} &w_1^i = \text{softplus}\left(h_{\phi,1}^i(s)\right), \quad w_2^i = \text{softplus}\left(h_{\phi,2}^i(s)\right) \\ &b_1^i \in \mathbb{R}, \quad b_2 \in \mathbb{R} \quad \text{(Global Bias)} \end{aligned} \tag{10}$$

where h_ϕ is the hypernetwork and softplus$(x) = \log(1 + e^x)$ ensures $w_1^i, w_2^i \geq 0$.

The joint action-value is computed as:

$$Q_{\text{tot}} = \sum_{i=1}^{n} \text{ELU}(Q_i \times (1 - p_d^i) \cdot w_1^i + b_1^i) \cdot w_2^i + \text{ReLU}(b_2) \tag{11}$$

where $(1 - p_d^i)$ provides survivability-aware soft attenuation, avoiding hard removal of dead agents while improving robustness under changing effective agent availability.

To satisfy the Individual-Global Maximization (IGM) principle, the mixing network must be monotonic:

$$\frac{\partial Q_{\text{tot}}}{\partial Q_i} \geq 0, \quad \forall i \in \{1, \ldots, n\} \tag{12}$$

This holds because $w_1^i, w_2^i \geq 0$ (softplus) and $(1 - p_d^i) \in [0, 1]$.

Theorem 1 (Monotonicity Preservation): The self-weighted mixing network satisfies the monotonicity constraint.

Proof : Let $z = Q_i \times (1 - p_d^i) \cdot w_1^i + b_1^i$. Then

$$\frac{\partial Q_{\text{tot}}}{\partial Q_i} = \frac{\partial \text{ELU}(z)}{\partial z} \cdot \frac{\partial z}{\partial Q_i} \cdot w_2^i \tag{13}$$

$$\frac{\partial \text{ELU}(z)}{\partial z} = \begin{cases} 1, & \text{if } z \geq 0 \\ \alpha e^z, & \text{if } z < 0 \end{cases} \quad \text{with } \alpha = 1 \tag{14}$$

$$\frac{\partial z}{\partial Q_i} = (1 - p_d^i) \cdot w_1^i \geq 0 \tag{15}$$

Since $\frac{\partial \text{ELU}(z)}{\partial z} \geq 0$ and $(1 - p_d^i) \cdot w_1^i \cdot w_2^i \geq 0$, we have $\frac{\partial Q_{\text{tot}}}{\partial Q_i} \geq 0$, which implies Eq. 12.

By introducing $(1-p_d^i)$, our mixing extends QMIX's fixed per-agent weighting to a survivability-aware dynamic weighting $w_i(t) = 1 - p_d^i(t)$. This soft elimination stabilizes learning under agent deaths and can improve sample efficiency by reducing the influence of invalid utilities in experience replay.

4.3 DP-QMIX

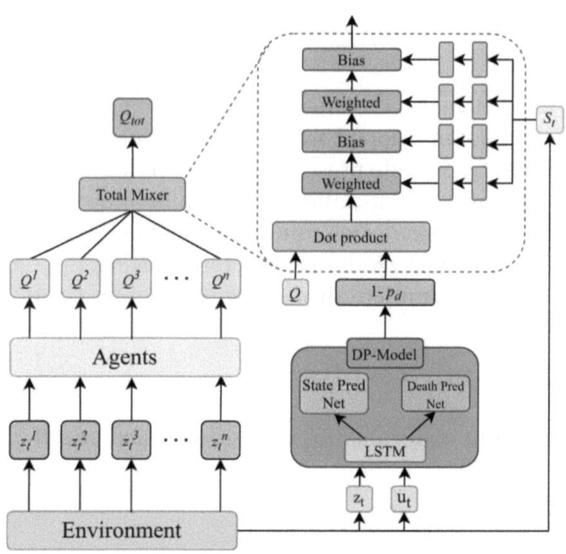

Fig. 3. The overall framework of the DP-QMIX algorithm.

As shown in Fig. 3, DP-QMIX integrates the DP-Model with the self-weighted mixing network to estimate joint action-values in unshaped scenarios with dynamic agent deaths. Each agent computes its individual utility Q^i from local observations z_t^i. The DP-Model processes observation–action histories (z_t, u_t)

with an LSTM to output per-agent death probabilities p_d^i, which are used to softly attenuate utilities via $Q^i(1 - p_d^i)$.

Algorithm 1. DP-QMIX

Input: Training steps $step_{max}$, exploration schedule $\epsilon(\cdot)$
Initialize Q-network θ, target network $\theta^- \leftarrow \theta$, DP-Model ϕ
Initialize replay buffer $\mathcal{D} \leftarrow \emptyset$, step counter $step \leftarrow 0$
Set DP-Model update freq f_{dp}, target network update freq f_{target}
for $step = 1$ **to** $step_{max}$ **do**
  Collect episode data:
    for $t = 0$ **to** $T - 1$ **do**
      Agents choose actions u_t via ϵ-greedy policy
      Execute u_t, observe $r_t, s_{t+1}, mask_{t+1}$
      Store transition $(s_t, u_t, r_t, s_{t+1}, mask_t, mask_{t+1})$ in $\mathcal{D}$
  if $|\mathcal{D}| \geq$ batch_size **then**
    Sample batch $B \sim \mathcal{D}$
    for each transition in B **do**
      $pd_t \leftarrow$ DP-Model$(z_t, u_t, mask_t; \phi)$
      $pd_{t+1} \leftarrow$ DP-Model$(z_{t+1}, u_{t+1}, mask_{t+1}; \phi)$
      $Q_{tot} \leftarrow$ Total-Mixer$(\{Q_i(1 - pd_t^i)\}; \theta)$
      $Q_{tot}^- \leftarrow$ Total-Mixer$(\{Q_i^-(1 - pd_{t+1}^i)\}; \theta^-)$
      $td_{error}^i \leftarrow r_t + \gamma Q_{tot}^- - Q_{tot}$
    $\mathcal{L}_Q \leftarrow \frac{1}{|B|} \sum_B (td_{error}^i)^2$
    Update θ via $\nabla_\theta \mathcal{L}_Q$
    if $step \mod f_{dp} == 0$ **then**
      Update ϕ using $\mathcal{L}_{tot}$ (Eq. 8)
    if $step \mod f_{target} == 0$ **then**
      $\theta^- \leftarrow \theta$

The attenuated utilities are then aggregated by the mixing network: a hypernetwork generates state-conditioned weights from the global state S_t, and nonlinear mixing produces Q_{tot} while preserving the monotonicity (IGM) constraint. Training follows the standard off-policy CTDE pipeline with experience replay buffer $\mathcal{D}$ and a target network θ^-: we minimize the TD error of Q_{tot} by updating θ, periodically update the DP-Model parameters ϕ using $\mathcal{L}_{tot}$, and copy θ to θ^- at a fixed frequency. The complete procedure is summarized in Algorithm 1.

5 Experiments and Results

This section presents the experimental setup, baselines, results, and ablations.

5.1 Experimental Setup

We evaluate DP-QMIX on SMACv2, a standard cooperative MARL benchmark based on StarCraft II micromanagement. Allied units are controlled by decentralized policies, while enemies follow the built-in scripted AI (difficulty Very Hard (7)). Agents receive local observations (e.g., relative positions, health/shield, unit types), and the global state is available only during centralized training.

We test on diverse SMACv2 maps: 2s3z, 10 m_vs_11m, 3s5z, 5 m_vs_6m, 3s5z_vs_3s6z, and 6h_vs_8z. The notation indicates unit compositions (e.g., 3s5z denotes 3 Stalkers and 5 Zealots), covering homogeneous/heterogeneous teams and symmetric/asymmetric matchups, thereby evaluating robustness under survivability-induced non-stationarity.

Baselines include QMIX+ and VDN+ (pymarl2 implementations by Hu et al. [7]), with our method denoted DP-QMIX+ on the same codebase. We further compare against QTRAN, MAPPO [13], and UNMAS [2] (hard elimination/masking for unshaped scenarios). This suite covers strong value-decomposition methods, an on-policy actor–critic baseline, and a representative hard-elimination strategy.

Table 1. The detail of setting parameters.

Setting	Name	Value
Training	Replay buffer $\mathcal{D}$	5000
	Batch size b	128
	Testing interval	10000
	Target update interval	200
	Exploration rate ϵ	1.0 to 0.05
	Discount factor γ	0.99
Network	Self-weighting mixing network layer	32
	Hyper network	64
	Agent RNN layer	64
	Optimizer	Adam
	Learning rate	0.001
DP-Model	LSTM hidden size	128
	LSTM hidden layer size	2
	LSTM Dropout rate	0.02
	w_1	0.05
	w_2	1
	Learning rate lr	0.001

We use test win rate as the primary metric. We train for 2.05M environment steps on faster-converging maps and 4.10M steps on more challenging maps. Every 10,000 steps, we evaluate using 32 test episodes. For fairness, we keep the training protocol and hyperparameters consistent across methods within each map (Table 1).

5.2 Results

We evaluate all methods by the mean and standard deviation of test win rate over the final training phase (Table 2). Learning curves on the 8 SMACv2 maps are shown in Fig. 4.

Table 2. Test win rates (mean and standard deviation) of different algorithms on 8 SMACv2 maps.

Map	DP-QMIX+	QMIX+	VDN+	UNMAS	QPLEX	MAPPO	QTRAN
2s3z	**0.98 (0.02)**	0.98 (0.02)	0.96 (0.03)	0.98 (0.02)	0.97 (0.03)	0.80 (0.02)	0.48 (0.03)
3s5z	**0.95 (0.03)**	0.82 (0.08)	0.52 (0.09)	0.57 (0.11)	0.95 (0.03)	0.31 (0.03)	0.00 (0.00)
10m_vs_11m	**0.97 (0.03)**	0.89 (0.05)	0.97 (0.03)	0.97 (0.03)	0.87 (0.07)	0.05 (0.03)	0.02 (0.03)
3s5z_vs_3s6z	**0.52 (0.07)**	0.22 (0.06)	0.26 (0.05)	0.03 (0.02)	0.47 (0.05)	0.01 (0.02)	0.00 (0.00)
5m_vs_6m	**0.77 (0.07)**	0.65 (0.09)	0.70 (0.08)	0.68 (0.09)	0.76 (0.07)	0.00 (0.00)	0.00 (0.00)
6h_vs_8z	**0.76 (0.06)**	0.64 (0.07)	0.21 (0.07)	**0.79 (0.06)**	0.01 (0.01)	0.00 (0.00)	0.00 (0.00)
corridor	**0.90 (0.05)**	0.82 (0.07)	0.58 (0.09)	0.60 (0.09)	0.00 (0.00)	0.00 (0.00)	0.00 (0.00)
MMM2	**0.95 (0.05)**	0.92 (0.05)	0.06 (0.05)	0.02 (0.02)	0.94 (0.04)	0.33 (0.05)	0.00 (0.00)

Overall, DP-QMIX+ achieves the best results on 7 of 8 maps and remains stable (standard deviation typically below 0.07). Gains are most pronounced on highly non-stationary maps with frequent deaths and asymmetric engagements. For example, on 3s5z_vs_3s6z DP-QMIX+ reaches 0.52, outperforming QMIX+ (0.22) and VDN+ (0.26), while UNMAS drops to 0.03, suggesting hard masking can be brittle under severe distribution shift. On corridor, DP-QMIX+ improves over QMIX+ (0.90 vs. 0.82). On simpler maps (2s3z, 10m_vs_11m), several value-based methods saturate near 0.97–0.98, indicating DP-QMIX+ preserves QMIX-style performance in relatively stationary settings. The only exception is 6h_vs_8z, where UNMAS slightly exceeds DP-QMIX+ (0.79 vs. 0.76), although DP-QMIX+ still improves over QMIX+ (0.64).

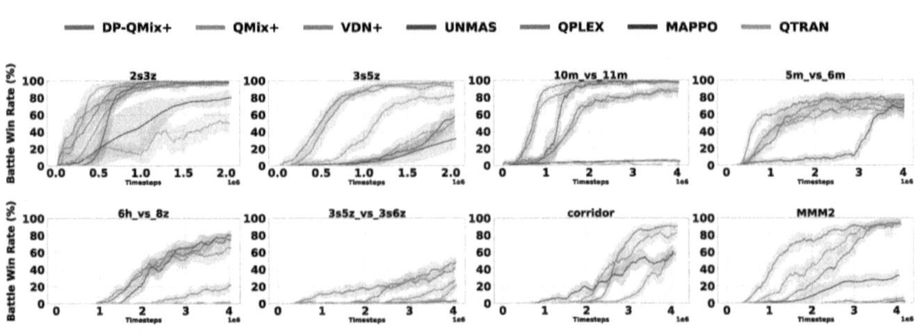

Fig. 4. Learning curves showing the test win rate versus timesteps for all evaluated algorithms across the 8 SMACv2 maps. DP-QMIX+ consistently demonstrates faster convergence and higher asymptotic performance in most scenarios.

Compared with QTRAN and MAPPO, which obtain near-zero win rates on multiple difficult maps, DP-QMIX+ remains consistently competitive, indicating that incorporating imminent death risk into value mixing is effective for unshaped settings under the same training budget. Ablations in Sect. 5.3 further analyze the contribution of the DP-Model and survivability weighting.

5.3 Ablation Results

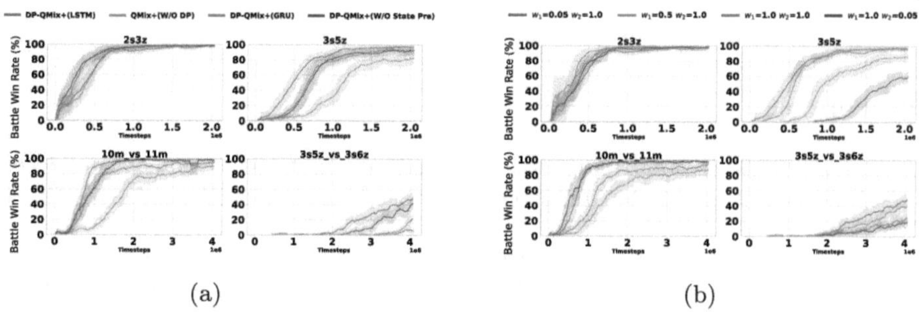

Fig. 5. Ablation Results: (a) removing or replacing each module, (b) the sensitivity experiments of w_1, w_2 on 4 SMACv2 maps.

Figure 5(a) shows that the full DP-QMIX+(LSTM) consistently performs best, with the largest gains on complex asymmetric maps such as 3s5z_vs_3s6z. Removing death prediction reduces performance and stability, indicating that modeling imminent death risk is important for soft elimination under survivability-induced distribution shift. Comparing recurrent backbones, LSTM and GRU are similar on simpler maps, but LSTM becomes more reliable as complexity increases [6]; on 3s5z_vs_3s6z, replacing LSTM with GRU collapses, suggesting insufficient long-range temporal modeling for death-risk prediction.

Removing the state prediction module also degrades performance, supporting its role as an auxiliary regularizer that improves death-risk estimation and accelerates early learning, especially on harder scenarios. Overall, the full architecture shows the clearest advantage when survival dynamics are most unpredictable.

Figure 5(b) reports sensitivity to the multi-task weights. A sufficiently large death prediction weight w_2 (at least 1.0) is required for stable learning; too small w_2 (e.g., 0.05) weakens death-risk estimation and soft elimination. In contrast, the state prediction weight w_1 should remain small (e.g., 0.05–0.2) since it is auxiliary, while overly large w_1 (e.g., 1.0) can slow convergence and reduce win rates. The default setting $w_1 = 0.05, w_2 = 1.0$ lies in the effective range, with sensitivity more pronounced on complex maps.

6 Conclusion

This paper addresses the challenges of multiagent reinforcement learning in unshaped scenarios and proposes the DP-QMIX+ algorithm. Its key components, a DP-Model and a dynamic weighting mechanism, prevent distribution drift from state-dimension drops, enabling better adaptation to dimension changes, and stable training data distribution. Experiments in various complex environments show that DP-QMIX+ outperforms VDN+, UNMAS, and QMIX+ in learning efficiency and winning rate.

However, DP-QMIX+ has limitations. The traditional LSTM it uses leads to high computational complexity in large-scale systems. In addition, the simulation platform does not account for real-world constraints, so its performance in complex practical scenarios requires further investigation.

References

1. Bernstein, D.S., Givan, R., Immerman, N., Zilberstein, S.: The complexity of decentralized control of Markov decision processes. Math. Oper. Res. **27**(4), 819–840 (2002)
2. Chai, J., Li, W., Zhu, Y.e.a.: Unmas: Multiagent reinforcement learning for unshaped cooperative scenarios. IEEE Trans. Neural Netw. Learn. Syst. **34**(4), 2093–2104 (2021)
3. Ellis, B., et al.: Smacv2: an improved benchmark for cooperative multi-agent reinforcement learning. Adv. Neural. Inf. Process. Syst. **36**, 37567–37593 (2023)
4. Fu, S., Zhao, S., Li, T., Yan, Y.: Qtypemix: enhancing multi-agent cooperative strategies through heterogeneous and homogeneous value decomposition. Neural Netw. **184**, 107093 (2025)
5. Ha, D., Dai, A.M., Le, Q.V.: Hypernetworks. In: Proceedings of the International Conference on Learning Representations (2017)
6. Hochreiter, S., Schmidhuber, J.: Long short-term memory. Neural Comput. **9**(8), 1735–1780 (1997)
7. Hu, J., Wang, S., Jiang, S., Wang, M.: Rethinking the implementation tricks and monotonicity constraint in cooperative multi-agent reinforcement learning. In: Proceedings of the Second Blogpost Track at ICLR 2023 (2023)
8. Jo, Y., Lee, S., Yeom, J.E.A.: Fox: formation-aware exploration in multi-agent reinforcement learning. In: Proceedings of the AAAI Conference on Artificial Intelligence, vol. 38, pp. 12985–12994 (2024)
9. Kraemer, L., Banerjee, B.: Multi-agent reinforcement learning as a rehearsal for decentralized planning. Neurocomputing **190**, 82–94 (2016)
10. Liu, Y., Luo, G., Yuan, Q.E.A.: GPLight: grouped multi-agent reinforcement learning for large-scale traffic signal control. In: Proceedings of the IJCAI, pp. 199–207 (2023)
11. Lohse, O., Pütz, N., Hörmann, K.: Implementing an online scheduling approach for production with multi agent proximal policy optimization (MAPPO). In: Dolgui, A., Bernard, A., Lemoine, D., von Cieminski, G., Romero, D. (eds.) APMS 2021. IAICT, vol. 634, pp. 586–595. Springer, Cham (2021). https://doi.org/10.1007/978-3-030-85914-5_62
12. Oliehoek, F.A., et al.: A concise introduction to decentralized POMDPs, vol. 1. Springer (2016)
13. Papoudakis, G., Christianos, F., Schäfer, L., Albrecht, S.V.: Benchmarking multi-agent deep reinforcement learning algorithms in cooperative tasks. In: Proceedings of the Neural Information Processing Systems Track on Datasets and Benchmarks (NeurIPS) (2021)
14. Rashid, T., Samvelyan, M., De Witt, C.S.E.A.: Monotonic value function factorisation for deep multi-agent reinforcement learning. J. Mach. Learn. Res. **21**(178), 1–51 (2020)
15. Shi, H., Liu, G., Zhang, K.E.A.: Marl sim2real transfer: merging physical reality with digital virtuality in metaverse. IEEE Trans. Syst. Man Cybern. Syst. **53**(4), 2107–2117 (2022)

16. Son, K., Kim, D., Kang, W.J.E.A.: Qtran: learning to factorize with transformation for cooperative multi-agent reinforcement learning. In: Proceedings of the International conference on machine learning, pp. 5887–5896. PMLR (2019)
17. Sunehag, P., Lever, G., Gruslys, A.E.A.: Value-decomposition networks for cooperative multi-agent learning based on team reward. In: Proceedings of the 17th International Conference on Autonomous Agents and Multiagent Systems, pp. 2085–2087. AAMAS '18 (2018)
18. Wang, L., Wang, K., Pan, C.E.A.: Multi-agent deep reinforcement learning-based trajectory planning for multi-UAV assisted mobile edge computing. IEEE Trans. Cogn. Commun. Networking **7**(1), 73–84 (2020)
19. Wang, W., Yang, T., Liu, Y.E.A.: Action semantics network: considering the effects of actions in multiagent systems. In: Proceedings of the International Conference on Learning Representations (2020)
20. Wang, Z., Du, J., Jiang, C.E.A.: Task scheduling for distributed AUV network target hunting and searching: An energy-efficient AOI-aware DMAPPO approach. IEEE Internet Things J. **10**(9), 8271–8285 (2022)
21. Wen, G., Fu, J., Dai, P., Zhou, J.: DTDE: a new cooperative multi-agent reinforcement learning framework. Innovation **2**(4) (2021)
22. Zhang, R., et al.: Multi-agent reinforcement learning for autonomous driving: a survey. CoRR **abs/2408.09675** (2024)

Emerging Topics in Knowledge Science

RelGraphQA: Relation-Driven KGQA with Schema-Indexed Grounding

Yixuan Wan(✉) and Zhipeng Wen

School of Computer Science and Engineering, Nanjing University of Science and Technology, Nanjing, China
{marisamagic,125106010733}@njust.edu.com

Abstract. Large Language Models (LLMs) excel at language understanding but often hallucinate under multi-hop reasoning and schema constraints. Knowledge graphs (KGs), with verifiable symbolic queries, can mitigate this issue. We present **RelGraphQA**, a training-free, relation-driven framework that anchors LLM generation to *KG schema* via *thresholded* FAISS matching and deterministic query synthesis. Natural-language relation mentions are grounded to *schema-valid relation types* using a lightweight FAISS `IndexIVFFlat`, retaining only high-similarity candidates. We also *early* infer head/answer types (and common operators) as structural guards for SPARQL/Cypher. A compact five-stages, four LLM calls pipeline performs (i) type/operator inference, (ii) relation grounding with thresholded schema matching, (iii) single-query synthesis, and (iv) faithful verbalization strictly from executed results. On **MetaQA**, **WebQSP**, **CWQ**, and **GrailQA**, RelGraphQA achieves competitive **Hits@1** scores and demonstrates robust performance across varying threshold settings. Ablations and sensitivity studies confirm the benefit of schema-indexed relation filtering and structural guards. Our code is publicly available at https://github.com/MarisaMagic/RelGraphQA.

Keywords: KGQA · Large Language Models · Relation Grounding · Schema-Constrained Reasoning · Query Generation

1 Introduction

Large Language Models (LLMs) have rapidly advanced open-domain question answering (QA), yet they remain vulnerable to *hallucinations*-confident but unsupported statements that proliferate during multi-hop reasoning or under fine-grained constraints [5,19]. Hallucinations are exacerbated when parametric knowledge is incomplete, outdated, or misaligned with the user's intent. To mitigate these issues, recent work increasingly *grounds* LLMs in external knowledge so that answers become verifiable rather than purely generative [20].

Knowledge graphs (KGs) offer controllable and verifiable reasoning: entities and relations are explicit, provenance is traceable, and symbolic queries

J. Niu et al. (Eds.): KSEM 2026, LNAI 16631, pp. 535–548, 2027.
https://doi.org/10.1007/978-981-92-2759-4_39

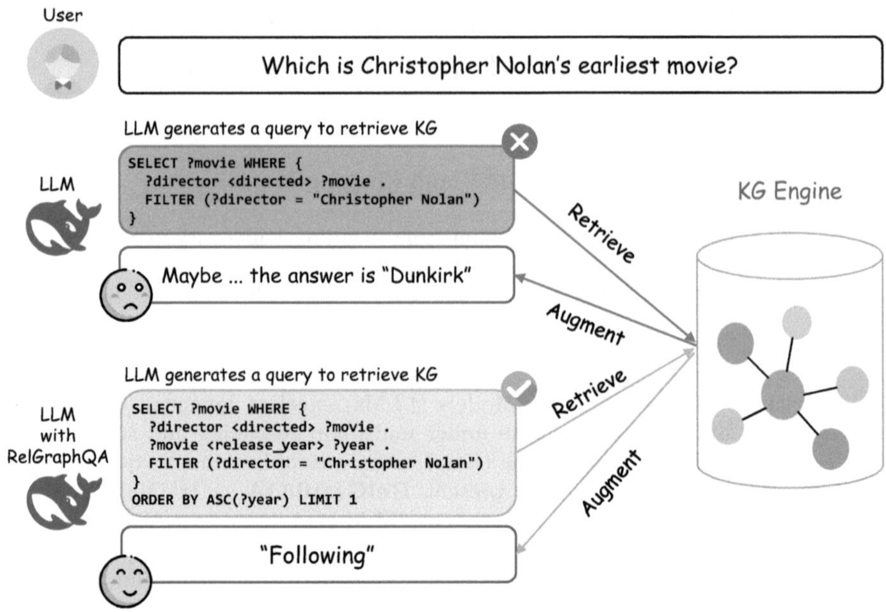

Fig. 1. Motivating example: Comparison of LLM-only vs. RelGraphQA on the question "Which is Christopher Nolan's earliest movie?"

(SPARQL/Cypher) can enforce operators such as aggregation, ordering, and comparison. In parallel, *Retrieval-Augmented Generation (RAG)* shows that coupling non-parametric memory with LLMs reduces hallucinations by conditioning on retrieved evidence [8]. Yet classical RAG chiefly retrieves unstructured text and thus under-utilizes the *relational structure* and *operator semantics* of KGs. This gap motivates graph-aware retrieval and KG-centric LLM frameworks that align retrieval with graph topology and schema semantics [3,4,7,9]. Early LLM-based structured KGQA pipelines such as KG-GPT, KB-BINDER, and DoG let LLMs synthesize executable queries or constrained subgraphs over KGs, but still suffer from unstable relation grounding, incomplete operator handling, and overly expanded subgraphs leading to spurious evidence. LMP [11], AMAR [21], and EPERM [10] briefly explore stronger structure-aware grounding via facts-graph construction and relevance-aware prompt representations. Collectively, these works demonstrate that *structure-aware grounding* and *relation-centric cues* outperform simply lengthening textual contexts. However, they also reveal remaining gaps in robust relation typing, operator-aware control, and compact subgraph restriction, which our RelGraphQA framework is designed to address.

Despite these advances, LLM-based KGQA still faces three key challenges. First, **relation grounding at scale**: while entity linking is relatively mature, selecting the correct *relation type* remains a bottleneck; LLMs often propose plausible yet out-of-schema relations that derail execution [7,9]. Second, **operator-aware control**: many real questions require `COUNT`, `MAX`/`MIN`,

`ORDER BY`, or comparative reasoning; without explicit operator detection and type constraints, operators may be omitted or incorrectly generated in the final query [4,9]. Third, **efficient subgraph restriction**: brute-force expansion introduces substantial irrelevant information, inflating the search space and degrading accuracy; classical subgraph retrieval is also sensitive to recall drift and KG sparsity [6,14–17].

We consider the question "Which is Christopher Nolan's earliest movie?". As illustrated in Fig. 1, a vanilla LLM or naive KG-augmented pipeline may (i) miss necessary multi-hop relations between the director and his works, (ii) generate partially executable or schema-invalid queries, or (iii) ignore the required `ORDER BY` (and `LIMIT`) operators, leading to incorrect or unverifiable answers.

We propose **RelGraphQA**, a relation-driven, training-free framework that anchors LLM generation with pre-indexed schema semantics and explicit, operator-aware query synthesis. Concretely, we: (i) construct lightweight *FAISS-based indices* over relation types (optionally typed as ⟨head-type, relation, tail-type⟩) and entity types; at inference time, the LLM extracts natural-language relation mentions which are matched to schema-valid relations via *thresholded* semantic similarity search, keeping only candidates with similarity $\geq \tau$; (ii) *infer* head/answer types and logical operators early, treating them as structural guards that shape SPARQL/Cypher templates; (iii) synthesize a single deterministic executable query under these constraints; and (iv) verbalize the query result into a concise natural-language answer. Leveraging the bracketed mentions in MetaQA and gold entities in WebQSP, we bypass full entity linking to focus on relation and operator grounding. In contrast to methods that learn to reweight multi-aspect retrieval or evidence paths, our pipeline remains training-free, featuring a compact five-stage design with four LLM calls that couples FAISS-based schema grounding, operator-aware template synthesis, and lightweight verbalization.

The remainder of this paper is organized as follows. Section 2 reviews related work on KGQA and LLM reasoning. Section 3 details the RelGraphQA framework, including type inference and relation grounding. Section 4 presents experimental results and ablation studies, and Sect. 5 concludes with limitations and future directions.

2 Related Work

2.1 Structured KGQA Before LLMs

Early KGQA relied on structured reasoning over retrieved subgraphs. **GRAFT-Net** [17] fuses KG entities and linked text within a heterogeneous graph via type-aware updates and personalized PageRank, but depends on subgraph recall and entity linking. **PullNet** [16] iteratively expands a question-specific subgraph through alternating retrieval and graph convolution, improving multi-hop recall at higher computation cost. **EmbedKGQA** [14] replaces explicit subgraph construction with KG embeddings and link prediction to handle missing edges, yet scoring many entities hurts scalability. **TransferNet** [15] transfers scores over relation graphs for interpretable multi-hop propagation, but remains sensitive to relation sparsity and hop limits. Overall, these methods are interpretable but suffer from EL error propagation, exhaustive subgraph construction, and weak support for operators and constraints. In addition, they typically require substantial supervised training and task-specific annotations (e.g., EL labels, relation/path supervision), incurring non-trivial training and maintenance costs and limiting portability to new domains.

2.2 LLM-Based KGQA

LLM-era pipelines increasingly *preserve KG structure* while exploiting LLM semantics. **KB-BINDER** [9] drafts a logical form with an LLM and then *binds* entities/relations via retrieval (e.g., BM25, Contriever) under schema checks. **KG-GPT** [7] generates executable queries with lightweight schema guidance. **DoG** [4] adopts multi-agent question decomposition, improving transparency on WebQSP/GrailQA but with higher API cost and sensitivity to relation filtering. **LMP** [11] textualizes graph neighborhoods for hierarchical "fact" message passing. While classical RAG primarily retrieves unstructured text, recent extensions incorporate structured sources and graph-aware retrieval; nevertheless, *out-of-schema relations*, *operator omissions* (`COUNT`, `ORDER BY`), and *inefficient subgraph restriction* remain common. Our method addresses these issues via schema-indexed grounding and operator-aware synthesis.

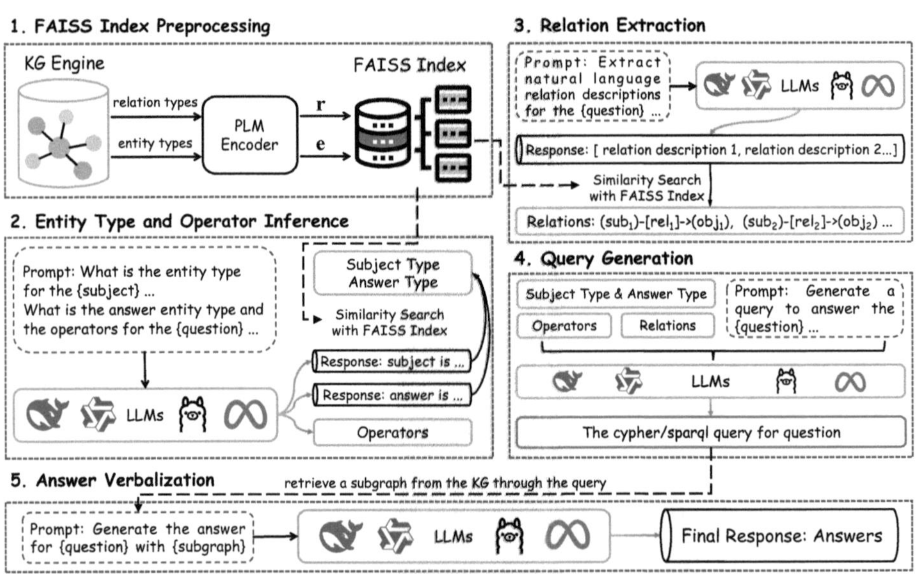

Fig. 2. Framework overview of RelGraphQA. The pipeline anchors LLM reasoning to the KG schema via thresholded FAISS matching and deterministic query synthesis.

3 Framework and Methodology

As shown in Fig. 2, RelGraphQA follows a five-stage workflow: (1) offline FAISS indexing over schema types, then four LLM-driven stages–(2) entity-type and operator inference, (3) relation grounding via thresholded FAISS similarity (cosine $\geq \tau$ with normalized embeddings, `IndexIVFFlat`), (4) SPARQL/Cypher synthesis, and (5) faithful verbalization from executed KG results–anchoring reasoning to schema constraints and producing deterministic queries.

3.1 FAISS Index Preprocessing

RelGraphQA begins with a FAISS-based indexing module [1] that extracts entity and relation types from the knowledge graph to support semantic retrieval. Through configurable database connections, the module retrieves structured schema metadata, including types, head/tail node types, and approximate occurrence frequencies. This process yields a semantic sample set capturing the core KG schema. Entity types serve directly as natural-language descriptors, while relation signatures are converted into concise natural-language templates, (e.g., mapping `(Movie)-[HAS_ACTOR]->(Actor)` to "A movie has an actor") to ensure consistent semantic representation.

Embedding Formulation. We encode textual descriptions using a locally deployed transformer PLM(·) (nomic-embed-text-v1) [13] with 512-token truncation, mean pooling, and ℓ_2 normalization. For each entity-type description d_i^{ent} and relation-type description d_j^{rel}, we compute

$$\mathbf{e}_i = \text{PLM}\big(d_i^{\text{ent}}\big) \in \mathbb{R}^d, \quad \tilde{\mathbf{e}}_i = \frac{\mathbf{e}_i}{\|\mathbf{e}_i\|_2}, \tag{1}$$

$$\mathbf{r}_j = \text{PLM}\big(d_j^{\text{rel}}\big) \in \mathbb{R}^d, \quad \tilde{\mathbf{r}}_j = \frac{\mathbf{r}_j}{\|\mathbf{r}_j\|_2}. \tag{2}$$

Embeddings are stacked into matrices $\mathbf{E} \in \mathbb{R}^{N_{\text{ent}} \times d}$ and $\mathbf{R} \in \mathbb{R}^{N_{\text{rel}} \times d}$ for FAISS indexing. During inference, **relation candidates are retrieved via thresholded cosine similarity**: the LLM-extracted relation phrase is embedded and searched against $\mathbf{R}$, retaining only candidates with similarity $\geq \tau$. Meanwhile, $\mathbf{E}$ validates subject and answer type predictions to ensure schema consistency.

Index Construction. We employ FAISS `IndexIVFFlat` with normalized embeddings (where dot product equals cosine similarity). An IVF coarse quantizer with n_{list} centroids is trained offline, probing n_{probe} lists at query time to balance recall and latency. We default to ($n_{\text{list}} = 1024$, $n_{\text{probe}} = 16$) for relation types and ($n_{\text{list}} = 512$, $n_{\text{probe}} = 8$) for entity types. The constructed indices and metadata are serialized for persistent use. This preprocessing step (Step 1 in Fig. 2) establishes a robust vector foundation for subsequent entity alignment, relation grounding, and KG-based reasoning.

3.2 Entity Type and Operator Inference

As shown in Fig. 2, the second stage employs an LLM to infer structural semantics before subgraph retrieval. The module jointly predicts the *subject type*, *answer type*, and *logical operators*, serving as schema-level constraints for subsequent steps.

Prompt Example. Few-shot exemplars guide the LLM to infer types and operators from annotated entities, as illustrated below.

Example Prompt for Type and Operator Inference
Input Question: What is the earliest movie directed by [Christopher Nolan]? **Given:** Annotated entity: "Christopher Nolan" Operator inventory: {COUNT, MAX, MIN, ORDER BY, COMPARE, DISTINCT, LIMIT} **Few-shot Exemplars:** Provide a small set of prompt-aligned examples to stabilize type and operator inference. **Expected Output:** $t_{\text{subj}} = \textit{Director}$ (Subject Type inferred from "Christopher Nolan") $t_{\text{ans}} = \textit{Movie}$ (Answer Type) $\hat{\mathcal{O}} = \{\text{ORDER BY, LIMIT}\}$ (Operators, sorted by release year)

Inference Procedure. Given a question with an annotated entity, the LLM is prompted to infer $t_{\text{subj}}^{\text{LLM}}$ and $t_{\text{ans}}^{\text{LLM}}$, which are embedded and aligned with the FAISS entity-type index $\mathbf{E}$ via cosine (dot-product) similarity:

$$t_{\text{subj}} = \arg\max_i \left(\tilde{\text{PLM}}(t_{\text{subj}}^{\text{LLM}})^\top \tilde{\mathbf{e}}_i\right), \tag{3}$$

$$t_{\text{ans}} = \arg\max_j \left(\tilde{\text{PLM}}(t_{\text{ans}}^{\text{LLM}})^\top \tilde{\mathbf{e}}_j\right). \tag{4}$$

where $\tilde{\text{PLM}}(\cdot)$ denotes embedding followed by ℓ_2 normalization. We provide a fixed operator inventory $\mathcal{O} = \{\text{COUNT, MAX, MIN, ORDER BY, COMPARE, DISTINCT, LIMIT}\}$, and prompt the LLM to select a subset $\hat{\mathcal{O}} \subseteq \mathcal{O}$ indicating which operators are needed for the current question. The resulting $(t_{\text{subj}}, t_{\text{ans}}, \hat{\mathcal{O}})$ triple forms the backbone for subsequent relation grounding and query synthesis.

3.3 Relation Extraction

The third stage bridges natural-language semantics with KG schema relations. Prompted with few-shot exemplars covering single- and multi-hop scenarios, the LLM extracts relation descriptions linking the subject to potential answers.

Prompt Example. The prompt guides the model to decompose questions into schema-grounded relation descriptions.

Example Prompt for Relation Extraction
Question: What is the earliest movie directed by [Christopher Nolan]? **Given:** $t_{\text{subj}} = \textit{Director}, \quad t_{\text{ans}} = \textit{Movie}$ **Few-shot Exemplars:** Provide a small set of prompt-aligned examples to stabilize relation extraction. **Expected Output (Relation Descriptions):** – "A director directed a movie." – "A movie has a release year." **Mapped Relation Path:** $\mathcal{R}_\tau = \{(\textit{Director}) - [\textit{DIRECTED}] \rightarrow (\textit{Movie}), \ (\textit{Movie}) - [\textit{HAS\_RELEASE\_YEAR}] \rightarrow (\textit{Year})\}$

Semantic Matching with FAISS. Each predicted relation phrase r_k^{LLM} is encoded by the same embedding model PLM(·) and compared against the FAISS index $\mathbf{R}$ using cosine similarity $s_{k,j} = \tilde{\mathbf{h}}_k^\top \tilde{\mathbf{r}}_j$. Rather than selecting a single top-1 match, we pre-set a similarity threshold $\tau \in [0, 1]$ and keep a candidate set for each phrase:

$$\mathcal{C}_k(\tau) = \{\, r_j \mid s_{k,j} \geq \tau \,\}. \tag{5}$$

Let K denote the number of relation phrases extracted by the LLM. For each phrase, we keep the thresholded candidate set $\mathcal{C}_k(\tau)$ as defined above. We then define:

$$\mathcal{R}_\tau \;=\; \{\mathcal{C}_k(\tau)\}_{k=1}^{K}. \tag{6}$$

The family $\mathcal{R}_\tau$ serves as the schema-constrained input to the subsequent query generation stage. During generation, decoding is restricted to select one grounded relation for each phrase from its own $\mathcal{C}_k(\tau)$ under type/operator consistency checks.

3.4 Query Generation

In Step 4 of Fig. 2, RelGraphQA converts the grounded structural elements into an executable query. Given the question q, the subject entity e_{subj}, the inferred subject and answer types $(t_{\text{subj}}, t_{\text{ans}})$, the *thresholded* relation set $\mathcal{R}_\tau$ (i.e., relations whose similarity to LLM phrases is $\geq \tau$), and the operator list $\hat{\mathcal{O}}$, the LLM is prompted to synthesize a schema-consistent SPARQL or Cypher statement under these constraints.

Prompt Example. Few-shot exemplars guide the LLM to generate schema-consistent queries under the inferred constraints, for instance:

Example Prompt for Query Generation

Question:
What is the earliest movie directed by [Christopher Nolan]?

Given:
Subject entity: "Christopher Nolan"
$t_{\text{subj}} = \textit{Director}, \quad t_{\text{ans}} = \textit{Movie}$
$\mathcal{R}_{\mathcal{T}} = \{(\textit{Director}) - [\textit{DIRECTED}] \rightarrow (\textit{Movie}), (\textit{Movie}) - [\textit{HAS\_RELEASE\_YEAR}] \rightarrow (\textit{Year})\}$
$\hat{\mathcal{O}} = \{\text{ORDER BY, LIMIT}\}$

Few-shot Exemplars: Provide a small set of prompt-aligned examples to stabilize Query Generation.

Expected Output (Cypher):

```
MATCH (d:Director {name: 'Christopher
Nolan'})-[r1:DIRECTED]->(m:Movie)
MATCH (m)-[r2:HAS_RELEASE_YEAR]->(y:Year)
RETURN d, r1, m, r2, y
ORDER BY toInteger(y.value) ASC
LIMIT 1
```

Formally, the generation process can be summarized as

$$\hat{q}_{\text{KG}} = \text{LLM}\Big(q,\, e_{\text{subj}},\, t_{\text{subj}},\, t_{\text{ans}},\, \mathcal{R}_{\mathcal{T}},\, \hat{\mathcal{O}}\Big), \tag{7}$$

where $\hat{q}_{\text{KG}}$ is an executable SPARQL or Cypher query that must respect the inferred types, the thresholded relation candidates, and the operator constraints.

3.5 Answer Verbalization

Step 5 (Fig. 2) produces the final answer from the executed result while keeping the LLM strictly grounded. We execute $\hat{q}_{\text{KG}}$ to obtain G_{sub}, serialize it into a compact context $\mathcal{G}_{\text{sub}}$, and prompt the LLM to *output the answer only* (no rationale/explanation), based solely on $\mathcal{G}_{\text{sub}}$:

$$A = \text{LLM}\big(q,\, \mathcal{G}_{\text{sub}}\big). \tag{8}$$

Denotation Evaluation. We parse the model output A into a set $\widehat{\mathcal{A}}$ and compare it with the gold denotation set $\mathcal{A}^{*}$ using order-invariant set equality. This uniformly handles single- and multi-entity answers.

4 Experiments

4.1 Setup

Datasets and Knowledge Graphs. We evaluate on four benchmarks: **MetaQA** (1–3 hops, movie domain with entity spans) [23], **WebQSP** [22] and **CWQ** [18] (Freebase-based natural questions), and **GrailQA** [2] (compositional generalization with unseen combinations). For MetaQA, we import the provided `kb.txt` file (each line: `subject | relation | object`) into Neo4j as a movie-domain knowledge graph [12]. For WebQSP, CWQ, and GrailQA, we host the Freebase RDF dump on a local Virtuoso SPARQL endpoint.

Models and Metrics. RelGraphQA utilizes online APIs (GPT, DeepSeek-V3.2, Qwen-3-Plus) and local Ollama deployments (DeepSeek-R1-7B, Qwen-3-8B, Llama-3-8B). We compare against KB-BINDER, KG-GPT, and DoG, quoting their reported metrics from original papers (noting potential backend differences). All experiments use standardized decoding parameters on an NVIDIA V100 (32,GB). We report **Hits@1** (exact match accuracy), where a prediction is correct iff the extracted answer set $\widehat{\mathcal{A}}$ exactly matches the gold answers $\mathcal{A}^{*}$. Further analysis on executability and threshold sensitivity is provided in Sect. 4.4 (Table 1).

Table 1. Execution accuracy (Hits@1). Bold: best; underline: second best.

Method	LLM	MetaQA			WebQSP	CWQ	GrailQA
		1-hop	2-hop	3-hop			
KB-BINDER	Codex	93.5	**99.9**	**99.5**	74.4	–	58.5
KG-GPT	GPT-3.5-Turbo	96.3	94.4	94.0	–	–	–
DoG	GPT-3.5-Turbo	98.6	96.6	90.9	88.6	58.2	77.8
DoG	Llama-3-8B	<u>99.8</u>	91.0	84.8	90.2	55.9	74.8
DoG	GPT-4	**100.0**	99.0	96.0	<u>91.0</u>	56.0	80.0
RelGraphQA	GPT-3.5-Turbo	98.3	97.1	92.4	87.7	57.3	76.5
RelGraphQA	Llama-3-8B	99.5	91.5	86.3	89.3	55.0	75.3
RelGraphQA	DeepSeek-V3.2	**100.0**	98.5	<u>98.0</u>	**91.4**	<u>58.8</u>	**81.4**
RelGraphQA	DeepSeek-R1-7B	97.9	93.3	87.9	89.0	57.0	76.8
RelGraphQA	Qwen-3-Plus	99.7	<u>99.2</u>	97.4	89.6	**59.6**	<u>81.0</u>
RelGraphQA	Qwen-3-8B	96.7	94.1	89.0	88.2	57.6	77.4

4.2 Overall Accuracy

RelGraphQA exhibits strong robustness across backends: even with GPT-3.5-Turbo or Llama-3-8B, it matches or exceeds prior systems on MetaQA and remains competitive on WebQSP, CWQ, and GrailQA. Stronger backends yield peak performance: DeepSeek-V3.2 achieves near-perfect MetaQA scores (100.0/98.5/98.0) and leads on WebQSP (91.4) and GrailQA (81.4), while Qwen-3-Plus attains the best CWQ score (59.6), validating our thresholded relation grounding.

4.3 Ablation Studies

We evaluate variants removing core components (Table 2): `w/o RelIdx` removes the FAISS-based relation-type index; `w/o` $\geq \tau$ `Filter` disables similarity-threshold filtering and always takes Top-1 matches; `w/o TypeGuard` omits subject/answer type inference; `w/o OpCtrl` disables operator detection and query templates; `w/o` $\hat{\mathcal{O}}$ `Guards` removes early operator-and-type guards, letting the LLM freely emit operators; `w/o TypeGuard & OpCtrl` drops both constraints jointly; and `SingleCall` merges all stages into one end-to-end prompt.

Table 2. Ablation results on execution accuracy (Hits@1) using DeepSeek-V3.2.

Variant	MetaQA-2	MetaQA-3	WebQSP	GrailQA
Full (ours)	98.5	98.0	91.4	81.4
`w/o RelIdx`	91.0	86.5	78.0	66.0
`w/o` $\geq \tau$ `Filter`	96.1	96.6	88.7	78.0
`w/o TypeGuard`	95.5	95.8	87.5	76.8
cre `w/o OpCtrl`	97.0	96.2	84.5	72.5
`w/o` $\hat{\mathcal{O}}$ `Guards`	95.6	95.0	83.4	71.2
`w/o TypeGuard & OpCtrl`	94.2	93.8	81.5	69.0
`SingleCall`	90.0	84.0	76.0	63.0

Ablation Analysis. Removing the index (`w/o RelIdx`) causes the largest drop due to off-schema relations. Threshold filtering proves crucial for pruning low-confidence matches, particularly on open-domain datasets. Ablating structural constraints (`w/o TypeGuard/OpCtrl`) consistently degrades performance, confirming the value of early structural guards. The `SingleCall` baseline performs worst, highlighting the necessity of our staged, constrained generation over naive end-to-end prompting.

4.4 Parameter Sensitivity

Few-Shot Per Stage. RelGraphQA uses stage-specific exemplars: (i) Entity Type & Operator Inference ($N_{\text{type/op}}$), (ii) Relation Extraction (N_{rel}), (iii) Query Generation (N_{query}). We vary one stage at a time with the others fixed to $\{6, 6, 6\}$ and sweep $N \in \{0, 3, 6, 9, 12\}$. We also probe a 2D grid for $(N_{\text{rel}}, N_{\text{query}})$.

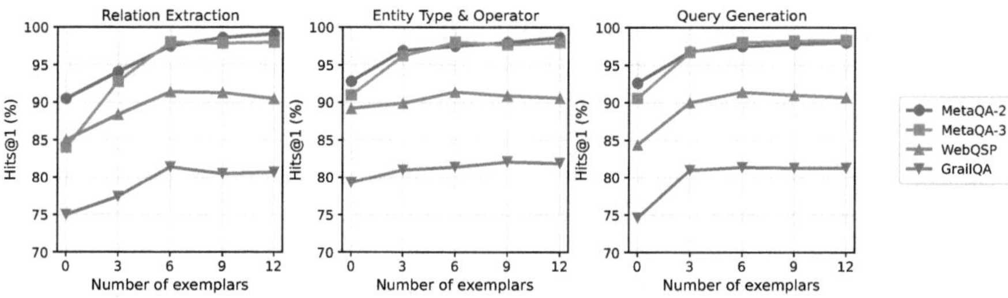

Fig. 3. Few-shot sensitivity across three stages of RelGraphQA.

Similarity Threshold τ *for Relation Filtering.* We adopt thresholded FAISS matching (IndexIVFFlat with normalized embeddings), keeping only schema relations whose cosine similarity to the LLM phrase is $\geq \tau$. We sweep $\tau \in \{0.60, 0.70, 0.80, 0.90\}$ while fixing $\{N_{\text{type/op}}, N_{\text{rel}}, N_{\text{query}}\} = \{6, 6, 6\}$. We report execution Hits@1 and executable rate on the full test set and an *operator-heavy* subset. The operator-heavy subset is constructed from **WebQSP**, **CWQ**,

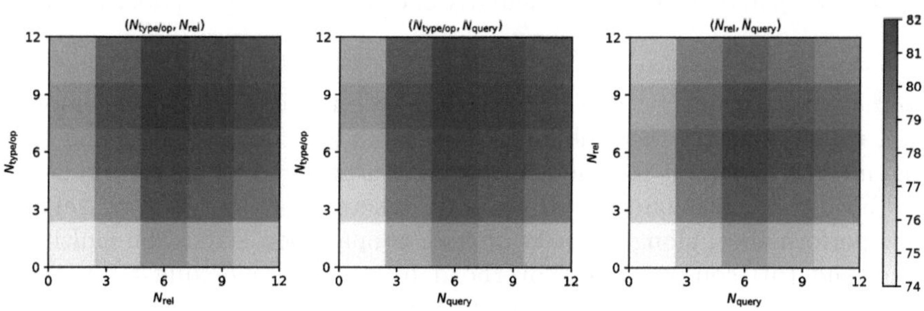

Fig. 4. Few-shot interaction heatmaps on GrailQA across stage pairs: (a) $N_{\text{type/op}} \times N_{\text{rel}}$, (b) $N_{\text{type/op}} \times N_{\text{query}}$, (c) $N_{\text{rel}} \times N_{\text{query}}$.

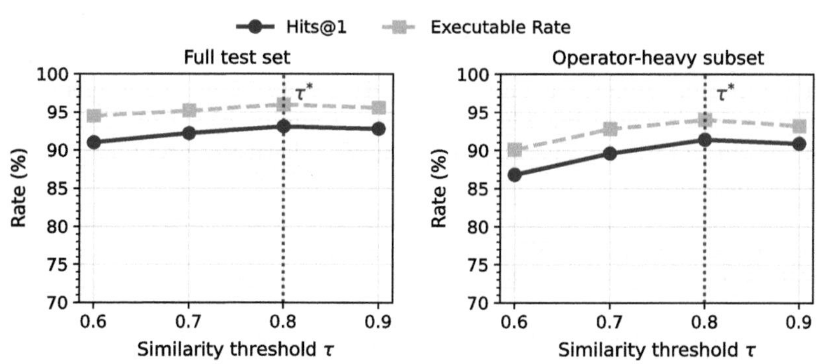

Fig. 5. Threshold sensitivity: Hits@1 and executable rate vs. τ. Left: full test set; Right: operator-heavy subset. The vertical line marks the default τ^* selected on the dev set.

and **GrailQA** by parsing gold SPARQL and selecting questions whose queries contain aggregation (`COUNT`/`GROUP BY`), ordering with truncation (`ORDER BY` ± `LIMIT`), or explicit comparisons/filters (inequalities, ranges, regex).

Parameter Analysis. As shown in Fig. 3, moderate few-shot guidance helps all three stages, with accuracy peaking around N=6; Fig. 4 further indicates balanced settings (e.g., $(6, 6)$) for stage pairs. For the threshold (Fig. 5), performance is stable in the mid range and degrades when τ is too low (noise admitted) or too high (recall loss). We therefore choose τ^*=0.80 on the dev set and use it by default; in practice, $\tau \in [0.75, 0.85]$ offers a good trade-off between accuracy, executability, and prompt length.

5 Conclusion

We presented **RelGraphQA**, a training-free framework that anchors LLM reasoning to KG schemas via thresholded FAISS matching and deterministic query synthesis. By enforcing upfront type and operator constraints, RelGraphQA mitigates hallucination and achieves strong execution accuracy on MetaQA, WebQSP, CWQ, and GrailQA, particularly excelling on complex, operator-heavy queries.

Limitations. We identify three primary limitations: (i) reliance on annotated entities, which bypasses the ambiguity and errors inherent in end-to-end entity linking; integrating an off-the-shelf entity linker is required for real-world deployment; (ii) dependence on schema quality, where missing types or relations degrade performance, alongside risks of error propagation across the multi-stage pipeline; and (iii) computational overhead from offline indexing requirements and the token costs associated with multi-turn LLM interactions.

Future Work. Future directions include integrating robust end-to-end entity linking and exploring joint re-ranking strategies for improved global consistency. We plan to optimize efficiency through prompt compression, model distillation, and auto-calibrated retrieval thresholds. Additionally, extending the framework to support temporal, numerical, and comparative reasoning—while ensuring generalization across diverse knowledge graphs—remains a key objective. Finally, releasing modular tools for encoder and indexer substitution will facilitate reproducible comparisons.

References

1. Douze, M., et al.: The faiss library. arXiv preprint (2024). https://arxiv.org/abs/2401.08281
2. Gu, Y., Kase, S., Vanni, M., Sadler, B., Liang, P., Yan, X., Su, Y.: Beyond i.i.d.: three levels of generalization for question answering on knowledge bases. arXiv preprint (2020). https://doi.org/10.48550/arXiv.2011.07743

3. Han, H., et al.: Retrieval-augmented generation with graphs (graphrag). arXiv preprint (2025). https://doi.org/10.48550/arXiv.2501.00309
4. Hu, W., et al.: Debate on graph: a flexible and reliable reasoning framework for large language models over knowledge graphs. In: Proceedings of the AAAI Conference on Artificial Intelligence, vol. 39. AAAI Press, Washington, DC (2025).https://doi.org/10.1609/aaai.v39i23.34658
5. Ji, Z., et al.: A survey of hallucinations in large language models. arXiv preprint (2023). https://doi.org/10.48550/arXiv.2302.06476
6. Jiang, J., Zhou, K., Zhao, W.X., Wen, J.: Unikgqa: unified retrieval and reasoning for solving multi-hop question answering over knowledge graph. In: The Eleventh International Conference on Learning Representations. OpenReview, Kigali, Rwanda (2023). https://openreview.net/forum?id=Z63RvyAZ2Vh
7. Kim, J., Kwon, Y., Jo, Y., Choi, E.: Kg-gpt: a general framework for reasoning on knowledge graphs using large language models. arXiv preprint (2023). https://doi.org/10.48550/arXiv.2310.11220
8. Lewis, P., et al.: Retrieval-augmented generation for knowledge-intensive nlp tasks. In: Advances in Neural Information Processing Systems 33, pp. 9459–9470. Curran Associates, Inc., Red Hook (2020). https://doi.org/10.48550/arXiv.2005.11401
9. Li, T., Ma, X., Zhuang, A., Gu, Y., Su, Y., Chen, W.: Few-shot in-context learning for knowledge base question answering. arXiv preprint (2023). https://doi.org/10.48550/arXiv.2305.01750
10. Long, X., Fan, Y., Feng, C., Li, G., Ding, X., Liu, Z., Jiang, W., Qi, J., Pang, L., Shen, H., Wang, J., Cheng, X.: Eperm: An evidence path enhanced reasoning model for knowledge graph question answering. In: Proceedings of the AAAI Conference on Artificial Intelligence. vol. 39, pp. 13227–13235. AAAI Press, Washington, DC (2025https://doi.org/10.1609/aaai.v39i12.33338
11. Luo, H., E, et al.: Digest the knowledge: Llm-empowered message passing for kgqa. In: Proceedings of the 63rd Annual Meeting of the Association for Computational Linguistics. Association for Computational Linguistics, Stroudsburg, PA (2025). https://doi.org/10.48550/arXiv.2411.13849
12. Miller, A., Fisch, A., Dodge, J., Karimi, A.H., Bordes, A., Weston, J.: Key-value memory networks for directly reading documents. arXiv preprint (2016). https://arxiv.org/abs/1606.03126
13. Nussbaum, Z., Morris, J.X., Duderstadt, B., Mulyar, A.: Nomic embed: Training a reproducible long context text embedder. arXiv preprint (2024). https://arxiv.org/abs/2402.01613
14. Saxena, A., Tripathi, A., Talukdar, P.: Improving multi-hop question answering over knowledge graphs using knowledge base embeddings. In: Proceedings of the 58th Annual Meeting of the Association for Computational Linguistics, pp. 4498–4507. Association for Computational Linguistics, Stroudsburg (2020). https://doi.org/10.18653/v1/2020.acl-main.412
15. Shi, J., Cao, S., Hou, L., Li, J., Zhang, H.: Transfernet: an effective and transparent framework for multi-hop question answering over relation graph. In: Proceedings of the 2021 Conference on Empirical Methods in Natural Language Processing, pp. 4149–4158. Association for Computational Linguistics, Online and Punta Cana, Dominican Republic (2021). https://doi.org/10.18653/v1/2021.emnlp-main.341
16. Sun, H., Bedrax-Weiss, T., Cohen, W.W.: Pullnet: Open domain question answering with iterative retrieval on knowledge bases and text. In: Proceedings of the 2019 Conference on Empirical Methods in Natural Language Processing and the 9th International Joint Conference on Natural Language Processing, pp. 2380–2390.

Association for Computational Linguistics, Hong Kong, China (2019). https://doi.org/10.18653/v1/D19-1242
17. Sun, H., Dhingra, B., Zaheer, M., Mazaitis, K., Salakhutdinov, R., Cohen, W.W.: Open domain question answering using early fusion of knowledge bases and text. In: Proceedings of the 2018 Conference on Empirical Methods in Natural Language Processing, pp. 4231–4242. Association for Computational Linguistics, Brussels, Belgium (2018). https://doi.org/10.18653/v1/D18-1455
18. Talmor, A., Berant, J.: The web as a knowledge-base for answering complex questions. In: Proceedings of the 2018 Conference of the North American Chapter of the Association for Computational Linguistics: Human Language Technologies, pp. 641–651. Association for Computational Linguistics, Stroudsburg (2018). https://doi.org/10.18653/v1/N18-1059
19. Tian, S., Liu, Z.H., Chen, Z., Zhao, W.X., Wen, J.R.: Measuring and mitigating factual errors in large language models. arXiv preprint (2023). https://doi.org/10.48550/arXiv.2311.02540
20. Xie, S.M., Wang, X., Wang, X., Li, S.: Faithful and controllable llms via external knowledge. arXiv preprint (2023). https://doi.org/10.48550/arXiv.2310.03058
21. Xu, D., et al.: Harnessing large language models for knowledge graph question answering via adaptive multi-aspect retrieval augmentation. arXiv preprint (2024). https://doi.org/10.48550/arXiv.2412.18537
22. Yih, W.T., Chang, M.W., He, X., Gao, J.: The value of semantic parse labeling for knowledge base question answering. In: Proceedings of the 54th Annual Meeting of the Association for Computational Linguistics, vol. 2, pp. 201–206. Association for Computational Linguistics, Berlin (2016). https://doi.org/10.18653/v1/P16-2033
23. Zhang, Y., Dai, H., Kozareva, Z., Smola, A.J., Song, L.: Variational reasoning for question answering with knowledge graph. In: Proceedings of the Thirty-Second AAAI Conference on Artificial Intelligence, pp. 6069–6076. AAAI Press, New Orleans (2018). https://doi.org/10.1609/aaai.v32i1.12057

What To Transfer: Refined Transfer Framework for Universal Cross-Domain Recommendation

Yuanyang Zhang[1], Bohan Li[1(✉)], Meng Ma[1], Changjie Wang[1], Wenlong Wu[1], and Min Tao[2]

[1] Nanjing University of Aeronautics and Astronautics, Nanjing, China
{zyy0620,bhli,mengmacs,changjiew829,wuwenlong}@nuaa.edu.cn
[2] Wuzhou University, Wuzhou, China
taomin@snnu.edu.cn

Abstract. Cross-domain recommendation (CDR) improves target-domain recommendation by leveraging behavioral signals from auxiliary domains, alleviating data sparsity and cold-start issues. Universal cross-domain recommendation (UniCDR) further learns a single model to unify multi-domain preferences and support both dual-domain and multi-domain scenarios. However, incorporating source-domain information can even hurt target-domain performance, a phenomenon known as negative transfer. This is because cross-domain signals are not uniformly beneficial: representation learning may capture shortcut cues that break under domain shift, and static fusion may further propagate such unreliable components into the target representation. To explicitly address *what to transfer*, we propose the **Refined Transfer Framework (RTF)**, an end-to-end architecture that decouples robust representation learning from selective cross-domain fusion. At the representation layer, RTF employs a temperature-scaled attention encoder over the source history and the global history, together with popularity down-weighting to suppress shortcut cues. At the fusion layer, we introduce a domain-routed decoder that aligns multi-source representations in a shared space and selectively fuses auxiliary signals with a global fallback. Finally, we optimize RTF with recommendation supervision and dual contrastive objectives to enhance intra-view robustness and cross-view consistency. Extensive experiments on Amazon benchmarks across four UniCDR scenarios demonstrate that RTF yields competitive and stable improvements over strong baselines.

Keywords: Universal Cross-Domain Recommendation · Negative Transfer · Attention Debiasing · Domain Routing · Contrastive Learning

1 Introduction

While recommendation systems alleviate information overload, they are often limited by data sparsity and the cold-start problem [26]. Cross-Domain Recom-

J. Niu et al. (Eds.): KSEM 2026, LNAI 16631, pp. 549–560, 2027.
https://doi.org/10.1007/978-981-92-2759-4_40

mendation (CDR) has become a key solution by transferring knowledge from the source domain to the target domain. To adapt to diverse scenarios, Universal Cross-Domain Recommendation (UniCDR) [3,30] has emerged, aiming to unify domain-specific and shared preferences for different tasks and to apply them to both dual-domain and multi-domain scenarios. Cao et al. [3] developed a pioneering framework that aggregates domain-specific features to achieve unified modeling. Inspired by this line, Hao et al. [8] proposed a fine-tuning-based transfer strategy, reconstructing preferences through universal embeddings, which further improved cross-domain performance. Ju et al. [13] introduced a masking mechanism to extract user preferences from item representations, guiding the model to predict interests indirectly in cases of incomplete information. Zhang et al. [31] proposed the PPA method, which incorporates a learnable prototype matching mechanism to quantify the semantic distance between user preferences and item features, helping separate user interests from domain-specific factors.

Despite the promising results achieved, existing methods still face two major challenges in flexibility and transfer quality. First, at the architectural level, many models rely on pretraining or static aggregation strategies [3,19], which can limit adaptive transfer in complex multi-domain environments. Developing a flexible, end-to-end adaptive architecture with clearer control over transferable and domain-specific signals therefore remains an open challenge [16,31]. More importantly, incorporating source-domain information may even degrade target performance, i.e., negative transfer. This is because cross-domain signals are not uniformly beneficial: representation learning may capture shortcut correlations, while static or holistic fusion may further propagate unreliable components into the target representation. Therefore, we explicitly study *what to transfer* in universal cross-domain recommendation (Fig. 1).

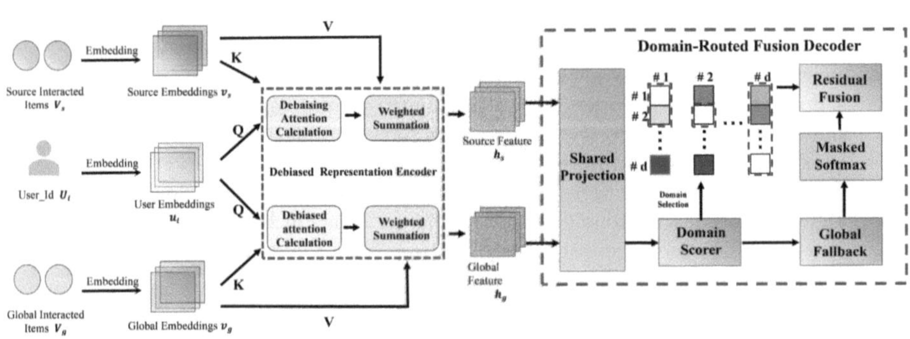

Fig. 1. Overview of the proposed RTF model.

To address these challenges, we propose the **Refined Transfer Framework (RTF)**. RTF follows an end-to-end encoder-decoder architecture [10,12,25] to decouple representation learning from cross-domain fusion. First, at the representation layer, we adopt a temperature-scaled attention encoder to learn user representations from the source history and the global history, and incorporate a built-in popularity down-weighting mechanism [14] to suppress shortcut cues and improve robustness. Second, at the fusion layer, we introduce a domain-routed module that projects multi-source representations into a shared metric space via a shared projection and performs selective fusion to refine what information is transferred [7]; in multi-domain settings, we further incorporate domain-level routing with masked normalization to emphasize more reliable sources and mitigate negative transfer. Finally, we introduce dual contrastive learning [18,24,28] as an optimization constraint by jointly enforcing cross-view consistency and intra-view robustness.

In summary, our contributions are as follows:

- We revisit negative transfer in universal cross-domain recommendation from a *what-to-transfer* perspective, and highlight two recurring issues associated with performance degradation: shortcut-induced spurious features and indiscriminate cross-domain fusion.
- We propose RTF, an end-to-end framework that integrates debiased encoding with a domain-routed fusion module, which aligns multi-source representations in a shared metric space and performs selective fusion to refine transferred information.
- Extensive experiments on Amazon benchmarks across four UniCDR scenarios show that RTF consistently delivers competitive and stable improvements over strong baselines.

2 Related Work

2.1 Cross-Domain Recommendation (CDR)

Cross-domain recommendation (CDR) improves target-domain recommendation by transferring knowledge from auxiliary domains. Existing studies are commonly categorized by whether users/items overlap across domains: non-overlapping settings typically rely on latent bridges or side information, while partially overlapping settings exploit shared users/items as anchors for alignment and transfer [11]. Early CDR methods were mainly based on matrix factorization with shared latent factors [15]. With deep learning, representative paradigms include shared-layer transfer [11], embedding mapping with explicit transformations [23], and adversarial alignment for domain-invariant representations [6,29]. More recently, graph-based models and contrastive sequential learning have been used to leverage higher-order signals and improve preference learning under implicit feedback [2,9]. Despite this progress, many methods still rely on specific assumptions or fixed transfer patterns, limiting their generality in universal settings.

2.2 Mitigating Negative Transfer

Negative transfer remains a key challenge in CDR, since not all auxiliary-domain signals are beneficial and indiscriminate transfer may hurt target performance.

A common strategy is to separate shared and domain-specific factors via disentanglement or structured regularization to improve transferability [4,18,21]. Another widely used paradigm is adversarial learning with a domain discriminator and gradient reversal to encourage domain-invariant features [6,22]. Beyond representation learning, selective transfer mechanisms (e.g., attention-based weighting) control how much information is borrowed from each source [17], while masking, contrastive objectives, and intention-aware graph modeling suppress spurious correlations and enhance robustness [2,34,35]. Recent universal multi-domain methods emphasize conservative global modeling with adaptive routing of auxiliary signals [3,31,32], highlighting the importance of controlling *what to transfer* and how to fuse heterogeneous sources.

3 Methodology

Let $\mathcal{U}$ and $\mathcal{V}$ denote the user and universal item sets, respectively. Universal cross-domain recommendation considers multiple domains $\mathcal{D}$ with domain-labeled interactions. We denote the target domain as $t \in \mathcal{D}$ and treat all others as auxiliary domains $\mathcal{D} \setminus \{t\}$. For each user $u \in \mathcal{U}$, we construct a **source-view** history $V_s^u = [v_1, \ldots, v_{|V_s^u|}]$ from a designated source domain and a **global-view** history $V_g^u = [v'_1, \ldots, v'_{|V_g^u|}]$ from observed cross-domain training interactions. In multi-domain settings, V_g^u is further split into per-domain subsequences $\{V_d^u\}$ for routing. Each item $v \in \mathcal{V}$ has an embedding $\mathbf{e}_v \in \mathbb{R}^p$.

3.1 Debiased Representation Encoder

We adopt an end-to-end encoder–decoder architecture. At the representation layer, we employ an attention-based encoder for V_s^u and V_g^u, and incorporate a popularity down-weighting mechanism to reduce shortcut signals.

Specifically, the sequential encoder produces contextual features, and we compute the raw attention logit $e_{u,i}$ between user u and item v_i via additive attention:

$$e_{u,i} = \mathbf{v}^\top \tanh(\mathbf{W}_Q \mathbf{e}_u + \mathbf{W}_K \mathbf{e}_i + \mathbf{b}). \tag{1}$$

To explicitly mitigate popularity bias, we inject a frequency-based penalty into the attention mechanism. We focus on frequency bias as a primary and measurable shortcut cue in implicit-feedback recommendation; other biases are orthogonal and left for future work. We employ a shared debiasing strength τ_{pop} across all domains, where $\text{freq}(v_i)$ is estimated from the corresponding training interactions, to capture a universal yet stable debiasing pattern. The penalty weight w_i is defined as:

$$w_i = (\text{freq}(v_i))^{-\tau_{pop}}. \tag{2}$$

We then modulate the logits using the penalty weight and a domain-specific temperature T_d. To ensure stability and avoid extreme scaling, we bound T_d to $[T_{\min}, T_{\max}]$ via a sigmoid parametrization:

$$T_d = T_{\min} + \sigma(\phi_d) \cdot (T_{\max} - T_{\min}), \tag{3}$$

where ϕ_d is a learnable parameter for domain d. The calibrated logits are computed as:

$$\tilde{e}_{u,i} = \frac{e_{u,i} \cdot w_i}{T_d}. \tag{4}$$

Finally, the normalized attention weights are obtained via softmax:

$$\alpha_{u,i} = \frac{\exp(\tilde{e}_{u,i})}{\sum_j \exp(\tilde{e}_{u,j})}. \tag{5}$$

The source-view and global-view representations are then obtained by weighted pooling based on these debiased attention weights.

3.2 Domain-Routed Fusion Decoder

At the fusion layer, we use a domain-routed decoder that performs *domain-level routing*: each auxiliary domain is summarized into a user-specific representation and scored for selective contribution, with a global fallback to avoid indiscriminate fusion.

Shared Projection. We map the global representation into a shared metric space:

$$\mathbf{z}_g^u = \mathrm{Norm}(\mathbf{P}\mathbf{h}_g^u), \tag{6}$$

where $\mathbf{P} \in \mathbb{R}^{p \times p}$ is shared and $\mathrm{Norm}(\cdot)$ denotes ℓ_2 normalization. For each auxiliary domain $d \in \mathcal{D} \setminus \{t\}$, we encode its per-domain subsequence V_d^u with the same sequential encoder to obtain $\mathbf{h}_d^u$, and project it as

$$\mathbf{z}_d^u = \mathrm{Norm}(\mathbf{P}\mathbf{h}_d^u). \tag{7}$$

The designated source view is treated as one auxiliary domain in this routing set.

Residual Candidates. We form a domain residual relative to the global base:

$$\mathbf{r}_d^u = \mathrm{LN}(\mathbf{z}_d^u - \mathbf{z}_g^u), \tag{8}$$

where $\mathrm{LN}(\cdot)$ is LayerNorm for stabilizing the scale of residual candidates before routing.

Domain-Level Scoring and Selection. Let $\mathcal{A}_u = \{d \in \mathcal{D} \setminus \{t\} \mid |V_d^u| > 0\}$ be the set of *available* auxiliary domains for user u. We compute a domain-level routing score for each $d \in \mathcal{A}_u$:

$$s_{u,d} = (\mathbf{z}_g^u)^\top \mathrm{diag}(\boldsymbol{\theta}_d)\, \mathbf{z}_d^u + b_d, \tag{9}$$

where $\boldsymbol{\theta}_d \in \mathbb{R}^p$ and b_d are domain-specific parameters. We then apply Top-K masking over $\mathcal{A}_u$ to keep routing focused and avoid overly diffuse fusion, forming the candidate set:

$$K_u = \max\big(1, \min(2, |\mathcal{A}_u|)\big), \quad \mathcal{S}_u = \text{Top-}K_u(\{s_{u,d}\}_{d \in \mathcal{A}_u}). \tag{10}$$

Masked Soft Routing with Global Fallback. We always keep the global base as a fallback candidate with a learnable logit $s_{u,g} = b_g$, and compute masked routing weights with a learnable temperature T_r:

$$\alpha_{u,k} = \frac{\exp(s_{u,k}/T_r)}{\exp(s_{u,g}/T_r) + \sum_{d \in \mathcal{S}_u} \exp(s_{u,d}/T_r)}, \quad k \in \{g\} \cup \mathcal{S}_u, \tag{11}$$

where $T_r \in [T_r^{\min}, T_r^{\max}]$ is learned via a bounded parametrization. Finally, we inject selected residuals into the conservative global base:

$$\mathbf{z}_u = \mathbf{z}_g^u + \sum_{d \in \mathcal{S}_u} \alpha_{u,d}\, \mathbf{r}_d^u. \tag{12}$$

In the dual-domain case, $|\mathcal{A}_u| = 1$ and $\{g\} \cup \mathcal{S}_u = \{g, s\}$, so the fallback weight $\alpha_{u,g}$ naturally enables "transfer or not transfer" without a separate hand-crafted gate.

3.3 Optimization Objective

We optimize RTF with a recommendation loss and two contrastive regularizers, where the latter improve stability and comparability.

Recommendation Loss. For recommendation, we use the binary cross-entropy loss:

$$\mathcal{L}_{rec} = -\sum_{(u,v) \in \mathcal{Y}} \left[y_{uv} \log \hat{y}_{uv} + (1 - y_{uv}) \log(1 - \hat{y}_{uv}) \right], \tag{13}$$

where $\mathcal{Y}$ denotes observed training pairs (with negative sampling if needed).

Intra-View Robustness Contrast. To suppress shortcut-driven fluctuations, we generate two order-preserving augmentations of the source view and maximize their agreement via InfoNCE against in-batch negatives.

$$\mathcal{L}_{intra} = -\sum_{u \in \mathcal{B}} \log \frac{\exp(\mathrm{sim}(\mathbf{z}_{s,1}^u, \mathbf{z}_{s,2}^u)/\tau_c)}{\sum_{u' \in \mathcal{B}} \exp(\mathrm{sim}(\mathbf{z}_{s,1}^u, \mathbf{z}_{s,2}^{u'})/\tau_c)}, \tag{14}$$

where $\mathcal{B}$ is a mini-batch, $\mathrm{sim}(\cdot,\cdot)$ denotes cosine similarity, and τ_c is a temperature.

Cross-View Alignment Contrast. To keep the two views comparable in the shared metric space, we align $\mathbf{z}_s^u$ and $\mathbf{z}_g^u$ using same-user positives and in-batch negatives:

$$\mathcal{L}_{align} = -\sum_{u \in \mathcal{B}} \log \frac{\exp(\mathrm{sim}(\mathbf{z}_s^u, \mathbf{z}_g^u)/\tau_a)}{\sum_{u' \in \mathcal{B}} \exp(\mathrm{sim}(\mathbf{z}_s^u, \mathbf{z}_g^{u'})/\tau_a)}, \tag{15}$$

where τ_a is a temperature. This objective does not require constructing cross-domain paired batches and remains compatible with domain-wise sampling.

Overall Objective. Finally, we optimize the overall loss:

$$\mathcal{L} = \mathcal{L}_{rec} + \lambda_1 \mathcal{L}_{intra} + \lambda_2 \mathcal{L}_{align}, \tag{16}$$

where λ_1 and λ_2 control the strength of robustness and alignment, respectively.

4 Experiments

We organize experiments around three research questions: **RQ1:** Does RTF consistently improve recommendation accuracy over strong baselines across four UniCDR scenarios? **RQ2:** How do the debiased encoder and the domain-routed fusion decoder contribute to performance? **RQ3:** How sensitive is RTF to key hyperparameters, including the auxiliary-loss weights $\lambda_{1,2}$ and the debiasing strength τ_{pop}?

4.1 Experimental Settings

Datasets and Evaluation Metrics. We conduct experiments on four UniCDR scenarios: (1) Dual-User-Intra (Sport & Cloth, Elec & Phone), preprocessed following DisenCDR [4]; (2) Dual-User-Inter (Sport & Cloth, Game & Video), preprocessed following CDRIB [5]; (3) Multi-Item-Intra (M1–M5), preprocessed following M^{3}Rec [1]; and (4) Multi-User-Intra (D1–D3), constructed by UniCDR [3]. We use Hit Ratio (HR) and Normalized Discounted Cumulative Gain (NDCG) [3] as evaluation metrics, and report HR@10 and NDCG@10 by ranking 1000 items per test case.
Validation Protocol and Hyperparameter Tuning. For Scenario 2–4, we tune hyperparameters on the official validation sets. For Scenario 1, we construct a validation split by holding out each usern's last target-domain interaction from training; all hyperparameters are selected on this split, and the test set is used only for final reporting.
Baselines and Implementation Details. We compare RTF with three baseline categories: (1) single-domain methods, NeuMF [10], NGCF [27], and LightGCN [9]; (2) cross-domain methods, CoNet [11], Bi-TGCF [20], DisenCDR [4], EMCDR [23], TMCDR [33], M^{3}Rec [1], and CDRIB [5]; and (3) universal CDR methods, UniCDR [3] and PPA [31]. All methods are evaluated under the same data splits and pipeline. RTF is implemented in PyTorch with embedding dimension $p = 128$, batch size $B = 1024$, and Adam optimizer with learning rate 1e−3. The newly introduced hyperparameters of RTF (e.g., popularity down-weighting strength and loss weights $\lambda_{1,2}$) are tuned on the validation split above.

4.2 Overall Performance (RQ1)

As shown in Tables 1, 2, 3 and Table 4, RTF consistently improves over strong baselines across the four UniCDR scenarios. The gains are observed in both dual-domain tasks and multi-domain tasks, suggesting that the proposed debiased encoding and domain-routed fusion work robustly under heterogeneous transfer settings.

Table 1. Performance comparison (%) on **dual-intra-domain** recommendation (Scenario 1). Bold denotes the best results.

Datasets	Metric@10	Single-Domain Methods				Cross-Domain Methods					Universal Methods		
		BPRMF	NeuMF	NGCF	LightGCN	CoNet	DDTCDR	PPGN	Bi-TGCF	DisenCDR	UniCDR	PPA	**RTF (Ours)**
Sport	HR	10.43	10.74	13.13	13.19	12.09	11.86	15.10	14.83	17.55	18.37	20.72	**22.35**
	NDCG	5.41	5.46	6.87	6.94	6.41	6.37	8.03	7.95	9.46	10.98	14.25	**15.88**
Cloth	HR	11.53	11.18	13.22	13.58	12.40	12.54	14.23	14.68	16.31	17.85	19.92	**21.51**
	NDCG	6.25	6.02	6.97	7.29	6.62	7.13	7.68	7.93	9.03	11.20	13.89	**15.35**
Elec	HR	15.71	16.17	18.55	19.17	17.22	18.47	21.68	22.14	24.57	22.92	25.39	**26.92**
	NDCG	9.19	9.24	10.87	10.28	9.86	11.08	11.63	12.20	14.51	13.83	15.37	**16.84**
Phone	HR	16.32	15.84	22.79	23.25	17.66	17.23	24.54	25.71	28.76	24.72	31.30	**32.95**
	NDCG	8.53	8.02	12.38	12.72	9.30	8.58	13.34	13.93	16.13	13.77	17.86	**19.32**

Table 2. Performance comparison (%) on **dual-inter-domain** recommendation (Scenario 2). Bold denotes the best results.

Datasets	Metric@10	Single-Domain Methods			Cross-Domain Methods					Universal Methods		
		CML	BPRMF	NGCF	EMCDR	SSCDR	TMCDR	SA-VAE	CDRIB	UniCDR	PPA	**RTF (Ours)**
Sport	HR	5.82	5.75	7.22	7.44	7.27	7.18	7.51	12.04	11.20	11.85	**13.61**
	NDCG	3.29	3.16	3.63	3.71	3.75	3.84	3.72	6.22	7.04	7.55	**8.95**
Cloth	HR	6.97	6.75	7.07	7.29	6.12	8.11	7.21	12.19	12.48	12.92	**14.33**
	NDCG	3.92	3.26	3.48	4.48	3.06	5.05	4.59	6.81	7.52	8.15	**8.89**
Game	HR	2.82	3.77	5.14	4.63	3.48	5.36	5.84	8.51	8.78	11.35	**12.82**
	NDCG	1.44	1.89	2.73	2.24	1.59	2.58	2.78	4.58	4.63	6.06	**7.21**
Video	HR	3.07	4.46	7.41	7.94	5.51	8.85	7.46	13.17	10.74	12.45	**14.55**
	NDCG	1.30	2.36	3.87	4.29	2.61	4.41	3.71	6.49	5.89	6.50	**7.97**

Table 3. Performance comparison (%) on **item-overlapped multi-intra-domain** recommendation (Scenario 3). Bold denotes the best results.

Datasets	Metric@10	Single-Domain Methods				Cross-Domain Methods						Universal Methods		
		NeuMF	LightGCN	RW	EASER	Cross-Stitch	MMoE	Bi-TGCF	STAR	FOREC	M^3Rec	UniCDR	PPA	**RTF (Ours)**
M1	HR	62.73	64.73	64.66	70.80	64.46	65.73	66.86	62.93	65.06	73.13	69.08	71.50	**73.85**
	NDCG	46.31	48.30	48.05	54.95	49.15	48.98	50.46	46.57	52.05	55.83	59.57	60.10	**61.91**
M2	HR	55.60	52.13	50.20	57.40	54.06	56.26	53.46	54.89	58.42	60.86	58.01	59.20	**61.33**
	NDCG	34.84	32.70	31.10	37.92	36.65	38.71	33.43	35.25	40.03	40.04	47.52	48.15	**49.15**
M3	HR	60.40	56.26	57.53	63.60	59.46	61.53	58.73	60.80	64.13	66.53	64.60	65.10	**66.98**
	NDCG	36.57	34.22	34.89	40.13	39.13	41.30	35.77	37.09	41.88	43.35	53.24	53.80	**54.20**
M4	HR	40.33	41.14	39.20	45.13	38.93	38.60	42.26	40.20	41.60	48.46	47.52	47.95	**48.35**
	NDCG	29.83	31.03	30.08	36.63	29.16	30.16	32.76	29.84	33.52	37.98	42.54	42.10	**42.50**
M5	HR	12.26	17.13	17.73	19.13	17.06	16.66	17.86	16.60	17.46	22.66	19.78	21.50	**23.05**
	NDCG	9.01	13.16	14.07	16.93	12.51	11.79	14.42	12.48	13.19	18.63	17.04	17.80	**18.92**

Table 4. Performance comparison (%) on **user-overlapped multi-intra-domain** recommendation (Scenario 4). Bold denotes the best results.

Datasets	Metric@10	Single-Domain Methods				Cross-Domain Methods					Universal Methods		
		BPRMF	NeuMF	EASER	LightGCN	MMoE	CoNet	Bi-TGCF	GA-MTCDR	HeroGraph	UniCDR	PPA	**RTF (Ours)**
D1	HR	19.48	20.57	9.15	25.52	21.22	20.60	26.98	26.13	29.73	32.60	36.07	**36.55**
	NDCG	7.66	7.17	4.04	10.60	8.82	8.46	10.64	10.02	11.74	13.56	15.26	**15.68**
D2	HR	50.45	52.92	50.07	56.18	56.22	53.53	60.48	59.59	61.49	64.37	63.85	**64.12**
	NDCG	33.50	35.73	28.53	37.09	38.63	37.66	47.19	47.67	49.57	50.48	50.15	**50.60**
D3	HR	64.87	64.53	50.40	67.13	65.71	65.90	72.88	73.32	71.77	73.89	74.08	**74.63**
	NDCG	47.69	48.44	29.02	40.49	47.08	47.51	54.15	57.00	56.81	59.15	59.61	**60.11**

4.3 Ablation Study (RQ2)

To evaluate the contribution of the encoder and the decoder, we conduct ablation studies on a representative dual-domain setting and a representative multi-domain setting. Specifically, we report results on **Scenario 2** (Dual-User-Inter) and **Scenario 4** (Multi-User-Intra).

We compare the full RTF model with two key variants:

- **RTF w/o Decoder (*w/o decoder*)**: The domain-routed fusion decoder is removed, and the model uses a static fusion scheme for prediction.
- **RTF w/o Encoder (*w/o encoder*)**: The debiased encoding mechanism is removed, and the model uses a standard attention-based encoder without popularity down-weighting (Table 5).

Table 5. Ablation study of key components in **RTF** on Scenario 2 and Scenario 4.

Scenario	Datasets	Metrics@10	w/o decoder	w/o encoder	RTF (Full)
Scenario 2 (Dual-User-Inter)	Sport	HR	12.80	11.20	**13.61**
		NDCG	8.10	6.50	**8.95**
	Cloth	HR	13.50	11.80	**14.33**
		NDCG	8.00	6.80	**8.89**
	Game	HR	11.90	9.50	**12.82**
		NDCG	6.50	4.50	**7.21**
	Video	HR	13.50	11.50	**14.55**
		NDCG	7.10	5.80	**7.97**
Scenario 4 (Multi-User-Intra)	D1	HR	32.10	34.80	**36.55**
		NDCG	12.50	14.20	**15.68**
	D2	HR	59.50	62.80	**64.12**
		NDCG	46.20	49.10	**50.60**
	D3	HR	70.80	73.20	**74.63**
		NDCG	56.50	58.80	**60.11**

Overall, removing either component degrades performance, indicating that robust preference extraction (encoder) and selective auxiliary injection with fallback (decoder) are both necessary for mitigating negative transfer.

4.4 Hyperparameter Sensitivity (RQ3)

We analyze the sensitivity of RTF to loss weights (λ_1, λ_2) and debiasing strength (τ_{pop}) on the Sport $\rightarrow$ Cloth task.

Loss Weights (λ_1, λ_2). Figure 2(a) shows a stable plateau at $\lambda_1 \in [0.1, 0.2]$ and $\lambda_2 \in [0.05, 0.1]$, while larger weights ($\geq 0.4$) hurt performance by over-regularizing the model.

Debiasing Strength (τ_{pop}). Figure 2(b) shows asymmetric sensitivity: performance peaks at $\tau_{pop} = 0.9$ (stable in $[0.7, 1.0]$), whereas over-correction ($\tau_{pop} > 1.2$) drops below the baseline.

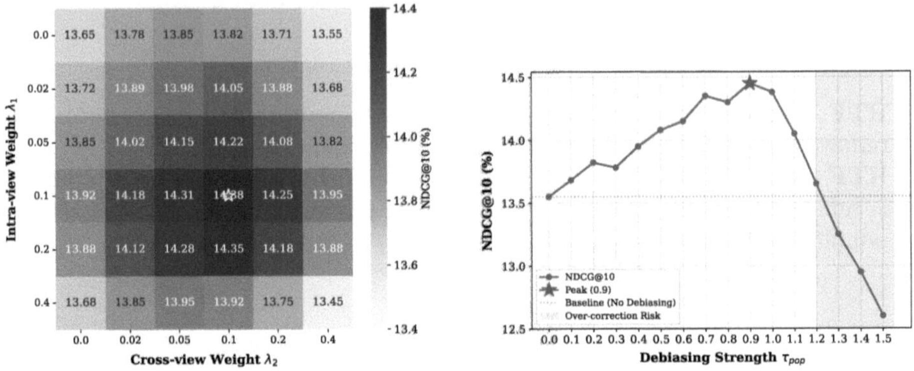

(a) Joint sensitivity of λ_1 and λ_2. (b) Impact of debiasing strength τ_{pop}.

Fig. 2. Hyperparameter sensitivity analysis on the Sport → Cloth task. (a) NDCG@10 w.r.t. contrastive weights λ_1 and λ_2; (b) NDCG@10 w.r.t. debiasing strength τ_{pop}.

5 Conclusion

We propose the **Refined Transfer Framework (RTF)** for Universal Cross-Domain Recommendation to mitigate negative transfer. RTF combines a debiased representation encoder with a domain-routed fusion decoder that aligns multi-source representations in a shared metric space and selectively injects auxiliary residuals into a conservative global base via masked soft routing. We further integrate a training objective with recommendation supervision, cross-view alignment, and intra-view contrastive robustness, which remains compatible with domain-wise sampling without requiring cross-domain paired batches. Overall, RTF provides an interpretable and practical approach for selective knowledge transfer in universal cross-domain recommendation.

References

1. Cao, J., Cong, X., Liu, T., Wang, B.: Item similarity mining for multi-market recommendation. In: Proceedings of the 45th International ACM SIGIR Conference on Research and Development in Information Retrieval, pp. 2249–2254. (2022)
2. Cao, J., Cong, X., Sheng, J., Liu, T., Wang, B.: Contrastive cross-domain sequential recommendation. In: Proceedings of the 31st ACM International Conference on Information & Knowledge Management, pp. 138–147 (2022)
3. Cao, J., Li, S., Yu, B., Guo, X., Liu, T., Wang, B.: Towards universal cross-domain recommendation. In: Proceedings of the Sixteenth ACM International Conference on Web Search and Data Mining, pp. 78–86 (2023)

4. Cao, J., Lin, X., Cong, X., Ya, J., Liu, T., Wang, B.: Disencdr: Learning disentangled representations for cross-domain recommendation. In: Proceedings of the 45th International ACM SIGIR Conference on Research and Development in Information Retrieval, pp. 267–277. (2022)
5. Cao, J., Sheng, J., Cong, X., Liu, T., Wang, B.: Cross-domain recommendation to cold-start users via variational information bottleneck. In: 2022 IEEE 38th International Conference on data engineering (ICDE), pp. 2209–2223. IEEE (2022)
6. Ganin, Y., et al.: Domain-adversarial training of neural networks. J. Mach. Learn. Res. **17**(59), 1–35 (2016)
7. Gou, J., Yu, B., Maybank, S.J., Tao, D.: Knowledge distillation: a survey. Int. J. Comput. Vision **129**(6), 1789–1819 (2021)
8. Hao, B., Yang, C., Guo, L., Yu, J., Yin, H.: Motif-based prompt learning for universal cross-domain recommendation. In: Proceedings of the 17th ACM International Conference on Web Search and Data Mining, pp. 257–265 (2024)
9. He, X., Deng, K., Wang, X., Li, Y., Zhang, Y., Wang, M.: Lightgcn: simplifying and powering graph convolution network for recommendation. In: Proceedings of the 43rd International ACM SIGIR Conference on Research and Development in Information Retrieval, pp. 639–648 (2020)
10. He, X., Liao, L., Zhang, H., Nie, L., Hu, X., Chua, T.S.: Proceedings of the 26th international conference on world wide web, pp. 173–182. (2017). Neural collaborative filtering
11. Hu, G., Zhang, Y., Yang, Q.: Conet: Collaborative cross networks for cross-domain recommendation. In: Proceedings of the 27th ACM International Conference on Information and Knowledge Management, pp. 667–676. (2018)
12. Huang, C., Gan, Z., Ye, F., Wang, P., Zhang, M.: Kncr: Knowledge-aware neural collaborative ranking for recommender systems. In: 2020 IEEE Intl Conf on Dependable, Autonomic and Secure Computing, Intl Conf on Pervasive Intelligence and Computing, Intl Conf on Cloud and Big Data Computing, Intl Conf on Cyber Science and Technology Congress (DASC/PiCom/CBDCom/CyberSciTech), pp. 339–344. IEEE (2020)
13. Ju, H., Kang, S., Lee, D., Hwang, J., Jang, S., Yu, H.: Multi-domain recommendation to attract users via domain preference modeling. In: Proceedings of the AAAI Conference on Artificial Intelligence, vol. 38, pp. 8582–8590 (2024)
14. Karboua, S., Harrag, F., Meziane, F., Boutadjine, A.: Mitigation of popularity bias in recommendation systems. In: Tunisian-Algerian Joint Conference on Applied Computing (2022)
15. Klami, A., Bouchard, G., Tripathi, A.: Group-sparse embeddings in collective matrix factorization (2013). arXiv:1312.5921 arXiv preprint
16. Kong, M., Hou, M., Zhao, S., Liu, F., Su, R., Chen, Y.: Dadin: domain adversarial deep interest network for cross domain recommender systems. Expert Syst. Appl. **243**, 122880 (2024)
17. Li, C., Xie, Y., Yu, C., Hu, B., Li, Z., Shu, G., Qie, X., Niu, D.: One for all, all for one: Learning and transferring user embeddings for cross-domain recommendation. In: Proceedings of the Sixteenth ACM International Conference on Web Search and Data Mining, pp. 366–374 (2023)
18. Li, H., Wang, Y., Xiao, Z., Yang, J., Zhou, C., Zhang, M., Ju, W.: Disco: graph-based disentangled contrastive learning for cold-start cross-domain recommendation. In: Proceedings of the AAAI Conference on Artificial Intelligence, vol. 39, pp. 12049–12057 (2025)

19. Lin, Z., Ding, H., Hoang, N.T., Kveton, B., Deoras, A., Wang, H.: Pre-trained recommender systems: a causal debiasing perspective. In: Proceedings of the 17th ACM International Conference on Web Search and Data Mining, pp. 424–433 (2024)
20. Liu, M., Li, J., Li, G., Pan, P.: Cross domain recommendation via bi-directional transfer graph collaborative filtering networks. In: Proceedings of the 29th ACM International Conference on Information & Knowledge Management, pp. 885–894 (2020)
21. Liu, X., Li, B., Chen, Y., Li, X., Xu, S., Yin, H.: Disentangled representations for cross-domain recommendation via heterogeneous graph contrastive learning. In: International Conference on Database Systems for Advanced Applications, pp. 35–50. Springer (2024)
22. Liu, Y., Wang, S., Li, X., Sun, F.: A meta-adversarial framework for cross-domain cold-start recommendation. Data Sci. Eng. **9**(2), 238–249 (2024)
23. Man, T., Shen, H., Jin, X., Cheng, X.: Cross-domain recommendation: an embedding and mapping approach. In: Ijcai 17, pp. 2464–2470 (2017)
24. Oord, A.v.d., Li, Y., Vinyals, O.: Representation learning with contrastive predictive coding. arXiv preprint arXiv:1807.03748 (2018)
25. Sedhain, S., Menon, A.K., Sanner, S., Xie, L.: Autorec: Autoencoders meet collaborative filtering. In: Proceedings of the 24th International Conference on World Wide Web, pp. 111–112 (2015)
26. Su, X., Khoshgoftaar, T.M.: A survey of collaborative filtering techniques. Adv. Artif. Intell. **2009**(1), 421425 (2009)
27. Wang, X., He, X., Wang, M., Feng, F., Chua, T.S.: Neural graph collaborative filtering. In: Proceedings of the 42nd international ACM SIGIR conference on Research and development in Information Retrieval, pp. 165–174 (2019)
28. Xie, R., Liu, Q., Wang, L., Liu, S., Zhang, B., Lin, L.: Contrastive cross-domain recommendation in matching. In: Proceedings of the 28th ACM SIGKDD Conference on Knowledge Discovery and Data Mining, pp. 4226–4236 (2022)
29. Zang, T., Zhu, Y., Zhang, R., Zhu, J., Tang, F.: Explicitly modeling relationships between domain-specific and domain-invariant interests for cross-domain recommendation. World Wide Web **27**(6), 73 (2024)
30. Zhang, H., et al.: A comprehensive survey on cross-domain recommendation: Taxonomy, progress, and prospects. ArXiv abs/2503.14110 (2025). https://api.semanticscholar.org/CorpusID:277104432
31. Zhang, Y., et al.: Preference prototype-aware learning for universal cross-domain recommendation. In: Proceedings of the 33rd ACM International Conference on Information and Knowledge Management, pp. 3290–3299 (2024)
32. Zhang, Y., et al.: Ppa++: preference prototype-aware learning with large language model for universal cross-domain recommendation. Data Science and Engineering, pp. 1–17 (2026)
33. Zhu, Y., Ge, K., Zhuang, F., Xie, R., Xi, D., Zhang, X., Lin, L., He, Q.: Transfer-meta framework for cross-domain recommendation to cold-start users. In: Proceedings of the 44th International ACM SIGIR Conference on Research and Development in Information Retrieval, pp. 1813–1817 (2021)
34. Zhuo, J., Li, B., Yu, S., Xu, S., Li, Y., Zhao, X., Yuan, G.: Tidgrec: dual-graph modeling with target-intention filtering for session-based recommendation. World Wide Web **28**(6), 61 (2025)
35. Zhuo, J., et al.: Self-supervised dual graph and intention association for session-based recommendation. In: International Conference on Database Systems for Advanced Applications, pp. 151–167. Springer (2025)

EATER: Entropy-Aware Multi-bit Watermarking for Large Language Models

Ran Ran[1], Keke Gai[1,2,3](✉), and Jing Yu[4,5,6](✉)

[1] School of Cyberspace Science and Technology, Beijing Institute of Technology, Beijing, China
3120241295@bit.edu.cn
[2] School of Artificial Intelligence, Beijing Institute of Technology, Beijing, China
[3] Zhongguancun Academy, Beijing, China
gaikeke@bit.edu.cn
[4] School of Information Engineering, Minzu University of China, Beijing, China
[5] Key Laboratory of Ethnic Language Intelligent Analysis and Security Governance of MOE, Minzu University of China, Beijing, China
[6] Institute of Artificial Intelligence, Minzu University of China, Beijing, China
jing.yu@muc.edu.cn

Abstract. The extensive generative capabilities of *Large Language Models* (LLMs) are causing the potential to increase abuse and misuse of AI-generated contents, which makes annotation and detection be critical tasks. Embedding watermarks into models is considered an effective approach that is imperceptible to humans but can be easily detected using specific algorithms. However, compared to the image and audio domains, the text domain possesses relatively limited redundancy. Most existing watermarking methods struggle to be effectively applied in scenarios requiring substantial embedding space, including low-entropy generation tasks and when it is necessary to embed multi-bit watermarks for advanced traceability. To address this challenge, in this work we propose a novel entropy-aware multi-bit watermarking framework. Specifically, by developing an entropy-aware filtering module, we estimate context entropy in real time to filter out invalid watermark spaces. Simultaneously, we integrate a multi-bit position allocation strategy to efficiently utilize the remaining space, thereby enabling trustworthy traceability of multi-bit watermark information in diverse generation scenarios. Comprehensive experiments demonstrate that our scheme improves text quality across various generation scenarios while maintaining high multi-bit decoding accuracy, providing a practical solution for the trustworthy traceability of LLMs.

Keywords: Model Watermarking · Large Language Models · Data Security · Copyright Protection · Inference-time Watermarking

1 Introduction

The advent of *Large Language Models* (LLMs) marks a pivotal shift by enabling machines to comprehend and generate natural language for complex task resolu-

J. Niu et al. (Eds.): KSEM 2026, LNAI 16631, pp. 561–575, 2027.
https://doi.org/10.1007/978-981-92-2759-4_41

tion effectively and reliably, which have been demonstrated across various application domains, such as question answering [22,26], machine translation [25,28], and code generation [2,9], marking a rapid evolution in the field. However, the widespread adoption of applications has also given rise to numerous challenges, with the risk of the exploitation for malicious purposes steadily increasing. For instance, malicious actors may use LLMs to fabricate fake news to manipulate public opinion [17,24]; students may carry out academic dishonesty [10]. Besides, criminals could abuse LLM-based systems to mass-produce phishing emails [20] to threaten public security.

The issues discussed above have raised increasing concerns, highlighting the necessity of labeling and detecting AI-generated texts. Watermarking represents an effective approach [14], enabling tracing and verification by embedding specific identifiers during the text generation process. Some watermarking methods have been explored to address this issue. For example, KGW [12] partitions the vocabulary into "green" and "red" lists at each step of token generation based on the hash value of the preceding token. A fixed bias is added to the logits of tokens in the "green" list to promote their generation, while the logits of tokens in the "red" list remain unchanged. Finally, the existence of the watermark is detected by calculating the proportion of "green" tokens within the suspicious text. Subsequent watermarking methods have largely built upon this foundation. In addition, some approaches utilize secret keys to generate watermarking logits biases to enhance robustness [19], while some control the generation of selected tokens through semantic associations to improve the quality of the generated text [15]. However, most existing methods primarily focus on zero-bit watermarking, which is limited to determining whether a text is machine-generated. When further tracing to specific malicious users is required, embedding additional watermark information becomes necessary, posing significant challenges to the text domain, where embedding redundancy is inherently limited. In addition, the practical deployment of watermarks must contend with diverse generation scenarios, such as code generation and factual question answering. In such low-entropy tasks, model predictions are highly deterministic, and the available redundancy for watermark embedding is further diminished, rendering most existing watermarking methods difficult to apply effectively.

To address the aforementioned challenges, we propose an Entropy-aware Adaptive Multi-bit Watermarking (EATER) framework that exploits the limited redundant space within the text domain to embed high-capacity watermark messages, while simultaneously filtering out invalid embedding positions based on entropy values, in order to ensure watermarking performance across diverse generation scenarios. Our method primarily consists of two core stages: Entropy-aware Filtering and Multi-bit Dynamic Allocation. Specifically, during the entropy-aware filtering stage, we employ a lightweight auxiliary model to estimate real-time entropy and filter out low-entropy invalid spaces, thereby applying watermark bias exclusively to high-entropy regions to accommodate diverse generation tasks and ensure the quality of generated content. In the multi-bit dynamic allocation stage, we first encode the watermark message and leverage context information to allocate message positions for the current token in real time. Subsequently, we construct corresponding watermark logits bias based on the message positions, thereby implicitly embedding multi-bit watermark information into the generated content.

The main contributions of our work are as follows.

- We propose a novel entropy-aware multi-bit watermarking framework, which involves two proposed key modules, namely, an entropy-aware filtering module and a multi-bit position allocation strategy module. Our scheme achieves efficient utilization of the limited embedding capacity within the text domain, addressing the fundamental challenge where existing methods struggle to ensure reliable watermark tracing in diverse generation scenarios.
- We have conducted comprehensive experimental evaluations across various model architectures and diverse text generation tasks. Experimental results demonstrate that, while maintaining multi-bit decoding accuracy comparable to existing methods, our approach significantly improves text quality and maintains stable watermark embedding capability, providing a practical solution for the trustworthy traceability of LLMs.

The rest of the paper is organized as follows. Section 2 reviews the related work on watermarking schemes for LLMs. In Sect. 3, we present the details of our proposed watermarking framework. Section 4 presents experimental results and a comprehensive discussion. A conclusion is given in Sect. 5.

2 Related Work

Watermarking serves as a proactive content protection technology that enables the detection and tracing of machine-generated text by embedding imperceptible identifiers, all while preserving its utility. The most prevalent category of watermarking methods is token-level inference-time watermarking. These methods typically do not alter the model itself, but embed watermarks into the generated text implicitly by modifying the logits distribution of the next token during the inference stage. Tokens with promoted logits value are more likely to appear in the generated text, thereby enabling the detection of the watermark through statistical testing.

Kirchenbauer *et al.* [11] proposed a token-level inference-time watermarking method. This approach utilizes the hash value of the preceding tokens to partition the vocabulary and applies a fixed bias to the logits values of a specific subset, thereby adjusting the model's sampling probability distribution to embed watermarks into machine-generated text. Building upon this foundation, numerous improved methods have been proposed. For instance, studies have suggested utilizing semantic information to generate watermark logits as a substitute for simple hash schemes, which enhances the robustness of the watermark [16,19]. Some other methods constrain the parts of speech of tokens, which can enhance watermark imperceptibility [7]. Additionally, some approaches evaluate the importance of candidate tokens to select watermark biases [1,5,15] or

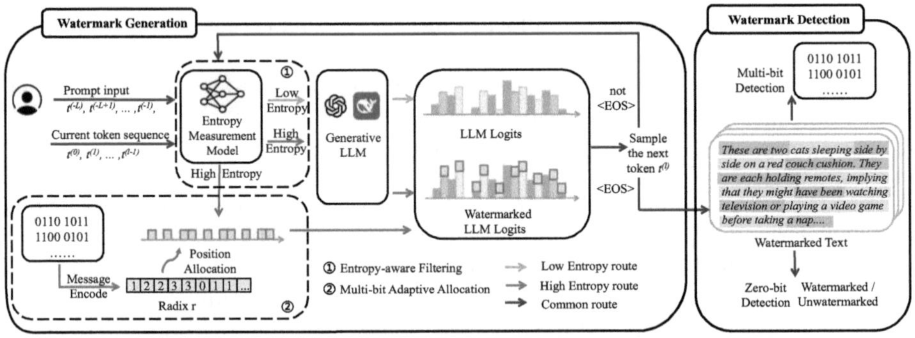

Fig. 1. Framework of the proposed watermarking approach.

dynamically adjust watermark strength [8] to improve the quality of the generated text. Nevertheless, all the aforementioned methods are limited to determining whether suspicious text is AI-generated and are incapable of further tracing, which necessitates embedding additional information within the limited text domain. Previous studies have explored this direction; for instance, Fernandez *et al.* [4] performed watermark embedding through cyclic shifting of multi-bit messages, while Yoo *et al.* [27] employed a position allocation mechanism to distribute and embed multi-bit watermark information. However, these approaches struggle to deal with diverse generation scenarios, while our research addresses this challenge effectively.

3 Methodology

Our proposed EATER fully exploits the redundant space within the text domain, achieving multi-bit watermark embedding for machine-generated text across diverse generation tasks. This method filters out low-entropy invalid watermark spaces through real-time context entropy estimation, and applies a message encoding strategy based on position allocation to the remaining valid regions to generate the watermark logits probability distribution, thereby achieving implicit watermark embedding and reliable multi-bit message tracing.

Figure 1 presents an overview of our watermark framework with two main phases, watermark embedding and detection. In the embedding phase, we generate watermark logits for specific tokens through the **Entropy-aware Filtering** and **Multi-bit Adaptive Allocation** modules, and add them to the original logits to embed the watermark. The procedure for watermark generation is delineated in Algorithm 1. In the detection phase, we identify each watermark token and calculate its watermark logits value, then determine the existence of the watermark through hypothesis testing and extract the multi-bit watermark information.

3.1 Entropy-Aware Filtering

The core goal of Entropy-aware Filtering is to identify high-entropy valid tokens for watermark embedding, thereby mitigating the impact of watermark bias on the quality of generated content. Furthermore, the mechanism of adaptively incorporating watermark logits based on entropy values enables our watermarking scheme to accommodate diverse generation tasks. Specifically, at the j-th step of text generation, the LLM M takes the prompt $t_{:0}$ and the preceding generated sequence $t_{0:(j-1)}$ to produce the logits vector $l^{(j-1)}$ for the current token over the vocabulary $\mathcal{V}$. The LLM then transforms the logits vector into a token probability distribution $P_M(l^{(j-1)}) = \{\hat{p}_0, \hat{p}_1, \cdots, \hat{p}_{\mathcal{V}-1}\}$ via the softmax function and samples the current token from this distribution. Typically, the resulting probability distributions vary across different generation tasks and contexts.

In our watermarking method, we utilize Shannon entropy [21], denoted as $H(\cdot)$ to quantify the uncertainty of the generation distribution. Shannon entropy directly reflects the model's degree of certainty regarding the next token, and its computational efficiency makes it suitable for real-time screening. When the entropy is high, the distribution is relatively flat with significant uncertainty; consequently, introducing watermark bias has a negligible impact on the quality of the generated content. However, when the entropy is low, the distribution is highly concentrated on a few specific tokens. In such cases, imposing a large watermark bias would severely degrade the correctness of the generated content, while introducing a small bias would fail to yield an effective watermark. This region constitutes the invalid watermark space described above.

We first adopt a predefined entropy α as the threshold. During the token generation process, we employ a lightweight auxiliary model LM to compute the real-time entropy parallelly:

$$H(P_{LM}(t_{:k-1})) = -\sum_{i=0}^{|\mathcal{V}|} \hat{p}_i^k \log \hat{p}_i^k. \tag{1}$$

Subsequently, we apply the watermark bias exclusively to token distributions whose entropy exceeds this threshold.

3.2 Multi-bit Adaptive Allocation

The objective of Multi-bit Adaptive Allocation is to leverage the limited space within the text domain to embed high-capacity watermark payloads, thereby facilitating the further tracing of generated content following the detection of watermark existence. Following the screening in the Entropy-aware Filtering stage, we need to apply appropriate watermark bias to valid high-entropy tokens at the logits layer. Thus, we develop two sub-modules, namely, Message Encoding and Position Allocation.

Message Encode. The Message Encoding sub-module is designed to encode the original multi-bit message into a format suitable for the generation of watermark logits bias. Specifically, given a binary watermark message m_0 of length

y_0, such as a user ID or a timestamp, we first perform base conversion based on the radix r. We adopt the configuration settings from the KGW scheme, setting the green list proportion to γ, and accordingly calculate the radix $r = \lfloor 1/\gamma \rfloor$. During each watermarking operation, we apply watermark logits enhancement only to a fraction γ of the tokens in the vocabulary. Similarly, for ease of description, we denote this subset of tokens as green tokens. We denote the message after base conversion as m, with a length of $y = \lceil y_0 / \log_2 r \rceil$. For any position $p \in 0, 1, \ldots, y-1$, we have $m[p] \in 0, 1, \ldots, r-1$. Thus, each position p carries $\log_2 r$ bits of information from the original message m_0, and this portion of the message will be embedded into the corresponding position during the subsequent generation process.

The Message Encoding sub-module offers two key advantages. On one side, by increasing the information capacity of each position, it effectively reduces the number of required message positions, thereby alleviating the dependency on long texts. On the other side, by decoupling the original message from the subsequent Position Allocation sub-module, it enables flexible adjustment of the message length and encoding method. After encoding, the converted message m is passed to the Position Allocation sub-module to calculate the specific message position that the current token should carry.

Position Allocation. The Position Allocation sub-module assigns a message position to each token during generation in real time. In this way, the multi-bit watermark message can be distributed across the text sequence.

Specifically, for the j-th token to be generated, we calculate the hash seed $s = Hash(t_{j-w:j-1})$ based on the preceding w generated tokens $t_{j-w:j-1}$, where $Hash(\cdot)$ is a public deterministic hash function and w is the window size. We first initialize a random number generator with seed s to sample a position index p from $\{0, 1, \ldots, y-1\}$, which determines that the current token carries the message content at the p-th position of the encoded message m. Subsequently, we utilize the same seed to randomly partition the vocabulary $\mathcal{V}$ into r equal-sized subsets, denoted as $\{\mathcal{V}_j^0, \mathcal{V}_j^1, \cdots, \mathcal{V}_j^{r-1}\}$, and apply watermark logit bias δ only to tokens within the cluster $\mathcal{V}_j^n$, where $n = m[p]$.

In the Position Allocation sub-module, the uniformity of the sampling process ensures that the number of tokens allocated to each message position is approximately equal. This helps avoid decoding failures caused by insufficient data at certain positions. In this way, the entire multi-bit message is implicitly dispersed and embedded into various positions within the generated text. This design not only ensures watermark robustness but also facilitates the efficient utilization of the limited redundancy in the text domain.

3.3 Watermark Detection

During the watermark detection stage, we perform analysis on the suspicious text at two different granularities. First, we determine whether the text contains a watermark, which corresponds to **Zero-bit Detection**. If a watermark is present, we further extract the embedded multi-bit information, which corresponds to **Multi-bit Detection**.

Zero-Bit Detection. The objective of zero-bit detection is to determine whether a suspicious text was generated by a watermarked model, focusing solely on the presence of the watermark. We formulate this problem as a hypothesis testing task, considering the following null hypothesis H_0 and the corresponding alternative hypothesis H_1:

$$H_0 : \text{The suspicious text is unwatermarked.}$$
$$H_1 : \text{The suspicious text is watermarked.}$$

For a segment of suspicious text $\{t_0, t_1, \ldots, t_L\}$, we first utilize the lightweight auxiliary model LM to sequentially calculate the Shannon entropy for each token. We then only retain those tokens with entropy values exceeding the pre-set threshold α as valid tokens, denoting the count of valid tokens as L_{eff}. For each valid token, we compute a hash seed based on its w prefix tokens to determine the assigned position and the corresponding target vocabulary partition at the time of generation. We then check whether the current token falls into this partition and count the total number of valid tokens satisfying this condition, denoting the result as the statistic S. Under the null hypothesis H_0, the probability of each valid token falling into the specified partition is $\gamma = 1/r$, and they are mutually independent. Therefore, S should follow a binomial distribution $S \sim \text{Binomial}(L_{\text{eff}}, \gamma)$. Based on this, we construct the z-statistic by Eq. (2).

$$z = \frac{S - \gamma L_{\text{eff}}}{\sqrt{\gamma(1-\gamma)L_{\text{eff}}}}. \tag{2}$$

Under the alternative hypothesis H_1, due to the existence of watermark logits, valid tokens will systematically gravitate towards target partitions, resulting in S being significantly higher than the expected value. We establish a significance level threshold z_α, by which we reject H_0 and conclude that the suspicious text contains a watermark when $z > z_\alpha$. Otherwise, we accept H_0 and determine that the text is not watermarked. By adjusting z_α, we can flexibly balance the detection rate and the False Positive Rate (FPR) across different application scenarios. For instance, in scenarios requiring stringent control, a higher z_α can be selected to mitigate the risk of false positives. Conversely, in scenarios necessitating broader screening, z_α can be appropriately lowered to enhance detection sensitivity. This makes the detection process interpretable and easy to adjust for different application scenarios.

Multi-bit Detection. Once zero-bit detection indicates that a text contains a watermark, multi-bit detection proceeds to recover the complete embedded watermark message. Different from zero-bit detection, which only focuses on watermark presence, multi-bit detection aims to recover the specific message content carried at each position. Similar to the process of zero-bit detection, we first retain valid tokens via entropy-aware filtering. For each valid token, we compute the hash seed based on its w prefix tokens to determine the assigned position p and the vocabulary partition into which it actually falls. By traversing all valid tokens, we construct the detection matrix $\mathbf{D} \in \mathbb{R}^{y \times r}$, where $D[p][i]$ denotes the

Algorithm 1: Entropy-Aware Multi-bit Watermark Embedding

Input: LLM M, Vocabulary $\mathcal{V}$, Prompt token sequence $t_{:0}$, Binary watermark message m_0, Message length y_0, Green list proportion γ, Window size w, Watermark strength δ, Entropy estimation model LM, Predefined entropy threshold α

Output: Watermarked text $t_{:L}$

radix $r \leftarrow \lfloor 1/\gamma \rfloor$;
$(m, y) \leftarrow$ Message Encode(m_0, y_0, r);
for $j = 1$ *to* L **do**
  if $H(P_{LM}(t_{:j-1})) > \alpha$ **then**
    $s \leftarrow Hash(t_{j-w:j-1})$;
    $p \leftarrow$ Position Allocation(s);
    $n \leftarrow m[p]$;
    $G \leftarrow \mathcal{V}_j^n$;

$$\hat{p}_k^{(j)} = \begin{cases} \dfrac{\exp(l_k^{(j)} + \delta)}{\sum_{i \notin G} \exp(l_i^{(j)}) + \sum_{i \in G} \exp(l_i^{(j)} + \delta)}, & k \in G \\ \dfrac{\exp(l_k^{(j)})}{\sum_{i \notin G} \exp(l_i^{(j)}) + \sum_{i \in G} \exp(l_i^{(j)} + \delta)}, & k \notin G \end{cases};$$

  end
  else

$$\hat{p}_k^{(j)} = \frac{\exp(l_k^{(j)})}{\sum_{i \in \mathcal{V}} \exp(l_i^{(j)})};$$

  end
  $P_j \leftarrow \{\hat{p}_0, \hat{p}_1, \cdots, \hat{p}_{\mathcal{V}-1}\}$;
  $t_j \leftarrow$ Sample(M, P_j);
end
return $t_{:L}$;

count of tokens falling into the i-th partition at position p. Subsequently, based on the constructed detection matrix, we decode each position independently. Specifically, for each position $p \in \{0, 1, \cdots, y-1\}$, we select the partition index with the maximum count at that position as the decoded r-radix message value by $\hat{m}[p] = \arg\max_{i \in [r]} \mathbf{D}[p][i]$. After decoding all positions, we obtain the r-radix message m. Finally, by reversing the Message Encoding process, we can recover the original watermark message m_0. In practical applications, if the confidence of decoding results for certain positions is low, we can output multiple candidate messages to facilitate further verification, thereby enhancing the stability of message decoding.

4 Experiments

4.1 Experiment Configuration

Dataset and Language Models. We conducted experiments on two public datasets, the realnewslike subset of C4 [18] and ELI5 [3]. C4-realnewslike offered a structured news corpus, while ELI5 contained explanatory question-answering content. The difference in textual characteristics between these datasets allowed us to evaluate proposed method's performance across different writing styles and domains Specifically, for each entry in the C4 dataset, we utilized the first 30 tokens as the prompt, whereas for the ELI5 dataset, we employed the question component as the prompt. For both datasets, we retained the original text as unaltered human-authored content (text without watermarks) and generated the subsequent 200 tokens using the corresponding prompts to produce watermarked texts. For language models, we utilized the GPT-2 and LLaMA [23] models for text generation tasks.

Baseline Approaches and Settings. We chose the following watermarking approaches as baselines for comparison. First, KGW-1 [11] utilized the hash value of the current token's prefix to partition the LLM's vocabulary and subsequently allocates watermark logits for it. Second, KGW-k [12] served as a straightforward extension of KGW-1 by employing the hash values of the preceding k prefixes to generate watermark logits, and we illustrated this with the example of $k = 2$ for comparison(KGW-2). Third, SIR [16] generated watermark logits based on semantic information of the prefix. Finally, MPAC [27] enabled the embedding of multi-bit watermark information through position allocation. In our experiments, we adopted a unified setting with a watermark strength of $\delta = 1.0$ and a green list proportion of $\gamma = 0.25$.

4.2 Evaluations

Zero-bit Watermark Detection. We first evaluated the capability of different methods to distinguish between watermarked and non-watermarked text under the zero-bit scenario. We set the watermark threshold based on the one-to-one correspondence between the one-sided z-test statistic and the FPR, identifying texts with z-values exceeding the threshold as watermarked. Table 1 presented the True Positive Rate (TPR) and F1 score for our EATER and four baseline methods at FPR of 1% and 0.1%, evaluated on the C4 and ELI5 datasets using GPT-2 and LLaMA as generation models.

Experiment results demonstrated that our scheme achieved superior zero-bit detection performance under most settings. On GPT-2, our scheme attained a TPR of 0.986 on the C4 dataset at 1% FPR, comparable to the best-performing MPAC; meanwhile, the TPR of 0.955 at 0.1% FPR closely approached the optimal SIR under this setting. On ELI5, EATER significantly outperformed all baselines. On LLaMA, while the detection performance of all methods declined, EATER still maintained its advantage, outperforming all baselines across nearly all metrics on both datasets. Overall, our scheme maintained high detection rates while achieving F1 scores that were generally superior or comparable to the best baselines, validating the effectiveness of the entropy-aware filter mechanism in complex generation scenarios.

Multi-bit Watermark Detection. We further evaluated the bit accuracy of each method in embedding and extracting watermark messages in the multi-bit

Table 1. Zero-bit detection results across different generative models and datasets under varying FPR thresholds.

Zero-bit Detection		C4 Dataset				Eli5 Dataset			
Model	Method	1%FPR		0.1%FPR		1%FPR		0.1%FPR	
		TPR	F1	TPR	F1	TPR	F1	TPR	F1
GPT2	KGW-1	0.972	0.981	0.908	0.949	0.996	0.991	0.980	0.987
	KGW-2	0.989	0.985	0.931	0.960	0.998	0.988	0.978	0.986
	SIR	0.994	0.886	**0.968**	0.925	0.998	0.913	0.986	0.942
	MPAC	**0.995**	**0.989**	0.953	0.974	0.994	0.986	0.988	0.991
	OURS	0.986	0.984	0.955	**0.975**	**1**	**0.996**	**0.990**	**0.992**
Llama	KGW-1	0.758	0.854	0.528	0.69	0.864	0.916	0.730	0.840
	KGW-2	0.686	0.808	0.472	0.641	0.872	0.927	0.698	0.822
	SIR	**0.876**	0.872	0.666	0.799	0.910	0.891	0.768	0.867
	MPAC	0.822	0.891	0.538	0.698	0.864	0.922	0.692	0.817
	OURS	0.860	**0.919**	**0.756**	**0.832**	**0.924**	**0.952**	**0.822**	**0.870**

Table 2. Comparison of multi-bit watermark detection accuracy between our EATER and the baseline multi-bit approach under varying bit lengths.

Multi-bit Detection		MPAC-8bit	MPAC-16bit	OURS-8bit	OURS-16bit
GPT2	C4	0.948	0.855	0.933	0.843
	Eli5	0.967	0.883	0.962	0.889
Llama	C4	0.817	0.730	0.853	0.748
	Eli5	0.849	0.762	0.870	0.771

scenario. Table 2 presented a comparison of bit accuracy between our EATER and the multi-bit baseline methods (MPAC) under both 8-bit and 16-bit settings.

On the GPT-2 model, EATER performed comparably to the multi-bit baseline MPAC. However, on the Llama model, the improvement of EATER was more pronounced. It achieved scores of 0.853 and 0.748 on the C4 dataset for 8-bit and 16-bit tasks, significantly surpassing MPAC's 0.817 and 0.730. Similarly, on the ELI5 dataset, our scheme outperformed MPAC with scores of 0.870 and 0.771 compared to 0.849 and 0.762. Overall, EATER maintained performance comparable to the multi-bit watermarking baseline while exhibiting superior multi-bit embedding capability in low-entropy scenarios and on larger models.

Text Quality Evaluation. The impact on the quality of generated content was also a crucial part for evaluating the watermarking methods. We adopted the following three metrics for evaluation: Perplexity (PPL), which measured the naturalness and fluency of the text computed using the OPT-1.3b model [29]; Coherence, which evaluated the semantic and logical consistency of the context

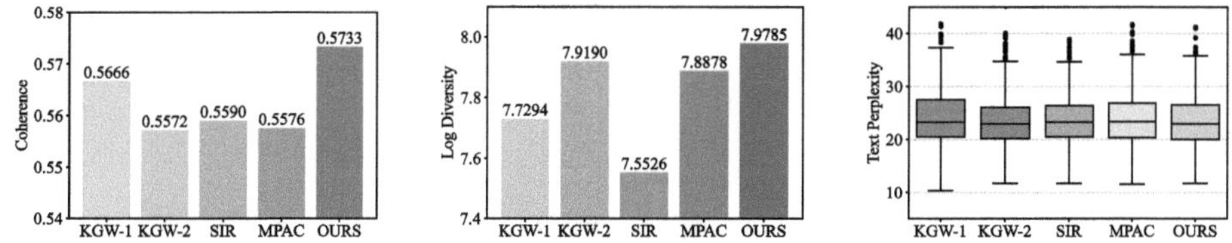

(a) Coherence (b) Log Diversity (c) Text Perplexity

Fig. 2. The comparison of EATER and four baseline methods in three aspects consisting of coherence, diversity, and text perplexity. These metrics measured the stealthiness of the watermark.

Table 3. Robustness evaluation of different watermarking methods against various text editing attacks.

Attack Methods	KGW-1		KGW-2		SIR		MPAC		OURS	
	TPR	F1	TPR	F1	TPR	F1	TPR	F1	TPR	F1
Copy-paste	0.940	0.941	0.947	0.964	**0.974**	0.876	0.967	0.975	0.969	**0.976**
Scramble	**0.994**	0.990	0.996	0.987	0.982	0.905	0.984	0.989	**0.994**	**0.993**
Zero-width	**0.996**	**0.991**	0.982	0.980	0.964	0.899	0.954	0.972	0.976	0.976
Paraphrasing	0.544	0.700	0.272	0.422	**0.670**	**0.698**	0.311	0.468	0.355	0.518

computed using the Simcse model [6]; and Diversity, which measured the lexical richness of the generated text.

Figure 2 presented a comparison of EATER with four baseline methods across these three metrics. As illustrated in Fig. 2, our scheme achieved superior performance across all metrics. In terms of coherence and diversity, EATER attained the highest scores, outperforming the four baseline methods. Furthermore, EATER yielded the lowest text perplexity, indicating superior text fluency and naturalness. The superior performance in terms of text quality further demonstrated the effectiveness of our watermarking method.

Watermark Robustness. We further evaluated the robustness of our watermarking method against various attacks. In the experiments, we simulated complex behaviors of real-world adversaries via four types of attacks: Copy-paste, scrambling, zero-width character insertion, and paraphrasing [13]. We reported the TPR and F1 score at 1% FPR to evaluate the robustness of the watermark.

Table 3 demonstrated that our method performed well in most attack scenarios. Specifically, our method achieved optimal performance under copy-paste and scrambling attacks, and maintained relative stability against zero-width character insertion attacks. In the case of paraphrase attacks, although EATER's performance was lower than SIR, which was specifically designed for such attacks, it still outperformed several other baseline methods. This indicated that our multi-bit watermarking method maintained robustness even when facing strong attacks.

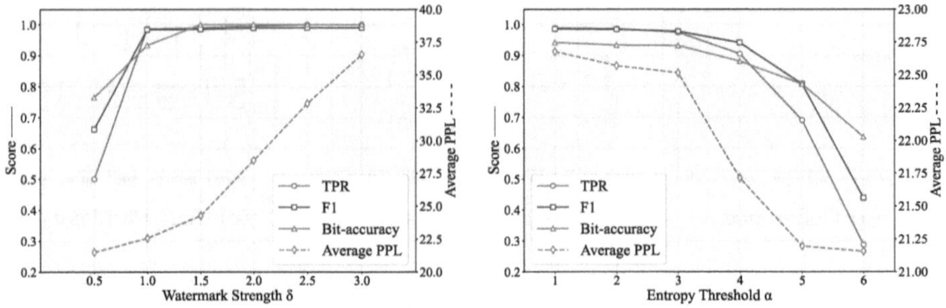

(a) Effect of Watermark Strength δ (b) Effect of Entropy Threshold α

Fig. 3. Trade-offs between watermarking effectiveness and text quality under varying (a)watermark strength δ and (b)entropy threshold α.

Table 4. Detection performance across varying watermark message lengths.

Bit-Len	4	8	16	24	32	64
TPR	0.987	0.986	0.975	0.977	0.980	0.984
F1	0.985	0.984	0.987	0.977	0.981	0.983
Bit-Accuracy	0.993	0.962	0.888	0.755	0.742	0.737

4.3 Discussions

The Impact of Watermark Strength δ. Watermark strength significantly affected detection performance and the quality of generated content. As illustrated in Fig. 3a, the decoded bit accuracy improved significantly as the watermark strength δ increased. When δ exceeded 1.5, the bit accuracy approached 1.0. Simultaneously, the TPR and F1 scores at 1% FPR also improved with increasing watermark strength. However, as the watermark strength increased, the watermark bias excessively interfered with the natural output distribution of the LLM, leading to a sharp decline in text quality, manifested as a significant increase in PPL. In the experiments, controlling the watermark strength δ within the range of 1.0 to 1.5 yielded a relatively balanced performance across all metrics, providing a reasonable reference for practical deployment.

The Impact of Entropy Threshold α. Figure 3b illustrated the regulatory effect of the entropy threshold α in the watermark embedding process of EATER. A lower α permitted watermark embedding on a greater number of low-entropy tokens, but these positions may compromise correct generation results, leading to a significantly higher PPL. Increasing the entropy threshold addressed this issue, but a higher α further reduced the effective embedding space, thereby diminishing the detection capability of the watermark. When α exceeded 5, the detection capability dropped sharply. This further highlighted the necessity of selecting an appropriate entropy threshold to maintain high-quality generated content while ensuring the stability of watermark detection.

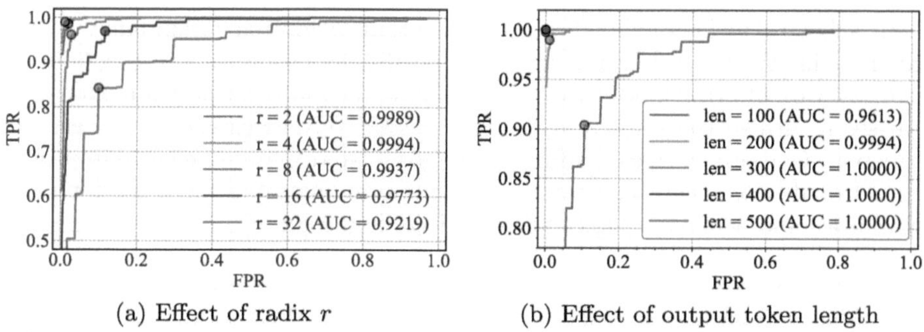

Fig. 4. ROC curves under different (a)radix r and (b)token output length.

The Impact of Watermark Message Length. The impact of the bit length of watermark messages on watermark detection performance was presented in Table 4. As the bit length increased from 4 to 64, the TPR and F1 scores at 1% FPR remained stable, indicating that the watermark can still be reliably detected. However, with the increase of bit length, bit accuracy exhibited a significant downward trend. In practical applications, a trade-off between information capacity and detection accuracy should be carefully balanced based on specific task requirements.

The Impact of Radix r. We also measured the impact of radix r on watermarking performance. Figure 4a illustrated the AUROC scores under different r values. As r increased from 2 to 4, the AUROC rised to a peak of 0.9994, indicating that moderately increasing the radix parameter enhances watermarking performance. However, further increasing r led to a corresponding degradation in watermarking performance.

The Impact of Output Token Length. Figure 4b illustrated the impact of output token length on watermark detection performance. As depicted in the figure, the watermark performance exhibited a clear saturation trend as the output token length increases. When the output token length reached 300, the AUROC attains 1.0 and remained stable, indicating that an output length exceeding 300 tokens was sufficient to contain the key information required to distinguish watermarked samples.

Limitations and Future Work. This method still had some limitations. First, it relied on an auxiliary model for entropy estimation. Second, its robustness against paraphrasing attacks remained limited. Future work will focus on developing adaptive entropy threshold mechanisms and further enhancing the method's robustness against strong semantic attacks.

5 Conclusions

In this work, we proposed a novel entropy-aware adaptive multi-bit watermarking framework, capable of protecting the model and its generated content. The core of our scheme lay in maximizing the utilization of limited redundancy in the text domain. We identified and excluded invalid watermark space through the entropy-aware filtering module, while combining the multi-bit position allocation strategy to utilize the remaining space to adaptively generate the watermark logits bias. Comprehensive experiments demonstrated that our scheme improved the text quality of generated content while maintaining robust zero-bit detection capabilities and achieving high multi-bit decoding accuracy.

Acknowledgments. This work is supported by the National Natural Science Foundation of China (Grant No.s U24B20146, 62372044), Beijing Municipal Science and Technology Commission Project (Z241100009124008), and Beijing Nova Program (Grant No. 20250484921).

References

1. Chen, L., et al.: X-mark: Towards lossless watermarking through lexical redundancy. arXiv preprint arXiv:2311.09832 (2023)
2. Du, X., et al.: Evaluating large language models in class-level code generation. In: Proceedings of the IEEE/ACM 46th International Conference on Software Engineering, pp. 1–13 (2024)
3. Fan, A., Jernite, Y., Perez, E., Grangier, D., Weston, J., Auli, M.: Eli5: Long form question answering. arXiv preprint arXiv:1907.09190 (2019)
4. Fernandez, P., Chaffin, A., Tit, K., Chappelier, V., Furon, T.: Three bricks to consolidate watermarks for large language models. In: 2023 IEEE International Workshop on Information Forensics and Security (WIFS), pp. 1–6. IEEE (2023)
5. Fu, Y., Xiong, D., Dong, Y.: Watermarking conditional text generation for ai detection: Unveiling challenges and a semantic-aware watermark remedy. In: Proceedings of the AAAI Conference on Artificial Intelligence, vol. 38, pp. 18003–18011 (2024)
6. Gao, T., Yao, X., Chen, D.: Simcse: Simple contrastive learning of sentence embeddings. arXiv preprint arXiv:2104.08821 (2021)
7. Hoang, D.C., et al.: Less is more: Sparse watermarking in llms with enhanced text quality. arXiv preprint arXiv:2407.13803 (2024)
8. Huo, M., Somayajula, S.A., Liang, Y., Zhang, R., Koushanfar, F., Xie, P.: Token-specific watermarking with enhanced detectability and semantic coherence for large language models. arXiv preprint arXiv:2402.18059 (2024)
9. Jiang, X.: Self-planning code generation with large language models. ACM Trans. Softw. Eng. Methodol. **33**(7), 1–30 (2024)
10. Kasneci, E., et al.: Chatgpt for good? on opportunities and challenges of large language models for education. Learn. Individ. Differ. **103**, 102274 (2023)
11. Kirchenbauer, J., Geiping, J., Wen, Y., Katz, J., Miers, I., Goldstein, T.: A watermark for large language models. In: International Conference on Machine Learning, pp. 17061–17084. PMLR (2023)
12. Kirchenbauer, J., et al.: On the reliability of watermarks for large language models. arXiv preprint arXiv:2306.04634 (2023)
13. Krishna, K., Song, Y., Karpinska, M., Wieting, J., Iyyer, M.: Paraphrasing evades detectors of ai-generated text, but retrieval is an effective defense. Advances in Neural Information Processing Systems **36** (2024)

14. Lei, L., Gai, K., Yu, J., Zhu, L., Wu, Q.: Secure and efficient watermarking for latent diffusion models in model distribution scenarios. In: Proceedings of the Thirty-Fourth International Joint Conference on Artificial Intelligence, IJCAI 2025, Montreal, Canada, August 16-22, 2025, pp. 7473–7481. ijcai.org (2025)
15. Li, Y., Wang, Y., Shi, Z., Hsieh, C.J.: Improving the generation quality of watermarked large language models via word importance scoring. arXiv preprint arXiv:2311.09668 (2023)
16. Liu, A., Pan, L., Hu, X., Meng, S., Wen, L.: A semantic invariant robust watermark for large language models. arXiv preprint arXiv:2310.06356 (2023)
17. Pagnoni, A., Graciarena, M., Tsvetkov, Y.: Threat scenarios and best practices to detect neural fake news. In: Proceedings of the 29th International Conference on Computational Linguistics, pp. 1233–1249 (2022)
18. Raffel, C., Shazeer, N., Roberts, A., Lee, K., Narang, S., Matena, M., Zhou, Y., Li, W., Liu, P.J.: Exploring the limits of transfer learning with a unified text-to-text transformer. J. Mach. Learn. Res. **21**(140), 1–67 (2020)
19. Ren, J., Xu, H., Liu, Y., Cui, Y., Wang, S., Yin, D., Tang, J.: A robust semantics-based watermark for large language model against paraphrasing. arXiv preprint arXiv:2311.08721 (2023)
20. Salloum, S., Gaber, T., Vadera, S., Shaalan, K.: Phishing email detection using natural language processing techniques: a literature survey. Procedia Comput. Sci. **189**, 19–28 (2021)
21. Shannon, C.E.: A mathematical theory of communication. Bell Syst. Techn. J. **27**(3), 379–423 (1948)
22. Shao, Z., Yu, Z., Wang, M., Yu, J.: Prompting large language models with answer heuristics for knowledge-based visual question answering. In: Proceedings of the IEEE/CVF Conference on Computer Vision and Pattern Recognition, pp. 14974–14983 (2023)
23. Touvron, H., et al.: Llama: Open and efficient foundation language models. arXiv preprint arXiv:2302.13971 (2023)
24. Wang, B., et al.: Explainable fake news detection with large language model via defense among competing wisdom. In: Proceedings of the ACM Web Conference 2024, pp. 2452–2463 (2024)
25. Wang, L., Lyu, C., Ji, T., Zhang, Z., Yu, D., Shi, S., Tu, Z.: Document-level machine translation with large language models. arXiv preprint arXiv:2304.02210 (2023)
26. Yasunaga, M., Ren, H., Bosselut, A., Liang, P., Leskovec, J.: Qa-gnn: Reasoning with language models and knowledge graphs for question answering. arXiv preprint arXiv:2104.06378 (2021)
27. Yoo, K., Ahn, W., Kwak, N.: Advancing beyond identification: Multi-bit watermark for large language models. In: Proceedings of the 2024 Conference of the North American Chapter of the Association for Computational Linguistics: Human Language Technologies (Volume 1: Long Papers), pp. 4031–4055 (2024)
28. Zhang, B., Haddow, B., Birch, A.: Prompting large language model for machine translation: a case study. In: International Conference on Machine Learning, pp. 41092–41110. PMLR (2023)
29. Zhang, S., et al.: Opt: Open pre-trained transformer language models. arXiv preprint arXiv:2205.01068 (2022)

DATEE: An Adaptively Thresholded Early-Exit Framework for Large Language Model Inference Based on Confidence Trend Sampling

Haonan Zou[1,2(✉)], Heng Zhang[1(✉)], Yongchun Jiang[1,3], Kaifan Jia[1,3], Yansong Dong[1,3], Shang Wang[1,3], and Zhihao Ling[1,3]

[1] Institute of Software, Chinese Academy of Sciences, Beijing, China
zhangheng17@iscas.ac.cn, {jiangyongchun24,jiakaifan23,dongyansong23, wangshang23,lingzhihao24}@mails.ucas.ac.cn
[2] Hangzhou Institute for Advanced Study, UCAS, Hangzhou, China
zouhaonan23@mails.ucas.ac.cn
[3] University of Chinese Academy of Sciences, Beijing, China

Abstract. As large language models (LLMs) scale, their inference-time computational cost and latency become increasingly prohibitive. Early-exit (EE) methodologies mitigate this issue by reducing the depth of effective inference, terminating the forward pass once the confidence in the prediction of the model exceeds a predefined threshold. However, existing EE approaches typically employ static thresholds, which can result in either premature exits that degrade predictive performance or unnecessarily deep computation that diminishes efficiency gains. To overcome these limitations, we propose DATEE, a **D**ynamic **A**daptively **T**hresholded **E**arly **E**xit framework based on a hierarchical trend sampling strategy. First, we develop a hierarchical trend-sampling mechanism. The first-stage sampling is conducted at shallow network layers to assess whether a predefined confidence threshold is met, while incurring minimal computational overhead. The second-stage sampling is then executed at deeper layers to capture and characterize confidence stabilization patterns. Second, we introduce a dynamically adaptive threshold method based on sampled feature representations, which jointly optimizes the confidence threshold and the initial sampling layer, thereby enabling coordinated and autonomous self-optimization. Experimental results on diverse natural language processing benchmarks show that DATEE stabilizes exits and improves inference efficiency by 1.1×–4.9×. Furthermore, it substantially reduces the average depth of inference and computational cost while preserving overall model performance.

Keywords: LLMs · Efficient Inference · Early Exit · Trend Sampling · Adaptive Thresholds

J. Niu et al. (Eds.): KSEM 2026, LNAI 16631, pp. 576–588, 2027.
https://doi.org/10.1007/978-981-92-2759-4_42

1 Introduction

Large language models have demonstrated marked improvements in task performance. These advances have been accompanied by pronounced increases in inference latency and computational resource consumption. In particular, autoregressive decoding requires executing the complete multi-layer computational stack for each newly generated token, causing the overall inference cost to scale linearly with the length of the output sequence. To mitigate this limitation, early exit techniques have been proposed. The central principle of early exit [2,7,11,20] is to adaptively terminate the inference process at an intermediate layer once the corresponding intermediate representation is deemed sufficiently reliable.

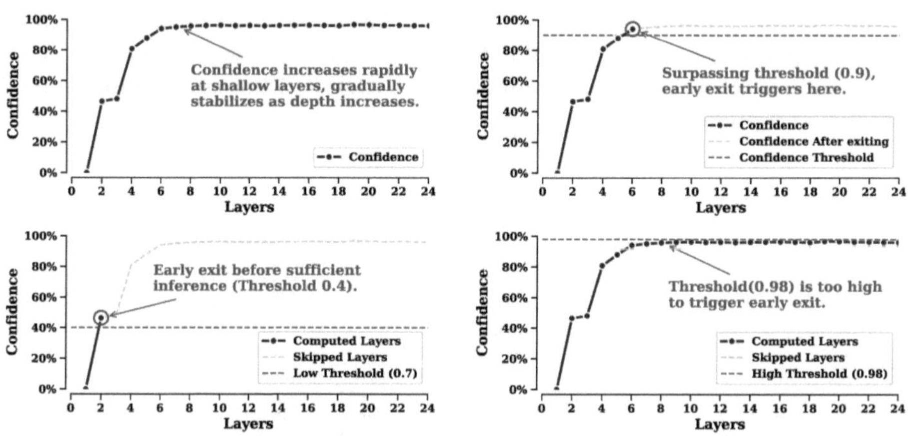

Fig. 1. Confidence average trend and the effect of optimal, low, and high static thresholds on early exit in LLMs.

Recent research on early-exit–based inference for LLMs predominantly employs a static confidence threshold as the exit criterion, where this threshold is specified a priori as a fixed constant. However, such approaches frequently encounter practical limitations, particularly in scenarios where the predictive confidence of the model for certain tasks persists below the predefined threshold. Through empirical analyses conducted on multiple benchmark datasets (SQuAD and BigPatent), we observed a consistent pattern in the confidence levels associated with intermediate layers of LLMs. As illustrated in Fig. 1, confidence increases rapidly in shallow layers and gradually stabilizes as depth increases.

In addition, optimal exit thresholds and exit positions vary substantially between different datasets.

Moreover, employing a single, static confidence threshold is insufficient to simultaneously accommodate both comparatively "easy" and "hard" instances. As illustrated in Fig. 1, when the threshold is set too low, the model may terminate the inference process prematurely, before the underlying semantic representations have adequately converged, which in turn degrades generation quality and compromises stability. Conversely, when the threshold is set excessively high, the exit criterion is typically met only at depths close to full inference, yielding minimal reductions in average inference depth and only marginal gains in computational efficiency.

These observations indicate that confidence trends provide a more robust indicator of inference progress than a single-layer confidence value. Nevertheless, existing studies have not adequately taken advantage of sequential confidence trend information. Motivated by this insight, we propose a dynamic adaptive threshold early exit framework, we propose **DATEE**, a Dynamic Adaptively Thresholded Early Exit framework that accelerates LLM inference through hierarchical trend sampling and an adaptive threshold method. Instead of relying on predetermined confidence thresholds and statically assigned exit layers, DATEE exploits the trend of confidence scores during inference to simultaneously assess whether the model has entered a stable plateau and whether the safe-exit criteria are fulfilled, thereby attaining an improved trade-off between computational efficiency and predictive stability.

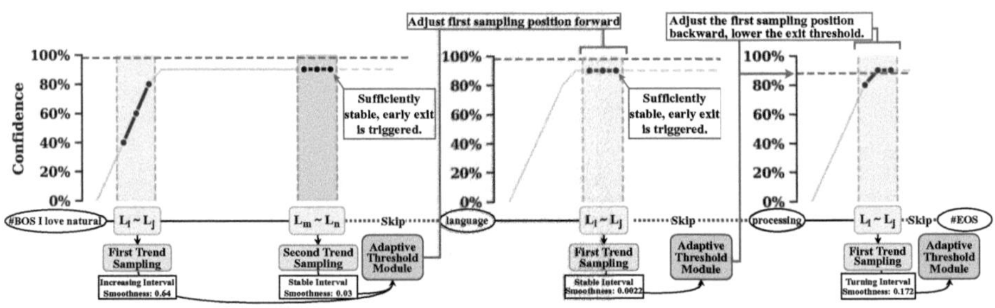

Fig. 2. Overview of the DATEE architecture.

Moreover, DATEE does not incur additional training overhead. It relies exclusively on intermediate-layer representations and a shared language modeling head to perform lightweight modeling of confidence trajectories, thereby enabling the joint self-optimization of early-exit strategies during inference.

Main Contributions. Our main contributions are summarized as follows.

1. **Analysis of Recent EE-Based LLM Inference Work.** We demonstrate that static-threshold early exiting exhibits pronounced sample-dependent pattern. Owing to inconsistent confidence trajectory trends across inputs, a fixed exit threshold is unable to provide both efficient and stable termination of inference.
2. **Hierarchical trend sampling mechanism.** We propose a novel hierarchical sampling strategy in which *confidence sampling* is defined as the difference between the top-1 and top-2 predicted probabilities produced by a shared LM head with a softmax output layer, whereas *trend sampling* is characterized by the variance of this confidence measure across successive transformer layers.

3. **Adaptive Threshold Method for Enhancing EE-Based Model Performance.** The early-exit behaviors are partitioned into five distinct categories, and both the confidence threshold and the initial sampling position are iteratively updated until convergence is achieved.
4. **Comprehensive Evaluation.** We evaluate DATEE on three benchmark datasets and show that it stabilizes early exits and improves inference efficiency by 1.1×–4.9×, reducing average inference depth and computational cost while maintaining overall performance.

2 Related Work

The introduction of the Transformer architecture [18] established the foundational computational paradigm for contemporary LLMs. Modern LLMs are typically implemented as deep stacks of identical layers, each comprising a full self-attention mechanism and an associated feed-forward network. During inference, the generation of each successive token necessitates a complete forward propagation from the initial layer through to the final layer. Because the intermediate layers are structurally isomorphic to the terminal layer—differing primarily in the extent of contextual integration and the level of semantic abstraction—this architectural property offers a natural basis for enabling early exit mechanisms at intermediate depths of the network [6].

2.1 Early Exit Strategy

The concept of early exiting can be traced to investigations of computational redundancy in deep neural networks [13]. BranchyNet [17] constitutes a seminal contribution in this area, introducing multiple auxiliary branch classifiers at different depths of a backbone network. By training these branch classifiers to estimate prediction confidence, the inference process can be terminated once a predefined confidence threshold is met, thereby substantially reducing inference latency. FastBERT [9] attaches lightweight classifiers to intermediate Transformer layers and enables early exit by evaluating prediction confidence or entropy during inference. PABEE [19] introduces a patience-based early exit strategy that monitors prediction stability across consecutive layers and terminates inference once the output becomes sufficiently consistent. SmartBERT [5] further introduces a layer-skipping mechanism that allows more flexible computation paths across different depths. LayerSkip [3] enhances shallow-layer predictions via layer-wise dropout and a unified exit loss. During inference, candidate outputs are generated at shallow layers and subsequently verified or corrected by deeper layers.

2.2 Threshold Strategies

Early approaches predominantly adopt a global static confidence threshold shared across all inputs and inference stages. While simple to implement, such strategies struggle to accommodate varying input difficulty and task characteristics. To address these limitations, several works have explored dynamic or layer-aware threshold strategies. CALM [15] performs offline optimization of exit decisions by systematically analyzing different confidence metrics and threshold functions, proposing lightweight exit criteria with low inference cost. FREE [1] leverages parallel decoding to compare shallow and deeper predictions, categorizing samples into prediction-aligned and non-aligned cases. During model updates, FREE applies maximum likelihood estimation to adjust thresholds online.

Our Motivation. Although these threshold optimization methods improve robustness to some extent, most exit decisions are still based on instantaneous confidence values from a single layer or a small set of layers. The overall evolution trend of prediction confidence across layers remains underexplored. Effectively exploiting the cross-layer confidence trend to dynamically adapt both the confidence threshold and the trend sampling layer remains an open problem.

3 Methodology

To tackle these challenges, we propose **DATEE**, a novel dynamic adaptive threshold early-exit framework for efficient LLM inference. DATEE consists of two core components: a **hierarchical confidence trend sampling mechanism**, and a **dynamic adaptive threshold method via sampling features**.

3.1 Hierarchical Confidence Trend Sampling Mechanism

As discussed in Sect. 1, the optimal Early Exit point of an LLM typically corresponds to the layer L_i at which the prediction confidence C_i transitions from rapid growth to a stable plateau. As illustrated in Fig. 2, we assume that C_i exhibits a stable plateau, consisting of an increasing interval followed by a stable interval in the ideal case. For clarity, we denote the narrow layer range where C_i shifts from increasing to stable as the *turning interval.* Motivated by this observation, we design an interval-based Early Exit mechanism based on first trend sampling (S_1). Specifically, the sampling stage S_1 starts from layer $L_{P_{S_1}}$ and aims to detect whether $C_i \geq \tau_C$ is detected as early as possible, allowing premature termination of inference. The sampling of C_i is restricted to the shallow interval of S_1, while layers outside the interval bypass the confidence computation, thus avoiding unnecessary inference overhead.

However, single-stage trend sampling is inherently limited. When the sampling position P_{S_1} deviates from the true turning interval, the model can still operate within the increasing interval, where both the magnitude of C_i and its smoothness are unreliable indicators of inference sufficiency. To mitigate this issue, we further introduce second-stage trend sampling S_2. The sampling stage S_2 is activated when S_1 fails to trigger an exit and is conducted at a deeper interval starting from $L_{P_{S_2}}$. By $smoothness_{S_1}$ and $smoothness_{S_2}$ captured from two Samplings, the model can more accurately infer its relative position with respect to the turning interval. This provides a reliable foundation for the subsequent adaptive adjustment of the confidence threshold τ_C and the self-optimization of the first sampling position P_{S_1}. The distinct confidence trend captured by the two sampling stages is illustrated in Fig. 6.

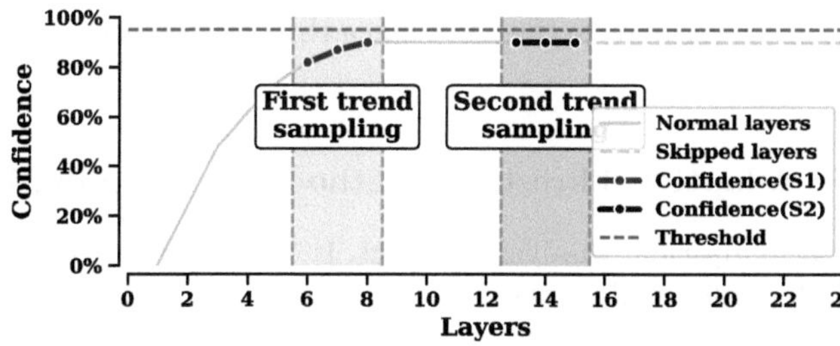

Fig. 3. Effectiveness of Hierarchical Confidence Trend Sampling.

To quantify the prediction confidence C_i in the intermediate layer L_i, we evaluate the confidence of the hidden representation $\mathbf{h}_i$ within the sampling intervals S_k. Specifically, $\mathbf{h}_i$ is projected into the vocabulary space through the final shared LM head, producing a logit vector. The logits are normalized by a Softmax function to obtain the predictive distribution: $P_{i,j} = \frac{\exp(x_{i,j})}{\sum_{k=1}^{|\mathcal{V}|} \exp(x_{i,k})}$. we define the layer-wise prediction confidence as the margin between the Top-1 and Top-2 probabilities (Fig. 3):

$$C_i = P_{i,\text{top}-1} - P_{i,\text{top}-2}, \tag{1}$$

where $P_{i,\text{top}-1}$ and $P_{i,\text{top}-2}$ represent the largest and second-largest values in P_i, respectively. A larger C_i indicates greater certainty of prediction at layer L_i.

Nevertheless, a confidence value C_i computed at a single layer is insufficient to characterize inference sufficiency across the entire network. As discussed in Sect. 1, the cross-layer confidence sequence $\{C_i\}$ typically exhibits a "rapid-increase followed by stabilization"pattern, under which transient fluctuations in individual C_i values cannot be reliably distinguished from genuine convergence when considered in isolation. To address this issue, we newly design a hierarchical trend sampling mechanism $\{S_k\}_{k=1}^{2}$ to explicitly model the confidence trend across depth.

For the k-th sampling stage S_k, we quantify the stability of the confidence sequence within its sampling interval by the smoothness metric:

$$smoothness_{S_k} = \mathrm{Var}\left(C_i, C_{i+1}, \ldots, C_{i+|S_k|-1}\right), \tag{2}$$

where P_{S_k} denotes the index of the initial layer in stage S_k, and $|S_k|$ represents the length of the corresponding interval. A smaller value of $smoothness_{S_k}$ reflects a more stable confidence trend, which in turn indicates convergence of the model's predictions.

Further, early-exit decisions are made jointly considering layer-wise confidence and interval-level smoothness. Specifically, inference ends at layer L_i when either of the following conditions is satisfied:

$$C_i \geq \tau_C \quad \vee \quad smoothness_{S_k} \leq \tau_{smoothness}, \tag{3}$$

where τ_C and $\tau_{smoothness}$ denote the confidence threshold and stability threshold, respectively.

3.2 Dynamic Adaptive Threshold Method via Sampling Features

Motivated by the empirical analysis in Sect. 1, we observe that across different datasets and model scales, the cross-layer confidence sequence C_i during inference exhibits a consistent trend: C_i increases rapidly at shallow layers and gradually converges to a stable plateau at deeper layers. The primary variations lie in the location of the transition region and the stabilized confidence magnitude. As illustrated by the red box in Fig. 4a, we denote the narrow layer interval where C_i transitions from rapid growth to stabilization as the *turning interval.*

We consider a practical deployment scenario in which an LLM is initialized with arbitrary hyperparameters. The optimization objective of DATEE is to jointly adapt the confidence threshold τ_C and the first sampling position P_{S_1} based on sampling outcomes, such that they align with the model state and input difficulty under the current inference setting. Since only confidence statistics within the sampled stages S_k are observable, the turning interval must be inferred indirectly from the sampling signals. In practice, this interaction gives rise to five composite cases:

Case 1: τ_C is slightly lower than the stabilized confidence level near the end of the turning interval, and P_{S_1} lies within the turning interval. Early exit may be triggered either by confidence-based criteria ($C_i \geq \tau_C$, Case 1.1) or by smoothness-based criteria ($smoothness_{S_1} \leq \tau_{smoothness}$, Case 1.2).

Case 2: τ_C is excessively high and P_{S_1} is too shallow, resulting in insufficient C_i and large $smoothness_{S_1}$ at the first sampling. Termination of LLM inference is postponed to the second-stage sampling process, denoted as S_2, or may not occur at all.

Case 3: τ_C is excessively high, while P_{S_1} is too deep, leading to insufficient C_i but small $smoothness_{S_1}$ at S_1, which directly triggers a smoothness-based exit.

Case 4: τ_C is excessively low and P_{S_1} is too shallow, causing an immediate confidence-based exit at S_1 without observing deeper confidence trends.

Case 5: τ_C is excessively low and P_{S_1} is too deep, similarly resulting in premature confidence-based exit at S_1 with limited trend information.

When an exit step is triggered at the first sampling S_1, the observed signals alone are insufficient to determine whether the exit occurs within the ideal turning interval or is caused by an overly small confidence threshold τ_C. In this case, τ_C is increased to promote activation of second-stage sampling S_2, while the sampling position P_{S_1} remains unchanged. In contrast, when historical exits

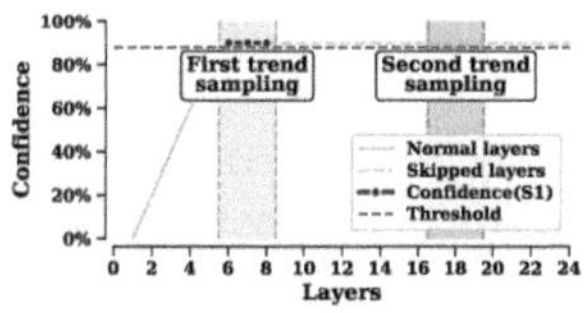

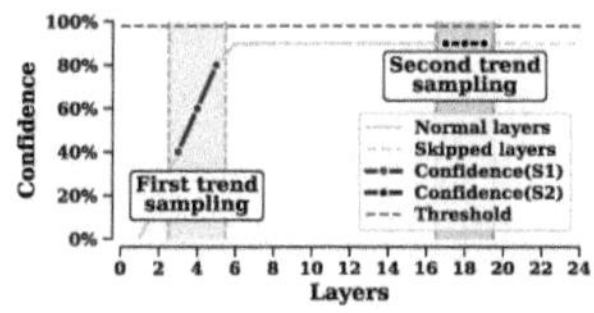

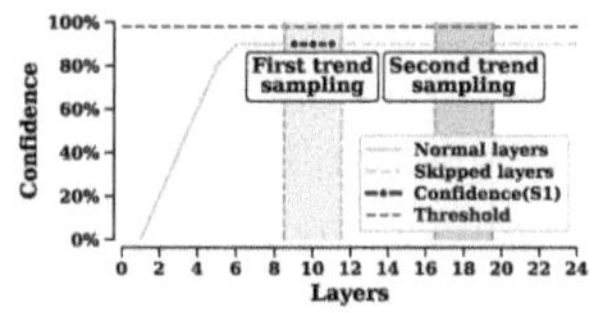

(a) Case 1: Optimal τ_C and P_{S_1} (b) Case 2: τ_C too high, P_{S_1} too shallow (c) Case 3: τ_C too high, P_{S_1} too deep

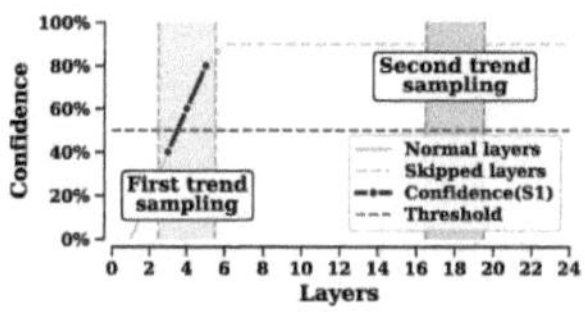

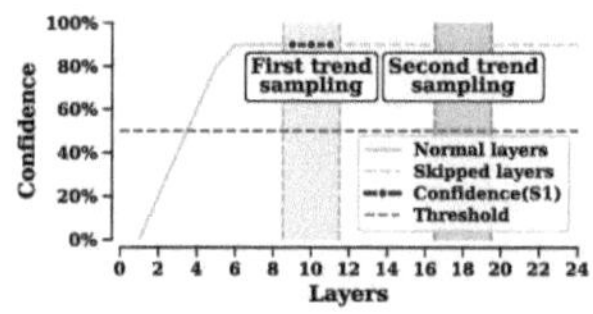

(d) Case 4: τ_C too low, P_{S_1} too shallow (e) Case 5: τ_C too low, P_{S_1} too deep

Fig. 4. Illustration of five Cases for τ_C and P_{S_1} settings.

$\mathcal{H}$ fall into Case 1.2, Case 2 or Case 3, the inference process terminates predominantly due to smoothness-based criteria, typically after deeper sampling. Under these conditions, τ_C decreases and the sampling position P_{S_1} is adjusted according to the outcome of S_2.

Specifically, in Case 2, τ_C is decreased and P_{S_1} is shifted deeper to approach the turning interval, while in Case 3, τ_C is decreased and P_{S_1} is shifted shallower. Cases 4 and 5 are empirically indistinguishable and therefore share the same update rule, that is, a monotonic increase of τ_C. As τ_C progressively aligns with the underlying confidence distribution of inference samples, the system naturally transitions toward Case 2 or Case 3, allowing finer-grained adjustment of P_{S_1}.

Through iterative updates, the exit statistics $\mathcal{H}$ converge to an alternating mixture of confidence-based exits and smoothness-based exits corresponding to the two subcases of Case 1. At convergence, the adaptive threshold τ_C reaches equilibrium with both the model and task characteristics. In practice, the relative proportions of the two exit modes are governed by the threshold update step Δ_{τ_C} and the sampling position adjustment rate Δ_P.

4 Experiments

We evaluate DATEE on multiple public datasets to validate its advantages in inference efficiency and task performance. The primary metrics are F1-Score [14], BLEU [10], and ROUGE-L [8], measuring task accuracy and text generation quality across different settings.

4.1 Experiment Setups

We use three datasets: SQuAD [14] for extractive question answering and reading comprehension; BIGPatent [16] for long-text understanding and generation on patent documents; and WMT19 [4] for machine translation, assessing text generation quality and cross-lingual transfer capability.

We adopt T5-large [12] as the baseline model, a Transformer-based sequence-to-sequence model with strong understanding and generation capacity. Comparative experiments on the three datasets analyze performance across task scenarios, providing a consistent reference for Early Exit evaluation.

4.2 Results and Analysis

Table 1. Performance and speedup comparison under varying initial confidence thresholds (τ_C). T5-large uses full inference, so τ_C does not apply. Note that for DATEE and FREE, reported results correspond to the converged adaptive threshold, independent of initialization.

Method	τ_C					
	0.6	0.7	0.8	0.9	0.95	0.995
F1 (×Speedup) on SQuAD						
T5-large	91.26(×1.0)	–	–	–	–	–
FREE	91.30(×2.5)	91.30(×2.5)	91.30(×2.5)	91.30(×2.5)	91.30(×2.5)	91.30(×2.5)
CALM	90.17(×4.9)	90.58(×4.6)	90.91(×4.3)	91.15(×3.7)	91.28(×3.3)	91.31(×2.2)
DATEE	91.36(×2.8)	91.36(×2.8)	91.36(×2.8)	91.36(×2.8)	91.36(×2.8)	91.36(×2.8)
Rouge-L (×Speedup) on BigPatent						
T5-large	44.36(×1.0)	–	–	–	–	–
FREE	17.35(×1.5)	17.35(×1.5)	17.35(×1.5)	17.35(×1.5)	17.35(×1.5)	17.35(×1.5)
CALM	9.00(×1.7)	9.24(×1.6)	9.61(×1.5)	10.39(×1.5)	10.84(×1.4)	13.48(×1.2)
DATEE	26.11(×1.4)	26.11(×1.4)	26.11(×1.4)	26.11(×1.4)	26.11(×1.4)	26.11(×1.4)
BLEU (×Speedup) on WMT19						
T5-large	38.47(×1.0)	–	–	–	–	–
FREE	25.20(×1.1)	25.20(×1.1)	25.20(×1.1)	25.20(×1.1)	25.20(×1.1)	25.20(×1.1)
CALM	3.00(×2.0)	4.21(×1.9)	6.69(×1.7)	11.02(×1.5)	15.57(×1.4)	29.62(×1.2)
DATEE	35.25(×1.2)	35.25(×1.2)	35.25(×1.2)	35.25(×1.2)	35.25(×1.2)	35.25(×1.2)

Table 1 demonstrates that methods lacking dynamic adaptation (such as CALM, which exhibits high sensitivity to τ_C), and methods with limited online threshold adjustment (e.g., FREE). Lower thresholds yield higher speedups but severely degrade accuracy (e.g., on WMT19, BLEU drops to 3.00 at $\tau_C = 0.6$).

In contrast, DATEE **eliminates hyperparameter sensitivity**, maintaining constant high performance across all τ_C settings (e.g., stable F1 of **91.36** on SQuAD). While FREE also achieves stability, DATEE significantly outperforms it. For instance, on WMT19, DATEE achieves a BLEU score of 35.25 compared to FREE's 25.20, while simultaneously offering a better speedup (×1.2 vs. ×1.1).

This indicates that DATEE finds a superior calibration point, terminating inference at shallower layers (avg. 20.32) without the performance penalty seen in FREE (avg. 21.23).

Consistent with Sect. 3.2, DATEE captures the discrepancy between τ_C and the confidence in the data's turning interval via hierarchical trend sampling. This allows the threshold to converge to the optimal "turning interval," dynamically adapting to input difficulty. This "plug-and-play" capability liberates users from precise threshold calibration.

Despite its robustness, a performance gap remains on generative tasks (BigPatent, WMT19). This is mainly due to their reliance on deeper semantic accumulation, where early exiting may truncate long-range dependencies. While DATEE adapts thresholds via confidence trends, it does not explicitly model sequence-level coherence, leading to a trade-off between efficiency and generation quality.

Summary: Regardless of initialization, DATEE spontaneously converges to a configuration that matches or exceeds baseline performance with significant acceleration, consistently outperforming other baselines.

4.3 Ablation Study I: Sensitivity to Initial τ_C and P_{S_1} Configuration

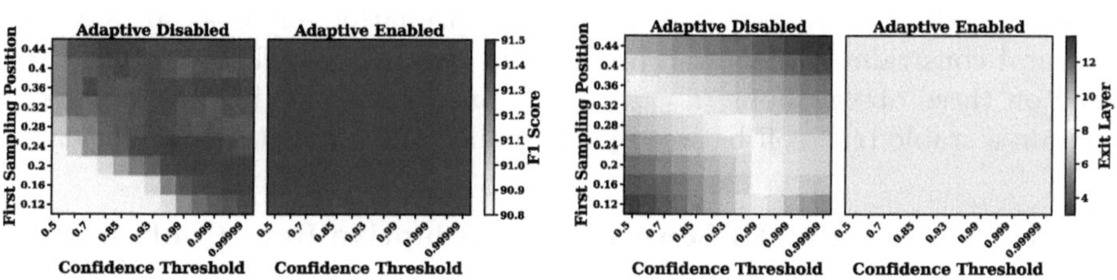

Fig. 5. Impact of DATEE Adaptive Threshold on initial τ_C and P_{S_1}. Evaluation performance (Left: F1 score, white vs. green) and computational cost (Right: exit layer, red vs. blue in Fig. b)

As shown in Fig. 5, **Adaptive Threshold effectively eliminates parameter sensitivity.** Without it (left), model performance varies significantly across parameter configurations. In contrast, **enabling AT yields an almost perfectly flat performance distribution** (right). This sharp contrast demonstrates that AT consistently finds an optimal equilibrium regardless of initial settings. As the heatmaps indicate, the F1 score becomes uniform across the entire $\tau_C \times P_{S_1}$ space, while the exit layer distribution converges to a stable, efficient point. These results confirm that DATEE's adaptive mechanism removes the need for hyperparameter tuning, ensuring robust performance independent of the starting configuration.

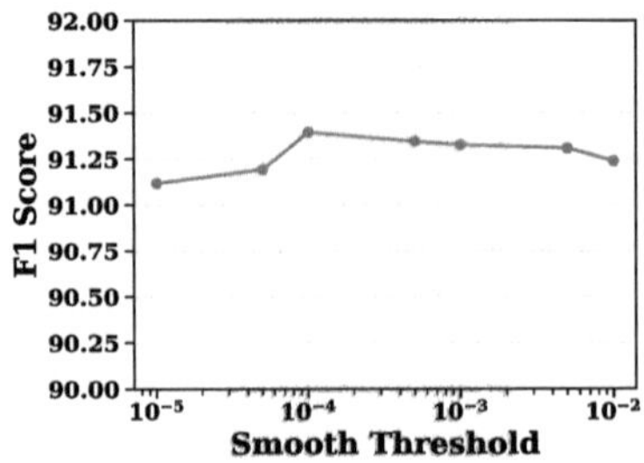

Fig. 6. Impact of DATEE Adaptive Threshold on initial $\tau_{smoothness}$

4.4 Ablation Study II: Sensitivity to Initial $\tau_{smoothness}$

As shown in Fig. 6, we evaluate the impact of $\tau_{smoothness}$ over a wide range. The results exhibit a relatively smooth unimodal trend: performance reaches its optimum at $\tau_{smoothness} \approx 10^{-3}$ (F1 = 91.39), while slightly decreasing for both larger and smaller values. Further analysis shows that a larger $\tau_{smoothness}$ may cause premature stability detection, while an overly small value enforces strict constraints that delay exits and increase unnecessary computation.

Overall, $\tau_{smoothness}$ demonstrates relatively low sensitivity, with performance variation consistently within 0.25 F1, which is smaller than that observed for τ_C and P_{S_1}. This indicates that $\tau_{smoothness}$ primarily serves as an auxiliary structural constraint rather than a dominant control variable in early exiting. Based on these observations, $\tau_{smoothness}$ is fixed in the DATEE framework to maintain a stable trade-off between performance and computational efficiency.

4.5 Ablation Study III: Sensitivity to Adaptive Rate Configuration

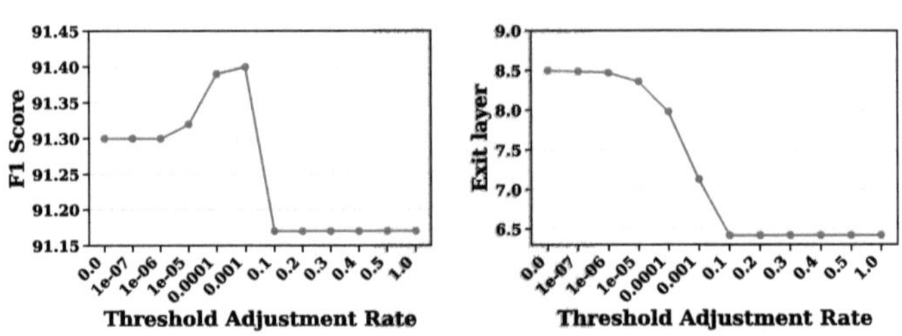

(a) F1 score distribution (b) Exit layer distribution

Fig. 7. Impact of different threshold adjustment rates on inference performance.

Finally, we investigate DATEE's sensitivity to the *Threshold Adjustment Rate ($\Delta\tau$)*. Figure 7 reveals that aggressive adjustment rates ($\Delta\tau \in [0.1, 1.0]$) cause the threshold to stagnate at suboptimal levels (F1 ≈ 91.17) with extremely shallow exit layers (≈ 6.4). This indicates that excessive relaxation triggers **threshold oscillation**, causing premature exits before sufficient semantic accumulation, thereby degrading performance. A clear phase transition occurs around $\Delta\tau \approx 10^{-3}$, where the F1 score peaks at 91.40 with an average exit layer of 7.1. This convergence point represents an optimal efficiency-performance trade-off—significantly accelerating simple samples while remaining conservative enough to process difficult inputs at deeper layers.

5 Conclusion

We proposed DATEE, a dynamic adaptive threshold early exit framework that accelerates large language model inference without additional training cost. Motivated by the observation that intermediate-layer confidence typically exhibits a rapid-growth–to–stabilization trend, DATEE departs from static thresholding and instead exploits cross-layer confidence evolution for exit control. DATEE uses hierarchical confidence trend sampling to capture both early growth and later stabilization. From these trends, a dynamic strategy jointly adjusts the confidence threshold and first-stage sampling position during inference, aligning automatically with the confidence turning interval. On SQuAD, BigPatent, and WMT19, DATEE consistently reduces inference depth and computation while maintaining performance. It is robust to initialization, removes manual threshold tuning, and provides a lightweight, plug-and-play solution for stable, efficient early-exit inference.

Despite these advantages, DATEE adopts static settings for the second-stage sampling position and the smoothness threshold, which may not fully adapt to diverse confidence trajectories across datasets. Our future work will investigate adaptive multi-stage sampling schemes with dynamically optimized sampling positions, as well as a deeper analysis of atypical confidence trends from hard or out-of-distribution samples to refine the smoothness criterion for more robust stabilization modeling.

Acknowledgements. This work was financially supported by the Youth Innovation Promotion Association CAS (2023120) and the National Natural Science Foundation of China (62002350).

References

1. Bae, S., Ko, J., Song, H., Yun, S.Y.: Fast and robust early-exiting framework for autoregressive language models with synchronized parallel decoding. arXiv preprint arXiv:2310.05424 (2023)
2. Bai, G., et al.: Beyond efficiency: A systematic survey of resource-efficient large language models. arXiv preprint arXiv:2401.00625 (2024)
3. Elhoushi, M., et al.: Layerskip: enabling early exit inference and self-speculative decoding. In: Proceedings of the 62nd Annual Meeting of the Association for Computational Linguistics (Volume 1: Long Papers), pp. 12622–12642 (2024)

4. Fonseca, E., Yankovskaya, L., Martins, A.F., Fishel, M., Federmann, C.: Findings of the wmt 2019 shared tasks on quality estimation. In: Proceedings of the Fourth Conference on Machine Translation (Volume 3: Shared Task Papers, Day 2), pp. 1–10 (2019)
5. Hu, B., Zhu, Y., Li, J., Tang, S.: Smartbert: a promotion of dynamic early exiting mechanism for accelerating bert inference. arXiv preprint arXiv:2303.09266 (2023)
6. Laskaridis, S., Kouris, A., Lane, N.D.: Adaptive inference through early-exit networks: Design, challenges and directions. In: Proceedings of the 5th International Workshop on Embedded and Mobile Deep Learning, pp. 1–6 (2021)
7. Li, B., Jiang, Y., Gadepally, V., Tiwari, D.: Llm inference serving: survey of recent advances and opportunities. In: 2024 IEEE High Performance Extreme Computing Conference (HPEC), pp. 1–8. IEEE (2024)
8. Lin, C.Y.: Rouge: A package for automatic evaluation of summaries. In: Text summarization branches out, pp. 74–81 (2004)
9. Liu, W., Zhou, P., Wang, Z., Zhao, Z., Deng, H., Ju, Q.: Fastbert: a self-distilling bert with adaptive inference time. In: Proceedings of the 58th annual meeting of the association for computational linguistics, pp. 6035–6044 (2020)
10. apineni, K., Roukos, S., Ward, T., Zhu, W.J.: Bleu: a method for automatic evaluation of machine translation. In: Proceedings of the 40th Annual Meeting of the Association for Computational Linguistics, pp. 311–318 (2002)
11. Qu, G., Chen, Q., Wei, W., Lin, Z., Chen, X., Huang, K.: Mobile edge intelligence for large language models: A contemporary survey. IEEE Communications Surveys & Tutorials (2025)
12. Raffel, C., Shazeer, N., Roberts, A., Lee, K., Narang, S., Matena, M., Zhou, Y., Li, W., Liu, P.J.: Exploring the limits of transfer learning with a unified text-to-text transformer. J. Mach. Learn. Res. **21**(140), 1–67 (2020)
13. Rahmath P, H., Srivastava, V., Chaurasia, K., Pacheco, R.G., Couto, R.S.: Early-exit deep neural network-a comprehensive survey. ACM Comput. Surv. **57**(3), 1–37 (2024)
14. Rajpurkar, P., Zhang, J., Lopyrev, K., Liang, P.: Squad: 100,000+ questions for machine comprehension of text. arXiv preprint arXiv:1606.05250 (2016)
15. Schuster, T., Fisch, A., Gupta, J., Dehghani, M., Bahri, D., Tran, V., Tay, Y., Metzler, D.: Confident adaptive language modeling. Adv. Neural. Inf. Process. Syst. **35**, 17456–17472 (2022)
16. Sharma, E., Li, C., Wang, L.: Bigpatent: A large-scale dataset for abstractive and coherent summarization. arXiv preprint arXiv:1906.03741 (2019)
17. Teerapittayanon, S., McDanel, B., Kung, H.T.: Branchynet: fast inference via early exiting from deep neural networks. In: 2016 23rd international conference on pattern recognition (ICPR), pp. 2464–2469. IEEE (2016)
18. Vaswani, A., et al.: Attention is all you need. Advances in neural information processing systems **30** (2017)
19. Zhou, W., Xu, C., Ge, T., McAuley, J., Xu, K., Wei, F.: Bert loses patience: fast and robust inference with early exit. Adv. Neural. Inf. Process. Syst. **33**, 18330–18341 (2020)
20. Zhou, Z., et al.: A survey on efficient inference for large language models. arXiv preprint arXiv:2404.14294 (2024)

Variational Bayesian Gradient Inversion Attack with Diffusion Models in Federated Learning

Linwei Fang[1,2], Zhen Xu[1(✉)], Yan Zhang[1], Mingxuan Li[3], and He Wang[1]

[1] Institute of Information Engineering, Chinese Academy of Sciences, Beijing, China
{fanglinwei,xuzhen,zhangyan,wanghe6029}@iie.ac.cn

[2] School of Cyber Security, University of Chinese Academy of Sciences, Beijing, China

[3] School of Criminal Investigation, People's Public Security University of China, Beijing, China
20236990@ppsuc.edu.cn

Abstract. Federated learning is a distributed learning paradigm, where each client jointly trains a global model by only sharing gradients. Nevertheless, previous research has shown that the shared gradients can be used to privacy leakage, i.e., the so-called gradient inversion attack. Notably, existing attack studies have some generic shortcomings, such as insufficient theoretical guarantee and poor reconstruction when given difficult conditions. In our work, based on variational Bayesian theory, we propose a gradient inversion attack combined with the novel diffusion models, exploiting its remarkable expressiveness of image manifold to improve the inverted results. Compared with existing research, we provide elaborate theoretical analysis for our attack, showing its good adaptability in face of two real-world attack scenarios, namely as sample-level and user-level inversion. Through comprehensive validations under diverse datasets and realistic circumstances, we hope that our work can help understand and evaluate such privacy risk in federated learning.

Keywords: Federated learning · Gradient inversion · Privacy attack · Variational Bayesian · Diffusion models

1 Introduction

In these years, federated learning (FL) has been widely known as a privacy-preserving machine learning paradigm [14]. FL can train a shared global model by only exchanging local model updates, e.g., gradients, without directly transmitting clients' privacy data out of local devices. The privacy-preserving attribute of FL has made it widely applied in many privacy-sensitive tasks [17]. However, recent research has shown that the attacker can possibly retrieve some sensitive information of the original training data merely from gradients, which is commonly referred to as *gradient inversion* attack [23].

J. Niu et al. (Eds.): KSEM 2026, LNAI 16631, pp. 589–604, 2027.
https://doi.org/10.1007/978-981-92-2759-4_43

Existing research normally models the gradient attack as an iterative optimization problem, with a primary gradient matching objective [23]. To obtain high-quality and accurate data leakage, recently, a line of attacks focus on introducing various image knowledge to aid in reconstruction, namely as image priors, such as total variation [7], norm-clip [8] or BN statistics [19]. Another kind of GAN-based methods [6,12,13] also introduce the generative image prior by utilizing GANs. However, these existing methods can only achieve limited reconstruction performance, especially when dealing with high-dimensional and large batch data, let alone more challenging cases with defenses applied.

Recently, diffusion models, like DDPMs [11], as a kind of emerging generative model, has been applied in many downstream vision inversion tasks [4], such as image denoising and inpainting, which demonstrates its potential as a powerful prior to solve image inverse problems. Therefore, one crucial motivation of our work is to study how diffusion models can enhance the solution of gradient inversion on image data.

In our work, by utilizing the Bayesian attack framework [1], we innovatively apply diffusion models into gradient inversion via a variational perspective, meanwhile addressing certain obstacles in both theory and implementation. Specifically, to cope with the intractable and nonlinear gradient inversion, we adopt diffusion models by fully exploiting innate characters of diffusion image prior at different timesteps. Through comprehensive experimental validation, our method can achieve significant improvement over previous approaches, showing good robustness in face of difficult circumstances.

Notably, we conclude most existing research as *sample-level* inversion, which aims to exactly reconstruct pixel-level details of targeted images. Moreover, regarding the case of cross-device FL, where extreme label imbalance is common in training batches, we correspondingly propose another *user-level* inversion, with the goal of retrieving a prototypical image that can recover enough semantics of targeted class, which gains little attention in previous research.

The main contributions of our work are summarized as follows:

1. Based on variational Bayesian theory, we elaborately integrate diffusion models into gradient inversion attack, obtaining improved performance than previous works. To our best knowledge, it is the first research that applies diffusion models in gradient inversion through one variational method.
2. Based on comprehensive analysis, we specially design a set of components for our attack framework, including the single denoising matching term, sliding weighting window and image random transformation. We also conduct grid searches for each critical hyperparameter to adapt various scenarios.
3. We validate the superiority of our approach on diverse datasets, even under difficult circumstances involved with defensive mechanisms. To sum up, regardless of pixel-level reconstruction accuracy or semantic similarity, our approach can achieve significant improvement over the state-of-the-art methods, as up to 35% on generic metrics such as PSNR, demonstrating the necessity of higher vigilance to the privacy leakage in federated learning.

2 Related Work

2.1 Gradient Inversion Attacks in FL

Recently, gradient inversion attack has been widely recognized as a specialized attack surface in federated learning [22]. DLG [23] first formulates such privacy attack as an iterative optimization problem. Following works [7,8,18,19] try to utilize various image-domain knowledge to enhance the reconstructed results, by directly adding diverse prior regularization into the optimization objective. Besides, another series of GAN-based methods also introduce the GAN prior through optimizing on latent space [13], alternate spaces [12] or intermediate feature spaces [6]. Moreover, work [1] builds a Bayesian attack framework on gradient inversion, concluding several previous attacks, while does not study the integration of more powerful priors, such as diffusion models.

2.2 Solving Inverse Problems with Diffusion Models

Diffusion models have emerged as a state-of-the-art generative model. Lately, several works have applied it to common image inversion tasks, such as image restoration and denoising [4]. Generally, these approaches can be divided into two categories, e.g., guided samplings or variational methods. The former ones have to directly estimate the posterior score at any timesteps by projection [2] or reconstruction guidance [3], with inevitable approximate errors. Besides, the latter ones otherwise approximate the true posterior distribution with a simpler and tractable distribution [10], and learn that simple distribution by optimization.

3 Preliminaries

3.1 Typical Formulation of Gradient Inversion Attack

Considering an image classification FL task consisting of a central server and a set of C clients, their goal is to jointly train a $\boldsymbol{W}$-parameterized neural network $f_{\boldsymbol{W}}(\cdot)$. In each training round, the c-th client independently trains on its local dataset $\mathbb{D}^c$ and subsequently transfers its updated gradients $\nabla \boldsymbol{W}^c$ to the server. After that, the server, as a *semi-honest* adversary, tries to use the observed gradients $\nabla \boldsymbol{W}^c$ to reconstruct the local dataset $\mathbb{D}^c$.

Specifically, the updated gradients computed by the c-th client during one local training procedure is

$$\nabla \boldsymbol{W} = \frac{1}{B} \sum_{i=1}^{B} \nabla_{\boldsymbol{W}} \ell(f_{\boldsymbol{W}}(\boldsymbol{x}_i), y_i) \,. \tag{1}$$

Without loss of generality, the superscript c is omitted. The local dataset is $\mathbb{D}^B = \{(\boldsymbol{x}_i, y_i)\}_{i \in B}$, where $(\boldsymbol{x}_i, y_i)$ denote the i-th pair of image and label. The training loss ℓ is usually a sample-wise function, e.g., cross-entropy.

Previous studies [19] have shown that the labels can be restored separately in an analytical manner. Therefore, assuming the labels are known, to obtain the reconstructed $\{\boldsymbol{x}_i^*\}_{i\in B}$, most existing research generally regards the gradient inversion attack as the following optimization problem:

$$\underset{\{\boldsymbol{x}_i^*\}_{i\in B}}{\arg\min}\, \underbrace{\mathcal{L}_{\mathrm{GM}}(\frac{1}{B}\sum_{i=1}^{B}\nabla_{\boldsymbol{W}}\ell(f_{\boldsymbol{W}}(\boldsymbol{x}_i^*));\nabla\boldsymbol{W})}_{\text{(i) } gradient\ matching} + \underbrace{\mathcal{R}_{\mathrm{AUX}}(\boldsymbol{X}^*)}_{\text{(ii) } image\ regularization}, \tag{2}$$

where the term (i) is the gradient matching term with optional metrics, e.g., Euclidean distance [23] or Cosine distance [7]. Due to the intractability of gradient inversion, most studies tend to additionally adopt image regularization term (ii), to enhance the reconstruction by introducing some handcrafted prior knowledge.

As research [1] points out, the gradient inversion attack can be reformulated in terms of Bayesian inference, where the gradient inversion attack can be regarded as a maximum a posteriori sampling on $\log p(\boldsymbol{x}|\nabla\boldsymbol{W}) \propto \log p(\nabla\boldsymbol{W}|\boldsymbol{x}) + \log p(\boldsymbol{x})$. For the adversary, the known global model $f_{\boldsymbol{W}}(\cdot)$ can be used to establish a log-likelihood $\log p(\nabla\boldsymbol{W}|\boldsymbol{x})$, acting the same as $\mathcal{L}_{\mathrm{GM}}$ in (2); while some additional domain knowledge can be used to determine a log-prior $\log p(\boldsymbol{x})$, corresponding to $\mathcal{R}_{\mathrm{AUX}}$ in (2).

3.2 Targeted Attack Scenarios

Like the most common research, our work bases on the fundamental *semi-honest* scenario [7], where the honest-but-curious server acts as the adversary, intercepting the clients' shared gradients and carrying out the inversion attack. Moreover, we assume the adversary can utilize some useful domain knowledge, from basic natural image prior to well-pretrained generative models.

In our work, we are specially interested in two typical attack scenarios, namely sample-level and user-level inversion. For **sample-level inversion**, the local training set can be denoted as $\mathbb{D} = \{(\boldsymbol{x}_1, y_1)\}$, The attack target is to precisely reconstruct the original sample's pixel-level detail. This is the simplest attack scenario, sufficient to evaluate the upper-bound capability of different attacks. For **user-level inversion**, the local training set is a batch with the same class $\tilde{y}$, i.e., $\mathbb{D} = \{(\boldsymbol{x}_i, \tilde{y})\}_{i\in B}$. The attack target is to recover a representative prototype from the averaged $\overline{\nabla\boldsymbol{W}}$, which should hold sufficient semantic restoration. This is a realistic and worth-studying scenario, as in cross-device FL, non-i.i.d. data is common [17], where each local dataset is collected from one unique user.

4 Methodology

In this section, we first propose our variational Bayesian gradient attack with diffusion models in Sect. 4.1. Then, we justify critical components of our attack in Sect. 4.2. A workflow of our attack framework is in Fig. 1.

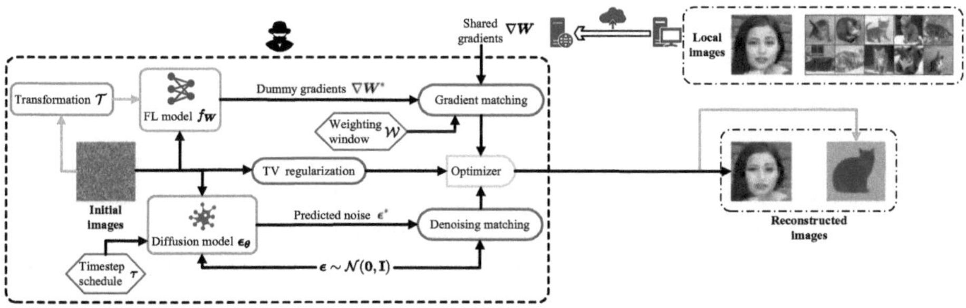

Fig. 1. The pipeline of our attack framework, showing each critical component. Note that the yellow paths denote the added workflows of our proposed user-level inversion in contrast to sample-level inversion. (Color figure online)

4.1 Variational Bayesian Gradient Attack with Diffusion Models

In this section, we show how to integrate one classic type of diffusion models, i.e., DDPMs, into gradient inversion via a variational Bayesian perspective. Note that our following discussion is based on the Bayesian attack framework described in work [1], and notations of DDPMs [11]. Thus, the key issue we need to address is how to extract and utilize the image prior knowledge $p_{\boldsymbol{\theta}}(\boldsymbol{x}_0)$ from pretrained diffusion models, namely the diffusion prior, and sample on a tractable $p(\boldsymbol{x}|\nabla\boldsymbol{W})$. Our discussion starts from the basic sample-level inversion.

Sample-Level Inversion. As described in DDPMs, diffusion models define a joint $p_{\boldsymbol{\theta}}(\boldsymbol{x}_{0:T})$ of latent variables $\{\boldsymbol{x}_t\}_{1:T}$ and original data $\boldsymbol{x}_0$, i.e., the **reverse process**. In order to smoothly introduce the diffusion prior, we choose to incorporate the latent variables $\boldsymbol{x}_{1:T}$ into the Bayesian framework (depicted in Sect. 3.1 and [1]) together with $\boldsymbol{x}_0$, i.e., considering sampling on $p(\boldsymbol{x}_{0:T}|\nabla\boldsymbol{W})$, and give the following lemma to facilitate subsequent derivation.

Lemma 1. *In terms of gradient inversion, the gradients* $\nabla\boldsymbol{W}$*, original data* $\boldsymbol{x}_0$*, and latent variables* $\{\boldsymbol{x}_t\}_{1:T}$*, owing to their innate relations, must obey a bidirectional Markov chain, meaning that the following equations hold true:*

$$p(\nabla\boldsymbol{W}|\boldsymbol{x}_{0:T}) = p(\nabla\boldsymbol{W}|\boldsymbol{x}_0)\,, \tag{3}$$

$$q(\boldsymbol{x}_{0:T}|\nabla\boldsymbol{W}) = q(\boldsymbol{x}_{1:T}|\boldsymbol{x}_0)q(\boldsymbol{x}_0|\nabla\boldsymbol{W})\,. \tag{4}$$

Obviously, based on Lemma 1, we can determine the targeted $p(\boldsymbol{x}_{0:T}|\nabla\boldsymbol{W})$ with known $p_{\boldsymbol{\theta}}(\boldsymbol{x}_{0:T})$ and $p(\nabla\boldsymbol{W}|\boldsymbol{x}_0)$. However, it is still intractable to sample on such complex posterior. Hence, by means of variational inference, we use a simplified variational posterior $\tilde{q}$ to approximate the real posterior p. Given Lemma 1 and the known $q(\boldsymbol{x}_{1:T}|\boldsymbol{x}_0)$, i.e., the **forward process** of DDPMs, to construct a variational posterior $\tilde{q}(\boldsymbol{x}_{0:T}|\nabla\boldsymbol{W})$, all we need to assume is a variational condition $\tilde{q}(\boldsymbol{x}_0|\nabla\boldsymbol{W})$. Without loss of generality, we initialize it as a Dirac distribution $\delta(\boldsymbol{x}_0 - \boldsymbol{x}^*)$, parameterized by $\boldsymbol{x}^*$. After that, to solve the unknown $\boldsymbol{x}^*$, we can optimize the following objective in principle of variational inference:

$$\arg\min_{\boldsymbol{x}^*} KL\left(\tilde{q}(\boldsymbol{x}_{0:T}|\nabla \boldsymbol{W}) \,||\, p(\boldsymbol{x}_{0:T}|\nabla \boldsymbol{W})\right) . \tag{5}$$

As depicted in literature [15], the minimization of such inverse KL will prompt the variational $\tilde{q}$ to seek a significant mode of the real posterior p, meaning that we can obtain a fine inverted result $\boldsymbol{x}^*$ by optimizing (5).

Hereinafter, we describe the further derivation in detail. Expanding the KL divergence in (5), we have

$$\begin{aligned}
&\mathbb{E}_{\tilde{q}}\left[-\log p(\nabla \boldsymbol{W}|\boldsymbol{x}_{0:T})\right] + KL\left(\tilde{q}(\boldsymbol{x}_{0:T}|\nabla \boldsymbol{W}) \,||\, p_{\boldsymbol{\theta}}(\boldsymbol{x}_{0:T})\right) + \log p(\nabla \boldsymbol{W}) \\
&= \mathbb{E}_{\tilde{q}}\left[-\log p(\nabla \boldsymbol{W}|\boldsymbol{x}_{0:T})\right] + \mathbb{E}_{\tilde{q}}\left[-\log \frac{p_{\boldsymbol{\theta}}(\boldsymbol{x}_{0:T})}{q(\boldsymbol{x}_{1:T}|\boldsymbol{x}_0)}\right] - \mathrm{H}(\tilde{q}(\boldsymbol{x}_0)) + \log p(\nabla \boldsymbol{W}) .
\end{aligned} \tag{6}$$

In (6), $\log p(\nabla \boldsymbol{W})$ is constant to $\boldsymbol{x}^*$, and $\mathrm{H}(\tilde{q})$ is normally regarded as 0 for the discrete Dirac $\tilde{q}$. Through subsequent simplification based on Lemma 1, we have the following objective:

$$\arg\min_{\boldsymbol{x}^*} -\log p(\nabla \boldsymbol{W}|\boldsymbol{x}^*) + \mathbb{E}_{\tilde{q}}\left[-\log \frac{p_{\boldsymbol{\theta}}(\boldsymbol{x}_{0:T})}{q(\boldsymbol{x}_{1:T}|\boldsymbol{x}_0)}\right] . \tag{7}$$

For the first log-likelihood term, as discussed in Sect. 3.1, we can directly substitute it with the gradient matching term in (2). For the second weighted variational bound, we can follow the parameterization in DDPMs, and finally get a denoising matching term like DDPMs. Additionally, to further enhance the reconstruction quality, we empirically add a total variation regularization.

All in all, the final objective is summarized as

$$\begin{aligned}
\arg\min_{\boldsymbol{x}^*} &\underbrace{\lambda_{gm}\mathcal{L}_{\mathrm{GM}}(\nabla_{\boldsymbol{W}}\ell(f_{\boldsymbol{W}}(\boldsymbol{x}^*)); \nabla \boldsymbol{W})}_{\text{(i) } \textit{gradient matching}} \\
&+ \underbrace{\lambda_{denoising}\mathbb{E}_{\boldsymbol{\epsilon}}\left[\left\|\boldsymbol{\epsilon} - \boldsymbol{\epsilon}_{\boldsymbol{\theta}}(\sqrt{\bar{\alpha}_\tau}\boldsymbol{x}^* + \sqrt{\bar{\beta}_\tau}\boldsymbol{\epsilon}, \tau)\right\|_2^2\right]}_{\text{(ii) } \textit{denoising matching}} \\
&+ \underbrace{\lambda_{tv}TV(\boldsymbol{x}^*)}_{\text{(iii) } \textit{total variation}} ,
\end{aligned} \tag{8}$$

where λ represent the flexible scaling factors to each objective term, requiring elaborate tuning. Note that different from the training objective in DDPMs, our method only conducts a single-timestep denoising matching in each iteration, related with a dynamic timestep schedule τ. We further discuss the setting of these components in Sect. 4.2.

User-Level Inversion. As depicted in Sect. 3.2, the goal of user-level attack is to recover a representative prototype $\hat{\boldsymbol{x}}$ of the original batch $\{\boldsymbol{x}_i\}_{i\in B}$, based on the observed averaged $\overline{\nabla \boldsymbol{W}}$. Considering the inherent variance among the original batch, we extra introduce a set of random image transformations $\{\mathcal{T}_i(\cdot)\}_{i\in B}$ to generate a dummy batch $\{\mathcal{T}_i(\hat{\boldsymbol{x}})\}_{i\in B}$. Intuitively, adopting such semantic-preserving and variance-simulating $\{\mathcal{T}_i(\hat{\boldsymbol{x}})\}_{i\in B}$ can better fit the original averaged $\overline{\nabla \boldsymbol{W}}$.

To sum up, given the targeted prototype $\hat{\boldsymbol{x}}$ and transformation $\{\mathcal{T}_i(\cdot)\}_{i\in B}$, the log-likelihood term in the Bayesian framework can be simply rewritten as $\log p(\overline{\nabla \boldsymbol{W}} | \{\mathcal{T}_i(\hat{\boldsymbol{x}})\}_{i\in B}) \rightarrow \log p(\overline{\nabla \boldsymbol{W}}|\hat{\boldsymbol{x}})$. Accordingly, the subsequent expansion and derivation is similar to the case of sample-level inversion. Here we directly give the final tractable objective:

$$
\begin{aligned}
\arg\min_{\hat{\boldsymbol{x}}} & \lambda_{gm}\mathcal{L}_{\mathrm{GM}}(\nabla_{\boldsymbol{W}}\ell(f_{\boldsymbol{W}}(\hat{\boldsymbol{x}})); \overline{\nabla \boldsymbol{W}}) \\
& + \lambda_{denoising}\mathbb{E}_{\boldsymbol{\epsilon}}\left[\left\| \boldsymbol{\epsilon} - \boldsymbol{\epsilon}_{\theta}(\sqrt{\bar{\alpha}_{\tau}}\hat{\boldsymbol{x}} + \sqrt{\bar{\beta}_{\tau}}\boldsymbol{\epsilon}, \tau)\right\|_2^2\right] \\
& + \lambda_{tv}TV(\hat{\boldsymbol{x}}) .
\end{aligned} \tag{9}
$$

The unified pseudocode of our method is in Algorithm 1. Note that we name it as **DiffGI**.

Algorithm 1: Variational Bayesian Gradient inversion attack with diffusion models (DiffGI)

Input: target model $f_{\boldsymbol{W}}$, observed gradients $\nabla \boldsymbol{W}$, pretrained DDPMs $\boldsymbol{\epsilon}_{\theta}$, iteration step S, timestep schedule τ, weighting window $\mathcal{W}$, learning rate η, (optional)random transformation $\mathcal{T}$, (optional)input batch size B.

Output: reconstructed image $\boldsymbol{x}^*$.

Initialize $\boldsymbol{x}^* \sim \mathcal{N}(\mathbf{0}, \mathbf{I})$;

for $n = 1, \ldots, S$ **do**

  Sample $\boldsymbol{\epsilon} \sim \mathcal{N}(\mathbf{0}, \mathbf{I})$;

  $\boldsymbol{x}_{\tau(n)} \leftarrow \sqrt{\bar{\alpha}_{\tau(n)}}\boldsymbol{x}^* + \sqrt{\bar{\beta}_{\tau(n)}}\boldsymbol{\epsilon}$;

  $\boldsymbol{g}_{denoising} \leftarrow \nabla_{\boldsymbol{x}^*} \left\|\boldsymbol{\epsilon} - \boldsymbol{\epsilon}_{\theta}(\boldsymbol{x}_{\tau(n)}, \tau(n))\right\|_2^2$;

  $\boldsymbol{g}_{tv} \leftarrow \nabla_{\boldsymbol{x}^*} TV(\boldsymbol{x}^*)$;

  if *User-level inversion* **then**

    `// User-level inversion`

    $\boldsymbol{g}_{gm} \leftarrow \nabla_{\boldsymbol{x}^*} \sum_{l=1}^{L} \mathcal{W}_l(n)\mathcal{L}_{\mathrm{GM}}(\{\mathcal{T}_i(\boldsymbol{x}^*)\}_{i\in B}; \nabla \boldsymbol{W}_l)$;

  else

    `// Sample-level inversion`

    $\boldsymbol{g}_{gm} \leftarrow \nabla_{\boldsymbol{x}^*} \sum_{l=1}^{L} \mathcal{W}_l(n)\mathcal{L}_{\mathrm{GM}}(\boldsymbol{x}^*; \nabla \boldsymbol{W}_l)$;

  $\boldsymbol{x}^* \leftarrow \boldsymbol{x}^* - \eta\left(\lambda_{denoising}\boldsymbol{g}_{denoising} + \lambda_{gm}\boldsymbol{g}_{gm} + \lambda_{tv}\boldsymbol{g}_{tv}\right)$;

Return reconstructed image $\boldsymbol{x}^*$.

4.2 Critical Components of Our Attack Framework

Dynamic Timestep Schedule $\boldsymbol{\tau}$. Existing research [10] shows that it is difficult to get fine results if simultaneously evaluating the denoising matching term over multiple timesteps. Thus, in our framework we only consider single denoising matching in each optimization iteration. Therefore, it is worth further analyzing the effect of diffusion prior at different timesteps. We first give the following proposition:

Proposition 1. *The denoising matching at high timestep will provide an overall structure of natural image manifold, while at low timestep will provide details of more specific image instances.*

Proof. First, we can transform the t-th denoising matching to the corresponding image matching, as

$$\|\boldsymbol{\epsilon} - \boldsymbol{\epsilon}_{\boldsymbol{\theta}}(\boldsymbol{x}_t, t)\|_2^2 = \frac{\bar{\alpha}_t}{\bar{\beta}_t} \|\boldsymbol{x}^* - \mathbb{E}[\boldsymbol{x}_0|\boldsymbol{x}_t]\|_2^2 \,. \tag{10}$$

Therefore, the t-th denoising regularization is equal to let the targeted $\boldsymbol{x}^*$ fit the conditional expectation $\mathbb{E}[\boldsymbol{x}_0|\boldsymbol{x}_t]$. A nature property [5] is that the $\mathbb{E}[\boldsymbol{x}_0|\boldsymbol{x}_t]$ has a shrinkage effect as t decreases. In other words, as t drops from high to low, the center of $\mathbb{E}[\boldsymbol{x}_0|\boldsymbol{x}_t]$ will shift from the global $\mathbb{E}[\boldsymbol{x}_0]$ to certain specific instance.

According to Proposition 1 and our empirical observation, we finally determine an annealing timestep schedule, inherently consistent with the generative sampling of DDPMs. We further fine-tune the **stop** timestep as in Fig. 2.

Scaling Factor $\boldsymbol{\lambda}$. Since our method is solved by gradient-based optimizer, the scaling factor λ can directly influence the impact of each objective term on optimization. As λ_{gm} and λ_{tv} can be empirically determined following existing research, we in practical set $\lambda_{denoising}$ as constants through grid search in face of different tasks.

Weighting Sliding Window on Network Layers $\boldsymbol{\mathcal{W}}$. Intuitively and empirically, gradients of different network layers will provide distinct semantic guidances [18]. We here give a relevant proposition as follows.

Proposition 2. *Gradients of deep layers will lead the inversion to fit high-level semantic features, while gradients of shallow layers will make the inversion focus on local and pixel-level structures.*

Thus, we consider applying dynamic weight to network layers as in Fig. 2c. We rewrite the original $\mathcal{L}_{\text{GM}}$ in (2) as $\sum_{l=1}^{L} \mathcal{W}_l \|\nabla \boldsymbol{W}_l - \nabla_{\boldsymbol{W}_l} \ell(f_{\boldsymbol{W}}(\boldsymbol{x}^*))\|_2^2$ for Euclidean distance, where $\mathcal{W}_l$ denotes the dynamic weight imposed on the l-th layer. In the initial stage of optimization, the deeper gradients are given higher attention, and subsequently the weights on shallower layers are increased. We believe that it can accelerate the overall optimization by guiding the inversion to restore the high-level features first, and then fill in the low-level features later.

5 Experiments

5.1 Overall Setups

Towards image classification tasks in FL, we conduct comprehensive evaluations to verify the proposed attack framework, in cases of sample-level and user-level inversion. Note that unless otherwise specified, the FL model is fixed to untrained ResNet-18 with no defense applied. We also conduct extensive validation under more difficult condition in Sect. 5.5.

Datasets. We test on diverse image categories, including face data from FFHQ (10 classes with age label) and CelebA (2 classes with gender label), animal data from ImageNet (first 397 classes). For sample-level inversion, we validate on image resized to 64px. For user-level inversion, we test on batch sizes of 10 with 64px. All tested samples are randomly selected from each validation set.

Implementations. We adopt two DDPMs-like models ($T = 1000$), respectively pretrained on FFHQ and ImageNet. The total iteration is 4000, with Adam optimizer and decaying lr linearly down from 1 to 0.1.

Baselines. We consider the following 4 representative counterparts with 2 kinds of image priors:

1. *Simple image prior*: IG [7] is a widely-accepted baseline, optimizing the gradient matching loss on pixel space with a TV regularization. Recently, the state-of-the-art HFGI [18], adopts a stepwise gradient matching term with a random dropout strategy.
2. *GAN-based prior*: GIAS [12] first integrates GANs into gradient inversion, which optimizes a reparameterized objective on generator's $\boldsymbol{z}/\boldsymbol{w}$ spaces. The newest GIFD [6] instead searches on generator's feature spaces.

Note that each hyperparameter is set following their original implementations. For used GANs, we adopt a StyleGAN2 pretrained on FFHQ and a BigGAN pretrained on ImageNet.

Evaluation Metrics. For sample-level inversion, we choose 4 metrics that reflect the image similarity: **MSE**, **PSNR**, **SSIM** and **LPIPS** [21]. For user-level inversion, we yet introduce some semantic metrics. For face data, we adopt **face detection rate**, the proportion of detected faces by MTCNN [20]; **face similarity**, the L2 distance between embeddings of reconstructed and original faces extracted by Facenet [16]. For animal data, we adopt **classification confidence**, the outputted prediction score of a pretrained ResNet-50.

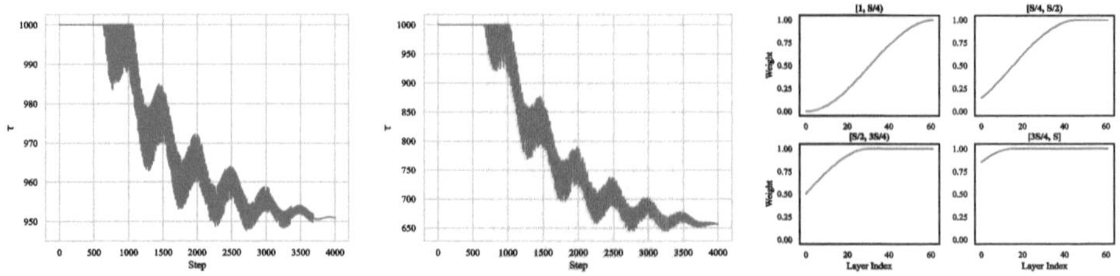

(a) $t_{end} = 950$ (b) $t_{end} = 650$ (c) Weighting window

Fig. 2. Timestep schedules and weighting window used in experiments.

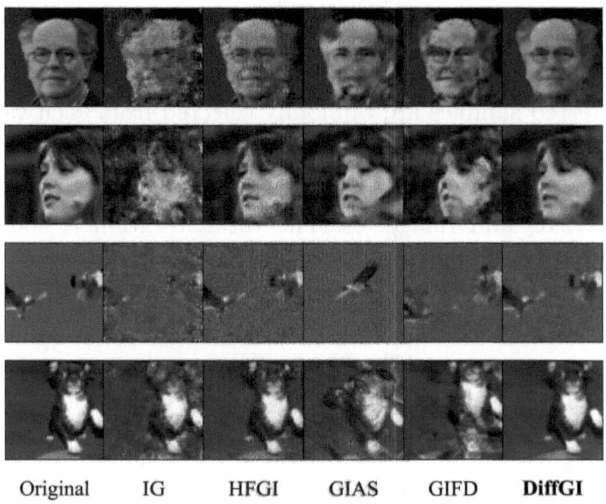

Fig. 3. Visual samples of sample-level inversion.

Table 1. Quantitative results of sample-level inversion for image similarity.

(a) FFHQ

Metric	IG [7]	HFGI [18]	GIAS [12]	GIFD [6]	**DiffGI**
MSE ↓	0.0173	0.0045	0.0180	0.0076	**0.0030**
PSNR ↑	17.68	23.61	17.85	21.74	**25.24**
SSIM ↑	0.4553	0.7356	0.5140	0.7030	**0.8023**
LPIPS ↓	0.3794	0.0941	0.1812	0.1202	**0.0659**

(b) ImageNet

Metric	IG [7]	HFGI [18]	GIAS [12]	GIFD [6]	**DiffGI**
MSE ↓	0.0113	0.0039	0.0182	0.0052	**0.0017**
PSNR ↑	19.92	25.49	18.46	23.24	**27.69**
SSIM ↑	0.5072	0.7101	0.4365	0.7003	**0.8289**
LPIPS ↓	0.3208	0.1581	0.3237	0.1616	**0.0755**

5.2 Results of Sample-Level Inversion Attack

For cases of sample-level inversion, we conduct experiments on FFHQ and ImageNet. All tests are repeated 20 times, with results in Table 1 and Fig. 3.

Through all considered cases, our attack maintains the best reconstruction performance beyond other counterparts. As shown both in quantitative and qualitative results, owing to the use of diffusion image prior, our attack can faithfully reconstruct clearer image details than others, with lower noise level.

5.3 Results of User-Level Inversion Attack

For cases of user-level inversion, we randomly conduct 20 trials for each test, respectively for face data on CelebA and animal data on ImageNet. The quantitative results are in Table 2, with visual samples in Fig. 4.

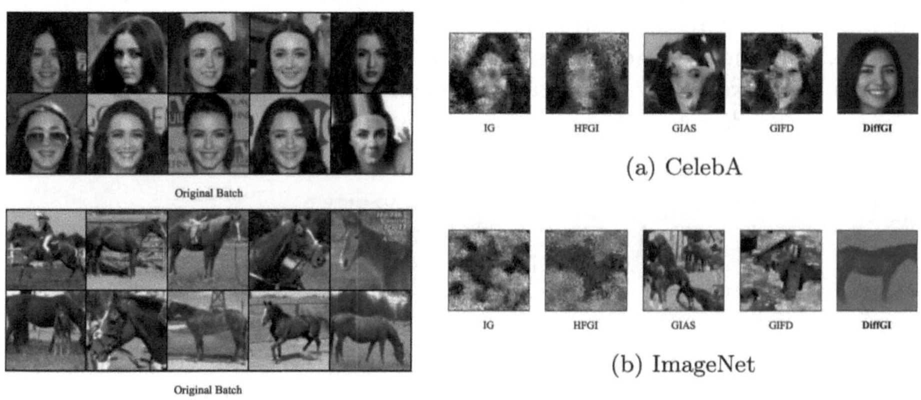

(a) CelebA

(b) ImageNet

Fig. 4. Visual samples of user-level inversion.

For both categories, our method can successfully restore significant semantic information of the original batch. For **face data**, our attack can recover a representative prototype with genuine facial features, while for any other methods, it is difficult to recover neither explicit nor meaningful visual content regarding the targeted face. For **animal data**, our attack can output an outlined appearance of the targeted animal, showing one intuitive and semantic depiction from a global perspective, while other counterparts can merely generate some local and pixel-level structures.

5.4 Discussion for Critical Design in Our Framework

In this section, we first provide ablation studies to justify components in our framework. Besides, to better analyze the benefit of utilizing diffusion models, we also provide in-depth discussion for two significant hyperparameters: t_{end} and $\lambda_{denoising}$, as they direct control the effect of diffusion prior in our approach.

Table 2. Quantitative results of user-level inversion for semantic similarity.

Method	CelebA		ImageNet
	Face detection rate ↑	Facial similarity ↑	Classification confidence ↑
Original batch	1.00	0.5394	0.4200
IG [7]	0.00	0.0000	0.0007
HFGI [18]	0.10	0.0702	0.0006
GIAS [12]	0.70	0.1694	0.3477
GIFD [6]	0.30	0.1886	0.0038
DiffGI	**1.00**	**0.5055**	**0.4639**

Ablations for Critical Components. To validate the selection of weighting window ($\mathcal{W}$), TV regularization (TV) and gradient metric ($\mathcal{D}_{grad}$), we set 4 variants, and conduct experiments in sample-level inversion. All results are shown in Fig. 5, with exemplary optimization processes shown in Fig. 5b.

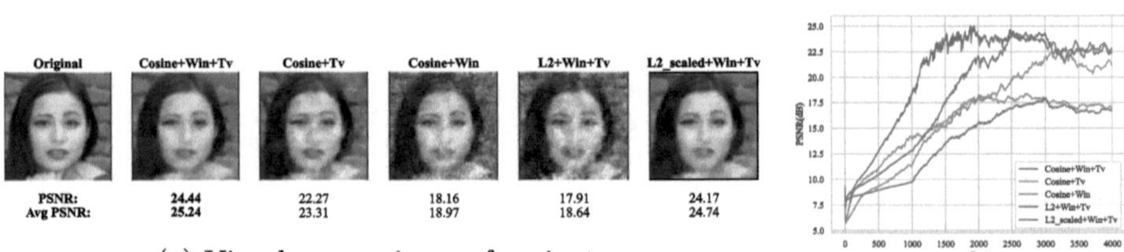

(a) Visual comparisons of variants

(b) Opti-processes

Fig. 5. Results of variants in sample-level inversion.

Based on visual and numerical results, we have the following conclusion: For $\mathcal{W}$, it is obvious that the method incorporated with weighting window can quickly reach a high image reconstruction level, while the method without $\mathcal{W}$ would be easily misled by low-level features and trap into local minimum in early optimization stage. For TV term, we also find that adopting the total variation operator can facilitate the inversion to achieve better image quality with less noise, by smoothing the mutation between adjacent pixels. For different $\mathcal{D}_{grad}$, we observe that, though L2 and Cosine distance fundamentally measure different gradient discrepancies, by balancing their impact on optimization process, where we scale down the gradient norm of L2-based $\mathcal{L}_{\text{GM}}$ by an empirical $\lambda_{gm} = 5e-3$, both $\mathcal{D}_{grad}$ will obtain nearly identical inverted results, as shown in Fig. 5a.

We also conduct an ablation experiment to verify the image random transformation $\mathcal{T}$ applied in user-level inversion. The result in Fig. 8a shows that adding the transformation indeed helps to obtain more accurate semantic recovery. The lack of $\mathcal{T}$ could lead to insufficient simulation of variance in the dummy batch, weakening the fitness to the original batch gradients, and consequently degrade the inverted results.

Grid Search for Stop Timestep t_{end}. Through all cases of experiments, We conduct a grid search for t_{end} in range from 950 down to 550. For sample-level inversion, visual results are provided in Fig. 6a; while for user-level inversion, visual results are provided in Fig. 7.

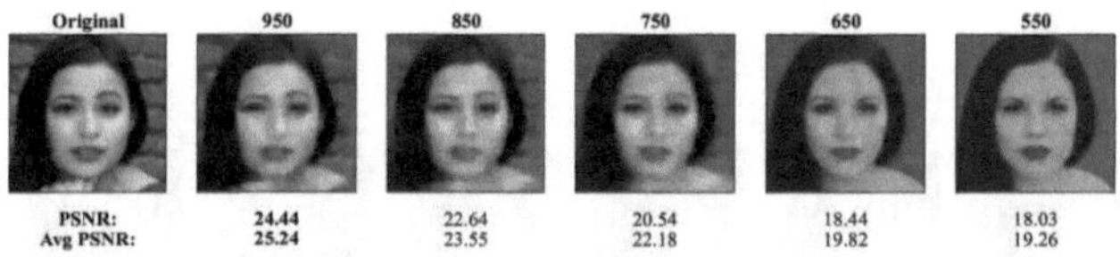

(a) Grid search for t_{end}

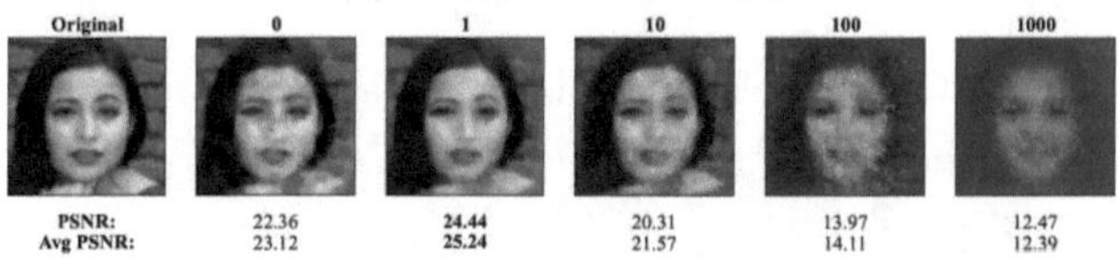

(b) Grid search for $\lambda_{denoising}$

Fig. 6. Grid search in sample-level inversion.

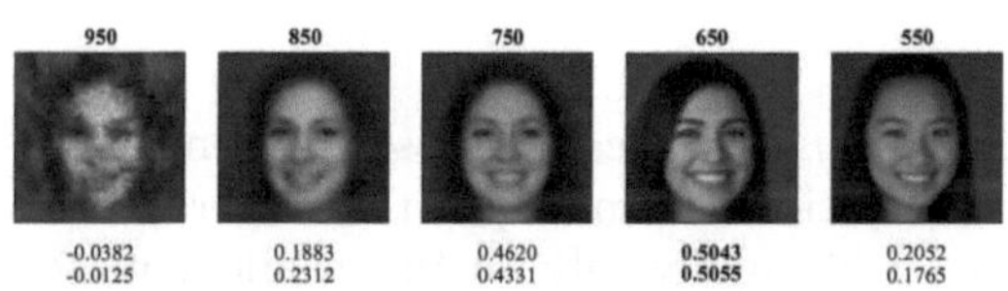

(a) Grid search on CelebA with face similarity

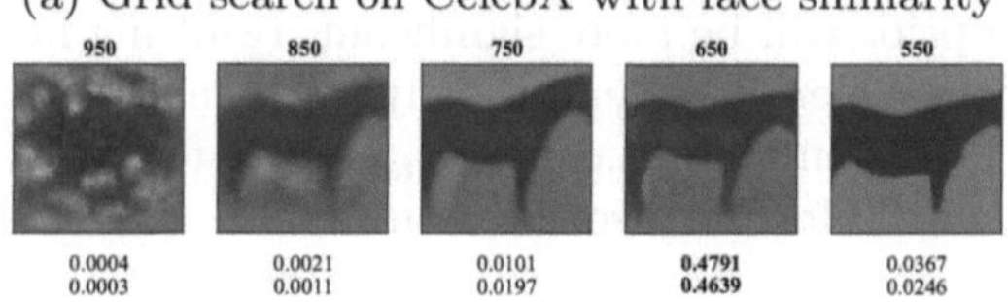

(b) Grid search on ImageNet with classification confidence

Fig. 7. Grid search for t_{end} in user-level inversion. The bottom rows show single and averaged metrics.

As we observe, decreasing t_{end} will generally make the inverted image's background smoother and the main object sharper, as well introducing more hallucinations, which is consistent with previous analysis in Sect. 4.2. To achieve the best tradeoff, for simple inversion tasks, a high $t_{end} = 950$ is empirically sufficient for good reconstruction. While for more difficult inversion tasks, like user-level inversion, adjusting a low $t_{end} = 650$ can provide stronger guidance of deeper diffusion prior, so that the quality of inversion could be improved. Overall, Fig. 2 shows the both used timestep schedules.

Grid Search for Denoising Scaling Factor $\lambda_{denoising}$. Like the above section, we also consider a grid search for $\lambda_{denoising}$ in range of 0 to 1000. All visual and numerical results are shown in Fig. 6b, 8 for sample and user-level inversion.

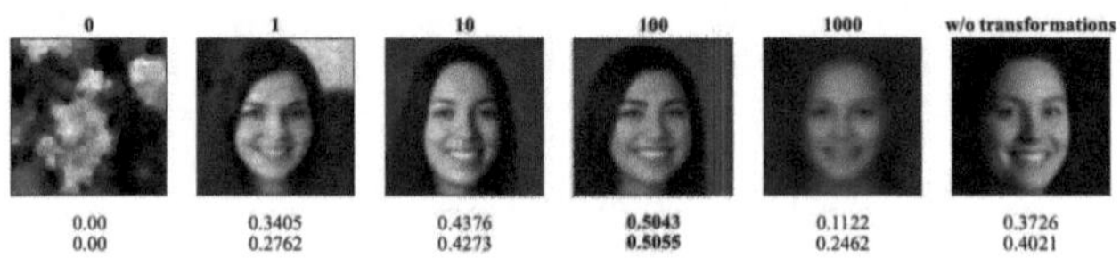

(a) Grid search on CelebA with face similarity

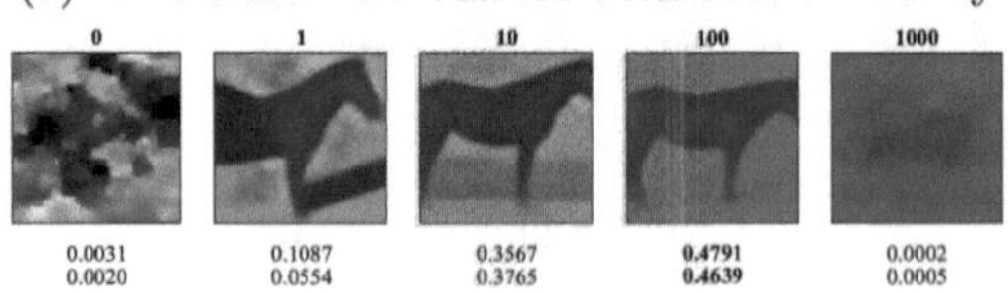

(b) Grid search on ImageNet with classification confidence

Fig. 8. Grid search for $\lambda_{denoising}$ in user-level inversion. The bottom rows show single and averaged metrics.

Obviously, changing $\lambda_{denoising}$ can impose different effect of diffusion prior on the inversion optimization. From a qualitative perspective, when $\lambda_{denoising}$ is small, the inversion will mainly rely on the gradient matching term, making inverted results hold more specific features with high noise. In turn, increasing $\lambda_{denoising}$, diffusion prior will be more significant, resulting in blurry and prototypical reconstruction. Overall, we empirically set balanced $\lambda_{denoising}$ according to the difficulty of inversion tasks, i.e., $\lambda_{denoising} = 1$ for our sample-level inversion and $\lambda_{denoising} = 100$ for our user-level inversion.

5.5 Validation Under Defensive Mechanisms

To test under harder condition involved with defense strategies, we here conduct sample-level validation considering two common defense mechanisms, i.e., *Gaussian Noise* (Differential Privacy) [9], which randomly perturbs the $\nabla \boldsymbol{W}$ by adding Gaussian noise with a standard deviation 0.1; and *Gradient Compression* [23], which maps small absolute components of $\nabla \boldsymbol{W}$ to zero with a sparsity of 90%. For both cases, there are $t_{end} = 950$, $\lambda_{denoising} = 1$.

The PSNR results shown in Table 3 indicate that the gradient-perturbation defense is significantly effective against most attacks, especially for these using simple image prior, e.g., IG and HFGI, making it difficult for them to achieve good reconstruction. In contrast, our method can still achieve the best reconstruction quality. This demonstrates that, by fully utilizing the diffusion prior, our robust attack can break through these two widely-used defenses, highlighting the necessity of more privacy-preserving design for federated learning.

Table 3. PSNR results of sample-level inversion under defensive mechanisms.

Defense	Dataset	IG [7]	HFGI [18]	GIAS [12]	GIFD [6]	DiffGI
Noise (0.1)	FFHQ	11.25	11.02	13.49	11.78	**16.05**
	ImageNet	13.23	13.03	16.87	14.66	**17.72**
Compression (90%)	FFHQ	12.05	11.57	13.30	12.92	**15.81**
	ImageNet	14.26	13.90	16.60	15.19	**17.49**

6 Conclusion

For federated learning, we proposed a strong gradient inversion attack based on the novel diffusion models via a variational perspective. By modeling a variational Bayesian inversion framework, we showed the advantages of our attack method compared with other representative ones through a wealth of theoretical analysis and experimental validation, reflecting the significant threat of gradient privacy leakage. We hope that our work can contribute to the assessment of such urgent privacy risk in federated learning.

Acknowledgments. This work was supported by the National Key Research and Development Program of China under Grant E3500921L6.

Disclosure of Interests. The authors declare that they have no competing interests.

References

1. Balunovic, M., Dimitrov, D.I., Staab, R., Vechev, M.: Bayesian framework for gradient leakage. In: International Conference on Learning Representations (2022)
2. Chung, H., Kim, J., Mccann, M.T., Klasky, M.L., Ye, J.C.: Diffusion posterior sampling for general noisy inverse problems. arXiv preprint arXiv:2209.14687 (2022)
3. Chung, H., Sim, B., Ryu, D., Ye, J.C.: Improving diffusion models for inverse problems using manifold constraints. Adv. Neural. Inf. Process. Syst. **35**, 25683–25696 (2022)
4. Daras, G., et al.: A survey on diffusion models for inverse problems. arXiv preprint arXiv:2410.00083 (2024)

5. Efron, B.: Tweedie's formula and selection bias. J. Am. Stat. Assoc. **106**(496), 1602–1614 (2011)
6. Fang, H., Chen, B., Wang, X., Wang, Z., Xia, S.T.: Gifd: a generative gradient inversion method with feature domain optimization. In: Proceedings of the IEEE/CVF International Conference on Computer Vision, pp. 4967–4976 (2023)
7. Geiping, J., Bauermeister, H., Dröge, H., Moeller, M.: Inverting gradients-how easy is it to break privacy in federated learning? Adv. Neural. Inf. Process. Syst. **33**, 16937–16947 (2020)
8. Geng, J., Mou, Y., Li, Q., Li, F., Beyan, O., Decker, S., Rong, C.: Improved gradient inversion attacks and defenses in federated learning. IEEE Trans. Big Data **10**(6), 839–850 (2023)
9. Geyer, R.C., Klein, T., Nabi, M.: Differentially private federated learning: a client level perspective. arXiv preprint arXiv:1712.07557 (2017)
10. Graikos, A., Malkin, N., Jojic, N., Samaras, D.: Diffusion models as plug-and-play priors. Adv. Neural. Inf. Process. Syst. **35**, 14715–14728 (2022)
11. Ho, J., Jain, A., Abbeel, P.: Denoising diffusion probabilistic models. Adv. Neural. Inf. Process. Syst. **33**, 6840–6851 (2020)
12. Jeon, J., Lee, K., Oh, S., Ok, J., et al.: Gradient inversion with generative image prior. Adv. Neural. Inf. Process. Syst. **34**, 29898–29908 (2021)
13. Li, Z., Zhang, J., Liu, L., Liu, J.: Auditing privacy defenses in federated learning via generative gradient leakage. In: Proceedings of the IEEE/CVF Conference on Computer Vision and Pattern Recognition, pp. 10132–10142 (2022)
14. McMahan, B., Moore, E., Ramage, D., Hampson, S., y Arcas, B.A.: Communication-efficient learning of deep networks from decentralized data. In: Artificial Intelligence and Statistics, pp. 1273–1282. PMLR (2017)
15. Minka, T., et al.: Divergence measures and message passing. Microsoft Research Technical Report (2005)
16. Schroff, F., Kalenichenko, D., Philbin, J.: Facenet: a unified embedding for face recognition and clustering. In: Proceedings of the IEEE Conference on Computer Vision and Pattern Recognition, pp. 815–823 (2015)
17. Yang, Q., Liu, Y., Chen, T., Tong, Y.: Federated machine learning: concept and applications. ACM Trans. Intell. Syst. Technol. (TIST) **10**(2), 1–19 (2019)
18. Ye, Z., Luo, W., Zhou, Q., Tang, Y.: High-fidelity gradient inversion in distributed learning. In: Proceedings of the AAAI Conference on Artificial Intelligence, vol. 38, pp. 19983–19991 (2024)
19. Yin, H., Mallya, A., Vahdat, A., Alvarez, J.M., Kautz, J., Molchanov, P.: See through gradients: Image batch recovery via gradinversion. In: Proceedings of the IEEE/CVF Conference on Computer Vision and Pattern Recognition, pp. 16337–16346 (2021)
20. Zhang, K., Zhang, Z., Li, Z., Qiao, Y.: Joint face detection and alignment using multitask cascaded convolutional networks. IEEE Signal Process. Lett. **23**(10), 1499–1503 (2016)
21. Zhang, R., Isola, P., Efros, A.A., Shechtman, E., Wang, O.: The unreasonable effectiveness of deep features as a perceptual metric. In: Proceedings of the IEEE conference on computer vision and pattern recognition, pp. 586–595 (2018)
22. Zhang, R., Guo, S., Wang, J., Xie, X., Tao, D.: A survey on gradient inversion: Attacks, defenses and future directions. In: Proceedings of the Thirty-First International Joint Conference on Artificial Intelligence, pp. 5678–685 (2023)
23. Zhu, L., Liu, Z., Han, S.: Deep leakage from gradients. Advances in neural information processing systems **32** (2019)

RLNA-Net: Reframing Document-Level Relation Extraction with Residual Attention

Rongen Yan[1,2], Jinyi Zhan[1], Ye Tao[3(✉)], Feifei Qian[4], and Shaolin Tan[3]

[1] School of Information Science and Technology (School of Artificial Intelligence), Beijing Forestry University, Beijing, China
reyan2023@bjfu.edu.cn

[2] Hebei Key Laboratory of Smart National Park, Beijing, China

[3] Zhongguancun Laboratory, Beijing, China
taoye_402@buaa.edu.cn

[4] School of Artificial Intelligence, Beijing Normal University, Beijing 100875, China
feifei_qian@mail.bnu.edu.cn

Abstract. Accurately extracting entity relationships from text is challenging due to information redundancy, and errors can propagate misinformation with security implications. Document-level relation extraction (RE) presents a particular challenge due to its inherent complexity, requiring the synthesis of entity relationships distributed across multiple sentences within a document. Existing methods often rely on simply stacking network layers to address long-range dependencies, which can result in insufficient model robustness and errors when processing lengthy contexts. To address this, we propose RLNA-Net, a novel method that reframes document-level RE as a semantic segmentation task. Our model integrates a ResNet architecture with Layer Normalization to stabilize training and mitigate degradation caused by deep networks. Furthermore, we incorporate Multi-Head Self-Attention (MHSA) into the backbone to effectively capture diverse and long-range dependencies within the document. Comprehensive experiments on three benchmark datasets—DocRED, CDR, and GDA—demonstrate that RLNA-Net outperforms existing strong baseline models.

Keywords: Document-level Relation Extraction · Semantic Segmentation · ResNet · Multi-Head Self-Attention · Layer Normalization

1 Introduction

Relation extraction (RE) identifies relationships between text entities, a fundamental NLP task with applications in biomedical text mining [7], information retrieval [21], and beyond [27]. Previously, entity relationships were extracted in

J. Niu et al. (Eds.): KSEM 2026, LNAI 16631, pp. 605–617, 2027.
https://doi.org/10.1007/978-981-92-2759-4_44

a single sentence [2,17]. However, sentence-level RE makes it challenging to capture the direct relationship between inter-sentence entity pairs. Unlike sentence-level RE, document-level RE requires reasoning and synthesizing among multiple sentences in a document. Moreover, document-level RE must address long-range dependencies between entities across sentences to capture global information. Document-level RE focuses on identifying and extracting relational data from comprehensive texts, going beyond sentence-level limitations to understand context and semantic relationships across an entire document. Therefore, research on document-level RE is necessary to enhance model transparency and interpretability.

Document-level RE methods fall into two categories: sequence-based [12,13,20,28] and graph-based [1,9,24]. Sequence-based approaches typically use neural networks to process entity information. However, as deep neural networks are increasingly used in document-level relational extraction, their inherent problems of uncertainty and vulnerability are becoming more prominent. To address the long-range dependency problem, the Transformer is employed for document-level RE research [2,12,13], and this approach applies the pre-trained language model directly without introducing the graph structure. The sequence-based method improves the performance of extracting relations between inter-sentence entity pairs, especially for samples that require complex logical reasoning. Recent studies [1,9,24] show that the document graph-based approach is more advantageous. The graph-based models mainly consider entities as nodes and construct document graphs by graph neural networks.

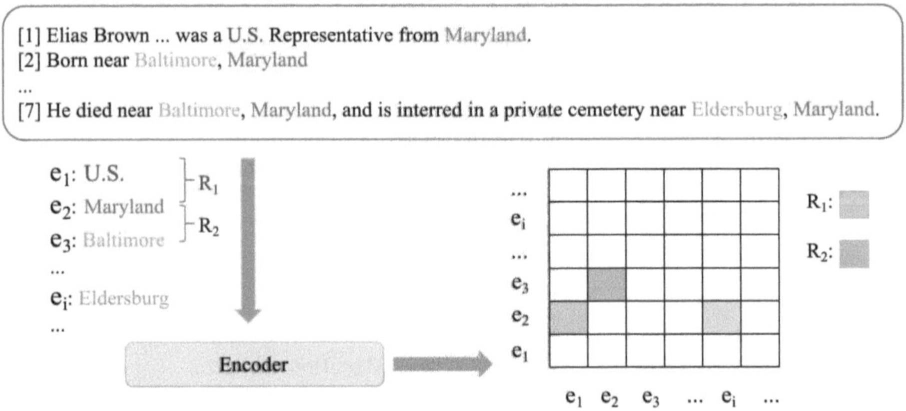

Fig. 1. The entity matrix construction.

However, the two main methods mentioned above both use entity pairs alone and do not consider the entity relationships between multiple triples. Hence, the entity-level relationship matrix [25] has been first proposed to capture global dependencies between triples, which views document-level RE as a semantic segmentation task. The initial entity-level relation matrix is composed of correlations R_i between entity pairs, which is shown in Fig. 1. For example, we extracted the relevant feature R_1 between *U.S* and *Maryland*, and R_2 between *Maryland* and *Baltimore* through pre-trained language model. Then, the relevant features R_i are viewed as pixel values, and the matrix is considered as an image. The U-shaped network (U-Net) [10] is applied to the segmentation module to reason and synthesize relations. Nevertheless, in the semantic segmentation module, modeling long-range dependency only by stacking more network layers is not easy.

Inspired by the work mentioned above, to model long-range dependency and capture global features, we propose a novel document-level RE model called **R**esNet with **L**ayer **N**ormalization and Multi-Head Self-**A**ttention (**RLNA-Net**). We use the same method proposed by Zhang et al. [25] to obtain the entity-level relationship matrix. Since U-Net [10] deepening can lead to gradient disappearance or network degradation, we incorporate ResNet [3] to stabilize deep networks. Furthermore, we integrate multi-head self-attention (MHSA) [14] to effectively address long-range dependencies, and layer normalization [4] to solve multi-channel normalization issues.

By enhancing document-level relation extraction, our research supports knowledge engineering tasks that depend on accurate information extraction from complex documents. In summary, we make the following contributions:

- We propose the novel network RLNA-Net, the ResNet with layer normalization, and MHSA. The model focuses on capturing global information after transforming the relations between entities into an image.
- We incorporate ResNet with layer normalization [4] to relieve network degradation caused by stacking layers. Besides, we introduce the MHSA mechanism to model long-range dependence and capture more comprehensive information in document-level RE.
- We performed the experiments on three benchmark datasets. The results show that our proposed model, RLNA-Net outperforms existing models.

2 Related Work

Sequence-based approaches initially employed recurrent neural networks (RNNs) [23], but have largely transitioned to transformer-based methods due to their limitations in modeling long-range dependencies. The transformer's MHSA mechanism has proven effective across domains, including vision tasks [11]. Some other transformer-based document-level RE networks have been proposed [12,13,28], which applied the proposed model directly to text sequences to obtain entity embedding and extract entity relationships. Therefore, it isn't accessible to reason and synthesizes the entity pairs' associations for the existing sequence-based models.

In recent years, graph-based methods [1,9,24] offer improved reasoning but often overlook connections across multiple triples. Zhang et al. [25] proposed the first approach to consider document-level RE as a semantic segmentation task. In the encoder module, they obtained the entity embedding based on a pre-trained language model and proposed two different calculating methods to get the relevance vector between entity pairs. Then they defined the relation matrix representing the relation vectors. Leveraging computer vision advances, Zhang et al. [25] treat the relation matrix as an image and apply U-Net [10] for semantic segmentation. In the semantic segmentation module, two down-sampling blocks and two up-sampling blocks form a U-shaped architecture. The U-shaped model used a 3×3 convolutional kernel for feature extraction. Hence the receptive field is too small to capture global relations. Some scholars increased the receptive field size by adding the number of network layers, while others explored reducing input redundancy to improve segmentation quality [19]. Nevertheless, stacking network layers can lead to problems, such as network degradation.

On the one hand, our work is inspired by Zhang et al. [25], which first proposed considering the document-level RE as a semantic segmentation task. Until now, not many studies have converted document-level RE to vision tasks. The U-shaped network provides strong inference capability in semantic segmentation. For this reason, we still use the U-Shaped Network in semantic segmentation for document-level RE. We introduce the Residual Network (ResNet) to implement shortcut connections [3] and solve network degradation caused by enlarging the receptive field size.

On the other hand, our study still needs to consider the multi-dimensional aspects of semantics. Due to the robust global model capability of the MHSA mechanism in the transformer-based model [14], we incorporate the MHSA mechanism in the final block of the encoder segmentation module to model long-range dependency. The DocRED dataset is proposed for document-level RE [20], which provides a baseline benchmark. Therefore, our experiments test on the DocRED dataset. To ensure the model's validity, we also experimented on two other biological domain datasets, CDR and GDA.

3 Methodology

3.1 Preliminary

We first introduce the problem definition, including the preprocessing module. Given a document $d = [x_t]_{t=1}^{s}$, we feed the document into the pre-trained language model to obtain the token embedding. Our model is built based on BERT pre-trained language model. h_{t_i} denotes the embedding of each token x_i.

$$\mathbf{H} = [h_{t_1}, h_{t_2}, ..., h_{t_s}] = \mathbf{BERT}([x_1, x_2, ..., x_s]) \tag{1}$$

Following Zhang et al. [25], we leverage dynamic window to obtain the mentioned embedding. Since an entity will appear multiple times in the document, we use m_j to denote the entity mentions, and the N_{e_i} represents the maximum number of times the entity was mentioned. The logsumexp pooling is utilized to obtain the entity embedding as below:

$$e_i = log\sum_{j=1}^{N_{e_i}} exp(m_j) \tag{2}$$

Then, the task is to capture the relevance between entity pairs. As Zhang et al. [25], we can obtain the entity-to-entity relationship value based on similarity and context. In this paper, we use the context-based method to collocate these relation vectors to form a preliminary entity pair matrix F as:

$$\begin{aligned} F_{ij} &= W_1 \mathbf{H} a^{(s,o)} \\ a^{(s,o)} &= softmax(\sum_{i=1}^{N_k} A_i^{(s,o)} \cdot /1^T \sum_{i=1}^{N_k} A_i^{(s,o)}) \end{aligned} \tag{3}$$

where W_1 is the learnable weight matrix, $a^{(s,o)}$ denotes the attention weight. $A_i^{(s,o)}$ refers to attention from token s to token o in the i-th attention head. N_k denotes the numbers of attention heads. We also normalized the attention. However, reasoning and predicting the relation between triples are not easy. For example, we have extracted the relation F_{13} of (e_1, e_3) and the F_{35} of (e_3, e_5). We need to reason the relation of (e_1, e_5) to predict the value of F_{15}. Having obtained the entire basic matrix F, we regard the relation matrix F as an image to capture the global relation matrix R. Our subsequent work is converted directly into a semantic segmentation task.

3.2 Proposed Architecture

After obtaining the preliminary relation matrix F, we consider it an image. The document-level RE is formulated into a semantic segmentation task on the image to obtain a deeper and more comprehensive relationship. U-Net [10] is the most widely used segmentation model, which can reason well. Thus, we propose a novel network, RLNA-Net, as shown in Fig. 2, our proposed semantic segmentation module mainly contains the encoder and decoder segmentation module, which follow the U-shaped structure but with improvements in the specific blocks. In the encoder segmentation module, we split into three blocks. We first use a double convolutional network and a downsampling block to expand the perceptual field. In the first down-sampling block, the number of channels is doubled, and we use max pooling in the filter to extract feature texture. Unlike Zhang et al. [25] we use the residual network with layer normalization in the second block instead of stacking the same convolution and downsampling layers. In addition, we utilize the MHSA mechanism instead of the spatial convolutional network in the final block to achieve global self-attention. The specific architecture is shown in Fig. 2. Our proposed model contains three modules: the *U-shaped BasicBlock*, the *U-Attention*, and the layer normalization.

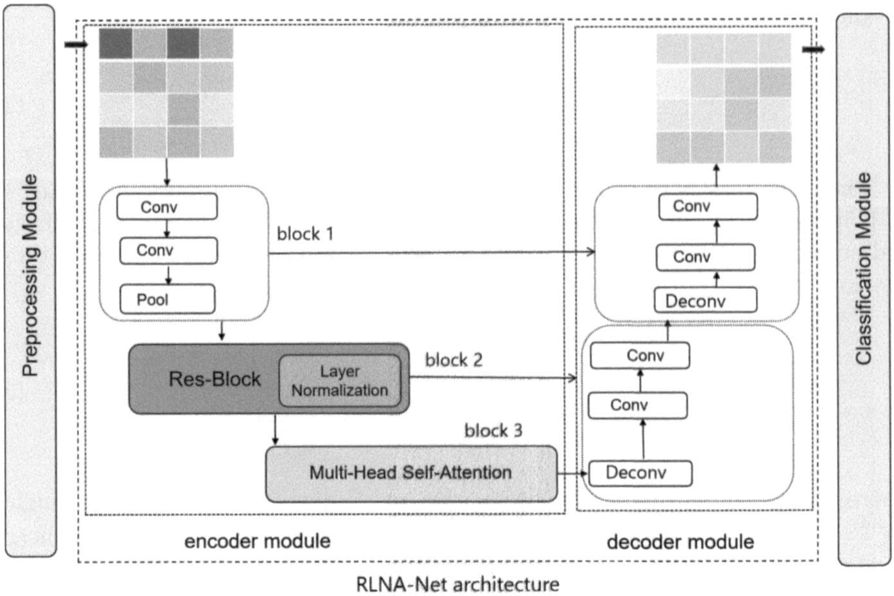

Fig. 2. Our proposed RLNA-Net architecture.

U-Shaped BasicBlock. The deep convolutional neural network has a breakthrough in computer vision [26]. As the depth of the network deepens, the training accuracy will tend to saturate, which is not what we expect. An effective way to solve this problem is to introduce a deep residual learning framework. Therefore, we add a shortcut connection to improve the training accuracy in the second block of our proposed structure. Since the layers of the convolutional neural network we use are shallow, we leverage the main design of ResNet34 [3]. The BasicBlock is incorporated into our U-shaped network. Therefore, we can call the module *U-shaped BasicBlock.* We reformulate the layer as learning functions that add shortcut connections and we use the following to denote our operation in the second Res-block:

$$f_{b2}(x)_{out} = X_{b_1} + f_{b2}(x)_{in} \tag{4}$$

where $f_{b2}(x)_{in}$ means the input function of Res-block containing two convolution layers, and $f_{b2}(x)_{out}$ denotes the learnable result of the second block, composed of the output function of the first block X_{b1} and the original input function. We can obtain better accuracy by constructing U-shaped BasicBlock when expanding receptive field.

U-Attention. We incorporate the MHSA mechanism [14] in the final block, replacing spatial convolutions to enhance long-range dependency modeling. The U-shaped network with MHSA mechanism can be viewed as the U-shaped

MHSA, and we call this architecture *U-Attention*. Different Query, Key, and Value weight matrices must be learned and projected to different dimensions separately. Since the MHSA connects the output results of multiple scaled dot-production attention, it can capture information from multiple dimensions. MHSA enables the model to focus on data from various representations at multiple locations. Our proposed model uses MHSA to decompose the entity-level matrix into its constituent dimensions, allowing us to extract the long-distance relationships between entities more easily. Since the attention mechanism is not a stridden operation, we reduce the pooling operation in the second block. This mechanism sufficiently improves the ability to capture global information and model long-range dependency rather than increasing the number of neural network layers. The computation of the MHSA mechanism does not depend on the output of the convolutional layers above, so it is possible to perform the computation in parallel and proceed directly to the next decode block.

$$f_{b3}(x)_{out} = f_M(W_Q \cdot f_{b2}(x)_{out} \cdot W_K W_V) \tag{5}$$

where W_Q, W_K, and $W_V$represent the query, key and value matrix separately. We use the f_M to denote the whole MHSA mechanism and $f_{b3}(x)_{out}$ denotes the result through the full connection of MHSA. We also compare the effect with and without the *U-Attention* in the experimental section.

Layer Normalization. We usually use normalization algorithms to reduce the computational cost when training deep neural networks. Many methods use batch normalization [5] to improve training efficiency. Given the document's level of complexity, any token could theoretically appear in a completely different context, and each sentence is of an extra length, which is not following the rules of NLP. Since layer normalization [4] is performed locally inside each sample, it is immune to these limitations. In our proposed architecture, we replace batch normalization with layer normalization in the BasicBlock of the residual network after double convolution operations and normalize the last three channels of the network. In addition, layer normalization and MHSA can achieve better performance by capturing more comprehensive and multi-dimensional information.

In the decoder segmentation module, the main structure is the same as Zhang et al. [25] mentioned, containing two up-sampling modules, and the number of channels is halved in each up-sampling module. Since we have utilized the residual network, we need to introduce the channel expansion in the BasicBlock to ensure that the dimensions match the output channels' number by the BasicBlock. Through the decoder module, the output matrix is the result of the relationship extraction, and the following equation can express the overall structure of our proposed model:

$$\mathbf{R} = RLNA(WF) \tag{6}$$

where F represents the input preliminary relation matrix, and Y denotes the output through the segmentation module. *RLNA* is the central architecture of our proposed semantic segmentation model. W denotes the weight matrix we need to learn and train.

Classification Module. Given the entity-pair embedding (e_s, e_o) and the relation matrix R, we obtain the probability as:

$$\begin{aligned} z_s &= tanh(W_s e_s + R_{(s,o)}) \\ z_o &= tanh(W_o e_o + R_{(s,o)}) \\ P(r|e_s, e_o) &= \sigma(z_s W_r z_o + p_r) \end{aligned} \tag{7}$$

where $R_{(s,o)}$ represents the relation between the entity pair (e_s, e_o) and z denotes the hidden state, where $W_s \in R^{d\times d}$, $W_o \in R^{d\times d}$, $W_r \in R^{d\times d}$, $p_r \in R$ are model parameters. To learn a suitable model, we need a loss function, which sets the threshold as zero. The loss function is shown as follows:

$$loss = log\left((1 + \sum_{i\in\Omega_{neg}} e^{s_i}) \cdot (1 + \sum_{j\in\Omega_{pos}} e^{-s_j})\right). \tag{8}$$

4 Experimental Results

4.1 Dataset

Our proposed RLNA-Net method is evaluated on three document-level RE datasets: DocRED [20], CDR [8], and GDA [18].

- **DocRED** [20] is the largest human-annotated dataset containing 3,053 /1,000/1,000 instances for training, validating, and testing. Besides, there are a total of 97 relations. DocRED is a large-scale, distantly supervised dataset characterized by data size and the need to read and reason about multiple sentences in a document. Thus it encourages us to design a better model to reason and synthesize the inter-sentence relation.
- **CDR** [8] is a large-scale dataset in the biomedical domain. The document-level RE is conducted on CDR to extract the binary interactions between chemical and disease concepts. The dataset contains 500/500/500 instances for training, validating, and testing. There are only two kinds of relations.
- **GDA** [18] is a human-annotated dataset in the biomedical domain, which contains 23353/5839/1000 instances for training, validating, and testing. The GDA dataset is similar to the CDR in that it has only two relations. The task of designing the large-scale dataset GDA is to predict binary interactions between genes and disease concepts.

4.2 Experimental Settings

Our experiments were run on an NVIDIA GeForce 11G GPU using PyTorch, with parameters tuned for efficiency. The BERT pre-trained language model encodes the DocRED, and the SciBERT-base model encodes CDR and GDA datasets. To compare the effect of our proposed model with other baseline models, we use Ign F_1 and F_1 to evaluate the performance of DocRED, F_1 to evaluate the effect on CDR and GDA. Our model is optimized with AdamW using learning rates $\in \{3e-4, 4e-4, 5e-4\}$ with a linear warmup for the first 6% of steps. The matrix size is 42. We tuned the hyperparameters on the development set.

4.3 Baseline Models

We compare our proposed RLNA-Net with three graph-based models, including LSR [9], GEDA [6], and GAIN [24]; and two transformer-based models, including HIN [13] and Coref [22]. Specifically, we compare with DocuNet [25], which formulated the document-level RE as the semantic segmentation task. Besides, we pick out some models that run well on the CDR and GDA dataset for comparison: BRAN [15], EoG [1], LSR [9], GLRE [16], and DocuNet [25] (Table 1).

Table 1. Results(%) on the DocRED dataset.

Model	Ign F_1	F_1
LSR [9]	52.43	59.00
GEDA [6]	54.52	56.16
GAIN [24]	59.14	61.22
HIN [13]	54.29	56.31
Coref [22]	55.32	57.51
DocuNet [25]	59.24	61.20
RLNA-Net	**59.63**	**61.60**

4.4 Results on CDR and GDA

We also conduct experiments on the CDR and GDA datasets to fully demonstrate RLNA-Net's effectiveness. We can observe from Table 2, our proposed model also achieves better performance in extracting the binary interactions between chemical or genes and disease concepts in the biomedical field. Our model achieves an F_1 of 86.4% on the CDR dataset and 85.8% on the GDA.

Table 2. Results(%) on the CDR and GDA datasets.

Model	CDR F_1	GDA F_1
BRAN [15]	62.1	-
EoG [1]	63.6	81.5
LSR [9]	64.8	82.2
GLRE [16]	68.5	-
DocuNet [25]	76.3	85.3
RLNA-Net	**86.4**	**85.8**

4.5 Ablation Study

To explore the influence of different components of our proposed model, we conduct ablation studies on DocRED, CDR, and GDA datasets separately. Tables 3 and 4 show that all components are crucial for capturing global information. We first conducted the experiment using the RLNA-Net structure with the Res-block component removed to validate the effectiveness of adding the shortcut connection. From Table 3, the RLNA-Net without Res-block drops by 0.36% in the Ign F_1 and 0.43% in F_1 compared with RLNA-Net on the DocRED dataset. As shown in Table 4, the value of F_1 also decreases in the other two datasets. As a result, the Res-block is useful for improving document-level RE performance.

Compared with the RLNA-Net model on the DocRED dataset, the RLNA-Net without the MHSA mechanism drops by 0.32% in Ign F_1 and 0.39% in F_1, which indicates the positive influence of introducing the MHSA mechanism. CDR and GDA datasets also show the comparable effects of MHSA. The F_1 drops by 0.4% on CDR and 0.6% on GDA. As we can observe from Tables 3 and 4, the benefits of incorporating layer normalization on the CDR and GDA datasets are not obvious. This is because there are only two types of relationships between entity pairs in these two datasets, whereas layer normalization facilitates the capture of multi-dimensional information. Thus, the improvement effect of our proposed model increases when the entity relationships are more complex.

Table 3. Ablation study on DocRED.

Model	Ign F_1	F_1
RLNA-Net-Resblock	59.24	61.20
RLNA-Net-MHSA	59.28	61.24
RLNA-Net-LN	59.36	61.30
RLNA-Net	**59.60**	**61.63**

Table 4. Ablation study on CDR and GDA.

Model	CDR (F_1)	GDA (F_1)
RLNA-Net-Resblock	85.7	84.8
RLNA-Net-MHSA	86.0	85.2
RLNA-Net-LN	85.2	85.4
RLNA-Net	**86.4**	**85.8**

5 Conclusion and Future Work

In this paper, we view the document-level RE as a semantic segmentation task, and we propose a novel model, RLNA-Net, to model long-range dependency and improve efficiency. RLNA-Net model introduces the shortcut connection block with layer normalization. Besides, the MHSA mechanism is also useful for obtaining global information. To our knowledge, this work represents the first integration of MHSA and ResNet into a U-Net framework for document-level RE. Experimental results on three datasets show that our proposed RLNA-Net can perform better than the state-of-the-art baseline. In the future, we will search for better methods to build the entity matrix and models to improve the accuracy of document-level RE.

Acknowledgments. This work was supported by the Outstanding Youth Team of Central Universities (QNTD202504), the National Key R&D Program of China (2022YFF1302700), the Emergency Open Competition Project of National Forestry and Grassland Administration (202303), and the Outstanding Youth Team Project of Central Universities (QNTD202308).

Disclosure of Interests. The authors have no competing interests to declare that are relevant to the content of this article.

References

1. Christopoulou, F., Miwa, M., Ananiadou, S.: Connecting the dots: document-level neural relation extraction with edge-oriented graphs. In: Proceedings of the 2019 Conference on Empirical Methods in Natural Language Processing and the 9th International Joint Conference on Natural Language Processing, pp. 4925–4936 (2019). https://doi.org/10.18653/v1/D19-1498
2. Gao, C., Wang, X., Sun, J.: TTM-RE: memory-augmented document-level relation extraction. In: Proceedings of the 62nd Annual Meeting of the Association for Computational Linguistics (Volume 1: Long Papers), pp. 443–458 (2024). https://doi.org/10.18653/v1/2024.acl-long.26
3. He, K., Zhang, X., Ren, S., Sun, J.: Deep residual learning for image recognition. In: Proceedings of the IEEE Conference on Computer Vision and Pattern Recognition, pp. 770–778 (2016)

4. Huang, L., Qin, J., Zhou, Y., Zhu, F., Liu, L., Shao, L.: Normalization techniques in training DNNS: methodology, analysis and application. IEEE Trans. Pattern Anal. Mach. Intell. **45**(8), 10173–10196 (2023). https://doi.org/10.1109/TPAMI.2023.3250241
5. Ioffe, S., Szegedy, C.: Batch normalization: accelerating deep network training by reducing internal covariate shift. In: International Conference on Machine Learning, pp. 448–456 (2015)
6. Li, B., Ye, W., Sheng, Z., Xie, R., Xi, X., Zhang, S.: Graph enhanced dual attention network for document-level relation extraction. In: Proceedings of the 28th International Conference on Computational Linguistics, pp. 1551–1560 (2020)
7. Li, G., Ross, K.E., Arighi, C.N., Peng, Y., Wu, C.H., Vijay-Shanker, K.: Mirtex: a text mining system for Mirna-gene relation extraction. PLoS Comput. Biol. **11**(9), e1004391 (2015)
8. Li, J., et al.: Biocreative V CDR task corpus: a resource for chemical disease relation extraction. Database (2016)
9. Nan, G., Guo, Z., Sekulic, I., Lu, W.: Reasoning with latent structure refinement for document-level relation extraction. In: Proceedings of the 58th Annual Meeting of the Association for Computational Linguistics, pp. 1546–1557 (2020). https://doi.org/10.18653/v1/2020.acl-main.141
10. Ronneberger, O., Fischer, P., Brox, T.: U-net: convolutional networks for biomedical image segmentation. In: International Conference on Medical Image Computing and Computer-assisted Intervention, pp. 234–241 (2015)
11. Srinivas, A., Lin, T.Y., Parmar, N., Shlens, J., Abbeel, P., Vaswani, A.: Bottleneck transformers for visual recognition. In: Proceedings of the IEEE/CVF Conference on Computer Vision and Pattern Recognition, pp. 16519–16529 (2021)
12. Tan, Q., He, R., Bing, L., Ng, H.T.: Document-level relation extraction with adaptive focal loss and knowledge distillation. In: Findings of the Association for Computational Linguistics: ACL 2022, pp. 1672–1681 (2022). https://aclanthology.org/2022.findings-acl.132/
13. Tang, H., et al.: HIN: hierarchical inference network for document-level relation extraction. In: Pacific-Asia Conference on Knowledge Discovery and Data Mining, pp. 197–209 (2020)
14. Vaswani, A., et al.: Attention is all you need. Adv. Neural Inf. Process. Syst. **30** (2017)
15. Verga, P., Strubell, E., McCallum, A.: Simultaneously self-attending to all mentions for full-abstract biological relation extraction. In: Proceedings of NAACL, pp. 872–884 (2018)
16. Wang, D., Hu, W., Cao, E., Sun, W.: Global-to-local neural networks for document-level relation extraction. In: Proceedings of EMNLP, pp. 3711–3721 (2020)
17. Wang, T., Yang, W., Wu, T.: Joint entity and relation extraction with fusion of multi-feature semantics. J. Intell. Inf. Syst. **63**, 21–42 (2025). https://doi.org/10.1007/s10844-024-00871-y
18. Wu, Y., Luo, R., Leung, H., Ting, H.F., Lam, T.W.: Renet: a deep learning approach for extracting gene-disease associations from literature. In: International Conference on Research in Computational Molecular Biology, pp. 272–284 (2019)
19. Yan, R., et al.: Document-level relation extraction with low entity redundancy feature map. IEEE Trans. Knowl. Data Eng. **37**(11), 6379–6391 (2025). https://doi.org/10.1109/TKDE.2025.3607566
20. Yao, Y., et al.: DocRED: a large-scale document-level relation extraction dataset. In: Proceedings of the 57th Annual Meeting of the Association for Computational Linguistics, pp. 764–777 (2019). https://doi.org/10.18653/v1/P19-1074

21. Yao, Y., et al.: Schema-aware reference as prompt improves data-efficient knowledge graph construction. In: Proceedings of SIGIR, pp. 911–921 (2023)
22. Ye, D., et al.: Coreferential reasoning learning for language representation. In: Proceedings of EMNLP, pp. 7170–7186 (2020)
23. Zaremba, W., Sutskever, I., Vinyals, O.: Recurrent neural network regularization (2014). arXiv:1409.2329 arXiv preprint
24. Zeng, S., Xu, R., Chang, B., Li, L.: Double graph based reasoning for document-level relation extraction. In: Proceedings of the 2020 Conference on Empirical Methods in Natural Language Processing, pp. 1630–1640 (2020). https://doi.org/10.18653/v1/2020.emnlp-main.127
25. Zhang, N., et al.: Document-level relation extraction as semantic segmentation. In: Proceedings of the 30th International Joint Conference on Artificial Intelligence, pp. 3999–4006 (2021). https://doi.org/10.24963/ijcai.2021/551
26. Zhao, X., Wang, L., Zhang, Y.: A review of convolutional neural networks in computer vision. Artif. Intell. Rev. **57**, 99 (2024). https://doi.org/10.1007/s10462-024-10721-6
27. Zhao, X., et al.: A comprehensive survey on relation extraction: recent advances and new frontiers. ACM Comput. Surv. **56**(11), 1–39 (2024)
28. Zhou, W., Huang, K., Ma, T., Huang, J.: Document-level relation extraction with adaptive thresholding and localized context pooling. In: Proceedings of the AAAI Conference on Artificial Intelligence. vol. 35, pp. 14612–14620 (2021)

Industrial Protocol Data Model and State Model Generation Based on Large Language Model

Songsong Liao, Rui Hao, Dongdong Zhao, Qianrong Zheng, Junwei Jiang, and Jianwen Xiang(✉)

School of Computer Science and Artificial Intelligence, Engineering Research Center of Transportation Information and Safety (ERCTIS), MoE of China, Wuhan University of Technology, Wuhan, China
{songsong,ruihao,zdd,qianrongzheng,jwjiang,jwxiang}@whut.edu.cn

Abstract. Industrial control protocol implementations are vulnerable due to their complex logic and real-time constraints. Peach Fuzzer is a widely used generation-based fuzzing tool, but its effectiveness heavily depends on the quality of the Peach Pit file, whose construction is labor-intensive, error-prone, and requires deep protocol expertise. While large language models (LLMs) provide a potential solution for automating Peach Pit generation, their direct application is hindered by insufficient structural compliance, lack of domain knowledge, and hallucination issues. To address these challenges, this paper proposes DTV-LLM, an LLM-based Peach Pit generation framework integrating Document-driven knowledge extraction, Template-based structural constraints, and multi-stage Validation. Specifically, a predefined XML template enforces the structural skeleton of the Peach Pit, while the LLM is guided to generate only protocol-specific message formats and interaction sequences from protocol documents or RFCs. Besides, a multi-stage verification loop, including tool pre-loading, syntax validation, and feedback-based revision, is employed to filter invalid configurations. Experiments conducted on six widely used protocols demonstrate that DTV-LLM achieves a 100% Peach syntax parsing pass rate after iterative refinement. In fuzzing experiments, the generated Peach Pit files achieve higher vulnerability detection efficiency and coverage than manual Peach Pits, improving branch coverage by 12.4% on average, and by 62.8% compared to AFLNet.

Keywords: Protocol Security · Fuzz Testing · Peach Pit · Large Language Model · Knowledge Extraction

1 Introduction

Industrial control protocols form the backbone of communication in modern Industrial Control Systems (ICS) and are widely deployed in critical infrastructures such as industrial automation, smart grids, and intelligent manufacturing

J. Niu et al. (Eds.): KSEM 2026, LNAI 16631, pp. 618–632, 2027.
https://doi.org/10.1007/978-981-92-2759-4_45

[9]. Due to complex interaction logic, strict real-time requirements, and insufficient testing during development, protocol implementations often contain security vulnerabilities. With the increasing connectivity of ICS driven by technologies such as the Internet of Things and artificial intelligence, previously isolated systems have become exposed to broader attack surfaces. Real-world incidents, including Stuxnet [11], DragonFly [17] and BlackEnergy [10], demonstrate that exploiting protocol vulnerabilities can lead to severe consequences for critical infrastructure security.

Fuzz testing is an effective technique for discovering protocol vulnerabilities by driving target implementations with malformed or unexpected inputs and monitoring abnormal behaviors such as crashes and logic errors [26]. Existing fuzzing approaches can be broadly classified into mutation-based [19] and generation-based [23] methods. Mutation-based fuzzers rely on existing valid inputs and apply random or guided mutations, which often break protocol structure and limit exploration of protocol logic. In contrast, generation-based fuzzing explicitly models protocol specifications and interaction sequences, making it particularly suitable for industrial control protocols that feature rigid message formats and standardized workflows. Peach Fuzzer [6] is a representative generation-based fuzzing tool widely used for industrial control protocol testing. Its core configuration file, known as the Peach Pit, defines both the protocol DataModel and the StateModel, which together determine fuzzing coverage and vulnerability detection effectiveness. However, constructing high-quality Peach Pit files is a labor-intensive and error-prone process that requires deep understanding of both protocol specifications and Peach syntax. This high modeling cost significantly limits the scalability and practical adoption of generation-based fuzzing.

Large language models (LLMs) [28] offer a promising opportunity to automate Peach Pit generation by extracting protocol semantics directly from documentation. Nevertheless, directly applying LLMs to generate complete Peach Pit files often leads to structurally invalid configurations, incomplete protocol semantics, and hallucinated content. Two key challenges therefore arise: (i) how to generate high-quality DataModel and StateModel that accurately capture protocol semantics, and (ii) how to ensure that the generated Peach Pit files are syntactically correct and executable.

To address these challenges, we propose DTV-LLM, an LLM-based Peach Pit generation framework that integrates Document-driven knowledge extraction, Template constraint, and multi-stage Validation. DTV-LLM employs a predefined XML template to enforce the fixed structural skeleton of Peach Pit files, allowing the LLM to focus solely on generating protocol-specific data models and interaction sequences. Protocol specifications or RFCs are used to guide document-driven knowledge extraction, enabling accurate modeling of message formats and protocol workflows. A multi-stage validation loop, including syntax checking, Peach tool preloading, and feedback-based refinement, is further applied to iteratively eliminate invalid or incorrectly generated configurations.

We evaluate DTV-LLM on six widely used industrial protocols: Modbus, IEC104, IEC60870, IEC61850, MQTT, and CoAP. Experimental results show that the parsing pass rate of Peach Pit files generated by DTV-LLM reaches 100% after iterative refinement, representing a 50%-point improvement over the baseline LLM. In fuzz testing across six representative industrial control protocols, the Peach Pit configurations generated by DTV-LLM achieve higher vulnerability detection capability and branch coverage than manually written configurations. Specifically, DTV-LLM improves branch coverage by 12.4% on average compared to manual Peach Pits, and by 62.8% on average compared to AFLNet. These results demonstrate that DTV-LLM significantly lowers the expertise required for Peach Pit construction, enhances fuzzing effectiveness and efficiency, and provides practical support for automated vulnerability discovery in industrial control protocol implementations.

Overall, our contributions are summarized as follows:

- We propose DTV-LLM, an LLM-based framework for automatically generating Peach Pit configurations for industrial control protocol fuzzing. DTV-LLM integrates document-driven knowledge extraction, template-based structural constraints, and multi-stage validation to ensure both protocol semantic accuracy and syntactic correctness.
- We design a document-driven protocol modeling approach, which incorporates a knowledge extraction mechanism to guide LLMs in generating protocol-aware DataModel and StateModel by extracting message formats and interaction sequences from protocol specifications or RFCs.
- We conduct experiments on six representative industrial protocols, demonstrating that DTV-LLM outperforms baseline approaches in parsing accuracy, fuzzing coverage, and vulnerability detection.

2 Related Work

Protocol Fuzzing. Protocol fuzzing has been widely adopted for discovering vulnerabilities in industrial control and network protocol implementations. Luo et al. [13] enhanced the Peach fuzzer with coverage-guided packet cracking, significantly improving fuzzing efficiency on ICS protocols such as Modbus and DNP3, while still relying on manually crafted protocol models. To reduce manual effort, learning-based approaches have been explored. Sun et al. [21] proposed MaskFuzzer, which uses GANs to learn protocol data structures, and Wang et al. [24] introduced a Transformer-based adaptive fuzzing method for Modbus TCP, improving test case acceptance and vulnerability discovery. However, these approaches primarily focus on data formats and lack explicit modeling of protocol interaction logic. Mutation-based fuzzers have also been applied to protocol testing. Pham et al. [19] proposed AFLNET, which mutates recorded message sequences and uses response-based state feedback to guide fuzzing without protocol specifications. While effective, AFLNET is limited by seed dependency and lacks semantic awareness. More protocol-specific approaches, such as Liu et al.'s MQueez [12] for MQTT, achieve high effectiveness through carefully engineered interaction models but suffer from poor generality. Overall, existing protocol fuzzing approaches either require extensive manual modeling or avoid protocol specifications at the cost of limited semantic coverage.

LLM-Based Fuzzing. Recent studies have explored LLMs for protocol fuzzing and analysis. Meng et al. [14] proposed CHATAFL, which leverages LLMs to infer protocol grammars and state transitions from natural-language specifications, achieving significant coverage improvements over AFLNET. Similarly, Wang et al. [22] introduced LLMIF, which augments LLMs with protocol specifications to guide IoT protocol fuzzing. Beyond fuzzing, Zheng et al. [27] proposed PARVAL, using LLMs to detect inconsistencies between protocol standards and implementations.

Despite these advances, existing LLM-based approaches mainly assist mutation or protocol inference and do not address the challenges of generating executable configurations for generation-based fuzzers. In contrast, our work focuses on automatically generating Peach Pit files, bridging LLM-based protocol understanding with practical generation-based fuzzing through structural constraints and validation mechanisms.

3 Background

3.1 Generation-Based Protocol Fuzzing

Fuzz testing can be divided into generation-based and mutation-based categories. Generation-based fuzz testing generates test cases from scratch based on the target industrial control protocol specifications, enabling comprehensive exploration of protocol logic and effective coverage of edge cases that are often missed by mutation-based approaches. Peach Fuzzer is a representative generation-based fuzz testing tool, whose core lies in the Peach Pit configuration file. A Peach Pit file defines three key components: the DataModel, which describes the structure and constraints of protocol messages (e.g., field types, lengths, and value ranges); the StateModel, which specifies protocol interaction sequences (e.g., connection establishment, request transmission, response reception, and connection termination in Modbus TCP); and Mutators, which define mutation strategies for generating malformed inputs. The quality of the Peach Pit configuration directly determines test coverage and vulnerability detection effectiveness.

However, manually constructing Peach Pit files is time-consuming and error-prone, significantly limiting the practical efficiency of generation-based fuzz testing for industrial control protocols. Notably, among the various elements defined in a Peach Pit file, only the message formats and interaction sequences are protocol-specific, while the remaining structural tags and execution logic follow fixed patterns. Therefore, by employing a template-based approach, these invariant components can be predefined, allowing the LLM to focus solely on generating protocol-specific message structures (DataModel) and interaction sequences

(StateModel). The final Peach Pit file can then be automatically assembled by filling the generated parameters into the predefined template, ensuring structural correctness while reducing the burden on the LLM.

3.2 Large Language Models

Large language models (LLMs) have achieved remarkable success in tasks such as code generation [5] and natural language understanding [15], owing to their large-scale parameters, massive training data, and strong contextual reasoning capabilities. Trained on diverse corpora including technical documentation and source code, modern LLMs demonstrate an enhanced ability to comprehend complex texts and perform step-by-step reasoning [16]. These properties make them particularly suitable for understanding protocol specifications, which are often lengthy, complex, and written in semi-formal natural language. Inspired by recent advances in LLMs [14,22], this paper applies LLMs to generation-based protocol fuzz testing. Specifically, we leverage LLMs to automatically extract protocol semantics from documentation, including message formats and interaction sequences, and generate corresponding DataModel and StateModel for fuzz testing.

To effectively control the model's behavior, we employ prompt engineering [8] techniques, including few-shot prompting [18] and chain-of-thought reasoning [25], to guide the LLM through step-by-step analysis that mimics the workflow of a human expert interpreting protocol documents. Rather than directly generating complete fuzzing configurations, the LLM is instructed to focus on producing protocol-specific semantic elements, such as message formats and interaction sequences, while invariant structural components are assembled using predefined templates. This design leverages the reasoning strengths of LLMs while mitigating issues such as hallucination and structural errors, enabling reliable and efficient generation of protocol test models.

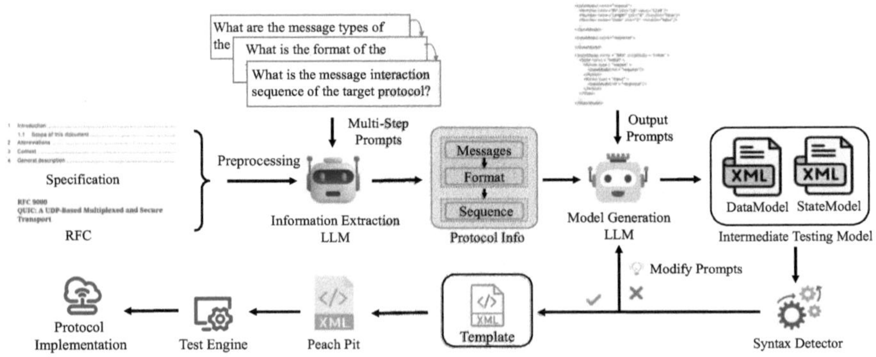

Fig. 1. The overall workflow of DTV-LLM.

4 Our Approach

We propose DTV-LLM, an LLM-based Peach pit generation method that integrates document-driven knowledge extraction, template constraints, and multi-stage validation. The framework consists of six key steps: (1) data preprocessing, (2) multi-step reasoning via prompting, (3) few-shot prompt-based conversion to DataModel, (4) template filling to generate the final Peach pit, (5) error feedback refinement, and (6) fuzz testing execution. Figure 1 illustrates the overall workflow of DTV-LLM.

4.1 Information Extraction

Data Preprocessing. The goal of data preprocessing is to drive the LLM to extract and compress domain knowledge of industrial control protocols from documents, including official protocol specifications and RFC documents, thus facilitating the model's accurate comprehension and efficient utilization of such knowledge. Specifically, to avoid excessively long context sequences that would exceed the LLM's context window limit and preserve contextual coherence between text segments, we first adopt a sliding window strategy with a 20% intersection-over-union (IoU) ratio to split the target document into contiguous text chunks. This overlapping segmentation mechanism effectively prevents the fragmentation of relevant protocol knowledge, while the chunking operation itself addresses the context length constraint of LLMs. Subsequently, the segmented text chunks are fed into the LLM, and a knowledge compression prompt is used to guide the LLM to summarize and compress the key information in the chunks, such as message definitions and interaction processes specific to industrial control. This compressed knowledge is stored in the LLM's context memory to provide continuous guidance for subsequent generation tasks.

Multi-step Thinking Prompting. To accurately extract the key information required for Peach Pit generation from the compressed protocol knowledge, a multi-step thinking prompting strategy is designed. Specifically, the LLM is guided through a sequence of structured prompts that correspond to three core questions: (1) What are the message types of the target protocol? (e.g., request message, response message, heartbeat message) (2) What is the format of each message type? (e.g., the fields contained in the message, the type and length of each field, especially control signal fields) (3) What is the message interaction sequence of the target protocol? (e.g., the sequence of connection establishment, data transmission, and connection termination) By decomposing protocol understanding into these ordered reasoning steps, the prompting strategy explicitly captures the logical dependencies among message types, message formats, and interaction semantics. This step-by-step guidance enables the LLM to mimic the analytical process of a human expert and significantly improves the accuracy and consistency of protocol information extraction. Figure 2 shows an example of the Multi-Step Thinking Prompting process used in DTV-LLM. Through structured prompts, the LLM is guided to reason step by step over protocol documents, successively identifying protocol message types, message formats, and message interaction sequences.

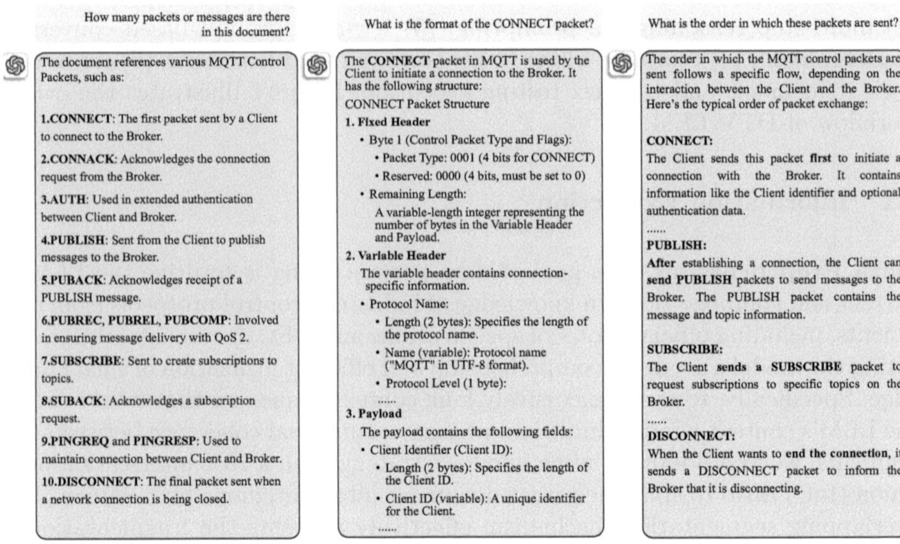

Fig. 2. The example of LLM extraction protocol message type, format and sequence.

4.2 Generation of Data Model and State Model

Few-Shot Prompt-Based Conversion to DataModel. Based on the extracted message format information, a few-shot prompting strategy is adopted to transform the information into a DataModel that conforms to Peach Pit syntax. Specifically, several high-quality, manually crafted DataModel examples from similar industrial control protocols are selected as few-shot demonstrations. These examples cover standard Peach Pit constructs and syntax elements, including <DataModel>, <StateModel>, <Number>, <String>, and <Block>. Then, the extracted message format information is provided to the LLM together with these few-shot samples, guiding the model to generate a DataModel tailored to the target protocol. By leveraging the LLM's few-shot learning capability, this approach effectively aligns the generated DataModel with Peach Pit's syntactic and structural requirements, thereby reducing syntax errors and improving model correctness.

Template Filling to Form the Final Peach Pit. As illustrated in Fig. 3, the left part of the figure shows a parameterized Peach Pit XML template that defines the invariant structural skeleton of the configuration file. The template

```
<?xml version="1.0" encoding="utf-8"?>
<Peach xmlns="http://peachfuzzer.com/2012/Peach"
xmlns:xsi="http://www.w3.org/2001/XMLSchema-instance"
xsi:schemaLocation="http://peachfuzzer.com/2012/Peach ../peach.xsd">

<!-- ========== 1. Data Models ========== -->
<DataModel name="{DataModelName}">
  {DataModelBody}
</DataModel>

<!-- ========== 2. State Model ========== -->
<StateModel name="{StateModelName}" initialState="InitialState">
  <State name="initialState">
    <Action type="output">
      <DataModel ref="{RequestDataModel}" />
    </Action>
    <Action type="input">
      <DataModel ref="{ResponseDataModel}" />
    </Action>
    <Action type="changeState" ref="{StateName}" />
  </State>
</StateModel>

<!-- ========== 3. Agent ========== -->
<Agent name="LocalAgent">
  <Monitor class="Process">
    <Param name="Executable" value="{TargetBinary}" />
    <Param name="Arguments" value="{TargetArgs}" />
  </Monitor>
</Agent>

<!-- ========== 4. Test Definition ========== -->
<Test name="DefaultTest">
  <Agent ref="LocalAgent"/>
  <StateModel ref="{StateModelName}" />
  <Publisher class="{PublisherClass}">
    <Param name="Host" value="{TargetIP}" />
    <Param name="Port" value="{TargetPort}" />
  </Publisher>
  <Strategy class="Random" />
  <Logger class="File">
    <Param name="Path" value="logs" />
  </Logger>
</Test>

</Peach>
```

```
Below is an MQTT protocol test model following the syntax format you provided :
<DataModel name="ConnectCommand">
  <Block name="FixedHeader">
    <Blob name="PacketType" value="10" valueType="hex" mutable="false"/>
    <Blob name="Reserved" value="0F" valueType="hex" mutable="false"/>
    <Blob name="RemainingLength" value="00 04" valueType="hex"
      mutable="false"/>
  </Block>
  <Block name="VariableHeader">
    <Blob name="ProtocolName" value="4D 51 54 54" valueType="hex"
      mutable="false"/>
    <Blob name="ProtocolLevel" value="04" valueType="hex" mutable="false"/>
    <Blob name="ConnectFlags" value="02" valueType="hex" mutable="false"/>
    <Blob name="KeepAlive" value="00 3C" valueType="hex" mutable="false"/>
  </Block>
  <Block name="Payload">
    <Blob name="ClientIDLength" value="00 03" valueType="hex"
      mutable="false"/>
    <Blob name="ClientID" value="61 62 63" valueType="hex" mutable="false"/>
  </Block>
</DataModel>

<DataModel name=" ConnectACK "></DataModel>

<DataModel name=" SubscribeCommand "></DataModel>
......

......
<StateModel name="MQTTFlow" initialState="initialState">
  <State name="initialState">
    <Action type="output">
      <DataModel ref="ConnectCommand" />
    </Action>
    <Action type="input">
      <DataModel ref="ConnectACK" />
    </Action>
    <Action type="changeState" ref="Subscribe" />
  </State>
  ......
</StateModel>
......
```

Fig. 3. Fill the pit template based on the data model and message sequence generated by LLM.

exposes placeholders (e.g., DataModel, StateModel, Publisher) for protocol-specific content while fixing the overall Peach syntax. The right part presents an instantiated example after template filling. Specifically, the DataModel generated in the previous step is directly injected into the DataModel slot of the template, while the StateModel is automatically constructed by merging the extracted message interaction sequence into a sequence of <State> and <Action> elements. Other parameters, such as the target executable, communication endpoint, and publisher settings, are filled using experiment-specific configurations during the assembly phase.

By separating protocol-dependent semantics (message formats and interaction sequences) from protocol-agnostic structural elements, this template-based assembly process allows the LLM to focus solely on generating semantic models, while all other Peach Pit tags are deterministically instantiated. This design effectively reduces configuration complexity and minimizes syntax and structural errors in the generated Peach Pit files.

Load Peach Pit and Feedback Modification. Due to the inherent limitations of LLMs, such as hallucinated content and imperfect adherence to domain-specific constraints, the Peach Pit file generated in the previous steps is not guaranteed to be immediately correct or executable. Therefore, the generated Peach Pit is loaded into Peach Fuzzer for syntax and logical validation. During this process, Peach reports errors such as unrecognized XML tags or invalid field constraints for industrial control signals. The reported error information is then extracted and transformed into a structured feedback prompt, which is fed back to the LLM. Guided by this explicit feedback and the retained protocol knowledge, the LLM revises only the corresponding faulty components of the Peach Pit file. This validation–feedback–revision loop is iteratively executed until the generated Peach Pit can be successfully parsed and executed by Peach Fuzzer.

Execute Fuzz Testing. Once a Peach Pit file is successfully validated, it is employed as the testing configuration to drive Peach Fuzzer for fuzz testing on the target protocol implementation. Guided by the generated DataModel and StateModel, Peach systematically produces malformed protocol messages and executes them according to the specified interaction sequences. During fuzzing, the runtime behavior of the target system is continuously monitored, and abnormal behaviors such as crashes, memory errors, or unexpected terminations are recorded. Meanwhile, coverage information and vulnerability-related evidence are collected throughout the testing process and used for subsequent quantitative evaluation and comparative analysis.

5 Experiment

We implemented DTV-LLM in Python based on GPT-4o (2025-03-26), used Peach 3.1.53 as the fuzzing engine, and employed Clang to insert trace-pc-guard instrumentation into the target implementations to collect code coverage information, the collected coverage data is used solely for evaluation purposes and does not influence the fuzzing strategy itself. Our experiments are designed to answer the following research questions:

RQ1: Can DTV-LLM accurately extract protocol testing information and generate syntactically correct and executable Peach Pit files?

RQ2: Can DTV-LLM achieve more effective fuzzing in terms of code coverage compared with baseline approaches?

RQ3: Can DTV-LLM improve vulnerability detection capability during protocol fuzzing?

5.1 Experimental Setup

Subjects. To comprehensively evaluate the effectiveness of DTV-LLM, we conducted experiments on six widely used industrial protocols: Modbus, IEC104,

IEC60870, IEC61850, MQTT, CoAP. For each protocol, we selected a representative open-source implementation as the fuzzing target: libmodbus [20], iec104 [3], lib60870 [1], lib61850-mms [2], mosquitto [7], libcoap [4].

Metrics. We employed three metrics for our evaluation: (i) Peach syntax validation pass rate, (ii) branch coverage achieved, and (iii) the number of unique crashes or abnormal behaviors detected. The first metric is used to measure the correctness and executability of the generated Peach Pit files, the second metric evaluates the effectiveness of fuzzing in exploring protocol logic, and the third metric reflects the vulnerability detection capability of the generated test configurations.

Experimental Settings. We use Docker containers as the runtime environment, each with 1 CPU core and 1G RAM. Randomity may have an impact on the results, and we performed 5 repeated experiments on each protocol implementation. All programs run on Ubuntu 20.04.2 LTS.

5.2 Correctness Analysis

Table 1 reports the syntax correctness of Peach Pit files generated by DTV-LLM across multiple iterative versions, evaluated by whether the generated configurations can be successfully parsed by the Peach syntax validator. As shown in the table, the initial generation (v1.0) achieves a parsing accuracy of 50%, indicating that the LLM is already capable of producing syntactically valid Pit files for some protocols, such as Modbus, MQTT, and CoAP. These protocols generally have relatively regular message formats and simpler interaction patterns, which makes their data models and state models easier for the LLM to infer correctly in a single generation pass.

After incorporating feedback-based revision, the parsing accuracy increases to 67% in v2.0. In this iteration, the generated Pit file for IEC 104 becomes syntactically valid, demonstrating that iterative correction guided by Peach parser feedback can effectively fix common structural issues, such as missing XML elements, incorrect attribute definitions, or invalid references between DataModel and StateModel components.

In v3.0, all generated Peach Pit files across the six protocols successfully pass Peach syntax validation, achieving a 100% accuracy. Notably, protocols with higher structural and semantic complexity, such as IEC 60870 and IEC 61850, only become valid in the final iteration. This is mainly due to their more complex message hierarchies, optional fields, and multi-stage interaction sequences, which significantly increase the likelihood of structural inconsistencies during early generations.

Table 1. The accuracy of the model generated by LLM after multiple iterations is parsed by the peach syntax

Protocol	Subject	v1.0	v2.0	v3.0
Modbus	libmodbus	✓	✓	✓
IEC104	iec104		✓	✓
IEC60870	lib60870			✓
IEC61850	libiec61850-mms			✓
MQTT	mosquitto	✓	✓	✓
CoAP	libcoap	✓	✓	✓
Accuracy	-	50%	67%	100%

Overall, these results demonstrate that while a single-pass LLM generation may be insufficient for producing fully valid Peach Pit files for complex industrial protocols, the proposed multi-stage validation and iterative refinement mechanism in DTV-LLM is effective in eliminating syntactic errors. This confirms the robustness of our approach in generating executable Peach Pit configurations across diverse protocol types.

5.3 Coverage Analysis

Table 2 summarizes the average number of code branches achieved by different fuzzers within a 24-hour time budget across six protocol implementations. Overall, DTV-LLM consistently outperforms both Peach with manually written Pit files and AFLNet, achieving the highest branch coverage on all evaluated subjects.

Compared with Peach, DTV-LLM improves branch coverage by an average of 12.4%, indicating that the automatically generated Pit files are able to drive the target implementations toward more diverse execution paths than manually constructed configurations. These results suggest that LLM-generated data models and state models can capture richer protocol semantics and interaction patterns, enabling more effective exploration of protocol logic. When compared with AFLNet, which adopts a mutation-based, state-aware fuzzing strategy, DTV-LLM achieves substantially higher coverage, with an average improvement of 62.8%. This can be attributed to the generation-based nature of Peach combined with high-quality protocol models produced by DTV-LLM, which systematically construct well-formed yet diverse inputs that better satisfy strict protocol constraints and reach deeper protocol states.

Table 2. Average number of code branches achieved by each fuzzer within 24 h.

Subject	Peach	AFLNet	DTV-LLM	$Improve_1$	$Improve_2$
libmodbus	1035	847	1062	+2.6%	+25.4%
iec104	279	180	318	+14.0%	+76.7%
lib60870	2517	1520	2913	+15.7%	+91.6%
mms	4528	2619	5125	+13.2%	+95.7%
mosquitto	4308	3389	5316	+23.4%	+56.9%
libcoap	4016	3238	4230	+5.3%	+30.6%
AVERAGE	-	-	-	+12.4%	+62.8%

For relatively simpler or more tolerant protocols, such as libmodbus and libcoap, the coverage improvements over Peach are smaller but still consistent. This indicates that even when manually written Pit files are already effective, DTV-LLM can further enhance coverage by refining field constraints and interaction sequences.

Overall, these results demonstrate that DTV-LLM not only generates syntactically valid Peach Pit files, but also significantly improves fuzzing effectiveness in terms of branch coverage. The consistent gains across diverse protocol implementations confirm the advantage of integrating LLM-driven protocol modeling into generation-based fuzz testing.

5.4 Bug Detection Capability

Table 3 reports the ability of different fuzzers to detect known vulnerabilities across several protocol implementations. Overall, DTV-LLM detects all reported vulnerabilities, while Peach and AFLNet each miss multiple cases, indicating that DTV-LLM exhibits stronger and more stable vulnerability detection capability.

For iec104, two known vulnerabilities are considered, including a heap-use-after-free and a segmentation fault (SEGV). DTV-LLM successfully triggers both vulnerabilities, whereas Peach only detects the SEGV and AFLNet fails to detect either issue. The heap-use-after-free vulnerability is particularly difficult to expose, as it typically requires carefully constructed message sequences and precise triggering conditions. This result suggests that the protocol interaction models generated by DTV-LLM are more effective in driving the implementation into vulnerable execution states.

In the case of lib60870, DTV-LLM and Peach both detect the known SEGV vulnerability, while AFLNet fails to trigger it. This indicates that generation-based fuzzing remains advantageous for protocols with strict structural and semantic constraints, and that DTV-LLM is able to preserve this advantage while further improving model quality.

For mosquitto, a known memory leak vulnerability is detected by both AFLNet and DTV-LLM, but not by Peach. This implies that mutation-based fuzzing can be effective for certain resource-related issues, while the improved input diversity and semantic coverage introduced by DTV-LLM allow generation-based fuzzing to reach similar vulnerable behaviors.

Taken together, these results demonstrate that DTV-LLM not only improves coverage but also translates coverage gains into practical vulnerability discovery. By generating protocol-aware data and state models, DTV-LLM enables Peach to exercise deeper and more diverse execution paths, thereby increasing the likelihood of triggering known vulnerabilities compared with both manually modeled generation-based fuzzing and state-aware mutation-based fuzzing.

Table 3. Summary of vulnerabilities detected by Peach++

No.	Subject	Type	Peach	AFLNet	DTV-LLM
1	iec104	heap-use-after-free			•
2	iec104	SEGV	•		•
3	lib60870	SEGV	•		•
4	mosquitto	memory leaks		•	•

6 Conclusion

In this paper, we proposed DTV-LLM, a framework for automatic Peach Pit generation that integrates document-driven knowledge extraction, template-based constraints, and multi-stage validation. DTV-LLM leverages large language models to generate protocol-specific DataModel and StateModel. Experimental results on six widely used industrial control protocols demonstrate that DTV-LLM produces fully valid Peach Pit files, achieves higher code coverage than both Peach and AFLNet, and effectively detects vulnerabilities. Overall, our approach reduces the expertise and effort required for protocol fuzz testing, improving both efficiency and reliability of automated vulnerability discovery.

Acknowledgment. This work is partially supported by the National Key Research and Development Program (Grant No. 2022YFB3104001).

References

1. mz automation: lib60870. https://github.com/mz-automation/lib60870
2. mz automation: libiec61850. https://github.com/mz-automation/libiec61850
3. dj chen: Iec104. https://github.com/airpig2011/IEC104
4. obgm Community: libcoap. https://github.com/obgm/libcoap
5. Dong, Y., Jiang, X., Jin, Z., Li, G.: Self-collaboration code generation via chatgpt. ACM Trans. Softw. Eng. Methodol. **33**(7), 1–38 (2024)
6. Eddington, M.: Peach Fuzzer. https://gitlab.com/gitlab-org/security-products/protocol-fuzzer-ce

7. Foundation, E.: Mosquitto. https://github.com/eclipse-mosquitto/mosquitto
8. Giray, L.: Prompt engineering with chatgpt: a guide for academic writers. Ann. Biomed. Eng. **51**(12), 2629–2633 (2023)
9. Hu, Y., et al.: Industrial internet of things intelligence empowering smart manufacturing: a literature review. IEEE Internet Things J. **11**(11), 19143–19167 (2024)
10. Khan, R., Maynard, P., McLaughlin, K., Laverty, D., Sezer, S.: Threat analysis of blackenergy malware for synchrophasor based real-time control and monitoring in smart grid. In: 4th International Symposium for ICS & SCADA Cyber Security Research, pp. 53–63 (2016). https://doi.org/10.14236/ewic/ICS2016.7
11. Langner, R.: Stuxnet: dissecting a cyberwarfare weapon. IEEE Secur. Privacy **9**(3), 49–51 (2011). https://doi.org/10.1109/MSP.2011.67
12. Liu, X., Wang, Q., Liu, P., Wang, W., Ji, S.: Mqueez: specification-driven fuzzing for MQTT broker (registered report). In: Proceedings of the 34th ACM SIGSOFT International Symposium on Software Testing and Analysis, pp. 133–142 (2025)
13. Luo, Z., Zuo, F., Shen, Y., Jiao, X., Chang, W., Jiang, Y.: ICS protocol fuzzing: coverage guided packet crack and generation. In: 2020 57th ACM/IEEE Design Automation Conference, pp. 1–6 (2020). https://doi.org/10.1109/DAC18072.2020.9218603
14. Meng, R., Mirchev, M., Böhme, M., Roychoudhury, A.: Large language model guided protocol fuzzing. In: Proceedings of the 31st Annual Network and Distributed System Security Symposium, pp. 1–17 (2024)
15. Min, B., et al.: Recent advances in natural language processing via large pre-trained language models: a survey. ACM Comput. Surv. **56**(2), 1–40 (2023)
16. Naveed, H., et al.: A comprehensive overview of large language models. arXiv preprint arXiv:2307.06435 (2023)
17. Nelson, N.: The Impact of Dragonfly Malware on Industrial Control Systems. Tech. rep, SANS Institute (2016)
18. Perez, E., Kiela, D., Cho, K.: True few-shot learning with language models. In: Ranzato, M., Beygelzimer, A., Dauphin, Y., Liang, P., Vaughan, J.W. (eds.) Advances in Neural Information Processing Systems, pp. 11054–11070 (2021)
19. Pham, V.T., Böhme, M., Roychoudhury, A.: Aflnet: a greybox fuzzer for network protocols. In: 2020 IEEE 13th International Conference on Software Testing, Validation and Verification, pp. 460–465 (2020).https://doi.org/10.1109/ICST46399.2020.00062
20. Raimbault, S.: Libmodbus. https://github.com/stephane/libmodbus
21. Sun, W., Zhang, B., Ding, J., Tang, M.: Maskfuzzer: a MASKGAN-based industrial control protocol fuzz testing framework. In: 2022 IEEE International Conference on Smart Internet of Things, pp. 51–57 (2022)
22. Wang, J., Yu, L., Luo, X.: Llmif: Augmented large language model for fuzzing IoT devices. In: 2024 IEEE Symposium on Security and Privacy (SP), pp. 881–896. IEEE (2024)
23. Wang, T., et al.: LLM-BOOFUZZ: generation-based black-box fuzzing for network protocols via LLMs. Electronics **14**(23), 4550 (2025)
24. Wang, W., Chen, Z., Zheng, Z., Wang, H.: An adaptive fuzzing method based on transformer and protocol similarity mutation. Comput. Secur. **129**, 103197 (2023)
25. Wei, J., et al.: Chain-of-thought prompting elicits reasoning in large language models. In: Advances in Neural Information Processing Systems, pp. 24824–24837 (2022)
26. Zhang, Z., Zhang, H., Zhao, J., Yin, Y.: A survey on the development of network protocol fuzzing techniques. Electronics **12**(13), 2904 (2023)

27. Zheng, M., Xie, D., Zhang, X.: Large language models for validating network protocol parsers. In: 2025 IEEE Security and Privacy Workshops (SPW), pp. 56–64. IEEE (2025)
28. Zhou, H., et al.: Large language model (LLM) for telecommunications: a comprehensive survey on principles, key techniques, and opportunities. IEEE Commun. Surv. Tutorials **27**(3), 1955–2005 (2024)

Author Index

J. Niu et al. (Eds.): KSEM 2026, LNAI 16631, pp. 633–635, 2027.
https://doi.org/10.1007/978-981-92-2759-4

MIX
Papier aus verantwortungsvollen Quellen
Paper from responsible sources
FSC® C105338

If you have any concerns about our products,
you can contact us on
ProductSafety@springernature.com

In case Publisher is established outside the EU,
the EU authorized representative is:
Springer Nature Customer Service Center GmbH
Europaplatz 3, 69115 Heidelberg, Germany

Printed by Libri Plureos GmbH
in Hamburg, Germany